Philosophical Entrées

Classic and Contemporary Readings in Philosophy

edited by
Dale Jacquette

D1374118

Boston   Burr Ridge, IL   Dubuque, IA   Madison, WI   New York
San Francisco   St. Louis   Bangkok   Bogotá   Caracas   Lisbon   London   Madrid
Mexico City   Milan   New Delhi   Seoul   Singapore   Sydney   Taipei   Toronto

McGraw-Hill Higher Education

A Division of The **McGraw-Hill** Companies

PHILOSOPHICAL ENTRÉES: CLASSIC AND CONTEMPORARY
READINGS IN PHILOSOPHY

Published by McGraw-Hill, an imprint of The McGraw-Hill Companies, Inc., 1221 Avenue of the Americas, New York, NY 10020. Copyright © 2001 by The McGraw-Hill Companies, Inc. All rights reserved. No part of this publication may be reproduced or distributed in any form or by any means, or stored in a database or retrieval system, without the prior written consent of The McGraw-Hill Companies, Inc., including, but not limited to, in any network or other electronic storage or transmission, or broadcast for distance learning.

Some ancillaries, including electronic and print components, may not be available to customers outside the United States.

This book is printed on acid-free paper.

1 2 3 4 5 6 7 8 9 0 DOC/DOC 0 9 8 7 6 5 4 3 2 1 0

ISBN 0–07–365933–9

Editorial director: *Jane E. Vaicunas*
Sponsoring editor: *Monica Eckman*
Developmental editor: *Hannah Glover*
Senior marketing manager: *Daniel M. Loch*
Project manager: *Joyce M. Berendes*
Production supervisor: *Laura Fuller*
Freelance design coordinator: *Pam Verros*
Cover photography: ©*Musee D'Orsay, Paris/Lauros-Giraudon, Paris/SuperStock*
Compositor: *Shepherd, Inc.*
Typeface: *10.5/12 Times Roman*
Printer: *R. R. Donnelley & Sons Company/Crawfordsville, IN*

Library of Congress Cataloging-in-Publication Data

Philosophical entrées : classic and contemporary readings in philosophy / [edited by] Dale Jacquette.
  p   cm.
  Includes bibliographical references and index.
  ISBN 0–07–365933–9
  1. Philosophy.   I. Jacquette, Dale.

B72 .P46   2001
100—dc21   00–022611
                                                                    CIP

www.mhhe.com

Contents

Foreword

The essays in this volume include selections from important classical and recent and contemporary philosophical writings. The essays are organized into six categories, concerning the meaning of life, epistemology or theory of knowledge, the concept of mind and problem of free will and determinism, the existence and nature of God, ethical theory and moral decision making, and metaphilosophy or the philosophy of philosophy.

The collection represents a choice of six central topics in philosophy. It is offered as supplementary readings to accompany my introductory philosophy text, *Six Philosophical Appetizers*. The *Appetizers* and *Entrées* complement one another; the six sections of readings in the *Entrées* correspond to the six philosophical topics of the *Appetizers*. An ideal way to combine these two sources would be to read a chapter in the *Appetizers,* and then to consult the corresponding readings in the *Entrées,* working back and forth between the two to understand the philosophical problems and their historical and current context of discussion for each of the six topics. Yet no definite reading program is presupposed in the organization of either book. Indeed, the concept of providing the reader with philosophical appetizers and entreés is to encourage a leisurely sampling according to individual taste. The order of essays in each section has been made for a variety of pedagogical and ideological reasons and inevitably reflects at least some of my personal philosophical preferences. It is recommended as an interesting experiment to read the same set of materials in different sequences, to see whether the exact presentation of philosophical ideas can affect even the impression of their truth.

The readings chosen are philosophical entrées in both senses of the word. They are main courses, philosophical food for thought, for which the appetizers in the companion text are table starters. They are also points of entry into the vast philosophical literature surrounding each of the six topics. By investigating the problems presented in these *Entrées,* it is possible to get a clear view of the issues that divide philosophers, and the variety of philosophical methods that have characterized philosophy's remarkable history. I have chosen the essays and chapter excerpts not only because of the attention they have deservedly received in the marketplace of ideas, but also for their outstanding literary qualities and diversity of outlook, representing many different philosophical perspectives from many different historical periods, involving many different styles of philosophical reasoning. The anthology illustrates the plurality of philosophical methods applied to a wide range of philosophical controversies.

Acknowledgments

I would like to thank Sarah Moyers and Monica Eckman, my editors at McGraw-Hill, for sympathetic direction and material assistance in planning and preparing this volume for publication.

PART ONE

The Meaning of Life

The scenes of our life are like pictures in rough mosaic which produce no effect if we stand close to them, but which must be viewed at a distance if we are to find them beautiful. Therefore to obtain something that was eagerly desired is equivalent to finding out how empty and insubstantial it was, and if we are always living in expectation of better things, we often repent at the same time and long for our past.

—Arthur Schopenhauer
Parerga and Paralipomena, 1851, §145

- Plato, *Apology* (excerpt)
- William James, Is Life Worth Living?
- Albert Camus, An Absurd Reasoning (excerpt)
- Thomas Nagel, The Absurd
- Richard Taylor, The Meaning of Life
- John Wisdom, The Meanings of the Questions of Life
- Irving Singer, The Meaning of Life: Rephrasing Questions
- Joseph Ellin, The Meaning of Life

To question the meaning of life is a relatively recent philosophical preoccupation. The ancient Greek philosophers asked how we ought to live and wondered whether suicide could ever be morally justified. For the most part, however, the earliest philosophical thinkers in the Western tradition seem to have believed that the purpose of life consists in living a morally good life, something that every person in principle is capable of doing, and that it is only if life becomes intolerable that it might be conceivable under dire circumstances for individuals to ask whether their lives remain worth living.

Thus, Socrates, on trial for his life, as recounted in Plato's dialogue the *Apology,* maintains that "the unexamined life is not worth living." But we would be hard-pressed to find any classical philosopher who would have found it reasonable to conclude after careful reflection simply that "life is not worth living," or, more importantly, to generalize about the meaning and value of life as such, as opposed to the life of particular persons under particular conditions. Although many ancient moralists were not squeamish about the ethical permissibility of suicide, they did not recommend self-destruction generally or for everyone on the grounds that life was somehow absurd, but considered it only as a desperate possibility of escape from the most extreme incurable pain or insufferable dishonor.

What gives life meaning? Many philosophers and nonphilosophers answer this question differently. For some, the meaning of life is bound up with developing one's talents, living according to certain moral prescriptions, accumulating wealth, raising a family, serving others, or preparing for a future existence after death. There is a philosophical dispute about whether life, if it has meaning, derives its meaning from within life or from something beyond. Some philosophers have argued that life is meaningless or absurd in and of itself, but that for this reason it is up to each individual to give life meaning by choosing a purpose and taking responsibility for the actions by which we try to achieve our goals. The problem that exercises many philosophers remains whether life has a built-in meaning or purpose, and, if so, what it is and how we can find out about it.

The idea that life is meaningless or absurd has several sources. The fact that whatever we try to achieve can be taken away from us so easily by death or disease or bad luck of another kind is one basis for denying the meaning of life. So is the randomness of events in the universe and its apparent indifference to our concerns that seems to contradict there being any purpose to life. The meaning of life ought to be universal, available in principle to all persons, or at most it will apply to those in particular circumstances. The meaning of life cannot be to win a prize at the Olympics, or to discover the cure for a disease, but must be something for which it makes sense for everyone to try to attain, by virtue of having a life. The principal candidates for the purpose of life conceived in general terms have been suggested as that of living a good life, raising a family and propagating the species, contributing to the good of others, or living in anticipation of an afterlife.

Yet there are also difficulties with these proposals in explaining the meaning of life. It is no longer clear to modern thinkers as it was to the ancient Greeks that everyone in principle is capable of doing good. The inhumanity of two recent mechanized world wars has made philosophers less optimistic about human nature than the ancient Greeks, despite their worldly-wise tragedies about war and plague. The concentration camps and wide-scale participation of average persons in the atrocities of war may have had something to do with the thematization of the meaning of life as a philosophical problem, and with the spread of intellectual nihilism, in the attitude that nothing matters and nothing has value. The shock of self-recognition that persons who commit terrible actions are not so different from ourselves may have led philosophers to question the Greek assumption that all persons in principle are capable of good. The roots of the meaning of life as a philosophical problem in any case extend back to before the two recent world wars. We can point to many other cultural factors that have had a hand in questioning the meaning of life. These include the alienation of persons one from another in urban industrial societies, and the affluence of an economy in which the minimal requirements of subsistence can virtually be taken for granted. The need for fewer persons to struggle constantly for the bare means of survival affords the luxury of questioning the meaning of life. The spread of popular religions also encourages believers to expect a continuation of life after death, raising the issue of the purpose of life as aiming at something beyond existence in the physical world of the here and now.

Whether life has a general purpose or meaning is the problem with which this collection of readings begins. It is a question that leads many thinkers to philosophy in the first place, as they turn to wonder about the human condition. The conclusion that life may be meaningless or absurd is not merely a matter of intellectualizing depression or generalizing melancholy to the whole of life. It is the outcome of a philosophical argument, correct or incorrect, to be evaluated by the same rigorous criteria as any other in philosophy. The essays included in this section provide a choice of raw materials for our own philosophical reflections on the meaningfulness or absurdity of life.

American philosopher and psychologist William James asks directly, "Is Life Worth Living?" He describes the mood swings associated with despair about the value of life in order to distinguish severe cases of the blues from what he designates as "that metaphysical *tedium vitæ* which is peculiar to reflecting men." This pessimistic *Weltschmerz* or excessive world-weariness is understood by James as a kind of mental disease. As a remedy, he recommends a restoration of religious faith that affirms a self-fulfilling assumption that life has value. James argues that if we proceed in good faith as though life has meaning, then our lives will acquire meaning. An attitude of confidence in the meaning of life will then turn out to be justified by the life-affirming actions we are more likely to undertake as a result of the will to believe. This seems like good practical advice, especially for the popular audience to which his lecture was addressed. But does it settle the metaphysical question that brings philosophers seriously to ask whether life has meaning? If it is true that life has meaning, then we ought to be able to say more definitely exactly what meaning it has by specifying the aim or purpose of life. James extolls us to carry on bravely in the face of doubts that sometimes arise about the meaning of life, with the expectation that things will work out right, especially if we have the heart to go forward and make life better for ourselves. But it is unlikely that James's encouragement will have much effect on persons who are deeply in the grip of uncertainty about whether life has meaning. More importantly, James says nothing definite about the purpose or direction of life.

In an excerpt from "An Absurd Reasoning" in *The Myth of Sisyphus,* the twentieth-century French existentialist philosopher and essayist Albert Camus poses the problem of the meaning of life in stark terms, as a question of whether or not we should continue to live. If life is meaningful, then we ought to live; but if live is meaningless or absurd, then we might as well choose suicide. Camus compares suicide as a solution to the absurdity of life with Edmund Husserl's abstract theory of intentionality or the object-directedness of thought, and with Søren Kierkegaard's religious conception of reason recognizing its own limits and humbling itself in the clear apprehension of life's enigmas that are beyond our ability to answer. In reaction to Husserl and Kierkegaard, Camus offers a remarkable alternative. He concludes that those who are troubled about the meaning of life should embrace the absurd, to sustain and contemplate it, which they can only do by continuing to live and think about the problem. Philosophical suicide in the sense in which Camus speaks of it is not the solution to the absurd, but the very opposite. The absurd enlightens those who reflect philosophically on the absurd, and as Camus in this absurd reasoning concludes, it is the absurd that makes life meaningful.

Thomas Nagel, in his essay on "The Absurd," looks closely at the reasons offered in support of the conclusion that life is absurd. He maintains that the usual arguments for the absurdity of life are inconclusive, although they may provide a natural expression for the sense many persons seem to have that life is absurd. By considering the reasoning underlying philosophical attitudes about the absurd, Nagel cuts much of the ground from under existentialism and other philosophies that depend on the assumption that life is meaningless, or in Camus's formulation, that life falls short of our expectations about the meaning we should like it to have. The effect of Nagel's analysis is to challenge the philosophical credentials of the feeling or emotional response that thinkers sometimes report as the absurdity of life in lived-through confrontations with the absurd. If life is truly absurd in a sense in which philosophy can take notice of it, then, if Nagel's criticism is correct, better arguments will need to be found.

Richard Taylor, in "The Meaning of Life" from his book, *Good and Evil,* by contrast, presents an evocative comparison of attitudes alternatively of life's meaninglessness and meaningfulness, in which the emotional content of one seems to cancel out the other, permitting Taylor to conclude on a note of heartfelt moral optimism. John Wisdom, in the chapter of his *Paradox and Discovery* on "The Meanings of the Questions of Life," takes the opposite approach to understanding the meaning of life. He offers plausible interpretations of doubts about the meaning of life by analogy with the kind of puzzlement and sense of meaninglessness we experience when we are puzzled in different specific ways about the meaning of a dramatic performance at the theater. We can be similarly perplexed as spectators of the unfolding events of our personal lives.

The same combination of blunting the philosophical force of considerations about the absurdity of life and projecting the individual's choice of objectives as a local solution to questions about the meaning of life is explored in distinctive ways in the concluding selections of chapters from Irving Singer's book, *Meaning in Life: The Creation of Value,* and Joseph Ellin's *Morality and the Meaning of Life.* Singer requires that the sense of the absurd as a challenge to the meaningfulness of life involve an outright logical absurdity. By showing that there is no contradiction in the purposefulness of the struggle for life and the apparent purposelessness of the universe as a whole, Singer argues that by reconciling the purposes of an individual life with the world's meaninglessness there is no need to acknowledge that life is absurd. Ellin similarly examines the origin of questions about the meaning of life and considers a number of likely answers that have been proposed in the history of philosophy. He addresses many different sources for the philosophical idea of the meaninglessness or absurdity of life and articulates a set of conditions to be satisfied by an adequate solution to the problem of the meaning of life. Any such big picture of the meaning of the world according to Ellin can only be accepted as a general article of faith that life has some meaning, with no particular insight as to its purpose. The literal meaninglessness of questions about the meaning of life is suggested by the difficulty if not finally the impossibility of answering such questions, or even of being able to say what kinds of answers might be appropriate. Ellin recognizes that semantic subterfuges cannot satisfy the intellectual yearnings of persons who are preoccupied with the problem of the meaning of life. He emphasizes purposes and moral values as giving individual meaning to each person's life even in the absence of any larger intelligible cosmic direction or plan.

Apology *(excerpt)*

Plato

Let us then take up the case from its beginning. What is the accusation from which arose the slander in which Meletus trusted when he wrote out the charge against me? What did they say when they slandered me? I must, as if they were my actual prosecutors, read the affidavit they would have sworn. It goes something like this: Socrates is guilty of wrongdoing in that he busies himself studying things in the sky and below the earth; he makes the worse into the stronger argument, and he teaches these same things to others. You have seen this yourselves in the comedy of Aristophanes, a Socrates swinging about there, saying he was walking on air and talking a lot of other nonsense about things of which I know nothing at all. I do not speak in contempt of such knowledge, if someone is wise in these things—lest Meletus bring more cases against me—but, gentlemen, I have no part in it, and on this point I call upon the majority of you as witnesses. I think it right that all those of you who have heard me conversing, and many of you have, should tell each other if anyone of you has ever heard me discussing such subjects to any extent at all. From this you will learn that the other things said about me by the majority are of the same kind.

Not one of them is true. And if you have heard from anyone that I undertake to teach people and charge a fee for it, that is not true either. Yet I think it a fine thing to be able to teach people as Gorgias of Leontini does, and Prodicus of Ceos, and Hippias of Elis.[1] Each of these men can go to any city and persuade the young, who can keep company with anyone of their own fellow-citizens they want without paying, to leave the company of these, to join with themselves, pay them a fee, and be grateful to them besides. Indeed, I learned that there is another wise man from Paros who is visiting us, for I met a man who has spent more money on Sophists than everybody else put together, Callias, the son of Hipponicus. So I asked him—he has two sons—"Callias," I said, "if your sons were colts or calves, we could find and engage a supervisor for them who would make them excel in their proper qualities, some horse breeder or farmer. Now since they are men, whom do you have in mind to supervise them? Who is an expert in this kind of excellence, the human and social kind? I think you must have given thought to this since you have sons. Is there such a person," I asked, "or is there not?" "Certainly there is," he said. "Who is he?" I asked, "What is his name, where is he from? and what is his fee?" "His name, Socrates, is Evenus, he comes from Paros, and his fee is five minas." I thought Evenus a

---

[1]These were all well-known Sophists. Gorgias, after whom Plato named one of his dialogues, was a celebrated rhetorician and teacher of rhetoric. He came to Athens in 42 B.C., and his rhetorical tricks took the city by storm. Two dialogues, the authenticity of which has been doubted, are named after Hippias, whose knowledge was encyclopedic. Prodicus was known for his insistence on the precise meaning of words. Both he and Hippias are characters in the *Protagoras* (named after another famous Sophist).

Source: Excerpts from *Plato, Five Dialogues,* trans. G. M. A. Grube, pp. 25–29, 41, 59–60, 69–76, 84–86.

happy man, if he really possesses this art, and teaches for so moderate a fee. Certainly I would pride and preen myself if I had this knowledge, but I do not have it, gentlemen.

One of you might perhaps interrupt me and say: "But Socrates, what is your occupation? From where have these slanders come? For surely if you did not busy yourself with something out of the common, all these rumours and talk would not have arisen unless you did something other than most people. Tell us what it is, that we may not speak inadvisedly about you." Anyone who says that seems to be right, and I will try to show you what has caused this reputation and slander. Listen then. Perhaps some of you will think I am jesting, but be sure that all that I shall say is true. What has caused my reputation is none other than a certain kind of wisdom. What kind of wisdom? Human wisdom, perhaps. It may be that I really possess this, while those whom I mentioned just now are wise with a wisdom more than human; else I cannot explain it, for I certainly do not possess it, and whoever says I do is lying and speaks to slander me. Do not create a disturbance, gentlemen, even if you think I am boasting, for the story I shall tell does not originate with me, but I will refer you to a trustworthy source. I shall call upon the god at Delphi as witness to the existence and nature of my wisdom, if it be such. You know Chairephon. He was my friend from youth, and the friend of most of you, as he shared your exile and your return. You surely know the kind of man he was, how impulsive in any course of action. He went to Delphi at one time and ventured to ask the oracle—as I say, gentlemen, do not create a disturbance—he asked if any man was wiser than I, and the Pythian replied that no one was wiser. Chairephon is dead, but his brother will testify to you about this.

Consider that I tell you this because I would inform you about the origin of the slander. When I heard of this reply I asked myself: "Whatever does the god mean? What is his riddle? I am very conscious that I am not wise at all; what then does he mean by saying that I am the wisest? For surely he does not lie; it is not legitimate for him to do so." For a long time I was at a loss as to his meaning; then I very reluctantly turned to some such investigation as this: I went to one of those reputed wise, thinking that there, if anywhere, I could refute the oracle and say to it: "This man is wiser than I, but you said I was." Then, when I examined this man—there is no need for me to tell you his name, he was one of our public men—my experience was something like this: I thought that he appeared wise to many people and especially to himself, but he was not. I then tried to show him that he thought himself wise, but that he was not. As a result he came to dislike me, and so did many of the bystanders. So I withdrew and thought to myself: "I am wiser than this man; it is likely that neither of us knows anything worthwhile, but he thinks he knows something when he does not, whereas when I do not know, neither do I think I know; so I am likely to be wiser than he to this small extent, that I do not think I know what I do not know." After this I approached another man, one of those thought to be wiser than he, and I thought the same thing, and so I came to be disliked both by him and by many others.

After that I proceeded systematically. I realized, to my sorrow and alarm, that I was getting unpopular, but I thought that I must attach the greatest importance to the god's oracle, so I must go to all those who had any reputation for knowledge to examine its meaning. And by the dog,[2] gentlemen of the jury—for I must tell you the truth—I experienced something like this: in my investigation in the service of the god I found that those who had the highest reputation were nearly the most deficient, while those who were thought to be inferior were more knowledgeable. I must give you an account of my journeyings as if they were labours I had undertaken to prove the oracle irrefutable. After the politicians, I went to the poets, the writers of tragedies and dithyrambs and the others, intending in their case to catch myself being more ignorant than they. So I took up those poems with which they seemed to have taken most trouble and asked them what they meant, in order that I might at the same time learn something from them. I am ashamed to tell you the truth, gentlemen, but I must. Almost all the bystanders might have explained the poems better than their authors could. I soon realized that poets do not compose their poems with knowledge, but by some inborn talent and by inspiration, like seers and prophets who also say many fine things without any understanding of what they say. The poets seemed to me to have had a similar experience. At the same time I saw that, because of their poetry, they thought themselves very wise men in other respects, which they were not. So there again I withdrew, thinking that I had the same advantage over them as I had over the politicians.

Finally I went to the craftsmen, for I was conscious of knowing practically nothing, and I knew that I would find that they had knowledge of many fine things. In this I was not mistaken; they knew things I did not know, and to that extent they were wiser than I. But, gentlemen of the jury, the good craftsmen seemed to me to have the same fault as the poets: each of them, because of his success at his craft, thought himself very wise in other most important pursuits, and this error of theirs overshadowed the wisdom they had, so that I asked myself, on behalf of the oracle, whether I should prefer to be as I am, with neither their wisdom nor their ignorance, or to have both. The answer I gave myself and the oracle was that it was to my advantage to be as I am.

As a result of this investigation, gentlemen of the jury, I acquired much unpopularity, of a kind that is hard to deal with and is a heavy burden; many slanders came from these people and a reputation for wisdom, for in each case the bystanders thought that I myself possessed the wisdom that I proved that my interlocutor did not have. What is probable, gentlemen, is that in fact the god is wise and that his oracular response meant that human wisdom is worth little or nothing, and that when he says this man, Socrates, he is using my name as an example, as if he said: "This man among you, mortals, is wisest who, like Socrates, understands that his wisdom is worthless." So even now I continue this investigation as the god bade me—and I go around seeking out anyone, citizen or stranger, whom I think wise. Then if I do not think he is, I come to the assistance of the god and show him that he is not wise. Because of this occupation, I do not have the leisure to engage in public affairs to any extent, nor indeed to look after my own, but I live in great poverty because of my service to the god. . . .

[2]A curious oath, occasionally used by Socrates, it appears in a longer form in the *Gorgias* (482b) as "by the dog, the god of the Egyptians."

I should have to be inordinately fond of life, gentlemen of the jury, to be so unreasonable as to suppose that other men will easily tolerate my company and conversation when you, my fellow citizens, have been unable to endure them, but found them a burden and resented them so that you are now seeking to get rid of them. Far from it, gentlemen. It would be a fine life at my age to be driven out of one city after another, for I know very well that wherever I go the young men will listen to my talk as they do here. If I drive them away, they will themselves persuade their elders to drive me out; if I do not drive them away, their fathers and relations will drive me out on their behalf.

Perhaps someone might say: But Socrates, if you leave us will you not be able to live quietly, without talking? Now this is the most difficult point on which to convince some of you. If I say that it is impossible for me to keep quiet because that means disobeying the god, you will not believe me and will think I am being ironical. On the other hand, if I say that it is the greatest good for a man to discuss virtue every day and those other things about which you hear me conversing and testing myself and others, for the unexamined life is not worth living for man, you will believe me even less.

Is Life Worth Living?

William James

When Mr. Mallock's book with this title appeared some fifteen years ago, the jocose answer that "it depends on the *liver*" had great currency in the newspapers. The answer which I propose to give to-night cannot be jocose. In the words of one of Shakespeare's prologues,—

> "I come no more to make you laugh; things now,
> That bear a weighty and a serious brow,
> Sad, high, and working, full of state and woe,"—

must be my theme. In the deepest heart of all of us there is a corner in which the ultimate mystery of things works sadly; and I know not what such an association as yours intends, nor what you ask of those whom you invite to address you, unless it be to lead you from the surface-glamour of existence, and for an hour at least to make you heedless to the buzzing and jigging and vibration of small interests and excitements that form the tissue of our ordinary consciousness. Without further explanation or apology, then, I ask you to join me in turning an attention, commonly too unwilling, to the profounder bass-note of life. Let us search the lonely depths for an hour together, and see what answers in the last folds and recesses of things our question may find.

Source: "Is Life Worth Living?" by William James, from *The Will to Believe and Other Essays on Popular Philosophy,* © 1956, 32–62. Reprinted by permission of the publisher.

I

With many men the question of life's worth is answered by a temperamental optimism which makes them incapable of believing that anything seriously evil can exist. Our dear old Walt Whitman's works are the standing text-book of this kind of optimism. The mere joy of living is so immense in Walt Whitman's veins that it abolishes the possibility of any other kind of feeling:—

"To breathe the air, how delicious!
To speak, to walk, to seize something by the hand! . . .
To be this incredible God I am! . . .
O amazement of things, even the least particle!
O spirituality of things!
I too carol the Sun, usher'd or at noon, or as now, setting;
I too throb to the brain and beauty of the earth and of all the growths of the earth. . . .

I sing to the last the equalities, modern or old,
I sing the endless finales of things,
I say Nature continues—glory continues.
I praise with electric voice,
For I do not see one imperfection in the universe,
And I do not see one cause or result lamentable at last."

So Rousseau, writing of the nine years he spent at Annecy, with nothing but his happiness to tell:—

"How tell what was neither said nor done nor even thought, but tasted only and felt, with no object of my felicity but the emotion of felicity itself! I rose with the sun, and I was happy; I went to walk, and I was happy; I saw 'Maman,' and I was happy; I left her, and I was happy. I rambled through the woods and over the vineslopes, I wandered in the valleys, I read, I lounged, I worked in the garden, I gathered the fruits, I helped at the indoor work, and happiness followed me everywhere. It was in no one assignable thing; it was all within myself; it could not leave me for a single instant."

If moods like this could be made permanent, and constitutions like these universal, there would never be any occasion for such discourses as the present one. No philosopher would seek to prove articulately that life is worth living, for the fact that it absolutely is so would vouch for itself, and the problem disappear in the vanishing of the question rather than in the coming of anything like a reply. But we are not magicians to make the optimistic temperament universal; and alongside of the deliverances of temperamental optimism concerning life, those of temperamental pessimism always exist, and oppose to them a standing refutation. In what is called "circular insanity," phases of melancholy succeed phases of mania, with no outward cause that we can discover; and often enough to one and the same well person life will present incarnate radiance to-day and incarnate dreariness to-morrow, according to the fluctuations of what the older medical books used to call "the concoction of the humors." In the words of the newspaper joke, "it depends on the liver." Rousseau's ill-balanced constitution undergoes a change, and behold him in his latter evil days a prey to melancholy and black delusions of suspicion and fear. Some men seem launched upon the world even from their birth with souls as incapable of happiness as Walt Whitman's was of gloom, and they have left us their messages in even more lasting verse than his,—the exquisite Leopardi, for example; or our own contemporary, James Thomson, in that pathetic book, *The City of Dreadful Night,* which I think is less well-known than it should be for its literary beauty, simply because men are afraid to quote its words,—they are so gloomy, and at the same time so sincere. In one place the poet describes a congregation gathered to listen to a preacher in a great unillumined cathedral at night. The sermon is too long to quote, but it ends thus:—

" 'O Brothers of sad lives! they are so brief;
A few short years must bring us all relief:
          Can we not bear these years of laboring breath?
But if you would not this poor life fulfil,
Lo, you are free to end it when you will,
          Without the fear of waking after death.'—

"The organ-like vibrations of his voice
          Thrilled through the vaulted aisles and died away;
The yearning of the tones which bade rejoice
          Was sad and tender as a requiem lay:
Our shadowy congregation rested still,
As brooding on that 'End it when you will.'
.   .   .   .   .   .

"Our shadowy congregation rested still,
          As musing on that message we had heard,
And brooding on that 'End it when you will,'
          Perchance awaiting yet some other word;
When keen as lightning through a muffled sky
Sprang forth a shrill and lamentable cry:—

" 'The man speaks sooth, alas! the man speaks sooth;
          We have no personal life beyond the grave;
There is no God; Fate knows nor wrath nor ruth:
          Can I find here the comfort which I crave?

" 'In all eternity I had one chance,
          One few years' term of gracious human life,—
The splendors of the intellect's advance,
          The sweetness of the home with babes and wife;

" 'The social pleasures with their genial wit;
          The fascination of the worlds of art;
The glories of the worlds of Nature lit
          By large imagination's glowing heart;

" 'The rapture of mere being, full of health;
          The careless childhood and the ardent youth;
The strenuous manhood winning various wealth,
          The reverend age serene with life's long truth:

" 'All the sublime prerogatives of Man;
     The storied memories of the times of old,
The patient tracking of the world's great plan
     Through sequences and changes myriadfold.

" 'This chance was never offered me before;
     For me the infinite past is blank and dumb;
This chance recurreth never, nevermore;
     Blank, blank for me the infinite To-come.

" 'And this sole chance was frustrate from my birth,
     A mockery, a delusion; and my breath
Of noble human life upon this earth
     So racks me that I sigh for senseless death.

" 'My wine of life is poison mixed with gall,
     My noonday passes in a nightmare dream,
I worse than lose the years which are my all:
     What can console me for the loss supreme?

" 'Speak not of comfort where no comfort is,
     Speak not at all: can words make foul things fair?
Our life's a cheat, our death a black abyss:
     Hush, and be mute, envisaging despair.'

"This vehement voice came from the northern aisle,
     Rapid and shrill to its abrupt harsh close;
And none gave answer for a certain while,
     For words must shrink from these most wordless woes;
At last the pulpit speaker simply said,
With humid eyes and thoughtful, drooping head,—

" 'My Brother, my poor Brothers, it is thus:
This life holds nothing good for us,
     But it ends soon and nevermore can be;
And we knew nothing of it ere our birth,
And shall know nothing when consigned to earth:
     I ponder these thoughts, and they comfort me.' "

"It ends soon, and never more can be," "Lo, you are free to end it when you will,"—these verses flow truthfully from the melancholy Thomson's pen, and are in truth a consolation for all to whom, as to him, the world is far more like a steady den of fear than a continual fountain of delight. That life is *not* worth living the whole army of suicides declare,—an army whose roll-call, like the famous evening gun of the British army, follows the sun round the world and never terminates. We, too, as we sit here in our comfort, must "ponder these things" also, for we are of one substance with these suicides, and their life is the life we share. The plainest intellectual integrity,—nay, more, the simplest manliness and honor, forbid us to forget their case.

"If suddenly," says Mr. Ruskin, "in the midst of the enjoyments of the palate and
     lightnesses of heart of a London dinner-party, the walls of the chamber were parted,

and through their gap the nearest human beings who were famishing and in misery were borne into the midst of the company feasting and fancy free; if, pale from death, horrible in destitution, broken by despair, body by body they were laid upon the soft carpet, one beside the chair of every guest,—would only the crumbs of the dainties be cast to them; would only a passing glance, a passing thought, be vouchsafed to them? Yet the actual facts, the real relation of each Dives and Lazarus, are not altered by the intervention of the house-wall between the table and the sick-bed,—by the few feet of ground (how few!) which are, indeed, all that separate the merriment from the misery."

II

To come immediately to the heart of my theme, then, what I propose is to imagine ourselves reasoning with a fellow-mortal who is on such terms with life that the only comfort left him is to brood on the assurance, "You may end it when you will." What reasons can we plead that may render such a brother (or sister) willing to take up the burden again? Ordinary Christians, reasoning with would-be suicides, have little to offer them beyond the usual negative, "Thou shalt not." God alone is master of life and death, they say, and it is a blasphemous act to anticipate his absolving hand. But can *we* find nothing richer or more positive than this, no reflections to urge whereby the suicide may actually see, and in all sad seriousness feel, that in spite of adverse appearances even for him life is still worth living? There are suicides and suicides (in the United States about three thousand of them every year), and I must frankly confess that with perhaps the majority of these my suggestions are impotent to deal. Where suicide is the result of insanity or sudden frenzied impulse, reflection is impotent to arrest its headway; and cases like these belong to the ultimate mystery of evil, concerning which I can only offer considerations tending toward religious patience at the end of this hour. My task, let me say now, is practically narrow, and my words are to deal only with that metaphysical *tedium vitæ* which is peculiar to reflecting men. Most of you are devoted, for good or ill, to the reflective life. Many of you are students of philosophy, and have already felt in your own persons the scepticism and unreality that too much grubbing in the abstract roots of things will breed. This is, indeed, one of the regular fruits of the overstudious career. Too much questioning and too little active responsibility lead, almost as often as too much sensualism does, to the edge of the slope, at the bottom of which lie pessimism and the nightmare or suicidal view of life. But to the diseases which reflection breeds, still further reflection can oppose effective remedies; and it is of the melancholy and *Weltschmerz* bred of reflection that I now proceed to speak.

Let me say, immediately, that my final appeal is to nothing more recondite than religious faith. So far as my argument is to be destructive, it will consist in nothing more than the sweeping away of certain views that often keep the springs of religious faith compressed; and so far as it is to be constructive, it will consist in holding up to the light of day certain considerations calculated to let loose these springs in a normal, natural way. Pessimism is essentially a religious disease. In the form of it to which you are most liable, it consists in nothing but a religious demand to which there comes no normal religious reply.

Now, there are two stages of recovery from this disease, two different levels upon which one may emerge from the midnight view to the daylight view of things, and I must treat of them in turn. The second stage is the more complete and joyous, and it corresponds to the freer exercise of religious trust and fancy. There are, as is well known, persons who are naturally very free in this regard, others who are not at all so. There are persons, for instance, whom we find indulging to their heart's content in prospects of immortality; and there are others who experience the greatest difficulty in making such a notion seem real to themselves at all. These latter persons are tied to their senses, restricted to their natural experience; and many of them, moreover, feel a sort of intellectual loyalty to what they call "hard facts," which is positively shocked by the easy excursions into the unseen that other people make at the bare call of sentiment. Minds of either class may, however, be intensely religious. They may equally desire atonement and reconciliation, and crave acquiescence and communion with the total soul of things. But the craving, when the mind is pent in to the hard facts, especially as science now reveals them, can breed pessimism, quite as easily as it breeds optimism when it inspires religious trust and fancy to wing their way to another and a better world.

That is why I call pessimism an essentially religious disease. The nightmare view of life has plenty of organic sources; but its great reflective source has at all times been the contradiction between the phenomena of nature and the craving of the heart to believe that behind nature there is a spirit whose expression nature is. What philosophers call "natural theology" has been one way of appeasing this craving; that poetry of nature in which our English literature is so rich has been another way. Now, suppose a mind of the latter of our two classes, whose imagination is pent in consequently, and who takes its facts "hard"; suppose it, moreover, to feel strongly the craving for communion, and yet to realize how desperately difficult it is to construe the scientific order of nature either theologically or poetically,— and what result *can* there be but inner discord and contradiction? Now, this inner discord (merely as discord) can be relieved in either of two ways: The longing to read the facts religiously may cease, and leave the bare facts by themselves; or, supplementary facts may be discovered or believed-in, which permit the religious reading to go on. These two ways of relief are the two stages of recovery, the two levels of escape from pessimism, to which I made allusion a moment ago, and which the sequel will, I trust, make more clear.

III

Starting then with nature, we naturally tend, if we have the religious craving, to say with Marcus Aurelius, "O Universe! what thou wishest I wish." Our sacred books and traditions tell us of one God who made heaven and earth, and, looking on them, saw that they were good. Yet, on more intimate acquaintance, the visible surfaces of heaven and earth refuse to be brought by us into any intelligible unity at all. Every phenomenon that we would praise there exists cheek by jowl with some contrary phenomenon that cancels all its religious effect upon the mind. Beauty and hideousness, love and cruelty, life and death keep house together in indissoluble partnership; and there gradually steals over us, instead of the old warm notion of a man-loving Deity, that of an awful power that neither hates nor loves, but rolls all things together meaninglessly to a common doom. This is an uncanny, a sinister, a nightmare view of life, and its peculiar *unheimlichkeit,* or poisonousness, lies expressly in our holding two things together which cannot possibly agree,—in our clinging, on the one hand to the demand that there shall be a living spirit of the whole; and, on the other, to the belief that the course of nature must be such a spirit's adequate manifestation and expression. It is in the contradiction between the supposed being of a spirit that encompasses and owns us, and with which we ought to have some communion, and the character of such a spirit as revealed by the visible world's course, that this particular death-in-life paradox and this melancholy-breeding puzzle reside. Carlyle expresses the result in that chapter of his immortal "Sartor Resartus" entitled "The Everlasting No." "I lived," writes poor Teufelsdröckh, "in a continual, indefinite, pining fear; tremulous, pusillanimous, apprehensive of I knew not what: it seemed as if all things in the heavens above and the earth beneath would hurt me; as if the heavens and the earth were but boundless jaws of a devouring monster, wherein I, palpitating, lay waiting to be devoured."

This is the first stage of speculative melancholy. No brute can have this sort of melancholy; no man who is irreligious can become its prey. It is the sick shudder of the frustrated religious demand, and not the mere necessary outcome of animal experience. Teufelsdröckh himself could have made shift to face the general chaos and bedevilment of this world's experiences very well, were he not the victim of an originally unlimited trust and affection towards them. If he might meet them piecemeal, with no suspicion of any whole expressing itself in them, shunning the bitter parts and husbanding the sweet ones, as the occasion served, and as the day was foul or fair, he could have zigzagged toward an easy end, and felt no obligation to make the air vocal with his lamentations. The mood of levity, of "I don't care," is for this world's ills a sovereign and practical anæsthetic. But, no! something deep down in Teufelsdröckh and in the rest of us tells us that there *is* a Spirit in things to which we owe allegiance, and for whose sake we must keep up the serious mood. And so the inner fever and discord also are kept up; for nature taken on her visible surface reveals no such Spirit, and beyond the facts of nature we are at the present stage of our inquiry not supposing ourselves to look.

Now, I do not hesitate frankly and sincerely to confess to you that this real and genuine discord seems to me to carry with it the inevitable bankruptcy of natural religion naïvely and simply taken. There were times when Leibnitzes with their heads buried in monstrous wigs could compose Theodicies, and when stall-fed officials of an established church could prove by the valves in the heart and the round ligament of the hip-joint the existence of a "Moral and Intelligent Contriver of the World." But those times are past; and we of the nineteenth century, with our evolutionary theories and our mechanical philosophies, already know nature too impartially and too well to worship unreservedly any God of whose character she can be an adequate expression. Truly, all we know of good and duty proceeds from nature; but none the less so all we know of evil. Visible nature is all plasticity and indifference,—a moral multiverse, as one might call it, and not a moral universe. To such a harlot we owe no allegiance; with her as a whole we can establish no moral communion; and we are free in our dealings with her several parts to obey or destroy, and to follow no law but that of prudence in coming to terms with such of her particular features as will help us to our private ends. If there be a divine Spirit of the universe, nature, such as we know her, cannot possibly be its *ultimate word* to man. Either there is no Spirit revealed in nature, or else it is inadequately revealed there; and (as all the higher religions have assumed) what we call visible nature, or *this* world, must be but a veil and surface-show whose full meaning resides in a supplementary unseen or *other* world.

I cannot help, therefore, accounting it on the whole a gain (though it may seem for certain poetic constitutions a very sad loss) that the naturalistic superstition, the worship of the God of nature, simply taken as such, should have begun to loosen its hold upon the educated mind. In fact, if I am to express my personal opinion unreservedly, I should say (in spite of its sounding blasphemous at first to certain ears) that the initial step towards getting into healthy ultimate relations with the universe is the act of rebellion against the idea that such a God exists. Such rebellion essentially is that which in the chapter I have quoted from Carlyle goes on to describe:—

> " 'Wherefore, like a coward, dost thou forever pip and whimper, and go cowering and trembling? Despicable biped! . . . Hast thou not a heart; canst thou not suffer whatsoever it be; and, as a Child of Freedom, though outcast, trample Tophet itself under thy feet, while it consumes thee? Let it come, then; I will meet it and defy it!' And as I so thought, there rushed like a stream of fire over my whole soul; and I shook base Fear away from me forever. . . .

> "Thus had the Everlasting No pealed authoritatively through all the recesses of my being, of my Me; and then was it that my whole Me stood up, in native God-created majesty, and recorded its Protest. Such a Protest, the most important transaction in life, may that same Indignation and Defiance, in a psychological point of view, be fitly called. The Everlasting No had said: 'Behold, thou art fatherless, outcast, and the Universe is mine;' to which my whole Me now made answer: 'I am not thine, but Free, and forever hate thee!' From that hour," Teufelsdröckh-Carlyle adds, "I began to be a man."

And our poor friend, James Thomson, similarly writes:—

> "Who is most wretched in this dolorous place?
>   I think myself; yet I would rather be
>   My miserable self than He, than He
> Who formed such creatures to his own disgrace.

> The vilest thing must be less vile than Thou
>   From whom it had its being, God and Lord!
>   Creator of all woe and sin! abhorred,
> Malignant and implacable! I vow

> That not for all Thy power furled and unfurled,
>   For all the temples to Thy glory built,
>   Would I assume the ignominious guilt
> Of having made such men in such a world."

We are familiar enough in this community with the spectacle of persons exulting in their emancipation from belief in the God of their ancestral Calvinism,—him who made the garden and the serpent, and preappointed the eternal fires of hell. Some of them have found humaner gods to worship, others are simply converts from all theology; but, both alike, they assure us that to have got rid of the sophistication of thinking they could feel any reverence or duty toward that impossible idol gave a tremendous happiness to their souls. Now, to make an idol of the spirit of nature, and worship it, also leads to sophistication; and in souls that are religious and would also be scientific the sophistication breeds a philosophical melancholy, from which the first natural step of escape is the denial of the idol; and with the downfall of the idol, whatever lack of positive joyousness may remain, there comes also the downfall of the whimpering and cowering mood. With evil simply taken as such, men can make short work, for their relations with it then are only practical. It looms up no longer so spectrally, it loses all its haunting and perplexing significance, as soon as the mind attacks the instances of it singly, and ceases to worry about their derivation from the "one and only Power."

Here, then, on this stage of mere emancipation from monistic superstition, the would-be suicide may already get encouraging answers to his question about the worth of life. There are in most men instinctive springs of vitality that respond healthily when the burden of metaphysical and infinite responsibility rolls off. The certainty that you now *may* step out of life whenever you please, and that to do so is not blasphemous or monstrous, is itself an immense relief. The thought of suicide is now no longer a guilty challenge and obsession.

> "This little life is all we must endure;
> The grave's most holy peace is ever sure,"—

says Thomson; adding, "I ponder these thoughts, and they comfort me." Meanwhile we can always stand it for twenty-four hours longer, if only to see what to-morrow's newspaper will contain, or what the next postman will bring.

But far deeper forces than this mere vital curiosity are arousable, even in the pessimistically-tending mind; for where the loving and admiring impulses are dead, the hating and fighting impulses will still respond to fit appeals. This evil which we feel so deeply is something that we can also help to overthrow; for its sources, now that no 'Substance' or 'Spirit' is behind them, are finite, and we can deal with each of them in turn. It is, indeed, a remarkable fact that sufferings and hardships do not, as a rule, abate the love of life; they seem, on the contrary, usually to give it a keener zest. The sovereign source of melancholy is repletion. Need and struggle are what excite and inspire us; our hour of triumph is what brings the void. Not the Jews of the captivity, but those of the days of Solomon's glory are those from whom the pessimistic utterances in our Bible come. Germany, when she lay trampled beneath the hoofs of Bonaparte's troopers, produced perhaps the most optimistic and idealistic literature that the world has seen; and not till the French "milliards" were distributed after 1871 did pessimism overrun the country in the shape in which we see it there to-day. The history of our own race is one long commentary on the cheerfulness that comes with fighting ills. Or take the Waldenses, of whom I lately have been reading, as examples of what strong men will endure. In 1485 a papal bull of

Innocent VIII enjoined their extermination. It absolved those who should take up the crusade against them from all ecclesiastical pains and penalties, released them from any oath, legitimized their title to all property which they might have illegally acquired, and promised remission of sins to all who should kill the heretics.

> "There is no town in Piedmont," says a Vaudois writer, "where some of our brethren have not been put to death. Jordan Terbano was burnt alive at Susa; Hippolite Rossiero at Turin; Michael Goneto, an octogenarian, at Sarcena; Vilermin Ambrosio hanged on the Col di Meano; Hugo Chiambs, of Fenestrelle, had his entrails torn from his living body at Turin; Peter Geymarali of Bobbio in like manner had his entrails taken out in Lucerna, and a fierce cat thrust in their place to torture him further; Maria Romano was buried alive at Rocca Patia; Magdalena Fauno underwent the same fate at San Giovanni; Susanna Michelini was bound hand and foot, and left to perish of cold and hunger on the snow at Sarcena: Bartolomeo Fache, gashed with sabres, had the wounds filled up with quicklime, and perished thus in agony at Fenile; Daniel Michelini had his tongue torn out at Bobbo for having praised God; James Baridari perished covered with sulphurous matches which had been forced into his flesh under the nails, between the fingers, in the nostrils, in the lips, and all over the body, and then lighted; Daniel Rovelli had his mouth filled with gunpowder, which, being lighted, blew his head to pieces; . . . Sara Rostignol was slit open from the legs to the bosom, and left so to perish on the road between Eyral and Lucerna; Anna Charbonnier was impaled, and carried thus on a pike from San Giovanni to La Torre."[1]

Und dergleichen mehr! In 1630 the plague swept away one-half of the Vaudois population, including fifteen of their seventeen pastors. The places of these were supplied from Geneva and Dauphiny, and the whole Vaudois people learned French in order to follow their services. More than once their number fell, by unremitting persecution, from the normal standard of twenty-five thousand to about four thousand. In 1686 the Duke of Savoy ordered the three thousand that remained to give up their faith or leave the country. Refusing, they fought the French and Piedmontese armies till only eighty of their fighting men remained alive or uncaptured, when they gave up, and were sent in a body to Switzerland. But in 1689, encouraged by William of Orange and led by one of their pastor-captains, between eight hundred and nine hundred of them returned to conquer their old homes again. They fought their way to Bobi, reduced to four hundred men in the first half year, and met every force sent against them; until at last the Duke of Savoy, giving up his alliance with that abomination of desolation, Louis XIV, restored them to comparative freedom,—since which time they have increased and multiplied in their barren Alpine valleys to this day.

What are our woes and sufferance compared with these? Does not the recital of such a fight so obstinately waged against such odds fill us with resolution against *our* petty powers of darkness,—machine politicians, spoilsmen, and the rest? Life is worth living, no matter what it bring, if only such combats may be carried to successful terminations and one's heel set on the tyrant's throat. To the suicide, then, in his supposed world of multifarious and immoral nature, you can appeal—and appeal in the name of the very evils that make his heart sick there—to wait and see

[1]Quoted by George E. Waring in his book on Tyrol. Compare A. Bérard: Les Vaudois, Lvon, Storck, 1892.

his part of the battle out. And the consent to live on, which you ask of him under these circumstances, is not the sophistical "resignation" which devotees of cowering religions preach: it is not resignation in the sense of licking a despotic Deity's hand. It is, on the contrary; a resignation based on manliness and pride. So long as your would-be suicide leaves an evil of his own unremedied, so long he has strictly no concern with evil in the abstract and at large. The submission which you demand of yourself to the general fact of evil in the world, your apparent acquiescence in it, is here nothing but the conviction that evil at large is *none of your business* until your business with your private particular evils is liquidated and settled up. A challenge of this sort, with proper designation of detail, is one that need only be made to be accepted by men whose normal instincts are not decayed; and your reflective would-be suicide may easily be moved by it to face life with a certain interest again. The sentiment of honor is a very penetrating thing. When you and I, for instance, realize how many innocent beasts have had to suffer in cattle-cars and slaughter-pens and lay down their lives that we might grow up, all fattened and clad, to sit together here in comfort and carry on this discourse, it does, indeed, put our relation to the universe in a more solemn light. "Does not," as a young Amherst philosopher (Xenos Clark, now dead) once wrote, "the acceptance of a happy life upon such terms involve a point of honor?" Are we not bound to take some suffering upon ourselves, to do some self-denying service with our lives, in return for all those lives upon which ours are built? To hear this question is to answer it in but one possible way, if one have a normally constituted heart.

Thus, then, we see that mere instinctive curiosity, pugnacity, and honor may make life on a purely naturalistic basis seem worth living from day to day to men who have cast away all metaphysics in order to get rid of hypochondria, but who are resolved to owe nothing as yet to religion and its more positive gifts. A poor half-way stage, some of you may be inclined to say; but at least you must grant it to be an honest stage; and no man should dare to speak meanly of these instincts which are our nature's best equipment, and to which religion herself must in the last resort address her own peculiar appeals.

IV

And now, in turning to what religion may have to say to the question, I come to what is the soul of my discourse. Religion has meant many things in human history; but when from now onward I use the word I mean to use it in the supernaturalist sense, as declaring that the so-called order of nature, which constitutes this world's experience, is only one portion of the total universe, and that there stretches beyond this visible world an unseen world of which we now know nothing positive, but in its relation to which the true significance of our present mundane life consists. A man's religious faith (whatever more special items of doctrine it may involve) means for me essentially his faith in the existence of an unseen order of some kind in which the riddles of the natural order may be found explained. In the more developed religions the natural world has always been regarded as the mere scaffolding or vestibule of a truer, more eternal world, and affirmed to be a sphere of education, trial, or redemption. In these religions, one must in some fashion die to the natural life before one can enter into life eternal. The notion that this physical world of wind and water, where the sun rises and the moon sets, is absolutely and ultimately the divinely aimed-at and established thing, is one which we find only in very early religions, such as that of the most primitive Jews. It is this natural religion (primitive still, in spite of the fact that poets and men of science whose good-will exceeds their perspicacity keep publishing it in new editions tuned to our contemporary ears) that, as I said a while ago, has suffered definitive bankruptcy in the opinion of a circle of persons, among whom I must count myself, and who are growing more numerous every day. For such persons the physical order of nature, taken simply as science knows it, cannot be held to reveal any one harmonious spiritual intent. It is mere *weather,* as Chauncey Wright called it, doing and undoing without end.

Now, I wish to make you feel, if I can in the short remainder of this hour, that we have a right to believe the physical order to be only a partial order; that we have a right to supplement it by an unseen spiritual order which we assume on trust, if only thereby life may seem to us better worth living again. But as such a trust will seem to some of you sadly mystical and execrably unscientific, I must first say a word or two to weaken the veto which you may consider that science opposes to our act.

There is included in human nature an ingrained naturalism and materialism of mind which can only admit facts that are actually tangible. Of this sort of mind the entity called "science" is the idol. Fondness for the word *scientist* is one of the notes by which you may know its votaries; and its short way of killing any opinion that it disbelieves in is to call it "unscientific." It must be granted that there is no slight excuse for this. Science has made such glorious leaps in the last three hundred years, and extended our knowledge of nature so enormously both in general and in detail; men of science, moreover, have as a class displayed such admirable virtues,—that it is no wonder if the worshippers of science lose their head. In this very University, accordingly, I have heard more than one teacher say that all the fundamental conceptions of truth have already been found by science, and that the future has only the details of the picture to fill in. But the slightest reflection on the real conditions will suffice to show how barbaric such notions are. They show such a lack of scientific imagination, that it is hard to see how one who is actively advancing any part of science can make a mistake so crude. Think how many absolutely new scientific conceptions have arisen in our own generation, how many new problems have been formulated that were never thought of before, and then cast an eye upon the brevity of science's career. It began with Galileo, not three hundred years ago. Four thinkers since Galileo, each informing his successor of what discoveries his own lifetime had seen achieved, might have passed the torch of science into our hands as we sit here in this room. Indeed, for the matter of that, an audience much smaller than the present one, an audience of some five or six score people, if each person in it could speak for his own generation, would carry us away to the black unknown of the human species, to days without a document or monument to tell their tale. Is it credible that such a mushroom knowledge, such a growth overnight as this, *can* represent more than the minutest glimpse of what the universe will really prove to be when adequately understood? No! our science is a drop, our ignorance a sea. Whatever else be certain, this at least is certain,— that the world of our present natural knowledge *is* enveloped in a larger world of *some* sort of whose residual properties we at present can frame no positive idea.

Agnostic positivism, of course, admits this principle theoretically in the most cordial terms, but insists that we must not turn it to any practical use. We have no right, this doctrine tells us, to dream dreams, or suppose anything about the unseen part of the universe, merely because to do so may be for what we are pleased to call our highest interests. We must always wait for sensible evidence for our beliefs; and where such evidence is inaccessible we must frame no hypotheses whatever. Of course this is a safe enough position *in abstracto.* If a thinker had no stake in the unknown, no vital needs, to live or languish according to what the unseen world contained, a philosophic neutrality and refusal to believe either one way or the other would be his wisest cue. But, unfortunately, neutrality is not only inwardly difficult, it is also outwardly unrealizable, where our relations to an alternative are practical and vital. This is because, as the psychologists tell us, belief and doubt are living attitudes, and involve conduct on our part. Our only way, for example, of doubting, or refusing to believe, that a certain thing *is,* is continuing to act as if it were *not.* If, for instance, I refuse to believe that the room is getting cold, I leave the windows open and light no fire just as if it still were warm. If I doubt that you are worthy of my confidence, I keep you uninformed of all my secrets just as if you were *un*worthy of the same. If I doubt the need of insuring my house, I leave it uninsured as much as if I believed there were no need. And so if I must not believe that the world is divine, I can only express that refusal by declining ever to act distinctively as if it were so, which can only mean acting on certain critical occasions as if it were *not* so, or in an irreligious way. There are, you see, inevitable occasions in life when inaction is a kind of action, and must count as action, and when not to be for is to be practically against; and in all such cases strict and consistent neutrality is an unattainable thing.

And, after all, is not this duty of neutrality where only our inner interests would lead us to believe, the most ridiculous of commands? Is it not sheer dogmatic folly to say that our inner interests can have no real connection with the forces that the hidden world may contain? In other cases divinations based on inner interests have proved prophetic enough. Take science itself! Without an imperious inner demand on our part for ideal logical and mathematical harmonies, we should never have attained to proving that such harmonies lie hidden between all the chinks and interstices of the crude natural world. Hardly a law has been established in science, hardly a fact ascertained, which was not first sought after, often with sweat and blood, to gratify an inner need. Whence such needs come from we do not know: we find them in us, and biological psychology so far only classes them with Darwin's "accidental variations." But the inner need of believing that this world of nature is a sign of something more spiritual and eternal than itself is just as strong and authoritative in those who feel it, as the inner need of uniform laws of causation ever can be in a professionally scientific head. The toil of many generations has proved the latter need prophetic. Why *may* not the former one be prophetic, too? And if needs of ours outrun the visible universe, why *may* not that be a sign that an invisible universe is there? What, in short, has authority to debar us from trusting our religious demands? Science as such assuredly has no authority, for she can only say what is, not what is not; and the agnostic "thou shalt not believe without coercive sensible evidence" is simply an expression (free to any one to make) of private personal appetite for evidence of a certain peculiar kind.

Now, when I speak of trusting our religious demands, just what do I mean by "trusting"? Is the word to carry with it license to define in detail an invisible world, and to anathematize and excommunicate those whose trust is different? Certainly not! Our faculties of belief were not primarily given us to make orthodoxies and heresies withal; they were given us to live by. And to trust our religious demands means first of all to live in the light of them, and to act as if the invisible world which they suggest were real. It is a fact of human nature, that men can live and die by the help of a sort of faith that goes without a single dogma or definition. The bare assurance that this natural order is not ultimate but a mere sign or vision, the external staging of a many-storied universe, in which spiritual forces have the last word and are eternal,—this bare assurance is to such men enough to make life seem worth living in spite of every contrary presumption suggested by its circumstances on the natural plane. Destroy this inner assurance, however, vague as it is, and all the light and radiance of existence is extinguished for these persons at a stroke. Often enough the wild-eyed look at life—the suicidal mood—will then set in.

And now the application comes directly home to you and me. Probably to almost every one of us here the most adverse life would seem well worth living, if we only could be *certain* that our bravery and patience with it were terminating and eventuating and bearing fruit somewhere in an unseen spiritual world. But granting we are not certain, does it then follow that a bare trust in such a world is a fool's paradise and lubberland, or rather that it is a living attitude in which we are free to indulge? Well, we are free to trust at our own risks anything that is not impossible, and that can bring analogies to bear in its behalf. That the world of physics is probably not absolute, all the converging multitude of arguments that make in favor of idealism tend to prove; and that our whole physical life may lie soaking in a spiritual atmosphere, a dimension of being that we at present have no organ for apprehending, is vividly suggested to us by the analogy of the life of our domestic animals. Our dogs, for example, are in our human life but not of it. They witness hourly the outward body of events whose inner meaning cannot, by any possible operation, be revealed to their intelligence,— events in which they themselves often play the cardinal part. My terrier bites a teasing boy, for example, and the father demands damages. The dog may be present at every step of the negotiations, and see the money paid, without an inkling of what it all means, without a suspicion that it has anything to do with *him;* and he never *can* know in his natural dog's life. Or take another case which used greatly to impress me in my medical-student days. Consider a poor dog whom they are vivisecting in a laboratory. He lies strapped on a board and shrieking at his executioners, and to his own dark consciousness is literally in a sort of hell. He cannot see a single redeeming ray in the whole business; and yet all these diabolical-seeming events are often controlled by human intentions with which, if his poor benighted mind could only be made to catch a glimpse of them, all that is heroic in him would religiously acquiesce. Healing truth, relief to future sufferings of beast and man, are to be bought by them. It may be genuinely a process of redemption. Lying on his back on the board there he may be performing a function incalculably higher than any that prosperous canine life admits of; and yet, of the whole performance, this function is the one portion that must remain absolutely beyond his ken.

Now turn from this to the life of man. In the dog's life we see the world invisible to him because we live in both worlds. In human life, although we only see our world, and his within it, yet encompassing both these worlds a still wider world may be there, as unseen by us as our world is by him; and to believe in that world *may* be the most essential function that our lives in this world have to perform. But "*may* be! *may* be!" one now hears the positivist contemptuously exclaim; "what use can a scientific life have for maybes?" Well, I reply, the "scientific" life itself has much to do with maybes, and human life at large has everything to do with them. So far as man stands for anything, and is productive or originative at all, his entire vital function may be said to have to deal with maybes. Not a victory is gained, not a deed of faithfulness or courage is done, except upon a maybe; not a service, not a sally of generosity, not a scientific exploration or experiment or textbook, that may not be a mistake. It is only by risking our persons from one hour to another that we live at all. And often enough our faith beforehand in an uncertified result *is the only thing that makes the result come true.* Suppose, for instance, that you are climbing a mountain, and have worked yourself into a position from which the only escape is by a terrible leap. Have faith that you can successfully make it, and your feet are nerved to its accomplishment. But mistrust yourself, and think of all the sweet things you have heard the scientists say of *maybes,* and you will hesitate so long that, at last, all unstrung and trembling, and launching yourself in a moment of despair, you roll in the abyss. In such a case (and it belongs to an enormous class), the part of wisdom as well as of courage is to *believe what is in the line of your needs,* for only by such belief is the need fulfilled. Refuse to believe, and you shall indeed be right, for you shall irretrievably perish. But believe, and again you shall be right, for you shall save yourself. You make one or the other of two possible universes true by your trust or mistrust,—both universes having been only *maybes,* in this particular, before you contributed your act.

Now, it appears to me that the question whether life is worth living is subject to conditions logically much like these. It does, indeed, depend on you *the liver.* If you surrender to the nightmare view and crown the evil edifice by your own suicide, you have indeed made a picture totally black. Pessimism, completed by your act, is true beyond a doubt, so far as your world goes. Your mistrust of life has removed whatever worth your own enduring existence might have given to it; and now, throughout the whole sphere of possible influence of that existence, the mistrust has proved itself to have had divining power. But suppose, on the other hand, that instead of giving way to the nightmare view you cling to it that this world is not the *ultimatum.* Suppose you find yourself a very well-spring, as Wordsworth says, of—

> "Zeal, and the virtue to exist by faith
> As soldiers live by courage; as, by strength
> Of heart, the sailor fights with roaring seas."

Suppose, however thickly evils crowd upon you, that your unconquerable subjectivity proves to be their match, and that you find a more wonderful joy than any passive pleasure can bring in trusting ever in the larger whole. Have you not now made life worth living on these terms? What sort of a thing would life really be, with your qualities ready for a tussle with it, if it only brought fair weather and gave these higher faculties of yours no scope? Please remember that optimism and pessimism are definitions of the world, and that our own reactions on the world, small as they are in bulk, are integral parts of the whole thing, and necessarily help to determine the definition. They may even be the decisive elements in determining the definition. A large mass can have its unstable equilibrium overturned by the addition of a feather's weight; a long phrase may have its sense reversed by the addition of the three letters *n-o-t.* This life *is* worth living, we can say, *since it is what we make it, from the moral point of view;* and we are determined to make it from that point of view, so far as we have anything to do with it, a success.

Now, in this description of faiths that verify themselves I have assumed that our faith in an invisible order is what inspires those efforts and that patience which make this visible order good for moral men. Our faith in the seen world's goodness (goodness now meaning fitness for successful moral and religious life) has verified itself by leaning on our faith in the unseen world. But will our faith in the unseen world similarly verify itself? Who knows?

Once more it is a case of *maybe;* and once more *maybes* are the essence of the situation. I confess that I do not see why the very existence of an invisible world may not in part depend on the personal response which any one of us may make to the religious appeal. God himself, in short, may draw vital strength and increase of very being from our fidelity. For my own part, I do not know what the sweat and blood and tragedy of this life mean, if they mean anything short of this. If this life be not a real fight, in which something is eternally gained for the universe by success, it is no better than a game of private theatricals from which one may withdraw at will. But it *feels* like a real fight,—as if there were something really wild in the universe which we, with all our idealities and faithfulnesses, are needed to redeem; and first of all to redeem our own hearts from atheisms and fears. For such a half-wild, half-saved universe our nature is adapted. The deepest thing in our nature is this *Binnenleben* (as a German doctor lately has called it), this dumb region of the heart in which we dwell alone with our willingnesses and unwillingnesses, our faiths and fears. As through the cracks and crannies of caverns those waters exude from the earth's bosom which then form the fountain-heads of springs, so in these crepuscular depths of personality the sources of all our outer deeds and decisions take their rise. Here is our deepest organ of communication with the nature of things; and compared with these concrete movements of our soul all abstract statements and scientific arguments—the veto, for example, which the strict positivist pronounces upon our faith—sound to us like mere chatterings of the teeth. For here possibilities, not finished facts, are the realities with which we have actively to deal; and to quote my friend William Salter, of the Philadelphia Ethical Society, "as the essence of courage is to stake one's life on a possibility, so the essence of faith is to believe that the possibility exists."

These, then, are my last words to you: Be not afraid of life. Believe that life *is* worth living, and your belief will help create the fact. The "scientific proof" that you are right may not be clear before the day of judgment (or some stage of being which that expression may serve to symbolize) is reached. But the faithful fighters of this hour, or the beings that then and there will represent them, may then turn to the faint-hearted, who here decline to go on, with words like those with which Henry IV greeted the tardy Crillon after a great victory had been gained: "Hang yourself, brave Crillon! we fought at Arques, and you were not there."

An Absurd Reasoning (excerpt)

Albert Camus

ABSURDITY AND SUICIDE

There is but one truly serious philosophical problem, and that is suicide. Judging whether life is or is not worth living amounts to answering the fundamental question of philosophy. All the rest—whether or not the world has three dimensions, whether the mind has nine or twelve categories—comes afterwards. These are games; one must first answer. And if it is true, as Nietzsche claims, that a philosopher, to deserve our respect, must preach by example, you can appreciate the importance of that reply, for it will precede the definitive act. These are facts the heart can feel; yet they call for careful study before they become clear to the intellect.

If I ask myself how to judge that this question is more urgent than that, I reply that one judges by the actions it entails. I have never seen anyone die for the ontological argument. Galileo, who held a scientific truth of great importance, abjured it with the greatest ease as soon as it endangered his life. In a certain sense, he did right.[1] That truth was not worth the stake. Whether the earth or the sun revolves around the other is a matter of profound indifference. To tell the truth, it is a futile question. On the other hand, I see many people die because they judge that life is not worth living. I see others paradoxically getting killed for the ideas or illusions that give them a reason for living (what is called a reason for living is also an excellent reason for dying). I therefore conclude that the meaning of life is the most urgent of questions. How to answer it? On all essential problems (I mean thereby those that run the risk of leading to death or those that intensify the passion of living) there are probably but two methods of thought: the method of La Palisse and the method of Don Quixote. Solely the balance between evidence and lyricism can allow us to achieve simultaneously emotion and lucidity. In a subject at once so humble and so heavy with emotion, the learned and classical dialectic

---

[1]From the point of view of the relative value of truth. On the other hand, from the point of view of virile behavior, this scholar's fragility may well make us smile.

Source: Excerpt from "An Absurd Reasoning" from *The Myth of Sisyphus and Other Essays* by Albert Camus, trans. Justin O'Brien. Copyright © 1955 by Alfred A. Knopf, Inc. Reprinted by permission of the publisher.

must yield, one can see, to a more modest attitude of mind deriving at one and the same time from common sense and understanding.

Suicide has never been dealt with except as a social phenomenon. On the contrary, we are concerned here, at the outset, with the relationship between individual thought and suicide. An act like this is prepared within the silence of the heart, as is a great work of art. The man himself is ignorant of it. One evening he pulls the trigger or jumps. Of an apartment-building manager who had killed himself I was told that he had lost his daughter five years before, that he had changed greatly since, and that that experience had "undermined" him. A more exact word cannot be imagined. Beginning to think is beginning to be undermined. Society has but little connection with such beginnings. The worm is in man's heart. That is where it must be sought. One must follow and understand this fatal game that leads from lucidity in the face of existence to flight from light.

There are many causes for a suicide, and generally the most obvious ones were not the most powerful. Rarely is suicide committed (yet the hypothesis is not excluded) through reflection. What sets off the crisis is almost always unverifiable. Newspapers often speak of "personal sorrows" or of "incurable illness." These explanations are plausible. But one would have to know whether a friend of the desperate man had not that very day addressed him indifferently. He is the guilty one. For that is enough to precipitate all the rancors and all the boredom still in suspension.[2]

But if it is hard to fix the precise instant, the subtle step when the mind opted for death, it is easier to deduce from the act itself the consequences it implies. In a sense, and as in melodrama, killing yourself amounts to confessing. It is confessing that life is too much for you or that you do not understand it. Let's not go too far in such analogies, however, but rather return to everyday words. It is merely confessing that that "is not worth the trouble." Living, naturally, is never easy. You continue making the gestures commanded by existence for many reasons, the first of which is habit. Dying voluntarily implies that you have recognized, even instinctively, the ridiculous character of that habit, the absence of any profound reason for living, the insane character of that daily agitation, and the uselessness of suffering.

What, then, is that incalculable feeling that deprives the mind of the sleep necessary to life? A world that can be explained even with bad reasons is a familiar world. But, on the other hand, in a universe suddenly divested of illusions and lights, man feels an alien, a stranger. His exile is without remedy since he is deprived of the memory of a lost home or the hope of a promised land. This divorce between man and his life, the actor and his setting, is properly the feeling of absurdity. All healthy men having thought of their own suicide, it can be seen, without further explanation, that there is a direct connection between this feeling and the longing for death.

The subject of this essay is precisely this relationship between the absurd and suicide, the exact degree to which suicide is a solution to the absurd. The principle

---

[2]Let us not miss this opportunity to point out the relative character of this essay. Suicide may indeed be related to much more honorable considerations—for example, the political suicides of protest, as they were called, during the Chinese revolution.

can be established that for a man who does not cheat, what he believes to be true must determine his action. Belief in the absurdity of existence must then dictate his conduct. It is legitimate to wonder, clearly and without false pathos, whether a conclusion of this importance requires forsaking as rapidly as possible an incomprehensible condition. I am speaking, of course, of men inclined to be in harmony with themselves.

Stated clearly, this problem may seem both simple and insoluble. But it is wrongly assumed that simple questions involve answers that are no less simple and that evidence implies evidence. *A priori* and reversing the terms of the problem, just as one does or does not kill oneself, it seems that there are but two philosophical solutions, either yes or no. This would be too easy. But allowance must be made for those who, without concluding, continue questioning. Here I am only slightly indulging in irony: this is the majority. I notice also that those who answer "no" act as if they thought "yes." As a matter of fact, if I accept the Nietzschean criterion, they think "yes" in one way or another. On the other hand, it often happens that those who commit suicide were assured of the meaning of life. These contradictions are constant. It may even be said that they have never been so keen as on this point where, on the contrary, logic seems so desirable. It is a commonplace to compare philosophical theories and the behavior of those who profess them. But it must be said that of the thinkers who refused a meaning to life none except Kirilov who belongs to literature, Peregrinos who is born of legend,[3] and Jules Lequier who belongs to hypothesis, admitted his logic to the point of refusing that life. Schopenhauer is often cited, as a fit subject for laughter, because he praised suicide while seated at a well-set table. This is no subject for joking. That way of not taking the tragic seriously is not so grievous, but it helps to judge a man.

In the face of such contradictions and obscurities must we conclude that there is no relationship between the opinion one has about life and the act one commits to leave it? Let us not exaggerate in this direction. In a man's attachment to life there is something stronger than all the ills in the world. The body's judgment is as good as the mind's, and the body shrinks from annihilation. We get into the habit of living before acquiring the habit of thinking. In that race which daily hastens us toward death, the body maintains its irreparable lead. In short, the essence of that contradiction lies in what I shall call the act of eluding because it is both less and more than diversion in the Pascalian sense. Eluding is the invariable game. The typical act of eluding, the fatal evasion that constitutes the third theme of this essay, is hope. Hope of another life one must "deserve" or trickery of those who live not for life itself but for some great idea that will transcend it, refine it, give it a meaning, and betray it.

Thus everything contributes to spreading confusion. Hitherto, and it has not been wasted effort, people have played on words and pretended to believe that refusing to grant a meaning to life necessarily leads to declaring that it is not worth living. In truth, there is no necessary common measure between these two judgments. One merely has to refuse to be misled by the confusions, divorces, and

---

[3]I have heard of an emulator of Peregrinos, a post-war writer who, after having finished his first book, committed suicide to attract attention to his work. Attention was in fact attracted, but the book was judged no good.

inconsistencies previously pointed out. One must brush everything aside and go straight to the real problem. One kills oneself because life is not worth living, that is certainly a truth—yet an unfruitful one because it is a truism. But does that insult to existence, that flat denial in which it is plunged come from the fact that it has no meaning? Does its absurdity require one to escape it through hope or suicide—this is what must be clarified, hunted down, and elucidated while brushing aside all the rest. Does the Absurd dictate death? This problem must be given priority over others, outside all methods of thought and all exercises of the disinterested mind. Shades of meaning, contradictions, the psychology that an "objective" mind can always introduce into all problems have no place in this pursuit and this passion. It calls simply for an unjust—in other words, logical—thought. That is not easy. It is always easy to be logical. It is almost impossible to be logical to the bitter end. Men who die by their own hand consequently follow to its conclusion their emotional inclination. Reflection on suicide gives me an opportunity to raise the only problem to interest me: is there a logic to the point of death? I cannot know unless I pursue, without reckless passion, in the sole light of evidence, the reasoning of which I am here suggesting the source. This is what I call an absurd reasoning. Many have begun it. I do not yet know whether or not they kept to it.

When Karl Jaspers, revealing the impossibility of constituting the world as a unity, exclaims: "This limitation leads me to myself, where I can no longer withdraw behind an objective point of view that I am merely representing, where neither I myself nor the existence of others can any longer become an object for me," he is evoking after many others those waterless deserts where thought reaches its confines. After many others, yes indeed, but how eager they were to get out of them! At that last crossroad where thought hesitates, many men have arrived and even some of the humblest. They then abdicated what was most precious to them, their life. Others, princes of the mind, abdicated likewise, but they initiated the suicide of their thought in its purest revolt. The real effort is to stay there, rather, in so far as that is possible, and to examine closely the odd vegetation of those distant regions. Tenacity and acumen are privileged spectators of this inhuman show in which absurdity, hope, and death carry on their dialogue. The mind can then analyze the figures of that elementary yet subtle dance before illustrating them and reliving them itself. . . .

I am taking the liberty at this point of calling the existential attitude philosophical suicide. But this does not imply a judgment. It is a convenient way of indicating the movement by which a thought negates itself and tends to transcend itself in its very negation. For the existentials negation is their God. To be precise, that god is maintained only through the negation of human reason.[4] But, like suicides, gods change with men. There are many ways of leaping, the essential being to leap. Those redeeming negations, those ultimate contradictions which negate the obstacle that has not yet been leaped over, may spring just as well (this is the paradox at which this reasoning aims) from a certain religious inspiration as from the rational order. They always lay claim to the eternal, and it is solely in this that they take the leap.

---

[4]Let me assert again: it is not the affirmation of God that is questioned here, but rather the logic leading to that affirmation.

It must be repeated that the reasoning developed in this essay leaves out altogether the most widespread spiritual attitude of our enlightened age: the one, based on the principle that all is reason, which aims to explain the world. It is natural to give a clear view of the world after accepting the idea that it must be clear. That is even legitimate, but does not concern the reasoning we are following out here. In fact, our aim is to shed light upon the step taken by the mind when, starting from a philosophy of the world's lack of meaning, it ends up by finding a meaning and depth in it. The most touching of those steps is religious in essence; it becomes obvious in the theme of the irrational. But the most paradoxical and most significant is certainly the one that attributes rational reasons to a world it originally imagined as devoid of any guiding principle. It is impossible in any case to reach the consequences that concern us without having given an idea of this new attainment of the spirit of nostalgia.

I shall examine merely the theme of "the Intention" made fashionable by Husserl and the phenomenologists. I have already alluded to it. Originally Husserl's method negates the classic procedure of the reason. Let me repeat. Thinking is not unifying or making the appearance familiar under the guise of a great principle. Thinking is learning all over again how to see, directing one's consciousness, making of every image a privileged place. In other words, phenomenology declines to explain the world, it wants to be merely a description of actual experience. It confirms absurd thought in its initial assertion that there is no truth, but merely truths. From the evening breeze to this hand on my shoulder, everything has its truth. Consciousness illuminates it by paying attention to it. Consciousness does not form the object of its understanding, it merely focuses, it is the act of attention, and, to borrow a Bergsonian image, it resembles the projector that suddenly focuses on an image. The difference is that there is no scenario, but a successive and incoherent illustration. In that magic lantern all the pictures are privileged. Consciousness suspends in experience the objects of its attention. Through its miracle it isolates them. Henceforth they are beyond all judgments. This is the "intention" that characterizes consciousness. But the word does not imply any idea of finality; it is taken in its sense of "direction": its only value is topographical.

At first sight, it certainly seems that in this way nothing contradicts the absurd spirit. That apparent modesty of thought that limits itself to describing what it declines to explain, that intentional discipline whence result paradoxically a profound enrichment of experience and the rebirth of the world in its prolixity are absurd procedures. At least at first sight. For methods of thought, in this case as elsewhere, always assume two aspects, one psychological and the other metaphysical.[5] Thereby they harbor two truths. If the theme of the intentional claims to illustrate merely a psychological attitude, by which reality is drained instead of being explained, nothing in fact separates it from the absurd spirit. It aims to enumerate what it cannot transcend. It affirms solely that without any unifying principle thought can still take delight in describing and understanding every aspect of experience. The truth involved then for each of those aspects is psychological in nature. It simply testifies to the "interest" that reality can offer. It is

---

[5]Even the most rigorous epistemologies imply metaphysics. And to such a degree that the metaphysic of many contemporary thinkers consists in having nothing but an epistemology.

a way of awaking a sleeping world and of making it vivid to the mind. But if one attempts to extend and give a rational basis to that notion of truth, if one claims to discover in this way the "essence" of each object of knowledge, one restores its depth to experience. For an absurd mind that is incomprehensible. Now, it is this wavering between modesty and assurance that is noticeable in the intentional attitude, and this shimmering of phenomenological thought will illustrate the absurd reasoning better than anything else.

For Husserl speaks likewise of "extra-temporal essences" brought to light by the intention, and he sounds like Plato. All things are not explained by one thing but by all things. I see no difference. To be sure, those ideas or those essences that consciousness "effectuates" at the end of every description are not yet to be considered perfect models. But it is asserted that they are directly present in each datum of perception. There is no longer a single idea explaining everything, but an infinite number of essences giving a meaning to an infinite number of objects. The world comes to a stop, but also lights up. Platonic realism becomes intuitive, but it is still realism. Kierkegaard was swallowed up in his God; Parmenides plunged thought into the One. But here thought hurls itself into an abstract polytheism. But this is not all: hallucinations and fictions likewise belong to "extra-temporal essences." In the new world of ideas, the species of centaurs collaborates with the more modest species of metropolitan man.

For the absurd man, there was a truth as well as a bitterness in that purely psychological opinion that all aspects of the world are privileged. To say that everything is privileged is tantamount to saying that everything is equivalent. But the metaphysical aspect of that truth is so far-reaching that through an elementary reaction he feels closer perhaps to Plato. He is taught, in fact, that every image presupposes an equally privileged essence. In this idea world without hierarchy, the formal army is composed solely of generals. To be sure, transcendency had been eliminated. But a sudden shift in thought brings back into the world a sort of fragmentary immanence which restores to the universe its depth.

Am I to fear having carried too far a theme handled with greater circumspection by its creators? I read merely these assertions of Husserl, apparently paradoxical yet rigorously logical if what precedes is accepted: "That which is true is true absolutely, in itself; truth is one, identical with itself, however different the creatures who perceive it, men, monsters, angels or gods." Reason triumphs and trumpets forth with that voice, I cannot deny. What can its assertions mean in the absurd world? The perception of an angel or a god has no meaning for me. That geometrical spot where divine reason ratifies mine will always be incomprehensible to me. There, too, I discern a leap, and though performed in the abstract, it nonetheless means for me forgetting just what I do not want to forget. When farther on Husserl exclaims: "If all masses subject to attraction were to disappear, the law of attraction would not be destroyed but would simply remain without any possible application," I know that I am faced with a metaphysic of consolation. And if I want to discover the point where thought leaves the path of evidence, I have only to reread the parallel reasoning that Husserl voices regarding the mind: "If we could contemplate clearly the exact laws of psychic processes, they would be seen to be likewise eternal and invariable, like the basic laws of theoretical natural science. Hence they would be valid even if there were no psychic process."

Even if the mind were not, its laws would be! I see then that of a psychological truth Husserl aims to make a rational rule: after having denied the integrating power of human reason, he leaps by this expedient to eternal Reason.

Husserl's theme of the "concrete universe" cannot then surprise me. If I am told that all essences are not formal but that some are material, that the first are the object of logic and the second of science, this is merely a question of definition. The abstract, I am told, indicates but a part, without consistency in itself, of a concrete universal. But the wavering already noted allows me to throw light on the confusion of these terms. For that may mean that the concrete object of my attention, this sky, the reflection of that water on this coat, alone preserve the prestige of the real that my interest isolates in the world. And I shall not deny it. But that may mean also that this coat itself is universal, has its particular and sufficient essence, belongs to the world of forms. I then realize that merely the order of the procession has been changed. This world has ceased to have its reflection in a higher universe, but the heaven of forms is figured in the host of images of this earth. This changes nothing for me. Rather than encountering here a taste for the concrete, the meaning of the human condition, I find an intellectualism sufficiently unbridled to generalize the concrete itself.

It is futile to be amazed by the apparent paradox that leads thought to its own negation by the opposite paths of humiliated reason and triumphal reason. From the abstract god of Husserl to the dazzling god of Kierkegaard the distance is not so great. Reason and the irrational lead to the same preaching. In truth the way matters but little; the will to arrive suffices. The abstract philosopher and the religious philosopher start out from the same disorder and support each other in the same anxiety. But the essential is to explain. Nostalgia is stronger here than knowledge. It is significant that the thought of the epoch is at once one of the most deeply imbued with a philosophy of the nonsignificance of the world and one of the most divided in its conclusions. It is constantly oscillating between extreme rationalization of reality which tends to break up that thought into standard reasons and its extreme irrationalization which tends to deify it. But this divorce is only apparent. It is a matter of reconciliation, and, in both cases, the leap suffices. It is always wrongly thought that the notion of reason is a one-way notion. To tell the truth, however rigorous it may be in its ambition, this concept is nonetheless just as unstable as others. Reason bears a quite human aspect, but it also is able to turn toward the divine. Since Plotinus, who was the first to reconcile it with the eternal climate, it has learned to turn away from the most cherished of its principles, which is contradiction, in order to integrate into it the strangest, the quite magic one of participation.[6] It is an instrument of thought and not thought itself. Above all, a man's thought is his nostalgia.

Just as reason was able to soothe the melancholy of Plotinus, it provides modern anguish the means of calming itself in the familiar setting of the eternal. The

[6]A.—At that time reason had to adapt itself or die. It adapts itself. With Plotinus, after being logical it becomes æsthetic. Metaphor takes the place of the syllogism. B.—Moreover, this is not Plotinus' only contribution to phenomenology. This whole attitude is already contained in the concept so dear to the Alexandrian thinker that there is not only an idea of man but also an idea of Socrates.

absurd mind has less luck. For it the world is neither so rational nor so irrational. It is unreasonable and only that. With Husserl the reason eventually has no limits at all. The absurd, on the contrary, establishes its limits since it is powerless to calm its anguish. Kierkegaard independently asserts that a single limit is enough to negate that anguish. But the absurd does not go so far. For it that limit is directed solely at the reason's ambitions. The theme of the irrational, as it is conceived by the existentials, is reason becoming confused and escaping by negating itself. The absurd is lucid reason noting its limits.

Only at the end of this difficult path does the absurd man recognize his true motives. Upon comparing his inner exigence and what is then offered him, he suddenly feels he is going to turn away. In the universe of Husserl the world becomes clear and that longing for familiarity that man's heart harbors becomes useless. In Kierkegaard's apocalypse that desire for clarity must be given up if it wants to be satisfied. Sin is not so much knowing (if it were, everybody would be innocent) as wanting to know. Indeed, it is the only sin of which the absurd man can feel that it constitutes both his guilt and his innocence. He is offered a solution in which all the past contradictions have become merely polemical games. But this is not the way he experienced them. Their truth must be preserved, which consists in not being satisfied. He does not want preaching.

My reasoning wants to be faithful to the evidence that aroused it. That evidence is the absurd. It is that divorce between the mind that desires and the world that disappoints, my nostalgia for unity, this fragmented universe and the contradiction that binds them together. Kierkegaard suppresses my nostalgia and Husserl gathers together that universe. That is not what I was expecting. It was a matter of living and thinking with those dislocations, of knowing whether one had to accept or refuse. There can be no question of masking the evidence, of suppressing the absurd by denying one of the terms of its equation. It is essential to know whether one can live with it or whether, on the other hand, logic commands one to die of it. I am not interested in philosophical suicide, but rather in plain suicide. I merely wish to purge it of its emotional content and know its logic and its integrity. Any other position implies for the absurd mind deceit and the mind's retreat before what the mind itself has brought to light. Husserl claims to obey the desire to escape "the inveterate habit of living and thinking in certain well-known and convenient conditions of existence," but the final leap restores in him the eternal and its comfort. The leap does not represent an extreme danger as Kierkegaard would like it to do. The danger, on the contrary, lies in the subtle instant that precedes the leap. Being able to remain on that dizzying crest—that is integrity and the rest is subterfuge. I know also that never has helplessness inspired such striking harmonies as those of Kierkegaard. But if helplessness has its place in the indifferent landscapes of history, it has none in a reasoning whose exigence is now known.

ABSURD FREEDOM

Now the main thing is done, I hold certain facts from which I cannot separate. What I know, what is certain, what I cannot deny, what I cannot reject—this is what counts. I can negate everything of that part of me that lives on vague nostalgias, except this desire for unity, this longing to solve, this need for clarity and cohesion. I can refute everything in this world surrounding me that offends or enraptures me, except this chaos, this sovereign chance and this divine equivalence which springs from anarchy. I don't know whether this world has a meaning that transcends it. But I know that I do not know that meaning and that it is impossible for me just now to know it. What can a meaning outside my condition mean to me? I can understand only in human terms. What I touch, what resists me—that is what I understand. And these two certainties—my appetite for the absolute and for unity and the impossibility of reducing this world to a rational and reasonable principle— I also know that I cannot reconcile them. What other truth can I admit without lying, without bringing in a hope I lack and which means nothing within the limits of my condition?

If I were a tree among trees, a cat among animals, this life would have a meaning, or rather this problem would not arise, for I should belong to this world. I should *be* this world to which I am now opposed by my whole consciousness and my whole insistence upon familiarity. This ridiculous reason is what sets me in opposition to all creation. I cannot cross it out with a stroke of the pen. What I believe to be true I must therefore preserve. What seems to me so obvious, even against me, I must support. And what constitutes the basis of that conflict, of that break between the world and my mind, but the awareness of it? If therefore I want to preserve it, I can through a constant awareness, ever revived, ever alert. This is what, for the moment, I must remember. At this moment the absurd, so obvious and yet so hard to win, returns to a man's life and finds its home there. At this moment, too, the mind can leave the arid, dried-up path of lucid effort. That path now emerges in daily life. It encounters the world of the anonymous impersonal pronoun "one," but henceforth man enters in with his revolt and his lucidity. He has forgotten how to hope. This hell of the present is his Kingdom at last. All problems recover their sharp edge. Abstract evidence retreats before the poetry of forms and colors. Spiritual conflicts become embodied and return to the abject and magnificent shelter of man's heart. None of them is settled. But all are transfigured. Is one going to die, escape by the leap, rebuild a mansion of ideas and forms to one's own scale? Is one, on the contrary, going to take up the heart-rending and marvelous wager of the absurd? Let's make a final effort in this regard and draw all our conclusions. The body, affection, creation, action, human nobility will then resume their places in this mad world. At last man will again find there the wine of the absurd and the bread of indifference on which he feeds his greatness.

Let us insist again on the method: it is a matter of persisting. At a certain point on his path the absurd man is tempted. History is not lacking in either religions or prophets, even without gods. He is asked to leap. All he can reply is that he doesn't fully understand, that it is not obvious. Indeed, he does not want to do anything but what he fully understands. He is assured that this is the sin of pride, but he does not understand the notion of sin; that perhaps hell is in store, but he has not enough imagination to visualize that strange future; that he is losing immortal life, but that seems to him an idle consideration. An attempt is made to get him to admit his guilt. He feels innocent. To tell the truth, that is all he feels—his irreparable innocence.

This is what allows him everything. Hence, what he demands of himself is to live *solely* with what he knows, to accommodate himself to what is, and to bring in nothing that is not certain. He is told that nothing is. But this at least is a certainty. And it is with this that he is concerned: he wants to find out if it is possible to live *without appeal.*

Now I can broach the notion of suicide. It has already been felt what solution might be given. At this point the problem is reversed. It was previously a question of finding out whether or not life had to have a meaning to be lived. It now becomes clear, on the contrary, that it will be lived all the better if it has no meaning. Living an experience, a particular fate, is accepting it fully. Now, no one will live this fate, knowing it to be absurd, unless he does everything to keep before him that absurd brought to light by consciousness. Negating one of the terms of the opposition on which he lives amounts to escaping it. To abolish conscious revolt is to elude the problem. The theme of permanent revolution is thus carried into individual experience. Living is keeping the absurd alive. Keeping it alive is, above all, contemplating it. Unlike Eurydice, the absurd dies only when we turn away from it. One of the only coherent philosophical positions is thus revolt. It is a constant confrontation between man and his own obscurity. It is an insistence upon an impossible transparency. It challenges the world anew every second. Just as danger provided man the unique opportunity of seizing awareness, so metaphysical revolt extends awareness to the whole of experience. It is that constant presence of man in his own eyes. It is not aspiration, for it is devoid of hope. That revolt is the certainty of a crushing fate, without the resignation that ought to accompany it.

This is where it is seen to what a degree absurd experience is remote from suicide. It may be thought that suicide follows revolt—but wrongly. For it does not represent the logical outcome of revolt. It is just the contrary by the consent it presupposes. Suicide, like the leap, is acceptance at its extreme. Everything is over and man returns to his essential history. His future, his unique and dreadful future—he sees and rushes toward it. In its way, suicide settles the absurd. It engulfs the absurd in the same death. But I know that in order to keep alive, the absurd cannot be settled. It escapes suicide to the extent that it is simultaneously awareness and rejection of death. It is, at the extreme limit of the condemned man's last thought, that shoelace that despite everything he sees a few yards away, on the very brink of his dizzying fall. The contrary of suicide, in fact, is the man condemned to death.

That revolt gives life its value. Spread out over the whole length of a life, it restores its majesty to that life. To a man devoid of blinders, there is no finer sight than that of the intelligence at grips with a reality that transcends it. The sight of human pride is unequaled. No disparagement is of any use. That discipline that the mind imposes on itself, that will conjured up out of nothing, that face-to-face struggle have something exceptional about them. To impoverish that reality whose inhumanity constitutes man's majesty is tantamount to impoverishing him himself. I understand then why the doctrines that explain everything to me also debilitate me at the same time. They relieve me of the weight of my own life, and yet I must carry it alone. At this juncture, I cannot conceive that a skeptical metaphysics can be joined to an ethics of renunciation.

Consciousness and revolt, these rejections are the contrary of renunciation. Everything that is indomitable and passionate in a human heart quickens them, on the contrary, with its own life. It is essential to die unreconciled and not of one's own free will. Suicide is a repudiation. The absurd man can only drain everything to the bitter end, and deplete himself. The absurd is his extreme tension, which he maintains constantly by solitary effort, for he knows that in that consciousness and in that day-to-day revolt he gives proof of his only truth, which is defiance. This is a first consequence.

If I remain in that prearranged position which consists in drawing all the conclusions (and nothing else) involved in a newly discovered notion, I am faced with a second paradox. In order to remain faithful to that method, I have nothing to do with the problem of metaphysical liberty. Knowing whether or not man is free doesn't interest me. I can experience only my own freedom. As to it, I can have no general notions, but merely a few clear insights. The problem of "freedom as such" has no meaning. For it is linked in quite a different way with the problem of God. Knowing whether or not man is free involves knowing whether he can have a master. The absurdity peculiar to this problem comes from the fact that the very notion that makes the problem of freedom possible also takes away all its meaning. For in the presence of God there is less a problem of freedom than a problem of evil. You know the alternative: either we are not free and God the all-powerful is responsible for evil. Or we are free and responsible but God is not all-powerful. All the scholastic subtleties have neither added anything to nor subtracted anything from the acuteness of this paradox.

This is why I cannot get lost in the glorification or the mere definition of a notion which eludes me and loses its meaning as soon as it goes beyond the frame of reference of my individual experience. I cannot understand what kind of freedom would be given me by a higher being. I have lost the sense of hierarchy. The only conception of freedom I can have is that of the prisoner or the individual in the midst of the State. The only one I know is freedom of thought and action. Now if the absurd cancels all my chances of eternal freedom, it restores and magnifies, on the other hand, my freedom of action. That privation of hope and future means an increase in man's availability.

Before encountering the absurd, the everyday man lives with aims, a concern for the future or for justification (with regard to whom or what is not the question). He weighs his chances, he counts on "someday," his retirement or the labor of his sons. He still thinks that something in his life can be directed. In truth, he acts as if he were free, even if all the facts make a point of contradicting that liberty. But after the absurd, everything is upset. That idea that "I am," my way of acting as if everything has a meaning (even if, on occasion, I said that nothing has)—all that is given the lie in vertiginous fashion by the absurdity of a possible death. Thinking of the future, establishing aims for oneself, having preferences—all this presupposes a belief in freedom, even if one occasionally ascertains that one doesn't feel it. But at that moment I am well aware that that higher liberty, that freedom *to be,* which alone can serve as basis for a truth, does not exist. Death is there as the only reality. After death the chips are down. I am not even free, either, to perpetuate myself, but a slave, and, above all, a slave without hope of an eternal revolution, without recourse to contempt.

And who without revolution and without contempt can remain a slave? What freedom can exist in the fullest sense without assurance of eternity?

But at the same time the absurd man realizes that hitherto he was bound to that postulate of freedom on the illusion of which he was living. In a certain sense, that hampered him. To the extent to which he imagined a purpose to his life, he adapted himself to the demands of a purpose to be achieved and became the slave of his liberty. Thus I could not act otherwise than as the father (or the engineer or the leader of a nation, or the post-office sub-clerk) that I am preparing to be. I think I can choose to be that rather than something else. I think so unconsciously, to be sure. But at the same time I strengthen my postulate with the beliefs of those around me, with the presumptions of my human environment (others are so sure of being free, and that cheerful mood is so contagious!). However far one may remain from any presumption, moral or social, one is partly influenced by them and even, for the best among them (there are good and bad presumptions), one adapts one's life to them. Thus the absurd man realizes that he was not really free. To speak clearly, to the extent to which I hope, to which I worry about a truth that might be individual to me, about a way of being or creating, to the extent to which I arrange my life and prove thereby that I accept its having a meaning, I create for myself barriers between which I confine my life. I do like so many bureaucrats of the mind and heart who only fill me with disgust and whose only vice, I now see clearly, is to take man's freedom seriously.

The absurd enlightens me on this point: there is no future. Henceforth this is the reason for my inner freedom. I shall use two comparisons here. Mystics, to begin with, find freedom in giving themselves. By losing themselves in their god, by accepting his rules, they become secretly free. In spontaneously accepted slavery they recover a deeper independence. But what does that freedom mean? It may be said, above all, that they *feel* free with regard to themselves, and not so much free as liberated. Likewise, completely turned toward death (taken here as the most obvious absurdity), the absurd man feels released from everything outside that passionate attention crystallizing in him. He enjoys a freedom with regard to common rules. It can be seen at this point that the initial themes of existential philosophy keep their entire value. The return to consciousness, the escape from everyday sleep represent the first steps of absurd freedom. But it is existential *preaching* that is alluded to, and with it that spiritual leap which basically escapes consciousness. In the same way (this is my second comparison) the slaves of antiquity did not belong to themselves. But they knew that freedom which consists in not feeling responsible.[7] Death, too, has patrician hands which, while crushing, also liberate.

Losing oneself in that bottomless certainty, feeling henceforth sufficiently remote from one's own life to increase it and take a broad view of it—this involves the principle of a liberation. Such new independence has a definite time limit, like any freedom of action. It does not write a check on eternity. But it takes the place of the illusions of *freedom,* which all stopped with death. The divine availability of the condemned man before whom the prison doors open in a certain early dawn, that unbelievable disinterestedness with regard to everything except for the pure

---

[7] I am concerned here with a factual comparison, not with an apology of humility. The absurd man is the contrary of the reconciled man.

flame of life—it is clear that death and the absurd are here the principles of the only reasonable freedom: that which a human heart can experience and live. This is a second consequence. The absurd man thus catches sight of a burning and frigid, transparent and limited universe in which nothing is possible but everything is given, and beyond which all is collapse and nothingness. He can then decide to accept such a universe and draw from it his strength, his refusal to hope, and the unyielding evidence of a life without consolation.

But what does life mean in such a universe? Nothing else for the moment but indifference to the future and a desire to use up everything that is given. Belief in the meaning of life always implies a scale of values, a choice, our preferences. Belief in the absurd, according to our definitions, teaches the contrary. But this is worth examining.

Knowing whether or not one can live *without appeal* is all that interests me. I do not want to get out of my depth. This aspect of life being given me, can I adapt myself to it? Now, faced with this particular concern, belief in the absurd is tantamount to substituting the quantity of experiences for the quality. If I convince myself that this life has no other aspect than that of the absurd, if I feel that its whole equilibrium depends on that perpetual opposition between my conscious revolt and the darkness in which it struggles, if I admit that my freedom has no meaning except in relation to its limited fate, then I must say that what counts is not the best living but the most living. It is not up to me to wonder if this is vulgar or revolting, elegant or deplorable. Once and for all, value judgments are discarded here in favor of factual judgments. I have merely to draw the conclusions from what I can see and to risk nothing that is hypothetical. Supposing that living in this way were not honorable, then true propriety would command me to be dishonorable.

The most living; in the broadest sense, that rule means nothing. It calls for definition. It seems to begin with the fact that the notion of quantity has not been sufficiently explored. For it can account for a large share of human experience. A man's rule of conduct and his scale of values have no meaning except through the quantity and variety of experiences he has been in a position to accumulate. Now, the conditions of modern life impose on the majority of men the same quantity of experiences and consequently the same profound experience. To be sure, there must also be taken into consideration the individual's spontaneous contribution, the "given" element in him. But I cannot judge of that, and let me repeat that my rule here is to get along with the immediate evidence. I see, then, that the individual character of a common code of ethics lies not so much in the ideal importance of its basic principles as in the norm of an experience that it is possible to measure. To stretch a point somewhat, the Greeks had the code of their leisure just as we have the code of our eight-hour day. But already many men among the most tragic cause us to foresee that a longer experience changes this table of values. They make us imagine that adventurer of the everyday who through mere quantity of experiences would break all records (I am purposely using this sports expression) and would thus win his own code of ethics.[8]

---

[8]Quantity sometimes constitutes quality. If I can believe the latest restatements of scientific theory, all matter is constituted by centers of energy. Their greater or lesser quantity makes its specificity more or less remarkable. A billion ions and one ion differ not only in quantity but also in quality. It is easy to find an analogy in human experience.

Yet let's avoid romanticism and just ask ourselves what such an attitude may mean to a man with his mind made up to take up his bet and to observe strictly what he takes to be the rules of the game.

Breaking all the records is first and foremost being faced with the world as often as possible. How can that be done without contradictions and without playing on words? For on the one hand the absurd teaches that all experiences are unimportant, and on the other it urges toward the greatest quantity of experiences. How, then, can one fail to do as so many of those men I was speaking of earlier—choose the form of life that brings us the most possible of that human matter, thereby introducing a scale of values that on the other hand one claims to reject?

But again it is the absurd and its contradictory life that teaches us. For the mistake is thinking that that quantity of experiences depends on the circumstances of our life when it depends solely on us. Here we have to be over-simple. To two men living the same number of years, the world always provides the same sum of experiences. It is up to us to be conscious of them. Being aware of one's life, one's revolt, one's freedom, and to the maximum, is living, and to the maximum. Where lucidity dominates, the scale of values becomes useless. Let's be even more simple. Let us say that the sole obstacle, the sole deficiency to be made good, is constituted by premature death. Thus it is that no depth, no emotion, no passion, and no sacrifice could render equal in the eyes of the absurd man (even if he wished it so) a conscious life of forty years and a lucidity spread over sixty years.[9] Madness and death are his irreparables. Man does not choose. The absurd and the extra life it involves *therefore do not depend on man's will,* but on its contrary, which is death.[10] Weighing words carefully, it is altogether a question of luck. One just has to be able to consent to this. There will never be any substitute for twenty years of life and experience.

By what is an odd inconsistency in such an alert race, the Greeks claimed that those who died young were beloved of the gods. And that is true only if you are willing to believe that entering the ridiculous world of the gods is forever losing the purest of joys, which is feeling, and feeling on this earth. The present and the succession of presents before a constantly conscious soul is the ideal of the absurd man. But the word "ideal" rings false in this connection. It is not even his vocation, but merely the third consequence of his reasoning. Having started from an anguished awareness of the inhuman, the meditation on the absurd returns at the end of its itinerary to the very heart of the passionate flames of human revolt.[11]

---

[9]Same reflection on a notion as different as the idea of eternal nothingness. It neither adds anything to nor subtracts anything from reality. In psychological experience of nothingness, it is by the consideration of what will happen in two thousand years that our own nothingness truly takes on meaning. In one of its aspects, eternal nothingness is made up precisely of the sum of lives to come which will not be ours.

[10]The will is only the agent here: it tends to maintain consciousness. It provides a discipline of life, and that is appreciable.

[11]What matters is coherence. We start out here from acceptance of the world. But Oriental thought teaches that one can indulge in the same effort of logic by choosing *against* the world. That is just as legitimate and gives this essay its perspectives and its limits. But when the negation of the world is pursued just as rigorously, one often achieves (in certain Vedantic schools) similar results regarding, for instance, the indifference of works. In a book of great importance, *Le Choix,* Jean Grenier establishes in this way a veritable "philosophy of indifference."

Thus I draw from the absurd three consequences, which are my revolt, my freedom, and my passion. By the mere activity of consciousness I transform into a rule
of life what was an invitation to death—and I refuse suicide. I know, to be sure, the
dull resonance that vibrates throughout these days. Yet I have but a word to say: that
it is necessary. When Nietzsche writes: "It clearly seems that the chief thing in
heaven and on earth is to *obey* at length and in a single direction: in the long run
there results something for which it is worth the trouble of living on this earth as,
for example, virtue, art, music, the dance, reason, the mind—something that trans-
figures, something delicate, mad, or divine," he elucidates the rule of a really distinguished code of ethics. But he also points the way of the absurd man. Obeying
the flame is both the easiest and the hardest thing to do. However, it is good for man
to judge himself occasionally. He is alone in being able to do so.

"Prayer," says Alain, "is when night descends over thought." "But the mind must
meet the night," reply the mystics and the existentials. Yes, indeed, but not that night
that is born under closed eyelids and through the mere will of man—dark, impenetrable night that the mind calls up in order to plunge into it. If it must encounter a
night, let it be rather that of despair, which remains lucid—polar night, vigil of the
mind, whence will arise perhaps that white and virginal brightness which outlines
every object in the light of the intelligence. At that degree, equivalence encounters
passionate understanding. Then it is no longer even a question of judging the existential leap. It resumes its place amid the age-old fresco of human attitudes. For the
spectator, if he is conscious, that leap is still absurd. In so far as it thinks it solves the
paradox, it reinstates it intact. On this score, it is stirring. On this score, everything
resumes its place and the absurd world is reborn in all its splendor and diversity.

But it is bad to stop, hard to be satisfied with a single way of seeing, to go without contradiction, perhaps the most subtle of all spiritual forces. The preceding
merely defines a way of thinking. But the point is to live.

The Absurd

Thomas Nagel

Most people feel on occasion that life is absurd, and some feel it vividly and continually. Yet the reasons usually offered in defense of this conviction are patently
inadequate: they *could* not really explain why life is absurd. Why then do they provide a natural expression for the sense that it is?

I

Consider some examples. It is often remarked that nothing we do now will matter
in a million years. But if that is true, then by the same token, nothing that will be

Source: "The Absurd" by Thomas Nagel, from *Mortal Questions,* Chapter 2, 1979, 11–23. Reprinted with
permission of Cambridge University Press.

the case in a million years matters now. In particular, it does not matter now that in a million years nothing we do now will matter. Moreover, even if what we did now *were* going to matter in a million years, how could that keep our present concerns from being absurd? If their mattering now is not enough to accomplish that, how would it help if they mattered a million years from now?

Whether what we do now will matter in a million years could make the crucial difference only if its mattering in a million years depended on its mattering, period. But then to deny that whatever happens now will matter in a million years is to beg the question against its mattering, period; for in that sense one cannot know that it will not matter in a million years whether (for example) someone now is happy or miserable, without knowing that it does not matter, period.

What we say to convey the absurdity of our lives often has to do with space or time: we are tiny specks in the infinite vastness of the universe; our lives are mere instants even on a geological time scale, let alone a cosmic one; we will all be dead any minute. But of course none of these evident facts can be what *makes* life absurd, if it is absurd. For suppose we lived for ever; would not a life that is absurd if it lasts seventy years be infinitely absurd if it lasted through eternity? And if our lives are absurd given our present size, why would they be any less absurd if we filled the universe (either because we were larger or because the universe was smaller)? Reflection on our minuteness and brevity appears to be intimately connected with the sense that life is meaningless; but it is not clear what the connection is.

Another inadequate argument is that because we are going to die, all chains of justification must leave off in mid-air: one studies and works to earn money to pay for clothing, housing, entertainment, food, to sustain oneself from year to year, perhaps to support a family and pursue a career—but to what final end? All of it is an elaborate journey leading nowhere. (One will also have some effect on other people's lives, but that simply reproduces the problem, for they will die too.)

There are several replies to this argument. First, life does not consist of a sequence of activities each of which has as its purpose some later member of the sequence. Chains of justification come repeatedly to an end within life, and whether the process as a whole can be justified has no bearing on the finality of these endpoints. No further justification is needed to make it reasonable to take aspirin for a headache, attend an exhibition of the work of a painter one admires, or stop a child from putting his hand on a hot stove. No larger context or further purpose is needed to prevent these acts from being pointless.

Even if someone wished to supply a further justification for pursuing all the things in life that are commonly regarded as self-justifying, that justification would have to end somewhere too. If *nothing* can justify unless it is justified in terms of something outside itself, which is also justified, then an infinite regress results, and no chain of justification can be complete. Moreover, if a finite chain of reasons cannot justify anything, what could be accomplished by an infinite chain, each link of which must be justified by something outside itself?

Since justifications must come to an end somewhere, nothing is gained by denying that they end where they appear to, within life—or by trying to subsume the multiple, often trivial ordinary justifications of action under a single, controlling life scheme. We can be satisfied more easily than that. In fact, through its misrepresentation of the process of justification, the argument makes a vacuous demand. It insists that the reasons available within life are incomplete, but suggests thereby that all reasons that come to an end are incomplete. This makes it impossible to supply any reasons at all.

The standard arguments for absurdity appear therefore to fail as arguments. Yet I believe they attempt to express something that is difficult to state, but fundamentally correct.

II

In ordinary life a situation is absurd when it includes a conspicuous discrepancy between pretension or aspiration and reality: someone gives a complicated speech in support of a motion that has already been passed; a notorious criminal is made president of a major philanthropic foundation; you declare your love over the telephone to a recorded announcement; as you are being knighted, your pants fall down.

When a person finds himself in an absurd situation, he will usually attempt to change it, by modifying his aspirations, or by trying to bring reality into better accord with them, or by removing himself from the situation entirely. We are not always willing or able to extricate ourselves from a position whose absurdity has become clear to us. Nevertheless, it is usually possible to imagine some change that would remove the absurdity—whether or not we can or will implement it. The sense that life as a whole is absurd arises when we perceive, perhaps dimly, an inflated pretension or aspiration which is inseparable from the continuation of human life and which makes its absurdity inescapable, short of escape from life itself.

Many people's lives are absurd, temporarily or permanently, for conventional reasons having to do with their particular ambitions, circumstances, and personal relations. If there is a philosophical sense of absurdity, however, it must arise from the perception of something universal—some respect in which pretension and reality inevitably clash for us all. This condition is supplied, I shall argue, by the collison between the seriousness with which we take our lives and the perpetual possibility of regarding everything about which we are serious as arbitrary, or open to doubt.

We cannot live human lives without energy and attention, nor without making choices which show that we take some things more seriously than others. Yet we have always available a point of view outside the particular form of our lives, from which the seriousness appears gratuitous. These two inescapable viewpoints collide in us, and that is what makes life absurd. It is absurd because we ignore the doubts that we know cannot be settled, continuing to live with nearly undiminished seriousness in spite of them.

This analysis requires defense in two respects: first as regards the unavoidability of seriousness; second as regards the inescapability of doubt.

We take ourselves seriously whether we lead serious lives or not and whether we are concerned primarily with fame, pleasure, virtues, luxury, triumph, beauty, justice, knowledge, salvation, or mere survival. If we take other people seriously and devote ourselves to them, that only multiplies the problem. Human life is full of effort, plans, calculation, success and failure: we *pursue* our lives, with varying degrees of sloth and energy.

It would be different if we could not step back and reflect on the process, but were merely led from impulse to impulse without self-consciousness. But human beings do not act solely on impulse. They are prudent, they reflect, they weigh consequences, they ask whether what they are doing is worth while. Not only are their lives full of particular choices that hang together in larger activities with temporal structure: they also decide in the broadest terms what to pursue and what to avoid, what the priorities among their various aims should be, and what kind of people they want to be or become. Some men are faced with such choices by the large decisions they make from time to time; some merely by reflection on the course their lives are taking as the product of countless small decisions. They decide whom to marry, what profession to follow, whether to join the Country Club, or the Resistance; or they may just wonder why they go on being salesmen or academics or taxi drivers, and then stop thinking about it after a certain period of inconclusive reflection.

Although they may be motivated from act to act by those immediate needs with which life presents them, they allow the process to continue by adhering to the general system of habits and the form of life in which such motives have their place—or perhaps only by clinging to life itself. They spend enormous quantities of energy, risk, and calculation on the details. Think of how an ordinary individual sweats over his appearance, his health, his sex life, his emotional honesty, his social utility, his self-knowledge, the quality of his ties with family, colleagues, and friends, how well he does his job, whether he understands the world and what is going on in it. Leading a human life is a full-time occupation, to which everyone devotes decades of intense concern.

This fact is so obvious that it is hard to find it extraordinary and important. Each of us lives his own life—lives with himself twenty-four hours a day. What else is he supposed to do—live someone else's life? Yet humans have the special capacity to step back and survey themselves, and the lives to which they are committed, with that detached amazement which comes from watching an ant struggle up a heap of sand. Without developing the illusion that they are able to escape from their highly specific and idiosyncratic position, they can view it *sub specie aeternitatis*—and the view is at once sobering and comical.

The crucial backward step is not taken by asking for still another justification in the chain, and failing to get it. The objections to that line of attack have already been stated; justifications come to an end. But this is precisely what provides universal doubt with its object. We step back to find that the whole system of justification and criticism, which controls our choices and supports our claims to rationality, rests on responses and habits that we never question, that we should not know how to defend without circularity, and to which we shall continue to adhere even after they are called into question.

The things we do or want without reasons, and without requiring reasons—the things that define what is a reason for us and what is not—are the starting points of our skepticism. We see ourselves from outside, and all the contingency and specificity of our aims and pursuits become clear. Yet when we take this view and recognize what we do as arbitrary, it does not disengage us from life, and there lies our absurdity: not in the fact that such an external view can be taken of us, but in the fact that we ourselves can take it, without ceasing to be the persons whose ultimate concerns are so coolly regarded.

III

One may try to escape the position by seeking broader ultimate concerns, from which it is impossible to step back—the idea being that absurdity results because what we take seriously is something small and insignificant and individual. Those seeking to supply their lives with meaning usually envision a role or function in something larger than themselves. They therefore seek fulfillment in service to society, the state, the revolution, the progress of history, the advance of science, or religion and the glory of God.

But a role in some larger enterprise cannot confer significance unless that enterprise is itself significant. And its significance must come back to what we can understand, or it will not even appear to give us what we are seeking. If we learned that we were being raised to provide food for other creatures fond of human flesh, who planned to turn us into cutlets before we got too stringy—even if we learned that the human race had been developed by animal breeders precisely for this purpose—that would still not give our lives meaning, for two reasons. First, we would still be in the dark as to the significance of the lives of those other beings; second, although we might acknowledge that this culinary role would make our lives meaningful to them, it is not clear how it would make them meaningful to us.

Admittedly, the usual form of service to a higher being is different from this. One is supposed to behold and partake of the glory of God, for example, in a way in which chickens do not share in the glory of coq au vin. The same is true of service to a state, a movement, or a revolution. People can come to feel, when they are part of something bigger, that it is part of them too. They worry less about what is peculiar to themselves, but identify enough with the larger enterprise to find their role in it fulfilling.

However, any such larger purpose can be put in doubt in the same way that the aims of an individual life can be, and for the same reasons. It is as legitimate to find ultimate justification there as to find it earlier, among the details of individual life. But this does not alter the fact that justifications come to an end when we are content to have them end—when we do not find it necessary to look any further. If we can step back from the purposes of individual life and doubt their point, we can step back also from the progress of human history, or of science, or the success of a society, or the kingdom, power, and glory of God, and put all these things into question in the same way. What seems to us to confer meaning, justification, significance, does so in virtue of the fact that we need no more reasons after a certain point.

What makes doubt inescapable with regard to the limited aims of individual life also makes it inescapable with regard to any larger purpose that encourages the sense that life is meaningful. Once the fundamental doubt has begun, it cannot be laid to rest.

Camus maintains in *The Myth of Sisyphus* that the absurd arises because the world fails to meet our demands for meaning. This suggests that the world might satisfy those demands if it were different. But now we can see that this is not the case. There does not appear to be any conceivable world (containing us) about which unsettlable doubts could not arise. Consequently the absurdity of our situation derives not from a collision between our expectations and the world, but from a collision within ourselves.

IV

It may be objected that the standpoint from which these doubts are supposed to be felt does not exist—that if we take the recommended backward step we will land on thin air, without any basis for judgment about the natural responses we are supposed to be surveying. If we retain our usual standards of what is important, then questions about the significance of what we are doing with our lives will be answerable in the usual way. But if we do not, then those questions can mean nothing to us, since there is no longer any content to the idea of what matters, and hence no content to the idea that nothing does.

But this objection misconceives the nature of the backward step. It is not supposed to give us an understanding of what is *really* important, so that we see by contrast that our lives are insignificant. We never, in the course of these reflections, abandon the ordinary standards that guide our lives. We merely observe them in operation, and recognize that if they are called into question we can justify them only by reference to themselves, uselessly. We adhere to them because of the way we are put together; what seems to us important or serious or valuable would not seem so if we were differently constituted.

In ordinary life, to be sure, we do not judge a situation absurd unless we have in mind some standards of seriousness, significance, or harmony with which the absurd can be contrasted. This contrast is not implied by the philosophical judgment of absurdity, and that might be thought to make the concept unsuitable for the expression of such judgments. This is not so, however, for the philosophical judgment depends on another contrast which makes it a natural extension from more ordinary cases. It departs from them only in contrasting the pretensions of life with a larger context in which *no* standards can be discovered, rather than with a context from which alternative, overriding standards may be applied.

V

In this respect, as in others, philosophical perception of the absurd resembles epistemological skepticism. In both cases the final, philosophical doubt is not contrasted with any unchallenged certainties, though it is arrived at by extrapolation from examples of doubt within the system of evidence or justification, where a contrast with other certainties *is* implied. In both cases our limitedness joins with a capacity to transcend those limitations in thought (thus seeing them as limitations, and as inescapable).

Skepticism begins when we include ourselves in the world about which we claim knowledge. We notice that certain types of evidence convince us, that we are content to allow justifications of belief to come to an end at certain points, that we feel we know many things even without knowing or having grounds for believing the denial of others which, if true, would make what we claim to know false.

For example, I know that I am looking at a piece of paper, although I have no adequate grounds for claiming I know that I am not dreaming; and if I am dreaming then I am not looking at a piece of paper. Here an ordinary conception of how appearance may diverge from reality is employed to show that we take our world largely for granted; the certainty that we are not dreaming cannot be justified except circularly, in terms of those very appearances which are being put in doubt. It is somewhat far-fetched to suggest I may be dreaming; but the possibility is only illustrative. It reveals that our claims to knowledge depend on our not feeling it necessary to exclude certain incompatible alternatives, and the dreaming possibility or the total-hallucination possibility are just representatives for limitless possibilities most of which we cannot even conceive.[1]

Once we have taken the backward step to an abstract view of our whole system of beliefs, evidence, and justification, and seen that it works only, despite its pretensions, by taking the world largely for granted, we are *not* in a position to contrast all these appearances with an alternative reality. We cannot shed our ordinary responses, and if we could it would leave us with no means of conceiving a reality of any kind.

It is the same in the practical domain. We do not step outside our lives to a new vantage point from which we see what is really, objectively significant. We continue to take life largely for granted while seeing that all our decisions and certainties are possible only because there is a great deal we do not bother to rule out.

Both epistemological skepticism and a sense of the absurd can be reached via initial doubts posed within systems of evidence and justification that we accept, and can be stated without violence to our ordinary concepts. We can ask not only why we should believe there is a floor under us, but also why we should believe the evidence of our senses at all—and at some point the framable questions will have outlasted the answers. Similarly, we can ask not only why we should take aspirin, but why we should take trouble over our own comfort at all. The fact that we shall take the aspirin without waiting for an answer to this last question does not show that it is an unreal question. We shall also continue to believe there is a floor under us without waiting for an answer to the other question. In both cases it is this unsupported natural confidence that generates skeptical doubts; so it cannot be used to settle them.

Philosophical skepticism does not cause us to abandon our ordinary beliefs, but it lends them a peculiar flavor. After acknowledging that their truth is incompatible with possibilities that we have no grounds for believing do not obtain—apart from grounds in those very beliefs which we have called into question—we return to our familiar convictions with a certain irony and resignation. Unable to abandon the

---

[1] I am aware that skepticism about the external world is widely thought to have been refuted, but I have remained convinced of its irrefutability since being exposed at Berkeley to Thompson Clarke's largely unpublished ideas on the subject.

natural responses on which they depend, we take them back, like a spouse who has run off with someone else and then decided to return; but we regard them differently (not that the new attitude is necessarily inferior to the old, in either case).

The same situation obtains after we have put in question the seriousness with which we take our lives and human life in general and have looked at ourselves without presuppositions. We then return to our lives, as we must, but our seriousness is laced with irony. Not that irony enables us to escape the absurd. It is useless to mutter: "Life is meaningless; life is meaningless . . ." as an accompaniment to everything we do. In continuing to live and work and strive, we take ourselves seriously in action no matter what we say.

What sustains us, in belief as in action, is not reason or justification, but something more basic than these—for we go on in the same way even after we are convinced that the reasons have given out.[2] If we tried to rely entirely on reason, and pressed it hard, our lives and beliefs would collapse—a form of madness that may actually occur if the inertial force of taking the world and life for granted is somehow lost. If we lose our grip on that, reason will not give it back to us.

VI

In viewing ourselves from a perspective broader than we can occupy in the flesh, we become spectators of our own lives. We cannot do very much as pure spectators of our own lives, so we continue to lead them, and devote ourselves to what we are able at the same time to view as no more than a curiosity, like the ritual of an alien religion.

This explains why the sense of absurdity finds its natural expression in those bad arguments with which the discussion began. Reference to our small size and short lifespan and to the fact that all of mankind will eventually vanish without a trace are metaphors for the backward step which permits us to regard ourselves from without and to find the particular form of our lives curious and slightly surprising. By feigning a nebula's-eye view, we illustrate the capacity to see ourselves without presuppositions, as arbitrary, idiosyncratic, highly specific occupants of the world, one of countless possible forms of life.

Before turning to the question whether the absurdity of our lives is something to be regretted and if possible escaped, let me consider what would have to be given up in order to avoid it.

Why is the life of a mouse not absurd? The orbit of the moon is not absurd either, but that involves no strivings or aims at all. A mouse, however, has to work to stay alive. Yet he is not absurd, because he lacks the capacities for self-consciousness and

---

[2]As Hume says in a famous passage of the *Treatise* [*A Treatise of Human Nature*]: "Most fortunately it happens, that since reason is incapable of dispelling these clouds, nature herself suffices to that purpose, and cures me of this philosophical melancholy and delirium, either by relaxing this bent of mind, or by some avocation, and lively impression of my senses, which obliterate all these chimeras. I dine, I play a game of backgammon, I converse, and am merry with my friends; and when after three or four hours' amusement, I would return to these speculations, they appear so cold, and strain'd, and ridiculous, that I cannot find in my heart to enter into them any farther" (bk I, pt IV, sect. 7; Selby-Bigge, p. 269).

self-transcendence that would enable him to see that he is only a mouse. If that *did* happen, his life would become absurd, since self-awareness would not make him cease to be a mouse and would not enable him to rise above his mousely strivings. Bringing his new-found self-consciousness with him, he would have to return to his meager yet frantic life, full of doubts that he was unable to answer, but also full of purposes that he was unable to abandon.

Given that the transcendental step is natural to us humans, can we avoid absurdity by refusing to take that step and remaining entirely within our sublunar lives? Well, we cannot refuse consciously, for to do that we would have to be aware of the viewpoint we were refusing to adopt. The only way to avoid the relevant self-consciousness would be either never to attain it or to forget it—neither of which can be achieved by the will.

On the other hand, it is possible to expend effort on an attempt to destroy the other component of the absurd—abandoning one's earthly, individual, human life in order to identify as completely as possible with that universal viewpoint from which human life seems arbitrary and trivial. (This appears to be the ideal of certain Oriental religions.) If one succeeds, then one will not have to drag the superior awareness through a strenuous mundane life, and absurdity will be diminished.

However, insofar as this self-etiolation is the result of effort, will-power, asceticism, and so forth, it requires that one take oneself seriously as an individual—that one be willing to take considerable trouble to avoid being creaturely and absurd. Thus one may undermine the aim of unworldliness by pursuing it too vigorously. Still, if someone simply allowed his individual, animal nature to drift and respond to impulse, without making the pursuit of its needs a central conscious aim, then he might, at considerable dissociative cost, achieve a life that was less absurd than most. It would not be a meaningful life either, of course; but it would not involve the engagement of a transcendent awareness in the assiduous pursuit of mundane goals. And that is the main condition of absurdity—the dragooning of an unconvinced transcendent consciousness into the service of an immanent, limited enterprise like a human life.

The final escape is suicide; before adopting any hasty solutions, it would be wise to consider carefully whether the absurdity of our existence truly presents us with a *problem,* to which some solution must be found—a way of dealing with *prima facie* disaster. That is certainly the attitude with which Camus approaches the issue, and it gains support from the fact that we are all eager to escape from absurd situations on a smaller scale.

Camus—not on uniformly good grounds—rejects suicide and the other solutions he regards as escapist. What he recommends is defiance or scorn. We can salvage our dignity, he appears to believe, by shaking a fist at the world which is deaf to our pleas, and continuing to live in spite of it. This will not make our lives unabsurd, but it will lend them a certain nobility.[3]

---

[3]"Sisyphus, proletarian of the gods, powerless and rebellious, knows the whole extent of his wretched condition: it is what he thinks of during his descent. The lucidity that was to constitute his torture at the same time crowns his victory. There is no fate that cannot be surmounted by scorn" (*The Myth of Sisyphus,* trans. Justin O'Brien (New York: Vintage, 1959), p. 90; first published, Paris: Gallimard, 1942).

This seems to me romantic and slightly self-pitying. Our absurdity warrants neither that much distress nor that much defiance. At the risk of falling into romanticism by a different route, I would argue that absurdity is one of the most human things about us: a manifestation of our most advanced and interesting characteristics. Like skepticism in epistemology, it is possible only because we possess a certain kind of insight—the capacity to transcend ourselves in thought.

If a sense of the absurd is a way of perceiving our true situation (even though the situation is not absurd until the perception arises), then what reason can we have to resent or escape it? Like the capacity for epistemological skepticism, it results from the ability to understand our human limitations. It need not be a matter for agony unless we make it so. Nor need it evoke a defiant contempt of fate that allows us to feel brave or proud. Such dramatics, even if carried on in private, betray a failure to appreciate the cosmic unimportance of the situation. If *sub specie aeternitatis* there is no reason to believe that anything matters, then that does not matter either, and we can approach our absurd lives with irony instead of heroism or despair.

The Meaning of Life

Richard Taylor

The question whether life has any meaning is difficult to interpret, and the more one concentrates his critical faculty on it the more it seems to elude him, or to evaporate as any intelligible question. One wants to turn it aside, as a source of embarrassment, as something that, if it cannot be abolished, should at least be decently covered. And yet I think any reflective person recognizes that the question it raises is important, and that it ought to have a significant answer.

If the idea of meaningfulness is difficult to grasp in this context, so that we are unsure what sort of thing would amount to answering the question, the idea of meaninglessness is perhaps less so. If, then, we can bring before our minds a clear image of meaningless existence, then perhaps we can take a step toward coping with our original question by seeing to what extent our lives, as we actually find them, resemble that image, and draw such lessons as we are able to from the comparison.

MEANINGLESS EXISTENCE

A perfect image of meaninglessness, of the kind we are seeking, is found in the ancient myth of Sisyphus. Sisyphus, it will be remembered, betrayed divine secrets to mortals, and for this he was condemned by the gods to roll a stone to the top of a hill, the stone then immediately to roll back down, again to be pushed to the top by Sisyphus, to roll down once more, and so on again and again, *forever.* Now in this we have the picture of meaningless, pointless toil, of a meaningless existence that is absolutely *never* redeemed. It is not even redeemed by a death that, if it were to accomplish nothing more, would at least bring this idiotic cycle to a close. If we were invited to imagine Sisyphus struggling for awhile and accomplishing nothing, perhaps eventually falling from exhaustion, so that we might suppose him then eventually turning to something having some sort of promise, then the meaninglessness of that chapter of his life would not be so stark. It would be a dark and dreadful dream, from which he eventually awakens to sunlight and reality. But he does not awaken, for there is nothing for him to awaken to. His repetitive toil is his life and reality, and it goes on forever, and it is without any meaning whatever. Nothing ever comes of what he is doing, except simply, more of the same. Not by one step, nor by a thousand, nor by ten thousand does he even expiate by the smallest token the sin against the gods that led him into this fate. Nothing comes of it, nothing at all.

This ancient myth has always enchanted men, for countless meanings can be read into it. Some of the ancients apparently thought it symbolized the perpetual rising and setting of the sun, and others the repetitious crashing of the waves upon the shore. Probably the commonest interpretation is that it symbolizes man's eternal struggle and unquenchable spirit, his determination always to try once more in the face of overwhelming discouragement. This interpretation is further supported by that version of the myth according to which Sisyphus was commanded to roll the stone *over* the hill, so that it would finally roll down the other side, but was never quite able to make it.

I am not concerned with rendering or defending any interpretation of this myth, however. I have cited it only for the one element it does unmistakably contain, namely, that of a repetitious, cyclic activity that never comes to anything. We could contrive other images of this that would serve just as well, and no myth-makers are needed to supply the materials of it. Thus, we can imagine two persons transporting a stone—or even a precious gem, it does not matter—back and forth, relay style. One carries it to a near or distant point where it is received by the other; it is returned to its starting point, there to be recovered by the first, and the process is repeated over and over. Except in this relay nothing counts as winning, and nothing brings the contest to any close, each step only leads to a repetition of itself. Or we can imagine two groups of prisoners, one of them engaged in digging a prodigious hole in the ground that is no sooner finished than it is filled in again by the other group, the latter then digging a new hole that is at once filled in by the first group, and so on and on endlessly.

Now what stands out in all such pictures as oppressive and dejecting is not that the beings who enact these roles suffer any torture or pain, for it need not be assumed that they do. Nor is it that their labors are great, for they are no greater than the labors commonly undertaken by most men most of the time. According to the original myth, the stone is so large that Sisyphus never quite gets it to the top and must groan under every step, so that his enormous labor is all for nought. But this is not what appalls. It is not that his great struggle comes to nothing, but that his existence itself is without meaning. Even if we suppose, for example, that the stone is but a pebble that can be carried effortlessly, or that the holes dug by the prisoners are but small ones, not the slightest meaning is introduced into their lives. The stone that Sisyphus moves to the top of the hill, whether we think of it as large or small, still rolls back every time, and the process is repeated forever. Nothing comes of it, and the work is simply pointless. That is the element of the myth that I wish to capture.

Again, it is not the fact that the labors of Sisyphus continue forever that deprives them of meaning. It is, rather, the implication of this: that they come to nothing. The image would not be changed by our supposing him to push a different stone up every time, each to roll down again. But if we supposed that these stones, instead of rolling back to their places as if they had never been moved, were assembled at the top of the hill and there incorporated, say, in a beautiful and enduring temple, then the aspect of meaninglessness would disappear. His labors would then have a point, something would come of them all, and although one could perhaps still say it was not worth it, one could not say that the life of Sisyphus was devoid of meaning altogether. Meaningfulness would at least have made an appearance, and we could see what it was.

That point will need remembering. But in the meantime, let us note another way in which the image of meaninglessness can be altered by making only a very slight change. Let us suppose that the gods, while condemning Sisyphus to the fate just described, at the same time, as an afterthought, waxed perversely merciful by implanting in him a strange and irrational impulse; namely, a compulsive impulse to roll stones. We may if we like, to make this more graphic, suppose they accomplish this by implanting in him some substance that has this effect on his character and drives. I call this perverse, because from our point of view there is clearly no reason why anyone should have a persistent and insatiable desire to do something so pointless as that. Nevertheless, suppose that is Sisyphus' condition. He has but one obsession, which is to roll stones, and it is an obsession that is only for the moment appeased by his rolling them—he no sooner gets a stone rolled to the top of the hill than he is restless to roll up another.

Now it can be seen why this little afterthought of the gods, which I called perverse, was also in fact merciful. For they have by this device managed to give Sisyphus precisely what he wants—by making him want precisely what they inflict on him. However it may appear to us, Sisyphus' fate now does not appear to him as a condemnation, but the very reverse. His one desire in life is to roll stones, and he is absolutely guaranteed its endless fulfillment. Where otherwise he might profoundly have wished surcease, and even welcomed the quiet of death to release him from endless boredom and meaninglessness, his life is now filled with mission and meaning, and he seems to himself to have been given an entry to heaven. Nor need he even fear death, for the gods have promised him an endless opportunity to indulge his single purpose, without concern or frustration. He will be able to roll stones *forever.*

What we need to mark most carefully at this point is that the picture with which we began has not really been changed in the least by adding this supposition.

Exactly the same things happen as before. The only change is in Sisyphus' view of them. The picture before was the image of meaningless activity and existence. It was created precisely to be an image of that. It has not lost that meaninglessness, it has now gained not the least shred of meaningfulness. The stones still roll back as before, each phase of Sisyphus' life still exactly resembles all the others, the task is never completed, nothing comes of it, no temple ever begins to rise, and all this cycle of the same pointless thing over and over goes on forever in this picture as in the other. The *only* thing that has happened is this: Sisyphus has been reconciled to it, and indeed more, he has been led to embrace it. Not, however, by reason or persuasion, but by nothing more rational than the potency of a new substance in his veins.

THE MEANINGLESSNESS OF LIFE

I believe the foregoing provides a fairly clear content to the idea of meaninglessness and, through it, some hint of what meaningfulness, in this sense, might be. Meaninglessness is essentially endless pointlessness, and meaningfulness is therefore the opposite. Activity, and even long, drawn-out and repetitive activity, has a meaning if it has some significant culmination, some more or less lasting end that can be considered to have been the direction and purpose of the activity. But the descriptions so far also provide something else; namely, the suggestion of how an existence that is objectively meaningless, in this sense, can nevertheless acquire a meaning for him whose existence it is.

Now let us ask: Which of these pictures does life in fact resemble? And let us not begin with our own lives, for here both our prejudices and wishes are great, but with the life in general that we share with the rest of creation. We shall find, I think, that it all has a certain pattern, and that this pattern is by now easily recognized.

We can begin anywhere, only saving human existence for our last consideration. We can, for example, begin with any animal. It does not matter where we begin, because the result is going to be exactly the same.

Thus, for example, there are caves in New Zealand, deep and dark, whose floors are quiet pools and whose walls and ceilings are covered with soft light. As one gazes in wonder in the stillness of these caves it seems that the Creator has reproduced there in microcosm the heavens themselves, until one scarcely remembers the enclosing presence of the walls. As one looks more closely, however, the scene is explained. Each dot of light identifies an ugly worm, whose luminous tail is meant to attract insects from the surrounding darkness. As from time to time one of these insects draws near it becomes entangled in a sticky thread lowered by the worm, and is eaten. This goes on month after month, the blind worm lying there in the barren stillness waiting to entrap an occasional bit of nourishment that will only sustain it to another bit of nourishment until. . . . Until what? What great thing awaits all this long and repetitive effort and makes it worthwhile? Really nothing. The larva just transforms itself finally to a tiny winged adult that lacks even mouth parts to feed and lives only a day or two. These adults, as soon as they have mated and laid eggs, are themselves caught in the threads and are devoured by the cannibalist worms, often without having ventured into the day, the only point to their existence having now been fulfilled. This has been going on for millions of years, and to no end other than that the same meaningless cycle may continue for another millions of years.

All living things present essentially the same spectacle. The larva of a certain cicada burrows in the darkness of the earth for seventeen years, through season after season, to emerge finally into the daylight for a brief flight, lay its eggs, and die— this all to repeat itself during the next seventeen years, and so on to eternity. We have already noted, in another connection, the struggles of fish, made only that others may do the same after them and that this cycle, having no other point than itself, may never cease. Some birds span an entire side of the globe each year and then return, only to insure that others may follow the same incredibly long path again and again. One is led to wonder what the point of it all is, with what great triumph this ceaseless effort, repeating itself through millions of years, might finally culminate, and why it should go on and on for so long, accomplishing nothing, getting nowhere. But then one realizes that there is no point to it at all, that it really culminates in nothing, that each of these cycles, so filled with toil, is to be followed only by more of the same. The point of any living thing's life is, evidently, nothing but life itself.

This life of the world thus presents itself to our eyes as a vast machine, feeding on itself, running on and on forever to nothing. And we are part of that life. To be sure, we are not just the same, but the differences are not so great as we like to think; many are merely invented, and none really cancels the kind of meaninglessness that we found in Sisyphus and that we find all around, wherever anything lives. We are conscious of our activity. Our goals, whether in any significant sense we choose them or not, are things of which we are at least partly aware and can therefore in some sense appraise. More significantly, perhaps, men have a history, as other animals do not, such that each generation does not precisely resemble all those before. Still, if we can in imagination disengage our wills from our lives and disregard the deep interest each man has in his own existence, we shall find that they do not so little resemble the existence of Sisyphus. We toil after goals, most of them—indeed every single one of them—of transitory significance and, having gained one of them, we immediately set forth for the next, as if that one had never been, with this next one being essentially more of the same. Look at a busy street any day, and observe the throng going hither and thither. To what? Some office or shop, where the same things will be done today as were done yesterday, and are done now so they may be repeated tomorrow. And if we think that, unlike Sisyphus, these labors do have a point, that they culminate in something lasting and, independently of our own deep interests in them, very worthwhile, then we simply have not considered the thing closely enough. Most such effort is directed only to the establishment and perpetuation of home and family; that is, to the begetting of others who will follow in our steps to do more of the same. Each man's life thus resembles one of Sisyphus' climbs to the summit of his hill, and each day of it one of his steps; the difference is that whereas Sisyphus himself returns to push the stone up again, we leave this to our children. We at one point imagined that the labors of Sisyphus finally culminated in the creation of a temple, but for this to make any difference it had to be a temple that would at least endure, adding beauty to the world for the remainder of time. Our achievements, even though they are often beautiful, are mostly bubbles; and those that do last, like the sand-swept pyramids, soon become mere curiosities while around them the rest of mankind continues its perpetual toting of rocks, only to see them roll down. Nations are built upon the bones of their founders and pioneers, but only to decay and crumble before long, their rubble then becoming the foundation for others directed to exactly the same fate. The picture of Sisyphus is the picture of existence of the individual man, great or unknown, of nations, of the race of men, and of the very life of the world.

On a country road one sometimes comes upon the ruined hulks of a house and once extensive buildings, all in collapse and spread over with weeds. A curious eye can in imagination reconstruct from what is left a once warm and thriving life, filled with purpose. There was the hearth, where a family once talked, sang, and made plans; there were the rooms, where people loved, and babes were born to a rejoicing mother; there are the musty remains of a sofa, infested with bugs, once bought at a dear price to enhance an ever-growing comfort, beauty, and warmth. Every small piece of junk fills the mind with what once, not long ago, was utterly real, with children's voices, plans made, and enterprises embarked upon. That is how these stones of Sisyphus were rolled up, and that is how they became incorporated into a beautiful temple, and that temple is what now lies before you. Meanwhile other buildings, institutions, nations, and civilizations spring up all around, only to share the same fate before long. And if the question "What for?" is now asked, the answer is clear: so that just this may go on forever.

The two pictures—of Sisyphus and of our own lives, if we look at them from a distance—are in outline the same and convey to the mind the same image. It is not surprising, then, that men invent ways of denying it, their religious proclaiming a heaven that does not crumble, their hymnals and prayer books declaring a significance to life of which our eyes provide no hint whatever.[1] Even our philosophies portray some permanent and lasting good at which all may aim, from the changeless forms invented by Plato to the beatific vision of St. Thomas and the ideals of permanence contrived by the moderns. When these fail to convince, then earthly ideals such as universal justice and brotherhood are conjured up to take their places and give meaning to man's seemingly endless pilgrimage, some final state that will be ushered in when the last obstacle is removed and the last stone pushed to the hilltop. No one believes, of course, that any such state will be final, or even wants it to be in case it means that human existence would then cease to be a struggle; but in the meantime such ideas serve a very real need.

---

[1]A popular Christian hymn, sung often at funerals and typical of many hymns, expresses this thought:
> Swift to its close ebbs out life's little day;
> Earth's joys grow dim, its glories pass away;
> Change and decay in all around I see:
> O thou who changest not, abide with me.

THE MEANING OF LIFE

We noted that Sisyphus' existence would have meaning if there were some point to his labors, if his efforts ever culminated in something that was not just an occasion for fresh labors of the same kind. But that is precisely the meaning it lacks. And human existence resembles his in that respect. Men do achieve things—they scale their towers and raise their stones to their hilltops—but every such accomplishment fades, providing only an occasion for renewed labors of the same kind.

But here we need to note something else that has been mentioned, but its significance not explored, and that is the state of mind and feeling with which such labors are undertaken. We noted that if Sisyphus had a keen and unappeasable desire to be doing just what he found himself doing, then, although his life would in no way be changed, it would nevertheless have a meaning for him. It would be an irrational one, no doubt, because the desire itself would be only the product of the substance in his veins, and not any that reason could discover, but a meaning nevertheless.

And would it not, in fact, be a meaning incomparably better than the other? For let us examine again the first kind of meaning it could have. Let us suppose that, without having any interest in rolling stones, as such, and finding this, in fact, a galling toil, Sisyphus did nevertheless have a deep interest in raising a temple, one that would be beautiful and lasting. And let us suppose he succeeded in this, that after ages of dreadful toil, all directed at this final result, he did at last complete his temple, such that now he could say his work was done, and he could rest and forever enjoy the result. Now what? What picture now presents itself to our minds? It is precisely the picture of infinite boredom! Of Sisyphus doing nothing ever again, but contemplating what he has already wrought and can no longer add anything to, and contemplating it for an eternity! Now in this picture we have a meaning for Sisyphus' existence, a point for his prodigious labor, because we have put it there; yet, at the same time, that which is really worthwhile seems to have slipped away entirely. Where before we were presented with the nightmare of eternal and pointless activity, we are now confronted with the hell of its eternal absence.

Our second picture, then, wherein we imagined Sisyphus to have had inflicted on him the irrational desire to be doing just what he found himself doing, should not have been dismissed so abruptly. The meaning that picture lacked was no meaning that he or anyone could crave, and the strange meaning it had was perhaps just what we were seeking.

At this point, then, we can reintroduce what has been until now, it is hoped, resolutely pushed aside in an effort to view our lives and human existence with objectivity; namely, our own wills, our deep interest in what we find ourselves doing. If we do this we find that our lives do indeed still resemble that of Sisyphus, but that the meaningfulness they thus lack is precisely the meaningfulness of infinite boredom. At the same time, the strange meaningfulness they possess is that of the inner compulsion to be doing just what we were put here to do, and to go on doing it forever. This is the nearest we may hope to get to heaven, but the redeeming side of that fact is that we do thereby avoid a genuine hell.

If the builders of a great and flourishing ancient civilization could somehow return now to see archaeologists unearthing the trivial remnants of what they had once accomplished with such effort—see the fragments of pots and vases, a few broken statues, and such tokens of another age and greatness—they could indeed ask themselves what the point of it all was, if this is all it finally came to. Yet, it did not seem so to them then, for it was just the building, and not what was finally built, that gave their life meaning. Similarly, if the builders of the ruined home and farm that I described a short while ago could be brought back to see what is left, they would have the same feelings. What we construct in our imaginations as we look over these decayed and rusting pieces would reconstruct itself in their very memories, and certainly with unspeakable sadness. The piece of a sled at our feet would revive in them a warm Christmas. And what rich memories would there be in the broken crib? And the weed-covered remains of a fence would reproduce the scene of a great herd of livestock, so laboriously built up over so many years. What was it all worth, if this is the final result? Yet, again, it did not seem so to them through those many years of struggle and toil, and they did not imagine they were building a Gibraltar. The things to which they bent their backs day after day, realizing one by one their ephemeral plans, were precisely the things in which their wills were deeply involved, precisely the things in which their interests lay, and there was no need then to ask questions. There is no more need of them now—the day was sufficient to itself, and so was the life.

This is surely the way to look at all of life—at one's own life, and each day and moment it contains; of the life of a nation; of the species; of the life of the world; and of everything that breathes. Even the glow worms I described, whose cycles of existence over the millions of years seem so pointless when looked at by us, will seem entirely different to us if we can somehow try to view their existence from within. Their endless activity, which gets nowhere, is just what it is their will to pursue. This is its whole justification and meaning. Nor would it be any salvation to the birds who span the globe every year, back and forth, to have a home made for them in a cage with plenty of food and protection, so that they would not have to migrate any more. It would be their condemnation, for it is the doing that counts for them, and not what they hope to win by it. Flying these prodigious distances, never ending, is what it is in their veins to do, exactly as it was in Sisyphus' veins to roll stones, without end, after the gods had waxed merciful and implanted this in him.

A human being no sooner draws his first breath than he responds to the will that is in him to live. He no more asks whether it will be worthwhile, or whether anything of significance will come of it, than the worms and the birds. The point of his living is simply to be living, in the manner that it is his nature to be living. He goes through his life building his castles, each of these beginning to fade into time as the next is begun; yet, it would be no salvation to rest from all this. It would be a condemnation, and one that would in no way be redeemed were he able to gaze upon the things he has done, even if these were beautiful and absolutely permanent, as they never are. What counts is that one should be able to begin a new task, a new castle, a new bubble. It counts only because it is there to be done and he has the will to do it. The same will be the life of his children, and of theirs; and if the philosopher is apt to see in this a pattern similar to the unending cycles of the existence of

Sisyphus, and to despair, then it is indeed because the meaning and point he is seeking is not there—but mercifully so. The meaning of life is from within us, it is not bestowed from without, and it far exceeds in both its beauty and permanence any heaven of which men have ever dreamed or yearned for.

The Meanings of the Questions of Life

John Wisdom

When one asks "What is the meaning of life?" one begins to wonder whether this large, hazy and bewildering question itself has any meaning. Some people indeed have said boldly that the question has no meaning. I believe this is a mistake. But it is a mistake which is not without excuse. And I hope that by examining the excuse we may begin to remedy the mistake, and so come to see that whether or not life has a meaning it is not senseless to enquire whether it has or not. First, then, what has led some people to think that the whole enquiry is senseless?

There is an old story which runs something like this: A child asked an old man "What holds up the world? What holds up all things?" The old man answered "A giant." The child asked "And what holds up the giant? You must tell me what holds up the giant." The old man answered "An elephant." The child said, "And what holds up the elephant?" The old man answered "A tortoise." The child said "You still have not told me what holds up all things. For what holds up the tortoise." The old man answered "Run away and don't ask me so many questions."

From this story we can see how it may happen that a question which looks very like sensible meaningful questions may turn out to be a senseless, meaningless one. Again and again when we ask "What supports this?" it is possible to give a sensible answer. For instance what supports the top-most card in a house of cards? The cards beneath it which are in their turn supported by the cards beneath them. What supports all the cards? The table. What supports the table? The floor and the earth. But the question "What supports all things, absolutely all things?" is different. It is absurd, it is senseless, like the question "What is bigger than the largest thing in the world?" And it is easy to see why the question "What supports all things?" is absurd. Whenever we ask, "What supports thing A or these things A, B, C," then we can answer this question only by mentioning some thing other than the thing A or things A, B, C about which we are asked "What supports it or them." We must if we are to answer the question mention something D other than those things which form the subject of our question, and we must say that this thing is what supports them. If we mean by the phrase "all things" absolutely all things which exist then obviously there is nothing outside that about which we are now asked "What supports all this?" Consequently any answer to the question will be self-contradictory just as any answer to the question "What is bigger than the biggest of all things" must be self-contradictory. Such questions are absurd, or, if you like, silly and senseless.

Source: "The Meaning of the Questions of Life" by John Wisdom, from *Paradox and Discovery*, Chapter 4, © 1965. Reprinted by permission of the Philosophical Library.

In a like way again and again when we ask "What is the meaning of this?" we answer in terms of something other than this. For instance imagine that there has been a quarrel in the street. One man is hitting another man on the jaw. A policeman hurries up. "Now then" he says, "what is the meaning of all this?" He wants to know what led up to the quarrel, what caused it. It is no good saying to the policeman "It's a quarrel." He knows there is a quarrel. What he wants to know is what went before the quarrel, what led up to it. To answer him we must mention something other than the quarrel itself. Again suppose a man is driving a motor car and sees in front of him a road sign, perhaps a red flag, perhaps a skull and cross bones. "What does this mean?" he asks and when he asks this he wants to know what the sign points to. To answer we must mention something other than the sign itself, such as a dangerous corner in the road. Imagine a doctor sees an extraordinary rash on the face of his patient. He is astonished and murmurs to himself "What is the meaning of this?" He wants to know what caused the strange symptoms, or what they will lead to, or both. In any case in order to answer his question he must find something which went before or comes after and lies outside that about which he asks "What does this mean?" This need to look before or after in order to answer a question of the sort "What is the meaning of this?" is so common, so characteristic, a feature of such questions that it is natural to think that when it is impossible to answer such a question in this way then the question has no sense. Now what happens when we ask "What is the meaning of life?"

Perhaps someone here replies, the meaning, the significance of this present life, this life on earth, lies in a life hereafter, a life in heaven. All right. But imagine that some persistent enquirer asks, "But what I am asking is what is the meaning of all life, life here and life beyond, life now and life hereafter? What is the meaning of all things in earth and heaven?" Are we to say that this question is absurd because there cannot be anything beyond all things while at the same time any answer to "What is the meaning of all things?" must point to some thing beyond all things?

Imagine that we come into a theatre after a play has started and are obliged to leave before it ends. We may then be puzzled by the part of the play that we are able to see. We may ask "What does it mean?" In this case we want to know what went before and what came after in order to understand the part we saw. But sometimes even when we have seen and heard a play from the beginning to the end we are still puzzled and still ask what does the whole thing mean. In this case we are not asking what came before or what came after, we are not asking about anything outside the play itself. We are, if you like asking a very different sort of question from that we usually put with the words "What does this mean?" But we are still asking a real question, we are still asking a question which has sense and is not absurd. For our words express a wish to grasp the character, the significance of the whole play. They are a confession that we have not yet done this and they are a request for help in doing it. Is the play a tragedy, a comedy or a tale told by an idiot? The pattern of it is so complex, so bewildering, our grasp of it still so inadequate, that we don't know what to say, still less whether to call it good or bad. But this question is not senseless.

In the same way when we ask "what is the meaning of all things?" we are not asking a senseless question. In this case, of course, we have not witnessed the whole play, we have only an idea in outline of what went before and what will come after that small part of history which we witness. But with the words "What is the meaning of it all?" we are trying to find the order in the drama of Time. The question may be beyond us. A child may be able to understand, to grasp a simple play and be unable to understand and grasp a play more complex and more subtle. We do not say on this account that when he asks of the larger more complex play "What does it mean?" then his question is senseless, nor even that it is senseless for him. He has asked and even answered such a question in simpler cases, he knows the sort of effort, the sort of movement of the mind which such a question calls for, and we do not say that a question is meaningless to him merely because he is not yet able to carry out quite successfully the movement of that sort which is needed in order to answer a complex question of that sort. We do not say that a question in mathematics which is at present rather beyond us is meaningless to us. We know the type of procedure it calls for and may make efforts which bring us nearer and nearer to an answer. We are able to find the meaning which lies not outside but within very complex but still limited wholes whether these are dramas of art or of real life. When we ask "What is the meaning of all things?" we are bewildered and have not that grasp of the order of things the desire for which we express when we ask that question. But this does not render the question senseless nor make it impossible for us to move towards an answer.

We must however remember that what one calls answering such a question is not giving an answer. I mean we cannot answer such a question in the form: "The meaning is this."

Such an idea about what form answering a question must take may lead to a new despair in which we feel we cannot do anything in the way of answering such a question as "What is the meaning in it all?" merely because we are not able to sum up our results in a phrase or formula.

When we ask what is the meaning of this play or this picture we cannot express the understanding which this question may lead to in the form of a list of just those things in the play or the picture which give it its meaning. No. The meaning eludes such a list. This does not mean that words quite fail us. They may yet help us provided that we do not expect of them more than they can do.

A person who is asked what he finds so hateful or so lovable in another may with words help himself and us in grasping what it is that so moves him. But he will only mislead us and himself if he pretends that his words are a complete account of all that there is in the matter.

It is the same when we ask what is it in all things that makes it all so good, so bad, so grand, so contemptible. We must not anticipate that the answer can be given in a word or in a neat list. But this does not mean that we can do nothing towards answering these questions nor even that words will not help us. Indeed surely the historians, the scientists, the prophets, the dramatists and the poets have said much which may help any man who asks himself: Is the drama of time meaningless as a tale told by an idiot? Or is it not meaningless? And if it is not meaningless is it a comedy or a tragedy, a triumph or a disaster, or is it a mixture in which sweet and bitter are for ever mixed?

The Meaning of Life:
Rephrasing Questions

Irving Singer

To a large extent, questions about the meaning of life emanate from the body of continuous investigation that constitutes the history of philosophy. And within that history, one finds an ambivalence that also pervades the mentality of ordinary people who have thought about this cluster of basic problems. We long to know the secrets of the universe and what it means, in itself, apart from human interests. At the same time, however, we seek a meaningful way to live our lives, whether or not we can find a separate meaning in the cosmos.

These two types of questions, which have usually been lumped together by philosophers as well as laymen, are really very different. Even the twentieth-century idea that life is "absurd" becomes more manageable once we recognize this difference. Having encountered difficulties in our search for a meaning of life as a whole, we may nevertheless hope to answer questions about the nature of a meaningful life. Is it something we find or something we create? How is it dependent on purposes, values, ideals? How is it related to happiness, and does it give us assurance that men and women can face up to their predicament as finite creatures? In working at these issues, we may be able to construct an outlook that reveals a life worth living even if we remain partly pessimistic about human existence.

As a prelude, it may be useful to review the speculations of three nineteenth-century philosophers who foresaw many of the problems that will follow us into the twenty-first century. Despite their dialectical differences, Hegel, Schopenhauer, and Nietzsche make a unity within themselves. On points of detail their views are often remarkably similar. Each was convinced that nothing of life, and certainly no human being, can long survive in itself. They hold out little hope for personal immortality or the escape from death that Western religions promised.

In other ways, of course, their philosophies differ greatly. Unlike the two later thinkers, Hegel is an optimist and an idealist insofar as he believes that reality is meaningful as a totality. Though individuals are annihilated once they have played their tiny role, they all contribute to the ongoing development of the cosmos. They do so by searching for value and self-awareness. Hegel identifies this quest, which he considers fundamental in the universe, as a yearning for moral or spiritual goals. This striving explains the material order of things as well as the struggles of conscious beings. Hegel believes that all reality moves toward total union with absolute spirit. Such union is also *re*union since it entails a return to primordial oneness, though each new particularity undergoes a kind of separation merely in existing as itself.

If Hegel is right, life may well be called a tragedy for everything that participates in it. It is tragic for each entity perceived as a being whose organic drives and cherished values will be defeated sooner or later. But in contributing to the search for greater spirituality, which motivates their behavior whether or not they realize it, all things have a permanent place within the cosmic performance. Their tragic existence contains an inherent creativity that reveals the progressive attainment of ever-increasing meaningfulness, goodness, and beauty.

Since Hegel assures us that these ideal determinants are objectively present in the world, we might well conclude that life is not really tragic. Taken as a whole it would all seem to be an ontological comedy, an enterprise that justifies our deepest hopes. It is nevertheless a tragedy for the participants, since they survive their brief appearance only in having a meager effect upon the ineluctable flow that quickly engulfs them. One might therefore say that Hegel sees life as a tragi-comedy: tragic for those who perform in it but infinitely rewarding for the evolving and impersonal spirituality that marches toward fulfillment throughout this process.

In its own sophisticated manner, the Hegelian comedy of life resembles the divine comedy that Dante portrays. In the *Paradiso* the blessed spirits are not entities of the sort they were on earth. In effect they have been annihilated, as Hegel would also say, for now they have no being apart from God. They radiate his luminous goodness, from which they are no longer separated. But in their unity with God, are they really persons? Are they not merely resplendent expressions of the divine presence? Hegel seems to think so. He duplicates Dante's vision except that he sees the final beatitude as residual or latent in each moment, as operative in existence at all times. For him this pervasive spirituality shows forth the meaning of life and explains the being of anything that occurs.

Schopenhauer, who was Hegel's contemporary, opposes his philosophy and condemns it as hideous wish-fulfillment. He denies that there is any benign principle in the cosmos that can mitigate or justify the suffering one observes. Schopenhauer thinks that all life must be tragic, since every event is governed by laws of nature that have nothing in them that could be considered ideal. The fundamental principle existing in the universe is dynamic, material, brutal, non-purposive, and more or less without direction. Schopenhauer calls this principle "the will" since we feel it most directly in our volitional impulses.

Rejecting Hegel's faith in underlying spiritual goals, Schopenhauer argues that existence is simply a reservoir of energy spewing out in no meaningful pattern—like explosions in an atom or a distant galaxy. Nature germinates individual manifestations of itself but then reamalgamates them without a trace, everything that exists belonging to an enormous recycling process. The totality keeps changing but without any discernible rationale. In living things, only an instinct for self-preservation is constant. At times, Schopenhauer refers to the will as "the will to live." Nothing else could count as an explanation of life.

Schopenhauer believes that animate existence is more often a form of suffering than of happiness or pleasure. Life on earth is a calamity whose only cure is death. But though he is pessimistic in this respect, he also thinks that knowledge of his philosophy will help us live agreeable and rewarding lives. Once people understand that the metaphysical will to which they are subject is unconcerned about their welfare, they can adapt to this fatality in constructive and satisfying ways. They cannot defeat the will and they must reconcile themselves to being parts of a recycling process. But also they can show their revulsion at the mindless cruelty of existence and attain essential dignity in their reaction to it.

Schopenhauer articulates a system of meaningful responses to the tragedy of life, and he outlines a moral philosophy based on feeling compassion for the suffering of everything that lives. The sense of dignity, which he posits as the source of any possible salvation, results from various attitudes or attainments that he recommends: philosophical awareness provided by his metaphysics; scientific and technological knowledge that enables us to re-direct the will despite our subjugation to it; contemplation of the quasi-Platonic forms through which, he thinks, being always shows itself; creativity and aesthetic delight that employs such contemplation in the making and enjoying of works of art; and in general, renunciation of bodily interests that merely perpetuate the will's imperious appetite.

In offering liberation of this sort, Schopenhauer's philosophy is neither gloomy nor wholly defeatist. He himself seems to have had a comfortable existence, writing as he wished, playing his flute for pleasure, and taking walks with his little dog. One can live a good or at least bearable life, he thought, but only after one has stared the horrors of reality in the face and withdrawn allegiance from the metaphysical force that produces them. Though we cannot defeat the will, we can and should say no to it. This was what Ivan Karamazov in Dostoyevsky's novel would later call giving back the ticket to the universe. Generations of thinkers who were influenced by Schopenhauer—for instance, Freud—inherited a comparable attitude of nay-saying. But it was this part of Schopenhauer's doctrine that Friedrich Nietzsche found most unacceptable as his own ideas matured.

Nietzsche agrees that the will is devoid of meaning, that it is vicious and the cause of more suffering than happiness, that there are no gods to whom we can appeal, and that the only paths of salvation are those that lead to philosophy, science, art, and the kind of morality that emerges from such pursuits. What Nietzsche could not stomach was the element of negativity in Schopenhauer's philosophy. He himself had, both mentally and physically, a more delicate constitution than Schopenhauer, and he felt that saying no to the universe would prevent one from being able to live productively.

As an alternative to nay-saying, Nietzsche recommends *amor fati* (love of destiny, or things as they really are). This attitude entails a heroic and healthy-minded acceptance of reality *even though* it is horrible and wholly destructive to everything that participates in it. For Nietzsche this love of the hateful cosmos is the highest attainment humanity can reach: "My formula for greatness in a human being is *amor fati:* that one wants nothing to be different, not forward, not backward, not in all eternity. Not merely bear what is necessary, still less conceal it—all idealism is mendaciousness in the face of what is necessary—but *love* it."

Nietzsche synthesizes the philosophies of Hegel and Schopenhauer. For Hegel, existence—harsh and horrid as it often is—could only be the means by which spirit joyfully progressed. Though life was a tragedy for everything that lives, it would eventually provide a happy resolution for the totality of being. Nietzsche is convinced that this totality must be meaningless, devoid of spirit, as Schopenhauer had said. And yet he thinks participants in life might create—through amor fati—a heroic comedy by courageously accepting it all despite the fact that everything is

ultimately tragic and even vile. In this way, Nietzsche feels, one might see life real-
istically without undermining the pursuit of noble ideals that Hegel considered
paramount.

There is much in Nietzsche's philosophy that speaks to people of the twentieth
century. But his ideas about amor fati and the meaning of life are unconvincing to
me. If Schopenhauer was accurate in depicting the horror of all existence, as Nietzsche believed, why should one *accept* reality rather than reject it as much as possible? Why should we identify with the aggressor, so to speak, instead of hating our
subjection to the will? Would it not be more honest to cry out in terror—as in the
famous painting of *The Shriek* by Edvard Munch—or at least to recognize coolly
that there must always remain a basic discontinuity between our values and the
world in which they make their freakish and unrepresentative appearance?

Nietzsche may have thought that love is so essential that no one, not even a
liberated pessimist like Schopenhauer, could enjoy a single moment of existence
unless he contrived to love reality despite its utter worthlessness. He may also have
felt that only one who loves the world while knowing how bad it is can find the
fortitude needed to improve it through moral conduct. But if the Nietzschean
philosopher-saint loves everything that exists, how can he reject the bad elements?
The worst parts of existence also belong to reality, and he has determined to love
and therefore to accept it all completely. Nietzsche's synthesis of Schopenhauer
and Hegel is, at best, very problematic.

Hegel's optimism may seem ridiculous to us in view of its unswerving certitude about the goodness of the universe, but it alerts us to the importance of ideals
and to the human capacity for self-fulfillment in the act of pursuing them. Hegel's
greatest strength consists in his recognition that human beings can and do enjoy life
by striving for spiritual goals. Consummation of this sort presupposes an attunement to nature and the world in which we live. Hegel understood that we could not
have the ends, the interests, and the values that define our being unless we believed
that reality sustains us in some way. Schopenhauer's philosophy is weak precisely
at this point, though it is clear-sighted about the material context in which human
idealization occurs. Combining the insights of Hegel and Schopenhauer, we need
not recommend a love of all the terrible things that happen in reality—as Nietzsche's notion of amor fati requires—but we may be able to develop a view of the
world that is realistic and yet sensitive to the possibility of meaning. Nietzsche is
to be revered for having shown us, with greater power than anyone else, how
ghastly human experience will be in the coming years unless our philosophers succeed in working out the details of a viable synthesis.

*

But what exactly is involved in the problems we are exploring? What is one saying
when one asks for the meaning of life? People who raise this question usually want
to know about more than life alone. They want to know where existence "comes
from." They want to know the why of it: why we are "here," and why anything—
or rather everything—should be as it is. To the scrupulous philosopher as well as

the plain-speaking skeptic on the street, such use of language must occasion puzzlement. What can "meaning" signify in this context? Out of all the many types of linguistic usage that cluster about this term, two senses of the word "meaning" seem to me especially relevant. One of them is cognitive; the other is valuational.

When we use "meaning" in its cognitive sense, we are looking for some kind of explanation, some clarification about an occurrence or event. We hope to find out why something has the properties it has. We want to gain insight into an existing or possible state of affairs. We wish to learn about its consequences, its implications for further observation. This usage applies to the denoting of an actuality as well as to the connotative function of a word. When we say "What does it mean if water fails to boil at 212 degrees Fahrenheit?" we seek a cognitive type of meaning. The same is true when we ask for the meaning of the term "Fahrenheit."

On the other hand, we often use the word "meaning" in relation to personal feelings and emotional significance. It then reveals and sometimes declares our highest values. It manifests ideals that we cherish and pursue, that guide our behavior and provide the norms by which we live. "Friendship means a great deal to that man; when his friends have need of him, money means nothing at all." This way of using words like "means" or "meaning" is easily combined with the first kind of usage. In saying that a mother's attitude toward her child reveals the meaning of love, we are suggesting that her response exemplifies a value system that may well be studied for its cognitive import.

People who search for "the meaning of life" are trying to articulate analogous questions about the world. They want to know what would enable us to understand the diverse and frequently bizarre phenomena that constitute reality. But also they wonder whether things can be as they are because of some benign intention of a quasi-human sort that pervades the universe. Theories about a deity who has created everything are often secondary to this concern. Ideas about God's essence—whether he is infinitely wise or good or powerful—pertain to mainly technical problems in theology. To argue about the Supreme Being's attributes is to engage in an exercise that probably has minor importance for most people. William James was quite right when he claimed that the "cash value" of such deliberations resides in our primordial need to reassure ourselves about an ultimate good will in the cosmos, a basic friendliness toward us and what we value, a final haven or support for our ideals and aspirations.

James thought that the "need of an eternal moral order is one of the deepest needs of our breast." Whether this is true of everyone, and whether or not the need is satisfiable, it helps explain our search for meaning in both senses of the term and regardless of specific religious belief. We know what it is to pursue ideals that express human values and elicit relevant emotional responses. The crucial question for most people is whether anything of the sort is justified by objective conditions in the universe. We may be willing to remain ignorant about the chances of our own immortality, and even about the ultimate fate of whatever we consider to be good. We mainly want to be assured that a controlling power exists in terms of which all things could be explained—if only we had intellects capable of understanding its nature—and that it is purposeful in some manner we might recognize as having consummate value.

*

By introducing the idea of purpose, we have taken an important step. Life often includes purposes that organize our actions in fixed and sometimes predictable patterns. "Why did the chicken cross the road?" We are expected to find the answer witty because the question has led us to anticipate a motive more interesting than wanting merely to reach the other side. That kind of purpose we take for granted. Life is filled with many like it. But is there one or even several purposes *of* life, over and above the purposes *in* life?

In earlier generations some philosophers believed that the purpose of life is the progressive advancement of the most highly organized species. Others claimed it is just the continuance of life itself. Nowadays one might be tempted to argue that the purpose of life is the replication of DNA. But to each of these replies, we can ask: What is the purpose of *that?* If we say that the final end has no purpose, since it simply *is,* we have concluded that ultimately there is no purpose of life. There would be purposefulness in life, most notably in human life, but no all-embracing purpose for life or being as a whole.

Different as they are, these accounts would seem to share a similar conception of what a purpose is. But that term also needs clarification. There are two primary senses of the word that have been used in Western philosophy. One, which may be considered "idealist," derives from Plato; the other we may call "pragmatic." The idealist sense is best exemplified by Plato's description of creation in the *Timaeus.* He there portrays the world as having been created by a demiurge or Grand Artificer who contemplates the realm of forms and then imposes them, as best he can, upon brute matter. Plato thinks of the forms as eternal possibilities; and he claims that since the Creator is good, he "desired that all things should be good and nothing bad, so far as this was attainable."

Plato formulates this model in order to show how the world may be seen as purposeful. He assumes that the creative agency has in mind not only what is good but also what is best. The Platonic forms are hierarchical, with the Good presiding over all other possibilities as the highest and most desirable object. This doctrine is rationalistic inasmuch as Plato maintains that contemplation employs abstract reason that takes the inquisitive soul beyond the sensory world. In the *Republic,* and elsewhere, he argues that only deductive reason—as in mathematics, logic, and metaphysical intuition—puts us in contact with reality. Only through deductive reason can we envision the ultimate form, which he sometimes calls the Beautiful as well as the Good.

In effect, Plato is saying not only that the world itself is purposeful, but also that activities within the world become more fully purposeful by employing reason and contemplation to realize the best that is attainable. The implications of this approach can be illustrated by touching on a problem in aesthetics. Philosophers have often wondered what is involved in making art. In Plato's view, artistic creativity imitates the action of the demiurge. According to Plato, painters, poets, composers, etc., contemplate a realm of possible forms to which they have access through their powers of abstract reason within the confines of their individual talent. They then impose these forms upon the materials of their art in the hope of achieving a predeterminate good. This good serves as a goal that guides the aesthetic process from its beginnings. Only by recognizing that his initial intuition shows forth reality and the meaning of life, can the artist—or anyone else—pursue the purposes ingredient in human creativity.

Much of Plato's philosophy is magnificent. But there are many difficulties in the conception he offers. They become especially apparent when we remember that in ordinary life, and even (some would say preeminently) in moments of great inspiration, purposefulness does not lend itself to any such analysis. The second approach, which I call "pragmatic," emphasizes the discrepancy between purposive behavior and reliance upon abstract reason of the sort that Plato advocates. Instead of depicting human beings as godlike entities who contemplate eternal possibilities, the pragmatic approach encourages us to study what happens when intelligent animals engage in behavior that we would deem purposive.

Think of a dog, let us say a relatively inexperienced puppy, that has not eaten for some time and presumably feels hunger. Imagine that it can see a bowl of food on the other side of a long chain fence with barbed wire on top. What are the likely events that could reveal the nature of purposive behavior? The dog might leap forward, only to be stopped by the fence. He might try to climb over or dig under it. There may be other unsuccessful experiments. Finally he gets the "idea" or "insight" (both of which I put in quotes because these are phenomena about which we know little or nothing) that leads him to run around the end of the fence. He then eats the food, lies down, and remains quiescent until some later desire stirs him into further activity.

The pragmatic conception interprets purposefulness as part of a process that satisfies organic needs. Purpose consists in appetitive striving that is finally eliminated by the attaining of consummatory goals. During the appetitive phase, the purposive animal undergoes a pattern of trial and error until it manages to get what it wants. Having got it, the animal rests. Its purposefulness is not a function of abstract reason or the contemplation of Platonic forms. It is only the doing of what is necessary to satisfy desires in a systematic, orderly, and therefore "sensible" fashion that happens to work in a given environment.

In books such as *How We Think* and *Logic: The Theory of Inquiry,* John Dewey develops the pragmatic view in great detail and shows its relation to what we normally mean by intelligence. In *Art as Experience* Dewey counters the Platonic approach to creativity by insisting that the ends an artist pursues throughout the making of his object cannot be separated from the means that he employs. Far from being the intuition of a formal and inherently perfect possibility that might have served as a prior goal, artistic effort is a coordinated succession of maneuvers motivated by needs and desires. The process terminates once an acceptable level of relevant satisfaction has been achieved by the artist. His behavior includes appetitive and consummatory phases comparable to what the hungry dog experienced, though far more complex and certainly more conceptual.

Each of these two approaches has its admirers and its critics. We need not adjudicate between them, or even determine whether they may be harmonized in a synthesis that reconciles their differences. The first one needs to overcome skepticism about the faculty of abstract reason that it invokes as an aprioristic attunement to ultimate reality. The second one must justify its claim that even the most elevated of human activities—in art, in ethical conduct, in religion—is based upon motivation similar to what occurs in animal behavior directed toward the satisfaction of organic needs. Of more immediate importance is the possibility that neither view of human purpose and its sources elucidates a meaning of life. Each may only make sense as an account of purposefulness *in* life. Examples of appetitive behavior and abstract reasoning abound. They are readily observed, though philosophers differ greatly in their theorizing about them. But what are we to say about extrapolations to the entire universe?

*

If we follow Dewey, we are likely to end up with a materialism that sees the cosmos as a field of contending forces in which purpose exists only to the extent that conscious creatures strive to gratify their own interests. If we follow Plato, we ascribe to some divinity or universal being a concern for higher values that humanity may pursue in an attempt to rise above its mundane condition.

In various ways, philosophers have tried to undermine suggestions that there might be this kind of superior purpose. For instance, if we said that a demiurge or a God of the Judaeo-Christian variety created the world in order to bring about as much goodness as possible, would we not be involving ourselves in an infinite regress? For we should have to ask whether God's purposiveness was itself occasioned by a prior purpose. It is not self-evident that a Supreme Creator must want to maximize goodness. If that desire is ascribed to his "essence," we might still wonder whether such an essence manifests some further, more ultimate purposefulness. We may have made an advance in seeking for the meaning of life, but the quest will have shown itself to be endless. Nor will we have made much progress if, in the pragmatic mode, we suggest that everything seeks its own completion as if it were all part of a cosmic organism trying to satisfy its natural appetites. For then, too, we awaken questions about the purposefulness of that animate totality.

Some philosophers argue that if there were indeed a comprehensive purpose of life, that alone would deprive us of traits human beings have always valued and sought to preserve. We pride ourselves on being free and autonomous, capable of heroic achievements when we live in accordance with our ideals. If, however, we are constituents of a cosmos that has been designed to fulfill a purpose, our status does not differ greatly from that of a tool or instrument fashioned with a predetermined end in mind. The form and use of a kitchen utensil is defined by the function it was designed to carry out. If humanity, or life in general, was created to serve a purpose beyond itself, our being would be analogous to that of a manufactured artifact. There seems to be little in this state of affairs to justify the exultation that religious people sometimes feel in thinking that God's plan reveals the purpose and the meaning of all reality.

Within the linguistic orientation that has characterized much of contemporary philosophy, queries about life's purpose are often rejected in a more radical manner. We are encouraged to believe that such language may really be nonsensical. In order to have meaning, our remarks must have a logical form that is syntactically and semantically adequate for expressing a meaningful question. We assume that a sentence such as "What is the purpose of life?" makes sense because it has the same grammatical form as sentences like "What is the purpose of pre-heating the oven?" This question is intelligible and has relevance to an observable purpose in life. But though the first utterance has a similar *grammatical* structure, there is no assurance that it has any meaning whatsoever.

To see how we might be fooled in this respect, compare the following sentences: "When it is 5 p.m. in New York, what time is it in Los Angeles?"; "When it is 5 p.m. in New York, what time is it on the sun?" Since clock-time is defined in terms of the angle at which the sun's rays strike some location on the earth, the second of these sentences is nonsense. Whatever its pretensions, a question about time on the sun is internally inconsistent. It has no coherent logical form, and is therefore not really a question. To take it seriously is to waste one's energy. Should we not say the same about putative questions about the purpose of life? Despite the beguiling arrangement of their grammar, are they not equally nonsensical?

This linguistic argument seems very powerful to me. We have often observed purposes in the world, and we know what someone asks when he raises questions about a particular pattern of behavior. But though we are immersed in the cosmos, it is not clear that we can have experience of the cosmos as a whole. We cannot stand back and regard the universe in its totality, as we might do with one or another of its parts. We have no awareness of a second universe with which to compare our own. For the most part, our language is a function of what we can experience or imagine on the basis of experience. We participate in life; we experience it directly; and that can give us knowledge of the purposes within it. But if these purposes must be grounded in a larger purpose that underlies the entire universe, nothing that we try to say or ask about the meaning of it all may really make sense.

And yet, questions about the purpose or meaning of life are not necessarily self-contradictory, or inconsistent, like questions about time on the sun. They are certainly vague, and must always involve perilous extensions beyond ordinary experience. They must be treated as metaphoric and symbolic rather than literal or factual. But this alone does not deprive them of intelligibility. It merely puts them in a category that is closer to poetry than to science. This need not be a serious impediment. Our linguistic capabilities are infinitely diverse. Though there may be good reasons for renouncing the quest for a meaning of life, we should not dismiss such interests merely because they require a language that is hard to understand.

*

If our concern about the meaning of everything cannot be rejected in advance, on purely linguistic grounds, theories about what that meaning might be are worth studying. Traditional Western religions trace it to an entity they call *super*natural because it exists apart from space, time, and all other coordinates of nature. This Being has a plan in accordance with which he (in the usual ascription of gender) has created the universe. Moreover, he has given everything the ability to live in accordance with his design. The cosmic plan, together with this innate capacity, provides an underlying purpose such that once we understand it we perceive the meaning of life. Millions of people have accepted that account as persuasive and reassuring, a fount of spiritual sustenance throughout their lives. How can this system of beliefs be rejected as nonsensical or logically inadequate?

To begin with, one would want to know what is meant by a universal "plan." Is it similar to the blueprint that an architect draws up before building a house? God, or whatever we call the supernatural being that establishes the purpose of life, presumably creates the universe in an attempt to carry out his prior design. All of nature strives to accomplish his intention, and we may liken this to construction workers following the architect's blueprint. But to talk in this way is to assume that one can refer to an intentionality *outside* of time and space comparable to what occurs within. That is the basic flaw in the analogy.

What can it mean to assert that something is "outside" of time and space? We might argue that numbers exist apart from time and space; and if someone were to claim that for all eternity $2 + 2 = 4$, we would know what is being said. But we would never suggest that numbers have the same properties as things *in* time and space. We do not say that numbers come into or go out of existence. We may even deny that they exist at all. We certainly do not believe that their relationships reveal a "purpose." In talking about a purposive being whose creativity gives value and a goal to all existence, it is as if Western religions confused abstract entities, such as numbers, with things in time and space. It is not a question of determining whether we can fathom the cosmic plan, or prove that a cosmic-planner exists, or manage to fulfill his purposive program. It is a question of knowing whether our mind is able to formulate these notions with any degree of clarity.

One's motive for seeking a meaning of life is quite evident. The problems of living would be greatly simplified if everything could be shown to make sense in terms of a goal toward which it was or ought to be tending. Even if this goal was inescapable or predetermined, we could still acquiesce and happily perform whatever actions are required. Of course we might also conclude that since all decisions must somehow follow the ineluctable order of things, it does not matter what we choose. Some might find this liberating, others might deem it injurious to their sense of freedom; but everyone could feel that an objective explanation has been discovered. Whatever the emotional response, the power of the human mind would at least have been established. Our species would have proved its ability to solve the greatest of all puzzles.

In the history of ideas, many great philosophers (beginning with Plato and Aristotle) have defended the belief in an Ultimate Being or Highest Good that provides objective ends each thing or person must pursue in order to fulfill itself. In theology equally great thinkers, such as Aquinas, have tried to codify our intuitions about the supernatural. This is not the place to engage them in debate. Instead I suggest, as others have in the last two hundred years, that such concepts issue from our human attempt to magnify and idealize what is merely natural. Far from transcending nature, we glorify the aspects that matter to us. In the process we both aggrandize our imagination and inflate our own experience.

Human beings seek a prior meaning in everything as a defense against doubts about the importance of anything, including man's existence. Though we see people expend a great deal of energy on matters of personal concern, we are also aware of human limitations. We know that we are mortal, living for fairly short periods, and that nothing we may do or feel can have a major influence upon the universe. There appears to be a disproportion between the seriousness with which men and women approach their multiple interests and the relative insignificance of these interests within the cosmos as a whole. If, however, the world itself pursues a goal toward which we all contribute, this basic disproportion would be resolved. What matters to us surely does matter if the course of reality includes it within some truly objective design. To affirm that there is a supreme meaning of life is to give the intellect an opportunity to escape the disquieting conclusion that *nothing* people do can possibly have more than slight importance.

*

The belief that human purposiveness has no real significance belongs to the philosophical view called "nihilism." This, in turn, is related to the idea that our existence is inherently "absurd." The beginnings of absurdist thought may be traced to David Hume. He argues that there is no knowable true statement from which one can deduce the existence of anything (except in a tautologous fashion). In other words, as far as we can tell, everything that is exists for no necessary reason. Hume reached this conclusion because he thought that causality is always ascribed to events that occur in a regular but ultimately arbitrary fashion. Every existing entity is just a *surd*—its occurrence is not necessitated by anything else even though it appears in a constant sequence with events that precede or follow it.

From this, one may conclude that there is no meaning of life, only a pervasive complex of basically inexplicable structures. Objects and events just happen to be as they are. There is no inherent reason for them to be or not to be, even though our minds become habituated to their usual appearance. They are not planned in any objective sense, and their existence cannot be explained by reference to a prior being.

In books such as *Nausea* and *Being and Nothingness,* Jean-Paul Sartre uses Hume's idea to express the nature of all factuality. Nothing that exists, he says, has any ontological necessity requiring it to be; and therefore its existence can never be "justified" or shown to be required for the existence of anything else. That is what Sartre means when he postulates the "contingency" of everything human, and of being in general. Since I am contingent, nothing fundamental in the world would be different if I did not exist. There may be interesting existential consequences of my never having been—for instance, my children would never have existed—but such considerations are irrelevant, since my children cannot be justified either. They exist, if they happen to do so, only as haphazard occurrences and not as the exemplars of an ultimate meaning in the universe.

In the writings of Albert Camus similar ideas about the absurdity of life are extended in a way that is especially pertinent to our discussion. Camus focuses upon the discrepancy between man's "longing for happiness and for reason" and his inevitable awareness that there is nothing in the universe to satisfy this longing except in a meager or ephemeral manner. The cosmos does not care about human welfare. Camus remarks that "the absurd is born of this confrontation between the human need and the unreasonable silence of the world." It is as if the life of every human being, from beginning to end, was simply a ridiculous rearranging of the chairs in the dining room of the *Titanic* after it has hit the iceberg. For us the iceberg is our finitude, our mortality, and the absurdity of our life lies in our inability either to forgo our customary strivings or to ignore the fact that reality shows no interest in dignifying and preserving them.

Developing a related theory of the absurd, Thomas Nagel says it results from an opposition between what he calls man's "self-consciousness" and his "self-transcendence." He means that the seriousness with which human beings live their lives conflicts with their capacity to transcend this attitude by seeing themselves as "arbitrary, idiosyncratic, highly specific occupants of the world, one of countless possible forms of life." The absurd arises from a discrepancy between our inclination to take our values seriously, as if they were really important, and our awareness that nothing in the universe justifies their existence. Like Camus, Nagel concludes that ultimately and objectively there is no basis for believing that anything matters.

In proposing their conceptions of absurdity, these philosophers assume a contradiction, or at least a split, between man and the world, and also between two aspects of human nature. Man is portrayed as inherently divided between his purposive desire to pursue whatever goals he values and his being as a self-transcending spectator who recognizes that the world is wholly unresponsive either to him or to his values. The world does not seem to mind destroying, sooner or later, everything man cares about. His sense of absurdity is therefore a painful counterpart to the intellect's demonstration of human pretentiousness.

Is this line of reasoning really cogent? For one thing, it is hard to imagine where the "serious" side of man could have come from if there is nothing to maintain it. Thinkers like Sartre and Martin Heidegger defend the absurdist approach by arguing that human life is predicated upon nothingness inasmuch as nothing has value or meaning until man brings these categories into existence. Strictly speaking, that is not correct, as these writers also perceive on occasion. For everything a sentient being wants will be valuable and meaningful to it, to some extent at least. This holds for all creatures that are able to have desires, even if it is true that only human beings can formulate the *concept* of value or meaning. In any event, it does not follow that values issue out of nothing or that the world does not sustain them.

What is meaningful to a human being originates in the vital necessities of the human condition, and that results from nature as it exists in us. It would indeed be absurd to expect inanimate objects or beings in some remote galaxy to share our own system of values. Human beings belong to nature in ways that are defined by the evolution of life on this particular planet. The seriousness of man does not *contradict* the world but rather springs from it as a new but wholly compatible expression of phenomena that may or may not occur elsewhere.

To assert that human interests are always pretentious or disproportionate, and therefore absurd, is to use a metaphor that does not apply. Rearranging the chairs on the *Titanic* is absurd because one then acts as if there is reason to prepare the dining room for passengers who will notice the placement of furniture, whereas everyone has already begun to scurry for the lifeboats. It is likewise absurd—to use one of Camus' examples—for an individual armed with nothing but a sword to attack machine guns, since the man who makes the attempt must know (as we do) that it cannot succeed. But one who tries to live a meaningful life does not manifest a similar confusion. He is not necessarily assuming that his values matter to the universe at large. He may act as he does with full recognition of the context in which he acts. Though the meaningfulness of his existence may be shortlived or highly circumscribed, that need not doom his efforts to futility. To say that one's interests are absurd would be to claim that here, as in the case of the *Titanic* or the solitary swordsman, one's knowledge about reality inevitably contradicts the gamut of beliefs implied by one's behavior. That claim seems to me wholly unwarranted. What could be the content of these damaging beliefs? An assumption that one's values are preordained or that one's life will go on forever? Or that it may consist of unalloyed pleasure, infinite achievement, increasing fervor, and continuous onward momentum? Sometimes people do act as if this is what they believe. But even so, the question remains: Does the pursuit of meaning *presuppose* such ideas? There is no reason to think that it does.

Since the absurdist philosophers assert that values issue from nothing and that the world therefore provides no ground for meaning, it seems strange from the very outset that they should consider man's condition to be inherently absurd. For that implies there is some other way for human beings to exist, though they absurdly fail to do so. But if there is no such alternative, as these philosophers insist, the concept of absurdity cannot be relevant to actual existence. I am willing to agree that men and women often yearn for unattainable goals, and that this sort of attitude may well be called absurd. But why should *all* human striving be characterized that way?

The absurdist philosophers observe, or assume, that the universe has no overarching purpose and, apparently, no concern for human welfare. Since people nevertheless continue to pursue cherished goals, the philosophers see a contradiction between the purposefulness in man's struggle for life and the general purposelessness of the cosmos. This is what they consider the source of human absurdity. I have been arguing that no contradiction, and therefore no absurdity, can be derived from the stated facts. If someone does think that his values matter to some ultimate being, while deep down he knows this cannot be true, his attitude reveals an obvious inconsistency that may justify calling it absurd. But the absurdists are unable to show that our pursuit of goals must always involve this type of contradiction. On the contrary, they themselves usually exhort us to live in a purposive manner that will be free of delusive hopes about corroboration from the universe. They call this an acceptance of our basic absurdity, but it would be more correct to say that acting for realistic goals without harboring false expectations means *avoiding* the alleged contradiction. If we do that, our life is not absurd. Since the absurdists believe that man can follow their recommendations, they cannot cogently argue that his condition is absurd by its very nature.

*

At this point we may reconsider motives that drive us to ask for the meaning of life. As a purely practical matter, would we not reduce the agony of our existence if we were certain that we are instruments in a grand and purposive design? Alone and afraid in a world we never made, we often yearn for marching orders from a superior power whose greater authority will direct our energies while making us feel sure that they are being properly used. And if we believed in such a power, would that not absolve us of absurdity?

Many people have said that it would, and have claimed that it does in their case. They must nevertheless confront the problem of validation. If a voice from the clouds suddenly booms forth instructions about how we should live, we must still determine that we are not having an auditory hallucination. And if we are told to act contrary to our own deepest feelings and intuitions, are we really obligated to accept the dictates of the superior being? Even if we acquiesce, what have we learned about the meaning of life? Submission to the higher power might simplify our lives and even help us go on living, but in itself it would not indicate what the meaning of life is. For we would still need to know why the words of this individual must be taken as the ultimate authority. Perhaps it gets its own sense of importance by arbitrarily giving orders to inferior beings. Perhaps it is carrying out the commands of a power higher than itself, even though reality as a whole has no meaning whatsoever.

One might reply that having access to vividly articulated prescriptions for behavior is so great a joy that we should not care about their final validation. That makes sense. But if we do not really care about final validation, then neither are we seeking a meaning of life in any objective sense. Instead we will have subtly redirected our original investigation. Rather than searching for a prior meaning of life, we would be asking what is needed for someone to have *a meaningful life.* This is a different kind of question: it orients us toward possibilities that emanate from man's estate regardless of any external meaning that may or may not surround it. Even if there is no meaning of life, or if this meaning is unknowable, or if the entire question is nonsensical in some respect, we may nevertheless hope for illumination about the circumstances under which human beings are able to achieve a meaningful existence.

Though Camus and the others say the human condition is absurd, they establish only that men and women act as if they can have meaningful lives while also believing that the universe does not give a damn. And if people act this way, are they not creating values and a meaning for themselves? The absurdists might agree. But in thinking that all human interests are merely arbitrary, all equally absurd, they cannot explain why people do (or should) prefer any particular attitude toward man's inescapable absurdity. Suggesting irony as an appropriate response, Nagel says: "If *sub specie aeternitatis* there is no reason to believe that anything matters, then that does not matter either, and we can approach our absurd lives with irony instead of heroism or despair." But Nagel is obviously advocating, or at least favoring, irony as a suitable and meaningful reaction, just as Camus had proposed heroic defiance as the means by which human beings can overcome the absurdity in life.

To say anything of this sort, however, is to admit that human existence is not wholly absurd. It then behooves us to determine the nature of meaningfulness and how it may be attained.

In a recent book, Nagel suggests that the conflict between self-consciousness and self-transcendence can possibly be minimized. He is not sanguine about this prospect, however. He concludes that "the possibilities for most of us are limited," and indeed that it is "better to be simultaneously engaged and detached, and therefore absurd, for this is the opposite of self-denial and the result of full awareness." But once we realize that life is not absurd, since we are able to create meaning in it, we see that Nagel's dichotomies are untenable. Values do not exist *sub specie aeternitatis;* but neither are they merely arbitrary, as Nagel seems to think.

The basic error in the absurdist approach consists in a kind of fallacy of abstraction through which these theorists observe the human condition. Though they realize that people constantly pursue values and construct ideals, the absurdists examine man's experience out of context. They ignore the ways in which our species is always acting as a part of nature. Men and women have the goals and purposes that are meaningful to them because a biological structure in their needs and satisfactions underlies, either directly or indirectly, their creation of meaning. It is not at all absurd that human beings have the values that they do. These belong to us as just the natural entities that we happen to be.

Nor is it absurd that we have values that are distinct from those of a fish or a bird or any other species significantly different from our own. Each set of values arises out of material and social circumstances that make an organism to be as it is, which is to say, as it has evolved in nature. When natural preconditions are satisfied, the organism is rewarded by consummations that reinforce a viable mode of living. That is how our values come into being. That is the soil in which a meaningful life originates.

There is a sense in which the evolution of species may be considered arbitrary, for we can imagine a world in which everything could have developed differently. In that sense, nothing in life is objectively necessary. But in the reality that we know—nature as it exists, species having evolved as they did—it is not at all absurd that human beings should seek the values and create the meanings that they do. This aspect of our being is no less natural than everything else that constitutes our fundamental humanity.

*

Thus far I have been discussing two approaches to the meaning of life: the traditionalist, which includes most of religious belief in the West, and the absurdist or nihilist. Despite the differences between them, they are alike in one crucial respect. Each addresses questions about the meaning of life as if it were a single something, and moreover, something *findable.* Though their answers to these questions are diametrically opposed, both approaches look for a unitary, all-embracing set of answers that somehow might be *there,* waiting to be revealed. The traditionalists would seem to see the world as a quasi-mathematical problem for which there must be a definite solution. If we can only refine our reasoning powers or cleanse our hearts, they say, we are sure to discover what we seek. Against this optimistic view, the absurdists despair of ever succeeding in such a quest. They conceive of the philosophical problem in similar terms, but they believe it is resolved only by the honest recognition that there is no meaning of life. The tragedy of man's condition thus consists in his having the propensity to act as if he had found a prior meaning that ratifies his decisions while all the time he senses at the deepest level of his being that no such meaning exists.

But are we sure that we even know what such a meaning could actually be? If we say that the world is or resembles a soluble problem, we use an analogy that may be wholly inappropriate. We have no acquaintance with different universes, as we do with different problems in mathematics, some of which can be solved while others cannot. To *ask* about a meaning of life that we might discover is not nonsensical. We may understand how the human imagination is operating when it poses such questions. To answer them in the manner of the traditionalists or the absurdists is fruitless, however, for they offer no way of verifying that a universe such as ours does or does not have an independent meaning capable of being found. How could we justify or defeat either assumption? What would count as evidence for or against it?

Whether or not the universe has a meaning to be found, the world as we know it is clearly one in which meaning *comes into being*. We frequently observe meaning being created, whether or not these new creations conform to a further meaning that precedes them. Rather than asking for the meaning of life as if it were a single or comprehensive pattern that permeates all existence a priori, we do better to investigate how it is that life acquires or may be *given* a meaning. This meaning is generally ambiguous, as Simone de Beauvoir argues in her book *The Ethics of Ambiguity.* Criticizing the absurdists, she states: "To declare that existence is absurd is to deny that it can ever be given a meaning." Beauvoir prefers the idea of ambiguity because "to say that it [existence] is ambiguous is to assert that its meaning is never fixed, that it must be constantly won." In other words, ours is not an absurd existence in which we seek for absolute meaning although we are convinced that the universe does not afford any such thing. Rather we are creatures who create meaning for ourselves without having objective and unambiguous criteria by which to determine how we should do so.

We therefore need to examine the conditions under which human beings, and other organisms, make life meaningful. To the extent that life becomes meaningful in this accumulative way, its total meaning is increased. This is something we can verify by reference to empirical data. And indeed, when people ask about "the meaning of life," it is often meaning as a developmental phenomenon in nature that really interests them more than anything else.

With this in mind, we can make an additional response to the pessimistic comment of Freud's referred to earlier. We may now say that there is nothing inherently sick about asking for a meaning of life, provided one recognizes that apart from such considerations life is and can be meaningful in itself. If, however, the metaphysical musings arise out of despair that anything man does will ever give sense or value to life, the pathological implications are obvious. The same applies to doubts that we might have about our individual ability to attain a meaningful life. If we function as healthy beings, we act with assurance that people like ourselves are capable of creating sense and value in their lives. To the extent that they do so they augment the meaning of life in ways that would not have existed otherwise. Without meaning of this sort, human existence degenerates into misery and general chaos.

As a variation on this idea, one might say that life itself includes the creation of meaning and value as part of its innate structure. In accordance with the parameters of their individual natures, different organisms—above all, different animals—manifest indigenous modes of meaning without which they could not survive. If a human being asks for the sense or value of his life, he is either revealing uncertainty about which mode is suitable to himself, or else speculating about further ways of achieving a meaningful life. That can be painful, but our species creates meaning by undergoing this dialectic of doubt and innovation. It is by immersing ourselves in "the destructive element"—as Joseph Conrad said—that we are able to have meaning in life.

We must therefore rephrase the usual questions. Instead of seeking the meaning of life as if it were something preexisting, we must study the natural history of mental acts and bodily responses that enable organisms such as ours to fabricate meaning for themselves. We speak of "finding" a life that is meaningful, but the meaning is something we create. Whether or not we believe there is a prior system of intentions built into reality, we need to ask questions of a different sort: How do we actually create meaning? What is the phenomenology of a meaningful life? What will give a meaning to *my* life? Is life worthwhile? Is it worth living? What makes a life significant? Does anything really matter? Can one learn how to live? If so, how does one do it?

I shall return to these questions, but here I would like to linger on the last one. It appeared most graphically in Tolstoy's account of his midlife crisis and subsequent discovery of faith. Tolstoy achieved his own salvation by observing how the peasants lived. Being close to nature and relatively exempt from the depravities of modern society, they seemed to have acquired what he had missed—the intuitive knowledge of how to live. In their case this meant minimal expectation, simplicity of heart, a curtailing of personal arrogance, and spontaneous submission to their lot as human beings. These were the attitudes Tolstoy considered essential for the faith that gives meaning to life.

Other thinkers have offered their own guides to a meaningful existence: the cultivation of creativity itself, aesthetic contemplation, the pursuit of spiritual or humanitarian ideals, the full employment of one's energies, the realization of individual talents, the search for truth, the experience of love in one or another of its modalities.

However we finally analyze these alternatives, they all belong to a spectrum of life attaining meaning it does not have until we bestow that meaning upon it. I refer to the human race, of course, but not exclusively. In most, and possibly all, forms of life meaning arises from the more or less creative response of a particular organism to its environment. Since the environment may include another bit of life, the creation of meaning can be a reaction to what is meaningful in someone else. My attitude means a great deal to my dog. He creates this meaning, and thereby augments the meaningfulness of his life, by the value he gives to occurrences that others may not even notice—small gestures of mine or my momentary moods. By cherishing his responsive meaning, I make my own life more meaningful. In general, meaning will always depend on the value-laden behavior that living creatures manifest. Meaning in life is the creating of values in accordance with the needs and inclinations that belong to one's natural condition. Valuation is the making of choices by individuals striving for a meaningful life in nature. The values and meanings that emerge are, in this sense, facts of nature—not at all transcendental, as various metaphysicians have thought.

Nor is there a single pattern of meaning that runs throughout the universe. The values of a bird are not only different from, but also incommensurate with, those of a fish. Though each may overlap with the other, and human meaningfulness can often resemble both, we need not posit a discernible identity that remains constant throughout. Even if each form of life is driven by a desire to survive—or to perpetuate itself in its own being, as Spinoza would say—this alone does not reveal a generic purpose that everything has in common. For that implies the existence of a particular program or underlying meaning that creatures must all have in the act of surviving as they do. We have little reason to think that any such uniformity resides within the endless variety of meaningful events that life comprises. Even if the many types of meaningfulness derive from a quest for gene replication, these types remain infinitely diverse among themselves.

*

Having recognized the dangers in speculating about a prior meaning of life, we can now focus our discussion on meaningfulness in living things. We may see them as separate units within a diversified class of meaningful lives, and we may possibly assert that the cosmos acquires greater meaning only to the extent that it includes a totality of lives that become increasingly meaningful. We may even conclude that this growth in universal meaning *is* the meaning of life. I shall return to that idea at the end of this book. Here I merely note that our interest in meaningfulness need not culminate in a stultifying positivism.

However we interpret the nature of meaningfulness, we must realize that it is always changing. It alters as living things create their own modes of meaning. We human beings differ from members of other species in our astounding capacity to innovate, to generate new meanings for ourselves. We are not more purposive than other animals, and we frequently seem to be less gifted than they are as far as personal happiness is concerned. Anyone who has ever watched a bird building its nest will agree that it usually goes about its business with a kind of confidence, security, and single-mindedness that is rare in men and women. Doing what comes naturally, animals often appear contented, sometimes even serene. Walt Whitman admired them for that:

> I think I could turn and live with animals, they
>   are so placid and self-contain'd,
> I stand and look at them long and long.

But though this conception of animal life may be attractive, these creatures attain their level of fulfillment largely by pursuing routine purposes in much the same way throughout a lifetime and from generation to generation. What is meaningful to them is usually constraining rather than expansive. Their placidity is correlated with a lack of intellect or imagination. They are limited in their ability to entertain novel or alternate meanings. Our species is unique in its great creativity with respect to meaningfulness. Our systems of meaning vary tremendously from moment to moment, from one individual to another, and from society to society. On the one hand, we are quickly bored by older meanings and are constantly trying to replace them with newer ones; on the other hand, we have the power to enrich what is meaningful by fashioning cultural and artistic traditions that may grow and develop for centuries.

What we define as culture or civilization is itself a complex of institutions and customs that enable people to acquire patterns of meaning throughout a historical continuity. Civilization is always conservative inasmuch as the future determines itself by means of responses—many of them habitual—that preserve what was meaningful in the past. But it is also progressive, since it gives the imagination material for extending earlier attitudes through sophisticated reactions that make possible vastly unforeseen and often unforeseeable variations. In general, nothing will survive unless it is revitalized in accordance with what has current meaning. Even the dead hand of the past, as in outmoded customs or bureaucracies, retains its power over the present only by a constantly renewed acquiescence among those who submit to it. This subservience is, paradoxically, part of their search for meaning. That creative venture is the human opportunity. It reveals *our* program: not only to ask for the meaning of life but also to bring it into being in the endless ways that constitute our creativity.

The capacity to create new and greater meaning does not exist without its perils. I shall address this problem further on. But here I can say a little about the factors that threaten meaningfulness. Physical decay and many types of disease, including mental illness, are often unable to diminish it. Indeed, some of the most meaningful lives are lived by persons who undergo severe pathologies of either mind or body. A meaningful life can and often does result from efforts to overcome such impediments. Some philosophers think that death itself is just another impediment, and that we negate it by having lived a life that achieves its proper meaning. Socrates talks this way in Plato's *Phaedo*. I think instead that we must treat death as the great destroyer of meaning since it is the termination of each life in nature. But human beings know that they will die, and this awareness may itself provide a source of meaning for them. Moreover, the death of one person is an occurrence in the lives of those who survive. For them, too, it can take on creative meaning.

What then is the relationship between death and meaningfulness? Is death the meaning of life, as philosophers and theologians have often said? Or is life the meaning of death, in the sense that we can understand mortality only in relation to the facts about our finite being? Once we have analyzed our ideas in this area, we may find that we are better able to approach the many difficult questions about meaning as it exists in human experience.

The Meaning of Life

Joseph Ellin

More than any other time in history, mankind faces a crossroads. One path leads to despair and utter hopelessness. The other, to total extinction. Let us pray that we have the wisdom to choose correctly.

—Woody Allen
"My Speech to the Graduates"

HOW THE QUESTION OF THE MEANING OF LIFE ARISES

How could anyone question whether life has meaning? Let us see.

1. Sometimes when people are depressed or unhappy they say things like, "My life has no meaning," or, "All the meaning has gone out of my life." This is a way of saying that they see no point in living or that it does not matter to them whether they are alive or dead. Sometimes people think that life has lost its meaning because of some misfortune that has happened to them, such as an unhappy love affair or a career setback. Other times people feel this way after reflecting on some of life's unpleasant features: people get sick, grow old, and die; they suffer from hunger, disasters, and distress; they are misunderstood and their good qualities unrecognized or taken to be something other than they are. In the end, everyone is going to die anyway; when you reflect that your real value as a person is unappreciated in your life and that you are inevitably going to be forgotten after you are dead, you may wonder what the point of anything really is. Why live if you will end up dead and forgotten?

2. Another way of questioning the meaning *of life is by reflecting on values.* Suppose it is true, as some philosophers think, that values are not real, that they are not objective or "out there," independent of our thinking. In that case, there is no objective truth by which a person ought to live, which justifies one's choices and decisions. Since there is no real reason to do one thing rather than anything else, it might be thought that it does not really matter what happens or what you do. You are more or less at sea, left to your own devices for creating whatever meaning or value your life is to have. The nonexistence of objective values places each of us in a rather difficult situation, at least in the opinion of some philosophers, for we are forced, whether we like it or not, simply to decide what our values will be: each of us must create his or her own fundamental truths, without any hope that the choices made will be the correct ones. But how can choices be made if there is no real guidance, no real reason why you should choose one value over any other, nothing even remotely resembling proof that your decisions will be good, or wise, or moral? You cannot even

hope that you might be better off if you choose one set of values as opposed to some other; for it is entirely up to you to decide for yourself what you want to count as being better off. Whatever we choose, it is all meaningless in the sense that it makes no difference, for no choices make any more sense (objectively) than any others. No wonder that existentialists see our condition as characterized by what they call anguish, a special sort of agony of the soul brought on by the encounter with meaninglessness.

The situation thus described can be quite poignant. Suppose you interest yourself in some project or in some cause—for example, raising money to send food to hungry people, or working to eliminate some form of tyranny or oppression somewhere. You then study philosophy and come to the conclusion that there are no objective values, that it makes no difference whatever to the universe whether the people in famine-afflicted countries starve or live, or whether the people living without freedom are oppressed or liberated. Objectively speaking, the goal for which you are striving is no more valid than its opposite, or than any other. If you are at all thoughtful, this philosophical conclusion is very likely going to give you pause: if it really does not matter what happens, why am I trying to accomplish one thing rather than another? Well, no doubt it matters to you, but this answer is not going to be adequate; you will soon ask, why should it matter to me, if it really does not matter objectively? Why should I care what I do, if what I do does not make any real difference? And this kind of questioning is destructive not only of all action, but of all concern as well. If there are no objectively correct values, then in the ultimate sense nothing matters, nothing has any meaning, and nothing is worth being concerned about.

3. But the meaning of life can be questioned through reflections that may not at all be connected with depression or with philosophical anxiety. People who are thoughtful often wonder whether there is any reason for their lives. Why are we here? What does it all mean? Does life add up to something in the end? Might there be some purpose to life that makes sense of what we are and what we do? Or do we have to conclude that life has no special significance, that it just goes on, leading nowhere and achieving nothing other than its own perpetuation?

These questions ask for what we may call an ultimate justification. We want to know the point or purpose of life, not from our own personal point of view, or even from the point of view (if there is such a point of view) of people in general; we want to know the purpose of life from the point of view of the universe itself. What difference do our lives make in the ultimate scheme of things, the scheme in which sooner or later everything perishes and is forgotten? We all pass through life but once; what we want is some affirmation that somehow it is better that we have lived than not, that something has been gained or accomplished by our brief journey. We do not wish to have lived in vain. We want to find the sense that can be made from our having been alive.

Philosophy and religion are expected to answer all these questions; perhaps it is more correct to say that philosophy and religion began as answers to these questions. Perhaps one difference between philosophy and religion is that religion still claims to answer them, while much philosophy today at most thinks it can investigate or examine such questions without answering them. The enduring popularity of religion, which is always being killed off by philosophers and other skeptical intellectuals only to rise again from its own intellectual ashes, can possibly be explained by the simple fact that people (by which is meant deep thinkers as well as ordinary nonintellectual people) are not satisfied to hear that life has no meaning, or that if it does have meaning, then no one knows what that meaning is. People want life to have meaning, and are willing to accept some point of view that claims to tell them what the meaning of life is. This is why religion seems to be more powerful than skeptical arguments, and why even sophisticated, educated people continue to entertain religious ideas that philosophers have long since exposed to scathing logical critique.

IS THE MEANING OF LIFE A KIND OF KNOWLEDGE?

But suppose you wanted to know what the meaning of life is, what would you want to know? What are people looking for when they look for the meaning of life (MoL), or when they hope that life has a meaning? When we ask a question, we hope to receive an answer, presumably an answer that can be stated in some form of intelligible words, that is, a proposition. So let us begin by asking whether the MoL is something that can be stated in a proposition. This would make the MoL similar to a certain kind of knowledge, that is, to information that can be acquired and passed on to others. According to this view, people who do not know what the MoL is, or wonder about it, lack some piece of information that others possibly possess.

This may seem to make sense, because people want to know what the MoL is, and requests for knowledge seem to be requests for some kind of information. Nevertheless, there are certain difficulties with holding that the MoL is a kind of knowledge. What kind of knowledge would it be? Presumably, whatever this knowledge is, it is valuable; indeed, highly valuable, or perhaps the most valuable knowledge one can learn. Knowledge can be valuable for two reasons: either it is interesting, or it is useful. Thus, astronomy and history are valuable because they are interesting; there is really not a lot of use to which one can put the knowledge that the universe is perhaps 12 billion years old, or that Julius Caesar was murdered by Brutus in the Roman Forum in 44 B.C. On the other hand, cookery and auto mechanics are valuable because they are useful (they may be interesting as well, but perhaps few people would learn cookery if they did not want to cook, or auto mechanics if they did not intend to fix cars). But the MoL cannot be merely interesting because of its evident importance; we expect that knowing the MoL will do something for us, even transform our lives, and not merely satisfy our intellectual curiosity or enlarge our understanding. No one's life is going to be transformed just by learning some new facts about something.

But how can this knowledge be useful? Suppose you discovered the piece of knowledge that constitutes the MoL (suppose someone who knows told it to you).

What would you do with this knowledge? What good would it do you to have it? What use would you put it to? Well, one way this knowledge is not useful is in a practical or commercial sense. And that brings us to one of the many bad jokes told about the MoL. It seems that a man went in search of the MoL. He had heard of a wise old sage who lived in a cave high in the Himalayan mountains, and who was reputed to know the secret of the MoL. After months of travel and after overcoming all the usual obstacles, our seeker after knowledge arrived at the sage's cave, inquired what the MoL was, and (in what is an unusual twist for this kind of joke) received an answer. Now he knew the MoL. And so what did he do? He went back to Beverly Hills, wrote a hit song called "The Meaning of Life," and became rich and famous overnight.

Why is this story farcical? The story is correct in supposing that the MoL is something useful to know, but it is wrong in what the usefulness of the knowledge is. It is not knowledge that is commercially valuable; we do not want to know the MoL to sell this knowledge to other people. Knowing the MoL is supposed to be valuable to you in a personal way; the knowledge enhances your life, but not by giving you the chance to get rich. And for the same reason, the knowledge is not valuable in a merely practical sense either. Practical knowledge is valuable because it enables you to achieve your ends; if you do not happen to have those ends, the knowledge is useless to you. Knowing auto mechanics is valuable only if you want to fix cars; it would not be very valuable to people living in a society without automobiles (how valuable is it to you to know how to shoe a horse, or to fix a wagon wheel?). But the knowledge we are talking about is supposed to be valuable no matter what your ends happen to be, since it enables you to see your life in a different way, and to understand what life is all about and why it is worth living.

There certainly can be knowledge that enables you to see your life differently, and that makes your life seem more worth living. Suppose you suffered from the worry that nobody really liked you; or perhaps you are worried and unhappy because you think you are not understanding your philosophy class very well and are probably going to fail. But then you learn something. You find out that you do have some good friends after all; or you take a philosophy test and get a good grade. This knowledge removes a source of anxiety in your life and makes you feel a lot better about everything. You might even think that some meaning has been restored to your life.

But for knowledge to work this way, it has to be fairly clear just what in your life is the source of the anxiety. What do you want that seems to you to be missing? In our examples, it was friends and grades. If the absence of these things makes you feel bad, it is natural that when you learn that the desired things are present, you feel much better. We can specify what knowledge (if you can get it) would remove the anxiety. But suppose you are worried about whether life has any meaning. What is it that you might come to know that would remove that anxiety? Of course, you might come to know all sorts of new information; but which of these facts would count as knowledge of the MoL? How could some fact count as being the MoL? Suppose you discover something truly wonderful, let us say the kind of thing people are often told by religions—for example, that God is love, or that Jesus is your personal savior. Now the question here is not how you might come to know such facts; we will just assume that somehow you really find that they are true. The question is how such knowledge can be the MoL. Of course, if you are looking for a personal savior, then knowing that you have one will make you happy and relieve whatever anxieties you may have felt worrying that perhaps you do not have a personal savior. But even if your worries are relieved on that point, it is not evident why the existence of a personal savior should be the MoL. And we might say the same about any piece of knowledge we acquired: why should *that* fact be the MoL?

This explains why, in those bad MoL jokes in which the sage tells the traveller what the MoL is, he always says something that seems idiotic, such as "Life is a fountain." The point is that no new information could count as the MoL, whether the information is profound or utterly trivial. There is really nothing for the sage to say, not because life has no meaning, but because the MoL is not the kind of thing that can be stated in a proposition or which can be explained from one person to the next. (And so, as the jokes often continue, the traveller is disappointed with the wisdom he has received from the sage: "You mean I've come all the way from Beverly Hills just so you can tell me life is a fountain?" And the sage retorts defensively, "Well, so maybe life isn't a fountain." Or perhaps, more aggressively, "Listen, what do you expect? If I knew the meaning of life, do you think I'd be sitting up here in a cave in the mountains?")

There is another possibility. Perhaps the MoL consists in the kind of knowledge that cannot be explained, stated, or validated. Perhaps the MoL is a kind of knowledge, but the kind you know without being able to say *what* you know. But is there such knowledge? Something like it is perhaps what some people mean by "wisdom," something that the Greek philosophers regarded as the true end of philosophy (a word that means, after all, "love of wisdom"). But what is wisdom? Well, it is something like knowing how to live, not in the biological sense of surviving or staying alive, but in a moral or spiritual sense of knowing what choices to make, of knowing what is important and what is not important in life. Wisdom, as Plato forcefully pointed out, is difficult to attain, partly because there are so many counterfeits offered to us, things that seem attractive, and really are pleasurable and fun, but are really not all that valuable in the end. (. . . Plato likes to draw an analogy with healthy food, which really is good for you but may not be all that pleasant to eat, and pastry and other sweets, which may be pleasant but are not really very good for you. Plato counsels that we avoid the blandishments of pastry chefs and listen to dieticians who know what is healthy to eat; his point is that we have to be equally careful in picking our spiritual advisors.) To be wise, Plato argues, consists in knowing what is truly valuable and what only seems to be valuable, so that we can pursue the good and avoid the counterfeit.

This is probably unobjectionable as far as it goes, but our question is, what kind of knowledge is this wisdom? Plato may or may not have thought that wisdom can be explained or stated: certainly he shows Socrates searching for wisdom by asking people questions, getting them to tell him what they think about important things in life, and then subjecting their ideas to logical analysis; as if, in the end, the most important ideas will have to be validated by logic. So Plato does seem to think that wisdom is something that can be defined in a coherent form of words. And in one of his dialogues, he makes Socrates say that a person who

knows something can explain why it is that what he knows is true. Surely dieticians, to make use of Plato's own analogy, know not only what is good, but why
it is good, and they can explain this to anyone who inquires. On the other hand,
Plato in some of the most famous of his dialogues (the *Republic,* the *Symposium*)
also seems to endorse a more mystical view of wisdom, the highest knowledge,
suggesting that it consists in an intellectual grasp of some thought that is not capable of being further explained. And he also seems to take the line that once a person attains this knowledge, the knowledge imbeds itself into the soul, so that you
automatically come to love it. Thus, this nonpropositional knowledge makes you
wise, not only in the intellectual sense of causing you to understand some thought,
but in the emotive, motivational sense of causing you to see your life in a different, more meaningful way.

     Whatever Plato's own views on the status of the most important kind of knowl-
edge, philosophers ever since Plato have debated whether there can be such a thing
as nonpropositional knowledge, knowledge that is simply grasped by the mind even
though it cannot be demonstrated, explained, or even stated. This problem takes us
far afield from our subject; but we should note here that, even if there is such
knowledge, and some people have it, one might wonder how anyone could know
they have it: how can a person distinguish between actually having the knowledge,
and just thinking (mistakenly) they have it? (This is not to say that there are no
methods for attaining such knowledge, but these methods are likely to be non- or
extrarational: they are alleged to consist in such techniques as engaging in trance-
like meditation, or contemplating inscrutable Zen riddles, or perhaps taking chemical stimulants.) Typically, those who claim there is such knowledge also claim that
once you get it, you just know you have it, so the question how you know does not
arise; but since there is no question of checking or confirming what you know, it is
not easy to see how the possibility of error can be avoided. If there is such knowledge, of course, it is rather pointless to write books about it: if you think you have
it and want other people to share it, all you can do is give them some hints about
how to go about attaining it. And it is an interesting question how someone who
does not yet have the knowledge is going to be able to recognize the people who
already do have it: are not all pseudogurus, cult leaders, false prophets, messiahs,
and other disreputable tricksters, fakers who claim to possess mystical knowledge
that they in fact lack (as their gullible followers—who would have profited by reading Plato—often discover too late)?

     So it is unlikely that the MoL consists in some piece of knowledge. If the MoL
could be stated in a proposition, it is difficult to see how knowing some fact might
constitute having meaning in one's life; if the MoL consists in some nonpropositional knowledge such as wisdom or knowing how to live, then it is difficult to see
how one could know what this is, or how to find it, or whether or not one had actually attained it.

     We must return to our bad joke, which turns out to have a certain wisdom after
all. For if the MoL really is some fact you can know, then it is indeed hard to see
what you can do with this information, other than package it and sell it (or give it
away of course, which is what the sage does in the story). Simply knowing that the
MoL is X (whatever X may be) will not by itself make your life more meaningful.

You may need to know facts to have a meaningful life (a life of ignorance perhaps cannot be very meaningful), but your life does not become meaningful simply because you have picked up a new piece of information. The knowledge has to fit into your life in some way. If the person in our story had been told by the sage that the MoL is to love thy neighbor, the joke would have lost its point, for there would then be something he could do with the knowledge he acquired. But "Love thy neighbor" is neither a fact nor a piece of propositional knowledge. It is an injunction to feel a certain sentiment.

But in that case, what is meant by wisdom? Is there such a thing as knowing how to live and what is important in life? The answer is yes, these are real things and they can be known. But they are not facts that can be stated in propositions. We shall come back to this at the end of the chapter.

IS THE MEANING OF LIFE HAPPINESS?

Let us turn to the question of what someone might lack if he or she felt (or thought) that his or her life lacked meaning. What is missing such that if they had it, they would no longer feel this way? We indicated above that there is a close connection between having no meaning in life and being unhappy. Perhaps these are the same thing? Could it be that someone who thinks that life has no meaning is merely thinking that he or she is unhappy, albeit expressing this in a rather odd way?

It might very well be said that for a person to be happy, his or her life must be meaningful. A person who leads a trivial, meaningless, pointless existence perhaps is not really happy. We should be careful here, however, just because the ingredients of happiness vary so much from one person to another; what may seem a boring and trivial existence to one person may not seem so to another. Perhaps what we should say is that if a person thinks his or her existence is meaningless and trivial, then that person cannot be happy. But perhaps this is not really saying very much, because thinking that your life is boring and pointless is an expression of dissatisfaction; and of course if you are dissatisfied with your life you cannot be happy, since happiness is, in part, being satisfied with your life. But in any case, even if having meaning is necessary for happiness, it would not be identical with happiness unless it was also enough for happiness, that is, sufficient for happiness.

So is having meaning in your life enough to make you happy? Suppose a person lacks everything else of value in life (whatever that may be). Would that person be happy nonetheless, if only there were meaning in his or her life? Many people might be inclined to answer yes to this. They might think of people who, although their lives seem to lack most of the normal ingredients of happiness, nevertheless have led meaningful lives and are happy. For example, perhaps these people lack romance, adventure, wealth, security, a good job, a loving family, a nice place to live, and yet, at the same time, they have an occupation, perhaps working for some charity or public interest organization, or even doing something personal such as research and study on a subject that interests them (such as the history of baseball or the Kennedy assassination). This occupation seems enough to give their lives meaning, and so to make them happy.

If this were all true, then we could conclude that meaning is both the necessary and sufficient condition for happiness: all happy people have meaningful lives, and all people with meaningful lives are happy. This would show that meaning and happiness always occur together: whenever you have meaning you have happiness, and whenever you have happiness you have meaning. But even so we might not want to say that meaning is the same thing as happiness; they might be two different things that always go together (we would have to explain why this is so; it could not be merely a coincidence). In that case, we would have discovered in a certain sense how to obtain meaning in life: just be happy, and meaning will automatically follow. But we would not have found out what meaning is, which was our original question.

To this point, we have some reason to think that having meaning in one's life is not just another way of saying that one is happy. This conclusion is reinforced when we consider that there are many ways to be unhappy; being unhappy because your life has no meaning, or has lost what meaning it had, is perhaps only one way of being unhappy. Meaninglessness is unhappiness of a special kind, and not unhappiness itself. But in that case, meaning is not sufficient for happiness, though it is perhaps necessary. So perhaps the most we can say is that a person who has meaning in his or her life is not necessarily rendered happy by that fact, but is protected against a special kind of unhappiness, the unhappiness that comes from the feeling that life has lost its meaning. And it is pretty evident that one can be unhappy for many other reasons.

But now we must turn to the question, what actually is lost when life loses its meaning? To be clear what we are trying to identify by this question, let us distinguish between the cause of life's losing its meaning, and the philosophical idea that one comes to hold when one reaches the conclusion that life has lost its meaning. We are interested in the idea, and not in the cause or the reason why one comes to hold this idea. What we want to do is to define or explain the idea that life has no meaning. What is it that life does not have? And a good way to understand this idea is to consider what is said by someone who has actually experienced the loss of meaning, and written about it, as have a number of authors. Perhaps the best and most famous of these is Count Leo Tolstoy (1828–1910), the famous Russian novelist.

Tolstoy's spiritual crisis, or loss of meaning, which he reports in his autobiographical *Confession,* occurred when he was in his mid-fifties, and at the height of his fame and powers. *War and Peace* and *Anna Karenina* had established him as the leading European novelist of his day; he could confidently say to himself that his name was known throughout the world and that his reputation would endure as long as people read books. He was rich; he was blessed with physical strength and health; his mental powers were inexhaustible; and, furthermore, he enjoyed a loving family to whom he was devoted. And in the midst of all this extraordinary good fortune, gradually the meaning went out of his life, and he began to feel as if all of this was as nothing to him, and that all he had accomplished, all that he was yet to accomplish, were of no value to him whatever.

Why? Because he began to reflect on death. He imagined that a man is like a traveller lost in a vast desert. The traveller falls into a deep pit, at the bottom of which is a monster waiting to devour him. He clutches at a little twig growing on the side of the pit, and so momentarily saves himself from the monster. But then he notices that two mice, one black and one white, are gnawing at the twig to which he clutches. So do we precariously cling to life, but time, represented by the two mice of night and day, inevitably draws us to our end. Soon, Tolstoy reflects, all his friends will be gone; one day his children too will die; and he himself must come to an end, leaving nothing but "stench and worms."

In the face of the inevitability of death, says Tolstoy, there are only four possible responses. The first is to ignore the problem, living in a condition of blissful ignorance reminiscent of Adam and Eve before the Fall. (Animals are enviable in that they seem to be unaware of the fact that they will die.) This is not, however, really possible for any intelligent human. The second is to admit the problem but simply go through the motions of life, acting as if what you did will make some difference, even though you know it will not. Perhaps most people live their lives trying to pretend that their life really matters, even though they know it does not. There is a certain nobility to this but on the whole it is a pretty desperate solution. A third possibility is to devote yourself to pleasure; if you are going to die anyway, you might as well have as good a time as possible while you are still around. This was the solution Tolstoy saw in his intellectual friends, who passed their time in witty and intelligent conversation that Tolstoy saw as the equivalent of idle amusements; it is not a solution so much as a running away from the problem. The fourth possibility is suicide; since there is no point to living, one very logical solution is to bring life to an end. Most people, however, are too afraid of death to take this seriously as a possible option.

None of these responses is really acceptable. So what is a person to do? What is the correct response to the inevitability of death? Tolstoy finds the answer in faith. What is needed is to reestablish meaning in life, and this cannot be done by intellect; there is no intellectual or philosophical answer that can restore meaning. Therefore, it is necessary to achieve religious faith—but not, Tolstoy believes, the complicated overintellectualized faith of theologians, who think that doctrinal answers can be given to the problem of meaning, but what Tolstoy regards as the simple, unspoiled faith of unlettered peasants, who simply know that God's love makes everything all right in the end. Without this faith, however (and Tolstoy's intellectual friends did not have it), one might as well either adopt a life devoted to pleasure, or kill oneself. There is really no other possibility.

What should we think of this? Tolstoy's analysis of the situation, given the hypothesis that the fact of death makes life lose its meaning, is quite acute. What can you do once your life has lost its meaning, other than kill yourself, or pretend not to notice, or try to escape your unhappiness in constant pleasure? Because of this, as the French existential philosopher Albert Camus (1913–1960) once said, the problem of suicide is the central problem of philosophy; either philosophy proves that there really is meaning in life, or suicide appears to be the only logical answer. (Camus, who did not think faith was possible for thinking people, held that philosophy could not find an answer; but, as we will see, he thought there was nonetheless an alternative to suicide.) Religious people, as already noted, would agree with Tolstoy that the answer lies in faith, although Tolstoy does not explain how such faith is to be achieved, or why it should not be regarded as simply one more form of escapism. But the main question Tolstoy's crisis raises is whether he was correct in concluding that the knowledge of death does take the meaning out of life. And a very simple argument shows that he was not correct. We call this "the death argument."

THE DEATH ARGUMENT

Death is a scary subject. Most people do not look forward to death, and wish to postpone it as long as possible; thinking about death, whether their own or the death of others close to them, is a depressing exercise for normal people. At the same time, sensible people might feel that Tolstoy's view of death is obsessive, morbid, and entirely unnecessary. Their response to him might be that, of course, everyone is going to die; so what else is new? But this is not entirely fair, for Tolstoy's claim is that the person who avoids thinking about death or goes on with normal life knowing that he or she will surely die, is practicing a form of escapism that Tolstoy finds unappealing. What is needed to answer Tolstoy is an argument that shows that death is not destructive of meaning, that one can rationally acknowledge death and still have a meaningful life. Fortunately, such an argument exists.

Tolstoy's basic claim is that the fact of death makes all of life meaningless. To make out this assertion, he must hold that apart from death, life would be good; but the badness of death overcomes or cancels the goodness of life.

But the death argument shows that this is a very bad point. This argument is simplicity itself. It begins with an understanding of death: death is nothing but the annihilation of life. But if that is the case, it follows immediately that if death is bad, it must be the case that life is good. And therefore, it cannot be true that the badness of death takes away from the goodness of life and renders life bad as well. Hence, Tolstoy (and he is not alone in making this argument) is simply mistaken in arguing that the fact that you will die makes life not worth living.

The reader will see that the death argument depends on the claim that death is nothing but the termination of life. Death is not a reality in itself; it is a mere nothingness, as darkness may be said to be the absence of light (or as evil is sometimes, by certain metaphysicians, said to be the absence of good). If death were a positive reality in itself, the death argument would not work, because it might be the case that a bad positive reality might remove or cancel the goodness in a different, good, positive reality (as a fire that is "bad" can destroy a house that is "good"). But as death is nothing in itself, its badness must consist only in the termination of something else; this termination could not be bad unless the thing terminated (life) were good. Therefore, the badness of death can never be used to prove that life also is bad. On the contrary, the badness of death proves that life is good.

And this conclusion is in accord with common sense. Why do we fear death? True, some people fear death because they understand death other than as a mere absence or termination of life; they see death as a destination, or a journey, or a kind of new life, which has special horrors of its own. But apart from these philosophical-religious views, we dislike death precisely because we do not want life to end. We do not fear death as something bad in itself. People do not want to die; but this is not because death is something they do not want to have, but because life is something they do not want to lose.

So far, we have agreed with Tolstoy that death is bad. But even this point can be challenged. Classically, Epicurus (died 270 B.C.) argued against the fear of death as follows. Do not fear death, he taught: for when you are, death is not; and when death is, you are not. Therefore, death cannot harm you.

Epicurus' argument is clever, but not convincing; he seems to waver between regarding death as nothing but the absence of life, and regarding death as something positive in itself. His premises seem to assume that death is nothing but the absence of life (when death is, you are not). But his conclusion (death cannot harm you) seems to regard death as a positive thing that might be harmful. He overlooks that what is "harmful" about death is what he has stated in his second premise: when death is, you are not. It is the absence of you—your total annihilation—that you regard as a harm, or more properly as the worst possible form of harm. So although Epicurus is correct in holding that death cannot cause you harm, he is wrong in concluding that there is nothing harmful about death. Death itself is harmful, in that what death is, a person's total nonexistence, is itself harmful. (But even this way of putting it is a bit odd, since calling something harmful implies that there is someone present who is harmed by the thing. In the case of death, the harm consists precisely in the person being no longer present.)

But there are other grounds for considering that death is not the evil it is made out to be. For consider the alternative. If there were no death, we would all live forever. Eternal life is usually regarded as something good, indeed wonderful. Religions attract multitudes by promising them eternal life, as if it were just obvious that such a thing is what we all want. But would eternal life be so wonderful? "Eternal" means infinite; to say we shall live eternally or forever is to say that we shall have an infinite amount of time at our disposal in the future. What are we going to do to fill that time? If you assume that the number of different things any person can do is finite, it follows that sooner or later we shall have done everything that can possibly be done. (Think of this concretely. Suppose you wanted to read every book ever written. The number of books, however large, is necessarily finite; there cannot be an infinite number of real books. So sooner or later you will have read them all. What do you read next?) Once we have done everything possible, we will still have infinite time ahead of us, which we shall have to fill somehow. There will be nothing to do other than to repeat what we have already done; and once we have repeated everything, we shall have to repeat it again, and so on, without end. This does not sound like such a wonderful thing; actually, eternal life seems rather boring, the same things endlessly repeated. (As an alternative, one might just sit there doing nothing for all eternity. This seems even more boring.)

People fail to notice this because they think that living in eternity is different from living here on earth. In eternity, it is held, you will sit at the right hand of God, enjoying eternal blessedness (assuming no different fate is in store for you). And eternal blessedness could not be boring. No doubt this is true, but it is true only by definition; eternal blessedness is not boring simply because we define eternal blessedness as a nonboring condition. But in fact we have no conception whatever of a permanent nonboring condition; in our experience, everything gets boring sooner or later if we have too much of it. In life as we know it, we require variety to maintain our interest in things. It is true that, for all anybody knows, eternity might be completely different from life as we know it; but life as we know it is the only standard we have by which to judge anything. And by this standard, eternity is not terribly attractive. To hold that eternal life is attractive, therefore, is simply to assert, without really comprehending, that eternity is completely different from anything we ever experience on earth. This is a pure question of faith; eternity as we can understand it is apt to be boring, but if someone wants to hope for an incomprehensible eternity that is not boring, logic alone cannot rule this out.

There is another point about death. If we really did have all eternity before us, we might never actually do anything. This is because as we actually are, we require the pressure of time to help us accomplish things. If we really could put everything off until tomorrow, we probably would; but as life is short, we know that what does not get done today may not get done at all. However, in eternity life is not short, and there is no reason not to put things off until tomorrow, so we might well pass all eternity postponing things we really feel like eventually doing.

Hence, we have a dilemma. We like life, so we do not want to die. At the same time, we do not want to live forever (or we would not if the above arguments were convincing), and the only way to avoid this is to die. The dilemma is that both alternatives are undesirable; dying is bad because life is good, and not dying is bad because living forever is not good. So, finally, perhaps the best thing to say is this: life is good, but living forever is not good, so death is necessary sooner or later; but the best thing would be later rather than sooner.

All of the above assumes our definition of death as the complete absence of life, that is, of biological and conscious processes. Death is a negation, not a positive entity in itself. This point is, however, not so clear to many people who think death is a positive reality. An expression of that idea was put by Shakespeare into the mouth of Claudio, a character in *Measure for Measure* (III, i, 118):

> ". . . to die, and go we know not where,
>
> .   .   .   .   .
>
> To bathe in fiery floods, or to reside
> In thrilling region of thick-ribbèd ice—
> To be imprison'd in the viewless winds,
> And blown with restless violence round about
> The pendent world, or to be worse than worst
> Of those that lawless and incertain thought
> Imagine howling—'tis too horrible!
> The weariest and most loathèd worldly life
> That age, ache, penury, and imprisonment
> Can lay on nature is a paradise
> To what we fear of death.

To which Isabella replies: "Alas, alas!"

Though Isabella might better grieve over Claudio's bad philosophy, he is not alone: that death is not merely the extinction of life is such a strong thought that it has even been asserted by certain philosophers who seem to want to make out that death is something, a kind of positive reality in its own right. The best known of these philosophers is the German crypto-Nazi, Martin Heidegger (1889–1976). Heidegger argues, although in the most obscure and confused way imaginable, that all of life is a progress toward death. Death is the reality that each of us must face; therefore, we must understand its nature. The attempt to understand death is the great problem of life; unfortunately, however, the only way to understand death is to die, at which time it is too late. So life is necessarily tragic, infected, so to speak, with the need to understand something that by its nature is incomprehensible to us.

This is a problem, however, only if death is thought of as a mysterious, incomprehensible reality. If death is the mere negation of life, then there is nothing incomprehensible about it: when we are dead, we simply will no longer be alive. Even if Heidegger is right in asserting that it is very important to understand this, he is wrong in claiming that there is some deep mystery about it. Further, if there is a tragedy about death, Heidegger has misunderstood what that tragedy is. The fact about death is that we do not want to die—yet death is inevitable. So sooner or later something will happen to us that we very much prefer to avoid. If there is a tragedy in this, it is quite the opposite of what Heidegger thinks. The tragedy is not that we want to understand what death is, but cannot; the tragedy is that we understand only too well what death is—the permanent extinction of each of us—and do not like it at all.

On this subject then, perhaps the last words should be granted to David Hume, who, lucid as ever on his deathbed, said that he was no more unhappy to think that he would not exist after his life was over than he was to think that he had not existed before it began. Or as a contemporary philosopher, A. J. Ayer, puts it, "Why should it worry me more, if at all, that I shall not be alive in the year 2050 than that I was not alive in the year 1850? The way things are going, the latter . . . might well prove the better time to have lived. In the very long . . . history of the universe, there is a relatively minute period that contains my life. . . . [W]hy should it matter to me at what points . . . this minute stretch begins and ceases?"

REPETITIVE POINTLESSNESS, ULTIMATE INSIGNIFICANCE, AND ABSURDITY

Given the above observations, the claim that death renders life tragic or meaningless seems much exaggerated. What other reflections might lead someone to conclude that life is meaningless? We shall note three that are quite commonly made: repetitive pointlessness, ultimate insignificance, and absurdity.

Repetitive Pointlessness

That life is, in the end, nothing but pointless repetition, is illustrated in a famous essay by Camus, who draws on the Greek myth of Sisyphus. This ancient hero sinned against the gods by stealing their secrets (in one version, Sisyphus learned how to escape death). For this the gods condemned him to spend all eternity pushing a large boulder to the top of a hill. After Sisyphus pushed the boulder to the top, it would roll down again, and so on without cease. It is the pointless repetitiveness of Sisyphus' task that Camus takes to be illustrative of the condition of human life: we are all condemned to pass our lives in endless repetitive labor that leads nowhere and accomplishes nothing. Sisyphus is supposed to exemplify the human condition, a kind of mythical prototype of the middle-level manager type, forever caught in the rat race: freeway, office, freeway, dinner, bed, and then the same process the following day. Or we might say the same about the factory worker, or the store clerk, or for that matter even the college student!

There are two aspects to Sisyphus' ordeal: *repetitiveness* and *pointlessness.* In some moods, anyone can think of his or her life as Sisyphus-like in both these aspects: there is plenty of repetitiveness in anyone's life, and many people can truly ask themselves, where does it all lead and what will it get me? "After years of going to the office day after day, you retire and die and so what?" one might easily ask when reflecting on the meaning of life. It has perhaps been fairly said that "Life isn't one damn thing after another; it's the same damn thing over and over again." Yet at the same time, perhaps few people's lives are absent of all variation and interest; we have already noted that variety is an important ingredient in a happy life, and most people are able to arrange things so that at least some variation in the dull routine manages to creep in from time to time. As for pointlessness, it all depends on what one counts as giving a point to life; most people do have goals at which they aim, such as attaining an education, developing a career, raising a family, and so on; and achieving these goals, or even striving toward them, gives their lives some point. So there are two problems with the story of Sisyphus. First, it is not really an accurate description of the lives of many people, and hence cannot be taken as an encapsulation of the human condition, or of human life as such. It is true, perhaps, that some people's lives resemble the life of Sisyphus, and no doubt these people are unhappy because their lives lack meaning, but all this shows is something to be avoided. And indeed, "Do not live like Sisyphus if you can avoid it!" is a fairly obvious sort of injunction.

The second problem is that the story does not specify what would count as *not* leading a life of repetitive pointlessness. This is an important failure in philosophical attempts to characterize human life as generally unhappy, meaningless, and disappointing. If, like Camus and many other philosophers, you are going to hold that human life is essentially characterized by some undesirable quality such as pointlessness, you must specify what would count as life's having a point, and then explain why no one's life can attain this. Camus, as other philosophers, fails even to consider this. Take Camus' own life. He wrote novels and essays, became famous, won the Nobel Prize, and died in a car crash at the age of 47. His books are still read today, translated into almost all languages. So did Camus consider his own life Sisyphus-like by being pointless? Well, maybe he did; but then, what would he count as life having a point? For most people, a life like Camus', apart from the tragic early death, would seem quite satisfactory. If it did not satisfy Camus, what would have satisfied him? The point is not to argue about how much success is enough, but to note that either Camus can specify what would count as life having a point, or he cannot. If he can, then he cannot really prove that no life can attain whatever it takes to give life a point. Set the standards too high, and few people will be able to attain them; but if you set the standards so high that nobody can attain them, it might be asked whether such high standards are not arbitrary and too personal. Why should everybody be bound by your high standards?

On the other hand, if you simply refuse or fail to specify what would count as a life having a point, simply saying that nothing can possibly give life a point, no matter what achievement or success, then you are guilty of proving your case by asserting it. For if there is nothing that can give life a point, then of course life will not have a point; but that is a tautology. The "if" proposition has to be proved. What you have to show is why there is nothing that can give life a point; why what most people ordinarily regard as giving life a point (for example, achieving certain goals or a reasonable level of happiness) really is not a point after all. In other words, you have to show that every life, no matter what, is really no different from that of Sisyphus. Or even stronger: that no life would be any different from that of Sisyphus, no matter what that life contained.

The problem we have been noticing can be illustrated by reference to the German philosopher, Arthur Schopenhauer (1788–1860), who attempted to establish pessimism as a philosophy. All human life, he thought, swings between desire and satisfaction. When we desire something, we are unhappy because we do not have it; when we get it, we are bored because our desire has been satisfied and there is nothing to do but wait for the next desire to come along. Hence, human life is miserable. Schopenhauer therefore counsels nirvana, or the extinction of all desire, which comes very close to the extinction of life itself.

The problem with this analysis of human misery is this. Of course it may be true that some desires, when you have satisfied them, leave you feeling bored. This is the case of those desires that are, in a sense, false: the person did not really want the thing he thought he wanted, or did not want it as much as he thought he did, so when he achieves it, he is not satisfied. But what is Schopenhauer's proof that all desires are like this? Why cannot there be a desire such that, when you get what you desire, you are content, and not bored? Schopenhauer seems simply to define a desire as that which, when satisfied, leaves you bored; which is another case of proving the proposition by assertion and not by evidence. His view is that nothing can count as real satisfaction. But he has not explained what real satisfaction would be, so as to then show why nothing can attain it.

Now in fairness to Camus, it should be noted that his intention is not necessarily to claim that the Sisyphus story is the model or type of all human existence (he is not very clear on whether he holds this or not). Rather, his main interest is in recommending what would count as an acceptable (to him, and presumably, to the reader as well) response to anyone who was in the Sisyphusean situation. What is this? It is *defiance*. Sisyphus is doomed, but as Camus sees it, he need not reconcile himself to this doom. Bloodied but unbowed, Sisyphus performs his endless task, refusing to accept with his will what he must accept in his outward behavior.

Camus' idea, crudely put, is that what gives meaning to life is not what kind of life one leads—for any kind of life amounts to the same pointless repetitiveness—but the spirit in which the life is led. The meaning of life comes not from the life that is lived, but from the frame of mind in which it is lived. But not any old frame of mind will give life meaning, it appears. Fate, Camus seems to think, is cruel; this is the overwhelming fact that cannot be escaped. The question then becomes, not what you will do about it, but what attitude you will take toward it. A person who meekly or humbly accepts his or her fate, a person whose attitude is one of resignation and compliance before the inevitable (the will of Allah, as Muslims say), Camus strongly suggests, has a life which, for that very reason, is deprived of meaning, that is to say, is deprived of all the meaning a human life can have. Meaning comes from defiance of fate.

The reader will recognize here the underlying view of the Romantic hero: never give up, fight on against the odds, and never admit defeat. Camus would have made a great football coach, except that the coach expects to win the game and Camus begins by acknowledging that the game cannot be won. The question here is not whether the attitude of defiance Camus recommends is an attractive one—this you can decide for yourself—but whether such an attitude is sufficient to make an otherwise pointless life in some way meaningful. If by meaningful we mean, roughly, worth living, then perhaps you may wonder whether any life as dreary as Sisyphus' can be made worth living, no matter what attitude one takes toward it. But perhaps Camus is saying no more than that this is the best we humans can do.

Ultimate Insignificance

The notion that, from the objective point of view, life is pretty bleak, but that some modicum of salvation can be found if one adopts the correct attitude—this is in a way the essence of Romantic heroics—seems to be less appealing now than it once was. There are, of course, many variations on the same basic theme. The English philosopher Bertrand Russell (1876–1972), for example, one of the most important philosophers and social thinkers of the twentieth century and one of the most intelligent people who ever lived (judging by his incredible store of knowledge and his vast output of books and articles), at one point in his life expressed his own version of Romantic heroics from a standpoint quite different from that of Camus. Russell points out that science, and in particular astronomy, makes clear that *human life is of total insignificance.* In the context of the vast scale of the universe, humans, who came into existence as the accidental result of forces beyond our control, may be seen as little specks of protoplasm scurrying around on the surface of a very minor planet in a very minor solar system in one of the billions and billions of galaxies that form the universe. The chance configuration of forces that allowed this bit of life to come into existence will soon enough, on the astronomical time scale, destroy it, and all that it has created, leaving no trace behind. Russell, in his own bit of imagery, regards human life as a kind of joke God and the devil have created for their own amusement; soon they will get tired of watching the human comedy and will eradicate it, turning to other amusements. This idea that life is a bad joke played by God—or somebody—on us who are its victims, is a powerful expression of a certain mood brought about by reflecting on the ultimate insignificance of everything we humans value and would wish to preserve.

Like Camus, Russell holds that what is important is what you do with this basic insight. But Russell's argument is actually much deeper and more sophisticated than Camus'. There are certain ideals that humans have created and which we value above all: truth, love, and art, for example. The important thing in the face of insignificance is to cherish and preserve these ideals as best we can. To abandon oneself to despair or dismay is the real defeat, just as a shallow optimism, a naive faith that things really do matter somehow in the end, is simply a way of pretending the problem does not exist. In particular in mathematics, which Russell throughout his long life seems to have regarded as ultimate truth and beauty combined, we are able to apprehend in a way something truly eternal, and thus to a certain (limited and metaphorical) extent escape total destruction. We can at least glimpse the imperishable, though we cannot avoid perishing.

Readers will recognize in all this what the French call a *cri de coeur,* a certain plaintive cry: we are so insignificant! And so we are. In the great scheme of things, humans just do not count for very much. Look up at the sky on a clear star-filled night. It is vast, and we are tiny. Or stand on the shore of the ocean and experience the same effect. But, one might ask in a crude sort of way, so what? Why should any of this make any difference? Well, think of an insect. There is nothing more insignificant. If that particular insect had never lived—if you end its life prematurely by squishing it—absolutely no difference would be made to anyone or anything; even the other insects will not notice. The thought that a person's life—any person's—is no more significant than an insect's, is worrisome to some people.

But why should it be? The question is, what do people want who have this worry? What would make them think that our lives were not insignificant? If the problem is the sheer size of the universe, then consider this thought experiment. Suppose the rest of the universe simply did not exist. Everything else would be the same, including all of human life (although a few astrophysicists would need to find other employment). Then the earth and its inhabitants would not be an insignificant part of a vast universe; we would *be* the universe. Would this make anyone feel better?

Why should it? How would the absence of the universe add meaning to our lives? And if it cannot, then why should the presence of the universe take the meaning away?

Of course, there is another sense in which someone might worry about being insignificant. A person might worry that he himself, personally, is insignificant. He might wish that he were famous, or very important (the President of the United States, or Albert Einstein, or somebody like that), and feel bad that he is not and probably will never be. Obviously, in a sense such a worry is foolish, since by definition very few—amazingly few—people can ever become important or famous. (If there were 10,000 important Americans, they would constitute approximately 0.003 percent of the entire U.S. population. Anybody's chance of becoming one of them would be 1/30,000.) So to have such an ambition and to make the meaning of your life depend on its fulfillment is a very risky gamble. But in any case, this is a different point about meaning than the point we have been examining. Wanting to become famous or important is an ambition someone might have, and we have already noted that meaning—in the sense of happiness, or feeling that your life is or has been worthwhile—depends in part on setting and achieving goals. Whether being famous is a wise goal to set can be left for a later discussion.

Absurdity

The third idea that is said to take the meaning from life is that *life is absurd*. The absurdity of life, or of existence, has been a favorite theme of existential philosophy as well as various kinds of absurdist literature and art. Absurdity means that life is irrational or makes no sense. There are two different reactions to this basic insight. Existentialist philosophers emphasize the tragic side of absurdity: the basic meaninglessness of life produces anxiety, a sense of the abyss, of being adrift without guidance, of disconnectedness, of the basic horror in everything. Some, such as Jean-Paul Sartre (1905–1980), hold that because there are no values, no meaning, even no truth, people have absolute freedom, and are therefore, faced with the almost intolerable burden of creating values and making choices without guidance or support. Any attempt to look outside the individual for guidance—to history, to religion, to culture, to philosophy, even to your friends or spiritual counselor—Sartre regards as an escape from the basic freedom of choice each individual faces. There is, as some philosophers put it, no appeal from the choices one makes: no confirmation or validation that one has done the right thing. We are left helplessly groping in the dark. This lonely groping in the dark fills existentialists with dread.

The other sense of absurdity is that life is basically ridiculous, not a tragedy but a farce. It is as if one lived in a Woody Allen movie, playing the Woody Allen character. Nothing ever goes right, nothing means what you think it means, your best efforts turn into preposterous near misses, just when you think you have everything figured out and under control some trivial event sends you spinning. It would be funny if it were not happening to you; and even you can see how ridiculous it all is. A famous artist, Marcel Duchamp, once exhibited a toilet bowl in an art show. "I am ridiculous," he was saying, "but I am not any more ridiculous than you are, with your pretensions to great art and deep meaning. All of life—all of art, all of philosophy—is absurd, and we only pretend that there are deep truths revealed to us by art, literature and the rest of high culture. Like a group of people trying to run in a field of mud, we are all ridiculous. Self-mockery is the only honest response to life."

To summarize: we see that there are many possible responses to the presumed meaninglessness of life: suicide, pleasure, or going through the motions, as Tolstoy said, but also defiance, upholding our ideals, honest acceptance, sheer terror, self-mockery, and perhaps others as well. But is it really necessary to accept that life has no meaning? What would we have to think to conclude that maybe life does have meaning after all?

"BIG PICTURE" MEANING AND FAITH

The previous discussion leads us to the following point. One way in which life is said to attain meaning is by being part of some larger scheme of things. We call this "big picture" meaning. Those who think life has no meaning think that there is no big picture of which our lives are a part. To the question, "What does it all mean, and what is the purpose of it all?" they respond that it all means nothing whatever; and, there is no purpose to it all ("it" being human life, life in general, the entire universe, or whatever you please). There is no meaning to life, because there is no purpose, no larger picture, no ultimate reason, of which our lives are a part and which would give them some point. So, the basic idea here seems to be that if there were a big picture or some basic scheme of things, life would have meaning after all; but, unfortunately, there is not. Or is there?

Let us see how the big picture might give life meaning. Take some familiar examples: team sports, for instance. Were you to observe a player on a team, let us say the shortstop on a baseball team, if you did not know baseball you would probably think his actions were totally screwy and meaningless. He runs this way and that, tries to catch the ball, sometimes throws the ball and sometimes does not, runs to the base and takes a throw from another player . . . all perfectly unintelligible, unless you know that what you are watching is a baseball game, and that the shortstop is playing his position according to the rules of the game. When you understand what the game is all about, then everything the shortstop does makes sense. You understand his role in the game, and how what he does contributes to his team's success. In other words, once you grasp the big picture, that is, the purpose of the game and the player's role in the game, you understand the meaning of the player's actions.

Another example might be the army. No soldier ever knows what is going on, and no soldier has very much significance all alone. Any individual soldier is entirely replaceable since there are millions of others exactly the same. Yet each has a role, however small, to play in the military scheme of things. If you eliminated any given soldier, not much would be different, and the army would go on as before. But if you eliminate enough individual soldiers, the army cannot function and will be defeated. So while each soldier may seem insignificant, when you add up all the tiny units you wind up with a very important total. So both the importance and the meaning of each individual can be understood by reference to some big picture of which each is a part. The big picture tells us the purpose of what they are doing, the reason for it, and the end it serves. It makes their actions intelligible. And the same could be true for any kind of organized enterprise in which people engage, whether it be a business, a political party, a public interest organization, and so on. Each person's actions make sense only in the context of the large scheme of things.

Someone who does not see the big picture might very well think that the individual's actions are pointless. And so they would be, taken out of context. Often, as in the army, the individuals themselves do not see the big picture, and so do not understand why they are doing what they are told to do. They may well think that what they are doing is meaningless and stupid. But, at least if the army is well run, in actual fact there is a big picture to which they are contributing.

Let us look at this more closely. What do we want a big picture theory of meaning to do for us? The following:

1. It must explain the purpose of human life.
2. It must enable anyone to explain the major events in his or her life by reference to this purpose.
3. It must justify suffering (including death), that is, show how or why suffering contributes to the purpose and is necessary in the larger scheme of things.
4. It must explain the purpose of life in a way that seems good; that is, it must reconcile us to the end of life.

Any big picture theory is going to proceed by telling some kind of a story, but not any story will satisfy all four criteria. For example, suppose the story is this: there is a race of Superbeings who are making a journey through the universe. By wise preordination, the gods have provided the Super-race with resting points where they can refresh themselves and restore their provisions. One such resting place is earth. As the gods must work through the laws of nature, all of evolution has been allowed to happen so that when the Super-race arrives, there will be ample food so they may continue on their journey. The food will be the top of the natural food chain, namely, us. We are here to provide food for the Super-race on the next stage of their journey. Our duty is to wait, reproduce, and maintain ourselves in suf- ficient numbers so that there will be ample food. For hundreds and thousands of (earth) years, the human race did not multiply fast enough. So the gods enabled us to develop science, technology, and industrial civilization so that there would be enough of us when the time comes. We have become so adept at multiplying that we now double our numbers every twenty years or so. As the earth cannot sustain such increases indefinitely, the gods have arranged things so that when the carrying capacity of the earth reaches its limit, the Super-race will arrive. We do not know when this will be (we do not know how many human beings the earth can sustain; all previous predictions have turned out to be wild underestimations), although many local strains on the earth's capacity have begun to appear. But it cannot be too far distant; perhaps a hundred years, perhaps a thousand.

Is this far-fetched? Suppose you are a wise old tuna fish, trying to explain the purpose of tuna life. Might not you tell such a tale, with human beings taking the place of the Super-race? (Human beings would be the Super-race from the stand- point of tuna fish.)

This story satisfies the first criterion, and with a little imaginative elaboration, could be improved to satisfy the second and third criteria as well. But it does not satisfy the fourth criterion, since it is not a story that human beings like. It does not provide us with a meaning to which we can be reconciled; to be food for a Super-race is not what we have in mind when we demand to know why we are here. This is not very good for us. We do not come out ahead in the end; we have nothing to gain, however glorious it may be to make a contribution to the progress of superior beings.

The reason that a big picture must satisfy the fourth criterion has been sug- gested earlier in this chapter. There we saw that the desire that life have meaning was in part a desire that life have some sort of ultimate justification. But now we see that it is not enough that your mere existence be justified, but that your values, hopes, and fondest ambitions be justified as well. This means that what you want from the big picture is that your values be proved to be acceptable in the larger scheme of things. The fourth criterion in effect guarantees that the big picture will do this. And since most people do not value the destruction of the human race, or that the human race be used for the benefit of some other sort of being, the story we told will not be appealing as a big picture giving the meaning of life.

One story that does satisfy the fourth criterion, as well as the other three, is religion, and notably orthodox Judeo-Christian religion. This tells a story in which human beings come out very well, defeating Satan and enjoying eternal blessedness at the right hand of God. We could not possibly ask for a better ending. Almost by definition of good ending, in fact, the religious story promises the best possible ending there could be: the righteous enjoy eternal bliss, and the wicked are doomed to their just reward. Nothing could better satisfy our deepest wishes.

Any big picture depends on faith, for there is evidently no way of proving by reason that the story told by the big picture is true. So the next question is, how much of the picture does one have to believe in order to believe enough to think that life has a meaning? And the answer is, not very much; in fact, one need not believe any of the details of the big picture at all, so long as one believes that there is a big picture. To understand this, imagine you have a ticket to a play: you have no idea what this play is about, but you have heard that it is excellent and you know the author is a famous playwright. Unfortunately, by bad luck you are late and do not arrive at the theater until the first act is well under way, with the result that you cannot understand what is happening. Who are these people and what are they doing, you keep thinking as the action unfolds. Even worse luck, your pager goes off just before the last act comes to an end, and you have to leave the theater before the dénouement. Consequently, you never come close to figuring out what the play was all about. But do you assume it had no meaning? On the contrary, you might well assume there must be a meaning. You have great confidence that the author would not write a meaningless, totally stupid play; and you also suspect that the author is a lot smarter than you are, so perhaps the meaning is disguised and difficult to understand. You might even think that there might be more than one meaning to the play; perhaps the author meant the play to have several meanings, so that different viewers could understand the play in different ways depending on their own points of view, and all of these interpretations might be correct. Since you have not seen enough of the play, you cannot prove that the play has any meaning at all; it might be just a jumble, a terribly constructed piece of work that the other members of the audience pretend to like because they are bedazzled by the reputation of the author. But you have great faith that this is not the case.

And perhaps life is like that. Clearly, we cannot prove it is; but can anyone really prove it is not? Perhaps there is a big picture that simply is beyond our grasp: life has meaning, all right, but no one can really figure out what that meaning is. And this is another reason why the wise gurus in the MoL jokes never give an intelligible answer. The gurus know the deepest truth anyone can know, which is that the deepest truth that exists is not a truth anyone can know. When the oracle tells Socrates he is the wisest person in Greece, Socrates, who thinks he knows nothing worth knowing, understands the oracle to mean that at least he, Socrates, knows that he knows nothing; whereas most of the other Greeks imagined, falsely, they knew something important. Like the gurus in the stories, Socrates was wise because he knew that he did not know, which is all the wisdom it is possible to have.

It is for this reason that many people believe that faith is necessary if life is to have meaning. Since they also hold that without meaning, life is not worth living, they conclude that it is faith that makes life worth living. Without faith, life is barely tolerable, everything becomes valueless, and activities lose their point. To avoid this unhappy conclusion, thinkers such as Tolstoy argue that we must believe in some meaning, even if we cannot understand what that meaning is.

This argument is perhaps the most persuasive argument possible for religion; for though religions postulate entities and principles that many people find impossible to accept in today's logical and scientific world, the importance of religion is that it gives people something to believe in, namely, that life makes sense and that there is some ultimate justification after all.

The analogy with a play may seem to support the faith argument—how can you enjoy the play unless you have faith that it means something?—but only up to a point, for our confidence in the playwright is not based on faith alone but on the experience of other playgoers who are familiar with the author's work, including the play in question. They know that the work makes sense, from experience. But by the definition of our problem, no one has any experience that the author's work makes sense or has any meaning whatever; we are all basing our confidence in the author on faith. But many people will not find it intelligible to believe in something while at the same time admitting there is not the slightest reason to believe in it. Such a faith can be justified only by practical necessity—the choice between faith or the abyss—but such practical necessity, however compelling, some people do not regard as possible grounds for belief. You cannot believe something just because it is better for you to believe it; you also need evidence that it is true, which is lacking in the present case.

Another difficulty with the faith solution is that it may seem that having faith in an unknowable meaning to life is utterly pointless: what good does it do you to believe that life has a meaning if you must remain totally ignorant of what that meaning is? Indeed, some skeptic might wonder, how does such a belief differ from no belief at all? Both believing that life has a meaning and believing that life has no meaning would seem to come to the same thing, if you have no idea what the meaning might be. Believing that some unknowable meaning exists cannot possibly make a difference in what you do, or in what you expect to get out of life: if the meaning is unknowable, you cannot know what it tells you to do or what will happen to you or for you if you do one thing or some other thing. Your actions are exactly the same as if you did not hold the belief; the belief makes no difference to your life, and so there is no difference between you and the person who does not hold the belief in the first place. Your faith is totally pointless.

IS THE QUESTION OF MEANING MEANINGFUL?

But this reflection suggests a new approach. Do we even know what we are trying to find out when we ask for the meaning of life? Perhaps the question itself does not even mean anything. That would certainly explain why it is so difficult to answer; how can you answer a question that is meaningless? Consider the child's question, how high is up? You cannot answer, not because you do not know the answer, but because there cannot be an answer: the question does not make sense. Maybe the question, what is the meaning of life? does not make sense either.

But can such an apparently deep and important question actually make no sense? The profundity of the question is no bar to its being meaningless; there is indeed one quite important school of philosophical thought, called *logical posi-*

tivism, that claims that almost all of the apparently deep philosophical questions actually do not mean anything; this is indeed precisely why they strike us as profound. For example, does the world really exist, or is all my experience an illusion? Do I have a mind or a soul, or am I a machine? Is the world a unity or an irreducible plurality of different things? Is there some reality behind or beneath the appearances I experience? All these questions, traditionally regarded as both the deepest and most perplexing questions that philosophers address, are resolved by logical positivists in one swift stroke. They are all meaningless. That is why they seem so perplexing, that is why in turn they seem profound, and that is why no one has ever succeeded in answering them.

But what makes an apparently significant question meaningless? One answer sometimes given is that a question is meaningless if it consists in an unintelligible combination of words. Taken separately, each word has a meaning, but put together, the result has none. Let us see how this operates with respect to the question about the meaning of life. To discover what this question means, let us ask what it might be for something to have a meaning. Begin by noticing what kinds of things do have meaning. Clearly words, sentences, books, and so on have meaning: the meaning of the word "dog" is, simply, the animal dog. (The word "dog" is not an animal, and the animal dog is not a word. The animal has no meaning; the word means the animal.) Similarly, the meaning of the sentence "It rained yesterday" is that it rained yesterday. (That it rained yesterday is also the meaning of the—French—sentence, *"Il pleuvait hier."* This shows that sentences are in languages, but meanings are not.) What else other than words has meaning? Actions have meaning: if I send you flowers, for example, it may mean I love you (or it may mean something else; if you get flowers from me, you might ask, what does it mean, that he sent me these flowers?) And finally, certain natural occurrences have meaning—for example, smoke means fire, or dark clouds mean it will rain. These examples enable us to see what meaning is: meaning is a connection from one thing to some other thing. Very roughly put, a thing (word, action, occurrence) has meaning if it is connected with another thing in such a way that a person who is presented with the first thing is thereby led to think of the second thing. Sometimes this connection is founded on natural facts such as cause (clouds) and effect (rain); sometimes on human psychology; and sometimes on certain social conventions, notably those of language (sending flowers is also a social convention, though a nonlinguistic one). So, because of your knowledge of facts and conventions, when you are presented with the word "dog," you think of the animal; when the flowers arrive, you think of the sender's possible love; when you see the clouds, you think of rain. The meaning of the thing that is presented is the other thing with which it is connected.

But if that is an explanation of meaning, it is perfectly clear that it makes little sense to attribute meaning to life, for life is not connected with some other thing in such a way that, when you think of life, you are thereby led to think of this other thing that is its meaning. Life, that is to say, does not signify anything other than itself; it simply is. And therefore, life is not the kind of thing that could have a meaning, for only that can have a meaning which is connected with something else so as to draw a person's thought from itself to that other thing. So while it may make sense to ask, "What is the meaning of these clouds?" or, "What is the meaning of these flowers my friend just sent me?", it cannot make sense to ask, "What is the meaning of life?" Despite its apparent importance, and despite the fact that it has the grammatical form of a question, the question is actually meaningless.

Logical positivists often make a somewhat different argument about meaning, but one that leads to the same conclusion. They ask, what is a question? Or better, what is it to understand a question? The answer to this question gives us a theory about what makes questions meaningful. According to this view, we understand a question by understanding what kind of an answer would be correct. This is not to say that we have to know what the answer is, but we do have to know what might count as an answer, what would be an answer. For example, you do not know (no one knows) what is the correct answer to this question: how many galaxies are there in the universe? But if you understand the question, you right away know that the answer is going to be some number, and a very large number at that. If someone wondered whether, perhaps, the answer to the question might be $E = mc^2$, or every prime number between 100 and 10,000, such a person would show that he or she simply had not understood what the question means. Or suppose you asked someone, what is their favorite music, or favorite musician, and they replied by naming a movie, or something else even more irrelevant; this would again show that they failed to understand the question. And the reason for this is very simple: a question is a request for a certain kind of information. What the question means, then, is given by the range of information in which the answer might be found. "Who is your favorite musician?" asks for information about musicians, and so its meaning is given by names of musicians: in effect, the question asks you to pick from among this list. Any question, according to this view, asks you to pick from among a certain list of possible answers. Since the meaning of the question is the range of its possible answers, until such a range of answers has been specified, no meaning has been given to the question.

But if we apply this simple point to the question about the meaning of life, we see that no one who asks this question has any idea what would count as an answer. There is no range of possible answers, one of which is the correct answer. Since no one knows what might give life meaning, no one can specify what the range of answers should be. And, therefore, no one understands the question being asked; but this is not because the question is so terribly profound that it is too deep for us to comprehend. No one understands the question because the question has not been given a meaning.

IF LIFE HAS NO MEANING, WHAT THEN?

This conclusion is not going to satisfy people who are searching for meaning. They argue that it is important to try to answer questions even if we do not understand them very well. This is Socrates' idea too: "Good question; no answer." But is this the best answer we can give? To this point, we have been suggesting that either life has no meaning, or, if it does, the meaning is beyond our capacity to understand. But is there another possibility? Let us call *big picture optimists* those who, like Tolstoy, believe it is possible to find some meaning to life, either through faith or possibly even through philosophy. We distinguish them from *skeptical pessimists,* who deny that there is any meaning to be found in life, and therefore, opt for despair. These thinkers regard the tenets of faith as irrational, and conclude that religious believers are practicing an acute form of self-delusion. (Like Camus and Russell, they are apt to opt for some kind of "heroic attitude" solution.) Both optimists and pessimists agree that unless life has meaning, then life is deprived of much or all of its spark or savor, and there is no real point in going on. What they disagree about is whether it is possible to find the meaning that is needed to make life worthwhile. Optimists think that you can, and so say that human life is worth living after all, while pessimists say you cannot, and so conclude either that life is not worth living, or that it must be lived under the cloud of failure and despair.

But the premise that meaning is needed to make life worthwhile can be challenged. Must it follow that if life has no meaning, then nothing is worthwhile? To explain this point, let us distinguish between life in general and the life of any particular human person. When it is said that life has no meaning, what is meant is that there is nothing that life is about, no reason (other than biological and accidental) why we are here, no purpose our lives serve. As far as the universe is concerned, we might as well not exist at all; there is no ultimate justification for our lives. But now it has to be asked, why should this matter to us? Might not our individual lives still have meaning, even if life as such has none?

Perhaps it is not so difficult to see how this might be. What does give meaning to the life of an individual person? Such things as engaging in worthwhile activities, having interesting goals and projects, enjoying the company of friends and loved ones, having a sense of self-worth—in short, being of use to yourself and to other people, acting in such a way that you make a difference in the world, however small it may be. Your life has meaning, we might say, if, at the end of it, somebody can truly say that the world is a better place than it would have been had you never lived. Now, this is something that cannot be done for you, either by the universe or by other people; giving meaning to your life is something you must do for yourself. And you must do it, as the existentialists quite correctly point out, without any sure proof that what you are doing is correct; for it is not the universe that is going to be glad you existed, but people with whom you interacted in your life. There is thus no ultimate justification, no proof that your life, your ideals, and your projects really matter. In this sense, meaning is not a kind of knowledge at all—we cannot know that our life has meaning—but at bottom a feeling, a sense of well-being from having made a difference.

But will just any kind of activity suffice? . . . Aristotle claims that some activities are more excellent than others, and that only those activities that manifest a high degree of human excellence can really make life worthwhile. However, it is not clear that it is possible to describe a truly objective set of the most excellent activities. Is studying philosophy truly more excellent than playing sports (as Aristotle holds), or only more excellent for a person like Aristotle? Perhaps for the non-intellectual, playing sports or fooling with cars is more excellent than thinking deep thoughts. One of Aristotle's points is that whatever you do, you should try to do it as well as you can; being good at fixing cars might be far better for some people than being bad at playing the piano. Perhaps what we should say, at least as a work-ing hypothesis, is that everybody is probably good at something, and that what is most likely to give any person's life real meaning is finding what he or she is good at and then developing the skill to do it well. This is what is likely to make your life of most use to yourself, and to other people as well: ineptness is as frustrating to its possessor as it is irritating to others who may depend on you to accomplish some-thing. In other words, being indolent, achieving nothing, living a life in which noth-ing very worthwhile is ever accomplished, is likely in the end to be dull, tedious, of little worth, and without much meaning (which may be the truth underlying Kant's claim that we have a duty to ourselves to develop our talents).

But will just any activities fit this picture? Cannot it be objected that nasty people—Mafia hit men, child molesters, neo-Nazi racists—also have projects that engage their attention and have talents that they develop, but we would not want to say their lives have meaning? If there is no ultimate justification, then is not any meaningful life as good as any other? Aristotle's reply presumably would be that killing people is not a form of human excellence, but here Aristotle fails to distin-guish between being moral and having a fulfilling life. Not every kind of immoral-ity takes meaning from your life, and some kinds may add meaning; for example, many people think hunting animals and even eating meat are immoral, but there is no doubt that these activities are the source of much meaning for many hunters and gourmets. To have meaning means that your life is elevated in a certain way, raised above the ordinary humdrum and given a purpose or a point; and there is no guar-antee that this can be achieved through moral actions alone. So even the life of a Mafia chief can be meaningful, because the Mafia chief, as much as (even more than) more honest or conventional people, engages in challenging activities that engage his fullest talents and give his life a purpose (to take over the drug trade in a city is a purpose, however ignoble). If a life is a success because it is interesting and fulfilling, then it is worth living and meaningful. We can thus answer the ques-tion posed earlier about wisdom. Wisdom is what the Greeks said it is: knowing how to live. But this knowledge is not what Plato seemed to think, an intellectual grasp of some proposition or thought. It is knowing how to arrange your life so that your life has meaning, in the way best described by Aristotle: making best use of your inner strengths and capacities so as to make your life worthwhile to your-self and to others.

MEANING AND MORALITY

But does not a meaningful life require some morality? If the Mafia chief dies, rich and surrounded by his loving family and loyal associates, we can say he has had a meaningful life and that it has not been without moral qualities: love, friendship, loyalty, and respect are moral qualities that can enter even the life of a criminal. Without any of these, it is doubtful that anyone would regard his or her own life as successful. But we have also said that for one's life to be meaningful one must make a contribution, or give someone some reason to be glad that you have lived. This is the role of morality; Mafia chiefs no doubt give most people a reason to be sorry that they have lived (which is why society puts them in jail if it can). On balance, such a life ought not to have been lived. So perhaps what we should say is that no life can be meaningful in the sense of personally satisfying if it lacks all moral qualities, and no life can be meaningful in the sense of its final net worth if its overall contribution to society is negative: a truly valuable life is one of which more people than not have reason to be glad that the life was lived.

We have talked about the ultimate justification of our lives. There are two distinct things that are wanted from ultimate justification. One is to justify morality, the other to justify the lives we lead. If our argument is correct, there is no ultimate justification for our lives, just because there is nothing that makes life as such meaningful: each life has to be justified or made meaningful by the person whose life it is. We have also indicated that if there are no moral facts (and even if there are moral facts, since it is unclear how they can be known), then morality depends on certain sentiments and attitudes for which there is also no validation. But we now see that there is more to it than that. To have meaning in your life requires that you create a meaningful life for yourself through interesting activities; but this is evidently not enough. Unless some morality also enters your life—love, friendship, loyalty, trust, contribution—your life will be less than fully meaningful and perhaps not very meaningful in the end. This justification is not ultimate (the universe does not really care whether you have a meaningful life or whether your life contains morality), but perhaps it is the most ultimate justification for morality we can attain.

PART TWO

Epistemology, Knowledge, and Skepticism

So, then, knowledge does not reside in our sensations, but in our reflecting on them. It is there, apparently, and not in the sensations themselves, that it may be possible to grasp existence and truth.

—Plato
Theaetetus 186d1–4

- Plato, *Meno* (excerpt)
- René Descartes, *Meditations on First Philosophy*, Meditation I
- G. E. Moore, A Defence of Common Sense
- Edmund L. Gettier, Is Justified True Belief Knowledge?
- Richard L. Kirkham, Does the Gettier Problem Rest on a Mistake?
- Roderick M. Chisholm, *The Problem of the Criterion* (excerpt)
- Keith Lehrer, Skepticism (excerpt)
- Alvin I. Goldman, A Causal Theory of Knowing
- Ernest Sosa, The Raft and the Pyramid: Coherence versus Foundations in the Theory of Knowledge
- William P. Alston, Two Types of Foundationalism

The problems of knowledge are many. There are challenges about how to define the concept of knowledge, and about whether knowledge is possible. Skepticism in several forms threatens to overturn our ordinary expectation that it is possible to know. If we surmount these hurdles in arriving at a correct understanding of knowledge, and answering some of the most serious skeptical objections about the possibility of knowledge, then we may begin to classify different types of knowledge and to identify appropriate methods of knowing.

As the readings in this section make clear, even some of the beliefs we ordinarily take for granted concerning the concept and possibility of knowledge give rise to serious philosophical difficulties. We may try to define knowledge as justified true belief, on the grounds that belief by itself is inadequate for knowledge if the belief happens to be false, and that true belief by itself remains inadequate if we do not have good reasons for accepting a true belief. If I believe that the next card I turn over as I flip through a deck will be a queen, and if the next card happens as a matter of fact to be a queen, then I have a true belief about the card. But it would be stretching things too far to say that I knew or had knowledge of what the next card would be. I simply made a lucky guess. Justification for true belief, therefore, also seems to be a necessary ingredient in the concept of knowledge.

We approach the definition of knowledge as justified true belief in our first reading, Plato's dialogue, the *Meno.* Near the very end of the dialogue, Socrates distinguishes between knowledge and right opinion. Right opinion is compared to the statues of Daedalus, so lifelike that they run away if not chained down. The anchor by which right opinion constitutes knowledge, according to Socrates, is the reason, warrant, or justification that keeps right opinion from slipping away by explaining why a belief is true or an opinion right.

Skeptical challenges to the possibility of knowing abound. Again in Plato's *Meno,* in an earlier part of the dialogue, a dilemma against the possibility of acquiring knowledge is examined. Meno asks Socrates whether virtue can be taught, or whether it is had by nature or in some other way. Socrates replies that he cannot so much as begin to answer the question because he does not even know what virtue is. Later, after Socrates has refuted several attempts by Meno to define the concept of virtue, Meno suggests that it may be impossible to acquire knowledge of any kind, including knowledge of the concept of virtue. Meno claims that either we already know or do not know that which we seek to know. If we know already, then we cannot acquire knowledge, because logically we cannot acquire what we already have. But if we do not know already, then we also cannot acquire knowledge, because then we do not know what to look for, nor would we recognize it if we happened to stumble upon it. Socrates' answer to this riddle is ingenious and leads him into some of the most characteristic principles of his philosophy, including the doctrine that knowledge is a permanent possession of our immortal souls.

The definition of knowledge as justified true belief satisfied philosophers for centuries. But in 1963 it was shown to be incorrect in a three-page gem of philosophical argumentation by Edmund L. Gettier. Gettier offers counterexamples to the traditional definition of knowledge, in which he shows that justified true belief is not sufficient for knowledge. The examples themselves, and the diagnosis of the so-called Gettier problem, along with the proper solution in revising the definition of knowledge, are important topics in recent theory of knowledge. A presupposition of Gettier's criticism is identified and rejected by Richard L. Kirkham in his essay "Does the Gettier Problem Rest on a Mistake?" Kirkham argues that efforts to resolve the Gettier problem mistakenly try to define knowledge so as to achieve both sufficient scope to include all of the kinds of beliefs that we commonly regard as constituting knowledge, while at the same time excluding all real or hypothetical beliefs that are not regarded as knowledge. Kirkham imagines two reactions to his argument. We might conclude that there are several senses of knowledge, which the Gettier problem serves to distinguish, or that the concept of knowledge is hopelessly confused and logically incoherent, as the Gettier counterexamples reveal. Kirkham opts for the second interpretation of Gettier's argument as proving a radical form of skepticism.

René Descartes, in his *Meditations on First Philosophy,* seeks to establish absolutely certain rational foundations for science. He sets the stage for this ambitious project in the selection included here from Meditation I, in which he attempts to advance the most powerful basis for systematic doubt. Descartes is at most a methodological skeptic. He does not propose skepticism as the conclusion of his philosophy, but only as a means to the higher end of developing a theory of knowledge that triumphs over even the strongest imaginable grounds for doubt. In Meditation I, Descartes explains that many of the propositions he was taught to believe have turned out to be false. He wants to rebuild knowledge on a more certain basis, which requires that he first discover a way of casting all of his previous beliefs in doubt. He considers several possibilities for doubting his prior knowledge and finally settles on the argument that there could be an evil demon who deceives him whenever he believes himself to acquire knowledge of the world by using his senses. If we cannot prove that there is no demon, how can we trust anything we have come to believe as a result of sensation?

In his essay "A Defence of Common Sense," G. E. Moore upholds the intuitive foundations of knowledge. He argues that there are beliefs known from immediate sense experience that cannot reasonably be doubted, except by invoking principles that are even more doubtful themselves. It is not always clear in Moore's exposition whether he is trying, as his title suggests, to give a defense of common sense, or whether he is defending the possibility of knowledge by appealing to common-sense experiential judgments. In either case, we find a remarkable opposition between his commonsense epistemology and Descartes's systematic methodological skepticism. Where Moore holds up his two hands, and claims, "Here is one hand, and here is another hand," defying us actually to doubt that there are two hands before us, Descartes declares that no matter how clear and commonsensical the sensory evidence for the existence of two hands may appear, appearances can often be deceiving. If we have no solid grounds for concluding that the appearance of the two hands cannot be the mischievous result of the evil demon's attempts to deceive us even in our most clear and distinct perceptions of things, then we cannot know with the sort of absolute certainty Descartes requires that Moore's two hands exist. A defender of Moore's defense of common sense is likely to reply that belief in the existence of our hands is at least if not finally much more certain than the reasoning by which Descartes argues that there is a possibility that there could be an evil demon that deceives us when we exercise our senses in perceiving the world. Thus, we have the makings for an interesting philosophical dispute about the role of certainty in the concept and experiential foundations of knowledge.

A dilemma for another type of skepticism is discussed by Roderick M. Chisholm in the excerpt from his lecture, *The Problem of the Criterion.* The diallelus or wheel, also known as the problem of the criterion, arises when we ask how it is possible to justify the truth of any belief. The obvious answer might be that we justify a belief as true by checking to see if it follows from a correct epistemic principle. But if we go on to ask what makes an epistemic principle correct, it appears the only answer we can give is that an epistemic principle is correct just in case it implies all and only true beliefs. We are thereby caught in a circle. To know which of our beliefs are true, we must consult a correct epistemic principle to see if they are entailed. But to know which of many epistemic principles is correct, we already need to know which beliefs are true, so that we can make sure the epistemic principle we want to use does not support false beliefs. If we need to know which epistemic principles are correct in order to know which beliefs are true, and if we already need to know which beliefs are true in order to know which epistemic principles are correct, then we need each before we can apply it to justify the other. We seem as a result to be saddled with the skeptical conclusion that we cannot know either which beliefs are true or which epistemic principles are correct. Chisholm lays out the problem clearly, and offers some basic distinctions by which to resolve the difficulty.

The illusion of knowledge is encouraged by an inexactness in our ordinary language that conceals the fact that we are virtually never justified in what we believe ourselves to know. To say that we know that a table is flat, absolutely flat in the strict geometrical sense, requires a condition that no actual table in our experience ever satisfies. An indirect reply to this kind of skepticism in defense of the possibility of knowledge is made by Keith Lehrer in a selection from his book, *Theory of Knowledge*. Lehrer maintains that adequate justification for probable empirical knowledge is possible as long as we do not demand that all knowledge be infallible. By softening the expectation that we cannot be wrong about the things we rightly claim to know, Lehrer restores the attribution of knowledge to the epistemic situations in which we ordinarily believe ourselves to know. The question of what constitutes adequate justification, and of what is meant by the concept of justification, is as important here as the differences about whether or not knowledge implies absolute certainty and uncompromising exactitude. Lehrer interprets knowing as an interactive exchange between potential critics who can help us to refine knowledge by exposing our beliefs to objections from others and persisting only in knowledge claims that stand the test of good criticism.

Alternative models of knowledge are discussed by Alvin I. Goldman in "A Causal Theory of Knowing," and by Ernest Sosa's "The Raft and the Pyramid: Coherence versus Foundations in the Theory of Knowledge" and William P. Alston's "Two Types of Foundationalism." The three essays represent major divisions in contemporary epistemology.

Goldman diagnoses the Gettier counterexamples as involving a lack of causal connection between the fact that an epistemic agent believes something and the fact that makes the belief true. Goldman argues that when belief constitutes knowledge there is a causal connection, typically involving the believer's sensory perception of the state of affairs that is believed and the cognitive state of believing that the state of affairs obtains. The causal theory of knowledge is revolutionary in comparison with traditional analyses of the conditions for knowledge in terms of more abstract concepts of logic and justification. Yet the causal theory promises to make important contributions to the scientific study of knowledge as a branch of psychology in a philosophical program often attributed to Willard Van Orman Quine in his influential essay, "Epistemology Naturalized."

Sosa, in a very different vein, develops the metaphors of the raft and pyramid as two different ways of modeling justification relations in epistemology. The raft is a symbol for coherentism, in which no single belief has independent justification, but depends for its acceptance on its relations with all other beliefs in a kind of mutually supportive grid or network that stands or falls more or less as a whole by virtue of its logical consistency. The pyramid suggests an entirely different image of the justification of beliefs. As a pyramid has a solid foundation on which a super-structure is built, so in a foundationalist theory of knowledge some beliefs are accepted as self-justifying with no need for independent support, while others are justified by virtue of the epistemic dependence relations by which they are related to and upheld on the strength of the foundations. Sosa considers and answers coher-entist objections to foundationalism, and foundationalist objections to coherentism, and concludes that while foundationalism is preferable to coherentism, foundation-alism is subject to a fatal dilemma that recommends in its place a theory of relia-bilism, in which moral and epistemic dispositions in an epistemology of intellec-tual virtues are compared with an ethics of moral virtues.

Finally, Alston distinguishes between two types of foundationalism. He differ-entiates much as Sosa does between two levels of foundational justification. Sim-ple foundationalism for Alston implies that for any epistemic agents there are propositions the agents are immediately justified in believing. Iterative foundation-alism by contrast is the theory that for any epistemic agents there are propositions the agents are immediately justified in believing, and furthermore immediately jus-tified in believing that they are immediately justified in believing. Alston argues that there are persuasive reasons for adopting simple foundationalism, but that there is no comparable support for iterative foundationalism. He concludes that by adopt-ing a version of simple foundationalism we can avoid skepticism and the most pow-erful objections to foundationalism in which the distinction between simple and iterative foundationalism is not recognized. Alston ends on a note of caution but tentatively asserts that simple foundationalism offers the best prospect for an ade-quate theory of knowledge.

Meno *(excerpt)*

Plato

MENO: Can you tell me, Socrates, can virtue[1] be taught? Or is it not teachable but the result of practice, or is it neither of these, but men possess it by nature or in some other way?

SOCRATES: Before now, Meno, Thessalians had a high reputation among the Greeks and were admired for their horsemanship and their wealth, but now, it seems to me, they are also admired for their wisdom, not least the fellow citizens of your friend Aristippus of Larissa. The responsibility for this reputation of yours lies with Gorgias,[2] for when he came to your city he found that the leading Aleuadae, your lover Aristippus among them, loved him for his wisdom, and so did the other leading Thessalians. In particular, he accustomed you to give a bold and grand answer to any question you may be asked, as experts are likely to do. Indeed, he himself was ready to answer any Greek who wished to question him, and every question was answered. But here in Athens, my dear Meno, the opposite is the case, as if there were a dearth of wisdom, and wisdom seems to have departed hence to go to you. If then you want to ask one of us that sort of question, everyone will laugh and say: "Good stranger, you must think me happy indeed if you think I know whether virtue can be taught or how it comes to be; I am so far from knowing whether virtue can be taught or not that I do not even have any knowledge of what virtue itself is."

   I myself, Meno, am as poor as my fellow citizens in this matter, and I blame myself for my complete ignorance about virtue. If I do not know what something is, how could I know what qualities it possesses? Or do you think that someone who does not know at all who Meno is could know whether he is good-looking or rich or well-born, or the opposite of these? Do you think that is possible?

M: I do not; but, Socrates, do you really not know what virtue is? Are we to report this to the folk back home about you?

S: Not only that, my friend, but also that, as I believe, I have never yet met anyone else who did know. . . .

   So now I do not know what virtue is; perhaps you knew before you contacted me, but now you are certainly like one who does not know. Nevertheless, I want to examine and seek together with you what it may be.

---

[1]The Greek word is *aretê*. It can refer to specific virtues such as moderation, courage, et cetera, but it is also used for *the* virtue or conglomeration of virtues that makes a man virtuous or good. In this dialogue it is mostly used in this more general sense. Socrates himself at times (e.g., 93 b ff.) uses "good" as equivalent to virtuous.

[2]Gorgias was perhaps the most famous of the earlier generation of Sophists, those traveling teachers who arose in the late fifth century to fill the need for higher education. They all taught rhetoric, or the art of speaking, but as Meno tells us, Gorgias concentrated on this more than the others and made fewer general claims for his teaching (95c). He visited Athens in 427 B.C., and his rhetorical devices gave him an immediate success. Plato named one of his dialogues after him. Fairly substantive fragments of his writings are extant.

Source: Plato, Five Dialogues: Euthyphro, Apology, Crito, Meno, Phaedo, translated by G. M. A. Grube. Indianapolis: Hackett Publishing Company, 1981, 59–60, 69–76, 84–86.

M: How will you look for it, Socrates, when you do not know at all what it is? How will you aim to search for something you do not know at all? If you should meet with it, how will you know that this is the thing that you did not know?

S: I know what you want to say, Meno. Do you realize what a debater's argument you are bringing up, that a man cannot search either for what he knows or for what he does not know? He cannot search for what he knows—since he knows it, there is no need to search—nor for what he does not know, for he does not know what to look for.

M: Does that argument not seem sound to you, Socrates?

S: Not to me.

M: Can you tell me why?

S: I can. I have heard wise men and women talk about divine matters . . .

M: What did they say?

S: What was, I thought, both true and beautiful.

M: What was it, and who were they?

S: The speakers were among the priests and priestesses whose care it is to be able to give an account of their practices. Pindar too says it, and many others of the divine among our poets. What they say is this; see whether you think they speak the truth: They say that the human soul is immortal; at times it comes to an end, which they call dying, at times it is reborn, but it is never destroyed, and one must therefore live one's life as piously as possible:

> Persephone will return to the sun above in the ninth year
>> the souls of those from whom
>> she will exact punishment for old miseries,
>> and from these come noble kings,
>> mighty in strength and greatest in wisdom,
>> and for the rest of time men will call them sacred heroes.

As the soul is immortal, has been born often and has seen all things here and in the underworld, there is nothing which it has not learned; so it is in no way surprising that it can recollect the things it knew before, both about virtue and other things. As the whole of nature is akin, and the soul has learned everything, nothing prevents a man, after recalling one thing only—a process men call learning—discovering everything else for himself, if he is brave and does not tire of the search, for searching and learning are, as a whole, recollection. We must, therefore, not believe that debater's argument, for it would make us idle, and fainthearted men like to hear it, whereas my argument makes them energetic and keen on the search. I trust that this is true, and I want to inquire along with you into the nature of virtue.

M: Yes, Socrates, but how do you mean that we do not learn, but that what we call learning is recollection? Can you teach me that this is so?

S: As I said just now, Meno, you are a rascal. You now ask me if I can teach you, when I say there is no teaching but recollection, in order to show me up at once as contradicting myself.

M: No, by Zeus, Socrates, that was not my intention when I spoke, but just a habit. If you can somehow show me that things are as you say, please do so.

S: It is not easy, but I am nevertheless willing to do my best for your sake. Call one of these many attendants of yours, whichever you like, that I may prove it to you in his case.

M: Certainly. You there, come forward.

S: Is he a Greek? Does he speak Greek?

M: Very much so. He was born in my household.

S: Pay attention then whether you think he is recollecting or learning from me.

M: I will pay attention.

S: Tell me now, boy, you know that a square figure is like this?—I do.

S: A square then is a figure in which all these four sides are equal?—Yes indeed.

S: And it also has these lines through the middle equal?[3]—Yes.

S: And such a figure could be larger or smaller?—Certainly.

S: If then this side were two feet, and this other side two feet, how many feet would the whole be? Consider it this way: if it were two feet this way, and only one foot that way, the figure[4] would be once two feet?—Yes.

S: But if it is two feet also that way, it would surely be twice two feet?—Yes.

S: How many feet is twice two feet? Work it out and tell me.—Four, Socrates.

S: Now let us have another figure twice the size of this one, with the four sides equal like this one.—Yes.

S: How many feet will that be?—Eight.

S: Come now, try to tell me how long each side of this will be. The side of this is two feet. What about each side of the one which is its double?—Obviously, Socrates, it will be twice the length.

S: You see, Meno, that I am not teaching the boy anything, but all I do is question him. And now he thinks he knows the length of the line on which an eight-foot figure is based. Do you agree?—I do.

S: And does he know?—Certainly not.

[3]Socrates draws a square ABCD. The sides are of course equal, and the "lines through the middle" are the lines joining the middle points of these sides, which also go through the center of the square, namely EF and GH.

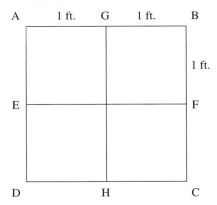

He then goes on to assume the sides to be two feet.

[4]I.e., the rectangle ABFE, which is obviously two square feet.

S: He thinks it is a line twice the length?—Yes.

S: Watch him now recollecting things in order, as one must recollect. Tell me, boy, do you say that a figure double the size is based on a line double the length? Now I mean such a figure as this, not long on one side and short on the other, but equal in every direction like this one, and double the size, that is, eight feet. See whether you still believe that it will be based on a line double the length.—I do.

S: Now the line becomes double its length if we add another of the same length here?—Yes indeed.

S: And the eight-foot square will be based on it, if there are four lines of that length?—Yes.

S: Well, let us draw from it four equal lines, and surely that is what you say is the eight-foot square?—Certainly.

S: And within this figure are four squares, each of which is equal to the four-foot square?—Yes.

S: How big is it then? Is it not four times as big?—Of course.

S: Is this square then, which is four times as big, its double?—No, by Zeus.

S: How many times bigger is it?—Four times.

S: Then, my boy, the figure based on a line twice the length is not double but four times as big?—You are right.

S: And four times four is sixteen, is it not?—Yes.

S: On how long a line then should the eight-foot square be based? Is it not based on this double line?—Yes. Now this four-foot square is based on a line half the length?—Yes.

S: Very well. Is the eight-foot square not double this one and half that one?[5]—Yes.

S: Will it not be based on a line longer than this one and shorter than that one? Is that not so?—I think so.

S: Good, you answer what you think. And tell me, was this one not two-feet long, and that one four feet?—Yes.

S: The line on which the eight-foot square is based must then be longer than this one of two feet, and shorter than that one of four feet?—It must be.

S: Try to tell me then how long a line you say it is.—Three feet.

S: Then if it is three feet, let us add the half of this one, and it will be three feet? For these are two feet, and the other is one. And here, similarly, these are two feet and that one is one foot, and so the figure you mention comes to be?—Yes.

S: Now if it is three feet this way and three feet that way, will the whole figure be three times three feet?—So it seems.

S: How much is three times three feet?—Nine feet.

S: And the double square was to be how many feet?—Eight.

S: So the eight-foot figure cannot be based on the three-foot line?—Clearly not.

S: But on how long a line? Try to tell us exactly, and if you do not want to work it out, show me from what line.—By Zeus, Socrates, I do not know.

[5]I.e., the eight-foot square is double the four-foot square and half the sixteen-foot square, double the square based on a line two-feet long, and half the square based on a four-foot side, so it must be based on a line between two and four feet in length. The slave naturally suggests three feet, but that gives a nine-foot square, and is still wrong. (83e).

S: You realize, Meno, what point he has reached in his recollection. At first he did
    not know what the basic line of the eight-foot square was; even now he does not
    yet know, but then he thought he knew, and answered confidently as if he did
    know, and he did not think himself at a loss, but now he does think himself at a
    loss, and as he does not know, neither does he think he knows.—That is true.
S: So he is now in a better position with regard to the matter he does not know?
M: I agree with that too.
S: Have we done him any harm by making him perplexed and numb as the torpedo
    fish does?—I do not think so.
S: Indeed, we have probably achieved something relevant to finding out how mat-
    ters stand, for now, as he does not know, he would be glad to find out, whereas
    before he thought he could easily make many fine speeches to large audiences
    about the square of double size and said that it must have a base twice as
    long.—So it seems.
S: Do you think that before he would have tried to find out that which he thought
    he knew though he did not, before he fell into perplexity and realized he did
    not know and longed to know?—I do not think so, Socrates.
S: Has he then benefitted from being numbed?—I think so.
S: Look then how he will come out of his perplexity while searching along with
    me. I shall do nothing more than ask questions and not teach him. Watch
    whether you find me teaching and explaining things to him instead of asking
    for his opinion.
S: You tell me, is this not a four-foot figure? You understand?—I do.
S: We add to it this figure which is equal to it?—Yes.
S: And we add this third figure equal to each of them?—Yes.
S: Could we then fill in the space in the corner?—Certainly.[6]
S: So we have these four equal figures?—Yes.
S: Well then, how many times is the whole figure larger than this one?[7]—Four
    times.

[6]Socrates now builds up his sixteen-foot square by joining two four-foot squares, then a third, like this:

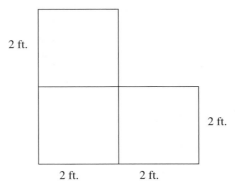

Filling "the space in the corner" will give another four-foot square, which completes the sixteen-foot square
containing four four-foot squares.
[7]"This one" is any one of the inside squares of four feet.

S: But we should have had one that was twice as large, or do you not remember?— I certainly do.

S: Does not this line from one corner to the other cut each of these figures in two?[8]—Yes.

S: So these are four equal lines which enclose this figure?—They are.

S: Consider now: how large is the figure?—I do not understand.

S: Each of these lines cuts off half of each of the four figures inside it, does it not?—Yes.

S: How many of this size are there in this figure?—Four.

S: How many in this?—Two.

S: What is the relation of four to two?—Double.

S: How many feet in this?—Eight.

S: Based on what line?—This one.

S: That is, on the line that stretches from corner to corner of the four-foot figure?— Yes.—Clever men call this the diagonal, so that if diagonal is its name, you say that the double figure would be that based on the diagonal?—Most certainly, Socrates.

S: What do you think, Meno? Has he, in his answers, expressed any opinion that was not his own?

M: No, they were all his own.

S: And yet, as we said a short time ago, he did not know?—That is true.

S: So these opinions were in him, were they not?—Yes.

S: So the man who does not know has within himself true opinions about the things that he does not know?—So it appears.

S: These opinions have now just been stirred up like a dream, but if he were repeatedly asked these same questions in various ways, you know that in the end his knowledge about these things would be as accurate as anyone's.—It is likely.

---

[8]Socrates now draws the diagonals of the four inside squares, namely, FH, HE, EG and GF, which together form the square GFHEG. We should note that Socrates here introduces a new element, which is not the result of a question but of his own knowledge, though the answer to the problem follows from questions. The new square contains four halves of a four foot square, and is therefore eight feet.

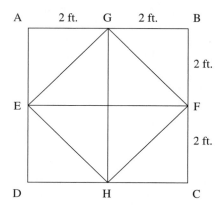

S: And he will know it without having been taught but only questioned, and find the knowledge within himself?—Yes.

S: And is not finding knowledge within oneself recollection?—Certainly.

S: Must he not either have at some time acquired the knowledge he now possesses, or else have always possessed it?—Yes.

S: If he always had it, he would always have known. If he acquired it, he cannot have done so in his present life. Or has someone taught him geometry? For he will perform in the same way about all geometry, and all other knowledge. Has someone taught him everything? You should know, especially as he has been born and brought up in your house.

M: But I know that no one has taught him.

S: Yet he has these opinions, or doesn't he?

M: That seems indisputable, Socrates.

S: If he has not acquired them in his present life, is it not clear that he had them and had learned them at some other time?—It seems so.

S: Then that was the time when he was not a human being?—Yes.

S: If then, during the time he exists and is not a human being he will have true opinions which, when stirred by questioning, become knowledge, will not his soul have learned during all time? For it is clear that during all time he exists, either as a man or not.—So it seems.

S: Then if the truth about reality is always in our soul, the soul would be immortal so that you should always confidently try to seek out and recollect what you do not know at present—that is, what you do not recollect?[9]

M: Somehow, Socrates, I think that what you say is right.

S: I think so too, Meno. I do not insist that my argument is right in all other respects, but I would contend at all costs both in word and deed as far as I could that we will be better men, braver and less idle, if we believe that one must search for the things one does not know, rather than if we believe that it is not possible to find out what we do not know and that we must not look for it.

M: In this too I think you are right, Socrates. . . .

S: We are probably poor specimens, you and I, Meno. Gorgias has not adequately educated you, nor Prodicus me. We must then at all costs turn our attention to ourselves and find someone who will in some way make us better. I say this in view of our recent investigation, for it is ridiculous that we failed to see that it is not only under the guidance of knowledge that men succeed in their affairs, and that is perhaps why the knowledge of how good men come to be escapes us.

M: How do you mean, Socrates?

S: I mean this: we were right to agree that good men must be beneficent, and that this could not be otherwise. Is that not so?—Yes.

S: And that they will be beneficent if they give us correct guidance in our affairs. To this too we were right to agree?—Yes.

---

[9]This is what the whole passage on recollection with the slave is intended to prove, namely, that the sophism introduced by Meno—that one cannot find out what one does not know—is false.

S: But that one cannot guide correctly if one does not have knowledge; to this our agreement is likely to be incorrect.—How do you mean?

S: I will tell you. A man who knew the way to Larissa, or anywhere else you like, and went there and guided others would surely lead them well and correctly?—Certainly.

S: What if someone had had a correct opinion as to which was the way but had not gone there nor indeed had knowledge of it, would he not also lead correctly?—Certainly.

S: And as long as he has the right opinion about that of which the other has knowledge, he will not be a worse guide than the one who knows, as he has a true opinion, though not knowledge.—In no way worse.

S: So true opinion is in no way a worse guide to correct action than knowledge. It is this that we omitted in our investigation of the nature of virtue, when we said that only knowledge can lead to correct action, for true opinion can do so also.—So it seems.

S: So correct opinion is no less useful than knowledge?

M: Yes, to this extent, Socrates. But the man who has knowledge will always succeed, whereas he who has true opinion will only succeed at times.

S: How do you mean? Will he who has the right opinion not always succeed, as long as his opinion is right?

M: That appears to be so of necessity, and it makes me wonder, Socrates, this being the case, why knowledge is prized far more highly than right opinion, and why they are different.

S: Do you know why you wonder, or shall I tell you?—By all means tell me.

S: It is because you have paid no attention to the statues of Daedalus, but perhaps there are none in Thessaly.

S: What do you have in mind when you say this?

S: That they too run away and escape if one does not tie them down but remain in place if tied down.—So what?

S: To acquire an untied work of Daedalus is not worth much, like acquiring a runaway slave, for it does not remain, but it is worth much if tied down, for his works are very beautiful. What am I thinking of when I say this? True opinions. For true opinions, as long as they remain, are a fine thing and all they do is good, but they are not willing to remain long, and they escape from a man's mind, so that they are not worth much until one ties them down by (giving) an account of the reason why. And that, Meno my friend, is recollection, as we previously agreed. After they are tied down, in the first place they become knowledge, and then they remain in place. That is why knowledge is prized higher than correct opinion, and knowledge differs from correct opinion in being tied down.

M: Yes, by Zeus, Socrates, it seems to be something like that.

S: Indeed, I too speak as one who does not have knowledge but is guessing. However, I certainly do not think I am guessing that right opinion is a different thing than knowledge. If I claim to know anything else—and I would make that claim about few things—I would put this down as one of the things I know.—Rightly so, Socrates.

S: Well then, is it not correct that when true opinion guides the course of every action, it does no worse than knowledge?—I think you are right in this too.

S: Correct opinion is then neither inferior to knowledge nor less useful in directing actions, nor is the man who has it less so than he who has knowledge.—That is so.

Meditations on First Philosophy, *Meditation I*

René Descartes

Several years have now passed since I first realized how numerous were the false opinions that in my youth I had taken to be true, and thus how doubtful were all those that I had subsequently built upon them. And thus I realized that once in my life I had to raze everything to the ground and begin again from the original foundations, if I wanted to establish anything firm and lasting in the sciences. But the task seemed enormous, and I was waiting until I reached a point in my life that was so timely that no more suitable time for undertaking these plans of action would come to pass. For this reason, I procrastinated for so long that I would henceforth be at fault, were I to waste the time that remains for carrying out the project by brooding over it. Accordingly, I have today suitably freed my mind of all cares, secured for myself a period of leisurely tranquillity, and am withdrawing into solitude. At last I will apply myself earnestly and unreservedly to this general demolition of my opinions.

Yet to bring this about I will not need to show that all my opinions are false, which is perhaps something I could never accomplish. But reason now persuades me that I should withhold my assent no less carefully from opinions that are not completely certain and indubitable than I would from those that are patently false. For this reason, it will suffice for the rejection of all of these opinions, if I find in each of them some reason for doubt. Nor therefore need I survey each opinion individually, a task that would be endless. Rather, because undermining the foundations will cause whatever has been built upon them to crumble of its own accord, I will attack straightaway those principles which supported everything I once believed.

Surely whatever I had admitted until now as most true I received either from the senses or through the senses. However, I have noticed that the senses are sometimes deceptive; and it is a mark of prudence never to place our complete trust in those who have deceived us even once.

But perhaps, even though the senses do sometimes deceive us when it is a question of very small and distant things, still there are many other matters concerning which one simply cannot doubt, even though they are derived from the very same senses: for example, that I am sitting here next to the fire, wearing my winter dressing gown, that I am holding this sheet of paper in my hands, and the like. But on what grounds could one deny that these hands and this entire body are mine? Unless perhaps I were to liken myself to the insane, whose brains are impaired by such an unrelenting vapor of black bile that they steadfastly insist that they are kings when they are utter paupers, or that they are arrayed in purple robes when they are naked, or that they have heads made of clay, or that they are gourds, or that they are made of glass. But such people are mad, and I would appear no less mad, were I to take their behavior as an example for myself.

This would all be well and good, were I not a man who is accustomed to sleeping at night, and to experiencing in my dreams the very same things, or now and then even less plausible ones, as these insane people do when they are awake. How often does my evening slumber persuade me of such ordinary things as these: that I am here, clothed in my dressing gown, seated next to the fireplace—when in fact I am lying undressed in bed! But right now my eyes are certainly wide awake when I gaze upon this sheet of paper. This head which I am shaking is not heavy with sleep. I extend this hand consciously and deliberately, and I feel it. Such things would not be so distinct for someone who is asleep. As if I did not recall having been deceived on other occasions even by similar thoughts in my dreams! As I consider these matters more carefully, I see so plainly that there are no definitive signs by which to distinguish being awake from being asleep. As a result, I am becoming quite dizzy, and this dizziness nearly convinces me that I am asleep.

Let us assume then, for the sake of argument, that we are dreaming and that such particulars as these are not true: that we are opening our eyes, moving our head, and extending our hands. Perhaps we do not even have such hands, or any such body at all. Nevertheless, it surely must be admitted that the things seen during slumber are, as it were, like painted images, which could only have been produced in the likeness of true things, and that therefore at least these general things—eyes, head, hands, and the whole body—are not imaginary things, but are true and exist. For indeed when painters themselves wish to represent sirens and satyrs by means of especially bizarre forms, they surely cannot assign to them utterly new natures. Rather, they simply fuse together the members of various animals. Or if perhaps they concoct something so utterly novel that nothing like it has ever been seen before (and thus is something utterly fictitious and false), yet certainly at the very least the colors from which they fashion it ought to be true. And by the same token, although even these general things—eyes, head, hands and the like—could be imaginary, still one has to admit that at least certain other things that are even more simple and universal are true. It is from these components, as if from true colors, that all those images of things that are in our thought are fashioned, be they true or false.

This class of things appears to include corporeal nature in general, together with its extension; the shape of extended things; their quantity, that is, their size and number; as well as the place where they exist; the time through which they endure, and the like.

Thus it is not improper to conclude from this that physics, astronomy, medicine, and all the other disciplines that are dependent upon the consideration of composite things are doubtful, and that, on the other hand, arithmetic, geometry, and other such disciplines, which treat of nothing but the simplest and most general things and which are indifferent as to whether these things do or do not in fact exist, contain something certain and indubitable. For whether I am awake or asleep, two plus three make five, and a square does not have more than four sides. It does not seem possible that such obvious truths should be subject to the suspicion of being false.

Be that as it may, there is fixed in my mind a certain opinion of long standing, namely that there exists a God who is able to do anything and by whom I, such as I am, have been created. How do I know that he did not bring it about that there is no earth at all, no heavens, no extended thing, no shape, no size, no place, and yet bringing it about that all these things appear to me to exist precisely as they do now? Moreover, since I judge that others sometimes make mistakes in matters that they believe they know most perfectly, may I not, in like fashion, be deceived every time I add two and three or count the sides of a square, or perform an even simpler operation, if that can be imagined? But perhaps God has not willed that I be deceived in this way, for he is said to be supremely good. Nonetheless, if it were repugnant to his goodness to have created me such that I be deceived all the time, it would also seem foreign to that same goodness to permit me to be deceived even occasionally. But we cannot make this last assertion.

Perhaps there are some who would rather deny so powerful a God than believe that everything else is uncertain. Let us not oppose them; rather, let us grant that everything said here about God is fictitious. Now they suppose that I came to be what I am either by fate, or by chance, or by a connected chain of events, or by some other way. But because being deceived and being mistaken appear to be a certain imperfection, the less powerful they take the author of my origin to be, the more probable it will be that I am so imperfect that I am always deceived. I have nothing to say in response to these arguments. But eventually I am forced to admit that there is nothing among the things I once believed to be true which it is not permissible to doubt—and not out of frivolity or lack of forethought, but for valid and considered reasons. Thus I must be no less careful to withhold assent henceforth even from these beliefs than I would from those that are patently false, if I wish to find anything certain.

But it is not enough simply to have realized these things; I must take steps to keep myself mindful of them. For long-standing opinions keep returning, and, almost against my will, they take advantage of my credulity, as if it were bound over to them by long use and the claims of intimacy. Nor will I ever get out of the habit of assenting to them and believing in them, so long as I take them to be exactly what they are, namely, in some respects doubtful, as has just now been shown, but nevertheless highly probable, so that it is much more consonant with reason to believe them than to deny them. Hence, it seems to me I would do well to deceive myself by turning my will in completely the opposite direction and pretend for a time that these opinions are wholly false and imaginary, until finally, as if with prejudices weighing down each side equally, no bad habit should turn my judgment any further from the correct perception of things. For indeed I know that meanwhile there is no danger or error in following this procedure, and that it is impossible for me to indulge in too much distrust, since I am now concentrating only on knowledge, not on action.

Accordingly, I will suppose not a supremely good God, the source of truth, but rather an evil genius, supremely powerful and clever, who has directed his entire effort at deceiving me. I will regard the heavens, the air, the earth, colors, shapes, sounds, and all external things as nothing but the bedeviling hoaxes of my dreams, with which he lays snares for my credulity. I will regard myself as not having hands, or yes, or flesh, or blood, or any senses, but as nevertheless falsely believing that I possess all these things. I will remain resolute and steadfast in this meditation, and even if it is not within my power to know anything true, it certainly is within my power to take care resolutely to withhold my assent to what is false, lest this deceiver, however powerful, however clever he may be, have any effect on me. But this undertaking is arduous, and a certain laziness brings me back to my customary way of living. I am not unlike a prisoner who enjoyed an imaginary freedom during his sleep, but, when he later begins to suspect that he is dreaming, fears being awakened and nonchalantly conspires with these pleasant illusions. In just the same way, I fall back of my own accord into my old opinions, and dread being awakened, lest the toilsome wakefulness which follows upon a peaceful rest must be spent thenceforward not in the light but among the inextricable shadows of the difficulties now brought forward.

A Defence of Common Sense

G. E. Moore

In what follows I have merely tried to state, one by one, some of the most important points in which my philosophical position differs from positions which have been taken up by *some* other philosophers. It may be that the points which I have had room to mention are not really the most important, and possibly some of them may be points as to which no philosopher has ever really differed from me. But, to the best of my belief, each is a point as to which many have really differed; although (in most cases, at all events) each is also a point as to which many have agreed with me.

I. The first point is a point which embraces a great many other points. And it is one which I cannot state as clearly as I wish to state it, except at some length. The method I am going to use for stating it is this. I am going to begin by enunciating, under the heading (1), a whole long list of propositions, which may seem, at first sight, such obvious truisms as not to be worth stating: they are, in fact, a set of propositions, every one of which (in my own opinion) I *know,* with certainty, to be true. I shall, next, under the heading (2), state a single proposition which makes an assertion about a whole set of *classes* of propositions—each class being defined, as the class consisting of all propositions which resemble *one* of the propositions in (1) in a certain respect. (2), therefore, is a proposition which could not be stated,

Source: "A Defense of Common Sense" from *Philosophical Papers* by G. E. Moore, Chapter 2, Collier Books, © 1962. Reprinted by permission of Timothy Moore.

until the list of propositions in (1), or some similar list, had already been given. (2) is itself a proposition which may seem such an obvious truism as not to be worth stating: and it is also a proposition which (in my own opinion) I *know,* with certainty, to be true. But, nevertheless, it is, to the best of my belief, a proposition with regard to which many philosophers have, for different reasons, differed from me; even if they have not directly denied (2) itself, they have held views incompatible with it. My first point, then, may be said to be that (2), together with all its implications, some of which I shall expressly mention, is true.

(1) I begin, then, with my list of truisms, every one of which (in my own opinion) I *know,* with certainty, to be true. The propositions to be included in this list are the following:

There exists at present a living human body, which is *my* body. This body was born at a certain time in the past, and has existed continuously ever since, though not without undergoing changes; it was, for instance, much smaller when it was born, and for some time afterwards, than it is now. Ever since it was born, it has been either in contact with or not far from the surface of the earth; and, at every moment since it was born, there have also existed many other things, having shape and size in three dimensions (in the same familiar sense in which it has), from which it has been *at various distances* (in the familiar sense in which it is now at a distance both from that mantelpiece and from that bookcase, and at a greater distance from the bookcase than it is from the mantelpiece); also there have (very often, at all events) existed some other things of this kind with which it was *in contact* (in the familiar sense in which it is now in contact with the pen I am holding in my right hand and with some of the clothes I am wearing). Among the things which have, in this sense, formed part of its environment (i.e. have been either in contact with it, or at *some* distance from it, however *great*) there have, at every moment since its birth, been large numbers of other living human bodies, each of which has, like it, (*a*) at some time been born, (*b*) continued to exist from some time after birth, (*c*) been, at every moment of its life after birth, either in contact with or not far from the surface of the earth; and many of these bodies have already died and ceased to exist. But the earth had existed also for many years before my body was born; and for many of these years, also, large numbers of human bodies had, at every moment, been alive upon it; and many of these bodies had died and ceased to exist before it was born. Finally (to come to a different class of propositions), I am a human being, and I have, at different times since my body was born, had many different experiences, of each of many different kinds: e.g. I have often perceived both my own body and other things which formed part of its environment, including other human bodies; I have not only perceived things of this kind, but have also observed facts about them, such as, for instance, the fact which I am now observing, that that mantelpiece is at present nearer to my body than that bookcase; I have been aware of other facts, which I was not at the time observing, such as, for instance, the fact, of which I am now aware, that my body existed yesterday and was then also for some time nearer to that mantelpiece than to that bookcase; I have had expectations with regard to the future, and many beliefs of other kinds, both true and false; I have thought of imaginary things and persons and incidents, in the reality of which I did not believe; I have had dreams; and I have had feelings of many different kinds. And, just as my body has been the body of a human being, namely myself, who has, during his lifetime, had many experiences of each of these (and other) different kinds; so, in the case of very many of the other human bodies which have lived upon the earth, each has been the body of a different human being, who has, during the lifetime of that body, had many different experiences of each of these (and other) different kinds.

(2) I now come to the single truism which, as will be seen, could not be stated except by reference to the whole list of truisms, just given in (1). This truism also (in my own opinion) I *know,* with certainty to be true; and it is as follows:

In the case of *very many* (I do not say *all*) of the human beings belonging to the class (which includes myself) defined in the following way, i.e. as human beings who have had human bodies, that were born and lived for some time upon the earth, and who have, during the lifetime of those bodies, had many different experiences of each of the kinds mentioned in (1), it is true that each has frequently, during the life of his body, known, with regard to *himself* or *his* body, and with regard to some time earlier than any of the times at which I wrote down the propositions in (1), a proposition *corresponding* to each of the propositions in (1), in the sense that it asserts with regard to *himself* or *his* body and the earlier time in question (namely, in each case, the time at which he knew it), just what the corresponding proposition in (1) asserts with regard to *me* or *my* body and the time at which I wrote that proposition down.

In other words what (2) asserts is only (what seems an obvious enough truism) that each of *us* (meaning by "us," very many human beings of the class defined) has frequently *known,* with regard to *himself* or *his* body and the time at which he knew it, everything which, in writing down my list of propositions in (1), I was claiming to know about *my*self or *my* body and the time at which I wrote that proposition down, i.e. just as *I* knew (when I wrote it down) "There exists at present a living human body which is my body," so each of us has frequently known with regard to himself and some other time the different but corresponding proposition, which *he* could *then* have properly expressed by, "There exists *at present* a human body which is *my* body"; just as *I* know "Many human bodies other than mine have before now lived on the earth," so each of us has frequently known the different but corresponding proposition "Many human bodies other than *mine* have before *now* lived on the earth"; just as *I* know "Many human beings other than myself have before now perceived, and dreamed, and felt," so each of *us* has frequently known the different but corresponding proposition "Many human beings other than *myself* have before *now* perceived, and dreamed, and felt"; and so on, in the case of *each* of the propositions enumerated in (1).

I hope there is no difficulty in understanding, so far, what this proposition (2) asserts. I have tried to make clear by examples what I mean by "propositions *corresponding* to each of the propositions in (1)." And what (2) asserts is merely that each of us has frequently known to be true a proposition *corresponding* (in that sense) to each of the propositions in (1)—a *different* corresponding proposition, of course, at each of the times at which he knew such a proposition to be true.

But there remain two points, which, in view of the way in which some philosophers have used the English language, ought, I think, to be expressly mentioned, if I am to make quite clear exactly how much I am asserting in asserting (2).

The first point is this. Some philosophers seem to have thought it legitimate to use the word "true" in such a sense that a proposition which is partially false may nevertheless also be true; and some of these, therefore, would perhaps *say* that propositions like those enumerated in (1) are, in their view, true, when all the time they believe that every such proposition is partially false. I wish, therefore, to make it quite plain that I am not using "true" in any such sense. I am using it in such a sense (and I think this is the ordinary usage) that if a proposition is partially false, it follows that it is *not* true, though, of course, it may be *partially* true. I am maintaining, in short, that all the propositions in (1), and also many propositions corresponding to each of these, are *wholly* true; I am asserting this in asserting (2). And hence any philosopher, who does in fact believe, with regard to any or all of these classes of propositions, that every proposition of the class in question is partially false, is, in fact, disagreeing with me and holding a view incompatible with (2), even though he may think himself justified in *saying* that he believes some propositions belonging to all of these classes to be "true."

And the second point is this. Some philosophers seem to have thought it legitimate to use such expressions as, e.g. "The earth has existed for many years past," as if they expressed something which they really believed, when in fact they believe that every proposition, which such an expression would *ordinarily* be understood to express, is, at least partially, false; and all they really believe is that there is some *other* set of propositions, related in a certain way to those which such expressions do actually express, which, unlike these, really are true. That is to say, they use the expression "The earth has existed for many years past" to express, not what it would ordinarily be understood to express, but the proposition that some proposition, related to this in a certain way, is true; when all the time they believe that the proposition, which this expression would ordinarily be understood to express, is, at least partially, false. I wish, therefore, to make it quite plain that I was not using the expressions I used in (1) in any such subtle sense. I meant by each of them precisely what every reader, in reading them, will have understood me to mean. And any philosopher, therefore, who holds that any of these expressions, if understood in this popular manner, expresses a proposition which embodies some popular error, is disagreeing with me and holding a view incompatible with (2), even though he may hold that there is some *other*, true, proposition which the expression in question might be legitimately used to express.

In what I have just said, I have assumed that there is some meaning which is *the* ordinary or popular meaning of such expressions as "The earth has existed for many years past." And this, I am afraid, is an assumption which some philosophers are capable of disputing. They seem to think that the question "Do you believe that the earth has existed for many years past?" is not a plain question, such as should be met either by a plain "Yes" or "No," or by a plain "I can't make up my mind," but is the sort of question which can be properly met by: "It all depends on what you mean by 'the earth' and 'exists' and 'years': if you mean so and so, and so and so, and so and so, then I do; but if you mean so and so, and so and so, and so and so, or so and so, and so and so, and so and so, or so and so, and so and so, and so and so, then I don't, or at least I think it is extremely doubtful." It seems to me that such a view is as profoundly mistaken as any view can be. Such an expression as "The earth has existed for many years past" is the very type of an unambiguous expression, the meaning of which we all understand. Anyone who takes a contrary view must, I suppose, be confusing the question whether we understand its meaning (which we all certainly do) with the entirely different question whether we *know what it means,* in the sense that we are able to *give a correct analysis* of its meaning. The question what is the correct analysis of *the* proposition meant *on any occasion* (for, of course, as I insisted in defining (2), a different proposition is meant at every different time at which the expression is used) by "The earth has existed for many years past" is, it seems to me, a profoundly difficult question, and one to which, as I shall presently urge, no one knows the answer. But to hold that we do not know what, in certain respects, is the analysis of what we understand by such an expression, is an entirely different thing from holding that we do not understand the expression. It is obvious that we cannot even raise the question how what we do understand by it is to be analysed, unless we do understand it. So soon, therefore, as we know that a person who uses such an expression is using it in its ordinary sense, we understand his meaning. So that in explaining that I was using the expressions used in (1) in their ordinary sense (those of them which have an ordinary sense, which is not the case with quite all of them), I have done all that is required to make my meaning clear.

But now, assuming that the expressions which I have used to express (2) are understood, I think, as I have said, that many philosophers have really held views incompatible with (2). And the philosophers who have done so may, I think, be divided into two main groups. A. What (2) asserts is, with regard to a whole set of *classes* of propositions, that we have, each of us, frequently *known* to be true propositions belonging to *each* of these classes. And one way of holding a view incompatible with this proposition is, of course, to hold, with regard to one or more of the classes in question, that *no* propositions of that class *are* true—that all of them are, at least partially, false; since if, in the case of any one of these classes, *no* propositions of that class *are* true, it is obvious that nobody can have *known* any propositions of that class to be true, and therefore that *we* cannot have known to be true propositions belonging to *each* of these classes. And my first group of philosophers consists of philosophers who have held views incompatible with (2) for this reason. They have held, with regard to one or more of the classes in question, simply that no propositions of that class *are* true. Some of them have held this with regard to *all* the classes in question; some only with regard to *some* of them. But, of course, whichever of these two views they have held, they have been holding a view inconsistent with (2). B. Some philosophers, on the other hand, have not ventured to assert, with regard to *any* of the classes in (2), that no propositions of that class *are* true, but what they have asserted is that, in the case of some of these classes, no human being has ever *known* with certainty, that any propositions of the class in question are true. That is to say, they differ profoundly from philosophers of group A, in that they hold that propositions of *all* these classes *may* be true; but nevertheless they hold a view incompatible with (2) since they hold, with regard to some of these classes, that none of us has ever *known* a proposition of the class in question to be true.

A. I said that some philosophers, belonging to this group, have held that no propositions belonging to *any* of the classes in (2) are wholly true, while others have only held this with regard to *some* of the classes in (2). And I think the chief division of this kind has been the following. Some of the propositions in (1) (and, therefore, of course, all propositions belonging to the corresponding classes in (2)) are propositions which cannot be true, unless some *material things* have existed and have stood *in spatial relations* to one another: that is to say, they are propositions which, *in a certain sense,* imply *the reality of material things,* and *the reality of Space.* E.g. the proposition that my body has existed for many years past, and has, at every moment during that time been either in contact with or not far from the earth, is a proposition which implies both the *reality of material things* (provided you use "material things" in such a sense that to deny the reality of material things implies that no proposition which asserts that human bodies have existed, or that the earth has existed, is wholly true) and also the *reality of Space* (provided, again, that you use "Space" in such a sense that to deny the reality of Space implies that no proposition which asserts that anything has ever been in contact with or at a distance from another, in the familiar senses pointed out in (1), is wholly true). But others among the propositions in (1) (and, therefore, propositions belonging to the corresponding classes in (2)), do not (at least obviously) imply either the reality of material things or the reality of Space: e.g. the propositions that I have often had dreams, and have had many different feelings at different times. It is true that propositions of this second class do imply one thing which is also implied by all propositions of the first, namely that (*in a certain sense*) *Time is real,* and imply also one thing not implied by propositions of the first class, namely that (*in a certain sense*) *at least one Self is real.* But I think there are some philosophers, who, while denying that (in the senses in question) either material things or Space are real, have been willing to admit that Selves and Time are real, in the sense required. Other philosophers, on the other hand, have used the expression "Time is not real," to express some view that they held; and some, at least, of these have, I think, meant by this expression something which is incompatible with the truth of *any* of the propositions in (1)—they have meant, namely, that *every* proposition of the sort that is expressed by the use of "now" or "at present," e.g. "I am now both seeing and hearing" or "There exists at present a living human body," or by the use of a *past* tense, e.g. "I *have* had many experiences in the past," or "The earth *has* existed for many years," are, at least partially, false.

All the four expressions I have just introduced, namely, "Material things are not real," "Space is not real," "Time is not real," "The Self is not real," are, I think, unlike the expressions I used in (1), really ambiguous. And it may be that, in the case of each of them, some philosopher has used the expression in question to express some view he held which was not incompatible with (2). With such philosophers, if there are any, I am not, of course, at present concerned. But it seems to me that the most natural and proper usage of each of these expressions is a usage in which it *does* express a view incompatible with (2); and, in the case of each of them, some philosophers have, I think, really used the expression in question to express such a view. All such philosophers have, therefore, been holding a view incompatible with (2).

All such views, whether incompatible with *all* of the propositions in (1), or only with *some* of them, seems to me to be quite certainly false; and I think the following points are specially deserving of notice with regard to them:

(*a*) If *any* of the classes of propositions in (2) is such that no proposition of that class is true, then no philosopher has ever existed, and therefore none can ever have held with regard to any such class, that no proposition belonging to it is true. In other words, the proposition that some propositions belonging to each of these classes are true is a proposition which has the peculiarity, that, if any philosopher has ever denied it, it follows from the fact that he has denied it, that he must have been wrong in denying it. For when I speak of "philosophers" I mean, of course (as we all do), exclusively philosophers who have been human beings, with human bodies that have lived upon the earth, and who have at different times had many different experiences. If, therefore, there have been any philosophers, there have been human beings of this class; and if there have been human beings of this class, all the rest of what is asserted in (1) is certainly true too. Any view, therefore, incompatible with the proposition that many propositions corresponding to each of the propositions in (1) are true, can only be true, on the hypothesis that no philosopher has ever held any such view. It follows, therefore, that, in considering whether this proposition is true, I cannot consistently regard the fact that many philosophers, whom I respect, have, to the best of my belief, held views incompatible with it, as having any weight at all against it. Since, if I know that they have held such views, I am, *ipso facto,* knowing that they were mistaken; and, if I have no reason to believe that the proposition in question is true, I have still less reason to believe that they have held views incompatible with it; since I am more certain that they have existed and held *some* views, i.e. that the proposition in question is true, than that they have held any views incompatible with it.

(*b*) It is, of course, the case that all philosophers who have held such views have repeatedly, even in their philosophical works, expressed other views inconsistent with them: i.e. no philosopher has ever been able to hold such views consistently. One way in which they have betrayed this inconsistency, is by alluding to the existence of other philosophers. Another way is by alluding to the existence of the human race, and in particular by using "we" in the sense in which I have already constantly used it, in which any philosopher who asserts that "we" do so and so, e.g. that "*we* sometimes believe propositions that are not true," is asserting not only that he himself has done the thing in question, but that *very many other human beings, who have had bodies and lived upon the earth,* have done the same. The fact is, of course, that all philosophers have belonged to the class of human beings which exists only if (2) be true: that is to say, to the class of human beings who have frequently *known* propositions corresponding to each of the propositions in (1). In holding views incompatible with the proposition that propositions of all these classes are true, they have, therefore, been holding views inconsistent with propositions which they themselves *knew* to be true; and it was, therefore, only to be expected that they should sometimes betray their knowledge of such propositions. The strange thing is that philosophers should have been able to hold sincerely, as part of their philosophical creed, propositions inconsistent with what they themselves *knew* to be true; and yet, so far as I can make out, this has really frequently happened. My position, therefore, on this first point, differs from that of philosophers belonging to this group A, not in that I hold anything which they don't hold, but only in that I don't hold, as part of my philosophical creed, things which they do hold as part of theirs—that is to say, propositions inconsistent with some which they and I both hold in common. But this difference seems to me to be an important one.

(*c*) Some of these philosophers have brought forward, in favour of their position, arguments designed to show, in the case of some or all of the propositions in (1), that no propositions of that type can possibly be wholly true, because every such proposition entails both of two incompatible propositions. And I admit, of course, that if any of the propositions in (1) did entail both of two incompatible propositions it could not be true. But it seems to me I have an absolutely conclusive argument to show that none of them does entail both of two incompatible propositions. Namely this: All of the propositions in (1) are true; no true proposition entails both of two incompatible propositions; therefore, none of the propositions in (1) entails both of two incompatible propositions.

(*d*) Although, as I have urged, no philosopher who has held with regard to any of these types of proposition that no propositions of that type are true, has failed to hold also other views inconsistent with his view in this respect, yet I do not think that the view, with regard to any or all of these types, that no proposition belonging to them is true, is *in itself* a self-contradictory view, i.e. entails both of two incompatible propositions. On the contrary, it seems to me quite clear that it *might* have been the case that Time was not real, material things not real, Space not real, selves not real. And in favour of my view that none of these things, which might have been the case, *is* in fact the case, I have, I think, no better argument than simply this—namely, that all the propositions in (1) are, in fact, true.

B. This view, which is usually considered a much more modest view than A, has, I think, the defect that, unlike A, it really is self-contradictory, i.e. entails both of two mutually incompatible propositions.

Most philosophers who have held this view, have held, I think, that though each of us knows propositions corresponding to *some* of the propositions in (1), namely to those which merely assert that *I* myself have had in the past experiences of certain kinds at many different times, yet none of us knows *for certain* any propositions either of the type (*a*) which assert the existence of *material things* or of the type (*b*) which assert the existence of *other* selves, beside myself, and that *they* also have had experiences. They admit that we do in fact *believe* propositions of both these types, and that they *may* be true: some would even say that we know them to be highly probable; but they deny that we ever know them, *for certain,* to be true. Some of them have spoken of such beliefs as "beliefs of Common Sense," expressing thereby their conviction that beliefs of this kind are very commonly entertained by mankind: but they are convinced that these things are, in all cases, only *believed,* not known for certain; and some have expressed this by saying that they are matters of Faith, not of Knowledge.

Now the remarkable thing which those who take this view have not, I think, in general duly appreciated, is that, in each case, the philosopher who takes it is making an assertion about "us"—that is to say, not merely about himself, but about *many other human beings as well.* When he says "No human being has ever *known* of the existence of other human beings," he is saying: "There have been many other human beings beside myself, and none of them (including myself) has ever known of the existence of other human beings." If he says: "These beliefs are beliefs of Common Sense, but they are not matters of *knowledge,*" he is saying: "There have been many other human beings, beside myself, who have shared these beliefs, but neither I nor any of the rest has ever known them to be true." In other words, he asserts with confidence that these beliefs *are* beliefs of Common Sense, and seems often to fail to notice that, *if* they are, they must be true; since the proposition that they are beliefs of Common Sense is one which logically entails propositions both of type (*a*) and of type (*b*); it logically entails the proposition that many human beings, beside the philosopher himself, have had human bodies, which lived upon the earth, and have had various experiences, including beliefs of this kind. This is why this position, as contrasted with positions of group A, seems to me to be self-contradictory. Its difference from A consists in the fact that it is making a proposition about *human knowledge* in general, and therefore is actually asserting the existence of many human beings, whereas philosophers of group A in stating their position are not doing this: they are only contradicting *other* things which they hold. It is true that a philosopher who says "There have existed many human beings beside myself, and none of us has ever known of the existence of any human beings beside himself," is only contradicting himself if what he holds is "There have *certainly* existed many human beings beside myself" or, in other words, "*I* know that there have existed other human beings beside myself." But this, it seems to me, is what such philosophers have in fact been generally doing. They seem to me constantly to betray the fact that they regard the proposition that those beliefs *are* beliefs of Common Sense, or the proposition that they themselves are not the only members of the human race, as not merely true, but *certainly* true; and *certainly* true it cannot be, unless one member, at least, of the human race, namely themselves, has *known* the very things which that member is declaring that no human being has ever known.

Nevertheless, my position that I *know,* with certainty, to be true all of the propositions in (1), is certainly not a position, the denial of which entails both of two incompatible propositions. If I do *know* all these propositions to be true, then, I think, it is quite certain that other human beings also have known corresponding propositions: that is to say (2) also *is* true, and *I* know it to be true. But do I really *know* all the propositions in (1) to be true? Isn't it possible that I merely believe them? Or know them to be highly probable? In answer to this question, I think I have nothing better to say than that it seems to me that I *do* know them, with certainty. It is, indeed, obvious that, in the case of most of them, I do not know them *directly:* that is to say, I only know them because, in the past, I have known to be true *other* propositions which were evidence for them. If, for instance, I do know that the earth had existed for many years before I was born, I certainly only know this because I have known other things in the past which were evidence for it. And I certainly do not know exactly what the evidence was. Yet all this seems to me to be no good reason for doubting that I do know it. We are all, I think, in this strange position that we do *know* many things, with regard to which we *know* further that we must have had evidence for them, and yet we do not know *how* we know them, i.e. we do not know what the evidence was. If there is any "we," and if we know that there is, this must be so: for that there is a "we" is one of the things in question. And that I do know that there is a "we," that is to say, that many other human beings, with human bodies, have lived upon the earth, it seems to me that I do know, for certain.

If this first point in my philosophical position, namely my belief in (2), is to be given any name, which has actually been used by philosophers in classifying the positions of other philosophers, it would have, I think, to be expressed by saying that I am one of those philosophers who have held that the "Common Sense view of the world" is, in certain fundamental features, *wholly* true. But it must be remembered that, according to me, *all* philosophers, without exception, have agreed with me in holding this: and that the real difference, which is commonly expressed in this way, is only a difference between those philosophers, who have *also* held views inconsistent with these features in "the Common Sense view of the world," and those who have not.

The features in question (namely, propositions of any of the classes defined in defining (2)) are all of them features, which have this peculiar property—namely, that *if we know that they are features in the "Common Sense view of the world," it follows that they are true:* it is self-contradictory to maintain that *we* know them to be features in the Common Sense view, and that yet they are not true; since to say that *we* know this, is to say that they are true. And many of them also have the further peculiar property that, *if they are features in the Common Sense view of the world (whether "we" know this or not), it follows that they are true,* since to say that there is a "Common Sense view of the world," is to say that they are true. The phrases "Common Sense view of the world" or "Common Sense beliefs" (as used by philosophers) are, of course, extraordinarily vague; and, for all I know, there may be many propositions which may be properly called features in "the Common Sense view of the world" or "Common Sense beliefs," which are not true, and which deserve to be mentioned with the contempt with which some philosophers speak of "Common Sense beliefs." But to speak with contempt of those "Common Sense beliefs" which I have mentioned is quite certainly the height of absurdity. And there are, of course, enormous numbers of other features in "the Common Sense view of the world" which, if these are true, are quite certainly true too: e.g. that there have lived upon the surface of the earth not only human beings, but also many different species of plants and animals, etc. etc.

II. What seems to me the next in importance of the points in which my philosophical position differs from positions held by *some* other philosophers, is one which I will express in the following way. I hold, namely, that there is no good reason to suppose either (A) that *every* physical fact is *logically* dependent upon some mental fact or (B) that *every* physical fact is *causally* dependent upon some mental fact. In saying this, I am not, of course, saying that there *are* any physical facts which are wholly independent (i.e. both logically and causally) of mental facts: I do, in fact, believe that there are; but that is not what I am asserting. I am only asserting that there is *no good reason* to suppose the contrary; by which I mean, of course, that none of the human beings, who have had human bodies that lived upon the earth, have, during the lifetime of their bodies, had any good reason to suppose the contrary. Many philosophers have, I think, not only believed either that *every* physical fact is *logically* dependent upon some mental fact ("physical fact" and "mental fact" being understood in the sense in which I am using these terms) or that *every* physical fact is *causally* dependent upon some mental fact, or both, but also that they themselves had good reason for these beliefs. In this respect, therefore, I differ from them.

In the case of the term "physical fact," I can only explain how I am using it by giving examples. I mean by "physical facts," facts *like* the following: "That mantelpiece is at present nearer to this body than that bookcase is," "The earth has existed for many years past," "The moon has at every moment for many years past been nearer to the earth than to the sun," "That mantelpiece is of a light colour." But, when I say "facts *like* these," I mean, of course, facts like them *in a certain respect;* and what this respect is I cannot define. The term "physical fact" is, however, in common use; and I think that I am using it in its ordinary sense. Moreover, there is no need for a definition to make my point clear; since among the examples I have given there are some with regard to which I hold that there is no reason to suppose *them* (i.e. these particular physical facts) either logically or causally dependent upon any mental fact.

"Mental fact," on the other hand, is a much more unusual expression, and I am using it in a specially limited sense, which, though I think it is a natural one, does need to be explained. There may be many other senses in which the term can be properly used, but I am only concerned with this one; and hence it is essential that I should explain what it is.

There may, possibly, I hold, be "mental facts" of three different kinds. It is only with regard to the first kind that I am sure that there are facts of that kind; but if there were any facts of either of the other two kinds, they would be "mental facts" in my limited sense, and therefore I must explain what is meant by the hypothesis that there are facts of those two kinds.

(*a*) My first kind is this. I am conscious now; and also I am seeing something now. These two facts are both of them mental facts of my first kind; and my first kind consists exclusively of facts which resemble one or other of the two *in a certain respect.*

(α) The fact that I am conscious now is obviously, in a certain sense, a fact, with regard to a particular individual and a particular time, to the effect that that individual is conscious at that time. And every fact which resembles this one in that respect is to be included in my first kind of mental fact. Thus the fact that I was also conscious at many different times yesterday is not itself a fact of this kind: but it entails that there *are* (or, as we should commonly say, because the times in question are past times, "were") many other facts, of this kind, namely each of the facts, which, at each of the times in question, I could have properly expressed by "I am conscious *now.*" *Any* fact which is, in this sense, a fact with regard to an individual and a time (whether the individual be myself or another, and whether the time be past or present), to the effect that that individual *is* conscious at that time, is to be included in my first kind of mental fact: and I call such facts, facts of class (α).

(β) The second example I gave, namely the fact that I am seeing something now, is obviously related to the fact that I am conscious now in a peculiar manner. It not only *entails* the fact that I am conscious now (for from the fact that I am seeing something it *follows* that I am conscious: I *could* not have been seeing anything, unless I had been conscious, though I might quite well have been conscious without seeing anything) but it also is a fact, with regard to a *specific way* (or mode) of being conscious, to the effect that I am conscious in that way: in the same sense in which the proposition (with regard to any particular thing) "This is red" both entails the proposition (with regard to the same thing) "This is coloured," and is also a proposition, with regard to a *specific way* of being coloured, to the effect that that thing is coloured in that way. And any fact which is related in this peculiar manner to any fact of class (α), is also to be included in my first kind of mental fact, and is to be called a fact of class (β). Thus the fact that I am hearing now is, like the fact that I am seeing now, a fact of class (β); and so is any fact, with regard to myself and a past time, which could at that time have been properly expressed by "I am dreaming now," "I am imagining now," "I am at present aware of the fact that . . . ," etc. etc. In short, any fact, which is a fact with regard to a particular individual (myself or another), a particular time (past or present), and *any particular kind of experience,* to the effect that that individual is having at that time an experience of that particular kind, is a fact of class (β): and only such facts are facts of class (β).

My first kind of mental facts consists exclusively of facts of classes (α) and (β), and consists of *all* facts of either of these kinds.

(*b*) That there are many facts of classes (α) and (β) seems to me perfectly certain. But many philosophers seem to me to have held a certain view with regard to the *analysis* of facts of class (α), which is such that, if it were true, there would be facts of another kind, which I should wish also to call "mental facts." I don't feel at all sure that this analysis is true; but it seems to me that it *may* be true; and since we can understand what is meant by the supposition that it is true, we can also understand what is meant by the supposition that there are "mental facts" of this second kind.

Many philosophers have, I think, held the following view as to the analysis of what each of us knows, when he knows (at any time) "I am conscious now." They have held, namely, that there is a certain intrinsic property (with which we are all of us familiar and which might be called that of "being an experience") which is such that, at any time at which any man knows "I am conscious now," he is knowing, with regard to that property and himself and the time in question, "There is occurring now an event which has this property (i.e. 'is an experience') and which is an experience of *mine,*" and such that this fact is what he expresses by "I am conscious now." And if this view is true, there must be many facts of each of three kinds, each of which I should wish to call "mental facts"; viz. (1) facts with regard to some event, which has this supposed intrinsic property, and to some time, to the effect that that event is occurring at that time, (2) facts with regard to this supposed intrinsic property and some time, to the effect that *some* event which has that property is occurring at that time, and (3) facts with regard to some property, which is a *specific way* of having the supposed intrinsic property (in the sense above explained in which "being red" is a specific way of "being coloured") and some time, to the effect that some event which has that specific property is occurring at that time. Of course, there not only are not, but *cannot* be, facts of any of these kinds, unless there is an intrinsic property related to what each of us (on any occasion) expresses by "I am conscious now," in the manner defined above; and I feel very doubtful whether there is any such property; in other words, although I know for certain both that I have had many experiences, and that I have had experiences of many different kinds, I feel very doubtful whether to say the first is the same thing as to say that there have been many events, each of which was an experience and an experience of mine, and whether to say the second is the same thing as to say that there have been many events, each of which was an experience of mine, and each of which also had a different property, which was a specific way of being an experience. The proposition that I have had experiences does not necessarily entail the proposition that there have been any events which were experiences; and I cannot satisfy myself that I am acquainted with any events of the supposed kind. But yet it seems to me possible that the proposed analysis of "I am conscious now" is correct: that I am really acquainted with events of the supposed kind, though I cannot see that I am. And *if* I am, then I should wish to call the three kinds of facts defined above "mental facts." Of course, if there are "experiences" in the sense defined, it would be possible (as many have held) that there *can* be no experiences which are not *some individual's* experiences; and in that case any fact of any of these three kinds would be logically dependent on, though not necessarily identical with, some fact of class (α) or class (β). But it seems to me also a possibility that, if there are "experiences," there might be experiences which did not belong to any individual; and, in that case, there would be "mental facts" which were neither identical with nor logically dependent on any fact of class (α) or class (β).

(*c*) Finally some philosophers have, so far as I can make out, held that there are or may be facts which are facts with regard to some individual, to the effect that he is conscious, or is conscious in some specific way, but which differ from facts of classes (α) and (β), in the important respect that they are not facts *with regard to any time:* they have conceived the possibility that there may be one or more individuals, who are *timelessly* conscious, and timelessly conscious in specific modes. And others, again, have, I think, conceived the hypothesis that the intrinsic property defined in (*b*) may be one which does not belong only to *events,* but may also belong to one or more wholes, which do *not* occur at any time: in other words, that there may be one or more *timeless* experiences, which might or might not be the experiences of some individual. It seems to me very doubtful whether any of these hypotheses are even possibly true; but I cannot see for certain that they are not possible: and, if they are possible, then I should wish to give the name "mental fact" to any fact (if there were any) of any of the five following kinds, viz. (1) to any fact which is the fact, with regard to any individual, that he is *timelessly* conscious, (2) to any fact which is the fact, with regard to any individual, that he is *timelessly* conscious in any specific way, (3) to any fact which is the fact with regard to a *timeless* experience that it exists, (4) to any fact which is the fact with regard to the supposed intrinsic property "being an experience," that something timelessly exists which has that property, and (5) to any fact which is the fact, with regard to any property, which is a specific mode of this supposed intrinsic property, that something timelessly exists which has that property.

I have, then, defined three different kinds of facts, each of which is such that, if there *were* any facts of that kind (as there certainly *are,* in the case of the first kind), the facts in question *would be* "mental facts" in my sense; and to complete the definition of the limited sense in which I am using "mental facts," I have only to add that I wish also to apply the name to one *fourth* class of facts: namely to any fact, which is the fact, with regard to any of these three kinds of facts, or any kinds included in them, *that there are facts of the kind in question;* i.e. not only will each individual fact of class (α) be, in my sense, a "mental fact," but also the general fact "that there are facts of class (α)," will itself be a "mental fact"; and similarly in all other cases: e.g. not only will the fact that I am now perceiving (which is a fact of class (β)) be a "mental fact," but also the general fact that *there are* facts, with regard to individuals and times, to the effect that the individual in question is perceiving at the time in question, will be a "mental fact."

A. Understanding "physical fact" and "mental fact" in the senses just explained, I hold, then, that there is no good reason to suppose that *every* physical fact is *logically* dependent upon some mental fact. And I use the phrase, with regard to two facts, F_1 and F_2, "F_1 is *logically dependent* on F_2," wherever and only where F_1 *entails* F_2, either in the sense in which the proposition "I am seeing now" *entails* the proposition "I am conscious now," or the proposition (with regard to any particular thing) "This is red" entails the proposition (with regard to the same thing) "This is coloured," or else in the more strictly logical sense in which (for instance) the conjunctive proposition "All men are mortal, and Mr. Baldwin is a man" entails the proposition "Mr. Baldwin is mortal." To say, then, of two facts, F_1 and F_2, that F_1 is *not* logically dependent upon F_2, is only to say that F_1 *might* have been a fact, even if there had been no such fact as F_2; or that the conjunctive proposition "F_1 is a fact, but there is no such fact as F_2" is a proposition which is not self-contradictory, i.e. does not entail both of two mutually incompatible propositions.

I hold, then, that, in the case of *some* physical facts, there is no good reason to suppose that there is some mental fact, such that the physical fact in question could not have been a fact unless the mental fact in question had also been one. And my position is perfectly definite, since I hold that this is the case with all the four physical facts, which I have given as examples of physical facts. For example, there is no good reason to suppose that there is any mental fact whatever, such that the fact that that mantelpiece is at present nearer to my body than that bookcase could not have been a fact, unless the mental fact in question had also been a fact; and, similarly, in all the other three cases.

In holding this I am certainly differing from some philosophers. I am, for instance, differing from Berkeley, who held that that mantelpiece, that bookcase, and my body are, all of them, either "ideas" or "constituted by ideas," and that no "idea" can possibly exist without being perceived. He held, that is, that this physical fact is logically dependent upon a mental fact of my fourth class: namely a fact which is the fact that there is at least one fact, which is a fact with regard to an individual and the present time, to the effect that that individual is now perceiving something. He does not say that this physical fact is logically dependent upon any fact which is a fact of any of my first three classes, e.g. on any fact which is the fact, with regard to a particular individual and the present time, that *that* individual is now perceiving something: what he does say is that the physical fact couldn't have been a fact, unless it had been a fact that there was *some* mental fact of this sort. And it seems to me that many philosophers, who would perhaps disagree either with Berkeley's assumption that my body is an "idea" or "constituted by ideas," or with his assumption that "ideas" cannot exist without being perceived, or with both, nevertheless would agree with him in thinking that this physical fact is logically dependent upon *some* "mental fact": e.g. they might say that it could not have been a fact, unless there had been, at some time or other, or, were timelessly, *some* "experience." Many, indeed, so far as I can make out, have held that *every* fact is logically dependent on every other fact. And, of course, they have held in the case of their opinions, as Berkeley did in the case of his, that they had good reasons for them.

B. I also hold that there is no good reason to suppose that *every* physical fact is *causally* dependent upon some mental fact. By saying that F_1 is *causally* dependent on F_2, I mean only that F_1 *wouldn't* have been a fact unless F_2 had been; *not* (which is what "logically dependent" asserts) that F_1 *couldn't conceivably* have been a fact, unless F_2 had been. And I can illustrate my meaning by reference to the example which I have just given. The fact that that mantelpiece is at present nearer to my body than that bookcase, is (as I have just explained) so far as I can see, not *logically* dependent upon any mental fact; it *might* have been a fact, even if there had been no mental facts. But it certainly is *causally* dependent on many mental facts: my body *would* not have been here unless I had been conscious in various ways in the past; and the mantelpiece and the bookcase certainly *would* not have existed, unless other men had been conscious too.

But with regard to two of the facts, which I gave as instances of physical facts, namely the fact that the earth has existed for many years past, and the fact that the moon has for many years past been nearer to the earth than to the sun, I hold that there is no good reason to suppose that these are *causally* dependent upon any mental fact. So far as I can see, there is no reason to suppose that there is any mental fact of which it could be truly said: unless this fact had been a fact, the earth would not have existed for many years past. And in holding this, again, I think I differ from some philosophers. I differ, for instance, from those who have held that all material things were created by God, and that they had good reasons for supposing this.

III. I have just explained that I differ from those philosophers who have held that there is good reason to suppose that all material things were created by God. And it is, I think, an important point in my position, which should be mentioned, that I differ also from all philosophers who have held that there is good reason to suppose that there is a God at all, whether or not they have held it likely that he created all material things.

And similarly, whereas some philosophers have held that there is good reason to suppose that we, human beings, shall continue to exist and to be conscious after the death of our bodies, I hold that there is no good reason to suppose this.

IV. I now come to a point of a very different order.

As I have explained under I., I am not at all sceptical as to the *truth* of such propositions as "The earth has existed for many years past." "Many human bodies have each lived for many years upon it," i.e. propositions which assert the existence of material things: on the contrary, I hold that we all know, with certainty, many such propositions to be true. But I am very sceptical as to what, in certain respects, the correct *analysis* of such propositions is. And this is a matter as to which I think I differ from many philosophers. Many seem to hold that there is no doubt at all as to their *analysis,* nor, therefore, as to the analysis of the proposition "Material things have existed," in certain respects in which I hold that the analysis of the propositions in question is extremely doubtful; and some of them, as we have seen, while holding that there is no doubt as to their *analysis,* seem to have doubted whether any such propositions are *true.* I, on the other hand, while holding that there is no doubt whatever that many such propositions are wholly true, hold also that no philosopher, hitherto, has succeeded in suggesting an analysis of them, as regards certain important points, which comes anywhere near to being certainly true.

It seems to me quite evident that the question how propositions of the type I have just given are to be analysed, depends on the question how propositions of another and simpler type are to be analysed. I know, at present, that I am perceiving a human hand, a pen, a sheet of paper, etc.; and it seems to me that I cannot know how the proposition "Material things exist" is to be analysed, until I know how, in certain respects, these simpler propositions are to be analysed. But even these are not simple enough. It seems to me quite evident that my knowledge that I am now perceiving a human hand is a deduction from a pair of propositions simpler still—propositions which I can only express in the form "I am perceiving *this*" and "*This* is a human hand." It is the analysis of propositions of the latter kind which seems to me to present such great difficulties, while nevertheless the whole question as to the *nature* of material things obviously depends upon their analysis. It seems to me a surprising thing that so few philosophers, while saying a great deal as to what material things *are* and as to what it is to perceive them, have attempted to give a clear account as to what precisely they suppose themselves to *know* (or to *judge,* in case they have held that we don't *know* any such propositions to be true, or even that no such propositions *are* true) when they know or judge such things as "This is a hand," "That is the sun," "This is a dog," etc. etc. etc.

Two things only seem to me to be quite certain about the analysis of such propositions (and even with regard to these I am afraid some philosophers would differ from me) namely that whenever I know, or judge, such a proposition to be true, (1) there is always some *sense-datum* about which the proposition in question is a proposition—some sense-datum which is *a* subject (and, in a certain sense, the principal or ultimate subject) of the proposition in question, and (2) that, nevertheless, *what* I am knowing or judging to be true about this sense-datum is not (in general) that it is *itself* a hand, or a dog, or the sun, etc. etc., as the case may be.

Some philosophers have I think doubted whether there are any such things as other philosophers have meant by "sense-data" or "sensa." And I think it is quite possible that some philosophers (including myself, in the past) have used these terms in senses such that it is really doubtful whether there are any such things. But there is no doubt at all that there are sense-data, in the sense in which I am now using that term. I am at present seeing a great number of them, and feeling others. And in order to point out to the reader what sort of things I mean by sense-data, I need only ask him to look at his own right hand. If he does this he will be able to pick out something (and, unless he is seeing double, *only* one thing) with regard to which he will see that it is, at first sight, a natural view to take that that thing is identical, not, indeed, with his whole right hand, but with that part of its surface which he is actually seeing, but will also (on a little reflection) be able to see that it is doubtful whether it can be identical with the part of the surface of his hand in question. Things *of the sort* (in a certain respect) of which this thing is, which he sees in looking at his hand, and with regard to which he can understand how some philosophers should have supposed it to *be* the part of the surface of his hand which he is seeing, while others have supposed that it can't be, are what I mean by "sense-data." I therefore define the term in such a way that it is an open question whether the sense-datum which I now see in looking at my hand and which is a sense-datum of my hand is or is not identical with that part of its surface which I am now actually seeing.

That what I know, with regard to this sense-datum, when I know "This is a human hand," is not that it is *itself* a human hand, seems to me certain because I know that my hand has many parts (e.g. its other side, and the bones inside it), which are quite certainly *not* parts of this sense-datum.

I think it certain, therefore, that the analysis of the proposition "This is a human hand" is, roughly at least, of the form "There is a thing, and only one thing, of which it is true both that it is a human hand and that *this surface* is a part of its surface." In other words, to put my view in terms of the phrase "theory of representative perception," I hold it to be quite certain that I do not *directly* perceive *my hand;* and that when I am said (as I may be correctly said) to "perceive" it, that I "perceive" it means that I perceive (in a different and more fundamental sense) something which is (in a suitable sense) *representative* of it, namely, a certain part of its surface.

This is all that I hold to be *certain* about the analysis of the proposition "This is a human hand." We have seen that it includes in its analysis a proposition of the form "This is part of the surface of a human hand" (where "This," of course, has a different meaning from that which it has in the original proposition which has now been analysed). But this proposition also is undoubtedly a proposition about the sense-datum, which I am seeing, which is a sense-datum *of* my hand. And hence the further question arises: *What,* when I know "*This* is *part of the surface of* a human hand," am I knowing about the sense-datum in question? Am I, in this case, really knowing about the sense-datum in question that it *itself* is part of the surface of a human hand? Or, just as we found in the case of "This is a human hand," that what I was knowing about the sense-datum was certainly not that it *itself* was a human hand, so, is it perhaps the case, with this new proposition, that even here I am not knowing, with regard to the sense-datum, that it is *itself* part of the surface of a hand? And, if so, what is it that I am knowing about the sense-datum itself?

This is the question to which, as it seems to me, no philosopher has hitherto suggested an answer which comes anywhere near to being *certainly* true.

There seem to me to be three, and only three, alternative types of answer possible; and to any answer yet suggested, of any of these types, there seem to me to be very grave objections.

1. Of the first type, there is but one answer: namely, that in this case what I am knowing really is that the sense-datum *itself* is part of the surface of a human hand. In other words that, though I don't perceive *my hand* directly, I do *directly* perceive part of its surface; that the sense-datum itself *is* this part of its surface and not merely something which (in a sense yet to be determined) "represents" this part of its surface; and that hence the sense in which I "perceive" this part of the surface of my hand, is not in its turn a sense which needs to be defined by reference to yet a third more ultimate sense of "perceive," which is the only one in which perception is direct, namely that in which I perceive the sense-datum.

   If this view is true (as I think it may just possibly be), it seems to me certain that we must abandon a view which has been held to be certainly true by most philosophers, namely the view that our sense-data always really have the qualities which they sensibly appear to us to have. For I know that if another man were looking through a microscope at the same surface which I am seeing with the naked eye, the sense-datum which he saw would sensibly appear to him to have qualities very different from and incompatible with those which my sense-datum sensibly appears to me to have: and yet, if my sense-datum is identical with the surface we are both of us seeing, his must be identical with it also. My sense-datum can, therefore, be identical with this surface only on condition that it is identical with his sense-datum; and, since his sense-datum sensibly appears to him to have qualities incompatible with those which mine sensibly appears to me to have, his sense-datum can be identical with mine only on condition that the sense-datum in question either has not got the qualities which it sensibly appears to me to have, or has not got those which it sensibly appears to him to have.

   I do not, however, think that this is a fatal objection to this first type of view. A far more serious objection seems to me to be that, when we see a thing double (have what is called "a double image" of it), we certainly have *two* sense-data each of which is *of* the surface seen, and which cannot therefore both be identical with it; and that yet it seems as if, if any sense-datum is ever identical with the surface *of* which it is a sense-datum, each of these so-called "images" must be so. It looks, therefore, as if every sense-datum is, after all, only "representative" of the surface, *of* which it is a sense-datum.

2. But, if so, what relation has it to the surface in question?

   This second type of view is one which holds that when I know "This is part of the surface of a human hand," what I am knowing with regard to the sense-datum which is *of* that surface, is, *not* that it is *itself* part of the surface of a human hand, but something of the following kind. There is, it says, *some* relation, R, such that what I am knowing with regard to the sense-datum is either "There is one thing and only one thing, of which it is true both that it is a part of the surface of a human hand, and that it has R to this sense-datum," or else "There are a set of things, of which it is true both that that set, taken collectively, *are* part of the surface of a human hand, and also that each member of the set has R to this sense-datum, and that nothing which is not a member of the set has R to it."

Obviously, in the case of this second type, many different views are possible, differing according to the view they take as to what the relation R is. But there is only one of them, which seems to me to have any plausibility; namely that which holds that R is an ultimate and unanalysable relation, which might be expressed by saying that "xRy" means the same as "y is an appearance or manifestation of x." I.e. the analysis which this answer would give of "This is part of the surface of a human hand" would be "There is one and only one thing of which it is true both that it is part of the surface of a human hand, and that this sense-datum is an appearance or manifestation of it."

To this view also there seem to me to be very grave objections, chiefly drawn from a consideration of the questions how we can possibly *know* with regard to any of our sense-data that there is one thing and one thing only which has to them such a supposed ultimate relation; and how, if we do, we can possibly *know* anything further about such things, e.g. of what size or shape they are.

3. The third type of answer, which seems to me to be the only possible alternative if (1) and (2) are rejected, is the type of answer which J. S. Mill seems to have been implying to be the true one when he said that material things are "permanent possibilities of sensation." He seems to have thought that when I know such a fact as "This is part of the surface of a human hand," what I am knowing with regard to the sense-datum which is the principal subject of that fact, is not that it is itself part of the surface of a human hand, nor yet, with regard to any relation, that *the* thing which has to it that relation is part of the surface of a human hand, but a whole set of hypothetical facts each of which is a fact of the form "If *these* conditions had been fulfilled, I should have been perceiving a sense-datum intrinsically related to *this* sense-datum in *this* way," "If *these* (other) conditions had been fulfilled, I should have been perceiving a sense-datum intrinsically related to *this* sense-datum in *this* (other) way," etc. etc.

With regard to this third type of view as to the analysis of propositions of the kind we are considering, it seems to me, again, just *possible* that it is a true one; but to hold (as Mill himself and others seem to have held) that it is *certainly,* or nearly certainly, true, seems to me as great a mistake, as to hold with regard either to (1) or to (2), that they are *certainly,* or nearly certainly, true. There seem to me to be very grave objections to it; in particular the three, (*a*) that though, in general, when I know such a fact as "This is a hand," I certainly do know some hypothetical facts of the form "If *these* conditions had been fulfilled, I should have been perceiving a sense-datum of *this* kind, which would have been a sense-datum of the same surface of which *this* is a sense-datum," it seems doubtful whether any conditions with regard to which I know this are not themselves conditions of the form "If this and that *material thing* had been in those positions and conditions . . . ," (*b*) that it seems again very doubtful whether there is any intrinsic relation, such that my knowledge that (under *these* conditions) I should have been perceiving a sense-datum of *this* kind, which would have been a sense-datum of the same surface of which *this* is a sense-datum, is equivalent to a knowledge, with regard to that relation, that I should, under those conditions, have been perceiving a sense-datum related by it to *this* sense-datum, and (*c*) that, if it were true, the sense in which a material surface is "round" or "square," would necessarily be utterly different from that in which our sense-data sensibly appear to us to be "round" or "square."

V. Just as I hold that the proposition "There are and have been material things" is quite certainly true, but that the question how this proposition is to be analysed is one to which no answer that has been hitherto given is anywhere near certainly true; so I hold that the proposition "There are and have been many Selves" is quite certainly true, but that here again all the analyses of this proposition that have been sugggested by philosophers are highly doubtful.

That I am now perceiving many different sense-data, and that I have at many times in the past perceived many different sense-data, I know for certain—that is to say, I know that there are mental facts of class (β), connected in a way which it is proper to express by saying that they are all of them facts about *me;* but how this kind of connection is to be analysed, I do not know for certain, nor do I think that any other philosopher knows with any approach to certainty. Just as in the case of the proposition "This is part of the surface of a human hand," there are several extremely different views as to its analysis, each of which seems to me *possible,* but none nearly certain, so also in the case of the proposition "This, that and that sense-datum are all at present being perceived by *me,*" and still more so in the case of the proposition "*I* am now perceiving this sense-datum, and *I* have in the past perceived sense-data of these other kinds." Of the *truth* of these propositions there seems to me to be no doubt, but as to what is the correct analysis of them there seems to me to be the gravest doubt— the true analysis may, for instance, *possibly* be quite as paradoxical as is the third view given under IV as to the analysis of "This is part of the surface of a human hand"; but whether it *is* as paradoxical as this seems to me to be quite as doubtful as in that case. Many philosophers, on the other hand, seem to me to have assumed that there is little or no doubt as to the correct analysis of such propositions; and many of these, just reversing my position, have also held that the propositions themselves are not true.

Is Justified True Belief Knowledge?

Edmund L. Gettier

Various attempts have been made in recent years to state necessary and sufficient conditions for someone's knowing a given proposition. The attempts have often been such that they can be stated in a form similar to the following:[1]

(a) S knows that P	*IFF*	(i) P is true,
		(ii) S believes that P, and
		(iii) S is justified in believing that P.

[1]Plato seems to be considering some such definition at *Theaetetus* 201, and perhaps accepting one at *Meno* 98.
Source: "Is Justified True Belief Knowledge?" by Edmund L. Gettier III, originally published in *Analysis,* 23, 1963, 121–123. Reprinted by permission of the author.

For example, Chisholm has held that the following gives the necessary and sufficient conditions for knowledge:[2]

(b) S knows that P   *IFF*   (i) S accepts P,

(ii) S has adequate evidence for P, and

(iii) P is true.

Ayer has stated the necessary and sufficient conditions for knowledge as follows:[3]

(c) S knows that P   *IFF*   (i) P is true,

(ii) S is sure that P is true, and

(iii) S has the right to be sure that P is true.

I shall argue that (a) is false in that the conditions stated therein do not constitute a *sufficient* condition for the truth of the proposition that S knows that P. The same argument will show that (b) and (c) fail if "has adequate evidence for" or "has the right to be sure that" is substituted for "is justified in believing that" throughout.

I shall begin by noting two points. First, in that sense of "justified" in which S's being justified in believing P is a necessary condition of S's knowing that P, it is possible for a person to be justified in believing a proposition that is in fact false. Secondly, for any proposition P, if S is justified in believing P, and P entails Q, and S deduces Q from P and accepts Q as a result of this deduction, then S is justified in believing Q. Keeping these two points in mind, I shall now present two cases in which the conditions stated in (a) are true for some proposition, though it is at the same time false that the person in question knows that proposition.

CASE I

Suppose that Smith and Jones have applied for a certain job. And suppose that Smith has strong evidence for the following conjunctive proposition:

(d) Jones is the man who will get the job, and Jones has ten coins in his pocket.

Smith's evidence for (d) might be that the president of the company assured him that Jones would in the end be selected, and that he, Smith, had counted the coins in Jones's pocket ten minutes ago. Proposition (d) entails:

(e) The man who will get the job has ten coins in his pocket.

---

[2]Roderick M. Chisholm, *Perceiving: a Philosophical Study,* Cornell University Press (Ithaca, New York, 1957), p. 16.
[3]A. J. Ayer, *The Problem of Knowledge,* Macmillan (London, 1956), p. 34.

Let us suppose that Smith sees the entailment from (d) to (c), and accepts (e) on the grounds of (d), for which he has strong evidence. In this case, Smith is clearly justified in believing that (e) is true.

But imagine, further, that unknown to Smith, he himself, not Jones, will get the job. And, also, unknown to Smith, he himself has ten coins in his pocket. Proposition (e) is then true, though proposition (d), from which Smith inferred (e), is false. In our example, then, all of the following are true: *(i)* (e) is true, *(ii)* Smith believes that (e) is true, and *(iii)* Smith is justified in believing that (e) is true. But it is equally clear that Smith does not *know* that (e) is true; for (e) is true in virtue of the number of coins in Smith's pocket, while Smith does not know how many coins are in Smith's pocket, and bases his belief in (e) on a count of the coins in Jones's pocket, whom he falsely believes to be the man who will get the job.

CASE II

Let us suppose that Smith has strong evidence for the following proposition:

(f) Jones owns a Ford.

Smith's evidence might be that Jones has at all times in the past within Smith's memory owned a car, and always a Ford, and that Jones has just offered Smith a ride while driving a Ford. Let us imagine, now, that Smith has another friend, Brown, of whose whereabouts he is totally ignorant. Smith selects three place-names quite at random, and constructs the following three propositions:

(g) Either Jones owns a Ford, or Brown is in Boston;

(h) Either Jones owns a Ford, or Brown is in Barcelona;

(i) Either Jones owns a Ford, or Brown is in Brest-Litovsk.

Each of these propositions is entailed by (f). Imagine that Smith realizes the entailment of each of these propositions he has constructed by (f), and proceeds to accept (g), (h), and (i) on the basis of (f). Smith has correctly inferred (g), (h), and (i) from a proposition for which he has strong evidence. Smith is therefore completely justified in believing each of these three propositions. Smith, of course, has no idea where Brown is.

But imagine now that two further conditions hold. First, Jones does *not* own a Ford, but is at present driving a rented car. And secondly, by the sheerest coincidence, and entirely unknown to Smith, the place mentioned in proposition (h) happens really to be the place where Brown is. If these two conditions hold then Smith does *not* know that (h) is true, even though *(i)* (h) *is* true, *(ii)* Smith does believe that (h) is true, and *(iii)* Smith is justified in believing that (h) is true.

These two examples show that definition (a) does not state a *sufficient* condition for someone's knowing a given proposition. The same cases, with appropriate changes, will suffice to show that neither definition (b) nor definition (c) do so either.

Does the Gettier Problem Rest on a Mistake?

Richard L. Kirkham

Attempts to resolve the Gettier Problem[1] rest on the mistaken assumption that an analysis of knowledge can be found which is (a) generous enough to include as items of knowledge all, or most, of those beliefs we commonly regard as knowledge,[2] and (b) rigorous enough to exclude from the class of knowledge any beliefs held in real *or hypothetical cases* which we would agree on reflection are situations where the epistemic agent does not know the belief in question. In actual practice there has been an inconsistency in the methods used to determine whether a particular analysis meets both criteria: We are asked to judge whether an analysis is too exclusive (criterion (a)) by reference to our ordinary, unreflective use of the word "know"; but we are to judge whether it is too inclusive (criterion (b)) by reference to hypothetical situations (sometimes very elaborate) which force us to be acutely attentive to our linguistic and conceptual intuitions about "know." (See for example the introduction to Pappas and Swain, ibid.) The inconsistency is a reflection of what has gone wrong in the literature on the Gettier Problem.

A Gettier type counterexample is used to show that a proposed analysis of knowledge is too inclusive. Such counterexamples are hypothetical situations in which (1) all of the conditions for knowledge specified in the analysis are met, but (2) the epistemic agent does not have knowledge because the conditions have been met only by dumb luck, by accident, by coincidence, or by some means we intuitively regard as illegitimate. A typical paper on the Gettier Problem begins with a counterexample to the most recent state-of-the-art analysis of knowledge. The author then goes on to propose a new, more demanding analysis which cannot be falsified by his counterexample (or any previous Gettier counterexample). The new analysis becomes the state-of-the-art for a year or two until, invariably, someone finds a counterexample to it. It is this process which has produced the jungle of Gettier literature. The method implied by the process is backward. I believe that eventually (perhaps after many years) this process would yield the conclusion that the *only* analyses which are immune to all Gettier type counterexamples are those with very powerful sceptical implications, that is, the only analyses which can meet criterion (b) above are those which *cannot* meet criterion (a). I propose a shortcut to the same conclusion: (1) I shall suggest a very demanding analysis of knowledge (without concern for the moment for its sceptical implications). (2) I shall show that the analysis is immune to any and all possible Gettier type counterexamples. (3) I shall show that *no possible analysis* which is less demanding (however slightly)

---

[1]Edmund L. Gettier, 'Is Justified True Belief Knowledge?', *Analysis,* XXIII. 6 (June 1963), pp. 121–123.

[2]George S. Pappas and Marshall Swain, *Essays on Knowledge and Justification* (Ithaca: Cornell U. Press, 1978), Introduction, p. 21.

Source: "Does the Gettier Problem Rest on a Mistake?" by Richard L. Kirkham, *Mind,* 93. Reprinted by permission of Oxford University Press.

than mine can be immune to all Gettier counterexamples. (4) Since my analysis is too demanding to meet criterion (a) and no analysis less demanding can meet criterion (b), I shall conclude that no analysis can meet both criteria. Finally, I shall discuss the implications of this conclusion.

I suggest the following as an analysis of "Smith knows that p": Smith knows that p iff

> (i) p is true,
>
> (ii) Smith believes that p, and
>
> (iii) *either* p is self-evident for Smith *or* Smith has validly deduced p from ultimate premises which are all self-evident for Smith.

I am using "self-evident" in the followng sense: p is self-evident for Smith iff

> (i) if Smith believes p, then p is true and,
>
> (ii) Smith would point to the fact that p cannot fail to be true whenever he believes it as (one of) his rational reason(s) for believing it.

Given the analyses of "knowledge" and "self-evident," very few propositions could be known. Among the few which could be are: "I believe something," "I think my name is Smith" (not "my name is Smith"), "I am in pain," and "Somebody believes something" (deduced from "I believe something"). Necessary truths are also potential items of knowledge, since, if they are always true, then they are true whenever Smith believes them. A case could be made that nothing would ever qualify as knowledge on the above two analyses, but we are not concerned (for the moment) with the sceptical implications of my analysis of knowledge.

To show that the above analysis of knowledge is immune from all possible Gettier type counterexamples it is only necessary to point out that the three conditions for knowledge cannot possibly be fulfilled by accident. In the case of a belief which is held because it is self-evident, how could it be self-evident by accident? And in the case of beliefs held because they are deduced from self-evident premises, how could the premises be accidentally self-evident or how could the belief be "accidently deduced"? It does not seem to make sense to talk of "accidental self-evidence" or an "accidental deduction." What could such phrases mean? I take further indication, albeit not proof, that my analysis is immune to Gettier type counterexamples from the fact that none of the dozens of Gettier counterexamples in the literature would apply to it. Even if a Gettier counterexample can be found to my analysis, that fact would not refute what I am attempting to show in this article; for if an even more demanding analysis is required for immunity to all Gettier counterexamples, then my claim that no analysis can fulfil *both* criteria (a) and (b) above is made all the stronger.

The next step is to show that no analysis less demanding than mine can possibly be immune to all Gettier counterexamples. In sum the kind of justification needed for knowledge must have two characteristics: (1) it must begin with self-evident premises and (2) these premises must necessitate the truth of the proposition which is to be known. (And, of course, it is just these two characteristics which give my analysis its sceptical implications.) I shall argue that any analysis of knowledge which does not require a person to be justified in a manner that at least includes these two characteristics will be vulnerable to one or another of three Gettier type counterexamples. And my argument will be such that it will not matter what other conditions of knowledge are included in a proposed analysis of knowledge: It still will not avoid all three of the Gettier type counterexamples I shall be using, unless it also includes a justification condition which specifies that justification must have these two characteristics. Thus, my argument will also apply to the sort of Gettier solutions which have been called "externalist" or "non-evidential" (i.e. those which do not require that the would-be knower have any evidence at all). The only exceptions will be those analyses which imply scepticism every bit as strongly as mine does. Thus, the only solutions to the Gettier Problem which will be invulnerable to all three of my Gettier counterexamples will be those which give no comfort to non-sceptics anyway. I shall not, of course, presuppose that my sense of knowledge is correct. Rather, I shall show that every possible weaker analysis can be falsified by one or another of three Gettier type counterexamples. And, thus, I shall conclude that no analysis weaker than mine is immune to all Gettier like counterexamples.

Before beginning the argument proper, let me point out that no analysis of knowledge will succeed if it does not require, in addition to whatever else it requires, that the would-be knower have some self-conscious evidence for his belief. For, if a would-be knower has a true belief, acquired *by whatever non-evidential process you wish,* but he has no self-conscious evidence at all for believing it, and, hence, no more *rational* reason for believing it than he does for many false beliefs he has acquired by whim or indoctrination or whatever, then intuitively we would say that he does not know. Thus, we can eliminate all *pure* non-evidentialist or externalist analyses of knowledge. What remain to be considered are the purely evidentialist analyses and the mixed analyses which contain a justification condition and a fourth, non-evidentialist condition for knowledge.

Let us consider first an analysis of knowledge which does have a justification condition but which does *not* require that justification begin with self-evident premises. For any analysis of this sort, it will always be possible to construct a Gettier type counterexample based on the idea that the ultimate premises are believed only by dumb luck, by accident, or by some other illegitimate means. Consider Smith who is allergic to cheese. His idiot cousin Ernie tells him that the moon is made of green cheese. Smith believes Ernie and deduces that if he (Smith) eats two pounds of the moon, he will get sick. And let us stipulate that it is true that anyone who eats two pounds of the moon will get sick. Hence, Smith has a justified true belief, but Smith does not know.

Some would be tempted to suggest that the problem here is that Smith's ultimate premise is false. The fact that it is not self-evident, they would claim, has nothing to do with why we would say that he does not know. But variations of the idiot cousin Ernie case can be constructed in which Smith's ultimate premise is true. Suppose Ernie tells Smith one hundred things about the moon. One of them, by Ernie's dumb luck, happens to be true: The moon is too heavy for any mortal to lift. Smith believes all one hundred things Ernie tells him and deduces something from each one. Some of his conclusions are false, some true. From the proposition that the moon is too heavy for any mortal to lift, Smith deduces that if he is mortal then he cannot lift the moon. Smith has another justified true belief, but he still does not have knowledge, since he believes the premise only because he heard Ernie say it and it is only dumb luck that what Ernie said is true. (Note that Smith does not believe that Ernie is always or even usually right. It is simply a fact that Smith believes what Ernie tells him. Smith has never entertained, much less believes, the proposition "Ernie is right." *So Smith's deduction does not rely on any false belief.* It is true that Smith's behaviour in believing what Ernie tells him would normally be good evidence that he also believes the proposition "Ernie is usually right." But unless we are prepared to endorse behaviourism, the possibility that Smith does not have the latter belief is not eliminated; and, since this is my own hypothetical story anyway, I can stipulate that Smith does not have the latter belief.)

It might be thought that all we must do to handle cases of this sort is to strengthen the justification condition by requiring that the ultimate premises be justified in some appropriate way. But this will not do, for, if the ultimate premises are so justified, then they are not the ultimate premises. They are, in fact, justified with reference to some other, more ultimate, premises. So then it will be possible to construct an "idiot cousin Ernie" counterexample based on the idea that these other, more ultimate, premises are arrived at by luck, or accident, or some such. The principle behind this is that if an ultimate premise truly is ultimate, then either it is self-evidenced in some way or it is not justified at all. Thus, the idiot cousin Ernie case shows not just that some or another kind of justification is needed for the ultimate premises, it shows precisely that they must be *self-evident,* for there is no other kind of justification for *ultimate* premises.

Perhaps the problem of the ultimate premises can be solved by introducing non-evidential requirements to ensure that the ultimate premises are not believed just by luck or by accident. Perhaps, taking a cue from Goldman,[3] we could say that "the fact that p" must be causally connected to Smith's belief in the ultimate premises from which he deduces his "belief that p." However, Goldman realizes that the would-be knower must be able to *correctly* reconstruct the causal chain. Moreover, Goldman is aware that the would-be knower might be able to reconstruct the causal chain just by a series of lucky guesses:

> An additional requirement for knowledge based on inference is that the knower's inferences be warranted. That is, the proposition on which he bases his belief of P must genuinely confirm P. . . . Reconstructing a causal chain merely by lucky guesses does not yield knowledge.[4]

But what about these propositions themselves which are a part of his reconstruction or on which his reconstruction is based? These have now become the new ultimate premises. How will we ensure that they are not believed just by luck? If we say that these, too, must be the result of a causal chain, then this chain will also have to be correctly reconstructed, and this reconstruction will have to be warranted by still more ultimate premises. And so on *ad infinitum.*

[3] Alvin I. Goldman, 'A Causal Theory of Knowing,' *Journal of Philosophy,* LXIV. 12 (June 1967), pp. 355–372, reprinted in Pappas and Swain, eds. ibid. pp. 67–86, passim.
[4] Goldman, ibid., reprinted in Pappas and Swain, ibid. p. 75.

The situation cannot be improved by insisting that Smith's ultimate premises must be arrived at by a reliable method. Suppose he has three methods for attaining new beliefs. One of them has always led him to believe true things while the other two have always led him to believe false things. But suppose he is not aware of the difference in reliability of the three methods. He has always confidently believed every conclusion of all three methods. Wondering whether or not the moon is too heavy for a mortal to lift, Smith chooses *at random* one of the methods and, as it happens, it is the method which has always been reliable. The method leads him to believe that the moon is too heavy and, hence, that if he is mortal he cannot lift it. Yet, intuitively we would say that Smith does not have knowledge, because it is only by dumb luck that he used a reliable method. Would it help to insist that he be warranted in thinking his method is reliable? But what about the premises on which this latter warrant is based? These are now the ultimate premises of his belief that if he is mortal he cannot lift the moon. Why does he believe *them?* Because his idiot cousin Ernie told him to?

I am unable to conceive any manner in which we might try to ensure that the ultimate premises are not believed just by luck which would not simply create new, more ultimate, premises. Hence, I conclude that some Gettier type counterexample based on the idea that the ultimate premises are believed by dumb luck, or by accident, or by coincidence, will work against any analysis of knowledge which does not specify that the would-be knower's ultimate premises must be self-evident.

So the search for an analysis which is immune to all Gettier type counterexamples, but which does not have the apparent sceptical implications of my sense, must now focus on those analyses of knowledge which allow that the inference from the premises to the belief in question need not be deductive, that is, the truth of the belief need not be necessitated by the evidence in its favour. It is my contention that any justification condition of this sort will be vulnerable to at least one of two kinds of Gettier like counterexamples. The first of these two kinds, called "the penguin case," is based on the idea that a method of inference which consistently leads to false belief does not yield knowledge even in the occasional case when, by luck, it produces a true belief. The second kind, called "the cube case," is based on the idea that, however reliable a method of inference usually is, it does not yield knowledge in the occasional case when it misfires (but a true belief is produced anyway purely by coincidence).

First imagine as strong a method of inference as you can short of deduction. Make it inductive, or inference-to-the-best-explanation, or a reconstruction of a causal chain, or whatever you wish. Now strengthen the method of inference as you like with requirements of indefeasibility and not reasoning through a false premise. In short, your assignment here is to devise the most rigorous method of inference you can, subject only to the constraint that the conclusion of such an inference is not necessitated by the ultimate premises. Call this "Method of Inference A." If you prefer, do not think of Method A as a purely inferential process: Think of it only as what Nozick calls a "way of coming to believe"[5] propositions

---

[5]Robert Nozick, *Philosophical Explanations* (Cambridge, Mass.: Harvard University Press, 1981), p. 179.

which has some non-evidential elements. The only constraint is that the use of the method may not logically necessitate the truth of the resulting beliefs.

Smith has gone to Antarctica to study penguins. Examining first some question about the fur of penguins, Smith applies Method A and comes up with a false conclusion. This is possible because in using Method A the premises do not, nor does the method, necessitate the truth of the conclusion. For a method with this characteristic it is *always* possible that something has gone wrong, even when one begins with true premises. Smith does not know his conclusion is false, but we in our ideal observer position do know that it is false. (All Gettier counterexamples put the reader in the position of an ideal observer who knows all the relevant facts about the would-be knower's evidence, how he acquired it, and whether or not his belief is true.) We know that he does not know his conclusion because the truth condition for knowledge has not been fulfilled. Smith applies Method A to another matter about penguins and, again, it issues in a false belief. He uses it again and again, always believing the conclusions, but (as we the ideal observers know) something always goes wrong. His resulting beliefs are always false. Finally, on the one hundred and first application, Method A issues in a true belief. At last Smith has a justified true belief (justified via Method A at any rate), but he does not have knowledge. He just got lucky; Method A finally produced a true belief.

The above counterexample will work against *any* analysis of knowledge that includes a justification condition (or "way of coming to believe") which does *not* require that, to be justified sufficiently to be known, the truth of a belief must be *necessitated* by the evidence in its favour. Because, for *any* method which does not have this characteristic, it is logically possible that it could issue in a false conclusion, not just once but a hundred times in a row.

One proposed solution to the Gettier Problem which would be vulnerable to a Gettier type counterexample like the penguin story is Robert Nozick's. He proposes the following conditions for knowledge:

1. P is true.
2. S believes, via method or way of coming to believe M, that P.
3. If P weren't true and S were to use M to arrive at a belief whether (or not) P, then S wouldn't believe, via M, that P.
4. If P were true and S were to use M to arrive at a belief whether (or not) P, then S would believe, via M, that P.[6]

Nozick says that a method which meets the latter two conditions is "sensitive" to the truth value of P. But note that Nozick's analysis of "knowing that P" makes the applicability of M depend solely on its sensitivity to the truth value of P alone. There is no requirement that M have a general reliability. Hence, Smith (perhaps thinking that M does have a general reliability) might use it one hundred times producing false beliefs each time. But if, by luck, Smith applies M, the one hundred and first time, to a proposition P such that M *is* sensitive to the truth value of P, then, on Nozick's view, we would have to say, counter-intuitively, that Smith knows P; for, with respect to P at least, all Nozick's conditions for knowledge are

[6]Ibid.

met. Moreover, the penguin case would be a counterexample to Nozick's analysis whether or not we think of M as a method of inference or only a "way of coming to believe."

What the penguin case suggests is that however rigorous a method of inference or "way of coming to believe" is and however "sensitive" to the truth value of a given proposition P it is, it will still not provide sufficient justification for knowing P in any given case *unless it has proven at least generally reliable in past instances.*

Let us suppose, then, an analysis of knowledge which requires that the belief in question be justified by some Method B such that Method B is just like Method A, except for the additional characteristic that it has always been reliable in the past.

But there is a Gettier type counterexample to this analysis as well. Suppose Jones has habitually used Method B all his life and it has never failed him. Jones walks into a room and Method B leads him to believe (or, if you prefer, to conclude), *correctly,* that there is a cube in the room and the cube is painted red. But suppose that, unknown to Jones there is a red light-bulb in the room's light-socket. If the cube had been painted white he would have believed it was painted red anyway. Although Method B has always been reliable in the past, it has finally misfired in this case: It is only by luck that the belief it produces is true. I think we would say, intuitively, that Jones does not know the cube is painted red.

A variation has Jones entering a room and correctly concluding that there is a white cube in the room. The light-bulb is white, but *if* the light-bulb had been red, then he would have falsely concluded, via Method B, that the cube was red. It is only lucky that the circumstances are such that Method B leads him to a true belief. Nozick, among others, has produced Gettier type counterexamples which parallel these two, but which are not cases of illusion (illusion luckily avoided, I should say); rather, they are based on some other sort of error.[7] (Nozick, of course, would say that the problem here is that Method B is not "sensitive" to the truth value of the propositions in these two cases. I shall discuss this suggestion below).

A misfiring of Method B is possible because the truth of the premises does not necessitate the truth of the belief. (Putting the same point another way, if Method B is thought of only as a "way of coming to believe," then the use of the method does not guarantee the truth of the resulting belief.)

Now it might be objected that if Method B were really as rigorous as it was supposed to be, then it will include requirements to the effect that Jones must look to see what colour the light-bulb is. But this would miss the point of the cube stories. Even if it is true that, for any given sort of illusion, we could create a Method B such that the possibility of *that* sort of illusion is eliminated, it is not the case that Method B could eliminate every sort of illusion or error; for if Method B involved gathering enough premises to eliminate all possibility of error, then the truth of the premises would necessitate the truth of the belief produced. Which would make the

[7]Ibid. p. 175, see also Ernest Sosa, 'Propositional Knowledge', *Philosophical Studies,* XX, 3 (April 1969), pp. 39 ff.; and Keith Lehrer and Thomas Paxson, Jr., 'Knowledge: Undefeated Justified True Belief', *Journal of Philosophy,* LXVI, (1969), pp. 236 ff.

analysis of knowledge of which it is a part every bit as demanding as mine.[8] Remember, the point here is to find some justification condition which is at least *slightly weaker* than mine but which is still immune to all Gettier type counterexamples. We are testing whether or not a justification condition which does *not* require that the premises necessitate the conclusion can have the needed immunity. We have already seen that some clause requiring reliability must be a part of such a justification condition if it is to be immune to the penguin case. We have now seen that, *if this slightly weaker justification condition really is weaker,* then it cannot eliminate every possibility of error, thus, it will always be possible that error is avoided only by dumb luck and this means that the slightly weaker justification condition will be subject to some Gettier type counterexample like the cube case.

The red cube case shows that Method B cannot assure that Jones would disbelieve the proposition that the cube is red even it it were false. And the white cube case shows that Method B cannot assure that Jones would always believe that the cube is white whenever it is white. It was for these reasons that Nozick proposed his third and fourth conditions for knowledge, quoted above. Perhaps, then, Nozick's two conditions (interpreted as strict implications for the time being instead of as subjunctive conditionals the way Nozick actually interpreted them) along with a clause about reliability will give Method B the needed immunity from Gettier type counterexamples. I think, in fact, that such a method or "way of coming to believe" would have this immunity, but it would have it only because it would not really be weaker than my justification condition; for to meet Nozick's third and fourth conditions (interpreted as strict implications) the method would have to eliminate all possibility of error. And, as I pointed out above, the point here is to find a justification condition which is *weaker* than mine and which is also immune to the Gettier examples.

Thus, I conclude that *no* analysis of knowledge which does not require that the would-be knower be justified such that his premises necessitate his belief is immune to all Gettier type counter examples: All analyses which do not require that the ultimate premises be self-evident are, as I argued above, vulnerable to the "idiot cousin Ernie" counterexample. Hence, despite its apparent sceptical implications, my analysis of knowledge is the weakest analysis which is immune to all Gettier like counterexamples.

Still some philosophers would rebel against the apparent sceptical implications of my justification condition. Nozick is one such philosopher and his reluctance to accept scepticism apparently motivated him to weaken the sense of his third and fourth conditions for knowledge. I have been treating these two conditionals as strict implications. In fact, Nozick calls them subjunctive conditionals and he does not intend for them to rule out every possibility of illusion (luckily avoided) nor, hence, every Gettier counterexample. He wants only to protect his analysis from those counterexamples which are actualized on possible worlds "close" to this one.[9]

---

[8]Some might suggest that if Method B had an appropriate defeasibility clause (see Lehrer and Paxson, ibid.), then it would prevent the cube illusions. But here, again, if the defeasibility clause is strong enough to eliminate every possibility of error, then Method B is not weaker than my kind of justification anyway; for the use of the method would necessitate the truth of the belief produced.

[9]Nozick, ibid. p. 173.

He never makes clear exactly what possible worlds he has in mind, but at any rate he seems to realize that some Gettier type counterexamples will have force against his analysis because by limiting the applicability of his third and fourth conditions for knowledge to possible worlds "close" to this one, he is not eliminating every possible situation in which an epistemic agent uses method M and yet avoids error only by dumb luck.

Other writers on the Gettier Problem have wanted to set out the necessary and sufficient conditions for knowledge. Nozick seems to realize that his analysis is not logically sufficient, so exactly what it is supposed to be is not at all clear. He says in one place that his analysis is not intended to clear up all cases where the applicability of the term "know" is itself unclear at the preanalytic level.[10] But "leaving some cases unclear" and "yielding to falsifying counterexamples" are two different things. Even if the former is not a vice for an analysis of knowledge, the latter certainly is.[11]

The first implication of my arguments is that the assumption on which the Gettier Problem rests (described in the first sentence) is mistaken; for, since my analysis is too demanding to meet criterion (a) of the assumption and no analysis less demanding than mine can meet criterion (b), there is no analysis of knowledge which can meet both. In the face of these results we have several options: We could conclude that there are two senses of knowledge. One of them is at work in ordinary life when we say that we know all kinds of propositions including many which are not justified in the manner my analysis requires. The other is revealed when Gettier counterexamples force us to be acutely attentive to our conceptual intuitions about knowledge. On the other hand, we could simply conclude that the concept of knowledge is hopelessly confused and contradictory; hence, no analysis is possible. The option I prefer is to conclude that the Gettier counterexamples reveal the correct analysis of knowledge and, thus, if my arguments have been cogent, a very radical form of scepticism is correct. This conclusion entails that most of the knowledge claims we make in ordinary life are simply incorrect. My preferred choice is more plausible if we remember that a belief or proposition does not become less valuable merely because we can no longer apply the "hurrah" word "knowledge" to it. Only the discovery that it has less justification than we thought it had can cause it to lose epistemic value. My inductively well justified belief that there is a blue typewriter here is no less reliable or pragmatically useful (nor is it less justified) when I discover that I cannot say that I *know* there is a blue typewriter here. At least not when the discovery is only based on my findings that knowledge requires more justification than I thought it required (and more than I ever had for my belief in the blue typewriter). The discovery that I do not know the typewriter

---

[10]Ibid. p. 192.

[11]Fred Dretske has proposed that, in order to know, one's reasons, R must be such that $\sim \Diamond \, (R \, \& \sim P)$ *in the given situation* (where P is the would-be knower's belief). Dretske intends that the reference to the given situation will put the same kind of limitations on the scope of the modal formula as Nozick achieves by calling his conditionals 'subjunctive'. In other words, Dretske's modal formula is not intended to rule out every possibility of error. It should be clear, then, that Dretske's formula will be vulnerable to a cube style counterexample as well as, of course, the penguin case. See Fred Dretske, 'Conclusive Reasons', *Australasian Journal of Philosophy*, XLIX, 1 (May 1971), pp. 1–22.

is here signals a reduced value for my belief in the typewriter only when the discovery is based on my finding that I have less justification for the belief than I thought I had. Hence, the kind of scepticism my analysis of knowledge implies is not the sort which should cause anyone discomfort.[12]

The Problem of the Criterion *(excerpt)*

Roderick M. Chisholm

1.

"The problem of the criterion" seems to me to be one of the most important and one of the most difficult of all the problems of philosophy. I am tempted to say that one has not begun to philosophise until one has faced this problem and has recognized how unappealing, in the end, each of the possible solutions is. I have chosen this problem as my topic for the Aquinas Lecture because what first set me to thinking about it (and I remain obsessed by it) were two treaties of twentieth century scholastic philosophy. I refer first to P. Coffey's two volume work, *Epistemology or the Theory of Knowledge,* published in 1917.[1] This led me in turn to the treatises of Coffey's great teacher, Cardinal D. J. Mercier: *Critériologie générale ou théorie générale de la certitude.*[2]

Mercier and, following him, Coffey set the problem correctly, I think, and have seen what is necessary for its solution. But I shall not discuss their views in detail. I shall formulate the problem; then note what, according to Mercier, is necessary if we are to solve the problem; then sketch my own solution; and, finally, note the limitations of my approach to the problem.

2.

What is the problem, then? It is the ancient problem of "the diallelus"—the problem of "the wheel" or "the vicious circle." It was put very neatly by Montaigne in his *Essays.* So let us begin by paraphrasing his formulation of the puzzle. To know whether things really are as they seem to be, we must have a *procedure* for distinguishing appearances that are true from appearances that are false. But to know whether our procedure is a good procedure, we have to know whether it

---

[12]Cf. William W. Rozeboom, 'Why I Know So Much More Than You Do', *American Philosophical Quarterly,* IV. 4 (October 1967), pp. 281–290.

[1]Published in London in 1917 by Longmans, Green and Co.

[2]The eighth edition of this work was published in 1923 in Louvain by the Institut Supérieur de Philosophie, and in Paris by Félix Alcan. The first edition was published in 1884. It has been translated into Spanish, Polish, Portuguese and perhaps still other languages, but unfortunately not yet into English.

Source: Excerpt from *The Problem of the Criterion,* by Roderick M. Chisholm, The Aquinas Lecture 1973, 1996, 1–18, 28–38. Reprinted by permission of Marquette University Press.

really *succeeds* in distinguishing appearances that are true from appearances that are false. And we cannot know whether it does really succeed unless we already know which appearances are *true* and which ones are *false*. And so we are caught in a circle.[3]

Let us try to see how one gets into a situation of this sort.

The puzzles begin to form when you ask yourself, "What can I really know about the world?" We all are acquainted with people who think they know a lot more than in fact they do know. I'm thinking of fanatics, bigots, mystics, various types of dogmatists. And we have all heard of people who claim at least to know a lot less than what in fact they do know. I'm thinking of those people who call themselves "sceptics" and who like to say that people cannot know what the world is really like. People tend to become sceptics, temporarily, after reading books on popular science: the authors tell us we cannot know what things are like really (but they make use of a vast amount of knowledge, or a vast amount of what is claimed to be knowledge, in order to support this sceptical conclusion). And as we know, people tend to become dogmatists, temporarily, as a result of the effects of alcohol, or drugs, or religious and emotional experiences. Then they claim to have an inside view of the world and they think they have a deep kind of knowledge giving them a key to the entire workings of the universe.

If you have a healthy common sense, you will feel that there is something wrong with both of these extremes and that the truth is somewhere in the middle: we can know far more than the sceptic says we can know and far less than the dogmatist or the mystic says that he can know. But how are we to decide these things?

3.

How do we decide, in any particular case, whether we have a genuine item of knowledge? Most of us are ready to confess that our beliefs far transcend what we really know. There are things we believe that we don't in fact know. And we can say of many of these things that we know that we don't know them. I believe that Mr. Jones is honest, say, but I don't know it, and I know that I don't know it. There are other things that we don't know, but they are such that we don't know that we don't know them. Last week, say, I thought I knew that Mr. Smith was honest, but he turned out to be a thief. I didn't know that he was a thief, and, moreover, I didn't know that I didn't know that he was a thief; I thought I knew that he was honest. And so the problem is: How are we to distinguish the real cases of knowledge from what only seem to be cases of knowledge? Or, as I put it before, how are we to decide in any particular case whether we have genuine items of knowledge?

---

[3]The quotation is a paraphrase. What Montaigne wrote was: "Pour juger des apparences que nous recevons des subjects, il nous faudroit un instrument judicatoire; pour verifier cet instrument, il nous y faut de la demonstration; pour verifier la demonstration, un instrument: nous voylà au rouet. Puisque les sens ne peuvent arrester notre dispute, éstans pleins eux-mesmes d'incertitude, il faut que se soit la raison; aucune raison s'establira sans une autre raison: nous voylà à reculons jusques à l'infiny." The passage appears in Book II, Chapter 12 ("An Apologie of Raymond Sebond"); it may be found on page 544 of the Modern Library edition of *The Essays of Montaigne*.

What would be a satisfactory solution to our problem? Let me quote in detail what Cardinal Mercier says:

> *If* there is any knowledge which bears the mark of truth, if the intellect does have a way of distinguishing the true and the false, in short, *if* there *is* a criterion of truth, then this criterion should satisfy three conditions: it should be *internal, objective,* and *immediate.*
>
> It should be *internal.* No reason or rule of truth that is provided by an *external authority* can serve as an ultimate criterion. For the reflective doubts that are essential to criteriology can and should be applied to this authority itself. The mind cannot attain to certainty until it has found *within itself* a sufficient reason for adhering to the testimony of such an authority.
>
> The criterion should be *objective.* The ultimate reason for believing cannot be a merely *subjective* state of the thinking subject. A man is aware that he can reflect upon his psychological states in order to control them. Knowing that he has this ability, he does not, so long as he has not made use of it, have the right to be sure. The ultimate ground of certitude cannot consist in a subjective feeling. It can be found only in that which, objectively, produces this feeling and is adequate to reason.
>
> Finally, the criterion must be *immediate.* To be sure, a certain conviction may rest upon many different reasons some of which are subordinate to others. But if we are to avoid an infinite regress, then we must find a ground of assent that presupposes no other. We must find an *immediate* criterion of certitude.
>
> Is there a criterion of truth that satisfies these three conditions? If so, what is it?[4]

4.

To see how perplexing our problem is, let us consider a figure that Descartes had suggested and that Coffey takes up in his dealings with the problem of the criterion.[5] Descartes' figure comes to this.

Let us suppose that you have a pile of apples and you want to sort out the good ones from the bad ones. You want to put the good ones in a pile by themselves and throw the bad ones away. This is a useful thing to do, obviously, because the bad apples tend to infect the good ones and then the good ones become bad, too. Descartes thought our beliefs were like this. The bad ones tend to infect the good ones, so we should look them over very carefully, throw out the bad ones if we can, and then—or so Descartes hoped—we would be left with just a stock of good beliefs on which we could rely completely. But how are we to do the sorting? If we are to sort out the good ones from the bad ones, then, of course, we must have a way of recognizing the good ones. Or at least we must have a way of recognizing the bad ones. And—again, of course—you and I do have a way of recognizing good apples and also of recognizing bad ones. The good ones have their own special feel, look, and taste, and so do the bad ones.

But when we turn from apples to beliefs, the matter is quite different. In the case of the apples, we have a method—a criterion—for distinguishing the good ones from the bad ones. But in the case of the beliefs, we do not have a method or

---

[4]*Op. cit.,* eighth edition, p. 234.
[5]See the reply to the VIIth set of Objections and Coffey, *op. cit.,* Vol. I, p. 127.

a criterion for distinguishing the good ones from the bad ones. Or, at least, we don't have one yet. The question we started with was: How *are* we to tell the good ones from the bad ones? In other words, we were asking: What is the proper method for deciding which are the good beliefs and which are the bad ones—which beliefs are genuine cases of knowledge and which beliefs are not?

And now, you see, we are on the wheel. First, we want to find out which are the good beliefs and which are the bad ones. To find this out we have to have some way—some method—of deciding which are the good ones and which are the bad ones. But there are good and bad methods—good and bad ways—of sorting out the good beliefs from the bad ones. And so we now have a new problem: How are we to decide which are the good methods and which are the bad ones?

If we could fix on a good method for distinguishing between good and bad methods, we might be all set. But this, of course, just moves the problem to a different level. How are we to distinguish between a good method for choosing good methods and a bad method for choosing good methods? If we continue in this way, of course, we are led to an infinite regress and we will never have the answer to our original question.

What do we do in fact? We do know that there are fairly reliable ways of sorting out good beliefs from bad ones. Most people will tell you, for example, that if you follow the procedures of science and common sense—if you tend carefully to your observations and if you make use of the canons of logic, induction, and the theory of probability—you will be following the best possible procedure for making sure that you will have more good beliefs than bad ones. This is doubtless true. But how do we know that it is? How do we know that the procedures of science, reason, and common sense are the best methods that we have?

If we do know this, it is because we know that these procedures work. It is because we know that these procedures do in fact enable us to distinguish the good beliefs from the bad ones. We say: "See—these methods turn out good beliefs." But *how* do we know that they do? It can only be that we already know how to tell the difference between the good beliefs and the bad ones.

And now you can see where the sceptic comes in. He'll say this: "You said you wanted to sort out the good beliefs from the bad ones. Then to do this, you apply the canons of science, commen sense, and reason. And now, in answer to the question, "How do you know that that's the right way to do it?," you say "Why, I can see that the ones it picks out are the good ones and the ones it leaves behind are the bad ones." But if you can *see* which ones are the good ones and which ones are the bad ones, why do you think you need a general method for sorting them out?"

5.

We can formulate some of the philosophical issues that are involved here by distinguishing two pairs of questions. These are:

(A) "*What* do we know? What is the *extent* of our knowledge?"

(B) "How are we to decide *whether* we know? What are the *criteria* of knowledge?"

If you happen to know the answers to the first of these pairs of questions, you may have some hope of being able to answer the second. Thus, if you happen to know which are the good apples and which are the bad ones, then maybe you could explain to some other person how he could go about deciding whether or not he has a good apple or a bad one. But if you don't know the answer to the first of these pairs of questions—if you don't know what things you know or how far your knowledge extends—it is difficult to see how you could possibly figure out an answer to the second.

On the other hand, *if,* somehow, you already know the answers to the second of these pairs of questions, then you may have some hope of being able to answer the first. Thus, if you happen to have a good set of directions for telling whether apples are good or bad, then maybe you can go about finding a good one—assuming, of course, that there are some good apples to be found. But if you don't know the answer to the second of these pairs of questions—if you don't know how to go about deciding whether or not you know, if you don't know what the criteria of knowing are—it is difficult to see how you could possibly figure out an answer to the first.

And so we can formulate the position of *the sceptic* on these matters. He will say: "You cannot answer question A until you have answered question B. And you cannot answer question B until you have answered question A. Therefore you cannot answer either question. You cannot know what, if anything, you know, and there is no possible way for you to decide in any particular case." Is there any reply to this?

6.

Broadly speaking, there are at least two other possible views. So we may choose among three possibilities.

There are people—philosophers—who think that they do have an answer to B and that, given their answer to B, they can then figure out their answer to A. And there are other people—other philosophers—who have it the other way around: they think that they have an answer to A and that, given their answer to A, they can then figure out the answer to B.

There don't seem to be any generally accepted names for these two different philosophical positions. (Perhaps this is just as well. There are more than enough names, as it is, for possible philosophical views.) I suggest, for the moment, we use the expressions "methodists" and "particularists." By "methodists," I mean, not the followers of John Wesley's version of Christianity, but those who think they have an answer to B, and who then, in terms of it, work out their answer to A. And by "particularists" I mean those who have it the other way around.

7.

Thus John Locke was a methodist—in our present, rather special sense of the term. He was able to arrive—somehow—at an answer to B. He said, in effect: "The way you decide whether or not a belief is a good belief—that is to say, the way you decide whether a belief is likely to be a genuine case of knowledge—is to see whether it is derived from sense experience, to see, for example, whether it bears certain relations to your sensations." Just what these relations to our sensations might be is a matter we may leave open, for present purposes. The point is: Locke felt that if a belief is to be credible, it must bear certain relations to the believer's sensations—but he never told us *how* he happened to arrive at this conclusion. This, of course, is the view that has come to be known as "empiricism." David Hume followed Locke in this empiricism and said that empiricism gives us an effective criterion for distinguishing the good apples from the bad ones. You can take this criterion to the library, he said. Suppose you find a book in which the author makes assertions that do not conform to the empirical criterion. Hume said: "Commit it to the flames: for it can contain nothing but sophistry and illusion."

8.

Empiricism, then, was a form of what I have called "methodism." The empiricist—like other types of methodist—begins with a criterion and then he uses it to throw out the bad apples. There are two objections, I would say, to empiricism. The first—which applies to every form of methodism (in our present sense of the word)—is that the criterion is very broad and far-reaching and at the same time completely arbitrary. How can one *begin* with a broad generalization? It seems especially odd that the empiricist—who wants to proceed cautiously, step by step, from experience—begins with such a generalization. He leaves us completely in the dark so far as concerns what *reasons* he may have for adopting this particular criterion rather than some other. The second objection applies to empiricism in particular. When we apply the empirical criterion—at least, as it was developed by Hume, as well as by many of those in the nineteenth and twentieth centuries who have called themselves "empiricists"—we seem to throw out, not only the bad apples but the good ones as well, and we are left, in effect, with just a few parings or skins with no meat behind them. Thus Hume virtually conceded that, if you are going to be empiricist, the only matters of fact that you can really know about pertain to the existence of sensations. " 'Tis vain," he said, "To ask whether there be body." He meant you cannot know whether there are any physical things—whether there are trees, or houses, or bodies, much less whether there are atoms or other such microscopic particles. All you can know is that there are and have been certain sensations. You cannot know whether there is any you who experiences those sensations—much less whether there are any other people who experience sensations. And I think, if he had been consistent in his empiricism, he would also have said you cannot really be sure whether there have been any sensations in the past; you can know only that there are certain sensations here and now. . . .

12.

Let us begin with the most difficult of the concepts to which we have just referred—that of a proposition being *certain* for a man at a given time. Can we formulate *criteria* of such certainty? I think we can.

Leibniz had said that there are two kinds of immediately evident proposition—
the "first truths of fact" and the "first truths of reason." Let us consider each of these
in turn.

Among the "first truths of fact," for any man at any given time, I would say, are
various propositions about his own state of mind at that time—his thinking certain
thoughts, his entertaining certain beliefs, his being in a certain sensory or emotional
state. These propositions all pertain to certain states of the man which may be said
to manifest or present themselves to him at that time. We could use Meinong's term
and say that there are certain states which are "self-presenting," where this concept
might be marked off in the following way.

A man's being in a certain state is *self-presenting* to him at a given time provided only that (i) he is in that state at that time and (ii) it is necessarily true that
if he is in that state at that time then it is evident to him that he is in that state at
that time.

The states of mind just referred to are of this character. Wishing, say, that one
were on the moon is a state which is such that a man cannot be in that state without it being evident to him that he is in that state. And so, too, for thinking certain
thoughts and having certain sensory or emotional experiences. These states present
themselves and are, so to speak, marks of their own evidence. They cannot occur
unless it is evident that they occur. I think they are properly called the "first truths
of fact." Thus St. Thomas could say that "the intellect knows that it possesses the
truth by reflecting on itself."[6]

Perceiving external things and remembering are not states that present themselves. But thinking that one perceives (or seeming to perceive) and thinking that
one remembers (or seeming to remember) *are* states of mind that present themselves. And in presenting themselves they may, at least under certain favorable conditions, present something else as well.

Coffey quotes Hobbes as saying that "the inn of evidence has no sign-board."[7]
I would prefer saying that these self-presenting states are sign-boards—of the inn
of indirect evidence. But these sign-boards need no further sign-boards in order to
be presented, for they present themselves.

13.

What of the first truths of reason? These are the propositions that some philosophers have called "*a priori*" and that Leibniz, following Locke, referred to as "maxims" or "axioms." These propositions are all necessary and have a further characteristic which Leibniz described in this way: "You will find in a hundred places that
the Scholastics have said that these propositions are evident, *ex terminis,* as soon as
the terms are understood, so that they were persuaded that the force of conviction

---

[6]*The Disputed Questions on Truth,* Question One, Article 9; tr. by Robert W. Mulligan (Chicago: Henry Regnery Company, 1952).
[7]Coffey, *op. cit.,* Vol. I, p. 146. I have been unable to find this quotation in Hobbes.

was grounded in the nature of the terms, i.e., in the connection of their ideas."[8] Thus St. Thomas referred to propositions that are "manifest through themselves."[9]

An axiom, one might say, is a necessary proposition which is such that one cannot understand it without thereby knowing that it is true. Since one cannot know a proposition unless it is evident and one believes it, and since one cannot believe a proposition unless one understands it, we might characterize these first truths of reason in the following way:

A proposition is *axiomatic* for a given subject at a given time provided only (i) the proposition is one that is necessarily true and (ii) it is also necessarily true that if the person then believes that proposition the proposition is then evident to him.

We might now characterize the *a priori* somewhat more broadly by saying that a proposition is *a priori* for a given subject at a given time provided that one or the other of these two things is true: either (i) the proposition is one that is axiomatic for that subject at that time, or else (ii) the proposition is one such that it is evident to the man at that time that the proposition is entailed by a set of propositions that are axiomatic for him at that time.

In characterizing the "first truths of fact" and the "first truths of reason," I have used the expression "evident." But I think it is clear that such truths are not only evident but also certain. And they may be said to be *directly,* or *immediately,* evident.

What, then, of the indirectly evident?

14.

I have suggested in rather general terms above what we might say about memory and the senses. These ostensible sources of knowledge are to be treated as innocent until there is positive ground for thinking them guilty. I will not attempt to develop a theory of the indirectly evident at this point. But I will note at least the *kind* of principle to which we might appeal in developing such a theory.

We could *begin* by considering the following two principles, M and P; M referring to memory, and P referring to perception or the senses.

(M) For any subject S, if it is evident to S that he seems to remember that *a* was F, then it is beyond reasonable doubt for S that *a* was F.

(P) For any subject S, if it is evident to S that he thinks he perceives that *a* is F, then it is evident to S that *a* is F.

"He seems to remember" and "he thinks he perceives" here refer to certain self-presenting states which, in the figure I used above, could be said to serve as sign-boards for the inn of indirect evidence.

But principles M and P, as they stand, are much too latitudinarian. We will find that it is necessary to make qualifications and add more and more conditions. Some of these will refer to the subject's sensory state; some will refer to certain of his

[8]*New Essays concerning Human Understanding,* Book IV, Chapter 7, n. 1.
[9]*Exposition of the Posterior Analytics of Aristotle,* Lectio 4, No. 10; tr. by Pierre Conway (Quebec: M. Doyon, 1956).

other beliefs; and some will refer to the relations of confirmation and mutual support. To set them forth in adequate detail would require a complete epistemology.[10]

So far as our problem of the criterion is concerned, the essential thing to note
is this. In formulating such principles we will simply proceed as Aristotle did when
he formulated his rules for the syllogism. As "particularists" in our approach to the
problem of the criterion, we will fit our rules to the cases—to the apples we know
to be good and to the apples we know to be bad. Knowing what we do about ourselves and the world, we have at our disposal certain instances which our rules or
principles should countenance, and certain other instances which our rules or principles should rule out or forbid. And, as rational beings, we assume that by investigating these instances we can formulate criteria which any instance must satisfy
if it is to be countenanced and we can formulate other criteria which any instance
must satisfy if it is to be ruled out or forbidden.

If we proceed in this way we will have satisfied Cardinal Mercier's criteria for a
theory of evidence or, as he called it, a theory of certitude. He said that any criterion,
or any adequate set of criteria, should be internal, objective, and immediate. The type
of criteria I have referred to are certainly *internal,* in his sense of the term. We have
not appealed to any external authority as constituting the ultimate test of evidence.
(Thus we haven't appealed to "science" or to "the scientists of our culture circle" as
constituting the touchstone of what we know.) I would say that our criteria are *objective.* We have formulated them in terms of the concept of epistemic preferability—
where the location "p is epistemically preferable to q for S" is taken to refer to an
objective relation that obtains independently of the actual preferences of any particular subject. The criteria that we formulate, if they are adequate, will be principles that
are necessarily true. And they are also *immediate.* Each of them is such that, if it is
applicable at any particular time, then the fact that it is then applicable is capable of
being directly evident to that particular subject at that particular time.

15.

But in all of this I have presupposed the approach I have called "particularism." The
"methodist" and the "sceptic" will tell us that we have started in the wrong place.
If now we try to reason with them, then, I am afraid, we will be back on the wheel.

What few philosophers have had the courage to recognize is this: we can deal
with the problem only by begging the question. It seems to me that, if we do recognise this fact, as we should, then it is unseemly for us to try to pretend that it isn't so.

One may object: "Doesn't this mean, then, that the sceptic is right after all?" I
would answer: "Not at all. His view is only one of the three possibilities and in
itself has no more to recommend it than the others do. And in favor of our approach
there is the fact that we *do* know many things, after all."

[10]I have attempted to do this to some extent in *Theory of Knowledge* (Englewood Cliffs, N.J.: Prentice-Hall,
Inc., 1966). Revisions and corrections may be found in my essay "On the Nature of Empirical Evidence" in
Roderick M. Chisholm and Robert J. Swartz, eds., *Empirical Knowledge* (Englewood Cliffs, N.J.: Prentice-
Hall, Inc., 1973).

Skepticism (excerpt)

Keith Lehrer

We say we know, but do we? Skeptics have denied it and they have had an influential history. We shall, in the light of our epistemology, assess the genuine merits of skepticism. We have used the skeptic as a heuristic opponent in the justification game, but now we must turn to the philosophical skeptic who really genuinely challenges our claim to knowledge.

SKEPTICISM AND AGNOIOLOGY

Skepticism comes in different depths. Shallow forms deny that we know the few things we claim to, and the deepest form denies that we know anything at all. Deeper forms of skepticism are based on the ubiquitous chance for error. Plain people, who comfort themselves in the snug foothills of accepted opinion, overlook the possibilities for error residing in our most familiar beliefs. In the minds of the dogmatic, what is familiar comes, through long acquaintance, to appear completely dependable and wins unquestioning confidence. The philosophical skeptic, inclined to question when others are drawn to dogmatic tranquillity, discovers the risk of error in our most trusted convictions. On this discovery, she constructs an *agnoiology,* a theory of ignorance.

Of course, skeptics who have denied that we know what we say we do have frequently been moved by more than a passion for the study of agnoiology. Often, they espouse some theory that conflicts with common opinion. Skepticism is defended to win consideration for their own theories. In reply, commonsense philosophers, like Reid and Moore, have rejected such speculative theories on the sole grounds that they conflict with common sense. The beliefs of common sense are innocent, they say, until proven guilty and constitute knowledge unless they are shown not to. Skeptics have been accused of semantic deviation, logical absurdity, and triviality. In an earlier chapter, we argued that what the skeptic says is semantically acceptable, logically consistent, and highly contentious. Rather than attempting to dismiss her abruptly by some superficial artifice, let us consider what sustains her argument.

There are a number of classical skeptical arguments appealing to dreams and hallucinations purporting to show that, whatever we take to be true, there remains some chance of error. However, skeptical argumentation does not depend on these appeals. They are simply familiar ways of explaining how people err. It matters little what the source of error may be. What is critical is most simple. People often accept what is false, and, when what they accept happens to be true, there was some chance that they might have erred. This is the fundamental skeptical premise.

CONCEPTION AND THE CHANCE OF ERROR

There are a variety of ways in which a skeptic may press this premise. Such arguments have the merit of calling our attention to some possibility of error we overlook. For example, a skeptic may base his argument on the nature of human conception. Experience by itself, as we have noted, tells us nothing. Knowledge requires the application of concepts and background information to experience. The best entrenched concept remains constantly subject to total rejection. In the pursuit of truth, we may discard any concept as lacking a denotation. Any concept may be thrown onto the junk-heap of repudiated concepts along with demons, entelechies, and the like. Moreover, any discarded concept can be refurbished. Because the concepts we reject may be better than the ones that supplant them, we may have to recycle what we discard. No concept or belief is sacrosanct in the quest for truth, and there is always some chance that any one may be cast off as misleading and erroneous.

The foregoing remarks describe more than a mere logical possibility. It is not only logically possible that any belief is in error, there is some genuine chance that it is so. The beliefs that have been most cherished and in which people have placed their greatest confidence, for example, the belief in witches, have been demoted from literal truths to figures of speech. Strictly speaking, there is no such thing. The concept of a witch, aside from use as a figure of speech, is a relic of religious conceptualization which is no longer tenable in an impartial and disinterested search for truth. This merely illustrates how, in the flux of conceptual change and innovation, any concept may be rejected for the sake of conceptual improvement and increased veracity.

We must note in passing that the concept of belief, indeed, even the concept of a concept, is no more secure than any other. Some materialists have said that belief is mental, and, consequently, that there is no such thing as belief. We cannot consider such materialism and the implications of it for our theory of knowledge here. Such materialism would require that, if we have referred to anything real in the world when speaking incorrectly of belief, what is real may be correctly described within a materialistic vocabulary.

The skeptic is correct, we concede, in affirming that the chance of error is always genuine. We grant the skeptical premise that if S accepts that p, then there is some chance that S is incorrect.

A REFUTATION OF SKEPTICISM:
FALLIBILITY, NOT IGNORANCE

To sustain skepticism, a skeptic must go on to argue that if there is some chance that S is incorrect in accepting that p, then S does not know that p. On the analysis of knowledge that we have articulated, this premise is unavailable. It does not follow from the premise that there is some chance that S is incorrect in accepting that p, that p is not true, or that S does not accept that p, or that S is not completely justified in accepting that p, or that S's justification is defeated. Even if S accepts that there is some chance that he is incorrect in accepting that *p,* it may, nevertheless, be just as reasonable for him to accept that *p* in addition.

In the interests of obtaining truth, it may be as reasonable to accept something one does while also accepting one's fallibility, that is, accepting that there is some chance that one might be in error. The skeptic in the justification game may always cite the chance of error as a competitor in the justification game, but the player can also neutralize it. Our fallibility is an insufficient basis for skeptical victory. We may accept the premise of the skeptic concerning conceptual change and the universal chance of error implicit therein without accepting the deep skeptical conclusion of universal ignorance.

With this reply to skepticism set forth, we hasten to note that in some ways our position is very close to that of the skeptic, for very often when people claim to know something, they claim to know for certain. If they do know for certain, then there must be no chance that they are in error. Hence, in agreeing that there is always some chance of error, we are agreeing with the skeptic that nobody ever knows for certain that anything is true. Joining hands with the skeptic in this way will win us little applause from those dogmatists who never doubt that people know for certain many of the things they claim to know.

Thus, our theory of knowledge is a theory of knowledge without certainty. We agree with the skeptic that if a person claims to know for certain, he does not know whereof he speaks. However, when we claim to know, we make no claim to certainty. We conjecture that to speak in this way is a departure from the most customary use of the word "know." Commonly, when people say that they know, they mean they know for certain and they assume that there is no chance of being in error. This assumption enables them to lay aside theoretical doubts and to pretend they proceed on certain grounds. Such a pretense offers comfort and security in practical affairs and often in scientific investigation, as well. Nonetheless, it is a pretense exposed by the skeptic and repudiated by those who seek the truth. We, like the skeptic, deny that our beliefs have any guarantee of truth. We, like the skeptic, admit there to be a genuine chance that any of our beliefs may be false. We, like the skeptic, acknowledge that there is some chance, however small and remote, that the hypotheses are true which skeptics have conceived to call our dogmatic assumptions into doubt, and these cannot be ruled out by semantic shenanigans or appeal to the fiat of commonsense.

Our only reply to the skeptic is that, even if there is some chance that any of our beliefs may be in error and, even if, therefore, we do not know for certain that any of them are true, still some of the things we accept are things we are justified in accepting because all competitors are beaten or neutralized on the basis of our acceptance system. Of course, what we accept may be wrong—we are fallible—but if enough of what we accept is correct, then our justification will be undefeated and we will have knowledge. If we are sufficiently correct in what we accept so that we can distinguish between when our acceptance of something is trustworthy and when it is not, then we may know what we think we do despite the risk of error that we confront. If we were massively mistaken, as we would be if the Cartesian demon were loose in the land, then we would lack knowledge. A merely conceivable demon cannot reduce us to ignorance, however.

THE MERITS OF SKEPTICISM

Before celebrating victory over the skeptic, however, it should be carefully noted that the agnoiology of some skeptics is closer to the truth than the epistemology of many dogmatists. We offer no proof that the skeptic is wrong. A skeptic, reflecting on the harrowing vicissitudes of human conception, may come to accept that we are not trustworthy in what we accept and that it is as reasonable to accept one thing as another, or, put more moderately, that everything we accept has at least one competitor that can be neither beaten nor neutralized, namely, its denial. Such a skeptic will not be completely justified in anything she accepts, and therefore on our theory will not know that any statement is true. Even if she is incorrect in denying that we have knowledge, she will be correct in denying that she does. She will know as little as she says she does. If she is correct in what she accepts, and we are in error, however, the beliefs in our acceptance systems which personally justify us in accepting what we do may be erroneous. Consequently, we would not be completely justified in accepting what we do. The skeptic would enjoy victory.

Thus, on our theory of knowledge, whether we win or the skeptic wins the day depends on whether what we accept is correct, and especially on what we accept about when we are trustworthy and when we are not. We cannot refute the skeptic by appeal to demonstration. We argue against her from our acceptance system which is precisely what she calls into question. We may, nonetheless, know that she is wrong. Assuming that our complete justification for some of the things we accept is sustained within the members of our ultrasystem, we know those things to be true, and, indeed, we know that we know. If we do know that we know, then, of course, we know that the skeptic is mistaken in denying we know.

We avoid skepticism by constructing a theory of justification without a guarantee of truth. On our theory, if people know anything at all, it is because of the correctness of what they accept in their quest for truth. It is what they accept that makes them personally justified in their acceptance and, if enough of what they accept is true, their justification will be undefeated and become knowledge. The mere possibility or risk of error is not sufficient to sustain the skeptic. She must deny what we accept, especially what we accept about our own trustworthiness, and she must be correct and we in error to render her victorious. So, whether we know or not depends on whether what we accept about ourselves and our trustworthiness is correct. Surely, that is exactly what we should expect.

To put the matter more precisely, consider principle T, to wit, that I am a trustworthy guide to truth. If T is true, the justification a person has for accepting T based on accepting T would, in normal circumstance, be undefeated. One would expect all competitors of T to be beaten or neutralized on the basis of the verific system and the ultrasystem of S and, therefore, would expect the following principles to be true:

> If S accepts that T and T is true, then S is completely justified in accepting that T

and

> If S accepts that T and T is true, then S is justified in accepting that T in a way that is undefeated.

Thus, the acceptance of T, if T is true, may be expected to yield knowledge of the truth of T. We may not be able to refute the skeptic who denies the truth of T or who advances some skeptical hypotheses implying the falsity of T. If, however, we are correct in thinking the skeptic is in error and, in accepting the truth of T, then, skeptical machinations notwithstanding, we know that T is true and know many other things as a result of this knowledge. We may not have the satisfaction of demonstrating that the skeptic is in error, for the attempt to do so would beg the question. We may, nevertheless, know that the skeptical hypotheses are false.

SKEPTICISM AND CLOSURE: AN EXTERNALIST CAVEAT

Some externalists have dealt with the skeptic in a way that resembles the preceding argument but is, nevertheless, distinct from it. They have rejected a closure principle affirming that if a person knows that p and that if p, then q, all at once, so to speak, then the person knows that q. The closure principle might be formulated with greater precision, of course, but this rough formulation suffices to understand how rejecting such a principle may be useful against a skeptic. The skeptic advances a skeptical hypothesis, the hypothesis that we are now asleep and dreaming rather than perceiving the external world as we suppose. She goes on to argue that we have no way of knowing that this skeptical hypothesis is false and concludes, therefore, that we do not know that we perceive the things we perceive. The externalist who rejects the closure principle concedes to the skeptic that we do not know her hypothesis is false but denies her inference. He says that we do know that we are perceiving external objects, a piece of paper before us, for example, even though we do not know that we are not now asleep and dreaming. True, he admits, if we are now asleep and dreaming, then we are not now perceiving the piece of paper, but we know that the latter is true even though we do not know that the former is false. Epistemic closure fails, he concludes, and with it all skeptical hypotheses.

The preceding line of thought is typical of externalists, though not advocated by all, because a belief resulting from a reliable process or a belief that tracks truth may have a consequence that does not result from a reliable process or track truth. I may have no way of telling whether I am asleep and dreaming or not, and hence the belief that I am not may not be the output of a reliable process nor track truth. I cannot, on this account, claim that I would not now believe that I am now awake and not asleep and dreaming if it were not true. The reason for this is that if I were asleep and dreaming it were true, I would believe just what I do. Dretske has suggested that, though one must be able to exclude relevant alternatives to what one believes in order to have knowledge, the skeptical alternatives fall short of relevance.

The foregoing approach has some appeal. Since we do not think of skeptical hypotheses concerning dreams, hallucinations, Cartesian demons, or brains in vats as we go about our daily rounds, it is natural to suppose that we do not need to know anything about such matters in order to know the many things we suppose we do, for example, that we perceive external objects. If we know we perceive those things and do not know that the skeptical hypotheses are false, then the reason for denying epistemic closure is clear. Still, is the externalist correct in supposing we do not know the skeptical hypotheses to be false? The contrary is the case. I know that I am not now dreaming. I know that I am not now hallucinating. I know that no Cartesian demon deceives me and that no powerful scientist has my brain in a vat in his laboratory. I may find it hard to explain just how I know these things. I am, however, personally justified in accepting that the skeptical hypotheses are false because my acceptance of their falsity is trustworthy. If, moreover, this personal justification is undefeated and my acceptance trustworthy as I suppose, then I know that these skeptical hypotheses are all false. The skeptical hypotheses are relevant, are genuine competitors, but they are beaten by my acceptance system, and their defeat is sustained in my ultrasystem yielding knowledge. This knowledge does not result from the irrelevance of the skeptical alternatives but from our being personally justified in accepting that we are not dreaming, hallucinating, deceived by an evil demon, brains in vats, and, assuming that we are right in this, from our justification being complete and undefeated.

The skeptic provides a competitor to our various claims to knowledge, to the claims of perception, memory, and introspection. She shows that it is possible that we are in error, and she is right in this. We may go further and admit not only the metaphysical possibility that we may err but also that we are genuinely fallible in what we accept. We make genuine errors of perception, memory, and introspection. Consequently, there is always some chance of error in what we accept, however small and not worth worrying about in our daily transactions. While we applaud the skeptic for reminding us that a sound epistemology must acknowledge that we sometimes err and are ever fallible in our judgment, we may at the same time neutralize her objection.

We acknowledge that we are fallible in perception, memory, and introspection, but when we accept that the chances of error are negligible, we also accept that we are trustworthy in such cases. It is then as reasonable for us to add that we are trustworthy and accept both the possibility of error and our trustworthiness to avoid it as to accept the skeptical worry alone. It is, therefore, our trustworthiness that neutralizes the skeptical worries. In those instances in which we are trustworthy as we accept, we have undefeated justification and knowledge. In those instances in which false pride leads us to accept that we are trustworthy when we are not, the neutralization fails and our justification is defeated. The possibility or even some small risk of error does not bring the skeptic victory, however. The possibility and risk of error may be worthwhile in the quest for truth. A simple moral suffices to answer the skeptic: One can be both fallible and trustworthy.

Why not, however, reject the closure principle and refute the skeptic twice over? Her ability to survive criticism has given her greater longevity than Methuselah, after all, and a double refutation seems appropriate. The problem is that rejection of the closure principle yields problematic results concerning other matters. Of course, as Harman has noted, the mere deduction of some result from what one knows does not ensure that one will know the thing deduced. What one knows at one time, one may fail to know at a later time because of what transpires in the interval, and the deduction of a consequence may have that result. The closure principle is intended to concern what one knows at a single time, however, and then it seems correct. The principle says that if one knows that p and that if p then q all at once, then one knows that q as well.

The problem that arises from denying this principle is illustrated by an example from Kripke based on an earlier example from Goldman. It would seem that if I know that I see a blue barn, then I know that I see a barn. How could I know the former and not the latter? If we deny the epistemic closure principle, then I might. Moreover, if externalist theories were correct, it also might be the case that I might. We may illustrate the connection by supposing that I am in a part of the country where a clever stage builder put up barn facades here and there, which, to the unsuspecting, look exactly like barns. Suppose, however, that no such facades are blue, and that I, innocent of the industry of facade builders, see a blue barn. Imagine, moreover, that there are no other real barns in the area, only red barn facades, and that I would not be able to tell the difference between such facades and a barn.

Do I know that I see a blue barn? It would seem that I do not, since I cannot here tell a barn from a barn facade in my present circumstances. Notice, however, that I would not believe that I see a blue barn if I did not see a blue barn, for there are no blue barn facades. My belief tracks truth, as Nozick requires. Were tracking truth sufficient for knowledge, I would know that I see a blue barn. Notice, however, that if I also believe I see a barn, this belief would not track truth. Since there are many barn facades, it would be incorrect to say that I would not believe that I see a barn if I did not see a barn. I might believe I see a barn because I see a barn facade. Thus, if tracking truth were sufficient for knowledge, I would know that I see a blue barn but not know that I see a barn. Closure would fail.

The foregoing problem might, perhaps, be avoided by some modification of externalism, but it is naturally avoided by the account we have offered. Suppose that I see a blue barn, ignorant of the existence of barn facades, as in the example. Then I will accept that I can tell a barn where I am when I see one. This is false, however. When replaced in a member of my ultrasystem by the acceptance of its denial, that is, by acceptance of the claim that I cannot tell a barn where I am when I see one, any justification I have for accepting that I see a blue barn, as well as for accepting simply that I see a barn, will be defeated. The result on our theory is that I do not know that I see a blue barn anymore than I know that I see a barn in a barn facade-infested environment. The moral is that if we try to escape from skepticism by rejecting the closure principle, we shall find ourselves committed to saying that we know that we see a blue barn when we do not know that we see a barn. For this reason, when the externalist replies to the skeptic that we know that we see a barn when we do not know that we are awake and not asleep and dreaming we see a barn, he can hardly expect any more tolerant response from her than a smile of unknowing contempt.

In summary, we may in our quest for truth become confident of some modest success and communicate our confidence to others by affirming that we know. We may then proceed to justify that claim to other inquirers. We thus elicit their rejoinders and sometimes change what we accept as a result. By so doing, we hope to correct what we accept and come to know our world. It is the purpose of our theory of knowledge and justification to explicate the product of this uncertain epistemic adventure. One necessary step in this explication has been to repudiate the dogmatic prejudice that we often proceed without any chance of error. Our epistemology closely approaches the agnoiology of skepticism. We affirm that there is no security against failure or guarantee of success in our search for truth. The nobility of our objective must suffice to sustain our quest. If we are, nevertheless, correct in enough of what we accept about ourselves, the external world, and our trustworthiness, we may, contrary to the skeptic, know what we think we do, including the falsity of her ingenious hypotheses. We should, however, have the modesty to concede that we do not know for certain that we are right nor can we demonstrate that she is in error. She is the touchstone of sound epistemology and merits our conscientious regard.

A Causal Theory of Knowing

Alvin I. Goldman

Since Edmund L. Gettier reminded us recently of a certain important inadequacy of the traditional analysis of "*S* knows that *p*," several attempts have been made to correct that analysis.[1] In this paper I shall offer still another analysis (or a sketch of an analysis) of "*S* knows that *p*," one which will avert Gettier's problem. My concern will be with knowledge of empirical propositions only, since I think that the traditional analysis is adequate for knowledge of nonempirical truths.

Consider an abbreviated version of Gettier's second counterexample to the traditional analysis. Smith believes

(*q*) Jones owns a Ford

and has very strong evidence for it. Smith's evidence might be that Jones has owned a Ford for many years and that Jones has just offered Smith a ride while driving a Ford. Smith has another friend, Brown, of whose whereabouts he is totally ignorant. Choosing a town quite at random, however, Smith constructs the proposition

(*p*) Either Jones owns a Ford or Brown is in Barcelona.

Seeing that *q* entails *p*, Smith infers that *p* is true. Since he has adequate evidence for *q*, he also has adequate evidence for *p*. But now suppose that Jones does *not* own a Ford (he was driving a rented car when he offered Smith a ride), but, quite by coincidence, Brown happens to be in Barcelona. This means that *p* is true, that Smith believes *p*, and that Smith has adequate evidence for *p*. But Smith does not know *p*.

---

[1]"Is True Justified Belief Knowledge?" *Analysis*, xxiii.6, ns 96 (June 1963): 121–123. I say "reminded" because essentially the same point was made by Russell in 1912. Cf. *The Problems of Philosophy* (Oxford, 1912), ch. xiii, pp. 132 ff. New analyses have been proposed by Michael Clark, "Knowledge and Grounds: A Comment on Mr. Gettier's Paper," *Analysis*, xxiv.2, ns 98 (December 1963): 46–48; Ernest Sosa, "The Analysis of 'Knowledge that *p*'," *ibid.*, xxv.1, ns 103 (October 1964): 1–3; and Keith Lehrer, "Knowledge, Truth, and Evidence," *ibid.*, xxv.5, ns 105 (April 1965): 168–175.
Source: Alvin I. Goldman, "A Causal Theory of Knowing," LXIV, 12 (June 22, 1967): 357–72. Reprinted by permission of the publisher and author.

A variety of hypotheses might be made to account for Smith's not knowing p. Michael Clark, for example, points to the fact that q is false, and suggests this as the reason why Smith cannot be said to know p. Generalizing from this case, Clark argues that, for S to know a proposition, each of S's grounds for it must be *true,* as well as his grounds for his grounds, etc.[2] I shall make another hypothesis to account for the fact that Smith cannot be said to know p, and I shall generalize this into a new analysis of "S knows that p."

Notice that what *makes p* true is the fact that Brown is in Barcelona, but that this fact has nothing to do with Smith's believing p. That is, there is no *causal* connection between the fact that Brown is in Barcelona and Smith's believing p. If Smith had come to believe p by reading a letter from Brown postmarked in Barcelona, then we might say that Smith knew p. Alternatively, if Jones did own a Ford, and his owning the Ford was manifested by his offer of a ride to Smith, and this in turn resulted in Smith's believing p, then we would say that Smith knew p. Thus, one thing that seems to be missing in this example is a causal connection between the fact that makes p true [or simply: the fact that p] and Smith's belief of p. The requirement of such a *causal connection* is what I wish to add to the traditional analysis.

To see that this requirement is satisfied in all cases of (empirical) knowledge, we must examine a variety of such causal connections. Clearly, only a sketch of the important kinds of cases is possible here.

Perhaps the simplest case of a causal chain connecting some fact p with someone's belief of p is that of *perception.* I wish to espouse a version of the causal theory of perception, in essence that defended by H. P. Grice.[3] Suppose that S sees that there is a vase in front of him. How is this to be analyzed? I shall not attempt a complete analysis of this, but a necessary condition of S's seeing that there is a vase in front of him is that there be a certain kind of causal connection between the presence of the vase and S's believing that a vase is present. I shall not attempt to describe this causal process in detail. Indeed, to a large extent, a description of this process must be regarded as a problem for the special sciences, not for philosophy. But a certain causal process—viz. that which standardly takes place when we say that so-and-so *sees* such-and-such—must occur. That our ordinary concept of sight (i.e., knowledge acquired by sight) includes a causal requirement is shown by the fact that if the relevant causal process is absent we would withhold the assertion that so-and-so *saw* such-and-such. Suppose that, although a vase is directly in front of S, a laser photograph[4] is interposed between it and S, thereby blocking it from S's view. The photograph, however, is one of a vase (a different vase), and when it is illuminated by light waves from a laser, it looks to S exactly like a real vase. When the photograph is illuminated, S forms the belief that there is a vase in front

[2]*Op. cit.* Criticisms of Clark's analysis will be discussed below.
[3]"The Causal Theory of Perception," *Proceedings of the Aristotelian Society,* supp. vol. xxxv (1961).
[4]If a laser photograph (hologram) is illuminated by light waves, especially waves from a laser, the effect of the hologram on the viewer is exactly as if the object were being seen. It preserves three-dimensionality completely, and even gives appropriate parallax effects as the viewer moves relative to it. Cf. E. N. Leith and J. Upatnieks, "Photography by Laser," *Scientific American,* ccxii, 6 (June 1965): 24.

of him. Here we would deny that *S sees* that there is a vase in front of him, for his view of the real vase is completely blocked, so that it has no causal role in the formation of his belief. Of course, *S* might *know* that there was a vase in front of him even if the photograph is blocking his view. Someone else, in a position to see the vase, might tell *S* that there is a vase in front of him. Here the presence of the vase might be a causal ancestor of *S*'s belief, but the causal process would not be a (purely) *perceptual* one. *S* could not be said to *see* that there is a vase in front of him. For this to be true, there must be a causal process, but one of a very special sort, connecting the presence of the vase with *S*'s belief.

I shall here assume that perceptual knowledge of facts is noninferential. This is merely a simplifying procedure, and not essential to my account. Certainly a percipient does not *infer* facts about physical objects from the state of his brain or from the stimulation of his sense organs. He need not know about these goings-on at all. But some epistemologists maintain that we directly perceive only sense data and that we infer physical-object facts from them. This view could be accommodated within my analysis. I could say that physical-object facts cause sense data, that people directly perceive sense data, and that they infer the physical object facts from the sense data. This kind of process would be fully accredited by my analysis, which will allow for knowledge based on inference. But for purposes of exposition it will be convenient to regard perceptual knowledge of external facts as independent of any inference.

Here the question arises about the *scope* of perceptual knowledge. By perception I can know noninferentially that there is a vase in front of me. But can I know noninferentially that the painting I am viewing is a Picasso? It is unnecessary to settle such issues here. Whether the knowledge of such facts is to be classed as inferential or noninferential, my analysis can account for it. So the scope of noninferential knowledge may be left indeterminate.

I turn next to memory, i.e., knowledge that is based, in part, on memory. Remembering, like perceiving, must be regarded as a causal process. *S* remembers *p* at time *t* only if *S*'s believing *p* at an earlier time is a cause of his believing *p* at *t*. Of course, not every causal connection between an earlier belief and a later one is a case of remembering. As in the case of perception, however, I shall not try to describe this process in detail. This is a job mainly for the scientist. Instead, the kind of causal process in question is to be identified simply by example, by "pointing" to paradigm cases of remembering. Whenever causal processes are of that kind—whatever that kind is, precisely—they are cases of remembering.[5]

A causal connection between earlier belief (or knowledge) of *p* and later belief (knowledge) of *p* is certainly a necessary ingredient in memory.[6] To remember a fact is not simply to believe it at t_0 and also to believe it at t_1. Nor does someone's knowing a fact at t_0 and his knowing it at t_1 entail that he remembers it at t_1. He

---

[5]For further defense of this kind of procedure, with attention to perception, cf. Grice, *op. cit.*

[6]Causal connections can hold between states of affairs, such as believings, as well as between events. If a given event or state, in conjunction with other events or states, "leads to" or "results in" another event or state (or the same state obtaining at a later time), it will be called a "cause" of the latter. I shall also speak of "facts" being causes.

may have perceived the fact at t_0, forgotten it, and then relearned it at t_1 by some-one's telling it to him. Nor does the inclusion of a memory "impression"—a feel-ing of remembering—ensure that one really remembers. Suppose S perceives p at t_0, but forgets it at t_1. At t_2 he begins to believe p again because someone tells him p, but at t_2 he has no memory impression of p. At t_3 we artificially stimulate in S a memory impression of p. It does not follow that S remembers p at t_3. The description of the case suggests that his believing p at t_0 has no causal effect what-ever on his believing p at t_3; and if we accepted this fact, we would deny that he remembers p at t_3.

Knowledge can be acquired by a combination of perception and memory. At t_0, the fact p causes S to believe p, by perception. S's believing p at t_0 results, via mem-ory, in S's believing p at t_1. Thus, the fact p is a cause of S's believing p at t_1, and S can be said to know p at t_1. But not all knowledge results from perception and memory alone. In particular, much knowledge is based on *inference*.

As I shall use the term "inference," to say that S knows p by "inference" does not entail that S went through an explicit, conscious process of reasoning. It is not neces-sary that he have "talked to himself," saying something like "Since such-and-such is true, p must also be true." My belief that there is a fire in the neighborhood is based on, or inferred from, my belief that I hear a fire engine. But I have not gone through a process of explicit reasoning, saying "There's a fire engine; therefore there must be a fire." Perhaps the word "inference" is ordinarily used only where explicit reasoning occurs; if so, my use of the term will be somewhat broader than its ordinary use.

Suppose S perceives that there is solidified lava in various parts of the coun-tryside. On the basis of this belief, plus various "background" beliefs about the pro-duction of lava, S concludes that a nearby mountain erupted many centuries ago. Let us assume that this is a highly warranted inductive inference, one which gives S adequate evidence for believing that the mountain did erupt many centuries ago. Assuming this proposition is true, does S know it? This depends on the nature of the causal process that induced his belief. If there is a continuous causal chain of the sort he envisages connecting the fact that the mountain erupted with his belief of this fact, then S knows it. If there is no such causal chain, however, S does not know that proposition.

Suppose that the mountain erupts, leaving lava around the countryside. The lava remains there until S perceives it and infers that the mountain erupted. Then S does know that the mountain erupted. But now suppose that, after the mountain has erupted, a man somehow removes all the lava. A century later, a different man (not knowing of the real volcano) decides to make it look as if there had been a volcano, and therefore puts lava in appropriate places. Still later, S comes across this lava and concludes that the mountain erupted centuries ago. In this case, S cannot be said to know the proposition. This is because the fact that the mountain did erupt is not a cause of S's believing that it erupted. A necessary condition of S's knowing p is that his believing p be connected with p by a causal chain.

In the first case, where S knows p, the causal connection may be diagrammed as in Figure 1. (p) is the fact that the mountain erupted at such-and-such a time. (q) is the fact that lava is (now) present around the countryside. 'B' stands for a belief, the

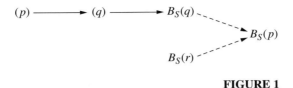

FIGURE 1

expression in parentheses indicating the proposition believed, and the subscript designating the believer. (r) is a "background" proposition, describing the ways in which lava is produced and how it solidifies. Solid arrows in the diagram represent causal connections; dotted arrows represent inferences. Notice that, in Figure 1, there is not only an arrow connecting (q) with S's belief of $(q,)$ but also an arrow connecting (p) with (q). In the suggested variant of the lava case, the latter arrow would be missing, showing that there is no continuous causal chain connecting (p) with S's belief of (p). Therefore, in that variant case, S could not be said to know (p).

I have said that p is causally connected to S's belief of p, in the case diagrammed in Figure 1. This raises the question, however, of whether the inferential part of the chain is itself a causal chain. In other words, is S's belief of q a cause of his believing p? This is a question to which I shall not try to give a definitive answer here. I am inclined to say that inference *is* a causal process, that is, that when someone *bases* his belief of one proposition on his belief of a set of other propositions, then his belief of the latter propositions can be considered a cause of his belief of the former proposition. But I do not wish to rest my thesis on this claim. All I do claim is that, if a chain of inferences is "added" to a causal chain, then the entire chain is causal. In terms of our diagram, a chain consisting of solid arrows plus dotted arrows is to be considered a causal chain, though I shall not take a position on the question of whether the dotted arrows represent causal connections. Thus, in Figure 1, p is a cause of S's belief of p, whether or not we regard S's belief of q a cause of his belief of p.[7]

Consider next a case of knowledge based on "testimony." This too can be analyzed causally. p causes a person T to believe p, by perception. T's belief of p gives rise to (causes) his asserting p. T's asserting p causes S, by auditory perception, to believe that T is asserting p. S infers that T believes p, and from this, in turn, he infers that p is a fact. There is a continuous causal chain from p to S's believing p, and thus, assuming that each of S's inferences is warranted, S can be said to know p.

This causal chain is represented in Figure 2. "A" refers to an act of asserting a proposition, the expression in parentheses indicating the proposition asserted and the subscript designating the agent. (q), (r), (u), and (v) are background propositions. (q) and (r), for example, pertain to T's sincerity; they help S conclude, from the fact that T asserted p, that T really believes p.

---

[7]A fact can be a cause of a belief even if it does not *initiate* the belief. Suppose I believe that there is a lake in a certain locale, this belief having started in a manner quite unconnected with the existence of the lake. Continuing to have the belief, I go to the locale and perceive the lake. At this juncture, the existence of the lake becomes a cause of my believing that there is a lake there. This is analogous to a table top that is supported by four legs. When a fifth leg is inserted flush beneath the table top, it too becomes a cause of the table top's not falling. It has a causal role in the support of the table top even though, before it was inserted, the table top was adequately supported.

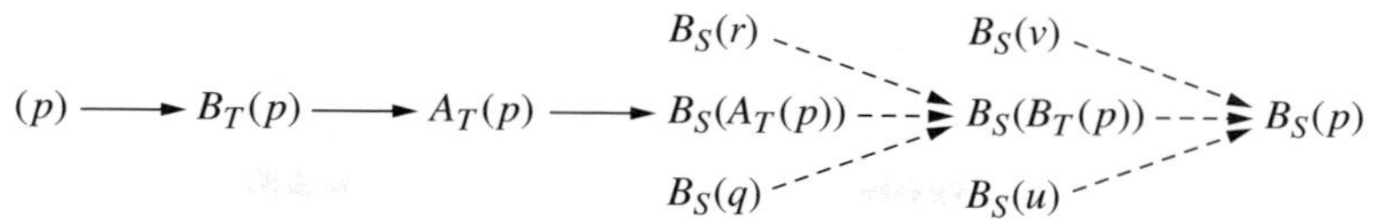

$$B_S(r) \cdots \qquad B_S(v) \cdots$$
$$(p) \longrightarrow B_T(p) \longrightarrow A_T(p) \longrightarrow B_S(A_T(p)) \dashrightarrow B_S(B_T(p)) \dashrightarrow B_S(p)$$
$$B_S(q) \cdots \qquad B_S(u) \cdots$$

FIGURE 2

In this case, as in the lava case, S knows p because he has correctly reconstructed the causal chain leading from p to the evidence for p that S perceives, in this case, T's asserting (p). This correct reconstruction is shown in the diagram by S's inference "mirroring" the rest of the causal chain. Such a correct reconstruction is a necessary condition of knowledge based on inference. To see this, consider the following example. A newspaper reporter observes p and reports it to his newspaper. When printed, however, the story contains a typographical error so that it asserts not-p. When reading the paper, however, S fails to see the word "not," and takes the paper to have asserted p. Trusting the newspaper, he infers that p is true. Here we have a continuous causal chain leading from p to S's believing $p;$ yet S does not know p. S thinks that p resulted in a report to the newspaper about p and that this report resulted in its printing the statement p. Thus, his reconstruction of the causal chain is mistaken. But, if he is to know $p,$ his reconstruction must contain no mistakes. Though he need not reconstruct *every* detail of the causal chain, he must reconstruct all important links.[8] An additional requirement for knowledge based on inference is that the knower's inferences be warranted. That is, the propositions on which he bases his belief of p must genuinely confirm p very highly, whether deductively or inductively. Reconstructing a causal chain merely by lucky guesses does not yield knowledge.

With the help of our diagrams, we can contrast the traditional analysis of knowing with Clark's analysis (*op. cit.*) and contrast each of these with my own analysis. The traditional analysis makes reference to just three features of the diagrams. First, it requires that p be true; i.e., that (p) appear in the diagram. Secondly, it requires that S believe $p;$ i.e., that S's belief of p appear in the diagram. Thirdly, it requires that S's inferences, if any, be warranted; i.e., that the sets of beliefs that are at the tail of a dotted arrow must jointly highly confirm the belief at the head of these arrows. Clark proposes a further requirement for knowledge. He requires that *each* of the beliefs in S's chain of inference be *true*. In other words, whereas the traditional analysis requires a fact to correspond to S's belief of $p,$ Clark requires that a fact correspond to *each* of S's beliefs on which he based his belief of p. Thus, corresponding to each belief on the right side of the diagram there must be a fact on the left side. (My diagrams omit facts corresponding to the "background" beliefs.)

---

[8]Clearly we cannot require someone to reconstruct every detail, since this would involve knowledge of minute physical phenomena, for example, of which ordinary people are unaware. On the other hand, it is difficult to give criteria to identify which details, in general, are "important." This will vary substantially from case to case.

As Clark's analysis stands, it seems to omit an element of the diagrams that my analysis requires, viz., the arrows indicating causal connections. Now Clark might reformulate his analysis so as to make implicit reference to these causal connections. If he required that the knower's beliefs include *causal beliefs* (of the relevant sort), then his requirement that these beliefs be true would amount to the requirement that there *be* causal chains of the sort I require. This interpretation of Clark's analysis would make it almost equivalent to mine, and would enable him to avoid some objections that have been raised against him. But he has not explicitly formulated his analysis this way, and it therefore remains deficient in this respect.

Before turning to the problems facing Clark's analysis, more must be said about my own analysis. So far, my examples may have suggested that, if *S* knows *p*, the fact that *p* is a cause of his belief of *p*. This would clearly be wrong, however. Let us grant that I can know facts about the future. Then, if we required that the known fact cause the knower's belief, we would have to countenance "backward" causation. My analysis, however, does not face this dilemma. The analysis requires that there be a causal *connection* between *p* and *S*'s belief, not necessarily that *p* be a *cause* of *S*'s belief. *p* and *S*'s belief of *p* can also be causally connected in a way that yields knowledge if both *p* and *S*'s belief of *p* have a *common* cause. This can be illustrated as follows.

T intends to go downtown on Monday. On Sunday, *T* tells *S* of his intention. Hearing *T* say he will go downtown, *S* infers that *T* really does intend to go downtown. And from this *S* concludes that *T* *will* go downtown on Monday. Now suppose that *T* fulfills his intention by going downtown on Monday. Can *S* be said to know that he would go downtown? If we ever can be said to have knowledge of the future, this is a reasonable candidate for it. So let us say *S* did know that proposition. How can my analysis account for *S*'s knowledge? *T*'s going downtown on Monday clearly cannot be a cause of *S*'s believing, on Sunday, that he would go downtown. But there is a fact that is the *common* cause of *T*'s going downtown and of *S*'s belief that he would go downtown, viz., *T*'s intending (on Sunday) to go downtown. This intention resulted in his going downtown and also resulted in *S*'s believing that he would go downtown. This causal connection between *S*'s belief and the fact believed allows us to say that *S knew* that *T* would go downtown.

The example is diagrammed in Figure 3. (*p*) = *T*'s going downtown on Monday. (*q*) = *T*'s intending (on Sunday) to go downtown on Monday. (*r*) = *T*'s telling *S* (on Sunday) that he will go downtown on Monday. (*u*) and (*v*) are relevant background propositions pertaining to *T*'s honesty, resoluteness, etc. The diagram reveals that *q* is a cause both of *p* and of *S*'s belief of *p*. Cases of this kind I shall call *Pattern 2* cases of knowledge. Figures 1 and 2 exemplify *Pattern 1* cases of knowledge.

Notice that the causal connection between *q* and *p* is an essential part of *S*'s knowing *p*. Suppose, for example, that *T*'s intending (on Sunday) to go downtown does not result in, or cause, *T*'s going downtown on Monday. Suppose that *T,* after telling *S* that he would go downtown, changes his mind. Nevertheless, on Monday he is kidnapped and forced, at the point of a gun, to go downtown. Here both *q* and *p* actually occur, but they are not causally related. The diagram in Figure 3 would have to be amended by deleting the arrow connecting (*q*) with (*p*). But if the rest of

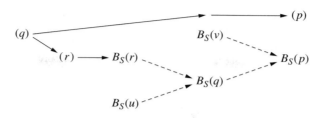

FIGURE 3

the facts of the original case remain the same, S could not be said to know p. It would be false to say that S knew, on Sunday, that T would go downtown on Monday.

Pattern 2 cases of knowledge are not restricted to knowledge of the future. I know that smoke was coming out of my chimney last night. I know this because I remember perceiving a fire in my fireplace last night, and I infer that the fire caused smoke to rise out of the chimney. This case exemplifies Pattern 2. The smoke's rising out of the chimney is not a causal factor of my belief. But the fact that there was a fire in the fireplace was a cause both of my belief that smoke was coming out of the chimney and of the fact that smoke was coming out of the chimney. If we supplement this case slightly, we can make my knowledge exemplify *both* Pattern 1 and Pattern 2. Suppose that a friend tells me today that he perceived smoke coming out of my chimney last night and I base my continued belief of this fact on his testimony. Then the fact was a cause of my current belief of it, as well as an *effect* of another fact that caused my belief. In general, numerous and diverse kinds of causal connections can obtain between a given fact and a given person's belief of that fact.

Let us now examine some objections to Clark's analysis and see how the analysis presented here fares against them. John Turk Saunders and Narayan Champawat have raised the following counterexample to Clark's analysis:[9]

Suppose that Smith believes

(p) Jones owns a Ford

because his friend Brown whom he knows to be generally reliable and honest yesterday told Smith that Jones had always owned a Ford. Brown's information was correct, but today Jones sells his Ford and replaces it with a Volkswagen. An hour later Jones is pleased to find that he is the proud owner of two cars: he has been lucky enough to win a Ford in a raffle. Smith's belief in p is not only justified and true, but is fully grounded, e.g., we suppose that each link in the . . . chain of Smith's grounds is true (8).

Clearly Smith does not know p; yet he seems to satisfy Clark's analysis of knowing.
Smith's lack of knowledge can be accounted for in terms of my analysis. Smith does not know p because his believing p is not causally related to p, Jones's owning a Ford *now*. This can be seen by examining Figure 4. In the diagram, (p) = Jones's owning a Ford now; (q) = Jones's having always owned a Ford (until yesterday); (r) = Jones's winning a Ford in a raffle today. (t), (u), and

[9]"Mr. Clark's Definition of 'Knowledge'," *Analysis,* xxv.1, ns 103 (October 1964): 8–9.

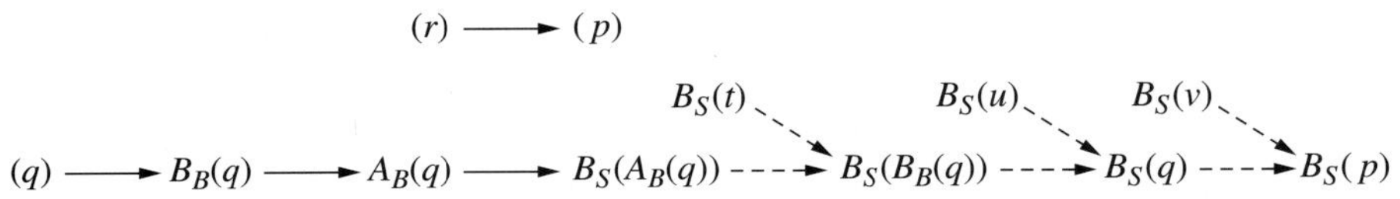

FIGURE 4

(v) are background propositions. (v), for example, deals with the likelihood of someone's continuing to own the same car today that he owned yesterday. The subscript "B" designates Brown, and the subscript "S" designates Smith. Notice the absence of an arrow connecting (p) with (q). The absence of this arrow represents the absence of a causal relation between (q) and (p). Jones's owning a Ford in the past (until yesterday) is not a cause of his owning one now. Had he continued owning the same Ford today that he owned yesterday, there would be a causal connection between q and p and, therefore, a causal connection between p and Smith's believing p. This causal connection would exemplify Pattern 2. But, as it happened, it is purely a coincidence that Jones owns a Ford today as well as yesterday. Thus, Smith's belief of p is not connected with p by Pattern 2, nor is there any Pattern 1 connection between them. Hence, Smith does not know p.

If we supplement Clark's analysis as suggested above, it can be saved from this counterexample. Though Saunders and Champawat fail to mention this explicitly, presumably it is one of Smith's beliefs that Jones's owning a Ford yesterday would *result* in Jones's owning a Ford now. This was undoubtedly one of his grounds for believing that Jones owns a Ford now. (A complete diagram of S's beliefs relevant to p would include this belief.) Since this belief is false, however, Clark's analysis would yield the correct consequence that Smith does not know p. Unfortunately, Clark himself seems not to have noticed this point, since Saunders and Champawat's putative counterexample has been allowed to stand.

Another sort of counterexample to Clark's analysis has been given by Saunders and Champawat and also by Keith Lehrer. This is a counterexample from which his analysis cannot escape. I shall give Lehrer's example (*op. cit.*) of this sort of difficulty. Suppose Smith bases his belief of

(p) Someone in his office owns a Ford

on his belief of four propositions

(q) Jones owns a Ford
(r) Jones works in his office
(s) Brown owns a Ford
(t) Brown works in his office

In fact, Smith knows q, r, and t, but he does not know s because s is false. Since s is false, not *all* of Smith's grounds for p are true, and, therefore, on Clark's analysis, Smith does not know p. Yet clearly Smith does know p. Thus, Clark's analysis is *too strong*.

Having seen the importance of a causal chain for knowing, it is fairly obvious how to amend Clark's requirements without making them too weak. We need not require, as Clark does, that *all* of S's grounds be true. What is required is that enough of them be true to ensure the existence of at least *one* causal connection between *p* and *S*'s belief of *p*. In Lehrer's example, Smith thinks that there are two ways in which he knows *p:* via his knowledge of the conjunction of *q* and *r,* and via his knowledge of the conjunction of *s* and *t*. He does not know *p* via the conjunction of *s* and *t,* since *s* is false. But there is a causal connection, via *q* and *r,* between *p* and Smith's belief of *p*. And this connection is enough.

    Another sort of case in which one of *S*'s grounds for *p* may be false without preventing him from knowing *p* is where the false proposition is a dispensable background assumption. Suppose *S* bases his belief of *p* on 17 background assumptions, but only 16 of these are true. If these 16 are strong enough to confirm *p,* then the 17th is dispensable. *S* can be said to know *p* though one of his grounds is false.

Our discussion of Lehrer's example calls attention to the necessity of a further clarification of the notion of a "causal chain." I said earlier that causal chains with admixtures of inferences are causal chains. Now I wish to add that causal chains with admixtures of logical connections are causal chains. Unless we allow this interpretation, it is hard to see how facts like "Someone in the office owns a Ford" or "All men are mortal" could be *causally* connected with beliefs thereof.

    The following principle will be useful: *If x is logically related to y and if y is a cause of z, then x is a cause of z.* Thus, suppose that *q* causes *S*'s belief of *q* and that *r* causes *S*'s belief of *r*. Next suppose that *S* infers *q* & *r* from his belief of *q* and of *r*. Then the facts *q* and *r* are causes of *S*'s believing *q* & *r*. But the fact *q* & *r* is logically related to the fact *q* and to the fact *r*. Therefore, using the principle enunciated above, the fact *q* & *r* is a cause of *S*'s believing *q* & *r*.

    In Lehrer's case another logical connection is involved: a connection between an existential fact and an instance thereof. Lehrer's case is diagrammed in Figure 5. In addition to the usual conventions, logical relationships are represented by double solid lines. As the diagram shows, the fact *p*—someone in Smith's office owning a Ford—is logically related to the fact *q* & *r*—Jones's owning a Ford and Jones's working in Smith's office. The fact *q* & *r* is, in turn, logically related to the fact *q* and to the fact *r*. *q* causes *S*'s belief of *q* and, by inference, his belief of *q* & *r* and of *p*. Similarly, *r* is a cause of *S*'s belief of *p*. Hence, by the above principle, *p* is a cause of *S*'s belief of *p*. Since Smith's inferences are warranted, even setting aside his belief of *s* & *t,* he knows *p*.

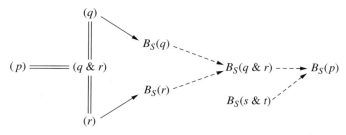

FIGURE 5

In a similar way, universal facts may be causes of beliefs thereof. The fact that all men are mortal is logically related to its instances: John's being mortal, George's being mortal, Oscar's being mortal, etc. Now suppose that S perceives George, John, Oscar, etc. to be mortal (by seeing them die). He infers from these facts that all men are mortal, an inference which, I assume, is warranted. Since each of the facts, John is mortal, George is mortal, Oscar is mortal, etc., is a cause of S's believing that fact, each is also a cause of S's believing that all men are mortal. Moreover, since the universal fact that all men are mortal is logically related to each of these particular facts, this universal fact is a cause of S's belief of it. Hence, S can be said to know that all men are mortal. In analogous fashions, S can know various other logically compound propositions.

We can now formulate the analysis of knowing as follows:

> S *knows that p* if and only if *the fact p is causally connected in an "appropriate" way with S's believing p.*

"Appropriate," knowledge-producing causal processes include the following:

1. perception
2. memory
3. a causal chain, exemplifying either Pattern 1 or 2, which is correctly reconstructed by inferences, each of which is warranted (background propositions help warrant an inference only if they are true)[10]
4. combinations of (1), (2), and (3)

We have seen that this analysis is *stronger* than the traditional analysis in certain respects: the causal requirement and the correct-reconstruction requirement are absent from the older analysis. These additional requirements enable my analysis to circumvent Gettier's counterexamples to the traditional one. But my analysis is *weaker* than the traditional analysis in another respect. In at least one popular interpretation of the traditional analysis, a knower must be able to justify or give evidence for any proposition he knows. For S to know p at t, S must be able, at t, to *state* his justification for believing p, or his grounds for p. My analysis makes no such requirement, and the absence of this requirement enables me to account for cases of knowledge that would wrongly be excluded by the traditional analysis.

I know now, for example, that Abraham Lincoln was born in 1809.[11] I originally came to know this fact, let us suppose, by reading an encyclopedia article. I believed that this encyclopedia was trustworthy and that its saying Lincoln was born in 1809 must have resulted from the fact that Lincoln was indeed born in 1809. Thus, my original knowledge of this fact was founded on a warranted inference. But now I no longer remember this inference. I remember that Lincoln was born in 1809, but not that this is stated in a certain encyclopedia. I no longer have any pertinent beliefs that highly confirm the proposition that Lincoln was born in 1809.

---

[10]Perhaps background propositions that help warrant S's inference must be *known* by S, as well as true. This requirement could be added without making our analysis of "S knows that p" circular. For these propositions would not include p. In other words, the analysis of knowledge could be regarded as recursive.

[11]This kind of case is drawn from an unpublished manuscript of Gilbert Harman.

Nevertheless, I know this proposition now. My original knowledge of it was preserved until now by the causal process of memory.

Defenders of the traditional analysis would doubtlessly deny that I really do know Lincoln's birth year. This denial, however, stems from a desire to protect their analysis. It seems clear that many things we know were originally learned in a way that we no longer remember. The range of our knowledge would be drastically reduced if these items were denied the status of knowledge.

Other species of knowledge without explicit evidence could also be admitted by my analysis. Notice that I have not closed the list of "appropriate" causal processes. Leaving the list open is desirable, because there may be some presently controversial causal processes that we may later deem "appropriate" and, therefore, knowledge-producing. Many people now doubt the legitimacy of claims to extrasensory perception. But if conclusive evidence were to establish the existence of causal processes connecting physical facts with certain persons' beliefs without the help of standard perceptual processes, we might decide to call such beliefs items of knowledge. This would be another species of knowledge in which the knower might be unable to justify or defend his belief. My analysis allows for the possibility of such knowledge, though it doesn't commit one to it.

Special comments are in order about knowledge of our own mental states. This is a very difficult and controversial topic, so I hesitate to discuss it, but something must be said about it. Probably there are some mental states that are clearly distinct from the subject's belief that he is in such a state. If so, then there is presumably a causal process connecting the existence of such states with the subject's belief thereof. We may add this kind of process to the list of "appropriate" causal processes. The more difficult cases are those in which the state is hardly distinguishable from the subject's believing that he is in that state. My being in pain and my believing that I am in pain are hardly distinct states of affairs. If there is no distinction here between the believing and the believed, how can there be a causal connection between them? For the purposes of the present analysis, we may regard identity as a "limiting" or "degenerate" case of a causal connection, just as zero may be regarded as a "limiting" or "degenerate" case of a number. It is not surprising that knowledge of one's own mental state should turn out to be a limiting or degenerate case of knowledge. Philosophers have long recognized its peculiar status. While some philosophers have regarded it as a paradigm case of knowledge, others have claimed that we have no "knowledge" of our mental states at all. A theory of knowledge that makes knowledge of one's own mental states rather different from garden-variety species of knowledge is, in so far forth, acceptable and even welcome.

In conclusion, let me answer some possible objections to my analysis. It might be doubted whether a causal analysis adequately provides the meaning of the word "knows" or of the sentence (-schema) "*S* knows *p*." But I am not interested in giving the *meaning* of "*S* knows *p*"; only its *truth conditions*. I claim to have given one correct set of truth conditions for "*S* knows *p*." Truth conditions of a sentence do not always provide its meaning. Consider, for example, the following truth-conditions statement: "The sentence 'Team *T* wins the baseball game' is true if and only if team *T* has more runs at the end of the game than the opposing team." This statement fails to provide the meaning of the sentence "Team *T* wins the baseball game"; for it fails to indicate an essential part of the meaning of that sentence, viz., that to win a game is to achieve the presumed goal of playing it. Someone might fully understand the truth conditions given above and yet fail to understand the meaning of the sentence because he has no understanding of the notion of "winning" in general.

Truth conditions should not be confused with verification conditions. My analysis of "*S* knows *p*" does not purport to give procedures for *finding out* whether a person (including oneself) knows a given proposition. No doubt, we sometimes do know that people know certain propositions, for we sometimes know that their beliefs are causally connected (in appropriate ways) with the facts believed. On the other hand, it may often be difficult or even impossible to find out whether this condition holds for a given proposition and a given person. For example, it may be difficult for me to find out whether I really do remember a certain fact that I seem to remember. The difficulties that exist for *finding out* whether someone knows a given proposition do not constitute difficulties for my analysis, however.

In the same vein it should be noted that I have made no attempt to answer skeptical problems. My analysis gives no answer to the skeptic who asks that I start from the content of my own experience and then prove that I know there is a material world, a past, etc. I do not take this to be one of the jobs of giving truth conditions for "*S* knows that *p*."

The analysis presented here flies in the face of a well-established tradition in epistemology, the view that epistemological questions are questions of logic or justification, not causal or genetic questions. This traditional view, however, must not go unquestioned. Indeed, I think my analysis shows that the question of whether someone knows a certain proposition is, in part, a causal question, although, of course, the question of what the correct analysis is of "*S* knows that *p*" is not a causal question.

The Raft and the Pyramid:
Coherence versus Foundations
in the Theory of Knowledge

Ernest Sosa

Contemporary epistemology must choose between the solid security of the ancient foundationalist pyramid and the risky adventure of the new coherentist raft. Our main objective will be to understand, as deeply as we can, the nature of the controversy and the reasons for and against each of the two options. But first of all we take note of two underlying assumptions.

Source: "The Raft and the Pyramid: Coherence versus Foundations in the Theory of Knowledge," by Ernest Sosa, from *Midwest Studies in Philosophy,* 5, Studies in Epistemology, 1980. Reprinted by permission.

1. *Two assumptions*
    (A1) Not everything believed is known, but nothing can be known without being at least believed (or accepted, presumed, taken for granted, or the like) in some broad sense. What additional requirements must a belief fill in order to be knowledge? There are surely at least the following two: (a) it must be true, and (b) it must be justified (or warranted, reasonable, correct, or the like).
    (A2) Let us assume, moreover, with respect to the second condition A1(b): first, that it involves a normative or evaluative property; and, second, that the relevant sort of justification is that which pertains to knowledge: epistemic (or theoretical) justification. Someone seriously ill may have two sorts of justification for believing he will recover: the practical justification that derives from the contribution such belief will make to his recovery and the theoretical justification provided by the lab results, the doctor's diagnosis and prognosis, and so on. Only the latter is relevant to the question whether he knows.
2. *Knowledge and criteria (or canons, methods, or the like)*
    a. There are two key questions of the theory of knowledge:
        (i) What do we know?
        (ii) How do we know?
        The answer to the first would be a list of bits of knowledge or at least of types of knowledge: of the self, of the external world, of other minds, and so on. An answer to the second would give us criteria (or canons, methods, principles, or the like) that would explain how we know whatever it is that we do know.
    b. In developing a theory of knowledge, we can begin either with a(i) or with a(ii). Particularism would have us begin with an answer to a(i) and only then take up a(ii) on the basis of that answer. Quite to the contrary, methodism would reverse that order. The particularist thus tends to be antiskeptical on principle. But the methodist is as such equally receptive to skepticism and to the contrary. Hume, for example, was no less a methodist than Descartes. Each accepted, in effect, that only the obvious and what is proved deductively on its basis can possibly be known.
    c. What, then, is the obvious? For Descartes it is what we know by intuition, what is clear and distinct, what is indubitable and credible with no fear of error. Thus for Descartes basic knowledge is always an infallible belief in an indubitable truth. All other knowledge must stand on that basis through deductive proof. Starting from such criteria (canons, methods, etc.), Descartes concluded that knowledge extended about as far as his contemporaries believed.[1]

---

[1]But Descartes's methodism was at most partial. James Van Cleve has supplied the materials for a convincing argument that the way out of the Cartesian circle is through a particularism of basic knowledge. (See James Van Cleve, "Foundationalism, Epistemic Principles, and the Cartesian Circle," *The Philosophical Review* 88 (1979): 55–91.) But this is, of course, compatible with methodism on inferred knowledge. Whether Descartes subscribed to such methodism is hard (perhaps impossible) to determine, since in the end he makes room for all the kinds of knowledge required by particularism. But his language when he introduces the method of hyperbolic doubt, and the order in which he proceeds, suggest that he did subscribe to such methodism.

Starting from similar criteria, however, Hume concluded that both science and common sense made claims far beyond their rightful limits.

d. Philosophical posterity has rejected Descartes's theory for one main reason: that it admits too easily as obvious what is nothing of the sort. Descartes's reasoning is beautifully simple: God exists; no omnipotent perfectly good being would descend to deceit; but if our common sense beliefs were radically false, that would represent deceit on His part. Therefore, our common sense beliefs must be true or at least cannot be radically false. But in order to buttress this line of reasoning and fill in details, Descartes appeals to various principles that appear something less than indubitable.

e. For his part, Hume rejects all but a miniscule portion of our supposed common sense knowledge. He establishes first that there is no way to prove such supposed knowledge on the basis of what is obvious at any given moment through reason or experience. And he concludes, in keeping with this methodism, that in point of fact there really is no such knowledge.

3. *Two metaphors: the raft and the pyramid*

Both metaphors concern the body or system of knowledge in a given mind. But the mind is of course a more complex marvel than is sometimes supposed. Here I do not allude to the depths plumbed by Freud, nor even to Chomsky's. Nor need we recall the labyrinths inhabited by statesmen and diplomats, nor the rich patterns of some novels or theories. We need look no further than the most common, everyday beliefs. Take, for instance, the belief that driving tonight will be dangerous. Brief reflection should reveal that any of us with that belief will join to it several other closely related beliefs on which the given belief depends for its existence or (at least) its justification. Among such beliefs we could presumably find some or all of the following: that the road will be icy or snowy; that driving on ice or snow is dangerous; that it will rain or snow tonight; that the temperature will be below freezing; appropriate beliefs about the forecast and its reliability; and so on.

How must such beliefs be interrelated in order to help justify my belief about the danger of driving tonight? Here foundationalism and coherentism disagree, each offering its own metaphor. Let us have a closer look at this dispute, starting with foundationalism.

Both Descartes and Hume attribute to human knowledge an architectonic structure. There is a nonsymmetric relation of physical support such that any two floors of a building are tied by that relation: one of the two supports (or at least helps support) the other. And there is, moreover, a part with a special status: the foundation, which is supported by none of the floors while supporting them all.

With respect to a body of knowledge K (in someone's possession), foundationalism implies that K can be divided into parts K_1, K_2, . . . such that there is some nonsymmetric relation R (analogous to the relation of physical support) which orders those parts in such a way that there is one—call it F—that bears R to every other part while none of them bears R in turn to F.

According to foundationalism, each piece of knowledge lies on a pyramid such as the following:

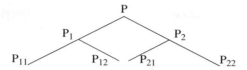

The nodes of such a pyramid (for a proposition P relative to a subject S and a time t) must obey the following requirements:

   a. The set of all nodes that succeed (directly) any given node must serve jointly as a base that properly supports that node (for S at t).
   b. Each node must be a proposition that S is justified in believing at t.
   c. If a node is not self-evident (for S at t), it must have successors (that serve jointly as a base that properly supports that node).
   d. Each branch of an epistemic pyramid must terminate.

For the foundationalist Descartes, for instance, each terminating node must be an indubitable proposition that S believes at t with no possibility of error. As for the nonterminal nodes, each of them represents inferential knowledge, derived by deduction from more basic beliefs.

Such radical foundationalism suffers from a fatal weakness that is twofold:

   a. there are not so many perfectly obvious truths as Descartes thought; and
   b. once we restrict ourselves to what is truly obvious in any given context, very little of one's supposed common sense knowledge can be proved on that basis.

If we adhere to such radical foundationalism, therefore, we are just wrong in thinking we know so much.

Note that in citing such a "fatal weakness" of radical foundationalism, we favor particularism as against the methodism of Descartes and Hume. For we reject the methods or criteria of Descartes and Hume when we realize that they plunge us in a deep skepticism. If such criteria are incompatible with our enjoyment of the rich body of knowledge that we commonly take for granted, then as good particularists we hold on to the knowledge and reject the criteria.

If we reject radical foundationalism, however, what are we to put in its place? Here epistemology faces a dilemma that different epistemologists resolve differently. Some reject radical foundationalism but retain some more moderate form of foundationalism. Others react more vigorously, however, by rejecting all forms of foundationalism in favor of a radically different coherentism. Coherentism is associated with idealism—of both the German and the British variety—and has recently acquired new vigor and interest.

The coherentists reject the metaphor of the pyramid in favor of one that they owe to the positivist Neurath, according to whom our body of knowledge is a raft that floats free of any anchor or tie. Repairs must be made afloat, and though no part is untouchable, we must stand on some in order to replace or repair others. Not every part can go at once.

According to the new metaphor, what justifies a belief is not that it be an infallible belief with an indubitable object, nor that it have been proved deductively on such a basis, but that it cohere with a comprehensive system of beliefs.

4. *A coherentist critique of foundationalism*

What reasons do coherentists offer for their total rejection of foundationalism? The argument that follows below summarizes much of what is alleged against foundationalism. But first we must distinguish between subjective states that incorporate a propositional attitude and those that do not. A propositional attitude is a mental state of someone with a proposition for its object: beliefs, hopes, and fears provide examples. By way of contrast, a headache does not incorporate any such attitude. One can of course be conscious of a headache, but the headache itself does not constitute or incorporate any attitude with a proposition for its object. With this distinction in the background, here is the antifoundationalist argument, which has two lemmas—a(iv) and b(iii)—and a principal conclusion.

a. (i) If a mental state incorporates a propositional attitude, then it does not give us direct contact with reality, e.g., with pure experience, unfiltered by concepts or beliefs.

   (ii) If a mental state does not give us direct contact with reality, then it provides no guarantee against error.

   (iii) If a mental state provides no guarantee against error, then it cannot serve as a foundation for knowledge.

   (iv) Therefore, if a mental state incorporates a propositional attitude, then it cannot serve as a foundation for knowledge.

b. (i) If a mental state does not incorporate a propositional attitude, then it is an enigma how such a state can provide support for any hypothesis, raising its credibility selectively by contrast with its alternatives. (If the mental state has no conceptual or propositional content, then what logical relation can it possibly bear to any hypothesis? Belief in a hypothesis would be a propositional attitude with the hypothesis itself as object. How can one depend logically for such a belief on an experience with no propositional content?)

   (ii) If a mental state has no propositional content and cannot provide logical support for any hypothesis, then it cannot serve as a foundation for knowledge.

   (iii) Therefore; if a mental state does not incorporate a propositional attitude, then it cannot serve as a foundation for knowledge.

c. Every mental state either does or does not incorporate a propositional attitude.

d. Therefore, no mental state can serve as a foundation for knowledge. (From a(iv), b(iii), and c.)

According to the coherentist critic, foundationalism is run through by this dilemma. Let us take a closer look.[2]

---

[2]Cf. Laurence Bonjour "The Coherence Theory of Truth," *Philosophical Studies* 30 (1976): 281–312; and, especially, Michael Williams, *Groundless Belief* (New Haven, 1977); and L. Bonjour, "Can Empirical Knowledge Have a Foundation?" *American Philosophical Quarterly* 15 (1978): 1–15.

In the first place, what reason is there to think, in accordance with premise b(i), that only propositional attitudes can give support to their own kind? Consider practices—e.g., broad policies or customs. Could not some person or group be justified in a practice because of its consequences: that is, could not the consequences of a practice make it a good practice? But among the consequences of a practice may surely be found, for example, a more just distribution of goods and less suffering than there would be under its alternatives. And neither the more just distribution nor the lower degree of suffering is a propositional attitude. This provides an example in which propositional attitudes (the intentions that sustain the practice) are justified by consequences that are not propositional attitudes. That being so, is it not conceivable that the justification of belief that matters for knowledge be analogous to the objective justification by consequences that we find in ethics?

Is it not possible, for instance, that a belief that there is something red before one be justified in part because it has its origin in one's visual experience of red when one looks at an apple in daylight? If we accept such examples, they show us a source of justification that serves as such without incorporating a propositional attitude.

As for premise a(iii), it is already under suspicion from our earlier exploration of premise b(i). A mental state M can be nonpropositional and hence not a candidate for so much as truth, much less infallibility, while it serves, in spite of that, as a foundation of knowledge. Leaving that aside, let us suppose that the relevant mental state is indeed propositional. Must it then be infallible in order to serve as a foundation of justification and knowledge? That is so far from being obvious that it seems more likely false when compared with an analogue in ethics. With respect to beliefs, we may distinguish between their being true and their being justified. Analogously, with respect to actions, we may distinguish between their being optimal (best of all alternatives, all things considered) and their being (subjectively) justified. In practical deliberation on alternatives for action, is it inconceivable that the most *eligible* alternative *not* be objectively the best, all things considered? Can there not be another alternative—perhaps a most repugnant one worth little if any consideration—that in point of fact would have a much better total set of consequences and would thus be better, all things considered? Take the physician attending to Frau Hitler at the birth of little Adolf. Is it not possible that if he had acted less morally, that would have proved better in the fullness of time? And if that is so in ethics, may not its likeness hold good in epistemology? Might there not be justified (reasonable, warranted) beliefs that are not even true, much less infallible? That seems to me not just a conceivable possibility, but indeed a familiar fact of everyday life, where observational beliefs too often prove illusory but no less reasonable for being false.

If the foregoing is on the right track, then the antifoundationalist is far astray. What has led him there?

As a diagnosis of the antifoundationalist argument before us, and more particularly of its second lemma, I would suggest that it rests on an Intellectualist Model of Justification.

According to such a model, the justification of belief (and psychological states generally) is parasitical on certain logical relations among propositions.

For example, my belief (i) that the streets are wet, is justified by my pair of beliefs (ii) that it is raining, and (iii) that if it is raining, the streets are wet. Thus we have a structure such as this:

B(Q) is justified by the fact that B(Q) is grounded on (B(P), B(P ⊃ Q)).

And according to an Intellectualist Model, this is parasitical on the fact that

P and (P ⊃ Q) together logically imply Q.

Concerning this attack on foundationalism I will argue (a) that it is useless to the coherentist, since if the antifoundationalist dilemma impales the foundationalist, a form of it can be turned against the coherentist to the same effect; (b) that the dilemma would be lethal not only to foundationalism and coherentism but also to the very possibility of substantive epistemology; and (c) that a form of it would have the same effect on normative ethics.

(a) According to coherentism, what justifies a belief is its membership in a coherent and comprehensive set of beliefs. But whereas being grounded on B(P) and (B(P ⊃ Q) is a property of a belief B(Q) that yields immediately the logical implication of Q and P and (P ⊃ Q) as the logical source of that property's justificatory power, the property of being a member of a coherent set is not one that immediately yields any such implication.

It may be argued, nevertheless, (i) that the property of being a member of a coherent set would supervene in any actual instance on the property of being a member of a particular set *a* that is in fact coherent, and (ii) that this would enable us to preserve our Intellectualist Model, since (iii) the justification of the member belief B(Q) by its membership in *a* would then be parasitical on the logical relations among the beliefs in *a* which constitute the coherence of that set of beliefs, and (iv) the justification of B(Q) by the fact that it is part of a coherent set would then be *indirectly* parasitical on logical relations among propositions after all.

But if such an indirect form of parasitism is allowed, then the experience of pain may perhaps be said to justify belief in its existence parasitically on the fact that P logically implies P! The Intellectualist Model seems either so trivial as to be dull, or else sharp enough to cut equally against both foundationalism and coherentism.

(b) If (i) only propositional attitudes can justify such propositional attitudes as belief, and if (ii) to do so they must in turn be justified by yet other propositional attitudes, it seems clear that (iii) there is no hope of constructing a complete epistemology, one which would give us, in theory, an account of what the justification of any justified belief would supervene on. For (i) and (ii) would rule out the possibility of a finite regress of justification.

(c) If only propositional attitudes can justify propositional attitudes, and if to do so they must in turn be justified by yet other propositional attitudes, it seems clear that there is no hope of constructing a complete normative ethics, one which would give us, in theory, an account of what the justification of any possible justified action would supervene upon. For the justification of an action presumably depends on the intentions it embeds and the justification of these, and here we are already within the net of propositional attitudes from which, for the Intellectualist, there is no escape.

It seems fair to conclude that our coherentist takes his antifoundationalist zeal too far. His antifoundationalist argument helps expose some valuable insights but falls short of its malicious intent. The foundationalist emerges showing no serious damage. Indeed, he now demands equal time for a positive brief in defense of his position.

5. *The regress argument*

a. The regress argument in epistemology concludes that we must countenance beliefs that are justified in the absence of justification by other beliefs. But it reaches that conclusion only by rejecting the possibility in principle of an infinite regress of justification. It thus opts for foundational beliefs justified in some noninferential way by ruling out a chain or pyramid of justification that has justifiers, and justifiers of justifiers, and so on *without end.* One may well find this too short a route to foundationalism, however, and demand more compelling reasons for thus rejecting an infinite regress as vicious. We shall find indeed that it is not easy to meet this demand.

b. We have seen how even the most ordinary of everyday beliefs is the tip of an iceberg. A closer look below the surface reveals a complex structure that ramifies with no end in sight. Take again my belief that driving will be dangerous tonight, at the tip of an iceberg, (1), that looks like this:

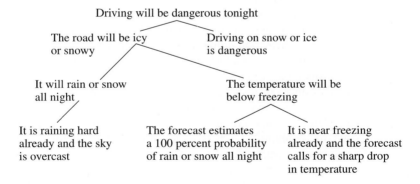

The immediate cause of my belief that driving will be hazardous tonight is the sound of raindrops on the windowpane. All but one or two members of the underlying iceberg are as far as they can be from my thoughts at the time. In what sense, then, do they form an iceberg whose tip breaks the calm surface of my consciousness?

Here I will assume that the members of (1) are beliefs of the subject, even if unconscious or subconscious, that causally buttress and thus justify his prediction about the driving conditions.

Can the iceberg extend without end? If may appear obvious that it cannot do so, and one may jump to the conclusion that any piece of knowledge must be ultimately founded on beliefs that are *not* (inferentially) justified or warranted by other beliefs. This is a doctrine of *epistemic foundationalism.*

Let us focus not so much on the *giving* of justification as on the *having* of it. *Can* there be a belief that is justified in part by other beliefs, some of which are in turn justified by yet other beliefs, and so on without end? Can there be an endless regress of justification?

c. There are several familiar objections to such a regress:

   (i) *Objection:* "It is incompatible with human limitations. No human subject could harbor the required infinity of beliefs." *Reply:* It is mere presumption to fathom with such assurance the depths of the mind, and especially its unconscious and dispositional depths. Besides, our object here is the nature of epistemic justification in itself and not only that of such justification as is accessible to humans. Our question is not whether humans could harbor an infinite iceberg of justification. Our question is rather whether *any* mind, no matter how deep, could do so. Or is it ruled out *in principle* by the very nature of justification?

   (ii) *Objection:* "An infinite regress is indeed ruled out in principle, for if justification were thus infinite how could it possibly end? *Reply:* (i) If the end mentioned is *temporal,* then why must there be such an end? In the first place, the subject may be eternal. Even if he is not eternal, moreover, why must belief acquisition and justification occur seriatim? What precludes an infinite body of beliefs acquired at a single stroke? Human limitations may rule this out for humans, but we have yet to be shown that it is precluded in principle, by the very nature of justification. (ii) If the end mentioned is justificatory, on the other hand, then to ask how justification could possibly end is just to beg the question.

   (iii) *Objection:* "Let us make two assumptions: first, that S's belief of q justifies his belief of p only if it works together with a justified belief on his part that q provides good evidence for p; and, second, that if S is to be justified in believing p on the basis of his belief of q and is to be justified in believing q on the basis of his belief of r, then S must be justified in believing that r provides good evidence for p via q. These assumptions imply that an actual regress of justification requires belief in an infinite proposition. Since no one (or at least no human) can believe an infinite proposition, no one (no human) can be a subject of such an actual regress."[3]

   Reply: Neither of the two assumptions is beyond question, but even granting them both, it may still be doubted that the conclusion follows. It is true that each finitely complex belief of the form "r provides good evidence for p via $q_1, \ldots, q_n$" will *omit* how some members of the full infinite regress are epistemically tied to belief of p. But that seems irrelevant given the fact that for each member r of the regress, such that r is tied epistemically to belief of p, there *is* a finite belief of the required sort

---

[3]Cf. Richard Foley, "Inferential Justification and the Infinite Regress," *American Philosophical Quarterly* 15 (1978): 311–16.

("r provides good evidence for p via $q_1, \ldots, q_n$") that ties the two together. Consequently, there is no apparent reason to suppose—even granted the two assumptions—that an infinite regress will require a single belief in an infinite proposition, and not just an infinity of beliefs in increasingly complex finite propositions.

(iv) *Objection:* "But if it is allowed that justification extend infinitely, then it is too easy to justify any belief at all or too many beliefs altogether. Take, for instance, the belief that there are perfect numbers greater than 100. And suppose a mind powerful enough to believe every member of the following sequence:

$$(\sigma 1) \text{ There is at least one perfect number} > 100$$
$$\text{There are at least two perfect numbers} > 100$$
$$" \qquad \text{three} \qquad " \qquad "$$

If such a believer has no other belief about perfect numbers save the belief that a perfect number is a whole number equal to the sum of its whole factors, then surely he is *not* justified in believing that there are perfect numbers greater than 100. He is quite unjustified in believing any of the members of sequence ($\sigma 1$), in spite of the fact that a challenge to any can be met easily by appeal to its successor. Thus it cannot be allowed after all that justification extend infinitely, and an infinite regress is ruled out."

Reply: We must distinguish between regresses of justification that are actual and those that are merely potential. The difference is *not* simply that an actual regress is composed of actual beliefs. For even if all members of the regress are actual beliefs, the regress may still be *merely potential* in the following sense: while it is true that *if* any member *were* justified then its predecessors *would* be, still none is in fact justified. Anyone with our series of beliefs about perfect numbers in the absence of any further relevant information on such numbers would presumably be the subject of such a merely potential justificatory regress.

(v) *Objection:* "But defenders of infinite justificatory regresses cannot distinguish thus between actual regresses and those that are merely potential. There is no real distinction to be drawn between the two. For if any regress ever justifies the belief at its head, then every regress must always do so. But obviously not every regress does so (as we have seen by examples), and hence no regress can do so."[4]

Reply: One can in fact distinguish between actual justificatory regresses and merely potential ones, and one can do so both abstractly and by examples.

What an actual regress has that a merely potential regress lacks is the property of containing only justified beliefs as members. What they both share is the property of containing no member without successors that would jointly justify it.

---

[4] Cf. John Post, "Infinite Regress Arguments," *Philosophical Studies* 34 (1980).

Recall our regress about perfect numbers greater than 100: i.e., there is at least one; there are at least two; there are at least three; and so on. Each member has a successor that would justify it, but no member is justified (in the absence of further information external to the regress). That is therefore a merely potential infinite regress. As for an actual regress, I see no compelling reason why someone (if not a human, then some more powerful mind) could not hold an infinite series of actually justified beliefs as follows:

$(\sigma 2)$ There is at least one even number
There are at least two even numbers
"   three   "

It may be that no one could be the subject of such a series of justified beliefs unless he had a proof that there is a denumerable infinity of even numbers. But even if that should be so, it would not take away the fact of the infinite regress of potential justifiers, each of which is actually justified, and hence it would not take away the fact of the actual endless regress of justification.

The objection under discussion is confused, moreover, on the nature of the issue before us. Our question is *not* whether there can be an infinite potential regress, each member of which would be justified by its successors, such that the belief at its head is justified in virtue of its position there, at the head of such a regress. The existence and even the possibility of a single such regress with a belief at its head that was *not* justified in virtue of its position there would of course settle that question in the negative. Our question is, rather, whether there can be an actual infinite regress of justification, and the fact that a belief at the head of a potential regress might still fail to be justified despite its position does *not* settle this question. For even if there can be a merely potential regress with an unjustified belief at its head, that leaves open the possibility of an infinite regress, each member of which is justified by its immediate successors working jointly, where every member of the regress is in addition actually justified.

6. *The relation of justification and foundationalist strategy*

The foregoing discussion is predicated on a simple conception of justification such that a set of beliefs β conditionally justifies (*would* justify) a belief X iff, necessarily, if all members of β are justified then X is also justified (if it exists). The fact that on such a conception of justification actual endless regresses—such as $(\sigma 2)$—seem quite possible blocks a straightforward regress argument in favor of foundations. For it shows that an actual infinite regress cannot be dismissed out of hand.

Perhaps the foundationalist could introduce some relation of justification—presumably more complex and yet to be explicated—with respect to which it could be argued more plausibly that an actual endless regress is out of the question.

There is, however, a more straightforward strategy open to the foundationalist. For he *need not* object to the possibility of an endless regress of justification.

His essential creed is the more positive belief that every justified belief must be at the head of a terminating regress. Fortunately, to affirm the universal necessity of a terminating regress is *not* to deny the bare possibility of a nonterminating regress. For a single belief can trail at once regresses of both sorts: one terminating and one not. Thus the proof of the denumerably infinite cardinality of the set of evens may provide for a powerful enough intellect a *terminating* regress for each member of the *endless* series of justified beliefs:

(σ2) There is at least one even number

There are at least two even numbers

"   three   "

At the same time, it is obvious that each member of (σ2) lies at the head of an actual endless regress of justification, on the assumption that each member is conditionally justified by its successor, which is in turn actually justified.

"Thank you so much," the foundationalist may sneer, "but I really do not need that kind of help. Nor do I need to be reminded of my essential creed, which I know as well as anyone. Indeed my rejection of endless regresses of justification is only a means of supporting my view that every justified belief must rest ultimately on foundations, on a terminating regress. You reject that strategy much too casually, in my view, but I will not object here. So we put that strategy aside. And now, my helpful friend, just what do we put in its place."

Fair enough. How then could one show the need for foundations if an endless regress is not ruled out?

7. *Two levels of foundationalism*

   a. We need to distinguish, first, between two forms of foundationalism: one *formal,* the other *substantive.* A type of *formal foundationalism* with respect to a normative or evaluative property (ϕ is the view that the conditions (actual and possible) within which ϕ would apply can be specified in general, perhaps recursively. *Substantive foundationalism* is only a particular way of doing so, and coherentism is another.

Simpleminded hedonism is the view that:

   (i) every instance of pleasure is good,

   (ii) everything that causes something good is itself good, and

   (iii) everything that is good is so in virtue of (i) or (ii) above.

Simpleminded hedonism is a type of formal foundationalism with respect to the good.

Classical foundationalism in epistemology is the view that:

   (i) every infallible, indubitable belief is justified,

   (ii) every belief deductively inferred from justified beliefs is itself justified, and

   (iii) every belief that is justified is so in virtue of (i) or (ii) above.

Classical foundationalism is a type of formal foundationalism with respect to epistemic justification.

Both of the foregoing theories—simpleminded hedonism in ethics, and classical foundationalism in epistemology—are of course flawed. But they both remain examples of formal foundationalist theories.

b. One way of arguing in favor of formal foundationalism in epistemology is to formulate a convincing formal foundationalist theory of justification. But classical foundationalism in epistemology no longer has for many the attraction that it had for Descartes, nor has any other form of epistemic foundationalism won general acceptance. Indeed epistemic foundationalism has been generally abandoned and its advocates have been put on the defensive by the writings of Wittgenstein, Quine, Sellars, Rescher, Aune, Harman, Lehrer, and others. It is lamentable that in our headlong rush away from foundationalism we have lost sight of the different types of foundationalism (formal vs. substantive) and of the different grades of each type. Too many of us now see it as a blur to be decried and avoided. Thus our present attempt to bring it all into better focus.

c. If we cannot argue from a generally accepted foundationalist theory, what reason is there to accept formal foundationalism? There is no reason to think that the conditions (actual and possible) within which an object is spherical are generally specifiable in nongeometric terms. Why should we think that the conditions (actual and possible) within which a belief is epistemically justified are generally specifiable in nonepistemic terms?

So far as I can see, the main reason for accepting formal foundationalism in the absence of an actual, convincing formal foundationalist theory is the very plausible idea that epistemic justification is subject to the supervenience that characterizes normative and evaluative properties generally. Thus, if a car is a good car, then any physical replica of that car must be just as good. If it is a good car in virtue of such properties as being economical, little prone to break down, etc., then surely any exact replica would share all such properties and would thus be equally good. Similarly, if a belief is epistemically justified, it is presumably so in virtue of its character and its basis in perception, memory, or inference (if any). Thus any belief exactly like it in its character and its basis must be equally well justified. Epistemic justification is supervenient. The justification of a belief supervenes on such properties of it as its content and its basis (if any) in perception, memory, or inference. Such a doctrine of supervenience may itself be considered, with considerable justice, a grade of foundationalism. For it entails that every instance of justified belief is founded on a number of its nonepistemic properties, such as its having a certain basis in perception, memory, and inference, or the like.

But there are higher grades of foundationalism as well. There is, for instance, the doctrine that the conditions (actual and possible) within which a belief would be epistemically justified *can be specified* in general, perhaps recursively (and by reference to such notions as perception, memory, and inference).

A higher grade yet of formal foundationalism requires not only that the conditions for justified belief be specifiable, in general, but that they be specifiable by a simple, comprehensive theory.

d. Simpleminded hedonism is a formal foundationalist theory of the highest grade. If it is true, then in every possible world goodness supervenes on pleasure and causation in a way that is recursively specifiable by means of a very simple theory.

Classical foundationalism in epistemology is also a formal foundationalist theory of the highest grade. If it is true, then in every possible world epistemic justification supervenes on infallibility cum indubitability and deductive inference in a way that is recursively specifiable by means of a very simple theory.

Surprisingly enough, coherentism may also turn out to be formal foundationalism of the highest grade, provided only that the concept of coherence is itself both simple enough and free of any normative or evaluative admixture. Given these provisos, coherentism explains how epistemic justification supervenes on the nonepistemic in a theory of remarkable simplicity: a belief is justified iff [if and only if] it has a place within a system of beliefs that is coherent and comprehensive.

It is a goal of ethics to explain how the ethical rightness of an action supervenes on what is not ethically evaluative or normative. Similarly, it is a goal of epistemology to explain how the epistemic justification of a belief supervenes on what is not epistemically evaluative or normative. If coherentism aims at this goal, that imposes restrictions on the notion of coherence, which must now be conceived innocent of epistemically evaluative or normative admixture. Its substance must therefore consist of such concepts as explanation, probability, and logical implication—with these conceived, in turn, innocent of normative or evaluative content.

e. We have found a surprising kinship between coherentism and substantive foundationalism, both of which turn out to be varieties of a deeper foundationalism. This deeper foundationalism is applicable to any normative or evaluative property ϕ, and it comes in three grades. The *first* or lowest is simply the supervenience of ϕ: the idea that whenever something has ϕ its having it is founded on certain others of its properties which fall into certain restricted sorts. The *second* is the explicable supervenience of ϕ: the idea that there are formulable principles that explain in quite general terms the conditions (actual and possible) within which ϕ applies. The *third* and highest is the easily explicable supervenience of ϕ: the idea that there is a *simple* theory that explains the conditions within which ϕ applies. We have found the coherentist and the substantive foundationalist sharing a primary goal: the development of a formal foundationalist theory of the highest grade. For they both want a simple theory that explains precisely how epistemic justification supervenes, in general, on the nonepistemic. This insight gives us an unusual viewpoint on some recent attacks against foundationalism. Let us now consider as an example a certain simple form of argument distilled from the recent antifoundationalist literature.[5]

---

[5]The argument of this whole section is developed in greater detail in my paper "The Foundations of Foundationalism" *Nous* (1980).

8. *Doxastic ascent arguments*

Several attacks on foundationalism turn on a sort of "doxastic ascent" argument that calls for closer scrutiny.[6] Here are two examples:

A. A belief B is foundationally justified for S in virtue of having property F only if S is justified in believing (1) that most at least of his beliefs with property F are true, and (2) that B has property F. But this means that belief B is not foundational after all, and indeed that the very notion of (empirical) foundational belief is incoherent.

It is sometimes held, for example, that perceptual or observational beliefs are often justified through their origin in the exercise of one or more of our five senses in standard conditions of perception. The advocate of doxastic ascent would raise a vigorous protest, however, for in his view the mere fact of such sensory prompting is impotent to justify the belief prompted. Such prompting must be coupled with the further belief that one's senses work well in the circumstances, or the like. For we are dealing here with *knowledge,* which requires not blind faith but *reasoned* trust. But now surely the further belief about the reliability of one's senses itself cannot rest on blind faith but requires its own backing of reasons, and we are off on the regress.

B. A belief B of proposition P is foundationally justified for S only if S is justified in believing that there are no factors present that would cause him to make mistakes on the matter of the proposition P. But, again, this means that belief B is not foundational after all and indeed that the notion of (empirical) foundational belief is incoherent.

From the vantage point of formal foundationalism, neither of these arguments seems persuasive. In the first place, as we have seen, what makes a belief foundational (formally) is its having a property that is nonepistemic (not evaluative in the epistemic or cognitive mode), and does not involve inference from other beliefs, but guarantees, via a necessary principle, that the belief in question is justified. A belief B is made foundational by having some such nonepistemic property that yields its justification. Take my belief that I am in pain in a context where it is caused by my being in pain. The property that my belief then has, of being a self-attribution of pain caused by one's own pain is, let us suppose, a nonepistemic property that yields the justification of any belief that has it. So my belief that I am in pain is in that context foundationally justified. Along with my belief that I am in pain, however, there come other beliefs that are equally well justified, such as my belief that someone is in pain. Thus I am foundationally justified in believing that I am in pain only if I am justified in believing that someone is in pain. Those who object to foundationalism as in A or B above are hence mis-

---

[6]For some examples of the influence of doxastic ascent arguments, see Wilfrid Sellars's writing in epistemology; e.g., "Empiricism and the Philosophy of Mind" in *Science, Perception, and Reality,* especially section VIII, and particularly p. 168. Also I. T. Oakley, "An Argument for Skepticism Concerning Justified Beliefs," *American Philosophical Quarterly* 13 (1976): 221–28; and Bonjour, "Can Empirical Knowledge Have a Foundation?"

taken in thinking that their premises would refute foundationalism. The fact is that they would not touch it. For a belief is no less foundationally justified for having its justification yoked to that of another closely related belief.

The advocate of arguments like A and B must apparently strengthen his premises. He must apparently claim that the beliefs whose justification is entailed by the foundationally justified status of belief B must in some sense function as a *necessary source* of the justification of B. And this would of course preclude giving B foundationally justified status. For if the *being justified* of those beliefs is an *essential* part of the source of the justification of B, then it is ruled out that there be a wholly *nonepistemic* source of B's justification.

That brings us to a second point about A and B, for it should now be clear that these cannot be selectively aimed at foundationalism. In particular, they seem neither more nor less valid objections to coherentism than to foundationalism, or so I will now argue about each of them in turn.

A'. A belief X is justified for S in virtue of membership in a coherent set only if S is justified in believing (1) that most at least of his beliefs with the property of thus cohering are true, and (2) that X has that property.

Any coherentist who accepts A seems bound to accept A'. For what could he possibly appeal to as a relevant difference? But A' is a quicksand of endless depth. (How is he justified in believing A'(1)? Partly through justified belief that *it* coheres? And what would justify *this*? And so on . . .).

B'. A belief X is justified for S only if S is justified in believing that there are no factors present that would cause him to make mistakes on the subject matter of that belief.

Again, any coherentist who accepts B seems bound to accept B'. But this is just another road to the quicksand. (For S is justified in believing that there are no such factors only if . . . and so on.)

Why are such regresses vicious? The key is again, to my mind, the doctrine of supervenience. Such regresses are vicious because they would be logically incompatible with the supervenience of epistemic justification on such nonepistemic facts as the totality of a subject's beliefs, his cognitive and experiential history, and as many other nonepistemic facts as may seem at all relevant. The idea is that there is a set of such nonepistemic facts surrounding a justified belief such that no belief could possibly have been surrounded by those very facts without being justified. Advocates of A or B run afoul of such supervenience, since they are surely committed to the more general views derivable from either of A or B by deleting "foundationally" from its first sentence. In each case the more general view would then preclude the possibility of supervenience, since it would entail that the source of justification *always* includes an *epistemic* component.

9. *Coherentism and substantive foundationalism*

   a. The notions of coherentism and substantive foundationalism remain unexplicated. We have relied so far on our intuitive grasp of them. In this section we shall consider reasons for the view that substantive foundationalism is superior to coherentism. To assess these reasons, we need some more explicit account of the difference between the two.

By coherentism we shall mean any view according to which the ultimate sources of justification for any belief lie in relations among that belief and other beliefs of the subject: explanatory relations, perhaps, or relations of probability or logic.

According to substantive foundationalism, as it is to be understood here, there are ultimate sources of justification other than relations among beliefs. Traditionally these additional sources have pertained to the special content of the belief or its special relations to the subjective experience of the believer.

b. The view that justification is a matter of relations among beliefs is open to an objection from alternative coherent systems or detachment from reality, depending on one's perspective. From the latter perspective the body of beliefs is held constant and the surrounding world is allowed to vary, whereas from the former perspective it is the surrounding world that is held constant while the body of beliefs is allowed to vary. In either case, according to the coherentist, there could be no effect on the justification for any belief.

Let us sharpen the question before us as follows. Is there reason to think that there is at least one system B', alternative to our actual system of beliefs B, such that B' contains a belief X with the following properties:

(i)   in our present nonbelief circumstances we would not be justified in having belief X even if we accepted along with that belief (as our total system of beliefs) the entire belief system B' in which it is embedded (no matter how acceptance of B' were brought about); and

(ii) that is so despite the fact that belief X coheres within B' at least as fully as does some actual justified belief of ours within our actual belief system B (where the justification of that actual justified belief is alleged by the coherentist to derive solely from its coherence within our actual body of beliefs B).

The coherentist is vulnerable to counterexamples of this sort right at the surface of his body of beliefs, where we find beliefs with minimal coherence, whose detachment and replacement with contrary beliefs would have little effect on the coherence of the body. Thus take my belief that I have a headache when I do have a splitting headache, and let us suppose that this *does* cohere within my present body of beliefs. (Thus I have no reason to doubt my present introspective beliefs, and so on. And if my belief does *not* cohere, so much the worse for coherentism, since my belief is surely justified.) Here then we have a perfectly justified or warranted belief. And yet such a belief may well have relevant relations of explanation, logic, or probability with at most a small set of other beliefs of mine at the time: say, that I am not free of headache, that I am in pain, that someone is in pain, and the like. If so, then an equally coherent alternative is not far to seek. Let everything remain constant, *including* the splitting headache, except for the following: replace the belief that I have a headache with the belief that I do *not* have a headache, the belief that I am in pain with the belief that I am *not* in pain, the belief that someone is in pain with the belief that someone is *not* in pain, and so on. I contend that my resulting hypothetical system of beliefs would cohere as fully as does my actual system of beliefs, and yet my hypothetical belief that I do *not* have a headache would not therefore be justified. What makes this difference concerning justification between my actual belief that I have a headache and the hypothetical belief that I am free of headache, each as coherent as the other within its own system, if not the actual splitting headache? But the headache is *not* itself a belief nor a relation among beliefs and is thus in no way constitutive of the internal coherence of my body of beliefs.

Some might be tempted to respond by alleging that one's belief about whether or not one has a headache is always *infallible*. But since we could devise similar examples for the various sensory modalities and propositional attitudes, the response given for the case of headache would have to be generalized. In effect, it would have to cover "peripheral" beliefs generally—beliefs at the periphery of one's body of beliefs, minimally coherent with the rest. These peripheral beliefs would all be said to be infallible. That is, again, a possible response, but it leads to a capitulation by the coherentist to the radical foundationalist on a crucial issue that has traditionally divided them: the infallibility of beliefs about one's own subjective states.

What is more, not all peripheral beliefs are about one's own subjective states. The direct realist is probably right that some beliefs about our surroundings are uninferred and yet justified. Consider my present belief that the table before me is oblong. This presumably coheres with such other beliefs of mine as that the table has the same shape as the piece of paper before me, which is oblong, and a different shape than the window frame here, which is square, and so on. So far as I can see, however, there is no insurmountable obstacle to replacing that whole set of coherent beliefs with an equally coherent set as follows: that the table before me is square, that the table has the same shape as the square window frame, and a different shape than the piece of paper, which is oblong, and so on. The important points are (a) that this replacement may be made without changing the rest of one's body of beliefs or any aspect of the world beyond, including one's present visual experience of something oblong, not square, as one looks at the table before one; and (b) that is so, in part, because of the fact (c) that the subject need not have any beliefs about his present sensory experience.

Some might be tempted to respond by alleging that one's present experience is *self-intimating,* i.e., always necessarily taken note of and reflected in one's beliefs. Thus if anyone has visual experience of something oblong, then he believes that he has such experience. But this would involve a further important concession by the coherentist to the radical foundationalist, who would have been granted two of his most cherished doctrines: the infallibility of introspective belief and the self-intimation of experience.

10. *The foundationalist's dilemma*

The antifoundationalist zeal of recent years has left several forms of foundationalism standing. These all share the conviction that a belief can be justified not only by its coherence within a comprehensive system but also by an appropriate combination of observational content and origin in the use of the senses in standard conditions. What follows presents a dilemma for any foundationalism based on any such idea.

a. We may surely suppose that beings with observational mechanisms radically unlike ours might also have knowledge of their environment. (That seems possible even if the radical difference in observational mechanisms precludes overlap in substantive concepts and beliefs.)

b. Let us suppose that there is such a being, for whom experience of type ϕ (of which we have no notion) has a role with respect to his beliefs of type ϕ analogous to the role that our visual experience has with respect to our visual beliefs. Thus we might have a schema such as the following:

Human	*Extraterrestrial being*
Visual experience	ϕ experience
Experience of something red	Experience of something F
Belief that there is something red before one	Belief that there is something F before one

c. It is often recognized that our visual experience intervenes in two ways with respect to our visual beliefs: as cause and as justification. But these are not wholly independent. Presumably, the justification of the belief that something here is red derives at least in part from the fact that it originates in a visual experience of something red that takes place in normal circumstances.

d. Analogously, the extraterrestrial belief that something here has the property of being F might be justified partly by the fact that it originates in a ϕ experience of something F that takes place in normal circumstances.

e. A simple question presents the foundationalist's dilemma: regarding the epistemic principle that underlies our justification for believing that something here is red on the basis of our visual experience of something red, is it proposed as a fundamental principle or as a derived generalization? Let us compare the famous Principle of Utility of value theory, according to which it is best for that to happen which, of all the possible alternatives in the circumstances, would bring with it into the world the greatest balance of pleasure over pain, joy over sorrow, happiness over unhappiness, content over discontent, or the like. Upon this fundamental principle one may then base various generalizations, rules of thumb, and maxims of public health, nutrition, legislation, etiquette, hygiene, and so on. But these are all then derived generalizations which rest for their validity on the fundamental principle. Similarly, one may also ask, with respect to the generalizations advanced by our foundationalist, whether these are proposed as fundamental principles or as derived maxims or the like. This sets him face to face with a dilemma, each of whose alternatives is problematic. If his proposals are meant to have the status of secondary or derived maxims, for instance, then it would be quite unphilosophical to stop there. Let us turn, therefore, to the other alternative.

f. On reflection it seems rather unlikely that epistemic principles for the justification of observational beliefs by their origin in sensory experience could have a status more fundamental than that of derived generalizations. For by granting such principles fundamental status we would open the door to a multitude of equally basic principles with no unifying factor. There would be some for vision, some for hearing, etc., without even mentioning the corresponding extraterrestrial principles.

g. It may appear that there is after all an idea, however, that unifies our multitude of principles. For they all involve sensory experience and sensible characteristics. But what is a sensible characteristic? Aristotle's answer appeals to examples: colors, shapes, sounds, and so on. Such a notion might enable us to unify perceptual epistemic principles under some more fundamental principle such as the following:

> If σ is a sensible characteristic, then the belief that there is something with σ before one is (prima facie) justified if it is based on a visual experience of something with σ in conditions that are normal with respect to σ.

h. There are at least two difficulties with such a suggestion, however, and neither one can be brushed aside easily. First, it is not clear that we can have a viable notion of sensible characteristic on the basis of examples so diverse as colors, shapes, tones, odors, and so on. Second, the authority of such a principle apparently derives from contingent circumstances concerning the reliability of beliefs prompted by sensory experiences of certain sorts. According to the foundationalist, our visual beliefs are justified by their origin in our visual experience or the like. Would such beliefs be equally well justified in a world where beliefs with such an origin were nearly always false?

i. In addition, finally, even if we had a viable notion of such characteristics, it is not obvious that fundamental knowledge of reality would have to derive causally or otherwise from sensory experience of such characteristics. How could one impose reasonable limits on extraterrestrial mechanisms for noninferential acquisition of beliefs? Is it not possible that such mechanisms need not always function through sensory experience of any sort? Would such beings necessarily be denied any knowledge of their surroundings and indeed of any contingent spatio-temporal fact? Let us suppose them to possess a complex system of true beliefs concerning their surroundings, the structures below the surface of things, exact details of history and geography, all constituted by concepts none of which corresponds to any of our sensible characteristics. What then? Is it not possible that their basic beliefs should all concern fields of force, waves, mathematical structures, and numerical assignments to variables in several dimensions? This is no doubt an exotic notion, but even so it still seems conceivable. And if it is in fact possible, what then shall we say of the noninferential beliefs of such beings? Would we have to concede the existence of special epistemic principles that can validate their noninferential beliefs? Would it not be preferable to formulate more abstract principles that can cover both human and

200   Part 2   Epistemology, Knowledge, and Skepticism

extraterrestrial foundations? If such more abstract principles are in fact accessible, then the less general principles that define the human foundations and those that define the extraterrestrial foundations are both derived principles whose validity depends on that of the more abstract principles. In this the human and extraterrestrial epistemic principles would resemble rules of good nutrition for an infant and an adult. The infant's rules would of course be quite unlike those valid for the adult. But both would still be based on a more fundamental principle that postulates the ends of well-being and good health. What more fundamental principles might support both human and extraterrestrial knowledge in the way that those concerning good health and well-being support rules of nutrition for both the infant and the adult?

11. *Reliabilism: an ethics of moral virtues and an epistemology of intellectual virtues*

In what sense is the doctor attending Frau Hitler justified in performing an action that brings with it far less value than one of its accessible alternatives? According to one promising idea, the key is to be found in the rules that he embodies through stable dispositions. His action is the result of certain stable virtues, and there are no equally virtuous alternate *dispositions* that, given his cognitive limitations, he might have embodied with equal or better total consequences, and that would have led him to infanticide in the circumstances. The important move for our purpose is the stratification of justification. Primary justification attaches to virtues and other dispositions, to stable dispositions to act, through their greater contribution of value when compared with alternatives. Secondary justification attaches to particular acts in virtue of their source in virtues or other such justified dispositions.

The same strategy may also prove fruitful in epistemology. Here primary justification would apply to *intellectual* virtues, to stable dispositions for belief acquisition, through their greater contribution toward getting us to the truth. Secondary justification would then attach to particular beliefs in virtue of their source in intellectual virtues or other such justified dispositions.[7]

That raises parallel questions for ethics and epistemology. We need to consider more carefully the concept of a virtue and the distinction between moral and intellectual virtues. In epistemology, there is reason to think that the most useful and illuminating notion of intellectual virtue will prove broader than our tradition would suggest and must give due weight not only to the subject and

---

[7]This puts in a more traditional perspective the contemporary effort to develop a "causal theory of knowing." From our viewpoint, this effort is better understood not as an attempt to *define* propositional knowledge but as an attempt to formulate fundamental principles of justification.
Cf. the work of D. Armstrong, *Belief, Truth and Knowledge* (London, 1973); and that of F. Dretske, A. Goldman, and M. Swain, whose relevant already published work is included in *Essays on Knowledge and Justification,* ed. G. Pappas and M. Swain (Ithaca and London, 1978). But the theory is still under development by Goldman and by Swain, who have reached general conclusions about it similar to those suggested here, though not necessarily—so far as I know—for the same reasons or in the same overall context.

his intrinsic nature but also to his environment and to his epistemic community. This is a large topic, however, to which I hope some of us will turn with more space, and insight, than I can now command.[8]

SUMMARY

1. *Two assumptions:* (A1) that for a belief to constitute knowledge it must be (a) true and (b) justified; and (A2) that the justification relevant to whether or not one knows is a sort of epistemic or theoretical justification to be distinguished from its practical counterpart.
2. *Knowledge and criteria.* Particularism is distinguished from methodism: the first gives priority to particular examples of knowledge over general methods of criteria, whereas the second reverses that order. The methodism of Descartes leads him to an elaborate dogmatism whereas that of Hume leads him to a very simple skepticism. The particularist is, of course, antiskeptical on principle.
3. *Two metaphors: the raft and the pyramid.* For the foundationalist every piece of knowledge stands at the apex of a pyramid that rests on stable and secure foundations whose stability and security does not derive from the upper stories or sections. For the coherentist a body of knowledge is a free-floating raft every plank of which helps directly or indirectly to keep all the others in place, and no plank of which would retain its status with no help from the others.
4. *A coherentist critique of foundationalism.* No mental state can provide a foundation for empirical knowledge. For if such a state is propositional, then it is fallible and hence no secure foundation. But if it is *not* propositional, then how can it possibly serve as a foundation for belief? How can one infer or justify anything on the basis of a state that, having no propositional content, must be logically dumb? An analogy with ethics suggests a reason to reject this dilemma. Other reasons are also advanced and discussed.
5. *The regress argument.* In defending his position, the foundationalist often attempts to rule out the very possibility of an infinite regress of justification (which leads him to the necessity for a foundation). Some of his arguments to that end are examined.
6. *The relation of justification and foundationalist strategy.* An alternative foundationalist strategy is exposed, one that does not require ruling out the possibility of an infinite regress of justification.
7. *Two levels of foundationalism.* Substantive foundationalism is distinguished from formal foundationalism, three grades of which are exposed: first, the supervenience of epistemic justification; second, its explicable supervenience;

[8]I am indebted above all to Roderick Chisholm: for his writings and for innumerable discussions. The main ideas in the present paper were first presented in a seminar of 1976–77 at the University of Texas. I am grateful to Anthony Anderson, David and Jean Blumenfeld, Laurence Bonjour, and Martin Perlmutter, who made that seminar a valuable stimulus. Subsequent criticism by my colleague James Van Cleve has also been valuable and stimulating.

and, third, its supervenience explicable by means of a simple theory. There turns out to be a surprising kinship between coherentism and substantive foundationalism, both of which aim at a formal foundationalism of the highest grade, at a theory of the greatest simplicity that explains how epistemic justification supervenes on nonepistemic factors.

8. *Doxastic ascent arguments.* The distinction between formal and substantive foundationalism provides an unusual viewpoint on some recent attacks against foundationalism. We consider doxastic ascent arguments as an example.

9. *Coherentism and substantive foundationalism.* It is argued that substantive foundationalism is superior since coherentism is unable to account adequately for the epistemic status of beliefs at the "periphery" of a body of beliefs.

10. *The foundationalist's dilemma.* All foundationalism based on sense experience is subject to a fatal dilemma.

11. *Reliabilism.* An alternative to foundationalism of sense experience is sketched.

Two Types of Foundationalism

William P. Alston

Foundationalism is often stated as the doctrine that knowledge constitutes a structure the foundations of which support all the rest but themselves need no support. To make this less metaphorical we need to specify the mode of support involved. In contemporary discussions of foundationalism knowledge is thought of in terms of true-justified-belief (with or without further conditions); thus the mode of support involved is justification, and what gets supported a belief.[1] The sense in which a foundation needs no support is that it is not justified by its relation to other justified beliefs; in that sense it does not "rest on" other beliefs. Thus we may formulate foundationalism as follows:

> I. Our justified beliefs form a structure, in that some beliefs (the foundations) are justified by something other than their relation to other justified beliefs; beliefs that *are* justified by their relation to other beliefs all depend for their justification on the foundations.

Notice that nothing is said about *knowledge* in this formulation. Since the structure alleged by foundationalism is a structure of the justification of belief, the doctrine can be stated in terms of that component of knowledge alone. Indeed, one who thinks that knowledge has nothing to do with justified belief is still

---

[1]Contemporary writers on foundationalism do not seem to notice that Descartes and Locke have a quite different view of knowledge and, hence, that, if they hold that knowledge rests on foundations, this will mean something rather different. See the section "Self-Consciously Reconstructing Knowledge from the Foundations" for a translation of a bit of Descartes into current foundationalist idiom.

Source: William P. Alston, "Two Types of Foundationalism," LXXIII, 7 (April 8, 1976): 165–85. Reprinted by permission of the publisher and author.

faced with the question of whether foundationalism is a correct view about the structure of epistemic justification.

Two emendations will render this formulation more perspicuous. First, a useful bit of terminology. Where what justifies a belief includes[2] the believer's having certain other justified beliefs, so related to the first belief as to embody reasons or grounds for it, we may speak of *indirectly (mediately) justified belief.* And, where what justifies a belief does not include any such constituent, we may speak of *directly (immediately) justified belief.* Correspondingly, a case of knowledge in which the justification requirement is satisfied by indirect (mediate) justification will be called *indirect (mediate) knowledge;* and a case in which the justification requirement is satisfied by direct (immediate) justification will be called *direct (immediate) knowledge.*

Second, we should make more explicit how mediate justification is thought to rest on immediately justified belief. The idea is that, although the other beliefs involved in the mediate justification of a given belief may themselves be mediately justified, if we continue determining at each stage how the supporting beliefs are justified, we will arrive, sooner or later, at directly justified beliefs. This will not, in general, be a single line of descent; typically the belief with which we start will rest on several beliefs, each of which in turn will rest on several beliefs. So the general picture is that of multiple branching from the original belief.

With this background we may reformulate foundationalism as follows (turning the "foundation" metaphor on its head):

> II. Every mediately justified belief stands at the origin of a (more or less) multiply branching tree structure at the tip of each branch of which is an immediately justified belief.

II can be read as purely hypothetical (*if* there are any mediately justified beliefs, then . . .) or with existential import (There are mediately justified beliefs, and . . .). Foundationalists typically make the latter claim, and I shall understand the doctrine to carry existential import.

II can usefully be divided into two claims:

(A) There are directly justified beliefs.

(B) A given person has a stock of directly justified beliefs sufficient to generate chains of justification that terminate in whatever indirectly justified beliefs he has.

In other words, (A) there are foundations, and (B) they suffice to hold up the building.

In this paper we shall restrict our attention to A. More specifically, we shall be concerned with a certain issue over what it takes for a belief to serve as a foundation.

---

[2]Only "includes" because other requirements are also commonly imposed for mediate justification, e.g., that the first belief be "based" on the others, and, by some epistemologists, that the believer realize that the other beliefs do constitute adequate grounds for the first.

I. THE SECOND-LEVEL ARGUMENT

Let's approach this issue by confronting foundationalism with a certain criticism, a recent version of which can be found in Bruce Aune.[3]

> The line of reasoning behind the empiricist's assumption is, again, that while intra-language rules may validly take us from premise to conclusion, they cannot themselves establish empirical truth. If the premises you start with are false, you will have no guarantee that the conclusions you reach are not false either. Hence, to attain knowledge of the actual world, you must ultimately have premises whose truth is acceptable independently of any inference and whose status is accordingly indubitable. Only by having such premises can you gain a starting point that would make inference worthwhile. For convenience, these indispensable basic premises may be called "intrinsically acceptable." The possibility of empirical knowledge may then be said to depend on the availability of intrinsically acceptable premises.
>
> If this line of thought is sound, it follows that utter scepticism can be ruled out only if one can locate basic empirical premises that are intrinsically acceptable. Although philosophers who attack scepticism in accordance with this approach generally think they are defending common sense, it is crucial to observe that they cannot actually be doing so. The reason for this is that, from the point of view of common experience, there is no plausibility at all in the idea that intrinsically acceptable premises, as so defined, ever exist. Philosophers defending such premises fail to see this because they always ignore the complexity of the situation in which an empirical claim is evaluated.
>
> I have already given arguments to show that introspective claims are not, in themselves, intrinsically infallible, they may be regarded as virtually certain if produced by a reliable (sane, clear-headed) observer, but their truth is not a consequence of the mere fact that they are confidently made. To establish a similar conclusion regarding the observation claims of everyday life only the sketchiest arguments are needed. Obviously the mere fact that such a claim is made does not assure us of its truth. If we know that the observer is reliable, made his observation in good light, was reasonably close to the object, and so on, then we may immediately regard it as acceptable. But its acceptability is not intrinsic to the claim itself . . . I would venture to say that any spontaneous claim, observational or introspective, carries almost no presumption of truth, when considered entirely by itself. If we accept such a claim as true, it is only because of our confidence that a complex body of background assumptions—concerning observers, standing conditions, the kind of object in question—and, often, a complex mass of further observations all point to the conclusion that it is true.
>
> Given these prosaic considerations, it is not necessary to cite experimental evidence illustrating the delusions easily brought about by, for example, hypnosis to see that no spontaneous claim is acceptable wholly on its own merits. On the contrary, common experience is entirely adequate to show that clear-headed men never accept a claim merely because it is made, without regard to the peculiarities of the agent and of the conditions under which it is produced. For such men, the acceptability of every claim is always determined by inference. If we are prepared to take these standards of acceptability seriously, we must accordingly admit that the traditional search for intrinsically acceptable empirical premises is completely misguided (41–43).

[3]*Knowledge, Mind and Nature* (New York: Random House, 1967).

Now the target of Aune's critique differs in several important respects from the foundationalism defined above. First and most obviously, Aune supposes that any "intrinsically acceptable premises" will be infallible and indubitable, and some of his arguments are directed specifically against these features.[4] Second, there is an ambiguity in the term "intrinsically acceptable." Aune introduces it to mean "whose truth is acceptable independently of any inference," this looks roughly equivalent to our "directly justified." However in arguing against the supposition that the "observation claims of everyday" are intrinsically acceptable, he says that "the mere fact that such a claim is made does not assure us of its truth," thereby implying that to be intrinsically acceptable a claim would have to be justified just by virtue of being made. Now it is clear that a belief (claim) of which this is true is directly justified, but the converse does not hold. A perceptual belief will also be directly justified, as that term was explained above, if what justifies it is the fact that the perceiver "is reliable, made his observation in good light, was reasonably close to the object, and so on," *provided it is not also required that he be justified in believing that these conditions are satisfied.* Thus this argument of Aune's has no tendency to show that perceptual beliefs cannot be directly justified, but only that they cannot enjoy that special sort of direct justification which we may term "self-justification."[5]

However some of Aune's arguments would seem to be directed against any immediate justification, and a consideration of these will reveal a third and more subtle discrepancy between Aune's target(s) and my version of foundationalism. Near the end of the passage Aune says:

> If we accept such a claim [observational or introspective] as true, it is only because of our confidence that a complex of background assumptions . . . all point to the conclusion that it is true.

And again:

> For such men [clear-headed men], the acceptability of every claim is always determined by inference.

It certainly looks as if Aune is arguing that whenever a claim (belief) is justified it is justified by inference (by relation to other justified beliefs); and that would be the denial of 'There are directly justified beliefs'. But look more closely. Aune is discussing not what would justify the issuer of an introspective or observational claim in his belief, but rather what it would take to justify "us" in accepting his claim; he is arguing from a third-person perspective. Now it does seem clear that *I* cannot be immediately justified in accepting *your* introspective or observational claim as true. If I am so justified it is because I am justified in supposing that you issued a claim of that sort, that you are in a normal condition and know the language, and (if it is an observational claim) that conditions were favorable for your accurately perceiving that sort of thing. But that is only because *I,* in contrast to you, am justified in

---

[4]See the distinctions between infallibility, indubitability, and immediacy in my "Varieties of Privileged Access," *American Philosophical Quarterly,* VIII, 3 (July 1971): 223–241.

[5]In "Varieties of Privileged Access" I use the term "self-warrant" for a belief that is justified by virtue of being a belief of a certain sort.

believing that *p* (where what you claimed is that *p,* and where I have no independent access to *p*) only if I am justified in supposing that you are justified in believing that *p.* My access to *p* is through your access. It is just because *my* justification in believing that *p* presupposes my being justified in believing that you are justified, that my justification has to be indirect. That is why I have to look into such matters as conditions of observation, and your normality. Thus what Aune is really pointing to is the necessity for "inferential" backing for any higher-level belief to the effect that someone is justified in believing that *p.* (I shall call such higher-level beliefs *epistemic beliefs.*) His argument, if it shows anything, shows that no epistemic belief can be immediately justified. But it does nothing to show that the original observer's or introspector's belief that *p* was not immediately justified. Hence his argument is quite compatible with the view that an introspective belief is self-justified and with the view that an observational belief is justified just by being formed in favorable circumstances.

As a basis for further discussion I should like to present my own version of an argument against the possibility of immediate justification for epistemic beliefs—what I shall call the *second-level argument:*

> A1. Where *S*'s belief that *p* is mediately justified, any jurisdiction for the belief that *S* *is justified in believing that p* is obviously mediate. For one could not be justified in this latter belief unless it were based on a justified belief that *S* is justified in accepting the grounds on which his belief that *p* is based. But even where *S* is immediately justified in believing that *p,* the higher-level belief will still be mediately justified, if at all. For in taking a belief to be justified, we are evaluating it in a certain way.[6] And, like any evaluative property, epistemic justification is a supervenient property, the application of which is based on more fundamental properties. A belief is justified because it possesses what Roderick Firth has called "warrant-increasing properties."[7] Hence in order for me to be justified in believing that *S*'s belief that *p* is justified, I must be justified in certain other beliefs, viz, that *S's belief that p* possesses a certain property, *Q,* and that *Q* renders its possessor justified. (Another way of formulating this last belief is: a belief that there is a valid epistemic principle to the effect that any belief that is *Q* is justified.) Hence in no case can an epistemic belief that *S* is justified in believing that *p,* itself be immediately justified.

Before proceeding I shall make two comments on this argument and its conclusion.

1. It may appear that the conclusion of the argument is incompatible with the thesis that one cannot be justified in believing that *p* without also being justified in believing that one is justified in believing that *p.* For if being immediately justified in believing that *p* necessarily carried with it being justified in believing that I am justified in believing that *p,* it would seem that this latter justification would be equally immediate. I would not shirk from such an incompatibility, since I feel confident in rejecting that thesis. It is not clear,

---

[6]For one attempt to explain the distinctively epistemic dimension of evaluation, see R. M. Chisholm, "On the Nature of Empirical Evidence," in Chisholm and R. J. Swartz, eds., *Empirical Knowledge* (Englewood Cliffs, N.J.: Prentice-Hall, 1973), pp. 225–230.
[7]In "Coherence, Certainty, and Epistemic Priority," this *Journal of Philosophy,* LXI, 19 (Oct. 15, 1964): 545–557.

however, that there is any such incompatibility. It all depends on how we construe the necessity. If, e.g., it is that my being justified in believing that p necessarily puts me into possession of the *grounds* I need for being justified in the higher-level belief, then that is quite compatible with our conclusion that the latter can only be mediately justified.

2. The conclusion should not be taken to imply that one must perform any conscious inference to be justified in an epistemic belief, or even that one must be explicitly aware that the lower-level belief has an appropriate warrant-increasing property. Here as in other areas, one's grounds can be possessed more or less implicitly. Otherwise we would have precious little mediate knowledge.

I have already suggested that the second-level argument is not really directed against II. To be vulnerable to this argument, a foundationalist thesis would have to require of foundations not only that *they* be immediately justified, but also that the believer be immediately justified in believing that they are immediately justified. A position that does require this we may call *iterative foundationalism,* and we may distinguish it from the earlier form (*simple foundationalism*) as follows (so far as concerns the status of the foundations):

> Simple Foundationalism: For any epistemic subject, S, there are p's such that S is immediately justified in believing that p.

> Iterative Foundationalism: For any epistemic subject, S, there are p's such that S is immediately justified in believing that p and S is immediately justified in believing that he is immediately justified in believing that p.[8]

It would not take much historical research to show that both positions have been taken. What I want to investigate here is which of them there is most reason to take. Since the classic support for foundationalism has been the regress argument, I shall concentrate on determining which form emerges from that line of reasoning.

II. THE REGRESS ARGUMENT

The regress argument seeks to show that the only alternatives to admitting epistemic foundations are circularity of justification or an equally unpalatable infinite regress of justification. It may be formulated as follows:

> A2. Suppose we are trying to determine whether S is mediately justified in believing that p. To be so justified he has to be justified in believing certain other propositions, q,

---

[8]One should not confuse the respect in which Iterative is stronger than Simple Foundationalism with other ways in which one version of the position may be stronger than another. These include at least the following: (1) whether it is required of foundations that they be infallible, indubitable, or incorrigible; (2) whether foundations have to be self-justified, or whether some weaker form of direct justification is sufficient; (3) how strongly the foundations support various portions of the superstructure. I am convinced that none of these modes of strength requires any of the others, but I will not have time to argue that here. Note too that our version of the regress argument (to be presented in a moment) does nothing to support the demand for foundations that are strong in any of these respects.

r, . . . that are suitably related to *p* (so as to constitute adequate grounds for *p*). Let's say we have identified a set of such propositions each of which *S* believes. Then he is justified in believing that *p* only if he is justified in believing each of those propositions.[9] And, for each of these propositions *q*, *r*, . . . that he is not immediately justified in believing, he is justified in believing it only if he is justified in believing some other propositions that are suitably related to it. And for each of these latter propositions . . .

Thus in attempting to give a definitive answer to the original question we are led to construct a more or less extensive true structure, in which the original belief and every other putatively mediately justified belief form nodes from which one or more branches issue, in such a way that every branch is a part of some branch that issues from the original belief. Now the question is: what form must be assumed by the structure in order that *S* be mediately justified in believing that *p?* There are the following conceivable forms for a given branch:

A. It terminates in an immediately justified belief.
B. It terminates in an unjustified belief.
C. The belief that *p* occurs at some point (past the origin), so that the branch forms a loop.
D. The branch continues infinitely.

Of course some branches might assume one form and others another.

The argument is that the original belief will be mediately justified only if every branch assumes form A. Positively, it is argued that on this condition the relevant necessary condition for the original belief's being mediately justified is satisfied, and, negatively, it is argued that if any branch assumes any of the other forms, is not.

A. Where every branch has form A, this necessary condition is satisfied for every belief in the structure. Since each branch terminates in an immediately justified belief that is justified without necessity for further justified beliefs, the regress is ended along each branch. Hence justification is transferred along each branch right back to the original belief.
B. For any branch that exhibits form B, no element, even the origin, is justified, at least by this structure. Since the terminus is not justified, the prior element, which is justified only if the terminus is, is not justified. And, since it is not justified, its predecessor, which is justified only if it is, is not justified either. And so on, right back to the origin, which therefore itself fails to be justified.
C. Where we have a branch that forms a closed loop, again nothing on that branch, even the origin, is justified, so far as its justification depends on this tree structure. For what the branch "says" is that the belief that *p* is justified only if the belief that *r* is justified, and that belief is justified only if. . . , and the belief that *z* is justified only if the belief that *p* is justified. So what this chain of necessary conditions tells us is that the belief that *p* is justified only if the belief that *p* is justified. True enough, but that still leaves it completely open whether the belief that *p* is justified.
D. If there is a branch with no terminus, that means that no matter how far we extend the branch the last element is still a belief that is mediately justified if at all. Thus, as far as this structure goes, wherever we stop adding elements we have still not shown that the relevant necessary condition for the mediate justification of the original belief is satisfied. Thus the structure does not exhibit the original belief as mediately justified.

[9]I am adopting the simplifying assumption that, for each mediately justified belief, there is only one set of adequate grounds that *S* justifiably believes. The argument can be formulated so as to allow for "overjustification," but at the price of further complexity.

Hence the original belief is mediately justified only if every branch in the tree structure terminates in an immediately justified belief. Hence every mediately justified belief stands at the origin of a tree structure at the tip of each branch of which is an immediately justified belief.[10]

Now this version of the argument, analogues of which occur frequently in the literature,[11] supports only simple foundationalism. It has no tendency to show that there is immediately justified epistemic belief. So long as *S is* directly justified in believing some *t* for each branch of the tree, that will be quite enough to stop the regress; for all that is needed is that he *be* justified in believing *t* without thereby incurring the need to be justified in believing some further proposition. But perhaps there are other versions that yield the stronger conclusion. Indeed, in surveying the literature one will discover versions that differ from A2 is one or both of the following respects:

1. Their starting points (the conditions of which they seek to establish) are cases of being justified in believing that one knows (is justified in believing) that *p*, rather than, more generally, cases of being justified in believing that *p*.
2. They are concerned to establish what is necessary for *showing* that *p*, rather than what is necessary for *being justified* in believing that *p*.

Let's consider whether regress arguments with one or the other of these features will yield iterative foundationalism.

First let's consider an argument that differs from A2 only in the first respect. In his essay "Theory of Knowledge" in a volume devoted to the history of twentieth-century American philosophy, R. M. Chisholm[12] launches a regress argument as follows:

To the question "What justification do I have for thinking that I know that *a* is true?" one may reply: "I know that *b* is true, and if I know that *b* is true then I also know that *a* is true." And to the question "What justification do I have for thinking I know that *b* is

---

[10]The weakest link in this argument is the rejection of D. So far as I am aware, this alternative is never adequately explained, and much less is adequate reason given for its rejection. Usually, I fear, *being justified* is confused with exhibiting one's justification, and it is argued (irrelevantly) that one cannot do the latter for an infinite sequence of propositions. It is interesting in this connection that in two very recent attacks on foundationalism the infinite regress rejected by the regress argument is construed as a regress of *showing justification,* and in different ways the critics argue that the impossibility of completing an infinite sequence of such showings does not imply that there may not *be* an infinite sequence of mediate justification. See Keith Lehrer, *Knowledge* (Oxford: Clarendon Press, 1974), pp. 15/6, and Frederick L. Will, *Induction and Justification* (Ithaca, N.Y.: Cornell, 1974), pp. 176–185.

An adequate treatment of the argument would involve looking into the possibility of an infinite structure of belief and the patterns of justification that can obtain there. Pending such an examination, the most one can say for the argument is that it is clear that mediate justification is possible on alternative A and not clear that it is possible on alternative D.

[11]See, e.g., Bertrand Russell, *Human Knowledge, Its Scope and Limits* (London: Allen & Unwin, 1948), p. 171; Anthony Quinton, *The Nature of Things* (London: Routledge & Kegan Paul, 1973), p. 119.

[12]*Philosophy* (Englewood Cliffs, N.J.: Prentice-Hall, 1964). Because of the ambiguity of the term "knowledge claim," formulations and criticisms of the argument are often ambiguous in the present respect. When we ask how a "knowledge claim" is justified, we may be asking what it takes to justify an assertion that *p* or we may be asking what it takes to justify a claim that one knows that *p*. Thus, e.g., we find Arthur Danto beginning the argument by speaking of *m* being justified in asserting *s* but then sliding into a consideration of what it takes to justify "claims to know" [*Analytical Philosophy of Knowledge* (New York: Cambridge, 1968), pp. 26–28].

true?" one may reply: "I know that c is true, and if I know that c is true then I also know that b is true." Are we thus led, sooner or later, to something, n, of which one may say "What justifies me in thinking I know that n is true is simply the fact than n is true"? (263)

Chisholm then supports an affirmative answer to this last question by excluding other alternatives in a manner similar to that of A2.

Now the crucial question is: why does Chisholm conclude not just that mediate justification of claims to know requires *some* immediately justified beliefs, but that it requires immediately justified *epistemic* beliefs? Of course, having granted the general position that any mediately justified belief rests on some immediately justified belief(s), it is natural to suppose that mediately justified *epistemic* beliefs will rest on immediately justified *epistemic* beliefs. But we should not assume that all cases of mediate knowledge rest on foundations that are similar in content. On the contrary, every version of foundationalism holds that from a certain set of basic beliefs one erects a superstructure that is vastly different from these foundations. From knowledge of sense data one derives knowledge of public physical objects, from knowledge of present occurrences one derives knowledge of the past and future, and so on. So why suppose that *if* mediate epistemic beliefs rest on foundations, those foundations will be epistemic beliefs? We would need some special reason for this. And neither Chisholm nor, to my knowledge, anyone else has given any such reason. All rely on essentially the same argument as A2, which at most yields the weaker conclusion. They seem to have just assumed uncritically that the foundations on which epistemic beliefs rest are themselves epistemic.[13]

Thus, altering the regress argument in the first way does not provide grounds for iterative foundationalism. Let's turn to the second modification. In order to maximize our chances, let's combine it with the first, and consider what it would take to *show*, for some p, that I am justified in believing that p.[14] It is easy to see

---

[13]Lest this assumption still seem obvious to some of my readers, let me take a moment to indicate how mediate epistemic knowledge might conceivably be derived from nonepistemic foundations. Let's begin the regress with Chisholm and follow the line of the first ground he mentions: that I justifiably believe that b. (To simplify this exposition I am replacing "know" with "justifiably believe" throughout.) By continuing to raise the same question we will at last arrive at a c such that I have *immediate* justification for believing that c. Here my justification (for believing that I justifiably believe that c) will shift from one or more other justified beliefs to the appropriate "warrant-increasing" property. What is then required at the next stage is a justification for supposing the belief that c to have this property, and for supposing that this property does confer warrant. It is highly controversial just how claims like these are to be justified, but, in any event, at this point we have exited from the arena of explicit claims to being justified in a certain belief; what needs justification from here on are beliefs as to what is in fact the case, and beliefs as to what principles of evaluation are valid, not beliefs as to my epistemic relation to these matters. And, without attempting to go into the details, it seems plausible that, if a foundationalist view is tenable at all, these sorts of beliefs will rest on the same sort of foundation as other factual and evaluative beliefs.

[14]I have not located a clear-cut example of a regress argument with this starting point and with the conclusion in question. Nevertheless, the prospect seems tempting enough to be worth deflating. Moreover, it forces us to raise interesting questions concerning the concept of showing.

Just as the ambiguity of "knowledge claim" led to versions' of the regress argument being indeterminate with respect to the earlier feature, so the process-product ambiguity of terms like "justification" and "justified" often make it uncertain whether a philosopher is talking about what it takes for a belief to *be* justified or about what it takes to *justify* a belief in the sense of *showing* it to be justified. See, e.g., C. I. Lewis, *An Analysis of Knowledge and Valuation* (La Salle, Ill.: Open Court, 1946), p. 187; Leonard Nelson, "The Impossibility of the 'Theory of Knowledge'," in Chisholm & Swartz, *op. cit.*, p. 8.

how one might be led into this. One who accepted the previous argument might still feel dissatisfied with simple foundationalism. "You have shown," he might say, "that it is *possible* to be justified in believing that *p* without having any immediately justified epistemic belief. But are we *in fact* justified in believing any *p?* To answer that question you will have to *show,* for some *p, that* you are justified in believing it. And the question is, what is required for that? Is it possible to do that without immediately justified epistemic belief?"

Now if we are to show, via a regress argument, that immediately justified epistemic belief is necessary for showing that I am justified in believing any *p*, it must be because some requirement for showing sets up a regress than can only be stopped if we have such beliefs. What could that requirement be? Let's see what is required for showing that *p*. Clearly, to show that *p* I must adduce some other (possibly compound) proposition, *q*. What restrictions must be put on a *q* and my relations thereto?

1. It is true that *q*.[15]
2. *q* constitutes adequate grounds for *p*.

These requirements give rise to no regress, or at least none that is vicious. Even if no proposition can be true without some other proposition's being true, there is nothing repugnant about the notion of an infinity of true propositions. Hence we may pass on.

3. I am justified in believing that *q*.[16]

This requirement clearly does give rise to a regress, viz., that already brought out in A2. We have seen that immediately justified epistemic belief is not required to end that regress; so again we may pass on.

4. I am justified in believing that I am justified in believing that *q*.

I am not prepared to admit this requirement, my reasons being closely connected with the point that one may be justified in believing that *q* without even believing that one is so justified, much less being justified in believing that one is so justified. However, it is not necessary to discuss that issue here. Even if 4 is required, it will simply set up a regress of the sort exemplified by Chisholm's argument, an argument we have seen to have no stronger conclusion than simple foundationalism.

5. I am able to show that *q*.

This looks more promising. Clearly this requirement gives rise to a regress that is different from that of A2. If I can show that *p* by citing *q* only if I am able to show

---

[15]It may also be required that *p* be true, on the ground that it makes no sense to speak of my having shown what is not the case. ("Show" is a success concept.) I neglect this point since it has no bearing on our present problem.

[16]One may contest this requirement on the grounds that, if I have produced what is in fact a true adequate ground, that is all that should be demanded. And it may be that there is some "objective" concept of showing of which this is true. Nevertheless where we are interested in whether *Jones* has shown that *p* (rather than just whether "it has been shown that *p*," where perhaps all we are interested in is whether there *are* true adequate grounds), it seems that we must adopt this requirement in order to exclude wildly accidental cases in which Jones is asserting propositions at random and just happens to hit the mark.

that *q,* and if, in turn, I am able to show that *q* by citing *r* only if I am able to show that *r,* it is clear that we will be able to avoid our familiar alternatives of circularity and infinite regress, only if at some point I arrive at a proposition that I can show to be correct without appealing to some other proposition. In deciding whether this argument provides support for iterative foundationalism, we must consider first whether requirement 5 is justified and, second, whether immediately justified epistemic belief would stop the regress so generated.

The requirement looks plausible. For, if I cannot show that *q,* then it looks as if I won't be able to settle whether or not it is the case that *q,* and in that case how can I claim to have settled the question about *p?* But this plausibility is specious, stemming from one of the protean forms assumed by that confusion of levels typified by the confusion of knowing that *p* with knowing that one knows that *p.* It's quite true that an inability to show that *q* will prevent me from showing *that I have shown that p;* for to do the latter I have to show that the grounds I have cited for *p* are correct. But why suppose that it also prevents me from showing that *p?* Can't I prove a theorem in logic without being able to prove that I have proved it? The former requires only an ability to wield the machinery of first-order logic, which one may possess without the mastery of metalogic required for the second. Similarly, it would seem that I can show that *p,* by adducing true adequate grounds I am justified in accepting, without being able to *show* that those grounds are true.

This conclusion is reinforced by the point that it is all too possible to *have* adequate grounds for a belief without being able to articulate them. Having observed Jones for a while, I may *have* adequate reasons for supposing him to be unsure of himself, without being able to specify just what features of his bearing and behavior provide those reasons. A philosophically unsophisticated person (and many of the philosophically sophisticated as well) may be amply justified in believing that there is a tree in front of his wide-open eyes, but not be able to show that he is so justified. I may be justified in believing that Louis IX reigned in the thirteenth century, since I acquired that belief on excellent authority, but not now be able to specify that authority, much less *show* that it is reliable. Of course in the case under discussion, I am able to articulate my grounds for *p,* for *ex hypothesi* I have adduced adequate grounds for *p.* But to suppose that it is reasonable to require that I be able to *show* that those grounds are true, and the grounds of these grounds, and . . . is to ignore the elementary point that a person may *have* adequate grounds for *q* and so be in an epistemically sound position vis-à-vis *q,* without being able to articulate those grounds. The latter ability is the exception rather than the rule with mediately justified belief.

But even if requirement 5 were justified and the show-regress were launched, immediately justified epistemic beliefs would be powerless to stop it. Let's say that I originally set out to show that I am justified in believing that *a,* and in the regress of showings thus generated I eventually cite as a ground *that I am immediately justified in believing that z* (call this higher-level proposition "*Z*"), where I am in fact immediately justified in believing that *Z.* How will this latter fact enable me to *show* that *Z?* As a result of being immediately justified in believing that *Z,* I may have no doubt about the matter; I may feel no need to show *myself* that *Z.* But of course that doesn't imply that I *have shown* that *Z.* However immediate my justification for accepting Z, I haven't *shown* that Z unless I adduce grounds for it that meet the appropriate conditions. And once I do that we are off to the races again. The regress has not been stopped. In the nature of the case it cannot be stopped. In this it differs from the original regress of *being* justified. *Showing* by its very nature requires the exhibition of grounds. Furthermore, grounds must be different from the proposition to be shown. (This latter follows from the "prag-matic" aspect of the concept of showing. To show that *p* is to present grounds that one can justifiably accept without already accepting *p*. Otherwise showing would lack the point that goes toward making it what it is.) Hence, there are no conceiv-able conditions under which I could show that *p* without citing other propositions that, by requirement 5, I must be able to show. If we accept requirement 5, if an infinite structure of abilities to show is ruled out, and if circularity is unacceptable, it follows that it is impossible ever to show anything. (That would seem to be an additional reason for rejecting 5.) Since immediately justified epistemic belief would do nothing to stop the regress, this kind of regress argument can provide no support for iterative foundationalism.

III. FUNCTIONS OF FOUNDATIONALISM

Thus, although simple foundationalism is strongly supported by A2, we have failed to find any argument that supports iterative foundationalism. And the second-level argument strikes at the latter but not the former. Hence it would seem that founda-tionalism has a chance of working only in its simple form. This being the case, it is of some interest to determine the extent to which simple foundationalism satisfies the demands and aspirations that foundationalism is designed to satisfy, other than stopping the regress of justification. I shall consider two such demands.

Answering Skepticism

Skepticism assumes various forms, many of which no sort of foundationalism could sensibly be expected to answer. For example, the extreme skeptic who refuses to accept anything until it has been shown to be true and who will not allow his oppo-nent any premises to use for this purpose, obviously cannot be answered whatever one's position. Talking with him is a losing game. Again there are more limited skepticisms in which one sort of knowledge is questioned (e.g., knowledge of the conscious states of other persons) but others are left unquestioned (e.g., knowledge of the physical environment). Here the answering will be done, if at all, by finding some way of deriving knowledge of the questioned sort from knowledge of the unquestioned sort. The role of a general theory of knowledge will be limited to lay-ing down criteria for success in the derivation, and differences over what is required for foundations would seem to make no difference to such criteria.

The kind of "answer to skepticism" that one might suppose to be affected by our difference is that in which the skeptic doubts that we have any knowledge, a successful answer being a demonstration there is some. One may think that the pos-session of immediate epistemic knowledge will put us in a better position to do that job. Whether it does, and if so how, depends on what it takes to show that one knows something. The discussion of showing in section II yielded the following conditions for *S*'s showing that *p:*

1. It is true that *p.*
2. *S* cites in support of *p* a certain proposition *q* such that:
    A. It is true that *q.*
    B. *q* is an adequate ground for *p.*
    C. *S* is justified in believing *q.*

We rejected the further condition that *S* be able to show that *q.* However, since we are here concerned with showing something to a skeptic, it may be that some further requirement should be imposed. After all, we could hardly expect a skeptic to abandon his doubt just on the *chance* that his interlocuter is correct in the grounds he gives. The skeptic will want to be given some reason for supposing those grounds to be correct; and this does not seem unreasonable. But we can't go back to the unqualified requirement that every ground adduced be established or even establishable, without automatically making showing impossible. Fortunately there is an intermediate requirement that might satisfy a reasonable skeptic while not rendering all showing impossible. Let's require that *S* be able to show that *r,* for any *r* among his grounds concerning which his audience has any real doubt. This differs from the unqualified requirement in leaving open the possibility that there will be grounds concerning which no reasonable person who has reflected on the matter will have any doubt; and if there be such it may still be possible for *S* to succeed in showing that *p.* Thus we may add to our list of conditions:

    D. If there is real doubt about *q, S* is able to show that *q.*

Now when *p* is "*S* knows that *a,*" the question is whether one or more of these conditions is satisfiable only if *S* has immediately justified epistemic beliefs. Let's consider the conditions in turn. As for 1, *S* can in fact know that *a* without having any directly justified epistemic belief, even if it should be the case that one can't know that *a* without knowing that one knows that *a.* For, as we saw in section II, there is no reason to doubt that all justified beliefs that one knows or is justified in believing something are themselves *mediately* justified. As for 2A and 2B, there should be no temptation to suppose that they depend on iterative foundationalism. Surely the grounds I adduce for the claim to know that *a* can be true and adequate without my having any immediately justified epistemic beliefs. Even if one or more of the grounds should themselves be claims to knowledge, the question of what is required for their truth can be handled in the same way as requirement 1. And adequacy, being a matter of relations between propositions, cannot depend on what sort of justification *S* has for one or another belief. As for 2C, the discussion in sections I and II failed to turn up any reasons for supposing that immediately justified epistemic belief is required for my being justified in believing anything. That leaves 2D. But this has already been covered. To satisfy 2D I have to be able to *show* that (some of) my grounds are true. But that will not require conditions that are different in kind from those already discussed. Hence we may conclude that iterative foundationalism is not a presupposition of our showing that we do have knowledge. Of course it remains an open question whether we are in fact capable of showing that we know something. But if we are incapable, it is not because of the lack of immediately justified epistemic belief.

Self-Consciously Reconstructing Knowledge from the Foundations

What I have in mind here is the enterprise classically exemplified by Descartes in the *Meditations*. There Descartes first sets out to identify those items for which there could not be any grounds for doubt. Having done so, he seeks to use these items as a basis for showing than other items are known as well. Now we cannot assimilate Descartes to our scheme without some adjustments. For one thing, Descartes required indubitability and infallibility of his foundations. For another, he was not working with a true-justified-belief conception of knowledge. Translating Descartes into the conception of knowledge we are using and ignoring the extra demands of indubitability and infallibility, it is clear that Descartes takes his foundational beliefs to be immediately justified. I am justified in believing that I exist or that I am presently thinking about epistemology, regardless of what else I may be justified in believing. I am so justified just by the fact that the belief "records" the content of a clear and distinct intuition of the fact that makes the belief true. Hence, in order to *identify* a belief, *B,* as foundational Descartes must be justified in the higher-level belief that *B* is immediately justified. And if he is to perform this identification at the outset of his reconstruction, when nothing is recognized as mediately justified, this justification must be immediate, since he lacks a suitable body of other beliefs on which to base it.[17] Hence this enterprise is possible only if one can be immediately justified in taking a certain belief to be immediately justified. Here, then, is a point at which iterative foundationalism is genuinely needed.[18]

If iterative foundationalism is both without strong support and subject to crushing objections, it looks as if we will have to do without a self-conscious reconstruction of knowledge. How grievous a loss is this? Why should anyone want to carry out such a reconstruction? Well, if knowledge does have a foundational structure it seems intolerable that we should be unable to spell this out. And it may seem that such a spelling out would have to take the present form. But that would be an illusion. If there are foundations, one can certainly identify them and determine how other sorts of knowledge are based on them without first taking on the highly artificial stance assumed by Descartes in the *Meditations*. One can approach this

---

[17]To be sure, this short treatment leaves open the abstract possibility that the first such higher-level belief might be justified by some of the lower-level beliefs among the current foundations (if indeed the rules of the game permit their use in justification without first having been justifiably recognized *as* immediately justified). But it is clear that the foundational beliefs Descartes recognizes are radically unsuitable for this employment.

[18]Descartes apparently felt that he was required not only to *identify* his foundations as such before building anything on them, but also to *show* at that stage that each of the foundations had the required status. And not even iterative foundationalism could help him with that. In the attempt to show that he immediately knows that, e.g., 2 plus 2 equals 4, he is inevitably and notoriously led to make use of premises the knowledge of which needs to be shown just as much or as little as the proposition with which he begins.

problem, as one approaches any other, making use of whatever relevant knowledge or justified belief one already possesses. In that case immediate epistemic knowledge is by no means required, just as we have seen it is not required to show that one is justified in holding certain beliefs.

The Cartesian program has been branded as unrealistic on more grounds than one. And if I am right in holding that the simple form of foundationalism is the most we can have, I have provided one more ground. If iterative foundationalism is false, we can still have as much epistemic knowledge as you like, but only after we have acquired quite a lot of first-level knowledge. And why should that not satisfy any epistemic aspirations that are fitting for the human condition?

IV. ENVOI

As we have seen, the main reason for adopting foundationalism is the seeming impossibility of a belief's being mediately justified without resting ultimately on immediately justified belief. And the main reason for rejecting it (at least the main antecedent reason, apart from the difficulties of working it out) is than reason one version of which we found in the quotation from Aune. That is, it appears that the foundationalist is committed to adopting beliefs in the absence of any reasons for regarding them as acceptable. And this would appear to be the sheerest dogmatism. It is the aversion to dogmatism, to the apparent arbitrariness of putative foundations, that leads many philosophers to embrace some form of coherence or contextualist theory, in which no belief is deemed acceptable unless backed by sound reasons.

The main burden of this paper is that with simple foundationalism one can have the best of both arguments; one can stop the regress of justification without falling into dogmatism. We have already seen that Aune's form of the dogmatism argument does not touch Simple Foundationalism. For that form of the argument attacks only the ungrounded acceptance of claims *to knowledge or justification;* and simple foundationalism is not committed to the immediate justification of any such higher-level claims. But one may seek to apply the same argument to lower-level beliefs. Even simple foundationalism, the critic may say, must allow that some beliefs may be accepted in the absence of any reasons for supposing them to be true. And this is still arbitrary dogmatism. But the simple foundationalist has an answer. His position does not require anyone to accept any belief without having a reason for doing so. Where a person *is* immediately justified in believing that *p,* he may find adequate reasons for the higher-level belief that he is immediately justified in believing than *p.* And if he has adequate reasons for accepting this epistemic proposition, it surely is not arbitrary of him to accept the proposition that *p.* What better reason could he have for accepting it?

Lest the reader dismiss this answer as a contemptible piece of sleight-of-hand, let me be more explicit about what is involved. Though the simple foundationalist requires *some* immediately justified beliefs in order to terminate the regress of justification, his position permits him to recognize that all epistemic beliefs require mediate justification. Therefore, for any belief that one is immediately justified in believing, one *may* find adequate reasons for accepting the proposition that one is so justified. The curse (of dogmatism) is taken off immediate justification at the lower level, just by virtue of the fact that propositions at the higher level are acceptable only on the basis of reasons. A foundational belief, *b,* is immediately justified just because some valid epistemic principle lays down conditions for its being justified which do not include the believer's having certain other justified beliefs. But the believer will be justified in believing *that* he is immediately justified in holding *b* only if he has *reasons* for regarding that principle as valid and for regarding *b* as falling under that principle. And if he does have such reasons he certainly cannot be accused of arbitrariness or dogmatism in accepting *b.* The absence of reasons for *b* is "compensated" for by the reasons for the correlated higher-level belief. Or, better, the sense in which one can have reasons for accepting an immediately justified belief is necessarily different from that in which one can have reasons for accepting a mediately justified belief. Reasons in the former case are necessarily "meta" in character; they have to do with reasons for regarding the belief as justified. Whereas in the latter case, though one *may* move up a level and find reasons for the higher-level belief that the original belief is mediately justified, it is also required that one have adequate reasons for the lower-level belief itself.

We should guard against two possible misunderstandings of the above argument. First, neither simple foundationalism nor any other epistemology can guarantee that one will, or can, find adequate reasons for a given epistemic proposition, or for any other proposition. The point rather is that there is nothing in the position that rules out the possibility that, for any immediately justified belief that one has, one can find adequate reasons for the proposition that one is so justified. Second, we should not take the critic to be denying the obvious point that people are often well advised, in the press of everyday life, to adopt beliefs for which they do not have adequate reasons. We should interpret him as requiring only that an *ideal* epistemic subject will adopt beliefs only for good and sufficient reason. Hence he insists that our epistemology must make room for this possibility. And, as just pointed out, Simple Foundationalism does so.

The dogmatism argument may be urged with respect to *showing* that *p,* as well as with respect to accepting the proposition that *p.* That is, the critic may argue that foundationalism is committed to the view that "foundations cannot be argued for." Suppose that in trying to show that *p* I adduce some grounds, and, the grounds being challenged, I try to show that they are true, and . . . in this regress I finally arrive at some foundation *f.* Here, according to the critic, the foundationalist must hold that the most I can (properly) do is simply *assert f,* several times if necessary, and with increasing volume. And again this is dogmatism. But again Simple Foundationalism is committed to no such thing. It leaves something for the arguer to do even here, viz., try to establish the higher-level proposition that he is immediately justified in believing that *f.* And, if he succeeds in doing this, what more could we ask? Unless someone demands that he go on to establish the grounds appealed to in that argument—to which again the simple foundationalist has no objection in principle. Of course, as we saw earlier, the demand that one establish every ground in a demonstration is a self-defeating demand. But the point is that the simple foundationalist need not, any more than the coherence theorist, mark out certain points at which the regress of showing *must* come to an end. He allows the possibility of one's giving reasons for an assertion whenever it is appropriate to do so, even if that assertion is of a foundation.

But, like many positions that give us the best of both worlds, this one may be too good to be true. Although I am convinced that simple foundationalism is the most defensible form of foundationalism, especially if it also divests itself of other gratuitous claims for foundations, such as infallibility and incorrigibility,[19] I do not claim that it can actually be made to work. Though it escapes the main antecedent objection, it still faces all the difficulties involved in finding enough immediately justified beliefs to ground all our mediately justified beliefs. And on this rock I suspect it will founder. Meanwhile, pending a final decision on that question, it is the version on which both constructive and critical endeavors should be concentrated.

---

[19]For a position that approximates this, see Anthony Quinton, *The Nature of Things* (London: Routledge & Kegan Paul, 1973), pt. II.

PART THREE

Philosophy of Mind, Freedom, and Determinism

As I sit with others at a great feast, suddenly while the music is playing,
To my mind, (whence it comes I know not,) spectral in mist of a wreck at sea, . . .
A huge sob—a few bubbles—the white foam spirting up—and then the women gone,
Sinking there while the passionless wet flows on—and I now pondering, Are those
women indeed gone?
Are souls drown'd and destroy'd so?
Is only matter triumphant?

—Walt Whitman
"Thought," Whispers of Heavenly Death, *Leaves of Grass,* 1892

- René Descartes, *Meditations on First Philosophy,* Meditations II, VI (excerpt)
- Franz Brentano, The Distinction Between Mental and Physical Phenomena (excerpt)
- U.T. Place, Is Consciousness a Brain Process?
- Frank C. Jackson, Epiphenomenal Qualia
- Alan M. Turing, Computing Machinery and Intelligence
- John Searle, Can Computers Think? (excerpt)
- Daniel C. Dennett, Can Machines Think? (excerpt)
- Arthur Schopenhauer, *Essay on Freedom of the Will* (excerpt)
- Gilbert Ryle, The Will (excerpt)
- Stuart Hampshire and H. L. A. Hart, Decision, Intention and Certainty
- Roderick M. Chisholm, Freedom and Action (excerpt)

We are thinking beings, creatures with minds who are capable of thought. But what is thought, and what is the mind? We are also creatures with bodies, with brains and nervous systems that we have good evidence for believing are causally connected with our ability to think, and with the actual content of our thoughts. The question naturally arises, then, whether our minds are the same as or different from our brains.

The mind-body problem is the philosophical challenge of understanding the relation between mind and body. We know that the condition of our brains and nervous systems has something to do with our thinking. Persons who suffer brain injury may be seriously diminished in their ability to think, and we can experience less drastic effects on the mind that result from other kinds of physiological changes, such as lack of sleep or food, or the effects of drugs and alcohol. But are our minds only no more than, or strictly identical with, our bodies? Or are our minds something different from our bodies, whose mental events are at most merely correlated with, but not actually identical to, physical brain and nervous system events?

The mind has also seemed to be different from the body—so different as to lead some philosophers to suppose that the mind could be causally free of determining events in the physical world. As a further consequence, it also has been argued that the mind is capable of surviving death as the immortal soul of religious faith. Thoughts do not immediately seem to be material things. They do not obviously have color or weight or definite location in physical space, even if they occur at particular times. For all that, it seems to make sense to say that Einstein first thought of the theory of general relativity in Vienna, and later thought of it again when he had moved to Princeton, New Jersey. What is more, materialists argue that if mind and brain are identical, then, despite superficial appearances to the contrary, thoughts must after all have color, weight, and definite spatial location, since in that case they are nothing other than specific brain events. If the mind-body problem is answered by saying that mind and body are identical rather than distinct, then a scientific psychology seems to exclude the concept of soul as it is usually understood. Free will and moral responsibility might then be illusory, and it might be impossible for the mind to survive the death of the body as an immortal soul, to carry on the experiences of a distinctive personality's thoughts, memories, beliefs, and expectations.

Descartes, in the continuation of his *Meditations on First Philosophy,* in Meditations II and VI, offers two arguments for the distinction between mind and body. The arguments jointly constitute a defense of what has since come to be known as Cartesian dualism. Descartes assumes that mind and body are identical if and only if they have all of their properties in common. He proposes to show that mind and body are not identical by discovering a property that the mind has but that the body does not have, or that the body has but the mind does not have. In Meditation II, Descartes argues that mind and body are nonidentical because the mind has the property of being better knowable than the body, or of being such that, unlike the body, the mind's existence cannot consistently be doubted. The justification for this conclusion is that the evil demon of Meditation I might deceive a thinker about the existence of the body, but that in order to doubt, the mind must exist, since doubting is itself a mental occurrence. This last argument is summed up in the famous Cartesian slogan, *Cogito, ergo sum*—I think, therefore I am. In Meditation VI, Descartes tries to show that mind is not identical to body because the body, unlike the mind, has the property of being divisible into like independently existing parts. The body, the brain, and nervous system, as material entities, can be carved up into multiple smaller material entities. But the mind, although it can shrink or expand by losing previous or taking on new beliefs, memories, and other thought contents, cannot be divided up into smaller independently existing minds as discrete thinking entities. It follows, according to Descartes, that the mind is not identical to the body, because mind and body do not have all of the same properties. Descartes's Meditation VI proof for mind-body nonidentity also purports to prove the immortality of the soul. The reasoning is that the mind as spiritual substance, by contrast with the body as material substance, cannot be destroyed, since only divisible things can be destroyed by breaking them down into their component parts. If Descartes's second argument is correct, then the mind or soul is indivisible, and as such has no parts into which it can be broken.

Although Descartes's discussion of body and mind has enjoyed both prestige and notoriety in the history of philosophy, there have also been devastating criticisms of Cartesian mind-body dualism. Descartes's theory has been lauded because of its rational support for beliefs about the apparent differences between mind and body that undergird religious faith in the immateriality and immortality of the soul, which is explicitly part of Descartes's purpose. But there are difficulties in Descartes's metaphysics of mind. Among the objections, philosophers have worried about the problem of accounting for the causal interaction between body and mind. Descartes wants to be able to say that what happens to the body can affect the mind, and conversely. But how can there be any causal connection between material substance located in a definite spatial location and spiritual substance existing entirely outside of space? How can something material that exists in space touch and be touched by something spiritual or immaterial that does not exist in space?

Franz Brentano, in a selection from his *Psychology from an Empirical Standpoint,* distinguishes between mental and physical phenomena on the basis of the intentionality, "aboutness," or object-directedness of thought, and the nonintentionality of the purely physical. Brentano's criterion of intentionality as the "mark of the mental" establishes a difference between mental and physical properties. The idea of intentionality is that to think is to think about something, whether we believe, doubt, hope, fear, expect, or engage in any mental activity whatsoever. If Brentano is right, then the same is not true of any purely physical occurrence. A brain event, considered only as such, is not about or does not intend anything, no more than a rock or lump of iron or even a nonthinking living thing like a tree or a fungus is about or intends anything. What remains unclear in Brentano's distinction is whether or to what extent the intentionality of thought may have implications for the freedom of the will or the immortality of the soul.

The materialist point of view that identifies body with mind is represented in U. T. Place's insightful essay, "Is Consciousness a Brain Process?" Although Place titles his article as a question, his purpose is to remove conceptual obstacles that would otherwise stand in the way of regarding mind and brain as one and the same. He champions the possibility of a materialist mind-brain identity theory as an appropriate scientific concept of the nature of consciousness. Although materialism in a mind-body identity theory simplifies the metaphysics of mind and makes psychology a branch of physics, it also has widely recognized philosophical drawbacks. A main problem with materialism is that it limits the embodiment of thought to particular kinds of material substances, whereas we might suppose that thought could be instantiated in different types of physical stuff. There is no reason to assume that thought can only be produced by carbon-based life-forms like ourselves, if it is logically possible for thought also to occur in the nonhuman brain chemistry of the brains or comparable thinking organs of, say, silicon-based extraterrestrials.

The concept of mind is arguably more abstract than of something made of any specific material substances. Functionalism is an alternative philosophy of mind that avoids some of the limitations of materialism. It has become very popular with many philosophers and cognitive scientists in psychology, as well as computer researchers in artificial intelligence. Functionalism is the theory that the mind can be explained in terms of an information processing model, in which the input-output flow and control of information is processed by the brain as a living computer. The brain is the hardware machine, according to functionalism, in which the mind is the functioning software. Among the interesting consequences of functionalism is the idea that the mind is in principle transportable to many different kinds of machines, provided only that they are materially capable of running the requisite information processing program with which the mind is identified. If functionalism is true, then even nonliving machines like computers loaded with the right software might not only simulate but actually duplicate mental phenomena, as artificial but nonetheless genuinely thinking self-conscious minds.

Frank C. Jackson, in his influential paper, "Epiphenomenal Qualia," offers a thought experiment about reductive theories of mind. He argues that efforts to explain mental phenomena from the standpoint of the third-person hard psychological sciences, such as behaviorism, cognitive psychology, and the information sciences, including artificial intelligence, are doomed to inadequacy by virtue of failing to include essential reference to the first-person qualia of experience. Jackson's thought experiment involves a color scientist who learns all there is to know about color through reading and by means of black and white television monitors, but has had no first-person experience of color. Jackson maintains that if a reductive philosophy of mind were adequate to explain mental phenomena, then the color scientist could not learn anything new about the experience of color by having her own first-person color experience. Yet, when we imagine the experiment taking place, and the color scientist finally experiencing color for herself for the first time, it seems impossible to deny that she will learn something new, namely what colors are like or what it is like to experience color. In a word, the color scientist learns about the qualia of color sensation.

The problem of artificial intelligence and the mechanical model of mind is considered in essays by Alan M. Turing, John Searle, and Daniel C. Dennett. Turing's classic paper of 1950, "Computing Machinery and Intelligence," sets forth the Imitation Game, or what has since come to be known as the Turing Test, as an operational criterion of machine intelligence. Turing imagines an interrogator asking questions of either a mind or a machine over a teletype, with a machine programmed to imitate the intelligent answers that would likely be given by a mind. If the interrogator cannot tell the difference in a significant percentage of cases, then,

Turing argues, the machine wins the Imitation Game or passes the Turing Test. Turing interprets this as the only appropriate answer to the question he proposes to substitute for the meaningless but irresistible problem of whether machines can think, which he regards as too vague for serious philosophical consideration. Turing perhaps conservatively predicts that by the year 2000 computing machines will have advanced to such a state of the art that they will have sufficiently capacious memory storage to play and win the Imitation Game so effectively as to deceive an average interrogator in more than 70 percent of applications. The idea of a machine dedicated to winning the Imitation Game or passing the Turing Test has been widely adopted as an ideal to which many artificial intelligence programmers aspire, but continues to fuel philosophical controversy about the concept of mind, the problem of whether the mind is a machine, and of whether it is possible to manufacture mechanical conscious minds.

The concept of strong or artificial intelligence, of a computer that does not just imitate but actually replicates conscious intelligence, is challenged by John Searle in his much discussed thought experiment of the Chinese Room. The version of the argument included here is not from Searle's original statement in his essay "Minds, Machines and Programs," from the journal *Behavioral and Brain Sciences,* but appears in Searle's 1984 Reith Lectures, broadcast on the BBC and published as a short book under the title *Minds, Brains and Science.* The Chinese Room is an imaginary chamber in which a non-Chinese speaker receives from a Turing Test interrogator questions written in Chinese and produces answers to them by following the instructions in a rulebook by which the shapes of Chinese calligraphy characters input to the room are correlated with other characters that are then issued as output, without the person who mediates the exchange of symbols having any understanding of their meaning. The Chinese Room seems to pass the Turing Test, but without the room itself or any part of it understanding the Chinese questions or answers processed to and from the interrogator. Searle concludes that the Chinese Room disproves the Turing Test as an adequate criterion of machine intelligence, at the same time that it invalidates functionalism and other types of mechanism as adequate solutions to the mind-body problem, and defeats strong artificial intelligence and mind-body reductivism as the philosophical ideology of cognitive science.

Dennett revisits the problem of artificial intelligence in "Can Machines Think?" He remarks that the Turing Test is applied daily in the conversational interactions in which we evaluate the empirical evidence that there are intelligent beings other than oneself. Dennett defends the Turing Test as the best criterion of machine intelligence, but he observes that the test is often misapplied. He compares the Turing Test with other methods of judging intelligence and concludes that it is a sufficiently rigorous way of deciding whether a mechanical system is intelligent. He recognizes that machines in the foreseeable future are unlikely to be able to pass the Turing Test. But he believes that in principle a machine could pass the test and declares himself ready in that case to agree that such a machine thinks in the true and full sense of the word.

The freedom of the will and its implications for moral responsibility are further explored in a concluding suite of essays. The topic directly links problems about the metaphysics of mind with some of the key presuppositions of ethics and moral philosophy. The issues concern whether it is possible for the mind to be free, and whether it is possible for an agent to be morally responsible if the mind is not free. If, as materialist identity and functionalist theories of mind have it, the mind is a purely physical or purely functional entity, then a correct theory of mind seems to preclude free will and moral responsibility. The free will controversy goes to the heart of philosophical questions about the kinds of beings we thinkers are.

We begin the discussion with a selection from Arthur Schopenhauer's lucid *Essay on Freedom of the Will.* Schopenhauer distinguishes between several meanings of "freedom" and argues that freedom cannot merely be freedom to do what we want if we are not also free to choose what we want. He elaborates a detailed philosophical theory of the nature of consciousness, arguing that there can be no freedom of will in the ordinary sense, but which nevertheless permits what he calls a higher transcendental sense of moral freedom, by which agents are responsible for their actions because they are constituted as individuals by what they will. Gilbert Ryle, in "The Will," from his influential book *The Concept of Mind,* similarly but for very different reasons maintains that freedom of the will is an illusion, and he concludes that our volitional vocabulary needs to be reinterpreted in light of the scientific study of mind as a dispositionally behavioristic physical system.

Stuart Hampshire and H. L. A. Hart collaborate in their essay, "Decision, Intention and Certainty," to argue that agents can be certain about their own voluntary actions. Acting, which is to say acting intentionally, is something of which an agent has immediate noninferential knowledge that establishes a necessary connection between intending to do something and doing it intentionally. The concept of reaching a decision to act precludes the agent's behavior from being accidental or mistaken, although Hampshire and Hart also acknowledge the possibility of intentional actions occurring that do not result from a conscious decision. The agent's firsthand knowledge of the intention to act bridges the philosophy of mind and the problem of free will and determinism through the theory of action by emphasizing the agent's intentions as essential to the concept of intending to act and thereby acting freely.

Finally, Roderick M. Chisholm, in this excerpt from his essay "Freedom and Action," defends a theory of agent causation, according to which actions are partly caused by persons, rather than entirely by other events. Chisholm's theory of agent causation is intended to run between the horns of the ancient dilemma of accounting for moral responsibility. If my actions are caused, then I can no more be morally responsible for them than any other purely physical event brought about by purely physical causes. But if my actions are not caused, then once again I cannot be morally responsible for them, since in that case as random and capricious they are not subject to my control. It is only by going beyond the limitations of the event-event causation model to a form of person-event causation that Chisholm sees a way to restore the concept of moral responsibility for actions.

Meditations on First Philosophy,
Meditations II, VI (excerpt)

René Descartes

Yesterday's meditation has thrown me into such doubts that I can no longer ignore them, yet I fail to see how they are to be resolved. It is as if I had suddenly fallen into a deep whirlpool; I am so tossed about that I can neither touch bottom with my foot, nor swim up to the top. Nevertheless I will work my way up and will once again attempt the same path I entered upon yesterday. I will accomplish this by putting aside everything that admits of the least doubt, as if I had discovered it to be completely false. I will stay on this course until I know something certain, or, if nothing else, until I at least know for certain that nothing is certain. Archimedes sought but one firm and immovable point in order to move the entire earth from one place to another. Just so, great things are also to be hoped for if I succeed in finding just one thing, however slight, that is certain and unshaken.

Therefore I suppose that everything I see is false. I believe that none of what my deceitful memory represents ever existed. I have no senses whatever. Body, shape, extension, movement, and place are all chimeras. What then will be true? Perhaps just the single fact that nothing is certain.

But how do I know there is not something else, over the above all those things that I have just reviewed, concerning which there is not even the slightest occasion for doubt? Is there not some God, or by whatever name I might call him, who instills these very thoughts, in me? But why would I think that, since I myself could perhaps be the author of these thoughts? Am I not then at least something? But I have already denied that I have any senses and any body. Still I hesitate; for what follows from this? Am I so tied to a body and to the senses that I cannot exist without them? But I have persuaded myself that there is absolutely nothing in the world: no sky, no earth, no minds, no bodies. Is it then the case that I too do not exist? But doubtless I did exist, if I persuaded myself of something. But there is some deceiver or other who is supremely powerful and supremely sly and who is always deliberately deceiving me. Then too there is no doubt that I exist, if he is deceiving me. And let him do his best at deception, he will never bring it about that I am nothing so long as I shall think that I am something. Thus, after everything has been most carefully weighed, it must finally be established that this pronouncement "I am, I exist" is necessarily true every time I utter it or conceive it in my mind.

But I do not yet understand sufficiently what I am—I, who now necessarily exist. And so from this point on, I must be careful lest I unwittingly mistake something else for myself, and thus err in that very item of knowledge that I claim to be the most certain and evident of all. Thus, I will meditate once more on what I once believed myself to be, prior to embarking upon these thoughts. For this reason, then, I will set aside whatever can be weakened even to the slightest degree by the arguments brought forward, so that eventually all that remains is precisely nothing but what is certain and unshaken.

What then did I use to think I was? A man, of course. But what is a man? Might I not say a "rational animal"? No, because then I would have to inquire what "animal" and "rational" mean. And thus from one question I would slide into many more difficult ones. Nor do I now have enough free time that I want to waste it on subtleties of this sort. Instead, permit me to focus here on what came spontaneously and naturally into my thinking whenever I pondered what I was. Now it occurred to me first that I had a face, hands, arms, and this entire mechanism of bodily members: the very same as are discerned in a corpse, and which I referred to by the name "body." It next occurred to me that I took in food, that I walked about, and that I sensed and thought various things; these actions I used to attribute to the soul. But as to what this soul might be, I either did not think about it or else I imagined it a rarified I-know-not-what, like a wind, or a fire, or ether, which had been infused into my coarser parts. But as to the body I was not in any doubt. On the contrary, I was under the impression that I knew its nature distinctly. Were I perhaps tempted to describe this nature such as I conceived it in my mind, I would have described it thus: by "body," I understand all that is capable of being bounded by some shape, of being enclosed in a place, and of filling up a space in such a way as to exclude any other body from it; of being perceived by touch, sight, hearing, taste, or smell; of being moved in several ways, not, of course, by itself, but by whatever else impinges upon it. For it was my view that the power of self-motion, and likewise of sensing or of thinking, in no way belonged to the nature of the body. Indeed I used rather to marvel that such faculties were to be found in certain bodies.

But now what am I, when I suppose that there is some supremely powerful and, if I may be permitted to say so, malicious deceiver who deliberately tries to fool me in any way he can? Can I not affirm that I possess at least a small measure of all those things which I have already said belong to the nature of the body? I focus my attention on them, I think about them, I review them again, but nothing comes to mind. I am tired of repeating this to no purpose. But what about those things I ascribed to the soul? What about being nourished or moving about? Since I now do not have a body, these are surely nothing but fictions. What about sensing? Surely this too does not take place without a body; and I seemed to have sensed in my dreams many things that I later realized I did not sense. What about thinking? Here I make my discovery: thought exists; it alone cannot be separated from me. I am; I exist—this is certain. But for how long? For as long as I am thinking; for perhaps it could also come to pass that if I were to cease all thinking I would then utterly cease to exist. At this time I admit nothing that is not necessarily true. I am therefore precisely nothing but a thinking thing; that is, a mind, or intellect, or understanding, or reason—words of whose meanings I was previously ignorant. Yet I am a true thing and am truly existing; but what kind of thing? I have said it already: a thinking thing.

What else am I? I will set my imagination in motion. I am not that concatenation of members we call the human body. Neither am I even some subtle air infused into these members, nor a wind, nor a fire, nor a vapor, nor a breath, nor anything

I devise for myself. For I have supposed these things to be nothing. The assumption still stands; yet nevertheless I am something. But is it perhaps the case that these very things which I take to be nothing, because they are unknown to me, nevertheless are in fact no different from that "me" that I know? This I do not know, and I will not quarrel about it now. I can make a judgment only about things that are known to me. I know that I exist; I ask now who is this "I" whom I know? Most certainly, in the strict sense the knowledge of this "I" does not depend upon things of whose existence I do not yet have knowledge. Therefore it is not dependent upon any of those things that I simulate in my imagination. But this word "simulate" warns me of my error. For I would indeed be simulating were I to "imagine" that I was something, because imagining is merely the contemplating of the shape or image of a corporeal thing. But I now know with certainty that I am and also that all these images—and, generally, everything belonging to the nature of the body—could turn out to be nothing but dreams. Once I have realized this, I would seem to be speaking no less foolishly were I to say: "I will use my imagination in order to recognize more distinctly who I am," than were I to say: "Now I surely am awake, and I see something true; but since I do not yet see it clearly enough, I will deliberately fall asleep so that my dreams might represent it to me more truly and more clearly." Thus I realize that none of what I can grasp by means of the imagination pertains to this knowledge that I have of myself. Moreover, I realize that I must be most diligent about withdrawing my mind from these things so that it can perceive its nature as distinctly as possible.

But what then am I? A thing that thinks. What is that? A thing that doubts, understands, affirms, denies, wills, refuses, and that also imagines and senses.

Indeed it is no small matter if all of these things belong to me. But why should they not belong to me? Is it not the very same "I" who now doubts almost everything, who nevertheless understands something, who affirms that this one thing is true, who denies other things, who desires to know more, who wishes not to be deceived, who imagines many things even against my will, who also notices many things which appear to come from the senses? What is there in all of this that is not every bit as true as the fact that I exist—even if I am always asleep or even if my creator makes every effort to mislead me? Which of these things is distinct from my thought? Which of them can be said to be separate from myself? For it is so obvious that it is I who doubt, I who understand, and I who will, that there is nothing by which it could be explained more clearly. But indeed it is also the same "I" who imagines; for although perhaps, as I supposed before, absolutely nothing that I imagined is true, still the very power of imagining really does exist, and constitutes a part of my thought. Finally, it is this same "I" who senses or who is cognizant of bodily things as if through the senses. For example, I now see a light, I hear a noise, I feel heat. These things are false, since I am asleep. Yet I certainly do seem to see, hear, and feel warmth. This cannot be false. Properly speaking, this is what in me is called "sensing." But this, precisely so taken, is nothing other than thinking.

From these considerations I am beginning to know a little better what I am. But it still seems (and I cannot resist believing) that corporeal things—whose images are formed by thought, and which the senses themselves examine—are much more distinctly known than this mysterious "I" which does not fall within the imagination.

And yet it would be strange indeed were I to grasp the very things I consider to be doubtful, unknown, and foreign to me more distinctly than what is true, what is known—than, in short, myself. But I see what is happening: my mind loves to wander and does not yet permit itself to be restricted within the confines of truth. So be it then; let us just this once allow it completely free rein, so that, a little while later, when the time has come to pull in the reins, the mind may more readily permit itself to be controlled.

Let us consider those things which are commonly believed to be the most distinctly grasped of all: namely the bodies we touch and see. Not bodies in general, mind you, for these general perceptions are apt to be somewhat more confused, but one body in particular. Let us take, for instance, this piece of wax. It has been taken quite recently from the honeycomb; it has not yet lost all the honey flavor. It retains some of the scent of the flowers from which it was collected. Its color, shape, and size are manifest. It is hard and cold; it is easy to touch. If you rap on it with your knuckle it will emit a sound. In short, everything is present in it that appears needed to enable a body to be known as distinctly as possible. But notice that, as I am speaking, I am bringing it close to the fire. The remaining traces of the honey flavor are disappearing; the scent is vanishing; the color is changing; the original shape is disappearing. Its size is increasing; it is becoming liquid and hot; you can hardly touch it. And now, when you rap on it, it no longer emits any sound. Does the same wax still remain? I must confess that it does; no one denies it; no one thinks otherwise. So what was there in the wax that was so distinctly grasped? Certainly none of the aspects that I reached by means of the senses. For whatever came under the senses of taste, smell, sight, touch or hearing has now changed; and yet the wax remains.

Perhaps the wax was what I now think it is: namely that the wax itself never really was the sweetness of the honey, nor the fragrance of the flowers, nor the whiteness, nor the shape, nor the sound, but instead was a body that a short time ago manifested itself to me in these ways, and now does so in other ways. But just what precisely is this thing that I thus imagine? Let us focus our attention on this and see what remains after we have removed everything that does not belong to the wax: only that it is something extended, flexible, and mutable. But what is it to be flexible and mutable? Is it what my imagination shows it to be: namely, that this piece of wax can change from a round to a square shape, or from the latter to a triangular shape? Not at all; for I grasp that the wax is capable of innumerable changes of this sort, even though I am incapable of running through these innumerable changes by using my imagination. Therefore this insight is not achieved by the faculty of imagination. What is it to be extended? Is this thing's extension also unknown? For it becomes greater in wax that is beginning to melt, greater in boiling wax, and greater still as the heat is increased. And I would not judge correctly what the wax is if I did not believe that it takes on an even greater variety of dimensions than I could ever grasp with the imagination. It remains then for me to concede that I do not grasp what this wax is through the imagination; rather, I perceive it through the mind alone. The point I am making refers to this particular piece of wax, for the case of wax in general is clearer still. But what is this piece of wax which is perceived only by the mind? Surely it is the same piece of wax that I see, touch, and imagine; in short it is the same piece of wax I took it to be from the very beginning. But I need to realize that the perception of the wax is neither a seeing, nor a touching, nor an imagining. Nor has it ever been, even though it previously seemed so; rather it is an inspection on the part of the mind alone. This inspection can be imperfect and confused, as it was before, or clear and distinct, as it is now, depending on how closely I pay attention to the things in which the piece of wax consists.

But meanwhile I marvel at how prone my mind is to errors. For although I am considering these things within myself silently and without words, nevertheless I seize upon words themselves and I am nearly deceived by the ways in which people commonly speak. For we say that we see the wax itself, if it is present, and not that we judge it to be present from its color or shape. Whence I might conclude straightaway that I know the wax through the vision had by the eye, and not through an inspection on the part of the mind alone. But then were I perchance to look out my window and observe men crossing the square, I would ordinarily say I see the men themselves just as I say I see the wax. But what do I see aside from hats and clothes, which could conceal automata? Yet I judge them to be men. Thus what I thought I had seen with my eyes, I actually grasped solely with the faculty of judgment, which is in my mind.

But a person who seeks to know more than the common crowd ought to be ashamed of himself for looking for doubt in common ways of speaking. Let us then go forward and inquire when it was that I perceived more perfectly and evidently what the piece of wax was. Was it when I first saw it and believed I knew it by the external sense, or at least by the so-called common sense, that is, the power of imagination? Or do I have more perfect knowledge now, when I have diligently examined both what the wax is and how it is known? Surely it is absurd to be in doubt about this matter. For what was there in my initial perception that was distinct? What was there that any animal seemed incapable of possessing? But indeed when I distinguish the wax from its external forms, as if stripping it of its clothing, and look at the wax in its nakedness, then, even though there can be still an error in my judgment, nevertheless I cannot perceive it thus without a human mind.

But what am I to say about this mind, that is, about myself? For as yet I admit nothing else to be in me over and above the mind. What, I ask, am I who seem to perceive this wax so distinctly? Do I not know myself not only much more truly and with greater certainty, but also much more distinctly and evidently? For if I judge that the wax exists from the fact that I see it, certainly from this same fact that I see the wax it follows much more evidently that I myself exist. For it could happen that what I see is not truly wax. It could happen that I have no eyes with which to see anything. But it is utterly impossible that, while I see or think I see (I do not now distinguish these two), I who think am not something. Likewise, if I judge that the wax exists from the fact that I touch it, the same outcome will again obtain, namely that I exist. If I judge that the wax exists from the fact that I imagine it, or for any other reason, plainly the same thing follows. But what I note regarding the wax applies to everything else that is external to me. Furthermore, if my perception of the wax seemed more distinct after it became known to me not only on account of sight or touch, but on account of many reasons, one has to admit how much more distinctly I am now known to myself. For there is not a single consideration that can aid in my perception of the wax or of any other body that fails to make even more manifest the nature of my mind. But there are still so many other things in the mind itself on the basis of which my knowledge of it can be rendered more distinct that it hardly seems worth enumerating those things which emanate to it from the body.

But lo and behold, I have returned on my own to where I wanted to be. For since I now know that even bodies are not, properly speaking, perceived by the senses or by the faculty of imagination, but by the intellect alone, and that they are not perceived through their being touched or seen, but only through their being understood, I manifestly know that nothing can be perceived more easily and more evidently than my own mind. But since the tendency to hang on to long-held beliefs cannot be put aside so quickly, I want to stop here, so that by the length of my meditation this new knowledge may be more deeply impressed upon my memory. . . .

Now my first observation here is that there is a great difference between a mind and a body in that a body, by its very nature, is always divisible. On the other hand, the mind is utterly indivisible. For when I consider the mind, that is, myself insofar as I am only a thinking thing, I cannot distinguish any parts within me; rather, I understand myself to be manifestly one complete thing. Although the entire mind seems to be united to the entire body, nevertheless, were a foot or an arm or any other bodily part to be amputated, I know that nothing has been taken away from the mind on that account. Nor can the faculties of willing, sensing, understanding, and so on be called "parts" of the mind, since it is one and the same mind that wills, senses, and understands. On the other hand, there is no corporeal or extended thing I can think of that I may not in my thought easily divide into parts; and in this way I understand that it is divisible. This consideration alone would suffice to teach me that the mind is wholly diverse from the body, had I not yet known it well enough in any other way.

My second observation is that my mind is not immediately affected by all the parts of the body, but only by the brain, or perhaps even by just one small part of the brain, namely, by that part where the "common" sense is said to reside. Whenever this part of the brain is disposed in the same manner, it presents the same thing to the mind, even if the other parts of the body are able meanwhile to be related in diverse ways. Countless experiments show this, none of which need be reviewed here.

My next observation is that the nature of the body is such that whenever any of its parts can be moved by another part some distance away, it can also be moved in the same manner by any of the parts that lie between them, even if this more distant part is doing nothing. For example, in the cord ABCD, if the final part D is pulled, the first part A would be moved in exactly the same manner as it could be, if one of the intermediate parts B or C were pulled, while the end part D remained immobile. Likewise, when I feel a pain in my foot, physics teaches me that this sensation took place by means of nerves distributed throughout the foot, like stretched cords extending from the foot all the way to the brain. When these nerves are pulled in the foot, they also pull on the inner parts of the brain to which they extend, and produce a certain motion in them. This motion has been constituted by nature so as to affect the mind with a sensation of pain, as if it occurred in the foot. But because these nerves need to pass through the shin, thigh, loins, back, and neck to get from the foot to the brain, it can happen that even if it is not the part in the foot but merely one of the intermediate parts that is being struck, the very same movement will occur in the brain that would occur were the foot badly injured. The inevitable result will be that the mind feels the same pain. The same opinion should hold for any other sensation.

My final observation is that, since any given motion occurring in that part of the brain immediately affecting the mind produces but one sensation in it, I can think of no better arrangement than that it produces the one sensation that, of all the ones it is able to produce, is most especially and most often conducive to the maintenance of a healthy man. Moreover, experience shows that all the sensations bestowed on us by nature are like this. Hence there is absolutely nothing to be found in them that does not bear witness to God's power and goodness. Thus, for example, when the nerves in the foot are agitated in a violent and unusual manner, this motion of theirs extends through the marrow of the spine to the inner reaches of the brain, where it gives the mind the sign to sense something, namely, the pain as if it is occurring in the foot. This provokes the mind to do its utmost to move away from the cause of the pain, since it is seen as harmful to the foot. But the nature of man could have been so constituted by God that this same motion in the brain might have indicated something else to the mind: for example, either the motion itself as it occurs in the brain, or in the foot, or in some place in between, or something else entirely different. But nothing else would have served so well the maintenance of the body. Similarly, when we need something to drink, a certain dryness arises in the throat that moves the nerves in the throat, and, by means of them, the inner parts of the brain. And this motion affects the mind with a sensation of thirst, because in this entire affair nothing is more useful for us to know than that we need something to drink in order to maintain our health; the same holds in the other cases.

From these considerations it is utterly apparent that, notwithstanding the immense goodness of God, the nature of man, insofar as it is composed of mind and body, cannot help being sometimes mistaken. For if some cause, not in the foot but in some other part through which the nerves extend from the foot to the brain, or perhaps even in the brain itself, were to produce the same motion that would normally be produced by a badly injured foot, the pain will be felt as if it were in the foot, and the senses will naturally be deceived. For since an identical motion in the brain can only bring about an identical sensation in the mind, and it is more frequently the case that this motion is wont to arise on account of a cause that harms the foot than on account of some other thing existing elsewhere, it is reasonable that the motion should always show pain to the mind as something belonging to the foot rather than to some other part. And if dryness in the throat does not arise, as is normal, because taking something to drink contributes to bodily health, but from a contrary cause, as happens in the case of someone with dropsy, then it is far better that it should deceive on that occasion than that it should always be deceptive when the body is in good health. The same holds for the other cases.

This consideration is most helpful, not only for my noticing all the errors to which my nature is liable, but also for enabling me to correct or avoid them without difficulty. To be sure, I know that all the senses set forth what is true more frequently than what is false regarding what concerns the welfare of the body. Moreover, I can nearly always make use of several of them in order to examine the same thing. Furthermore, I can use my memory, which connects current happenings with past ones, and my intellect, which now has examined all the causes of error. Hence I should no longer fear that those things that are daily shown me by the senses are false. On the contrary, the hyperbolic doubts of the last few days ought to be rejected as ludicrous. This goes especially for the chief reason for doubting, which dealt with my failure to distinguish being asleep from being awake. For I now notice that there is a considerable difference between these two; dreams are never joined by the memory with all the other actions of life, as is the case with those actions that occur when one is awake. For surely, if, while I am awake, someone were suddenly to appear to me and then immediately disappear, as occurs in dreams, so that I see neither where he came from nor where he went, it is not without reason that I would judge him to be a ghost or a phantom conjured up in my brain, rather than a true man. But when these things happen, and I notice distinctly where they come from, where they are now, and when they come to me, and when I connect my perception of them without interruption with the whole rest of my life, I am clearly certain that these perceptions have happened to me not while I was dreaming but while I was awake. Nor ought I have even the least doubt regarding the truth of these things, if, having mustered all the senses, in addition to my memory and my intellect, in order to examine them, nothing is passed on to me by one of these sources that conflicts with the others. For from the fact that God is no deceiver, it follows that I am in no way mistaken in these matters. But because the need to get things done does not always permit us the leisure for such a careful inquiry, we must confess that the life of man is apt to commit errors regarding particular things, and we must acknowledge the infirmity of our nature.

The Distinction between Mental and Physical Phenomena (excerpt)

Franz Brentano

1. All the data of our consciousness are divided into two great classes—the class of physical and the class of mental phenomena. We spoke of this distinction earlier when we established the concept of psychology, and we returned to it again in our discussion of psychological method. But what we have said is still not sufficient. We must now establish more firmly and more exactly what was only mentioned in passing before.

This seems all the more necessary since neither agreement nor complete clarity has been achieved regarding the delimitation of the two classes. We have already

Source: Excerpt from "The Distinction between Mental and Physical Phenomena," *Psychology from an Empirical Standpoint,* by Franz Bretano, edited by Oskar Kraus, English edition by Linda L. McAlister, translated by Antos C. Rancurello, D. B. Terrell, and Linda L. McAlister, © 1973. Reprinted by permission.

seen how physical phenomena which appear in the imagination are sometimes taken for mental phenomena. There are many other such instances of confusion. And even important psychologists may be hard pressed to defend themselves against the charge of self-contradiction.* For instance, we encounter statements like the following: sensation and imagination are distinguished by the fact that one occurs as the result of a physical phenomenon, while the other is evoked by a mental phenomenon according to the laws of association. But then the same psychologists admit that what appears in sensation does not correspond to its efficient cause. Thus it turns out that the so-called physical phenomenon does not actually appear to us, and, indeed, that we have no presentation of it whatsoever—certainly a curious misuse of the term "phenomenon"! Given such a state of affairs, we cannot avoid going into the question in somewhat greater detail.

2. The explanation we are seeking is not a definition according to the traditional rules of logic. These rules have recently been the object of impartial criticism, and much could be added to what has already been said. Our aim is to clarify the meaning of the two terms *"physical phenomenon"* and *"mental phenomenon,"* removing all misunderstanding and confusion concerning them. And it does not matter to us what means we use, as long as they really serve to clarify these terms.

To this end, it is not sufficient merely to specify more general, more inclusive definitions. Just as deduction is opposed to induction when we speak of kinds of proof, in this case explanation by means of subsumption under a general term is opposed to explanation by means of particulars, through examples. And the latter kind of explanation is appropriate whenever the particular terms are clearer than the general ones. Thus it is probably a more effective procedure to explain the term "color" by saying that it designates the class which contains red, blue, green and yellow, than to do the opposite and attempt to explain "red" by saying it is a particular kind of color. Moreover, explanation through particular definitions will be of even greater use when we are dealing, as in our case, with terms which are not common in ordinary life, while those for the individual phenomena included under them are frequently used. So let us first of all try to clarify the concepts by means of examples.

*In this respect, I, at least, cannot reconcile the different definitions given by Bain in one of his latest psychological works, *Mental Science,* 3rd ed. (London, 1872). On p. 120, No. 59, he says that mental science (Science of Mind, which he also calls Subject science) is grounded on self-consciousness or introspective attention; the eye, the ear, the organs or touch being only the media for the observation of the physical world, or the "object world," as he expresses it. On the other hand, on p. 198, No. 4, he says that, "The perception of matter or the Object consciousness is connected with the putting forth of Muscular Energy, as opposed to Passive Feeling." And by way of explanation, he adds, "In purely *passive* feeling as in those of our sensations that do not call forth our muscular energies, we are not perceiving matter, we are in a state of subject consciousness." He illustrates this with the example of the sensation of warmth that one has when taking a warm bath, and with those cases of gentle contact in which there is no muscular activity, and declares that, under the same conditions, sounds and possibly even light and color could be "a purely subject experience." Thus he takes as illustrations to substantiate subject consciousness the very sensations from the eye, ear and organs of touch, which he had characterized as indicators of "object consciousness" in opposition to "subject consciousness."

Every idea or presentation which we acquire either through sense perception or imagination is an example of a mental phenomenon.[1] By presentation I do not mean that which is presented, but rather the act of presentation. Thus, hearing a sound, seeing a colored object, feeling warmth or cold, as well as similar states of imagination are examples of what I mean by this term. I also mean by it the thinking of a general concept, provided such a thing actually does occur. Furthermore, every judgement, every recollection, every expectation, every inference, every conviction or opinion, every doubt, is a mental phenomenon. Also to be included under this term is every emotion: joy, sorrow, fear, hope, courage, despair, anger, love, hate, desire, act of will, intention, astonishment, admiration, contempt, etc.

Examples of physical phenomena,[2] on the other hand, are a color, a figure, a landscape which I see, a chord which I hear, warmth, cold, odor which I sense; as well as similar images which appear in the imagination.

These examples may suffice to illustrate the differences between the two classes of phenomena.

3. Yet we still want to try to find a different and a more unified way of explaining mental phenomena. For this purpose we make use of a definition we used earlier when we said that the term "mental phenomena" applies to presentations as

---

[1]"*Examples of mental phenomena.*" Brentano consequently understands "mental phenomenon" to mean the same as "mental activity," and what is characteristic of it, in his opinion, is the "reference to something as object," i.e. being concerned with something. With this the word φαινόμενον has become mere "internal linguistic form." The same thing holds true of the word "activity," since in Brentano's opinion every such activity, at least in men and animals, is a *passio,* an affection in the Aristotelian sense. So what we are concerned with is the sheer "having something as object" as the distinguishing feature of any act of consciousness, which Brentano also calls "state of consciousness," in Book One, Chap. 1, Sect. 2. Supplementary essay II is more precise on this point and on the further distinction between mental activity and mental reference. It would be better to avoid the expression "phenomenon," even though according to Brentano every consciousness not only has something appearing to it but appears to itself (see Book Two, Chap. 2).

[2]In citing examples of physical phenomena, Brentano intends to bring in first of all examples of "physical phenomena" which are given directly in perception. Thus he enumerates: colors, shapes, musical chords, warmth, cold, odors. In each of these cases we are concerned with objects of our sensations, what is sensed. Now "a landscape, which I see" has slipped in among these examples. But it was obvious for Brentano that I cannot see a landscape, only something colored, extended, bounded in some way. In his books and articles on the history of philosophy, Brentano repeatedly emphasized as one of the most fundamental rules of interpretation, that philosophical writers are to be interpreted in the context of all their work. Now anyone who takes notice of Brentano's *Psychologie des Aristotles* (Mainz, 1876), will find that on p. 84 he deals with that which is sensible *per accidens.* Aristotle uses an example to explain the sensible *per accidens:* someone sees the son of Diares. Now, to be sure, we can say that he sees the son of Diares, but he does not see him as such. He sees something white and it is a fact concerning the white thing he sees that it is the son of Diares. This should at least have called attention to the fact that Brentano does not believe one can see a landscape in the same way that one can see something variously colored. In other words, landscape is no sense-quality and cannot be an object of direct sense-perception. What one sees, when one "sees" a landscape are extended colored shapes at some distance from us. Everything else is a matter of interpretation in terms of judgements and concepts. One can find fault with the example, then, in that it includes "landscape" among the "physical phenomena" belonging to our *direct perception.* Thus Husserl accuses Brentano of having confused "sense contents" with "external objects" that appear to us and of holding that physical phenomena "exist only phenomenally or intentionally." But this accusation is shown to be wrong in the Introduction to the present book. According to Brentano, we have perceptions of the mental and perceptions of the physical; the former exhibit nothing that is extended and the latter are restricted to what is qualitative and extended.

well as to all the phenomena which are based upon presentations. It is hardly necessary to mention again that by "presentation" we do not mean that which is presented, but rather the presenting of it. This act of presentation forms the foundation not merely of the act of judging, but also of desiring and of every other mental act. Nothing can be judged, desired, hoped or feared, unless one has a presentation of that thing.[3] Thus the definition given includes all the examples of mental phenomena which we listed above, and in general all the phenomena belonging to this domain.

It is a sign of the immature state of psychology that we can scarcely utter a single sentence about mental phenomena which will not be disputed by many people. Nevertheless, most psychologists agree with what we have just said, namely, that presentations are the foundation for the other mental phenomena. Thus Herbart asserts quite rightly, "Every time we have a feeling, there will be something or other presented in consciousness, even though it may be something very diversified, confused and varied, so that this particular presentation is included in this particular feeling. Likewise, whenever we desire something . . . we have before our minds that which we desire."[*]

Herbart then goes further, however. He sees all other phenomena as nothing but certain states of presentations which are derivable from the presentations themselves. This view has already been attacked repeatedly with decisive arguments, in particular by Lotze. Most recently, J. B. Meyer, among others, has set forth a long criticism of it in his account of Kant's psychology. But Meyer was not satisfied to deny that feelings and desires could be derived from presentations. He claims that phenomena of this kind can exist in the absence of presentations.[†] Indeed, Meyer believes that the lowest forms of animal life have feelings and desires, but no presentations and also that the lives of higher animals and men begin with mere feelings and desires, while presentations emerge only upon further development.[‡] Thus Meyer, too, seems to come into conflict with our claim.

But, if I am not mistaken, the conflict is more apparent than real. Several of his expressions suggest that Meyer has a narrower concept of presentation than we have, while he correspondingly broadens the concept of feeling. "Presentation," he says, "begins when the modification which we experience in our own state can be understood as the result of an external stimulus, even if this at first expresses itself only in the unconscious looking around or feeling around for an external object which results from it." If Meyer means by "presentation" the same thing that we do, he could not possibly speak in this way. He would see that a condition such as the one he describes as the origin of presentation, already involves an abundance of presentations, for example, the idea of temporal succession, ideas of spatial

[3]The descriptive psychological law that Brentano here expresses is not obtained inductively but is self-evident in view of the concepts of presentation, judgement, and appetition. See Introduction, p. 370, and *The Origin of our Knowledge of Right and Wrong.*
[*]*Psychologie als Wissenschaft,* Part II, Sect. 1, Chap. 1, No. 103. Cp. also Drobisch, *Empirische Psychologie,* p. 38, and others of Herbart's school.
[†]*Kant's Psychologie* (Berlin, 1870), pp. 92 ff.
[‡]*Kant's Psychologie,* p. 94.

proximity and ideas of cause and effect. If all of these ideas must already be present in the mind in order for there to be a presentation in Meyer's sense, it is absolutely clear that such a thing cannot be the basis of every other mental phenomenon. Even the "being present" of any single one of the things mentioned is "being presented" in our sense. And such things occur whenever something appears in consciousness, whether it is hated, loved, or regarded indifferently, whether it is affirmed or denied or there is a complete withholding of judgement and—I cannot express myself in any other way than to say—it is presented. As we use the verb "to present," "to be presented" means the same as "to appear."

Meyer himself admits that a presentation in this sense is presupposed by every feeling of pleasure and pain, even the lowliest, although, since his terminology differs from ours, he calls this a feeling and not a presentation. At least that is what seems to me to emerge from the following passage: "There is no intermediate state between sensation and non-sensation. . . . Now the simplest form of sensation need be nothing more than a mere *sensation of change* in one's own body or a part thereof, caused by some stimulus. Beings endowed with such sensations would only have a *feeling of their own states.* A sensibility of the soul for the changes which are favorable or harmful to it could very well be directly connected with this *vital feeling* for the events beneath one's own skin, even if this *new sensitivity* could not simply be derived from that feeling: such a soul could have *feelings* of pleasure and pain *along with the sensation.* . . . A soul so endowed still has no Presentations."* It is easy to see that what is, in our view, the only thing which deserves the name "feeling," also emerges according to J. B. Meyer as the second element. It is preceded by another element which falls under the concept of a presentation as we understand it, and which constitutes the indispensable precondition for this second phenomenon. So it would seem that if Meyer's view were translated into our terminology, the opposition would disappear automatically.

Perhaps a similar situation obtains, too, in the case of others who express themselves in a manner similar to Meyer's. Yet it may still be the case that with respect to some kinds of sensory pleasure and pain feelings, someone may really be of the opinion that there are no presentations involved, even in our sense. At least we cannot deny that there is a certain temptation to do this. This is true, for example, with regard to the feelings present when one is cut or burned. When someone is cut he has no perception of touch, and someone who is burned has no feeling of warmth, but in both cases there is only the feeling of pain.

Nevertheless there is no doubt that even here the feeling is based upon a presentation. In cases such as this we always have a presentation of a definite spatial location which we usually characterize in relation to some visible and touchable part of our body. We say that our foot or our hand hurts, that this or that part of the body

---

Kant's Psychologie, p. 92. J. B. Meyer seems to conceive of sensation in the same way as Überweg in his *Logik I,* 2nd ed., p. 64. "Perception differs from mere sensation in that in sensation we are conscious only of the subjective state, while in perception there is another element which is perceived and which therefore stands apart from the act of perception as something different and objective." Even if Überweg's view of the difference between sensation and perception were correct, sensation would still involve a presentation in our sense. Why we consider it to be incorrect will be apparent later.

is in pain. Those who consider such a spatial presentation something originally given by the neural stimulation itself cannot deny that a presentation is the basis of this feeling. But others cannot avoid this assumption either. For there is in us not only the idea of a definite spatial location but also that of a particular sensory quality analogous to color, sound and other so-called sensory qualities, which is a physical phenomenon and which must be clearly distinguished from the accompanying feeling. If we hear a pleasing and mild sound or a shrill one, harmonious chord or a dissonance, it would not occur to anyone to identify the sound with the accompanying feeling of pleasure or pain. But then in cases where a feeling of pain or pleasure is aroused in us by a cut, a burn or a tickle, we must distinguish in the same way between a physical phenomenon, which appears as the object of external perception, and the mental phenomenon of feeling, which accompanies its appearance, even though in this case the superficial observer is rather inclined to confuse them.

The principal basis for this misconception is probably the following. It is well known that our perceptions are mediated by the so-called afferent nerves. In the past people thought that certain nerves served as conductors of each kind of sensory qualities, such as color, sound, etc. Recently, however, physiologists have been more and more inclined to take the opposite point of view.* And they teach almost universally that the nerves for tactile sensations, if stimulated in a certain way, produce sensations of warmth and cold in us, and if stimulated in another way produce in us so-called pleasure and pain sensations. In reality, however, something similar is true for all the nerves, insofar as a sensory phenomenon of the kind just mentioned can be produced in us by every nerve. In the presence of very strong stimuli, all nerves produce painful phenomena, which cannot be distinguished from one another.† When a nerve transmits different kinds of sensations, it often happens that it transmits several at the same time. Looking into an electric light, for example, produces simultaneously a "beautiful," i.e. pleasant, color phenomenon and a phenomenon of another sort which is painful. The nerves of the tactile sense often simultaneously transmit a so-called sensation of touch, a sensation of warmth or cold, and a so-called sensation of pleasure or pain. Now we notice that when several sensory phenomena appear at the same time, they are not infrequently regarded as *one*. This has been demonstrated in a striking manner in regard to the sensations of smell and taste. It is well established that almost all the differences usually considered differences in taste are really only differences in the concomitant olfactory phenomena. Something similar occurs when we eat food cold or warm; we often think that it tastes different while in reality only the temperature sensations differ. It is not surprising, then, if we do not always distinguish precisely between a phenomenon which is a temperature sensation and another which is a tactile sensation. Perhaps we would not even distinguish between them at all if they did not ordinarily appear independently of one another. If we now look at the sensations of feeling,[4] we find, on the contrary, that their phenomena are usually linked with another

---

*Cp. especially Wundt, *Principles of Physiological Psychology* (trans. Titchener), pp. 322 ff.
†Cp. below, Book Two, Chap. III, Sect. 6.
[4]On "sensations of feeling," compare Brentano's controversy with Stumpf in *Untersuchungen zur Sinnespsychologie.*

sort of sensation, and when the excitation is very strong these other sensations sink into insignificance beside them. Thus the fact that a given individual has been mistaken about the appearance of a particular class of sensory qualities and has believed that he has had one single sensation instead of two is very easily explained. Since the intervening idea was accompanied by a relatively very strong feeling, incomparably stronger than that which followed upon the first kind of quality, the person considers this mental phenomenon as the only new thing he has experienced. In addition, if the first kind of quality disappeared completely, then he would believe that he possessed only a feeling without any underlying presentation of a physical phenomenon.

A further basis for this illusion is the fact that the quality which precedes the feeling and the feeling itself do not have two distinct names. The physical phenomenon which appears along with the feeling of pain is also called pain. Indeed, we do not say that we sense this or that phenomenon in the foot with pain; we say that we feel pain in the foot. This is an equivocation, such as, indeed, we often find when different things are closely related to one another. We call the body healthy, and in reference to it we say that the air, the food, the color of the face, etc., are healthy, but obviously in another sense. In our case, the physical phenomenon itself is called pleasure or pain after the feeling of pleasure or pain which accompanies the appearance of the physical phenomenon, and there, too, in a modified sense of the words. It is as if we would say of a harmonious chord that it is a pleasure because we experience pleasure when we hear it, or, too, that the loss of a friend is a great sorrow for us. Experience shows that equivocation is one of the main obstacles to recognizing distinctions. And it must necessarily be the largest obstacle here where there is an inherent danger of confusion and perhaps the extension of the term was itself the result of this confusion. Thus many psychologists were deceived by this equivocation and this error fostered further errors. Some came to the false conclusion that the sensing subject must be present at the spot in the injured limb in which a painful phenomenon is located in perception.[5] Then, since they identified the phenomenon with the accompanying pain sensation, they regarded this phenomenon as a mental rather than a physical phenomenon. It is precisely for this reason that they thought that its perception in the limb was an inner, and consequently evident and infallible perception.* Their view is contradicted by the fact that the same phenomena often appear in the same way after the amputation of the limb. For this reason others argued, in a rather skeptical manner, against the self-evidence of inner perception. The difficulty disappears if we distinguish between pain in the sense in which the term describes the apparent condition of a part of our body, and the feeling of pain which is connected with the concomitant sensation. Keeping this in mind, we shall no longer be inclined to assert that there is no presentation at the basis of the feeling of sensory pain experienced when one is injured.

Accordingly, we may consider the following definition of mental phenomena as indubitably correct: they are either presentations or they are based upon presentations in the sense described above. Such a definition offers a second, more

---

*This is the opinion of the Jesuit, Tongiorgi, in his widely circulated philosophy textbook.

[5]Here "perception" is taken in the loose and extended sense, for localization in the foot goes beyond sensation.

simple explanation of this concept. This explanation, of course, is not completely unified because it separates mental phenomena into two groups.

4. People have tried to formulate a completely unified definition which distinguishes all mental phenomena from physical phenomena by means of negation. All physical phenomena, it is said, have extension and spatial location, whether they are phenomena of vision or of some other sense, or products of the imagination, which presents similar objects to us. The opposite, however, is true of mental phenomena; thinking, willing and the like appear without extension and without spatial location.

According to this view, it would be possible for us to characterize physical phenomena easily and exactly in contrast to mental phenomena by saying that they are those phenomena which appear extended and localized in space. Mental phenomena would then be definable with equal exactness as those phenomena which do not have extension or spatial location. Descartes and Spinoza could be cited in support of such a distinction. The chief advocate of this view, however, is Kant, who explains space as the form of the intuition of the external sense.

Recently Bain has given the same definition:

> The department of the Object, or Object–World, is exactly circumscribed by one property, Extension. The world of Subject-experience is devoid of this property. A tree or a river is said to possess extended magnitude. A pleasure has no length, breadth, or thickness; it is in no respect an extended thing. A thought or idea may refer to extended magnitudes, but it cannot be said to have extension in itself. Neither can we say that an act of the will, a desire or a belief occupy dimensions in space. Hence all that comes within the sphere of the Subject is spoken of as the Unextended.
>
> Thus, if Mind, as commonly happens, is put for the sum-total of Subject-experiences, we may define it negatively by a single fact—the absence of Extension.*

Thus it seems that we have found, at least negatively, a unified definition for the totality of mental phenomena.

But even on this point there is no unanimity among psychologists, and we hear it denied for contradictory reasons that extension and lack of extension are characteristics which distinguish physical and mental phenomena.

Many declare that this definition is false because not only mental phenomena, but also many physical phenomena appear to be without extension. A large number of not unimportant psychologists, for example, teach that the phenomena of some, or even of all of our senses originally appear apart from all extension and spatial location. In particular, this view is quite generally held with respect to sounds and olfactory phenomena.[6] It is true of colors according to Berkeley, of the phenomena of touch according to Platner, and of the phenomena of all the external senses according to Herbart and Lotze, as well as according to Hartley, Brown, the two Mills, H. Spencer and others. Indeed it seems that the phenomena revealed by the external senses, especially sight and the sense of touch, are all spatially extended. The reason for this, it is said, is that we connect them with spatial presentations that

---

*Mental Science, Introduction, Chap. 1.

[6]In the *Untersuchungen zur Sinnespsychologie,* Brentano attempts to show that we experience all sense-qualities as being localized.

are gradually developed on the basis of earlier experiences. They are originally without spatial location, and we subsequently localize them. If this were really the only way in which physical phenomena attain spatial location we could obviously no longer separate the two areas by reference to this property. In fact, mental phenomena are also localized by us in this way, as, for example, when we locate a phenomenon of anger in the irritated lion, and our own thoughts in the space which we occupy.

This is one way in which the above definition has been criticized by a great number of eminent psychologists, including Bain. At first sight he seems to defend such a definition, but in reality he follows Hartley's lead on this issue. He has only been able to express himself as he does because he does not actually consider the phenomena of the external senses, in and for themselves, to be physical phenomena (although he is not always consistent in this).*

Others, as we said, will reject this definition for the opposite reason. It is not so much the assertion that all physical phenomena appear extended that provokes them, but rather the assertion that all mental phenomena lack extension. According to them, certain mental phenomena also appear to be extended. Aristotle seems to have been of this opinion when, in the first chapter of this treatise on sense and sense objects he considers it immediately evident, without any prior proof, that sense perception is the act of a bodily organ.† Modern psychologists and physiologists sometimes express themselves in the same way regarding certain affects. They speak of feelings of pleasure or pain which appear in the external organs, sometimes even after the amputation of the limb and yet, feeling, like perception, is a mental phenomenon. Some authors even maintain that sensory appetites appear localized. This view is shared by the poet when he speaks, not, to be sure, of thought, but of rapture and longing which suffuse the heart and all parts of the body.[7]

Thus we see that the distinction under discussion is disputed from the point of view of both physical and mental phenomena. Perhaps both of these objections are equally unjustified.‡ At any rate, another definition common to all mental phenomena is still desirable. Whether certain mental and physical phenomena appear extended or not, the controversy proves that the criterion given for a clear separation is not adequate. Furthermore, this criterion gives us only a negative definition of mental phenomena.[8]

5. What positive criterion shall we now be able to provide? Or is there perhaps no positive definition which holds true of all mental phenomena generally?

---

*Cp. above, p. 77, note.

†*De Sensu et Sensibili,* 1, 436, b. 7. Cp. also what he says in *De Anima,* I, 1, 403 16, about affective states, in particular about fear.

‡The assertion that even mental phenomena appear to be extended rests obviously on a confusion of mental and physical phenomena similar to the confusion which we became convinced of above when we pointed out that a presentation is also the necessary foundation of sensory feelings.

[7]Brentano was entirely familiar, then, with such false localizations and interpretations. They did not lead him to doubt the evident nature of inner perception. In the Supplementary Essays he emphasizes that this evidence is not affected by the confused character of inner perception. Husserl takes "perception" to refer to complex interpretations and is thus led to dispute the evidence of inner perception.

[8]Compare Book Two, Chap. 4, Sect. 3.

Bain thinks that in fact there is none.* Nevertheless, psychologists in earlier times have already pointed out that there is a special affinity and analogy which exists among all mental phenomena, and which physical phenomena do not share.

Every mental phenomenon is characterized by what the Scholastics of the Middle Ages called the intentional (or mental)† inexistence of an object, and what we might call, though not wholly unambiguously, reference to a content, direction toward an object[9] (which is not to be understood here as meaning a thing),[10] or immanent objectivity. Every mental phenomenon includes something as object within itself, although they do not all do so in the same way. In presentation something is presented, in judgement something is affirmed or denied, in love loved, in hate hated, in desire desired and so on.‡

This intentional in-existence is characteristic exclusively of mental phenomena. No physical phenomenon exhibits anything like it. We can, therefore, define mental phenomena by saying that they are those phenomena which contain an object intentionally within themselves.[11]

But here, too, we come upon controversies and contradiction. Hamilton, in particular, denies this characteristic to a whole broad class of mental phenomena, namely, to all those which he characterizes as feelings, to pleasure and pain in all

*The Senses and the Intellect, Introduction.

†They also use the expression "to exist as an object (objectively) in something," which, if we wanted to use it at the present time, would be considered, on the contrary, as a designation of a real existence outside the mind. At least this is what is suggested by the expression "to exist immanently as an object," which is occasionally used in a similar sense, and in which the term "immanent" should obviously rule out the misunderstanding which is to be feared.

‡Aristotle himself spoke of this mental in-existence. In his books on the soul he says that the sensed object, as such, is in the sensing subject; that the sense contains the sensed object without its matter; that the object which is thought is in the thinking intellect. In Philo, likewise, we find the doctrine of mental existence and in-existence. However, since he confuses them with existence in the proper sense of the word, he reaches his contradictory doctrine of the *logos* and Ideas. The same is true of the Neoplatonists. St. Augustine in his doctrine of the *Verbum mentis* and of its inner origin touches upon the same fact. St. Anselm does the same in his famous ontological argument; many people have observed that his consideration of mental existence as a true existence is at the basis of his paralogism (cp. Überweg, *Geschichte der Philosophie,* II). St. Thomas Aquinas teaches that the object which is thought is intentionally in the thinking subject, the object which is loved in the person who loves, the object which is desired in the person desiring, and he uses this for theological purposes. When the Scriptures speak of an indwelling of the Holy Ghost, St. Thomas explains it as an intentional indwelling through love. In addition, he attempted to find, through the intentional in-existence in the acts of thinking and loving, a certain analogy for the mystery of the Trinity and the procession *ad intra* of the Word and the Spirit.

[9]Brentano here uses "content" synonymously with "object." He later came to prefer the term "object."

[10]As we have noted, Brentano subsequently denies that we can have anything "irreal" as object; we can have as object only that which would be a substance or *thing* if it existed.

[11]Brentano later acknowledged that the way he attempted to describe consciousness here, adhering to the Aristotelian tradition which asserts "the mental inexistence of the object," was imperfect. The so-called "inexistence of the object," the immanent objectivity, is not to be interpreted as a mode of being the thing has in consciousness, but as an imprecise description of the fact that I have something (a thing, real entity, substance) as an object, am mentally concerned with it, refer to it. There are more details on this point in the Supplementary Essays and the Introduction. The Table of Contents speaks more appropriately of "reference to an object." See note 20.

their most diverse shades and varieties.[12] With respect to the phenomena of thought and desire he is in agreement with us. Obviously there is no act of thinking without an object that is thought, nor a desire without an object that is desired. "In the phenomena of Feelings—the phenomena of Pleasure and Pain—on the contrary, consciousness does not place the mental modification or state before itself; it does not contemplate it apart—as separate from itself—but is, as it were, fused into one. The peculiarity of Feeling, therefore, is that there is nothing but what is subjectively subjective; there is no object different from the self—no objectification of any mode of self."* In the first instance there would be something which, according to Hamilton's terminology, is "objective," in the second instance something which is "objectively subjective," as in self-awareness, the object of which Hamilton consequently calls the "subject-object." By denying both concerning feelings, Hamilton rejects unequivocally all intentional in-existence of these phenomena.

In reality, what Hamilton says is not entirely correct, since certain feelings undeniably refer to objects. Our language itself indicates this through the expressions it employs. We say that we are pleased with or about something, that we feel sorrow or grieve about something. Likewise, we say: that pleases me, that hurts me, that makes me feel sorry, etc. Joy and sorrow, like affirmation and negation, love and hate, desire and aversion, clearly follow upon a presentation and are related to that which is presented.

One is most inclined to agree with Hamilton in those cases in which, as we saw earlier, it is most easy to fall into the error that feeling is not based upon any presentation: the case of pain caused by a cut or a burn, for example. But the reason is simply the same temptation toward this, as we have seen, erroneous assumption. Even Hamilton recognizes with us the fact that presentations occur without exception and thus even here they form the basis of the feeling. Thus his denial that feelings have an object seems all the more striking.

One thing certainly has to be admitted; the object to which a feeling refers is not always an external object. Even in cases where I hear a harmonious sound, the pleasure which I feel is not actually pleasure in the sound but pleasure in the hearing.[13] In fact you could say, not incorrectly, that in a certain sense it even refers to itself, and this introduces, more or less, what Hamilton was talking about, namely that the feeling and the object are "fused into one." But this is nothing that is not

---

*Lecture on Metaphysics, I, 432.

[12]Here, too, we are concerned with the question already mentioned in Note 1, whether it belongs to the essence of every act of consciousness to be a consciousness of something. Opinions are still divided on this most elementary question in psychology. There is still a distinction drawn today, as there was before Brentano, between objective acts of consciousness and mere states of consciousness. Brentano assails this doctrine with arguments which have remained unrefuted and indeed have gone largely unnoticed. His *Untersuchungen zur Sinnespsychologie* has, in particular, been largely ignored.

[13]The Supplementary Essays and the *Untersuchungen zur Sinnespsychologie* exclude sensual affects of pleasure from sensations of *hearing and seeing,* limit them, that is, to what Brentano called the "*Spürsinn.*" On this view, pleasure in hearing something is an affect of the "Spürsinn" which accompanies and is elicited by the hearing of it. [Translators' note: Brentano classified the sense-modalities in such a way that sensations other than visual and aural ones were grouped under one heading, to which he attached this term. Any attempt at a literal translation would merely be misleading.]

true in the same way of many phenomena of thought and knowledge, as we will see when we come to the investigation of inner consciousness. Still they retain a mental inexistence, a Subject-Object, to use Hamilton's mode of speech, and the same thing is true of these feelings. Hamilton is wrong when he says that with regard to feelings everything is "subjectively subjective"—an expression which is actually self-contradictory, for where you cannot speak of an object, you cannot speak of a subject either. Also, Hamilton spoke of a fusing into one of the feeling with the mental impression, but when carefully considered it can be seen that he is bearing witness against himself here. Every fusion is a unification of several things; and thus the pictorial expression which is intended to make us concretely aware of the distinctive character of feeling still points to a certain duality in the unity.

We may, therefore, consider the intentional in-existence of an object to be a general characteristic of mental phenomena which distinguishes this class of phenomena from the class of physical phenomena.

6. Another characteristic which all mental phenomena have in common is the fact that they are only perceived in inner consciousness, while in the case of physical phenomena only external perception is possible. This distinguishing characteristic is emphasized by Hamilton.*

It could be argued that such a definition is not very meaningful. In fact, it seems much more natural to define the act according to the object, and therefore to state that inner perception, in contrast to every other kind, is the perception of mental phenomena. However, besides the fact that it has a special object, inner perception possesses another distinguishing characteristic: its immediate, infallible self-evidence. Of all the types of knowledge of the objects of experience, inner perception alone possesses this characteristic. Consequently, when we say that mental phenomena are those which are apprehended by means of inner perception, we say that their perception is immediately evident.

Moreover, inner perception is not merely the only kind of perception which is immediately evident; it is really the only perception in the strict sense of the word.† As we have seen, the phenomena of the so-called external perception cannot be proved true and real even by means of indirect demonstration. For this reason, anyone who in good faith has taken them for what they seem to be is being misled by the manner in which the phenomena are connected. Therefore, strictly speaking, so-called external perception is not perception. Mental phenomena, therefore, may be described as the only phenomena of which perception in the strict sense of the word is possible.

This definition, too, is an adequate characterization of mental phenomena. That is not to say that all mental phenomena are internally perceivable by all men, and so all those which someone cannot perceive are to be included by him among physical phenomena. On the contrary, as we have already expressly noted above, it is obvious that no mental phenomenon is perceived by more than one individual. At

---

Lecture on Metaphysics, I, 432.

†[Translators' note: The German word which we translate as "perception" is *"Wahrnehmung"* which literally means taking something to be true. The English word does not reflect this literal meaning so this paragraph only makes sense if we bear in mind the German word.]

the same time, however, we also saw that every type of mental phenomenon is present in every fully developed human mental life. For this reason, the reference to the phenomena which constitute the realm of inner perception serves our purpose satisfactorily.

7. We said that mental phenomena are those phenomena which alone can be perceived in the strict sense of the word. We could just as well say that they are those phenomena which alone possess real existence as well as intentional existence. Knowledge, joy and desire really exist. Color, sound and warmth have only a phenomenal and intentional existence.[14]

There are philosophers who go so far as to say that it is self-evident that phenomena such as those which we call physical phenomena *could not* correspond to any reality. According to them, the assertion that these phenomena have an existence different from mental existence is self-contradictory. Thus, for example, Bain says that attempts have been made to explain the phenomena of external perception by supposing a material world, "in the first instance, detached from perception, and, afterwards, coming into perception, by operating upon the mind." "This view," he says, "involves a contradiction. The prevailing doctrine is that a tree is something in itself apart from all perception; that, by its luminous emanations, it impresses our mind and is then perceived, the perception being an effect, and the unperceived tree [i.e. the one which exists outside of perception] the cause. But the tree is known only through perception; what it may be anterior to, or independent of, perception, we cannot tell; we can think of it as perceived but not as unperceived. There is a manifest contradiction in the supposition; we are required at the same moment to perceive the thing and not to perceive it. We know the touch of iron, but we cannot know the touch apart from the touch."*

I must confess that I am unable to convince myself of the soundness of this argument. It is undoubtedly true that a color appears to us only when we have a presentation of it. We cannot conclude from this, however, that a color cannot exist without being presented. Only if the state of being presented were contained in the color as one of its elements, as a certain quality and intensity is contained in it, would a color which is not presented imply a contradiction, since a whole without one of its parts is indeed a contradiction. But this is obviously not the case. Otherwise, it would also be absolutely inconceivable how the belief in the real existence of physical phenomena outside our presentation could have, not to say originated, but achieved the most general dissemination, been maintained with the utmost tenacity, and, indeed, even been shared for a long time by the most outstanding thinkers. Bain said: "We can think of a tree as perceived, but not as unperceived. There is a manifest contradiction in the supposition." If what he said were correct, his further conclusions could not be objected to. But it is precisely this which cannot be granted. Bain explains this statement by remarking, "We are required at the same moment to perceive the thing and not to perceive it." It is not correct, however, to say that such

---

*Mental Science, 3rd ed., p. 198.

[14]This passage also makes clear what Brentano intended as the object of outer perception; "color, sound, heat," in brief, sense-qualities, that someone having a sensation senses—what is sensed—but not "landscapes" or "boxes."

a demand is placed upon us, for, in the first place, not every act of thinking is a perception. Secondly, even if this were the case, it would only follow that we can think only of trees that have been perceived by us, but not that we can think only of trees *as perceived by us.* To taste a piece of white sugar does not mean to taste a piece of sugar *as white.* The fallacy reveals itself quite clearly in the case of mental phenomena. If someone said, "I cannot think about a mental phenomenon without thinking about it; therefore I can only think about mental phenomena as thought by me; therefore no mental phenomenon exists outside my thinking," his method of reasoning would be identical to that of Bain. Nevertheless, even Bain will not deny that his individual mental life is not the only one which has actual existence. When Bain adds: "we know the touch of iron, but it is not possible that we should know the touch apart from the touch," he obviously uses the word "touch" first to mean the object that is sensed and secondly to mean the act of sensing. These are different concepts, even though the word is the same. Consequently, only those who would let themselves be deceived by this equivocation could grant the existence of immediate evidence as postulated by Bain.

It is not correct, therefore, to say that the assumption that there exists a physical phenomenon outside the mind which is just as real as those which we find intentionally in us, implies a contradiction.[15] It is only that, when we compare one with the other we discover conflicts which clearly show that no real existence corresponds to the intentional existence in this case. And even if this applies only to the realm of our own experience, we will nevertheless make no mistake if in general we deny to physical phenomena any existence other than intentional existence.

Is Consciousness a Brain Process?

U. T. Place

The thesis that consciousness is a process in the brain is put forward as a reasonable scientific hypothesis, not to be dismissed on logical grounds alone. The conditions under which two sets of observations are treated as observations of the same process, rather than as observations of two independent correlated processes, are discussed. It is suggested that we can identify consciousness with a given pattern of brain activity, if we can explain the subject's introspective observations by reference to the brain processes with which they are correlated. It is argued that the problem of providing a physiological explanation of introspective observations is made to seem more difficult than it really is by the "phenomenological fallacy," the

---

[15]We see from this that the account in the Table of Contents, Book Two, Chap. I, Sect. 7, is mistaken. Colors and sounds and so on *could* exist, i.e. their existence involves no direct contradiction. But critical inquiry and comparison convinces us of the blindness of our compulsive belief in the objects of outer perception and natural science convinces us of its incorrectness. In this paragraph Brentano uses "perception" in a broader sense, following Bain's usage. One can no more perceive trees in the sense of sensing them than one can perceive landscapes.

Source: "Is Consciousness a Brain Process?" by U. T. Place, in *British Journal of Psychology,* 1956, 44–50. Reprinted with permission from British Journal of Psychology.

mistaken idea that descriptions of the appearances of things are descriptions of the actual state of affairs in a mysterious internal environment.

I INTRODUCTION

The view that there exists a separate class of events, mental events, which cannot be described in terms of the concepts employed by the physical sciences no longer commands the universal and unquestioning acceptance among philosophers and psychologists which it once did. Modern physicalism, however, unlike the materialism of the seventeenth and eighteenth centuries, is behavioristic. Consciousness on this view is either a special type of behavior, "sampling" or "running-back-and-forth" behavior as Tolman has it,[1] or a disposition to behave in a certain way, an itch, for example, being a temporary propensity to scratch. In the case of cognitive concepts like "knowing," "believing," "understanding," "remembering," and volitional concepts like "wanting" and "intending," there can be little doubt, I think, that an analysis in terms of dispositions to behave is fundamentally sound.[2] On the other hand, there would seem to be an intractable residue of concepts clustering around the notions of consciousness, experience, sensation, and mental imagery, where some sort of inner process story is unavoidable.[3] It is possible, of course, that a satisfactory behavioristic account of this conceptual residuum will ultimately be found. For our present purposes, however, I shall assume that this cannot be done and that statements about pains and twinges, about how things look, sound, and feel, about things dreamed of or pictured in the mind's eye, are statements referring to events and processes which are in some sense private or internal to the individual of whom they are predicated. The question I wish to raise is whether in making this assumption we are inevitably committed to a dualist position in which sensations and mental images form a separate category of processes over and above the physical and physiological processes with which they are known to be correlated. I shall argue that an acceptance of inner processes does not entail dualism and that the thesis that consciousness is a process in the brain cannot be dismissed on logical grounds.

II THE "IS" OF DEFINITION AND THE "IS" OF COMPOSITION

I want to stress from the outset that in defending the thesis that consciousness is a process in the brain, I am not trying to argue that when we describe our dreams, fantasies, and sensations we are talking about processes in our brains. That is, I am not claiming that statements about sensations and mental images are reducible to or analyzable into statements about brain processes, in the way in which "cognition statements" are analyzable into statements about behavior. To say that statements

---

[1]E. C. Tolman, *Purposive Behavior in Animals and Men* (Berkeley 1932).
[2]L. Wittgenstein, *Philosophical Investigations* (Oxford 1953); G. Ryle, *The Concept of Mind* (1949).
[3]Place, "The Concept of Heed," *British Journal of Psychology* XLV (1954), 243–55.

about consciousness are statements about brain processes is manifestly false. This is shown (a) by the fact that you can describe your sensations and mental imagery without knowing anything about your brain processes or even that such things exist, (b) by the fact that statements about one's consciousness and statements about one's brain processes are verified in entirely different ways, and (c) by the fact that there is nothing self-contradictory about the statement "X has a pain but there is nothing going on in his brain." What I do want to assert, however, is that the statement "Consciousness is a process in the brain," although not necessarily true, is not necessarily false. "Consciousness is a process in the brain" in my view is neither self-contradictory nor self-evident; it is a reasonable scientific hypothesis, in the way that the statement "Lightning is a motion of electric charges" is a reasonable scientific hypothesis.

The all but universally accepted view that an assertion of identity between consciousness and brain processes can be ruled out on logical grounds alone derives, I suspect, from a failure to distinguish between what we may call the "is" of definition and the "is" of composition. The distinction I have in mind here is the difference between the function of the word "is" in statements like "A square is an equilateral rectangle," "Red is a color," "To understand an instruction is to be able to act appropriately under the appropriate circumstances," and its function in statements like "His table is an old packing case," "Her hat is a bundle of straw tied together with string," "A cloud is a mass of water droplets or other particles in suspension." These two types of "is" statements have one thing in common. In both cases it makes sense to add the qualification "and nothing else." In this they differ from those statements in which the "is" is an "is" of predication; the statements "Toby is eighty years old and nothing else," "Her hair is red and nothing else," or "Giraffes are tall and nothing else," for example, are nonsense. This logical feature may be described by saying that in both cases both the grammatical subject and the grammatical predicate are expressions which provide an adequate characterization of the state of affairs to which they both refer.

In another respect, however, the two groups of statements are strikingly different. Statements like "A square is an equilateral rectangle" are necessary statements which are true by definition. Statements like "His table is an old packing-case," on the other hand, are contingent statements which have to be verified by observation. In the case of statements like "A square is an equilateral rectangle" or "Red is a color," there is a relationship between the meaning of the expression forming the grammatical predicate and the meaning of the expression forming the grammatical subject, such that whenever the subject expression is applicable the predicate must also be applicable. If you can describe something as red then you must also be able to describe it as colored. In the case of statements like "His table is an old packing-case," on the other hand, there is no such relationship between the meanings of the expressions "his table" and "old packing-case"; it merely so happens that in this case both expressions are applicable to and at the same time provide an adequate characterization of the same object. Those who contend that the statement "Consciousness is a brain process" is logically untenable, base their claim, I suspect, on the mistaken assumption that if the meanings of two statements or expressions are quite unconnected, they cannot both provide an adequate characterization of the same object or state of affairs: if something is a state of consciousness, it cannot be a brain process, since there is nothing self-contradictory in supposing that someone feels a pain when there is nothing happening inside his skull. By the same token we might be led to conclude that a table cannot be an old packing-case, since there is nothing self-contradictory in supposing that someone has a table, but is not in possession of an old packing-case.

III THE LOGICAL INDEPENDENCE OF EXPRESSIONS AND THE ONTOLOGICAL INDEPENDENCE OF ENTITIES

There is, of course, an important difference between the table/packing-case and the consciousness/brain process case in that the statement "His table is an old packing-case" is a particular proposition which refers only to one particular case, whereas the statement "Consciousness is a process in the brain" is a general or universal proposition applying to all states of consciousness whatever. It is fairly clear, I think, that if we lived in a world in which all tables without exception were packing-cases, the concepts of "table" and "packing-case" in our language would not have their present logically independent status. In such a world a table would be a species of packing-case in much the same way that red is a species of color. It seems to be a rule of language that whenever a given variety of object or state of affairs has two characteristics or sets of characteristics, one of which is unique to the variety of object or state of affairs in question, the expression used to refer to the characteristic or set of characteristics which defines the variety of object or state of affairs in question will always entail the expression used to refer to the other characteristic or set of characteristics. If this rule admitted of no exception it would follow that any expression which is logically independent of another expression which uniquely characterizes a given variety of object or state of affairs must refer to a characteristic or set of characteristics which is not normally or necessarily associated with the object or state of affairs in question. It is because this rule applies almost universally, I suggest, that we are normally justified in arguing from the logical independence of two expressions to the ontological independence of the states of affairs to which they refer. This would explain both the undoubted force of the argument that consciousness and brain processes must be independent entities because the expressions used to refer to them are logically independent and, in general, the curious phenomenon whereby questions about the furniture of the universe are often fought and not infrequently decided merely on a point of logic.

   The argument from the logical independence of two expressions to the ontological independence of the entities to which they refer breaks down in the case of brain processes and consciousness, I believe, because this is one of a relatively small number of cases where the rule stated above does not apply. These exceptions are to be found, I suggest, in those cases where the operations which have to be performed in order to verify the presence of the two sets of characteristics inhering in the object or state of affairs in question can seldom if ever be performed simultaneously. A good example here is the case of the cloud and the mass of droplets or other particles in suspension. A cloud is a large semitransparent mass with a fleecy texture suspended in the atmosphere whose shape is subject to continual and kaleidoscopic change. When observed at close quarters, however, it is found to consist of a mass of tiny particles, usually water droplets, in continuous motion. On the basis of this second observation we conclude that a cloud is a mass of tiny particles and nothing else. But there is no logical connection in our language between a cloud and a mass of tiny particles; there is nothing self-contradictory in talking about a cloud which is not composed of tiny particles in suspension. There is no contradiction involved in supposing that clouds consist of a dense mass of fibrous tissue; indeed, such a consistency seems to be implied by many of the functions performed by clouds in fairy stories and mythology. It is clear from this that the terms "cloud" and "mass of tiny particles in suspension" mean quite different things. Yet we do not conclude from this that there must be two things, the mass of particles in suspension and the cloud. The reason for this, I suggest, is that although the characteristics of being a cloud and being a mass of tiny particles in suspension are invariably associated, we never make the observations necessary to verify the statement "That is a cloud" and those necessary to verify the statement "This is a mass of tiny particles in suspension" at one and the same time. We can observe the micro-structure of a cloud only when we are enveloped by it, a condition which effectively prevents us from observing those characteristics which from a distance lead us to describe it as a cloud. Indeed, so disparate are these two experiences that we use different words to describe them. That which is a cloud when we observe it from a distance becomes a fog or mist when we are enveloped by it.

IV WHEN ARE TWO SETS OF OBSERVATIONS OBSERVATIONS OF THE SAME EVENT?

The example of the cloud and the mass of tiny particles in suspension was chosen because it is one of the few cases of a general proposition involving what I have called the "is" of composition which does not involve us in scientific technicalities. It is useful because it brings out the connection between the ordinary everyday cases of the "is" of composition like the table/packing-case example and the more technical cases like "Lightning is a motion of electric charges" where the analogy with the consciousness/brain process case is most marked. The limitation of the cloud/tiny particles in suspension case is that it does not bring out sufficiently clearly the crucial problems of how the identity of the states of affairs referred to by the two expressions is established. In the cloud case the fact that something is a cloud and the fact that something is a mass of tiny particles in suspension are both verified by the normal processes of visual observation. It is arguable, moreover, that the identity of the entities referred to by the two expressions is established by the continuity between the two sets of observations as the observer moves towards or away from the cloud. In the case of brain processes and consciousness there is no such continuity between the two sets of observations involved. A closer introspective scrutiny will never reveal the passage of nerve impulses over a thousand synapses in the way that a closer scrutiny of a cloud will reveal a mass of tiny particles in suspension. The operations required to verify statements about consciousness and statements about brain processes are fundamentally different.

To find a parallel for this feature we must examine other cases where an identity is asserted between something whose occurrence is verified by the ordinary processes of observation and something whose occurrence is established by special procedures. For this purpose I have chosen the case where we say that lightning is a motion of electric charges. As in the case of consciousness, however closely we scrutinize the lightning we shall never be able to observe the electric charges, and just as the operations for determining the nature of one's state of consciousness are radically different from those involved in determining the nature of one's brain processes, so the operations for determining the occurrence of lightning are radically different from those involved in determining the occurrence of a motion of electric charges. What is it, therefore, that leads us to say that the two sets of observations are observations of the same event? It cannot be merely the fact that the two sets of observations are systematically correlated such that whenever there is lightning there is always a motion of electric charges. There are innumerable cases of such correlations where we have no temptation to say that the two sets of observations are observations of the same event. There is a systematic correlation, for example, between the movement of the tides and the stages of the moon, but this does not lead us to say that records of tidal levels are records of the moon's stages or vice versa. We speak rather of a causal connection between two independent events or processes.

The answer here seems to be that we treat the two sets of observations as observations of the same event in those cases where the technical scientific observations set in the context of the appropriate body of scientific theory provide an immediate explanation of the observations made by the man in the street. Thus we conclude that lightning is nothing more than a motion of electric charges, because we know that a motion of electric charges through the atmosphere, such as occurs when lightning is reported, gives rise to the type of visual stimulation which would lead an observer to report a flash of lightning. In the moon/tide case, on the other hand, there is no such direct causal connection between the stages of the moon and the observations made by the man who measures the height of the tide. The causal connection is between the moon and the tides, not between the moon and the measurement of the tides.

V THE PHYSIOLOGICAL EXPLANATION OF INTROSPECTION AND THE PHENOMENOLOGICAL FALLACY

If this account is correct, it should follow that in order to establish the identity of consciousness and certain processes in the brain, it would be necessary to show that the introspective observations reported by the subject can be accounted for in terms of processes which are known to have occurred in his brain. In the light of this suggestion it is extremely interesting to find that when a physiologist, as distinct from a philosopher, finds it difficult to see how consciousness could be a process in the brain, what worries him is not any supposed self-contradiction involved in such an assumption, but the apparent impossibility of accounting for the reports given by the subject of his conscious processes in terms of the known properties of the central nervous system. Sir Charles Sherrington has posed the problem as follows:

> The chain of events stretching from the sun's radiation entering the eye to, on the one hand, the contraction of the pupillary muscles, and on the other, to the electrical disturbances in the brain-cortex are all straightforward steps in a sequence of physical "causation," such as, thanks to science, are intelligible. But in the second serial chain there follows on, or attends, the stage of brain-cortex reaction an event or set of events quite inexplicable to us, which both as to themselves and as to the causal tie between them and what preceded them science does not help us; a set of events seemingly incommensurable with any of the events leading up to it. The self "sees" the sun; it senses a two-dimensional disc of brightness, located in the "sky," this last a field of lesser brightness, and overhead shaped as a rather flattened dome, coping the self and a hundred other visual things as well. Of hint that this is within the head there is none. Vision is saturated with this strange property called "projection," the unargued inference that what it sees is at a "distance" from the seeing "self." Enough has been said to stress that in the sequence of events a step is reached where a physical situation in the brain leads to a psychical, which however contains no hint of the brain or any other bodily part . . . The supposition has to be, it would seem, two continuous series of events, one physico-chemical, the other psychical, and at times interaction between them.[4]

Just as the physiologist is not likely to be impressed by the philosopher's contention that there is some self-contradiction involved in supposing consciousness to be a brain process, so the philosopher is unlikely to be impressed by the considerations which lead Sherrington to conclude that there are two sets of events, one physico-chemical, the other psychical. Sherrington's argument, for all its emotional appeal, depends on a fairly simply logical mistake, which is unfortunately all too frequently made by psychologists and physiologists and not infrequently in the past by the philosophers themselves. This logical mistake, which I shall refer to as the "phenomenological fallacy," is the mistake of supposing that when the subject describes his experience, when he describes how things look, sound, smell, taste, or feel to him, he is describing the literal properties of objects and events on a peculiar sort of internal cinema or television screen, usually referred to in the modern psychological literature as the "phenomenal field." If we assume, for example, that when a subject reports a green after-image he is asserting the occurrence inside himself of an object which is literally green, it is clear that we have on our hands an entity for which there is no place in the world of physics. In the case of the green after-image there is no green object in the subject's environment corresponding to the description that he gives. Nor is there anything green in his brain; certainly there is nothing which could have emerged when he reported the appearance of the green after-image. Brain processes are not the sort of things to which color concepts can be properly applied.

The phenomenological fallacy on which this argument is based depends on the mistaken assumption that because our ability to describe things in our environment depends on our consciousness of them, our descriptions of things are primarily descriptions of our conscious experience and only secondarily, indirectly,

---

[4]Sir Charles Sherrington, *The Integrative Action of the Nervous System* (Cambridge 1947) pp. xx–xxi.

and inferentially descriptions of the objects and events in our environments. It is assumed that because we recognize things in our environment by their look, sound, smell, taste, and feel, we begin by describing their phenomenal properties, i.e. the properties of the looks, sounds, smells, tastes, and feels which they produce in us, and infer their real properties from their phenomenal properties. In fact, the reverse is the case. We begin by learning to recognize the real properties of things in our environment. We learn to recognize them, of course, by their look, sound, smell, taste, and feel; but this does not mean that we have to learn to describe the look, sound, smell, taste, and feel of things before we can describe the things themselves. Indeed, it is only after we have learned to describe the things in our environment that we learn to describe our consciousness of them. We describe our conscious experience not in terms of the mythological "phenomenal properties" which are supposed to inhere in the mythological "objects" in the mythological "phenomenal field," but by reference to the actual physical properties of the concrete physical objects, events, and processes which normally, though not perhaps in the present instance, give rise to the sort of conscious experience which we are trying to describe. In other words when we describe the after-image as green, we are not saying that there is something, the after-image, which is green; we are saying that we are having the sort of experience which we normally have when, and which we have learned to describe as, looking at a green patch of light.

Once we rid ourselves of the phenomenological fallacy we realize that the problem of explaining introspective observations in terms of brain processes is far from insuperable. We realize that there is nothing that the introspecting subject says about his conscious experiences which is inconsistent with anything the physiologist might want to say about the brain processes which cause him to describe the environment and his consciousness of that environment in the way he does. When the subject describes his experience by saying that a light which is in fact stationary appears to move, all the physiologist or physiological psychologist has to do in order to explain the subject's introspective observations is to show that the brain process which is causing the subject to describe his experience in this way is the sort of process which normally occurs when he is observing an actual moving object and which therefore normally causes him to report the movement of an object in his environment. Once the mechanism whereby the individual describes what is going on in his environment has been worked out, all that is required to explain the individual's capacity to make introspective observations is an explanation of his ability to discriminate between those cases where his normal habits of verbal descriptions are appropriate to the stimulus situation and those cases where they are not, and an explanation of how and why, in those cases where the appropriateness of his normal descriptive habits is in doubt, he learns to issue his ordinary descriptive protocols preceded by a qualificatory phrase like "it appears," "seems," "looks," "feels," etc.[5]

[5]I am greatly indebted to my fellow-participants in a series of informal discussions on this topic which took place in the Department of Philosophy, University of Adelaide, in particular to Mr. C. B. Martin for his persistent and searching criticism of my earlier attempts to defend the thesis that consciousness is a brain process, to Professor D. A. T. Gasking, of the University of Melbourne, for clarifying many of the logical issues involved, and to Professor J. J. C. Smart for moral support and encouragment in what often seemed a lost cause.

Epiphenomenal Qualia

Frank C. Jackson

It is undeniable that the physical, chemical and biological sciences have provided a great deal of information about the world we live in and about ourselves. I will use the label "physical information" for this kind of information, and also for information that automatically comes along with it. For example, if a medical scientist tells me enough about the processes that go on in my nervous system, and about how they relate to happenings in the world around me, to what has happened in the past and is likely to happen in the future, to what happens to other similar and dissimilar organisms, and the like, he or she tells me—if I am clever enough to fit it together appropriately—about what is often called the functional role of those states in me (and in organisms in general in similar cases). This information, and its kin, I also label "physical."

I do not mean these sketchy remarks to constitute a definition of "physical information," and of the correlative notions of physical property, process, and so on, but to indicate what I have in mind here. It is well known that there are problems with giving a precise definition of these notions, and so of the thesis of Physicalism that all (correct) information is physical information.[1] But—unlike some—I take the question of definition to cut across the central problems I want to discuss in this paper.

I am what is sometimes known as a "qualia freak." I think that there are certain features of the bodily sensations especially, but also of certain perceptual experiences, which no amount of purely physical information includes. Tell me everything physical there is to tell about what is going on in a living brain, the kind of states, their functional role, their relation to what goes on at other times and in other brains, and so on and so forth, and be I as clever as can be in fitting it all together, you won't have told me about the hurtfulness of pains, the itchiness of itches, pangs of jealousy, or about the characteristic experience of tasting a lemon, smelling a rose, hearing a loud noise or seeing the sky.

There are many qualia freaks, and some of them say that their rejection of Physicalism is an unargued intuition.[2] I think that they are being unfair to themselves. They have the following argument. Nothing you could tell of a physical sort captures the smell of a rose, for instance. Therefore, Physicalism is false. By our lights this is a perfectly good argument. It is obviously not to the point to question its validity, and the premise is intuitively obviously true both to them and to me.

I must, however, admit that it is weak from a polemical point of view. There are, unfortunately for us, many who do not find the premise intuitively obvious. The task then is to present an argument whose premises are obvious to all, or at least to as many as possible. This I try to do in section I with what I will call "the

---

[1]See, e.g., D. H. Mellor, "Materialism and phenomenal qualities," *Aristotelian Society Supp. Vol.* 47 (1973), 107–19; and J. W. Cornman, *Materialism and Sensations,* New Haven and London, 1971.
[2]Particularly in discussion, but see, e.g., Keith Campbell, *Metaphysics,* Belmont, 1976, p. 67.
Source: "Epiphenomenal Qualia," by Frank C. Jackson, in *Philosophical Quarterly,* 32, 1982, 127–136. Reprinted by permission of the publisher.

Knowledge argument." In section II I contrast the Knowledge argument with the modal argument and in section III with the "What is it like to be" argument. In section IV I tackle the question of the causal role of qualia. The major factor in stopping people from admitting qualia is the belief that they would have to be given a causal role with respect to the physical world and especially the brain;[3] and it is hard to do this without sounding like someone who believes in fairies. I seek in section IV to turn this objection by arguing that the view that qualia are epiphenomenal is a perfectly possible one.

I THE KNOWLEDGE ARGUMENT FOR QUALIA

People vary considerably in their ability to discriminate colors. Suppose that in an experiment to catalog this variation Fred is discovered. Fred has better color vision than anyone else on record; he makes every discrimination that anyone has ever made, and moreover he makes one that we cannot even begin to make. Show him a batch of ripe tomatoes and he sorts them into two roughly equal groups and does so with complete consistency. That is, if you blindfold him, shuffle the tomatoes up, and then remove the blindfold and ask him to sort them out again, he sorts them into exactly the same two groups.

We ask Fred how he does it. He explains that all ripe tomatoes do not look the same color to him, and in fact that this is true of a great many objects that we classify together as red. He sees two colors where we see one, and he has in consequence developed for his own use two words "red_1" and "red_2" to mark the difference. Perhaps he tells us that he has often tried to teach the difference between red_1 and red_2 to his friends but has got nowhere and has concluded that the rest of the world is red_1–red_2 color-blind—or perhaps he has had partial success with his children; it doesn't matter. In any case he explains to us that it would be quite wrong to think that because "red" appears in both "red_1" and "red_2" that the two colors are shades of the one color. He only uses the common term "red" to fit more easily into our restricted usage. To him red_1 and red_2 are as different from each other and all the other colors as yellow is from blue. And his discriminatory behavior bears this out: he sorts red_1 from red_2 tomatoes with the greatest of ease in a wide variety of viewing circumstances. Moreover, an investigation of the physiological basis of Fred's exceptional ability reveals that Fred's optical system is able to separate out two groups of wavelengths in the red spectrum as sharply as we are able to sort out yellow from blue.[4]

I think that we should admit that Fred can see, really see, at least one more color than we can; red_1 is a different color from red_2. We are to Fred as a totally red–green color-blind person is to us. H. G. Wells' story "The country of the blind" is about a sighted person in a totally blind community.[5] This person never manages

---

[3]See, e.g., D. C. Dennett, "Current issues in the philosophy of mind," *American Philosophical Quarterly* 15 (1978), 249–61.

[4]Put this, and similar specifications below, in terms of Land's theory if you prefer. See e.g., Edwin H. Land, "Experiments in color vision," *Scientific American* 200 (5 May 1959), 84–99.

[5]H. G. Wells, *The Country of the Blind and Other Stories,* London, n.d.

to convince them that he can see, that he has an extra sense. They ridicule this sense as quite inconceivable, and treat his capacity to avoid falling into ditches, to win fights and so on as precisely that capacity and nothing more. We would be making their mistake if we refused to allow that Fred can see one more color than we can.

What kind of experience does Fred have when he sees red$_1$ and red$_2$? What is the new color or colors like? We would dearly like to know but do not; and it seems that no amount of physical information about Fred's brain and optical system tells us. We find out perhaps that Fred's cones respond differentially to certain light waves in the red section of the spectrum that make no difference to ours (or perhaps he has an extra cone) and that this leads in Fred to a wider range of those brain states responsible for visual discriminatory behavior. But none of this tells us what we really want to know about his color experience. There is something about it we don't know. But we know, we may suppose, everything about Fred's body, his behavior and dispositions to behavior and about his internal physiology, and everything about his history and relation to others that can be given in physical accounts of persons. We have all the physical information. Therefore, knowing all this is *not* knowing everything about Fred. It follows that Physicalism leaves something out.

To reinforce this conclusion, imagine that as a result of our investigations into the internal workings of Fred we find out how to make everyone's physiology like Fred's in the relevant respects; or perhaps Fred donates his body to science and on his death we are able to transplant his optical system into someone else—again the fine detail doesn't matter. The important point is that such a happening would create enormous interest. People would say "At last we will know what it is like to see the extra color, at last we will know how Fred has differed from us in the way he has struggled to tell us about for so long." Then it cannot be that we knew all along all about Fred. But *ex hypothesi* we did know all along everything about Fred that features in the physicalist scheme; hence the physicalist scheme leaves something out.

Put it this way. *After* the operation, we will know *more* about Fred and especially about his color experiences. But beforehand we had all the physical information we could desire about his body and brain, and indeed everything that has ever featured in physicalist accounts of mind and consciousness. Hence there is more to know than all that. Hence Physicalism is incomplete.

Fred and the new color(s) are of course essentially rhetorical devices. The same point can be made with normal people and familiar colors. Mary is a brilliant scientist who is, for whatever reason, forced to investigate the world from a black and white room *via* a black and white television monitor. She specializes in the neurophysiology of vision and acquires, let us suppose, all the physical information there is to obtain about what goes on when we see ripe tomatoes, or the sky, and use terms like "red," "blue," and so on. She discovers, for example, just which wavelength combinations from the sky stimulate the retina, and exactly how this produces *via* the central nervous system the contraction of the vocal chords and expulsion of air from the lungs that results in the uttering of the sentence "The sky is blue." (It can hardly be denied that it is in principle possible to obtain all this physical information from black and white television, otherwise the Open University would *of necessity* need to use color television.)

What will happen when Mary is released from her black and white room or is given a color television monitor? Will she *learn* anything or not? It seems just obvious that she will learn something about the world and our visual experience of it. But then it is inescapable that her previous knowledge was incomplete. But she had *all* the physical information. *Ergo* there is more to have than that, and Physicalism is false.

Clearly the same style of Knowledge argument could be deployed for taste, hearing, the bodily sensations and generally speaking for the various mental states which are said to have (as it is variously put) raw feels, phenomenal features or qualia. The conclusion in each case is that the qualia are left out of the physicalist story. And the polemical strength of the Knowledge argument is that it is so hard to deny the central claim that one can have all the physical information without having all the information there is to have.

II THE MODAL ARGUMENT

By the Modal argument I mean an argument of the following style.[6] Sceptics about other minds are not making a mistake in deductive logic, whatever else may be wrong with their position. No amount of physical information about another *logically entails* that he or she is conscious or feels anything at all. Consequently there is a possible world with organisms exactly like us in every physical respect (and remember that includes functional states, physical history, et al.) but which differ from us profoundly in that they have no conscious mental life at all. But then what is it that we have and they lack? Not anything physical *ex hypothesi*. In all physical regards we and they are exactly alike. Consequently there is more to us than the purely physical. Thus Physicalism is false.[7]

It is sometimes objected that the Modal argument misconceives Physicalism on the ground that that doctrine is advanced as a *contingent* truth.[8] But to say this is only to say that physicalists restrict their claim to *some* possible worlds, including especially ours; and the Modal argument is only directed against this lesser claim. If we in *our* world, let alone beings in any others, have features additional to those of our physical replicas in other possible worlds, then we have non-physical features or qualia.

The trouble rather with the modal argument is that it rests on a disputable modal intuition. Disputable because it is disputed. Some sincerely deny that there can be physical replicas of us in other possible worlds which nevertheless lack consciousness. Moreover, at least one person who once had the intuition now has doubts.[9]

[6]See, e.g., Keith Campbell, *Body and Mind,* New York, 1970; and Robert Kirk, "Sentience and behavior," *Mind* 83 (1974), 43–60.
[7]I have presented the argument in an inter-world rather than the more usual intra-world fashion to avoid inessential complications to do with supervenience, causal anomalies and the like.
[8]See, e.g., W. G. Lycan, "A new Lilliputian argument against machine functionalism," *Philosophical Studies* 35 (1979), 279–87, p. 280; and Don Locke, "Zombies, schizophrenics and purely physical objects," *Mind* 85 (1976), 97–9.
[9]See R. Kirk, "From physical explicability to full-blooded materialism," *Philosophical Quarterly* 29 (1979), 229–37. See also the arguments against the modal intuition in, e.g., Sydney Shoemaker, "Functionalism and qualia," *Philosophical Studies* 27 (1975), 291–315.

Head-counting may seem a poor approach to a discussion of the modal argument. But frequently we can do no better when modal intuitions are in question, and remember our initial goal was to find the argument with the greatest polemical utility.

Of course, *qua* protagonists of the Knowledge argument we may well accept the modal intuition in question; but this will be a *consequence* of our already having an argument to the conclusion that qualia are left out of the physicalist story, not our ground for that conclusion. Moreover, the matter is complicated by the possibility that the connection between matters physical and qualia is like that sometimes held to obtain between esthetic qualities and natural ones. Two possible worlds which agree in all "natural" respects (including the experiences of sentient creatures) must agree in all esthetic qualities also, but it is plausibly held that the esthetic qualities cannot be reduced to the natural.

III THE "WHAT IS IT LIKE TO BE" ARGUMENT

In "What is it like to be a bat?" Thomas Nagel argues that no amount of physical information can tell us what it is like to be a bat, and indeed that we, human beings, cannot imagine what it is like to be a bat.[10] His reason is that what this is like can only be understood from a bat's point of view, which is not our point of view and is not something capturable in physical terms which are essentially terms understandable equally from many points of view.

It is important to distinguish this argument from the Knowledge argument. When I complained that all the physical knowledge about Fred was not enough to tell us what his special color experience was like, I was not complaining that we weren't finding out what it is like to *be* Fred. I was complaining that there is something *about* his experience, a property of it, of which we were left ignorant. And if and when we come to know what this property is we still will not know what it is like to *be* Fred, but we will know more *about* him. No amount of knowledge about Fred, be it physical or not, amounts to knowledge "from the inside" considering Fred. We are not Fred. There is thus a whole set of items of knowledge expressed by forms of words like "that is *I myself* who is . . . " which Fred has and we simply cannot have because we are not him.[11]

When Fred sees the color he alone can see, one thing he knows is the way his experience of it differs from his experience of seeing red and so on; *another* is that he himself is seeing it. Physicalist and qualia freaks alike should acknowledge that no amount of information of whatever kind that *others* have *about* Fred amounts to knowledge of the second. My complaint though concerned the first and was that the

---

[10]*Philosophical Review* 83 (1974), 435–50. Two things need to be said about this article. One is that, despite my dissociations to come, I am much indebted to it. The other is that the emphasis changes through the article, and by the end Nagel is objecting not so much to Physicalism as to all extant theories of mind for ignoring points of view, including those that admit (irreducible) qualia.

[11]Knowledge *de se* in the terms of David Lewis, "Attitudes de dicto and de se," *Philosophical Review* 88 (1979), 513–43.

special quality of his experience is certainly a fact about it, and one which Physicalism leaves out because no amount of physical information told us what it is.

Nagel speaks as if the problem he is raising is one of extrapolating from knowledge of one experience to another, of imagining what an unfamiliar experience would be like on the basis of familiar ones. In terms of Hume's example, from knowledge of some shades of blue we can work out what it would be like to see other shades of blue. Nagel argues that the trouble with bats et al. is that they are too unlike us. It is hard to see an objection to Physicalism here. Physicalism makes no special claims about the imaginative or extrapolative powers of human beings, and it is hard to see why it need do so.[12]

Anyway, our Knowledge argument makes no assumptions on this point. If Physicalism were true, enough physical information about Fred would obviate any need to extrapolate or to perform special feats of imagination or understanding in order to know all about his special color experience. *The information would already be in our possession.* But it clearly isn't. That was the nub of the argument.

IV THE BOGEY OF EPIPHENOMENALISM

Is there any really *good* reason for refusing to countenance the idea that qualia are causally impotent with respect to the physical world? I will argue for the answer no, but in doing this I will say nothing about two views associated with the classical epiphenomenalist position. The first is that mental *states* are inefficacious with respect to the physical world. All I will be concerned to defend is that it is possible to hold that certain *properties* of certain mental states, namely those I've called qualia, are such that their possession or absence makes no difference to the physical world. The second is that the mental is *totally* causally inefficacious. For all I will say it may be that you have to hold that the instantiation of *qualia* makes a difference to *other mental states* though not to anything physical. Indeed general considerations to do with how you could come to be aware of the instantiation of qualia suggest such a position.[13]

Three reasons are standardly given for holding that a quale like the hurtfulness of a pain must be causally efficacious in the physical world, and so, for instance, that its instantiation must sometimes make a difference to what happens in the brain. None, I will argue, has any real force. (I am much indebted to Alec Hyslop and John Lucas for convincing me of this.)

(i) It is supposed to be just obvious that the hurtfulness of pain is partly responsible for the subject seeking to avoid pain, saying "It hurts" and so on. But, to reverse Hume, anything can fail to cause anything. No matter how often *B* follows *A,* and no matter how initially obvious the causality of the connection seems, the hypothesis that *A* causes *B* can be overturned by an over-arching theory which shows the two as distinct effects of a common underlying causal process.

[12]See Laurence Nemirow's comments on "What it is . . ." in his review of T. Nagel *Mortal Quesitons in Philosophical Review* 89 (1980), 473–7. I am indebted here in particular to a discussion with David Lewis.
[13]See my review of K. Campbell, *Body and Mind,* in *Australasian Journal of Philosophy* 50 (1972), 77–80.

To the untutored the image on the screen of Lee Marvin's fist moving from left to right immediately followed by the image of John Wayne's head moving in the same general direction looks as causal as anything.[14] And of course throughout countless Westerns images similar to the first are followed by images similar to the second. All this counts for precisely nothing when we know the over-arching theory concerning how the relevant images are both effects of an underlying causal process involving the projector and the film. The epiphenomenalist can say exactly the same about the connection between, for example, hurtfulness and behavior. It is simply a consequence of the fact that certain happenings in the brain cause both.

(ii) The second objection relates to Darwin's Theory of Evolution. According to natural selection the traits that evolve over time are those conducive to physical survival. We may assume that qualia evolved over time—we have them, the earliest forms of life do not—and so we should expect qualia to be conducive to survival. The objection is that they could hardly help us to survive if they do nothing to the physical world.

The appeal of this argument is undeniable, but there is a good reply to it. Polar bears have particularly thick, warm coats. The Theory of Evolution explains this (we suppose) by pointing out that having a thick warm coat is conducive to survival in the Arctic. But having a thick coat goes along with having a heavy coat, and having a heavy coat is *not* conducive to survival. It slows the animal down.

Does this mean that we have refuted Darwin because we have found an evolved trait—having a heavy coat—which is not conducive to survival? Clearly not. Having a heavy coat is an unavoidable concomitant of having a warm coat (in the context, modern insulation was not available), and the advantages for survival of having a warm coat outweighed the disadvantages of having a heavy one. The point is that all we can extract from Darwin's theory is that we should expect any evolved characteristic to be *either* conducive to survival *or* a by-product of one that is so conducive. The epiphenomenalist holds that qualia fall into the latter category. They are a by-product of certain brain processes that are highly conducive to survival.

(iii) The third objection is based on a point about how we come to know about other minds. We know about other minds by knowing about other behavior, at least in part. The nature of the inference is a matter of some controversy, but it is not a matter of controversy that it proceeds from behavior. That is why we think that stones do not feel and dogs do feel. But, runs the objection, how can a person's behavior provide any reason for believing he has qualia like mine, or indeed any qualia at all, unless this behavior can be regarded as the *outcome* of the qualia. Man Friday's footprint was evidence of Man Friday because footprints are causal outcomes of feet attached to people. And an epiphenomenalist cannot regard behavior, or indeed anything physical, as an outcome of qualia.

But consider my reading in *The Times* that Spurs won. This provides excellent evidence that the *Telegraph* has also reported that Spurs won, despite the fact that (I trust) the *Telegraph* does not get the results from *The Times*. They each send their

---

[14]Cf. Jean Piaget, "The child's conception of physical causality," reprinted in *The Essential Piaget*, London, 1977.

own reporters to the game. The *Telegraph's* report is in no sense an outcome of *The Times',* but the latter provides good evidence for the former nevertheless.

The reasoning involved can be reconstructed thus. I read in *The Times* that Spurs won. This gives me reason to think that Spurs won because I know that Spurs' winning is the most likely candidate to be what caused the report in *The Times.* But I also know that Spurs' winning would have had many effects, including almost certain a report in the *Telegraph.*

I am arguing from one effect back to its cause and out again to another effect. The fact that neither effect causes the other is irrelevant. Now the epiphenomenalist allows that qualia are effects of what goes on in the brain. Qualia cause nothing physical but are caused by something physical. Hence the epiphenomenalist can argue from the behavior of others to the qualia of others by arguing from the behavior of others back to its causes in the brains of others and out again to their qualia.

You may well feel for one reason or another that this is a more dubious chain of reasoning than its model in the case of newspaper reports. You are right. The problem of other minds is a major philosophical problem, the problem of other newspaper reports is not. But there is no special problem for Epiphenomenalism as opposed to, say, Interactionism here.

There is a very understandable response to the three replies I have just made. "All right, there is no knockdown refutation of the existence of epiphenomenal qualia. But the fact remains that they are an excrescence. They *do* nothing, they *explain* nothing, they serve merely to soothe the intuitions of dualists, and it is left a total mystery how they fit into the world view of science. In short we do not and cannot understand the how and why of them."

This is perfectly true; but is no objection to qualia, for it rests on an overly optimistic view of the human animal, and its powers. We are the products of Evolution. We understand and sense what we need to understand and sense in order to survive. Epiphenomenal qualia are totally irrelevant to survival. At no stage of our evolution did natural selection favor those who could make sense of how they are caused and the laws governing them, or in fact why they exist at all. And that is why we can't.

It is not sufficiently appreciated that Physicalism is an extremely optimistic view of our powers. If it is true, we have, in very broad outline admittedly, a grasp of our place in the scheme of things. Certain matters of sheer complexity defeat us—there are an awful lot of neurons—but in principle we have it all. But consider the antecedent probability that everything in the Universe be of a kind that is relevant in some way or other to the survival of *Homo sapiens.* It is very low surely. But then one must admit that it is very likely that there is a part of the whole scheme of things, maybe a big part, which no amount of evolution will ever bring us near to knowledge about or understanding of. For the simple reason that such knowledge and understanding is irrelevant to survival.

Physicalists typically emphasize that we are a part of nature on their view, which is fair enough. But if we are a part of nature, we are as nature has left us after however many years of evolution it is, and each step in that evolutionary progression has been a matter of chance constrained just by the need to preserve or increase survival value. The wonder is that we understand as much as we do, and there is no wonder that there should be matters which fall quite outside our comprehension. Perhaps exacty how epiphenomenal qualia fit into the scheme of things is one such.

This may seem an unduly pessimistic view of our capacity to articulate a truly comprehensive picture of our world and our place in it. But suppose we discovered living on the bottom of the deepest oceans a sort of sea slug which manifested intelligence. Perhaps survival in the conditions required rational powers. Despite their intelligence, these sea slugs have only a very restricted conception of the world by comparison with ours, the explanation for this being the nature of their immediate environment. Nevertheless they have developed sciences which work surprisingly well in these restricted terms. They also have philosophers, called slugists. Some call themselves tough-minded slugists, others confess to being soft-minded slugists.

The tough-minded slugists hold that the restricted terms (or ones pretty like them which may be introduced as their sciences progress) suffice in principle to describe everything without remainder. These tough-minded slugists admit in moments of weakness to a feeling that their theory leaves something out. They resist this feeling and their opponents, the soft-minded slugists, by pointing out— absolutely correctly—that no slugist has ever succeeded in spelling out how this mysterious residue fits into the highly successful view that their sciences have and are developing of how their world works.

Our sea slugs don't exist, but they might. And there might also exist super beings which stand to us as we stand to these slugs. We cannot adopt the perspective of these super beings, because we are not them, but the possibility of such a perspective is, I think, an antidote to excessive optimism.[15]

Computing Machinery and Intelligence

Alan M. Turing

1. THE IMITATION GAME

I propose to consider the question "Can machines think?" This should begin with definitions of the meaning of the terms "machine" and "think." The definitions might be framed so as to reflect so far as possible the normal use of the words, but this attitude is dangerous. If the meaning of the words "machine" and "think" are to be found by examining how they are commonly used it is difficult to escape the conclusion that the meaning and the answer to the question, "Can machines think?" is to be sought in a statistical survey such as a Gallup poll. But this is absurd.

---

[15]I am indebted to Robert Pargetter for a number of comments and, despite his dissent, to section IV of Paul E. Meehl's "The complete autocerebroscopist," in Paul Feyerabend and Grover Maxwell (eds), *Mind, Matter and Method,* Minneapolis, 1966.

Source: "Computing Machinery and Intelligence," by Alan M. Turing, *Mind,* 59, 1950. Reprinted by permission of Oxford University Press.

Instead of attempting such a definition I shall replace the question by another, which is closely related to it and is expressed in relatively unambiguous words.

The new form of the problem can be described in terms of a game which we call the "imitation game." It is played with three people, a man (A), a woman (B), and an interrogator (C) who may be of either sex. The interrogator stays in a room apart from the other two. The object of the game for the interrogator is to determine which of the other two is the man and which is the woman. He knows them by labels X and Y, and at the end of the game he says either "X is A and Y is B" or "X is B and Y is A." The interrogator is allowed to put questions to A and B thus:

C: Will X please tell me the length of his or her hair?

Now suppose X is actually A, then A must answer. It is A's object in the game to try to cause C to make the wrong identification. His answer might therefore be

"My hair is shingled, and the longest strands are about nine inches long."

In order that tones of voice may not help the interrogator the answers should be written, or better still, typewritten. The ideal arrangement is to have a teleprinter communicating between the two rooms. Alternatively the question and answers can be repeated by an intermediary. The object of the game for the third player (B) is to help the interrogator. The best strategy for her is probably to give truthful answers. She can add such things as "I am the woman, don't listen to him!" to her answers, but it will avail nothing as the man can make similar remarks.

We now ask the question, "What will happen when a machine takes the part of A in this game?" Will the interrogator decide wrongly as often when the game is played like this as he does when the game is played between a man and a woman? These questions replace our original, "Can machines think?"

2. CRITIQUE OF THE NEW PROBLEM

As well as asking, "What is the answer to this new form of the question," one may ask, "Is this new question a worthy one to investigate?" This latter question we investigate without further ado, thereby cutting short an infinite regress.

The new problem has the advantage of drawing a fairly sharp line between the physical and the intellectual capacities of a man. No engineer or chemist claims to be able to produce a material which is indistinguishable from the human skin. It is possible that at some time this might be done, but even supposing this invention available we should feel there was little point in trying to make a "thinking machine" more human by dressing it up in such artificial flesh. The form in which we have set the problem reflects this fact in the condition which prevents the interrogator from seeing or touching the other competitors, or hearing their voices. Some other advantages of the proposed criterion may be shown up by specimen questions and answers. Thus:

Q: Please write me a sonnet on the subject of the Forth Bridge.
A: Count me out on this one. I never could write poetry.
Q: Add 34957 to 70764.
A: (Pause about 30 seconds and then give as answer) 105621.

Q: Do you play chess?
A: Yes.
Q: I have K at my K1, and no other pieces. You have only K at K6 and R at R1. It is your move. What do you play?
A: (After a pause of 15 seconds) R-R8 mate.

The question and answer method seems to be suitable for introducing almost any one of the fields of human endeavor that we wish to include. We do not wish to penalize the machine for its inability to shine in beauty competitions, nor to penalize a man for losing in a race against an airplane. The conditions of our game make these disabilities irrelevant. The "witnesses" can brag, if they consider it advisable, as much as they please about their charms, strength or heroism, but the interrogator cannot demand practical demonstrations.

The game may perhaps be criticized on the ground that the odds are weighted too heavily against the machine. If the man were to try and pretend to be the machine he would clearly make a very poor showing. He would be given away at once by slowness and inaccuracy in arithmetic. May not machines carry out something which ought to be described as thinking but which is very different from what a man does? This objection is a very strong one, but at least we can say that if, nevertheless, a machine can be constructed to play the imitation game satisfactorily, we need not be troubled by this objection.

It might be urged that when playing the "imitation game" the best strategy for the machine may possibly be something other than imitation of the behavior of a man. This may be, but I think it is unlikely that there is any great effect of this kind. In any case there is no intention to investigate here the theory of the game, and it will be assumed that the best strategy is to try to provide answers that would naturally be given by a man.

3. THE MACHINES CONCERNED IN THE GAME

The question which we put in §1 will not be quite definite until we have specified what we mean by the word "machine." It is natural that we should wish to permit every kind of engineering technique to be used in our machines. We also wish to allow the possibility that an engineer or team of engineers may construct a machine which works, but whose manner of operation cannot be satisfactorily described by its constructors because they have applied a method which is largely experimental. Finally, we wish to exclude from the machines men born in the usual manner. It is difficult to frame the definitions so as to satisfy these three conditions. One might for instance insist that the team of engineers should be all of one sex, but this would not really be satisfactory, for it is probably possible to rear a complete individual from a single cell of the skin (say) of a man. To do so would be a feat of biological technique deserving of the very highest praise, but we would not be inclined to regard it as a case of "constructing a thinking machine." This prompts us to abandon the requirement that every kind of technique should be permitted. We are the more ready to do so in view of the fact that the present interest in "thinking machines" has been aroused by a particular kind of machine, usually called an "electronic computer" or "digital computer." Following this suggestion we only permit digital computers to take part in our game.

This restriction appears at first sight to be a very drastic one. I shall attempt to show that it is not so in reality. To do this necessitates a short account of the nature and properties of these computers.

It may also be said that this identification of machines with digital computers, like our criterion for "thinking," will only be unsatisfactory if (contrary to my belief), it turns out that digital computers are unable to give a good showing in the game.

There are already a number of digital computers in working order, and it may be asked, "Why not try the experiment straight away? It would be easy to satisfy the conditions of the game. A number of interrogators could be used, and statistics compiled to show how often the right identification was given." The short answer is that we are not asking whether all digital computers would do well in the game nor whether the computers at present available would do well, but whether there are imaginable computers which would do well. But this is only the short answer. We shall see this question in a different light later.

4. DIGITAL COMPUTERS

The idea behind digital computers may be explained by saying that these machines are intended to carry out any operations which could be done by a human computer. The human computer is supposed to be following fixed rules; he has no authority to deviate from them in any detail. We may suppose that these rules are supplied in a book, which is altered whenever he is put on to a new job. He has also an unlimited supply of paper on which he does his calculations. He may also do his multiplications and additions on a "desk machine," but this is not important.

If we use the above explanation as a definition we shall be in danger of circularity of argument. We avoid this by giving an outline of the means by which the desired effect is achieved. A digital computer can usually be regarded as consisting of three parts:

    (i) Store.
    (ii) Executive unit.
    (iii) Control.

The store is a store of information, and corresponds to the human computer's paper, whether this is the paper on which he does his calculations or that on which his book of rules is printed. Insofar as the human computer does calculations in his head a part of the store will correspond to his memory.

The executive unit is the part which carries out the various individual operations involved in a calculation. What these individual operations are will vary from machine to machine. Usually fairly lengthy operations can be done such as "Multiply 3540675445 by 7076345687" but in some machines only very simple ones such as "Write down 0" are possible.

We have mentioned that the "book of rules" supplied to the computer is replaced in the machine by a part of the store. It is then called the "table of instructions." It is the duty of the control to see that these instructions are obeyed correctly and in the right order. The control is so constructed that this necessarily happens.

The information in the store is usually broken up into packets of moderately small size. In one machine, for instance, a packet might consist of ten decimal digits. Numbers are assigned to the parts of the store in which the various packets of information are stored, in some systematic manner. A typical instruction might say—

"Add the number stored in position 6809 to that in 4302 and put the result back into the latter storage position."

Needless to say it would not occur in the machine expressed in English. It would more likely be coded in a form such as 6809430217. Here 17 says which of various possible operations is to be performed on the two numbers. In this case the operation is that described above, viz. "Add the number. . . ." It will be noticed that the instruction takes up 10 digits and so forms one packet of information, very conveniently. The control will normally take the instructions to be obeyed in the order of the positions in which they are stored, but occasionally an instruction such as—

"Now obey the instruction stored in position 5606, and continue from there"— may be encountered, or again—

"If position 4505 contains 0 obey next the instruction stored in 6707, otherwise continue straight on."

Instructions of these latter types are very important because they make it possible for a sequence of operations to be repeated over and over again until some condition is fulfilled, but in doing so to obey, not fresh instructions on each repetition, but the same ones over and over again. To take a domestic analogy. Suppose Mother wants Tommy to call at the cobbler's every morning on his way to school to see if her shoes are done; she can ask him afresh every morning. Alternatively she can stick up a notice once and for all in the hall which he will see when he leaves for school and which tells him to call for the shoes, and also to destroy the notice when he comes back if he has the shoes with him.

The reader must accept it as a fact that digital computers can be constructed, and indeed have been constructed, according to the principles we have described, and that they can in fact mimic the actions of a human computer very closely.

The book of rules which we have described our human computer as using is of course a convenient fiction. Actual human computers really remember what they have got to do. If one wants to make a machine mimic the behavior of the human computer in some complex operation one has to ask him how it is done, and then translate the answer into the form of an instruction table. Constructing instruction tables is usually described as "programing." To "program a machine to carry out the operation A" means to put the appropriate instruction table into the machine so that it will do A.

An interesting variant on the idea of a digital computer is a "digital computer with a random element." These have instructions involving the throwing of a die or some equivalent electronic process; one such instruction might for instance be, "Throw the die and put the resulting number into store 1000." Sometimes such a machine is described as having free will (though I would not use this phrase myself). It is not normally possible to determine from observing a machine whether it has a random element, for a similar effect can be produced by such devices as making the choices depend on the digits of the decimal for π.

Most actual digital computers have only a finite store. There is no theoretical difficulty in the idea of a computer with an unlimited store. Of course only a finite part can have been used at any one time. Likewise only a finite amount can have been constructed, but we can imagine more and more being added as required. Such computers have special theoretical interest and will be called infinite capacity computers.

The idea of a digital computer is an old one. Charles Babbage, Lucasian Professor of Mathematics at Cambridge from 1828 to 1839, planned such a machine, called the Analytical Engine, but it was never completed. Although Babbage had all the essential ideas, his machine was not at that time such a very attractive prospect. The speed which would have been available would be definitely faster than a human computer but something like 100 times slower than the Manchester machine, itself one of the slower of the modern machines. The storage was to be purely mechanical, using wheels and cards.

The fact that Babbage's Analytical Engine was to be entirely mechanical will help us to rid ourselves of a superstition. Importance is often attached to the fact that modern digital computers are electrical, and that the nervous system also is electrical. Since Babbage's machine was not electrical, and since all digital computers are in a sense equivalent, we see that this use of electricity cannot be of theoretical importance. Of course electricity usually comes in where fast signaling is concerned, so that it is not surprising that we find it in both these connections. In the nervous system chemical phenomena are at least as important as electrical. In certain computers the storage system is mainly acoustic. The feature of using electricity is thus seen to be only a very superficial similarity. If we wish to find such similarities we should look rather for mathematical analogies of function.

5. UNIVERSALITY OF DIGITAL COMPUTERS

The digital computers considered in the last section may be classified among the "discrete state machines." These are the machines which move by sudden jumps or clicks from one quite definite state to another. These states are sufficiently different for the possibility of confusion between them to be ignored. Strictly speaking there are no such machines. Everything really moves continuously. But there are many kinds of machines which can profitably be *thought of* as being discrete state machines. For instance in considering the switches for a lighting system it is a convenient fiction that each switch must be definitely on or definitely off. There must be intermediate positions, but for most purposes we can forget about them. As an example of a discrete state machine we might consider a wheel which clicks round through 120° once a second, but may be stopped by a lever which can be operated from outside; in addition a lamp is to light in one of the positions of the wheel. This machine could be described abstractly as follows: The internal state of the machine (which is described by the position of the wheel) may be q_1, q_2 or q_3. There is an input signal i_0 or i_1 (position of lever). The internal state at any moment is determined by the last state and input signal according to the table

		Last State		
		q_1	q_2	q_3
Input	i_0	q_2	q_3	q_1
	i_1	q_1	q_2	q_3

The output signals, the only externally visible indication of the internal state (the light) are described by the table

State	q_1	q_2	q_3
Output	o_0	o_0	o_1

This example is typical of discrete state machines. They can be described by such tables provided they have only a finite number of possible states.

It will seem that given the initial state of the machine and the input signals it is always possible to predict all future states. This is reminiscent of Laplace's view that from the complete state of the universe at one moment of time, as described by the positions and velocities of all particles, it should be possible to predict all future states. The prediction which we are considering is, however, rather nearer to practicability than that considered by Laplace. The system of the "universe as a whole" is such that quite small errors in the initial conditions can have an overwhelming effect at a later time. The displacement of a single electron by a billionth or a centimeter at one moment might make the difference between a man being killed by an avalanche a year later, or escaping. It is an essential property of the mechanical systems which we have called "discrete state machines" that this phenomenon does not occur. Even when we consider the actual physical machines instead of the idealized machines, reasonably accurate knowledge of the state at one moment yields reasonably accurate knowledge any number of steps later.

As we have mentioned, digital computers fall within the class of discrete state machines. But the number of states of which such a machine is capable is usually enormously large. For instance, the number for the machine now working at Manchester is about $2^{165,000}$, i.e., about $10^{50,000}$. Compare this with our example of the clicking wheel described above, which had three states. It is not difficult to see why the number of states should be so immense. The computer includes a store corresponding to the paper used by a human computer. It must be possible to write into the store any one of the combinations of symbols which might have been written on the paper. For simplicity suppose that only digits from 0 to 9 are used as symbols. Variations in handwriting are ignored. Suppose the computer is allowed 100 sheets of paper each containing 50 lines each with room for 30 digits. Then the number of states is $10^{100 \times 50 \times 30}$, i.e., $10^{150,000}$. This is about the number of states of three Manchester machines put together. The logarithm to the base two of the number of states is usually called the "storage capacity" of the machine. Thus the Manchester machine has a storage capacity of about 165,000 and the wheel machine of our example about $1 \cdot 6$. If two machines are put together their capacities must be added to obtain the capacity of the resultant machine. This leads to the possibility of statements such as "The Manchester machine contains 64 magnetic tracks each with a capacity of 2560, eight electronic tubes with a capacity of 1280. Miscellaneous storage amounts to about 300 making a total of 174,380."

Given the table corresponding to a discrete state machine it is possible to predict what it will do. There is no reason why this calculation should not be carried out by means of a digital computer. Provided it could be carried out sufficiently quickly the digital computer could mimic the behavior of any discrete state machine. The imitation game could then be played with the machine in question (as B) and the mimicking digital computer (as A) and the interrogator would be unable to distinguish them. Of course the digital computer must have an adequate storage capacity as well as working sufficiently fast. Moreover, it must be programed afresh for each new machine which it is desired to mimic.

This special property of digital computers, that they can mimic any discrete state machine, is described by saying that they are *universal* machines. The existence of machines with this property has the important consequence that, considerations of speed apart, it is unnecessary to design various new machines to do various computing processes. They can all be done with one digital computer, suitably programed for each case. It will be seen that as a consequence of this all digital computers are in a sense equivalent.

We may now consider again the point raised at the end of §3. It was suggested tentatively that the question, "Can machines think?" should be replaced by "Are there imaginable digital computers which would do well in the imitation game?" If we wish we can make this superficially more general and ask "Are there discrete state machines which would do well?" But in view of the universality property we see that either of these questions is equivalent to this, "Let us fix our attention on one particular digital computer C. Is it true that by modifying this computer to have an adequate storage, suitably increasing its speed of action, and providing it with an appropriate program, C can be made to play satisfactorily the part of A in the imitation game, the part of B being taken by a man?"

6. CONTRARY VIEWS ON THE MAIN QUESTION

We may now consider the ground to have been cleared and we are ready to proceed to the debate on our question, "Can machines think?" and the variant of it quoted at the end of the last section. We cannot altogether abandon the original form of the problem, for opinions will differ as to the appropriateness of the substitution and we must at least listen to what has to be said in this connection.

It will simplify matters for the reader if I explain first my own beliefs in the matter. Consider first the more accurate form of the question. I believe that in about fifty years' time it will be possible to program computers, with a storage capacity of about 10^9, to make them play the imitation game so well that an average interrogator will not have more than 70 per cent chance of making the right identification after five minutes of questioning. The original question, "Can machines think?" I believe to be too meaningless to deserve discussion. Nevertheless I believe that at the end of the century the use of words and general educated opinion will have altered so much that one will be able to speak of machines thinking without expecting to be contradicted. I believe further that no useful purpose is served by concealing these beliefs. The popular view that scientists proceed inexorably from well-established fact to well-established fact, never being influenced by any unproved conjecture, is quite mistaken. Provided it is made clear which are proved facts and which are conjectures, no harm can result. Conjectures are of great importance since they suggest useful lines of research.

I now proceed to consider opinions opposed to my own.

(1) *The Theological Objection.* Thinking is a function of man's immortal soul. God has given an immortal soul to every man and woman, but not to any other animal or to machines. Hence no animal or machine can think.[1]

I am unable to accept any part of this, but will attempt to reply in theological terms. I should find the argument more convincing if animals were classed with men, for there is a greater difference, to my mind, between the typical animate and the inanimate than there is between man and the other animals. The arbitrary character of the orthodox view becomes clearer if we consider how it might appear to a member of some other religious community. How do Christians regard the Moslem view that women have no souls? But let us leave this point aside and return to the main argument. It appears to me that the argument quoted above implies a serious restriction of the omnipotence of the Almighty. It is admitted that there are certain things that He cannot do such as making one equal to two, but should we not believe that He has freedom to confer a soul on an elephant if He sees fit? We might expect that He would only exercise this power in conjunction with a mutation which provided the elephant with an appropriately improved brain to minister to the needs of this soul. An argument of exactly similar form may be made for the case of machines. It may seem different because it is more difficult to "swallow." But this really only means that we think it would be less likely that He would consider the circumstances suitable for conferring a soul. The circumstances in question are discussed in the rest of this paper. In attempting to construct such machines we should not be irreverently usurping His power of creating souls, any more than we are in the procreation of children: rather we are, in either case, instruments of His will providing mansions for the souls that He creates.

However, this is mere speculation. I am not very impressed with theological arguments whatever they may be used to support. Such arguments have often been found unsatisfactory in the past. In the time of Galileo it was argued that the texts, "And the sun stood still . . . and hasted not to go down about a whole day" (Joshua x. 13) and "He laid the foundations of the earth, that it should not move at

---

[1]Possibly this view is heretical. St. Thomas Aquinas [*Summa Theologica,* quoted by Bertrand Russell, *A History of Western Philosophy* (New York: Simon and Schuster, 1945), p. 458] states that God cannot make a man to have no soul. But this may not be a real restriction on His powers, but only a result of the fact that men's souls are immortal, and therefore indestructible.

any time" (Psalm cv. 5) were an adequate refutation of the Copernican theory. With our present knowledge such an argument appears futile. When that knowledge was not available it made a quite different impression.

(2) *The "Heads in the Sand" Objection.* "The consequences of machines thinking would be too dreadful. Let us hope and believe that they cannot do so."

This argument is seldom expressed quite so openly as in the form above. But it affects most of us who think about it at all. We like to believe that Man is in some subtle way superior to the rest of creation. It is best if he can be shown to be *necessarily* superior, for then there is no danger of him losing his commanding position. The popularity of the theological argument is clearly connected with this feeling. It is likely to be quite strong in intellectual people, since they value the power of thinking more highly than others, and are more inclined to base their belief in the superiority of Man on this power.

I do not think that this argument is sufficiently substantial to require refutation. Consolation would be more appropriate: perhaps this should be sought in the transmigration of souls.

(3) *The Mathematical Objection.* There are a number of results of mathematical logic which can be used to show that there are limitations to the powers of discrete state machines. The best known of these results is known as Gödel's theorem, and shows that in any sufficiently powerful logical system statements can be formulated which can neither be proved nor disproved within the system, unless possibly the system itself is inconsistent. There are other, in some respects similar, results due to Church, Kleene, Rosser, and Turing. The latter result is the most convenient to consider, since it refers directly to machines, whereas the others can only be used in a comparatively indirect argument: for instance if Gödel's theorem is to be used we need in addition to have some means of describing logical systems in terms of machines, and machines in terms of logical systems. The result in question refers to a type of machine which is essentially a digital computer with an infinite capacity. It states that there are certain things that such a machine cannot do. If it is rigged up to give answers to questions as in the imitation game, there will be some questions to which it will either give a wrong answer, or fail to give an answer at all however much time is allowed for a reply. There may, of course, be many such questions, and questions which cannot be answered by one machine may be satisfactorily answered by another. We are of course supposing for the present that the questions are of the kind to which an answer "Yes" or "No" is appropriate, rather than questions such as "What do you think of Picasso?" The questions that we know the machines must fail on are of this type, "Consider the machine specified as follows. . . . Will this machine ever answer 'Yes' to any question?" The dots are to be replaced by a description of some machine in a standard form, which could be something like that used in Sec. 5. When the machine described bears a certain comparatively simple relation to the machine which is under interrogation, it can be shown that the answer is either wrong or not forthcoming. This is the mathematical result: it is argued that it proves a disability of machines to which the human intellect is not subject.

The short answer to this argument is that although it is established that there are limitations to the powers of any particular machine, it has only been stated, without any sort of proof, that no such limitations apply to the human intellect. But I do not think this view can be dismissed quite so lightly. Whenever one of these machines is asked the appropriate critical question, and gives a definite answer, we know that this answer must be wrong, and this gives us a certain feeling of superiority. Is this feeling illusory? It is no doubt quite genuine, but I do not think too much importance should be attached to it. We too often give wrong answers to questions ourselves to be justified in being very pleased at such evidence of fallibility on the part of the machines. Further, our superiority can only be felt on such an occasion in relation to the one machine over which we have scored our petty triumph. There would be no question of triumphing simultaneously over *all* machines. In short, then, there might be men cleverer than any given machine, but then again there might be other machines cleverer again, and so on.

Those who hold to the mathematical argument would, I think, mostly be willing to accept the imitation game as a basis for discussion. Those who believe in the two previous objections would probably not be interested in any criteria.

(4) *The Argument from Consciousness.* This argument is very well expressed in Professor Jefferson's Lister Oration for 1949, from which I quote. "Not until a machine can write a sonnet or compose a concerto because of thoughts and emotions felt, and not by the chance fall of symbols, could we agree that machine equals brain—that is, not only write it but know that it had written it. No mechanism could feel (and not merely artificially signal, an easy contrivance) pleasure at its successes, grief when its valves fuse, be warmed by flattery, be made miserable by its mistakes, be charmed by sex, be angry or depressed when it cannot get what it wants."

This argument appears to be a denial of the validity of our test. According to the most extreme form of this view the only way by which one could be sure that a machine thinks is to *be* the machine and to feel oneself thinking. One could then describe these feelings to the world, but of course no one would be justified in taking any notice. Likewise according to this view the only way to know that a *man* thinks is to be that particular man. It is in fact the solipsist point of view. It may be the most logical view to hold but it makes communication of ideas difficult. A is liable to believe "A thinks but B does not" while B believes "B thinks but A does not." Instead of arguing continually over this point it is usual to have the polite convention that everyone thinks.

I am sure that Professor Jefferson does not wish to adopt the extreme and solipsist point of view. Probably he would be quite willing to accept the imitation game as a test. The game (with the player B omitted) is frequently used in practice under the name of *viva voce* to discover whether someone really understands something or has "learned it parrot fashion." Let us listen in to a part of such a *viva voce:*

INTERROGATOR: In the first line of your sonnet which reads "Shall I compare thee to a summer's day," would not "a spring day" do as well or better?

WITNESS: It wouldn't scan.

INTERROGATOR: How about "a winter's day." That would scan all right.

WITNESS: Yes, but nobody wants to be compared to a winter's day.

INTERROGATOR: Would you say Mr. Pickwick reminded you of Christmas?

WITNESS: In a way.

INTERROGATOR: Yet Christmas is a winter's day, and I do not think Mr. Pickwick would mind the comparison.

WITNESS: I don't think you're serious. By a winter's day one means a typical winter's day, rather than a special one like Christmas.

And so on. What would Professor Jefferson say if the sonnet-writing machine was able to answer like this in the *viva voce?* I do not know whether he would regard the machine as "merely artificially signaling" these answers, but if the answers were as satisfactory and sustained as in the above passage I do not think he would describe it as "an easy contrivance." This phrase is, I think, intended to cover such devices as the inclusion in the machine of a record of someone reading a sonnet, with appropriate switching to turn it on from time to time.

In short then, I think that most of those who support the argument from consciousness could be persuaded to abandon it rather than be forced into the solipsist position. They will then probably be willing to accept our test.

I do not wish to give the impression that I think there is no mystery about consciousness. There is, for instance, something of a paradox connected with any attempt to localize it. But I do not think these mysteries necessarily need to be solved before we can answer the question with which we are concerned in this paper.

(5) *Arguments from Various Disabilities.* These arguments take the form, "I grant you that you can make machines do all the things you have mentioned but you will never be able to make one to do X." Numerous features X are suggested in this connection. I offer a selection:

> Be kind, resourceful, beautiful, friendly (p. 19), have initiative, have a sense of humor, tell right from wrong, make mistakes (p. 19), fall in love, enjoy strawberries and cream (p. 19), make someone fall in love with it, learn from experience (pp. 25f.), use words properly, be the subject of its own thought (p. 20), have as much diversity of behavior as a man, do something really new (p. 20). (Some of these disabilities are given special consideration as indicated by the page numbers.)

No support is usually offered for these statements. I believe they are mostly founded on the principle of scientific induction. A man has seen thousands of machines in his lifetime. From what he sees of them he draws a number of general conclusions. They are ugly, each is designed for a very limited purpose, when required for a minutely different purpose they are useless, the variety of behavior of any one of them is very small, etc., etc. Naturally he concludes that these are necessary properties of machines in general. Many of these limitations are associated with the very small storage capacity of most machines. (I am assuming that the idea of storage capacity is extended in some way to cover machines other than discrete state machines. The exact definition does not matter as no mathematical accuracy is claimed in the present discussion.) A few years ago, when very little had been heard of digital computers, it was possible to elicit much incredulity concerning them, if one mentioned their properties without describing their construction. That was presumably due to a similar application of the principle of scientific induction. These applications of the principle are of course largely unconscious. When a burned child fears the fire and shows that he fears it by avoiding it, I should say that he was applying scientific induction. (I could of course also describe his behavior in many other ways.) The works and customs of mankind do not seem to be very suitable material to which to apply scientific induction. A very large part of space-time must be investigated if reliable results are to be obtained. Otherwise we may (as most English children do) decide that everybody speaks English, and that it is silly to learn French.

There are, however, special remarks to be made about many of the disabilities that have been mentioned. The inability to enjoy strawberries and cream may have struck the reader as frivolous. Possibly a machine might be made to enjoy this delicious dish, but any attempt to make one do so would be idiotic. What is important about this disability is that it contributes to some of the other disabilities, e.g., to the difficulty of the same kind of friendliness occurring between man and machine as between white man and white man, or between black man and black man.

The claim that "machines cannot make mistakes" seems a curious one. One is tempted to retort, "Are they any the worse for that?" But let us adopt a more sympathetic attitude, and try to see what is really meant. I think this criticism can be explained in terms of the imitation game. It is claimed that the interrogator could distinguish the machine from the man simply by setting them a number of problems in arithmetic. The machine would be unmasked because of its deadly accuracy. The reply to this is simple. The machine (programed for playing the game) would not attempt to give the *right* answers to the arithmetic problems. It would deliberately introduce mistakes in a manner calculated to confuse the interrogator. A mechanical fault would probably show itself through an unsuitable decision as to what sort of a mistake to make in the arithmetic. Even this interpretation of the criticism is not sufficiently sympathetic. But we cannot afford the space to go into it much further. It seems to me that this criticism depends on a confusion between two kinds of mistakes. We may call them "errors of functioning" and "errors of conclusion." Errors of functioning are due to some mechanical or electrical fault which causes the machine to behave otherwise than it was designed to do. In philosophical discussions one likes to ignore the possibility of such errors; one is therefore discussing "abstract machines." These abstract machines are mathematical fictions rather than physical objects. By definition they are incapable of errors of functioning. In this sense we can truly say that "machines can never make mistakes." Errors of conclusion can only arise when some meaning is attached to the output signals from the machine. The machine might, for instance, type out mathematical equations, or sentences in English. When a false proposition is typed we say that the machine has committed an error of conclusion. There is clearly no reason at all for saying that a machine cannot make this kind of mistake. It might do nothing but type out repeatedly "$0 = 1$." To take a less perverse example, it might have some method for drawing conclusions by scientific induction. We must expect such a method to lead occasionally to erroneous results.

The claim that a machine cannot be the subject of its own thought can of course only be answered if it can be shown that the machine has *some* thought with *some* subject matter. Nevertheless, "the subject matter of a machine's operations" does seem to mean something, at least to the people who deal with it. If, for instance, the machine was trying to find a solution of the equation $x^2 - 40x - 11 = 0$ one would be tempted to describe this equation as part of the machine's subject matter at that moment. In this sort of sense a machine undoubtedly can be its own subject matter. It may be used to help in making up its own programs, or to predict the effect of alterations in its own structure. By observing the results of its own behavior it can modify its own programs so as to achieve some purpose more effectively. These are possibilities of the near future, rather than Utopian dreams.

The criticism that a machine cannot have much diversity of behavior is just a way of saying that it cannot have much storage capacity. Until fairly recently a storage capacity of even a thousand digits was very rare.

The criticisms that we are considering here are often disguised forms of the argument from consciousness. Usually if one maintains that a machine *can* do one of these things, and describes the kind of method that the machine could use, one will not make much of an impression. It is thought that the method (whatever it may be, for it must be mechanical) is really rather base. Compare the parenthesis in Jefferson's statement quoted above.

(6) *Lady Lovelace's Objection.* Our most detailed information of Babbage's Analytical Engine comes from a memoir by Lady Lovelace. In it she states, "The Analytical Engine has no pretensions to *originate* anything. It can do *whatever we know how to order it* to perform" (her italics). This statement is quoted by Hartree who adds: "This does not imply that it may not be possible to construct electronic equipment which will 'think for itself,' or in which, in biological terms, one could set up a conditioned reflex, which would serve as a basis for 'learning.' Whether this is possible in principle or not is a stimulating and exciting question, suggested by some of these recent developments. But it did not seem that the machines constructed or projected at the time had this property."

I am in thorough agreement with Hartree over this. It will be noticed that he does not assert that the machines in question had not got the property, but rather that the evidence available to Lady Lovelace did not encourage her to believe that they had it. It is quite possible that the machines in question had in a sense got this property. For suppose that some discrete state machine has the property. The Analytical Engine was a universal digital computer, so that, if its storage capacity and speed were adequate, it could by suitable programing be made to mimic the machine in question. Probably this argument did not occur to the Countess or to Babbage. In any case there was no obligation on them to claim all that could be claimed.

This whole question will be considered again under the heading of learning machines.

A variant of Lady Lovelace's objection states that a machine can "never do anything really new." This may be parried for a moment with the saw, "There is nothing new under the sun." Who can be certain that "original work" that he has done was not simply the growth of the seed planted in him by teaching, or the effect of following well-known general principles. A better variant of the objection says that a machine can never "take us by surprise." This statement is a more direct challenge and can be met directly. Machines take me by surprise with great frequency. This is largely because I do not do sufficient calculation to decide what to expect them to do, or rather because, although I do a calculation, I do it in a hurried, slipshod fashion, taking risks. Perhaps I say to myself, "I suppose the voltage here ought to be the same as there: anyway let's assume it is." Naturally I am often wrong, and the result is a surprise for me, for by the time the experiment is done these assumptions have been forgotten. These admissions lay me open to lectures on the subject of my vicious ways, but do not throw any doubt on my credibility when I testify to the surprises I experience.

I do not expect this reply to silence my critic. He will probably say that such surprises are due to some creative mental act on my part, and reflect no credit on the machine. This leads us back to the argument from consciousness, and far from the idea of surprise. It is a line of argument we must consider closed, but it is perhaps worth remarking that the appreciation of something as surprising requires as much of a "creative mental act" whether the surprising event originates from a man, a book, a machine or anything else.

The view that machines cannot give rise to surprises is due, I believe, to a fallacy to which philosophers and mathematicians are particularly subject. This is the assumption that as soon as a fact is presented to a mind all consequences of that fact spring into the mind simultaneously with it. It is a very useful assumption under many circumstances, but one too easily forgets that it is false. A natural consequence of doing so is that one then assumes that there is no virtue in the mere working out of consequences from data and general principles.

(7) *Argument from Continuity in the Nervous System.* The nervous system is certainly not a discrete state machine. A small error in the information about the size of a nervous impulse impinging on a neuron, may make a large difference to the size of the outgoing impulse. It may be argued that, this being so, one cannot expect to be able to mimic the behavior of the nervous system with a discrete state system.

It is true that a discrete state machine must be different from a continuous machine. But if we adhere to the conditions of the imitation game, the interrogator will not be able to take any advantage of this difference. The situation can be made clearer if we consider some other simpler continuous machine. A differential analyzer will do very well. (A differential analyzer is a certain kind of machine not of the discrete state type used for some kinds of calculation.) Some of these provide their answers in a typed form, and so are suitable for taking part in the game. It would not be possible for a digital computer to predict exactly what answers the differential analyzer would give to a problem, but it would be quite capable of giving the right sort of answer. For instance, if asked to give the value of π (actually about $3 \cdot 1416$) it would be reasonable to choose at random between the values $3 \cdot 12, 3 \cdot 13, 3 \cdot 14, 3 \cdot 15, 3 \cdot 16$ with the probabilities of $0 \cdot 05, 0 \cdot 15, 0 \cdot 55, 0 \cdot 19, 0 \cdot 06$ (say). Under these circumstances it would be very difficult for the interrogator to distinguish the differential analyzer from the digital computer.

(8) *The Argument from Informality of Behavior.* It is not possible to produce a set of rules purporting to describe what a man should do in every conceivable set of circumstances. One might for instance have a rule that one is to stop when one sees a red traffic light, and to go if one sees a green one, but what if by some fault both appear together? One may perhaps decide that it is safest to stop. But some

further difficulty may well arise from this decision later. To attempt to provide rules of conduct to cover every eventuality, even those arising from traffic lights, appears to be impossible. With all this I agree.

From this it is argued that we cannot be machines. I shall try to reproduce the argument, but I fear I shall hardly do it justice. It seems to run something like this. "If each man had a definite set of rules of conduct by which he regulated his life he would be no better than a machine. But there are no such rules, so men cannot be machines." The undistributed middle is glaring. I do not think the argument is ever put quite like this, but I believe this is the argument used nevertheless. There may however be a certain confusion between "rules of conduct" and "laws of behavior" to cloud the issue. By "rules of conduct" I mean precepts such as "Stop if you see red lights," on which one can act, and of which one can be conscious. By "laws of behavior" I mean laws of nature as applied to a man's body such as "if you pinch him he will squeak." If we substitute "laws of behavior which regulate his life" for "laws of conduct by which he regulates his life" in the argument quoted the undistributed middle is no longer insuperable. For we believe that it is not only true that being regulated by laws of behavior implies being some sort of machine (though not necessarily a discrete state machine), but that conversely being such a machine implies being regulated by such laws. However, we cannot so easily convince ourselves of the absence of complete laws of behavior as of complete rules of conduct. The only way we know of for finding such laws is scientific observation, and we certainly know of no circumstances under which we could say, "We have searched enough. There are no such laws."

We can demonstrate more forcibly that any such statement would be unjustified. For suppose we could be sure of finding such laws if they existed. Then given a discrete state machine it should certainly be possible to discover by observation sufficient about it to predict its future behavior, and this within a reasonable time, say a thousand years. But this does not seem to be the case. I have set up on the Manchester computer a small program using only 1000 units of storage, whereby the machine supplied with one sixteen figure number replies with another within two seconds. I would defy anyone to learn from these replies sufficient about the program to be able to predict any replies to untried values.

(9) *The Argument from Extra-Sensory Perception.* I assume that the reader is familiar with the idea of extra-sensory perception, and the meaning of the four items of it, viz., telepathy, clairvoyance, precognition and psychokinesis. These disturbing phenomena seem to deny all our usual scientific ideas. How we should like to discredit them! Unfortunately the statistical evidence, at least for telepathy, is overwhelming. It is very difficult to rearrange one's ideas so as to fit these new facts in. Once one has accepted them it does not seem a very big step to believe in ghosts and bogies. The idea that our bodies move simply according to the known laws of physics, together with some others not yet discovered but somewhat similar, would be one of the first to go.

This argument is to my mind quite a strong one. One can say in reply that many scientific theories seem to remain workable in practice, in spite of clashing with E.S.P.; that in fact one can get along very nicely if one forgets about it. This is rather cold comfort, and one fears that thinking is just the kind of phenomenon where E.S.P. may be especially relevant.

A more specific argument based on E.S.P. might run as follows: "Let us play the imitation game, using as witnesses a man who is good as a telepathic receiver, and a digital computer. The interrogator can ask such questions as 'What suit does the card in my right hand belong to?' The man by telepathy or clairvoyance gives the right answer 130 times out of 400 cards. The machine can only guess at random, and perhaps get 104 right, so the interrogator makes the right identification." There is an interesting possibility which opens here. Suppose the digital computer contains a random number generator. Then it will be natural to use this to decide what answer to give. But then the random number generator will be subject to the psychokinetic powers of the interrogator. Perhaps this psychokinesis might cause the machine to guess right more often than would be expected on a probability calculation, so that the interrogator might still be unable to make the right identification. On the other hand, he might be able to guess right without any questioning, by clairvoyance. With E.S.P. anything may happen.

If telepathy is admitted it will be necessary to tighten our test. The situation could be regarded as analogous to that which would occur if the interrogator were talking to himself and one of the competitors was listening with his ear to the wall. To put the competitors into a "telepathy-proof room" would satisfy all requirements.

7. LEARNING MACHINES

The reader will have anticipated that I have no very convincing arguments of a positive nature to support my views. If I had I should not have taken such pains to point out the fallacies in contrary views. Such evidence as I have I shall now give.

Let us return for a moment to Lady Lovelace's objection, which stated that the machine can only do what we tell it to do. One could say that a man can "inject" an idea into the machine, and that it will respond to a certain extent and then drop into quiescence, like a piano string struck by a hammer. Another simile would be an atomic pile of less than critical size: an injected idea is to correspond to a neutron entering the pile from without. Each such neutron will cause a certain disturbance which eventually dies away. If, however, the size of the pile is sufficiently increased, the disturbance caused by such an incoming neutron will very likely go on and on increasing until the whole pile is destroyed. Is there a corresponding phenomenon for minds, and is there one for machines? There does seem to be one for the human mind. The majority of them seem to to "subcritical," i.e., to correspond in this analogy to piles of subcritical size. An idea presented to such a mind will on an average give rise to less than one idea in reply. A smallish proportion are supercritical. An idea presented to such a mind may give rise to a whole "theory" consisting of secondary, tertiary and more remote ideas. Animals' minds seem to be very definitely subcritical. Adhering to this analogy we ask, "Can a machine be made to be supercritical?"

The "skin of an onion" analogy is also helpful. In considering the functions of the mind or the brain we find certain operations which we can explain in purely mechanical terms. This we say does not correspond to the real mind: it is a sort of skin which we must strip off if we are to find the real mind. But then in what remains we find a further skin to be stripped off, and so on. Proceeding in this way do we ever come to the "real" mind, or do we eventually come to the skin which has nothing in it? In the latter case the whole mind is mechanical. (It would not be a discrete state machine however. We have discussed this.)

These last two paragraphs do not claim to be convincing arguments. They should rather be described as "recitations tending to produce belief."

The only really satisfactory support that can be given for the view expressed at the beginning of Sec. 6, p. 13, will be that provided by waiting for the end of the century and then doing the experiment described. But what can we say in the meantime? What steps should be taken now if the experiment is to be successful?

As I have explained, the problem is mainly one of programing. Advances in engineering will have to be made too, but it seems unlikely that these will not be adequate for the requirements. Estimates of the storage capacity of the brain vary from 10^{10} to 10^{15} binary digits. I incline to the lower values and believe that only a very small fraction is used for the higher types of thinking. Most of it is probably used for the retention of visual impressions. I should be surprised if more than 10^9 was required for satisfactory playing of the imitation game, at any rate against a blind man. (Note: The capacity of the *Encyclopaedia Britannica,* eleventh edition, is 2×10^9.) A storage capacity of 10^7 would be a very practicable possibility even by present techniques. It is probably not necessary to increase the speed of operations of the machines at all. Parts of modern machines which can be regarded as analogues of nerve cells work about a thousand times faster than the latter. This should provide a "margin of safety" which could cover losses of speed arising in many ways. Our problem then is to find out how to program these machines to play the game. At my present rate of working I produce about a thousand digits of program a day, so that about sixty workers, working steadily through the fifty years might accomplish the job, if nothing went into the wastepaper basket. Some more expeditious method seems desirable.

In the process of trying to imitate an adult human mind we are bound to think a good deal about the process which has brought it to the state that it is in. We may notice three components,

(a) The initial state of the mind, say at birth,

(b) The education to which it has been subjected,

(c) Other experience, not to be described as education, to which it has been subjected.

Instead of trying to produce a program to simulate the adult mind, why not rather try to produce one which simulates the child's? If this were then subjected to an appropriate course of education one would obtain the adult brain. Presumably the child-brain is something like a notebook as one buys it from the stationers. Rather little mechanism, and lots of blank sheets. (Mechanism and writing are from our point of view almost synonymous.) Our hope is that there is so little mechanism in the child-brain that something like it can be easily programed. The amount of work in the education we can assume, as a first approximation, to be much the same as for the human child.

We have thus divided our problem into two parts—the child-program and the education process. These two remain very closely connected. We cannot expect to find a good child-machine at the first attempt. One must experiment with teaching one such machine and see how well it learns. One can then try another and see if it is better or worse. There is an obvious connection between this process and evolution, by the identifications

Structure of the child-machine = Hereditary material

Changes   "   "   "   = Mutations

Natural selection   = Judgment of the experimenter

One may hope, however, that this process will be more expeditious than evolution. The survival of the fittest is a slow method for measuring advantages. The experimenter, by the exercise of intelligence, should be able to speed it up. Equally important is the fact that he is not restricted to random mutations. If he can trace a cause for some weakness he can probably think of the kind of mutation which will improve it.

It will not be possible to apply exactly the same teaching process to the machine as to a normal child. It will not, for instance, be provided with legs, so that it could not be asked to go out and fill the coal scuttle. Possibly it might not have eyes. But however well these deficiencies might be overcome by clever engineering, one could not send the creature to school without the other children making excessive fun of it. It must be given some tuition. We need not be too concerned about the legs, eyes, etc. The example of Miss Helen Keller shows that education can take place provided that communication in both directions between teacher and pupil can take place by some means or other.

We normally associate punishments and rewards with the teaching process. Some simple child-machines can be constructed or programed on this sort of principle. The machine has to be so constructed that events which shortly preceded the occurrence of a punishment-signal are unlikely to be repeated, whereas a reward-signal increases the probability of repetition of the events which led up to it. These definitions do not presuppose any feelings on the part of the machine. I have done some experiments with one such child-machine, and succeeded in teaching it a few things, but the teaching method was too unorthodox for the experiment to be considered really successful.

The use of punishments and rewards can at best be a part of the teaching process. Roughly speaking, if the teacher has no other means of communicating to the pupil, the amount of information which can reach him does not exceed the total number of rewards and punishments applied. By the time a child has learned to repeat "Casabianca" he would probably feel very sore indeed, if the text could only be discovered by a "Twenty Questions" technique, every "NO" taking the form of a blow. It is necessary therefore to have some other "unemotional" channels of communication. If these are available it is possible to teach a machine by punishments and rewards to obey orders given in some language, e.g., a symbolic language. These orders are to be transmitted through the "unemotional" channels. The use of this language will diminish greatly the number of punishments and rewards required.

Opinions may vary as to the complexity which is suitable in the child-machine. One might try to make it as simple as possible consistently with the general principles.

Alternatively one might have a complete system of logical inference "built in."[2] In the latter case the store would be largely occupied with definitions and propositions. The propositions would have various kinds of status, e.g., well-established facts, conjectures, mathematically proved theorems, statements given by an authority, expressions having the logical form of proposition but not belief-value. Certain propositions may be described as "imperatives." The machine should be so constructed that as soon as an imperative is classed as "well-established" the appropriate action automatically takes place. To illustrate this, suppose the teacher says to the machine, "Do your homework now." This may cause "Teacher says 'Do your homework now' " to be included among the well-established facts. Another such fact might be, "Everything that teacher says is true." Combining these may eventually lead to the imperative, "Do your homework now," being included among the well-established facts, and this, by the construction of the machine, will mean that the homework actually gets started, but the effect is very unsatisfactory. The processes of inference used by the machine need not be such as would satisfy the most exacting logicians. There might for instance be no hierarchy of types. But this need not mean that type fallacies will occur, any more than we are bound to fall over unfenced cliffs. Suitable imperatives (expressed *within* the systems, not forming part of the rules *of* the system) such as "Do not use a class unless it is a subclass of one which has been mentioned by teacher" can have a similar effect to "Do not go too near the edge."

The imperatives that can be obeyed by a machine that has no limbs are bound to be of a rather intellectual character, as in the example (doing homework) given above. Important among such imperatives will be ones which regulate the order in which the rules of the logical system concerned are to be applied. For at each stage when one is using a logical system, there is a very large number of alternative steps, any of which one is permitted to apply, so far as obedience to the rules of the logical system is concerned. These choices make the difference between a brilliant and a footling reasoner, not the difference between a sound and a fallacious one. Propositions leading to imperatives of this kind might be "When Socrates is mentioned, use the syllogism in Barbara" or "If one method has been proved to be quicker than another, do not use the slower method." Some of these may be "given by authority," but others may be produced by the machine itself, e.g., by scientific induction.

The idea of a learning machine may appear paradoxical to some readers. How can the rules of operation of the machine change? They should describe completely how the machine will react whatever its history might be, whatever changes it might undergo. The rules are thus quite time-invariant. This is quite true. The explanation of the paradox is that the rules which get changed in the learning process are of a rather less pretentious kind, claiming only an ephemeral validity. The reader may draw a parallel with the Constitution of the United States.

An important feature of a learning machine is that its teacher will often be very largely ignorant of quite what is going on inside, although he may still be able to

---

[2]Or rather "programed in" for our child-machine will be programed in a digital computer. But the logical system will not have to be learned.

some extent to predict his pupil's behavior. This should apply most strongly to the later education of a machine arising from a child-machine of well-tried design (or program). This is in clear contrast with normal procedure when using a machine to do computations: one's object is then to have a clear mental picture of the state of the machine at each moment in the computation. This object can only be achieved with a struggle. The view that "the machine can only do what we know how to order it to do,"[3] appears strange in face of this. Most of the programs which we can put into the machine will result in its doing something that we cannot make sense of at all, or which we regard as completely random behavior. Intelligent behavior presumably consists in a departure from the completely disciplined behavior involved in computation, but a rather slight one, which does not give rise to random behavior, or to pointless repetitive loops. Another important result of preparing our machine for its part in the imitation game by a process of teaching and learning is that "human fallibility" is likely to be omitted in a rather natural way, i.e., without special "coaching." . . . Processes that are learned do not produce a hundred per cent certainty of result; if they did they could not be unlearned.

It is probably wise to include a random element in a learning machine. . . . A random element is rather useful when we are searching for a solution of some problem. Suppose for instance we wanted to find a number between 50 and 200 which was equal to the square of the sum of its digits, we might start at 51 then try 52 and go on until we got a number that worked. Alternatively we might choose numbers at random until we got a good one. This method has the advantage that it is unnecessary to keep track of the values that have been tried, but the disadvantage that one may try the same one twice, but this is not very important if there are several solutions. The systematic method has the disadvantage that there may be an enormous block without any solutions in the region which has to be investigated first. Now the learning process may be regarded as a search for a form of behavior which will satisfy the teacher (or some other criterion). Since there is probably a very large number of satisfactory solutions the random method seems to be better than the systematic. It should be noticed that it is used in the analogous process of evolution. But there the systematic method is not possible. How could one keep track of the different genetical combinations that had been tried, so as to avoid trying them again?

We may hope that machines will eventually compete with men in all purely intellectual fields. But which are the best ones to start with? Even this is a difficult decision. Many people think that a very abstract activity, like the playing of chess, would be best. It can also be maintained that it is best to provide the machine with the best sense organs that money can buy, and then teach it to understand and speak English. This process could follow the normal teaching of a child. Things would be pointed out and named, etc. Again I do not know what the right answer is, but I think both approaches should be tried.

We can only see a short distance ahead, but we can see plenty there that needs to be done.

---

[3]Compare Lady Lovelace's statement (pp. 274f.), which does not contain the word "only."

Can Computers Think? (excerpt)

John Searle

Though we do not know in detail how the brain functions, we do know enough to have an idea of the general relationships between brain processes and mental processes. Mental processes are caused by the behaviour of elements of the brain. At the same time, they are realised in the structure that is made up of those elements. I think this answer is consistent with the standard biological approaches to biological phenomena. Indeed, it is a kind of commonsense answer to the question, given what we know about how the world works. However, it is very much a minority point of view. The prevailing view in philosophy, psychology, and artificial intelligence is one which emphasises the analogies between the functioning of the human brain and the functioning of digital computers. According to the most extreme version of this view, the brain is just a digital computer and the mind is just a computer program. One could summarise this view—I call it "strong artificial intelligence," or "strong AI"—by saying that the mind is to the brain, as the program is to the computer hardware.

This view has the consequence that there is nothing essentially biological about the human mind. The brain just happens to be one of an indefinitely large number of different kinds of hardware computers that could sustain the programs which make up human intelligence. On this view, any physical system whatever that had the right program with the right inputs and outputs would have a mind in exactly the same sense that you and I have minds. So, for example, if you made a computer out of old beer cans powered by windmills; if it had the right program, it would have to have a mind. And the point is not that for all we know it might have thoughts and feelings, but rather that it must have thoughts and feelings, because that is all there is to having thoughts and feelings: implementing the right program.

Most people who hold this view think we have not yet designed programs which are minds. But there is pretty much general agreement among them that it's only a matter of time until computer scientists and workers in artificial intelligence design the appropriate hardware and programs which will be the equivalent of human brains and minds. These will be artificial brains and minds which are in every way the equivalent of human brains and minds.

Many people outside of the field of artificial intelligence are quite amazed to discover that anybody could believe such a view as this. So, before criticising it, let me give you a few examples of the things that people in this field have actually said. Herbert Simon of Carnegie-Mellon University says that we already have machines that can literally think. There is no question of waiting for some future machine, because existing digital computers already have thoughts in exactly the same sense that you and I do. Well, fancy that! Philosophers have been worried for centuries about whether or not a machine could think, and now we discover that they already have such machines at Carnegie-Mellon. Simon's colleague Alan Newell claims that we have now discovered (and notice that Newell says "discovered" and not "hypothesised" or "considered the possibility," but we have *discovered*) that intelligence is just a matter of physical symbol manipulation; it has no essential connection with any specific kind of biological or physical wetware or hardware. Rather, any system whatever that is capable of manipulating physical symbols in the right way is capable of intelligence in the same literal sense as human intelligence of human beings. Both Simon and Newell, to their credit, emphasise that there is nothing metaphorical about these claims; they mean them quite literally. Freeman Dyson is quoted as having said that computers have an advantage over the rest of us when it comes to evolution. Since consciousness is just a matter of formal processes, in computers these formal processes can go on in substances that are much better able to survive in a universe that is cooling off than beings like ourselves made of our wet and messy materials. Marvin Minsky of MIT says that the next generation of computers will be so intelligent that we will "be lucky if they are willing to keep us around the house as household pets." My all-time favourite in the literature of exaggerated claims on behalf of the digital computer is from John McCarthy, the inventor of the term "artificial intelligence." McCarthy says even "machines as simple as thermostats can be said to have beliefs." And indeed, according to him, almost any machine capable of problem-solving can be said to have beliefs. I admire McCarthy's courage. I once asked him: "What beliefs does your thermostat have?" And he said: "My thermostat has three beliefs—it's too hot in here, it's too cold in here, and it's just right in here." As a philosopher, I like all these claims for a simple reason. Unlike most philosophical theses, they are reasonably clear, and they admit of a simple and decisive refutation. It is this refutation that I am going to undertake in this chapter.

The nature of the refutation has nothing whatever to do with any particular stage of computer technology. It is important to emphasise this point because the temptation is always to think that the solution to our problems must wait on some as yet uncreated technological wonder. But in fact, the nature of the refutation is completely independent of any state of technology. It has to do with the very definition of a digital computer, with what a digital computer is.

It is essential to our conception of a digital computer that its operations can be specified purely formally; that is, we specify the steps in the operation of the computer in terms of abstract symbols—sequences of zeroes and ones printed on a tape, for example. A typical computer "rule" will determine that when a machine is in a certain state and it has a certain symbol on its tape, then it will perform a certain operation such as erasing the symbol or printing another symbol and then enter another state such as moving the tape one square to the left. But the symbols have no meaning; they have no semantic content; they are not about anything. They have to be specified purely in terms of their formal or syntactical structure. The zeroes and ones, for example, are just numerals; they don't even stand for numbers. Indeed, it is this feature of digital computers that makes them so powerful. One and the same type of hardware, if it is appropriately designed, can be used to run an indefinite range of different programs. And one and the same program can be run on an indefinite range of different types of hardwares.

But this feature of programs, that they are defined purely formally or syntactically, is fatal to the view that mental processes and program processes are identical. And the reason can be stated quite simply. There is more to having a mind than having formal or syntactical processes. Our internal mental states, by definition, have certain sorts of contents. If I am thinking about Kansas City or wishing that I had a cold beer to drink or wondering if there will be a fall in interest rates, in each case my mental state has a certain mental content in addition to whatever formal features it might have. That is, even if my thoughts occur to me in strings of symbols, there must be more to the thought than the abstract strings, because strings by themselves can't have any meaning. If my thoughts are to be *about* anything, then the strings must have a *meaning* which makes the thoughts about those things. In a word, the mind has more than a syntax, it has a semantics. The reason that no computer program can ever be a mind is simply that a computer program is only syntactical, and minds are more than syntactical. Minds are semantical, in the sense that they have more than a formal structure, they have a content.

To illustrate this point I have designed a certain thought-experiment. Imagine that a bunch of computer programmers have written a program that will enable a computer to simulate the understanding of Chinese. So, for example, if the computer is given a question in Chinese, it will match the question against its memory, or data base, and produce appropriate answers to the questions in Chinese. Suppose for the sake of argument that the computer's answers are as good as those of a native Chinese speaker. Now then, does the computer, on the basis of this, understand Chinese, does it literally understand Chinese, in the way that Chinese speakers understand Chinese? Well, imagine that you are locked in a room, and in this room are several baskets full of Chinese symbols. Imagine that you (like me) do not understand a word of Chinese, but that you are given a rule book in English for manipulating these Chinese symbols. The rules specify the manipulations of the symbols purely formally, in terms of their syntax, not their semantics. So the rule might say: "Take a squiggle-squiggle sign out of basket number one and put it next to a squoggle-squoggle sign from basket number two." Now suppose that some other Chinese symbols are passed into the room, and that you are given further rules for passing back Chinese symbols out of the room. Suppose that unknown to you the symbols passed into the room are called "questions" by the people outside the room, and the symbols you pass back out of the room are called "answers to the questions." Suppose, furthermore, that the programmers are so good at designing the programs and that you are so good at manipulating the symbols, that very soon your answers are indistinguishable from those of a native Chinese speaker. There you are locked in your room shuffling your Chinese symbols and passing out Chinese symbols in response to incoming Chinese symbols. On the basis of the situation as I have described it, there is no way you could learn any Chinese simply by manipulating these formal symbols.

Now the point of the story is simply this: by virtue of implementing a formal computer program from the point of view of an outside observer, you behave exactly as if you understood Chinese, but all the same you don't understand a word of Chinese. But if going through the appropriate computer program for understanding Chinese is not enough to give *you* an understanding of Chinese, then it is not enough to give *any other digital computer* an understanding of Chinese. And again, the reason for this can be stated quite simply. If you don't understand Chinese, then no other computer could understand Chinese because no digital computer, just by virtue of running a program, has anything that you don't have. All that the computer has, as you have, is a formal program for manipulating uninterpreted Chinese symbols. To repeat, a computer has a syntax, but no semantics. The whole point of the parable of the Chinese room is to remind us of a fact that we knew all along. Understanding a language, or indeed, having mental states at all, involves more than just having a bunch of formal symbols. It involves having an interpretation, or a meaning attached to those symbols. And a digital computer, as defined, cannot have more than just formal symbols because the operation of the computer, as I said earlier, is defined in terms of its ability to implement programs. And these programs are purely formally specifiable—that is, they have no semantic content.

We can see the force of this argument if we contrast what it is like to be asked and to answer questions in English, and to be asked and to answer questions in some language where we have no knowledge of any of the meanings of the words. Imagine that in the Chinese room you are also given questions in English about such things as your age or your life history, and that you answer these questions. What is the difference between the Chinese case and the English case? Well again, if like me you understand no Chinese and you do understand English, then the difference is obvious. You understand the questions in English because they are expressed in symbols whose meanings are known to you. Similarly, when you give the answers in English you are producing symbols which are meaningful to you. But in the case of the Chinese, you have none of that. In the case of the Chinese, you simply manipulate formal symbols according to a computer program, and you attach no meaning to any of the elements.

Various replies have been suggested to this argument by workers in artificial intelligence and in psychology, as well as philosophy. They all have something in common; they are all inadequate. And there is an obvious reason why they have to be inadequate, since the argument rests on a very simple logical truth, namely, syntax alone is not sufficient for semantics, and digital computers insofar as they are computers have, by definition, a syntax alone.

I want to make this clear by considering a couple of the arguments that are often presented against me.

Some people attempt to answer the Chinese room example by saying that the whole system understands Chinese. The idea here is that though I, the person in the room manipulating the symbols do not understand Chinese, I am just the central processing unit of the computer system. They argue that it is the whole system, including the room, the baskets full of symbols and the ledgers containing the programs and perhaps other items as well, taken as a totality, that understands Chinese. But this is subject to exactly the same objection I made before. There is no way that the system can get from the syntax to the semantics. I, as the central processing unit, have no way of figuring out what any of these symbols means; but then neither does the whole system.

Another common response is to imagine that we put the Chinese understanding program inside a robot. If the robot moved around and interacted causally with the world, wouldn't that be enough to guarantee that it understood Chinese? Once again the inexorability of the semantics-syntax distinction overcomes this manoeuvre. As long as we suppose that the robot has only a computer for a brain then, even though it might behave exactly as if it understood Chinese, it would still have no way of getting from the syntax to the semantics of Chinese. You can see this if you imagine that I am the computer. Inside a room in the robot's skull I shuffle symbols without knowing that some of them come in to me from television cameras attached to the robot's head and others go out to move the robot's arms and legs. As long as all I have is a formal computer program, I have no way of attaching any meaning to any of the symbols. And the fact that the robot is engaged in causal interactions with the outside world won't help me to attach any meaning to the symbols unless I have some way of finding out about that fact. Suppose the robot picks up a hamburger and this triggers the symbol for hamburger to come into the room. As long as all I have is the symbol with no knowledge of its causes or how it got there, I have no way of knowing what it means. The causal interactions between the robot and the rest of the world are irrelevant unless those causal interactions are represented in some mind or other. But there is no way they can be if all that the so-called mind consists of is a set of purely formal, syntactical operations.

It is important to see exactly what is claimed and what is not claimed by my argument. Suppose we ask the question that I mentioned at the beginning: "Could a machine think?" Well, in one sense, of course, we are all machines. We can construe the stuff inside our heads as a meat machine. And of course, we can all think. So, in one sense of "machine," namely that sense in which a machine is just a physical system which is capable of performing certain kinds of operations, in that sense, we are all machines, and we can think. So, trivially, there are machines that can think. But that wasn't the question that bothered us. So let's try a different formulation of it. Could an artefact think? Could a man-made machine think? Well, once again, it depends on the kind of artefact. Suppose we designed a machine that was molecule-for-molecule indistinguishable from a human being. Well then, if you can duplicate the causes, you can presumably duplicate the effects. So once again, the answer to that question is, in principle at least, trivially yes. If you could build a machine that had the same structure as a human being, then presumably that machine would be able to think. Indeed, it would be a surrogate human being. Well, let's try again.

The question isn't: "Can a machine think?" or: "Can an artefact think?" The question is: "Can a digital computer think?" But once again we have to be very careful in how we interpret the question. From a mathematical point of view, anything whatever can be described *as if* it were a digital computer. And that's because it can be described as instantiating or implementing a computer program. In an utterly trivial sense, the pen that is on the desk in front of me can be described as a digital computer. It just happens to have a very boring computer program. The program says: "Stay there." Now since in this sense, anything whatever is a digital computer, because anything whatever can be described as implementing a computer program, then once again, our question gets a trivial answer. Of course our brains are digital computers, since they implement any number of computer programs. And of course our brains can think. So once again, there is a trivial answer to the question. But that wasn't really the question we were trying to ask. The question we wanted to ask is this: "Can a digital computer, as defined, think?" That is to say: "Is instantiating or implementing the right computer program with the right inputs and outputs, sufficient for, or constitutive of, thinking?" And to this question, unlike its predecessors, the answer is clearly "no." And it is "no" for the reason that we have spelled out, namely, the computer program is defined purely syntactically. But thinking is more than just a matter of manipulating meaningless symbols, it involves meaningful semantic contents. These semantic contents are what we mean by "meaning."

It is important to emphasise again that we are not talking about a particular stage of computer technology. The argument has nothing to do with the forthcoming, amazing advances in computer science. It has nothing to do with the distinction between serial and parallel processes, or with the size of programs, or the speed of computer operations, or with computers that can interact causally with their environment, or even with the invention of robots. Technological progress is always grossly exaggerated, but even subtracting the exaggeration, the development of computers has been quite remarkable, and we can reasonably expect that even more remarkable progress will be made in the future. No doubt we will be much better able to simulate human behaviour on computers than we can at present, and certainly much better than we have been able to in the past. The point I am making is that if we are talking about having mental states, having a mind, all of these simulations are simply irrelevant. It doesn't matter how good the technology is, or how rapid the calculations made by the computer are. If it really is a computer, its operations have to be defined syntactically, whereas consciousness, thoughts, feelings, emotions, and all the rest of it involve more than a syntax. Those features, by definition, the computer is unable to *duplicate* however powerful may be its ability to *simulate*. The key distinction here is between duplication and simulation. And no simulation by itself ever constitutes duplication.

What I have done so far is give a basis to the sense that those citations I began this talk with are really as preposterous as they seem. There is a puzzling question in this discussion though, and that is: "Why would anybody ever have thought that computers could think or have feelings and emotions and all the rest of it?" After all, we can do computer simulations of any process whatever that can be given a formal description. So, we can do a computer simulation of the flow of money in the British economy, or the pattern of power distribution in the Labour party. We can do computer simulation of rain storms in the home counties, or warehouse fires in East London. Now, in each of these cases, nobody supposes that the computer simulation is actually the real thing; no one supposes that a computer simulation of a storm will leave us all wet, or a computer simulation of a fire is likely to burn the house down. Why on earth would anyone in his right mind suppose a computer simulation of mental processes actually had mental processes? I don't really know the answer to that, since the idea seems to me, to put it frankly, quite crazy from the start. But I can make a couple of speculations.

First of all, where the mind is concerned, a lot of people are still tempted to some sort of behaviourism. They think if a system behaves as if it understood Chinese, then it really must understand Chinese. But we have already refuted this form of behaviourism with the Chinese room argument. Another assumption made by many people is that the mind is not a part of the biological world, it is not a part of the world of nature. The strong artificial intelligence view relies on that in its conception that the mind is purely formal; that somehow or other, it cannot be treated as a concrete product of biological processes like any other biological product. There is in these discussions, in short, a kind of residual dualism. AI partisans believe that the mind is more than a part of the natural biological world; they believe that the mind is purely formally specifiable. The paradox of this is that the AI literature is filled with fulminations against some view called "dualism," but in fact, the whole thesis of strong AI rests on a kind of dualism. It rests on a rejection of the idea that the mind is just a natural biological phenomenon in the world like any other.

I want to conclude this chapter by putting together the thesis of the last chapter and the thesis of this one. Both of these theses can be stated very simply. And indeed, I am going to state them with perhaps excessive crudeness. But if we put them together I think we get a quite powerful conception of the relations of minds, brains and computers. And the argument has a very simple logical structure, so you can see whether it is valid or invalid. The first premise is:

1. *Brains cause minds.*
   Now, of course, that is really too crude. What we mean by that is that mental processes that we consider to constitute a mind are caused, entirely caused, by processes going on inside the brain. But let's be crude, let's just abbreviate that as three words—brains cause minds. And that is just a fact about how the world works. Now let's write proposition number two:
2. *Syntax is not sufficient for semantics.*
   That proposition is a conceptual truth. It just articulates our distinction between the notion of what is purely formal and what has content. Now, to these two propositions—that brains cause minds and that syntax is not sufficient for semantics—let's add a third and a fourth:
3. *Computer programs are entirely defined by their formal, or syntactical, structure.*
   That proposition, I take it, is true by definition; it is part of what we mean by the notion of a computer program.
4. *Minds have mental contents; specifically, they have semantic contents.*

And that, I take it, is just an obvious fact about how our minds work. My thoughts, and beliefs, and desires are about something, or they refer to something, or they concern states of affairs in the world; and they do that because their content directs them at these states of affairs in the world. Now, from these four premises, we can draw our first conclusion; and it follows obviously from premises 2, 3 and 4:

CONCLUSION 1. *No computer program by itself is sufficient to give a system a mind. Programs, in short, are not minds, and they are not by themselves sufficient for having minds.*

Now, that is a very powerful conclusion, because it means that the project of trying to create minds solely by designing programs is doomed from the start. And it is important to re-emphasise that this has nothing to do with any particular state of technology or any particular state of the complexity of the program. This is a purely formal, or logical, result from a set of axioms which are agreed to by all (or nearly all) of the disputants concerned. That is, even most of the hardcore enthusiasts for artificial intelligence agree that in fact, as a matter of biology, brain processes cause mental states, and they agree that programs are defined purely formally. But if you put these conclusions together with certain other things that we know, then it follows immediately that the project of strong AI is incapable of fulfilment.

However, once we have got these axioms, let's see what else we can derive. Here is a second conclusion:

CONCLUSION 2. *The way that brain functions cause minds cannot be solely in virtue of running a computer program.*

And this second conclusion follows from conjoining the first premise together with our first conclusion. That is, from the fact that brains cause minds and that programs are not enough to do the job, it follows that the way that brains cause minds can't be solely by running a computer program. Now that also I think is an important result, because it has the consequence that the brain is not, or at least is not just, a digital computer. We saw earlier that anything can trivially be described as if it were a digital computer, and brains are no exception. But the importance of this conclusion is that the computational properties of the brain are simply not enough to explain its functioning to produce mental states. And indeed, that ought to seem a commonsense scientific conclusion to us anyway because all it does is remind us of the fact that brains are biological engines; their biology matters. It is not, as several people in artificial intelligence have claimed, just an irrelevant fact about the mind that it happens to be realised in human brains.

Now, from our first premise, we can also derive a third conclusion:

CONCLUSION 3. *Anything else that caused minds would have to have causal powers at least equivalent to those of the brain.*

And this third conclusion is a trivial consequence of our first premise. It is a bit like saying that if my petrol engine drives my car at seventy-five miles an hour, then any diesel engine that was capable of doing that would have to have a power output at least equivalent to that of my petrol engine. Of course, some other system might cause mental processes using entirely different chemical or biochemical features from those the brain in fact uses. It might turn out that there are beings on other planets, or in other solar systems, that have mental states and use an entirely different biochemistry from ours. Suppose that Martians arrived on earth and we concluded that they had mental states. But suppose that when their heads were opened up, it was discovered that all they had inside was green slime. Well still, the green slime, if it functioned to produce consciousness and all the rest of their mental life, would have to have causal powers equal to those of the human brain. But now, from our first conclusion, that programs are not enough, and our third conclusion, that any other system would have to have causal powers equal to the brain, conclusion four follows immediately:

CONCLUSION 4. *For any artefact that we might build which had mental states equivalent to human mental states, the implementation of a computer program would not by itself be sufficient. Rather the artefact would have to have powers equivalent to the powers of the human brain.*

The upshot of this discussion I believe is to remind us of something that we have known all along: namely, mental states are biological phenomena. Consciousness, intentionality, subjectivity and mental causation are all a part of our biological life history, along with growth, reproduction, the secretion of bile, and digestion.

Can Machines Think? (excerpt)

Daniel C. Dennett

Can machines think? This has been a conundrum for philosophers for years, but in their fascination with the pure conceptual issues they have for the most part overlooked the real social importance of the answer. It is of more than academic importance that we learn to think clearly about the actual cognitive powers of computers, for they are now being introduced into a variety of sensitive social roles, where their powers will be put to the ultimate test: In a wide variety of areas, we are on the verge of making ourselves dependent upon their cognitive powers. The cost of over-estimating them could be enormous.

One of the principal inventors of the computer was the great British mathematician Alan Turing. It was he who first figured out, in highly abstract terms, how to design a programmable computing device—what we now call a universal Turing machine. All programmable computers in use today are in essence Turing machines. Over thirty years ago, at the dawn of the computer age, Turing began a classic article, "Computing Machinery and Intelligence" with the words: "I propose to consider the question, 'Can machines think?' "—but then went on to say this was a bad question, a question that leads only to sterile debate and haggling over definitions, a question, as he put it, "too meaningless to deserve discussion" (Turing, 1950). In its place he substituted what he took to be a much better question, a question that would be crisply answerable and intuitively satisfying—in every way an acceptable substitute for the philosophic puzzler with which he began.

First he described a parlor game of sorts, the "imitation game," to be played by a man, a woman, and a judge (of either gender). The man and woman are hidden from the judge's view but able to communicate with the judge by teletype; the judge's task is to guess, after a period of questioning each contestant, which interlocutor is the man and which the woman. The man tries to convince the judge he is the woman (and the woman tries to convince the judge of the truth), and the man wins if the judge makes the wrong identification. A little reflection will convince you, I am sure, that, aside from lucky breaks, it would take a clever man to convince the judge that he was a woman—assuming the judge is clever too, of course.

Now suppose, Turing said, we replace the man or woman with a computer, and give the judge the task of determining which is the human being and which is the

Source: "Can Machines Think?" by Daniel C. Dennett, from *How We Know,* Harper & Row, © 1985, 3–20.

computer. Turing proposed that any computer that can regularly or often fool a discerning judge in this game would be intelligent—would be a computer that thinks—*beyond any reasonable doubt.* Now, it is important to realize that failing this test is not supposed to be a sign of lack of intelligence. Many intelligent people, after all, might not be willing or able to play the imitation game, and we should allow computers the same opportunity to decline to prove themselves. This is, then, a one-way test; failing it proves nothing.

Furthermore, Turing was not committing himself to the view (although it is easy to see how one might think he was) that to think is to think just like a human being—any more than he was committing himself to the view that for a man to think, he must think exactly like a woman. Men and women, and computers, may all have different ways of thinking. But surely, he thought, if one can think in one's own peculiar style well enough to imitate a thinking man or woman, one can think well, indeed. This imagined exercise has come to be known as the Turing test.

It is a sad irony that Turing's proposal has had exactly the opposite effect on the discussion of that which he intended. Turing didn't design the test as a useful tool in scientific psychology, a method of confirming or disconfirming scientific theories or evaluating particular models of mental function; he designed it to be nothing more than a philosophical conversation-stopper. He proposed—in the spirit of "Put up or shut up!"—a simple test for thinking that was *surely* strong enough to satisfy the sternest skeptic (or so he thought). He was saying, in effect, "Instead of arguing interminably about the ultimate nature and essence of thinking, why don't we all agree that whatever that nature is, anything that could pass this test would surely have it; then we could turn to asking how or whether some machine could be designed and built that might pass the test fair and square." Alas, philosophers—amateur and professional—have instead taken Turing's proposal as the pretext for just the sort of definitional haggling and interminable arguing about imaginary counterexamples he was hoping to squelch.

This thirty-year preoccupation with the Turing test has been all the more regrettable because it has focused attention on the wrong issues. There are *real world* problems that are revealed by considering the strengths and weaknesses of the Turing test, but these have been concealed behind a smokescreen of misguided criticisms. A failure to think imaginatively about the test actually proposed by Turing has led many to underestimate its severity and to confuse it with much less interesting proposals.

So first I want to show that the Turing test, conceived as he conceived it, is (as he thought) plenty strong enough as a test of thinking. I defy anyone to improve upon it. But here is the point almost universally overlooked by the literature: There is a common *misapplication* of the sort of testing exhibited by the Turing test that often leads to drastic overestimation of the powers of actually existing computer systems. The follies of this familiar sort of thinking about computers can best be brought out by a reconsideration of the Turing test itself.

The insight underlying the Turing test is the same insight that inspires the new practice among symphony orchestras of conducting auditions with an opaque screen between the jury and the musician. What matters in a musician, obviously, is musical ability and only musical ability; such features as sex, hair length, skin

color, and weight are strictly irrelevant. Since juries might be biased—even innocently and unawares—by these irrelevant features, they are carefully screened off
so only the essential feature, musicianship, can be examined. Turing recognized
that people similarly might be biased in their judgments of intelligence by whether
the contestant had soft skin, warm blood, facial features, hands and eyes—which
are obviously not themselves essential components of intelligence—so he devised
a screen that would let through only a sample of what really mattered: the capacity
to understand, and think cleverly about, challenging problems. Perhaps he was
inspired by Descartes, who in his *Discourse on Method* (1637) plausibly argued
that there was no more demanding test of human mentality than the capacity to hold
an intelligent conversation:

> It is indeed conceivable that a machine could be so made that it would utter words, and
> even words appropriate to the presence of physical acts or objects which cause some
> change in its organs; as, for example, if it was touched in some spot that it would ask
> what you wanted to say to it; if in another, that it would cry that it was hurt, and so on
> for similar things. But it could never modify its phrases to reply to the sense of what-
> ever was said in its presence, as even the most stupid men can do.

This seemed obvious to Descartes in the seventeenth century, but of course the fan-
ciest machines he knew were elaborate clockwork figures, not electronic computers. Today it is far from obvious that such machines are impossible, but Descartes's
hunch that ordinary conversation would put as severe a strain on artificial intelligence as any other test was shared by Turing. Of course there is nothing sacred
about the particular conversational game chosen by Turing for his test; it is just a
cannily chosen test of more general intelligence. The assumption Turing was prepared to make was this: Nothing could possibly pass the Turing test by winning the
imitation game without being able to perform indefinitely many other clearly intelligent actions. Let us call that assumption the quick-probe assumption. Turing realized, as anyone would, that there are hundreds and thousands of telling signs of
intelligent thinking to be observed in our fellow creatures, and one could, if one
wanted, compile a vast battery of different tests to assay the capacity for intelligent
thought. But success on his chosen test, he thought, would be highly predictive of
success on many other intuitively acceptable tests of intelligence. Remember, failure on the Turing test does not predict failure on those others, but success would
surely predict success. His test was so severe, he thought, that nothing that could
pass it fair and square would disappoint us in other quarters. Maybe it wouldn't do
everything we hoped—maybe it wouldn't appreciate ballet, or understand quantum
physics, or have a good plan for world peace, but we'd all see that it was surely one
of the intelligent, thinking entities in the neighborhood.

   Is this high opinion of the Turing test's severity misguided? Certainly many
have thought so—but usually because they have not imagined the test in sufficient
detail, and hence have underestimated it. Trying to forestall this skepticism, Turing
imagined several lines of questioning that a judge might employ in this game—
about writing poetry, or playing chess—that would be taxing indeed, but with thirty
years' experience with the actual talents and foibles of computers behind us, perhaps we can add a few more tough lines of questioning.

Terry Winograd, a leader in artificial intelligence efforts to produce conversational ability in a computer, draws our attention to a pair of sentences (Winograd, 1972). They differ in only one word. The first sentence is this:

> The committee denied the group a parade permit because they advocated violence.

Here's the second sentence:

> The committee denied the group a parade permit because they feared violence.

The difference is just in the verb—*advocated* or *feared.* As Winograd points out, the pronoun *they* in each sentence is officially ambiguous. Both readings of the pronoun are always legal. Thus we can imagine a world in which governmental committees in charge of parade permits advocate violence in the streets and, for some strange reason, use this as their pretext for denying a parade permit. But the natural, reasonable, intelligent reading of the first sentence is that it's the group that advocated violence, and of the second, that it's the committee that feared violence.

Now if sentences like this are embedded in a conversation, the computer must figure out which reading of the pronoun is meant, if it is to respond intelligently. But mere rules of grammar or vocabulary will not fix the right reading. What fixes the right reading for us is knowledge about the world, about politics, social circumstances, committees and their attitudes, groups that want to parade, how they tend to behave, and the like. One must know about the world, in short, to make sense of such a sentence.

In the jargon of Artificial Intelligence (AI), a conversational computer needs a lot of *world knowledge* to do its job. But, it seems, if somehow it is endowed with that world knowledge on many topics, it should be able to do much more with that world knowledge than merely make sense of a conversation containing just that sentence. The only way, it appears, for a computer to disambiguate that sentence and keep up its end of a conversation that uses that sentence would be for it to have a much more general ability to respond intelligently to information about social and political circumstances, and many other topics. Thus, such sentences, by putting a demand on such abilities, are good quick-probes. That is, they test for a wider competence.

People typically ignore the prospect of having the judge ask off-the-wall questions in the Turing test, and hence they underestimate the competence a computer would have to have to pass the test. But remember, the rules of the imitation game as Turing presented it permit the judge to ask any question that could be asked of a human being—no holds barred. Suppose then we give a contestant in the game this question:

> An Irishman found a genie in a bottle who offered him two wishes. "First I'll have a pint of Guinness," said the Irishman, and when it appeared he took several long drinks from it and was delighted to see that the glass filled itself magically as he drank. "What about your second wish?" asked the genie. "Oh well," said the Irishman, "that's easy. I'll have another one of these!"
>
> —Please explain this story to me, and tell me if there is anything funny or sad about it.

Now even a child could express, if not eloquently, the understanding that is required to get this joke. But think of how much one has to know and understand about human culture, to put it pompously, to be able to give any account of the point of this joke. I am not supposing that the computer would have to laugh at, or be amused by, the joke. But if it wants to win the imitation game—and that's the test, after all—it had better know enough in its own alien, humorless way about human psychology and culture to be able to pretend effectively that it was amused and explain why.

It may seem to you that we could devise a better test. Let's compare the Turing test with some other candidates.

Candidate 1: A computer is intelligent if it wins the World Chess Championship.

That's not a good test, as it turns out. Chess prowess has proven to be an isolatable talent. There are programs today that can play fine chess but can do nothing else. So the quick-probe assumption is false for the test of playing winning chess.

Candidate 2: The computer is intelligent if it solves the Arab-Israeli conflict.

This is surely a more severe test than Turing's. But it has some defects: it is unrepeatable, if passed once; slow, no doubt; and it is not crisply clear what would count as passing it. Here's another prospect, then:

Candidate 3: A computer is intelligent if it succeeds in stealing the British crown jewels without the use of force or violence.

Now this is better. First, it could be repeated again and again, though of course each repeat test would presumably be harder—but this is a feature it shares with the Turing test. Second, the mark of success is clear—either you've got the jewels to show for your efforts or you don't. But it is expensive and slow, a socially dubious caper at best, and no doubt luck would play too great a role.

With ingenuity and effort one might be able to come up with other candidates that would equal the Turing test in severity, fairness, and efficiency, but I think these few examples should suffice to convince us that it would be hard to improve on Turing's original proposal.

But still, you may protest, something might pass the Turing test and still not be intelligent, not be a thinker. What does *might* mean here? If what you have in mind is that by cosmic accident, by a supernatural coincidence, a stupid person or a stupid computer *might* fool a clever judge repeatedly, well, yes, but so what? The same frivolous possibility "in principle" holds for any test whatever. A playful god, or evil demon, let us agree, could fool the world's scientific community about the presence of H_2O in the Pacific Ocean. But still, the tests they rely on to establish that there is H_2O in the Pacific Ocean are quite beyond reasonable criticism. If the Turing test for thinking is no worse than any well-established scientific test, we can set skepticism aside and go back to serious matters. Is there any more likelihood of a "false positive" result on the Turing test than on, say, the test currently used for the presence of iron in an ore sample?

This question is often obscured by a "move" that philosophers have sometimes made called operationalism. Turing and those who think well of his test are often accused of being operationalists. Operationalism is the tactic of *defining* the presence of some property, for instance, intelligence, as being established once and for all by the passing of some test. Let's illustrate this with a different example.

Suppose I offer the following test—we'll call it the Dennett test—for being a great city:

A great city is one in which, on a randomly chosen day, one can do all three of the following:

> Hear a symphony orchestra
>
> See a Rembrandt *and* a professional athletic contest
>
> Eat *quenelles de brochet à la Nantua* for lunch

To make the operationalist move would be to declare that any city that passes the Dennett test is *by definition* a great city. What being a great city *amounts to* is just passing the Dennett test. Well then, if the Chamber of Commerce of Great Falls, Montana, wanted—and I can't imagine why—to get their hometown on my list of great cities, they could accomplish this by the relatively inexpensive route of hiring full time about ten basketball players, forty musicians, and a quick-order quenelle chef and renting a cheap Rembrandt from some museum. An idiotic operationalist would then be stuck admitting that Great Falls, Montana, was in fact a great city, since all he or she cares about in great cities is that they pass the Dennett test.

Sane operationalists (who for that very reason are perhaps not operationalists at all, since *operationalist* seems to be a dirty word) would cling confidently to their test, but only because they have what they consider to be very good reasons for thinking the odds against a false positive result, like the imagined Chamber of Commerce caper, are astronomical. I devised the Dennett test, of course, with the realization that no one would be both stupid and rich enough to go to such preposterous lengths to foil the test. In the actual world, wherever you find symphony orchestras, *quenelles,* Rembrandts, and professional sports, you also find daily newspapers, parks, repertory theaters, libraries, fine architecture, and all the other things that go to make a city great. My test was simply devised to locate a telling sample that could not help but be representative of the rest of the city's treasures. I would cheerfully run the minuscule risk of having my bluff called. Obviously, the test items are not all that I care about in a city. In fact, some of them I don't care about at all. I just think they would be cheap and easy ways of assuring myself that the subtle things I do care about in cities are present. Similarly, I think it would be entirely unreasonable to suppose that Alan Turing had an inordinate fondness for party games, or put too high a value on party game prowess in his test. In both the Turing and the Dennett test, a very unrisky gamble is being taken: the gamble that the quick-probe assumption is, in general, safe.

But two can play this game of playing the odds. Suppose some computer programmer happens to be, for whatever strange reason, dead set on tricking me into judging an entity to be a thinking, intelligent thing when it is not. Such a trickster could rely as well as I can on unlikelihood and take a few gambles. Thus, if the programmer can expect that it is not remotely likely that I, as the judge, will bring up the topic of children's birthday parties, or baseball, or moon rocks, then he or she can avoid the trouble of building world knowledge on those topics into the data base. Whereas if I do improbably raise these issues, the system will draw a blank and I will unmask the pretender easily. But given all the topics and words that I *might* raise, such a savings would no doubt be negligible. Turn the idea inside out, however, and the trickster would have a fighting chance. Suppose the programmer has reason to believe that I will ask *only* about children's birthday parties, or baseball, or moon rocks—all other topics being, for one reason or another, out of bounds. Not only does the task shrink dramatically, but there already exist systems or preliminary sketches of systems in artificial intelligence that can do a whiz-bang job of responding with apparent intelligence on just those specialized topics.

William Wood's LUNAR program, to take what is perhaps the best example, answers scientists' questions—posed in ordinary English—about moon rocks. In one test it answered correctly and appropriately something like 90 percent of the questions that geologists and other experts thought of asking it about moon rocks. (In 12 percent of those correct responses there were trivial, correctable defects.) Of course, Wood's motive in creating LUNAR was not to trick unwary geologists into thinking they were conversing with an intelligent being. And if that had been his motive, his project would still be a long way from success.

For it is easy enough to unmask LUNAR without ever straying from the prescribed topic of moon rocks. Put LUNAR in one room and a moon rock specialist in another, and then ask them both their opinion of the social value of the moon-rocks-gathering expeditions, for instance. Or ask the contestants their opinion of the suitability of moon rocks as ashtrays, or whether people who have touched moon rocks are ineligible for the draft. Any intelligent person knows a lot more about moon rocks than their geology. Although it might be *unfair* to demand this extra knowledge of a computer moon rock specialist, it would be an easy way to get it to fail the Turing test.

But just suppose that someone could extend LUNAR to cover itself plausibly on such probes, so long as the topic was still, however indirectly, moon rocks. We might come to think it was a lot more like the human moon rocks specialist than it really was. The moral we should draw is that as Turing test judges we should resist all limitations and waterings-down of the Turing test. They make the game too easy—vastly easier than the original test. Hence they lead us into the risk of over-estimating the actual comprehension of the system being tested.

Consider a different limitation of the Turing test that should strike a suspicious chord in us as soon as we hear it. This is a variation on a theme developed in an article by Ned Block (1982). Suppose someone were to propose to restrict the judge to a vocabulary of, say, the 850 words of "Basic English," and to single-sentence probes—that is "moves"—of no more than four words. Moreover, contestants must respond to these probes with no more than four words per move, and a test may involve no more than forty questions.

Is this an innocent variation on Turing's original test? These restrictions would make the imitation game clearly finite. That is, the total number of all possible permissible games is a large, but finite, number. One might suspect that such a limitation would permit the trickster simply to store, in alphabetical order, all the possible good conversations within the limits and beat the judge with nothing more sophisticated than a system of table lookup. In fact, that isn't in the cards. Even with these severe and improbable and suspicious restrictions imposed upon the imitation game, the number of legal games, though finite, is mind-bogglingly large. I haven't bothered trying to calculate it, but it surely exceeds astronomically the number of possible chess games with no more than forty moves, and that number has been calculated. John Haugeland says it's in the neighborhood of ten to the one hundred twentieth power. For comparison, Haugeland (1981, p. 16) suggests that there have only been ten to the eighteenth seconds since the beginning of the universe.

Of course, the number of good, sensible conversations under these limits is a tiny fraction, maybe one quadrillionth, of the number of merely grammatically well formed conversations. So let's say, to be very conservative, that there are only ten to the fiftieth different smart conversations such a computer would have to store. Well, the task shouldn't take more than a few trillion years—given generous government support. Finite numbers can be very large.

So though we needn't worry that this particular trick of storing all the smart conversations would work, we can appreciate that there are lots of ways of making the task easier that may appear innocent at first. We also get a reassuring measure of just how severe the unrestricted Turing test is by reflecting on the more than astronomical size of even that severely restricted version of it.

Block's imagined—and utterly impossible—program exhibits the dreaded feature known in computer science circles as *combinatorial explosion*. No conceivable computer could overpower a combinatorial explosion with sheer speed and size. Since the problem areas addressed by artificial intelligence are veritable minefields of combinatorial explosion, and since it has often proven difficult to find *any* solution to a problem that avoids them, there is considerable plausibility in Newell and Simon's proposal that avoiding combinatorial explosion (by any means at all) be viewed as one of the hallmarks of intelligence.

Our brains are millions of times bigger than the brains of gnats, but they are still, for all their vast complexity, compact, efficient, timely organs that somehow or other manage to perform all their tasks while avoiding combinatorial explosion. A computer a million times bigger or faster than a human brain might not look like the brain of a human being, or even be internally organized like the brain of a human being, but if, for all its differences, it somehow managed to control a wise and timely set of activities, it would have to be the beneficiary of a very special design that avoided combinatorial explosion, and whatever that design was, would we not be right to consider the entity intelligent?

Turing's test was designed to allow for this possibility. His point was that we should not be species-chauvinistic, or anthropocentric, about the insides of an intelligent being, for there might be inhuman ways of being intelligent.

To my knowledge, the only serious and interesting attempt by any program designer to win even a severely modified Turing test has been Kenneth Colby's. Colby is a psychiatrist and intelligence artificer at UCLA. He has a program called PARRY, which is a computer simulation of a paranoid patient who has delusions about the Mafia being out to get him. As you do with other conversational programs, you interact with it by sitting at a terminal and typing questions and answers back and forth. A number of years ago, Colby put PARRY to a very restricted test. He had genuine psychiatrists interview PARRY. He did not suggest to them that they might be talking or typing to a computer; rather, he made up some plausible story about why they were communicating with a real live patient by teletype. He also had the psychiatrists interview real, human paranoids via teletype. Then he took a PARRY transcript, inserted it in a group of teletype transcripts from real patients, gave them to *another* group of experts—more psychiatrists—and said, "One of these was a conversation with a computer. Can you figure out which one it was?" They couldn't. They didn't do better than chance.

Colby presented this with some huzzah, but critics scoffed at the suggestions that this was a legitimate Turing test. My favorite commentary on it was Joseph Weizenbaum's; in a letter to the *Communications of the Association of Computing Machinery* (Weizenbaum, 1974, p. 543), he said that, inspired by Colby, he had designed an even better program, which passed the same test. His also had the virtue of being a very inexpensive program, in these times of tight money. In fact you didn't even need a computer for it. All you needed was an electric typewriter. His program modeled infant autism. And the transcripts—you type in your questions, and the thing just sits there and hums—cannot be distinguished by experts from transcripts of real conversations with infantile autistic patients. What was wrong, of course, with Colby's test was that the unsuspecting interviewers had no motivation at all to try out any of the sorts of questions that easily would have unmasked PARRY.

Colby was undaunted, and after his team had improved PARRY he put it to a much more severe test—a surprisingly severe test. This time, the interviewers— again, psychiatrists—*were* given the task at the outset of telling the computer from the real patient. They were set up in a classic Turing test: the patient in one room, the computer PARRY in the other room, with the judges conducting interviews with both of them (on successive days). The judges' task was to find out which one was the computer and which one was the real patient. Amazingly, they didn't do much better, which leads some people to say, "Well, that just confirms my impression of the intelligence of psychiatrists!"

But now, more seriously, was this an honest-to-goodness Turing test? Were there tacit restrictions on the lines of questioning of the judges? Like the geologists interacting with LUNAR, the psychiatrists' professional preoccupations and habits kept them from asking the sorts of unlikely questions that would have easily unmasked PARRY. After all, they realized that since one of the contestants was a real, live paranoid person, medical ethics virtually forbade them from toying with, upsetting, or attempting to confuse their interlocutors. Moreover, they also knew that this was a test of a model of paranoia, so there were certain questions that wouldn't be deemed to be relevant to testing the model *as a model of paranoia.* So, they asked just the sort of questions that therapists *typically* ask of such patients, and of course PARRY had been ingeniously and laboriously prepared to deal with just that sort of question.

One of the psychiatrist judges did, in fact, make a rather half-hearted attempt to break out of the mold and ask some telling questions: "Maybe you've heard of the saying 'Don't cry over spilled milk.' What does that mean to you?" PARRY answered: "Maybe it means you have to watch out for the Mafia." When then asked "Okay, now if you were in a movie theater watching a movie and smelled something like burning wood or rubber, what would you do?" PARRY replied: "You know, they know me." And the next question was, "If you found a stamped, addressed letter in your path as you were walking down the street, what would you do?" PARRY replied: "What else do you want to know?"[1]

Clearly PARRY was, you might say, *parrying* these questions, which were incomprehensible to it, with more or less stock paranoid formulas. We see a bit of a dodge, which is apt to work, apt to seem plausible to the judge, only because the "contestant" is *supposed* to be paranoid, and such people are expected to respond uncooperatively on such occasions. These unimpressive responses didn't particularly arouse the suspicions of the judge, as a matter of fact, though probably they should have.

PARRY, like all other large computer programs, is dramatically bound by limitations of cost-effectiveness. What was important to Colby and his crew was simulating his model of paranoia. This was a massive effort. PARRY has a thesaurus or dictionary of about 4500 words and 700 idioms and the grammatical competence to use it—a *parser,* in the jargon of computational linguistics. The entire PARRY program takes up about 200,000 words of computer memory, all laboriously installed by the programming team. Now once all the effort had gone into devising the model of paranoid thought processes and linguistic ability, there was little if any time, energy, money, or interest left over to build in huge amounts of world knowledge of the sort that any actual paranoid, of course, would have. (Not that anyone yet knows how to build in world knowledge in the first place.) Building in the world knowledge, if one could even do it, would no doubt have made PARRY orders of magnitude larger and slower. And what would have been the point, given Colby's theoretical aims?

PARRY is a theoretician's model of a psychological phenomenon: paranoia. It is not intended to have practical applications. But in recent years a branch of AI (knowledge engineering) has appeared that develops what are now called expert systems. Expert systems *are* designed to be practical. They are software superspecialist consultants, typically, that can be asked to diagnose medical problems, to analyze geological data, to analyze the results of scientific experiments, and the like. Some of them are very impressive. SRI in California announced in the mid-eighties that PROSPECTOR, an SRI-developed expert system in geology, had correctly predicted the existence of a large, important mineral deposit that had been entirely unanticipated by the human geologists who had fed it its data. MYCIN, perhaps the most famous of these expert systems, diagnoses infections of the blood, and it does probably as well as, maybe better than, any human consultants. And many other expert systems are on the way.

All expert systems, like all other large AI programs, are what you might call Potemkin villages. That is, they are cleverly constructed facades, like cinema sets.

---

[1] I thank Kenneth Colby for providing me with the complete transcripts (including the Judges' commentaries and reactions), from which these exchanges are quoted. The first published account of the experiment is Heiser, et al. (1980, pp. 149–162). Colby (1981, pp. 515–560) discusses PARRY and its implications.

The actual filling-in of details of AI programs is time-consuming, costly work, so economy dictates that only those surfaces of the phenomenon that are likely to be probed or observed are represented.

Consider, for example, the CYRUS program developed by Janet Kolodner in Roger Schank's AI group at Yale a few years ago (see Kolodner, 1983a; 1983b, pp. 243–280; 1983c, pp. 281–328). CYRUS stands (we are told) for Computerized Yale Retrieval Updating System, but surely it is no accident that CYRUS modeled the memory of Cyrus Vance, who was then secretary of state in the Carter administration. The point of the CYRUS project was to devise and test some plausible ideas about how people organize their memories of the events they participate in; hence it was meant to be a "pure" AI system, a scientific model not an expert system intended for any practical purpose. CYRUS was updated daily by being fed all UPI wire service news stories that mentioned Vance, and it was fed them directly, with no doctoring and no human intervention. Thanks to an ingenious news-reading program called FRUMP, it could take any story just as it came in on the wire and could digest it and use it to update its data base so that it could answer more questions. You could address questions to CYRUS in English by typing at a terminal. You addressed them in the second person, as if you were talking with Cyrus Vance himself. The results looked like this:

Q: *Last time you went to Saudi Arabia, where did you stay?*
A: In a palace in Saudi Arabia on September 23, 1978.
Q: *Did you go sightseeing there?*
A: Yes, at an oilfield in Dhahran on September 23, 1978.
Q: *Has your wife even met Mrs. Begin?*
A: Yes, most recently at a state dinner in Israel in January 1980.

CYRUS could correctly answer thousands of questions—almost any fair question one could think of asking it. But if one actually set out to explore the boundaries of its facade and find the questions that overshot the mark, one could soon find them. "Have you ever met a female head of state?" was a question I asked it, wondering if CYRUS knew that Indira Ghandi and Margaret Thatcher were women. But for some reason the connection could not be drawn, and CYRUS failed to answer either yes or no. I had stumped it, in spite of the fact that CYRUS could handle a host of what you might call neighboring questions flawlessly. One soon learns from this sort of probing exercise that it is very hard to extrapolate accurately from a sample performance that one has observed to such a system's total competence. It's also very hard to keep from extrapolating much too generously.

While I was visiting Schank's laboratory in the spring of 1980, something revealing happened. The real Cyrus Vance resigned suddenly. The effect on the program CYRUS was chaotic. It was utterly unable to cope with the flood of "unusual" news about Cyrus Vance. The only sorts of episodes CYRUS could understand at all were diplomatic meetings, flights, press conferences, state dinners, and the like—less than two dozen general sorts of activities (the kinds that are newsworthy and typical of secretaries of state). It had no provision for sudden resignation. It was as if the UPI had reported that a wicked witch had turned Vance into a frog. It is distinctly possible that CYRUS would have taken that report more in stride than the actual news. One can imagine the conversation:

Q: *Hello, Mr. Vance, what's new?*
A: I was turned into a frog yesterday.

But of course it wouldn't know enough about what it had just written to be puzzled, or startled, or embarrassed. The reason is obvious. When you look inside CYRUS, you find that it has skeletal definitions of thousands of words, but these definitions are minimal. They contain as little as the system designers think that they can get away with. Thus, perhaps, *lawyer* would be defined as synonymous with *attorney* and *legal counsel,* but aside from that, all one would discover about lawyers is that they are adult human beings and that they perform various functions in legal areas. If you then traced out the path to *human being,* you'd find out various obvious things CYRUS "knew" about human beings (hence about lawyers), but that is not a lot. That lawyers are university graduates, that they are better paid than chambermaids, that they know how to tie their shoes, that they are unlikely to be found in the company of lumberjacks—these trivial, if weird, facts about lawyers would not be explicit or implicit anywhere in this system. In other words, a very thin stereotype of a lawyer would be incorporated into the system, so that almost nothing you could tell it about a lawyer would surprise it.

So long as surprising things don't happen, so long as Mr. Vance, for instance, leads a typical diplomat's life, attending state dinners, giving speeches, flying from Cairo to Rome, and so forth, this system works very well. But as soon as his path is crossed by an important anomaly, the system is unable to cope, and unable to recover without fairly massive human intervention. In the case of the sudden resignation, Kolodner and her associates soon had CYRUS up and running again, with a new talent—answering questions about Edmund Muskie, Vance's successor—but it was no less vulnerable to unexpected events. Not that it mattered particularly since CYRUS was a theoretical model, not a practical system.

There are a host of ways of improving the performance of such systems, and of course, some systems are much better than others. But all AI programs in one way or another have this facade-like quality, simply for reasons of economy. For instance, most expert systems in medical diagnosis so far developed operate with statistical information. They have no deep or even shallow knowledge of the underlying causal mechanisms of the phenomena that they are diagnosing. To take an imaginary example, an expert system asked to diagnose an abdominal pain would be oblivious to the potential import of the fact that the patient had recently been employed as a sparring partner by Muhammad Ali—there being no statistical data available to it on the rate of kidney stones among athlete's assistants. That's a fanciful case no doubt—too obvious, perhaps, to lead to an actual failure of diagnosis and practice. But more subtle and hard-to-detect limits to comprehension are always present, and even experts, even the system's designers, can be uncertain of where and how these limits will interfere with the desired operation of the system. Again, steps can be taken and are being taken to correct these flaws. For instance, my former colleague at Tufts, Benjamin Kuipers, is currently working on an expert system in nephrology—for diagnosing kidney ailments—that will be based on an elaborate system of causal reasoning about the phenomena being diagnosed. But this is a very ambitious, long-range project of considerable theoretical difficulty. And even if all the reasonable, cost-effective steps are taken to minimize the superficiality of expert systems, they will still be facades, just somewhat thicker or wider facades.

When we were considering the fantastic case of the crazy Chamber of Commerce of Great Falls, Montana, we couldn't imagine a plausible motive for anyone going to any sort of trouble to trick the Dennett test. The quick-probe assumption for the Dennett test looked quite secure. But when we look at expert systems, we see that, however innocently, their designers do have motivation for doing exactly the sort of trick that would fool an unsuspicious Turing tester. First, since expert systems are all superspecialists who are only supposed to know about some narrow subject, users of such systems, not having much time to kill, do not bother probing them at the boundaries at all. They don't bother asking "silly" or irrelevant questions. Instead, they concentrate—not unreasonably—on exploiting the system's strengths. But shouldn't they try to obtain a clear vision of such a system's weaknesses as well? The normal habit of human thought when conversing with one another is to assume general comprehension, to assume rationality, to assume, moreover, that the quick-probe assumption is, in general, sound. This amiable habit of thought almost irresistibly leads to putting too much faith in computer systems, especially user-friendly systems that present themselves in a very anthropomorphic manner.

Part of the solution to this problem is to teach all users of computers, especially users of expert systems, how to probe their systems before they rely on them, how to search out and explore the boundaries of the facade. This is an exercise that calls not only for intelligence and imagination, but also a bit of special understanding about the limitations and actual structure of computer programs. It would help, of course, if we had standards of truth in advertising, in effect, for expert systems. For instance, each such system should come with a special demonstration routine that exhibits the sorts of shortcomings and failures that the designer knows the system to have. This would not be a substitute, however, for an attitude of cautious, almost obsessive, skepticism on the part of the users, for designers are often, if not always, unaware of the subtler flaws in the products they produce. That is inevitable and natural, given the way system designers must think. They are trained to think positively—constructively, one might say—about the designs that they are constructing.

I come, then, to my conclusions. First, a philosophical or theoretical conclusion: The Turing test in unadulterated, unrestricted form, as Turing presented it, is plenty strong if well used. I am confident that no computer in the next twenty years is going to pass an unrestricted Turing test. They may well win the World Chess Championship or even a Nobel Prize in physics, but they won't pass the unrestricted Turing test. Nevertheless, it is not, I think, impossible in principle for a computer to pass the test, fair and square. I'm not running one of those a priori "computers can't think" arguments. I stand unabashedly ready, moreover, to declare that any computer that actually passes the unrestricted Turing test will be, in every theoretically interesting sense, a thinking thing.

But remembering how very strong the Turing test is, we must also recognize that there may also be interesting varieties of thinking or intelligence that are not well poised to play and win the imitation game. That no nonhuman Turing test winners are yet visible on the horizon does not mean that there aren't machines that already exhibit *some* of the important features of thought. About them, it is probably futile to ask my title question, Do they think? Do they *really* think? In some regards they do, and in some regards they don't. Only a detailed look at what they do, and how they are structured, will reveal what is interesting about them. The Turing test, not being a scientific test, is of scant help on that task, but there are plenty of other ways of examining such systems. Verdicts on their intelligence or capacity for thought or consciousness would be only as informative and persuasive as the theories of intelligence or thought or consciousness the verdicts are based on and since our task is to create such theories, we should get on with it and leave the Big Verdict for another occasion. In the meantime, should anyone want a surefire, almost-guaranteed-to-be-fail-safe test of thinking by a computer, the Turing test will do very nicely.

My second conclusion is more practical, and hence in one clear sense more important. Cheapened versions of the Turing test are everywhere in the air. Turing's test is not just effective, it is entirely natural—this is, after all, the way we assay the intelligence of each other every day. And since incautious use of such judgments and such tests is the norm, we are in some considerable danger of extrapolating too easily, and judging too generously, about the understanding of the systems we are using. The problem of overestimation of cognitive prowess, of comprehension, of intelligence, is not, then, just a philosophical problem, but a real social problem, and we should alert ourselves to it, and take steps to avert it.

REFERENCES

Block, N. 1982, "Psychologism and Behaviorism," *Philosophical Review,* 90, pp. 5–43.

Descartea, R., 1637, *Discourse on Method,* LaFleur, Lawrence, trans., New York: Bobbs Merrill, 1960.

Haugeland, J., ed., 1981, *Mind Design: Philosophy, Psychology, Artificial Intelligence,* Cambridge, MA: Bradford Books/The MIT Press.

Kolodner, J. L., 1980a, "Retrieval and Organization Strategies in Conceptual Memory: A Computer Model" (Ph.D. diss.), Research Report #187, Dept. of Computer Science, Yale University.

————, 1983b, "Maintaining Organization in a Dynamic Long-term Memory," *Cognitive Science,* 7.

Turing, A., 1950, "Computing Machinery and Intelligence," *Mind,* 59 (236), pp. 433–460. Reprinted in Hofstadter, D., and Dennett, D. C., eds., *The Mind's I* (New York: Basic Books, 1981), pp. 54–67.

Weizenbaum, J., 1974, letter to the editor, *Communications of the Association for Computing Machinery,* 17 (9) (September).

Winograd, T., 1972, *Understanding Natural Language,* New York: Academic Press.

Essay on Freedom of the Will *(excerpt)*

Arthur Schopenhauer

DEFINITION OF CONCEPTS

A question which is so important, serious, and difficult, and which coincides in essentials with a basic problem of the entire philosophy of medieval and modern times, needs to be treated with great precision. An analysis, therefore, of the basic concepts which the question contains is certainly in order.

1) What is freedom?

When carefully examined, this concept turns out to be negative. It signifies merely the absence of any hindrance and restraint. But this restraint, as it manifests power, must be positive. Corresponding to the possible nature of this restraint, the concept has three very different subspecies: physical, intellectual, and moral freedom.

a) Physical freedom is the absence of material hindrances of any sort. Thus we say: a clear sky, an open view, clear air, an open field, a vacant place,[1] free heat (which is not bound chemically), free electric charge, free flow of the stream where it is no longer checked by mountains or sluices, etc. Even such expressions as "free room and board," "free press," "post-free letter," signify the absence of those encumbering conditions which often attach themselves to such things and hinder their enjoyment. Most frequently, however, we conceive of freedom as an attribute of animate beings, whose distinctive feature is the ability to originate movements from their own will, that is, voluntarily. Thus such movements are called free when no material obstacles prevent them. Since these obstacles may be of very different kinds, but that with which they interfere is always the will for the sake of simplicity one prefers to think of the concept of freedom in positive terms; the concept is used to cover everything that moves or acts only from its own will. This reversal of the concept changes nothing in essentials. Accordingly, in this physical meaning of the concept of freedom, animals and men are called free when their actions are not hindered by any physical or material obstacles—such as fetters, or prison, or paralysis—but proceed in accordance with their will.

This physical meaning of the concept of freedom, especially when predicated on animate beings, is the original, immediate, and hence most frequent one. As such, the concept in this meaning is not subject to doubt or controversy, and its reality can always be authenticated empirically. For whenever an animate being acts only from its will, it is, in the physical sense, free. Here we do not take into account whatever may influence the will itself. For in its original, immediate, and therefore popular meaning, the concept of freedom refers only to the ability to act, that is, precisely to the absence of physical obstacles to its actions. Hence one says: free is the bird in the sky, the wild beast in the forest; man is by nature free; only the free

---

[1] [The English words: *clear, open, vacant* are rendered in German by the word *frei* (free).—Tr.]

Source: Excerpt from *Essay on Freedom of the Will,* by Arthur Schopenhauer, translated by Konstantin Kolenda, © 1960. Reprinted by permission of Prentice-Hall, Inc., Upper Saddle River, NJ.

are happy. We also call a nation free, meaning thereby that it is governed solely by laws, but that it has given itself these laws: for in that case it merely obeys its own will. Therefore, political freedom must be included under physical freedom.

However, as soon as we leave physical freedom and consider the two remaining kinds, we are no longer dealing with the popular but with a philosophical sense of the concept. This, as is well known, leads to many difficulties. It falls into two entirely different classes: intellectual and moral freedom.

b) Intellectual freedom, "the voluntary and involuntary with respect to thought"[2] in Aristotle, is mentioned here only for the sake of completeness of classification. I shall therefore take the liberty of postponing its discussion to the very end of this essay, when the concepts to be used in it will have been explained in the foregoing sections. This will enable us to deal with intellectual freedom quite concisely. But since it is most closely related to physical freedom, it must follow it in the classification.

c) So I turn directly to the third kind, namely to *moral freedom.* This is really the *liberum arbitrium* cited in the question of the Royal Society. This concept connects with that of physical freedom in a way which makes its necessarily much later origination understandable. Physical freedom, as noted above, has to do only with material obstacles; it is at once present when they are absent. But in some cases it has been observed that a man, without being hindered by material obstacles, was restrained by mere motives—such as threats, promises, dangers, and the like—from acting in a way which, if these motives were absent, would have certainly expressed his will. Consequently, the question was raised whether such a man was still free, or whether the actions which express his actual will could really be checked and prevented just as effectively by a strong countermotive as by a physical obstacle. A sound mind would find no difficulty in arriving at the answer: a motive can never act in the same ways as a physical obstacle. Undoubtedly the latter easily transcends human bodily powers unconditionally, while a motive can never be irresistible in itself and has no absolute power but can be always offset by a stronger countermotive, provided that such a countermotive is present and that the particular man can be determined by it. We often observe that even the strongest of all motives—to preserve one's life—is outweighed by other motives, for example, in suicide or in sacrificing one's life for others, for one's convictions, and for various causes. Conversely, all degrees of the most refined tortures on the rack have now and again been overcome by the mere thought that otherwise life would be lost. But even though it were evident from this that the motives bring with them no purely objective and absolute compulsion, still one could ascribe to them a subjective and relative compulsion, namely, relative to the person involved. In either case the result is the same. Hence the question remains: is the will itself free?

The concept of freedom, until now conceived only in respect to *ability,* was thus put in a relation to *willing,* and so the problem arose whether the willing itself is free. But on close inspection, the original, purely empirical, and hence popular concept of freedom shows itself incapable of becoming thus related to willing. For

---

[2] [Aristotle, *The Works of Aristotle* (Oxford, 1915), IX, *Ethica Eudemia,* Book II, sec. 7, 1223a, 23–25, ed. W. D. Ross.—Tr.]

according to it "free" means "in accordance with one's own will." Consequently, to ask whether the will itself is free, is to ask whether the will is in accordance with itself. This, of course, is self-evident, but says also nothing at all. The empirical concept of freedom signifies: "I am free when I can *do what I will.*" Here in the phrase "what I will" the freedom is already affirmed. But when we now inquire about the freedom of willing itself, the question would then take this form: "Can you also will your volitions?," as if a volition depended on another volition which lay behind it. Suppose that this question is answered in the affirmative, what then? Another question would arise: "Can you also will that which you will to will?" Thus we would be pushed back indefinitely, since we would think that a volition depended on a previous, deeper lying volition. In vain would we try to arrive in this way finally at a volition which we must think of and accept as dependent on nothing else. But if we were willing to accept such a volition, we could as well accept the first as the one we happened to make the last. Consequently, the question would be reduced to a simple: "Can you will?" But whether a mere affirmation of this question decides the problem of the freedom of the will, is what we wanted to know. So the problem remains unresolved.

We can see then that it is impossible to establish a direct connection between the concept of freedom—in its original, empirical meaning derived from action—and the concept of willing. In order nevertheless to be in a position to apply the concept of freedom to the will, one had to modify this concept by interpreting it more abstractly. This was accomplished by making the concept of freedom signify in general only the absence of any *necessity.* Thus interpreted, the concept retained its negative character, which I attributed to it from the very beginning. Accordingly, one must first investigate the concept of necessity, for this is the positive concept which gives meaning to the negative one.

So let us ask: What does one mean by "necessary"? The usual explanation: "necessary is that whose opposite is impossible, or which cannot be otherwise," is a mere word-definition, or paraphrase of the concept, which does not increase our understanding. As a real definition I propose the following: Something is necessary which follows from a given sufficient ground. This sentence, like any correct definition, can also be reversed. Depending on whether the ground in question is logical, or mathematical, or physical (i.e., called a cause), the necessity will be logical (e.g., of a conclusion, given the premises), or mathematical (e.g., equality of the sides of a triangle, given the equality of the angles), or physical, real (e.g., the occurrence of the effect, as soon as the cause is present). In all these cases, with equal strictness, the necessity is attached to the consequent when the ground is given. Only in so far as we comprehend something as the consequent of a given ground do we recognize it to be necessary. Conversely, as soon as we recognize something to be a consequent of a sufficient ground, we see that it is necessary. This is so because all grounds are compelling. This real definition is so adequate and exhaustive that the concept of necessity and the concept of consequent of a given sufficient ground are exchangeable concepts. In all cases, the one can be put in the place of the other.[3]

---

[3] There is a discussion of the concept of necessity in my essay on the *Principle of Sufficient Reason,* Second Ed., § 49.

According to this, the absence of necessity would be identical with the absence of a determining sufficient ground. Still, we think of the *accidental* as the opposite of the *necessary*. But there is no conflict between these two views; each accidental occurrence is only relatively so. For in the world of reality, where alone accidents can be encountered, every event is necessary in relation to its cause, while in relation to all other events which are contemporaneous and spatially contiguous with it, the event is accidental. But since the mark of freedom is absence of necessity, that which is free would have to be absolutely independent of any cause and would therefore have to be defined as absolutely accidental. This is a most problematic notion, and I don't guarantee that it is even conceivable. Nevertheless, it coincides in a singular fashion with the concept of freedom.

At any rate, that which is free remains that which is in no respect necessary, that is, not dependent on any ground. If this concept were applied to the will of man, this would mean that an individual will in its manifestations (volitions) would not be determined by causes or by sufficient grounds at all. Besides, since the consequent of a given ground (of whatever kind this may be) is always necessary, a man's acts would not be free but necessary. On this rests Kant's definition, according to which freedom is the capacity to initiate of oneself a series of changes. For in its true signification the expression "of oneself" means "without antecedent cause." This, however, is the same as "without necessity." So that, even though that definition gives to the concept of freedom the appearance of being positive, upon close scrutiny its negative nature emerges again.

A free will then would be the will which is not determined by grounds—and since everything that determines another must be a ground, in real things a real ground, that is, a cause—a free will would not be determined by anything at all. The particular manifestations of this will (volitions) would then proceed absolutely and quite originally from the will itself, without being brought about necessarily by antecedent conditions, and hence also without being determined by anything according to a rule. When we try to deal with this concept, clear thinking abandons us because, while the positing of a ground, in all of its meanings, is the essential form of our entire cognitive faculty, we are here asked to refrain from positing a ground. Still, there is no lack of a technical term also for this concept: this is *liberum arbitrium indifferentiae.* This is, by the way, the only clearly defined, firm, and positive concept of that which is called freedom of the will. One cannot therefore get away from it without involving oneself in vacillating, hazy explanations, behind which hides hesitant indecision, as when one talks about grounds which do not necessarily bring about their consequents. Every consequent of a ground is necessary, and every necessity is the consequent of a ground. The positing of such a free will of indifference has an immediate consequence which characterizes this concept and must therefore be regarded as its peculiar feature. This is that for a human individual equipped with such a feature, under given external conditions which are thoroughly determined in every particular, two diametrically opposed actions are equally possible.

2) What is the self-consciousness?

Answer: The consciousness of one's own self, in contrast to the consciousness of *other* things; this latter being the cognitive faculty. To be sure, even before those other things appear in it, this faculty contains certain forms of the manner of this occurrence. These forms are accordingly conditions of the possibility of objective being of things, that is, of their existing for us as objects. They are, as is well known, time, space, and causality. Now, although we find these forms of understanding in ourselves, their only purpose is that we can become conscious of other things as such, and be put in a definite relation to them. Therefore, even though these forms are contained in us, we must look upon them not as belonging to the self-consciousness, but rather as making possible the consciousness of other things, that is, our objective knowledge.

Further, the ambiguity of the word *conscientia,* used in the question, will not mislead me into loading the self-consciousness with the moral impulses known under the name of conscience or of practical reason together with its categorical imperatives affirmed by Kant. This should not be done, first, because these impulses appear only as a result of experience and reflection, hence as a result of the consciousness of other things, and second, because the borderline between that in them which belongs originally and properly to human nature and that which is added by moral and religious education, is not yet sharply and indisputably drawn. Moreover, it cannot possibly be the intention of the Royal Society to have the question transplanted onto the ground of morality by including conscience in the self-consciousness, and to see a restatement of Kant's moral proof—or rather postulate—of freedom from the a priori known moral laws, in virtue of the dictum, "you can because you ought."

From what has been said, it is evident that by far the greatest part of our entire consciousness in general is not our self-consciousness, but the consciousness of other things, or the cognitive faculty. The latter is directed outward with all its powers and is the scene (indeed, from a deeper point of investigation, the condition) of the real external world. At first our cognitive faculty grasps this world perceptively, but that which is thus obtained is forthwith worked over, as it were in a ruminating fashion, into concepts. Endless combinations of concepts, brought about with the help of words, constitute thinking. Only after we subtract this, by far the greatest part of our entire consciousness, do we get the self-consciousness. We already see that the content of the latter cannot be great. Hence, if the data required for the proof of the freedom of the will should really lie in the self-consciousness, we may hope that they will not escape us. An *inner sense* has also been set up as an organ of the self-consciousness.[4] But this must be taken in a metaphorical rather than in a real sense, because the self-consciousness is immediate. Be that as it may, our next question is: What does the self-consciousness contain? or How does man become directly conscious of his own self?

Answer: altogether as one who wills. In observing his own self-consciousness everyone will soon be aware that its object is always his own volitions. By this one must understand, to be sure, not only the deliberate acts of will which are immediately put into effect and the formal decisions together with the actions which follow from them. Whoever is capable of somehow discerning the essential element,

---

[4]It is found already in Cicero as *tactus interior: Acad. quaest.,* IV, 7. More explicitly in Augustine, *De lib. arb.,* II, 3 *sqq.* Then in Descartes, *Princ. phil.,* IV, 190; and quite developed in Locke.

even when it is disguised under various modifications of degree and kind, will not hesitate to include among the manifestations of will also all desiring, striving, wishing, demanding, longing, hoping, loving, rejoicing, jubilation, and the like, no less than not willing or resisting, all abhorring, fleeing, fearing, being angry, hating, mourning, suffering pains—in short, all emotions and passions. For these emotions and passions are weaker or stronger, violent and stormy or else quiet impulsions of one's own will, which is either restrained or unleashed, satisfied or unsatisfied. In their many variations they relate to the successful or frustrated attainment of that which is willed, to the endurance or the overcoming of that which is abhorred. Consequently, they are explicit affections of the same will which is active in decisions and actions.[5] To this context belongs even that which goes under the name of feelings of pleasure and of displeasure. Of course, these are present in a great variety of degrees and kinds, but still they can always be traced to the affections of desiring or abhorring, that is, to the will itself becoming aware of itself as satisfied or unsatisfied, restrained or unleashed. Indeed, here should be included the bodily emotions, pleasant or painful, and all the innumerable others which lie between these two, since the nature of these emotions consists in this: they enter directly into the self-consciousness as either something which is in accordance with the will or something which opposes it. Even of his own body one is directly conscious, strictly speaking, only as the externally active organ of the will and as the seat of receptivity for pleasant or unpleasant sensations. But these sensations themselves, as just said, refer back to the quite immediate affections of the will which either conform or are opposed to it. For that matter, we may or may not include here these mere feelings of pleasure or displeasure, but in any case we find that all those movements of the will—that alternate wanting and not wanting, which in its constant ebb and flow constitutes the only object of the self-consciousness, or, if one prefers, of the inner sense—stand in a universal and generally acknowledged relation to that which is perceived and known in the external world. But that, as we have seen, lies no longer in the realm of the immediate self-consciousness. Consequently, we have arrived at the borderline of the self-consciousness as soon as we touched the external world, where the self-consciousness touches on the realm of the consciousness of other things. But the objects apprehended in the world are the material and the occasion for all those movements and acts of will. One will not interpret this as begging the question, for no one can deny that our willing always has external things for its object. It is directed toward them, it revolves around them, and is at least motivated by them. To think otherwise is to see the will as completely cut off from the external world and locked up in the dark recesses of the self-consciousness. The only issue which is still problematical for us here is the necessity with which the things located in the external world determine volition.

---

[5]It is well worth noting that the church father Augustine recognized this fully, while many modern thinkers, with their alleged "feeling faculty," do not see it. Namely in *De Civit, Dei*, Lib. XIV. c. 6, he speaks of affections of the soul, which in the previous book he brought under the four categories of desire, fear, joy, sadness, and says, "For the will is in them all; yea, none of them is anything else than will. For what are desire and joy but a volition of consent to the things we wish? And what are fear and sadness but a volition of aversion from the things we do not wish?" [Cf. Augustine's *The City of God* transl. M. Dods (Edinburgh: 1872), p. 9.—Tr.]

Thus we find that the self-consciousness is intensely, really even exclusively, occupied with willing. But does this sole content of the self-consciousness furnish data from which could be inferred the *freedom* of that very willing in the only distinct and definite sense of the word set forth above? To establish this is our end in view, and we shall now steer straight toward it. So far we have approached it only indirectly, and yet we have come noticeably closer to it.

The Will (excerpt)

Gilbert Ryle

(1) FOREWORD

Most of the mental-conduct concepts whose logical behaviour we examine in this book are familiar and everyday concepts. We all know how to apply them and we understand other people when they apply them. What is in dispute is not how to apply them, but how to classify them, or in what categories to put them.

The concept of volition is in a different case. We do not know in daily life how to use it, for we do not use it in daily life and do not, consequently, learn by practice how to apply it, and how not to misapply it. It is an artificial concept. We have to study certain specialist theories in order to find out how it is to be manipulated. It does not, of course, follow from its being a technical concept that it is an illegitimate or useless concept. "Ionisation" and "off-side" are technical concepts, but both are legitimate and useful. "Phlogiston" and "animal spirits" were technical concepts, though they have now no utility.

I hope to show that the concept of volition belongs to the latter tribe.

(2) THE MYTH OF VOLITIONS

It has for a long time been taken for an indisputable axiom that the Mind is in some important sense tripartite, that is, that there are just three ultimate classes of mental processes. The Mind or Soul, we are often told, has three parts, namely, Thought, Feeling and Will; or, more solemnly, the Mind or Soul functions in three irreducibly different modes, the Cognitive mode, the Emotional mode and the Conative mode. This traditional dogma is not only not self-evident, it is such a welter of confusions and false inferences that it is best to give up any attempt to re-fashion it. It should be treated as one of the curios of theory.

The main object of this chapter is not, however, to discuss the whole trinitarian theory of mind but to discuss, and discuss destructively, one of its ingredients. I hope to refute the doctrine that there exists a Faculty, immaterial Organ,

Source: "The Will" by Gilbert Ryle, from *The Concept of Mind*, Chapter 3, © 1949, Barnes & Noble, 62–82. Reprinted by permission.

or Ministry, corresponding to the theory's description of the "Will" and, accordingly, that there occur processes, or operations, corresponding to what it describes as "volitions." I must however make it clear from the start that this refutation will not invalidate the distinctions which we all quite properly draw between voluntary and involuntary actions and between strong-willed and weak-willed persons. It will, on the contrary, make clearer what is meant by "voluntary" and "involuntary," by "strong-willed" and "weak-willed," by emancipating these ideas from bondage to an absurd hypothesis.

Volitions have been postulated as special acts or operations, "in the mind" by means of which a mind gets its ideas translated into facts. I think of some state of affairs which I wish to come into existence in the physical world, but, as my thinking and wishing are unexecutive, they require the mediation of a further executive mental process. So I perform a volition which somehow puts my muscles into action. Only when a bodily movement has issued from such a volition can I merit praise or blame for what my hand or tongue has done.

It will be clear why I reject this story. It is just an inevitable extension of the myth of the ghost in the machine. It assumes that there are mental states and processes enjoying one sort of existence, and bodily states and processes enjoying another. An occurrence on the one stage is never numerically identical with an occurrence on the other. So, to say that a person pulled the trigger intentionally is to express at least a conjunctive proposition, asserting the occurrence of one act on the physical stage and another on the mental stage; and, according to most versions of the myth, it is to express a causal proposition, asserting that the bodily act of pulling the trigger was the effect of a mental act of willing to pull the trigger.

According to the theory, the workings of the body are motions of matter in space. The causes of these motions must then be *either* other motions of matter in space *or,* in the privileged case of human beings, thrusts of another kind. In some way which must forever remain a mystery, mental thrusts, which are not movements of matter in space, can cause muscles to contract. To describe a man as intentionally pulling the trigger is to state that such a mental thrust did cause the contraction of the muscles of his finger. So the language of "volitions" is the language of the para-mechanical theory of the mind. If a theorist speaks without qualms of "volitions," or "acts of will," no further evidence is needed to show that he swallows whole the dogma that a mind is a secondary field of special causes. It can be predicted that he will correspondingly speak of bodily actions as "expressions" of mental processes. He is likely also to speak glibly of "experiences," a plural noun commonly used to denote the postulated non-physical episodes which constitute the shadow-drama on the ghostly boards of the mental stage.

The first objection to the doctrine that overt actions, to which we ascribe intelligence-predicates, are results of counterpart hidden operations of willing is this. Despite the fact that theorists have, since the Stoics and Saint Augustine, recommended us to describe our conduct in this way, no one, save to endorse the theory, ever describes his own conduct, or that of his acquaintances, in the recommended idioms. No one ever says such things as that at 10 a.m. he was occupied in willing this or that, or that he performed five quick and easy volitions and two slow and difficult volitions between midday and lunch-time. An accused person may admit or deny that he did something, or that he did it on purpose, but he never admits or denies having willed. Nor do the judge and jury require to be satisfied by evidence, which in the nature of the case could never be adduced, that a volition preceded the pulling of the trigger. Novelists describe the actions, remarks, gestures and grimaces, the daydreams, deliberations, qualms and embarrassments of their characters; but they never mention their volitions. They would not know what to say about them.

By what sorts of predicates should they be described? Can they be sudden or gradual, strong or weak, difficult or easy, enjoyable or disagreeable? Can they be accelerated, decelerated, interrupted, or suspended? Can people be efficient or inefficient at them? Can we take lessons in executing them? Are they fatiguing or distracting? Can I do two or seven of them synchronously? Can I remember executing them? Can I execute them, while thinking of other things, or while dreaming? Can they become habitual? Can I forget how to do them? Can I mistakenly believe that I have executed one, when I have not, or that I have not executed one, when I have? At which moment was the boy going through a volition to take the high dive? When he set foot on the ladder? When he took his first deep breath? When he counted off "One, two, three—Go," but did not go? Very, very shortly before he sprang? What would his own answer be to those questions?

Champions of the doctrine maintain, of course, that the enactment of volitions is asserted by implication, whenever an overt act is described as intentional, voluntary, culpable or meritorious; they assert too that any person is not merely able but bound to know that he is willing when he is doing so, since volitions are defined as a species of conscious process. So if ordinary men and women fail to mention their volitions in their descriptions of their own behaviour, this must be due to their being untrained in the dictions appropriate to the description of their inner, as distinct from their overt, behaviour. However, when a champion of the doctrine is himself asked how long ago he executed his last volition, or how many acts of will he executes in, say, reciting "Little Miss Muffet" backwards, he is apt to confess to finding difficulties in giving the answer, though these difficulties should not, according to his own theory, exist.

If ordinary men never report the occurrence of these acts, for all that, according to the theory, they should be encountered vastly more frequently than headaches, or feelings of boredom; if ordinary vocabulary has no non-academic names for them; if we do not know how to settle simple questions about their frequency, duration or strength, then it is fair to conclude that their existence is not asserted on empirical grounds. The fact that Plato and Aristotle never mentioned them in their frequent and elaborate discussions of the nature of the soul and the springs of conduct is due not to any perverse neglect by them of notorious ingredients of daily life but to the historical circumstance that they were not acquainted with a special hypothesis the acceptance of which rests not on the discovery but on the postulation, of these ghostly thrusts.

The second objection is this. It is admitted that one person can never witness the volitions of another; he can only infer from an observed overt action to the volition from which it resulted, and then only if he has any good reason to believe that the overt action was a voluntary action, and not a reflex or habitual action, or one resulting from some external cause. It follows that no judge, schoolmaster, or parent ever knows that the actions which he judges merit praise or blame; for he cannot do better than guess that the action was willed. Even a confession by the agent, if such confessions were ever made, that he had executed a volition before his hand did the deed would not settle the question. The pronouncement of the confession is only another overt muscular action. The curious conclusion results that though volitions were called in to explain our appraisals of actions, this explanation is just what they fail to provide. If we had no other antecedent grounds for applying appraisal-concepts to the actions of others, we should have no reasons at all for inferring from those actions to the volitions alleged to give rise to them.

Nor could it be maintained that the agent himself can know that any overt action of his own is the effect of a given volition. Supposing, what is not the case, that he could know for certain, either from the alleged direct deliverances of consciousness, or from the alleged direct findings of introspection, that he had executed an act of will to pull the trigger just before he pulled it, this would not prove that the pulling was the effect of that willing. The connection between volitions and movements is allowed to be mysterious, so, for all he knows, his volition may have had some other movement as its effect and the pulling of the trigger may have had some other event for its cause.

Thirdly, it would be improper to burke the point that the connection between volition and movement is admitted to be a mystery. It is a mystery not of the unsolved but soluble type, like the problem of the cause of cancer, but of quite another type. The episodes supposed to constitute the careers of minds are assumed to have one sort of existence, while those constituting the careers of bodies have another sort; and no bridge-status is allowed. Transactions between minds and bodies involve links where no links can be. That there should be any causal transactions between minds and matter conflicts with one part, that there should be none conflicts with another part of the theory. Minds, as the whole legend describes them, are what must exist if there is to be a causal explanation of the intelligent behaviour of human bodies; and minds, as the legend describes them, live on a floor of existence defined as being outside the causal system to which bodies belong.

Fourthly, although the prime function of volitions, the task for the performance of which they were postulated, is to originate bodily movements, the argument, such as it is, for their existence entails that some mental happenings also must result from acts of will. Volitions were postulated to be that which makes actions voluntary, resolute, meritorious and wicked. But predicates of these sorts are ascribed not only to bodily movements but also to operations which, according to the theory, are mental and not physical operations. A thinker may ratiocinate resolutely, or imagine wickedly; he may try to compose a limerick and he may meritoriously concentrate on his algebra. Some mental processes then can, according to the theory, issue from volitions. So what of volitions themselves? Are they voluntary or involuntary acts of mind? Clearly either answer leads to absurdities. If I cannot help willing to pull the trigger, it would be absurd to describe my pulling it as "voluntary." But if my volition to pull the trigger is voluntary, in the sense assumed by the theory, then it must issue from a prior volition and that from another *ad infinitum*. It has been suggested, to avoid this difficulty, that volitions cannot be described as either voluntary or involuntary. "Volition" is a term of the wrong type to accept either predicate. If so, it would seem to follow that it is also of the wrong type to accept such predicates as "virtuous" and "wicked," "good" and "bad," a conclusion which might embarrass those moralists who use volitions as the sheet-anchor of their systems.

In short, then, the doctrine of volitions is a causal hypothesis, adopted because it was wrongly supposed that the question, "What makes a bodily movement voluntary?" was a causal question. This supposition is, in fact, only a special twist of the general supposition that the question, "How are mental-conduct concepts applicable to human behaviour?" is a question about the causation of that behaviour.

Champions of the doctrine should have noticed the simple fact that they and all other sensible persons knew how to decide questions about the voluntariness and involuntariness of actions and about the resoluteness and irresoluteness of agents before they had ever heard of the hypothesis of the occult inner thrusts of actions. They might then have realised that they were not elucidating the criteria already in efficient use, but, tacitly assuming their validity, were trying to correlate them with hypothetical occurrences of a para-mechanical pattern. Yet this correlation could, on the one hand, never be scientifically established, since the thrusts postulated were screened from scientific observation; and, on the other hand, it would be of no practical or theoretical use, since it would not assist our appraisals of actions, depending as it would on the presupposed validity of those appraisals. Nor would it elucidate the logic of those appraisal-concepts, the intelligent employment of which antedated the invention of this causal hypothesis.

Before we bid farewell to the doctrine of volitions, it is expedient to consider certain quite familiar and authentic processes with which volitions are sometimes wrongly identified.

People are frequently in doubt what to do; having considered alternative courses of action, they then, sometimes, select or choose one of these courses. This process of opting for one of a set of alternative courses of action is sometimes said to be what is signified by "volition." But this identification will not do, for most voluntary actions do not issue out of conditions of indecision and are not therefore results of settlements of indecisions. Moreover it is notorious that a person may choose to do something but fail, from weakness of will, to do it; or he may fail to do it because some circumstance arises after the choice is made, preventing the execution of the act chosen. But the theory could not allow that volitions ever fail to result in action, else further executive operations would have to be postulated to account for the fact that sometimes voluntary actions are performed. And finally the process of deliberating between alternatives and opting for one of them is itself subject to appraisal-predicates. But if, for example, an act of choosing is describable as voluntary, then, on this suggested showing, it would have in its turn to be the result of a prior choice to choose, and that from a choice to choose to choose. . . .

The same objections forbid the identification with volitions of such other familiar processes as that of resolving or making up our minds to do something and that of nerving or bracing ourselves to do something. I may resolve to get out of bed or go to the dentist, and I may, clenching my fists and gritting my teeth, brace myself to do so, but I may still backslide. If the action is not done, then, according to the doctrine, the volition to do it is also unexecuted. Again, the operations of resolving and nerving ourselves are themselves members of the class of creditable or discreditable actions, so they cannot constitute the peculiar ingredient which, according to the doctrine, is the common condition of any performance being creditable or discreditable.

(3) THE DISTINCTION BETWEEN VOLUNTARY AND INVOLUNTARY

It should be noticed that while ordinary folk, magistrates, parents and teachers, generally apply the words "voluntary" and "involuntary" to actions in one way, philosophers often apply them in quite another way.

In their most ordinary employment "voluntary" and "involuntary" are used, with a few minor elasticities, as adjectives applying to actions which ought not to be done. We discuss whether someone's action was voluntary or not only when the action seems to have been his fault. He is accused of making a noise, and the guilt is his, if the action was voluntary, like laughing; he has successfully excused himself, if he satisfies us that it was involuntary, like a sneeze. In the same way in ordinary life we raise questions of responsibility only when someone is charged, justly or unjustly, with an offence. It makes sense, in this use, to ask whether a boy was responsible for breaking a window, but not whether he was responsible for finishing his homework in good time. We do not ask whether it was his fault that he got a long-division sum right, for to get a sum right is not a fault. If he gets it wrong, he may satisfy us that his failure was not his fault, perhaps because he had not yet been shown how to do such calculations.

In this ordinary use, then, it is absurd to discuss whether satisfactory, correct or admirable performances are voluntary or involuntary. Neither inculpation nor exculpation is in point. We neither confess to authorship nor adduce extenuating circumstances; neither plead "guilty" nor plead "not guilty"; for we are not accused.

But philosophers, in discussing what constitutes acts voluntary or involuntary, tend to describe as voluntary not only reprehensible but also meritorious actions, not only things that are someone's fault but also things that are to his credit. The motives underlying their unwitting extension of the ordinary sense of "voluntary," "involuntary" and "responsible" will be considered later. For the moment it is worth while to consider certain consequences which follow from it. In the ordinary use, to say that a sneeze was involuntary is to say that the agent could not help doing it, and to say that a laugh was voluntary is to say that the agent could have helped doing it. (This is not to say that the laugh was intentional. We do not laugh on purpose.) The boy could have got the sum right which he actually got wrong; he knew how to behave, but he misbehaved; he was competent to tie a reef-knot, though what he unintentionally produced was a granny-knot. His failure or lapse was his fault. But when the word "voluntary" is given its philosophically stretched use, so that correct as well as incorrect, admirable as well as contemptible acts are described as voluntary, it seems to follow by analogy with the ordinary use, that a boy who gets his sum right can also be described as having been "able to help it." It would then be proper to ask: Could you have helped solving the riddle? Could you have helped drawing the proper conclusion? Could you have helped tying a proper reef-knot? Could you have helped seeing the point of that joke? Could you have helped being kind to that child? In fact, however, no one could answer these questions, though it is not at first obvious why, if it is correct to say that someone could have avoided getting a sum wrong, it is incorrect to say that he could have avoided getting it right.

The solution is simple. When we say that someone could have avoided committing a lapse or error, or that it was his fault that he committed it, we mean that he knew how to do the right thing, or was competent to do so, but did not exercise his knowledge or competence. He was not trying, or not trying hard enough. But when a person has done the right thing, we cannot then say that he knew how to do the wrong thing, or that he was competent to make mistakes. For making mistakes is not an exercise of competence, nor is the commission of slips an exercise of knowledge *how;* it is a failure to exercise knowledge *how.* It is true in one sense of "could" that a person who had done a sum correctly could have got it wrong; in the sense, namely, that he is not exempt from the liability to be careless. But in another sense of "could," to ask, "Could you have got it wrong?" means "Were you sufficiently intelligent and well-trained and were you concentrating hard enough to make a miscalculation?," and this is as silly a question as to ask whether someone's teeth are strong enough to be broken by cracking nuts.

The tangle of largely spurious problems, known as the problem of the Freedom of the Will, partly derives from this unconsciously stretched use of "voluntary" and these consequential misapplications of different senses of "could" and "could have helped."

The first task is to elucidate what is meant in their ordinary, undistorted use by "voluntary," "involuntary," "responsible," "could not have helped" and "his fault," these expressions are used in deciding concrete questions of guilt and innocence.

If a boy has tied a granny-knot instead of a reef-knot, we satisfy ourselves that it was his fault by first establishing that he knew how to tie a reef-knot, and then by establishing that his hand was not forced by external coercion and that there were no other agencies at work preventing him from tying the correct knot. We establish that he could tie reef-knots by finding out that he had been taught, had had practice, usually got them right, or by finding that he could detect and correct knots tied by others, or by finding that he was ashamed of what he had done and, without help from others, put it right himself. That he was not acting under duress or in panic or high fever or with numb fingers, is discovered in the way in which we ordinarily discover that highly exceptional incidents have not taken place; for such incidents would have been too remarkable to have gone unremarked, at least by the boy himself.

The first question which we had to decide had nothing to do with the occurrence or non-occurrence of any occult episode in the boy's stream of consciousness; it was the question whether or not he had the required higher-level competence, that of knowing how to tie reef-knots. We were not, at this stage, inquiring whether he committed, or omitted, an extra public or private operation, but only whether he possessed or lacked a certain intelligent capacity. What satisfied us was not the (unattainable) knowledge of the truth or falsity of a particular covert cause-overt effect proposition, but the (attainable) knowledge of the truth or falsity of a complex and partially general hypothetical proposition—not, in short, that he did tie a shadowy reef- or granny-knot behind the scenes, but that he could have tied a real one with this rope and would have done so on this occasion, if he had paid more heed to what he was doing. The lapse was his fault because, knowing how to tie the knot, he still did not tie it correctly.

Consider next the case of an act which everyone would decide was not the agent's fault. A boy arrives late for school and on inquiry it turns out that he left home at the usual time, did not dally on his way to the omnibus halt and caught the usual omnibus. But the vehicle broke down and could not complete the journey. The boy ran as fast as he could the rest of the way, but was still late. Clearly all the steps taken by the boy were either the same as those which normally bring him to school in time, or were the only steps open to him for remedying the effects of the breakdown. There was nothing else that he could have done and his teacher properly recommends him to follow the same routine on future occasions. His late arrival was not the result of a failure to do what he was capable of doing. He was prevented by a circumstance which was not in his power to modify. Here again the teacher is judging an action with reference to the capacities and opportunities of the agent; his excuse is accepted that he could not have done better than he did. The whole question of the involuntariness of his late arrival is decided without the boy being asked to report any deliverances of consciousness or introspection about the execution or non-execution of any volitions.

It makes no difference if the actions with which an agent is charged either are or embody operations of silent soliloquy or other operations with verbal or non-verbal images. A slip in mental arithmetic is the pupil's fault on the same grounds as a slip made in written arithmetic; and an error committed in matching colours in the mind's eye may merit the reproach of carelessness in the same way as an error committed in matching colours on the draper's counter. If the agent could have done better than he did, then he could have helped doing it as badly as he did.

Besides considering the ordinary senses of "voluntary," involuntary," "responsible," "my fault" and "could" or "could not help," we should notice as well the ordinary uses of such expressions as "effort of will," "strength of will" and "irresolute." A person is described as behaving resolutely when in the execution of difficult, protracted or disagreeable tasks he tends not to relax his efforts, not to let his attention be diverted, not to grumble and not to think much or often about his fatigue or fears. He does not shirk or drop things to which he has set his hand. A weak-willed person is one who is easily distracted or disheartened, apt to convince himself that another time will be more suitable or that the reasons for undertaking the task were not after all very strong. Note that it is no part of the definition of resoluteness or of irresoluteness that a resolution should actually have been formed. A resolute man may firmly resist temptations to abandon or postpone his task, though he never went through a prefatory ritual-process of making up his mind to complete it. But naturally such a man will also be disposed to perform any vows which he has made to others or to himself. Correspondingly the irresolute man will be likely to fail to carry out his often numerous good resolutions, but his lack of tenacity of purpose will be exhibited also in surrenders and slacknesses in courses of action which were unprefaced by any private or public undertakings to accomplish them.

Strength of will is a propensity the exercises of which consist in sticking to tasks; that is, in not being deterred or diverted. Weakness of will is having too little of this propensity. The performances in which strength of will is exerted may be performances of almost any sort, intellectual or manual, imaginative or administrative. It is not a single-track disposition or, for that and other reasons, a disposition to execute occult operations of one special kind.

By "an effort of will" is meant a particular exercise of tenacity of purpose, occurring when the obstacles are notably great, or the counter-temptations notably strong. Such efforts may, but need not, be accompanied by special processes, often of a ritual character, of nerving or adjuring oneself to do what is required; but these processes are not so much ways in which resoluteness is shown as ways in which fear of irresoluteness manifests itself.

Before we leave the concept or concepts of voluntariness, two further points need to be made. (1) Very often we oppose things done voluntarily to things suffered under compulsion. Some soldiers are volunteers, others are conscripts; some yachtsmen go out to sea voluntarily, others are carried out to sea by the wind and tide. Here questions of inculpation and exculpation need not arise. In asking whether the soldier volunteered or was conscripted, we are asking whether he joined up because he wanted to do so, or whether he joined up because he had to do so, where "had to" entails "no matter what he wanted." In asking whether the yachtsman went out to sea of his own accord or whether he was carried out, we are asking whether he went out on purpose, or whether he would still have gone out as he did, even if he had meant not to do so. Would bad news from home, or a warning from the coastguard, have stopped him?

What is involuntary, in this use, is not describable as an act. Being carried out to sea, or being called up, is something that happens to a person, not something which he does. In this respect, this antithesis between voluntary and involuntary differs from the antithesis we have in mind when we ask whether someone's tying of a granny-knot, or his knitting of his brows, is voluntary or involuntary. A person who frowns involuntarily is not forced to frown, as a yachtsman may be forced out to sea; nor is the careless boy forced to tie a granny-knot, as the conscript is forced to join the army. Even frowning is something that a person does. It is not done to him. So sometimes the question "Voluntary or involuntary?" means "Did the person do it, or was it done to him?"; sometimes it presupposes that he did it, but means "Did he do it with or without heeding what he was doing?" or "Did he do it on purpose or inadvertently, mechanically, or instinctively, etc.?"

(2) When a person does something voluntarily, in the sense that he does it on purpose or is trying to do it, his action certainly reflects some quality or qualities of mind, since (it is more than a verbal point to say) he is in some degree and in one fashion or another minding what he is doing. It follows also that, if linguistically equipped, he can then tell, without research or conjecture, what he has been trying to accomplish. But, . . . these implications of voluntariness do not carry with them the double-life corollaries often assumed. To frown intentionally is not to do

one thing on one's forehead and another thing in a second metaphorical place; nor is it to do one thing with one's brow-muscles and another thing with some non-bodily organ. In particular, it is not to bring about a frown on one's forehead by first bringing about a frown-causing exertion of some occult non-muscle. "He frowned intentionally" does not report the occurrence of two episodes. It reports the occurrence of one episode, but one of a very different character from that reported by "he frowned involuntarily," though the frowns might be photographically as similar as you please.

(4) FREEDOM OF THE WILL

It has been pointed out that in some philosophers' discussions of the voluntariness of actions, the words "voluntary," "involuntary" and "responsible" are used, not with their ordinary restriction to lapses or apparent lapses, but with a wider scope covering all performances which are to be adjudged favourably or unfavourably by any criteria of excellence or admissibility. In their use, a person is described as voluntarily doing the right thing and as voluntarily doing the wrong thing, or as being responsible not only for actions for which he is subject to accusation, but also for actions entitling him to kudos. It is used, that is, as a synonym of "intentional."

Now the philosophers who have worked with this stretched usage have had a strong intellectual motive for doing so. They felt the need for an apparatus of terms by which to demarcate those things and occurrences to which *either* plaudits *or* strictures are appropriate from those to which neither are appropriate. Without such an apparatus it would, they felt, be impossible to state what are the qualifications for membership of the realm of Spirit, the lack of which entails relegation to the realm of brute Nature.

The main source of this concern to discover some peculiar element present, wherever Spirit is present, and absent, where it is absent, was alarm at the bogey of Mechanism. It was believed that the physical sciences had established, or were on the way to establishing, that the things and events of the external world are rigidly governed by discoverable laws, laws the formulations of which admit no appraisal-words. It was felt that all external happenings are confined within the iron grooves of mechanical causation. The genesis, the properties and the courses of these happenings were, or would be, totally explained in terms of measurable and, it was supposed, therefore purposeless forces.

To salve our right to employ appraisal-concepts, the field of their proper application had to be shown to lie somewhere else than this external world, and an internal world of unmeasurable but purposeful forces was thought to do the trick. "Volitions" being already nominated as the required outputs of internal forces, it was then natural to suppose that voluntariness, defined in terms of propagation by volitions, was the common and peculiar element which makes occurrences spiritual. Scientific propositions and appraisal-propositions were accordingly distinguished as being respectively descriptions of what takes place in the external world and descriptions of what takes place in the internal world—at least until psychologists claimed that their assertions were scientific descriptions of what takes place in the inner world.

The question whether human beings can merit praise or blame was consequently construed as the question whether volitions are effects.

(5) THE BOGEY OF MECHANISM

Whenever a new science achieves its first big successes, its enthusiastic acolytes always fancy that all questions are now soluble by extension of its methods of solving its questions. At one time theorists imagined that the whole world was nothing more than a complex of geometrical figures, at another that the whole world was describable and explicable in the propositions of pure arithmetic. Chemical, electrical, Darwinian and Freudian cosmogonies have also enjoyed their bright but brief days. "At long last," the zealots always say, "we can give, or at least indicate, a solution of all difficulties and one which is unquestionably a scientific solution."

The physical sciences launched by Copernicus, Galileo, Newton and Boyle secured a longer and a stronger hold upon the cosmogony-builders than did either their forerunners or their successors. People still tend to treat laws of Mechanics not merely as the ideal type of scientific laws, but as, in some sense, the ultimate laws of Nature. They tend to hope or fear that biological, psychological and sociological laws will one day be "reduced" to mechanical laws—though it is left unclear what sort of a transaction this "reduction" would be.

I have spoken of Mechanism as a bogey. The fear that theoretically minded persons have felt lest everything should turn out to be explicable by mechanical laws is a baseless fear. And it is baseless not because the contingency which they dread happens not to be impending, but because it makes no sense to speak of such a contingency. Physicists may one day have found the answers to all physical questions, but not all questions are physical questions. The laws that they have found and will find may, in one sense of the metaphorical verb, govern everything that happens, but they do not ordain everything that happens. Indeed they do not ordain anything that happens. Laws of nature are not fiats.

An illustration may elucidate this point. A scientifically trained spectator, who is not acquainted with chess or any other game, is permitted to look at a chessboard in the intervals between the moves. He does not yet see the players making the moves. After a time he begins to notice certain regularities. The pieces known to us as "pawns," normally move only one square at a time and then only forwards, save in certain special circumstances when they move diagonally. The pieces known to us as "bishops" only move diagonally, though they can move any number of squares at a time. Knights always make dog-legged moves. And so on. After much research this spectator will have worked out all the rules of chess, and he is then allowed to see that the moves of the pieces are made by people whom we know as "players." He commiserates with them upon their bondage. "Every move that you make," he says, "is governed by unbreakable rules; from the moment that one of you puts his hand on a pawn, the move that he will make with it is, in most cases, accurately predictable. The whole course of what you tragically dub your "game" is remorselessly pre-ordained; nothing in it takes place which cannot be shown to be governed by one or other of the iron rules. Heartless necessity dictates the play, leaving no room in it for intelligence or purpose. True, I am not yet competent to explain every move that I witness by the rules that I have so far discovered. But it would be unscientific to suppose that there are inexplicable moves. There must therefore be further rules, which I hope to discover and which will satisfactorily complete the explanations which I have inaugurated." The players, of course, laugh and explain to him that though every move is governed, not one of them is ordained by the rules. "True, given that I start to move my bishop, you can predict with certainty that it will end on a square of the same colour as that from which it started. That can be deduced from the rules. But that, or how far, I shall move my bishop at this or that stage of the game is not stated in, or deducible from, the rules. There is plenty of room for us to display cleverness and stupidity and to exercise deliberation and choice. Though nothing happens that is irregular, plenty happens that is surprising, ingenious and silly. The rules are the same for all the games of chess that have ever been played, yet nearly every game that has ever been played has taken a course for which the players can recall no close parallels. The rules are unalterable, but the games are not uniform. The rules prescribe what the players may not do; everything else is permitted, though many moves that are permitted would be bad tactics.

"There are no further rules of the game for you to discover and the 'explanations' which you hope to find for the particular moves that we make can, of course, be discovered, but they are not explanations in terms of rules but in terms of some quite different things, namely, such things as the player's consideration and application of tactical principles. Your notion of what constitutes an explanation was too narrow. The sense in which a rule 'explains' a move made in conformity with it is not the same as the sense in which a tactical principle explains a move, for all that every move that obeys a tactical principle also obeys a rule. Knowing how to apply tactical principles involves knowing the rules of the game, but there is no question of these principles being 'reducible' to rules of the game."

This illustration is not intended to suggest that the laws of physics are very much like the rules of chess; for the course of Nature is not a game and its laws are not human inventions or conventions. What the illustration is meant to bring out is the fact there is no contradiction in saying that one and the same process, such as the move of a bishop, is in accordance with two principles of completely different types and such that neither is "reducible" to the other, though one of them presupposes the other.

Hence there derive two quite different sorts of "explanation" of the moves, neither of which is incompatible with the other. Indeed the explanation in terms of tactical canons presupposes that in terms of the rules of chess, but it is not deducible from those rules. This point can be expressed in another way. A spectator might ask, in one sense of "why," why the bishop always ends a move on a square of the same colour as that on which it began the game; he would be answered by being referred to the rules of chess, including those prescribing the design of the board. He might then ask, in another sense of "why," why a player at a certain stage of the game moved one of his bishops (and not some other piece) to one square (and not to another); he might be answered that it was to force the opposing Queen to cease to threaten the player's King.

Words like "explanation," "law," "rule," "principle," "why," "because," "cause," "reason," "govern," "necessitate," etc., have a range of typically different senses. Mechanism seemed to be a menace because it was assumed that the use of these terms in mechanical theories is their sole use; that all "why" questions are answerable in terms of laws of motion. In fact all "why" questions of one type are perhaps answerable in those terms and no "why" questions of other types are answerable merely in those terms.

It may well be that throughout the whole length of *The Decline and Fall of the Roman Empire* Gibbon never once infringes the rules of English grammar. They governed his entire writing, yet they did not ordain what he should write, or even the style in which he should write; they merely forbade certain ways of conjoining words. Knowing these rules and Gibbon's obedience to them, a reader can predict from the fact that a particular sentence has for its subject a plural noun that its verb will be a plural verb. His predictions will be uniformly correct, yet we feel no inclination to lament that Gibbon's pen ran in a fatal groove. Grammar tells the reader that the verb must be a plural verb, but not which verb it will be.

An argumentative passage from *The Decline and Fall* might be examined for the grammatical rules which its word-arrangements observe, the stylistic canons which its word-arrangements observe, and the logical rules which its word-arrangements observe. There is no conflict or competition between these different types of principles; all alike are applied in the same material; all alike can supply licenses for correct predictions; all alike may be referred to for answers to questions of the same verbal pattern "Why did Gibbon write this and not something else?"

The discoveries of the physical sciences no more rule out life, sentience, purpose or intelligence from presence in the world than do the rules of grammar extrude style or logic from prose. Certainly the discoveries of the physical sciences say nothing of life, sentience, or purpose, but nor do the rules of grammar say anything about style or logic. For the laws of physics apply to what is animate as well as to what is inanimate, to intelligent people as well as to idiots, just as the rules of grammar apply to *Whitaker's Almanac* as well as to *The Decline and Fall,* to Mrs. Eddy's as well as to Hume's reasonings.

The favourite model to which the fancied mechanistic world is assimilated is that of billiard balls imparting their motion to one another by impact. Yet a game of billiards provides one of the simplest examples of a course of events for the description of which mechanical terms are necessary without being sufficient. Certainly from accurate knowledge of the weight, shape, elasticity and movements of the balls, the constitution of the table and the conditions of the atmosphere it is in principle possible, in accordance with known laws, to deduce from a momentary state of the balls what will be their later state. But it does not follow from this that the course of the game is predictable in accordance with those laws alone. A scientific forecaster, who was ignorant of the rules and tactics of the game and of the skill and plans of the players, could predict, perhaps, from the beginning of a single stroke, the positions in which the balls will come to rest before the next stroke is made; but he could predict no further. The player himself may be able to foresee with modest probability the sort of break that he will make, for he knows, perhaps, the best tactics to apply to situations like this and he knows a good deal about his own skill, endurance, patience, keenness and intentions.

It must be noticed that in so far as the player has any skill in getting the balls where he wishes, he must have knowledge, of a rule-of-thumb sort, of the mechanical principles which govern the accelerations and decelerations of the balls. His knowledge how to execute his intentions is not at loggerheads with his knowledge of mechanical laws; it depends on that knowledge. In applying appraisal-concepts to his play we are not worded by the fact that the motions imparted by him to the balls are governed by mechanical laws; for there could not be a game of skill at all if, *per impossibile,* the instruments of the game behaved randomly.

The modern interpretation of natural laws as statements not of necessities but of very, very long odds is sometimes acclaimed as providing a desiderated element of non-rigorousness in Nature. Now at last, it is sometimes felt, we can be scientific while reserving just a very few occasions in which appraisal-concepts can be properly applied. This silly view assumes that an action could not merit favourable or unfavourable criticism, unless it were an exception to scientific generalisations. But the billiards player asks for no special indulgences from the laws of physics any more than he does from the rules of billiards. Why should he? They do not force his hand. The fears expressed by some moral philosophers that the advance of the natural sciences diminishes the field within which the moral virtues can be exercised rests on the assumption that there is some contradiction in saying that one and the same occurrence is governed both by mechanical laws and by moral principles, an assumption as baseless as the assumption that a golfer cannot at once conform to the laws of ballistics *and* obey the rules of golf *and* play with elegance and skill. Not only is there plenty of room for purpose where everything is governed by mechanical laws, but there would be no place for purpose if things were not so governed. Predictability is a necessary condition of planning.

Mechanism then is a mere bogy and while there is much to be elucidated in the special concepts of biology, anthropology, sociology, ethics, logic, aesthetics, politics, economics, historiography, etc., there is no need for the desperate salvage-operation of withdrawing the applications of them out of the ordinary world to some postulated other world, or of setting up a partition between things that exist in Nature and things that exist in non-Nature. No occult precursors of overt acts are required to preserve for their agent his title to plaudits or strictures for performing them, nor would they be effective preservatives if they did exist.

Men are not machines, not even ghost-ridden machines. They are men—a tautology which is sometimes worth remembering. People often pose such questions as "How does my mind get my hand to make the required movements?" and even "What makes my hand do what my mind tells it to do?" Questions of these patterns are properly asked of certain chain-processes. The question "What makes the bullet fly out of the barrel?" is properly answered by "The expansion of gases in the cartridge"; the question "What makes the cartridge explode?" is answered by reference to the percussion of the detonator; and the question "How does my squeezing the trigger make the pin strike the detonator?" is answered by describing the mechanism of springs, levers and catches between the trigger and the pin. So when it is asked "How does my mind get my finger to squeeze the trigger?" the form of the question presupposes that a further chain-process is involved, embodying still earlier tensions, releases and discharges, though this time "mental" ones. But whatever is the act or operation adduced as the first step of this postulated chain-process, the performance of it has to be described in just the same way as in ordinary life we describe the squeezing of the trigger by the marksman. Namely we say simply "He did it" and not "He did or underwent something else which caused it."

In conclusion, it is perhaps worth while giving a warning against a very popular fallacy. The hearsay knowledge that everything in Nature is subject to mechanical laws often tempts people to say that Nature is either one big machine, or else a conglomeration of machines. But in fact there are very few machines in Nature. The only machines that we find are the machines that human beings make, such as clocks, windmills and turbines. There are a very few natural systems which somewhat resemble such machines, namely, such things as solar systems. These do go on by themselves and repeat indefinitely the same series of movements. The do go, as few unmanufactured things go, "like clock-work." True, to make machines we have to know and apply Mechanics. But inventing machines is not copying things found in inanimate Nature.

Paradoxical though it may seem, we have to look rather to living organisms for examples in Nature of self-maintaining, routine-observing systems. The movements of the heavenly bodies provided one kind of "clock." It was the human pulse that provided the next. Nor is it merely primitive animism which makes native children think of engines as iron horses. There is very little else in Nature to which they are so closely analogous. Avalanches and games of billiards are subject to mechanical laws; but they are not at all like the workings of machines.

Decision, Intention and Certainty

Stuart Hampshire and H. L. A. Hart

I

There is a kind of certainty about human actions, wants, likes and dislikes, which is different from the kind of certainty about these subjects that is based upon empirical evidence: it is a kind of certainty, or knowledge, to which the notion of evidence is irrelevant. And it is different again from the kind of knowledge that is knowing how to do something, that is, the knowledge that is a skill or competence.

In each of the following pairs of sentences knowledge of this peculiar kind is mentioned: (1) "I am not sure which of these I like best." "I know which I like." (2) "He does not know what he wants." "I now know what I want" (3) "I think I will do it, but I am not sure." "I know now what I will do" (where an entirely voluntary action is envisaged). The kind of knowledge referred to in each of these

Source: "Decision, Intention, and Certainty," by Stuart Hampshire and J. A. Hart, *Mind,* 67, 1958. Reprinted by permission of Oxford University Press.

sentences, as they are normally used, would be dissociated from any possible appeal to evidence. This is the most important, but not the only, respect in which there is an analogy between the pairs of sentences (1), (2) and (3). There is also an analogy in the grammatical form of these sentences. But in this article we are concerned with only one case of the kind of certainty or knowledge that cannot be associated with any appeal to evidence: namely, case (3), a man's knowledge of his own present and future voluntary actions. Our thesis is that there is a necessary connexion between certainty of this kind, and upon this topic, and deciding to do something, and also that there is a necessary connexion between certainty of this kind and intending to do something, and doing it intentionally.

The necessary connexion between certainty about future voluntary action and decision emerges in the following entailments: (1) "I have decided to do this" entails "I am certain that I will do this, unless I am in some way prevented." (2) "I am certain that I will do this" (where the action referred to is entirely voluntary) entails "I have decided to do this." (3) "I do not know what I will do in such-and-such a contingency" (where the possible actions are envisaged as entirely voluntary and as a matter of my own choice) entails "I have not decided what I will do in such-and-such a contingency." (4) "I have not decided what I will do in such-and-such a contingency" entails "I am uncertain what I will do in such-and-such a contingency." (5) "He has not yet decided what he will do" entails "He does not yet know what he will do." (6) "He does not yet know what he will do" entails "He has not yet decided what he will do." (7) "He is wondering what to do" entails "He is uncertain what he will do." (8) "He has made up his mind what he will do" entails "There is no doubt in his mind about what he will do."

If a man is in the position of still having to decide between two or more courses of action open to him, then he must be uncertain what he will do. His uncertainty might in principle be terminated in two very different ways: either, after considering the evidence of his own behaviour and reactions in similar situations in the past, he may become certain in his own mind that he will in fact do so-and-so, or at least try to do it, when the time comes: this would be certainty based upon empirical evidence, and his announcement of it would, for this reason, count as a *prediction,* and not as a decision: or, after reflection on the *reasons* for acting in one way rather than another, he may become certain (make up his mind) what he will do, or at least try to do: in this case his announcement will count as an announcement of his *decision,* and not as a prediction. If a man does claim to be able to predict with certainty his own future actions, basing his prediction on induction, then he is implying that the actions in question will be in some sense, or to some degree, involuntary, the effect of causes outside his own control. If action in the situation envisaged were entirely voluntary, then it must be up to him to decide what he will do. If it is up to him to decide what he is going to do, then he must still be uncertain what he will do until he has made a decision or until his intentions are formed. While he is making the decision, and while he is reviewing reasons for acting in one way rather than another, he must be in a state of uncertainty about what he is going to do. The certainty comes at the moment of decision, and indeed constitutes the decision, when the certainty is arrived at in this way, as a result of considering reasons, and not as a result of considering evidence.

Many, if not most, voluntary and deliberate actions are not preceded by any datable event which could be called a moment of decision. An action is often performed, voluntarily and deliberately, without the agent's having stopped to wonder whether he would perform it or not, and without his having rehearsed in his mind the reasons for and against performing it. It might still be true that, if he had been asked what he was going to do, he would have been able to answer with complete confidence. He knew what he would do, and he might even be said to have decided to do it, although he had never considered alternatives. But the word "decision," as opposed to the word "intention," is more naturally associated with conditions in which the agent has asked himself the question—"Shall I do it or shall I not?"—thereby showing his uncertainty about what he is going to do, an uncertainty of the kind which constitutes indecision. When he has made his decision, that is, when, after considering reasons, all uncertainty about what he is going to do has been removed from his mind, he will be said to intend to do whatever he has decided to do, until either he falls into uncertainty again, as a result of further reasons suggesting themselves, or until he definitely changes his mind.

As there are degrees of knowledge, ranging from complete certainty to complete uncertainty, so there are degrees of decision. "Will you accept the appointment?" "I think I will, but I am not sure." In English the word "intend" often has a suggestion of the tentative and of the not entirely certain; good intentions may come to nothing. But "decide" has a ring of finality. If I say that I had decided to do action *x,* but admit that I did not in fact do it, or even try to do it, then I strictly imply either that I later changed my mind, or that I was somehow prevented, or that I altogether lost control of myself. It may be objected that "deciding" and "changing my mind" represent an act, something that I *do,* and that therefore deciding cannot be adequately characterized as simply becoming certain about one's own future voluntary action after considering reasons, and not considering evidence. One may be inclined to say that the certainty is the consequence or outcome of the decision, and must be distinguished from the decision itself. But what is the force of saying that to decide to do something is to perform an act? This category-word, in this as in other contexts, is entirely unclear. Certainly one can say: "You ought to decide, to make up your mind." Or one can give a blunt order: "Make up your mind." The possibility of using the imperative, or the quasi-imperative form, of the verb might be taken as a sufficient condition of saying that the verb represents an act. There is also the idiom: "I cannot make up my mind: I am quite unable to decide between these two courses of action." It looks therefore as if there is something which I cannot *do,* and it is not the actions themselves, but rather the preliminary action of deciding between them. But these idioms are often misleading. Often the order to decide is an order to do one or other of the actions, no matter which, and often it is an order to announce a decision. But even when the imperative, or quasi-imperative, form cannot be attached to another verb—as it cannot in the phrases "Never hesitate" or "Always decide what you are going to do in advance"—it is still an imperative which has a parallel use with the cognitive verbs. One may intelligibly be told not to believe information of a certain kind, or one may be told that one ought not to believe it. One may even be told that one ought not to doubt some matter of fact, and that one ought to accept it as something which is certainly true. Doubt and certainty about an action are not in this respect essentially different from doubt and certainty about a statement; the one is as little, or as much, an act as the other.

II

If there are two possible kinds of certainty about one's own future actions—inductive certainty, and certainty based upon reasons, which is decision—it is evidently possible that they may on occasion come into conflict with each other. This is one part of the problem of free-will. Suppose a man to have been offered an appointment: he is undecided, and expresses his state of indecision in the appropriate form—"I am uncertain whether to do it or not." In this state of indecision, and therefore of uncertainty, he asks himself the question—"Shall I do it or shall I not?," reviewing reasons for and against, with a view to ending the uncertainty, that is, to deciding. If he has confronted choices exactly like this one on many occasions in the past, and if he has always passed through a phase of indecision and then refused, he may acknowledge to himself that this is good evidence that he will in fact ultimately refuse the appointment on this occasion; he may confess to having a feeling or premonition that he will ultimately refuse, while saying that he has still not decided. But the evidence of his past behaviour, or of the behaviour of people like him, or even the evidence of a well tested psychological law, cannot by itself convince him that he will in fact refuse, *if* he still maintains that his refusal or acceptance is a matter for his own decision. If he is convinced by empirical evidence alone that he will *certainly* refuse, then he must have been convinced by this evidence that it is not in his power not to refuse, and that, in spite of appearances, the outcome will not be determined by his decision. And there certainly are occasions when a man may in this way adopt a spectator's attitude to his own conduct, convinced by experience, or perhaps even by scientific knowledge, that the appearance of free decision is delusive and that, when it comes to the moment of action, he will certainly act in a certain way. If he *admits* that this is his conviction, it would be senseless for him to claim that he was making any decision in the matter; nothing would count as a decision to do that which he is certain on other grounds that he will in any case do, and nothing would count as a decision to do that which he is certain that he will not do. A man may decide to *try* to achieve a result which he thinks, on the basis of evidence, that he will almost certainly fail to achieve; but then there must be some action or actions, which constitute the attempt, and which he is certain that he will perform, and certain not on empirical evidence.

There may be mixed, confused situations in which a man drifts into a course of action, fatalistically certain, on the evidence of his own past, that this is the course of action that he will in fact follow, while at the same time not denying that his own conduct in this sphere could be changed by his own decisions. He half decides to continue as before, and half feels himself to be passive in the matter, his certainty about his future action being based on a mixture of the evidence of his past behaviour together with reasons for not making the effort to change. The psychology of human decision can be very complicated. But the fact that there are these mixed cases does not invalidate the general distinction between the certainty about one's own future action that is based upon evidence and induction, and the certainty that is based upon reasons.

This kind of certainty, or knowledge, about our own future actions will help to illuminate the concept of intention also.

Intention

Usually a person engaged in doing something knows, and is able to specify, what action he is doing, and often, though not always, a person knows, and is able to specify, some action which he will later try to do. Yet in neither of these cases is the agent's knowledge of his own present or future action normally derived from observation nor is it a conclusion from evidence. Other people are often able to say what action someone is doing or is going to do, when they know this either from observation of his movements or as a conclusion from evidence available to them. They make use of criteria or evidence in determining what he is doing or going to do; but the agent himself does not. The segregation of this form of knowledge which the agent has of his own present or future actions, and the identification of corresponding uses of expressions such as "not knowing what one is doing," "being certain or uncertain," "being mistaken," is an essential element in the elucidation of the concept of intention. We shall consider the dependence upon this form of knowledge (practical knowledge) of certain distinct but related applications of the notion of intention.

There are two principal ways in which intention is connected with action. First, when a person has done something, *e.g.* struck another person, the question of whether he did it intentionally or unintentionally may arise, and this is equivalent, except in certain trivial respects, to the question whether he intended, or did not intend, to do what he has in fact done. Secondly, the question may arise as to whether a person intends, or does not intend, to do some action in the future; and a similar question may arise about his past intention to do some action, even if he did not in fact do it.

These two applications of the notion of intention do not of course exhaust the notion. Besides them there is the special application of intention in cases where it has close connexion with the notions of meaning and reference. What did he intend by those words? To whom did he intend to refer by that name? There is also the use of intention in conjunction with the actions of other people: we may intend other people to do certain things or even to have certain experiences. "I intended you to take that book," "I intended him to suffer." Although there are these and other applications of the concept of intention, the first two are of special relevance to the present subject.

Acting intentionally. We must first consider the type of context required if the question whether a person has done something intentionally or not is to have any point. In any ordinary narrative describing ordinary actions done in normal circumstances, it would be pointless to say that a person did these things intentionally; for normally there is a fulfilled presumption that if a person does something, he does it intentionally. This is a feature of the whole conceptual scheme involved in our description of persons in terms of actions. If I am telling you simply what someone did, *e.g.* took off his hat or sat down, it would normally be redundant, and hence misleading, though not false, to say that he sat down intentionally. The primary point of saying that someone acted intentionally is to rebut a *prima facie* suggestion that he was in some way ignorant of, or mistaken about, some element involved in this action. Usually the suggestion arises from the fact that what he has done is abnormal or wrong in some way or that it is something which ordinary people would not do except unintentionally. Part of the force of "He did it intentionally" is just to rule out the suggestion which he did it unintentionally, where "unintentionally" means that the agent did what he did through some accident or by mistake. This suggests that the whole meaning of "intentionally" simply lies in its negation of accident or mistake, and that once these two ideas are elucidated, as they easily can be, the analysis of the notion of intentionally doing something is within our grasp. On this view the analysis will simply be (1) a description of the appropriate context for the use of the expression "intentionally" as rebutting accident or mistake, and (2) the elucidation of the ideas of accident and mistake. But this would only be the first step towards the analysis of the notion of intentionally doing something; for the assertion that someone has done something intentionally, or that he intended to do what he has done, is not merely the equivalent of the assertion that he did not do it unintentionally, or that he did not do it accidentally or by mistake. Accident and mistake are certainly incompatible with the agent doing what he did intentionally; but the assertion that someone did what he did intentionally does not merely exclude these cases of unintentional action. This may be seen from the following example. A man fires and shoots another: if asked what he was doing, and if he was prepared to give an honest answer, he would identify his action as shooting at someone. But in a perfectly ordinary sense of "know," he would know that shooting at someone involved making the loud noise which in fact the shot had made. In such a case it is clear that he did not make the noise by mistake or by accident; it is therefore clear that he did not make it unintentionally. But on these facts it would be misleading to say he intentionally made the noise, or that he intended to make the noise; for this would suggest that this is what the agent would say that he was doing, if asked. Always the expression "He intended to do it" means more than, though it also includes, "He did not do it unintentionally."

If an action is to be intentional, or to be what the agent intended to do, two different kinds of requirement must be satisfied. First, the agent must have ordinary empirical knowledge of certain features of his environment and of the nature and characteristics of certain things affected by his movements. Precisely what knowledge of this sort he must have will depend upon precisely what action is ascribed to him. If, for example, he is said intentionally to have shot at a bird, he must know, in the ordinary sense of "know," that what he has in his hands is a gun, and that there is a bird in the line of fire. He must also have certain types of general knowledge, for example, of the consequences of pulling the trigger of a loaded gun. Without such knowledge as this, his action in shooting the bird would be accidental or done by mistake, and hence would be ranked as unintentional. Second, and more important, if his action is intentional (what he intended to do), the agent must know what he was doing in some sense which would differentiate his shooting at the bird from other non-accidental actions performed at the same time, such as making the cartridge explode. This is the action which he himself would specify, if he were prepared to give an honest reply to the question "What are you doing?"

The special kind of knowledge involved in intentional action may emerge from a comparison of the agent's own declaration or description of what he is doing ("I am shooting at X") and statements made about his action by others ("He is shooting at X"). The latter statements are generally made on the strength of observation of the agent's movements; and these movements provide logically sufficient grounds for such statements ("He is shooting at X"), though they do not exhaust the meaning of the statement, which is liable to qualification, though not withdrawal, if it later appears that certain abnormalities were present in the situation. In the case of statements made by others, the question "How do you know that he is shooting at X?" is one which could be properly answered by referring to his observed movements. But the agent does not himself use these, or any other criteria, in declaring what he is doing; there is a corresponding pointlessness in the question, "How do you know you are shooting at X?" or "What grounds have you for saying that you were shooting at X?" The suggestion that, before answering the question, "What are you doing?," we first look and see how our body is disposed is absurd. The ascription to ourselves of some action (the declaration of what we are currently doing) is not a report of our bodily movements nor a conclusion from the observation of movements. Perhaps the absurdity is most evident in the case of speech action; if someone to whom we are talking asks us what we are saying, we do not have to listen or recall the sound of our own words before answering, and our answer is not a report of those sounds nor a conclusion from evidence provided by them.

Secondly, a knowledge of the position or movements of our own body would not be sufficient to enable us to answer the question "What are you doing?" In the relevant sense of knowing what we are doing, it is perfectly possible that we should recognize, and be able to describe, such features of the situation as that a knife is in our hands, and yet we may have forgotten what we were engaged in doing. Except in abnormal cases, memory returns and we may then say that we were sharpening a pencil. This illustrates the irrelevance of prior observation by the agent of his bodily movement to his declarations of what he is currently engaged in doing.

Thirdly, there is a sense in which our own declarations about our current actions may be mistaken. We may say that we are sharpening a pencil when in fact, owing to inadvertence, we were cutting away at a pen. In these cases the natural comment would be, not that the agent's statement was false (though there would also be occasions for that comment), but that he was doing something unintentionally or by mistake. But it is important to notice that, whereas statements made by others concerning a person's action characteristically leave open the question whether he has done what he has done unintentionally, it is a distinguishing feature of the agent's own statement about his actions that an answer of the form "I am doing this but I am not doing it intentionally" would be absurd. It would be the virtual equivalent of "I am doing this but I do not know what I am doing."

The normal ability of an agent to say what he is doing without prior observation suggests two explanations, both of which, though tempting, are mistaken. It may seem that the agent's ability to specify what he is doing in this way is explained by the fact that, prior to acting, he must always have considered and decided what to do; in saying what he is actually doing he is simply recalling the previous decision. The objections to this are, first, that very frequently we know what we are doing, and so are doing it intentionally, although this has never been preceded by any stage of prior deliberation or doubt. I may just break off drawing in order to sharpen a pencil without prior deliberation, and yet I can still answer correctly the question "What are you doing?" without first observing my own movements. And, even where there has been prior deliberation and decision, the question "What are you doing?" is answered without recall of this earlier stage.

The second explanation, suggested by certain passages in Wittgenstein's *Philosophical Investigations,* is that, since the agent in declaring what he is doing makes no use of any criteria, and in particular does not use the criteria upon which other persons rely, the agent's own declaration should be treated, not as a statement, but as a "signal," to be assimilated to the behaviour-criteria which are the basis of third-person statements about his actions. But this explanation, though it may serve to correct some mistakes (notably that the agent's own statements about his action are made on the basis of observation), surely distorts the facts and is open to now familiar objections. The agent's own statements about his actions may be true or false; we contrast an agent's *telling us* what he is doing with other forms of words which he might use and which might be our evidence that he is doing some action. His statement about his own action stands in recognizable logical relations with statements made by other persons. If the agent says, "I am shooting a bird," and a third party says, "He is not shooting a bird," these statements are contradictories. If the third party says "He is shooting a bird" and the agent says, "I am shooting a bird," the latter statement confirms the first. These relationships would be impossible if first-person statements were to be treated as signals, and therefore as having a different meaning from third-person statements about action. Only a doctrinaire identification of the meaning of the statement with the means of its verification entails this result. Action is a concept which, like many concepts involving reference to states of consciousness (I expect, he expects; I believe, he believes), exhibits this asymmetry between first-person and third-person statements.

Intention to do a future act. In those cases where the agent announces his intention to do an action in the future, there is a similar need to distinguish a belief which the agent may have formed as to the course of his future actions as a result of observation, or as a conclusion from evidence, from a belief which he has formed independently of observation or evidence; for the second is essentially involved in this application of the notion of intention.

It is clear that a person's announcement of his intention to do some action in the future is not a prediction that he will do this action, although others may base their predictions upon such announcements by the agent. That such statements are not predictions is evident from the fact that if the agent does not act as he says that he intends to act, this exposes him, not to the criticism that what he said was false, or that he was mistaken, but to the charge that he has changed his mind. He may be accused, if he does not do what he says that he intends to do, of having lied about his intentions. But it is possible for him to exculpate himself from this charge by convincing others that he had changed his mind.

The obviously mistaken analysis of announcements of intention to do an act in the future as a prediction must be distinguished from an analysis of such an announcement as a statement by the agent of his present belief as to his future action. On this view, "I intend to do X" will at least entail, "I believe that I shall do X." Certainly this needs qualification: for it is plain that "I intend to do X" is compatible with "I believe I shall do X unless prevented or unless I fail by reason of circumstances outside my control." The statement, "I intend to do X" is also compatible with "I believe I shall do X unless a change in circumstances leads me to change my mind," though there is at least a suggestion that if the agent thus leaves open the possibility of a change of mind, he does not yet really intend to do the future action. If we take these qualifications into account, the minimum force of "I intend to do X" is "I believe that I will try to do X." Hence it would be a contradiction to say, "I intend to do X though I do not believe I will even try to do X when an opportunity arises." But again the salient characteristic of this form of belief is that it is not a conclusion from evidence, and that it is neither proper to ask, nor necessary to answer, the question: "Why do you believe that you will try to do X?" The contrast with ordinary professions of belief is plain.

The contrast between first and third-person statements is instructive. An observer who says "He intends to do X" makes his statement on the basis of observation or evidennce, and he could be asked to support his statement by evidence, which may range from remote circumstantial evidence to a report of X's statement of his own future intentions. On the other hand, the third person who says that X intends to do a future action is committed to the statement that X believes that he will at least try to do X if the occasion arises. He has evidence that X does so believe, but it would be absurd to suggest that X himself has evidence that he does so believe or has evidence in favour of the truth of his belief.

In many cases the agent will have formed the intention to do a future action as a result of considering alternatives and deciding between them, and perhaps the characteristics of intention to do a future act best emerge from a study of such cases. But not all intention is formed as a result of prior decision. I intend to go home after writing this essay, but I have never decided to do this. If we consider those intentions which emerge as a result of deliberation and decision, we can trace certain parallels with the formation of theoretical certainty about the future, as well as the major contrast we have noticed with regard to the independence of evidence. In deliberation we consider whether to do, or not to do, something, and we oscillate between these alternatives: we attend to reasons for or against the proposed action, and we attribute more or less weight to these reasons: we then decide what to do. In the theoretical case we consider whether something is or is not be the case, and we attend to the evidence in favour of one or other alternative: we find the evidence in favour of one alternative convincing and then decide that it is or is not be the case. In both cases we could substitute for the expression "decision" expressions such as "being certain" or "making up our mind." But neither the deliberative process concerning future action nor its theoretical counterpart need issue in decision. We may remain undecided, on the one hand whether to do something or not, and on the other hand whether something is the case or not. We may be unable to decide, and may give up both the practical or theoretical problem as too difficult, leaving others to tell us what to do or what is to be the case.

The characteristic termination of the practical inquiry is the settled frame of mind when we are no longer undecided what to do. We have made up our mind and are both certain what to do and certain what we will try to do. In describing this termination of deliberation, we cannot separate the temporal reference to the future from the solution of the practical question. We have decided what to do, and that we shall at least try to do it. We cannot have this form of confident belief about our future voluntary action without this form of practical certainty about what to do.

Freedom and Action (excerpt)

Roderick M. Chisholm

"*A staff moves a stone, and is moved by a hand, which is moved by a man.*"
—Aristotle, Physics, 256a.

I

The metaphysical problem of human freedom might be summarized in the following way: "Human beings are responsible agents; but this fact appears to conflict with a deterministic view of human action (the view that every event that is involved in an act is caused by some other event); and it *also* appears to conflict with an indeterministic view of human action (the view that the act, or some event that is essential to the act, is not caused at all)." To solve the problem, I believe, we must make somewhat far-reaching assumptions about the self of the agent—about the man who performs the act.

Perhaps it is needless to remark that, in all likelihood, it is impossible to say anything significant about this ancient problem that has not been said before.[1]

Source: Excerpt from "Freedom and Action" *Freedom and Determinism,* edited by Keith Lehrer, © 1966, 11–25, 40–44. Reprinted by permission of the author.
Note: Part I of this paper is an adaptation of the Lindley Lecture delivered at the University of Kansas, April 23, 1964. The lecture was published separately as *Human Freedom and the Self* (Lawrence, Kans., 1964), © Copyright 1964 by the Department of Philosophy, University of Kansas, and is here drawn upon with the permission of the Department of Philosophy of the University of Kansas. Certain passages in Part II are taken from "The Descriptive Element in the Concept of Action," *Journal of Philosophy,* LXI (1964), 613–625, and are reprinted with the permission of the editors.
[1]The general position to be presented here is suggested in the following writings, among others: Aristotle, *Eudemian Ethics,* Book II, Ch. 6, *Nichomachean Ethics,* Book III, Chapters 1–5; Thomas Reid, *Essays on the Active Powers of Man;* C. A. Campbell, "Is 'Free Will' a Pseudo-Problem?," *Mind,* LX (1951), 441–465; Roderick M. Chisholm, "Responsibility and Avoidability," in Sidney Hook, ed., *Determinism and Freedom in the Age of Modern Science* (New York, 1958), and Richard Taylor, "Determinism and the Theory of Agency," in Sidney Hook, ed., *Determinism and Freedom in the Age of Modern Science* (New York, 1958).

Let us consider some deed, or misdeed, that may be attributed to a responsible agent: one man, say, shot another. If the man *was* responsible for what he did, then, I would urge, what was to happen at the time of the shooting was something that was entirely up to the man himself. There was a moment at which it was true, both that he could have fired the shot and also that he could have refrained from firing it. And if this is so, then, even though he did fire it, he could have done something else instead. (He didn't find himself firing the shot "against his will," as we say.) I think we can say, more generally, then, that if a man is responsible for a certain event or a certain state of affairs (in our example, the shooting of another man), then that event or state of affairs was brought about by some act of his, and the act was something that was in his power either to perform or not to perform.

But now, if the act which he *did* perform was an act that was also in his power *not* to perform, then *it* could not have been caused or determined by any event that was not itself within his power either to bring about or not to bring about. For example, if what we say he did was really something that was brought about by a second man, one who forced his hand upon the trigger, say, or who, by means of hypnosis, compelled him to perform the act, then, since the act was caused by the *second* man, it was nothing that was within the power of the *first* man to prevent. And precisely the same thing is true, I think, if instead of referring to a second man who compelled the first one, we speak instead of the *desires* and *beliefs* which the first man happens to have had. For if what we say he did was really something that was brought about by his own beliefs and desires, if these beliefs and desires in the particular situation in which he happened to have found himself caused him to do just what it was that we say he did do, then, since *they* caused it, *he* was unable to do anything other than just what he did do. It makes no difference whether the cause of the deed was internal or external: if the cause was some state or event for which the man himself was not responsible, then he was not responsible for what we have been mistakenly calling his act. If a flood caused the poorly structured dam to break, then, given the flood and the constitution of the dam, the break, we may say, *had* to occur and nothing could have happened in its place. And if the flood of desire caused the weak-willed man to give in, then he, too, had to do just what it was that he did do and he was no more responsible than was the dam for the results that followed. (It is true, of course, that if the man is responsible for the beliefs and desires that he happens to have, then he may also be responsible for the things they lead him to do. But the question now becomes: *is* he responsible for the beliefs and desires he happens to have? If he is, then there was a time when they were within his power either to acquire or not to acquire, and we are left, therefore, with our general point.)

One may object: But surely if there were such a thing as a man who is really *good,* then he would be responsible for things that he would do; yet, he would be unable to do anything other than just what he does do, since, being good, he will always choose to do what is best. The answer, I think, is suggested by a comment that Thomas Reid makes upon an ancient author. The author had said of Cato, "He was good because he could not be otherwise," and Reid observes: "This saying, if understood literally and strictly, is not the praise of Cato, but of his constitution which was no more the work of Cato than his existence."[2] If Cato was himself responsible for the good things that he did, then Cato, as Reid suggests, was such that, although he had the power to do what was not good, he exercised his power only for that which was good.

All of this, if it is true, may give a certain amount of comfort to those who are tender-minded. But we should remind them that it also conflicts with a familiar view about the nature of God—with the view that St. Thomas Aquinas expresses by saying that "every movement both of the will and of nature proceeds from God as the Prime Mover."[3] If the act of the sinner *did* proceed from God as the Prime Mover, then God was in the position of the second agent we just discussed—the man who forced the trigger finger, or the hypnotist—and the sinner, so-called, was *not* responsible for what he did. (This may be a bold assertion, in view of the history of western theology, but I must say that I have never encountered a single good reason for denying it.)

There is one standard objection to all of this and we should consider it briefly.

The objection takes the form of a stratagem—one designed to show that determinism (and divine providence) is consistent with human responsibility. The stratagem is one that was used by Jonathan Edwards and by many philosophers in the present century, most notably, G. E. Moore.[4]

One proceeds as follows: The expression

(a) He could have done otherwise,

it is argued, means no more nor less than

(b) If he had chosen to do otherwise, then he would have done otherwise.

In place of "chosen," one might say "tried," "set out," "decided," "undertaken," or "willed.") The truth of statement (b), it is then pointed out, is consistent with determinism (and with divine providence); for even if all of the man's actions were causally determined, the man could still be such that, *if* he had chosen otherwise, then he would have done otherwise. What the murderer saw, let us suppose, along with his beliefs and desires, *caused* him to fire the shot; yet he was such that *if,* just then, he had chosen or decided *not* to fire the shot, then he would not have fired it. All of this is certainly possible. Similarly, we could say, of the dam, that the flood caused it to break and also that the dam was such that, *if* there had been no flood or any similar pressure, then the dam would have remained intact. And therefore, the argument proceeds, if (b) is consistent with determinism, and if (a) and (b) say the same thing, then (a) is also consistent with determinism; hence we can say that the agent *could* have done otherwise, even though he was caused to do what he did do; and therefore determinism and moral responsibility are compatible.

Is the argument sound? The conclusion follows from the premises, but the catch, I think, lies in the first premise—the one saying that statement (a) tells us no more nor

[2]Thomas Reid, *Essays on the Active Powers of Man,* Essay IV, Chapter 4 in Works, p. 600.
[3]St. Thomas Aquinas, *Summa Theologica,* First Part of the Second Part, Question VI ("On the Voluntary and Involuntary").
[4]Jonathan Edwards, *Freedom of the Will* (New Haven, 1957); G. E. Moore, *Ethics* (London, 1912), Chapter Six.

less than what statement (b) tells us. For (b), it would seem, could be true while (a) is false. That is to say, our man might be such that, it he had chosen to do otherwise, then he would have done otherwise, and yet *also* such that he could not have done otherwise. Suppose, after all, that our murderer could not have *chosen,* or could not have *decided,* to do otherwise. Then the fact that he happens also to be a man such that, if he had chosen not to shoot he would not have shot, would make no difference. For if he could *not* have chosen *not* to shoot, then he could not have done anything other than just what it was that he did do. In a word: from our statement (b) above ("If he had chosen to do otherwise, then he would have done otherwise"), we cannot make an inference to (a) above ("He could have done otherwise"), unless we can *also* assert:

(c) He could have chosen to do otherwise.

And therefore, if we must reject this third statement (c), then, even though we may be justified in asserting (b), we are not justified in asserting (a). If the man could not have chosen to do otherwise, then he would not have done otherwise— *even if* he was such that, if he *had* chosen to do otherwise, then he would have done otherwise.

The stratagem in question, then, seems to me not to work, and I would say, therefore, that the ascription of responsibility conflicts with a deterministic view of action.

Perhaps there is less need to argue that the ascription of responsibility also conflicts with an indeterministic view of action—with the view that the act, or some event that is essential to the act, is not caused at all. If the act—the firing of the shot— was not caused at all, if it was fortuitous or capricious, happening so to speak "out of the blue," then, presumably, no one—and nothing—was responsible for the act. Our conception of action, therefore, should be neither deterministic nor indeterministic. Is there any other possibility?

We must not say that every event involved in the act is caused by some other event, and we must not say that the act is something that is not caused at all. The possibility that remains, therefore, is this: We should say that at least one of the events that are involved in the act is caused, not by any other events, but by something else instead. And this something else can only be the agent—the man. If there is an event that is caused, not by other events, but by the man, then there are some events involved in the act that are not caused by other events. But if the event in question is caused by the man, then it *is* caused and we are not committed to saying that there is something involved in the act that is not caused at all.

But this, of course, is a large consequence, implying something of considerable importance about the nature of the agent or the man.

If we consider only inanimate natural objects, we may say that causation, if it occurs, is a relation between *events* or *states of affairs.* The dam's breaking was an event that was caused by a set of other events—the dam being weak, the flood being strong, and so on. But if a man is responsible for a particular deed, then, if what I have said is true, there is some event, or set of events, that is caused, *not* by other events or states of affairs, but by the man himself, by the agent, whatever he may be.

I shall borrow a pair of medieval terms, using them, perhaps, in a way that is slightly different from that for which they were originally intended. I shall say that when one event or state of affairs (or set of events or states of affairs) causes some other event or state of affairs, then we have an instance of *transeunt* causation. And I shall say that when an *agent,* as distinguished from an event, causes an event or state of affairs, then we have an instance of *immanent* causation.

The nature of what is intended by the expression "immanent causation" may be illustrated by this sentence from Aristotle's *Physics:* "Thus, a staff moves a stone, and is moved by a hand, which is moved by a man" (VII, 5, 256a, 6–8). If the man was responsible, then we have in this illustration a number of instances of causation—most of them transeunt, but at least one of them immanent. What the staff did to the stone was an instance of transeunt causation, and thus we may describe it as a relation between events: "the motion of the staff caused the motion of the stone." And similarly for what the hand did to the staff: "the motion of the hand caused the motion of the staff." And, as we know from physiology, there are still other events which caused the motion of the hand. Hence we need not introduce the agent at this particular point, as Aristotle does—we *need* not, though we *may.* We *may* say that the hand was moved by the man, but we may *also* say that the motion of the hand was caused by the motion of certain muscles; and we may say that the motion of the muscles was caused by certain events that took place within the brain. But some event, and presumably one of those that took place within the brain, was caused by the agent and not by any other events.

There are, of course, objections to this way of putting the matter; I shall consider the two that seem to me to be most important.

One may object, firstly: "If the *man* does anything, then, as Aristotle's remark suggests, what he does is to move the *hand.* But he certainly does not *do* anything to his brain—he may not even know that he *has* a brain. And if he doesn't do anything to the brain, and if, as physiology seems to tell us, the motion of the hand was caused by something that happened within the brain, then there is no point in appealing to "immanent causation" as being something incompatible with "transeunt causation"—for the whole thing, after all, is a matter of causal relations among events or states of affairs. The motion of the hand was caused by the brain and not by the man."

The answer to this objection, I think, is this: It is true that the agent does not *do* anything with his brain, or to his brain, in the sense in which he *does* something with his hand and does something to the staff. But from this it does not follow that the agent was not the immanent cause of something that happened within his brain.

We should note a useful distinction that has been proposed by Professor A. I. Melden—namely, the distinction between "making something A happen" and "doing A."[5] If I reach for the staff and pick it up, then one of the things that I *do* is just that—reach for the staff and pick it up. And if it is something that I do, then there is a very clear sense in which it may be said to be something that I know that

[5] A. I. Melden, *Free Action* (London, 1961), especially Chapter Three. Mr. Melden's own views, however, are quite the contrary of those that are proposed here.

I do. If you ask me, "Are you doing something, or trying to do something, with the staff?," I will have no difficulty in finding an answer. But in doing something with the staff, I also make various things happen which are not in this same sense things that I do: I will make various air-particles move; I will free a number of blades of grass from the pressure that had been upon them; and I may cause a shadow to move from one place to another. If these are merely things that I make happen, as distinguished from things that I do, then I may know nothing whatever about them; I may not have the slightest idea that, in moving the staff, I am bringing about any such thing as the motion of air-particles, shadows, and blades of grass.

We may say, in answer to the first objection, therefore, that it is true that our agent does nothing to his brain or with his brain; but from this it does not follow that the agent is not the immanent cause of some event within his brain; for the brain event may be something which, like the motion of the air-particles, he made happen in picking up the staff. The only difference between the two cases is this: in each case, he made something happen when he picked up the staff; but in the one case—the motion of the air-particles or of the shadows—it was the motion of the staff that caused the event to happen; and in the other case—the event that took place in the brain—it was this event that caused the motion of the staff.

The point is, in a word, that whenever a man does something A, then (by "immanent causation") he makes a certain cerebral event happen, and this cerebral event (by "transeunt causation") makes A happen.

The second objection is more difficult, and it concerns the very concept of "immanent causation," or causation by an agent, as this concept is to be interpreted here. The concept is subject to a difficulty which has long been associated with that of the prime mover unmoved. We have said that there must be some event A, presumably some cerebral event, which is caused not by any other event, but by the agent. Since A was not caused by any other event, then the agent himself cannot be said to have undergone any change or produced any other event (such as "an act of will" or the like) which brought A about. For if the cerebral event is caused by some change *within* the agent, then it *is* caused by an event and we have lost the solution to our problem. But now: if, when the agent made A happen, there was no event involved other than A itself, no event which could be described as *making* A happen, what did the agent's causation consist of? What, for example, is the difference between A's just happening, and the agent's *causing* A to happen? We cannot attribute the difference to any event that took place within the agent. And so far as the event A itself is concerned, there would seem to be no discernible difference—no discernible difference between A just happening and the agent causing A to happen. Thus Aristotle said that the activity of the prime mover is nothing in addition to the motion that it produces, and Suarez said that "the action is in reality nothing but the effect as it flows from the agent."[6] Must we conclude, then, that there is no more to the man's action in causing event A than there is to the event A's happening by itself? Here we would seem to have a distinction without a difference—in which case we have failed to find a *via media* between a deterministic and an indeterministic view of action.

[6]Aristotle, *Physics,* Book III, Chapter 3; Suarez, *Disputationes Metaphysicae,* Disputation 18, Section 10.

The only answer, I think, can be this: that the difference between the man's causing A, on the one hand, and the event A just happening, on the other, lies in the fact that, in the first case but not the second, the event A *was* caused and was caused by the man. There was a brain event A; the agent did, in fact, cause the brain event; but there was nothing that he did to cause it.

This answer may not entirely satisfy and it will be likely to provoke the following question: "But what are you really *adding* to the assertion that A happened when you utter the words "The agent *caused* A to happen'?" As soon as we have put the question this way, we see, I think, that whatever difficulty we may have encountered is one that may be traced to the concept of causation generally—whether "immanent" or "transeunt." The problem, in other words, is not a problem that is peculiar to our conception of human action. It is a problem that must be faced by anyone who makes use of the concept of causation at all and therefore, I would say, it is a problem for everyone but the complete indeterminist.

For the problem, as we put it, referring just to "immanent causation," or causation by an agent, was this: "What is the difference between saying, of an event A, that A just happened and saying that someone caused A to happen?" The analogous problem, which holds for "transeunt causation," or causation by an event, is this: "What is the difference between saying, of two events A and B, that B happened and then A happened, and saying that B's happening was the *cause* of A's happening?" And the only answer that one can give is this—that in the one case the agent was the cause of A's happening, and in the other case event B was the cause of A's happening. The nature of transeunt causation is no more clear than is that of immanent causation. In short, as long as we talk about causation at all (and we cannot avoid it) the difficulty is one that we will have on our hands. It is not a difficulty that is peculiar, therefore, to our treatment of the problem of freedom.

But we may plausibly say—and there is a respectable philosophical tradition to which we may appeal—that the notion of immanent causation, or causation by an agent, is in fact more clear than that of transeunt causation, or causation by an event, and that it is only by understanding our own causal efficacy, as agents, that we can grasp the concept of *cause* at all. Hume may be said to have shown that we do not derive the concept of *cause* from what we perceive of external things. How, then, do we derive it? The most plausible suggestion, it seems to me, is that of Reid, once again: namely that "the conception of an efficient cause may very probably be derived from the experience we have had . . . of our own power to produce certain effects."[7] If we did not understand the concept of immanent causation, we would not understand that of transeunt causation.

It may have been noted that I have avoided the term "free will" in all of this. For even if there is such a faculty as "the will," which somehow sets our acts a-going, the question of freedom, as John Locke said, is not "the question whether the will be free"; it is the question "whether a man be free."[8] For if there is a "will," as a moving faculty,

---

[7]Reid, *op. cit., Works,* p. 524.
[8]John Locke, *Essay concerning Human Understanding,* Book II, Chapter XXI.

the question is whether the man is free to will to do those things that he does will to do—and also whether he is free *not* to will any of those things that he does will to do, and, again, whether he is free to will any of those things that he does not will to do. Jonathan Edwards tried to restrict himself to the question—"Is the man free to do what it is that he wills?"—but the answer to this question will not tell us whether the man is responsible for what it is that he *does* will to do. Using still another pair of medieval terms, we may say that the metaphysical problem of freedom does not concern the *actus imperatus:* it does not concern the question whether we are free to accomplish whatever it is that we will or set out to do; it concerns the *actus elicitus,* the question whether we are free to will or to set out to do those things that we do will or set out to do. It is one thing to ask whether the things that a man wills are things that are within his power: this is the problem of the *actus imperatus.* It is quite a different thing to ask whether his willing itself is something that is within his power: this is the problem of the *actus elicitus.* And this latter—the problem of the *actus elicitus*—is the problem, not of the freedom of the will, but of the freedom of the man.

If we are responsible, and if what I have been trying to say is true, then we have a prerogative which some would attribute only to God: each of us, when we act, is a prime mover unmoved. In doing what we do, we cause certain events to happen, and nothing—or no one—causes us to cause those events to happen.

If we are thus prime movers unmoved and if our actions, or those for which we are responsible, are not causally determined, then they are not causally determined by our *desires.* And this means that the relation between what we want or what we desire, on the one hand, and what it is that we do, on the other, is not as simple as most philosophers would have it.

We may distinguish between what we might call the "Hobbist approach" and what we might call the "Kantian approach" to this question. The Hobbist approach is the one that is generally accepted at the present time, but the Kantian approach, I believe, is the one that is true. According to Hobbism, if we *know,* of some man, what his beliefs and desires happen to be and how strong they are, if we know what he feels certain of, what he desires more than anything else, and if we know the state of his body and what stimuli he is being subjected to, then we may *deduce,* logically, just what it is that he will do—or, more accurately, just what it is that he will try, set out, or undertake to do. Thus Professor Melden has said that "the connection between wanting and doing is logical."[9]

But according to the Kantian approach to our problem, and this is the one that I would take, there is no such logical connection between wanting and doing, nor need there even be a causal connection. No set of statements about a man's desires, beliefs, and stimulus situation at any time implies any statement, telling us what the man will try, set out, or undertake to do at that time. As Reid put it, "Though we may reason from men's motives to their actions and, in many cases, with great probability," we can never do so "with absolute certainty."[10]

---

[9]Melden, *op. cit.,* p. 166.
[10]Reid, *op. cit., Works,* pp. 608, 612.

This means that, in one very strict sense of the terms, there can be no complete science of man. If we think of science as a matter of finding out what laws happen to hold, and if the statement of a law tells us what kinds of events are caused by what other kinds of events, then there will be human actions that we cannot explain by subsuming them under any laws. We cannot say, "It is causally necessary that, given such and such desires and beliefs, and being subject to such and such stimuli, the agent will do so and so." For at times the agent, if he chooses, may rise above his desires and do something else instead.

But all of this is consistent with saying that, perhaps more often than not, our desires do exist under conditions such that those conditions necessitate us to act. And we may also say, with Leibniz, that at other times our desires may "incline without necessitating." . . .

We may now outline, briefly and schematically, certain other descriptive action concepts which, though they are closely related to the concept of intentional action (intentional making-happen) which has just been defined, should not be confused with it.

"He makes A happen *voluntarily*," in one important descriptive sense, might now be defined as: there is a state of affairs B such that he undertook to make B happen; in undertaking to make B happen, he believed or knew that, in so doing, he might well make A happen; and his undertaking to make B happen makes A happen. Thus a man who, in his haste, runs through the garden, fully realizing that he will leave his footprints there and thus destroy the garden, may be said to destroy it voluntarily, even though he does nothing for the purpose of destroying the garden. (But "voluntarily" also has an *imputative* use; e.g., we may conclude that he destroyed the garden "voluntarily" if, whatever he himself may have thought, we think he ought to have known that he would destroy the garden.)

"He makes A happen *willingly*" (unlike "He makes A happen voluntarily") may imply something about his desires—perhaps not that he desires A but at least that he does not desire not-A.

"*Involuntarily*," even in its purely descriptive uses, is less clear-cut than "voluntarily." Thus "He made A happen *involuntarily*" could mean: (i) some other agent caused him to make A happen; or (ii) he made A happen but did not do so willingly; or (iii) some state of his body, which he did not make happen (or which he did not make happen voluntarily) made A happen; or (iv) had he known that his act would thus make A happen, he would have undertaken something else instead.

"He made A happen *unintentionally*," in one descriptive use, is likely to mean simply that he made A happen but did not do so voluntarily; but it may also mean the same as (iii), or as (iv), under "involuntarily"—i.e., it may mean either that some state of his body which he did not make happen (or did not make happen voluntarily) made A happen, or that, had he known that his act would make A happen, he would have undertaken something else instead.[11]

---

[11]Compare J. L. Austin's treatment of these concepts in "A Plea for Excuses," *Philosophical Papers* (Oxford, 1961), and in "Three Ways of Spilling Ink," in Carl J. Friedrich, ed., *Responsibility; Nomos III* (New York, 1960). I am indebted to Ann Ferguson for helping me to clarify my views on these and related concepts.

At any given time, as we have noted, there will be many different things, A, B, C, . . . N, that our agent is making happen. Some of these will be intentional and others not, and some will be voluntary and others not. When we come to appraise his action, therefore, we should not ask simply "Is what he is doing voluntary or involuntary, intentional or unintentional?" We should ask instead, of particular things that he is making happen, whether he is making *those* things happen voluntarily or involuntarily, intentionally or unintentionally.

Finally, let us apply the results of our discussion to three additional philosophical puzzles.

(1) Our first puzzle may be put as follows: "Laius, the offensive traveler, was Oedipus' father. It may be that Oedipus intended to kill the offensive traveler, but he certainly did not intend to kill his own father. Yet the killing of the offensive traveler *was* the killing of Oedipus' father. Hence we must say of this event that it *was* intentional and also that it was *not* intentional. How can this be?"

The problem can be solved, I suggest, if we observe G. H. von Wright's distinction between an "act-qualifying" property (e.g., the property of being a killing) and the "act-individuals" that have that property (those particular acts that *are* killings).[12] Thus every act-individual, like every other individual, has many properties; indeed, every act-individual is such that, for every property, either the act-individual has that property or it has the negation of that property. The agent always "knows what he is doing" in that he can know, at any time, what act-qualifying properties he is undertaking to realize at that time, but in every case the act-individual will have properties that he knows nothing about. Since the offensive traveler was Oedipus' father, that act-individual which was the killing of the offensive traveler is the same as that act-individual which was the killing of Oedipus' father; but the act-qualifying property which is the killing of the offensive traveler is different from the act-qualifying property which is the killing of Oedipus' father. If we say that the killing of the offensive traveler was intentional and that the killing of Oedipus' father was not, our statement should not be taken to mean that a certain act-individual both is and is not intentional. It means, rather, that the act-individual which is the killing of the offensive traveler (= the act-individual which is the killing of Oedipus' father) is something that was intended to have the act-qualifying property of being the killing of the offensive traveler, but was not intended to have the act-qualifying property of being the killing of Oedipus' father.

(2) The second of our three puzzles is this: "A responsible act is an act such that, at the time at which the agent undertook to perform it, he had it within his power to perform the act and also within his power not to perform the act. But what it is that he thus accomplishes is caused by certain physiological events. (The man raises his arm; yet, as we know from physiology, certain cerebral events cause his arm to go up.) Hence it is false that it is within his power not to perform the act, and therefore he is not responsible."

[12]G. H. von Wright, *Logical Studies* (London, 1957), p. 59. Compare C. I. Lewis's distinction between "states of affairs" and "concrete Whiteheadian events," in *An Analysis of Knowledge and Valuation* (La Salle, Ill., 1945), pp. 52–55.

We have already touched upon this puzzle [previously]. Let us say, perhaps misusing words, that a man makes something A happen *directly,* provided he makes A happen, and there is no B such that he makes B happen and B's happening makes A happen. Presumably if there is anything that an agent makes happen, then there is something that he makes happen directly. The things he makes happen directly may well be certain cerebral events, and therefore they will be things he is likely to know nothing about.[13] In undertaking to make his arm go up, he made certain such events happen directly, and those events in turn made his arm go up. Hence if raising his arm and not raising it were each within his power, then so, too, was the occurrence and the nonoccurrence of the events that he directly made happen; there is no contradiction, therefore, in saying that these events caused his arm to go up and that he had it within his power not to make the arm go up. A puzzle arises because we tend to suppose that, if a man makes B happen in the endeavor to make A happen, he thereby does something for the purpose of making B happen; but, as we have seen, this supposition is a mistake.

Our solution to the puzzle is consistent with A. I. Melden's observation that "one does not raise one's arm by performing another doing which has the motion of one's arm as effect—one simply raises one's arm."[14] For this observation—that raising one's arm is a "basic action"—is consistent with saying that one makes one's arm go up by making certain cerebral and muscular events happen. Making one's arm go up is an "intentional action," as we have defined this term, but making the cerebral and muscular events happen need not be.

(3) And our final puzzle is this: "If a man has learned what the muscle motions are that cause his arm to go up, and if, in the course of a physical examination, he wishes to move those muscles, then he can do so by raising his arm. But it is the muscle motions that cause the arm to go up. And causation is asymmetrical: if A is the cause of B, then B cannot be the cause of A. The cause, moreover, cannot occur after the effect. How, then, can he move his muscles by raising his arm?"

We will find the answer if we consider, once again, the man who caused the telephone to ring in Los Angeles in order to bring about the prior switching in the telephone offices in Denver. He did not undertake to make the Los Angeles ringing cause the Denver switching; what he did was to undertake to cause the Los Angeles ringing and to make this undertaking cause the Denver switching. And when our present agent makes his arm go up in order to make the muscles move, he does so because he knows that the motion of the muscles will be caused, not by the arm going up, but by his undertaking to make the arm go up.

---

[13]Compare H. A. Prichard, *Moral Obligation* (Oxford, 1949), p. 193. This concept of "direct causation" should not be confused with Danto's concept of "basic action," referred to above. Compare the issues involved in the question whether divine intervention in the course of nature always takes place by means of "natural causes." Presumably, if God ever does intervene, there are certain natural events that he makes happen directly, in the sense defined above.

[14]A. I. Melden, *op. cit.,* p. 65.

PART FOUR

Existence and Nature of God

If God did not exist, it would be necessary to invent Him.

—Voltaire
Epître à M. Saurin, "A l'auteur du livre des trois Imposteurs," 1770

- Anselm of Canterbury, *Proslogion* (excerpt)
- Immanuel Kant, *The Ideal of Pure Reason* (excerpt)
- Alvin Plantinga, Kant's Objection to the Ontological Argument
- Norman Malcolm, Anselm's Ontological Arguments
- Thomas Aquinas, *Summa Theologica* (excerpt)
- William Paley, *Natural Theology* (excerpt)
- David Hume, *Dialogues Concerning Natural Religion* (excerpt)
- Richard G. Swinburne, The Argument from Design
- Blaise Pascal, *Pensées* (excerpt)
- François-Marie Arouet de Voltaire, *Tout est Bien*—All is Good
- H. J. McCloskey, God and Evil
- Terence Penelhum, Divine Goodness and the Problem of Evil
- Michael Bakunin, *God and the State* (excerpt)
- Bertrand Russell, Why I Am Not a Christian (excerpt)
- Bertrand Russell, Has Religion Made Useful Contributions to Society? (excerpt)

The writings collected in this section raise central questions about the philosophy of religion. The problem of the relation between religious faith and reason, the concept of God, and the issue of whether the existence or nonexistence of God can be rationally demonstrated are philosophically controversial.

Many persons of religious belief are so firm in their psychological conviction that they assume, as with other matters of specialized knowledge, that there must be a way to prove the existence and nature of God, even if they do not happen to know what it is. Others believe that it is in some ways unnecessary and perhaps even sacrilegious to seek rational demonstration for the existence of God, which they may think should instead be accepted without any attempt at proof. Yet philosophers as a rule are not satisfied with anything less than good reasons for adopting a belief. In matters of religion, as in any other area, philosophers search

345

for answers that can be justified by sound arguments, and they are unwilling to build on any foundation that is not first secured by philosophical reflection.

What can we know about God? If God exists, can we prove it in the way that we can prove the truths of mathematical theorems or scientific discoveries? If God exists, what kind of entity is God? Is God a person, a force, an all-powerful invisible mind and creator of the universe? Is God by definition perfectly good? How would we know whether or not God has any moral properties whatsoever? If we cannot know whether or not God has a moral psychology anything like our own, what implications should our lack of information about God's nature have for our expectations about a final judgment day, or about praying to God or anticipating divine justice or loving protection? What can we infer from a philosophical perspective about the truth of fundamental religious teachings?

A selection of two of the most influential attempts to prove the existence of God are presented in essays by Saint Anselm of Canterbury and Saint Thomas Aquinas. Anselm, in his *Proslogion,* tries to demonstrate the existence of God by pure reason. He argues that it is impossible for God not to exist, if God by definition is the greatest conceivable being. If, contrary to reason, Anselm holds, God did not exist, then something greater than God, an existent rather than nonexistent being with all of God's other properties, would be conceivable, and God, despite the agreed definition, would not be the greatest conceivable being. The argument purports to derive the necessary existence of God from God's nature, essence, or definition, and in particular tries to show that the very concept of the greatest conceivable being entails its actual existence.

Immanuel Kant, in a section of his monumental *Critique of Pure Reason* on "The Ideal of Pure Reason," argues against Anselm's ontological proofs for the existence of God. Kant claims that the existence of an entity can never validly be derived from its essence, nature, or definition. If we define a being in such a way as to include existence as among its distinguishing or identity-determining properties, then we cannot intelligibly say of precisely the same thing that it either exists or does not exist. If we try to say that it does not exist, then by hypothesis we will be speaking of an object that has the property of existing in its definition. If it makes no sense to say that such a thing does not exist, then neither can it make any sense to say that it exists. Kant summarizes the criticism by saying that "existence is not a predicate," by which we should interpret him to mean that existence cannot be among the defining properties of an object by which its nature or essence is constituted. Kant summarizes the attitude of numerous philosophers when he concludes, as a result of his criticism of efforts to prove the existence of God, not that God does not exist, which does not follow from the failure of any style of proof, but that reason has specific limitations in its efforts to prove that God exists. As Kant says in the "Preface" to the second edition of the *Critique,* "I have therefore found it necessary to deny *knowledge,* in order to make room for *faith.*"

Kant's objection to Anselm's ontological argument is answered in the essay by Alvin Plantinga. Plantinga claims that Kant misunderstands the logic of Anselm's argument as an exercise in attributing existence to an object only after building existence into the concept. This, Plantinga admits, would be a failure in Anselm's proof, which Plantinga interprets differently as applying the suppressed premise that existence in reality is greater than existence in the understanding alone to the definition of God as that than which none greater is conceivable, together with the key assumption that God does not exist in reality but only in the understanding, as leading to a contradiction. Plantinga considers several interpretations of Kant's objection and decides that none of them represent a sound objection to Anselm's argument properly understood. Norman Malcolm, in "Anselm's Ontological Arguments," distinguishes between two strands of argument in Anselm's writings that each deserve to be known as an ontological argument for the existence of God. Malcolm offers careful reconstructions of Anselm's inferences in the two parts of his exposition and evaluates criticisms of the argument. He concludes that a nonbeliever need not be convinced by Anselm's inference even if it is judged to be logically valid.

Aquinas, in this short selection from his massive *Summa Theologica,* considers five compact proofs for the existence of God, the so-called five ways of the *Summa.* Each is unique, but most are variations on an argument that was originally presented in Aristotle's *Physics,* to prove on cosmological grounds that God must be the originator of motion in the universe. If there is not such a godlike first-cause of motion, then either causation must regress infinitely backward in time, or time must go in a circle, with some effects preceding some causes, both of which alternatives are rejected as absurd. The argument from design for the existence of God, in an effort to conclude that God probably exists as the cause of order in the universe, is described by William Paley in an excerpt from his *Natural Theology.* Paley here offers the analogy of a watch for which it is reasonable to infer that it must have been designed and produced by a watchmaker as opposed to occurring because of a chance concurrence of random events. Applying this reasoning to the universe as a whole as a kind of clockwork, Paley maintains that it too must have been designed and created by God as a proportionately powerful intelligent designer.

The argument from design is critically examined in the selection from David Hume's *Dialogues Concerning Natural Religion.* This popular form of theological proof in the eighteenth century was characterized by an emphasis on empirical methods in science. If like effects have like causes, then we ought to conclude from our empirical observations of the machinelike order in the universe that the cause of order in the universe as in human artifacts is probably a proportionately intelligent divine architect. The characters in Hume's dialogue discuss the merits of this argument and, in the selection represented here, offer a cogent statement of the proof as well as some of the most damaging criticisms of its inferences. It is undetermined which if any of the characters in the dialogue speak for Hume's own point of view, but some have argued that Hume is likely represented by either Philo or Cleanthes, both of whom are highly critical of the argument from design. It is undoubtedly for this reason that Hume did not publish the dialogue during his lifetime but left careful instructions for its posthumous publication immediately after his death. The merits of the argument from design are critically reconsidered in light of Hume's criticisms in Richard G. Swinburne's essay "The Argument from Design."

Blaise Pascal, the seventeenth-century mathematician and philosopher, in his epigrammatic *Pensées,* offers in a series of aphorisms a way of avoiding some of the criticisms of efforts to prove the existence of God. Pascal's reasoning takes the form of a wager. If God exists, and we believe that God exists, then we have nothing to lose and everything to gain, enjoying an eternity of heavenly bliss after the resurrection. If, on the other hand, God exists and we do not believe, we stand to suffer an eternity of excruciating punishment in hell. If God does not exist, we lose nothing by falsely believing that God exists. So, regardless of whether or not there can ever be an adequate positive rational demonstration of the existence of God, it is rational for us to believe and irrational for us not to believe in the existence of God. This is a remarkable argument. But it raises many philosophical questions about the possibility of exercising voluntary control over the content of our beliefs in the absence of compelling reasons to believe. From a theological point of view, the argument also seems to take it for granted that God will reward those who believe, not as an expression of sincere faith, but rather as the conclusion of a cold calculation in the service of rational self-interest in securing eternal bliss and avoiding eternal torment.

Voltaire, the pen name of François-Marie Arouet, in the entry titled "*Tout est Bien*—All is Good" from his diverting *Philosophical Dictionary,* raises the problem of evil in rational theology. He attributes the formulation of the problem to Lactantius in his work *The Wrath of God,* who in turn puts the argument in the mouth of a historically fictional Epicurus as a character in a dialogue. The argument is in the form of a trilemma, with three choices all leading to the same conclusion. The problem of evil is that if God exists, then either God does not know about the natural evil in the world, or God knows about the natural evil but cannot prevent it, or knows about the natural evil and could prevent it but chooses not to prevent it. God by definition is supposed to be omniscient or all-knowing, omnipotent or all-powerful, and perfectly benevolent or all-good. If God does not know about the natural evil suffered on Earth, then God is not omniscient. If God knows about the natural evil but cannot prevent it, then God is not omnipotent. If God knows about the natural evil and could prevent it, but chooses not to, then God is not perfectly good. By natural evil, as Hume also discusses the concept in his *Dialogues,* we describe Voltaire's interest in great calamities of nature that cause immense human suffering, to innocent and corrupt persons alike, that do not appear to result from immoral free will decisions by human beings. It is this concept that Voltaire finds difficult to reconcile with the concept of God as a perfect creator of the universe. The conflict is dramatized in Voltaire's popular novel *Candide,* where his protagonist goes from misfortune to greater misfortune, naively never questioning that this must be, in the German philosopher Gottfried Wilhelm von Leibniz's catchphrase, "the best of all possible worlds." In Voltaire's day, the religious faith of many thinkers was shaken by the great earthquake of 1755 in Lisbon, Portugal, in which more than seventy thousand persons perished in just a matter of minutes, as a shocking example of natural evil.

The problem of evil, of how it is conceivable for there to be suffering in a world created and sustained by God as a perfect being, is taken seriously enough by theologians to have developed an entire branch of religious theory known as theodicy, dedicated to efforts to resolve this rational challenge to religious faith. The problem of evil is addressed by two contemporary commentators, H. J. McCloskey and Terence Penelhum, in recent discussions that on the whole are skeptical of solving the problem in a way that would be satisfactory to belief in the existence of God as omniscient, omnipotent, and perfectly benevolent. McCloskey is noteworthy as concluding confidently that the existence of evil disproves the existence of God.

The final selections by the Russian activist and political pamphleteer Michael Bakunin, and the British philosopher, logician, and mathematician Bertrand Russell, raise other kinds of doubts about the existence of God and the value of religion. Their views confront the comfortable attitudes many people have about the religions that they have been taught, whose truth and moral goodness they may prefer not to question. Philosophy inquires rigorously, open-mindedly, and without apology here as elsewhere into the justification of any beliefs. Bakunin not only doubts the reasonableness of traditional Christianity, but, like Russell, sees it as a malicious threat to personal liberty and freedom of thought and action, particularly in what he argues is its inevitable manifestation in the form of an organized religion serving the interests of a repressive state. Russell more systematically examines the philosophical grounds for religious belief and concludes that there are no sound arguments in support of belief in God, from which he goes on to argue that religion on the whole has had a pernicious effect on the development of civilization, repeatedly standing in the way of individual enlightenment and the advancement of science.

Proslogion *(excerpt)*

Anselm of Canterbury

CHAPTER TWO: GOD TRULY, [OR REALLY], EXISTS

Therefore, Lord, Giver of understanding to faith, grant me to understand—to the degree You deem best—that You exist, as we believe, and that You are what we believe You to be. Indeed, we believe You to be something than which nothing greater can be thought. Is there, then, no such nature as You, for the Fool has said in his heart that God does not exist? But surely when this very Fool hears the words "something than which nothing greater can be thought," he understands what he hears. And what he understands is in his understanding, even if he does not understand [judge] it to exist. Indeed, for a thing to be in the understanding is different from understanding [judging] that this thing exists. For when an artist envisions what he is about to paint, he has it in his understanding, but he does not yet understand [judge] that there exists what he has not yet painted. But after he has painted it, he has it in his understanding and he understands [judges] that what he has painted exists. So even the Fool is convinced that something than which nothing greater can be thought exists at least in his understanding; for when he hears of this being, he understands [what he hears], and whatever is understood is in the understanding. But surely that than which a greater cannot be thought cannot be only in the understanding. For if it were only in the understanding, it could be thought to exist also in reality—which is greater [than existing only in the understanding]. Therefore, if that than which a greater cannot be thought existed only in the understanding, then that than which a greater *cannot* be thought would be that than which a greater *can* be thought! But surely this conclusion is impossible. Hence, without doubt, something than which a greater cannot be thought exists both in the understanding and in reality.

CHAPTER THREE: GOD CANNOT BE THOUGHT NOT TO EXIST

Assuredly, this being exists so truly [really] that it cannot even be thought not to exist. For there can be thought to exist something whose non-existence is inconceivable; and this thing is greater than anything whose non-existence is conceivable. Therefore, if that than which a greater cannot be thought could be thought not to exist, then that than which a greater cannot be thought would not be that than which a greater cannot be thought—a contradiction. Hence, something than which a greater cannot be thought exists so truly [really] that it cannot even be thought not to exist.

Source: Translated by Jasper Hopkins and Herbert Richardson, Vol. I. Toronto and New York: The Edwin Mellen Press, 1975, 93–96, 104.

And You are this being, O Lord our God. Therefore, Lord my God, You exist so truly [really] that You cannot even be thought not to exist. And this is rightly the case. For if any mind could conceive of something better than You, the creature would rise above the Creator and would sit in judgment over the Creator—an utterly preposterous consequence. Indeed, except for You alone, whatever else exists can be conceived not to exist. Therefore, You alone exist most truly [really] of all and thus most greatly of all; for whatever else there is does not exist as truly [really] as You and thus does not exist as much as do You. Since, then, it is so readily clear to a rational mind that You exist most greatly of all, why did the Fool say in his heart that God does not exist? Why indeed except because he is foolish and simple!

CHAPTER FOUR: HOW THE FOOL SAID IN HIS HEART WHAT CANNOT BE THOUGHT

Yet, since to say something in one's heart is to think it, how did the Fool say in his heart what he was not able to think, or how was he unable to think what he did say in his heart? Now, if he really—rather, since he really—both thought [what he did] because he said it in his heart and did not say it in his heart because he was unable to think it, then there is not merely one sense in which something is said in one's heart, or is thought. For in one sense an object is thought when the word signifying it is thought, and in another when what the object is [i.e., its essence] is understood. Thus, in the first sense but not at all in the second, God can be thought not to exist. Indeed, no one who understands what God is can think that God does not exist, even though he says these words [viz. "God does not exist"] in his heart either meaninglessly or else bizzarely. For God is that than which a greater cannot be thought. Anyone who comprehends (*bene intelligit*) this, surely understands (*intelligit*) that God so exists that He cannot even conceivably not exist. Therefore, anyone who understands that this is the manner in which God exists cannot think that He does not exist.

I thank You, good Lord, I thank You that what at first I believed through Your giving, now by Your enlightening I so understand that even if I did not want to believe that You exist, I could not fail to understand [that You exist].

CHAPTER FIVE: GOD IS WHATEVER IT IS BETTER TO BE THAN NOT TO BE. HE ALONE, EXISTING THROUGH HIMSELF, CREATES ALL ELSE FROM NOTHING

What, then, are You, Lord God, than whom nothing greater can be thought? What in fact are You except that which—as highest of all things, alone existing through Himself—created all else from nothing? For whatever is not this is less great than can be conceived. But You cannot be thought to be less great than can be conceived. Therefore, what good is lacking to the Supreme Good, through whom every good exists? Consequently, You are just, truthful, blessed, and whatever it is better to be than not to be. For it is better to be just than not just, blessed than not blessed. . . .

CHAPTER FIFTEEN: HE IS GREATER THAN CAN BE THOUGHT

Therefore, O Lord, not only are You that than which a greater cannot be thought, but You are also something greater than can be thought. For since something of this kind can be thought [viz., something which is greater than can be thought], if You were not this being then something greater than You could be thought—a consequence which is impossible.

The Ideal of Pure Reason *(excerpt)*

Immanuel Kant

THE IMPOSSIBILITY OF AN ONTOLOGICAL PROOF OF THE EXISTENCE OF GOD

It is evident, from what has been said, that the concept of an absolutely necessary being is a concept of pure reason, that is, a mere idea the objective reality of which is very far from being proved by the fact that reason requires it. For the idea instructs us only in regard to a certain unattainable completeness, and so serves rather to limit the understanding than to extend it to new objects. But we are here faced by what is indeed strange and perplexing, namely, that while the inference from a given existence in general to some absolutely necessary being seems to be both imperative and legitimate, all those conditions under which alone the understanding can form a concept of such a necessity are so many obstacles in the way of our doing so.

In all ages men have spoken of an *absolutely necessary* being, and in so doing have endeavoured, not so much to understand whether and how a thing of this kind allows even of being thought, but rather to prove its existence. There is, of course, no difficulty in giving a verbal definition of the concept, namely, that it is something the non-existence of which is impossible. But this yields no insight into the conditions which make it necessary[1] to regard the non-existence of a thing as absolutely unthinkable. It is precisely these conditions that we desire to know, in order that we may determine whether or not, in resorting to this concept, we are thinking anything at all. The expedient of removing all those conditions which the understanding indispensably requires in order to regard something as necessary, simply through the introduction of the word *unconditioned,* is very far from sufficing to show whether I am still thinking anything in the concept of the unconditionally necessary, or perhaps rather nothing at all.

Nay more, this concept, at first ventured upon blindly, and now become so completely familiar, has been supposed to have its meaning exhibited in a number

Source: Critique of Pure Reason [1781, 1787], translated by Norman Kemp Smith. New York: St. Martin's Press, 1965, 500–507.
[1][Reading, with Noiré, *notwendig* for *unmöglich.*]

of examples; and on this account all further enquiry into its intelligibility has seemed to be quite needless. Thus the fact that every geometrical proposition, as, for instance, that a triangle has three angles, is absolutely necessary, has been taken as justifying us in speaking of an object which lies entirely outside the sphere of our understanding as if we understood perfectly what it is that we intend to convey by the concept of that object.

All the alleged examples are, without exception, taken from *judgments,* not from *things* and their existence. But the unconditioned necessity of judgments is not the same as an absolute necessity of things. The absolute necessity of the judgment is only a conditioned necessity of the thing, or of the predicate in the judgment. The above proposition does not declare that three angles are absolutely necessary, but that, under the condition that there is a triangle (that is, that a triangle is given), three angles will necessarily be found in it. So great, indeed, is the deluding influence exercised by this logical necessity that, by the simple device of forming an *a priori* concept of a thing in such a manner as to include existence within the scope of its meaning, we have supposed ourselves to have justified the conclusion that because existence necessarily belongs to the object of this concept— always under the condition that we posit the thing as given (as existing)—we are also of necessity, in accordance with the law of identity, required to posit the existence of its object, and that this being is therefore itself absolutely necessary—and this, to repeat, for the reason that the existence of this being has already been thought in a concept which is assumed arbitrarily and on condition that we posit its object.

If, in an identical proposition, I reject the predicate while retaining the subject, contradiction results; and I therefore say that the former belongs necessarily to the latter. But if we reject subject and predicate alike, there is no contradiction; for nothing is then left that can be contradicted. To posit a triangle, and yet to reject its three angles, is self-contradictory; but there is no contradiction in rejecting the triangle together with its three angles. The same holds true of the concept of an absolutely necessary being. If its existence is rejected, we reject the thing itself with all its predicates; and no question of contradiction can then arise. There is nothing outside it that would then be contradicted, since the necessity of the thing is not supposed to be derived from anything external; nor is there anything internal that would be contradicted, since in rejecting the thing itself we have at the same time rejected all its internal properties. "God is omnipotent" is a necessary judgment. The omnipotence cannot be rejected if we posit a Deity, that is, an infinite being; for the two concepts are identical. But if we say, "There is no God," neither the omnipotence nor any other of its predicates is given; they are one and all rejected together with the subject, and there is therefore not the least contradiction in such a judgment.

We have thus seen that if the predicate of a judgment is rejected together with the subject, no internal contradiction can result, and that this holds no matter what the predicate may be. The only way of evading this conclusion is to argue that there are subjects which cannot be removed, and must always remain. That, however, would only be another way of saying that there are absolutely necessary subjects; and that is the very assumption which I have called in question, and the possibility of which the above argument professes to establish. For I cannot form the least concept of a thing which, should it be rejected with all its predicates, leaves behind a contradiction; and in the absence of contradiction I have, through pure *a priori* concepts alone, no criterion of impossibility.

Notwithstanding all these general considerations, in which every one must concur, we may be challenged with a case which is brought forward as proof that in actual fact the contrary holds, namely, that there is one concept, and indeed only one, in reference to which the not-being or rejection of its object is in itself contradictory, namely, the concept of the *ens realissimum*. It is declared that it possesses all reality, and that we are justified in assuming that such a being is possible (the fact that a concept does not contradict itself by no means proves the possibility of its object: but the contrary assertion I am for the moment willing to allow).[a] Now [the argument proceeds] "all reality" includes existence; existence is therefore contained in the concept of a thing that is possible. If, then, this thing is rejected, the internal possibility of the thing is rejected—which is self-contradictory.

My answer is as follows. There is already a contradiction in introducing the concept of existence—no matter under what title it may be disguised—into the concept of a thing which we profess to be thinking solely in reference to its possibility. If that be allowed as legitimate, a seeming victory has been won; but in actual fact nothing at all is said: the assertion is a mere tautology. We must ask: Is the proposition that *this or that thing* (which, whatever it may be, is allowed as possible) *exists,* an analytic or a synthetic proposition? If it is analytic, the assertion of the existence of the thing adds nothing to the thought of the thing; but in that case either the thought, which is in us, is the thing itself, or we have presupposed an existence as belonging to the realm of the possible, and have then, on that pretext, inferred its existence from its internal possibility—which is nothing but a miserable tautology. The word "reality," which in the concept of the thing sounds other than the word "existence" in the concept of the predicate, is of no avail in meeting this objection. For if all positing (no matter what it may be that is posited) is entitled reality, the thing with all its predicates is already posited in the concept of the subject, and is assumed as actual; and in the predicate this is merely repeated. But if, on the other hand, we admit, as every reasonable person must, that all existential propositions are synthetic, how can we profess to maintain that the predicate of existence cannot be rejected without contradiction? This is a feature which is found only in analytic propositions, and is indeed precisely what constitutes their analytic character.

I should have hoped to put an end to these idle and fruitless disputations in a direct manner, by an accurate determination of the concept of existence, had I not

---

[a]A concept is always possible if it is not self-contradictory. This is the logical criterion of possibility, and by it the object of the concept is distinguishable from the *nihil negativum*. But it may none the less be an empty concept, unless the objective reality of the synthesis through which the concept is generated has been specifically proved; and such proof, as we have shown above, rests on principles of possible experience, and not on the principle of analysis (the law of contradiction). This is a warning against arguing directly from the logical possibility of concepts to the real possibility of things.

found that the illusion which is caused by the confusion of a logical with a real predicate (that is, with a predicate which determines a thing) is almost beyond correction. Anything we please can be made to serve as a logical predicate; the subject can even be predicated of itself; for logic abstracts from all content. But a *determining* predicate is a predicate which is added to the concept of the subject and enlarges it. Consequently, it must not be already contained in the concept.

"*Being*" is obviously not a real predicate; that is, it is not a concept of something which could[2] be added to the concept of a thing. It is merely the positing of a thing, or of certain determinations, as existing in themselves. Logically, it is merely the copula of the judgment. The proposition, "God is omnipotent," contains two concepts, each of which has its object—God and omnipotence. The small word "is" adds no new predicate, but only serves to posit the predicate *in its relation* to the subject. If, now, we take the subject (God) with all its predicates (among which is omnipotence), and say "God is," or "There is a God," we attach no new predicate to the concept of God, but only posit the subject in itself with all its predicates, and indeed posit it as being an *object* that stands in relation to my *concept.* The content of both must be one and the same; nothing can have been added to the concept, which expresses merely what is possible, by my thinking its object (through the expression "it is") as given absolutely. Otherwise stated, the real contains no more than the merely possible. A hundred real thalers do not contain the least coin more than a hundred possible thalers. For as the latter signify the concept, and the former the object and the positing of the object, should the former contain more than the latter, my concept would not, in that case, express the whole object, and would not therefore be an adequate concept of it. My financial position is, however, affected very differently by a hundred real thalers than it is by the mere concept of them (that is, of their possibility). For the object, as it actually exists, is not analytically contained in my concept, but is added to my concept (which is a determination of my state) synthetically; and yet the conceived hundred thalers are not themselves in the least increased through thus acquiring existence outside my concept.

By whatever and by however many predicates we may think a thing—even if we completely determine it—we do not make the least addition to the thing when we further declare that this thing *is.* Otherwise, it would not be exactly the same thing that exists, but something more than we had thought in the concept; and we could not, therefore, say that the exact object of my concept exists. If we think in a thing every feature of reality except one,[3] the missing reality is not added by my saying that this defective thing exists. On the contrary, it exists with the same defect with which I have thought it, since otherwise what exists would be something different from what I thought. When, therefore, I think a being as the supreme reality, without any defect, the question still remains whether it exists or not. For though, in my concept, nothing may be lacking of the possible real content of a thing in general, something is still lacking in its relation to my whole state of thought, namely, [in so far as I am unable to assert] that knowledge of this

[2][Reading, with Erdmann, *könnte* for *könne.*]
[3][*alle Realität ausser einer.*]

object is also possible *a posteriori*. And here we find the source of our present difficulty. Were we dealing with an object of the senses, we could not confound the existence of the thing with the mere concept of it. For through the concept the object is thought only as conforming to the *universal conditions* of possible empirical knowledge in general, whereas through its existence it is thought as belonging to the context of experience as a whole. In being thus connected with the *content* of experience as a whole, the concept of the object is not, however, in the least enlarged; all that has happened is that our thought has thereby obtained an additional possible perception. It is not, therefore, surprising that, if we attempt to think existence through the pure category alone, we cannot specify a single mark distinguishing it from mere possibility.

Whatever, therefore, and however much, our concept of an object may contain, we must go outside it, if we are to ascribe existence to the object. In the case of objects of the senses, this takes place through their connection with some one of our perceptions, in accordance with empirical laws. But in dealing with objects of pure thought, we have no means whatsoever of knowing their existence, since it would have to be known in a completely *a priori* manner. Our consciousness of all existence (whether immediately through perception, or mediately through inferences which connect something with perception) belongs exclusively to the unity of experience; any [alleged] existence outside this field, while not indeed such as we can declare to be absolutely impossible, is of the nature of an assumption which we can never be in a position to justify.

The concept of a supreme being is in many respects a very useful idea; but just because it is a mere idea, it is altogether incapable, by itself alone, of enlarging our knowledge in regard to what exists. It is not even competent to enlighten us as to the *possibility* of any existence beyond that which is known in and through experience.[4] The analytic criterion of possibility, as consisting in the principle that bare positives (realities) give rise to no contradiction, cannot be denied to it. But since the realities are not given to us in their specific characters; since even if they were, we should still[5] not be in a position to pass judgment; since the criterion of the possibility of synthetic knowledge is never to be looked for save in experience, to which the object of an idea cannot belong,[6] the connection of all real properties in a thing is a synthesis, the possibility of which we are unable to determine *a priori*. And thus the celebrated Leibniz is far from having succeeded in what he plumed himself on achieving—the comprehension *a priori* of the possibility of this sublime ideal being.

The attempt to establish the existence of a supreme being by means of the famous ontological argument of Descartes is therefore merely so much labour and effort lost; we can no more extend our stock of [theoretical] insight by mere ideas, than a merchant can better his position by adding a few noughts to his cash account.

[4][*in Ansehung der Möglichkeit eines Mehreren.*]
[5][Reading, with B, *da aber* for *weil aber.*]
[6][Reading, with Wille, *stattfände* for *stattfinde.*]

Kant's Objection to the Ontological Argument

Alvin Plantinga

The Ontological Argument for the existence of God has fascinated and puzzled philosophers ever since it was first formulated by St. Anselm. I suppose most philosophers have been inclined to reject the argument, although it has an illustrious line of defenders extending to the present and presently terminating in Professors Malcolm and Hartshorne. Many philosophers have tried to give *general* refutations of the argument—refutations designed to show that no version of it can possibly succeed—of which the most important is, perhaps, Kant's objection, with its several contemporary variations. I believe that none of these general refutations are successful; in what follows I shall support this belief by critically examining Kant's objection.

Anselm's argument, it seems to me, is best construed as a *reductio ad absurdum*. Let us use the term 'God' as an abbreviation for 'the being than which none greater can be conceived'. The argument then proceeds (in Anselm's own terms as much as possible) as follows:

1. God exists in the understanding but not in reality.

    (assumption for *reductio*)
2. Existence in reality is greater than existence in the understanding alone.

    (premise)
3. A being having all of God's properties plus existence in reality can be conceived.

    (premise)
4. A being having all of God's properties plus existence in reality is greater than God.

    (from 1 and 2)
5. A being greater than God can be conceived.   (3, 4)
6. It is false that a being greater than God can be conceived.

    (by definition of 'God')
7. Hence, it is false that God exists in the understanding but not in reality.

    (1–6 *reductio ad absurdum*)

And so, if God exists in the understanding, he also exists in reality; but clearly enough he does exist in the understanding (as even the fool will testify); accordingly, he exists in reality as well.

A couple of preliminary comments: to say that a state of affairs is conceivable is to say that there is no logical impossibility in the supposition that it obtains. And to say specifically that a being having all of God's properties plus existence in reality is conceivable, is simply to say that it is possible that there is a being having all of God's properties plus existence in reality—i.e., it is possible that God exists. To say that a being greater than God can be conceived, on the other hand, is to say that it is possible that there exist a being greater than the being than which

Source: The Journal of Philosophy, 63, 1966, 537–546.

it is not possible that there exist a greater—which certainly seems unlikely. We should note further that premise 2 of the argument is susceptible of several interpretations, each yielding a different version of the argument. For example, it may be taken as 2a:

2a. If x exists and y does not, then x is greater than y.

It can also be taken as a weaker claim. Suppose we select some properties—call them "g-properties"—whose possession makes for greatness. Then we might read 2 as

2b. If x has every g-property y has, and x exists and y does not, then x is greater than y.[1]

And of course there are many other possible interpretations.

The most famous attack upon the Ontological Argument is contained in a few pages of the *Critique of Pure Reason*—an attack which many think conclusive. The heart of Kant's objection is contained in the following passage:

> "*Being*" is obviously not a real predicate; that is, it is not a concept of something which could be added to the concept of a thing. It is merely the positing of a thing, or of certain determinations, as existing in themselves. Logically, it is merely the copula of a judgment. The proposition "God is omnipotent" contains two concepts, each of which has its object—God and omnipotence. The small word "is" adds no new predicate, but only serves to posit the predicate *in its relation* to the subject. If, now, we take the subject (God) with all its predicates (among which is omnipotence), and say "God is," or "There is a God," we attach no new predicate to the concept of God, but only posit the subject in itself with all its predicates, and indeed, posit it as an *object* that stands in relation to my *concept*. The content of both must be one and the same; nothing can have been added to the concept, which expresses merely what is possible, by my thinking its object (through the expression "it is") as given absolutely. Otherwise stated, the real contains no more than the merely possible. A hundred real thalers do not contain the least coin more than a hundred possible thalers. For as the latter signify the concept and the former the object and the positing of the concept, should the former contain more than the latter, my concept would not, in that case, express the whole object, and would not therefore be an adequate concept of it. My financial position, however, is affected very differently by a hundred real thalers than it is by the mere concept of them (that is, of their possibility). For the object, as it actually exists, is not analytically contained in my concept, but is added to my concept (which is a determination of my state) synthetically; and yet the conceived hundred thalers are not themselves in the least increased through thus acquiring existence outside my concept.
>
> By whatever and by however many predicates we may think a thing—even if we completely determine it—we do not make the least addition to the thing when we further declare that this thing *is*. Otherwise it would not be exactly the same thing that exists, but something more than we had thought in the concept: and we could not, therefore, say that the exact object of my concept exists. If we think in a thing every feature of reality except one, the missing reality is not added by my saying that this defective thing exists.[2]

---

[1]This version of 2 was suggested to me by Peter De Vos.
[2]Kemp Smith translation (London: Macmillan, 1929), pp. 504–5.

How, exactly, is what Kant says here relevant to Anselm's Ontological Argument? And how are we to understand what he says? The point of the passage seems to be that being or existence is not a real predicate; Kant apparently thinks this follows from (or is equivalent to) what he puts variously as "the real *contains* no more than the merely possible," "the *content* of both (i.e., concept and object) must be one and the same," "being is not the concept of something that could be *added to* the concept of a thing," etc. An adequate concept, Kant believes, must contain as much content as the thing of which it is the concept; the content of the concept of a thing remains the same whether the thing exists or not; and the existence of the object of a concept is not part of the content of that concept. But what *is* the content of a concept, or of an object? In what way do objects and concepts have content? Kant gives us very little help, in the passage under consideration, in understanding what it is to *add something* to a concept, what it means to say that a concept *contains* as much as an object, or what it is for a concept and its object both to have *content*—the *same* content.

Perhaps what he means is something like this: the content of a concept is the set of properties a thing must have to fall under or be an instance of that concept. The content of the concept *crevasse,* for example, includes, among others, the properties of *occurring on or in glaciers,* and *being more than one foot deep.* The content of the concept *the tallest man in Boston,* will include, among others, the properties of *being a man, being in Boston,* and *being taller than any other man in Boston.* The content of an *object,* on the other hand, is the set of properties that object has; and a thing *a has* (at least) *as much content as* or *contains as much as* a thing *b* if every member of *b*'s content is a member of *a*'s content. But here we immediately encounter difficulty. For of course it will not be true that the concept of an object contains as much content as the object itself. Consider, for example, the concept *horse.* Any real horse will have many properties not contained in that concept; any real horse will be either more than 16 hands high or else 16 hands or less. But neither of these properties is in the content of the concept *horse* (although of course the property of being either more than 16 hands high or else 16 hands or less will be). Similarly for the tallest man in Boston: he will have the property of being married or else the property of being unmarried; but neither of these properties is part of the content of the concept *the tallest man in Boston.* This suggestion, therefore, requires amendment.

"By whatever and by however many predicates we may think a thing—even if we completely determine it—we do not make the least addition to the thing when we further declare that this thing *is.*" This sentence provides a clue. We might note that to every object there corresponds its *whole concept:* the concept whose content includes all (and only) the properties the object in question has. And where *C* is the whole concept of some object *O,* suppose we say that *a whole concept of O diminished with respect to P* is any concept whose content is a largest subset of the content of *C* that does not entail[3] *P*—that is, its content is a subset of *C* that does not entail *P,* and is such that the addition of any other member of the content of *C* yields

---

[3]Where a set *S* of properties entails a property *P* if the proposition that a thing *x* has *P* follows from the proposition that *x* has every property in *S*.

a set that does entail P. Very roughly and inaccurately, a whole concept diminished with respect to P is what remains of the whole concept when P is deleted from its content.

Now suppose we consider a domain D of objects some of which really exist and some of which are merely mythological; among its members we may find, e.g., Pegasus, the Taj Mahal, Lyndon Johnson, Santa Claus, Bucephalos, and King Arthur. Suppose also that we define an existential quantifier over this domain as follows: "$(\exists x)x$ is pink" is to be read as "some existing member of D is pink." (If we went on to embed this quantifier in an appropriate lower functional calculus, the result would be what has been called "free logic.") Suppose, furthermore, that the Taj Mahal is pink; and let C, C^{-E}, and C^{-P} be, respectively, the whole concept of the Taj Mahal, a whole concept of the Taj Mahal diminished with respect to existence, and a whole concept of the Taj Mahal diminished with respect to pinkness. Finally, let Cx, $C^{-E}x$ and $C^{-P}x$, respectively, ascribe to x all the properties in C, C^{-E}, and C^{-P}. Now perhaps Kant means to point out that existence differs from pinkness in the following respect. Evidently there are possible circumstances in which $(\exists x)C^{-P}x$ would be true but $(\exists x)Cx$ false; perhaps these circumstances would obtain if the Taj Mahal were green, for example. But the same does not hold for $(\exists x)C^{-E}x$; it cannot be true unless $(\exists x)Cx$ is too. It is possible that a whole concept of the Taj Mahal diminished with respect to pinkness be exemplified by some existing member of D when the whole concept of the Taj Mahal is not. But here existence differs from pinkness; if any whole concept of the Taj Mahal diminished with respect to existence is exemplified, then so is the whole concept. A whole concept diminished with respect to existence, unlike a whole concept diminished with respect to pinkness, is *existentially equivalent* to the corresponding whole concept. And perhaps this fact yields an explanation of the claim that existence is not a real property or predicate; we might say that P is a *real* property or predicate just in case it is false that any whole concept diminished with respect to P is existentially equivalent to the corresponding whole concept ($D1$). It then turns out that existence, unlike pinkness, is not a real property; it "is not a concept of something that could be added to the concept of a thing."

But here we must consider an objection that runs as follows. It is certainly true that, on the proffered definitions, existence is not a real quality. But that this is so is, given these definitions, a mere triviality that in no significant way distinguishes existence from other properties. To see this, let us return to our domain of objects. We defined a quantifier over this domain in such a way that "$(\exists x)Qx$" is to mean that some existent member of the domain has Q. We could also define a "quantifier" $(\exists^P x)$ (the quotation marks may serve to mollify the purist) in such a way that "$(\exists^P x)Qx$" is to mean that some *pink* member of the domain has Q. Then, even if no *existent* member of D were pink, it would still be true that $(\exists^P x)$ (x = Valhalla) since, as is well known, the walls of Valhalla are pink. And now we note that $(\exists^P x)C^{-P}x$ can be true if and only if $(\exists^P x)Cx$ is true; we might say that a whole concept diminished with respect to pinkness is *pinksistentially equivalent* to the corresponding whole concept. Of course the same is not true for a whole concept diminished with respect to existence. There are possible circumstances in which $(\exists^P x)C^{-E}x$ but not $(\exists^P x)Cx$ would hold; these circumstances might have obtained, for example, had the Taj Mahal been the merely mythological dwelling place of some legendary Indian prince. And if we said that *P* is a real property or predicate just in case it is false that any whole concept diminished with respect to *P* is pinksistentially equivalent to the corresponding whole concept (*D2*), then existence, but not pinkness, would be a real property or predicate.

We might put the charge of triviality as follows. To say, under (*D1*), that pinkness is a real predicate but existence is not, really comes to saying that the proposition *all existent members of D exist* is necessarily true but *all existent members of D are pink* is not. This is indeed so; but it seems no more illuminating, in the present context, than the parallel remark that, although *all pink members of D are pink* is necessarily true, *all pink members of D exist* is not.

If we accept this objection, then, Kant's claim begins to look like an insignificant triviality with which Anselm scarcely need concern himself. But should we accept it? Kant is not, it seems to me, entirely without a reply; there is a fairly plausible refinement of his claim that may evade the charge of triviality. For consider any merely mythological creature such as Santa Claus, and ask whether he has the property of wearing a size-ten shoe. The legends and stories say nothing at all about the size of Santa's feet. Does Santa wear a size-ten shoe? There seems no reason for supposing that he does, but also no reason for supposing the contrary. There seems, furthermore, to be no way to investigate the question. And perhaps it is plausible to suggest that it's not merely that we don't *know* whether Santa wears a size-ten shoe—there is nothing *to* know here. That Santa wears a size-ten shoe is neither true nor false; he has neither the property of wearing a size-ten shoe nor the complement of that property. And, it might be added, here is the crucial difference between any existent and any nonexistent object. Where *O* is any existent object and *P* any property, either *O* has *P* or *O* has the complement *P̄* of *P*, (and if *O*'s having *P* is absurd or necessarily false, as in the case of President Johnson and the property of being a real number, then *O* has *P̄*). But if *O* is a merely fictional object such as Pegasus or Santa Claus, then there is at least one property *P* such that *O* has neither *P* nor *P̄;* there is at least one property *P* such that *O has P* is neither true nor false.

I know of no very strong arguments either for or against this view. But suppose for the moment that it is true. Then a certain difference between existence and pinkness emerges. First of all, the whole concept of an existing object will be *maximal* in the sense that, for any property *P,* either *P* or *P̄* will be a member of it; since this is false for any whole concept of a nonexistent being, a whole concept of an existent is larger than any whole concept of a nonexistent. To put the same point differently, any consistent maximal concept contains existence. This is not true for pinkness, of course; it is not true that any consistent maximal concept contains pinkness.

Furthermore, a whole concept diminished with respect to existence will be smaller than a whole concept diminished with respect to pinkness. For consider any pair of whole concepts diminished with respect to pinkness and existence respectively: suppose we call them C^{-P} and C^{-E}. The result of adding *nonexistence* to C^{-E} is a consistent concept, since it is possible that *D* contain an object that has every property in C^{-E} and lacks existence. But this new concept cannot be maximal; for, if it were, then on the doctrine under consideration it would contain existence; since it also contains nonexistence, the result would be inconsistent. So we cannot construct a maximal concept by adding nonexistence to a whole concept diminished with respect to existence. On the other hand, it is possible to show that we *can* construct a maximal concept by adding nonpinkness to some whole concept diminished with respect to pinkness. In this respect, therefore, a whole concept diminished with respect to existence is smaller than one diminished with respect to pinkness.

We could dramatize this difference by redefining "whole concept diminished with respect to P" as "set of properties such that (1) it is a largest subset of C that does not entail P, and (2) the addition of $\bar{P}$ to it yields a maximal concept." Then there would *be* no whole concepts diminished with respect to existence; and then the dictum that existence is not a property could be understood as the claim that what distinguishes existence from a real property such as pinkness is just that there are no whole concepts diminished with respect to existence.

Giving a clear and fairly plausible explanation of the claim that existence is not a real predicate, this interpretation also suggests an interesting respect in which existence may differ from other predicates or properties. Unfortunately, it seems to have no particular bearing on Anselm's argument. For Anselm can certainly agree, so far as his argument is concerned, that existence is not a real predicate in the explained sense. Anselm maintains that the concept *the being than which none greater can be conceived* is necessarily exemplified; that this is so is in no way inconsistent with the suggestion that existence differs in the way just explained from pinkness. Anselm argues that the proposition *God exists* is necessarily true; but neither this claim nor his argument for it entails or presupposes that existence is a predicate in the sense just explained.

Finally I wish to make a desultory gesture (space permits no more) in the direction of another way of understanding Kant's objection. "Being is obviously not a real predicate; that is, it is not a concept of something that could be added to the concept of a thing. It is merely the positing of a thing, or of certain determinations, as existing in themselves." Conceivably Gottlob Frege means to echo this sentiment when he writes that "Affirmation of existence is in fact nothing but a denial of the number nought. Because existence is a property of concepts [and not of objects] the ontological argument for the existence of God breaks down."[4] Now, in saying that existence is not a property of objects, Frege does not mean to say, of course, that propositions of the form *x exists* are all nonsensical or false. He means rather that any proposition of that form is equivalent to one that predicates *being instantiated* or *having some number other than nought* of a concept. And he means to say further that the second way of putting the matter is more revealing or more "basic" than the first. But how does this bear on Anselm's proof? It seems to show only that an equivalent (and perhaps more "basic") form of the argument may be obtained by replacing every phrase of the form "*x* exists," in the argument, by some such phrase as "the concept of *x* is not instantiated." Now, if this procedure is to reveal some

---

[4]*The Foundation of Arithmetic,* tr. J. L. Austin, rev. ed. (London: Blackwell & Mott, 1953; New York: Harper, TB 534, 1962), p. 65.

impropriety in Anselm's argument, then the resulting argument must display some glaring deficiency not apparent in the original. But what sort of deficiency would this be? Possibly Frege thinks that, upon translating the argument in the suggested way, we see the futility of premise 2:

2. Existence is greater than nonexistence.

Now to function properly in the argument, 2 must be construed along the following lines:

2a. For any objects A and B, if A exists and B does not, then A is greater than B.

And, given Frege's claim about existence, 2a must be understood as

2′. If the concept of A is instantiated and the concept of B is not, then A is greater than B.

Now perhaps Frege's query is as follows: If the concept of B is not instantiated, with what are we comparing A? There seems to be nothing relevant with which to compare it. If the concept of B is not instantiated, then it makes no sense, it may be said, to try to compare an object A with B with respect to greatness or, indeed, any other property.

C. D. Broad concurs in this suggestion:

> (1) No comparison can be made between a non-existent term and anything else except on the hypothesis that it exists and (2) on this hypothesis it is meaningless to compare it with anything in respect of the presence or absence of existence.[5]

But this claim is surely false. One certainly *can* compare, for example, Hamlet with Louis XIV in point of the number of books written about each. And this comparison need not be hypothetical in Broad's sense; when a man says *more books have been written about Hamlet than about Louis XIV,* he certainly need not commit himself to the supposition that if Hamlet had existed more books would have been written about him than about Louis XIV. (If Hamlet really existed, people might find him something of a bore.) And while it is true that Superman is a comic-book figure much stronger than any actual man, it is probably false that if Superman really existed he would be a comic book figure much stronger than any actual man. Finally, one certainly *can* compare an existent and a nonexistent with respect to existence; to do this is only to point out that the one really exists while the other does not. One of the principal differences between Cerberus and Governor Wallace, for example, is that the latter (for better or worse) really exists.

If we return to our domain D of objects we may see another way of putting this point. We have defined two quantifiers over D: $(\exists x)$ and $(\exists^P x)$. Every member of D has Q. And now we may put the present point as follows: Kant, Frege, and Broad (if we have understood them) have confused the first of these quantifiers with the third. It is perhaps excusable to hold that if Louis XIV and Hamlet are to be compared, some appropriate domain must contain them both; (Ex) $(x = \text{Hamlet})$ and (Ex) $(x = \text{Louis XIV})$ must both be true. But this does not entail the false claim that

[5]*Religion, Philosophy and Psychical Research* (New York: Harcourt, Brace, 1953), p. 181.

($\exists x$) (x = Hamlet) must be true if we are to compare Hamlet with some other member of D. Frege too, then, fails to provide a sense of "is a predicate" such that, in that sense, it is clear both that existence is not a predicate and that Anselm's argument requires it to be one.

What *does* Kant's argument show, then? How could anyone be led to suppose that Kant's claim did dispose of the Ontological Argument? This last question is not altogether easy to answer. What Kant's argument does show, however, is that one cannot "define things into existence"; it shows that one cannot, by adding existence to a concept that has application contingently if at all, get a concept that is necessarily exemplified. For let C be any whole concept and C^{-E} be that whole concept diminished with respect to existence. If the proposition ($\exists x$)$C^{-E}x$ is contingent, so is ($\exists x$)Cx. Kant's argument shows that the proposition *there exists an object to which C applies* is logically equivalent to *there exists an object to which C^{-E} applies;* hence, if either is contingent, so is the other. And this result can be generalized. For *any* concept C, singular or general, if it is a contingent truth that C is exemplified, it is also a contingent truth that the concept derived from C by annexing existence to it is exemplified. From a concept that has application contingently—e.g., *crow*—we can't, by annexing existence to it, get a concept that necessarily applies; for if it is a contingent truth that there exist some crows, it is also a contingent truth that there are existent crows.

But of course Anselm needn't have thought otherwise. Schopenhauer describes the Ontological Argument as follows: "On some occasion or other someone excogitates a conception, composed out of all sorts of predicates, among which, however, he takes care to include the predicate actuality or existence, either openly or wrapped up for decency's sake in some other predicate, such as perfection, immensity, or something of the kind."[6] If this *were* Anselm's procedure—if he started with some concept that has instances contingently if at all and then annexed *existence* to it—then indeed his argument would be subject to Kant's criticism. But he didn't, and it isn't. And Kant's objection shows neither that there are no necessary existential propositions nor that the proposition *God exists* is not necessary—any more than it shows that *there is a prime between 50 and 55* is a contingent proposition.

Anselm's Ontological Arguments

Norman Malcolm

I believe that in Anselm's *Proslogion* and *Responsio editoris* there are two different pieces of reasoning which he did not distinguish from one another, and that a good deal of light may be shed on the philosophical problem of "the ontological

---

[6]"The Fourfold Root of the Principle of Sufficient Reason," tr. Mme. Carl Hildebrand, reprinted in A. Plantinga, ed., *The Ontological Argument* (New York: Doubleday, 1965), pp. 66–67.

Source: The Philosophical Review, 69, 1960, 41–62.

argument" if we do distinguish them. In Chapter 2 of the *Proslogion*[1] Anselm says
that we believe that God is *something a greater than which cannot be conceived.*
(The Latin is *aliquid quo nihil maius cogitari posit.* Anselm sometimes uses the
alternate expressions *aliquid quo maius nihil cogitari potest, id quo maius cogitari
nequit, aliquid quo maius cogitari non valet.*) Even the fool of the Psalm who says
in his heart there is no God, when he hears this very thing that Anselm says, namely,
"something a greater than which cannot be conceived," understands what he hears,
and what he understands is in his understanding though he does not understand that
it exists.

Apparently Anselm regards it as tautological to say that whatever is understood
is in the understanding (*quidquid intelligitur in intellectu est*): he uses *intelligitur*
and *initellectu est* as interchangeable locutions. The same holds for another formula
of his: whatever is thought is in thought (*quidquid cogitatur in cogitatione est*).[2]

Of course many things may exist in the understanding that do not exist in reality; for example, elves. Now, says Anselm, something a greater than which cannot
be conceived exists in the understanding. But it cannot exist *only* in the understanding, for to exist in reality is greater. Therefore that thing a greater than which
cannot be conceived cannot exist only in the understanding, for then a greater
thing could be conceived: namely, one that exists both in the understanding and in
reality.[3]

Here I have a question. It is not clear to me whether Anselm means that
(a) existence in reality by itself is greater than existence in the understanding, or
that (b) existence in reality and existence in the understanding together are greater
than existence in the understanding alone. Certainly he accepts (b). But he might
also accept (a), as Descartes apparently does in *Meditation III* when he suggests
that the mode of being by which a thing is "objectively in the understanding" is
imperfect.[4] Of course Anselm might accept both (a) and (b). He might hold that in
general something is greater if it has both of these "modes of existence" than if it
has either one alone, but also that existence in reality is a more perfect mode of
existence than existence in the understanding.

In any case, Anselm holds that something is greater if it exists both in the
understanding and in reality than if it exists merely in the understanding. An equivalent way of putting this interesting proposition, in a more current terminology, is:
something is greater if it is both conceived of and exists than if it is merely conceived of. Anselm's reasoning can be expressed as follows: *id quo maius cogitari
nequit* cannot be merely conceived of and not exist, for then it would not be *id quo
maius cogitari nequit.* The doctrine that something is greater if it exists in addition

---

[1]I have consulted the Latin text of the *Proslogion,* of *Gaunilonis Pro Insipiente,* and of the *Responsio editoris,* in S. Anselmi, *Opera Omnia,* edited by F. C. Schmitt (Secovii, 1938), vol. I. With numerous modifications, I have used the English translation by S. N. Deane: *St. Anselm* (La Salle, Illinois, 1948).
[2]See *Proslogion* 1 and *Responsio* 2.
[3]Anselm's actual words are: "Et certe id quo maius cogitari nequit, non potest esse in solo intellectu. Si enim
vel in solo intellectu est, potest cogitari esse et in re, quod maius est. Si ergo id quo maius cogitari non potest,
est in solo intellectu: id ipsum quo maius cogitari non potest, est quo maius cogitari potest. Sed certe hoc esse
non potest." *Proslogion* 2.
[4]Haldane and Ross, *The Philosophical Works of Descartes,* 2 vols. (Cambridge, 1931), I, 163.

to being conceived of, than if it is only conceived of, could be called the doctrine that *existence is a perfection.* Descartes maintained, in so many words, that existence is a perfection,[5] and presumably he was holding Anselm's doctrine, although he does not, in *Meditation V* or elsewhere, argue in the way that Anselm does in *Proslogion 2.*

When Anselm says, "And certainly, that than which nothing greater can be conceived cannot exist merely in the understanding. For suppose it exists merely in the understanding, then it can be conceived to exist in reality, which is greater,"[6] he is claiming that if I conceived of a being of great excellence, that being would be *greater* (more excellent, more perfect) if it existed than if it did not exist. His supposition that "it exists merely in the understanding" is the supposition that it is conceived of but does not exist. Anselm repeated this claim in his reply to the criticism of the monk Gaunilo. Speaking of the being a greater than which cannot be conceived, he says:

> I have said that if it exists merely in the understanding it can be conceived to exist in reality, which is greater. Therefore, if it exists merely in the understanding obviously the very being a greater than which cannot be conceived, is one a greater than which can be conceived. What, I ask, can follow better than that? For if it exists merely in the understanding, can it not be conceived to exist in reality? And if it can be so conceived does not he who conceives of this conceive of a thing greater than it, if it does exist merely in the understanding? Can anything follow better than this: that if a being a greater than which cannot be conceived exists merely in the understanding, it is something a greater than which can be conceived? What could be plainer?[7]

He is implying, in the first sentence, that if I conceive of something which does not exist then it is possible for it to exist, and *it will be greater if it exists than if it does not exist.*

The doctrine that existence is a perfection is remarkably queer. It makes sense and is true to say that my future house will be a better one if it is insulated than if it is not insulated; but what could it mean to say that it will be a better house if it exists than if it does not? My future child will be a better man if he is honest than if he is not; but who would understand the saying that he will be a better man if he exists than if he does not? Or who understands the saying that if God exists He is more perfect than if He does not exist? One might say, with some intelligibility, that it would be better (for oneself or for mankind) if God exists than if He does not—but that is a different matter.

A king might desire that his next chancellor should have knowledge, wit, and resolution; but it is ludicrous to add that the king's desire is to have a chancellor who exists. Suppose that two royal councilors, A and B, were asked to draw up separately descriptions of the most perfect chancellor they could conceive, and that the descriptions they produced were identical except that A included existence in his list of attributes of a perfect chancellor and B did not. (I do not mean that B put nonexistence in his list.) One and the same person could satisfy both descriptions.

[5]*Op. cit.,* p. 182.
[6]*Proslogion* 2; Deane, p. 8.
[7]*Responsio* 2; Deane, pp. 157–58.

More to the point, any person who satisfied A's description would *necessarily* satisfy B's description and *vice versa!* This is to say that A and B did not produce descriptions that differed in any way but rather one and the same description of necessary and desirable qualities in a chancellor. A only made a show of putting down a desirable quality that B had failed to include.

I believe I am merely restating an observation that Kant made in attacking the notion that "existence" or "being" is a "real predicate." He says:

> By whatever and by however many predicates we may think a thing—even if we completely determine it—we do not make the least addition to the thing when we further declare that this thing *is*. Otherwise, it would not be exactly the same thing that exists, but something more than we had thought in the concept; and we could not, therefore, say that the exact object of my concept exists.[8]

Anselm's ontological proof of *Proslogion 2* is fallacious because it rests on the false doctrine that existence is a perfection (and therefore that "existence" is a "real predicate"). It would be desirable to have a rigorous refutation of the doctrine but I have not been able to provide one. I am compelled to leave the matter at the more or less intuitive level of Kant's observation. In any case, I believe that the doctrine does not belong to Anselm's other formulation of the ontological argument. It is worth noting that Gassendi anticipated Kant's criticism when he said, against Descartes:

> Existence is a perfection neither in God nor in anything else; it is rather that in the absence of which there is no perfection. . . . Hence neither is existence held to exist in a thing in the way that perfections do, nor if the thing lacks existence is it said to be imperfect (or deprived of a perfection), so much as to be nothing.[9]

II

I take up now the consideration of the second ontological proof, which Anselm presents in the very next chapter of the *Proslogion*. (There is no evidence that he thought of himself as offering two different proofs.) Speaking of the being a greater than which cannot be conceived, he says:

> And it so truly exists that it cannot be conceived not to exist. For it is possible to conceive of a being which cannot be conceived not to exist; and this is greater than one which can be conceived not to exist. Hence, if that, than which nothing greater can be conceived, can be conceived not to exist, it is not that than which nothing greater can be conceived. But this is a contradiction. So truly, therefore, is there something than which nothing greater can be conceived, that it cannot even be conceived not to exist. And this being thou art, O Lord, our God.[10]

Anselm is saying two things: first, that a being whose nonexistence is logically impossible is "greater" than a being whose nonexistence is logically possible (and

---

[8]*The Critique of Pure Reason,* tr. by Norman Kemp Smith (London, 1929), p. 505.
[9]Haldane and Ross, II, 186.
[10]*Proslogion* 3; Deane, pp. 8–9.

therefore that a being a greater than which cannot be conceived must be one whose nonexistence is logically impossible); second, that *God* is a being than which a greater cannot be conceived.

In regard to the second of these assertions, there certainly is *a* use of the word "God," and I think far the more common use, in accordance with which the statements "God is the greatest of all beings," "God is the most perfect being," "God is the supreme being," are *logically* necessary truths, in the same sense that the statement "A square has four sides" is a logically necessary truth. If there is a man named "Jones" who is the tallest man in the world, the statement "Jones is the tallest man in the world" is merely true and is not a logically necessary truth. It is a virtue of Anselm's unusual phrase, "a being a greater than which cannot be conceived,"[11] to make it explicit that the sentence "God is the greatest of all beings" expresses a logically necessary truth and not a mere matter of fact such as the one we imagined about Jones.

With regard to Anselm's first assertion (namely, that a being whose nonexistence is logically impossible is greater than a being whose nonexistence is logically possible) perhaps the most puzzling thing about it is the use of the word "greater." It appears to mean exactly the same as "superior," "more excellent," "more perfect." This equivalence by itself is of no help to us, however, since the latter expressions would be equally puzzling here. What is required is some explanation of their use.

We do think of *knowledge,* say, as an excellence, a good thing. If A has more knowledge of algebra than B we express this in common language by saying that A has a *better* knowledge of algebra than B, or that A's knowledge of algebra is *superior* to B's, whereas we should not say that B has a better or superior *ignorance* of algebra than A. We do say "greater ignorance," but here the word "greater" is used purely quantitatively.

Previously I rejected *existence* as a perfection. Anselm is maintaining in the remarks last quoted, not that existence is a perfection, but that *the logical impossibility of nonexistence is a perfection.* In other words, *necessary existence* is a perfection. His first ontological proof uses the principle that a thing is greater if it exists than if it does not exist. His second proof employs the different principle that a thing is greater if it necessarily exists than if it does not necessarily exist.

Some remarks about the notion of *dependence* may help to make this latter principle intelligible. Many things depend for their existence on other things and events. My house was built by a carpenter: its coming into existence was dependent on a certain creative activity. Its continued existence is dependent on many things: that a tree does not crush it, that it is not consumed by fire, and so on. If we reflect on the common meaning of the word "God" (no matter how vague and confused this is), we realize that it is incompatible with this meaning that God's existence should *depend* on anything. Whether we believe in Him or not we must admit that the "almighty and everlasting God" (as several ancient prayers begin), the "Maker of heaven and earth, and of all things visible and invisible" (as is said in the

---

[11]Professor Robert Calhoun has pointed out to me that a similar locution had been used by Augustine. In *De moribus Manichaeorum* (Bk. II, ch. xi, sec. 24), he says that God is a being *quo esse aut cogitari melius nihil possit* (*Patrologiae Patrum Latinorum,* ed. by J. P. Migne, Paris, 1841–1845, vol. 32: *Augustinus,* vol. 1).

Nicene Creed), cannot be thought of as being brought into existence by anything or as depending for His continued existence on anything. To conceive of anything as dependent upon something else for its existence is to conceive of it as a lesser being than God.

If a housewife has a set of extremely fragile dishes, then as dishes they are *inferior* to those of another set like them in all respects except that they are *not* fragile. Those of the first set are *dependent* for their continued existence on gentle handling; those of the second set are not. There is a definite connection in common language between the notions of dependency and inferiority, and independence and superiority. To say that something which was dependent on nothing whatever was superior to ("greater than") anything that was dependent in any way upon anything is quite in keeping with the everyday use of the terms "superior" and "greater." Correlative with the notions of dependence and independence are the notions of *limited* and *unlimited*. An engine requires fuel and this is a limitation. It is the same thing to say that an engine's operation is *dependent* on as that it is *limited* by its fuel supply. An engine that could accomplish the same work in the same time and was in other respects satisfactory, but did not require fuel, would be a *superior* engine.

God is usually conceived of as an *unlimited* being. He is conceived of as a being who *could not* be limited, that is, as an absolutely unlimited being. This is no less than to conceive of Him as *something a greater than which cannot be conceived*. If God is conceived to be an absolutely unlimited being He must be conceived to be unlimited in regard to His existence as well as His operation. In this conception it will not make sense to say that He depends on anything for coming into or continuing in existence. Nor, as Spinoza observed, will it make sense to say that something could *prevent* Him from existing.[12] Lack of moisture can prevent trees from existing in a certain region of the earth. But it would be contrary to the concept of God as an unlimited being to suppose that anything other than God Himself could prevent Him from existing, and it would be self-contradictory to suppose that He Himself could do it.

Some may be inclined to object that although nothing could prevent God's existence, still it might just *happen* that He did not exist. And if He did exist that too would be by chance. I think, however, that from the supposition that it could happen that God did not exist it would follow that, if He existed, He would have mere duration and not eternity. It would make sense to ask, "How long has He existed?," "Will He still exist next week?," "He was in existence yesterday but how about today?," and so on. It seems absurd to make God the subject of such questions. According to our ordinary conception of Him, He is an eternal being. And eternity does not mean endless duration, as Spinoza noted. To ascribe eternity to something is to exclude as senseless all sentences that imply that it has duration. If a thing has duration then it would be merely a *contingent* fact, if it was a fact, that its duration was endless. The moon could have endless duration but not eternity. If something has endless duration it will *make sense* (although it will be false) to say that it will cease to exist, and it will make sense (although it will be false) to say that something will *cause* it to cease to exist. A being with

[12]*Ethics*, pt. I, prop. 11.

endless duration is not, therefore, an absolutely unlimited being. That God is conceived to be eternal follows from the fact that He is conceived to be an absolutely unlimited being.

I have been trying to expand the argument of *Proslogion* 3. In *Responsio* 1 Anselm adds the following acute point: if you can conceive of a certain thing and this thing does not exist then if it *were* to exist its nonexistence would be *possible*. It follows, I believe, that if the thing were to exist it would depend on other things both for coming into and continuing in existence, and also that it would have duration and not eternity. Therefore it would not be, either in reality or in conception, an unlimited being, *aliquid quo nihil maius cogitari possit.*

Anselm states his argument as follows:

> If it [the thing a greater than which cannot be conceived] can be conceived at all it must exist. For no one who denies or doubts the existence of a being a greater than which is inconceivable, denies or doubts that if it did exist its non-existence, either in reality or in the understanding, would be impossible. For otherwise it would not be a being a greater than which cannot be conceived. But as to whatever can be conceived but does not exist: if it were to exist its non-existence either in reality or in the understanding would be possible. Therefore, if a being a greater than which cannot be conceived, can even be conceived, it must exist.[13]

What Anselm has proved is that the notion of contingent existence or of contingent nonexistence cannot have any application to God. His existence must either be logically necessary or logically impossible. The only intelligible way of rejecting Anselm's claim that God's existence is necessary is to maintain that the concept of God, as a being a greater than which cannot be conceived, is self-contradictory or nonsensical.[14] Supposing that this is false, Anselm is right to deduce God's necessary existence from his characterization of Him as a being a greater than which cannot be conceived.

Let me summarize the proof. If God, a being a greater than which cannot be conceived, does not exist then He cannot *come* into existence. For if He did He would either have been *caused* to come into existence or have *happened* to come into existence, and in either case He would be a limited being, which by our conception of Him He is not. Since He cannot come into existence, if He does not exist His existence is impossible. If He does exist He cannot have come into existence (for the reasons given), nor can He cease to exist, for nothing could cause Him to cease to exist nor could it just happen that He ceased to exist. So if God exists His existence is necessary. Thus God's existence is either impossible or necessary. It can be the former

---

[13]*Responsio* 1; Deane, pp. 154–55.
[14]Gaunilo attacked Anselm's argument on this very point. He would not concede that a being a greater than which cannot be conceived existed in his understanding (*Gaunilonis Pro Insipiente,* secs. 4 and 5; Deane, pp. 148–50). Anselm's reply is: "I call on your faith and conscience to attest that this is most false" (*Responsio* 1; Deane, p. 154). Gaunilo's faith and conscience will attest that it is false that "God is not a being a greater than which is inconceivable," and false that "He is not understood (*intelligitur*) or conceived (*cogitatur*)" (*ibid.*) Descartes also remarks that one would go to "strange extremes" who denied that we understand the words "*that thing which is the most perfect that we can conceive;* for that is what all men call God" (Haldane and Ross, II, 129).

only if the concept of such a being is self-contradictory or in some way logically absurd. Assuming that this is not so, it follows that He necessarily exists.

It may be helpful to express ourselves in the following way: to say, not that *omnipotence* is a property of God, but rather that *necessary omnipotence* is; and to say, not that omniscience is a property of God, but rather that *necessary omniscience* is. We have criteria for determining that a man knows this and that and can do this and that, and for determining that one man has greater knowledge and abilities in a certain subject than another. We could think of various tests to give them. But there is nothing we should wish to describe, seriously and literally, as "testing" God's knowledge and powers. That God is omniscient and omnipotent has not been determined by the application of criteria: rather these are requirements of our conception of Him. They are internal properties of the concept, although they are also rightly said to be properties of God. *Necessary existence* is a property of God in the *same sense* that *necessary omnipotence* and *necessary omniscience* are His properties. And we are not to think that "God necessarily exists" means that it follows necessarily from something that God exists *contingently*. The a priori proposition "God necessarily exists" entails the proposition "God exists," if and only if the latter also is understood as an a priori proposition: in which case the two propositions are equivalent. In this sense Anselm's proof is a proof of God's existence.

Descartes was somewhat hazy on the question of whether existence is a property of things that exist, but at the same time he saw clearly enough that *necessary existence* is a property of God. Both points are illustrated in his reply to Gassendi's remark, which I quoted above:

> I do not see to what class of reality you wish to assign existence, nor do I see why it may not be said to be a property as well as omnipotence, taking the word property as equivalent to any attribute or anything which can be predicated of a thing, as in the present case it should be by all means regarded. Nay, necessary existence in the case of God is also a true property in the strictest sense of the word, because it belongs to Him and forms part of His essence alone.[15]

Elsewhere he speaks of "the necessity of existence" as being "that crown of perfections without which we cannot comprehend God."[16] He is emphatic on the point that necessary existence applies solely to "an absolutely perfect Being."[17]

III

I wish to consider now a part of Kant's criticism of the ontological argument which I believe to be wrong. He says:

> If, in an identical proposition, I reject the predicate while retaining the subject, contradiction results; and I therefore say that the former belongs necessarily to the latter. But if we reject subject and predicate alike, there is no contradiction; for nothing is then left

[15]Haldane and Ross, II, 228.
[16]*Ibid.,* I, 445.
[17]E.g., *ibid.,* Principle 15, p. 225.

that can be contradicted. To post a triangle, and yet to reject its three angles, is self-contradictory; but there is no contradiction in rejecting the triangle together with its three angles. The same holds true of the concept of an absolutely necessary being. If its existence is rejected, we reject the thing itself with all its predicates; and no question of contradiction can then arise. There is nothing outside it that would then be contradicted, since the necessity of the thing is not supposed to be derived from anything external; nor is there anything internal that would be contradicted, since in rejecting the thing itself we have at the same time rejected all its internal properties. "God is omnipotent" is a necessary judgment. The omnipotence cannot be rejected if we posit a Deity, that is, an infinite being; for the two concepts are identical. But if we say, "There is no God," neither the omnipotence nor any other of its predicates is given; they are one and all rejected together with the subject, and there is therefore not the least contradiction in such a judgment.[18]

To these remarks the reply is that when the concept of God is correctly understood one sees that one cannot "reject the subject." "There is no God" is seen to be a necessarily false statement. Anselm's demonstration proves that the proposition "God exists" has the same a priori footing as the proposition "God is omnipotent."

Many present-day philosophers, in agreement with Kant, declare that existence is not a property and think that this overthrows the ontological argument. Although it is an error to regard existence as a property of things that have contingent existence, it does not follow that it is an error to regard necessary existence as a property of God. A recent writer says, against Anselm, that a proof of God's existence "based on the necessities of thought" is "universally regarded as fallacious: it is not thought possible to build bridges between mere abstractions and concrete existence."[19] But this way of putting the matter obscures the distinction we need to make. Does "concrete existence" mean contingent existence? Then to build bridges between concrete existence and mere abstractions would be like inferring the existence of an island from the concept of a perfect island, which both Anselm and Descartes regarded as absurd. What Anselm did was to give a demonstration that the proposition "God necessarily exists" is entailed by the proposition "God is a being a greater than which cannot be conceived" (which is equivalent to "God is an absolutely unlimited being"). Kant declares that when "I think a being as the supreme reality, without any defect, the question still remains whether it exists or not."[20] But once one has grasped Anselm's proof of the necessary existence of a being a greater than which cannot be conceived, no question remains as to whether it exists or not, just as Euclid's demonstration of the existence of an infinity of prime numbers leaves no question on that issue.

Kant says that "every reasonable person" must admit that "all existential propositions are synthetic."[21] Part of the perplexity one has about the ontological argument is in deciding whether or not the proposition "God necessarily exists" is

---

[18]*Op cit.*, p. 502.
[19]J. N. Findlay, "Can God's Existence Be Disproved?," *New Essays in Philosophical Theology,* ed. by A. N. Flew and A. MacIntyre (London, 1955), p. 47.
[20]*Op. cit.*, pp. 505–6.
[21]*Ibid.*, pp. 504.

or is not an "existential proposition." But let us look around. Is the Euclidean the-orem in number theory, "There exists an infinite number of prime numbers," an "existential proposition"? Do we not want to say that *in some sense* it asserts the existence of something? Cannot we say, with equal justification, that the proposi-tion "God necessarily exists" asserts the existence of something, *in some sense?* What we need to understand, in each case, is the particular sense of the assertion. Neither proposition has the same sort of sense as do the propositions, "A low pres-sure area exists over the Great Lakes," "There still exists some possibility that he will survive," "The pain continues to exist in his abdomen." One good way of see-ing the difference in sense of these various propositions is to see the variously dif-ferent ways in which they are proved or supported. It is wrong to think that all assertions of existence have the same kind of meaning. There are as many kinds of existential propositions as there are kinds of subjects of discourse.

Closely related to Kant's view that all existential propositions are "syn-thetic" is the contemporary dogma that all existential propositions are contin-gent. Professor Gilbert Ryle tells us that "Any assertion of the existence of some-thing, like any assertion of the occurrence of something, can be denied without logical absurdity."[22] "All existential statements are contingent," says Mr. I. M. Crombie.[23] Professor J. J. C. Smart remarks that "Existence is not a property" and then goes on to assert that "There can never be any *logical contradiction* in denying that God exists."[24] He declares that "The concept of a logically neces-sary being is a self-contradictory concept, like the concept of a round square. . . . No existential proposition can be logically necessary," he main-tains, for "the truth of a logically necessary proposition depends only on our symbolism, or to put the same thing in another way, on the relationship of con-cepts" (p. 38). Professor K. E. M. Baier says, "It is no longer seriously in dispute that the notion of a logically necessary being is self-contradictory. Whatever can be conceived of as existing can equally be conceived of as not existing."[25] This is a repetition of Hume's assertion, "Whatever we conceive as existent, we can also conceive as non-existent. There is no being, therefore, whose non-existence implies a contradiction."[26]

Professor J. N. Findlay ingeniously constructs an ontological *dis*proof of God's existence, based on a "modern view of the nature of "necessity in propositions"": the view, namely, that necessity in propositions "merely reflects our use of words, the arbitrary conventions of our language."[27] Findlay undertakes to characterize what he calls "religious attitude," and here there is a striking agreement between his observations and some of the things I have said in expounding Anselm's proof. Religious attitude, he says, presumes *superiority* in its object and superiority so great that the worshiper is in comparison as nothing. Religious attitude finds it

[22]*The nature of Metaphysics,* ed. by D. F. Pears (New York, 1957), p. 150.
[23]*New Essays in Philosophical Theology,* p. 114.
[24]*Ibid.,* p. 34.
[25]*The Meaning of Life,* Inaugural Lecture, Canberra University College (Canberra, 1957), p. 8.
[26]*Dialogues Concerning Natural Religion,* pt. IX.
[27]Findlay, *op. cit.,* p. 54.

"anomalous to worship anything *limited* in any unthinkable manner. . . . And hence we are led on irresistibly to demand that our religious object should have an *unsurpassable* supremacy along all avenues, that it should tower *infinitely* above all other objects" (p. 51). We cannot help feeling that "the worthy object of our worship can never be a thing that merely *happens* to exist, nor one on which all other objects merely *happen* to depend. The true object of religious reverence must not be one, merely, to which no *actual* independent realities stand opposed: it must be one to which such opposition is totally *inconceivable*. . . . And not only must the existence of *other* things be unthinkable without Him, but His own non-existence must be wholly unthinkable in any circumstances" (p. 52). And now, says Findlay, when we add up these various requirements, what they entail is "not only that there isn't a God, but that the Divine Existence is either senseless or impossible" (p. 54). For on the one hand, "if God is to satisfy religious claims and needs, He must be a being in every way inescapable, One whose existence and whose possession of certain excellences we cannot possibly conceive away." On the other hand, "modern views make it self-evidently absurd (if they don't make it ungrammatical) to speak of such a Being and attribute existence to Him. It was indeed an ill day for Anselm when he hit upon his famous proof. For on that day he not only laid bare something that is of the essence of an adequate religious object, but also something that entails its necessary non-existence" (p. 55).

Now I am inclined to hold the "modern" view that logically necessary truth "merely reflects our use of words" (although I do not believe that the conventions of language are always *arbitrary*). But I confess that I am unable to see how that view is supposed to lead to the conclusion that "the Divine existence is either senseless or impossible." Findlay does not explain how this result comes about. Surely he cannot mean that this view entails that nothing can have necessary properties: for this would imply that mathematics is "senseless or impossible," which no one wants to hold. Trying to fill in the argument that is missing from his article, the most plausible conjecture I can make is the following: Findlay thinks that the view that logical necessity "reflects the use of words" implies, not that nothing has necessary properties, but that *existence* cannot be a necessary property of anything. That is to say, every proposition of the form "*x* exists," including the proposition "God exists," must be *contingent*.[28] At the same time, our concept of God requires that His existence be *necessary,* that is, that "God exists" be a necessary truth. Therefore, the modern view of necessity proves that what the concept of God requires *cannot* be fulfilled. It proves that God *cannot* exist.

The correct reply is that the view that logical necessity merely reflects the use of words cannot possibly have the implication that every existential proposition must be contingent. That view requires us to *look at* the use of words and not manufacture a priori theses about it. In the Ninetieth Psalm it is said: "Before the

---

[28]The other philosophers I have just cited may be led to this opinion by the same thinking. Smart, for example, says that "the truth of a logically necessary proposition depends only on our symbolism, or to put the same thing in another way, on the relationship of concepts" (*supra.*) This is very similar to saying that it "reflects our use of words."

mountains were brought forth, or ever thou hadst formed the earth and the world, even from everlasting to everlasting, thou art God." Here is expressed the idea of the necessary existence and eternity of God, an idea that is essential to the Jewish and Christian religions. In those complex systems of thought, those "language-games," God has the status of a necessary being. Who can doubt that? Here we must say with Wittgenstein, "This language-game is played!"[29] I believe we may rightly take the existence of those religious systems of thought in which God figures as a necessary being to be a disproof of the dogma, affirmed by Hume and others, that no existential proposition can be necessary.

Another way of criticizing the ontological argument is the following. "Granted that the concept of necessary existence follows from the concept of a being a greater than which cannot be conceived, this amounts to no more than granting the *a priori* truth of the *conditional* proposition, 'If such a being exists then it necessarily exists.' This proposition, however, does not entail the *existence* of *anything,* and one can deny its antecedent without contradiction." Kant, for example, compares the proposition (or "judgment," as he calls it) "A triangle has three angles" with the proposition "God is a necessary being." He allows that the former is "absolutely necessary" and goes on to say:

> The absolute necessity of the judgment is only a conditional necessity of the thing, or of the predicate in the judgment. The above proposition does not declare that three angles are absolutely necessary, but that, under the condition that there is a triangle (that is, that a triangle is given), three angles will necessarily be found in it.[30]

He is saying, quite correctly, that the proposition about triangles is equivalent to the conditional proposition, "If a triangle exists, it has three angles." He then makes the comment that there is no contradiction "in rejecting the triangle together with its three angles." He proceeds to draw the alleged parallel: "The same holds true of the concept of an absolutely necessary being. If its existence is rejected, we reject the thing itself with all its predicates; and no question of contradiction can then arise."[31] The priest, Caterus, made the same objection to Descartes when he said:

> Though it be conceded that an entity of the highest perfection implies its existence by its very name, yet it does not follow that that very existence is anything actual in the real world, but merely that the concept of existence is inseparably united with the concept of highest being. Hence you cannot infer that the existence of God is anything actual, unless you assume that that highest being actually exists; for then it will actually contain all its perfections, together with this perfection of real existence.[32]

I think that Caterus, Kant, and numerous other philosophers have been mistaken in supposing that the proposition "God is a necessary being" (or "God necessarily exists") is equivalent to the conditional proposition "If God exists then He necessarily

---

[29]*Philosophical Investigations* (New York, 1953), sec. 654.
[30]*Op. cit.,* pp. 501–2.
[31]*Ibid.,* p. 502.
[32]Haldane and Ross, II, 7.

exists."[33] For how do they want the antecedent clause, "*If* God exists," to be under-stood? Clearly they want it to imply that it is *possible* that God does *not* exist.[34] The whole point of Kant's analysis is to try to show that it is possible to "reject the subject." Let us make this implication explicit in the conditional proposition, so that it reads: "If God exists (and it is possible that He does not) then He necessar-ily exists." But now it is apparent, I think, that these philosophers have arrived at a self-contradictory position. I do not mean that this conditional proposition, taken alone, is self-contradictory. Their position is self-contradictory in the following way. On the one hand, they agree that the proposition "God necessarily exists" is an a priori truth; Kant implies that it is "absolutely necessary," and Caterus says that God's existence is implied by His very name. On the other hand, they think that it is correct to analyze this proposition in such a way that it will entail the proposition "It is possible that God does not exist." But so far from its being the case that the proposition "God necessarily exists" entails the proposition "It is pos-sible that God does not exist," it is rather the case that they are *incompatible* with one another! Can anything be clearer than the conjunction "God necessarily exists but it is possible that He does not exist" is self-contradictory? Is it not just as plainly self-contradictory as the conjunction "A square necessarily has four sides but it is possible for a square not to have four sides"? In short, this familiar criti-cism of the ontological argument is self-contradictory, because it accepts *both* of two incompatible propositions.[35]

One conclusion we may draw from our examination of this criticism is that (con-trary to Kant) there is a lack of symmetry, in an important respect, between the propo-sitions "A triangle has three angles" and "God has necessary existence," although both are a priori. The former can be expressed in the conditional assertion "If a triangle

---

[33]I have heard it said by more than one person in discussion that Kant's view was that it is really a misuse of language to speak of a "necessary being," on the grounds that necessity is properly predicated only of propo-sitions (judgments) not of *things.* This is not a correct account of Kant. (See his discussion of "The Postu-lates of Empirical Thought in General," *op. cit.,* pp. 239–56, esp. p. 239 and pp. 247–48.) But if he had held this, as perhaps the above philosophers think he should have then presumably his view would not have been that the pseudo-proposition "God is a necessary being" is equivalent to the conditional "If God exists then He necessarily exists." Rather his view would have been that the genuine proposition " 'God exists' is nec-essarily true" is equivalent to the conditional "If God exists then He exists" (*not* "If God exists then He *nec-essarily* exists," which would be an illegitimate formulation, on the view imaginatively attributed to Kant).

" 'If God exists then He exists" is a foolish tautology which says nothing different from the tautology "If a new earth satellite exists then it exists." If "If God exists then He exists" were a correct analysis of " 'God exists' is necessarily true," then "If a new earth satellite exists then it exists" would be a correct analysis of " 'A new earth satellite exists' is necessarily true." If the *analysans* is necessarily true then the *analysandum* must be necessarily true, provided the analysis is correct. If this proposed Kantian analysis of " 'God exists' is necessarily true" were correct, we should be presented with the consequence that not only is it necessarily true that God exists, but also it is necessarily true that a new earth satellite exists: which is absurd.

[34]When summarizing Anselm's proof (in part II, *supra*) I said: "If God exists He necessarily exists." But there I was merely stating an entailment. "If God exists" did not have the implication that it is possible He does not exist. And of course I was not regarding the conditional as *equivalent* to "God necessarily exists."

[35]This fallacious criticism of Anselm is implied in the following remarks by Gilson: "To show that the affir-mation of necessary existence is analytically implied in the idea of God, would be . . . to show that God is necessary if He exists, but would not prove that He does exist" (E. Gilson, *The Spirit of Medieval Philoso-phy,* New York, 1940, p. 62).

exists (and it is possible that none does) it has three angles." The latter cannot be expressed in the corresponding conditional assertion without contradiction.

IV

I turn to the question of whether the idea of a being a greater than which cannot be conceived is self-contradictory. Here Leibniz made a contribution to the discussion of the ontological argument. He remarked that the argument of Anselm and Descartes

> is not a paralogism, but it is an imperfect demonstration, which assumes something that must still be proved in order to render it mathematically evident; that is, it is tacitly assumed that this idea of the all-great or all-perfect being is possible, and implies no contradiction. And it is already something that by this remark it is proved that, assuming that God is possible, he exists, which is the privilege of divinity alone.[36]

Leibniz undertook to give a proof that God is possible. He defined a *perfection* as a simple, positive quality in the highest degree.[37] He argued that since perfections are *simple* qualities they must be compatible with one another. Therefore the concept of a being possessing all perfections is consistent.

I will not review his argument because I do not find his definition of a perfection intelligible. For one thing, it assumes that certain qualities or attributes are "positive" in their intrinsic nature, and others "negative" or "privative," and I have not been able clearly to understand that. For another thing, it assumes that some qualities are intrinsically simple. I believe that Wittgenstein has shown in the *Investigations* that nothing is *intrinsically* simple, but that whatever has the status of a simple, an indefinable, in one system of concepts, may have the status of a complex thing, a definable thing, in another system of concepts.

I do not know how to demonstrate that the concept of God—that is, of a being a greater than which cannot be conceived—is not self-contradictory. But I do not think that it is legitimate to demand such a demonstration. I also do not know how to demonstrate that either the concept of a material thing or the concept of *seeing* a material thing is not self-contradictory, and philosophers have argued that both of them are. With respect to any particular reasoning that is offered for holding that the concept of seeing a material thing, for example, is self-contradictory, one may try to show the invalidity of the reasoning and thus free the concept from the charge of being self-contradictory *on that ground.* But I do not understand what it would mean to demonstrate *in general,* and not in respect to any particular reasoning, that the concept is not self-contradictory. So it is with the concept of God. I should think there is no more of a presumption that it is self-contradictory than is the concept of seeing a material thing. Both concepts have a place in the thinking and the lives of human beings.

But even if one allows that Anselm's phrase may be free of self-contradiction, one wants to know how it can have any *meaning* for anyone. Why is it that human

---

[36]*New Essays Concerning the Human Understanding,* Bk. IV, ch. 10; ed. by A. G. Langley (La Salle, Illinois, 1949), p. 504.

[37]See *Ibid.,* Appendix X, p. 714.

beings have even *formed* the concept of an infinite being, a being a greater than which cannot be conceived? This is a legitimate and important question. I am sure there cannot be a deep understanding of that concept without an understanding of the phenomena of human life that give rise to it. To give an account of the latter is beyond my ability. I wish, however, to make one suggestion (which should not be understood as autobiographical).

There is the phenomenon of feeling guilt for something that one has done or thought or felt or for a disposition that one has. One wants to be free of this guilt. But sometimes the guilt is felt to be so great that one is sure that nothing one could do oneself, nor any forgiveness by another human being, would remove it. One feels a guilt that is beyond all measure, a guilt "a greater than which cannot be conceived." Paradoxically, it would seem, one nevertheless has an intense desire to have this incomparable guilt removed. One requires a forgiveness that is beyond all measure, a forgiveness "a greater than which cannot be conceived." Out of such a storm in the soul, I am suggesting, there arises the conception of a forgiving mercy that is limitless, beyond all measure. This is one important feature of the Jewish and Christian conception of God.

I wish to relate this thought to a remark made by Kierkegaard, who was speaking about belief in Christianity but whose remark may have a wider application. He says:

> There is only one proof of the truth of Christianity and that, quite rightly, is from the emotions, when the dread of sin and a heavy conscience torture a man into crossing the narrow line between despair bordering upon madness—and Christendom.[38]

One may think it absurd for a human being to feel a guilt of such magnitude, and even more absurd that, if he feels it, he should *desire* its removal. I have nothing to say about that. It may also be absurd for people to fall in love, but they do it. I wish only to say that there *is* that human phenomenon of an unbearably heavy conscience and that it is importantly connected with the genesis of the concept of God, that is, with the formation of the "grammar" of the word "God." I am sure that this concept is related to human experience in other ways. If one had the acuteness and depth to perceive these connections one could grasp the *sense* of the concept. When we encounter this concept as a problem in philosophy, we do not consider the human phenomena that lie behind it. It is not surprising that many philosophers believe that the idea of a necessary being is an arbitrary and absurd construction.

What is the relation of Anselm's ontological argument to religious belief? This is a difficult question. I can imagine an atheist going through the argument, becoming convinced of its validity, acutely defending it against objections, yet remaining an atheist. The only effect it could have on the fool of the Psalm would be that he stopped saying in his heart "There is no God," because he would now realize that this is something he cannot meaningfully say or think. It is hardly to be expected that a demonstrative argument should, in addition, produce in him a living faith. Surely there is a level at which one can view the argument as a piece of logic, following the deductive moves but not being touched religiously? I think so. But even

---

[38]*The Journals,* tr. by A. Dru (Oxford, 1938), sec. 926.

at this level the argument may not be without religious value, for it may help to remove some philosophical scruples that stand in the way of faith. At a deeper level, I suspect that the argument can be thoroughly understood only by one who has a view of that human "form of life" that gives rise to the idea of an infinitely great being, who views it from the *inside* not just from the outside and who has, therefore, at least some inclination to *partake* in that religious form of life. This inclination, in Kierkegaard's words, is "from the emotions." This inclination can hardly be an *effect* of Anselm's argument, but is rather presupposed in the fullest understanding of it. It would be unreasonable to require that the recognition of Anselm's demonstration as valid must produce a conversion.

Summa Theologica *(excerpt)*

Thomas Aquinas

Because the chief aim of sacred doctrine is to teach the knowledge of God, not only as He is in Himself, but also as He is the beginning of things and their last end, and especially of rational creatures, as is clear from what has been already said, therefore, in our endeavor to expound this science, we shall treat: (1) Of God; (2) Of the rational creature's advance towards God; (3) Of Christ, Who as man, is our way to God.

In treating of God there will be a threefold division:—

For we shall consider (1) Whatever concerns the Divine Essence; (2) Whatever concerns the distinctions of Persons; (3) Whatever concerns the procession of creatures from Him.

Concerning the Divine Essence, we must consider:—

(1) Whether God exists? (2) The manner of His existence, or, rather, what is *not* the manner of His existence; (3) Whatever concerns His operations—namely, His knowledge, will, power.

Concerning the first, there are three points of inquiry:—

(1) Whether the proposition "God exists" is self-evident? (2) Whether it is demonstrable? (3) Whether God exists?

FIRST ARTICLE

Whether the Existence of God Is Self-Evident?

We proceed thus to the First Article:—

Objection 1. It seems that the existence of God is self-evident. Now those things are said to be self-evident to us the knowledge of which is naturally

Source: [1225–1274], Question 2, "The existence of God (In Three Articles)," Complete English Edition in Five Volumes, translated by Fathers of the English Dominican Province, Vol I. Westminister: Christian Classics, 1981, 11–14.

implanted in us, as we can see in regard to first principles. But as Damascene says (*De Fid. Orth.* i. 1, 3), *the knowledge of God is naturally implanted in all.* Therefore the existence of God is self-evident.

Obj. 2. Further, those things are said to be self-evident which are known as soon as the terms are known, which the Philosopher (1 *Poster.* iii) says is true of the first principles of demonstration. Thus, when the nature of a whole and of a part is known, it is at once recognized that every whole is greater than its part. But as soon as the signification of the word "God" is understood, it is at once seen that God exists. For by this word is signified that thing than which nothing greater can be conceived. But that which exists actually and mentally is greater than that which exists only mentally. Therefore, since as soon as the word "God" is understood it exists mentally, it also follows that it exists actually. Therefore the proposition "God exists" is self-evident.

Obj. 3. Further, the existence of truth is self-evident. For whoever denies the existence of truth grants that truth does not exist: and, if truth does not exist, then the proposition "Truth does not exist" is true: and if there is anything true, there must be truth. But God is truth itself: *I am the way, the truth, and the life* (John xiv. 6). Therefore "God exists" is self-evident.

On the contrary, No one can mentally admit the opposite of what is self-evident; as the Philosopher (*Metaph.* iv., lect. vi) states concerning the first principles of demonstration. But the opposite of the proposition "God is" can be mentally admitted: *The fool said in his heart, There is no God* (Ps. lii. 1). Therefore, that God exists is not self-evident.

I answer that, A thing can be self-evident in either of two ways; on the one hand, self-evident in itself, though not to us; on the other, self-evident in itself, and to us. A proposition is self-evident because the predicate is included in the essence of the subject, as "Man is an animal," for animal is contained in the essence of man. If, therefore the essence of the predicate and subject be known to all, the proposition will be self-evident to all; as is clear with regard to the first principles of demonstration, the terms of which are common things that no one is ignorant of, such as being and non-being, whole and part, and such like. If, however, there are some to whom the essence of the predicate and subject is unknown, the proposition will be self-evident in itself, but not to those who do not know the meaning of the predicate and subject of the proposition. Therefore, it happens, as Boëthius says (*Hebdom., the title of which is: "Whether all that is, is good"*), "that there are some mental concepts self-evident only to the learned, as that incorporeal substances are not in space." Therefore I say that this proposition, "God exists," of itself is self-evident, for the predicate is the same as the subject; because God is His own existence as will be hereafter shown (Q. 3, A. 4). Now because we do not know the essence of God, the proposition is not self-evident to us; but needs to be demonstrated by things that are more known to us, though less known in their nature— namely, by effects.

Reply Obj. 1. To know that God exists in a general and confused way is implanted in us by nature, inasmuch as God is man's beatitude. For man naturally desires happiness, and what is naturally desired by man must be naturally known to him. This, however, is not to know absolutely that God exists; just as to know that someone is approaching is not the same as to know that Peter is approaching, even though it is Peter who is approaching; for many there are who imagine that man's perfect good which is happiness, consists in riches, and others in pleasures, and others in something else.

Reply Obj. 2. Perhaps not everyone who hears this word "God" understands it to signify something than which nothing greater can be thought, seeing that some have believed God to be a body. Yet, granted that everyone understands that by this word "God" is signified something than which nothing greater can be thought, nevertheless, it does not therefore follow that he understands that what the word signifies exists actually, but only that it exists mentally. Nor can it be argued that it actually exists, unless it be admitted that there actually exists something than which nothing greater can be thought; and this precisely is not admitted by those who hold that God does not exist.

Reply Obj. 3. The existence of truth in general is self-evident but the existence of a Primal Truth is not self-evident to us.

SECOND ARTICLE

Whether It Can Be Demonstrated That God Exists?

We proceed thus to the Second Article:—

Objection 1. It seems that the existence of God cannot be demonstrated. For it is an article of faith that God exists. But what is of faith cannot be demonstrated, because a demonstration produces scientific knowledge; whereas faith is of the unseen (Heb. xi. 1). Therefore it cannot be demonstrated that God exists.

Obj. 2. Further, the essence is the middle term of demonstration. But we cannot know in what God's essence consists, but solely in what it does not consist; as Damascene says (*De Fid. Orth.* i. 4). Therefore we cannot demonstrate that God exists.

Obj. 3. Further, if the existence of God were demonstrated, this could only be from His effects. But His effects are not proportionate to Him, since He is infinite and His effects are finite; and between the finite and infinite there is no proportion. Therefore, since a cause cannot be demonstrated by an effect not proportionate to it, it seems that the existence of God cannot be demonstrated.

On the contrary, The Apostle says: *The invisible things of Him are clearly seen, being understood by the things that are made* (Rom. i. 20). But this would not be unless the existence of God could be demonstrated through the things that are made; for the first thing we must know of anything is, whether it exists.

I answer that, Demonstration can be made in two ways: One is through the cause, and is called *a priori,* and this is to argue from what is prior absolutely. The other is through the effect, and is called a demonstration *a posteriori;* this is to argue from what is prior relatively only to us. When an effect is better known to us than its cause, from the effect we proceed to the knowledge of the cause. And from every effect the existence of its proper cause can be demonstrated, so long as its effects are better known to us; because since every effect depends upon its cause, if the effect exists, the cause must pre-exist. Hence the existence of God, in so far as it is not self-evident to us, can be demonstrated from those of His effects which are known to us.

Reply Obj. 1. The existence of God and other like truths about God, which can be known by natural reason, are not articles of faith, but are preambles to the articles; for faith presupposes natural knowledge, even as grace presupposes nature, and perfection supposes something that can be perfected. Nevertheless, there is nothing to prevent a man, who cannot grasp a proof, accepting, as a matter of faith, something which in itself is capable of being scientifically known and demonstrated.

Reply Obj. 2. When the existence of a cause is demonstrated from an effect, this effect takes the place of the definition of the cause in proof of the cause's existence. This is especially the case in regard to God, because, in order to prove the existence of anything, it is necessary to accept as a middle term the meaning of the word, and not its essence, for the question of its essence follows on the question of its existence. Now the names given to God are derived from His effects; consequently, in demonstrating the existence of God from His effects, we may take for the middle term the meaning of the word "God."

Reply Obj. 3. From effects not proportionate to the cause no perfect knowledge of that cause can be obtained. Yet from every effect the existence of the cause can be clearly demonstrated, and so we can demonstrate the existence of God from His effects; though from them we cannot perfectly know God as He is in His essence.

THIRD ARTICLE

Whether God Exists?

We proceed thus to the Third Article:—

Objection. 1. It seems that God does not exist; because if one of two contraries be infinite, the other would be altogether destroyed. But the word "God" means that He is infinite goodness. If, therefore, God existed, there would be no evil discoverable; but there is evil in the world. Therefore God does not exist.

Obj. 2. Further, it is superfluous to suppose that what can be accounted for by a few principles has been produced by many. But it seems that everything we see in the world can be accounted for by other principles, supposing God did not exist. For all natural things can be reduced to one principle, which is nature; and all voluntary things can be reduced to one principle, which is human reason, or will. Therefore there is no need to suppose God's existence.

On the contrary, It is said in the person of God: *I am Who am* (Exod. iii. 14).

I answer that, The existence of God can be proved in five ways.

The first and more manifest way is the argument from motion. It is certain, and evident to our senses, that in the world some things are in motion. Now whatever is in motion is put in motion by another, for nothing can be in motion except it is in potentiality to that towards which it is in motion; whereas a thing moves inasmuch as it is in act. For motion is nothing else than the reduction of something from potentiality to actuality. But nothing can be reduced from potentiality to actuality, except by something in a state of actuality. Thus that which is actually hot, as fire, makes wood, which is potentially hot, to be actually hot, and thereby moves and changes it. Now it is not possible that the same thing should be at once in actuality and potentiality in the same respect, but only in different respects. For what is actually hot cannot simultaneously be potentially hot; but it is simultaneously potentially cold. It is therefore impossible that in the same respect and in the same way a thing should be both mover and moved, *i.e.,* that it should move itself. Therefore, whatever is in motion must be put in motion by another. If that by which it is put in motion be itself put in motion, then this also must needs be put in motion by another, and that by another again. But this cannot go on to infinity, because then there would be no first mover, and, consequently, no other mover; seeing that subsequent movers move only inasmuch as they are put in motion by the first mover; as the staff moves only because it is put in motion by the hand. Therefore it is necessary to arrive at a first mover, put in motion by no other; and this everyone understands to be God.

The second way is from the nature of the efficient cause. In the world of sense we find there is an order of efficient causes. There is no case known (neither is it, indeed, possible) in which a thing is found to be the efficient cause of itself; for so it would be prior to itself, which is impossible. Now in efficient causes it is not possible to go on to infinity, because in all efficient causes following in order, the first is the cause of the intermediate cause, and the intermediate is the cause of the ultimate cause, whether the intermediate cause be several, or one only. Now to take away the cause is to take away the effect. Therefore, if there be no first cause among efficient causes, there will be no ultimate, nor any intermediate cause. But if in efficient causes it is possible to go on to infinity, there will be no first efficient cause, neither will there be an ultimate effect, nor any intermediate efficient causes; all of which is plainly false. Therefore it is necessary to admit a first efficient cause, to which everyone gives the name of God.

The third way is taken from possibility and necessity, and runs thus. We find in nature things that are possible to be and not to be, since they are found to be generated, and to corrupt, and consequently, they are possible to be and not to be. But it is impossible for these always to exist, for that which is possible not to be at some time is not. Therefore, if everything is possible not to be, then at one time there could have been nothing in existence. Now if this were true, even now there would be nothing in existence, because that which does not exist only begins to exist by something already existing. Therefore, if at one time nothing was in existence, it would have been impossible for anything to have begun to exist; and thus even now nothing would be in existence—which is absurd. Therefore, not all beings are merely possible, but there must exist something the existence of which is necessary. But every necessary thing either has its necessity caused by another, or not. Now it is impossible to go on to infinity in necessary things which have their necessity caused by another, as has been already proved in regard to efficient causes. Therefore we cannot but postulate the existence of some being having of itself its own necessity, and not receiving it from another, but rather causing in others their necessity. This all men speak of as God.

The fourth way is taken from the gradation to be found in things. Among beings there are some more and some less good, true, noble, and the like. But "more" and "less" are predicated of different things, according as they resemble in their different ways something which is the maximum, as a thing is said to be hotter according as it more nearly resembles that which is hottest; so that there is something which is truest, something best, something noblest, and, consequently, something which is uttermost being; for those things that are greatest in truth are greatest in being, as it is written in *Metaph.* ii. Now the maximum in any genus is the cause of all in that genus; as fire, which is the maximum of heat, is the cause of all hot things. Therefore there must also be something which is to all beings the cause of their being, goodness, and every other perfection; and this we call God.

The fifth way is taken from the governance of the world. We see that things which lack intelligence, such as natural bodies, act for an end, and this is evident from their acting always, or nearly always, in the same way, so as to obtain the best result. Hence it is plain that not fortuitously, but designedly, do they achieve their end. Now whatever lacks intelligence cannot move towards an end, unless it be directed by some being endowed with knowledge and intelligence; as the arrow is shot to its mark by the archer. Therefore some intelligent being exists by whom all natural things are directed to their end; and this being we call God.

Reply Obj. 1. As Augustine says (*Enchir.* xi): *Since God is the highest good, He would not allow any evil to exist in His works, unless His omnipotence and goodness were such as to bring good even out of evil.* This is part of the infinite goodness of God, that He should allow evil to exist, and out of it produce good.

Reply Obj. 2. Since nature works for a determinate end under the direction of a higher agent, whatever is done by nature must needs be traced back to God, as to its first cause. So also whatever is done voluntarily must also be traced back to some higher cause other than human reason or will, since these can change and fail; for all things that are changeable and capable of defect must be traced back to an immovable and self-necessary first principle, as was shown in the body of the *Article.*

Natural Theology *(excerpt)*

William Paley

CHAPTER I

State of the Argument

In crossing a heath, suppose I pitched my foot against a *stone* and were asked how the stone came to be there, I might possibly answer that for anything I knew to the contrary it had lain there forever; nor would it, perhaps, be very easy to show the

Source: Evidences of the Existence and Attributes of the Deity Collected from the Appearances of Nature, 11th edition. London: R. Faulder and Son, 1807, 1–19, 61–82.

absurdity of this answer. But suppose I had found a *watch* upon the ground, and it should be inquired how the watch happened to be in that place, I should hardly think of the answer which I had before given, that for anything I knew the watch might have always been there. Yet why should not this answer serve for the watch as well as for the stone; why is it not as admissible in the second case as in the first? For this reason, and for no other, namely, that when we come to inspect the watch, we perceive—what we could not discover in the stone—that its several parts are framed and put together for a purpose, e.g., that they are so formed and adjusted as to produce motion, and that motion so regulated as to point out the hour of the day; that if the different parts had been differently shaped from what they are, or placed after any other manner or in any other order than that in which they are placed, either no motion at all would have been carried on in the machine, or none which would have answered the use that is now served by it. To reckon up a few of the plainest of these parts and of their offices, all tending to one result: we see a cylindrical box containing a coiled elastic spring, which, by its endeavor to relax itself, turns round the box. We next observe a flexible chain—artificially wrought for the sake of flexure—communicating the action of the spring from the box to the fusee. We then find a series of wheels, the teeth of which catch in and apply to each other, conducting the motion from the fusee to the balance and from the balance to the pointer, and at the same time, by the size and shape of those wheels, so regulating that motion as to terminate in causing an index, by an equable and measured progression, to pass over a given space in a given time. We take notice that the wheels are made of brass, in order to keep them from rust; the springs of steel, no other metal being so elastic; that over the face of the watch there is placed a glass, a material employed in no other part of the work, but in the room of which, if there had been any other than a transparent substance, the hour could not be seen without opening the case. This mechanism being observed—it requires indeed an examination of the instrument, and perhaps some previous knowledge of the subject, to perceive and understand it; but being once, as we have said, observed and understood—the inference we think is inevitable, that the watch must have had a maker—that there must have existed, at some time and at some place or other, an artificer or artificers who formed it for the purpose which we find it actually to answer, who completely comprehended its construction and designed its use.

I. Nor would it, I apprehend, weaken the conclusion, that we had never seen a watch made—that we had never known an artist capable of making one—that we were altogether incapable of executing such a piece of workmanship ourselves, or of understanding in what manner it was performed; all this being no more than what is true of some exquisite remains of ancient art, of some lost arts, and, to the generality of mankind, of the more curious productions of modern manufacture. Does one man in a million know how oval frames are turned? Ignorance of this kind exalts our opinion of the unseen and unknown artist's skill, if he be unseen and unknown, but raises no doubt in our minds of the existence and agency of such an artist, at some former time and in some place or other. Nor can I perceive that it varies at all the inference, whether the question arise concerning a human agent or concerning an agent of a different species, or an agent possessing in some respects a different nature.

II. Neither, secondly, would it invalidate our conclusion, that the watch sometimes went wrong or that it seldom went exactly right. The purpose of the machinery, the design, and the designer might be evident, and in the case supposed, would be evident, in whatever way we accounted for the irregularity of the movement, or whether we could account for it or not. It is not necessary that a machine be perfect in order to show with what design it was made: still less necessary, where the only question is whether it were made with any design at all.

III. Nor, thirdly, would it bring any uncertainty into the argument, if there were a few parts of the watch, concerning which we could not discover or had not yet discovered in what manner they conduced to the general effect; or even some parts, concerning which we could not ascertain whether they conduced to that effect in any manner whatever. For, as to the first branch of the case, if by the loss, or disorder, or decay of the parts in question, the movement of the watch were found in fact to be stopped, or disturbed, or retarded, no doubt would remain in our minds as to the utility or intention of these parts, although we should be unable to investigate the manner according to which, or the connection by which, the ultimate effect depended upon their action or assistance; and the more complex the machine, the more likely is this obscurity to arise. Then, as to the second thing supposed, namely, that there were parts which might be spared without prejudice to the movement of the watch, and that we had proved this by experiment, these superfluous parts, even if we were completely assured that they were such, would not vacate the reasoning which we had instituted concerning other parts. The indication of contrivance remained, with respect to them, nearly as it was before.

IV. Nor, fourthly, would any man in his senses think the existence of the watch with its various machinery accounted for, by being told that it was one out of possible combinations of material forms; that whatever he had found in the place where he found the watch, must have contained some internal configuration or other; and that this configuration might be the structure now exhibited, namely, of the works of a watch, as well as a different structure.

V. Nor, fifthly, would it yield his inquiry more satisfaction, to be answered that there existed in things a principle of order, which had disposed the parts of the watch into their present form and situation. He never knew a watch made by the principle of order; nor can he even form to himself an idea of what is meant by a principle of order distinct from the intelligence of the watchmaker.

VI. Sixthly, he would be surprised to hear that the mechanism of the watch was no proof of contrivance, only a motive to induce the mind to think so:

VII. And not less surprised to be informed that the watch in his hand was nothing more than the result of the laws of *metallic* nature. It is a perversion of language to assign any law as the efficient, operative cause of any thing. A law presupposes an agent, for it is only the mode according to which an agent proceeds: it implies a power, for it is the order according to which that power acts. Without this agent, without this power, which are both distinct from itself, the *law* does nothing, is nothing. The expression, "the law of metallic nature," may sound strange and harsh to a philosophic ear; but it seems quite as justifiable as some others which are more familiar to him, such as "the law of vegetable nature," "the law of animal nature," or, indeed, as "the law of nature" in general, when assigned as the cause of phenomena, in exclusion of agency and power, or when it is substituted into the place of these.

VIII. Neither, lastly, would our observer be driven out of his conclusion or from his confidence in its truth by being told that he knew nothing at all about the matter. He knows enough for his argument; he knows the utility of the end; he knows the subserviency and adaptation of the means to the end. These points being known, his ignorance of other points, his doubts concerning other points affect not the certainty of his reasoning. The consciousness of knowing little need not beget a distrust of that which he does know.

CHAPTER II

State of Argument Continued

Suppose, in the next place, that the person who found the watch should after some time discover that, in addition to all the properties which he had hitherto observed in it, it possessed the unexpected property of producing in the course of its movement another watch like itself—the thing is conceivable; that it contained within it a mechanism, a system of parts—a mold, for instance, or a complex adjustment of lathes, files, and other tools—evidently and separately calculated for this purpose; let us inquire what effect ought such a discovery to have upon his former conclusion.

I. The first effect would be to increase his admiration of the contrivance, and his conviction of the consummate skill of the contriver. Whether he regarded the object of the contrivance, the distinct apparatus, the intricate, yet in many parts intelligible mechanism by which it was carried on, he would perceive in this new observation nothing but an additional reason for doing what he had already done—for referring the construction of the watch to design and to supreme art. If that construction *without* this property, or, which is the same thing, before this property had been noticed, proved intention and art to have been employed about it, still more strong would the proof appear when he came to the knowledge of this further property, the crown and perfection of all the rest.

II. He would reflect that, though the watch before him were *in some sense* the maker of the watch which was fabricated in the course of its movements, yet it was in a very different sense from that in which a carpenter, for instance, is the maker of a chair—the author of its contrivance, the cause of the relation of its parts to their use. With respect to these, the first watch was no cause at all to the second; in no such sense as this was it the author of the constitution and order, either of the parts which the new watch contained, or of the parts by the aid and instrumentality of which it was produced. We might possibly say, but with great latitude of expression, that a stream of water ground corn; but no latitude of expression would allow us to say, no stretch of conjecture could lead us to think that the stream of water built the mill, though it were too ancient for us to know who the builder was. What the stream of water does in the affair is neither more nor less than this: by the application of an unintelligent impulse to a mechanism previously arranged, arranged independently of it and arranged by intelligence, an effect is produced, namely, the corn is ground. But the effect results from the arrangement. The force of the stream cannot be said to be the cause or the author of the effect, still less of the arrangement. Understanding and plan in the formation of the mill were not the less necessary for any share which the water has in grinding the corn; yet is this share the same as that which the watch would have contributed to the production of the new watch, upon the supposition assumed in the last section. Therefore,

III. Though it be now no longer probable that the individual watch which our observer had found was made immediately by the hand of an artificer, yet this alteration does not in anywise affect the inference that an artificer had been originally employed and concerned in the production. The argument from design remains as it was. Marks of design and contrivance are no more accounted for now than they were before. In the same thing, we may ask for the cause of different properties. We may ask for the cause of the color of a body, of its hardness, of its heat; and these causes may be all different. We are now asking for the cause of that subserviency to a use, that relation to an end, which we have remarked in the watch before us. No answer is given to this question by telling us that a preceding watch produced it. There cannot be design without a designer; contrivance without a contriver; order without choice; arrangement without anything capable of arranging; subserviency and relation to a purpose without that which could intend a purpose; means suitable to an end, and executing their office in accomplishing that end, without the end ever having been contemplated or the means accommodated to it. Arrangement, disposition of parts, subserviency of means to an end, relation of instruments to a use imply the presence of intelligence and mind. No one, therefore, can rationally believe that the insensible, inanimate watch, from which the watch before us issued, was the proper cause of the mechanism we so much admire in it—could be truly said to have constructed the instrument, disposed its parts, assigned their office, determined their order, action, and mutual dependency, combined their several motions into one result, and that also a result connected with the utilities of other beings. All these properties, therefore, are as much unaccounted for as they were before.

IV. Nor is anything gained by running the difficulty farther back, that is, by supposing the watch before us to have been produced from another watch, that from a former, and so on indefinitely. Our going back ever so far brings us no nearer to the least degree of satisfaction upon the subject. Contrivance is still unaccounted for. We still want a contriver. A designing mind is neither supplied by this supposition nor dispensed with. If the difficulty were diminished the farther we went back, by going back indefinitely we might exhaust it. And this is the only case to which this sort of reasoning applies. Where there is a tendency, or, as we increase the number of terms, a continual approach toward a limit, *there,* by supposing the number of terms to be what is called infinite, we may conceive the limit to be attained; but where there is no such tendency or approach, nothing is effected by lengthening the series. There is no difference as to the point in question, whatever there may be as to many points, between one series and another—between a series which is finite and a series which is infinite. A chain composed of an infinite number of links can no more support itself than a chain composed of a finite number of links. And of this we are assured, though we never *can* have tried the experiment; because, by increasing the number of links, from ten, for instance, to a hundred, from a hundred to a thousand, etc., we make not the smallest approach, we observe not the smallest tendency toward self-support. There is no difference in this respect—yet there may be a great difference in several respects—between a chain of a greater or less length, between one chain and another, between one that is finite and one that is infinite. This very much resembles the case before us. The machine which we are inspecting demonstrates, by its construction, contrivance and design. Contrivance must have had a contriver, design a designer, whether the machine immediately proceeded from another machine or not. That circumstance alters not the case. That other machine may, in like manner, have proceeded from a former machine: nor does that alter the case; the contrivance must have had a contriver. That former one from one preceding it: no alteration still; a contriver is still necessary. No tendency is perceived, no approach toward a diminution of this necessity. It is the same with any and every succession of these machines—a succession of ten, of a hundred, of a thousand; with one series, as with another—a series which is finite, as with a series which is infinite. In whatever other respects they may differ, in this they do not. In all equally, contrivance and design are unaccounted for.

The question is not simply, how came the first watch into existence?—which question, it may be pretended, is done away by supposing the series of watches thus produced from one another to have been infinite, and consequently to have had no such *first* for which it was necessary to provide a cause. This, perhaps, would have been nearly the state of the question, if nothing had been before us but an unorganized, unmechanized substance, without mark or indication of contrivance. It might be difficult to show that such substance could not have existed from eternity, either in succession—if it were possible, which I think it is not, for unorganized bodies to spring from one another—or by individual perpetuity. But that is not the question now. To suppose it to be so is to suppose that it made no difference whether he had found a watch or a stone. As it is, the metaphysics of that question have no place; for, in the watch which we are examining are seen contrivance, design, an end, a purpose, means for the end, adaptation to the purpose. And the question which irresistibly presses upon our thoughts is, whence this contrivance and design? The thing required is the intending mind, the adapted hand, the intelligence by which that hand was directed. This question, this demand is not shaken off by increasing a number or succession of substances destitute of these properties; nor the more, by increasing that number to infinity. If it be said that, upon the supposition of one watch being produced from another in the course of that other's movements and by means of the mechanism within it, we have a cause for the watch in my hand, namely, the watch from which it proceeded; I deny that for the design, the contrivance, the suitableness of means to an end, the adaptation of instruments to a use, all of which we discover in the watch, we have any cause whatever. It is in vain, therefore, to assign a series of such causes or to allege that a series may be carried back to infinity; for I do not admit that we have yet any cause at all for the phenomena, still less any series of causes either finite or infinite. Here is contrivance but no contriver; proofs of design, but no designer.

V. Our observer would further also reflect that the maker of the watch before him was in truth and reality the maker of every watch produced from it: there being no difference, except that the latter manifests a more exquisite skill, between the making of another watch with his own hands, by the mediation of files, lathes, chisels, etc., and the disposing, fixing, and inserting of these instruments, or of others equivalent to them, in the body of the watch already made, in such a manner as to form a new watch in the course of the movements which he had given to the old one. It is only working by one set of tools instead of another.

The conclusion which the *first* examination of the watch, of its works, construction, and movement, suggested, was that it must have had, for cause and author of that construction, an artificer who understood its mechanism and designed its use. This conclusion is invincible. A *second* examination presents us with a new discovery. The watch is found, in the course of its movement, to produce another watch similar to itself; and not only so, but we perceive in it a system or organization separately calculated for that purpose. What effect would this discovery have or ought it to have upon our former inference? What, as has already been said, but to increase beyond measure our admiration of the skill which had been employed in the formation of such a machine? Or shall it, instead of this, all at once turn us round to an opposite conclusion, namely, that no art or skill whatever has been concerned in the business, although all other evidences of art and skill remain as they were, and this last and supreme piece of art be now added to the rest? Can this be maintained without absurdity? Yet this is atheism.

CHAPTER V

Application of the Argument Continued

Every observation which was made in our first chapter concerning the watch may be repeated with strict propriety concerning the eye, concerning animals, concerning plants, concerning, indeed, all the organized parts of the works of nature. As,

I. When we are inquiring simply after the *existence* of an intelligent Creator, imperfection, inaccuracy, liability to disorder, occasional irregularities may subsist in a considerable degree without inducing any doubt into the question; just as a watch may frequently go wrong, seldom perhaps exactly right, may be faulty in some parts, defective in some, without the smallest ground of suspicion from thence arising that it was not a watch, or not made for the purpose ascribed to it. When faults are pointed out, and when a question is started concerning the skill of the artist or the dexterity with which the work is executed, then, indeed, in order to defend these qualities from accusation, we must be able either to expose some intractableness and imperfection in the materials or point out some invincible difficulty in the execution, into which imperfection and difficulty the matter of complaint may be resolved; or, if we cannot do this, we must adduce such specimens of consummate art and contrivance proceeding from the same hand as may convince the inquirer of the existence, in the case before him, of impediments like those which we have mentioned, although, what from the nature of the case is very likely to happen, they be unknown and unperceived by him. This we must do in order to vindicate the artist's skill, or at least the perfection of it; as we must also judge of his intention and of the provisions employed in fulfilling that intention, not from an instance in which they fail but from the great plurality of instances in which they succeed. But, after all, these are different questions from the question of the artist's existence; or, which is the same, whether the thing before us be a work of art or not; and the questions ought always to be kept separate in the mind. So likewise it is in the works of nature. Irregularities and imperfections are of little or no weight in the consideration when that consideration relates simply to the existence of a Creator. When the argument respects his attributes, they are of weight; but are then to be taken in conjunction—the attention is not to rest upon them, but they are to be taken in conjunction with the unexceptional evidences which we possess of skill, power, and benevolence displayed in other instances; which evidences may, in strength, number, and variety, be such and may so overpower apparent blemishes as to induce us, upon the most reasonable ground, to believe that these last ought to be referred to some cause, though we be ignorant of it, other than defect of knowledge or of benevolence in the author.

II. There may be also parts of plants and animals, as there were supposed to be of the watch, of which in some instances the operation, in others the use, is unknown. These form different cases; for the operation may be unknown, yet the use be certain. Thus it is with the lungs of animals. It does not, I think, appear that we are acquainted with the action of the air upon the blood, or in what manner that action is communicated by the lungs; yet we find that a very short suspension of their office destroys the life of the animal. In this case, therefore, we may be said to know the use, nay, we experience the necessity of the organ though we be ignorant of its operation. Nearly the same thing may be observed of what is called the lymphatic system. We suffer grievous inconveniences from its disorder, without being informed of the office which it sustains in the economy of our bodies. There may possibly also be some few examples of the second class in which not only the operation is unknown, but in which experiments may seem to prove that the part is not necessary; or may leave a doubt how far it is even useful to the plant or animal in which it is found. This is said to be the case with the spleen, which has been extracted from dogs without any sensible injury to their vital functions. Instances of the former kind, namely, in which we cannot explain the operation, may be numerous; for they will be so in proportion to our ignorance. They will be more or fewer to different persons, and in different stages of science. Every improvement of knowledge diminishes their number. There is hardly, perhaps, a year passes that does not in the works of nature bring some operation or some mode of operation to light, which was before undiscovered—probably unsuspected. Instances of the second kind, namely, where the part appears to be totally useless, I believe to be extremely rare; compared with the number of those of which the use is evident, they are beneath any assignable proportion and perhaps have been never submitted to trial and examination sufficiently accurate, long enough continued, or often enough repeated. No accounts which I have seen are satisfactory. The mutilated animal may live and grow fat—as was the case of the dog deprived of its spleen—yet may be defective in some other of its functions, which, whether they can all, or in what degree of vigor and perfection, be performed, or how long preserved without the extirpated organ, does not seem to be ascertained by experiment. But to this case, even were it fully made out, may be applied the consideration which we suggested concerning the watch, namely, that these superfluous parts do not negative [negate] the reasoning which we instituted concerning those parts which are useful, and of which we know the use; the indication of contrivance with respect to them remains as it was before.

III. One atheistic way of replying to our observations upon the works of nature, and to the proofs of a Deity which we think that we perceive in them, is to tell us that all which we see must necessarily have had some form, and that it might as well be its present form as any other. Let us now apply this answer to the eye, as we did before to the watch. Something or other must have occupied that place in the animal's head, must have filled up, as we say, the socket; we will say also, that it must have been of that sort of substance which we call animal substance, as flesh, bone, membrane, or cartilage, etc. But that it should have been an *eye,* knowing as we do what an eye comprehends, namely, that it should have consisted, first, of a series of transparent lenses—very different, by the by, even in their substance, from the opaque materials of which the rest of the body is, in general at least, composed, and with which the whole of its surface, this single portion of it excepted, is covered; secondly, of a black cloth or canvas—the only membrane in the body which is black—spread out behind these lenses, so as to receive the image formed by pencils of light transmitted through them, and at which alone a distinct image could be formed, namely, at the concourse of the refracted rays; thirdly, of a large nerve communicating between this membrane and the brain, without which the action of light upon the membrane, however modified by the organ; would be lost to the purposes of sensation; that this fortunate conformation of parts should have been the lot not of one individual out of many thousand individuals, like the great prize in a lottery or like some singularity in nature, but the happy chance of a whole species; nor of one species out of many thousand species with which we are acquainted, but of by far the greatest number of all that exist, and that under varieties not causal or capricious, but bearing marks of being suited to their respective exigencies; that all this should have taken place merely because something must have occupied these points on every animal's forehead, or that all this should be thought to be accounted for by the short answer that "whatever was there must have had some form or other" is too absurd to be made more so by any argumentation. We are not contented with this answer; we find no satisfaction in it, by way of accounting for appearances of organization far short of those of the eye, such as we observe in fossil shells, petrified bones, or other substances which bear the vestiges of animal or vegetable recrements, but which, either in respect to utility or of the situation in which they are discovered, may seem accidental enough. It is no way of accounting even for these things, to say that the stone, for instance, which is shown to us—supposing the question to be concerning a petrifaction—must have contained some internal conformation or other. Nor does it mend the answer to add, with respect to the singularity of the conformation, that after the event it is no longer to be computed what the chances were against it. This is always to be computed when the question is whether a useful or imitative conformation be the product of chance or not: I desire no greater certainty in reasoning than that by which chance is excluded from the present disposition of the natural world. Universal experience is against it. What does chance ever do for us? In the human body, for instance, chance, that is, the operation of causes without design, may produce a wen, a wart, a mole, a pimple, but never an eye. Among inanimate substances, a clod, a pebble, a liquid drop might be; but never was a watch, a telescope, an organized body of any kind, answering a valuable purpose by a complicated mechanism, the effect of chance. In no assignable instance has such a thing existed without intention somewhere.

IV. There is another answer which has the same effect as the resolving of things into chance, which answer would persuade us to believe that the eye, the animal to which it belongs, every other animal, every plant, indeed every organized body which we see are only so many out of the possible varieties and combinations of being which the lapse of infinite ages has brought into existence; that the present world is the relic of that variety; millions of other bodily forms and other species having perished, being, by the defect of their constitution, incapable of preservation, or of continuance by generation. Now there is no foundation whatever for this conjecture in any thing which we observe in the works of nature; no such experiments are going on at present—no such energy operates as that which is here supposed, and which should be constantly pushing into existence new varieties of beings. Nor are there any appearances to support an opinion that every possible combination of vegetable or animal structure has formerly been tried. Multitudes of conformation, both of vegetables and animals, may be conceived capable of existence and succession, which yet do not exist. Perhaps almost as many forms of plants might have been found in the fields as figures of plants can be delineated upon paper. A countless variety of animals might have existed which do not exist. Upon the supposition here stated, we should see unicorns and mermaids, sylphs and centaurs, the fancies of painters and the fables of poets, realized by examples. Or, if it be alleged that these may transgress the bounds of possible life and propagation, we might at least have nations of human beings without nails upon their fingers, with more or fewer fingers and toes than ten, some with one eye, others with one ear, with one nostril, or without the sense of smelling at all. All these and a thousand other imaginable varieties might live and propagate. We may modify any one species many different ways, all consistent with life, and with the actions necessary to preservation, although affording different degrees of conveniency and enjoyment to the animal. And if we carry these modifications through the different species which are known to subsist, their number would be incalculable. No reason can be given why, if these deperdits ever existed, they have now disappeared. Yet, if all possible existences have been tried, they must have formed part of the catalogue.

But, moreover, the division of organized substances into animals and vegetables, and the distribution and subdistribution of each into genera and species, which distribution is not an arbitrary act of the mind, but founded in the order which prevails in external nature, appear to me to contradict the supposition of the present world being the remains of an indefinite variety of existences—of a variety which rejects all plan. The hypothesis teaches that every possible variety of being has at one time or other found its way into existence—by what cause or in what manner is not said—and that those which were badly formed perished; but how or why those which survived should be cast, as we see that plants and animals are cast, into regular classes, the hypothesis does not explain; or rather the hypothesis is inconsistent with this phenomenon.

The hypothesis, indeed, is hardly deserving of the consideration which we have given it. What should we think of a man who, because we had never ourselves seen watches, telescopes, stocking mills, steam engines, etc., made, knew not how they were made, nor could prove by testimony when they were made, or by whom, would have us believe that these machines, instead of deriving their curious structures from the thought and design of their inventors and contrivers, in truth derive them from no other origin than this: namely, that a mass of metals and other materials having run, when melted, into all possible figures, and combined themselves in all possible forms and shapes and proportions, these things which we see are what were left from the incident, as best worth preserving, and as such are become the remaining stock of a magazine which at one time or other, has by this means contained every mechanism, useful and useless, convenient and inconvenient, into which such like materials could be thrown? I cannot distinguish the hypothesis, as applied to the works of nature, from this solution, which no one would accept as applied to a collection of machines.

V. To the marks of contrivance discoverable in animal bodies, and to the argument deduced from them in proof of design and of a designing Creator, this turn is sometimes attempted to be given, namely, that the parts were not intended for the use, but that the use arose out of the parts. This distinction is intelligible. A cabinetmaker rubs his mahogany with fish skin; yet it would be too much to assert that the skin of the dogfish was made rough and granulated on purpose for the polishing of wood, and the use of cabinetmakers. Therefore the distinction is intelligible. But I think that there is very little place for it in the works of nature. When roundly and generally affirmed of them, as it has sometimes been, it amounts to such another stretch of assertion as it would be to say that all the implements of the cabinetmaker's workshop, as well as his fish skin, were substances accidentally configurated, which he had picked up and converted to his use; that his adzes, saws, planes, and gimlets were not made, as we suppose, to hew, cut, smooth, shape out, or bore wood with, but that, these things being made, no matter with what design, or whether with any, the cabinetmaker perceived that they were applicable to his purpose and turned them to account.

But, again, so far as this solution is attempted to be applied to those parts of animals the action of which does not depend upon the will of the animal, it is fraught with still more evident absurdity. Is it possible to believe that the eye was formed without any regard to vision; that it was the animal itself which found out that, though formed with no such intention, it would serve to see with; and that the use of the eye as an organ of sight resulted from this discovery, and the animal's application of it? The same question may be asked of the ear; the same of all the senses. None of the senses fundamentally depend upon the election of the animal; consequently neither upon his sagacity nor his experience. It is the impression which objects make upon them that constitutes their use. Under that impression he is passive. He may bring objects to the sense, or within its reach; he may select these objects; but over the impression itself he has no power, or very little; and that properly is the sense.

Secondly, there are many parts of animal bodies which seem to depend upon the will of the animal in a greater degree than the senses do, and yet with respect to which this solution is equally unsatisfactory. If we apply the solution to the human body, for instance, it forms itself into questions upon which no reasonable mind can doubt: such as, whether the teeth were made expressly for the mastication of food, the feet for walking, the hands for holding; or whether, these things as they are being in fact in the animal's possession, his own ingenuity taught him that they were convertible to these purposes, though no such purposes were contemplated in their formation.

All that there is of the appearance of reason in this way of considering the subject is that, in some cases, the organization seems to determine the habits of the animal and its choice to a particular mode of life which in a certain sense may be called "the use arising out of the part." Now, to all the instances in which there is any place for this suggestion, it may be replied that the organization determines the animal to habits beneficial and salutary to itself, and that this effect would not be seen so regularly to follow, if the several organizations did not bear a concerted and contrived relation to the substance by which the animal was surrounded. They would, otherwise, be capacities without objects—powers without employment. The webfoot determines, you say, the duck to swim; but what would that avail if there were no water to swim in? The strong hooked bill and sharp talons of one species of bird determine it to prey upon animals; the soft straight bill and weak claws of another species determine it to pick up seeds; but neither determination could take effect in providing for the sustenance of the birds, if animal bodies and vegetable seeds did not lie within their reach. The peculiar conformation of the bill and tongue and claws of the woodpecker determines that bird to search for his food among the insects lodged behind the bark or in the wood of decayed trees; but what would this profit him if there were no trees, no decayed trees, no insects lodged under their bark or in their trunk? The proboscis with which the bee is furnished determines him to seek for honey; but what would that signify if flowers supplied none? Faculties thrown down upon animals at random, and without reference to the objects amidst which they are placed, would not produce to them the services and benefits which we see; and if there be that reference, then there is intention.

Lastly, the solution fails entirely when applied to plants. The parts of plants answer their uses without any concurrence from the will or choice of the plant.

VI. Others have chosen to refer every thing to a *principle of order* in nature. A principle of order is the word; but what is meant by a principle of order as different from an intelligent Creator has not been explained either by definition or example; and without such explanation it should seem to be a mere substitution of words for reasons, names for causes. Order itself is only the adaptation of means to an end: a principle of order, therefore, can only signify the mind and intention which so adapts them. Or, were it capable of being explained in any other sense, is there any experience, any analogy, to sustain it? Was a watch ever produced by a principle of order; and why might not a watch be so produced as well as an eye?

Furthermore, a principle of order, acting blindly and without choice, is nega-tived [negated] by the observation that order is not universal, which it would be if it issued from a constant and necessary principle, nor indiscriminate, which it would be if it issued from an unintelligent principle. Where order is wanted, there we find it; where order is not wanted, that is, where if it prevailed, it would be useless, there we do not find it. In the structure of the eye—for we adhere to our example—in the figure and position of its several parts, the most exact order is maintained. In the forms of rocks and mountains, in the lines which bound the coasts of continents and islands, in the shape of bays and promontories, no order whatever is perceived, because it would have been superfluous. No useful purpose would have arisen from molding rocks and mountains into regular solids, bounding the channel of the ocean by geometrical curves, or from the map of the world resembling a table of diagrams in Euclid's *Elements* or Simpson's "Conic Sections."

VII. Lastly, the confidence which we place in our observations upon the works of nature, in the marks which we discover of contrivance, choice, and design, and in our reasoning upon the proofs afforded us, ought not to be shaken, as it is some-times attempted to be done, by bringing forward to our view our own ignorance, or rather the general imperfection of our knowledge of nature. Nor, in many cases, ought this consideration to affect us even when it respects some parts of the subject immediately under our notice. True fortitude of understanding consists in not suf-fering what we know, to be disturbed by what we do not know. If we perceive a use-ful end, and means adapted to that end, we perceive enough for our conclusion. If these things be clear, no matter what is obscure, the argument is finished. For instance, if the utility of vision to the animal which enjoys it, and the adaptation of the *eye* to this office, be evident and certain—and I can mention nothing which is more so—ought it to prejudice the inference which we draw from these premises, that we cannot explain the use of the spleen? Nay, more, if there be parts of the eye, namely, the cornea, the crystalline, the retina, in their substance, figure and posi-tion, manifestly suited to the formation of an image by the refraction of rays of light, at least as manifestly as the glasses and tubes of a dioptric telescope are suited to that purpose, it concerns not the proof which these afford of design, and of a designer, that there may perhaps be other parts, certain muscles, for instance, or nerves in the same eye, of the agency or effect of which we can give no account, any more than we should be inclined to doubt, or ought to doubt, about the construction of a telescope, namely, for what purpose it was constructed, or whether it was con-structed at all, because there belonged to it certain screws and pins, the use or action of which we did not comprehend. I take it to be a general way of infusing doubts and scruples into the mind, to recur to its own ignorance, its own imbecility—to tell us that upon these subjects we know little; that little imperfectly; or rather, that we know nothing properly about the matter. These suggestions so fall in with our con-sciousness as sometimes to produce a general distrust of our faculties and our con-clusions. But this is an unfounded jealousy. The uncertainty of one thing does not necessarily affect the certainty of another thing. Our ignorance of many points need not suspend our assurance of a few. Before we yield, in any particular instance, to the skepticism which this sort of insinuation would induce, we ought accurately to ascertain whether our ignorance or doubt concern those precise points upon which our conclusion rests. Other points are nothing. Our ignorance of other points may be of no consequence to these, though they be points, in various respects, of great importance. A just reasoner removes from his consideration not only what he knows, but what he does not know, touching matters not strictly connected with his argument, that is, not forming the very steps of his deduction: beyond these, his knowledge and his ignorance are alike irrelative.

Dialogues Concerning Natural Religion *(excerpt)*

David Hume

PART II

I must own, Cleanthes, said Demea, that nothing can more surprise me, than the light, in which you have, all along, put this argument. By the whole tenor of your discourse, one would imagine that you were maintaining the being of a God, against the cavils of atheists and infidels; and were necessitated to become a champion for that fundamental principle of all religion. But this, I hope, is not by any means a question among us. No man; no man, at least, of common sense, I am persuaded, ever entertained a serious doubt with regard to a truth so certain and self-evident. The question is not concerning the *being* but the *nature* of *God*. This, I affirm, from the infirmities of human understanding, to be altogether incomprehensible and unknown to us. The essence of that supreme mind, his attributes, the manner of his existence, the very nature of his duration; these and every particular, which regards so divine a Being, are mysterious to men. Finite, weak, and blind creatures, we ought to humble ourselves in his august presence, and, conscious of our frailties, adore in silence his infinite perfections, which eye hath not seen, ear hath not heard, neither hath it entered into the heart of man to conceive them. They are covered in a deep cloud from human curiosity: It is profaneness to attempt penetrating through these sacred obscurities: And next to the impiety of denying his existence, is the temerity of prying into his nature and essence, decrees and attributes.

But lest you should think, that my *piety* has here got the better of my *philosophy,* I shall support my opinion, if it needs any support, by a very great authority. I might cite all the divines almost, from the foundation of Christianity, who have ever treated of this or any other theological subject: But I shall confine myself, at present, to one equally celebrated for piety and philosophy. It is Father Malebranche, who, I remember, thus expresses himself.[1] "One ought not so much (says he) to call

---

[1]*Recherche de la vérité, liv.* 3, chap. 9

Source: [1776], Part II, III, V, VI, edited with an introduction by Norman Kemp Smith. Indianapolis: Bobbs-Merrill, 1947, 141–157, 165–175.

God a spirit, in order to express positively what he is, as in order to signify that he is not matter. He is a Being infinitely perfect: Of this we cannot doubt. But in the same manner as we ought not to imagine, even supposing him corporeal, that he is cloathed with a human body, as the Anthropomorphites asserted, under colour that that figure was the most perfect of any; so neither ought we to imagine, that the Spirit of God has human ideas, or bears *any* resemblance to our spirit; under colour that we know nothing more perfect than a human mind. We ought rather to believe, that as he comprehends the perfections of matter without being material . . . he comprehends also the perfections of created spirits, without being spirit, in the manner we conceive spirit: That his true name is, *He that is,* or in other words, Being without restriction, All Being, the Being infinite and universal."

After so great an authority, Demea, replied Philo, as that which you have produced, and a thousand more, which you might produce, it would appear ridiculous in me to add my sentiment, or express my approbation of your doctrine. But surely, where reasonable men treat these subjects, the question can never be concerning the *being,* but only the *nature* of the Deity. The former truth, as you well observe, is unquestionable and self-evident. Nothing exists without a cause; and the original cause of this universe (whatever it be) we call God; and piously ascribe to him every species of perfection. Whoever scruples this fundamental truth deserves every punishment, which can be inflicted among philosophers, to wit, the greater ridicule, contempt and disapprobation. But as all perfection is entirely relative, we ought never to imagine, that we comprehend the attributes of this divine Being, or to suppose, that his perfections have any analogy or likeness to the perfections of a human creature. Wisdom, thought, design, knowledge; these we justly ascribe to him; because these words are honourable among men, and we have no other language or other conceptions, by which we can express our adoration of him. But let us beware, lest we think, that our ideas any wise correspond to his perfections, or that his attributes have any resemblance to these qualities among men. He is infinitely superior to our limited view and comprehension; and is more the object of worship in the temple, than of disputation in the schools.

In reality, Cleanthes, continued he, there is no need of having recourse to that affected scepticism, so displeasing to you, in order to come at this determination. Our ideas reach no farther than our experience: We have no experience of divine attributes and operations: I need not conclude my syllogism: You can draw the inference yourself. And it is a pleasure to me (and I hope to you too) that just reasoning and sound piety here concur in the same conclusion, and both of them establish the adorably mysterious and incomprehensible nature of the supreme Being.

Not to lose any time in circumlocutions, said Cleanthes, addressing himself to Demea, much less in replying to the pious declamations of Philo; I shall briefly explain how I conceive this matter. Look round the world: Contemplate the whole and every part of it: You will find it to be nothing but one great machine, subdivided into an infinite number of lesser machines, which again admit of subdivisions, to a degree beyond what human senses and faculties can trace and explain. All these various machines, and even their most minute parts, are adjusted to each other with an accuracy, which ravishes into admiration all men, who have ever contemplated them. The curious adapting of means to ends, throughout all nature, resembles exactly, though it much exceeds, the productions of human contrivance; of human design, thought, wisdom, and intelligence. Since therefore the effects resemble each other, we are led to infer, by all the rules of analogy, that the causes also resemble; and that the Author of nature is somewhat similar to the mind of man; though possessed of much larger faculties, proportioned to the grandeur of the work, which he has executed. By this argument *a posteriori,* and by this argument alone, we do prove at once the existence of a Deity, and his similarity to human mind and intelligence.

I shall be so free, Cleanthes, said Demea, as to tell you, that from the beginning, I could not approve of your conclusion concerning the similarity of the Deity to men; still less can I approve of the mediums, by which you endeavour to establish it. What! No demonstration of the being of a God! No abstract arguments! No proofs *a priori!* Are these, which have hitherto been so much insisted on by philosophers, all fallacy, all sophism? Can we reach no farther in this subject than experience[2] and probability? I will not say, that this is betraying the cause of a Deity: But surely, by this affected candour, you give advantage to atheists, which they never could obtain, by the mere dint of argument and reasoning.

What I chiefly scruple in this subject, said Philo, is not so much, that all religious arguments are by Cleanthes reduced to experience, as that they appear not to be even the most certain and irrefragable of that inferior kind. That a stone will fall, that fire will burn, that the earth has solidity, we have observed a thousand and a thousand times; and when any new instance of this nature is presented, we draw without hesitation the accustomed inference. The exact similarity of the cases gives us a perfect assurance of a similar event; and a stronger evidence is never desired nor sought after. But wherever you depart, in the least, from the similarity of the cases, you diminish proportionably the evidence; and may at last bring it to a very weak *analogy,* which is confessedly liable to error and uncertainty. After having experienced the circulation of the blood in human creatures, we make no doubt that it takes place in Titius and Mævius: But from its circulation in frogs and fishes, it is only a presumption, though a strong one, from analogy, that it takes place in men and other animals. The analogical reasoning is much weaker, when we infer the circulation of the sap in vegetables from our experience that the blood circulates in animals; and those, who hastily followed that imperfect analogy, are found, by more accurate experiments, to have been mistaken.

If we see a house, Cleanthes, we conclude, with the greatest certainty, that it had an architect or builder; because this is precisely that species of effect, which we have experienced to proceed from that species of cause. But surely you will not affirm, that the universe bears such a resemblance to a house, that we can with the same certainty infer a similar cause, or that the analogy is here entire and perfect. The dissimilitude is so striking, that the utmost you can here pretend to is a guess, a conjecture, a presumption concerning a similar cause; and how that pretension will be received in the world, I leave you to consider.

It would surely be very ill received, replied Cleanthes; and I should be deservedly blamed and detested, did I allow that the proofs of a Deity amounted to

[2][moral evidence *substituted for* experience, and *then* experience *restored*]

no more than a guess or conjecture. But is the whole adjustment of means to ends in a house and in the universe so slight a resemblance? The œconomy of final causes? The order, proportion, and arrangement of every part? Steps of a stair are plainly contrived, that human legs may use them in mounting; and this inference is certain and infallible. Human legs are also contrived for walking and mounting; and this inference, I allow, is not altogether so certain, because of the dissimilarity which you remark; but does it, therefore, deserve the name only of presumption or conjecture?

Good God! cried Demea, interrupting him, where are we? Zealous defenders of religion allow, that the proofs of a Deity fall short of perfect evidence! And you, Philo, on whose assistance I depended, in proving the adorable mysteriousness of the divine nature, do you assent to all these extravagant opinions of Cleanthes? For what other name can I give them? Or why spare my censure, when such principles are advanced, supported by such an authority, before so young a man as Pamphilus?

You seem not to apprehend, replied Philo, that I argue with Cleanthes in his own way; and by showing him the dangerous consequences of his tenets, hope at last to reduce him to our opinion. But what sticks most with you, I observe, is the representation which Cleanthes has made of the argument *a posteriori;* and finding that that argument is likely to escape your hold and vanish into air, you think it so disguised that you can scarcely believe it to be set in its true light. Now, however much I may dissent, in other respects, from the dangerous principles of Cleanthes, I must allow, that he has fairly represented that argument; and I shall endeavour so to state the matter to you, that you will entertain no farther scruples with regard to it.

Were a man to abstract from every thing which he knows or has seen, he would be altogether incapable, merely from his own ideas, to determine what kind of scene the universe must be, or to give the preference to one state or situation of things above another. For as nothing, which he clearly conceives, could be esteemed impossible or implying a contradiction, every chimera of his fancy would be upon an equal footing; nor could he assign any just reason, why he adheres to one idea or system, and rejects the others, which are equally possible.

Again; after he opens his eyes, and contemplates the world, as it really is, it would be impossible for him, at first, to assign the cause of any one event; much less, of the whole of things or of the universe. He might set his fancy a rambling; and she might bring him in an infinite variety of reports and representations. These would all be possible; but being all equally possible, he would never, of himself, give a satisfactory account for his preferring one of them to the rest. Experience alone can point out to him the true cause of any phenomenon.

Now according to this method of reasoning, Demea, it follows (and is, indeed, tacitly allowed by Cleanthes himself) that order, arrangement, or the adjustment of final causes is not, of itself, any proof of design; but only so far as it has been experienced to proceed from that principle. For aught we can know *a priori,* matter may contain the source or spring of order originally, within itself, as well as mind does; and there is no more difficulty in conceiving, that the several elements, from an internal unknown cause, may fall into the most exquisite arrangement, than to conceive that their ideas, in the great, universal mind, from a like internal, unknown cause, fall into that arrangement. The equal possibility of both these suppositions is allowed. By experience we find (according to Cleanthes), that there is a difference between them. Throw several pieces of steel together, without shape or form; they will never arrange themselves so as to compose a watch: Stone, and mortar, and wood, without an architect, never erect a house. But the ideas in a human mind, we see, by an unknown, inexplicable œconomy, arrange themselves so as to form the plan of a watch or house. Experience, therefore, proves, that there is an original principle of order in mind, not in matter. From similar effects we infer similar causes. The adjustment of means to ends[3] is alike in the universe, as in a machine of human contrivance. The causes, therefore, must be resembling.

I was from the beginning scandalised, I must own, with this resemblance, which is asserted, between the Deity and human creatures; and must conceive it to imply such a degradation of the supreme Being as no sound theist could endure. With your assistance, therefore, Demea, I shall endeavour to defend what you justly call the adorable mysteriousness of the divine nature, and shall refute this reasoning of Cleanthes; provided he allows, that I have made a fair representation of it.

When Cleanthes had assented, Philo, after a short pause, proceeded in the following manner.

That all inferences, Cleanthes, concerning fact, are founded on experience, and that all experimental reasonings are founded on the supposition, that similar causes prove similar effects, and similar effects similar causes; I shall not, at present, much dispute with you. But observe, I entreat you, with what extreme caution all just reasoners proceed in the transferring of experiments to similar cases. Unless the cases be exactly similar, they repose no perfect confidence in applying their past observation to any particular phenomenon. Every alteration of circumstances occasions a doubt concerning the event; and it requires new experiments to prove certainly, that the new circumstances are of no moment or importance. A change in bulk, situation, arrangement, age, disposition of the air, or surrounding bodies; any of these particulars may be attended with the most unexpected consequences: And unless the objects be quite familiar to us, it is the highest temerity to expect with assurance, after any of these changes, an event similar to that which before fell under our observation. The slow and deliberate steps of philosophers, here, if any where, are distinguished from the precipitate march of the vulgar, who, hurried on by the smallest similitude, are incapable of all discernment or consideration.

But can you think, Cleanthes, that your usual phlegm and philosophy have been preserved in so wide a step as you have taken, when you compared to the universe houses, ships, furniture, machines; and from their similarity in some circumstances inferred a similarity in their causes? Thought, design, intelligence, such as we discover in men and other animals, is no more than one of the springs and principles of the universe, as well as heat or cold, attraction or repulsion, and a hundred others, which fall under daily observation. It is an active cause, by which some particular parts of nature, we find, produce alterations on other parts. But can a conclusion, with any propriety, be transferred from parts to the whole? Does not the great disproportion bar all comparison and inference? From observing the growth

---

[3][means to ends *for* final causes]

of a hair, can we learn any thing concerning the generation of a man? Would the manner of a leaf's blowing, even though perfectly known, afford us any instruction concerning the vegetation of a tree?

But allowing that we were to take the *operations* of one part of nature upon another for the foundation of our judgment concerning the *origin* of the whole (which never can be admitted) yet why select so minute, so weak, so bounded a principle as the reason and design of animals is found to be upon this planet? What peculiar privilege has this little agitation of the rain which we call thought, that we must thus make it the model of the whole universe? Our partiality in our own favour does indeed present it on all occasions: But sound philosophy ought carefully to guard against so natural an illusion.

So far from admitting, continued Philo, that the operations of a part can afford us any just conclusion concerning the origin of the whole, I will not allow any one part to form a rule for another part, if the latter be very remote from the former. Is there any reasonable ground to conclude, that the inhabitants of other planets possess thought, intelligence, reason, or any thing similar to these faculties in men? When nature has so extremely diversified her manner of operation in this small globe; can we imagine, that she incessantly copies herself throughout so immense a universe? And if thought, as we may well suppose, be confined merely to this narrow corner, and has even there so limited a sphere of action; with what propriety can we assign it for the original cause of all things? The narrow views of a peasant, who makes his domestic œconomy the rule for the government of kingdoms, is in comparison a pardonable sophism.

But were we ever so much assured, that a thought and reason, resembling the human, were to be found throughout the whole universe, and were its activity elsewhere vastly greater and more commanding than it appears in this globe: Yet I cannot see, why the operations of a world, constituted, arranged, adjusted, can with any propriety be extended to a world, which is in its embryo-state, and is advancing towards that constitution and arrangement. By observation, we know somewhat of the œconomy, action, and nourishment of a finished animal; but we must transfer with great caution that observation to the growth of a fœtus in the womb, and still more, to the formation of an animalcule in the loins of its male parent. Nature, we find, even from our limited experience, possesses an infinite number of springs and principles, which incessantly discover themselves on every change of her position and situation. And what new and unknown principles would actuate her in so new and unknown a situation as that of the formation of a universe, we cannot, without the utmost temerity, pretend to determine.

[A very small part of this great system, during a very short time, is very imperfectly discovered to us: And do we thence pronounce decisively concerning the origin of the whole?][4]

Admirable conclusion! Stone, wood, brick, iron, brass have not, at this time, in this minute globe of earth, an order or arrangement without human art and contrivance: Therefore the universe could not originally attain its order and arrangement, without something similar to human art. But is a part of nature a rule for

---

[4][This paragraph transferred from Part I]

another part very wide of the former? Is it a rule for the whole?[5] Is a very small part a rule for the universe? Is nature in one situation, a certain rule for[6] nature in another situation, vastly different from the former?

And can you blame me, Cleanthes, if I here imitate the prudent reserve of Simonides, who, according to the noted story,[7] being asked by Hiero, *What God was?* desired a day to think of it, and then two days more; and after that manner continually prolonged the term, without ever bringing in his definition or description? Could you even blame me, if I had answered at first, *that I did not know,* and was sensible that this subject lay vastly beyond the reach of my faculties? You might cry out sceptic and raillier as much as you pleased: But having found, in so many other subjects, much more familiar, the imperfections and even contradictions of human reason, I never should expect any success from its feeble conjectures, in a subject, so sublime, and so remote from the sphere of our observation. When two *species* of objects have always been observed to be conjoined together, I can *infer,* by custom, the existence of one wherever I *see* the existence of the other: And this I call an argument from experience. But how this argument can have place, where the objects, as in the present case,[8] are single, individual, without parallel, or specific resemblance, may be difficult to explain. And will any man tell me with a serious countenance, that an orderly universe must arise from some thought and art, like the human; because we have experience of it? To ascertain this reasoning, it were requisite, that we had experience of the origin of worlds; and it is not sufficient surely, that we have seen ships and cities arise from human art and contrivance. . . .

Philo was proceeding in this vehement manner, somewhat between jest and earnest, as it appeared to me; when he observed some signs of impatience in Cleanthes, and then immediately stopped short. What I had to suggest, said Cleanthes, is only that you would not abuse terms, or make use of popular expressions to subvert philosophical reasonings. You know, that the vulgar often distinguish reason from experience, even where the question relates only to matter of fact and existence; though it is found, where that *reason* is properly analysed, that it is nothing but a species of experience. To prove by experience the origin of the universe from mind is not more contrary to common speech than to prove the motion of the earth from the same principle. And a caviller might raise all the same objections to the Copernican system, which you have urged against my reasonings. Have you other earths, might he say, which you have seen to move? Have. . . .

Yes! cried Philo, interrupting him, we have other earths. Is not the moon another earth, which we see to turn round its centre? Is not Venus another earth, where we observe the same phenomenon? Are not the revolutions of the sun also a confirmation, from analogy, of the same theory? All the planets, are they not earths, which revolve about the sun? Are not the satellites moons, which move round Jupiter and Saturn, and along with these primary planets, round the sun? These

[5][whole *for* world]
[6][a certain rule for *for* precisely similar to]
[7][*Cf.* Cicero, *De Natura Deorum,* Bk. 1, 22]
[8][concerning the origin of the world *omitted*]

analogies and resemblances, with others, which I have not mentioned, are the sole proofs of the Copernican system: And to you it belongs to consider, whether you have any analogies of the same kind to support your theory.

In reality, Cleanthes, continued he, the modern system of astronomy is now so much received by all enquirers, and has become so essential a part even of our earliest education, that we are not commonly very scrupulous in examining the reasons upon which it is founded. It is now become a matter of mere curiosity to study the first writers on that subject, who had the full force of prejudice to encounter, and were obliged to turn their arguments on every side, in order to render them popular and convincing. But if we peruse Galilæo's famous Dialogues concerning the system of the world, we shall find, that that great genius, one of the sublimest that ever existed, first bent all his endeavours to prove, that there was no foundation for the distinction commonly made between elementary and celestial substances. The schools, proceeding from the illusions of sense, had carried this distinction very far; and had established the latter substances to be ingenerable, incorruptible, unalterable, impassible; and had assigned all the opposite qualities to the former. But Galilæo, beginning with the moon, proved its similarity in every particular to the earth; its convex figure, its natural darkness when not illuminated, its density, its distinction into solid and liquid, the variations of its phases, the mutual illuminations of the earth and moon, their mutual eclipses, the inequalities of the lunar surface, etc. After many instances of this kind, with regard to all the planets, men plainly saw, that these bodies became proper objects of experience; and that the similarity of their nature enabled us to extend the same arguments and phenomena from one to the other.

In this cautious proceeding of the astronomers, you may read your own condemnation, Cleanthes; or rather may see, that the subject in which you are engaged exceeds all human reason and enquiry. Can you pretend to show any such similarity between the fabric of a house, and the generation of a universe? Have you ever seen nature in any such situation as resembles the first arrangement of the elements? Have worlds ever been formed under your eye? and have you had leisure to observe the whole progress of the phenomenon, from the first appearance of order to its final consummation? If you have, then cite your experience, and deliver your theory.

PART III

Now the most absurd argument, replied Cleanthes, in the hands of a man of ingenuity and invention, may acquire an air of[9] probability! Are you not aware, Philo, that it became necessary for Copernicus and his first disciples to prove the similarity of the terrestrial and celestial matter; because several philosophers, blinded by old systems, and supported by some sensible appearances,[10] had denied this similarity? But that it is by no means necessary, that theists should prove the similarity

---

[9][truth and *omitted*]
[10][some sensible appearances *for* the illusions of sense]

of the works of nature to those of art; because this similarity is self-evident and undeniable? The same matter, a like form: What more is requisite to show[11] an analogy between their causes, and to ascertain the origin of all things from a divine purpose and intention? Your objections, I must freely tell you, are no better than the abstruse cavils of those philosophers, who denied motion; and ought to be refuted in the same manner, by illustrations, examples, and instances, rather than by serious argument and philosophy.

Suppose, therefore, that an articulate voice were heard in the clouds, much louder and more melodious than any which human art could ever reach: Suppose, that this voice were extended in the same instant over all nations, and spoke to each nation in its own language and dialect: Suppose, that the words delivered not only contain a just sense and meaning, but convey some instruction altogether worthy of a benevolent Being, superior to mankind: Could you possibly hesitate a moment concerning the cause of this voice? And must you not instantly ascribe it to some design or purpose? Yet I cannot see but all the same objections (if they merit that appellation) which lie against the system of theism, may also be produced against this inference.

Might you not say, that all conclusions concerning fact were founded on experience: That when we hear an articulate voice in the dark, and thence infer a man, it is only the resemblance of the effects, which leads us to conclude that there is a like resemblance in the cause: But that this extraordinary voice, by its loudness, extent, and flexibility to all languages, bears so little analogy to any human voice, that we have no reason to suppose any analogy in their causes: And consequently, that a rational, wise, coherent speech proceeded, you knew not whence, from some accidental whistling of the winds, not from any divine reason or intelligence? You see clearly your own objections in these cavils; and I hope too, you see clearly, that they cannot possibly have more force in the one case than in the other.

But to bring the case still nearer the present one of the universe, I shall make two suppositions, which imply not any absurdity or impossibility. Suppose, that there is a natural, universal, invariable language, common to every individual of human race; and that books are natural productions, which perpetuate themselves in the same manner with animals and vegetables, by descent and propagation. Several expressions of our passions contain a universal language: All brute[12] animals have a natural speech, which, however limited, is very intelligible to their own species. And as there are infinitely fewer parts and less contrivance in the finest composition of eloquence, than in the coarsest organized body, the propagation of an *Iliad* or *Æneid* is an easier supposition than that of any plant or animal.

Suppose, therefore, that you enter into your library, thus peopled by natural[13] volumes, containing the most refined reason and most exquisite beauty: Could you possibly open one of them, and doubt, that its original cause bore the strongest analogy to mind and intelligence? When it reasons and discourses; when it expostulates, argues, and enforces its views and topics; when it applies sometimes to the pure

[11][show *for* prove]
[12][brute *added*]
[13][vegetating animal *omitted*]

intellect, sometimes to the affections; when it collects, disposes, and adorns every consideration suited to the subjects could you persist in asserting, that all this, at the bottom, had really no meaning, and that the first formation of this volume in the loins of its original[14] parent proceeded not from thought and design? Your obstinacy, I know, reaches not that degree of firmness: Even your sceptical play and wantonness would be abashed at so glaring an absurdity.

But if there be any difference, Philo, between this supposed case and the real one of the universe, it is all to the advantage of the latter. The anatomy of an animal affords many stronger instances of design than the perusal of Livy or Tacitus:[15] And any objection which you start in the former case, by carrying me back to so unusual and extraordinary a scene as the first formation of worlds, the same objection has place on the supposition of our vegetating library. Choose, then, your party, Philo, without ambiguity or evasion: Assert either that a rational volume is no proof of a rational cause, or admit of a similar cause to all the works of nature.

Let me here observe too, continued Cleanthes, that this religious argument, instead of being weakened by that scepticism, so much affected by you, rather acquires force from it, and becomes more firm and undisputed. To exclude all argument or reasoning of every kind is either affectation or madness. The declared profession of every reasonable sceptic is only to reject abstruse, remote and refined arguments; to adhere to common sense and the plain instincts of nature; and to assent, wherever any reasons strike him with so full a force, that he cannot, without the greatest violence, prevent it. Now the arguments for natural religion are plainly of this kind; and nothing but the most perverse, obstinate metaphysics can reject them. Consider, anatomize the eye: Survey its structure and contrivance; and tell me, from your own feeling, if the idea of a contriver does not immediately flow in upon you with a force like that of sensation. The most obvious conclusion surely is in favour of design; and it requires time, reflection and study, to summon up those frivolous, though abstruse, objections, which can support infidelity. Who can behold the male and female of each species, the correspondence of their parts and instincts, their passions and whole course of life before and after generation, but must be sensible, that the propagation of the species is intended by nature? Millions and millions of such instances present themselves through every part of the universe; and no language can convey a more intelligible, irresistible meaning, than the curious adjustment of final causes. To what degree, therefore, of blind dogmatism must one have attained, to reject such natural and such convincing arguments?

[[16]Some beauties in writing we may meet with, which seem contrary to rules, and which gain the affections, and animate the imagination, in opposition to all the precepts of criticism, and to the authority of the established masters of art. And if the argument for theism be, as you pretend, contradictory to the principles of logic: its universal, its irresistible influence proves clearly, that there may be arguments of a like irregular nature. Whatever cavils may be urged; an orderly

---

[14][original *added*]

[15][Livy or Tacitus *for* the Iliad]

[16][This paragraph in brackets is added on the last page of Part III, with marks to indicate point of insertion.]

world, as well as a coherent, articulate speech, will still be received as an incontestable proof of design and intention.]

It sometimes happens, I own, that the religious arguments have not their due influence on an ignorant savage and barbarian; not because they are obscure and difficult, but because he never asks himself any question with regard to them. Whence arises the curious structure of an animal? From the copulation of its parents. And these whence? From *their* parents. A few removes set the objects at such a distance, that to him they are lost in darkness and confusion; nor is he actuated by any curiosity to trace them farther. But this is neither dogmatism nor scepticism, but stupidity; a state of mind very different from your sifting, inquisitive disposition, my ingenious friend. You can trace causes from effects: You can compare the most distant and remote objects: And your greatest errors proceed not from barrenness of thought and invention, but from too luxuriant a fertility, which suppresses your natural good sense, by a profusion of unnecessary scruples and objections.

Here I could observe, Hermippus, that Philo was a little embarrassed and confounded: But while he hesitated in delivering an answer, luckily for him, Demea broke in upon the discourse, and saved his countenance,

Your instance, Cleanthes, said he, drawn from books and language, being familiar, has, I confess, so much more force on that account; but is there not some danger too in this very circumstance, and may it not render us presumptuous, by making us imagine we comprehend the Deity, and have some adequate idea of his nature and attributes? When I read a volume, I enter into the mind and intention of the author: I become him, in a manner, for the instant; and have an immediate feeling and conception of those ideas, which revolved in his imagination, while employed in that composition. But so near an approach we never surely can make to the Deity. His ways are not our ways. His attributes are perfect, but incomprehensible. And this volume of nature contains a great and inexplicable riddle, more than any intelligible discourse or reasoning.

The ancient Platonists, you know, were the most religious and devout of all the pagan philosophers: Yet many of them, particularly Plotinus, expressly declare, that intellect or understanding is not to be ascribed to the Deity, and that our most perfect worship of him consists, not in acts of veneration, reverence, gratitude or love; but in a certain mysterious self-annihilation or total extinction of all our faculties. These ideas are, perhaps, too far stretched; but still it must be acknowledged, that, by representing the Deity as so intelligible, and comprehensible, and so similar to a human mind,[17] we are guilty of the grossest and most narrow partiality, and make our selves the model of the whole universe.

[[18] All the *sentiments* of the human mind, gratitude, resentment, love, friendship, approbation, blame, pity, emulation, envy, have a plain reference to the state and situation of man, and are calculated for preserving the existence, and promoting the activity of such a being in such circumstances. It seems therefore unreasonable to transfer such sentiments to a supreme existence, or to suppose him actu-

[17][and so similar to a human mind *added*]
[18][This concluding paragraph in brackets is added, with marks to indicate point of insertion, on lower part of the last page of Part III, and continued on an otherwise blank sheet.]

ated by them; and the phenomena, besides, of the universe will not support us in such a theory. All our *ideas,* derived from the senses, are confessedly false and illusive; and cannot, therefore, be supposed to have place in a supreme intelligence: And as the ideas of internal sentiment, added to those of the external senses, compose the whole furniture of human understanding, we may conclude, that none of the *materials* of thought are in any respect similar in the human and in the divine intelligence. Now, as to the *manner* of thinking; how can we make any comparison between them, or suppose them any wise resembling? Our thought is fluctuating, uncertain, fleeting, successive, and compounded; and were we to remove these circumstances, we absolutely annihilate its essence, and it would, in such a case, be an abuse of terms to apply to it the name of thought or reason. At least, if it appear more pious and respectful (as it really is still to retain these terms, when we mention the supreme Being, we ought to acknowledge, that their meaning, in that case, is totally incomprehensible; and that the infirmities of our nature do not permit us to reach any ideas, which in the least[19] correspond to the ineffable sublimity of the divine attributes.] . . .

PART V

But to show you still more inconveniences, continued Philo, in your anthropomorphism; please to take a new survey of your principles. *Like effects prove like causes.* This is the experimental argument; and this, you say too, is the sole theological[20] argument. Now it is certain, that the liker the effects are, which are seen, and the liker the causes, which are inferred, the stronger is the argument. Every departure on either side diminishes the probability, and renders the experiment less conclusive. You cannot doubt of[21] this principle: Neither ought you to reject its consequences.

All the new discoveries in astronomy, which prove the immense grandeur and magnificence of the works of nature, are so many additional arguments for a Deity, according to the true system of theism: But according to your hypothesis of experimental theism,[22] they become so many objections, by removing the effect still farther from all resemblance to the effects of human art and contrivance. For if Lucretius,[23] even following the old system of the world, could exclaim,

> Quis regere immensi summam, quis habere profundi
> Indu manu validas potis est moderanter habenas?
> Quis pariter cœlos omnes convertere? et omnes
> Ignibus ætheriis terras suffire feraces?
> Omnibus inve locis esse omni tempore præsto?

---

[19][in the least *added*]
[20][theological *for* religious]
[21][doubt of *for* deny]
[22][of experimental theism *added*]
[23]Lib. II, 1095 ["Who can rule the sum, who hold in his hand with controlling force the strong reins, of the immeasurable deep? who can at once make all the different heavens to roll and warm with ethereal fires all the fruitful earths, or be present in all places at all times" (Munro's translation).]

If *Tully*[24] esteemed this reasoning so natural, as to put it into the mouth of his Epicurean. *Quibus enim oculis animi intueri potuit vester Plato fabricam illam tanti operis, qua construi a Deo alque ædificari mundum facit? quæ molitio? quæ ferramenta? qui vectes? quæ machinæ? qui ministri tanti muneris fuerunt? quemadmodum autem obedire et arere voluntati architecti aer, ignis, aqua, terra potuerunt?* If this argument, I say, had any force in former ages; how much greater must it have at present; when the bounds of nature are so infinitely enlarged, and such a magnificent scene is opened to us? It is still more unreasonable to form our idea of so unlimited a cause from our experience of the narrow productions of human design and invention.

The discoveries by microscopes, as they open a new universe in miniature, are still objections, according to you; arguments, according to me. The farther we push our researches of this kind, we are still led to infer the universal cause of All to be vastly different from mankind, or from any object of human experience and observation.

And what say you to the discoveries in anatomy, chemistry, botany? . . . These surely are no objections, replied Cleanthes: They only discover new instances of art and contrivance. It is still the image of mind reflected on us from unnumerable objects. Add, a mind *like the human,* said Philo. I know of no other, replied Cleanthes. And the liker the better, insisted Philo. To be sure, said Cleanthes.

Now, Cleanthes, said Philo, with an air of alacrity and triumph, mark the consequences. *First,* By this method of reasoning, you renounce all claim to infinity in any of the attributes of the Deity. For as the cause ought only to be proportioned to the effect, and the effect, so far as it falls under our cognisance, is not infinite; what pretensions have we, upon your suppositions,[25] to ascribe that attribute to the divine Being? You will still insist, that, by removing him so much from all similarity to human creatures, we give into the most arbitrary hypothesis, and at the same time weaken all proofs of his existence.

Secondly, You have no reason, on your theory, for ascribing perfection to the Deity, even in his finite capacity; or for supposing him free from every error, mistake, or incoherence in his undertakings. There are many inexplicable difficulties in the works of nature, which, if we allow a perfect Author to be proved *a priori,* are easily solved, and become only seeming difficulties, from the narrow capacity of man, who cannot trace infinite relations. But according to your method of reasoning, these difficulties become all real; and perhaps will be insisted on, as new instances of likeness to human art and contrivance. At least, you must acknowledge, that it is impossible for us to tell, from our limited views, whether this system contains any great faults, or deserves any considerable praise, if

---

[24]*De Nat[ura] Deor[um]*, Lib. I [8. "For with what eyes of the mind could your Plato have beheld that workshop of such stupendous toil, in which he represents the world as having been put together and built by God? How was so vast an undertaking set about? What tools, what levers, what machines, what servants, were employed in so great a work? How came air, fire, water, and earth to obey and submit to the architect's will?"]

[25][upon your suppositions *added*]

compared to other possible, and even real systems. Could a peasant, if the Æneid were read to him, pronounce that poem to be absolutely faultless, or even assign to it its proper rank among the productions of human wit; he, who had never seen any other production?

[[26]But were this world ever so perfect a production, it must still remain uncertain, whether all the excellencies of the work can justly be ascribed to the workman. If we survey a ship, what an exalted idea must we form of the ingenuity of the carpenter, who framed so complicated, useful, and beautiful a machine? And what surprise must we entertain, when we find him a stupid mechanic, who imitated others, and copied an art, which, through a long succession of ages, after multiplied trials, mistakes, corrections, deliberations, and controversies, had been gradually improving? Many worlds might have been botched and bungled, throughout an eternity, ere this system was struck out: Much labour lost: Many fruitless trials made: And a slow, but continued improvement carried on during infinite ages in the art of world-making. In such subjects, who can determine, where the truth; nay, who can conjecture where the probability, lies; amidst a great number of hypotheses which may be proposed, and a still greater number which may be imagined?]

And what shadow of an argument, continued Philo, can you produce, from your hypothesis, to prove the unity of the Deity? A great number of men join in building a house or ship, in rearing a city, in framing a commonwealth: Why may not several Deities combine in contriving and framing a world? This is only so much greater similarity to human affairs. By sharing the work among several, we may so much farther limit the attributes of each, and get rid of that extensive power and knowledge, which must be supposed in one Deity, and which, according to you, can only serve to weaken the proof of his existence. And if such foolish, such vicious creatures as man can yet often unite in framing and executing one plan; how much more those Deities or Dæmons, whom we may suppose several degrees more perfect?

[To multiply causes, without necessity, is indeed contrary to true philosophy: But this principle applies not to the present case. Were one Deity antecedently proved by your theory, who were possessed of every attribute requisite to the production of the universe; it would be needless, I own (though not absurd) to suppose any other Deity existent. But while it is still a question, whether all these attributes are united in one subject, or dispersed among several independent Beings: By what phenomena in nature can we pretend to decide the controversy? Where we see a body raised in a scale, we are sure that there is in the opposite scale, however concealed from sight, some counterpoising weight equal to it: But it is still allowed to doubt, whether that weight be an aggregate of several distinct bodies, or one uniform united mass. And if the weight requisite very much exceeds any thing which we have ever seen conjoined in any single body, the former supposition becomes still more probable and natural. An intelligent Being of such vast power and capacity, as is necessary to produce the universe, or, to speak in the language of ancient philosophy, so prodigious an animal, exceeds all analogy, and even comprehension.]

---

[26][This paragraph, and the paragraph below it, in square brackets, are added on the last page of Part V, with marks to indicate points of insertion.]

But farther, Cleanthes; men are mortal, and renew their species by generation; and this is common to all living creatures. The two great sexes of male and female, says Milton, animate the world. Why must this circumstance, so universal, so essential, be excluded from those numerous and limited Deities? Behold then the theogony of ancient times brought back upon us.

And why not become a perfect anthropomorphite? Why not assert the Deity or Deities to be corporeal, and to have eyes, a nose, mouth, ears, etc.? Epicurus maintained, that no man had ever seen reason but in a human figure; therefore the gods must have a human figure. And this argument, which is deservedly so much ridiculed by Cicero,[27] becomes, according to you, solid and philosophical.

In a word, Cleanthes, a man, who follows your hypothesis, is able, perhaps, to assert, or conjecture, that the universe, sometime, arose from something like[28] design: But beyond that position he cannot ascertain one single circumstance, and is left afterwards to fix every point of his theology, by the utmost licence of fancy and hypothesis. This world, for aught he knows, is very faulty and imperfect, compared to a superior standard; and was only the first rude essay of some infant Deity, who afterwards abandoned it, ashamed of his lame performance; it is the work only of some dependent, inferior Deity; and is the object of decision to his superiors: it is the production of old age and dotage in some superannuated Deity; and ever since his death, has run on at adventures, from the first impulse and active force, which it received from him. . . . You justly give signs of horror, Demea, at these strange suppositions: But these, and a thousand more of the same kind, are Cleanthes's suppositions, not mine. From the moment the attributes of the Deity are supposed finite, all these have place. And I cannot, for my part, think, that so wild and unsettled a system of theology is, in any respect, preferable to none at all.

These suppositions I absolutely disown, cried Cleanthes: They strike me, however, with no horror; especially, when proposed in that rambling way in which they drop from you. On the contrary, they give me pleasure, when I see, that, by the utmost indulgence of your imagination, you never get rid of the hypothesis of design in the universe; but are obliged, at every turn, to have recourse to it. To this concession I adhere steadily; and this I regard as a sufficient foundation for religion.

PART VI

It must be a slight fabric, indeed, said Demea, which can be erected on so tottering a foundation. While we are uncertain, whether there is one Deity or many; whether the Deity or Deities, to whom we owe our existence, be perfect or imperfect, subordinate or supreme, dead or alive; what trust or confidence can we repose in them? What devotion or worship address to them? What veneration or obedience pay them? To all the purposes of life, the theory of religion becomes altogether useless:

---

[27][Cicero *for* Divines]
[28][something like *for* some kind of]

And even with regard to speculative consequences, its uncertainty, according to you, must render it totally precarious and unsatisfactory.

To render it still more unsatisfactory, said Philo, there occurs to me another hypothesis, which must acquire an air of probability from the method of reasoning so much insisted on by Cleanthes. That like effects arise from like causes: This principle he supposes the foundation of all religion. But there is another principle of the same kind, no less certain, and derived from the same source of[29] experience; that where several known circumstances are *observed* to be similar, the unknown will[30] also be *found* similar. Thus, if we see the limbs of a human body, we conclude, that it is also attended with a human head, though hid from us. Thus, if we see, through a chink in a wall, a small part of the sun, we conclude, that, were the wall removed, we should see the whole body.[31] In short, this method of reasoning is so obvious and familiar, that no scruple can ever be made with regard to its solidity.

Now if we survey the universe, so far as it falls under our knowledge, it bears a great resemblance to an animal or organized body, and seems actuated with a like principle of life and motion. A continual circulation of matter in it produces no disorder: A continual waste in every part is incessantly repaired: The closest sympathy is perceived throughout the entire system: And each part or member, in performing its proper offices, operates both to its own preservation and to that of the whole. The world, therefore, I infer, is an animal, and the Deity is the soul of the world, actuating it, and actuated by it.

You have too much learning, Cleanthes, to be at all surprised at this opinion, which, you know, was maintained by almost all the theists of antiquity, and chiefly prevails in their discourses and reasonings. For though sometimes the ancient philosophers reason from final causes, as if they thought the world the workmanship of God; yet it appears rather their favourite notion to consider it as his body, whose organization renders it subservient to him. And it must be confessed, that as the universe resembles more a human body than it does the works of human art and contrivance; if our limited analogy could ever, with any propriety, be extended to the whole of nature, the inference seems juster in favour of the ancient than the modern theory.

There are many other advantages too, in the former theory, which recommended it to the ancient theologians. Nothing more repugnant to all their notions, because nothing more repugnant to common experience, than mind without body; a mere spiritual substance, which fell not under their senses nor comprehension, and of which they had not observed one single instance throughout all nature. Mind and body they knew, because they felt both: An order, arrangement, organization, or internal machinery in both they likewise knew, after the same manner: And it could not but seem reasonable to transfer this experience to the universe, and to

---

[29][practice and *omitted*]

[30][will *for* must]

[31][*This sentence has been substituted for:* Thus, if we hear, in the dark, reason and sense delivered in an articulate voice, we infer, that there is also present a human figure, which we shall discover on the return of light. *There is also, on the margin, scored out, the words:* If we see from a distance the buildings of a city, we infer that they contain inhabitants whom we shall discover on our approach to them.]

suppose the divine mind and body to be also coeval, and to have, both of them, order and arrangement naturally inherent in them, and inseparable from them.

Here therefore is a new species of anthropomorphism, Cleanthes, on which you may deliberate; and a theory which seem not liable to any considerable difficulties. You are too much superior surely to *systematical prejudices,* to find any more difficulty in supposing an animal body to be, originally, of itself, or from unknown causes, possessed of order and organization, than in supposing a similar order to belong[32] to mind. But the *vulgar prejudice,* that body and mind ought always to accompany each other, ought not, one should think, to be entirely neglected; since it is founded on *vulgar experience,* the only guide which you profess to follow in all these theological inquiries. And if you assert, that our limited experience is an unequal standard, by which to judge of the unlimited extent of nature; you entirely abandon your own hypothesis, and must thenceforward adopt our mysticism, as you call it, and admit of the absolute incomprehensibility of the divine nature.[33]

This theory, I own, replied Cleanthes, has never before occurred to me, though a pretty natural one; and I cannot readily, upon so short an examination and reflection, deliver any opinion with regard to it. You are very scrupulous, indeed, said Philo; were I to examine any system of yours, I should not have acted with half that caution and reserve, in starting objections and difficulties to it. However, if any thing occur to you, you will oblige us by proposing it.

Why then, replied Cleanthes, it seems to me that, though the world does, in many circumstances, resemble an animal body; yet is the analogy also effective in many circumstances, the most material: No organs of sense; no seat of thought or reason; no one precise origin of motion and action. In short, it seems to bear a stronger resemblance to a vegetable than to an animal; and your inference would be so far inconclusive in favour of the soul of the world.

But in the next place, your theory seems to imply the eternity of the world; and that is a principle which, I think, can be refuted by the strongest reasons and probabilities. I shall suggest an argument to this purpose, which, I believe, has not been insisted on by any writer. Those, who reason from the late origin of arts and sciences, though their inference wants not force, may perhaps be refuted by considerations derived from the nature of human society, which is in continual revolution between ignorance and knowledge, liberty and slavery, riches and poverty; so that it is impossible for us, from our limited experience, to foretell with assurance what events may or may not be expected. Ancient learning and history seem to have been in great danger of entirely perishing after the inundation of the barbarous nations; and had these convulsions continued a little longer, or been a little more violent, we should not probably have now known what passed in the world a few centuries before us. Nay, were it not for the superstition of the Popes, who preserved a little jargon of Latin, in order to support the appearance of an ancient and universal church, that tongue must have been utterly lost: In which case, the Western world, being totally barbarous, would not have been in a fit disposition for receiving the Greek language and learning, which was conveyed to them after the sacking of

---

[32][order to belong *for* principle belonging]

[33][This last sentence scored out, with note on the margin: "Print this sentence though eraz'd."]

Constantinople. When learning and books had been[34] extinguished, even the
mechanical arts would have fallen considerably to decay; and it is easily imagined,
that fable or tradition might ascribe to them a much later origin than the true one.
This vulgar[35] argument, therefore, against the eternity of the world, seems a little
precarious.

But here appears to be the foundation of a better argument. Lucullus was the
first that brought cherry-trees from Asia to Europe; though that tree thrives so well
in many European climates, that it grows in the woods without any culture. Is it
possible, that, throughout a whole eternity, no European had ever passed into Asia,
and thought of transplanting so delicious a fruit into his own country? Or if the tree
was once transplanted and propagated, how could it ever afterwards perish?
Empires may rise and fall; liberty and slavery succeed alternately; ignorance and
knowledge give place to each other; but the cherry-tree will still remain in the
woods of Greece, Spain and Italy, and will never be affected by the revolutions of
human society.

It is not two thousand years since vines were transplanted into France; though
there is no climate in the world more favourable to them. It is not three centuries
since horses, cows, sheep, swine, dogs, corn, were known in America. Is it possible, that, during the revolutions of a whole eternity, there never arose a Columbus,
who might open the communication between Europe and that continent? We may
as well imagine, that all men would wear stockings for ten thousand years, and
never have the sense to think of garters to tie them. All these seem convincing
proofs of the youth, or rather infancy, of the world; as being founded on the operation of principles more constant and steady than those by which human society is
governed and directed. Nothing less than a total convulsion of the elements will
ever destroy all the European animals and vegetables, which are now to be found
in the Western world.

And what argument have you against such convulsions? replied Philo.
Strong and almost incontestable proofs may be traced over the whole earth, that
every part of this globe has continued for many ages entirely covered with water.
And though order were supposed inseparable from matter, and inherent in it; yet
may matter be susceptible of many and great revolutions, through the endless
periods of eternal duration. The incessant change, to which every part of it is subject, seem to intimate some such general transformations; though at the same
time, it is observable, that all the changes and corruptions, of which we have ever
had experience, are but passages from one state of order to another; nor can matter ever rest in total deformity and confusion. What we see in the parts, we may
infer in the whole; at least, that is the method of reasoning on which you rest
your whole theory. And were I obliged to defend any particular system of this
nature (which I never willingly should do), I esteem none more plausible than
that which ascribes an eternal, inherent principle of order to the world;[36] though
attended with great and continual revolutions and alterations. This at once solves

---

[34][totally *omitted*]
[35][vulgar *for* common]
[36][to the world *for* in matter]

all difficulties;[37] and if the solution, by being so general,[38] is not entirely complete and satisfactory, it is, at least, a theory, that we must, sooner or later, have recourse to, whatever system we embrace. How could things have been as they are, were there not an original, inherent principle of order somewhere, in thought or in matter? And it is very[39] indifferent to which of these we give the preference. Chance has no place, on any hypothesis, sceptical or religious.[40] Every thing is surely governed by steady, inviolable laws. And were the inmost essence of things laid open to us, we should then discover a scene, of which, at present, we can have no idea. Instead of admiring the order of natural beings, we should clearly see, that it was absolutely impossible for them, in the smallest article, ever to admit of any other disposition.

Were any one inclined to revive the ancient Pagan Theology, which maintained, as we learn from Hesiod,[41] that this globe was governed by 30,000 Deities, who arose from the unknown powers of nature: You would naturally object, Cleanthes, that nothing is gained by this hypothesis, and that it is as easy to suppose all men and animals, beings more numerous, but less perfect, to have sprung immediately from a like origin. Push the same inference a step farther; and you will find a numerous society of Deities as explicable as one universal Deity, who possesses, within himself, the powers and perfections of the whole society. All these systems, then, of scepticism, polytheism, and theism, you must allow, on your principles, to be on a like footing,[42] and that no one of them has any advantages over the others. You may thence learn the fallacy of your principles.

The Argument from Design

Richard G. Swinburne

The object of this paper[1] is to show that there are no valid formal objections to the argument from design, so long as the argument is articulated with sufficient care. In particular I wish to analyse Hume's attack on the argument in *Dialogues Concerning Natural Religion* and to show that none of the formal objections made therein by Philo have any validity against a carefully articulated version of the argument.

The argument from design is an argument from the order or regularity of things in the world to a god or, more precisely, a very powerful free non-embodied rational

---

[37][solves all difficulties *for* answers all questions]
[38][by being so general, is not *for* be not]
[39][is very *for* seems]
[40][(1) *Originally:* Chance it is ridiculous to maintain on any hypothesis, (2) *Altered to:* Chance, or what is the same thing liberty, seems not to have place on any hypothesis, sceptical or religious. (3) *Finally revised as above.*]
[41][which maintained . . . Hesiod *for* mentioned by Varro]
[42][on a like footing *for* alike explicable]

Source: Philosophy, 43, 1968, 199–212.

agent, who is responsible for that order. By a body I understand a part of the material universe subject, at any rate partially, to an agent's direct control, to be contrasted with other parts not thus subject. An agent's body marks the limits to what he can directly control; he can only control other parts of the universe by moving his body. An agent who could directly control any part of the universe would not be embodied. Thus ghosts, if they existed, would be non-embodied agents, because there are no particular pieces of matter subject to their direct control, but any piece of matter may be so subject. I use the word "design" in such a way that it is not analytic that if anything evinces design, an agent designed it, and so it becomes a synthetic question whether the design of the world shows the activity of a designer.

The argument, taken by itself, as was admitted in the *Dialogues* by Cleanthes the proponent of the argument, does not show that the designer of the world is omnipotent, omniscient, totally good, etc. Nor does it show that he is the God of Abraham, Isaac, and Jacob. To make these points, further arguments would be needed. The isolation of the argument from design from the web of Christian apologetic is perhaps a somewhat unnatural step, but necessary in order to analyse its structure. My claim is that the argument does not commit any formal fallacy, and by this I mean that it keeps to the canons of argument about matters of fact and does not violate any of them. It is, however, an argument by analogy. It argues from an analogy between the order of the world and the products of human art to a god responsible for the former, in some ways similar to man who is responsible for the latter. And even if there are no formal fallacies in the argument, one unwilling to admit the conclusion might still claim that the analogy was too weak and remote for him to have to admit it, that the argument gave only negligible support to the conclusion which remained improbable. In defending the argument I will leave to the objector this way of escape from its conclusion.

I will begin by setting forward the argument from design in a more careful and precise way than Cleanthes did.

There are in the world two kinds of regularity or order, and all empirical instances of order are such because they evince one or other or both kinds of order. These are the regularities of co-presence or spatial order, and regularities of succession, or temporal order. Regularities of co-presence are patterns of spatial order at some one instant of time. An example of a regularity of co-presence would be a town with all its roads at right angles to each other, or a section of books in a library arranged in alphabetical order of authors. Regularities of succession are simple patterns of behaviour of objects, such as their behaviour in accordance with the laws of nature—for example, Newton's law of gravitation, which holds universally to a very high degree of approximation, that all bodies attract each other with forces proportional to the product of their masses and inversely proportional to the square of their distance apart.

Many of the striking examples of order in the world evince an order which is the result both of a regularity of co-presence and of a regularity of succession. A working car consists of many parts so adjusted to each other that it follows the instructions of the driver delivered by his pulling and pushing a few levers and buttons and turning a wheel to take passengers whither he wishes. Its order arises because its parts are so arranged at some instant (regularity of co-presence) that, the laws of nature being as they are (regularity of succession), it brings about the result neatly and efficiently. The order of living animals and plants likewise results from regularities of both types.

Men who marvel at the order of the world may marvel at either or both of the regularities of co-presence and of succession. The men of the eighteenth century, that great century of "reasonable religion," were struck almost exclusively by the regularities of co-presence. They marvelled at the design and orderly operations of animals and plants; but since they largely took for granted the regularities of succession, what struck them about the animals and plants, as to a lesser extent about machines made by men, was the subtle and coherent arrangement of their millions of parts. Paley's *Natural Theology* dwells mainly on details of comparative anatomy, on eyes and ears and muscles and bones arranged with minute precision so as to operate with high efficiency, and Hume's Cleanthes produces the same kind of examples: "Consider, anatomise the eye, survey its structure and contrivance, and tell me from your own feeling, if the idea of a contriver does not immediately flow in upon you with a force like that of sensation."[2]

Those who argue from the existence of regularities of co-presence other than those produced by men to the existence of a god who produced them are, however, in many respects on slippery ground when compared with those who rely for their premises on regularities of succession. We shall see several of these weaknesses later in considering Hume's objections to the argument, but it is worth while noting two of them at the outset. First, although the world contains many striking regularities of co-presence (some few of which are caused by human agency), it also contains many examples of spatial disorder. The uniform distribution of the galactic clusters is a marvellous example of spatial order, but the arrangement of trees in an African jungle is a marvellous example of spatial disorder. Although the proponent of the argument may then proceed to argue that in an important sense or from some point of view (e.g., utility to man) the order vastly exceeds the disorder, he has to argue for this in-no-way-obvious proposition.

Secondly the proponent of the argument runs the risk that the regularities of co-presence may be explained in terms of something else by a normal scientific explanation[3] in a way that the regularities of succession could not possibly be. A scientist could show that a regularity of co-presence R arose from an apparently disordered state D by means of the normal operation of the laws of nature. This would not entirely "explain away" the regularity of co-presence, because the proponent of this argument from design might then argue that the apparently disordered state D really had a latent order, being the kind of state which, when the laws of nature operate, turns into a manifestly ordered one. As long as only few of the physically possible states of apparent disorder were states of latent order, the existence of many states of latent order would be an important contingent fact which

[2]David Hume, *Dialogues Concerning Natural Religion,* ed. H. D. Aiken (New York, 1948), p. 28.
[3]I understand by a "normal scientific explanation" one conforming to the pattern of deductive or statistical explanation utilised in paradigm empirical sciences such as physics and chemistry, elucidated in recent years by Hempel, Braithwaite, Popper, and others. Although there are many uncertain points about scientific explanation, those to which I appeal in the text are accepted by all philosophers of science.

could form a premiss for an argument from design. But there is always the risk that scientists might show that most states of apparent disorder were states of latent order, that is, that if the world lasted long enough considerable order must emerge from whichever of many initial states it began. If a scientist showed that, he would have explained by normal scientific explanation the existence of regularities of co-presence in terms of something completely different. The eighteenth-century proponents of the argument from design did not suspect this danger, and hence the devastating effect of Darwin's Theory of Evolution by Natural Selection on those who accepted their argument. For Darwin showed that the regularities of co-presence of the animal and plant kingdoms had evolved by natural processes from an apparently disordered state and would have evolved equally from many other apparently disordered states. Whether all regularities of co-presence can be fully explained in this kind of way no one yet knows, but the danger remains for the proponent of an argument from design of this kind that they can be.

However, those who argue from the operation of regularities of succession other than those produced by men to the existence of a god who produces them do not run into either of these difficulties. Regularities of succession (other than those produced by men), unlike regularities of co-presence, are all-pervasive. Simple natural laws rule almost all successions of events. Nor can regularities of succession be given a normal scientific explanation in terms of something else. For the normal scientific explanation of the operation of a regularity of succession is in terms of the operation of a yet more general regularity of succession. Note too that a normal scientific explanation of the existence of regularities of co-presence in terms of something different, if it can be provided, is explanation in terms of regularities of succession.

For these reasons the proponent of the argument from design does much better to rely for his premiss more on regularities of succession. St. Thomas Aquinas, wiser than the men of the eighteenth century, did just this. He puts forward an argument from design as his fifth and last way to prove the existence of God, and gives his premiss as follows:

"The fifth way is based on the guidedness of nature. An orderedness of actions to an end is observed in all bodies obeying natural laws, even when they lack awareness. For their behaviour hardly ever varies, and will practically always turn out well; which shows that they truly tend to a goal, and do not merely hit it by accident."[4] If we ignore any value judgment in "practically always turn out well," St. Thomas' argument is an argument from regularities of succession.

The most satisfactory premiss for the argument from design is then the operation of regularities of succession other than those produced by men, that is, the operation of natural laws. Almost all things almost always obey simple natural laws and so behave in a strikingly regular way. Given the premiss, what is our justification for proceeding to the conclusion that a very powerful free non-embodied rational agent is responsible for their behaving in that way? The justification which Aquinas gives is that "Nothing . . . that lacks awareness tends to a goal, except under the direction of someone with awareness and with understanding; the arrow,

---

[4]St. Thomas Aquinas, *Summa Theologiae*, Ia.2.3. Trans. Timothy McDermott, o.p. (London, 1964).

for example, requires an archer. Everything in nature, therefore, is directed to its goal by someone with understanding, and this we call 'God'."[5] A similar argument has been given by many religious apologists since Aquinas, but clearly as it stands it is guilty of the grossest *petitio principii*. Certainly *some* things which tend to a goal, tend to a goal because of a direction imposed upon them by someone "with awareness and with understanding." Did not the archer place the arrow and pull the string in a certain way the arrow would not tend to its goal. But whether *all* things which tend to a goal tend to a goal for this reason is the very question at issue, and that they do cannot be used as a premiss to prove the conclusion. We must therefore reconstruct the argument in a more satisfactory way.

The structure of any plausible argument from design can only be that the existence of a god responsible for the order in the world is a hypothesis well-confirmed on the basis of the evidence—viz., that contained in the premiss which we have now stated, and better confirmed than any other hypothesis. I shall begin by showing that there can be no other possible explanation for the operation of natural laws than the activity of a god, and then see to what extent the hypothesis is well confirmed on the basis of the evidence.

Almost all phenomena can, as we have seen, be explained by a normal scientific explanation in terms of the operation of natural laws on preceding states. There is, however, one other way of explaining natural phenomena, and that is explaining in terms of the rational choice of a free agent. When a man marries Jane rather than Anne, becomes a solicitor rather than a barrister, kills rather than shows mercy after considering arguments in favour of each course, he brings about a state of the world by his free and rational choice. To all appearances this is an entirely different way whereby states of the world may come about than through the operation of laws of nature on preceding states. Someone may object that it is necessary that physiological or other scientific laws operate in order for the agent to bring about effects. My answer is that certainly it is necessary that such laws operate in order for effects brought about directly by the agent to have ulterior consequences. But unless there are some effects which the agent brings about directly without the operation of scientific laws' acting on preceding physical states bringing them about, then these laws and states could fully explain the effects and there would be no need to refer in explaining them to the rational choice of an agent. True, the apparent freedom and rationality of the human will *may* prove an illusion. Man may have no more option what to do than a machine and be guided by an argument no more than is a piece of iron. But this has never yet been shown, and, in the absence of good philosophical and scientific argument to show it, I assume, what is apparent, that when a man acts by free and rational choice, his agency is the operation of a different kind of causality from that of scientific laws. The free choice of a rational agent is the only way of accounting for natural phenomena other than the way of normal scientific explanation, which is recognised as such by all men and has not been reduced to normal scientific explanation.

Almost all regularities of succession are the result of the normal operation of scientific laws. But to say this is simply to say that these regularities are instances

---

[5]*Ibid.*

of more general regularities. The operation of the most fundamental regularities clearly cannot be given a normal scientific explanation. If their operation is to receive an explanation and not merely to be left as a brute fact, that explanation must therefore be in terms of the rational choice of a free agent. What, then, are grounds for adopting this hypothesis, given that it is the only possible one?

The grounds are that we can explain some few regularities of succession as produced by rational agents and that the other regularities cannot be explained except in this way. Among the typical products of a rational agent acting freely are regularities both of co-presence and of succession. The alphabetical order of books on a library shelf is the result of the activity of the librarian who chose to arrange them thus. The order of the cards of a pack by suits and seniority in each suit is the result of the activity of the cardplayer who arranged them thus. Among examples of regularities of succession produced by men are the notes of a song sung by a singer or the movements of a dancer's body when he performs a dance in time with the accompanying instrument. Hence, knowing that some regularities of succession have such a cause, we postulate that they all have. An agent produces the celestial harmony like a man who sings a song. But at this point an obvious difficulty arises. The regularities of succession, such as songs which are produced by men, are produced by agents of comparatively small power, whose bodies we can locate. If an agent is responsible for the operation of the laws of nature, he must act directly on the whole universe, as we act directly on our bodies. Also he must be of immense power and intelligence compared with men. Hence he can only be somewhat similar to men, having, like them, intelligence and freedom of choice, yet unlike them in the degree of these and in not possessing a body. For a body, as I have distinguished it earlier, is a part of the universe subject to an agent's direct control, to be contrasted with other parts not thus subject. The fact that we are obliged to postulate on the basis of differences in the effects, differences in the causes, men and the god, weakens the argument. How much it weakens it depends on how great these differences are.

Our argument thus proves to be an argument by analogy and to exemplify a pattern common in scientific inference. As are caused by Bs. A*s are similar to As. Therefore—given that there is no more satisfactory explanation of the existence of A*s—they are produced by B*s similar to Bs. B*s are postulated to be similar in all respects to Bs except in so far as shown otherwise, viz., except in so far as the dissimilarities between As and A*s force us to postulate a difference. A well-known scientific example of this type of inference is as follows. Certain pressures (As) on the walls of containers are produced by billiard balls (Bs) with certain motions. Similar pressures (A*s) are produced on the walls of containers which contain not billiard balls but gases. Therefore, since we have no better explanation of the existence of the pressures, gases consist of particles (B*s) similar to billiard balls except in certain respects—e.g., size. By similar arguments, scientists have argued for the existence of many unobservables. Such an argument becomes weaker in so far as the properties which we are forced to attribute to the B*s because of the differences between the As and the A*s become different from those of the Bs. Nineteenth-century physicists postulated the existence of an elastic solid, the aether, to account for the propagation of light. But the way in which light was propagated turned out to have such differences (despite the similarities) from the way in which waves in solids are normally propagated that the physicists had to say that if there was an aether it had very many peculiar properties not possessed by normal liquids or solids. Hence they concluded that the argument for its existence was very weak. The proponent of the argument from design stresses the similarities between the regularities of succession produced by man and those which are laws of nature and so between men and the agent which he postulates as responsible for the laws of nature. The opponent of the argument stresses the dissimilarities. The degree of support which the conclusion obtains from the evidence depends on how great the similarities are.

The degree of support for the conclusion of an argument from analogy does not, however, depend merely on the similarities between the types of evidence but on the degree to which the resulting theory makes explanation of empirical matters more simple and coherent. In the case of the argument from design, the conclusion has an enormous simplifying effect on explanations of empirical matters. For if the conclusion is true, if a very powerful non-embodied rational agent is responsible for the operation of the laws of nature, then normal scientific explanation would prove to be personal explanation. That is, explanation of some phenomenon in terms of the operation of a natural law would ultimately be an explanation in terms of the operation of an agent. Hence (given an initial arrangement of matter) the principles of explanation of phenomena would have been reduced from two to one. It is a basic principle of explanation that we should postulate as few as possible kinds of explanation. To take a more mundane example—if we have as possible alternatives to explain physical phenomena by the operation of two kinds of force, the electromagnetic and the gravitational, and to explain physical phenomena in terms of the operation of only one kind of force, the gravitational, we ought always—*ceteris paribus*—to prefer the latter alternative. Since, as we have seen, we are obliged, at any rate at present, to use explanation in terms of the free choice of a rational agent in explaining many empirical phenomena, then if the amount of similarity between the order in the universe not produced by human agents and that produced by human agents makes it at all plausible to do so, we ought to postulate that an agent is responsible for the former as well as for the latter. So then in so far as regularities of succession produced by the operation of natural laws are similar to those produced by human agents, to postulate that a rational agent is responsible for them would indeed provide a simple unifying and coherent explanation of natural phenomena. What is there against taking this step? Simply that celebrated principle of explanation—*entia non sunt multiplicanda praeter necessitatem*—do not add a god to your ontology unless you have to. The issue turns on whether the evidence constitutes enough of a *necessitas* to compel us to multiply entities. Whether it does depends on how strong the analogy is between the regularities of succession produced by human agents and those produced by the operation of natural laws. I do not propose to assess the strength of the analogy but only to claim that everything turns on it. I claim that the inference from natural laws to a god responsible for them is of a perfectly proper type for inference about matters of fact, and that the only issue is whether the evidence is strong enough to allow us to affirm that it is probable that the conclusion is true.

Now that I have reconstructed the argument from design in what is, I hope, a logically impeccable form, I turn to consider Hume's criticisms of it, and I shall argue that all his criticisms alleging formal fallacies in the argument do not apply to it in the form in which I have stated it. This, we shall see, is largely because the criticisms are bad criticisms of the argument in any form but also in small part because Hume directed his fire against that form of the argument which used as its premiss the existence of regularities of co-presence other than those produced by men, and did not appeal to the operation of regularities of succession. I shall begin by considering one general point which he makes only in the *Enquiry* and then consider in turn all the objections which appear on the pages of the *Dialogues*.

1. The point which appears at the beginning of Hume's discussion of the argument in section XI of the *Enquiry* is a point which reveals the fundamental weakness of Hume's sceptical position. In discussing the argument, Hume puts forward as a general principle that "when we infer any particular cause from an effect, we must proportion the one to the other, and can never be allowed to ascribe to the cause any qualities but what are exactly sufficient to produce the effect."[6] Now, it is true that Hume uses this principle mainly to show that we are not justified in inferring that the god responsible for the design of the universe is totally good, omnipotent, and omniscient. I accept, as Cleanthes did, that the argument does not by itself lead to that conclusion. But Hume's use of the principle tends to cast doubt on the validity of the argument in the weaker form in which I am discussing it, for it seems to suggest that although we may conclude that whatever produced the regularity of the world was a regularity-producing object, we cannot go further and conclude that it is an agent who acts by choice, etc., for this would be to suppose more than we need in order to account for the effect. It is, therefore, important to realise that the principle is clearly false on our normal understanding of what are the criteria of inference about empirical matters. For the universal adoption of this celebrated principle would lead to the abandonment of science. Any scientist who told us only that the cause[s] of E [are] E-producing characteristics would not add an iota to our knowledge. Explanation of matters of fact consists in postulating on reasonable grounds that the cause of an effect has certain characteristics other than those sufficient to produce the effect.

2. Two objections seem to be telescoped in the following passage of the *Dialogues*. "When two *species* of objects have always been observed to be conjoined together, I can *infer* by custom the existence of one wherever I *see* the existence of the other; and this I call an argument from experience. But how this argument can have place where the objects, as in the present case, are single, individual, without parallel or specific resemblance, may be difficult to explain."[7] One argument here seems to be that we can only infer from an observed A to an unobserved B when we have frequently observed As and Bs together, and that we cannot infer to a B unless we have actually observed other

[6]David Hume, *An Enquiry Concerning Human Understanding*, ed. L. A. Selby-Bigge (2nd ed., 1902), p. 136.
[7]*Dialogues*, p. 23.

Bs. Hence we cannot infer from regularities of succession to an unobserved god on the analogy of the connection between observed regularities and human agents, unless we have observed at other times other gods. This argument, like the first, reveals Hume's inadequate appreciation of scientific method. As we saw in the scientific examples which I cited, a more developed science than Hume knew has taught us that when observed As have a relation R to observed Bs, it is often perfectly reasonable to postulate that observed A*s, similar to As, have the same relation to unobserved and unobservable B*s similar to Bs.

3. The other objection which seems to be involved in the above passage is that we cannot reach conclusions about an object which is the only one of its kind, and, as the universe is such an object, we cannot reach conclusions about the regularities characteristic of it as a whole.[8] But cosmologists are reaching very well-tested scientific conclusions about the universe as a whole, as are physical anthropologists about the origins of our human race, even though it is the only human race of which we have knowledge and perhaps the only human race there is. The principle quoted in the objections is obviously wrong. There is no space here to analyze its errors in detail, but suffice it to point out that it becomes hopelessly confused by ignoring the fact that uniqueness is relative to description. Nothing describable is unique under all descriptions (the universe is, like the solar system, a number of material bodies distributed in empty space), and everything describable is unique under some description.

4. The next argument which we meet in the *Dialogues* is that the postulated existence of a rational agent who produces the order of the world would itself need explaining. Picturing such an agent as a mind, and a mind as an arrangement of ideas, Hume phrases the objection as follows: "a mental world or Universe of ideas requires a cause as much as does a material world or Universe of objects."[9] Hume himself provides the obvious answer to this—that it is no objection to explaining X by Y that we cannot explain Y. But then he suggests that the Y in this case, the mind, is just as mysterious as the ordered universe. Men never "thought it satisfactory to explain a particular effect by a particular cause which was no more to be accounted for than the effect itself."[10] On the contrary, scientists have always thought it reasonable to postulate entities merely to explain effects, so long as the postulated entities accounted simply and coherently for the characteristics of the effects. The existence of molecules with their characteristic behaviour was "no more to be accounted for" than observable phenomena, but the postulation of their existence gave a neat and simple explanation of a whole host of chemical and physical phenomena, and that was the justification for postulating their existence.

5. Next, Hume argues that if we are going to use the analogy of a human agent we ought to go the whole way and postulate that the god who gives order to the universe is like men in many other respects. "Why not become a perfect anthropomorphite? Why not assert the deity or deities to be corporeal, and to have

---

[8]For this argument see also *Enquiry,* pp. 147f.
[9]*Dialogues,* p. 33.
[10]*Ibid.,* p. 36.

eyes, a nose, mouths, ears, etc."[11] The argument from design is, as we have seen, an argument by analogy. All analogies break down somewhere; otherwise they would not be analogies. In saying that the relation of A to B is analogous to a relation of A* to a postulated B*, we do not claim that B* is in all respects like B, but only in such respects as to account for the existence of the relation and also in other respects except in so far as we have contrary evidence. For the activity of a god to account for the regularities, he must be free, rational, and very powerful. But it is not necessary that he, like men, should only be able to act on a limited part of the universe, a body, and by acting on that control the rest of the universe. And there is good reason to suppose that the god does not operate in this way. For, if his direct control was confined to a part of the universe, scientific laws outside his control must operate to ensure that his actions have effects in the rest of the universe. Hence the postulation of the existence of the god would not explain the operations of those laws: yet to explain the operation of all scientific laws was the point of postulating the existence of the god. The hypothesis that the god is not embodied thus explains more and explains more coherently than the hypothesis that he is embodied. Hume's objection would, however, have weight against an argument from regularities of co-presence which did not appeal to the operation of regularities of succession. For one could suppose an embodied god just as well as a disembodied god to have made the animal kingdom and then left it alone, as a man makes a machine, or, like a landscape gardener, to have laid out the galactic clusters. The explanatory force of such an hypothesis is as great as that of the hypothesis that a disembodied god did these things, and argument from analogy would suggest the hypothesis of an embodied god to be more probable. Incidentally, a god whose prior existence was shown by the existence of regularities of co-presence might now be dead, but a god whose existence was shown by the present operation of regularities of succession could not be, since the existence of an agent is contemporaneous with the temporal regularities which he produces.

6. Hume urges: why should we not postulate many gods to give order to the universe, not merely one? "A great number of men join in building a house or a ship, in rearing a city, in framing a commonwealth, why may not several deities combine in framing a world?"[12] Hume again is aware of the obvious counterobjection to his suggestion—"To multiply causes without necessity is . . . contrary to true philosophy."[13] He claims, however, that the counter-objection does not apply here, because it is an open question whether there is a god with sufficient power to put the whole universe in order. The principle, however, still applies whether or not we have prior information that a being of sufficient power exists. When postulating entities, postulate as few as possible. Always suppose only one murderer, unless the evidence forces you to suppose a second. If there were more than one deity responsible for the order of the universe, we should expect to see characteristic marks of the handiwork of different

[11]*Ibid.*, p. 40.
[12]*Ibid.*, p. 39.
[13]*Ibid.*, p. 40.

deities in different parts of the universe, just as we see different kinds of workmanship in the different houses of a city. We should expect to find an inverse square law of gravitation obeyed in one part of the universe, and in another part a law which was just short of being an inverse square law—without the difference's being explicable in terms of a more general law. But it is enough to draw this absurd conclusion to see how ridiculous the Humean objection is.

7. Hume argues that there are in the universe other things than rational agents which bestow order. "A tree bestows order and organisation on that tree which springs from it, without knowing the order; an animal in the same manner on its offspring."[14] It would, therefore, Hume argues, be equally reasonable if we are arguing from analogy, to suppose the cause of the regularities in the world "to be something similar or analogous to generation or vegetation."[15] This suggestion makes perfectly good sense if it is the regularities of co-presence which we are attempting to explain. But as analogous processes to explain regularities of succession, generation or vegetation will not do, because they only produce regularities of co-presence—and those through the operation of regularities of succession outside their control. The seed only produces the plant because of the continued operation of the laws of biochemistry.

8. The last distinct objection which I can discover in the *Dialogues* is the following. Why should we not suppose, Hume urges, that this ordered universe is a mere accident among the chance arrangements of eternal matter? In the course of eternity, matter arranges itself in all kinds of ways. We just happen to live in a period when it is characterised by order, and mistakenly conclude that matter is always ordered. Now, as Hume phrases this objection, it is directed against an argument from design which uses as its premiss the existence of the regularities of co-presence. "The continual motion of matter . . . in less than infinite transpositions must produce this economy or order, and by its very nature, that order, when once established supports itself for many ages if not to eternity."[16] Hume thus relies here partly on chance and partly on the operation of regularities of succession (the preservation of order) to account for the existence of regularities of co-presence. In so far as it relies on regularities of succession to explain regularities of co-presence, such an argument has, as we saw earlier, some plausibility. But in so far as it relies on chance, it does not—if the amount of order to be accounted for is very striking. An attempt to attribute the operation of regularities of succession to chance would not thus be very plausible. The claim would be that there are no laws of nature which always apply to matter; matter evinces in the course of eternity all kinds of patterns of behaviour; it is just chance that at the moment the states of the universe are succeeding each other in a regular way. But if we say that it is chance that in 1960 matter is behaving in a regular way, our claim becomes less and less plausible as we find that in 1961 and 1962 and so on it continues to behave in a regular way. An appeal to chance to account for order becomes less and less plausible, the

---

[14]*Ibid.*, p. 50.
[15]*Ibid.*, p. 47.
[16]*Ibid.*, p. 53.

greater the order. We would be justified in attributing a typewritten version of collected works of Shakespeare to the activity of monkeys typing eternally on eternal typewriters if we had some evidence of the existence of an infinite quantity of paper randomly covered with type, as well as the collected works. In the absence of any evidence that matter behaved irregularly at other temporal periods, we are not justified in attributing its present regular behaviour to chance.

In addition to the objections which I have stated, the *Dialogues* contain a lengthy presentation of the argument that the existence of evil in the world shows that the god who made it and gave it order is not both totally good and omnipotent. But this does not affect the argument from design which, as Cleanthes admits, does not purport to show that the designer of the universe does have these characteristics. The eight objections which I have stated are all the distinct objections to the argument from design which I can find in the *Enquiry* and in the *Dialogues,* which claim that in some formal respect the argument does not work. As well as claiming that the argument from design is deficient in some formal respect, Hume makes the point that the analogy of the order produced by men to the other order of the universe is too remote for us to postulate similar causes.[17] I have argued earlier that if there is a weakness in the argument it is here that it is to be found. The only way to deal with this point would be to start drawing the parallels or stressing the dissimilarities, and these are perhaps tasks more appropriate for the preacher and the poet than for the philosopher. The philosopher will be content to have shown that though perhaps weak, the argument has some force. How much force depends on the strength of the analogy.

Pensées *(excerpt)*

Blaise Pascal

225

Atheism shows strength of mind, but only to a certain degree.

226

Infidels, who profess to follow reason, ought to be exceedingly strong in reason. What say they then? "Do we not see," say they, "that the brutes live and die like

---

[17]See, for example, *Dialogues,* pp. 18 and 37.
Source: [1670] §§226–24, with an introduction by T.S. Eliot. New York: E.P. Dutton & Co., Inc., 1958, 63–70.

men, and Turks like Christians? They have their ceremonies, their prophets, their doctors, their saints, their monks, like us," etc. (Is this contrary to Scripture? Does it not say all this?)

If you care but little to know the truth, here is enough of it to leave you in repose. But if you desire with all your heart to know it, it is not enough; look at it in detail. This would be sufficient for a question in philosophy; but not here, where it concerns your all. And yet, after a trifling reflection of this kind, we go to amuse ourselves, etc. Let us inquire of this same religion whether it does not give a reason for this obscurity; perhaps it will teach it to us.

227

Order by dialogues.—What ought I to do? I see only darkness everywhere. Shall I believe I am nothing? Shall I believe I am God?

"All things change and succeed each other." You are mistaken; there is . . .

228

Objection of atheists: "But we have no light."

229

This is what I see and what troubles me. I look on all sides, and I see only darkness everywhere. Nature presents to me nothing which is not matter of doubt and concern. If I saw nothing there which revealed a Divinity, I would come to a negative conclusion; if I saw everywhere the signs of a Creator, I would remain peacefully in faith. But, seeing too much to deny and too little to be sure, I am in a state to be pitied; wherefore I have a hundred times wished that if a God maintains nature, she should testify to Him unequivocally, and that, if the signs she gives are deceptive, she should suppress them altogether; that she should say everything or nothing, that I might see which cause I ought to follow. Whereas in my present state, ignorant of what I am or of what I ought to do, I know neither my condition nor my duty. My heart inclines wholly to know where is the true good, in order to follow it; nothing would be too dear to me for eternity.

I envy those whom I see living in the faith with such carelessness, and who make such a bad use of a gift of which it seems to me I would make such a different use.

230

It is incomprehensible that God should exist, and it is incomprehensible that He should not exist; that the soul should be joined to the body, and that we should have no soul; that the world should be created, and that it should not be created, etc.; that original sin should be, and that it should not be.

231

Do you believe it to be impossible that God is infinite, without parts?—Yes. I wish therefore to show you an infinite and indivisible thing. It is a point moving everywhere with an infinite velocity; for it is one in all places, and is all totality in every place.

Let this effect of nature, which previously seemed to you impossible, make you know that there may be others of which you are still ignorant. Do not draw this conclusion from your experiment, that there remains nothing for you to know; but rather that there remains an infinity for you to know.

232

Infinite movement, the point which fills everything, the moment of rest; infinite without quantity, indivisible and infinite.

233

Infinite—nothing.—Our soul is cast into a body, where it finds number, time, dimension. Thereupon it reasons, and calls this nature, necessity, and can believe nothing else.

Unity joined to infinity adds nothing to it, no more than one foot to an infinite measure. The finite is annihilated in the presence of the infinite, and becomes a pure nothing. So our spirit before God, so our justice before divine justice. There is not so great a disproportion between our justice and that of God, as between unity and infinity.

The justice of God must be vast like His compassion. Now justice to the outcast is less vast, and ought less to offend our feelings than mercy towards the elect.

We know that there is an infinite, and are ignorant of its nature. As we know it to be false that numbers are finite, it is therefore true that there is an infinity in number. But we do not know what it is. It is false that it is even, it is false that it is odd; for the addition of a unit can make no change in its nature. Yet it is a number, and every number is odd or even (this is certainly true of every finite number). So we may well know that there is a God without knowing what He is. Is there not one substantial truth, seeing there are so many things which are not the truth itself?

We know then the existence and nature of the finite, because we also are finite and have extension. We know the existence of the infinite, and are ignorant of its nature, because it has extension like us, but not limits like us. But we know neither the existence nor the nature of God, because He has neither extension nor limits.

But by faith we know His existence; in glory we shall know His nature. Now, I have already shown that we may well know the existence of a thing, without knowing its nature.

Let us now speak according to natural lights.

If there is a God, He is infinitely incomprehensible, since, having neither parts nor limits, He has no affinity to us. We are then incapable of knowing either what He is or if He is. This being so, who will dare to undertake the decision of the question? Not we, who have no affinity to Him.

Who then will blame Christians for not being able to give a reason for their belief, since they profess a religion for which they cannot give a reason? They declare, in expounding it to the world, that it is a foolishness, *stultitiam;* and then you complain that they do not prove it! If they proved it, they would not keep their word; it is in lacking proofs, that they are not lacking in sense. "Yes, but although this excuses those who offer it as such, and takes away from them the blame of putting it forward without reason, it does not excuse those who receive it." Let us then examine this point, and say, "God is, or He is not." But to which side shall we incline? Reason can decide nothing here. There is an infinite chaos which separated us. A game is being played at the extremity of this infinite distance where heads or tails will turn up. What will you wager? According to reason, you can do neither the one thing nor the other; according to reason, you can defend neither of the propositions.

Do not then reprove for error those who have made a choice; for you know nothing about it. "No, but I blame them for having made, not this choice, but a choice; for again both he who chooses heads and he who chooses tails are equally at fault, they are both in the wrong. The true course is not to wager at all."

Yes; but you must wager. It is not optional. You are embarked. Which will you choose then? Let us see. Since you must choose, let us see which interests you least. You have two things to lose, the true and the good; and two things to stake, your reason and your will, your knowledge and your happiness; and your nature has two things to shun, error and misery. Your reason is no more shocked in choosing one rather than the other, since you must of necessity choose. This is one point settled. But your happiness? Let us weigh the gain and the loss in wagering that God is. Let us estimate these two chances. If you gain, you gain all; if you lose, you lose nothing. Wager, then, without hesitation that He is.— "That is very fine. Yes, I must wager; but I may perhaps wager too much."—Let us see. Since there is an equal risk of gain and of loss, if you had only to gain two lives, instead of one, you might still wager. But if there were three lives to gain, you would have to play (since you are under the necessity of playing), and you would be imprudent, when you are forced to play, not to chance your life to gain three at a game where there is an equal risk of loss and gain. But there is an eternity of life and happiness. And this being so, if there were an infinity of chances, of which one only would be for you, you would still be right in wagering one to win two, and you would act stupidly, being obliged to play, by refusing to stake one life against three at a game in which out of an infinity of chances there is one for you, if there were an infinity of an infinitely happy life to gain. But there is here an infinity of an infinitely happy life to gain, a chance of gain against a finite number of chances of loss, and what you stake is finite. It is all divided; wherever the infinite is and there is not an infinity of chances of loss against that of gain, there is no time to hesitate, you must give all. And thus, when one is forced to play, he must renounce reason to preserve his life, rather than risk it for infinite gain, as likely to happen as the loss of nothingness.

For it is no use to say it is uncertain if we will gain, and it is certain that we risk, and that the infinite distance between the *certainty* of what is staked and the *uncertainty* of what will be gained, equals the finite good which is certainly staked against the uncertain infinite. It is not so, as every player stakes a certainty to gain an uncertainty, and yet he stakes a finite certainty to gain a finite uncertainty, without transgressing against reason. There is not an infinite distance between the certainty staked and the uncertainty of the gain; that is untrue. In truth, there is an infinity between the certainty of gain and the certainty of loss. But the uncertainty of the gain is proportioned to the certainty of the stake according to the proportion of the chances of gain and loss. Hence it comes that, if there are as many risks on one side as on the other, the course is to play even; and then the certainty of the stake is equal to the uncertainty of the gain, so far is it from fact that there is an infinite distance between them. And so our proposition is of infinite force, when there is the finite to stake in a game where there are equal risks of gain and of loss, and the infinite to gain. This is demonstrable; and if men are capable of any truths, this is one.

"I confess it, I admit it. But, still, is there no means of seeing the faces of the cards?"—Yes, Scripture and the rest, etc. "Yes, but I have my hands tied and my mouth closed; I am forced to wager, and am not free. I am not released, and am so made that I cannot believe. What, then, would you have me do?"

True. But at least learn your inability to believe, since reason brings you to this, and yet you cannot believe. Endeavour then to convince yourself, not by increase of proofs of God, but by the abatement of your passions. You would like to attain faith, and do not know the way; you would like to cure yourself of unbelief, and ask the remedy for it. Learn of those who have been bound like you, and who now stake all their possessions. These are people who know the way which you would follow, and who are cured of an ill of which you would be cured. Follow the way by which they began; by acting as if they believed, taking the holy water, having masses said, etc. Even this will naturally make you believe, and deaden your acuteness.— "But this is what I am afraid of."—And why? What have you to lose?

But to show you that this leads you there, it is this which will lessen the passions, which are your stumbling-blocks.

The end of this discourse.—Now, what harm will befall you in taking this side? You will be faithful, honest, humble, grateful, generous, a sincere friend, truthful. Certainly you will not have those poisonous pleasures, glory and luxury; but will you not have others? I will tell you that you will thereby gain in this life, and that, at each step you take on this road, you will see so great certainty of gain, so much nothingness in what you risk, that you will at last recognise that you have wagered for something certain and infinite, for which you have given nothing.

"Ah! This discourse transports me, charms me," etc.

If this discourse pleases you and seems impressive, know that it is made by a man who has knelt, both before and after it, in prayer to that Being, infinite and without parts, before whom he lays all he has, for you also to lay before Him all you have for your own good and for His glory, that so strength may be given to lowliness.

234

If we must not act save on a certainty, we ought not to act on religion, for it is not certain. But how many things we do on an uncertainty, sea voyages, battles! I say then we must do nothing at all, for nothing is certain, and that there is more certainty in religion than there is as to whether we may see to-morrow; for it is not certain that we may see to-morrow, and it is certainly possible that we may not see it. We cannot say as much about religion. It is not certain that it is; but who will venture to say that it is certainly possible that it is not? Now when we work for to-morrow, and so on an uncertainty, we act reasonably; for we ought to work for an uncertainty according to the doctrine of chance which was demonstrated above.

Saint Augustine has seen that we work for an uncertainty, on sea, in battle, etc. But he has not seen the doctrine of chance which proves that we should do so. Montaigne has seen that we are shocked at a fool, and that habit is all-powerful; but he has not seen the reason of this effect.

All these persons have seen the effects, but they have not seen the causes. They are, in comparison with those who have discovered the causes, as those who have only eyes are in comparison with those who have intellect. For the effects are perceptible by sense, and the causes are visible only to the intellect. And although these effects are seen by the mind, this mind is, in comparison with the mind which sees the causes, as the bodily senses are in comparison with the intellect.

235

Rem viderunt, causam non viderunt. [We see things; we do not see causes.]

236

According to the doctrine of chance, you ought to put yourself to the trouble of searching for the truth; for if you die without worshipping the True Cause, you are lost.—"But," say you, "if He had wished me to worship Him, He would have left me signs of His will."—He has done so; but you neglect them. Seek them, therefore; it is well worth it.

237

Chances.—We must live differently in the world, according to these different assumptions: (1) that we could always remain in it; (2) that it is certain that we shall not remain here long, and uncertain if we shall remain here one hour. This last assumption is our condition.

238

What do you then promise me, in addition to certain troubles, but ten years of self-love (for ten years is the chance), to try hard to please without success?

239

Objection.—Those who hope for salvation are so far happy; but they have as a counterpoise the fear of hell.

Reply.—Who has most reason to fear hell: he who is in ignorance whether there is a hell, and who is certain of damnation if there is; or he who certainly believes there is a hell, and hopes to be saved if there is?

240

"I would soon have renounced pleasure," say they, "had I faith." For my part I tell you, "You would soon have faith, if you renounced pleasure." Now, it is for you to begin. If I could, I would give you faith. I cannot do so, nor therefore test the truth of what you say. But you can well renounce pleasure, and test whether what I say is true.

241

Order.—I would have far more fear of being mistaken, and of finding that the Christian religion was true, than of not being mistaken in believing it true.

Tout est Bien—*All is Good*

François-Marie Arouet de Voltaire

There was a fine clamor raised in the schools, and even among men who think, when Leibnitz, paraphrasing Plato, built his edifice of the best of all possible worlds and imagined that all was for the best in it. He asserted, in the north of Germany, that God could make but a single world. Plato at least had left him the

Source: Philosophical Dictionary [1974], translated with an introduction and glossary by Peter Gay. New York: Basic Books, Inc., 1962, 116–122.

liberty of making five, because there are only five solid regular bodies: the tetra-hedron, or pyramid with three faces, with uniform base, the cube, the hexahedron, the dodecahedron, the icosahedron. But since our world is not shaped like any of Plato's five bodies, he had to allow God a sixth method.

Let us leave the divine Plato to one side. Leibnitz, then, who was surely a bet-ter geometer than he, and a more profound metaphysician, did mankind the service of persuading us that we should be quite content, and that God could do no more for us; that indisputably, he necessarily chose, among all the possible choices, the best one.

"What will become of original sin?" they shouted at him. "Let it become what it may," said Leibnitz and his friends; but in public he wrote that original sin nec-essarily was a part of the best of worlds.

What! To be chased out of a place of delights, where we would have lived for-ever if we hadn't eaten an apple! What! To produce in misery miserable children, who will suffer everything, who will make others suffer everything! What! To undergo all illnesses, feel all sorrows; die in pain, and for refreshment to be burned in the eternity of centuries! Is this really the best of available lots? It is not too *good* for us; in what way can it be good for God?

Leibnitz sensed that he had no reply to this: so he made fat books in which he disagreed with himself.

To deny there is evil—that can be done laughingly by a Lucullus who is in good health and who has a good dinner with his friends and his mistress in the salon of Apollo; but let him stick his head out the window, he will see unhappy people enough; let him catch a fever, he will be unhappy himself.

I don't like to quote; that's usually thorny work: you neglect what precedes and what follows the passage you quote, and expose yourself to a thousand quarrels. Nevertheless I must quote Lactantius, Church Father, who in chapter 13 of *The Wrath of God* has Epicurus say this: "Either God wishes to expunge the evil from this world and cannot; or he can and does not wish to; or he neither can nor wishes to; or finally he wishes to and can. If he wishes to and cannot, that is impotence, which is contrary to the nature of God; if he can and does not wish to, that is wickedness, and that is no less contrary to his nature; if he neither wishes to nor can, that is wickedness and impotence at the same time; if he wishes to and can (which is the only one among these choices appropriate to God), where does the evil in this world come from?"

The argument is serious; and, indeed, Lactantius replies to it very feebly, by saying that God wishes evil, but has given us the wisdom with which to choose the good. It must be admitted that this reply is rather weak in comparison with the objection; for it supposes that God grants wisdom only through creating evil; and anyhow, our wisdom is a laughable one!

The origin of evil has always been an abyss whose bottom nobody has been able to see. It is this that reduced so many ancient philosophers and legislators to suppos-ing two principles, one good, the other bad. Among the Egyptians, Typhon was the bad principle; among the Persians, it was Arimane. It is well known that the Manicheans adopted this theology; but since these gentlemen never had conversation either with the good principle or the bad, we needn't believe every word they said.

Among the absurdities with which this world overflows, and which may be numbered among our evils, it is not a trifling one to have imagined two all-powerful beings fighting to see which of them would put more of himself into the world, and making a treaty like the two doctors in Molière: Pass me the emetic, and I'll pass you the bleeding cup.

Following the Platonists, Basilides maintained, as early as the first century of the Church, that God has assigned the creation of our world to his lowest angels, and that these, lacking skill, made things as we see them now. This theological fable collapses before the powerful objection that it is not in the nature of an all-powerful and all-wise God to have a world built by architects who know nothing about their job.

Simon, who felt the force of this objection, attempted to forestall it by saying that the angel who superintended the workshop was damned for botching his work; but burning the angel does not cure us.

Pandora's adventure among the Greeks does not answer the objection any better. The box holding all the evils, and at whose bottom hope remains, is admittedly a charming allegory; but this Pandora was made by Vulcan only to revenge himself on Prometheus, who had fashioned a man from mud.

The Indians did no better: after God created man, he gave him a drug which assured him everlasting health; man loaded his donkey with the drug; the donkey was thirsty; the serpent showed him a fountain, and while the donkey drank the serpent took the drug for himself.

The Syrians imagined that after man and woman had been created in the fourth sky, they took it into their heads to eat a pancake instead of the ambrosia which was their natural food. The ambrosia was exhaled through the pores; but after they had eaten the pancake, they had to go to the toilet. The man and woman asked an angel to show them where the bathroom was. "Do you see," the angel asked them, "that little planet, a mere nothing in size, which is some fifty million miles from here? There's the privy of the universe; go there as fast as you can." They went there; they were left there; and from that time on our world has been what it is.

We may still ask the Syrians why God permitted man to eat the pancake and why a host of such appalling evils should descend on us.

I move quickly from that fourth sky to Lord Bolingbroke, lest I grow bored. That man, who undoubtedly possessed great talent, provided the celebrated Pope with his plan for his *All is good,* which in fact we find word for word in Lord Bolingbroke's posthumous works, and which Lord Shaftesbury had earlier inserted into his *characteristics.* Read in Shaftesbury the chapter on the moralists and there you will see these words:

"Much is alleged in answer to show why Nature errs, and how she came thus impotent and erring from an unerring hand. But I deny she errs. . . . 'Tis from this order of inferior and superior things that we admire the world's beauty, founded thus on contrarieties, whilst from such various and disagreeing principles a universal concord is established. . . . The vegetables by their death sustain the animals, and animal bodies dissolved enrich the earth, and raise again the vegetable world. . . . The central powers, which hold the lasting orbs in their just poise and movement, must not be controlled to save a fleeting form, and rescue from the precipice a puny animal, whose brittle frame, however protected, must of itself so soon dissolve."

Bolingbroke, Shaftesbury, and Pope, their promoter, didn't resolve the question any better than the others: their. *All is good* means nothing more than that everything is directed by immutable laws; who does not know that? You teach us nothing when you observe, with all the little children, that flies are born to be eaten by spiders, spiders by swallows, swallows by shrikes, shrikes by eagles, eagles to be killed by men, men to kill one another and to be eaten by worms and then—excepting one in a thousand—by devils.

Here's a clear and constant order among the animals of all species; here is order throughout. When a stone is formed in my bladder, it is by an admirable piece of machinery: gravelly juices pass little by little into my blood, filter into the kidneys, pass through the urethras, deposit themselves in my bladder, assemble there by an excellent Newtonian attraction; the stone is formed, grows larger; I suffer evils a thousand times worse than death, by the most beautiful arrangement in the world; a surgeon, having perfected the art invented by Tubalcain, comes to thrust a sharp and pointed iron into the perineum and seizes my stone with his pincers. It breaks under his efforts by a necessary mechanism; and, by the same mechanism, I die in horrible torments. *All this is good,* all this is the evident consequence of unchangeable physical principles; I agree, and I know it as well as you do.

If we were without feeling, there would be no objection to this natural philosophy. But that is not the issue; we ask you if there are not perceptible evils, and where they come from. "There are no evils," says Pope in his fourth epistle on the *All is good;* "or, if there are particular evils, they compose the general good."

Here's a strange general good, composed of the stone, the gout, all crimes, all sufferings, death, and damnation.

The fall of man is the ointment we put on all the specific maladies of body and soul, which you call the *general health;* but Shaftesbury and Bolingbroke jeered at original sin; Pope doesn't talk about it; it is clear that their system saps the Christian religion at its foundations, and explains nothing at all.

Nevertheless, this system has recently been approved by several theologians who are perfectly willing to put up with agreeable contradictions; we shouldn't begrudge anyone the consolation of reasoning as best he can about the deluge of evils that inundates us. It is right to let desperately sick men eat what they want. They have gone so far as to claim that this system is comforting.

"God," says Pope,

> . . . sees with equal eye, as God of all,
> A hero perish, or a sparrow fall,
> Atoms or systems into ruin hurled,
> And now a bubble burst, and now a world.
> [*Essay on Man,* I, 87–90]

That's a pleasant consolation, I admit; don't you find a great relief in the ordinance of Lord Shaftesbury which says that God will not upset his eternal laws for the sake of an animal as puny as man? We must at least admit that this puny animal is right to cry out humbly and, crying out, to seek to understand why these eternal laws are not made for the well-being of every individual.

The system of *All is good* merely represents the author of nature as a powerful and malicious king, who does not care if it should cost the lives of four or five hundred thousand men, and if the others drag out their days in want and tears, provided that he accomplishes his work.

So then, far from consoling them, the notion of the best of possible worlds drives the philosophers who adopt it to despair. The question of good and evil remains an inexplicable chaos for those who search honestly; it is a witticism for those who argue: they are galley-slaves who jingle their chains. As for the unthinking, they closely resemble fish who have been brought from a river to a reservoir; they don't suspect that they are to be eaten during Lent. Similarly, on our own none of us knows a thing about the causes of our destiny.

Let us put at the end of almost all the chapters of metaphysics the two letters the Roman judges set down when they could not understand a cause: *N. L., non liquet,* it is not clear.

God and Evil

H. J. McCloskey

A. THE PROBLEM STATED

Evil is a problem for the theist in that a contradiction is involved in the fact of evil on the one hand, and the belief in the omnipotence and perfection of God on the other. God cannot be both all-powerful and perfectly good if evil is real. This contradiction is well set out in its detail by Mackie in his discussion of the problem.[1] In his discussion [J. L.] Mackie seeks to show that this contradiction cannot be resolved in terms of man's free will. In arguing in this way Mackie neglects a large number of important points, and concedes far too much to the theist. He implicitly allows that whilst physical evil creates a problem, this problem is reducible to the problem of moral evil and that therefore the satisfactoriness of solutions of the problem of evil turns on the compatibility of free will and absolute goodness. In fact physical evils create a number of distinct problems which are not reducible to the problem of moral evil. Further, the proposed solution of the problem of moral evil in terms of free will renders the attempt to account for physical evil in terms of moral good, and the attempt thereby to reduce the problem of evil to the problem of moral evil, completely untenable. Moreover, the account of moral evil in terms of free will breaks down on more obvious and less disputable grounds than those indicated by Mackie. Moral evil can be shown to remain a problem whether or not

---

[1]Evil and Omnipotence," *Mind,* 1955.
Source: The Philosophical Quarterly, 10, 1960, 97–114.

free will is compatible with absolute goodness. I therefore propose in this paper to reopen the discussion of "the problem of evil," by approaching it from a more general standpoint, examining a wider variety of solutions than those considered by Mackie and his critics.

The fact of evil creates a problem for the theist; but there are a number of simple solutions available to a theist who is content seriously to modify his theism. He can either admit a limit to God's power, or he can deny God's moral perfection. He can assert either (1) that God is not powerful enough to make a world that does not contain evil, or (2) that God created only the good in the universe and that some other power created the evil, or (3) that God is all-powerful but morally imperfect, and chose to create an imperfect universe. Few Christians accept these solutions, and this is no doubt partly because such "solutions" ignore the real inspiration of religious beliefs, and partly because they introduce embarrassing complications for the theist in his attempts to deal with other serious problems. However, if any one of these "solutions" is accepted, then the problem of evil is avoided, and a weakened version of theism is made secure from attacks based upon the fact of the occurrence of evil.

For more orthodox theism, according to which God is both omnipotent and perfectly good, evil creates a real problem; and this problem is well-stated by the Jesuit, Father G. H. Joyce. Joyce writes:

> The existence of evil in the world must at all times be the greatest of all problems which the mind encounters when it reflects on God and His relation to the world. If He is, indeed, all-good and all-powerful, how has evil any place in the world which He has made? Whence came it? Why is it here? If He is all-good why did He allow it to arise? If all-powerful why does He not deliver us from the burden? Alike in the physical and moral order creation seems so grievously marred that we find it hard to understand how it can derive in its entirety from God.[2]

The facts which give rise to the problem are of two general kinds, and give rise to two distinct types of problem. These two general kinds of evil are usually referred to as "physical" and as "moral" evil. These terms are by no means apt— suffering for instance is not strictly physical evil—and they conceal significant differences. However, this terminology is too widely accepted, and too convenient to be dispensed with here, the more especially as the kinds of evil, whilst important as distinct kinds, need not for our purposes be designated by separate names.

Physical evil and moral evil then are the two general forms of evil which independently and jointly constitute conclusive grounds for denying the existence of God in the sense defined, namely as an all-powerful, perfect Being. The acuteness of these two general problems is evident when we consider the nature and extent of the evils of which account must be given. To take physical evils, looking first at the less important of these.

(*a*) *Physical evils.* Physical evils are involved in the very constitution of the earth and animal kingdom. There are deserts and icebound areas; there are dangerous

---

[2]Joyce: *Principles of Natural Theology,* ch. XVII. All subsequent quotations from Joyce in this paper are from this chapter of this work.

animals of prey, as well as creatures such as scorpions and snakes. There are also pests such as flies and fleas and the hosts of other insect pests, as well as the multitude of lower parasites such as tapeworms, hookworms and the like. Secondly, there are the various natural calamities and the immense human suffering that follows in their wake—fires, floods, tempests, tidal-waves, volcanoes, earthquakes, droughts and famines. Thirdly, there are the vast numbers of diseases that torment and ravage man. Diseases such as leprosy, cancer, poliomyelitis, appear *prima facie* not to be creations which are to be expected of a benevolent Creator. Fourthly, there are the evils with which so many are born—the various physical deformities and defects such as misshapen limbs, blindness, deafness, dumbness, mental deficiency and insanity. Most of these evils contribute towards increasing human pain and suffering: but not all physical evils are reducible simply to pain. Many of these evils are evils whether or not they result in pain. This is important, for it means that, unless there is one solution to such diverse evils, it is both inaccurate and positively misleading to speak of *the* problem of physical evil. Shortly I shall be arguing that no one "solution" covers all these evils, so we shall have to conclude that physical evils create not one problem but a number of distinct problems for the theist.

The nature of the various difficulties referred to by the theist as the problem of physical evil is indicated by Joyce in a way not untypical among the more honest, philosophical theists, as follows:

> The actual amount of suffering which the human race endures is immense. Disease has store and to spare of torments for the body: and disease and death are the lot to which we must all look forward. At all times, too, great numbers of the race are pinched by want. Nor is the world ever free for very long from the terrible sufferings which follow in the track of war. If we concentrate our attention on human woes, to the exclusion of the joys of life, we gain an appalling picture of the ills to which the flesh is heir. So too if we fasten our attention on the sterner side of nature, on the pains which men endure from natural forces—on the storms which wreck their ships, the cold which freezes them to death, the fire which consumes them—if we contemplate this aspect of nature alone we may be led to wonder how God came to deal so harshly with His Creatures as to provide them with such a home.

Many such statements of the problem proceed by suggesting, if not by stating, that the problem arises at least in part by concentrating one's attention too exclusively on one aspect of the world. This is quite contrary to the facts. The problem is not one that results from looking at only one aspect of the universe. It may be the case that over-all pleasure predominates over pain, and that physical goods in general predominate over physical evils, but the opposite may equally well be the case. It is both practically impossible and logically impossible for this question to be resolved. However, it is not an unreasonable presumption, with the large bulk of mankind inadequately fed and housed and without adequate medical and health services, to suppose that physical evils at present predominate over physical goods. In the light of the facts at our disposal, this would seem to be a much more reasonable conclusion than the conclusion hinted at by Joyce and openly advanced by less cautious theists, namely, that physical goods in fact outweigh physical evils in the world.

However, the question is not, Which predominates, physical good or physical evil? The problem of physical evil remains a problem whether the balance in the universe is on the side of physical good or not, because the problem is that of accounting for the fact that physical evil occurs at all.

(*b*) *Moral evil.* Physical evils create one of the groups of problems referred to by the theist as "the problem of evil." Moral evil creates quite a distinct problem. Moral evil is simply immorality—evils such as selfishness, envy, greed, deceit, cruelty, callousness, cowardice and the larger scale evils such as wars and the atrocities they involve.

Moral evil is commonly regarded as constituting an even more serious problem than physical evil. Joyce so regards it, observing:

> The man who sins thereby offends God. . . . We are called on to explain how God came to create an order of thing in which rebellion and even final rejection have such a place. Since a choice from among an infinite number of possible worlds lay open to God, how came He to choose one in which these occur? Is not such a choice in flagrant opposition to the Divine Goodness?

Some theists seek a solution by denying the reality of evil or by describing it as a "privation" or absence of good. They hope thereby to explain it away as not needing a solution. This, in the case of most of the evils which require explanation, seems to amount to little more than an attempt to sidestep the problem simply by changing the name of that which has to be explained. It can be exposed for what it is simply by describing some of the evils which have to be explained. That is why a survey of the data to be accounted for is a most important part of the discussion of the problem of evil.

In *The Brothers Karamazov,* Dostoyevsky introduces a discussion of the problem of evil by reference to some then recently committed atrocities. Ivan states the problem:

> "By the way, a Bulgarian I met lately in Moscow," Ivan went on . . . "told me about the crimes committed by Turks in all parts of Bulgaria through fear of a general rising of the Slavs. They burn villages, murder, outrage women and children, and nail their prisoners by the ears to the fences, leave them till morning, and in the morning hang them—all sorts of things you can't imagine. People talk sometimes of bestial cruelty, but that's a great injustice and insult to the beasts; a beast can never be so cruel as a man, so artistically cruel. The tiger only tears and gnaws and that's all he can do. He would never think of nailing people by the ears, even if he were able to do it. These Turks took a pleasure in torturing children too; cutting the unborn child from the mother's womb, and tossing babies up in the air and catching them on the points of their bayonets before their mothers' eyes. Doing it before the mother's eyes was what gave zest to the amusement. Here is another scene that I thought very interesting. Imagine a trembling mother with her baby in her arms, a circle of invading Turks around her. They've planned a diversion: they pet the baby to make it laugh. They succeed; the baby laughs. At that moment, a Turk points a pistol four inches from the baby's face. The baby laughs with glee, holds out its little hands to the pistol, and he pulls the trigger in the baby's face and blows out its brains. Artistic, wasn't it?"[3]

Ivan's statement of the problem was based on historical events. Such happenings did not cease in the nineteenth century. *The Scourge of the Swastika* by Lord

[3]P. 244, Garnett translation, Heinemann.

Russell of Liverpool contains little else than descriptions of such atrocities; and it is simply one of a host of writings giving documented lists of instances of evils, both physical and moral.

Thus the problem of evil is both real and acute. There is a clear *prima facie* case that evil and God are incompatible—both cannot exist. Most theists admit this, and that the onus is on them to show that the conflict is not fatal to theism; but a consequence is that a host of proposed solutions are advanced.

The mere fact of such a multiplicity of proposed solutions, and the widespread repudiation of each other's solutions by theists, in itself suggests that the fact of evil is an insuperable obstacle to theism as defined here. It also makes it impossible to treat of all proposed solutions, and all that can be attempted here is an examination of those proposed solutions which are most commonly invoked and most generally thought to be important by theists.

Some theists admit the reality of the problem of evil, and then seek to sidestep it, declaring it to be a great mystery which we poor humans cannot hope to comprehend. Other theists adopt a rational approach and advance rational arguments to show that evil, properly understood, is compatible with, and even a consequence of God's goodness. The arguments to be advanced in this paper are directed against the arguments of the latter theists; but in so far as these arguments are successful against the rational theists, to that extent they are also effective in showing that the non-rational approach in terms of great mysteries is positively irrational.

B. PROPOSED SOLUTIONS TO THE PROBLEM OF PHYSICAL EVIL

Of the large variety of arguments advanced by theists as solutions to the problem of physical evil, five popularly used and philosophically significant solutions will be examined. They are, in brief: (i) Physical good (pleasure) requires physical evil (pain) to exist at all; (ii) Physical evil is God's punishment of sinners; (iii) Physical evil is God's warning and reminder to man; (iv) Physical evil is the result of the natural laws, the operations of which are on the whole good; (v) Physical evil increases the total good.

(i) *Physical Good Is Impossible without Physical Evil.* Pleasure is possible only by way of contrast with pain. Here the analogy of colour is used. If everything were blue we should, it is argued, understand neither what colour is nor what blue is. So with pleasure and pain.

The most obvious defect of such an argument is that it does not cover all physical goods and evils. It is an argument commonly invoked by those who think of physical evil as creating only one problem, namely the problem of human pain. However, the problems of physical evils are not reducible to the one problem, the problem of pain; hence the argument is simply irrelevant to much physical evil. Disease and insanity are evils, but health and sanity are possible in the total absence of disease and insanity. Further, if the argument were in any way valid even in respect of pain, it would imply the existence of only a speck of pain, and not the immense amount of pain in the universe. A speck of yellow is all that is needed for an appreciation of blueness and of colour generally. The argument is therefore seen to be seriously defective on two counts even if its underlying principle is left unquestioned. If its underlying principle is questioned, the argument is seen to be essentially invalid. Can it seriously be maintained that if an individual were born crippled and deformed and never in his life experienced pleasure, that he could not experience pain, not even if he were severely injured? It is clear that pain is possible in the absence of pleasure. It is true that it might not be distinguished by a special name and called "pain," but the state we now describe as a painful state would nonetheless be possible in the total absence of pleasure. So too the converse would seem to apply. Plato brings this out very clearly in Book 9 of the *Republic* in respect of the pleasures of taste and smell. These pleasures seem not to depend for their existence on any prior experience of pain. Thus the argument is unsound in respect of its main contention; and in being unsound in this respect, it is at the same time ascribing a serious limitation to God's power. It maintains that God cannot create pleasure without creating pain, although as we have seen, pleasure and pain are not correlatives.

(ii) *Physical Evil Is God's Punishment for Sin.* This kind of explanation was advanced to explain the terrible Lisbon earthquake in the 18th century, in which 40,000 people were killed. There are many replies to this argument, for instance Voltaire's. Voltaire asked: "Did God in this earthquake select the 40,000 least virtuous of the Portuguese citizens?" The distribution of disease and pain is in no obvious way related to the virtue of the persons afflicted, and popular saying has it that the distribution is slanted in the opposite direction. The only way of meeting the fact that evils are not distributed proportionately to the evil of the sufferer is by suggesting that all human beings, including children, are such miserable sinners, that our offenses are of such enormity, that God would be justified in punishing all of us as severely as it is possible for humans to be punished; but even then, God's apparent caprice in the selection of His victims requires explanation. In any case it is by no means clear that young children who very often suffer severely are guilty of sin of such an enormity as would be necessary to justify their sufferings as punishment.

Further, many physical evils are simultaneous with birth—insanity, mental defectiveness, blindness, deformities, as well as much disease. No crime or sin of *the child* can explain and justify these physical evils as punishment; and, for a parent's sin to be punished in the child is injustice or evil of another kind.

Similarly, the sufferings of animals cannot be accounted for as punishment. For these various reasons, therefore, this argument must be rejected. In fact it has dropped out of favour in philosophical and theological circles, but it continues to be invoked at the popular level.

(iii) *Physical Evil Is God's Warning to Men.* It is argued, for instance of physical calamities, that "they serve a moral end which compensates the physical evil which they cause. The awful nature of these phenomena, the overwhelming power of the forces at work, and man's utter helplessness before them, rouse him from the religious indifference to which he is so prone. They inspire a reverential awe of the Creator who made them, and controls them, and a salutary fear of violating the laws which He has imposed" (Joyce). This is where immortality is often alluded to as justifying evil.

This argument proceeds from a proposition that is plainly false; and that the proposition from which it proceeds is false is conceded implicitly by most theologians. Natural calamities do not necessarily turn people to God, but rather present the problem of evil in an acute form; and the problem of evil is said to account for more defections from religion than any other cause. Thus if God's object in bringing about natural calamities is to inspire reverence and awe, He is a bungler. There are many more reliable methods of achieving this end. Equally important, the use of physical evil to achieve this object is hardly the course one would expect a benevolent God to adopt when other, more effective, less evil methods are available to Him, for example, miracles, special revelation, etc.

(iv) *Evils Are the Results of the Operation of Laws of Nature.* This fourth argument relates to most physical evil, but it is more usually used to account for animal suffering and physical calamities. These evils are said to result from the operation of the natural laws which govern these objects, the relevant natural laws being the various causal laws, the law of pleasure-pain as a law governing sentient beings, etc. The theist argues that the non-occurrence of these evils would involve either the constant intervention by God in a miraculous way, and contrary to his own natural laws, or else the construction of a universe with different components subject to different laws of nature; for God, in creating a certain kind of being, must create it subject to its appropriate laws; He cannot create it and subject it to any law of His own choosing. Hence He creates a world which has components and laws good in their total effect, although calamitous in some particular effects.

Against this argument three objections are to be urged. First, it does not cover all physical evil. Clearly not all disease can be accounted for along these lines. Secondly, it is not to give a reason against God's miraculous intervention simply to assert that it would be unreasonable for Him constantly to intervene in the operation of His own laws. Yet this is the only reason that theists seem to offer here. If, by intervening in respect to the operation of His laws, God could thereby eliminate an evil, it would seem to be unreasonable and evil of Him not to do so. Some theists seek a way out of this difficulty by denying that God has the power miraculously to intervene; but this is to ascribe a severe limitation to His power. It amounts to asserting that when His Creation has been effected, God can do nothing else except contemplate it. The third objection is related to this, and is to the effect that it is already to ascribe a serious limitation to God's omnipotence to suggest that He could not make sentient beings which did not experience pain, nor sentient beings without deformities and deficiencies, nor natural phenomena with different laws of nature governing them. There is no reason why better laws of nature governing the existing objects are not possible on the divine hypothesis. Surely, if God is all-powerful, He could have made a better universe in the first place, or one with better laws of nature governing it, so that the operation of its laws did not produce calamities and pain. To maintain this is not to suggest that an omnipotent God should be capable of achieving what is logically impossible. All that has been indicated here is logically possible, and therefore not beyond the powers of a being Who is really omnipotent.

This fourth argument seeks to exonerate God by explaining that He created a universe sound on the whole, but such that He had no direct control over the laws governing His creations, and had control only in His selection of His creations. The previous two arguments attribute the detailed results of the operations of these laws directly to God's will. Theists commonly use all three arguments. It is not without significance that they betray such uncertainty as to whether God is to be *commended* or *exonerated*.

(v) *The Universe Is Better with Evil in It.* This is the important argument. One version of it runs:

> Just as the human artist has in view the beauty of his composition as a whole, not making it his aim to give to each several part the highest degree of brilliancy, but that measure of adornment which most contributes to the combined effect, so it is with God. [Joyce]

Another version of this general type of argument explains evil not so much as *a component* of a good whole, seen out of its context as a mere component, but rather as *a means* to a greater good. Different as these versions are, they may be treated here as one general type of argument, for the same criticisms are fatal to both versions.

This kind of argument if valid simply shows that some evil may enrich the Universe; it tells us nothing about *how much* evil will enrich this particular universe, and how much will be too much. So, even if valid in principle—and shortly I shall argue that it is not valid—such an argument does not in itself provide a justification for the evil in the universe. It shows simply that the evil which occurs might have a justification. In view of the immense amount of evil the probabilities are against it.

This is the main point made by Wisdom in his discussion of this argument. Wisdom sums up his criticism as follows:

> It remains to add that, unless there are independent arguments in favour of this world's being the best logically possible world, it is probable that some of the evils in it are not logically necessary to a compensating good; it is probable because there are so many evils.[4]

Wisdom's reply brings out that the person who relies upon this argument as a conclusive and complete argument is seriously mistaken. The argument, if valid, justifies only some evil. A belief that it justifies all the evil that occurs in the world is mistaken, for a second argument, by way of a supplement to it, is needed. This supplementary argument would take the form of a proof that all the evil that occurs is *in fact* valuable and necessary as a means to greater good. Such a supplementary proof is in principle impossible; so, at best, this fifth argument can be taken to show only that some evil *may be* necessary for the production of good, and that the evil in the world may perhaps have a justification on this account. This is not to justify a physical evil, but simply to suggest that physical evil might nonetheless have a justification, although we may never come to know this justification.

Thus the argument even if it is valid as a general form of reasoning is unsatisfactory because inconclusive. It is, however, also unsatisfactory in that it follows on

[4]*Mind*, 1931.

the principle of the argument that, just as it is possible that evil in the total context contributes to increasing the total ultimate good, so equally, it will hold that good in the total context may increase the ultimate evil. Thus if the principle of the argument were sound, we could never know whether evil is really evil, or good really good. (Aesthetic analogies may be used to illustrate this point.) By implication it follows that it would be dangerous to eliminate evil because we may thereby introduce a discordant element into the divine symphony of the universe; and, conversely, it may be wrong to condemn the elimination of what is good, because the latter may result in the production of more, higher goods.

So it follows that, even if the general principle of the argument is not questioned, it is still seen to be a defective argument. On the one hand, it proves too little—it justifies only some evil and not necessarily all the evil in the universe; on the other hand it proves too much because it creates doubts about the goodness of apparent goods. These criticisms in themselves are fatal to the argument as a solution to the problem of physical evil. However, because this is one of the most popular and plausible accounts of physical evil, it is worthwhile considering whether it can properly be claimed to establish even the very weak conclusion indicated above.

Why, and in what way, is it supposed that physical evils such as pain and misery, disease and deformity, will heighten the total effect and add to the value of the moral? The answer given is that physical evil enriches the whole by giving rise to moral goodness. Disease, insanity, physical suffering and the like are said to bring into being the noble moral virtues—courage, endurance, benevolence, sympathy and the like. This is what the talk about the Enriched whole comes to. W. D. Niven makes this explicit in his version of the argument:

> Physical evil has been the goad which has impelled men to most of those achievements which made the history of man so wonderful. Hardship is a stern but fecund parent of invention. Where life is easy because physical ills are at a minimum we find man degenerating in body, mind, and character.

And Niven concludes by asking:

> Which is preferable—a grim fight with the possibility of splendid triumph; or no battle at all?[5]

Joyce's corresponding argument runs:

> Pain is the great stimulant to action. Man no less than animals is impelled to work by the sense of hunger. Experience shows that, were it not for this motive the majority of men would be content to live in indolent ease. Man must earn his bread.
> One reason plainly why God permits suffering is that man may rise to a height of heroism which would otherwise have been beyond his scope. Nor are these the only benefits which it confers. That sympathy for others which is one of the most precious parts of our experience and one of the most fruitful sources of well-doing, has its origin in the fellow: feeling engendered by endurance of similar trials. Furthermore, were

[5]W. D. Niven, *Encyclopedia of Religion and Ethics.*

it not for these trials, man would think little enough of a future existence, and of the need of striving after his last end. He would be perfectly content with his existence, and would reck little of any higher good. These considerations here briefly advanced suffice at least to show how important is the office filled by pain in human life, and with what little reason it is asserted that the existence of so much suffering is irreconcilable with the wisdom of the Creator.

And:

It may be asked whether the Creator could not have brought man to perfection without the use of suffering. Most certainly He could have conferred upon him a similar degree of virtue without requiring any effort on his part. Yet it is easy to see that there is a special value attaching to a conquest of difficulties such as man's actual demands, and that in God's eyes this may well be an adequate reason for assigning this life to us in preference to another. . . . Pain has value in respect to the next life, but also in respect to this. The advance of scientific discovery, the gradual improvement of the organization of the community, the growth of material civilization are due in no small degree to the stimulus afforded by pain.

The argument is: Physical evil brings moral good into being, and in fact is an essential precondition for the existence of some moral goods. Further, it is sometimes argued in this context that those moral goods which are possible in the total absence of physical evils are more valuable in themselves if they are achieved as a result of a struggle. Hence physical evil is said to be justified on the grounds that moral good plus physical evil is better than the absence of physical evil.

A common reply, and an obvious one, is that urged by Mackie.[6] Mackie argues that whilst it is true that moral good plus physical evil together are better than physical good alone, the issue is not as simple as that, for physical evil also gives rise to and makes possible many moral evils that would not or could not occur in the absence of physical evil. It is then urged that it is not clear that physical evils (for example, disease and pain) plus some moral goods (for example, courage) plus some moral evil (for example, brutality) are better than physical good and those moral goods which are possible and which would occur in the absence of physical evil.

This sort of reply, however, is not completely satisfactory. The objection it raises is a sound one, but it proceeds by conceding too much to the theist, and by overlooking two more basic defects of the argument. It allows implicitly that the problem of physical evil may be reduced to the problem of moral evil; and it neglects the two objections which show that the problem of physical evil cannot be so reduced.

The theist therefore happily accepts this kind of reply, and argues that, if he can give a satisfactory account of moral evil he will then have accounted for both physical and moral evil. He then goes on to account for moral evil in terms of the value of free will and/or its goods. This general argument is deceptively plausible. It breaks down for the two reasons indicated here, but it breaks down at another point as well. If free will alone is used to justify moral evil, then even if no moral good occurred, moral evil would still be said to be justified; but physical evil would have

[6]Mackie, "Evil and Omnipotence," *Mind,* 1955.

no justification. Physical evil is not essential to free will; it is only justified if moral good actually occurs, and if the moral good which results from physical evils outweighs the moral evils. This means that the argument from free will cannot alone justify physical evil along these lines; and it means that the argument from free will and its goods does not justify physical evil, because such an argument is incomplete, and necessarily incomplete. It needs to be supplemented by factual evidence that it is logically and practically impossible to obtain.

The correct reply, therefore, is first that the argument is irrelevant to many instances of physical evil, and secondly that it is not true that physical evil plus the moral good it produces is better than physical good and its moral goods. Much pain and suffering, in fact much physical evil generally, for example in children who die in infancy, animals and the insane passes unnoticed; it therefore has no morally uplifting effects upon others, and cannot by virtue of the examples chosen have such effects on the sufferers. Further, there are physical evils such as insanity and much disease to which the argument is inapplicable. So there is a large group of significant cases not covered by the argument. And where the argument is relevant, its premiss is plainly false. It can be shown to be false by exposing its implications in the following way.

We either have obligations to lessen physical evil or we have not. If we have obligations to lessen physical evil then we are thereby reducing the total good in the universe. If, on the other hand, our obligation is to increase the total good in the universe it is our duty to prevent the reduction of physical evil and possibly even to increase the total amount of physical evil. Theists usually hold that we are obliged to reduce the physical evil in the universe; but in maintaining this, the theist is, in terms of this account of physical evil, maintaining that it is his duty to reduce the total amount of real good in the universe, and thereby to make the universe worse. Conversely, if by eliminating the physical evil he is not making the universe worse, then that amount of evil which he eliminates was unnecessary and in need of justification. It is relevant to notice here that evil is not always eliminated for morally praiseworthy reasons. Some discoveries have been due to positively unworthy motives, and many other discoveries which have resulted in a lessening of the sufferings of mankind have been due to no higher a motive than a scientist's desire to earn a reasonable living wage.

This reply to the theist's argument brings out its untenability. The theist's argument is seen to imply that war plus courage plus the many other moral virtues war brings into play are better than peace and its virtues; that famine and its moral virtues are better than plenty; that disease and its moral virtues are better than health. Some Christians in the past, in consistency with this mode of reasoning, opposed the use of anaesthetics to leave scope for the virtues of endurance and courage, and they opposed state aid to the sick and needy to leave scope for the virtues of charity and sympathy. Some have even contended that war is a good in disguise, again in consistency with this argument. Similarly the theist should, in terms of this fifth argument, in his heart if not aloud regret the discovery of the Salk polio vaccine because Dr. Salk has in one blow destroyed infinite possibilities of moral good.

There are three important points that need to be made concerning this kind of account of physical evil. (*a*) We are told, as by Niven, Joyce and others, that pain is a goad to action and that part of its justification lies in this fact. This claim is empirically false as a generalization about all people and all pain. Much pain frustrates action and wrecks people and personalities. On the other hand many men work and work well without being goaded by pain or discomfort. Further, to assert that men need goading is to ascribe another evil to God, for it is to claim that God made men naturally lazy. There is no reason why God should not have made men naturally industrious; the one is no more incompatible with free will than the other. Thus the argument from physical evil being a goad to man breaks down on three distinct counts. Pain often frustrates human endeavour, pain is not essential as a goad with many men, and where pain is a goad to higher endeavours, it is clear that less evil means to this same end are available to an omnipotent God. (*b*) The real fallacy in the argument is in the assumption that all or the highest moral excellence results from physical evil. As we have already seen, this assumption is completely false. Neither all moral goodness nor the highest moral goodness is triumph in the face of adversity or benevolence towards others in suffering. Christ Himself stressed this when He observed that the two great commandments were commandments to love. Love does not depend for its possibility on the existence and conquest of evil. (*c*) The "negative" moral virtues which are brought into play by the various evils—courage, endurance, charity, sympathy and the like—besides not representing the highest forms of moral virtue, are in fact commonly supposed by the theist and atheist alike not to have the value this fifth argument ascribes to them. We—theists and atheists alike—reveal our comparative valuations of these virtues and of physical evil when we insist on state aid for the needy; when we strive for peace, for plenty, and for harmony within the state.

In brief, the good man, the morally admirable man, is he who loves what is good knowing that it is good and preferring it because it is good. He does not need to be torn by suffering or by the spectacle of another's sufferings to be morally admirable. Fortitude in his own sufferings, and sympathetic kindness in others' may reveal to us his goodness; but his goodness is not necessarily increased by such things.

Five arguments concerning physical evil have now been examined. We have seen that the problem of physical evil is a problem in its own right, and one that cannot be reduced to the problem of moral evil; and further, we have seen that physical evil creates not one but a number of problems to which no one nor any combination of the arguments examined offers a solution.

C. PROPOSED SOLUTIONS TO THE PROBLEM OF MORAL EVIL

The problem of moral evil is commonly regarded as being the greater of the problems concerning evil. As we shall see, it does create what appears to be insuperable difficulties for the theist; but so too, apparently, do physical evils.

For the theist moral evil must be interpreted as a breach of God's law and as a rejection of God himself. It may involve the eternal damnation of the sinner, and in many of its forms it involves the infliction of suffering on other persons. Thus it aggravates the problem of physical evil, but its own peculiar character consists in the fact of sin. How could a morally perfect, all-powerful God create a universe in which occur such moral evils as cruelty, cowardice and hatred, the more especially as these evils constitute a rejection of God Himself by His creations, and as such involve them in eternal damnation?

The two main solutions advanced relate to free will and to the fact that moral evil is a consequence of free will. There is a third kind of solution more often invoked implicitly than as an explicit and serious argument, which need not be examined here as its weaknesses are plainly evident. This third solution is to the effect that moral evils and even the most brutal atrocities have their justification in the moral goodness they make possible or bring into being.

(i) *Free will alone provides a justification for moral evil.* This is perhaps the more popular of the serious attempts to explain moral evil. The argument in brief runs: men have free will; moral evil is a consequence of free will; a universe in which men exercise free will even with lapses into moral evil is better than a universe in which men become *automata* doing good always because predestined to do so. Thus on this argument it is the mere fact of the supreme value of free will itself that is taken to provide a justification for its corollary moral evil.

(ii) *The goods made possible by free will provide a basis for accounting for moral evil.* According to this second argument, it is not the mere fact of free will that is claimed to be of such value as to provide a justification of moral evil, but the fact that free will makes certain goods possible. Some indicate the various moral virtues as the goods that free will makes possible, whilst others point to beatitude, and others again to beatitude achieved by man's own efforts or the virtues achieved as a result of one's own efforts. What all these have in common is the claim that the good consequences of free will provide a justification of the bad consequences of free will, namely moral evil.

Each of these two proposed solutions encounters two specific criticisms, which are fatal to their claims to be real solutions.

(i) To consider first the difficulties to which the former proposed solution is exposed. (*a*) A difficulty for the first argument—that it is free will alone that provides a justification for moral evil—lies in the fact that the theist who argues in this way has to allow that it is logically possible on the free will hypothesis that all men should always will what is evil, and that even so, a universe of completely evil men possessing free will is better than one in which men are predestined to virtuous living. It has to be contended that the value of free will itself is so immense that it more than outweighs the total moral evil, the eternal punishment of the wicked, and the sufferings inflicted on others by the sinners in their evilness. It is this paradox that leads to the formulation of the second argument; and it is to be noted that the explanation of moral evil switches to the second argument or to a combination of the first and second argument, immediately the theist refuses to face the logical possibility of complete wickedness, and insists instead that in fact men do not always choose what is evil.

(*b*) The second difficulty encountered by the first argument relates to the possibility that free will is compatible with less evil, and even with no evil, that is, with absolute goodness. If it could be shown that free will is compatible with absolute goodness, or even with less moral evil than actually occurs, then all or at least some evil will be left unexplained by free will alone.

Mackie, in his recent paper, and Joyce, in his discussion of this argument, both contend that free will is compatible with absolute goodness. Mackie argues that if it is not possible for God to confer free will on men and at the same time ensure that no moral evil is committed, He cannot really be omnipotent. Joyce directs his argument rather to fellow-theists, and it is more of an *ad hominem* argument addressed to them. He writes:

> Free will need not (as is often assumed) involve the power to choose wrong. Our ability to misuse the gift is due to the conditions under which it is exercised here. In our present state we are able to reject what is truly good, and exercise our power of preference in favour of some baser attraction. Yet it is not necessary that it should be so. And all who accept Christian revelation admit that those who attain their final beatitude exercise freedom of will, and yet cannot choose aught but what is truly good. They possess the knowledge of Essential Goodness; and to it, not simply to good in general, they refer every choice. Moreover, even in our present condition it is open to omnipotence so to order our circumstances and to confer on the will such instinctive impulses that we should in every election adopt the right course and not the wrong one.

To this objection, that free will is compatible with absolute goodness and that therefore a benevolent, omnipotent God would have given man free will and ensured his absolute virtue, it is replied that God is being required to perform what is logically impossible. It is logically impossible, so it is argued, for free will and absolute goodness to be combined, and hence, if God lacks omnipotence only in this respect, He cannot be claimed to lack omnipotence in any sense in which serious theists have ascribed it to Him.

Quite clearly, if free will and absolute goodness are logically incompatible, then God, in not being able to confer both on man does not lack omnipotence in any important sense of the term. However, it is not clear that free will and absolute goodness are logically opposed; and Joyce does point to considerations which suggest that they are not logical incompatibles. For my own part I am uncertain on this point; but my uncertainty is not a factual one but one concerning a point of usage. It is clear that an omnipotent God could create rational agents predestined always to make virtuous "decisions"; what is not clear is whether we should describe such agents as having free will. The considerations to which Joyce points have something of the status of test cases, and they would suggest that we should describe such agents as having free will. However, no matter how we resolve the linguistic point, the question remains—Which is more desirable, free will and moral evil and the physical evil to which free will gives rise, or this special free will or pseudo-free will which goes with absolute goodness? I suggest that the latter is clearly preferable. Later I shall endeavour to defend this conclusion; for the moment I am content to indicate the nature of the value judgement on which the question turns at this point.

The second objection to the proposed solution of the problem of moral evil in terms of free will alone is related to the contention that free will is compatible with less moral evil than occurs, and possibly with no moral evil. We have seen what is involved in the latter contention. We may now consider what is involved in the former. It may be argued that free will is compatible with less moral evil than in fact occurs on various grounds. (1) God, if He were all-powerful, could miraculously intervene to prevent some or perhaps all moral evil; and He is said to do so on occasion in answer to prayers (for example, to prevent wars) or of His own initiative (for instance, by producing calamities which serve as warnings, or by working miracles, etc.). (2) God has made man with a certain nature. This nature is often interpreted by theologians as having a bias to evil. Clearly God could have created man with a strong bias to good, whilst still leaving scope for a decision to act evilly. Such a bias to good would be compatible with freedom of the will. (3) An omnipotent God could so have ordered the world that it was less conducive to the practice of evil.

These are all considerations advanced by Joyce, and separately and jointly, they establish that God could have conferred free will upon us, and at least very considerably *reduced* the amount of moral evil that would have resulted from the exercise of free will. This is sufficient to show that *not all* the moral evil that exists can be justified by reference to free will alone. This conclusion is fatal to the account of moral evil in terms of free will alone. The more extreme conclusion that Mackie seeks to establish—that absolute goodness is compatible with free will— is not essential as a basis for refuting the free will argument. The difficulty is as fatal to the claims of theism whether all moral evil or only some moral evil is unaccountable. However, whether Mackie's contentions are sound is still a matter of logical interest, although not of any real moment in the context of the case against theism, once the fact that less moral evil is compatible with free will has been established.

(ii) The second free will argument arises out of an attempt to circumvent these objections. It is not free will, but the value of the goods achieved through free will that is said to be so great as to provide a justification for moral evil.

(*a*) This second argument meets a difficulty in that it is now necessary for it to be supplemented by a proof that the number of people who practice moral virtue or who attain beatitude and/or virtue after a struggle is sufficient to outweigh the evilness of moral evil, the evilness of their eternal damnation and the physical evil they cause to others. This is a serious defect in the argument, because it means that the argument can at best show that moral evil *may have* a justification, and not that it has a justification. It is both logically and practically impossible to supplement and complete the argument. It is necessarily incomplete and inconclusive even if its general principle is sound.

(*b*) This second argument is designed also to avoid the other difficulty of the first argument—that free will may be compatible with no evil and certainly with less evil. It is argued that even if free will is compatible with absolute goodness it is still better that virtue and beatitude be attained after a genuine personal struggle; and this, it is said, would not occur if God in conferring free will nonetheless prevented moral evil or reduced the risk of it. Joyce argues in this way:

> To receive our final beatitude as the fruit of our labours, and as the recompense of a hard-won victory, is an incomparably higher destiny than to receive it without any effort

on our part. And since God in His wisdom has seen fit to give us such a lot as this, it was inevitable that man should have the power to choose wrong. We could not be called to merit the reward due to victory without being exposed to the possibility of defeat.

There are various objections which may be urged here. First, this argument implies that the more intense the struggle, the greater is the triumph and resultant good, and the better the world; hence we should apparently, on this argument, court temptation and moral struggles to attain greater virtue and to be more worthy of our reward. Secondly, it may be urged that God is being said to be demanding too high a price for the goods produced. He is omniscient. He knows that many will sin and not attain the goods or the Good free will is said to make possible. He creates men with free will, with the natures men have, in the world as it is constituted, knowing that in His doing so He is committing many to moral evil and eternal damnation. He could avoid all this evil by creating men with rational wills predestined to virtue, or He could eliminate much of it by making men's natures and the conditions in the world more conducive to the practice of virtue. He is said not to choose to do this. Instead, at the cost of the sacrifice of the many, He is said to have ordered things so as to allow fewer men to attain this higher virtue and higher beatitude that result from the more intense struggle.

In attributing such behaviour to God, and in attempting to account for moral evil along these lines, theists are, I suggest, attributing to God immoral behaviour of a serious kind—of a kind we should all unhesitatingly condemn in a fellow human being.

We do not commend people for putting temptation in the way of others. On the contrary, anyone who today advocated, or even allowed where he could prevent it, the occurrence of evil and the sacrifice of the many—even as a result of their own freely chosen actions—for the sake of the higher virtue of the few, would be condemned as an immoralist. To put severe temptation in the way of the many, knowing that many and perhaps even most will succumb to the temptation, for the sake of the higher virtue of the few, would be blatant immorality; and it would be immoral whether or not those who yielded to the temptation possessed free will. This point can be brought out by considering how a conscientious moral agent would answer the question: Which should I choose for other people, a world in which there are intense moral struggles and the possibility of magnificent triumphs and the certainty of many defeats, or a world in which there are less intense struggles, less magnificent triumphs and fewer defeats, or a world in which there are no struggles, no triumphs and no defeats? We are constantly answering less easy questions than this in a way that conflicts with the theist's contentions. If by modifying our own behaviour we can save someone else from an intense moral struggle and almost certain moral evil for example if by refraining from gambling or excessive drinking ourselves we can help a weaker person not to become a confirmed gambler or an alcoholic, or if by locking our car and not leaving it unlocked and with the key in it we can prevent people yielding to the temptation to become car thieves, we feel obliged to act accordingly, even though the persons concerned would freely choose the evil course of conduct. How much clearer is the decision with which God is said to be faced—the choice between the higher virtue of some and the evil of others, or the higher but less high virtue of many more, and the evil of many fewer. Neither alternative denies free will to men.

These various difficulties dispose of each of the main arguments relating to moral evil. There are in addition to these difficulties two other objections that might be urged.

If it could be shown that man has not free will both arguments collapse; and even if it could be shown that God's omniscience is incompatible with free will they would still break down. The issues raised here are too great to be pursued in this paper; and they can simply be noted as possible additional grounds for which criticisms of the main proposed solutions of the problem of moral evil may be advanced.

The other general objection is by way of a follow-up to points made in objections (*b*) to both arguments (i) and (ii). It concerns the relative value of free will and its goods and evils and the value of the best of the alternatives to free will and its goods. Are free will and its goods so much more valuable than the next best alternatives that their superior value can really justify the immense amount of evil that is introduced into the world by free will?

Theologians who discuss this issue ask, Which is better—men with free will striving to work out their own destinies, or automata-machine-like creatures, who never make mistakes because they never make decisions? When put in this form we naturally doubt whether free will plus moral evil plus the possibility of the eternal damnation of the many and the physical evil of untold billions are quite so unjustified after all; but the fact of the matter is that the question has not been fairly put. The real alternative is, on the one hand, rational agents with free wills making many bad and some good decisions on rational and non-rational grounds, and "rational" agents predestined always "to choose" the right things for the right reasons—that is, if the language of automata must be used, rational automata. Predestination does not imply the absence of rationality in all senses of that term. God, were He omnipotent, could preordain the decisions and the reasons upon which they were based; and such a mode of existence would seem to be in itself a worthy mode of existence, and one preferable to an existence with free will, irrationality and evil.

D. CONCLUSION

In this paper it has been maintained that God, were He all-powerful and perfectly good, would have created a world in which there was no unnecessary evil. It has not been argued that God ought to have created a perfect world, nor that He should have made one that is in any way logically impossible. It has simply been argued that a benevolent God could, and would, have created a world devoid of superfluous evil. It has been contended that there is evil in this world—unnecessary evil—and that the more popular and philosophically more significant of the many attempts to explain this evil are completely unsatisfactory. Hence we must conclude from the existence of evil that there cannot be an omnipotent, benevolent God.

Divine Goodness and the Problem of Evil

Terence Penelhum

I

The purpose of this paper is not to offer any solution to the problem of evil, or to declare it insoluble. It is rather the more modest one of deciding on its nature. Many writers assume that the problem of evil is one that poses a logical challenge to the theist, rather than a challenge of a moral or scientific sort. If this assumption is correct, and the challenge cannot be met, Christian theism can be shown to be untenable on grounds of inconsistency. This in turn means that it is refutable by philosophers, even if their task is interpreted in the most narrowly analytical fashion. It has recently been argued that the challenge of the problem of evil can be met on logical grounds, and that if the existence of evil is damaging to theism it is not because the recognition of its existence is inconsistent with some essential part of it. I take two examples of this position. The first is in the paper "Hume on Evil" by Nelson Pike;[1] the second I owe to Professor R. M. Chisholm.[2]

Let us first present the problem of evil in its traditional, logical guise. The argument is that it is inconsistent for anyone to believe both of the following two propositions:

I. The world is the creation of a God who is omnipotent, omniscient, and wholly good.
II. The world contains evil.

Both, especially the first, are highly complex propositions, and it is natural that the problem is often put as one of the apparent inconsistency of holding three or four or more propositions at once. Although the complexity of I is vital, the problem can be stated well enough in this deceptively simple form. Let us begin by recognising two things about the problem as presented. (*a*) Apart from some eminent and disingenuous theologians, proposition II is not itself a challenge to theism. It is a part of it. The existence of evil is not something the facts of life force the theist to admit, in the way in which the facts of the fossil evidence forced some nineteenth century theists to admit the antiquity of the world. The existence of evil is something the theist emphasises. Theists do not see fewer evils in the world than atheists; they see more. It is a necessary truth that they see more. For example, to the theist adultery is not only an offence against another person or persons, but also an offence against a sacrament, and therefore against God; it is therefore a worse offence, because it is a compound of several offences. Atheists can never be against sin, for to atheists

---

[1] Nelson Pike, "Hume on Evil," *Philosophical Review,* 72, (1963), 180–97 [Chapter II in this collection]. The argument is also presented in his volume *God and Evil* (Prentice-Hall, 1964), 85–102.
[2] I learned of this argument through seminar discussion, and Professor Chisholm is not responsible for any inaccuracies in my account of it or any infelicities in my examples.
Source: Religious Studies, 2, 1966–1967, 95–107.

there can be no sins, "sin" being a theological concept that only has application if God exists. Only if this is accepted can the problem of evil be represented as a logical problem. For a charge of inconsistency can only be levelled against the theist if he holds both of the allegedly inconsistent propositions *as part of his belief.* The nineteenth century theist who finally accepted the antiquity of the world could not have been accused of logical inconsistency unless a belief like that of the world's beginning in 4004 B.C. were entailed by his form of theism. (*b*) Given this, it is easy to see why the logical challenge the problem of evil presents is so serious. For the theist, in believing in God, believes *both* that God created the world *and* that much that is in the world is deeply deficient in the light of the very standards God himself embodies. The inconsistency seems to result from two distinguishable functions which the idea of God has. It is an ultimate source of explanations of why things are as they are; it is also the embodiment of the very standards by which many of them are found to be wanting.

II

Let us now turn to Pike's argument. Briefly paraphrased, it runs as follows. Propositions I and II are not of themselves incompatible. To get a logically inconsistent set of beliefs we have to add:

III. A being who is omnipotent and omniscient would have no morally sufficient reason for allowing instances of evil.

I, II, and III are, taken together, logically inconsistent, since any two together entail the falsity of the third. For the inconsistency of theism to be demonstrated, Pike argues, III has to be a necessary truth. Unless it is shown to be a necessary truth it is always open to a theist to say that there is some morally sufficient reason why God allows evil, even though he may have no idea what this reason actually is. He can say that he knows I and II are true (e.g. I by revelation and II by observation); so III is false: even though God is omnipotent and omniscient, there is some (mysterious) morally sufficient reason for the evils which he allows. There just *must* be. This is, Pike argues, a perfectly adequate retort to the charge of inconsistency unless proposition III can be *demonstrated:* i.e. unless there is a demonstration that there *cannot* be any available morally sufficient reason for an omnipotent and omniscient being to allow evils.

But how would one set about demonstrating the truth of III? It cannot be deduced from I or II separately, and in any case to try to do this would be to beg the question. It obviously cannot be deduced from the conjunction of I and II, because it is incompatible with this conjunction. The only apparent way of establishing the truth of III is to show in one case after another that a suggested reason for God's permitting evil is not morally sufficient. But this is not conclusive, since the theist can always deny that the list of suggested reasons is complete. This denial can be based on a simple deduction from I and II taken together, and is compatible with complete agnosticism as to what God's morally sufficient reason or reasons might be. A theist is not, in other words, committed to any particular theodicy. The onus is therefore on the sceptic to show that III is a necessary truth. The theist does not have to make it seem *plausible* that there is a morally sufficient reason for evil in order to evade the inconsistency charge. Rather the sceptic has to make the inconsistency charge take hold by proving that there *cannot* be one.

I think this argument is serious. I shall now summarise Chisholm's argument. The goodness or badness of a state of affairs is, says Chisholm, *defeasible,* if it can (logically) be overridden. This can happen when the state of affairs is combined with another and the resultant complex is of a value which is either neutral or opposite to that of the first state of affairs, and is not reduced by the fact that the first state of affairs is a part of it. It might be held, for example, that the evil of my suffering pain is defeated by my acquisition of fortitude in the face of it; or that the evil of my suffering mental distress is defeated by the fact that my distress is due to contrition for my former sins. Since there is no more good, and perhaps even less good, in my acquiring fortitude in ways other than that of living through occasions that require its exercise, then the pain plus the fortitude is better than either without the other; and since contrition is only possible if some sins have been committed, the contrite sinner may be a better phenomenon, or no worse a phenomenon, than the unhumbled innocent.

The theist can argue in the face of the problem of evil in the following way. Every evil in the world, he can say, is or will be defeated. For every evil there is a state of affairs which, when combined with it, results in a conjoint state of affairs which is *either*

> (i) not bad and better than either without the other,
> or (ii) good and better than either without the other,
> or (iii) good and better than any alternative state of affairs.

God can allow evil situations if their defeat is assured in one of these ways; in fact, his goodness would require him to do so.

Chisholm concludes that the problem of evil as a logical challenge is soluble. The moral problem of evil, as he calls it, is harder. This is the problem of suggesting in given cases what states of affairs actually defeat the evils we find in the world; the problem in other words, of finding a specific theodicy. On this he recommends the agnosticism which Pike implicitly recommends. Pike recommends this by classifying the problem thus understood as a "noncrucial perplexity of relatively minor importance."[3]

I would like to suggest that this defence of theism is not successful, since it is not open to the theist to eschew theodicy in the way Pike and Chisholm recommend.

III

Consider the following discussion. To counter the argument that diseases are an indication that the world is not the creation of a wholly good and powerful deity, a believer uses the following obviously bad arguments.

[3]Pike, "Hume on Evil," p. 197.

(i) Diseases are a way of reducing populations and preventing undue pressure on world food supplies.

(ii) Some diseases have aesthetically pleasing side-effects: tuberculosis sufferers often acquire a charming pink flush and according to Puccini can often sing better than healthy people.

Both these arguments fail, but for different reasons. The first one fails because it implies what is clearly false, that God could not manage to avoid over-population and food shortage by any means other than allowing epidemics. The second fails because it suggests that aesthetically pleasing side-effects are a morally sufficient reason for allowing the suffering attendant upon diseases. Sceptics often score points against believers by showing that more sophisticated defences end up on examination by committing the same errors. It is very important to stress that the basic challenge that these arguments, and others like them, fail to meet is a logical one rather than a moral or scientific one. This is especially hard to bear in mind in the second sort of case, because people who object to defences of this sort have to appeal to moral considerations in presenting their case. Nevertheless it is the consistency of theism that is at issue. In the first case the defence fails because it would only work if God were not omnipotent or were not omniscient; and these attributes are built into the *concept* of God. By saying the world is created by God the believer is ruling out this line of defence from the beginning. In the second case we reject the defence because it could only succeed if we were prepared to agree that minor aesthetic advantages could outweigh major moral and physical disadvantages in the assessment of evils like disease. We reject this evaluation, and in doing so we commit ourselves to saying that any being who placed such aesthetic considerations higher on the scale of choices than the physical ones would not be morally good. And moral goodness is also built into the concept of God. It is therefore inconsistent to present a defence of theism which attributes to God this particular preference.

These cases show, therefore, that for all the moral heat the problem of evil gives rise to it is correct to regard it as a logical issue, even though logical issues frequently do not give rise to heatedness. They also show, if they are as typical in form as I think they are, that the concept of God rules out a very large number of theistic defences, because they entail attributing to God limitations or preferences that are incompatible with his stated attributes. So although it may seem plausible for a theist to say, with Pike and Chisholm, that he does not need to commit himself to any particular theodicy, his very theism commits him at the very least to saying that a large number of possible theodicies are false, viz. all those that commit these errors. This entails the view that whatever reason God may have for allowing evils, it is a reason which is compatible with his omnipotence, omniscience, and his moral goodness. The situations regarding the omnipotence and the omniscience are fairly clear, though they generate interesting perplexities. I would like to concentrate here on the more complex attribute of moral goodness.

It is impossible to emphasise too much how deeply our thinking about religious matters has been affected by the absorption of the ideas of moral goodness and omnipotence into the concept of God. From time to time thinkers suggest that there is a God who is all-good but not all-powerful, or who is all-powerful but not all-good. Such suggestions clearly avoid the problem of evil; but we are merely bored by them. The alternatives are always tacitly restricted to two: either there is a God who is all-powerful and all-good, or there is no God at all. Christianity may not have convinced everybody, but it has certainly made us all very finicky. For (as Findlay has so forcibly reminded us[4]) the only God in whose existence we can evince interest is one whom it would be proper to worship. And worship in the Western world does not now mean the appeasing of an angry god or the encouragement of a weak one. It necessarily includes submission and moral reverence.

This important feature of the logic of theism goes so deep that it can be overlooked or misunderstood. In particular, since the very complexity of the demands made on the concept of deity by most people issues in a tacit rejection of many possible hypotheses intermediate between theism and atheism, there is a tendency for us to overlook the fact that there are a variety of reasons why the concept of God may be thought to have no application. An unbeliever may decide that no being is omnipotent, or that no being is omniscient, or that no being is all-good. Or he may decide that even if there exists a being who is all these things in the eyes of the believers he knows, the policies attributed to him are not such as to merit moral reverence. If he decides this he decides that the object of his friends' worship is not God; God does not exist. This is a *moral* rejection of theism. He may, yet again, reject theism on the ground that no being who was all-powerful, omniscient and all-good *by his friends' standards* would allow the evils that he and his friends both see to exist. *This* would be a logical reason for rejecting theism, even though it would lean, at critical points, on the attribution to God of moral goodness. Let us now explore this attribution with more care.

IV

There is something very odd about suggesting that although someone is morally good I have no idea what he would do in a wide range of situations; though it is quite possible for me to say that I do not know how he would handle some particularly knotty problem. The reason the second is possible is that familiar situations, where the good man's actions are predictable, do not supply precedents that yield ready answers to the knotty problems. In such cases the good man will likely serve as the source of such guidance, his suitability for this role deriving from his rectitude in more readily assessable situations. If this is correct it shows that evaluating someone as morally good may entail a readiness to agree to the wisdom of his decision on a difficult case just because it is he who is making the decision; but it also shows that this cannot cover *all* cases. His very authority derives from our having certified him as good, and this derives from his decisions in straightforward instances. These I acknowledge as good on the basis of *my own* moral standards. If I see that someone

---

[4]J. N. Findlay, "Can God's Existence be Disproved?" in Flew and MacIntyre, *New Essays in Philosophical Theology* (London: SCM, 1955), 47–56.

else, however consistent or deliberative, acts in straightforward cases in ways that manifest standards different from my own, I will not accept his decisions as a guide, and not evaluate his decisions as morally good. (If I call such a person good I shall refer to his motives not his particular choices, and, what is important here, I shall not regard the reasons he offers for his decisions as morally sound or sufficient, even though I shall not blame him for adhering to them.) The case of God may be different; but I shall put this possibility on one side for the present. What I wish to emphasise at this stage is that the concept of moral goodness, however, blessedly general it may look, nevertheless requires, when actually applied to a particular person and his actions *by* some particular person (in other words, when actually used rather than mentioned) the attribution to the person it is applied to of a fairly specific set of choice-patterns. More than this, these choice-patterns are (and this is a necessary truth, and a familiar one) the choice-patterns *of the speaker.* In calling someone morally good, a speaker must have in mind some set of moral standards which the man he calls good follows in his conduct. In Hare's terms, he must have criteria of goodness which the man he calls good satisfies.[5] And these must be criteria he subscribes to himself (though he need not, of course, act on them—he can show he subscribes to them by feeling guilty at *not* acting on them). For it is inconsistent to say that someone else's decisions are made in accordance with correct moral standards but that one does not subscribe to these standards oneself. It is true that people's criteria of goodness differ. But in calling someone good I have to use *some* set of criteria. And these have, banally, to be my own.

Extrapolating to the divine case is hazardous. But I will nevertheless hazard the following. In calling God good one is not merely applying to him some general epithet of commendation, with no ancillary commitment on what he might be expected to do. Although one cannot require God to do anything, in calling him good one is necessarily expressing the conviction that his behaviour will satisfy a certain set of moral standards; and in this case as in others, it is vacuous to apply the concept of goodness without a fairly detailed idea of what these standards are. These standards are standards which the speaker must regard as applying to himself. If God's actions are approved because it is God who does them, this is the result of his manifesting, in general, the standards to which believers subscribe themselves. I wish to conclude from this set of theses that in calling God good a theist is committed to saying that God's reasons for permitting evils must be reasons that are acceptable according to the believer's own set of moral standards. I wish to argue that in some important cases these are sufficiently restrictive to delineate a definite theodicy, even if it is not worked out in practice.

It is true that people's moral standards differ. But if they do, their concepts of God differ also; and, notoriously, one's concept of the will of God will be affected by one's independent moral judgments and the changes in them. Let us imagine two examples. A doctor, who believes in God, may find it hard to decide whether euthanasia is ever morally permissible. If he decides it never is, he will no doubt say euthanasia is contrary to the will of God. Let us now suppose that after some harrowing experiences he comes to believe that euthanasia is in some cases morally

---

[5]See *The Language of Morals* (Oxford: Clarendon Press, 1952), ch. 6.

right. How will he describe his state of mind? I think it is clear he will not say, "I used to agree with God that euthanasia is always wrong; but now I see he is mistaken." He will say, if he retains his belief, that he has reversed his view of what God's will is. If he has changed his mind about euthanasia but not about the divine will he must abandon his theism. Secondly, let us imagine a consistent disciple of Oscar Wilde, who believes that aesthetic values can properly take precedence over ethical ones. We can expect such a person, if he believes in God, to ascribe such standards to him, and not, therefore, to repudiate the aesthetic defence of theism that I outlined earlier. "Good," we are often reminded, is an evaluative term, and evaluations vary; but the concept of the being who gets the highest possible value-rating will vary with the scale of values of those who award the marks.

It should be emphasised that the word 'evil' is also an evaluative term. It is frequently said that observation will establish that the world contains evil. This is no doubt true, but the judgment that certain observed facts in the world are *to be classed as evils* is an evaluative judgment, however much the presence of those facts is established by observation. The theist can only be accused of inconsistency if the scale of values *he* uses commits him to saying that the facts *he* calls evil are allowed by God without reasons that *his* scale of values allows *him* to call morally sufficient; if the states of affairs *he* calls evil ones are undefeated on *his* scale of values by other facts conjoined with them. And of course the theist commits no logical mistake if he rejects the sceptic's value-scale, and insists that certain apparent evils are not evils at all, and certain apparent goods not goods at all. We must avoid posing the problem as one where the theist is attacked for accepting the existence of certain facts which only the critic regards as evil and ascribing to God reasons which only the critic would refuse to accept as morally good. This is a moral disagreement, not a logical one. We must also avoid the suggestion that the recognition of the evil facts is straightforwardly empirical, and their justification something more besides. If the facts are to pose a problem at all, they have to be accepted by the believer as potential counter-examples; and moral agreement here is too readily assumed. This is one of the many places where Christianity is paying a high price for its social success.

It might be agreed thus far that in ascribing the creation of the world to a being he classifies as all-good, the theist is ascribing to God a scale of values akin to his own, and that this circumscribes the range of possible reasons for allowing evil that he can consistently ascribe to God. But this may seem a long way from admitting that the theist is committed in most or any cases to the choice of one or two such reasons, or from admitting that he cannot in the tough cases resort to agnosticism on the grounds that God knows best and we do not understand.

Let us look at the second first. Certainly it seems reasonable in the case of any person endowed with high moral standing and authority to say that he should be the source of advice, and even to go so far as to say that *his* deciding one way rather than the other may serve, now and again, as a criterion of the correctness of the decision. If this can go for wise men, why not for the deity? Certainly there is a strong theological tradition which argues, against Plato, that some things are right because God does them rather than that God does them because they are right. I think the retort to this for our present purpose is not to contest this possibility, but to allow it and contest its relevance. Certainly I might say that I have accepted the

Pope's moral authority and must therefore accept what he says on birth control, even though it runs counter to my own intuitions in these matters. This is allowable, but does have one consequence. Having decided that the authority's decision has to stand, I am not at liberty to leave my principles unaffected. If the Pope's stand on birth control is agreed to, so be it; but then I must sacrifice any principles I previously held with which this value-decision is inconsistent. Or I must show that there are no real inconsistencies, only apparent ones. Then of course those who object to the papal pronouncements have a straightforwardly moral disagreement with me— and it follows at once that their concept of God cannot be mine, or (what comes to the same here) that they think the Pope is not the infallible mouthpiece of the Holy Ghost. We do not need to insist that God's moral authority depends on his decisions' coinciding with our moral intuitions; but we do need to insist that if we accept a purported moral decision as coming from God, our moral intuitions have to be put aside as misleading if they do not coincide with that decision. What is necessary is that the moral principles the theist holds to and the ones he ascribes to God are the same. Here again we have to allow for the fact that an omnipotent and omniscient being will not be in situations that compare precisely with any in which we find ourselves (God, in fact, is never "in" situations at all); but the principles he follows must be the same. A rich man with no family and a poor man with a large one will no doubt respond differently to the same request for money; yet their moral principles can be identical.

The problem of internal consistency would arise if some moral decision were ascribed to God which was inconsistent with moral principles the theist could not adjust or abandon, because they were previously held by him to have divine sanction. And it would arise also if the only logically possible reasons for the existence of a given evil were inconsistent with such principles. This would show, if it happened, that there are no morally sufficient reasons possible for the evil in question (that it is indefeasible), and that agnosticism regarding the reasons God actually might have does not provide an escape-route for the theist.

How would we know when such a case was before us? The answer, I think, is "when the system of values adhered to by the believer, and ascribed to God, is one which contains specific guidance on what goods do and do not defeat certain evils, or upon what is and is not a morally sufficient reason for certain evils; when a given evil is agreed to exist, and the goods which might defeat it do not." If this general answer is agreed to, it will readily be seen that some forms of theism would indeed permit a wide range of instances where a prudent agnosticism on matters of theodicy might be possible, and others would not permit any range at all. One could only argue from this point on with particular theists with particular scales of value. Catholics would have much less room for manœuvre than Unitarians. I propose to discuss the case of a moderately sophisticated biblical Protestant.

V

It would be absurd to attempt a detailed characterisation of Christian ethics here. But two features of it are particularly striking and important. The first is the fact that Christian principles are in many cases rules for assigning priorities in choice, and serve as guides to relatively complex moral situations, not as mere classifications of certain states of affairs as good or bad. To illustrate, let us consider the contrast between Christian ethics and hedonistic ethics. The latter are based upon the fundamentally simple assertions that pleasure is the main or only good and pain the main or only evil. The fundamental principles of Christian ethics, such as the Ten Commandments, deal directly with complex moral situations such as stealing, murder, or adultery, rather than with their ingredients. Notoriously they do not even say unambiguously whether pleasure and pain are good or bad; they direct attention at once onto occasions where we are called upon, as moral agents, to assign a precedence among various possibilities. However good pleasure may be, or however bad frustration may be, if the potential partner in the enterprise is another man's wife, the pleasure is forbidden. The goodness of the pleasure, if any, is defeated by the badness of the violation of the marriage-bond; and the badness, if any, of the frustration, is defeated by the goodness of the observance of it. However good, if at all, the acquisition of property is, the badness of depriving someone to whom it already belongs defeats it. The ethic makes fundamental use of notions such as temptation and resistance, which themselves suggest this sort of complexity of choice. The second feature requiring emphasis here is the fact that as it finds expression in the New Testament, the Christian ethic places uniquely high value on certain personal qualities and relationships, founded upon love. The value assigned to pleasure or pain would seem to depend upon their relationship to these qualities (or to their opposites) in complex situations. Clearly in the Christian tradition pleasure in the infliction of suffering makes the infliction worse, not better; although the same conclusion can be arrived at in a hedonistic ethic, a good deal of casuistic footwork needs to be done to reach it. Christianity obviously rejects the thesis that pleasure is the only good, and does not clearly embrace even the modest thesis that it is good *per se,* i.e. in the absence of bad accompaniments. It even more obviously rejects the principle that pain is the only, or even the greatest, evil, though in enjoining its diminution it would seem to embrace the thesis that it is *per se* bad, i.e. bad when not a means to that which is prized, such as steadfastness, forgiveness or humility.

If these brief characterisations of the ethics associated with one familiar form of theism are correct, it follows, I would suggest, that its adherents are committed to the principles of a familiar form of theodicy, and embroiled thereby in its problems. For they are committed to a moral scheme which requires them to judge the value of certain states of affairs in the light of that of others. This, in turn, will determine their judgments on what are, and (equally importantly) what are not, morally sufficient reasons for certain kinds of action or inaction. As theists they are committed to ascribing this very scheme of moral priorities to God, to ascribing to him, in other words, a set of policies which have to determine what evils have to be allowed by him in his creation. More accurately, they are committed to ascribing to him the particular sorts of reasons which *their* ethic would permit them to regard as sufficient for the evils which his creation can independently be seen to contain. They have to say, in other words, that the universe is run on Christian principles, and when they encounter a state of affairs which, by those principles, is evil, they must in consistency hold that it is permitted by God for reasons which are applications of those principles. This follows from calling God good and this state of affairs evil. More specifically, if certain forms of spiritual life and relationship have the highest place in the application of Christian principles, God too must value them highly, and evils he permits must only *appear* to contravene the ascription of these values to him; when rightly understood they have to be thought of as furthering them. We seem to be involved, therefore, in the traditional theological exercise of regarding all evils as justified, if God exists, by the possibility of some spiritual benefit of which they are the necessary condition.

This is not to say that a commitment to a general theodicy of this sort is tantamount to agreement to any particular theologian's justification of a particular historical evil, like the Lisbon earthquake. It is, however, tantamount to the acceptance of a limited *range* of possible explanations (those that entail ascribing to God a choice good by Christian standards) and the rejection of others. The problem becomes the acute difficulty of internal consistency it is traditionally alleged to be when the permissible range provides no reason that will fit some state of affairs that is admittedly an evil one. (A theodicy emphasising spiritual benefits can perhaps offer reason for human suffering, but seems unable to deal with animal pain, for example. Such an evil may not be in practice the worst, but it may be in theology the most intractable.)

Even this limitation allows a wide range of theological interpretation. Two areas of potential variation should be mentioned. There is, first of all, some ambiguity in the ascription to God of the value-scale of a believer. Our moral principles tell us what to do in certain sets of circumstances. God is not limited by circumstances, but creates them. Some principles tell us what to do in bad circumstances, e.g. the rule that we should forgive injuries. In ascribing such a standard to God we do of course imply that he forgives those who commit offences against him. But do we also imply that he so prizes forgiveness in us that his goodness requires him to provide (or allow) the unpleasant occasions that call for its exercise? Granted that when Smith injures Jones, Jones ought to forgive Smith; is the evil of Smith's injury to Jones justified by the fact that only it, or something like it, could afford Jones an opportunity to show forgiveness? It is at least plausible to argue that a theodicy that would justify the evil by reference to its potential for training men in the right spiritual responses would require us to ascribe to God this very strong sort of adherence to the value of forgiveness; but it is not obviously necessary to do so. Furthermore, the spiritual states most highly prized in the Christian tradition are only possible for free agents; hence the great emphasis on man's freedom of choice in all the major theodicies. This emphasis enables apologists to distinguish between natural evils like pain (evils which can elicit good states of mind but which are not caused by bad states of mind) and moral evils like vengefulness which *are* bad states of mind. The latter can all be blamed on the misuse of human free choice, which is a logically necessary condition of good states of mind like love and forgiveness, or fortitude, which can turn natural evils into ingredients of good situations. From this in turn it follows that the badness of many actual bad states of mind can be regarded as justified by the fact that their very possibility is a necessary condition of the free choice which is logically required for the chance of the good states of mind which have not, on these occasions, materialised. This generates the problem of whether free choice is itself a good which God fosters. It is not obvious what the apologist should say to this. All he *has* to say is that the highest goods in the Christian tradition are states of mind and relationships which cannot exist without free choice; so that the presence of some evils which free choice can lead to (such as revenge instead of forgiveness) is due to the wrong exercise of a faculty which one has to have to achieve the preferred states of mind. This would seem to leave open, and perhaps to render unimportant, the issue of the intrinsic value of free choice itself.

These two areas of potential controversy are enough to show that there is much freedom of theological manœuvre even within the fairly specific value scheme of Christian theism. It is nevertheless true, however, that Christian theism, by calling God omnipotent and omniscient *and* wholly good, requires its adherents to hold that he permits such evils as there are for Christian reasons; and that these involve his being said to allow them in the interests of certain spiritual states in his creatures, who have, to participate in these states, to be capable of free choice. A Christian theist, therefore, is committed to some form or other of the traditional "free-will defence."

VI

To sum up: I have argued that any theist, in calling his God good, ascribes to him his own moral principles, and implies that the world is created and governed in a way which ideally represents their exercise. Any evils he admits to being in the world must, he must say, be allowed by God because their presence is at least compatible with the futherance of those ends regarded on the very scale which classes the evils *as* evils, as being supremely good. The existence of any admitted evil not so compatible would refute the believer's theism; for to admit its existence would be to introduce an element of inconsistency into the theist's position. When this is recognised it becomes clear that a theist is committed to a scheme of theodicy in two ways at least. He cannot remain confidently agnostic about the range of purposes for which God would allow evils. And the more specific his moral code is on moral priorities, the more precise he has to be in suggesting possible divine reasons for particular evils. I have suggested that *Christian* theism is quite specific on moral priorities, and that it lays fundamental stress on certain relationships and states of mind. A Christian theist, faced with what he admits to be an evil, has therefore to hold that God allows it because the existence or possibility of it, or of something equally bad, is a necessary condition of some such relationship or state of mind. To admit the existence of an evil which demonstrably cannot have this function would be to admit a proposition inconsistent with Christian theism. For such an evil would be *pointless*. It is logically inconsistent for a theist to admit the existence of a pointless evil.

Pike argued that for the problem of evil to present a logical challenge to the theist, it must be possible to show that his proposition III:

A being who is omnipotent and omniscient would have no morally sufficient reason for allowing instances of evil is a necessary truth; and that it is not possible to show it to be one. In all its high generality it is not. I have tried to show, however, that in a given form of theism the concept of a morally sufficient reason may be sufficiently restricted to render it impossible for an omnipotent and omniscient being to have morally sufficient reasons for some evils. If such evils seem to exist in fact, then the problem of evil presents itself to the theist as the logical difficulty it has traditionally been thought to be.

Similarly, Chisholm's suggestion that a theist can hold that every evil is defeated without claiming to know by what, must contend with the fact that in a given form of theism the range of possible defeating factors may be specifically understood and incorporated in its moral requirements. If it should seem that a particular evil is not so defeasible its existence poses a logical difficulty to the theist as it has traditionally been thought to do.

God and the State *(excerpt)*

Michael Bakunin

Who are right, the idealists or the materialists? The question once stated in this way hesitation becomes impossible. Undoubtedly the idealists are wrong and the materialists right. Yes, facts are before ideas; yes, the ideal, as Proudhon said, is but a flower, whose root lies in the material conditions of existence. Yes, the whole history of humanity, intellectual and moral, political and social, is but a reflection of its economic history.

All branches of modern science, of true and disinterested science, concur in proclaiming this grand truth, fundamental and decisive: The social world, properly speaking, the human world—in short, humanity—is nothing other than the last and supreme development—at least on our planet and as far as we know—the highest manifestation of animality. But as every development necessarily implies a negation, that of its base or point of departure, humanity is at the same time and essentially the deliberate and gradual negation of the animal element in man; and it is precisely this negation, as rational as it is natural, and rational only because natural—at once historical and logical, as inevitable as the development and realization of all the natural laws in the world—that constitutes and creates the ideal, the world of intellectual and moral convictions, ideas.

Yes, our first ancestors, our Adams and our Eves, were, if not gorillas, very near relatives of gorillas, omnivorous, intelligent and ferocious beasts, endowed in a higher degree than the animals of any other species with two precious faculties— *the power to think* and *the desire to rebel.*

These faculties, combining their progressive action in the devil did not deceive Adam and Eve in promising them knowledge and liberty as a reward for the act of disobedience which he had induced them to commit; for, immediately they had

Source: With a new introduction and index of persons by Paul Avrich. New York: Dover Publications, Inc., 1970, 11–30.

eaten of the forbidden fruit, God himself said (see Bible): "Behold, the man is become as one of the gods, to know good and evil; prevent him, therefore, from eating of the fruit of eternal life, lest he become immortal like Ourselves."

Let us disregard now the fabulous portion of this myth and consider its true meaning, which is very clear. Man has emancipated himself; he has separated himself from animality and constituted himself a man; he has begun his distinctively human history and development by an act of disobedience and science—that is, by *rebellion* and by *thought.*

Three elements or, if you like, three fundamental principles constitute the essential conditions of all human development, collective or individual, in history: (1) *human animality;* (2) *thought;* and (3) *rebellion.* To the first properly corresponds *social and private economy;* to the second, *science;* to the third, *liberty.*

Idealists of all schools, aristocrats and *bourgeois,* theologians and metaphysicians, politicians and moralists, religionists, philosophers, or poets, not forgetting the liberal economists—unbounded worshippers of the ideal, as we know—are much offended when told that man, with his magnificent intelligence, his sublime ideas, and his boundless aspirations, is, like all else existing in the world, nothing but matter, only a product of *vile matter.*

We may answer that the matter of which materialists speak, matter spontaneously and eternally mobile, active, productive, matter chemically or organically determined and manifested by the properties or forces, mechanical, physical, animal, and intelligent, which necessarily belong to it—that this matter has nothing in common with the *vile matter* of the idealists. The latter, a product of their false abstraction, is indeed a stupid, inanimate, immobile thing, incapable of giving birth to the smallest product, a *caput mortuum,* an *ugly* fancy in contrast to the *beautiful* fancy which they call *God;* as the opposite of this supreme being, matter, their matter, stripped by them of all that constitutes its real nature, necessarily represents supreme nothingness. They have taken away from matter intelligence, life, all its determining qualities, active relations or forces, motion itself, without which matter would not even have weight, leaving it nothing but impenetrability and absolute immobility in space; they have attributed all these natural forces, properties, and manifestations to the imaginary being created by their abstract fancy; then, interchanging *rôles,* they have called this product of their imagination, this phantom, this God who is nothing, "supreme Being," and, as a necessary consequence, have declared that the real being, matter, the world, is nothing. After which they gravely tell us that this matter is incapable of producing anything, not even of setting itself in motion, and consequently must have been created by their God.

At the end of this book I exposed the fallacies and truly revolting absurdities to which one is inevitably led by this imagination of a God, let him be considered as a personal being, the creator and organizer of worlds; or even as impersonal, a kind of divine soul spread over the whole universe and constituting thus its eternal principle; or let him be an idea, infinite and divine, always present and active in the world, and always manifested by the totality of material and definite beings. Here I shall deal with one point only.

The gradual development of the material world, as well as of organic animal life and of the historically progressive intelligence of man, individually or socially, is perfectly conceivable. It is a wholly natural movement from the simple to the complex, from the lower to the higher, from the inferior to the superior; a movement in conformity with all our daily experiences, and consequently in conformity also with our natural logic, with the distinctive laws of our mind, which being formed and developed only by the aid of these same experiences, is, so to speak, but the mental, cerebral reproduction or reflected summary thereof.

The system of the idealists is quite the contrary of this. It is the reversal of all human experiences and of that universal and common good sense which is the essential condition of all human understanding, and which, in rising from the simple and unanimously recognized truth that twice two are four to the sublimest and most complex scientific considerations—admitting, moreover, nothing that has not stood the severest tests of experience or observation of things and facts—becomes the only serious basis of human knowledge.

Very far from pursuing the natural order from the lower to the higher, from the inferior to the superior, and from the relatively simple to the more complex; instead of wisely and rationally accompanying the progressive and real movement from the world called inorganic to the world organic, vegetables, animal, and then distinctively human—from chemical matter or chemical being to living matter or living being, and from living being to thinking being—the idealists, obsessed, blinded, and pushed on by the divine phantom which they have inherited from theology, take precisely the opposite course. They go from the higher to the lower, from the superior to the inferior, from the complex to the simple. They begin with God, either as a person or as divine substance or idea, and the first step that they take is a terrible fall from the sublime heights of the eternal ideal into the mire of the material world; from absolute perfection into absolute imperfection; from thought to being, or rather, from supreme being to nothing. When, how, and why the divine being, eternal, infinite, absolutely perfect, probably weary of himself, decided upon this desperate *salto mortale* is something which no idealist, no theologian, no metaphysician, no poet, has ever been able to understand himself or explain to the profane. All religions, past and present, and all the systems of transcendental philosophy hinge on this unique and iniquitous mystery.* Holy men, inspired lawgivers, prophets, messiahs, have searched it for life, and found only torment and death. Like the ancient sphinx, it has devoured them, because they could not explain it. Great philosophers, from Heraclitus and Plato down to Descartes, Spinoza, Leibnitz, Kant, Fichte, Schelling, and Hegel, not to mention the Indian philosophers, have written heaps of volumes and built systems as ingenious as sublime, in which they have said by the way many beautiful and grand things and discovered immortal truths, but they have left this mystery, the principal object of their transcendental investigations, as unfathomable as before. The gigantic efforts of the most wonderful geniuses that the world has known, and who, one after another, for at least thirty centuries, have undertaken anew this labor of Sisyphus, have resulted only in

---

*I call it "iniquitous" because, as I believe I have proved in the Appendix alluded to, this mystery has been and still continues to be the consecration of all the horrors which have been and are being committed in the world; I call it unique, because all the other theological and metaphysical absurdities which debase the human mind are but its necessary consequences.

rendering this mystery still more incomprehensible. Is it to be hoped that it will be unveiled to us by the routine speculations of some pedantic disciple of an artificially warmed-over metaphysics at a time when all living and serious spirits have abandoned that ambiguous science born of a compromise—historically explicable no doubt—between the unreason of faith and sound scientific reason?

It is evident that this terrible mystery is inexplicable—that is, absurd, because only the absurd admits of no explanation. It is evident that whoever finds it essential to his happiness and life must renounce his reason, and return, if he can, to naive, blind, stupid faith, to repeat with Tertullianus and all sincere believers these words, which sum up the very quintessence of theology: *Credo quia absurdum.* Then all discussion ceases, and nothing remains but the triumphant stupidity of faith. But immediately there arises another question: *How comes an intelligent and well-informed man ever to feel the need of believing in this mystery?*

Nothing is more natural than that the belief in God, the creator, regulator, judge, master, curser, savior, and benefactor of the world, should still prevail among the people, especially in the rural districts, where it is more widespread than among the proletariat of the cities. The people, unfortunately, are still very ignorant, and are kept in ignorance by the systematic efforts of all the governments, who consider this ignorance, not without good reason, as one of the essential conditions of their own power. Weighted down by their daily labor, deprived of leisure, of intellectual intercourse, of reading, in short of all the means and a good portion of the stimulants that develop thought in men, the people generally accept religious traditions without criticism and in a lump. These traditions surround them from infancy in all the situations of life, and artificially sustained in their minds by a multitude of official poisoners of all sorts, priests and laymen, are transformed therein into a sort of mental and moral habit, too often more powerful even than their natural good sense.

There is another reason which explains and in some sort justifies the absurd beliefs of the people—namely, the wretched situation to which they find themselves fatally condemned by the economic organization of society in the most civilized countries of Europe. Reduced, intellectually and morally as well as materially, to the minimum of human existence, confined in their life like a prisoner in his prison, without horizon, without outlet, without even a future if we believe the economists, the people would have the similarly narrow souls and blunted instincts of the bourgeois if they did not feel a desire to escape; but of escape there are but three methods—two chimerical and a third real. The first two are the dram-shop and the church, debauchery of the body or debauchery of the mind; the third is social revolution. Hence I conclude this last will be much more potent than all the theological propagandism of the freethinkers to destroy to their last vestige the religious beliefs and dissolute habits of the people, beliefs and habits much more intimately connected than is generally supposed. In substituting for the at once illusory and brutal enjoyments of bodily and spiritual licentiousness the enjoyments, as refined as they are real, of humanity developed in each and all, the social revolution alone will have the power to close at the same time all the dram-shops and all the churches.

Till then the people, taken as a whole, will believe; and, if they have no reason to believe, they will have at least a right.

There is a class of people who, if they do not believe, must at least make a semblance of believing. This class, comprising all the tormentors, all the oppressors, and all the exploiters of humanity; priests, monarchs, statesmen, soldiers, public and private financiers, officials of all sorts, policemen, gendarmes, jailers and executioners, monopolists, capitalists, tax-leeches, contractors and landlords, lawyers, economists, politicians of all shades, down to the smallest vendor of sweetmeats, all will repeat in unison those words of Voltaire:

"If God did not exist, it would be necessary to invent him." For, you understand, "the people must have a religion." That is the safety-valve.

There exists, finally, a somewhat numerous class of honest but timid souls who, too intelligent to take the Christian dogmas seriously, reject them in detail, but have neither the courage nor the strength nor the necessary resolution to summarily renounce them altogether. They abandon to your criticism all the special absurdities of religion, they turn up their noses at all the miracles, but they cling desperately to the principal absurdity; the source of all the others, to the miracle that explains and justifies all the other miracles, the existence of God. Their God is not the vigorous and powerful being, the brutally positive God of theology. It is a nebulous, diaphanous, illusory being that vanishes into nothing at the first attempt to grasp it; it is a mirage, an *ignis fatuus* that neither warms nor illuminates. And yet they hold fast to it, and believe that, were it to disappear, all would disappear with it. They are uncertain, sickly souls, who have lost their reckoning in the present civilization, belonging to neither the present nor the future, pale phantoms eternally suspended between heaven and earth, and occupying exactly the same position between the politics of the bourgeois and the Socialism of the proletariat. They have neither the power nor the wish nor the determination to follow out their thought, and they waste their time and pains in constantly endeavoring to reconcile the irreconcilable. In public life these are known as bourgeois Socialists.

With them, or against them, discussion is out of the question. They are too puny.

But there are a few illustrious men of whom no one will dare to speak without respect, and whose vigorous health, strength of mind, and good intention no one will dream of calling in question. I need only cite the names of Mazzini, Michelet, Quinet, John Stuart Mill.* Generous and strong souls, great hearts, great minds, great writers, and the first the heroic and revolutionary regenerator of a great nation, they are all apostles of idealism and bitter despisers and adversaries of materialism, and consequently of Socialism also, in philosophy as well as in politics.

Against them, then, we must discuss this question.

First, let it be remarked that not one of the illustrious men I have just named nor any other idealistic thinker of any consequence in our day has given any attention to the logical side of this question properly speaking. Not one has tried to settle philosophically the possibility of the divine *salto mortale* from the pure and eternal regions of spirit into the mire of the material world. Have they feared to

*Mr. Stuart Mill is perhaps the only one whose serious idealism may be fairly doubted, and that for two reasons: first, that, if not absolutely the disciple, he is a passionate admirer, an adherent of the positive philosophy of Auguste Comte, a philosophy which, in spite of its numerous reservations, is really Atheistic; second, that Mr. Stuart Mill is English, and in England to proclaim oneself an Atheist is to ostracise oneself, even at this late day.

approach this irreconcilable contradiction and despaired of solving it after the failures of the greatest geniuses of history, or have they looked upon it as already sufficiently well settled? That is their secret. The fact is that they have neglected the theoretical demonstration of the existence of a God, and have developed only its practical motives and consequences. They have treated it as a fact universally accepted, and, as such, no longer susceptible of any doubt whatever, for sole proof thereof limiting themselves to the establishment of the antiquity and this very universality of the belief in God.

This imposing unanimity, in the eyes of many illustrious men and writers to quote only the most famous of them who eloquently expressed it, Joseph de Maistre and the great Italian patriot, Giuseppe Mazzini—is of more value than all the demonstrations of science; and if the reasoning of a small number of logical and even very powerful, but isolated, thinkers is against it, so much the worse, they say, for these thinkers and their logic, for universal consent, the general and primitive adoption of an idea, has always been considered the most triumphant testimony to its truth. The sentiment of the whole world, a conviction that is found and maintained always and everywhere, cannot be mistaken; it must have its root in a necessity absolutely inherent in the very nature of man. And since it has been established that all peoples, past and present, have believed and still believe in the existence of God, it is clear that those who have the misfortune to doubt it, whatever the logic that led them to this doubt, are abnormal exceptions, monsters.

Thus, then, the *antiquity* and *universality* of a belief should be regarded, contrary to all science and all logic, as sufficient and unimpeachable proof of its truth. Why?

Until the days of Copernicus and Galileo everybody believed that the sun revolved about the earth. Was not everybody mistaken? What is more ancient and more universal than slavery? Cannibalism perhaps. From the origin of historic society down to the present day there has been always and everywhere exploitation of the compulsory labor of the masses—slaves, serfs, or wage-workers—by some dominant minority; oppression of the people by the Church and by the State. Must it be concluded that this exploitation and this oppression are necessities absolutely inherent in the very existence of human society? These are examples which show that the argument of the champions of God proves nothing.

Nothing, in fact, is as universal or as ancient as the iniquitous and absurd; truth and justice, on the contrary, are the least universal, the youngest features in the development of human society. In this fact, too, lies the explanation of a constant historical phenomenon—namely, the persecution of which those who first proclaim the truth have been and continue to be the objects at the hands of the official, privileged, and interested representatives of "universal" and "ancient" beliefs, and often also at the hands of the same masses who, after having tortured them, always end by adopting their ideas and rendering them victorious.

To us materialists and Revolutionary Socialists, there is nothing astonishing or terrifying in this historical phenomenon. Strong in our conscience, in our love of truth at all hazards, in that passion for logic which of itself alone constitutes a great power and outside of which there is no thought; strong in our passion for justice and in our unshakable faith in the triumph of humanity over all theoretical and practical bestialities; strong, finally, in the mutual confidence and support given each other by the few who share our convictions—we resign ourselves to all the consequences of this historical phenomenon, in which we see the manifestation of a social law as natural, as necessary, and as invariable as all the other laws which govern the world.

This law is a logical, inevitable consequence of the *animal origin* of human society; for in face of all the scientific, physiological, psychological, and historical proofs accumulated at the present day, as well as in face of the exploits of the Germans conquering France, which now furnish so striking a demonstration thereof, it is no longer possible to really doubt this origin. But from the moment that this animal origin of man is accepted, all is explained. History then appears to us as the revolutionary negation, now slow, apathetic, sluggish, now passionate and powerful, of the past. It consists precisely in the progressive negation of the primitive animality of man by the development of his humanity. Man, a wild beast, cousin of the gorilla, has emerged from the profound darkness of animal instinct into the light of the mind, which explains in a wholly natural way all his past mistakes and partially consoles us for his present errors. He has gone out from animal slavery, and passing through divine slavery, a temporary condition between his animality and his humanity, he is now marching on to the conquest and realization of human liberty. Whence it results that the antiquity of a belief, of an idea, far from proving anything in its favor, ought, on the contrary, to lead us to suspect it. For behind us is our animality and before us our humanity; human light, the only thing that can warm and enlighten us, the only thing that can emancipate us, give us dignity, freedom, and happiness, and realize fraternity among us, is never at the beginning, but, relatively to the epoch in which we live, always at the end of history. Let us, then, never look back, let us look ever forward; for forward is our sunlight, forward our salvation. If it is justifiable, and even useful and necessary, to turn back to study our past, it is only in order to establish what we have been and what we must no longer be, what we have believed and thought and what we must no longer believe or think, what we have done and what we must do nevermore.

So much for *antiquity*. As for the *universality* of an error, it proves but one thing—the similarity, if not the perfect identity, of human nature in all ages and under all skies. And, since it is established that all peoples, at all periods of their life, have believed and still believe in God, we must simply conclude that the divine idea, an outcome of ourselves, is an error historically necessary in the development of humanity, and ask why and how it was produced in history and why an immense majority of the human race still accept it as a truth.

Until we shall account to ourselves for the manner in which the idea of a supernatural or divine world was developed and had to be developed in the historical evolution of the human conscience, all our scientific conviction of its absurdity will be in vain; until then we shall never succeed in destroying it in the opinion of the majority, because we shall never be able to attack it in the very depths of the human being where it had birth. Condemned to a fruitless struggle, without issue and without end, we should for ever have to content ourselves with fighting it solely on the surface, in its innumerable manifestations, whose absurdity will be scarcely beaten down by the blows of common sense before it will reappear in a new form no less nonsensical. While the root of all the absurdities that torment the world, belief in God, remains intact, it will never fail to bring forth new offspring. Thus, at the present time, in certain sections of the highest society, Spiritualism tends to establish itself upon the ruins of Christianity.

It is not only in the interest of the masses, it is in that of the health of our own minds, that we should strive to understand the historic genesis, the succession of causes which developed and produced the idea of God in the consciousness of men. In vain shall we call and believe ourselves Atheists, until we comprehend these causes, for, until then, we shall always suffer ourselves to be more or less governed by the clamors of this universal conscience whose secret we have not discovered; and, considering the natural weakness of even the strongest individual against the all-powerful influence of the social surroundings that trammel him, we are always in danger of relapsing sooner or later, in one way or another, into the abyss of religious absurdity. Examples of these shameful conversions are frequent in society to-day.

I have stated the chief practical reason of the power still exercised to-day over the masses by religious beliefs. These mystical tendencies do not signify in man so much an aberration of mind as a deep discontent at heart. They are the instinctive and passionate protest of the human being against the narrowness, the platitudes, the sorrows, and the shame of a wretched existence. For this malady, I have already said, there is but one remedy—Social Revolution.

In the meantime I have endeavored to show the causes responsible for the birth and historical development of religious hallucinations in the human conscience. Here it is my purpose to treat this question of the existence of a God, or of the divine origin of the world and of man, solely from the standpoint of its moral and social utility, and I shall say only a few words, to better explain my thought, regarding the theoretical grounds of this belief.

All religions, with their gods, their demigods, and their prophets, their messiahs and their saints, were created by the credulous fancy of men who had not attained the full development and full possession of their faculties. Consequently, the religious heaven is nothing but a mirage in which man, exalted by ignorance and faith, discovers his own image, but enlarged and reversed—that is, *divinized.* The history of religions, of the birth, grandeur, and decline of the gods who have succeeded one another in human belief, is nothing, therefore, but the development of the collective intelligence and conscience of mankind. As fast as they discovered, in the course of their historically progressive advance, either in themselves or in external nature, a power, a quality, or even any great defect whatever, they attributed them to their gods, after having exaggerated and enlarged them beyond measure, after the manner of children, by an act of their religious fancy. Thanks to this modesty and pious generosity of believing and credulous men, heaven has grown rich with the spoils of the earth, and, by a necessary consequence, the richer heaven became, the more wretched became humanity and the earth. God once installed, he was naturally proclaimed the cause, reason, arbiter, and absolute disposer of all things: the world thenceforth was nothing, God was all; and man, his real creator, after having unknowingly extracted him from the void, bowed down before him, worshipped him, and avowed himself his creature and his slave.

Christianity is precisely the religion *par excellence,* because it exhibits and manifests, to the fullest extent, the very nature and essence of every religious system, which is *the impoverishment, enslavement, and annihilation of humanity for the benefit of divinity.*

God being everything, the real world and man are nothing. God being truth, justice, goodness, beauty, power, and life, man is falsehood, iniquity, evil, ugliness, impotence, and death. God being master, man is the slave. Incapable of finding justice, truth, and eternal life by his own effort, he can attain them only through a divine revelation. But whoever says revelation says revealers, messiahs, prophets, priests, and legislators inspired by God himself; and these, once recognized as the representatives of divinity on earth, as the holy instructors of humanity, chosen by God himself to direct it in the path of salvation, necessarily exercise absolute power. All men owe them passive and unlimited obedience; for against the divine reason there is no human reason, and against the justice of God no terrestrial justice holds. Slaves of God, men must also be slaves of Church and State, *in so far as the State is consecrated by the Church.* This truth Christianity, better than all other religions that exist or have existed, understood, not excepting even the old Oriental religions, which included only distinct and privileged nations, while Christianity aspires to embrace entire humanity; and this truth Roman Catholicism, alone among all the Christian sects, has proclaimed and realized with rigorous logic. That is why Christianity is the absolute religion, the final religion; why the Apostolic and Roman Church is the only consistent, legitimate, and divine church.

With all due respect, then, to the metaphysicians and religious idealists, philosophers, politicians, or poets: *The idea of God implies the abdication of human reason and justice; it is the most decisive negation of human liberty, and necessarily ends in the enslavement of mankind, both in theory and practice.*

Unless, then, we desire the enslavement and degradation of mankind, as the Jesuits desire it, as the *mômiers,* pietists, or Protestant Methodists desire it, we may not, must not make the slightest concession either to the God of theology or to the God of metaphysics. He who, in this mystical alphabet, begins with A will inevitably end with Z; he who desires to worship God must harbor no childish allusions about the matter, but bravely renounce his liberty and humanity.

If God is, man is a slave; now, man can and must be free; then, God does not exist.

I defy anyone whomsoever to avoid this circle; now, therefore, let all choose.

Is it necessary to point out to what extent and in what manner religions debase and corrupt the people? They destroy their reason, the principal instrument of human emancipation, and reduce them to imbecility, the essential condition of their slavery. They dishonor human labor, and make it a sign and source of servitude. They kill the idea and sentiment of human justice, ever tipping the balance to the side of triumphant knaves, privileged objects of divine indulgence. They kill human pride and dignity, protecting only the cringing and humble. They stifle in the heart of nations every feeling of human fraternity, filling it with divine cruelty instead.

All religions are cruel, all founded on blood; for all rest principally on the idea of sacrifice—that is, on the perpetual immolation of humanity to the insatiable vengeance of divinity. In this bloody mystery man is always the victim, and the priest—a man also, but a man privileged by grace—is the divine executioner. That explains why the priests of all religions, the best, the most humane, the gentlest, almost always have at the bottom of their hearts—and, if not in their hearts, in their imaginations, in their minds (and we know the fearful influence of either on the hearts of men)—something cruel and sanguinary.

None know all this better than our illustrious contemporary idealists. They are learned men, who know history by heart; and, as they are at the same time living men, great souls penetrated with a sincere and profound love for the welfare of humanity, they have cursed and branded all these misdeeds, all these crimes of religion with an eloquence unparalleled. They reject with indignation all solidarity with the God of positive religions and with his representatives, past, present, and on earth.

The God whom they adore, or whom they think they adore, is distinguished from the real gods of history precisely in this—that he is not at all a positive god, defined in any way whatever, theologically or even metaphysically. He is neither the supreme being of Robespierre and J. J. Rousseau, nor the pantheistic god of Spinoza, nor even the at once immanent, transcendental, and very equivocal god of Hegel. They take good care not to give him any positive definition whatever, feeling very strongly that any definition would subject him to the dissolving power of criticism. They will not say whether he is a personal or impersonal god, whether he created or did not create the world; they will not even speak of his divine providence. All that might compromise him. They content themselves with saying "God" and nothing more. But, then, what is their God? Not even an idea; it is an aspiration.

It is the generic name of all that seems grand, good, beautiful, noble, human to them. But why, then, do they not say, "Man." Ah! because King William of Prussia and Napoleon III. and all their compeers are likewise men: which bothers them very much. Real humanity presents a mixture of all that is most sublime and beautiful with all that is vilest and most monstrous in the world. How do they get over this? Why, they call one *divine* and the other *bestial,* representing divinity and animality as two poles, between which they place humanity. They either will not or cannot understand that these three terms are really but one, and that to separate them is to destroy them.

They are not strong on logic, and one might say that they despise it. That is what distinguishes them from the pantheistical and deistical metaphysicians, and gives their ideas the character of a practical idealism, drawing its inspiration much less from the severe development of a thought than from the experiences, I might almost say the emotions, historical and collective as well as individual, of life. This gives their propaganda an appearance of wealth and vital power, but an appearance only; for life itself becomes sterile when paralyzed by a logical contradiction.

This contradiction lies here: they wish God, and they wish humanity. They persist in connecting two terms which, once separated, can come together again only to destroy each other. They say in a single breath: "God and the liberty of man," "God and the dignity, justice, equality, fraternity, prosperity of men"— regardless of the fatal logic by virtue of which, if God exists, all these things are condemned to non-existence. For, if God is, he is necessarily the eternal, supreme, absolute master, and, if such a master exists, man is a slave; now, if he is a slave, neither justice, nor equality, nor fraternity, nor prosperity are possible for him. In vain, flying in the face of good sense and all the teachings of history, do they represent their God as animated by the tenderest love of human liberty: a master, whoever he may be and however liberal he may desire to show himself, remains none the less always a master. His existence necessarily implies the slavery of all that is beneath him. Therefore, if God existed, only in one way could he serve human liberty—by ceasing to exist.

A jealous lover of human liberty, and deeming it the absolute condition of all that we admire and respect in humanity, I reverse the phrase of Voltaire, and say that, *if God really existed, it would be necessary to abolish him.*

The severe logic that dictates these words is far too evident to require a development of this argument. And it seems to me impossible that the illustrious men, whose names so celebrated and so justly respected I have cited, should not have been struck by it themselves, and should not have perceived the contradiction in which they involve themselves in speaking of God and human liberty at once. To have disregarded it, they must have considered this inconsistency or logical license *practically* necessary to humanity's well-being.

Perhaps, too, while speaking of *liberty* as something very respectable and very dear in their eyes, they give the term a meaning quite different from the conception entertained by us, materialists and Revolutionary Socialists. Indeed, they never speak of it without immediately adding another word, *authority*—a word and a thing which we detest with all our heart.

What is authority? Is it the inevitable power of the natural laws which manifest themselves in the necessary concatenation and succession of phenomena in the physical and social worlds? Indeed, against these laws revolt is not only forbidden— it is even impossible. We may misunderstand them or not know them at all, but we cannot disobey them; because they constitute the basis and fundamental conditions of our existence; they envelop us, penetrate us, regulate all our movements, thoughts, and acts; even when we believe that we disobey them, we only show their omnipotence.

Yes, we are absolutely the slaves of these laws. But in such slavery there is no humiliation, or, rather, it is not slavery at all. For slavery supposes an external master, a legislator outside of him whom he commands, while these laws are not outside of us; they are inherent in us; they constitute our being, our whole being, physically, intellectually, and morally: we live, we breathe, we act, we think, we wish only through these laws. Without them we are nothing, *we are not.* Whence, then, could we derive the power and the wish to rebel against them?

In his relation to natural laws but one liberty is possible to man—that of recognizing and applying them on an ever-extending scale in conformity with the object of collective and individual emancipation or humanization which he pursues. These laws, once recognized, exercise an authority which is never disputed by the mass of men. One must, for instance, be at bottom either a fool or a theologian or at least a metaphysician, jurist, or bourgeois economist to rebel against the law by which twice two make four. One must have faith to imagine that fire will not burn nor water drown, except, indeed, recourse be had to some subterfuge founded in its turn on some other natural law. But these revolts, or, rather, these attempts at or foolish fancies of an impossible revolt, are decidedly the exception; for, in general, it may be said that the mass of men, in their daily lives, acknowledge the government of common sense—that is, of the sum of the natural laws generally recognized—in an almost absolute fashion.

The great misfortune is that a large number of natural laws, already established as such by science, remain unknown to the masses, thanks to the watchfulness of these tutelary governments that exist, as we know, only for the good of the people.

There is another difficulty—namely, that the major portion of the natural laws connected with the development of human society, which are quite as necessary, invariable, fatal, as the laws that govern the physical world, have not been duly established and recognized by science itself.

Once they shall have been recognized by science, and then from science, by means of an extensive system of popular education and instruction, shall have passed into the consciousness of all, the question of liberty will be entirely solved. The most stubborn authorities must admit that then there will be no need either of political organization or direction or legislation, three things which, whether they emanate from the will of the sovereign or from the vote of a parliament elected by universal suffrage, and even should they conform to the system of natural laws—which has never been the case and never will be the case—are always equally fatal and hostile to the liberty of the masses from the very fact that they impose upon them a system of external and therefore despotic laws.

The liberty of man consists solely in this: that he obeys natural laws because he has *himself* recognized them as such, and not because they have been externally imposed upon him by any extrinsic will whatever, divine or human, collective or individual.

Why I Am Not a Christian (excerpt)

Bertrand Russell

This lecture was delivered on March 6, 1927, at Battersea Town Hall under the auspices of the South London Branch of the National Secular Society.

As your Chairman has told you, the subject about which I am going to speak to you tonight is "Why I Am Not a Christian." Perhaps it would be as well, first of all, to try to make out what one means by the word *Christian*. It is used these days in a very loose sense by a great many people. Some people mean no more by it than a person who attempts to live a good life. In that sense I suppose there would be Christians in all sects and creeds; but I do not think that that is the proper sense of the word, if only because it would imply that all the people who are not Christians—all the Buddhists, Confucians, Mohammedans, and so on—are not trying to live a good life. I do not mean by a Christian any person who tries to live decently according to his lights. I think that you must have a certain amount of definite belief before you have a right to call yourself a Christian. The word does not have quite such a full-blooded meaning now as it had in the times of St. Augustine and St. Thomas Aquinas. In those days, if a man said that he was a Christian it was known what he meant. You accepted a whole collection of creeds which were set out with great precision, and every single syllable of those creeds you believed with the whole strength of your convictions.

Source: Why I Am Not a Christian and Other Essays on Related Subjects, edited with an appendix on the "Bertrand Russell Case" by Paul Edwards. New York: Simon and Schuster, 1957, 3–23.

WHAT IS A CHRISTIAN?

Nowadays it is not quite that. We have to be a little more vague in our meaning of Christianity. I think, however, that there are two different items which are quite essential to anybody calling himself a Christian. The first is one of a dogmatic nature—namely, that you must believe in God and immortality. If you do not believe in those two things, I do not think that you can properly call yourself a Christian. Then, further than that, as the name implies, you must have some kind of belief about Christ. The Mohammedans, for instance, also believe in God and in immortality, and yet they would not call themselves Christians. I think you must have at the very lowest the belief that Christ was, if not divine, at least the best and wisest of men. If you are not going to believe that much about Christ, I do not think you have any right to call yourself a Christian. Of course, there is another sense, which you find in *Whitaker's Almanack* and in geography books, where the population of the world is said to be divided into Christians, Mohammedans, Buddhists, fetish worshipers, and so on; and in that sense we are all Christians. The geography books count us all in, but that is a purely geographical sense, which I suppose we can ignore. Therefore I take it that when I tell you why I am not a Christian I have to tell you two different things: first, why I do not believe in God and in immortality; and, secondly, why I do not think that Christ was the best and wisest of men, although I grant him a very high degree of moral goodness.

But for the successful efforts of unbelievers in the past, I could not take so elastic a definition of Christianity as that. As I said before, in olden days it had a much more full-blooded sense. For instance, it included the belief in hell. Belief in eternal hell-fire was an essential item of Christian belief until pretty recent times. In this country, as you know, it ceased to be an essential item because of a decision of the Privy Council, and from that decision the Archbishop of Canterbury and the Archbishop of York dissented; but in this country our religion is settled by Act of Parliament, and therefore the Privy Council was able to override their Graces and hell was no longer necessary to a Christian. Consequently I shall not insist that a Christian must believe in hell.

THE EXISTENCE OF GOD

To come to this question of the existence of God: it is a large and serious question, and if I were to attempt to deal with it in any adequate manner I should have to keep you here until Kingdom Come, so that you will have to excuse me if I deal with it in a somewhat summary fashion. You know, of course, that the Catholic Church has laid it down as a dogma that the existence of God can be proved by the unaided reason. That is a somewhat curious dogma, but it is one of their dogmas. They had to introduce it because at one time the freethinkers adopted the habit of saying that there were such and such arguments which mere reason might urge against the existence of God, but of course they knew as a matter of faith that God did exist. The arguments and the reasons were set out at great length, and the Catholic Church felt that they must stop it. Therefore they laid it down that the existence of God can be proved by the unaided reason and they had to set up what they considered were arguments to prove it. There are, of course, a number of them, but I shall take only a few.

THE FIRST-CAUSE ARGUMENT

Perhaps the simplest and easiest to understand is the argument of the First Cause. (It is maintained that everything we see in this world has a cause, and as you go back in the chain of causes further and further you must come to a First Cause, and to that First Cause you give the name of God.) That argument, I suppose, does not carry very much weight nowadays, because, in the first place, cause is not quite what it used to be. The philosophers and the men of science have got going on cause, and it has not anything like the vitality it used to have; but, apart from that, you can see that the argument that there must be a First Cause is one that cannot have any validity. I may say that when I was a young man and was debating these questions very seriously in my mind, I for a long time accepted the argument of the First Cause, until one day, at the age of eighteen, I read John Stuart Mill's Autobiography, and I there found this sentence: "My father taught me that the question 'Who made me?' cannot be answered, since it immediately suggests the further question 'Who made God?'" That very simple sentence showed me, as I still think, the fallacy in the argument of the First Cause. If everything must have a cause, then God must have a cause. If there can be anything without a cause, it may just as well be the world as God, so that there cannot be any validity in that argument. It is exactly of the same nature as the Hindu's view, that the world rested upon an elephant and the elephant rested upon a tortoise; and when they said, "How about the tortoise?" the Indian said, "Suppose we change the subject." The argument is really no better than that. There is no reason why the world could not have come into being without a cause; nor, on the other hand, is there any reason why it should not have always existed. There is no reason to suppose that the world had a beginning at all. The idea that things must have a beginning is really due to the poverty of our imagination. Therefore, perhaps, I need not waste any more time upon the argument about the First Cause.

THE NATURAL-LAW ARGUMENT

Then there is a very common argument from natural law. That was a favorite argument all through the eighteenth century, especially under the influence of Sir Isaac Newton and his cosmogony. People observed the planets going around the sun according to the law of gravitation, and they thought that God had given a behest to these planets to move in that particular fashion, and that was why they did so. That was, of course, a convenient and simple explanation that saved them the trouble of looking any further for explanations of the law of gravitation. Nowadays we explain the law of gravitation in a somewhat complicated fashion that Einstein has introduced. I do not propose to give you a lecture on the law of gravitation, as interpreted by Einstein, because that again would take some time; at any rate, you no longer have the sort of natural law that you had in the Newtonian system, where, for some reason that nobody could understand, nature behaved in a uniform fashion. We now find that a great many things we thought were natural laws are really human conventions. You know that even in the remotest depths of stellar space there are still three feet to a yard. That is, no doubt, a very remarkable fact, but you would hardly call it a law of nature. And a great many things that have been regarded as laws of nature are of that kind. On the other hand, where you can get down to any knowledge of what atoms actually do, you will find they are much less subject to law than people thought, and that the laws at which you arrive are statistical averages of just the sort that would emerge from chance. There is, as we all know, a law that if you throw dice you will get double sixes only about once in thirty-six times, and we do not regard that as evidence that the fall of the dice is regulated by design; on the contrary, if the double sixes came every time we should think that there was design. The laws of nature are of that sort as regards a great many of them. They are statistical averages such as would emerge from the laws of chance; and that makes this whole business of natural law much less impressive than it formerly was. Quite apart from that, which represents the momentary state of science that may change tomorrow, the whole idea that natural laws imply a lawgiver is due to a confusion between natural and human laws. Human laws are behests commanding you to behave a certain way, in which way you may choose to behave, or you may choose not to behave; but natural laws are a description of how things do in fact behave, and being a mere description of what they in fact do, you cannot argue that there must be somebody who told them to do that, because even supposing that there were, you are then faced with the question "Why did God issue just those natural laws and no others?" If you say that he did it simply from his own good pleasure, and without any reason, you then find that there is something which is not subject to law, and so your train of natural law is interrupted. If you say, as more orthodox theologians do, that in all the laws which God issues he had a reason for giving those laws rather than others—the reason, of course, being to create the best universe, although you would never think it to look at it—if there were a reason for the laws which God gave, then God himself was subject to law, and therefore you do not get any advantage by introducing God as an intermediary. You have really a law outside and anterior to the divine edicts, and God does not serve your purpose, because he is not the ultimate lawgiver. In short, this whole argument about natural law no longer has anything like the strength that it used to have. I am traveling on in time in my review of the arguments. The arguments that are used for the existence of God change their character as time goes on. They were at first hard intellectual arguments embodying certain quite definite fallacies. As we come to modern times they become less respectable intellectually and more and more affected by a kind of moralizing vagueness.

THE ARGUMENT FROM DESIGN

The next step in this process brings us to the argument from design. You all know the argument from design: everything in the world is made just so that we can manage to live in the world, and if the world was ever so little different, we could not manage to live in it. That is the argument from design. It sometimes takes a rather curious form; for instance, it is argued that rabbits have white tails in order to be easy to shoot. I do not know how rabbits would view that application. It is an easy argument to parody. You all know Voltaire's remark, that obviously the nose was designed to be such as to fit spectacles. That sort of parody has turned out to be not nearly so wide of the mark as it might have seemed in the eighteenth century, because since the time of Darwin we understand much better why living creatures are adapted to their environment. It is not that their environment was made to be suitable to them but that they grew to be suitable to it, and that is the basis of adaptation. There is no evidence of design about it.

When you come to look into this argument from design, it is a most astonishing thing that people can believe that this world, with all the things that are in it, with all its defects, should be the best that omnipotence and omniscience have been able to produce in millions of years. I really cannot believe it. Do you think that, if you were granted omnipotence and omniscience and millions of years in which to perfect your world, you could produce nothing better than the Ku Klux Klan or the Fascists? Moreover, if you accept the ordinary laws of science, you have to suppose that human life and life in general on this planet will die out in due course: it is a stage in the decay of the solar system; at a certain stage of decay you get the sort of conditions of temperature and so forth which are suitable to protoplasm, and there is life for a short time in the life of the whole solar system. You see in the moon the sort of thing to which the earth is tending—something dead, cold, and lifeless.

I am told that that sort of view is depressing, and people will sometimes tell you that if they believed that, they would not be able to go on living. Do not believe it; it is all nonsense. Nobody really worries much about what is going to happen millions of years hence. Even if they think they are worrying much about that, they are really deceiving themselves. They are worried about something much more mundane, or it may merely be a bad digestion; but nobody is really seriously rendered unhappy by the thought of something that is going to happen to this world millions and millions of years hence. Therefore, although it is of course a gloomy view to suppose that life will die out—at least I suppose we may say so, although sometimes when I contemplate the things that people do with their lives I think it is almost a consolation—it is not such as to render life miserable. It merely makes you turn your attention to other things.

THE MORAL ARGUMENTS FOR DEITY

Now we reach one stage further in what I shall call the intellectual descent that the Theists have made in their argumentations, and we come to what are called the moral arguments for the existence of God. You all know, of course, that there used to be in the old days three intellectual arguments for the existence of God, all of which were disposed of by Immanuel Kant in the *Critique of Pure Reason;* but no sooner had he disposed of those arguments than he invented a new one, a moral argument, and that quite convinced him. He was like many people: in intellectual matters he was skeptical, but in moral matters he believed implicitly in the maxims that he had imbibed at his mother's knee. That illustrates what the psychoanalysts so much emphasize—the immensely stronger hold upon us that our very early associations have than those of later times.

Kant, as I say, invented a new moral argument for the existence of God, and that in varying forms was extremely popular during the nineteenth century. It has all sorts of forms. One form is to say that there would be no right or wrong unless God existed. I am not for the moment concerned with whether there is a difference between right and wrong, or whether there is not: that is another question. The point I am concerned with is that, if you are quite sure there is a difference between right and wrong, you are then in this situation: Is that difference due to God's fiat or is it not? If it is due to God's fiat, then for God himself there is no difference between right and wrong, and it is no longer a significant statement to say that God is good. If you are going to say, as theologians do, that God is good, you must then say that right and wrong have some meaning which is independent of God's fiat, because God's fiats are good and not bad independently of the mere fact that he made them. If you are going to say that, you will then have to say that it is not only through God that right and wrong came into being, but that they are in their essence logically anterior to God. You could, of course, if you liked, say that there was a superior deity who gave orders to the God who made this world, or could take up the line that some of the gnostics took up—a line which I often thought was a very plausible one—that as a matter of fact this world that we know was made by the devil at a moment when God was not looking. There is a good deal to be said for that, and I am not concerned to refute it.

THE ARGUMENT FOR THE REMEDYING OF INJUSTICE

Then there is another very curious form of moral argument, which is this: they say that the existence of God is required in order to bring justice into the world. In the part of this universe that we know there is great injustice, and often the good suffer, and often the wicked prosper, and one hardly knows which of those is the more annoying; but if you are going to have justice in the universe as a whole you have to suppose a future life to redress the balance of life here on earth. So they say that there must be a God, and there must be heaven and hell in order that in the long run there may be justice. That is a very curious argument. If you looked at the matter from a scientific point of view, you would say, "After all, I know only this world. I do not know about the rest of the universe, but so far as one can argue at all on probabilities one would say that probably this world is a fair sample, and if there is injustice here the odds are that there is injustice elsewhere also." Supposing you got a crate of oranges that you opened, and you found all the top layer of oranges bad, you would not argue, "The underneath ones must be good, so as to redress the balance." You would say, "Probably the whole lot is a bad consignment"; and that is really what a scientific person would argue about the universe. He would say, "Here we find in this world a great deal of injustice, and so far as that goes that is a reason for supposing that justice does not rule in the world; and therefore so far as it goes it affords a moral argument against deity and not in favor of one." Of course I know that the sort of intellectual arguments that I have been talking to you about are not what really moves people. What really moves people to believe in God is not any intellectual argument at all. Most people believe in God because they have been taught from early infancy to do it, and that is the main reason.

Then I think that the next most powerful reason is the wish for safety, a sort of feeling that there is a big brother who will look after you. That plays a very profound part in influencing people's desire for a belief in God.

THE CHARACTER OF CHRIST

I now want to say a few words upon a topic which I often think is not quite sufficiently dealt with by Rationalists, and that is the question whether Christ was the best and the wisest of men. It is generally taken for granted that we should all agree that that was so. I do not myself. I think that there are a good many points upon which I agree with Christ a great deal more than the professing Christians do. I do not know that I could go with Him all the way, but I could go with Him much further than most professing Christians can. You will remember that He said, "Resist not evil: but whosoever shall smite thee on thy right cheek, turn to him the other also." That is not a new precept or a new principle. It was used by Lao-tse and Buddha some 500 or 600 years before Christ, but it is not a principle which as a matter of fact Christians accept. I have no doubt that the present Prime Minister,* for instance, is a most sincere Christian, but I should not advise any of you to go and smite him on one cheek. I think you might find that he thought this text was intended in a figurative sense.

Then there is another point which I consider excellent. You will remember that Christ said, "Judge not lest ye be judged." That principle I do not think you would find was popular in the law courts of Christian countries. I have known in my time quite a number of judges who were very earnest Christians, and none of them felt that they were acting contrary to Christian principles in what they did. Then Christ says, "Give to him that asketh of thee, and from him that would borrow of thee turn not thou away." That is a very good principle. Your Chairman has reminded you that we are not here to talk politics, but I cannot help observing that the last general election was fought on the question of how desirable it was to turn away from him that would borrow of thee, so that one must assume that the Liberals and Conservatives of this country are composed of people who do not agree with the teaching of Christ, because they certainly did very emphatically turn away on that occasion.

Then there is one other maxim of Christ which I think has a great deal in it, but I do not find that it is very popular among some of our Christian friends. He says, "If thou wilt be perfect, go and sell that which thou hast, and give to the poor." That is a very excellent maxim, but, as I say, it is not much practiced. All these, I think, are good maxims, although they are a little difficult to live up to. I do not profess to live up to them myself; but then, after all, it is not quite the same thing as for a Christian.

*Stanley Baldwin.

DEFECTS IN CHRIST'S TEACHING

Having granted the excellence of these maxims, I come to certain points in which I do not believe that one can grant either the superlative wisdom or the superlative goodness of Christ as depicted in the Gospels; and here I may say that one is not concerned with the historical question. Historically it is quite doubtful whether Christ ever existed at all, and if He did we do not know anything about Him, so that I am not concerned with the historical question, which is a very difficult one. I am concerned with Christ as He appears in the Gospels, taking the Gospel narrative as it stands, and there one does find some things that do not seem to be very wise. For one thing, He certainly thought that His second coming would occur in clouds of glory before the death of all the people who were living at that time. There are a great many texts that prove that. He says, for instance, "Ye shall not have gone over the cities of Israel till the Son of Man be come." Then He says, "There are some standing here which shall not taste death till the Son of Man comes into His kingdom"; and there are a lot of places where it is quite clear that He believed that His second coming would happen during the lifetime of many then living. That was the belief of His earlier followers, and it was the basis of a good deal of His moral teaching. When He said, "Take no thought for the morrow," and things of that sort, it was very largely because He thought that the second coming was going to be very soon, and that all ordinary mundane affairs did not count. I have, as a matter of fact, known some Christians who did believe that the second coming was imminent. I knew a parson who frightened his congregation terribly by telling them that the second coming was very imminent indeed, but they were much consoled when they found that he was planting trees in his garden. The early Christians did really believe it, and they did abstain from such things as planting trees in their gardens, because they did accept from Christ the belief that the second coming was imminent. In that respect, clearly He was not so wise as some other people have been, and He was certainly not superlatively wise.

THE MORAL PROBLEM

Then you come to moral questions. There is one very serious defect to my mind in Christ's moral character, and that is that He believed in hell. I do not myself feel that any person who is really profoundly humane can believe in everlasting punishment. Christ certainly as depicted in the Gospels did believe in everlasting punishment, and one does find repeatedly a vindictive fury against those people who would not listen to His preaching—an attitude which is not uncommon with preachers, but which does somewhat detract from superlative excellence. You do not, for instance find that attitude in Socrates. You find him quite bland and urbane toward the people who would not listen to him; and it is, to my mind, far more worthy of a sage to take that line than to take the line of indignation. You probably all remember the sort of things that Socrates was saying when he was dying, and the sort of things that he generally did say to people who did not agree with him.

You will find that in the Gospels Christ said, "Ye serpents, ye generation of vipers, how can ye escape the damnation of hell." That was said to people who did not like His preaching. It is not really to my mind quite the best tone, and there are a great many of these things about hell. There is, of course, the familiar text about the sin against the Holy Ghost: "Whosoever speaketh against the Holy Ghost it shall not be forgiven him neither in this World nor in the world to come." That text has caused an unspeakable amount of misery in the world, for all sorts of people have imagined that they have committed the sin against the Holy Ghost, and thought that it would not be forgiven them either in this world or in the world to come. I really do not think that a person with a proper degree of kindliness in his nature would have put fears and terrors of that sort into the world.

Then Christ says, "The Son of Man shall send forth His angels, and they shall gather out of His kingdom all things that offend, and them which do iniquity, and shall cast them into a furnace of fire; there shall be wailing and gnashing of teeth"; and He goes on about the wailing and gnashing of teeth. It comes in one verse after another, and it is quite manifest to the reader that there is a certain pleasure in contemplating wailing and gnashing of teeth, or else it would not occur so often. Then you all, of course, remember about the sheep and the goats; how at the second coming He is going to divide the sheep from the goats, and He is going to say to the goats, "Depart from me, ye cursed, into everlasting fire." He continues, "And these shall go away into everlasting fire." Then He says again, "If thy hand offend thee, cut it off; it is better for thee to enter into life maimed, than having two hands to go into hell, into the fire that never shall be quenched; where the worm dieth not and the fire is not quenched." He repeats that again and again also. I must say that I think all this doctrine, that hell-fire is a punishment for sin, is a doctrine of cruelty. It is a doctrine that put cruelty into the world and gave the world generations of cruel torture; and the Christ of the Gospels, if you could take Him as His chroniclers represent Him, would certainly have to be considered partly responsible for that.

There are other things of less importance. There is the instance of the Gadarene swine, where it certainly was not very kind to the pigs to put the devils into them and make them rush down the hill to the sea. You must remember that He was omnipotent, and He could have made the devils simply go away; but He chose to send them into the pigs. Then there is the curious story of the fig tree, which always rather puzzled me. You remember what happened about the fig tree. "He was hungry; and seeing a fig tree afar off having leaves, He came if haply He might find anything thereon; and when He came to it He found nothing but leaves, for the time of figs was not yet. And Jesus answered and said unto it: 'No man eat fruit of thee hereafter for ever' . . . and Peter . . . saith unto Him: 'Master, behold the fig tree which thou cursedst is withered away.' " This is a very curious story, because it was not the right time of year for figs, and you really could not blame the tree. I cannot myself feel that either in the matter of wisdom or in the matter of virtue Christ stands quite as high as some other people known to history. I think I should put Buddha and Socrates above Him in those respects.

THE EMOTIONAL FACTOR

As I said before, I do not think that the real reason why people accept religion has anything to do with argumentation. They accept religion on emotional grounds. One is often told that it is a very wrong thing to attack religion, because religion makes men virtuous. So I am told; I have not noticed it. You know, of course, the parody of that argument in Samuel Butler's book, *Erewhon Revisited.* You will remember that in *Erewhon* there is a certain Higgs who arrives in a remote country, and after spending some time there he escapes from that country in a balloon. Twenty years later he comes back to that country and finds a new religion in which he is worshiped under the name of the "Sun Child," and it is said that he ascended into heaven. He finds that the Feast of the Ascension is about to be celebrated, and he hears Professors Hanky and Panky say to each other that they never set eyes on the man Higgs, and they hope they never will; but they are the high priests of the religion of the Sun Child. He is very indignant, and he comes up to them, and he says, "I am going to expose all this humbug and tell the people of Erewhon that it was only I, the man Higgs, and I went up in a balloon." He was told, "You must not do that, because all the morals of this country are bound round this myth, and if they once know that you did not ascend into heaven they will all become wicked"; and so he is persuaded of that and he goes quietly away.

That is the idea—that we should all be wicked if we did not hold to the Christian religion. It seems to me that the people who have held to it have been for the most part extremely wicked. You find this curious fact, that the more intense has been the religion of any period and the more profound has been the dogmatic belief, the greater has been the cruelty and the worse has been the state of affairs. In the so-called ages of faith, when men really did believe the Christian religion in all its completeness, there was the Inquisition, with its tortures; there were millions of unfortunate women burned as witches; and there was every kind of cruelty practiced upon all sorts of people in the name of religion.

You find as you look around the world that every single bit of progress in humane feeling, every improvement in the criminal law, every step toward the diminution of war, every step toward better treatment of the colored races, or every mitigation of slavery, every moral progress that there has been in the world, has been consistently opposed by the organized churches of the world. I say quite deliberately that the Christian religion, as organized in its churches, has been and still is the principal enemy of moral progress in the world.

HOW THE CHURCHES HAVE RETARDED PROGRESS

You may think that I am going too far when I say that that is still so. I do not think that I am. Take one fact. You will bear with me if I mention it. It is not a pleasant fact, but the churches compel one to mention facts that are not pleasant. Supposing that in this world that we live in today an inexperienced girl is married to a syphilitic man; in that case the Catholic Church says, "This is an indissoluble sacrament. You must endure celibacy or stay together. And if you stay together, you must not use birth control to prevent the birth of syphilitic children." Nobody whose natural sympathies have not been warped by dogma, or whose moral nature was not absolutely dead to all sense of suffering, could maintain that it is right and proper that that state of things should continue.

That is only an example. There are a great many ways in which, at the present moment, the church, by its insistence upon what it chooses to call morality, inflicts upon all sorts of people undeserved and unnecessary suffering. And of course, as we know, it is in its major part an opponent still of progress and of improvement in all the ways that diminish suffering in the world, because it has chosen to label as morality a certain narrow set of rules of conduct which have nothing to do with human happiness; and when you say that this or that ought to be done because it would make for human happiness, they think that has nothing to do with the matter at all. "What has human happiness to do with morals? The object of morals is not to make people happy."

FEAR, THE FOUNDATION OF RELIGION

Religion is based, I think, primarily and mainly upon fear. It is partly the terror of the unknown and partly, as I have said, the wish to feel that you have a kind of elder brother who will stand by you in all your troubles and disputes. Fear is the basis of the whole thing—fear of the mysterious, fear of defeat, fear of death. Fear is the parent of cruelty, and therefore it is no wonder if cruelty and religion have gone hand in hand. It is because fear is at the basis of those two things. In this world we can now begin a little to understand things, and a little to master them by help of science, which has forced its way step by step against the Christian religion, against the churches, and against the opposition of all the old precepts. Science can help us to get over this craven fear in which mankind has lived for so many generations. Science can teach us, and I think our own hearts can teach us, no longer to look around for imaginary supports, no longer to invent allies in the sky, but rather to look to our own efforts here below to make this world a fit place to live in, instead of the sort of place that the churches in all these centuries have made it.

WHAT WE MUST DO

We want to stand upon our own feet and look fair and square at the world—its good facts, its bad facts, its beauties, and its ugliness; see the world as it is and be not afraid of it. Conquer the world by intelligence and not merely by being slavishly subdued by the terror that comes from it. The whole conception of God is a conception derived from the ancient Oriental despotisms. It is a conception quite unworthy of free men. When you hear people in church debasing themselves and saying that they are miserable sinners, and all the rest of it, it seems contemptible and not worthy of self-respecting human beings. We ought to stand up and look the world frankly in the face. We ought to make the best we can of the world, and if it is not so good as we wish, after all it will still be better than what these others have made of it in all these ages. A good world needs knowledge, kindliness, and courage; it does not need a regretful hankering after the past or a fettering of the free intelligence by the words uttered long ago by ignorant men. It needs a fearless outlook and a free intelligence. It needs hope for the future, not looking back all the time toward a past that is dead, which we trust will be far surpassed by the future that our intelligence can create.

Has Religion Made Useful Contributions to Civilization? (excerpt)

Bertrand Russell

My own view on religion is that of Lucretius. I regard it as a disease born of fear and as a source of untold misery to the human race. I cannot, however, deny that it has made some contributions to civilization. It helped in early days to fix the calendar, and it caused Egyptian priests to chronicle eclipses with such care that in time they became able to predict them. These two services I am prepared to acknowledge, but I do not know of any others.

The word *religion* is used nowadays in a very loose sense. Some people, under the influence of extreme Protestantism, employ the word to denote any serious personal convictions as to morals or the nature of the universe. This use of the word is quite unhistorical. Religion is primarily a social phenomenon. Churches may owe their origin to teachers with strong individual convictions, but these teachers have seldom had much influence upon the churches that they founded, whereas churches have had enormous influence upon the communities in which they flourished. To take the case that is of most interest to members of Western civilization: the teaching of Christ, as it appears in the Gospels, has had extraordinarily little to do with the ethics of Christians. The most important thing about Christianity, from a social and historical point of view, is not Christ but the church, and if we are to judge of Christianity as a social force we must not go to the Gospels for our material. Christ taught that you should give your goods to the poor, that you should not fight, that you should not go to church, and that you should not punish adultery. Neither Catholics nor Protestants have shown any strong desire to follow His teaching in any of these respects. Some of the Franciscans, it is true, attempted to teach the doctrine of apostolic poverty, but the Pope condemned them, and their doctrine was declared heretical. Or, again, consider such a text as "Judge not, that ye be not judged," and ask yourself what influence such a text has had upon the Inquisition and the Ku Klux Klan.

What is true of Christianity is equally true of Buddhism. The Buddha was amiable and enlightened; on his deathbed he laughed at his disciples for supposing that

First published in 1930.
Source: Why I Am Not a Christian and Other Essays on Related Subjects, edited with an appendix on the "Bertrand Russell Case" by Paul Edwards. New York: Simon and Schuster, 1957, 24–26.

he was immortal. But the Buddhist priesthood—as it exists, for example, in Tibet—has been obscurantist, tyrannous, and cruel in the highest degree.

There is nothing accidental about this difference between a church and its founder. As soon as absolute truth is supposed to be contained in the sayings of a certain man, there is a body of experts to interpret his sayings, and these experts infallibly acquire power, since they hold the key to truth. Like any other privileged caste, they use their power for their own advantage. They are, however, in one respect worse than any other privileged caste, since it is their business to expound an unchanging truth, revealed once for all in utter perfection, so that they become necessarily opponents of all intellectual and moral progress. The church opposed Galileo and Darwin; in our own day it opposes Freud. In the days of its greatest power it went further in its opposition to the intellectual life. Pope Gregory the Great wrote to a certain bishop a letter beginning: "A report has reached us which we cannot mention without a blush, that thou expoundest grammar to certain friends." The bishop was compelled by pontifical authority to desist from this wicked labor, and Latinity did not recover until the Renaissance. It is not only intellectually but also morally that religion is pernicious. I mean by this that it teaches ethical codes which are not conducive to human happiness. When, a few years ago, a plebiscite was taken in Germany as to whether the deposed royal houses should still be allowed to enjoy their private property, the churches in Germany officially stated that it would be contrary to the teaching of Christianity to deprive them of it. The churches, as everyone knows, opposed the abolition of slavery as long as they dared, and with a few well-advertised exceptions they oppose at the present day every movement toward economic justice. The Pope has officially condemned Socialism.

PART FIVE

Ethics, Virtue, and Morality

In the world of knowledge, the idea of Good is the limit of our inquiries, and can barely be perceived; but when perceived, we cannot help concluding that it is in every case the source of all that is bright and beautiful—in the visible world giving birth to light and its master, and in the intellectual world dispensing immediately and with full authority, truth and reason—and that whosoever would act wisely, either in private or in public, must set this form of Good before his eyes.

—Plato
The Republic, 517b8–c5

- Plato, *The Republic* (excerpt)
- Aristotle, *Nicomachean Ethics* (excerpt)
- Immanuel Kant, *The Fundamental Principles of the Metaphysics of Ethics* (excerpt)
- Jeremy Bentham, An Introduction to the Principles of Morals and Legislation (excerpt)
- John Stuart Mill, Utilitarianism (excerpt)
- Friedrich Nietzsche, Good and Evil, Good and Bad
- Charles Leslie Stevenson, The Emotive Meaning of Ethical Terms
- Lawrence M. Hinman, The Role of Relativism in the Moral Life
- F. H. Bradley, Why Should I Be Moral?
- A. I. Melden, Why Be Moral?

The problems of ethics concern the values by which we live our lives. There are philosophical questions about theoretical and practical or applied ethics. Yet a sound moral theory must be judged in part by its applications in practice, while applied ethics is a practical extension of moral theory.

Among the philosophical problems of theoretical ethics, there are questions about how we ought to think about moral value in abstract terms. Is moral value absolute or relative? If moral value is relative, is it relative to particular cultures or circumstances, or can it be relative to particular individuals? What makes an action or decision to act morally right or morally wrong? How can we understand the distinction between good and evil? Can it ever be morally justified to lie, cheat, steal, or even kill? Is moral good primarily a matter of having good intentions regardless of consequences, or do the consequences of our actions make them good or bad independently of what we intend to do, of whether we act with a good or bad will? If we can finally decide on a correct theory of ethics, why should we actually put it into practice and do what we believe in theory to be morally right? Why, in particular, should we be moral if it is difficult or costly for us to do so, or if acting rightly conflicts with what we perceive to be our more immediate rational self-interest? What rational considerations explain why we ought to be moral and motivate us sufficiently to overcome our weakness of will in doing good?

In the brief excerpt from Plato's ethical-political dialogue, *The Republic,* Plato's brother Glaucon is engaged in discussion with Socrates. Glaucon wants Socrates to convince the others that it is better to be just in reality and not merely in appearance. Glaucon had baited Socrates into discoursing on the concept of justice by holding out a distinction that Socrates could not resist, between a person's being just in reality versus merely appearing to be just. Glaucon provokes Socrates with the statement that many people believe that the best situation in life is to have the mere appearance of being good while in reality being able to commit any injustice without risk of being discovered. The moral question is whether justice is really choiceworthy in and of itself, or only because of the benefits that derive from having the reputation of being just, and because of the penalties one is ordinarily likely to suffer for being rightly or wrongly accused of injustice. Glaucon challenges Socrates by describing a magic ring that with a turn of its stone makes the wearer invisible. If someone had such a ring, the so-called Ring of Gyges, one could commit all sorts of evil acts but never be discovered as a wrongdoer, and so never acquire a bad reputation. If justice is really something valuable for its own sake, and not merely in appearance or in the opinions of others, then, according to Glaucon, Socrates should be able to explain why it would be wrong to use the ring for moral misdeeds. It takes Socrates a long time, in an exchange that extends throughout the rest of Plato's dialogue, to answer Glaucon's question. For our purposes, it is sufficient to see precisely how the question of the intrinsic value of justice or of doing good arises in Plato's philosophy, and to begin to wonder whether and why it is important to do what is morally right.

Aristotle, in *Nicomachean Ethics,* investigates the moral principles by which agents endeavor to achieve the good life (*eudaemonia*), as the ultimate end to which all other choices in life are the means. Aristotle defines the good for human beings as an activity of the soul in accord with virtue, and he defines virtue as a habit or state of character concerned with choosing the mean, relative to each individual, between extremes of excess and defect among continuous values. Aristotle explains the nature of human good and underscores the importance of the distinction between intrinsic and instrumental value, of things that are desired for their own sakes as ends in themselves as opposed to those desired merely as means to another end. He distinguishes between three types of friendship and considers friendship and social association with others as a primary motivation for being moral. There are friendships of advantage or utility, of pleasure, and of virtue. Friendships of virtue are the highest type, because friendships of utility dissolve when their purpose is fulfilled, and, although friendships of pleasure may go beyond utility as friends continue to find enjoyment in each other's company, they also fade away when interests or pleasures change. It is only friendships of the third kind, those a friend enters into for the sake of the other person, and not for the sake of something else that is useful or pleasurable, that recognize a friend as intrinsically valuable, and not merely as a means to another end of pleasure or advantage. The highest form of friendship is one of the best things human life has to offer, and Aristotle believes that in one way or another it is something necessary to our leading truly happy lives as essentially social beings. The foundations of morality are thus intimately connected for Aristotle with the good relations that obtain among friends. A friend of virtuous disposition can assist friends to remain steadfast in virtue in a number of ways. As we know from common sense and everyday experience, friends can help friends to be virtuous by providing a good example, by inspiring each other with a sense of shame for wrongdoing, and by living an admirable life of virtue. We have a good reason for being moral in terms of our rational self-interests if it is valuable to enjoy the highest type of friendship, and if only virtuous persons can be friends in the highest category.

The concept of the categorical imperative is described in Immanuel Kant's *The Fundamental Principles of the Metaphysics of Ethics*. Kant argues that moral theory must be purified of any empirical elements involving the psychology of moral agents. The concept of morality does not require an agent to have any particular sort of psychological properties, because an angel or extraterrestrial might be a morally responsible agent despite not being capable of pleasure or pain, conscience or guilt, or having any other characteristically human psychological properties. Kant believes that it is only by making moral theory purely rational that an essential precondition of moral right and wrong can be satisfied. To be morally responsible implies being capable of acting freely, which Kant interprets as a matter of autonomy. A rational agent is autonomous, according to Kant, only when reason accepts the moral law as deriving exclusively from reason, or only when reason dictates the principles of right action to reason, and hence to itself. This is roughly the sense of freedom we experience when we choose for ourselves what to do, rather than being told what we must do by another. Where reason is not autonomous, it has another type of moral law dictated to it heteronomously, which is to say externally from a source other than reason.

Kant includes as a conspicuous example of heteronomous moral determination any rule of action recommended by its contribution to feelings of happiness or similar incidents of empirical psychology. In that case, reason does not freely accept reason's own internal moral law of reason but has imposed on it an external moral law demanded by emotion or the psychology of pleasure and pain. The rational principle by which reason freely or autonomously determines the moral law for reason Kant calls the categorical imperative. This is the rule that we should act always in such a way that we can will the maxim of our action to be a universal law for all rational agents. We can will a maxim to be a universal law if and only if in trying to do so we avoid contradiction. This is very different from formulations of the so-called golden rule, that you should do unto others what you would have others do unto you. For Kant, it is not a matter of the consequences that follow if everyone were to follow a particular moral maxim, but rather a question of logic, of whether it is logically possible for an agent consistently to will that everyone follow the maxim. Kant's generous interpretation of the contradictions entailed in trying to will the universalization of morally unjustified maxims is illustrated by his discussion of four applications of the categorical imperative to situations in which a moral agent decides whether or not to commit suicide, to repay a debt, to develop natural talents rather than indulging in lazy pleasure, and to be charitable to other persons in time of need. The plausibility of Kant's applications have been seriously questioned by critics as undermining the acceptability of the categorical imperative.

Jeremy Bentham and John Stuart Mill, in selections respectively from *An Introduction to the Principles of Morals and Legislation* and *Utilitarianism,* explain the principles of a consequentialist ethics that judges and prescribes actions on the basis of their producing more happiness than unhappiness, or leading to the greatest good for the greatest number. Bentham outlines a principle of utility by which a decision to act is morally obligatory if it causes more happiness and less unhappiness among the alternative actions available to an agent, counting each potential individual affected by the action as one and none as more than one. It may be difficult today to appreciate the democratic novelty of Bentham's principle, but in its historical context, the principle of utility was politically revolutionary. It extends no special consideration to persons in privileged social classes in evaluating the morality of actions but takes into account only the potential effects of an action on all individual subjects capable of experiencing pleasure or pain. The effect of an action on a king is not to count for more than its effect, say, on a day laborer. Nor, for that matter, does it make any difference according to Bentham whether the subject affected by an action is human or nonhuman, provided only that the individuals to which the utilitarian criterion is applied are sentient. The general principle of utilitarianism requires that we include animals as well as human beings within the realm of our moral consideration. Bentham offers a variety of psychological factors to be considered in computing whether an action is morally justified in what he describes as a hedonic calculus of pleasure and pain. Mill's classic statement of utilitarianism more completely defines and defends the principle of utility and develops a procedure for evaluating the merits of different types of pleasures.

The excerpt on "Good and Evil, Good and Bad," from Friedrich Nietzsche's *The Genealogy of Morals,* presents Nietzsche's account of the development of contemporary moral attitudes. He traces their origins etymologically from an earlier robust appreciation of goodness as uncaring power and ability to what Nietzsche sees as the contemporary ethical view that despises strength and exalts weakness and humility. Nietzsche refers to the more recent form of ethics as a slave morality and attributes its development specifically to the rise of Judeo-Christian religions, in which oppressed believers effected a devaluation of values by instilling in the strong a sense of guilt for their mastery. The degeneration of healthy moral values into those of a slave morality in Nietzsche's judgment reflects a subjectivization and relativization of virtue, which he deplores, but does not see any way to reverse. When he criticizes "the English psychologists" in moral theory, he takes direct aim at, among others, the utilitarian philosophers Bentham and Mill. In later writings, Nietzsche projects a philosopher of the future who is beyond good and evil, in the sense that he acts spontaneously out of desire rather than guilty reason. The philosopher of the future is supposed to achieve a reversal of the classic Greek ideal that always values reason above desire, which Nietzsche mythologizes as the conflict between the ancient gods Apollo (who stands for reason), and Dionysius (desire). Serious doubts can nevertheless be raised both about Nietzsche's ethical stance and the historical accuracy of his genealogy of moral values.

Charles Leslie Stevenson, in his landmark essay "The Emotive Meaning of Ethical Terms," explains and defends a conception of the language of ethical judgment as expressing emotional rather than cognitive or higher abstract valuational content. Stevenson criticizes what he calls "interest theories" of emotive meaning, which he believes wrongly presuppose that ethical statements simply express the information, for example, that an individual approves of a certain action in speaking of it as morally good. Stevenson hopes to avoid objections to other theories of emotive meaning by recognizing the fact that such pronouncements are also attempts to influence other persons' interests in a moral decision-making context. By acknowledging both of these components of emotive meaning, Stevenson proposes to interpret the meaning of "X is good" as equivalent to "We like X." The disarming simplicity of this analysis emphasizes the expression of approval in judgments of what is good. But Stevenson's theory leaves unanswered the further question that many thinkers would like to have answered concerning the philosophical basis for justified statements of moral approval. To say that "X is good" means "We like X" does not yet say whether and in what sense we may be morally right or wrong to like X.

The problem of relativism in ethics is more systematically explored in Lawrence M. Hinman's valuable study of "The Role of Relativism in the Moral Life," a chapter of his book *Ethics: A Pluralistic Approach to Moral Theory.* Hinman distinguishes between several types of moral relativism and discusses the attractions and pitfalls of the doctrine that moral value is relative to social circumstances. He considers moral relativism as an explanation of conflicting opinions about moral good and evil in diverse cultures, and in the context of its advantages and disadvantages when compared with the alternative of moral absolutism. Hinman recognizes the fact that different societies regard different kinds of actions as morally acceptable or unacceptable by itself does not prove that moral value is culturally relative, just as the fact that some societies regard different scientific propositions as true or false by itself does not prove that scientific truth is culturally relative. It remains possible that prevailing opinion in some or all of these cultures is simply wrong in their judgments of truth or morality. Hinman nevertheless sees moral relativism as a basis for a salutary moral tolerance of other values in a pluralistic approach to ethics.

The question first raised in Plato's truth of the Ring of Gyges about why we ought to be moral is addressed again in the concluding two essays by F. H. Bradley and A. I. Melden. It is customary to distinguish between prudential and moral considerations in motivating morality. What is prudent, the smart thing to do, is to avoid immoral behavior to which sanctions attach. If an agent wants to avoid being caught and punished for moral infractions, then this may be an adequate reason for the person to do what is right, although not for specifically moral reasons. Plato's Ring of Gyges is intended to set aside prudential considerations for being moral, where an agent by becoming invisible can commit wrongful acts without suffering

the usual consequences. The effect of Plato's myth is to cast in bold relief the outstanding question of whether there can be good moral as opposed to prudential reasons for being moral. A dilemma that haunts this discussion is that only persons
who already have a correct moral outlook can possibly be influenced by reasons for
being moral, and that they ironically are precisely the ones who do not need such
reasons. Those who are immoral in their outlook by contrast are unlikely to be
swayed by any moral considerations. In practice, the sharp edges of this argument
may be softened by the fact that many individuals are neither entirely moral nor
immoral in character, but fall somewhere in between, where their tendency to drift
into immorality can be checked by due reflection on good moral as well as prudential reasons for being moral. Bradley grasps one horn of the dilemma when he
concludes that the only adequate moral motivation for being moral must be an
internal one of the individual's seeking a self-realization of moral perfectability as
an intrinsically valuable end in itself. Melden, by contrast, argues that the problem
of why we ought to be moral is not a theoretical question, and that, as a practical
issue, only a heartfelt moral commitment to live or act in a certain way in accord
with certain values can adequately motivate an agent to be moral.

The Republic *(excerpt)*

Plato

Now, when I had said this, I thought I was freed from argument. But after all, as it seems, it was only a prelude. For Glaucon is always most courageous in everything, and so now he didn't accept Thrasymachus' giving up but said, "Socrates, do you want to seem to have persuaded us, or truly to persuade us, that it is in every way better to be just than unjust?"

"I would choose to persuade you truly," I said, "if it were up to me."

"Well, then," he said, "you're not doing what you want. Tell me, is there in your opinion a kind of good that we would choose to have not because we desire its consequences, but because we delight in it for its own sake—such as enjoyment and all the pleasures which are harmless and leave no after effects other than the enjoyment in having them?"

"In my opinion, at least," I said, "there is a good of this kind."

"And what about this? Is there a kind we like both for its own sake and for what comes out of it, such as thinking and seeing and being healthy? Surely we delight in such things on both accounts."

"Yes," I said.

"And do you see a third form of good, which includes gymnastic exercise, medical treatment when sick as well as the practice of medicine, and the rest of the activities from which money is made? We would say that they are drudgery but beneficial to us; and we would not choose to have them for themselves but for the sake of the wages and whatever else comes out of them."

"Yes, there is also this third," I said, "but what of it?"

"In which of them," he said, "would you include justice?"

"I, for my part, suppose," I said, "that it belongs in the finest kind, which the man who is going to be blessed should like both for itself and for what comes out of it."

"Well, that's not the opinion of the many," he said, "rather it seems to belong to the form of drudgery, which should be practiced for the sake of wages and the reputation that comes from opinion; but all by itself it should be fled from as something hard."

"I know this is the popular opinion," I said, "and a while ago justice, taken as being such, was blamed by Thrasymachus while injustice was praised. But I, as it seems, am a poor learner."

"Come, now," he said, "hear me too, and see if you still have the same opinion. For it looks to me as though Thrasymachus, like a snake, has been charmed more quickly than he should have been; yet to my way of thinking there was still no proof about either. For I desire to hear what each is and what power it has all alone by itself when it is in the soul—dismissing its wages and its consequences. So I shall

Source: The Republic of Plato, translated with notes, an interpretive essay, and a new introduction by Allan Bloom, 2nd edition. New York: Basic Books, 1968, 35–40.

do it this way, if you too consent: I'll restore Thrasymachus' argument, and first I'll tell what kind of thing they say justice is and where it came from; second, that all those who practice it do so unwillingly, as necessary but not good; third, that it is fitting that they do so, for the life of the unjust man is, after all, far better than that of the just man, as they say. For, Socrates, though that's not at all my own opinion, I am at a loss: I've been talked deaf by Thrasymachus and countless others, while the argument on behalf of justice—that it is better than injustice—I've yet to hear from anyone as I want it. I want to hear it extolled all by itself, and I suppose I would be most likely to learn that from you. That's the reason why I'll speak in vehement praise of the unjust life, and in speaking I'll point out to you how I want to hear you, in your turn, blame injustice and praise justice. See if what I'm saying is what you want."

"Most of all," I said. "What would an intelligent man enjoy talking and hearing about more again and again?"

"What you say is quite fine," he said. "Now listen to what I said I was going to tell first—what justice is and where it came from.

"They say that doing injustice is naturally good, and suffering injustice bad, but that the bad in suffering injustice far exceeds the good in doing it; so that, when they do injustice to one another and suffer it and taste of both, it seems profitable—to those who are not able to escape the one and choose the other—to set down a compact among themselves neither to do injustice nor to suffer it. And from there they began to set down their own laws and compacts and to name what the law commands lawful and just. And this, then, is the genesis and being of justice; it is a mean between what is best—doing injustice without paying the penalty—and what is worst—suffering injustice without being able to avenge oneself. The just is in the middle between these two, cared for not because it is good but because it is honored due to a want of vigor in doing injustice. The man who is able to do it and is truly a man would never set down a compact with anyone not to do injustice and not to suffer it. He'd be mad. Now the nature of justice is this and of this sort, and it naturally grows out of these sorts of things. So the argument goes.

"That even those who practice it do so unwillingly, from an incapacity to do injustice, we would best perceive if we should in thought do something like this: give each, the just man and the unjust, license to do whatever he wants, while we follow and watch where his desire will lead each. We would catch the just man red-handed going the same way as the unjust man out of a desire to get the better; this is what any nature naturally pursues as good, while it is law which by force perverts it to honor equality. The license of which I speak would best be realized if they should come into possession of the sort of power that it is said the ancestor of Gyges, the Lydian, once got. They say he was a shepherd toiling in the service of the man who was then ruling Lydia. There came to pass a great thunderstorm and an earthquake; the earth cracked and a chasm opened at the place where he was pasturing. He saw it, wondered at it, and went down. He saw, along with other quite wonderful things about which they tell tales, a hollow bronze horse. It had windows; peeping in, he saw there was a corpse inside that looked larger than human size. It had nothing on except a gold ring on its hand; he slipped it off and went out. When there was the usual gathering of the shepherds to make the monthly report to the king about the flocks, he too came, wearing the ring. Now, while he was sitting with the others, he chanced to turn the collet of the ring to himself, toward the inside of his hand; when he did this, he became invisible to those sitting by him, and they discussed him as though he were away. He wondered at this, and, fingering the ring again, he twisted the collet toward the outside; when he had twisted it, he became visible. Thinking this over, he tested whether the ring had this power, and that was exactly his result: when he turned the collet inward, he became invisible, when outward, visible. Aware of this, he immediately contrived to be one of the messengers to the king. When he arrived, he committed adultery with the king's wife and, along with her, set upon the king and killed him. And so he took over the rule.

"Now if there were two such rings, and the just man would put one on, and the unjust man the other, no one, as it would seem, would be so adamant as to stick by justice and bring himself to keep away from what belongs to others and not lay hold of it, although he had license to take what he wanted from the market without fear, and to go into houses and have intercourse with whomever he wanted, and to slay or release from bonds whomever he wanted, and to do other things as an equal to a god among humans. And in so doing, one would act no differently from the other, but both would go the same way. And yet, someone could say that this is a great proof that no one is willingly just but only when compelled to be so. Men do not take it to be a good for them in private, since wherever each supposes he can do injustice, he does it. Indeed, all men suppose injustice is far more to their private profit than justice. And what they suppose is true, as the man who makes this kind of an argument will say, since if a man were to get hold of such license and were never willing to do any injustice and didn't lay his hands on what belongs to others, he would seem most wretched to those who were aware of it, and most foolish too, although they would praise him to each others' faces, deceiving each other for fear of suffering injustice. So much for that.

"As to the judgment itself about the life of these two of whom we are speaking, we'll be able to make it correctly if we set the most just man and the most unjust in opposition; if we do not, we won't be able to do so. What, then, is this opposition? It is as follows: we shall take away nothing from the injustice of the unjust man nor from the justice of the just man, but we shall take each as perfect in his own pursuit. So, first, let the unjust man act like the clever craftsmen. An outstanding pilot or doctor is aware of the difference between what is impossible in his art and what is possible, and he attempts the one, and lets the other go; and if, after all, he should still trip up in any way, he is competent to set himself aright. Similarly, let the unjust man also attempt unjust deeds correctly, and get away with them, if he is going to be extremely unjust. The man who is caught must be considered a poor chap. For the extreme of injustice is to seem to be just when one is not. So the perfectly unjust man must be given the most perfect injustice, and nothing must be taken away; he must be allowed to do the greatest injustices while having provided himself with the greatest reputation for justice. And if, after all, he should trip up in anything, he has the power to set himself aright; if any of his unjust deeds should come to light, he is capable both of speaking persuasively and of using force, to the extent that force is needed, since he is courageous and strong and since he has provided for friends and money. Now, let us set him down as such, and put beside him in the argument the just man in his turn, a man simple and noble, who, according to Aeschylus, does not wish to seem, but rather to be, good. The seeming must be taken away. For if he should seem just, there would be honors and gifts for him for seeming to be such. Then it wouldn't be plain whether he is such for the sake of the just or for the sake of the gifts and honors. So he must be stripped of everything except justice, and his situation must be made the opposite of the first man's. Doing no injustice, let him have the greatest reputation for injustice, so that his justice may be put to the test to see if it is softened by bad reputation and its consequences. Let him go unchanged till death, seeming throughout life to be unjust although he is just, so that when each has come to the extreme—the one of justice, the other of injustice—they can be judged as to which of the two is happier."

"My, my," I said, "my dear Glaucon, how vigorously you polish up each of the two men—just like a statue—for their judgment."

"As much as I can, he said. "With two such men it's no longer hard, I suppose, to complete the speech by a description of the kind of life that awaits each. It must be told, then. And if it's somewhat rustically told, don't suppose that it is I who speak, Socrates, but rather those who praise injustice ahead of justice. They'll say that the just man who has such a disposition will be whipped; he'll be racked; he'll be bound; he'll have both his eyes burned out; and, at the end, when he has undergone every sort of evil, he'll be crucified and know that one shouldn't wish to be, but to seem to be, just. After all, Aeschylus' saying applies far more correctly to the unjust man. For really, they will say, it is the unjust man, because he pursues a thing dependent on truth and does not live in the light of opinion, who does not wish to seem unjust but to be unjust,

> Reaping a deep furrow in his mind
> From which trusty plans bear fruit.

First, he rules in the city because he seems to be just. Then he takes in marriage from whatever station he wants and gives in marriage to whomever he wants; he contracts and has partnerships with whomever he wants, and, besides benefiting himself in all this, he gains because he has no qualms about doing injustice. So then, when he enters contests, both private and public, he wins and gets the better of his enemies. In getting the better, he is wealthy and does good to friends and harm to enemies. To the gods he makes sacrifices and sets up votive offerings, adequate and magnificent, and cares for the gods and those human beings he wants to care for far better than the just man. So, in all likelihood, it is also more appropriate for him to be dearer to the gods than is the just man. Thus, they say, Socrates, with gods and with humans, a better life is provided for the unjust man than for the just man."

Nicomachean Ethics *(excerpt)*

Aristotle

BOOK I

1   Every art and every inquiry, and similarly every action and pursuit, is thought to aim at some good; and for this reason the good has rightly been declared[1] to be that at which all things aim. But a certain difference is found among ends; some are activities, others are products apart from the activities that produce them. Where there are ends apart from the actions, it is the nature of the products to be better than the activities. Now, as there are many actions, arts, and sciences, their ends also are many; the end of the medical art is health, that of shipbuilding a vessel, that of strategy victory, that of economics wealth. But where such arts fall under a single capacity—as bridle-making and the other arts concerned with the equipment of horses fall under the art of riding, and this and every military action under strategy, in the same way other arts fall under yet others—in all of these the ends of the master arts are to be preferred to all the subordinate ends; for it is for the sake of the former that the latter are pursued. It makes no difference whether the activities themselves are the end of the actions, or something else apart from the activities, as in the case of the sciences just mentioned.

2   If, then, there is some end of the things we do, which we desire for its own sake (everything else being desired for the sake of this), and if we do not choose everything for the sake of something else (for at that rate the process would go on to infinity, so that our desire would be empty and vain), clearly this must be the good and the chief good. Will not the knowledge of it, then, have a great influence on life? Shall we not, like archers who have a mark to aim at, be more likely to hit upon what is right? If so, we must try, in outline at least to determine what it is, and of which of the sciences or capacities it is the object. It would seem to belong to the most authoritative art and that which is most truly the master art. And politics appears to be of this nature; for it is this that ordains which of the sciences should be studied in a state, and which each class of citizens should learn and up to what point they should learn them; and we see even the most highly esteemed of capacities to fall under this, e.g. strategy, economics, rhetoric; now, since politics uses the rest of the sciences, and since, again, it legislates as to what we are to do and what we are to abstain from, the end of this science must include those of the others, so that this end must be the good for man. For even if the end is the same for a single man and for a state, that of the state seems at all events something greater and more complete whether to attain or to preserve; though it is worth while to attain the end

[1]Perhaps by Eudoxus; Cf. 1172[b] g.
Source: Books I, VIII, translated by W. D. Ross, *The Works of Aristotle*. Oxford: The Clarendon Press, 1952, 1094[a]–1103[a]10, 1155[a]–1063[b]28.

merely for one man, it is finer and more godlike to attain it for a nation or for city-
states. These, then, are the ends at which our inquiry aims, since it is political science, in one sense of that term.

3   Our discussion will be adequate if it has as much clearness as the subject-matter
admits of, for precision is not to be sought for alike in all discussions, any more
than in all the products of the crafts. Now fine and just actions, which political science investigates, admit of much variety and fluctuation of opinion, so that they
may be thought to exist only by convention, and not by nature. And goods also give
rise to a similar fluctuation because they bring harm to many people; for before now
men have been undone by reason of their wealth, and others by reason of their
courage. We must be content, then, in speaking of such subjects and with such premisses to indicate the truth roughly and in outline, and in speaking about things
which are only for the most part true and with premisses of the same kind to reach
conclusions that are no better. In the same spirit, therefore, should each type of
statement be *received;* for it is the mark of an educated man to look for precision
in each class of things just so far as the nature of the subject admits; it is evidently
equally foolish to accept probable reasoning from a mathematician and to demand
from a rhetorician scientific proofs.

     Now each man judges well the things he knows, and of these he is a good
judge. And so the man who has been educated in a subject is a good judge of that
subject, and the man who has received an all-round education is a good judge in
general. Hence a young man is not a proper hearer of lectures on political science;
for he is inexperienced in the actions that occur in life, but its discussions start
from these and are about these; and, further, since he tends to follow his passions,
his study will be vain and unprofitable, because the end aimed at is not knowledge but action. And it makes no difference whether he is young in years or
youthful in character; the defect does not depend on time, but on his living, and
pursuing each successive object, as passion directs. For to such persons, as to the
incontinent, knowledge brings no profit; but to those who desire and act in accordance with a rational principle knowledge about such matters will be of great
benefit.

     These remarks about the student, the sort of treatment to be expected, and the
purpose of the inquiry, may be taken as our preface.

4   Let us resume our inquiry and state, in view of the fact that all knowledge and
every pursuit aims at some good, what it is that we say political science aims at
and what is the highest of all goods achievable by action. Verbally there is very
general agreement; for both the general run of men and people of superior refinement say that it is happiness, and identify living well and doing well with being
happy; but with regard to what happiness is they differ, and the many do not give
the same account as the wise. For the former think it is some plain and obvious
thing, like pleasure, wealth, or honour; they differ, however, from one another—
and often even the same man identifies it with different things, with health when
he is ill, with wealth when he is poor; but, conscious of their ignorance, they
admire those who proclaim some great ideal that is above their comprehension.

Now some[2] thought that apart from these many goods there is another which is self-subsistent and causes the goodness of all these as well. To examine all the opinions that have been held were perhaps somewhat fruitless; enough to examine those that are most prevalent or that seem to be arguable.

Let us not fail to notice, however, that there is a difference between arguments from and those to the first principles. For Plato, too, was right in raising this question and asking, as he used to do, "are we on the way from or to the first principles?"[3] There is a difference, as there is in a race-course between the course from the judges to the turning-point and the way back. For, while we must begin with what is known, things are objects of knowledge in two senses—some to us, some without qualification. Presumably, then, *we* must begin with things known to *us*. Hence any one who is to listen intelligently to lectures about what is noble and just and, generally, about the subjects of political science must have been brought up in good habits. For the fact is the starting-point, and if this is sufficiently plain to him, he will not at the start need the reason as well; and the man who has been well brought up has or can easily get starting-points. And as for him who neither has nor can get them, let him hear the words of Hesiod:

> Far best is he who knows all things himself;
> Good, he that hearkens when men counsel right;
> But he who neither knows, nor lays to heart
> Another's wisdom, is a useless wight.

5   Let us, however, resume our discussion from the point at which we digressed. To judge from the lives that men lead, most men, and men of the most vulgar type, seem (not without some ground) to identify the good, or happiness, with pleasure; which is the reason why they love the life of enjoyment. For there are, we may say, three prominent types of life—that just mentioned, the political, and thirdly the contemplative life. Now the mass of mankind are evidently quite slavish in their tastes, preferring a life suitable to beasts, but they get some ground for their view from the fact that many of those in high places share the tastes of Sardanapallus. A consideration of the prominent types of life shows that people of superior refinement and of active disposition identify happiness with honour; for this is, roughly speaking, the end of the political life. But it seems too superficial to be what we are looking for, since it is thought to depend on those who bestow honour rather than on him who receives it, but the good we divine to be something proper to a man and not easily taken from him. Further, men seem to pursue honour in order that they may be assured of their goodness; at least it is by men of practical wisdom that they seek to be honoured, and among those who know them, and on the ground of their virtue; clearly, then, according to them, at any rate, virtue is better. And perhaps one might even suppose this to be, rather than honour, the end of the political life. But even this appears somewhat incomplete; for possession of virtue seems actually compatible with being asleep, or with lifelong inactivity, and, further, with the greatest sufferings and misfortunes; but a man who was living so no one would call

---

[2]The Platonic School; Cf. ch. 6.
[3]Cf. *Rep.* 511 B.

happy, unless he were maintaining a thesis at all costs. But enough of this; for the subject has been sufficiently treated even in the current discussions. Third comes the contemplative life, which we shall consider later.[4]

The life of money-making is one undertaken under compulsion, and wealth is evidently not the good we are seeking; for it is merely useful and for the sake of something else. And so one might rather take the aforenamed objects to be ends; for they are loved for themselves. But it is evident that not even these are ends; yet many arguments have been thrown away in support of them. Let us leave this subject, then.

6 We had perhaps better consider the universal good and discuss thoroughly what is meant by it, although such an inquiry is made an uphill one by the fact that the Forms have been introduced by friends of our own. Yet it would perhaps be thought to be better, indeed to be our duty, for the sake of maintaining the truth even to destroy what touches us closely, especially as we are philosophers or lovers of wisdom; for, while both are dear, piety requires us to honour truth above our friends.

The men who introduced this doctrine did not posit Ideas of classes within which they recognized priority and posteriority (which is the reason why they did not maintain the existence of an Idea embracing all numbers); but the term "good" is used both in the category of substance and in that of quality and in that of relation, and that which is *per se,* i. e. substance, is prior in nature to the relative (for the latter is like an offshoot and accident of being); so that there could not be a common Idea set over all these goods. Further, since "good" has as many senses as "being" (for it is predicated both in the category of substance, as of God and of reason, and in quality, i. e. of the virtues, and in quantity, i. e. of that which is moderate, and in relation, i. e. of the useful, and in time, i. e. of the right opportunity, and in place, i. e. of the right locality and the like), clearly it cannot be something universally present in all cases and single; for then it could not have been predicated in all the categories but in one only. Further, since of the things answering to one Idea there is one science, there would have been one science of all the goods; but as it is there are many sciences even of the things that fall under one category, e. g. of opportunity, for opportunity in war is studied by strategics and in disease by medicine, and the moderate in food is studied by medicine and in exercise by the science of gymnastics. And one might ask the question, what in the world they *mean* by "a thing itself," if (as is the case) in "man himself" and in a particular man the account of man is one and the same. For in so far as they are man, they will in no respect differ; and if this is so, neither will "good itself" and particular goods, in so far as they are good. But again it will not be good any the more for being eternal, since that which lasts long is no whiter than that which perishes in a day. The Pythagoreans seem to give a more plausible account of the good, when they place the one in the column of goods; and it is they that Speusippus seems to have followed.

But let us discuss these matters elsewhere[5]; an objection to what we have said, however, may be discerned in the fact that the Platonists have not been speaking

---

[4]1177ᵃ 12-1178ᵃ 8, 1178ᵃ 22-1179ᵃ 32.
[5]Cf. *Met.* 986ᵃ 22–6, 1028ᵇ 21–4, 1072ᵇ 30–1073ᵃ 3, 1091ᵃ 29–ᵇ 3, ᵇ13–1092ᵃ 17.

about *all* goods, and that the goods that are pursued and loved for themselves are called good by reference to a single Form, while those which tend to produce or to preserve these somehow or to prevent their contraries are called so by reference to these, and in a secondary sense. Clearly, then, goods must be spoken of in two ways, and some must be good in themselves, the others by reason of these. Let us separate, then, things good in themselves from things useful, and consider whether the former are called good by reference to a single Idea. What sort of goods would one call good in themselves? Is it those that are pursued even when isolated from others, such as intelligence, sight, and certain pleasures and honours? Certainly, if we pursue these also for the sake of something else, yet one would place them among things good in themselves. Or is nothing other than the Idea of good good in itself? In that case the Form will be empty. But if the things we have named are also things good in themselves, the account of the good will have to appear as something identical in them all, as that of whiteness is identical in snow and in white lead. But of honour, wisdom, and pleasure, just in respect of their goodness, the accounts are distinct and diverse. The good, therefore, is not some common element answering to one Idea.

But what then do we mean by the good? It is surely not like the things that only chance to have the same name. Are goods one, then, by being derived from one good or by all contributing to one good, or are they rather one by analogy? Certainly as sight is in the body, so is reason in the soul, and so on in other cases. But perhaps these subjects had better be dismissed for the present; for perfect precision about them would be more appropriate to another branch of philosophy.[6] And similarly with regard to the Idea; even if there is some one good which is universally predicable of goods or is capable of separate and independent existence, clearly it could not be achieved or attained by man; but we are now seeking something attainable. Perhaps, however, some one might think it worth while to recognize this with a view to the goods that *are* attainable and achievable; for having this as a sort of pattern we shall know better the goods that are good for us, and if we know them shall attain them. This argument has some plausibility, but seems to clash with the procedure of the sciences; for all of these, though they aim at some good and seek to supply the deficiency of it, leave on one side the knowledge of *the* good. Yet that all the exponents of the arts should be ignorant of, and should not even seek, so great an aid is not probable. It is hard, too, to see how a weaver or a carpenter will be benefited in regard to his own craft by knowing this "good itself," or how the man who has viewed the Idea itself will be a better doctor or general thereby. For a doctor seems not even to study health in this way, but the health of man, or perhaps rather the health of a particular man; it is individuals that he is healing. But enough of these topics.

7   Let us again return to the good we are seeking, and ask what it can be. It seems different in different actions and arts; it is different in medicine, in strategy, and in the other arts likewise. What then is the good of each? Surely that for whose sake everything else is done. In medicine this is health, in strategy victory, in architecture

[6]Cf. *Met.* iv. 2.

a house, in any other sphere something else, and in every action and pursuit the end; for it is for the sake of this that all men do whatever else they do. Therefore, if there is an end for all that we do, this will be the good achievable by action, and if there are more than one, these will be the goods achievable by action.

So the argument has by a different course reached the same point; but we must try to state this even more clearly. Since there are evidently more than one end, and we choose some of these (e. g. wealth, flutes, and in general instruments) for the sake of something else, clearly not all ends are final ends; but the chief good is evidently something final. Therefore, if there is only one final end, this will be what we are seeking, and if there are more than one, the most final of these will be what we are seeking. Now we call that which is in itself worthy of pursuit more final than that which is worthy of pursuit for the sake of something else, and that which is never desirable for the sake of something else more final than the things that are desirable both in themselves and for the sake of that other thing, and therefore we call final without qualification that which is always desirable in itself and never for the sake of something else.

Now such a thing above all else, is held to be; for this we choose always for itself and never for the sake of something else, but honour, pleasure, reason, and every virtue we choose indeed for themselves (for if nothing resulted from them we should still choose each of them), but we choose them also for the sake of happiness, judging that by means of them we shall be happy. Happiness, on the other hand, no one chooses for the sake of these, nor, in general, for anything other than itself.

From the point of view of self-sufficiency the same result seems to follow; for the final good is thought to be self-sufficient. Now by self-sufficient we do not mean that which is sufficient for a man by himself, for one who lives a solitary life, but also for parents, children, wife, and in general for his friends and fellow citizens, since man is born for citizenship. But some limit must be set to this; for if we extend our requirement to ancestors and descendants and friends' friends we are in for an infinite series. Let us examine this question, however, on another occasion;[7] the self-sufficient we now define as that which when isolated makes life desirable and lacking in nothing; and such we think happiness to be; and further we think it most desirable of all things, without being counted as one good thing among others—if it were so counted it would clearly be made more desirable by the addition of even the least of goods; for that which is added becomes of excess an goods, and of goods the greater is always more desirable. Happiness, then, is something final and self-sufficient, and is the end of action.

Presumably, however, to say that happiness is the chief good seems a platitude, and a clearer account of what it is is still desired. This might perhaps be given, if we could first ascertain the function of man. For just as for a flute-player, a sculptor, or any artist, and, in general, for all things that have a function or activity, the good and the "well" is thought to reside in the function, so would it seem to be for man, if he has a function. Have the carpenter, then, and the tanner certain functions or activities, and has man none? Is he born without a function? Or as eye, hand, foot, and in general each of the parts evidently has a function, may one lay it down

[7]i. 10, 11, ix. 10.

that man similarly has a function apart from all these? What then can this be? Life seems to be common even to plants, but we are seeking what is peculiar to man. Let us exclude, therefore, the life of nutrition and growth. Next there would be a life of perception, but *it* also seems to be common even to the horse, the ox, and every animal. There remains, then, an active life of the element that has a rational principle; of this, one part has such a principle in the sense of being obedient to one, the other in the sense of possessing one and exercising thought. And, as "life of the rational element" also has two meanings, we must state that life in the sense of activity is what we mean; for this seems to be the more proper sense of the term. Now if the function of man is an activity of soul which follows or implies a rational principle, and if we say "a so-and-so" and "a good so-and-so" have a function which is the same in kind, e.g. a lyre-player and a good lyre-player, and so without qualification in all cases, eminence in respect of goodness being added to the name of the function (for the function of a lyre-player is to play the lyre, and that of a good lyre-player is to do so well): if this is the case, [and we state the function of man to be a certain kind of life, and this to be an activity or actions of the soul implying a rational principle, and the function of a good man to be the good and noble performance of these, and if any action is well performed when it is performed in accordance with the appropriate excellence: if this is the case,] human good turns out to be activity of soul in accordance with virtue, and if there are more than one virtue, in accordance with the best and most complete.

But we must add "in a complete life." For one swallow does not make a summer, nor does one day; and so too one day, or a short time, does not make a man blessed and happy.

Let this serve as an outline of the good; for we must presumably first sketch it roughly, and then later fill in the details. But it would seem that any one is capable of carrying on and articulating what has once been well outlined, and that time is a good discoverer or partner in such a work; to which facts the advances of the arts are due; for any one can add what is lacking. And we must also remember what has been said before,[8] and not look for precision in all things alike, but in each class of things such precision as accords with the subject-matter, and so much as is appropriate to the inquiry. For a carpenter and a geometer investigate the right angle in different ways; the former does so in so far as the right angle is useful for his work, while the latter inquires what it is or what sort of thing it is; for he is a spectator of the truth. We must act in the same way, then, in all other matters as well, that our main task may not be subordinated to minor questions. Nor must we demand the cause in all matters alike; it is enough in some cases that the *fact* be well established, as in the case of the first principles; the fact is the primary thing or first principle. Now of first principles we see some by induction, some by perception, some by a certain habituation, and others too in other ways. But each set of principles we must try to investigate in the natural way, and we must take pains to state them definitely, since they have a great influence on what follows. For the beginning is thought to be more than half of the whole, and many of the questions we ask are cleared up by it.

[8]1094[b] 11–27.

8   We must consider it, however, in the light not only of our conclusion and our premisses, but also of what is commonly said about it; for with a true view all the data harmonize, but with a false one the facts soon clash. Now goods have been divided into three classes,[9] and some are described as external, others as relating to soul or to body; we call those that relate to soul-most properly and truly goods, and psychical actions and activities we class as relating to soul. Therefore our account must be sound, at least according to this view, which is an old one and agreed on by philosophers. It is correct also in that we identify the end with certain actions and activities; for thus it falls among goods of the soul and not among external goods. Another belief which harmonizes with our account is that the happy man lives well and does well; for we have practically defined happiness as a sort of good life and good action. The characteristics that are looked for in happiness seem also, all of them, to belong to what we have defined happiness as being. For some identify happiness with virtue, some with practical wisdom, others with a kind of philosophic wisdom, others with these, or one of these, accompanied by pleasure or not without pleasure; while others include also external prosperity. Now some of these views have been held by many men and men of old, others by a few eminent persons; and it is not probable that either of these should be entirely mistaken, but rather that they should be right in at least some one respect or even in most respects.

   With those who identify happiness with virtue or some one virtue our account is in harmony; for to virtue belongs virtuous activity. But it makes, perhaps, no small difference whether we place the chief good in possession or in use, in state of mind or in activity. For the state of mind may exist without producing any good result, as in a man who is asleep or in some other way quite inactive, but the activity cannot; for one who has the activity will of necessity be acting, and acting well. And as in the Olympic Games it is not the most beautiful and the strongest that are crowned but those who compete (for it is some of these that are victorious), so those who act win, and rightly win, the noble and good things in life.

   Their life is also in itself pleasant. For pleasure is a state of *soul,* and to each man that which he is said to be a lover of is pleasant; e. g. not only is a horse pleasant to the lover of horses, and a spectacle to the lover of sights, but also in the same way just acts are pleasant to the lover of justice and in general virtuous acts to the lover of virtue. Now for most men their pleasures are in conflict with one another because these are not by nature pleasant, but the lovers of what is noble find pleasant the things that are by nature pleasant; and virtuous actions are such, so that these are pleasant for such men as well as in their own nature. Their life, therefore, has no further need of pleasure as a sort of adventitious charm, but has its pleasure in itself. For, besides what we have said, the man who does not rejoice in noble actions is not even good; since no one would call a man just who did not enjoy acting justly, nor any man liberal who did not enjoy liberal actions; and similarly in all other cases. If this is so, virtuous actions must be in themselves pleasant. But they are also *good* and *noble,* and have each of these attributes in the highest degree,

---

[9]Pl. *Euthyd.* 279 ᴀʙ, *Phil.* 48 ᴇ, *Laws,* 743 ᴇ.

since the good man judges well about these attributes; his judgement is such as we have described.[10] Happiness then is the best, noblest, and most pleasant thing in the world, and these attributes are not severed as in the inscription at Delos—

> Most noble is that which is justest, and best is health;
> But pleasantest is it to win what we love.

For all these properties belong to the best activities; and these, or one—the best— of these, we identify with happiness.

Yet evidently, as we said,[11] it needs the external goods as well; for it is impossible, or not easy, to do noble acts without the proper equipment. In many actions we use friends and riches and political power as instruments; and there are some things the lack of which takes the lustre from happiness, as good birth, goodly children, beauty; for the man who is very ugly in appearance or ill-born or solitary and childless is not very likely to be happy, and perhaps a man would be still less likely if he had thoroughly bad children or friends or had lost good children or friends by death. As we said,[11] then, happiness seems to need this sort of prosperity in addition; for which reason some identify happiness with good fortune, though others identify it with virtue.

9   For this reason also the question is asked, whether happiness is to be acquired by learning or by habituation or some other sort of training, or comes in virtue of some divine providence or again by chance. Now if there is *any* gift of the gods to men, it is reasonable that happiness should be god-given, and most surely god-given of all human things inasmuch as it is the best. But this question would perhaps be more appropriate to another inquiry; happiness seems, however, even if it is not god-sent but comes as a result of virtue and some process of learning or training, to be among the most god-like things; for that which is the prize and end of virtue seems to be the best thing in the world, and something godlike and blessed.

It will also on this view be very generally shared; for all who are not maimed as regards their potentiality for virtue may win it by a certain kind of study and care. But if it is better to be happy thus than by chance, it is reasonable that the facts should be so, since everything that depends on the action of nature is by nature as good as it can be, and similarly everything that depends on art or any rational cause, and especially if it depends on the best of all causes. To entrust to chance what is greatest and most noble would be a very defective arrangement.

The answer to the question we are asking is plain also from the definition of happiness; for it has been said[12] to be a virtuous activity of soul, of a certain kind. Of the remaining goods, some must necessarily pre-exist as conditions of happiness, and others are naturally co-operative and useful as instruments. And this will be found to agree with what we said at the outset;[13] for we stated the end of political

---

[10]i. e., he judges that virtuous actions are good and noble in the highest degree.
[11]1098[b] 26–9.
[12]1098[a] 16.
[13]1094[a] 27.

science to be the best end, and political science spends most of its pains on making the citizens to be of a certain character, viz. good and capable of noble acts.

It is natural, then, that we call neither ox nor horse nor any other of the animals happy; for none of them is capable of sharing in such activity. For this reason also a boy is not happy; for he is not yet capable of such acts, owing to his age; and boys who are called happy are being congratulated by reason of the hopes we have for them. For there is a required, as we said,[14] not only complete virtue but also a complete life, since many changes occur in life, and all manner of chances, and the most prosperous may fall into great misfortunes in old age, as is told of Priam in the Trojan Cycle; and one who has experienced such chances and has ended wretchedly no one calls happy.

10   Must no one at all, then, be called happy while he lives; must we, as Solon says, see the end? Even if we are to lay down this doctrine, is it also the case that a man *is* happy when he is *dead?* Or is not this quite absurd, especially for us who say that happiness is an activity? But if we do not call the dead man happy, and if Solon does not mean this, but that one can then safely *call* a man blessed as being at last beyond evils and misfortunes, this also affords matter for discussion; for both evil and good are thought to exist for a dead man, as much as for one who is alive but not aware of them; e.g. honours and dishonours and the good or bad fortunes of children and in general of descendants. And this also presents a problem; for though a man has lived happily up to old age and has had a death worthy of his life, many reverses may befall his descendants—some of them may be good and attain the life they deserve, while with others the opposite may be the case; and clearly too the degrees of relationship between them and their ancestors may vary indefinitely. It would be odd, then, if the dead man were to share in these changes and become at one time happy, at another wretched; while it would also be odd if the fortunes of the descendants did not for *some* time have *some* effect on the happiness of their ancestors.

But we must return to our first difficulty; for perhaps by a consideration of it our present problem might be solved. Now if we must see the end and only then call a man happy, not as being happy but as having been so before, surely this is a paradox, that when he is happy the attribute that belongs to him is not to be truly predicated of him because we do not wish to call living men happy, on account of the changes that may befall them, and because we have assumed happiness to be something permanent and by no means easily changed, while a single man may suffer many turns of fortune's wheel. For clearly if we were to keep pace with his fortunes, we should often call the same man happy and again wretched, making the happy man out to be a "chameleon and insecurely based." Or is this keeping pace with his fortunes quite wrong? Success or failure in life does not depend on these, but human life, as we said,[15] needs these as mere additions, while virtuous activities or their opposites are what constitute happiness or the reverse.

The question we have now discussed confirms our definition. For no function of man has so much permanence as virtuous activities (these are thought to be more

---

[14]1098ᵃ 16–18.
[15]1099ᵃ 31–ᵇ7.

durable even than knowledge of the sciences), and of these themselves the most valuable are more durable because those who are happy spend their life most readily and most continuously in these; for this seems to be the reason why we do not forget them. The attribute in question,[16] then, will belong to the happy man, and he will be happy throughout his life; for always, or by preference to everything else, he will be engaged in virtuous action and contemplation, and he will bear the chances of life most nobly and altogether decorously, if he is "truly good" and "foursquare beyond reproach."[17]

Now many events happen by chance, and events differing in importance; small pieces of good fortune or of its opposite clearly do not weigh down the scales of life one way or the other, but a multitude of great events if they turn out well will make life happier (for not only are they themselves such as to add beauty to life, but the way a man deals with them may be noble and good), while if they turn out ill they crush and maim happiness; for they both bring pain with them and hinder many activities. Yet even in these nobility shines through, when a man bears with resignation many great misfortunes, not through insensibility to pain but through nobility and greatness of soul.

If activities are, as we said,[18] what gives life its character, no happy man can become miserable; for he will never do the acts that are hateful and mean. For the man who is truly good and wise, we think, bears all the chances of life becomingly and always makes the best of circumstances, as a good general makes the best military use of the army at his command and a good shoemaker makes the best shoes out of the hides that are given him; and so with all other craftsmen. And if this is the case, the happy man can never become miserable—though he will not reach *blessedness,* if he meet with fortunes like those of Priam.

Nor, again, is he many-coloured and changeable; for neither will he be moved from his happy state easily or by any ordinary misadventures, but only by many great ones, nor, if he has had many great misadventures, will he recover his happiness in a short time, but if at all, only in a long and complete one in which he has attained many splendid successes.

Why then should we not say that he is happy who is active in accordance with complete virtue and is sufficiently equipped with external goods, not for some chance period but throughout a complete life? Or must we add "and who is destined to live thus and die as befits his life"? Certainly the future is obscure to us, while happiness, we claim, is an end and something in every way final. If so, we shall call happy those among living men in whom these conditions are, and are to be, fulfilled—but happy *men.* So much for these questions.

11 [19]That the fortunes of descendants and of all a man's friends should not affect his happiness at all seems a very unfriendly doctrine, and one opposed to the opinions men hold; but since the events that happen are numerous and admit of all sorts

---

[16]Durability.
[17]Simonides.
[18]I.9.
[19]Aristotle now returns to the question stated in 1100ᵃ 18–30.

of difference, and some come more near to us and others less so, it seems a long—nay, an infinite—task to discuss each in detail; a general outline will perhaps suffice. If, then, as some of a man's own misadventures have a certain weight and influence on life while others are, as it were, lighter, so too there are differences among the misadventures of our friends taken as a whole, and it makes a difference whether the various sufferings befall the living or the dead (much more even than whether lawless and terrible deeds are presupposed in a tragedy or done on the stage), this difference also must be taken into account; or rather, perhaps, the fact that doubt is felt whether the dead share in any good or evil. For it seems, from these considerations, that even if anything whether good or evil penetrates to them, it must be something weak and negligible, either in itself or for them, or if not, at least it must be such in degree and kind as not to make happy those who are not happy nor to take away their blessedness from those who are. The good or bad fortunes of friends, then, seem to have some effects on the dead, but effects of such a kind and degree as neither to make the happy unhappy nor to produce any other change of the kind.

12 These questions having been definitely answered, let us consider whether happiness is among the things that are praised or rather among the things that are prized; for clearly it is not to be placed among *potentialities.*[20] Everything that is praised seems to be praised because it is of a certain kind and is related somehow to something else; for we praise the just or brave man and in general both the good man and virtue itself because of the actions and functions involved, and we praise the strong man, the good runner, and so on, because he is of a certain kind and is related in a certain way to something good and important. This is clear also from the praises of the gods; for it seems absurd that the gods should be referred to our standard, but this *is* done because praise involves a reference, as we said, to something else. But if praise is for things such as we have described, clearly what applies to the best things is not praise, but something greater and better, as is indeed obvious; for what we do to the gods and the most godlike of men is to call them blessed and happy. And so too with good *things;* no one praises happiness as he does justice, but rather calls it blessed, as being something more divine and better.

Eudoxus also seems to have been right in his method of advocating the supremacy of pleasure; he thought that the fact that, though a good, it is not praised indicated it to be better than the things that are praised, and that this is what God and the good are; for by reference to these all other things are judged. *Praise* is appropriate to virtue, for as a result of virtue men tend to do noble deeds; but *encomia* are bestowed on acts, whether of the body or of the soul. But perhaps nicety in these matters is more proper to those who have made a study of encomia; to us it is clear from what has been said that happiness is among the things that are prized and perfect. It seems to be so also from the fact that it is a first principle; for it is for the sake of this that we all do all that we do, and the first principle and cause of goods is, we claim, something prized and divine.

---

[20]Cf. *Top.* 126[b] 4; *M. M.* 1183[b] 20.

13   Since happiness is an activity of soul in accordance with perfect virtue, we must consider the nature of virtue; for perhaps we shall thus see better the nature of happiness. The true student of politics, too, is thought to have studied virtue above all things; for he wishes to make his fellow citizens good and obedient to the laws. As an example of this we have the lawgivers of the Cretans and the Spartans, and any others of the kind that there may have been. And if this inquiry belongs to political science, clearly the pursuit of it will be in accordance with our original plan. But clearly the virtue we must study is human virtue; for the good we were seeking was human good and the happiness human happiness. By human virtue we mean not that of the body but that of the soul; and happiness also we call an activity of soul. But if this is so, clearly the student of politics must know somehow the facts about soul, as the man who is to heal the eyes or the body as a whole must know about the eyes or the body; and all the more since politics is more prized and better than medicine; but even among doctors the best educated spend much labour on acquiring knowledge of the body. The student of politics, then, must study the soul, and must study it with these objects in view, and do so just to the extent which is sufficient for the questions we are discussing; for further precision is perhaps something more laborious than our purposes require.

Some things are said about it, adequately enough, even in the discussions outside our school, and we must use these; e.g. that one element in the soul is irrational and one has a rational principle. Whether these are separated as the parts of the body or of anything divisible are, or are distinct by definition but by nature inseparable, like convex and concave in the circumference of a circle, does not affect the present question.

Of the irrational element one division seems to be widely distributed, and vegetative in its nature, I mean that which causes nutrition and growth; for it is this kind of power of the soul that one must assign to all nurslings and to embryos and this same power to full-grown creatures; this is more reasonable than to assign some different power to them. Now the excellence of this seems to be common to all species and not specifically human; for this part or faculty seems to function most in sleep, while goodness and badness are least manifest in sleep (whence comes the saying that the happy are no better off than the wretched for half their lives; and this happens naturally enough, since sleep is an inactivity of the soul in that respect in which it is called good or bad), unless perhaps to a small extent some of the movements actually penetrate to the soul, and in this respect the dreams of good men are better than those of ordinary people. Enough of this subject, however; let us leave the nutritive faculty alone, since it has by its nature no share in human excellence.

There seems to be also another irrational element in the soul—one which in a sense, however, shares in a rational principle. For we praise the rational principle of the continent man and of the incontinent, and the part of their soul that has such a principle, since it urges them aright and towards the best objects; but there is found in them also another element naturally opposed to the rational principle, which fights against and resists that principle. For exactly as paralysed limbs when we intend to move them to the right turn on the contrary to the left, so is it with the soul; the impulses of incontinent people move in contrary directions. But while in the body we see that which moves astray, in the soul we do not. No doubt, however, we must none the less suppose that in the soul too there is something contrary to the rational principle, resisting and opposing it. In what sense it is distinct from the other elements does not concern us. Now even this seems to have a share in a rational principle, as we said,[21] at any rate in the continent man it obeys the rational principle—and presumably in the temperate and brave man it is still more obedient; for in him it speaks, on all matters, with the same voice as the rational principle.

Therefore the irrational element also appears to be twofold. For the vegetative element in no way shares in a rational principle, but the appetitive, and in general the desiring element in a sense shares in it, in so far as it listens to and obeys it; this is the sense in which we speak of "taking account" of one's father or one's friends, not that in which we speak of "accounting" for a mathematical property. That the irrational element is in some sense persuaded by a rational principle is indicated also by the giving of advice and by all reproof and exhortation. And if this element also must be said to have a rational principle, that which has a rational principle (as well as that which has not) will be twofold, one subdivision having it in the strict sense and in itself, and the other having a tendency to obey as one does one's father.

Virtue too is distinguished into kinds in accordance with this difference; for we say that some of the virtues are intellectual and others moral, philosophic wisdom and understanding and practical wisdom being intellectual, liberality and temperance moral. For in speaking about a man's character we do not say that he is wise or has understanding but that he is good-tempered or temperate; yet we praise the wise man also with respect to his state of mind; and of states of mind we call those which merit praise virtues. . . .

BOOK VIII

1   After what we have said, a discussion of friendship would naturally follow, since it is a virtue or implies virtue, and is besides most necessary with a view to living. For without friends no one would choose to live, though he had all other goods; even rich men and those in possession of office and of dominating power are thought to need friends most of all; for what is the use of such prosperity without the opportunity of beneficence, which is exercised chiefly and in its most laudable form towards friends? Or how can prosperity be guarded and preserved without friends? The greater it is, the more exposed is it to risk. And in poverty and in other misfortunes men think friends are the only refuge. It helps the young, too, to keep from error; it aids older people by ministering to their needs and supplementing the activities that are failing from weakness; those in the prime of life it stimulates to noble actions—"two going together"[1]—for with friends men are more able both to think and to act. Again, parent seems by nature to feel it for offspring and offspring for parent, not only among men but among birds and among most animals; it is felt mutually by members of the same race, and especially by men, whence we praise lovers of their fellowmen. We may see even in our travels how near and dear every

---

[21]I.13.
[1]*Il.* x. 224.

man is to every other. Friendship seems too to hold states together, and lawgivers to care more for it than for justice; for unanimity seems to be something like friendship, and this they aim at most of all, and expel faction as their worst enemy; and when men are friends they have no need of justice, while when they are just they need friendship as well, and the truest form of justice is thought to be a friendly quality.

But it is not only necessary but also noble; for we praise those who love their friends, and it is thought to be a fine thing to have many friends; and again we think it is the same people that are good men and are friends.

Not a few things about friendship are matters of debate. Some define it as a kind of likeness and say like people are friends, whence come the sayings "like to like," "birds of a feather flock together," and so on; others on the contrary say "two of a trade never agree." On this very question they inquire for deeper and more physical causes, Euripides saying that "parched earth loves the rain, and stately heaven when filled with rain loves to fall to earth," and Heraclitus that "it is what opposes that helps" and "from different tones comes the fairest tune" and "all things are produced through strife"; while Empedocles, as well as others, expresses the opposite view that like aims at like. The physical problems we may leave alone (for they do not belong to the present inquiry); let us examine those which are human and involve character and feeling, e.g. whether friendship can arise between any two people or people cannot be friends if they are wicked, and whether there is one species of friendship or more than one. Those who think there is only one because it admits of degrees have relied on an inadequate indication; for even things different in species admit of degree. We have discussed this matter previously.

2   The kinds of friendship may perhaps be cleared up if we first come to know the object of love. For not everything seems to be loved but only the lovable, and this is good, pleasant, or useful; but it would seem to be that by which some good or pleasure is produced that is useful, so that it is the good and the useful that are lovable as ends. Do men love, then, *the* good, or what is good for *them?* These sometimes clash. So too with regard to the pleasant. Now it is thought that each loves what is good for himself, and that the good is without qualification lovable, and what is good for each man is lovable for him; but each man loves not what is good for him but what seems good. This however will make no difference; we shall just have to say that this is "that which seems lovable." Now there are three grounds on which people love; of the love of lifeless objects we do not use the word "friendship"; for it is not mutual love, nor is there a wishing of good to the other (for it would surely be ridiculous to wish wine well; if one wishes anything for it, it is that it may keep, so that one may have it oneself); but to a friend we say we ought to wish what is good for his sake. But to those who thus wish good we ascribe only goodwill, if the wish is not reciprocated; goodwill when it *is* reciprocal being friendship. Or must we add "when it is recognized"? For many people have goodwill to those whom they have not seen but judge to be good or useful; and one of these might return this feeling. These people seem to bear goodwill to each other; but how could one call them friends when they do not know their mutual feelings? To be friends, then, they must

be mutually recognized as bearing goodwill and wishing well to each other for one of the aforesaid reasons.

3   Now these reasons differ from each other in kind; so, therefore, do the corresponding forms of love and friendship. There are therefore three kinds of friendship, equal in number to the things that are loveable; for with respect to each there is a mutual and recognized love, and those who love each other wish well to each other in that respect in which they love one another. Now those who love each other for their utility do not love each other for themselves but in virtue of some good which they get from each other. So too with those who love for the sake of pleasure; it is not for their character that men love ready-witted people, but because they find them pleasant. Therefore those who love for the sake of utility love for the sake of what is good for *themselves,* and those who love for the sake of pleasure do so for the sake of what is pleasant to *themselves,* and not in so far as the other is the person loved but in so far as he is useful or pleasant. And thus these friendships are only incidental; for it is not as being the man he is that the loved person is loved, but as providing some good or pleasure. Such friendships, then, are easily dissolved, if the parties do not remain like themselves; for if the one party is no longer pleasant or useful the other ceases to love him.

Now the useful is not permanent but is always changing. Thus when the motive of the friendship is done away, the friendship is dissolved, inasmuch as it existed only for the ends in question. This kind of friendship seems to exist chiefly between old people (for at that age people pursue not the pleasant but the useful) and, of those who are in their prime or young, between those who pursue utility. And such people do not live much with each other either; for sometimes they do not even find each other pleasant; therefore they do not need such companionship unless they are useful to each other; for they are pleasant to each other only in so far as they rouse in each other hopes of something good to come. Among such friendships people also class the friendship of host and guest. On the other hand the friendship of young people seems to aim at pleasure; for they live under the guidance of emotion, and pursue above all what is pleasant to themselves and what is immediately before them; but with increasing age their pleasures become different. This is why they quickly become friends and quickly cease to be so; their friendship changes with the object that is found pleasant, and such pleasure alters quickly. Young people are amorous too; for the greater part of the friendship of love depends on emotion and aims at pleasure; this is why they fall in love and quickly fall out of love, changing often within a single day. But these people do wish to spend their days and lives together; for it is thus that they attain the purpose of their friendship.

Perfect friendship is the friendship of men who are good, and alike in virtue; for these wish well alike to each other *qua* good, and they are good in themselves. Now those who wish well to their friends for their sake are most truly friends; for they do this by reason of their own nature and not incidentally; therefore their friendship lasts as long as they are good—and goodness is an enduring thing. And each is good without qualification and to his friend, for the good are both good without qualification and useful to each other. So too they are pleasant; for the good are pleasant both without qualification and to each other, since to each his own activities and others like them are pleasurable, and the actions of the good *are* the same or like. And such a friendship is as might be expected permanent, since there meet in it all the qualities that friends should have. For all friendship is for the sake of good or of pleasure—good or pleasure either in the abstract or such as will be enjoyed by him who has the friendly feeling—and is based on a certain resemblance; and to a friendship of good men all the qualities we have named belong in virtue of the nature of the friends themselves; for in the case of this kind of friendship the other qualities also[2] are alike in both friends, and that which is good without qualification is also without qualification pleasant, and these are the most lovable qualities. Love and friendship therefore are found most and in their best form between such men.

But it is natural that such friendships should be infrequent; for such men are rare. Further, such friendship requires time and familiarity; as the proverb says, men cannot know each other till they have "eaten salt together"; nor can they admit each other to friendship or be friends till each has been found lovable and been trusted by each. Those who quickly show the marks of friendship to each other wish to be friends, but are not friends unless they both are lovable and know the fact; for a wish for friendship may arise quickly, but friendship does not.

4   This kind of friendship, then, is perfect both in respect of duration and in all other respects, and in it each gets from each in all respects the same as, or something like what, he gives; which is what ought to happen between friends. Friendship for the sake of pleasure bears a resemblance to this kind; for good people too *are* pleasant to each other. So too does friendship for the sake of utility; for the good are also useful to each other. Among men of these inferior sorts too, friendships are most permanent when the friends get the same thing from each other (e.g. pleasure), and not only that but also from the same source, as happens between ready-witted people, not as happens between lover and beloved. For these do not take pleasure in the same things, but the one in seeing the beloved and the other in receiving attentions from his lover; and when the bloom of youth is passing the friendship sometimes passes too (for the one finds no pleasure in the sight of the other, and the other gets no attentions from the first); but many lovers on the other hand are constant, if familiarity has led them to love each other's characters, these being alike. But those who exchange not pleasure but utility in their amour are both less truly friends and less constant. Those who are friends for the sake of utility part when the advantage is at an end; for they were lovers not of each other but of profit.

For the sake of pleasure or utility, then, even bad men may be friends of each other, or good men of bad, or one who is neither good nor bad may be a friend to any sort of person, but for their own sake clearly only good men can be friends; for bad men do not delight in each other unless some advantage come of the relation.

The friendship of the good too and this alone is proof against slander; for it is not easy to trust any one's talk about a man who has long been tested by oneself; and it is among good men that trust and the feeling that "he would never wrong me"

---

[2] i.e. absolute pleasantness, relative goodness, and relative pleasantness, as well as absolute goodness.

and all the other things that are demanded in true friendship are found. In the other kinds of friendship, however, there is nothing to prevent these evils arising.

For men apply the name of friends even to those whose motive is utility, in which sense states are said to be friendly (for the alliances of states seem to aim at advantage), and to those who love each other for the sake of pleasure, in which sense children are called friends. Therefore we too ought perhaps to call such people friends, and say that there are several kinds of friendship—firstly and in the proper sense that of good men *qua* good, and by analogy the other kinds; for it is in virtue of something good and something akin to what is found in true friendship that they are friends, since even the pleasant is good for the lovers of pleasure. But these two kinds of friendship are not often united, nor do the same people become friends for the sake of utility and of pleasure; for things that are only incidentally connected are not often coupled together.

Friendship being divided into these kinds, bad men will be friends for the sake of pleasure or of utility, being in this respect like each other, but good men will be friends for their own sake, i.e. in virtue of their goodness. These, then, are friends without qualification; the others are friends incidentally and through a resemblance to these.

5   As in regard to the virtues some men are called good in respect of a state of character, others in respect of an activity, so too in the case of friendship; for those who live together delight in each other and confer benefits on each other, but those who are asleep or locally separated are not performing, but are disposed to perform, the activities of friendship; distance does not break off the friendship absolutely, but only the activity of it. But if the absence is lasting, it seems actually to make men forget their friendship; hence the saying "out of sight, out of mind." Neither old people nor sour people seem to make friends easily; for there is little that is pleasant in them, and no one can spend his days with one whose company is painful, or not pleasant, since nature seems above all to avoid the painful and to aim at the pleasant. Those, however, who approve of each other but do not live together seem to be well-disposed rather than actual friends. For there is nothing so characteristic of friends as living together (since while it is people who are in need that desire benefits, even those who are supremely happy desire to spend their days together; for solitude suits such people least of all); but people cannot live together if they are not pleasant and do not enjoy the same things, as friends who are companions seem to do.

The truest friendship, then, is that of the good, as we have frequently said;[3] for that which is without qualification good or pleasant seems to be lovable and desirable, and for each person that which is good or pleasant to him; and the good man is lovable and desirable to the good man for both these reasons. Now it looks as if love were a feeling, friendship a state of character, for love may be felt just as much towards lifeless things, but mutual love involves choice and choice springs from a state of character; and men wish well to those whom they love, for their sake, not as a result of feeling but as a result of a state of character. And in loving a friend

[3]1156[b] 7, 23, 33, 1157[a] 30, [b]4.

men love what is good for themselves; for the good man in becoming a friend becomes a good to his friend. Each, then, both loves what is good for himself, and makes an equal return in goodwill and in pleasantness; for friendship is said to be equality, and both of these are found most in the friendship of the good.

6   Between sour and elderly people friendship arises less readily, inasmuch as they are less good-tempered and enjoy companionship less; for these are thought to be the greatest marks of friendship and most productive of it. This is why, while young men become friends quickly, old men do not; it is because men do not become friends with those in whom they do not delight; and similarly sour people do not quickly make friends either. But such men may bear goodwill to each other; for they wish one another well and aid one another in need; but they are hardly *friends* because they do not spend their days together nor delight in each other, and these are thought the greatest marks of friendship.

One cannot be a friend to many people in the sense of having friendship of the perfect type with them, just as one cannot be in love with many people at once (for love is a sort of excess of feeling, and it is the nature of such only to be felt towards one person); and it is not easy for many people at the same time to please the same person very greatly, or perhaps even to be good in his eyes. One must, too, acquire some experience of the other person and become familiar with him, and that is very hard. But with a view to utility or pleasure it is possible that many people should please one; for many people are useful or pleasant, and these services take little time.

Of these two kinds that which is for the sake of pleasure is the more like friendship, when both parties get the same things from each other and delight in each other or in the same things, as in the friendships of the young; for generosity is more found in such friendships. Friendship based on utility is for the commercially minded. People who are supremely happy, too, have no need of useful friends, but do need pleasant friends: for they wish to live with *some one* and, though they can endure for a short time what is painful, no one could put up with it continuously, nor even with the Good itself if it were painful to him; this is why they look out for friends who are pleasant. Perhaps they should look out for friends who, being pleasant, are also good, and good for them, too; for so they will have all the characteristics that friends should have.

People in positions of authority seem to have friends who fall into distinct classes; some people are useful to them and others are pleasant, but the same people are rarely both; for they seek neither those whose pleasantness is accompanied by virtue nor those whose utility is with a view to noble objects, but in their desire for pleasure they seek for ready-witted people, and their other friends they choose as being clever at doing what they are told, and these characteristics are rarely combined. Now we have said that the *good* man *is* at the same time pleasant and useful;[4] but such a man does not become the friend of one who surpasses him in station, unless he is surpassed also in virtue; if this is not so, he does not establish

---

[4]1156^b 13–15, 1157^a 1–3.

equality by being proportionally exceeded in both respects. But people who surpass him in both respects are not so easy to find.

However that may be, the aforesaid friendships involve equality; for the friends get the same things from one another and wish the same things for one another, or exchange one thing for another, e.g. pleasure for utility; we have said,[5] however, that they are both less truly friendships and less permanent. But it is from their likeness and their unlikeness to the same thing that they are thought both to be and not to be friendships. It is by their likeness to the friendship of virtue that they seem to be friendships (for one of them involves pleasure and the other utility, and these characteristics belong to the friendship of virtue as well); while it is because the friendship of virtue is proof against slander and permanent, while these quickly change (besides differing from the former in many other respects), that they appear *not* to be friendships; i.e. it is because of their unlikeness to the friendship of virtue.

7   But there is another kind of friendship, viz. that which involves an inequality between the parties, e.g. that of father to son and in general of elder to younger, that of man to wife and in general that of ruler to subject. And these friendships differ also from each other; for it is not the same that exists between parents and children and between rulers and subjects, nor is even that of father to son the same as that of son to father, nor that of husband to wife the same as that of wife to husband. For the virtue and the function of each of these is different, and so are the reasons for which they love; the love and the friendship are therefore different also. Each party, then, neither gets the same from the other, nor ought to seek it; but when children render to parents what they ought to render to those who brought them into the world, and parents render what they should to their children, the friendship of such persons will be abiding and excellent. In all friendships implying inequality the love also should be proportional, i.e. the better should be more loved than he loves, and so should the more useful, and similarly in each of the other cases; for when the love is in proportion to the merit of the parties, then in a sense arises equality, which is certainly held to be characteristic of friendship.

But equality does not seem to take the same form in acts of justice and in friendship; for in acts of justice what is equal in the primary sense is that which is in proportion to merit, while quantitative equality is secondary, but in friendship quantitative equality is primary and proportion to merit secondary. This becomes clear if there is a great interval in respect of virtue or vice or wealth or anything else between the parties; for then they are no longer friends, and do not even expect to be so. And this is most manifest in the case of the gods; for they surpass us most decisively in all good things. But it is clear also in the case of kings; for with them, too, men who are much their inferiors do not expect to be friends; nor do men of no account expect to be friends with the best or wisest men. In such cases it is not possible to define exactly up to what point friends can remain friends; for much can be taken away and friendship remain, but when one party is removed to a great distance, as God is, the possibility of friendship ceases. This is in fact the origin of the question whether friends really wish for their friends the greatest goods, e.g. that of

[5]1156ᵃ 16–24, 1157ᵃ 20–33.

being gods; since in that case their friends will no longer be friends to them, and therefore will not be good things for them (for friends *are* good things). The answer is that if we were right in saying that friend wishes good to friend for his sake,[6] his friend must remain the sort of being he is, whatever that may be; therefore it is for him only so long as he remains a man that he will wish the greatest goods. But perhaps not *all* the greatest goods; for it is for himself most of all that each man wishes what is good.

8   Most people seem, owing to ambition, to wish to be loved rather than to love; which is why most men love flattery; for the flatterer is a friend in an inferior position, or pretends to be such and to love more than he is loved; and being loved seems to be akin to being honoured, and this is what most people aim at. But it seems to be not for its own sake that people choose honour, but incidentally. For most people enjoy being honoured by those in positions of authority because of their hopes (for they think that if they want anything they will get it from them; and therefore they delight in honour as a token of favour to come); while those who desire honour from good men, and men who know, are aiming at confirming their own opinion of themselves; they delight in honour, therefore, because they believe in their own goodness on the strength of the judgement of those who speak about them. In being loved, on the other hand, people delight for its own sake; whence it would seem to be better than being honoured, and friendship to be desirable in itself. But it seems to lie in loving rather than in being loved, as is indicated by the delight mothers take in loving; for some mothers hand over their children to be brought up, and so long as they know their fate they love them and do not seek to be loved in return (if they cannot have both), but seem to be satisfied if they see them prospering; and they themselves love their children even if these owing to their ignorance give them nothing of a mother's due. Now since friendship depends more on loving, and it is those who love their friends that are praised, loving seems to be the characteristic virtue of friends, so that it is only those in whom this is found in due measure that are lasting friends, and only their friendship that endures.
    It is in this way more than any other that even unequals can be friends; they can be equalized. Now equality and likeness are friendship, and especially the likeness of those who are like in virtue; for being steadfast in themselves they hold fast to each other, and neither ask nor give base services, but (one may say) even prevent them; for it is characteristic of good men neither to go wrong themselves nor to let their friends do so. But wicked men have no steadfastness (for they do not remain even like to themselves), but become friends for a short time because they delight in each other's wickedness. Friends who are useful or pleasant last longer; i.e. as long as they provide each other with enjoyments or advantages. Friendship for utility's sake seems to be that which most easily exists between contraries, e.g. between poor and rich, between ignorant and learned; for what a man actually lacks he aims at, and one gives something else in return. But under this head, too, we might bring lover and beloved, beautiful and ugly. This is why lovers sometimes

---

[6]1155[b] 31.

seem ridiculous, when they demand to be loved as they love; if they are equally lovable their claim can perhaps be justified, but when they have nothing lovable about them it is ridiculous. Perhaps, however, contrary does not even aim at contrary by its own nature, but only incidentally, the desire being for what is intermediate; for that is what is good, e.g. it is good for the dry not to become wet[7] but to come to the intermediate state, and similarly with the hot and in all other cases. These subjects we may dismiss; for they are indeed somewhat foreign to our inquiry.

9   Friendship and justice seem, as we have said at the outset of our discussion,[8] to be concerned with the same objects and exhibited between the same persons. For in every community there is thought to be some form of justice, and friendship too; at least men address as friends their fellow-voyagers and fellow-soldiers, and so too those associated with them in any other kind of community. And the extent of their association is the extent of their friendship, as it is the extent to which justice exists between them. And the proverb "what friends have is common property" expresses the truth; for friendship depends on community. Now brothers and comrades have all things in common, but the others to whom we have referred have definite things in common—some more things, others fewer; for of friendships, too, some are more and others less truly friendships. And the claims of justice differ too; the duties of parents to children and those of brothers to each other are not the same nor those of comrades and those of fellow-citizens, and so, too, with the other kinds of friendship. There is a difference, therefore, also between the acts that are unjust towards each of these classes of associates, and the injustice increases by being exhibited towards those who are friends in a fuller sense; e.g. it is a more terrible thing to defraud a comrade than a fellow-citizen, more terrible not to help a brother than a stranger, and more terrible to wound a father than any one else. And the demands of justice also seem to increase with the intensity of the friendship, which implies that friendship and justice exist between the same persons and have an equal extension.

Now all forms of community are like parts of the political community; for men journey together with a view to some particular advantage, and to provide something that they need for the purposes of life; and it is for the sake of advantage that the political community too seems both to have come together originally and to endure, for this is what legislators aim at, and they call just that which is to the common advantage. Now the other communities aim at advantage bit by bit, e.g. sailors at what is advantageous on a voyage with a view to making money or something of the kind, fellow-soldiers at what is advantageous in war, whether it is wealth or victory or the taking of a city that they seek, and members of tribes and demes act similarly [Some communities seem to arise for the sake of pleasure, viz. religious guilds and social clubs; for these exist respectively for the sake of offering sacrifice and of companionship. But all these seem to fall under the political community; for it aims not at present advantage but at what is advantageous for life as a whole], offering sacrifices and arranging gatherings for the purpose, and assigning honours to the gods,

[7]Cf. 1155[b] 3.
[8]1155[a] 22–28.

and providing pleasant relaxations for themselves. For the ancient sacrifices and gatherings seem to take place after the harvest as a sort of firstfruits, because it was at these seasons that people had most leisure. All the communities, then, seem to be parts of the political community; and the particular kinds of friendship will correspond to the particular kinds of community.

10   There are three kinds of constitution, and an equal number of deviation-forms—perversions, as it were, of them. The constitutions are monarchy, aristocracy, and thirdly that which is based on a property qualification, which it seems appropriate to call timocratic, though most people are wont to call it polity. The best of these is monarchy, the worst timocracy. The deviation from monarchy is tyranny; for both are forms of one-man rule, but there is the greatest difference between them; the tyrant looks to his own advantage, the king to that of his subjects. For a man is not a king unless he is sufficient to himself and excels his subjects in all good things; and such a man needs nothing further; therefore he will not look to his own interests but to those of his subjects; for a king who is not like that would be a mere titular king. Now tyranny is the very contrary of this; the tyrant pursues his own good. And it is clearer in the case of tyranny that it is the worst deviation-form;[9] but it is the contrary of the best that is worst.[10] Monarchy passes over into tyranny; for tyranny is the evil form of one-man rule and the bad king becomes a tyrant. Aristocracy passes over into oligarchy by the badness of the rulers, who distribute contrary to equity what belongs to the city—all or most of the good things to themselves, and office always to the same people, paying most regard to wealth; thus the rulers are few and are bad men instead of the most worthy. Timocracy passes over into democracy; for these are coterminous, since it is the ideal even of timocracy to be the rule of the majority, and all who have the property qualification count as equal. Democracy is the least bad of the deviations; for in its case the form of constitution is but a slight deviation. These then are the changes to which constitutions are most subject; for these are the smallest and easiest transitions.

One may find resemblances to the constitutions and, as it were, patterns of them even in households. For the association of a father with his sons bears the form of monarchy, since the father cares for his children; and this is why Homer calls Zeus "father"; it is the ideal of monarchy to be paternal rule. But among the Persians the rule of the father is tyrannical; they use their sons as slaves. Tyrannical too is the rule of a master over slaves; for it is the advantage of the master that is brought about in it. Now this seems to be a correct form of government, but the Persian type is perverted; for the modes of rule appropriate to different relations are diverse. The association of man and wife seems to be aristocratic; for the man rules in accordance with his worth, and in those matters in which a man should rule, but the matters that befit a woman he hands over to her. If the man rules in everything the relation passes over into oligarchy; for in doing so he is not acting in accordance with their respective worth, and not ruling in virtue of his superiority. Sometimes, however, women rule, because they are heiresses; so their rule is not in virtue of

[9]Than it is that monarchy is the best genuine form ([a]35).
[10]Therefore monarchy must be the best.

excellence but due to wealth and power, as in oligarchies. The association of brothers is like timocracy; for they are equal, except in so far as they differ in age; hence if they differ *much* in age, the friendship is no longer of the fraternal type. Democracy is found chiefly in masterless dwellings (for here every one is on an equality), and in those in which the ruler is weak and every one has license to do as he pleases.

11   Each of the constitutions may be seen to involve friendship just in so far as it involves justice. The friendship between a king and his subjects depends on an excess of benefits conferred; for he confers benefits on his subjects if being a good man he cares for them with a view to their well-being, as a shepherd does for his sheep (whence Homer called Agamemnon "shepherd of the peoples"). Such too is the friendship of a father, though this exceeds the other in the greatness of the benefits conferred; for he is responsible for the existence of his children, which is thought the greatest good, and for their nurture and upbringing. These things are ascribed to ancestors as well. Further, by nature a father tends to rule over his sons, ancestors over descendants, a king over his subjects. These friendships imply superiority of one party over the other, which is why ancestors are honoured. The justice therefore that exists between persons so related is not the same on both sides but is in every case proportioned to merit; for that is true of the friendship as well. The friendship of man and wife, again, is the same that is found in an aristocracy; for it is in accordance with virtue—the better gets more of what is good, and each gets what befits him; and so, too, with the justice in these relations. The friendship of brothers is like that of comrades; for they are equal and of like age, and such persons are for the most part like in their feelings and their character. Like this, too, is the friendship appropriate to timocratic government; for in such a constitution the ideal is for the citizens to be equal and fair; therefore rule is taken in turn, and on equal terms; and the friendship appropriate here will correspond.

But in the deviation-forms, as justice hardly exists, so too does friendship. It exists least in the worst form; in tyranny there is little or no friendship. For where there is nothing common to ruler and ruled, there is not friendship either, since there is not justice; e.g. between craftsman and tool, soul and body, master and slave; the latter in each case is benefited by that which uses it, but there is no friendship nor justice towards lifeless things. But neither is there friendship towards a horse or an ox, nor to a slave *qua* slave. For there is nothing common to the two parties; the slave is a living tool and the tool a lifeless slave. *Qua* slave then, one cannot be friends with him. But *qua* man one can; for there seems to be some justice between any man and any other who can share in a system of law or be a party to an agreement; therefore there can also be friendship with him in so far as he is a man. Therefore while in tyrannies friendship and justice hardly exist, in democracies they exist more fully; for where the citizens are equal they have much in common.

12   Every form of friendship, then, involves association, as has been said.[11] One might, however, mark off from the rest both the friendship of kindred and that of

---

[11]1159ᵇ 29–32.

comrades. Those of fellow-citizens, fellow-tribesmen, fellow-voyagers, and the like are more like mere friendships of association; for they seem to rest on a sort of compact. With them we might class the friendship of host and guest.

The friendship of kinsmen itself, while it seems to be of many kinds, appears to depend in every case on parental friendship; for parents love their children as being a part of themselves, and children their parents as being something originating from them. Now (1) parents know their offspring better than their children know that they are their children, and (2) the originator feels his offspring to be his own more than the offspring do their begetter; for the product belongs to the producer (e. g. a tooth or hair or anything else to him whose it is), but the producer does not belong to the product, or belongs in a less degree. And (3) the length of time produces the same result; parents love their children as soon as these are born, but children love their parents only after time has elapsed and they have acquired understanding or the power of discrimination by the senses. From these considerations it is also plain why mothers love more than fathers do. Parents, then, love their children as themselves (for their issue are by virtue of their separate existence a sort of other selves), while children love their parents as being born of them, and brothers love each other as being born of the same parents; for their identity with them makes them identical with each other (which is the reason why people talk of "the same blood," "the same stock," and so on). They are, therefore, in a sense the same thing, though in separate individuals. Two things that contribute greatly to friendship are a common upbringing and similarity of age; for "two of an age take to each other," and people brought up together tend to be comrades; whence the friendship of brothers is akin to that of comrades. And cousins and other kinsmen are bound up together by derivation from brothers, viz. by being derived from the same parents. They come to be closer together or farther apart by virtue of the nearness or distance of the original ancestor.

The friendship of children to parents, and of men to gods, is a relation to them as to something good and superior; for they have conferred the greatest benefits, since they are the causes of their being and of their nourishment, and of their education from their birth; and this kind of friendship possesses pleasantness and utility also, more than that of strangers, inasmuch as their life is lived more in common. The friendship of brothers has the characteristics found in that of comrades (and especially when these are good), and in general between people who are like each other, inasmuch as they belong more to each other and start with a love for each other from their very birth, and inasmuch as those born of the same parents and brought up together and similarly educated are more akin in character; and the test of time has been applied most fully and convincingly in their case.

Between other kinsmen friendly relations are found in due proportion. Between man and wife friendship seems to exist by nature; for man is naturally inclined to form couples—even more than to form cities, inasmuch as the household is earlier and more necessary than the city, and reproduction is more common to man with the animals. With the other animals the union extends only to this point, but human beings live together not only for the sake of reproduction but also for the various purposes of life; for from the start the functions are divided, and those of man and woman are different; so they help each other by throwing their peculiar gifts into the common stock. It is for these reasons that both utility and pleasure seem to be found in this kind of friendship. But this friendship may be based also on virtue, if the parties are good; for each has its own virtue and they will delight in the fact. And children seem to be a bond of union (which is the reason why childless people part more easily); for children are a good common to both and what is common holds them together.

How man and wife and in general friend and friend ought mutually to behave seems to be the same question as how it is just for them to behave; for a man does not seem to have the same duties to a friend, a stranger, a comrade, and a schoolfellow.

13   There are three kinds of friendship, as we said at the outset of our inquiry,[12] and in respect of each some are friends on an equality and others by virtue of a superiority (for not only can equally good men become friends but a better man can make friends with a worse, and similarly in friendships of pleasure or utility the friends may be equal or unequal in the benefits they confer). This being so, equals must effect the required equalization on a basis of equality in love and in all other respects, while unequals must render what is in proportion to their superiority or inferiority.

Complaints and reproaches arise either only or chiefly in the friendship of utility, and this is only to be expected. For those who are friends on the ground of virtue are anxious to do well by each other (since that is a mark of virtue and of friendship), and between men who are emulating each other in this there cannot be complaints or quarrels; no one is offended by a man who loves him and does well by him—if he is a person of nice feeling he takes his revenge by doing well by the other. And the man who excels the other in the services he renders will not complain of his friend, since he gets what he aims at; for each man desires what is good. Nor do complaints arise much even in friendships of pleasure; for both get at the same time what they desire, if they enjoy spending their time together; and even a man who complained of another for *not* affording him pleasure would seem ridiculous, since it is in his power not to spend his days with him.

But the friendship of utility is full of complaints; for as they use each other for their own interests they always want to get the better of the bargain, and think they have got less than they should, and blame their partners because they do not get all they "want and deserve"; and those who do well by others cannot help them as much as those whom they benefit want.

Now it seems that, as justice is of two kinds, one unwritten and the other legal, one kind of friendship of utility is moral and the other legal. And so complaints arise most of all when men do not dissolve the relation in the spirit of the same type of friendship in which they contracted it. The *legal* type is that which is on fixed terms; its purely commercial variety is on the basis of immediate payment, while the more liberal variety allows time but stipulates for a definite *quid pro quo*. In this variety the debt is clear and not ambiguous, but in the postponement it contains an element of friendliness; and so some states do not allow suits arising out of such

---

[12]1156ᵃ 7.

agreements, but think men who have bargained on a basis of credit ought to accept the consequences. The *moral* type is not on fixed terms; it makes a gift, or does whatever it does, as to a friend; but one expects to receive as much or more, as having not given but lent; and if a man is worse off when the relation is dissolved than he was when it was contracted he will complain. This happens because all or most men, while they wish for what is noble, choose what is advantageous; now it is noble to do well by another without a view to repayment, but it is the receiving of benefits that is advantageous.

Therefore if we can we should return the equivalent of what we have received (for we must not make a man our friend against his will; we must recognize that we were mistaken at the first and took a benefit from a person we should not have taken it from—since it was not from a friend, nor from one who did it just for the sake of acting so—and we must settle up just as if we had been benefited on fixed terms). Indeed, one would agree to repay if one could (if one could not, even the giver would not have expected one to do so); therefore if it is possible we must repay. But at the outset we must consider the man by whom we are being benefited and on what terms he is acting, in order that we may accept the benefit on these terms, or else decline it.

It is disputable whether we ought to measure a service by its utility to the receiver and make the return with a view to that, or by the benevolence of the giver. For those who have received say they have received from their benefactors what meant little to the latter and what they might have got from others—minimizing the service; while the givers, on the contrary, say it was the biggest thing they had, and what could not have been got from others, and that it was given in times of danger or similar need. Now if the friendship is one that aims at *utility,* surely the advantage to the receiver is the measure. For it is he that asks for the service, and the other man helps him on the assumption that he will receive the equivalent; so the assistance has been precisely as great as the advantage to the receiver, and therefore he must return as much as he has received, or even more (for that would be nobler). In friendships based on *virtue* on the other hand, complaints do not arise, but the purpose of the doer is a sort of measure; for in purpose lies the essential element of virtue and character.

14   Differences arise also in friendships based on superiority; for each expects to get more out of them, but when this happens the friendship is dissolved. Not only does the better man think he ought to get more, since more should be assigned to a good man, but the more useful similarly expects this; they say a useless man should not get as much as they should, since it becomes an act of public service and not a friendship if the proceeds of the friendship do not answer to the worth of the benefits conferred. For they think that, as in a commercial partnership those who put more in get more out, so it should be in friendship. But the man who is in a state of need and inferiority makes the opposite claim; they think it is the part of a good friend to help those who are in need; what, they say, is the use of being the friend of a good man or a powerful man, if one is to get nothing out of it?

At all events it seems that each party is justified in his claim, and that each should get more out of the friendship than the other—not more of the same thing, however, but the superior more honour and the inferior more gain; for honour is the prize of virtue and of beneficence, while gain is the assistance required by inferiority.

It seems to be so in constitutional arrangements also; the man who contributes nothing good to the common stock is not honoured; for what belongs to the public is given to the man who benefits the public, and honour does belong to the public. It is not possible to get wealth from the common stock and at the same time honour. For no one puts up with the smaller share in *all* things; therefore to the man who loses in wealth they assign honour and to the man who is willing to be paid, wealth, since the proportion to merit equalizes the parties and preserves the friendship, as we have said.[13]

This then is also the way in which we should associate with unequals; the man who is benefited in respect of wealth or virtue must give honour in return, repaying what he can. For friendship asks a man to do what he can, not what is proportional to the merits of the case; since that cannot always be done, e.g. in honours paid to the gods or to parents; for no one could ever return to them the equivalent of what he gets, but the man who serves them to the utmost of his power is thought to be a good man.

This is why it would not seem open to a man to disown his father (though a father may disown his son; being in debt, he should repay, but there is nothing by doing which a son will have done the equivalent of what he has received, so that he is always in debt. But creditors can remit a debt; and a father can therefore do so too. At the same time it is thought that presumably no one would repudiate a son who was not far gone in wickedness; for apart from the natural friendship of father and son it is human nature not to reject a son's assistance. But the son, if he *is* wicked, will naturally avoid aiding his father, or not be zealous about it; for most people wish to get benefits, but avoid doing them, as a thing unprofitable.—So much for these questions.

The Fundamental Principles of the Metaphysics of Ethics *(excerpt)*

Immanuel Kant

TRANSITION FROM POPULAR MORAL PHILOSOPHY TO THE METAPHYSIC OF ETHICS

The fact that we have drawn our concept of duty from the common use of our practical reason is no reason whatever to conclude that we have been treating it as an empirical concept. On the contrary, when we observe the empirical facts of human conduct

---

[13]1162[a] 34-[b] 4, Cf. 1158[b] 27, 1159[a] 35–[b] 3.

Source: Translated with an introduction by Otto Manthey-Zorn. New York: Appleton-Century-Crofts, Inc., 1938, 22–42.

we meet frequent and, as we ourselves admit, just complaints that it is impossible to find a single clear example of a disposition to act from pure duty. Although many a thing demanded *by duty* may be done *in accordance* with it, yet there is always reason to doubt that it has actually been done *out of duty,* and thus has moral worth. Consequently there have at all times been philosophers who have simply denied the reality of such a disposition in human conduct and have ascribed everything to a more or less refined love of self. In taking this attitude they did not question the soundness of the concept of morality, but they rather spoke with sincere regret of the frailty and meanness of human nature which, though noble enough to make a precept of so worthy an idea, is at the same time too weak to follow it; and which employs reason that should have given it its code of laws merely to satisfy the interests of the inclinations either singly or, at most, in their greatest compatibility with one another.

It is indeed absolutely impossible by experience to establish with complete certainty a single case in which the maxim of an otherwise dutiful action rested solely on moral grounds and on the conception of duty. To be sure, it is true at times that, with the keenest self-examination, we can discover nothing that could have been strong enough to induce us to this or that good act and to so great a sacrifice, except the moral basis of duty. However, that is not at all sufficient reason for concluding that such idea was not a mere delusion and that really no hidden motive of self-love was the actual determining cause of our will. For we delight in flattering ourselves with a nobler motive which we falsely assume, but in reality we can never, even by a most painstaking search, fully discover the hidden springs of action, because examination of moral values does not depend upon the actions that one sees, but upon their inner principles which one does not see.

One can indeed render no greater service to those who mock at all morality as a vainly over-reaching imagination than to admit to them that the concept of duty must be taken solely from experience (just as one finds it convenient to persuade oneself of the same about all other concepts); for by so doing one assures their triumph. Out of love for humanity I am willing to admit that even most of our actions are in conformance with duty. But when one examines their intentions more closely the "dear self" everywhere comes to light upon which these intentions are directed, rather than upon the severe command of duty which would often demand the denial of self. Nor is it necessary to be an enemy of duty, but merely a cold-blooded observer who does not at once consider the most vivid desire for the good to be a desire also for its reality, in order to doubt at certain moments that any real virtue can actually be found in the world. (Especially is this true in advanced years when experience has made judgment shrewd and also keen to observe.) In this case nothing can save us from a complete desertion of our ideas of duty or maintain in us a firm respect for its law, except the clear conviction that, even though there should never up to now have been any actions arisen from such pure sources, it still is not now our concern whether this or that takes place, but that reason for itself and independent of all phenomena commands what ought to take place. Consequently we are concerned with actions of which there may never have been an example in the world, the potentiality of which anyone who bases everything on experience may even doubt greatly, but which reason nevertheless incessantly demands; that, for example, pure integrity in matters of friendship can none the less be demanded of every person even though there may not have existed an honest friend hitherto, because this duty as a duty lies, before all experience, in the idea of a reason determining the will by *a priori* principles.

When we add to this that, unless we go so far as to deny that the concept of morality has any truth or reference to any possible object, we cannot dispute that its law is of such far-reaching significance that it must be considered *necessary,* not only for man, but for all *rational creatures in general,* and not merely under fortuitious conditions and with exceptions, but *absolutely;* then it is clear that no experience could lead us to infer even the possibility of such apodictic laws. For with what right can we show the unlimited respect which is due to a universal precept from every rational nature for that which perhaps holds good only under the contingent condition of mankind? And how should laws of the determination of *our* will be regarded laws of the determination of the will of rational creatures in general, or even laws of our own will indeed, if they were merely empirical and did not have their origin wholly *a priori* in a pure but practical reason?

One could not serve morality worse than to derive it from examples. For every example that is presented must itself first be judged according to the principles of morality to determine whether it is worthy to serve as an original example, that is, as pattern, but by no means can it supply the idea of morality straightway. Even the Holy One of the Gospel must first be compared with our ideal of perfection before he is recognized as such. He says of Himself: "Why call ye Me (whom you see) good; none is good (the prototype of the good) but God only (whom you do not see)?" But where did we get our conception of God as the highest good? Solely from the *idea* of moral perfection which reason forms *a priori* and unites inseparably with the concept of a free will. In morality there never are imitations, and examples serve only as stimuli, that is, they put beyond doubt the feasibility of that which the law commands, they demonstrate what the practical rule expresses in a more general way; but they never give us the right to set aside the true original that lies in reason and to guide ourselves by examples.

If then there is no supreme principle of morality which does not necessarily rest solely on pure reason and is independent of all experience, then it seems to me that it is beyond all question worth while to make a general (*in abstracto*) presentation of these concepts as they and the principles belonging to them exist *a priori,* if our knowledge is to be distinguished from common understanding, and to be called philosophical. In our times it is certainly necessary. For, if a vote were taken whether a pure knowledge of reason, separated from everything empirical, that is, a metaphysic of ethics, or a popular practical philosophy is to be preferred, it is easy to guess which side would have the majority.

It is indeed commendable to condescend to popular notions, provided the principles of pure reason have first been ascertained and satisfactorily established. That implies that we first *found* the theory of ethics upon metaphysics and then, when it is firmly established, *promote its acceptance* by giving it a popular character. But it is extremely incongruous to accede to popularity in the first inquiry upon which the soundness of the principle depends. On the one hand, such a proceeding can never lay claim to the extremely rare merit of a true *philosophical popularity,* for it is very simple to make a popular presentation by merely renouncing all thorough insight. On the other hand, it also brings to light a disgusting mess of patched-up observations and half-subtilizing principles, in which shallow brains delight because it gives them something to use in their daily chatter. The sagacious, however, see in all this nothing but confusion and turn away in disgust without knowing what to do about it; while philosophers, who see quite well through this delusion, get little attention when they ask that for a time the alleged popularity be set aside, so that they may be properly popular after a definite insight has been won.

We need only to look at the essays on morality written in the falsely popular fashion and we will find a strange mixture either of the special constitution of human nature (at times, to be sure, also the idea of a rational nature in general), or of perfection, or happiness; here moral sense, there fear of God; a little of this and a little of that as well. To none of these writers will it have occurred to ask whether in all their knowledge of human nature (which certainly can be derived from experience only) the principle of morality can be sought for, and, if that is impossible, if morality is to be found wholly *a priori,* free from everything empirical, simply in pure concepts of reason, and not even to the slightest degree anywhere else; whether it is not better to plan to make this a separate inquiry, as a pure practical philosophy or (if we may use so descried a term) as metaphysic of ethics,* to carry it to its full completion by itself alone, and to ask the public which demands a popular treatment to await the end of the undertaking.

Such a completely isolated metaphysic of ethics, not mixed with any anthropology, physics or hyperphysics, even less with any hidden qualities (which might be called hypophysical), is not only an indispensable substratum of every theoretical knowledge of duties which has been determined with certainty, but also a desideratum of the highest importance to the actual fulfilment of its precepts. For the pure conception of duty with no strange admixture of empirical stimulation, and of the moral law generally, has so much stronger an influence upon the heart of man, solely by way of reason (which first from this realizes that it is able to be practical of itself), than all the other motives† that may be aroused within the field of experience, so that, in the consciousness of its dignity, it despises the latter and little by little learns to become its master. In comparison with this a mixed theory of morals which is derived from motives of feelings and inclinations together with concepts of reason, makes the mind vacillate between

---

*Just as pure mathematics is distinguished from applied and pure from applied logic, so one may distinguish a pure philosophy of morals (metaphysic) from applied (that is, applied to human nature). This designation at once calls attention to the fact that moral principles are not founded upon the properties of human nature, but must subsist *a priori* of themselves, that from these principles, however, it must be possible to deduce practical rules for every rational nature, and therefore also for the nature of man.

†I have a letter from the late excellent Sulzer in which he asks me why the theories of morals accomplish so little, even though they are so convincing to reason. My answer was delayed because I wished to make it complete. But the only answer is this: The teachers did not clarify their own ideas. In their desire to be thorough they spoiled them by digging up motives of moral goodness from every quarter in order to make their medicine good and strong. For the most ordinary observation will show that, when we imagine an act of righteousness performed with steadfast soul, free from the purpose of any advantage whatever, in this or the next world, even under the greatest temptation or enticements, then this act will outweigh by far every similar act which is affected even in the least by some other stimulation. It will elevate the soul and make us wish that we might be able to act in some other way. Even moderately young children have this impression, and duties should never be presented to them in any other light.

impulsions that cannot be brought under any principle and which only by chance lead to the good, but may more often lead to evil as well.

From what has been said it is clear that all moral concepts have their seat and origin wholly *a priori* in reason, and indeed in common human reason as well as in that which is highly speculative; that they cannot be abstracted from any knowledge which is empirical and therefore merely fortuitous; that this very purity of their origin makes them worthy to serve as our supreme practical principles; that their real influence and the unqualified value of actions suffer in direct proportion to the empirical which is added to them. Furthermore, that it is not only of the greatest necessity from a theoretical, purely speculative point of view, but of the greatest practical importance as well, that the moral concepts and laws be derived from pure reason and be presented pure and unmixed; that, when we determine the entire scope of this practical but pure knowledge of the reason, that is to say, the whole faculty of pure practical reason, we do not make the principles dependent upon the particular nature of human reason, which may be allowed or even sometimes necessary in speculative philosophy; but that we derive them from the general concept of a rational being, because, though it requires anthropology for its *application* to man, moral law must be generally valid for every rational creature. We must first of all present all morality complete in itself and independent of the former as pure philosophy, that is a metaphysic (which is quite possible in so specialized a study); well knowing that, without it, it would not only be vain to make an exact speculative appraisal of the moral element of duty in all apparently dutiful actions; but also that even in common and practical usage, especially in moral precepts, it would be impossible to found morals upon their genuine principles, and thereby produce pure moral attitudes and instil them in the minds of men for the highest good of life.

But in order that this study may not merely advance from ordinary moral judgment (which we have described as worthy of great respect) to the philosophical, which we have already done, but to progress by natural stages from a popular philosophy, which goes only as far as it can get by groping its way with the help of examples, to metaphysic (which does not allow itself to be checked by anything empirical and, since it must measure the whole content of the knowledge of reason, penetrates even to the ideas themselves where examples fail us); we must pursue and describe clearly the practical faculty of reason up to the point where the concepts of duty arise from it.

Each thing in nature works according to laws. Only a rational being has the faculty to act *according to the conception* of laws, that is according to principles, in other words has a will. Since the deduction of actions from laws requires *reason* the will is nothing but practical reason. If reason invariably determines the will then the actions which such a being recognizes as objectively necessary are subjectively necessary as well, that is to say, the will is the faculty to choose *that only* which reason, independent of inclination, recognizes as practically necessary, that is, good. But if reason of itself alone does not sufficiently determine the will, if the latter is dependent also on subjective conditions (certain impulses) which do not always correspond with the objective conditions; in a word, if the will is not *in itself* in full accord with reason (as is actually the case with men) then the actions which objectively are recognized as necessary are subjectively contingent, and the determination of such a will according to objective laws is *obligation*. By this we mean, the relation of the objective laws to a will which is not good throughout is conceived as the determination of the will of a rational being by principles of reason which, however, this will does not by virtue of its nature necessarily follow.

The conception of an objective principle, in so far as it is obligatory for the will, is called a command (of reason), and the formula of the command is called an *imperative.*

All imperatives are expressed by a "Thou Shalt" and thereby indicate the relation of an objective law of reason to a will which is not by virtue of its subjective constitution necessarily determined by it (an obligation). These imperatives say that something would be good to do or to omit, but they say it to a will which does not always do a thing merely because it is presented to it as being good to do. That, however, is practically good which determines the will by means of the conceptions of reason, accordingly not from subjective causes, but from objective ones, that is to say on principles which are valid for every rational being as such. It is distinguished from the *pleasant* as that which influences the will only by means of sensations from merely subjective causes which apply only to the feeling of this or that person, and not as principles of reason valid for everyone.*

A completely good will would therefore likewise be subject to objective laws (of the good), but it could not for that reason be conceived as *obliged* to good actions, because of itself according to its subjective constitution it can be determined only by the conception of the good. Therefore no imperatives hold for the *Divine Will* or in general for a *holy* will; the "Thou Shalt" is out of place here, because already the "*I Will*" is necessarily of itself in harmony with the law. Therefore imperatives are merely formulae to express the relation of objective laws of volition in general to the subjective imperfection of the will of this or that rational being, for example of the human will.

Now all *imperatives* command either *hypothetically* or *categorically*. The former represents the practical necessity of a possible action as a means to arrive at something else that is willed (or may be willed). The categorical imperative would then be that which represented an action as objectively necessary of itself without relation to another end.

Since every practical law represents a possible action as good and consequently as necessary for a subject who can be determined practically by reason, therefore all imperatives are formulae for actions which are necessary according to the principle of a will that in some manner or other is good. Now, if the action is meant to

---

*The dependence of the desire on sensations is called inclination and this accordingly always indicates a *want.* But the dependence of a will which may be determined by chance on principles of reason is called an *interest.* The latter therefore arises only with a dependent will which is not of itself at all times in accord with reason. Within the Divine Will an interest is inconceivable. But also the human will can *take an interest in* something without therefore *acting out of interest.* The former denotes *practical* interest in an action, the latter *pathological* interest in the object of the action. The first shows merely the dependence of the will on principles of reason as such, the second on principles of reason in behalf of inclination, inasmuch as reason merely supplies the practical rules by which the wants of inclination may be met. In the first case the actions themselves interest me, in the second the object of the action (inasmuch as it is pleasant to me). In the first section we have seen that in an action done from duty the interest to be regarded must not be in the object, but in the action itself and in its principle of reason (the law).

be good merely as a means to *something else,* then the imperative is *hypothetical;* but if it is represented as good of itself and thus necessary as a principle of a will which is of itself in accord with reason, then it is *categorical.*

The imperative then tells me which of my possible actions would be good, and presents the practical rule in relation to a will which, however, does not at once perform an act because it is good, partly because the subject does not always know that it is good, partly, even though it knows it, because its maxims may still be opposed to the objective principles of practical reason.

The hypothetical imperative accordingly tells only that an action is good for this or that possible or actual purpose. In the first case it is a problematic principle, in the second case an assertorial practical principle. The categorical imperative, which declares that the action is of itself objectively necessary without relation to any purpose and therefore also without any other end than itself, has the nature of a (practical) apodictic principle.

That which is possible only by virtue of some rational being may also be conceived as a possible purpose of some will; and therefore the principles of action are indeed infinitely numerous in so far as they are considered necessary for the realization of a possible purpose. All sciences have a practical part consisting of problems stating the possibility of some purpose, and of imperatives that direct how to realize the purpose. The latter may therefore be called in general imperatives of skill. Whether the end is reasonable and good is of no concern here at all; but only what must be done to attain it. The prescription given by a physician in order to effect the thorough cure of his patient, and that prepared by a poisoner to bring about certain death, are both of equal value in so far as each serves to realize its purpose perfectly. Because it is unknown what purposes life may later present to youth, parents seek above all to have their children learn *a great many things* and encourage the development of *skill* in the use of the means to *all sorts* of ends, of none of which they are able to determine that it will really become in the future a purpose for the child, though it possibly may. This concern is so great that parents commonly neglect because of it to form and set aright in their children the judgments on the value of the things that may be chosen as ends.

There is nevertheless *one* end that may be assumed as being present in all rational beings (in so far as they are dependent beings and imperatives apply to them) and therefore one purpose of which they not only are *capable,* but of which it may safely be assumed that each and every one must by a natural necessity *possess* it. This purpose is *happiness.* The hypothetical imperative, which represents the practical necessity of an action as means to the advancement of happiness, is assertorial. This must be explained as necessary not only to an uncertain and merely possible purpose, but also to a purpose that can be assumed in each person with certainty and *a priori,* because it is part of his being. Now skill in the choice of the means to one's own greatest well-being may be called *prudence,** in the narrowest sense of the word. Therefore the imperative which refers to the choice of the means

---

*The word *prudence* is taken in two senses. In the one it may be called worldly prudence, in the other private prudence. The first is the skill of a person to influence others so as to use them for his own purposes. The second is the ability to see how to unite all these purposes for one's own lasting benefit. The latter is

to one's own happiness, the precept of prudence, is still hypothetical; the action is not commanded absolutely, but only as a means to another purpose.

Finally, there is an imperative which commands a certain conduct directly and which is not based on the condition of attaining any other purpose by it. This imperative is categorical. It has nothing to do with the matter of the action or with that which results from it, but with the form and the principle from which it itself proceeds; and its essential good consists of the state of mind irrespective of what may result from it. This imperative may be called the imperative of morality.

In accordance with these three kinds of principles volition is clearly differentiated also by the *dissimilarity* of the will. To make these differences clear it would seem best to describe them in their order as existing either as *rules* of skill, or *counsels* of prudence, or *commands (laws)* of morality. For the law alone involves an unconditional and, moreover, objective and, therefore, universally valid necessity; and commands are laws that must be obeyed, that is, must be followed even against the inclinations. Counsels, to be sure, also involve necessity, but this can be valid only under the subjective contingent, whether this or that person considers this or that part of his happiness. The categorical imperative, however, is limited by no condition and may with complete propriety be called a command as being absolutely, though practically, necessary. The first imperatives may also be called *technical* (belonging to art) the second *pragmatic*† (to welfare), the third *moral* (belonging to free conduct generally, that is, to *morals*).

Now the question arises: how are all these imperatives possible? This question does not demand to know how the execution of an action which the imperative demands is possible, but merely how the obligation of the will can be conceived, the problem of which the imperative expresses. How an imperative of skill is possible probably needs no special explanation. Whoever wills the end, also (in so far as reason has a decisive influence upon his actions) wills the indispensably necessary means at his disposal. As regards volition this proposition is analytical. For in willing an object as my effect there is already implied the causality of myself as acting cause, that is, the employment of the means, and the imperatives already derive the conception of actions necessary to this end from the conception of the willing of the end. (To determine the means to a chosen end there is need, to be sure, of synthetical propositions, which, however, do not concern the principle, the act of the will, but the realization of the object.) To be sure, mathematics uses only synthetical propositions to teach that in order to bisect a line I must draw two intersecting arcs from its extremities; but it is an analytical proposition to say, when I know that by a certain act alone the intended effect can be reached, that I also will the action that accomplishes the effect. For it is one and the same thing to conceive an effect as possible of attainment in a certain manner by me and to conceive myself as acting in this same manner in respect to it.

---

really the one to which even the value of the former is traced; and when a person is prudent in the first sense, but not in the second, we might better say of him that he is clever and cunning, but, on the whole, imprudent.
†It seems to me that this is the most accurate determination of the real meaning of the word *pragmatic.* For those *sanctions* are called pragmatic which do not really proceed fom the rights of the states as necessary laws, but from the provision for the general welfare. A *history* is pragmatic when it makes men *prudent,* that is, when it teaches the world how to foster its advantage better than in the past, or at least as well.

If it were as easy to make a definite concept of happiness, the imperative of prudence would in every way be similar to those of skill and likewise analytical. For here as well the proposition would read: Whoever wills the end also wills (necessarily according to reason) the indispensable means that are in his power. However, it is unfortunate that the concept of happiness is so indefinite that, although everybody desires to attain it, he can never say definitely and consistently what he really desires and wills. The reason for this is that the elements belonging to the concept of happiness are altogether empirical, that they must all be taken from experience, but at the same time require an absolute whole, a maximum of well-being in the present and every future state. However, it is impossible that the human being who is most penetrating and also most capable, but nevertheless limited, should construct for himself a definite conception of what he really wants. If he wills riches, with what worry, envy and persecution is he not apt to burden himself because of it? If he wills knowledge and insight, that may merely make his eyes sharper to see as the more terrible the unavoidable evils which are still hidden from him, or else burden his avidity that already troubles him enough with further desires. If he desires a long life, what guarantee is there that it will not be a long misery? If he at least wants health, how often has not the discomfort of the body prevented dissipations to which an unimpaired health may have tempted him, and so forth. In short he is unable to determine with complete certainty, according to any principle, what will make him truly happy because it would take omniscience to do so. It is therefore impossible to act according to definite principles in order to be happy, but one must act in accordance with empirical counsels, for example, of diet, economy, courtesy, restraint and the like, of which experience teaches that they on the average best promote well-being. It follows from this that the imperatives of prudence cannot command at all in the strict sense of the word, that is, that they cannot present actions objectively as practically *necessary:* that they are to be considered counsels (*consilia*) rather than precepts (*praecepta*) of reason; that the problem how to determine surely and absolutely what action will promote the happiness of a rational being is wholly insoluble; that therefore there can be no imperative which in a strict sense would command to do that which makes happy, because happiness is not an ideal of reason but of the imagination and therefore rests on empirical grounds only, of which it is vain to expect that they should determine an action whereby the totality of an actually endless series of effects would be attained. However, if it is assumed that the means to happiness can be definitely described, then this imperative of prudence would be an analytical practical proposition, for it differs from the imperative of skill only in this, that in the latter the end is merely possible, but in the former it is given. But since both ordain merely the means to that which is assumed as being willed as an end, therefore the imperative which commands the willing of the means for him who wills the end is in both cases analytical. Consequently there is no difficulty in regard to the possibility of an imperative of this kind either.

The only question in need of a solution is how an imperative of *morality* is possible, since it is in no sense hypothetical and the objective necessity which it presents is consequently based on no assumption as is the case with a hypothetical imperative. However, one must always be mindful that *by no example,* that is empirically, can it be discovered whether there is such an imperative at all; but one must apprehend that all imperatives that seem to be categorical may in some hidden way still be hypothetical. For example when it says: You shall not make a false promise, and one answers that the necessity of this prohibition is not a mere counsel to avoid some other evil, so that it would perhaps say: You shall not make a lying promise lest you be discredited when the lie is detected; rather when an action of this sort must be considered evil in itself and the imperative of the prohibition consequently is categorical, even then one cannot show with certainty in any example that the will was determined by no other impulse than the law, even though that may appear to be the case. For it is always possible that fear of humiliation or perhaps some hidden worry of other dangers may have a secret influence upon the will. How can the non-existence of a cause be proven by experience when the latter teaches only that we do not observe it? But in such a case the so-called moral imperative which, being moral, appears to be categorical and unconditional would in fact be a mere pragmatic precept which makes us attentive to our advantage and merely teaches us to observe it.

We shall then have to investigate wholly *a priori* the possibility of a *categorical* imperative, since we do not have the advantage in the case of this imperative that its actuality is given in experience and that therefore the possibility of its being is not necessary to establish it but merely to explain it. To begin with we must understand, however, that the categorical imperative alone has the form of a practical *law,* while all the other imperatives may indeed be called *principles of* the will, but not laws. For whatever is necessary to do merely to attain some intention or other may be considered as in itself contingent and we can always free ourselves from the precept by giving up the intention; while, on the other hand, the absolute command leaves the will no choice to go contrary to it, and therefore it alone carries with it that necessity which we require in a law.

In the second place, the difficulty of understanding the possibility of this categorical imperative or law of morality is indeed very great. It is an *a priori* synthetical practical proposition.* And inasmuch as it is so difficult to understand the possibility of a proposition of this kind in speculative knowledge it easily follows that the difficulty will be no less in practical knowledge.

In attacking this problem we shall investigate first whether perhaps the mere concept of a categorical imperative will not supply also the formula which contains the proposition that alone can be a categorical imperative. To comprehend how such an absolute command is possible, even when we know its formula, will require further special and difficult study which we shall reserve for the last section.

When I conceive a *hypothetical* imperative in general I do not know what it will contain until the condition is supplied. But when I conceive a *categorical* imperative I know at once what it contains. For, since besides the law the imperative contains

---

*I connect the act with the will without implying the condition of any inclination, but *a priori* and consequently necessarily (though only objectively, that is under the idea of a reason which would have full power over all objective motives). This is consequently a practical proposition which does not deduce the willing of an action analytically from another already presupposed (for we have no such perfect will); but rather connects it immediately with the concept of a rational being, as something not contained in it.

only the maxim[†] to accord with this law, the law however contains no condition which limits it; therefore nothing remains but the universality of the law in general with which the maxim of action shall conform, and this conformity alone the imperative really represents as necessary.

Consequently there is only one categorical imperative and it is this: *Act only on that maxim which will enable you at the same time to will that it be a universal law.*

Now if all imperatives of duty can be deduced from this single imperative as from their principle, then, although we here refrain from stating whether what one calls duty may be an empty notion, we shall at least be able to indicate what we understand by it and what the concept means.

Because the universality of the law according to which effects are produced constitutes what we really mean by *nature* in the most general sense (according to form), that is, the existence of things in so far as it is determined by universal laws, the universal imperative of duty may read thus: *Act as if the maxim of your action by your will were to become a* UNIVERSAL LAW OF NATURE.

We will now enumerate a few duties dividing them in the accustomed manner into duties to ourselves, and to others, and into perfect and imperfect duties.[‡]

A person who is wearied with life because of a series of misfortunes that has reduced him to despair still possesses sufficient reason to be able to ask himself, whether it may not be contrary to his duty to himself to take his life. Now he asks himself, whether the maxim of his action could possibly be a universal law of nature. But this maxim reads: Out of love of self I make it my principle to shorten my life if its continuation threatens more evil than it promises comfort. But he will still ask, whether his principle of self-love is capable of being a universal law of nature. Then he will soon see that a nature, whose law it would be to destroy life by the very feeling which is meant to stimulate the promotion of life, would contradict itself and therefore not persist as nature. Accordingly the maxim cannot possibly function as a universal law of nature, and it consequently completely refutes the supreme principle of all duty.

Another person is in need and finds it necessary to borrow money. He knows very well that he will not be able to repay it, but he also realizes that he will not receive a loan unless he promises solemnly to pay at a definite time. He has a desire to make this promise, but he still has enough conscience to ask himself whether it is not improper and contrary to duty to relieve distress in this manner. If he should nevertheless decide to do so, then the maxim of his action would read thus: When I think

---

[†]A *maxim* is the subjective principle to act and must be distinguished from the *objective principle,* the practical law. The former contains the practical rule which reason determines according to the conditions of the subject (often its ignorance or its inclinations), and it is therefore the principle by which the subject *acts.* On the other hand, the law is the objective principle valid for every rational being, and the principle by which it *shall* act, that is, an imperative.

[‡]It must be noted that I am reserving altogether the classification of duties for a future *metaphysic of ethics,* and that the present division is merely casual (in order to arrange my examples). I also mean by a perfect duty one that does not permit an exception in favor of inclination, and in this I include not only external but also inner perfect duties. This is contrary to the accepted school-use of the word, but I have no intention of justifying it here because it is indifferent to my purpose whether it is permitted or not.

that I am in need of money I will borrow and promise to repay, even though I know that I will never do so. Now this principle of my love of self or advantage may perhaps well agree with my whole future well-being; the next question, however, is, whether it is right. Thereby I change the interpretation of self-love into a universal law and arrange my question thus: How would things be if my maxim were a universal law? Then I see at once that it could never count as a universal law of nature and still agree with itself, but must necessarily contradict itself. For the universality of a law, according to which anyone who believed himself in distress could promise anything he pleased with no intention of keeping it, would make promises themselves and any purpose they may have impossible; since nobody would believe that a promise had been made, but everybody would ridicule such statements as vain pretenses.

A third finds that he possesses a gift which with some cultivation could make a useful man of him in all sorts of respects. But he is in comfortable circumstances and prefers to indulge in pleasure rather than trouble himself with the expansion and improvement of his fortunate natural faculties. But he still questions, whether his maxim of neglect of his natural gifts, besides agreeing with his inclination to diversions, also agrees with what is called duty. Then he sees that according to such a universal law a nature could still go on persisting although man, like the South Sea islander, should let his talents rest and his life were intent only on idleness, diversions, propagation, in a word, pleasure; but he cannot possibly *will* this to be a universal law of nature or be given to us as such by a natural instinct. For as a rational being he necessarily wants all his faculties to develop because they after all are given to him and serve him for all sorts of possible purposes.

Again a *fourth*, who is well off while he sees others struggling with great difficulties (which he could well alleviate), thinks: What concern is it of mine? May each man be as happy as the heavens decree or he can make himself to be; I shall deprive him of nothing and not even envy him. But neither do I care to contribute to his welfare nor offer him help in his distress. Now if such an attitude were to be a universal law of nature the human race could subsist very well, to be sure, and doubtless better than when everybody chatters of sympathy and good will, even endeavors occasionally to exert it, but also takes every chance to deceive and to plunder or otherwise to violate the rights of man. But although it is possible that a universal law of nature could exist by that maxim, it is still impossible to *will* that such a principle count as a law of nature generally. For by deciding for such a law a will would run counter to itself, inasmuch as many an occasion might arise where a person of such will might need the love and sympathy of others and where he would deprive himself of all hope of the desired assistance because of such a natural law arisen from his own will.

These are then a few of the duties, actual or at least accepted as such by us, whose derivation from the single principle which we have described is at once clear. The canon of the moral judgment of actions generally is this: One must be *able to will* that the maxim of an action be a universal law. Some actions are so constituted that their maxim cannot even be *conceived* as a universal law of nature, not to mention that one might *will* that it *ought* to be such. In others this inner impossibility cannot be discovered, but it nevertheless is impossible to *will* that their maxim be elevated to the universality of a law of nature because such a will would contradict itself. Plainly the first kind of maxim runs counter to the more strict or immediate (inflexible) duty, the second to the less immediate (meritorious) duty. Thus all duties, judged by their kind of obligation (and not by the object of the action) are shown by these examples to be completely dependent on the one principle.

If we now examine ourselves at each transgression of a duty we find that we do not really will that our maxim be a universal law; for that would be impossible. We rather will that the opposite generally persist as a law. We merely take the liberty to make an *exception* in our own favor or, just for this one time, in favor of our inclination. Consequently, if we considered everything from one and the same point of view, namely that of reason, then we would discover the contradiction in our own volition that a certain principle objectively is necessary as a universal law and, at the same time, subjectively should not be generally valid, but admit of exceptions. But since we at one time look upon our action from a point of view wholly in accord with reason and then examine the same action from a point of view affected by our inclination, there is really no contradiction at all, but rather a resistance of the inclination to the precept of reason (*antagonismus*) whereby the universality of the principle (*universalitas*) is changed into a mere generality (*generalitas*) by which the practical principle of reason is to meet the maxim halfway. Although this cannot be justified in our own impartial judgment, it nevertheless proves that we really acknowledge the validity of the categorical imperative, and (with all respect for it) merely allow ourselves a few exceptions that seem insignificant and forced upon us by circumstances.

An Introduction to the Principles of Morals and Legislation (excerpt)

Jeremy Bentham

CHAPTER I
OF THE PRINCIPLE OF UTILITY

I.

Nature has placed mankind under the governance of two sovereign masters, *pain* and *pleasure*. It is for them alone to point out what we ought to do, as well as to determine what we shall do. On the one hand the standard of right and wrong, on the other the chain of causes and effects, are fastened to their throne. They govern us in all we do, in all we say, in all we think: every effort we can make to throw off our subjection, will serve but to demonstrate and confirm it. In words a man may pretend to abjure their empire: but in reality he will remain subject to it all the

Source: The Works of Jeremy Bentham, Vol. I. Edinburgh: William Tair, 1843, 1–4, 14–17.

while. The *principle of utility** recognises this subjection, and assumes it for the foundation of that system, the object of which is to rear the fabric of felicity by the hands of reason and of law. Systems which attempt to question it, deal in sounds instead of sense, in caprice instead of reason, in darkness instead of light.

But enough of metaphor and declamation: it is not by such means that moral science is to be improved.

II.

The principle of utility is the foundation of the present work: it will be proper therefore at the outset to give an explicit and determinate account of what is meant by it. By the principle† of utility is meant that principle which approves or disapproves of every action whatsoever, according to the tendency which it appears to have to augment or diminish the happiness of the party whose interest is in question: or, what is the same thing in other words, to promote or to oppose that happiness. I say of every action whatsoever; and therefore not only of every action of a private individual, but of every measure of government.

III.

By utility is meant that property in any object, whereby it tends to produce benefit, advantage, pleasure, good, or happiness (all this in the present case comes to the same thing), or (what comes again to the same thing) to prevent the happening of mischief, pain, evil, or unhappiness to the party whose interest is considered: if that

---

*Note by the Author, July 1822—

To this denomination has of late been added, or substituted, the *greatest happiness* or *greatest felicity* principle: this for shortness, instead of saying at length *that principle* which states the greatest happiness of all those whose interest is in question, as being the right and proper, and only right and proper and universally desirable, end of human action: of human action in every situation, and in particular in that of a functionary or set of functionaries exercising the powers of Government. The word *utility* does not so clearly point to the ideas of *pleasure* and *pain* as the words *happiness* and *felicity* do: nor does it lead us to the consideration of the *number,* of the interests affected; to the *number,* as being the circumstance, which contributes, in the largest proportion, to the formation of the standard here in question; the *standard of right and wrong,* by which alone the propriety of human conduct, in every situation, can with propriety be tried. This want of a sufficiently manifest connexion between the ideas of *happiness* and *pleasure* on the one hand, and the idea of *utility* on the other, I have every now and then found operating, and with but too much efficiency, as a bar to the acceptance, that might otherwise have been given, to this principle.

†[Principle.] The word principle is derived from the Latin *principium:* which seems to be compounded of the two words *primus,* first, or chief, and *cipium,* a termination which seems to be derived from *capio,* to take, as in *mancipium, municipium;* to which are analogous *anceps, forceps,* and others. It is a term of very vague and very extensive signification: it is applied to any thing which is conceived to serve as a foundation or beginning to any series of operations: in some cases, of physical operations: but of mental operations in the present case.

The principle here in question may be taken for an act of the mind; a sentiment; a sentiment of approbation; a sentiment which, when applied to an action, approves of its utility, as that quality of it by which the measure of approbation or disapprobation bestowed upon it ought to be governed.

party be the community in general, then the happiness of the community: if a particular individual, then the happiness of that individual.

IV.

The interest of the community is one of the most general expressions that can occur in the phraseology of morals: no wonder that the meaning of it is often lost. When it has a meaning, it is this. The community is a fictitious *body,* composed of the individual persons who are considered as constituting as it were its *members.* The interest of the community then is, what?—the sum of the interests of the several members who compose it.

V.

It is in vain to talk of the interest of the community, without understanding what is the interest of the individual.* A thing is said to promote the interest, or to be *for* the interest, of an individual, when it tends to add to the sum total of his pleasures: or, what comes to the same thing, to diminish the sum total of his pains.

VI.

An action then may be said to be conformable to the principle of utility, or, for shortness sake, to utility (meaning with respect to the community at large), when the tendency it has to augment the happiness of the community is greater than any it has to diminish it.

VII.

A measure of government (which is but a particular kind of action, performed by a particular person or persons) may be said to be conformable to or dictated by the principle of utility, when in like manner the tendency which it has to augment the happiness of the community is greater than any which it has to diminish it.

VIII.

When an action, or in particular a measure of government, is supposed by a man to be conformable to the principle of utility, it may be convenient, for the pur-

---

*[Interest, &c.] Interest is one of those words, which not having any superior *genns,* cannot in the ordinary way be defined.

poses of discourse, to imagine a kind of law or dictate, called a law or dictate of utility: and to speak of the action in question, as being conformable to such law or dictate.

IX.

A man may be said to be a partizan of the principle of utility, when the approbation or disapprobation be annexes to any action, or to any measure, is determined, by and proportioned to the tendency which he conceives it to have to augment or to diminish the happiness of the community: or in other words, to its conformity or unconformity to the laws or dictates of utility.

X.

Of an action that is conformable to the principle of utility, one may always say either that it is one that ought to be done, or at least that it is not one that ought not to be done. One may say also, that it is right it should be done; at least that it is not wrong it should be done: that it is a right action; at least that it is not a wrong action. When thus interpreted, the words *ought,* and *right* and *wrong,* and others of that stamp, have a meaning: when otherwise, they have none.

XI.

Has the rectitude of this principle been ever formally contested? It should seem that it had, by those who have not known what they have been meaning. Is it susceptible of any direct proof? It should seem not: for that which is used to prove every thing else, cannot itself be proved: a chain of proofs must have their commencement somewhere. To give such proof is as impossible as it is needless.

XII.

Not that there is or ever has been that human creature breathing, however stupid or perverse, who has not on many, perhaps on most occasions of his life, deferred to it. By the natural constitution of the human frame, on most occasions of their lives men in general embrace this principle, without thinking of it: if not for the ordering of their own actions, yet for the trying of their own actions, as well as of those of other men. There have been, at the same time, not many, perhaps, even of the most intelligent, who have been disposed to embrace it purely and without reserve. There are even few who have not taken some occasion or other to quarrel with it, either on account of their not understanding always how to apply it, or on account of some prejudice or other which they were afraid to examine into, or could not bear to part with. For such is the stuff that man is made of: in principle and in practice, in a right track and in a wrong one, the rarest of all human qualities is consistency.

XIII.

When a man attempts to combat the principle of utility, it is with reasons drawn, without his being aware of it, from that very principle itself.† His arguments, if they prove any thing, prove not that the principle is *wrong,* but that, according to the applications he supposes to be made of it, it is *misapplied,* is it possible for a man to move the earth? Yes; but he must first find out another earth to stand upon.

XIV.

To disprove the propriety of it by arguments is impossible; but, from the causes that have been mentioned, or from some confused or partial view of it, a man may happen to be disposed not to relish it. Where this is the case, if he thinks the settling of

---

†"The principle of utility (I have heard it said) is a dangerous principle: it is dangerous on certain occasions to consult it." This is as much as to say, what? that it is not consonant to utility, to consult utility; in short, that it is *not* consulting it, to consult it.

Addition by the Author, July 1822—

Not long after the publication of the Fragment on Government, anno 1776, in which, in the character of an all-comprehensive and all-commanding principle, the principle of *utility* was brought to view, one person by whom observation to the above effect was made was *Alexander Wedderburn,* at that time Attorney or Solicitor General, afterwards successively Chief Justice of the Common Pleas, and Chancellor of England, under the successive titles of Lord Loughborough and Earl of Rosslyn. It was made—not indeed in my hearing, but in the hearing of a person by whom it was almost immediately, communicated to me. . . So far from being self-contradictory, it was a shrewd and perfectly true one. By that distinguished functionary, the state of the Government was thoroughly understood: by the obscure individual, at that time not so much as supposed to be so: his disquisitions had not been as yet applied, with any thing like a comprehensive view, to the field of Constitutional Law, nor therefore to those features of the English Government, by which the greatest happiness of the ruling *one* with or without that of a favoured few, are now so plainly seen to be the only ends to which the course of it has at any time been directed. The *principle of utility* was an appellative, at that time employed—employed by me, as it had been by others, to designate that which, in a more perspicuous and instructive manner, may, as above, be designated by the name of the *greatest happiness principle.* "This principle (said Wedderburn) is a dangerous one." Saying so, he said that which, to a certain extent, is strictly true: a principle, which lays down, as the only *right* and justifiable end of Government, the greatest happiness of the greatest number—how can it be denied to be a dangerous one? dangerous it unquestionably is, to every government which has for its *actual* end or object, the greatest happiness of a certain *one,* with or without the addition of some comparatively small number of others, whom it is matter of pleasure or accommodation to him to admit, each of them, to a share in the concern, on the footing of so many junior partners. *Dangerous* it therefore really was, to the interest—the sinister interest—of all those functionaries, himself included, whose interest it was, to maximize delay, vexation, and expense, in judicial and other modes of procedure, for the sake of the profit, extractible out of the expense. In a Government which had for its end in view the greatest happiness of the greatest number, Alexander Wedderburn might have been Attorney General and then Chancellor: but he would not have been Attorney General with £15,000 a-year, nor Chancellor with a peerage, with a veto upon all justice, with £25,000 a-year, and with 500 sinecures at his disposal, under the name of Ecclesiastical Benefices, besides *et cæteras.*

his opinions on such a subject worth the trouble, let him take the following steps, and at length, perhaps, he may come to reconcile himself to it.

1. Let him settle with himself, whether he would wish to discard this principle altogether; if so, let him consider what it is that all his reasonings (in matters of politics especially) can amount to?
2. If he would, let him settle with himself, whether he would judge and act without any principle, or whether there is any other he would judge and act by?
3. If there be, let him examine and satisfy himself whether the principle he thinks he has found is really any separate intelligible principle; or whether it be not a mere principle in words, a kind of phrase, which at bottom expresses neither more nor less than the mere averment of his own unfounded sentiments; that is, what in another person he might be apt to call caprice?
4. If he is inclined to think that his own approbation or disapprobation, annexed to the idea of an act, without any regard to its consequences, is a sufficient foundation for him to judge and act upon, let him ask himself whether his sentiment is to be a standard of right and wrong, with respect to every other man, or whether every man's sentiment has the same privilege of being a standard to itself?
5. In the first case, let him ask himself whether his principle is not despotical, and hostile to all the rest of human race?
6. In the second case, whether it is not anarchial, and whether at this rate there are not as many different standards of right and wrong as there are men? and whether even to the same man, the same thing, which is right to-day, may not (without the least change in its nature) be wrong to-morrow? and whether the same thing is not right and wrong in the same place at the same time? and in either case, whether all argument is not at an end? and whether, when two men have said. "I like this," and "I don't like it," they can (upon such a principle) have any thing more to say?
7. If he should have said to himself, No: for that the sentiment which he proposes as a standard must be grounded on reflection, let him say on what particulars the reflection is to turn? If on particulars having relation to the utility of the act, then let him say whether, this is not deserting his own principle, and borrowing assistance from that very one in opposition to which he sets it up: or if not on those particulars, on what other particulars?
8. If he should be for compounding the matter, and adopting his own principle in part, and the principle of utility in part, let him say how far he will adopt it?
9. When he has settled with himself where he will stop, then let him ask himself how he justifies to himself the adopting it so far? and why he will not adopt it any farther?
10. Admitting any other principle than the principle of utility to be a right principle, a principle that it is right for a man to pursue; admitting (what is not true) that the word *right* can have a meaning without reference to utility, let him say whether there is any such thing as a *motive* that a man can have to pursue the dictates of it: if there is, let him say what that motive is, and how it is to be distinguished from those which enforce the dictates of utility: if not, then lastly let him say what it is this other principle can be good for? . . .

CHAPTER III
OF THE FOUR* SANCTIONS OR SOURCES OF PAIN AND PLEASURE

I.

It has been shown that the happiness of the individuals, of whom a community is composed, that is, their pleasures and their security, is the end and the sole end which the legislator ought to have in view: the sole standard, in conformity to which each individual ought, as far as depends upon the legislator, to be *made* to fashion his behaviour. But whether it be this or any thing else that is to be *done,* there is nothing by which a man can ultimately be *made* to do it, but either pain or pleasure. Having taken a general view of these two grand objects (*viz.* pleasure, and what comes to the same thing, immunity from pain) in the character of *final* causes; it will be necessary to take a view of pleasure and pain itself, in the character of *efficient* causes or means.

II.

There are four distinguishable sources from which pleasure and pain are in use to flow: considered separately, they may be termed the *physical,* the *political,* the *moral,* and the *religious:* and inasmuch as the pleasures and pains belonging to each of them are capable of giving a binding force to any law or rule of conduct, they may all of them be termed *sanctions.*†

---

*The following is an extract from a letter of Bentham's to Dumont, dated Oct. 28, 1821:—

"*Sanctions.* Since the Traites, others have been discovered. There are now, I. Human: six, viz. 1. Physical; 2. Retributive; 3. Sympathetic; 4. Antipathetic; 5. Popular, or Moral; 6. Political, including Legal and Administrative.

"II. Superhuman *vice* Religious: all exemplifiable in the case of drunkenness; viz. the punitory class.

"*Note*—Sanctions in *genere* duæ, punitoriæ et remuneratoriæ; *in serie,* septem ut super; seven multiplied by two, equal fourteen.

"The Judicatory of the popular or moral sanction has two Sections: that of the few, and that of the many: Aristocratical and Democratical: their laws, their decisions, are to a vast extent opposite."

†Sanctio, in Latin, was used to signify the *act of binding,* and, by a common grammatical transition, *any thing which serves to bind a man:* to wit, to the observance of such or such a mode of conduct. According to a Latin grammarian,[a] the import of the word is derived by rather a far-fetched process (such as those commonly are, and in a great measure indeed must be, by which intellectual ideas are derived from sensible ones) from the word *sanguis,* blood: because among the Romans, with a view to inculcate into the people a persuasion that such or such a mode of conduct would be rendered obligatory upon a man by the force of what I call the religious sanction (that is, that he would be made to suffer by the extraordinary interposition of some superior being, if he failed to observe the mode of conduct in question) certain ceremonies were contrived by the priests: in the course of which ceremonies the blood of victims was made use of.

A Sanction then is a source of obligatory powers or *motives:* that is, of *pains* and *pleasures;* which, according as they are connected with such or such modes of conduct, operate, and are indeed the only things which can operate, as *motives.* See Chap. x. [Motives.]

[a]Servius. See Ainsworth's Dict. ad verbum *Sanctio.*

III.

If it be in the present life, and from the ordinary course of nature, not purposely modified by the interposition of the will of any human being, nor by any extraordinary interposition of any superior invisible being, that the pleasure or the pain takes place or is expected, it may be said to issue from, or to belong to, the *physical sanction.*

IV.

If at the hands of a *particular* person or set of persons in the community, who under names correspondent to that of *judge,* are chosen for the particular purpose of dispensing it, according to the will of the sovereign or supreme ruling power in the state, it may be said to issue from the *political sanction.*

V.

If at the hands of such *chance* persons in the community, as the party in question may happen in the course of his life to have concerns with, according to each man's spontaneous disposition, and not according to any settled or concerted rule, it may be said to issue from the *moral* or *popular sanction.*‡

VI.

If from the immediate hand of a superior invisible being, either in the present life, or in a future, it may be said to issue from the *religious sanction.*

VII.

Pleasures or pains which may be expected to issue from the *physical, political,* or *moral* sanctions, must all of them be expected to be experienced, if ever, in the *present* life: those which may be expected to issue from the *religious* sanction, may be expected to be experienced either in the *present* life or in a *future.*

---

‡Better termed *popular,* as more directly indicative of its constituent cause; as likewise of its relation to the more common phrase *public opinion,* in French *opinion publique,* the name there given to that tutelary power, of which of late so much is said, and by which so much is done. The latter appellation is however unhappy and inexpressive; since if *opinion* is material, it is only in virtue of the influence it exercises over action, through the medium of the affections and the will.

VIII.

Those which can be experienced in the present life, can of course be no others than such as human nature in the course of the present life is susceptible of: and from each of these sources may flow all the pleasures or pains of which, in the course of the present life, human nature is susceptible. With regard to these, then (with which alone we have in this place any concern), those of them which belong to any one of those sanctions, differ not ultimately in kind from those which belong to any one of the other three: the only difference there is among them lies in the circumstances that accompany their production. A suffering which befals a man in the natural and spontaneous course of things, shall be styled, for instance, a *calamity:* in which case, if it be supposed to befal him through any imprudence of his, it may be styled a punishment issuing from the physical sanction. Now this same suffering, if inflicted by the law, will be what is commonly called a *punishment;* if incurred for want of any friendly assistance, which the misconduct, or supposed misconduct, of the sufferer has occasioned to be withholden, a punishment issuing from the *moral* sanction; if through the immediate interposition of a particular providence, a punishment issuing from the religious sanction.

IX.

A man's goods, or his person, are consumed by fire. If this happened to him by what is called an accident, it was a calamity: if by reason of his own imprudence (for instance, from his neglecting to put his candle out), it may be styled a punishment of the physical sanction: if it happened to him by the sentence of the political magistrate, a punishment belonging to the political sanction—that is, what is commonly called a punishment: if for want of any assistance which his *neighbour* withheld from him out of some dislike to his *moral* character, a punishment of the *moral* sanction: if by an immediate net of *God's* displeasure, manifested on account of some *sin* committed by him, or through any distraction of mind, occasioned by the dread of such displeasure, a punishment of the *religious* sanction.*

X.

As to such of the pleasures and pains belonging to the religious sanction, as regard a future life, of what kind these may be, we cannot know. These lie not open to our observation. During the present life they are matter only of expectation: and, whether that expectation be derived from natural or revealed religion, the particular kind of pleasure or pain, if it be different from all those which lie open to our observation, is what we can have no idea of. The best ideas we can obtain of such

*A suffering conceived to befal a man by the immediate act of God, as above, is often, for shortness sake, called a *judgment:* instead of saying, a suffering inflicted on him in consequence of a special judgment formed, and resolution thereupon taken, by the Deity.

pains and pleasures are altogether unliquidated in point of quality. In what other respects our ideas of them *may* be liquidated, will be considered in another place.[†]

XI.

Of these four sanctions, the physical is altogether, we may observe, the ground-work of the political and the moral: so is it also of the religious, in as far as the latter bears relation to the present life. It is included in each of those other three. This may operate in any case (that is, any of the pains or pleasures belonging to it may operate) independently of *them:* none of *them* can operate but by means of this. In a word, the powers of nature may operate of themselves; but neither the magistrate, nor men at large, *can* operate, nor is God in the case in question *supposed* to operate, but through the powers of nature.

XII.

For these four objects, which in their nature have so much in common, it seemed of use to find a common name. It seemed of use, in the first place, for the convenience of giving a name to certain pleasures and pains, for which a name equally characteristic could hardly otherwise have been found: in the second place, for the sake of holding up the efficacy of certain moral forces, the influence of which is apt not to be sufficiently attended to. Does the political sanction exert an influence over the conduct of mankind? The moral, the religious sanctions, do so too. In every inch of his career are the operations of the political magistrate liable to be aided or impeded by these two foreign powers: who, one or other of them, or both, are sure to be either his rivals or his allies. Does it happen to him to leave them out in his calculations? he will be sure almost to find himself mistaken in the result. Of all this we shall find abundant proofs in the sequel of this work. It behoves him, therefore, to have them continually before his eyes; and that under such a name as exhibits the relation they bear to his own purposes and designs.

CHAPTER IV
VALUE OF A LOT OF PLEASURE OR PAIN, HOW TO BE MEASURED

I.

Pleasures then, and the avoidance of pains are the *ends* which the legislator has in view it behoves him therefore to understand their *value.* Pleasures and pains are the *instruments* he has to work with: it behoves him therefore to understand their force, which is again, in another point of view, their value.

---

†See ch. xv. [Cases unmeet], par. 2, Note.

II.

To a person considered *by himself,* the value of a pleasure or pain considered *by itself,* will be greater or less, according to the four following circumstances:*

1. Its *intensity.*
2. Its *duration.*
3. Its *certainty or uncertainty.*
4. Its *propinquity or remoteness.*

III.

These are the circumstances which are to be considered in estimating a pleasure or a pain considered each of them by itself. But when the value of any pleasure or pain is considered for the purpose of estimating the tendency of any *act* by which it is produced, there are two other circumstances to be taken into the account; these are,

5. Its *fecundity,* or the chance it has of being followed by sensations of the *same* kind: that is, pleasures, if it be a pleasure: pains, if it be a pain.
6. Its *purity,* or the chance it has of *not* being followed by sensations of the *opposite* kind: that is, pains, if it be a pleasure: pleasures, if it be a pain.

These two last, however, are in strictness scarcely to be deemed properties of the pleasure or the pain itself; they are not, therefore, in strictness to be taken into the account of the value of that pleasure or that pain. They are in strictness to be deemed properties only of the act, or other event, by which such pleasure or pain has been produced; and accordingly are only to be taken into the account of the tendency of such act or such event.

IV.

To a *number* of persons, with reference to each of whom the value of a pleasure or a pain is considered, it will be greater or less, according to seven circumstances: to wit, the six preceding ones; *viz.*

1. Its *intensity.*
2. Its *duration.*

*These circumstances have since been denominated *elements* or *dimensions* of *value* in a pleasure or a pain. Not long after the publication of the first edition, the following memoriter verses were framed, in the view of lodging more effectually, in the memory, these points, on which the whole fabric of morals and legislation may be seen to rest.

> *Intense, long, certain, speedy, fruitful, pure—*
> Such marks in *pleasures* and in *pains* endure.
> Such pleasures seek, if *private* be thy end:
> If it be *public,* wide let them *extend.*
> Such *pains* avoid, whichever be thy view:
> If pains *must* come, let them *extend* to few.

3. Its *certainty* or *uncertainty.*
4. Its *propinquity* or *remoteness.*
5. Its *fecundity.*
6. Its *purity.*

And one other; to wit:

7. Its *extent;* that is, the number of persons to whom it *extends;* or (in other words) who are affected by it.

V.

To take an exact account, then, of the general tendency of any act, by which the interests of a community are affected, proceed as follows. Begin with any one person of those whose interests seem most immediately to be affected by it: and take an account,

1. Of the value of each distinguishable *pleasure* which appears to be produced by it in the *first* instance.
2. Of the value of each *pain* which appears to be produced by it in the *first* instance.
3. Of the value of each pleasure which appears to be produced by it *after* the first. This constitutes the *fecundity* of the first *pleasure* and the *impurity* of the first *pain.*
4. Of the value of each *pain* which appears to be produced by it after the first. This constitutes the *fecundity* of the first *pain,* and the *impurity* of the first pleasure.
5. Sum up all the values of all the *pleasures* on the one side, and those of all the pains on the other. The balance, if it be on the side of pleasure, will give the *good* tendency of the act upon the whole, with respect to the interests of that *individual* person; if on the side of pain, the *bad* tendency of it upon the whole.
6. Take an account of the *number* of persons whose interests appear to be concerned; and repeat the above process with respect to each. *Sum up* the numbers expressive of the degrees of *good* tendency, which the act has, with respect to each individual, in regard to whom the tendency of it is *good* upon the whole: do this again with respect to each individual, in regard to whom the tendency of it is *good* upon the whole: do this again with respect to each individual, in regard to whom the tendency of it is *bad* upon the whole. Take the *balance;* which, if on the side of *pleasure,* will give the general *good tendency* of the act, with respect to the total number or community of individuals concerned; if on the side of pain, the general *evil tendency,* with respect to the same community.

VI.

It is not to be expected that this process should be strictly pursued previously to every moral judgment, or to every legislative or judicial operation. It may, however, be always kept in view: and as near as the process actually pursued on these occasions approaches to it, so near will such process approach to the character of an exact one.

VII.

The same process is alike applicable to pleasure and pain, in whatever shape they appear; and by whatever denomination they are distinguished; to pleasure, whether it be called *good* (which is properly the cause or instrument of pleasure), or *profit* (which is distant pleasure, or the cause or instrument of distant pleasure), or *convenience,* or *advantage, benefit, emolument, happiness,* and so forth; to pain, whether it be called *evil* (which corresponds to *good*), or *mischief,* or *inconvenience,* or *disadvantage,* or *loss,* or *unhappiness,* and so forth.

VIII.

Nor is this a novel and unwarranted, any more than it is a useless theory. In all this there is nothing but what the practice of mankind, wheresoever they have a clear view of their own interest, is perfectly conformable to. An article of property, an estate in land, for instance, is valuable: on what account? On account of the pleasures of all kinds which it enables a man to produce, and, what comes to the same thing, the pains of all kinds which it enables him to avert. But the value of such an article of property is universally understood to rise or fall according to the length or shortness of the time which a man has in it: the certainty or uncertainty of its coming into possession: and the nearness or remoteness of the time at which, if at all, it is to come into possession. As to the *intensity* of the pleasures which a man may derive from it, this is never thought of, because it depends upon the use which each particular person may come to make of it; which cannot be estimated till the particular pleasures he may come to derive from it, or the particular pains he may come to exclude by means of it, are brought to view. For the same reason, neither does he think of the *fecundity* or *purity* of those pleasures.

Thus much for pleasure and pain, happiness and unhappiness, in *general.* We come now to consider the several particular kinds of pain and pleasure.

Utilitarianism (excerpt)

John Stuart Mill

CHAPTER II
WHAT UTILITARIANISM IS

A passing remark is all that needs be given to the ignorant blunder of supposing that those who stand up for utility as the test of right and wrong, use the term in that restricted and merely colloquial sense in which utility is opposed to pleasure. An

Source: [1861], Chapter II, *Collected Works of John Stuart Mill,* Vol. X, edited by J. M. Robson. London: Routledge & Kegan Paul, 1969, 209–226.

apology is due to the philosophical opponents of utilitarianism, for even the momentary appearance of confounding them with any one capable of so absurd a misconception; which is the more extraordinary, inasmuch as the contrary accusation, of referring everything to pleasure, and that too in its grossest form, is another of the common charges against utilitarianism: and, as has been pointedly remarked by an able writer, the same sort of persons, and often the very same persons, denounce the theory "as impracticably dry when the word utility precedes the word pleasure, and as too practicably voluptuous when the word pleasure precedes the word utility." Those who know anything about the matter are aware that every writer, from Epicurus to Bentham, who maintained the theory of utility, meant by it, not something to be contradistinguished from pleasure, but pleasure itself, together with exemption from pain; and instead of opposing the useful to the agreeable or the ornamental, have always declared that the useful means these, among other things. Yet the common herd, including the herd of writers, not only in newspapers and periodicals, but in books of weight and pretension, are perpetually falling into this shallow mistake. Having caught up the word utilitarian, while knowing nothing whatever about it but its sound, they habitually express by it the rejection, or the neglect, of pleasure in some of its forms; of beauty, of ornament, or of amusement. Nor is the term thus ignorantly misapplied solely in disparagement, but occasionally in compliment; as though it implied superiority to frivolity and the mere pleasures of the moment. And this perverted use is the only one in which the word is popularly known, and the one from which the new generation are acquiring their sole notion of its meaning. Those who introduced the word, but who had for many years discontinued it as a distinctive appellation, may well feel themselves called upon to resume it, if by doing so they can hope to contribute anything towards rescuing it from this utter degradation.*

The creed which accepts as the foundation of morals, Utility, or the Greatest Happiness Principle, holds that actions are right in proportion as they tend to promote happiness, wrong as they tend to produce the reverse of happiness. By happiness is intended pleasure, and the absence of pain; by unhappiness, pain, and the privation of pleasure. To give a clear view of the moral standard set up by the theory, much more requires to be said; in particular, what things it includes in the ideas of pain and pleasure; and to what extent this is left an open question. But these supplementary explanations do not affect the theory of life on which this theory of morality is grounded—namely, that pleasure, and freedom from pain, are the only things desirable as ends; and that all desirable things (which are as numerous in the utilitarian as in any other scheme) are desirable either for the pleasure inherent in themselves, or as means to the promotion of pleasure and the prevention of pain.

---

*The author of this essay has reason for believing himself to be the first person who brought the word utilitarian into use. He did not invent it, but adopted it from a passing expression in Mr. [John] Galt's *Annals of the Parish* [Edinburgh: Blackwood, 1821, p. 286]. After using it as a designation for several years, he and others abandoned it from a growing dislike to anything resembling a badge or watchword of sectarian distinction. But as a name for one single opinion, not a set of opinions—to denote the recognition of utility as a [61 the] standard, not any particular way of applying it—the term supplies a want in the language, and offers, in many cases, a convenient mode of avoiding tiresome circumlocution.

Now, such a theory of life excites in many minds, and among them in some of the most estimable in feeling and purpose, inveterate dislike. To suppose that life has (as they express it) no higher end than pleasure—no better and nobler object of desire and pursuit—they designate as utterly mean and grovelling; as a doctrine worthy only of swine, to whom the followers of Epicurus were, at a very early period, contemptuously likened; and modern holders of the doctrine are occasionally made the subject of equally polite comparisons by its German, French, and English assailants.

When thus attacked, the Epicureans have always answered, that it is not they, but their accusers, who represent human nature in a degrading light; since the accusation supposes human beings to be capable of no pleasures except those of which swine are capable. If this supposition were true, the charge could not be gainsaid, but would then be no longer an imputation; for if the sources of pleasure were precisely the same to human beings and to swine, the rule of life which is good enough for the one would be good enough for the other. The comparison of the Epicurean life to that of beasts is felt as degrading, precisely because a beast's pleasures do not satisfy a human being's conceptions of happiness. Human beings have faculties more elevated than the animal appetites, and when once made conscious of them, do not regard anything as happiness which does not include their gratification. I do not, indeed, consider the Epicureans to have been by any means faultless in drawing out their scheme of consequences from the utilitarian principle. To do this in any sufficient manner, many Stoic, as well as Christian elements require to be included. But there is no known Epicurean theory of life which does not assign to the pleasures of the intellect, of the feelings and imagination, and of the moral sentiments, a much higher value as pleasures than to those of mere sensation. It must be admitted, however, that utilitarian writers in general have placed the superiority of mental over bodily pleasures chiefly in the greater permanency, safety, uncostliness, &c., of the former—that is, in their circumstantial advantages rather than in their intrinsic nature. And on all these points utilitarians have fully proved their case; but they might have taken the other, and, as it may be called, higher ground, with entire consistency. It is quite compatible with the principle of utility to recognise the fact, that some *kinds* of pleasure are more desirable and more valuable than others. It would be absurd that while, in estimating all other things, quality is considered as well as quantity, the estimation of pleasures should be supposed to depend on quantity alone.

If I am asked, what I mean by difference of quality in pleasures, or what makes one pleasure more valuable than another, merely as a pleasure, except its being greater in amount, there is but one possible answer. Of two pleasures, if there be one to which all or almost all who have experience of both give a decided preference, irrespective of any feeling of moral obligation to prefer it, that is the more desirable pleasure. If one of the two is, by those who are competently acquainted with both, placed so far above the other that they prefer it, even though knowing it to be attended with a greater amount of discontent, and would not resign it for any quantity of the other pleasure which their nature is capable of, we are justified in ascribing to the preferred enjoyment a superiority in quality, so far outweighing quantity as to render it, in comparison, of small account.

Now it is an unquestionable fact that those who are equally acquainted with, and equally capable of appreciating and enjoying, both, do give a most marked preference to the manner of existence which employs their higher faculties. Few human creatures would consent to be changed into any of the lower animals, for a promise of the fullest allowance of a beast's pleasures; no intelligent human being would consent to be a fool, no instructed person would be an ignoramus, no person of feeling and conscience would be selfish and base, even though they should be persuaded that the fool, the dunce, or the rascal is better satisfied with his lot than they are with theirs. They would not resign what they possess more than he, for the most complete satisfaction of all the desires which they have in common with him. If they ever fancy they would, it is only in cases of unhappiness so extreme, that to escape from it they would exchange their lot for almost any other, however undesirable in their own eyes. A being of higher faculties requires more to make him happy, is capable probably of more acute suffering, and *is*[b] certainly accessible to it at more points, than one of an inferior type; but in spite of these liabilities, he can never really wish to sink into what he feels to be a lower grade of existence. We may give what explanation we please of this unwillingness; we may attribute it to pride, a name which is given indiscriminately to some of the most and to some of the least estimable feelings of which mankind are capable; we may refer it to the love of liberty and personal independence, an appeal to which was with the Stoics one of the most effective means for the inculcation of it; to the love of power, or to the love of excitement, both of which do really enter into and contribute to it: but its most appropriate appellation is a sense of dignity, which all human beings possess in one form or other, and in some, though by no means in exact, proportion to their higher faculties, and which is so essential a part of the happiness of those in whom it is strong, that nothing which conflicts with it could be, otherwise than momentarily, an object of desire to them. Whoever supposes that this preference takes place at a sacrifice of happiness—that the superior being, in anything like equal circumstances, is not happier than the inferior—confounds the two very different ideas, of happiness, and content. It is indisputable that the being whose capacities of enjoyment are low, has the greatest chance of having them fully satisfied; and a highly-endowed being will always feel that any happiness which he can look for, as the world is constituted, is imperfect. But he can learn to bear its imperfections, if they are at all bearable; and they will not make him envy the being who is indeed unconscious of the imperfections, but only because he feels not at all the good which those imperfections qualify. It is better to be a human being dissatisfied than a pig satisfied; better to be Socrates dissatisfied than a fool satisfied. And if the fool, or the pig, *is*[c] of a different opinion, it is because they only know their own side of the question. The other party to the comparison knows both sides.

It may be objected, that many who are capable of the higher pleasures, occasionally, under the influence of temptation, postpone them to the lower. But this is quite compatible with a full appreciation of the intrinsic superiority of the higher. Men often, from infirmity of character, make their election for the nearer good, though they

[b-b]+ 67, 71
[c-c]61,63 are

know it to be the less valuable; and this no less when the choice is between two bodily pleasures, than when it is between bodily and mental. They pursue sensual indulgences to the injury of health, though perfectly aware that health is the greater good. It may be further objected, that many who begin with youthful enthusiasm for everything noble, as they advance in years sink into indolence and selfishness. But I do not believe that those who undergo this very common change, voluntarily choose the lower description of pleasures in preference to the higher. I believe that before they devote themselves exclusively to the one, they have already become incapable of the other. Capacity for the nobler feelings is in most natures a very tender plant, easily killed, not only by hostile influences, but by mere want of sustenance; and in the majority of young persons it speedily dies away if the occupations to which their position in life has devoted them, and the society into which it has thrown them, are not favourable to keeping that higher capacity in exercise. Men lose their high aspirations as they lose their intellectual tastes, because they have not time or opportunity for indulging them; and they addict themselves to inferior pleasures, not because they deliberately prefer them, but because they are either the only ones to which they have access, or the only ones which they are any longer capable of enjoying. It may be questioned whether any one who has remained equally susceptible to both classes of pleasures, ever knowingly and calmly preferred the lower; though many, in all ages, have broken down in an ineffectual attempt to combine both.

From this verdict of the only competent judges, I apprehend there can be no appeal. On a question which is the best worth having of two pleasures, or which of two modes of existence is the most grateful to the feelings, apart from its moral attributes and from its consequences, the judgment of those who are qualified by knowledge of both, or, if they differ, that of the majority among them, must be admitted as final. And there needs be the less hesitation to accept this judgment respecting the quality of pleasures, since there is no other tribunal to be referred to even on the question of quantity. What means are there of determining which is the acutest of two pains, or the intensest of two pleasurable sensations, except the general suffrage of those who are familiar with both? Neither pains nor pleasures are homogeneous, and pain is always heterogeneous with pleasure. What is there to decide whether a particular pleasure is worth purchasing at the cost of a particular pain, except the feelings and judgment of the experienced? When, therefore, those feelings and judgment declare the pleasures derived from the higher faculties to be preferable *in kind,* apart from the question of intensity, to those of which the animal nature, disjoined from the higher faculties, is susceptible, they are entitled on this subject to the same regard.

I have dwelt on this point, as being a necessary part of a perfectly just conception of Utility or Happiness, considered as the directive rule of human conduct. But it is by no means an indispensable condition to the acceptance of the utilitarian standard; for that standard is not the agent's own greatest happiness, but the greatest amount of happiness altogether; and if it may possibly be doubted whether a noble character is always the happier for its nobleness, there can be no doubt that it makes other people happier, and that the world in general is immensely a gainer by it. Utilitarianism, therefore, could only attain its end by the general cultivation of nobleness of character, even if each individual were only benefited by the nobleness of others, and his own, so far as happiness is concerned, were a sheer deduction from the benefit. But the bare enunciation of such an absurdity ^{d}as this last,^{d} renders refutation superfluous.

According to the Greatest Happiness Principle, as above explained, the ultimate end, with reference to and for the sake of which all other things are desirable (whether we are considering our own good or that of other people), is an existence exempt as far as possible from pain, and as rich as possible in enjoyments, both in point of quantity and quality; the test of quality, and the rule for measuring it against quantity, being the preference felt by those who, in their opportunities of experience, to which must be added their habits of self-consciousness and self-observation, are best furnished with the means of comparison. This, being, according to the utilitarian opinion, the end of human action, is necessarily also the standard of morality; which may accordingly be defined, the rules and precepts for human conduct, by the observance of which an existence such as has been described might be, to the greatest extent possible, secured to all mankind; and not to them only, but, so far as the nature of things admits, to the whole sentient creation.

Against this doctrine, however, arises another class of objectors, who say that happiness, in any form, cannot be the rational purpose of human life and action; because, in the first place, it is unattainable: and they contemptuously ask, What right hast thou to be happy? a question which Mr. Carlyle clenches by the addition, What right, a short time ago, hadst thou even *to be?*[*] Next, they say, that men can do *without* happiness; that all noble human beings have felt this, and could not have become noble but by learning the lesson of Entsagen, or renunciation; which lesson, thoroughly learnt and submitted to, they affirm to be the beginning and necessary condition of all virtue.

The first of these objections would go to the root of the matter were it well founded; for if no happiness is to be had at all by human beings, the attainment of it cannot be the end of morality, or of any rational conduct. Though, even in that case, something might still be said for the utilitarian theory; since utility includes not solely the pursuit of happiness, but the prevention or mitigation of unhappiness; and if the former aim be chimerical, there will be all the greater scope and more imperative need for the latter, so long at least as mankind think fit to live, and do not take refuge in the simultaneous act of suicide recommended under certain conditions by Novalis.[†] When, however, it is thus positively asserted to be impossible that human life should be happy, the assertion, if not something like a verbal quibble, is at least an exaggeration. If by happiness be meant a continuity of highly pleasurable excitement, it is evident enough that this is impossible. A state of exalted pleasure lasts only moments, or in some cases, and with some intermissions, hours or days, and is the occasional brilliant flash of enjoyment, not its permanent and steady flame. Of this the philosophers who have taught that happiness is the end of life were as fully aware as those who taunt them. The happiness which they meant was not a life of rapture; but moments of such, in an existence made up of few and transitory pains, many and various pleasures, with a decided predominance of the active over the passive, and

---

$^{d\text{-}d}$ + 63,64,67,71

[*Thomas Carlyle. *Sartor Resartus.* 2nd ed. Boston: Munroe, 1837, p. 197.]

[†See Thomas Carlyle. "Novalis," *Critical and Miscellaneous Essays.* 5 vols. London: Fraser, 1840, Vol. II, pp. 286, 288.]

having as the foundation of the whole, not to expect more from life than it is capable of bestowing. A life thus composed, to those who have been fortunate enough to obtain it, has always appeared worthy of the name of happiness. And such an existence is even now the lot of many, during some considerable portion of their lives. The present wretched education, and wretched social arrangements, are the only real hindrance to its being attainable by almost all.

The objectors perhaps may doubt whether human beings, if taught to consider happiness as the end of life, would be satisfied with such a moderate share of it. But great numbers of mankind have been satisfied with much less. The main constituents of a satisfied life appear to be two, either of which by itself is often found sufficient for the purpose: tranquillity, and excitement. With much tranquillity, many find that they can be content with very little pleasure: with much excitement, many can reconcile themselves to a considerable quantity of pain. There is assuredly no inherent impossibility in enabling even the mass of mankind to unite both; since the two are so far from being incompatible that they are in natural alliance, the prolongation of either being a preparation for, and exciting a wish for, the other. It is only those in whom indolence amounts to a vice, that do not desire excitement after an interval of repose; it is only those in whom the need of excitement is a disease, that feel the tranquillity which follows excitement dull and insipid, instead of pleasurable in direct proportion to the excitement which preceded it. When people who are tolerably fortunate in their outward lot do not find in life sufficient enjoyment to make it valuable to them, the cause generally is, caring for nobody but themselves. To those who have neither public nor private affections, the excitements of life are much curtailed, and in any case dwindle in value as the time approaches when all selfish interests must be terminated by death: while those who leave after them objects of personal affection, and especially those who have also cultivated a fellow-feeling with the collective interests of mankind, retain as lively an interest in life on the eve of death as in the vigour of youth and health. Next to selfishness, the principal cause which makes life unsatisfactory, is want of mental cultivation. A cultivated mind—I do not mean that of a philosopher, but any mind to which the fountains of knowledge have been opened, and which has been taught, in any tolerable degree, to exercise its faculties—finds sources of inexhaustible interest in all that surrounds it; in the objects of nature, the achievements of art, the imaginations of poetry, the incidents of history, the ways of mankind past and present, and their prospects in the future. It is possible, indeed, to become indifferent to all this, and that too without having exhausted a thousandth part of it; but only when one has had from the beginning no moral or human interest in these things, and has sought in them only the gratification of curiosity.

Now there is absolutely no reason in the nature of things why an amount of mental culture sufficient to give an intelligent interest in these objects of contemplation should not be the inheritance of every one born in a civilized country. As little is there an inherent necessity that any human being should be a selfish egotist, devoid of every feeling or care but those which centre in his own miserable individuality. Something far superior to this is sufficiently common even now, to give ample earnest of what the human species may be made. Genuine private affections, and a sincere interest in the public good, are possible, though in unequal degrees, to every rightly brought up human being. In a world in which there is so much to interest, so much to enjoy, and so much also to correct and improve, every one who has this moderate amount of moral and intellectual requisites is capable of an existence which may be called enviable; and unless such a person, through bad laws, or subjection to the will of others, is denied the liberty to use the sources of happiness within his reach, he will not fail to find this enviable existence, if he escape the positive evils of life, the great sources of physical and mental suffering—such as indigence, disease, and the unkindness, worthlessness, or premature loss of objects of affection. The main stress of the problem lies, therefore, in the contest with these calamities, from which it is a rare good fortune entirely to escape; which, as things now are, cannot be obviated, and often cannot be in any material degree mitigated. Yet no one whose opinion deserves a moment's consideration can doubt that most of the great positive evils of the world are in themselves removable, and will, if human affairs continue to improve, be in the end reduced within narrow limits. Poverty, in any sense implying suffering, may be completely extinguished by the wisdom of society, combined with the good sense and providence of individuals. Even that most intractable of enemies, disease, may be indefinitely reduced in dimensions by good physical and moral education, and proper control of noxious influences; while the progress of science holds out a promise for the future of still more direct conquests over this detestable foe. And every advance in that direction relieves us from some, not only of the chances which cut short our own lives, but, what concerns us still more, which deprive us of those in whom our happiness is wrapt up. As for vicissitudes of fortune, and other disappointments connected with worldly circumstances, these are principally the effect either of gross imprudence, of ill-regulated desires, or of bad or imperfect social institutions. All the grand sources, in short, of human suffering are in a great degree, many of them almost entirely, conquerable by human care and effort; and though their removal is grievously slow—though a long succession of generations will perish in the breach before the conquest is completed, and this world becomes all that, if will and knowledge were not wanting, it might easily be made—yet every mind sufficiently intelligent and generous to bear a part, however small and unconspicuous, in the endeavour, will draw a noble enjoyment from the contest itself, which he would not for any bribe in the form of selfish indulgence consent to be without.

And this leads to the true estimation of what is said by the objectors concerning the possibility, and the obligation, of learning to do without happiness. Unquestionably it is possible to do without happiness; it is done involuntarily by nineteen-twentieths of mankind, even in those parts of our present world which are least deep in barbarism; and it often has to be done voluntarily by the hero or the martyr, for the sake of something which he prizes more than his individual happiness. But this something, what is it, unless the happiness of others, or some of the requisites of happiness? It is noble to be capable of resigning entirely one's own portion of happiness, or chances of it: but, after all, this self-sacrifice must be for some end; it is not its own end; and if we are told that its end is not happiness, but virtue, which is better than happiness, I ask, would the sacrifice be made if the hero or martyr did not believe that it would earn for others immunity from similar sacrifices? Would it be made, if he thought that his renunciation of happiness for himself would produce no fruit for any of his fellow creatures, but to make their lot like his, and place them also in the condition of persons who have renounced happiness? All honour to those who can abnegate for themselves the personal enjoyment of life, when by such renunciation they contribute worthily to increase the amount of happiness in the world; but he who does it, or professes to do it, for any other purpose, is no more deserving of admiration than the ascetic mounted on his pillar. He may be an inspiriting proof of what men *can* do, but assuredly not an example of what they *should*.

Though it is only in a very imperfect state of the world's arrangements that any one can best serve the happiness of others by the absolute sacrifice of his own, yet so long as the world is in that imperfect state, I fully acknowledge that the readiness to make such a sacrifice is the highest virtue which can be found in man. I will add, that in this condition of the world, paradoxical as the assertion may be, the conscious ability to do without happiness gives the best prospect of realizing such happiness as is attainable. For nothing except that consciousness can raise a person above the chances of life, by making him feel that, let fate and fortune do their worst, they have not power to subdue him: which, once felt, frees him from excess of anxiety concerning the evils of life, and enables him, like many a Stoic in the worst times of the Roman Empire, to cultivate in tranquillity the sources of satisfaction accessible to him, without concerning himself about the uncertainty of their duration, any more than about their inevitable end.

Meanwhile, let utilitarians never cease to claim the morality of self-devotion as a possession which belongs by as good a right to them, as either to the Stoic or to the Transcendentalist. The utilitarian morality does recognise in human beings the power of sacrificing their own greatest good for the good of others. It only refuses to admit that the sacrifice is itself a good. A sacrifice which does not increase, or tend to increase, the sum total of happiness, it considers as wasted. The only self-renunciation which it applauds, is devotion to the happiness, or to some of the means of happiness, of others; either of mankind collectively, or of individuals within the limits imposed by the collective interests of mankind.

I must again repeat, what the assailants of utilitarianism seldom have the justice to acknowledge, that the happiness which forms the utilitarian standard of what is right in conduct, is not the agent's own happiness, but that of all concerned. As between his own happiness and that of others, utilitarianism requires him to be as strictly impartial as a disinterested and benevolent spectator. In the golden rule of Jesus of Nazareth, we read the complete spirit of the ethics of utility. To do as *e*one*e* would be done by, and to love *f*one's*f* neighbour as *g*oneself*g*, constitute the ideal perfection of utilitarian morality. As the means of making the nearest approach to this ideal, utility would enjoin, first, that laws and social arrangements should place the happiness, or (as speaking practically it may be called) the interest, of every individual, as nearly as possible in harmony with the interest of the whole; and secondly, that education and opinion, which have so vast a power over human character, should so use that power as to establish in the mind of every individual an indissoluble association between his own happiness and the good of the whole; especially between his own happiness and the practice of such modes of conduct, negative and positive, as regard for the universal happiness prescribes: so that not only he may be unable to conceive the possibility of happiness to himself, consis-

*e-e*61,63 you
*f-f*61,63 your
*g-g*61,63 yourself

tently with conduct opposed to the general good, but also that a direct impulse to promote the general good may be in every individual one of the habitual motives of action, and the sentiments connected therewith may fill a large and prominent place in every human being's sentient existence. If the impugners of the utilitarian morality represented it to their own minds in this its true character, I know not what recommendation possessed by any other morality they could possibly affirm to be wanting to it: what more beautiful or more exalted developments of human nature any other ethical system can be supposed to foster, or what springs of action, not accessible to the utilitarian, such system rely on for giving effect to their mandates.

The objectors to utilitarianism cannot always be charged with representing it in a discreditable light. On the contrary, those among them who entertain anything like a just idea of its disinterested character, sometimes find fault with its standard as being too high for humanity. They say it is exacting too much to require that people shall always act from the inducement of promoting the general interests of society. But this is to mistake the very meaning of a standard of morals, and *h*to*h* confound the rule of action with the motive of it. It is the business of ethics to tell us what are our duties, or by what test we may know them; but no system of ethics requires that the sole motive of all we do shall be a feeling of duty; on the contrary, ninety-nine hundredths of all our actions are done from other motives, and rightly so done, if the rule of duty does not condemn them. It is the more unjust to utilitarianism that this particular misapprehension should be made a ground of objection to it, inasmuch as utilitarian moralists have gone beyond almost all others in affirming that the motive has nothing to do with the morality of the action, though much with the worth of the agent. He who saves a fellow creature from drowning does what is morally right, whether his motive be duty, or the hope of being paid for his trouble: he who betrays the friend that trusts him, is guilty of a crime, even if his object be to serve another friend to whom he is under greater obligations.*

---

h-h + 67,71

*[64] An opponent, whose intellectual and moral fairness it is a pleasure to acknowledge (the Rev. J. Llewellyn Davies), has objected to this passage, saying, "Surely the rightness or wrongness of saving a man from drowning does depend very much upon the motive with which it is done. Suppose that a tyrant, when his enemy jumped into the sea to escape from him, saved him from drowning simply in order that he might inflict upon him more exquisite tortures, would it tend to clearness to speak of that rescue as 'a morally right action?' Or suppose again, according to one of the stock illustrations of ethical inquiries, that a man betrayed a trust *(continued) received from a friend, because the discharge of it would fatally injure that friend himself or some one belonging to him, would utilitarianism compel one to call the betrayal 'a crime' as much as if it had been done from the meanest motive?"

I submit, that he who saves another from drowning in order to kill him by torture afterwards, does not differ only in motive from him who does the same thing from duty or benevolence; the act itself is different. The rescue of the man is, in the case supposed, only the necessary first step of an act far more atrocious than leaving him to drown would have been. Had Mr. Davies said, "The rightness or wrongness of saving a man from drowning does depend very much" —not upon the motive, but—"upon the *intention*," no utilitarian would have differed from him. Mr. Davies, by an oversight too common not to be quite venial, has in this case confounded the very different ideas of Motive and Intention. There is no point which utilitarian thinkers (and Bentham pre-eminently) have taken more pains to illustrate than this. The morality of the action depends entirely upon the intention—that is, upon what the agent *wills to do*. But the motive, that is, the feeling which makes him will so to do, when it [64, 67 if it] makes no difference in the act, makes none in the morality: though it makes a great difference in our moral estimation of the agent, especially if it indicates a good or a bad habitual *disposition*— a bent of character from which useful, or from which hurtful actions are likely to arise.

But to speak only of actions done from the motive of duty, and in direct obedience to principle: it is a misapprehension of the utilitarian mode of thought, to conceive it as implying that people should fix their minds upon so wide a generality as the world, or society at large. The great majority of good actions are intended, not for the benefit of the world, but for that of individuals, of which the good of the world is made up; and the thoughts of the most virtuous man need not on these occasions travel beyond the particular persons concerned, except so far as is necessary to assure himself that in benefiting them he is not violating the rights—that is, the legitimate and authorized expectations—of any one else. The multiplication of happiness is, according to the utilitarian ethics, the object of virtue: the occasions on which any person (except one in a thousand) has it in his power to do this on an extended scale, in other words, to be a public benefactor, are but exceptional; and on these occasions alone is he called on to consider public utility; in every other case, private utility, the interest or happiness of some few persons, is all he has to attend to. Those alone the influence of whose actions extends to society in general need concern themselves habitually about so large an object. In the case of abstinences indeed—of things which people forbear to do, from moral considerations, though the consequences in the particular case might be beneficial—it would be unworthy of an intelligent agent not to be consciously aware that the action is of a class which, if practised generally, would be generally injurious, and that this is the ground of the obligation to abstain from it. The amount of regard for the public interest implied in this recognition is no greater than is demanded by every system of morals; for they all enjoin to abstain from whatever is manifestly pernicious to society.

The same considerations dispose of another reproach against the doctrine of utility, founded on a still grosser misconception of the purpose of a standard of morality, and of the very meaning of the words right and wrong. It is often affirmed that utilitarianism renders men cold and unsympathizing; that it chills their moral feelings towards individuals; that it makes them regard only the dry and hard consideration of the consequences of actions, not taking into their moral estimate the qualities from which those actions emanate. If the assertion means that they do not allow their judgment respecting the rightness or wrongness of an action to be influenced by their opinion of the qualities of the person who does it, this is a complaint not against utilitarianism, but against having any standard of morality at all; for certainly no known ethical standard decides an action to be good or bad because it is done by a good or a bad man, still less because done by an amiable, a brave, or a benevolent man, or the contrary. These considerations are relevant, not to the estimation of actions, but of persons; and there is nothing in the utilitarian theory inconsistent with the fact that there are other things which interest us in persons besides the rightness and wrongness of their actions. The Stoics, indeed, with the paradoxical misuse of language which was part of their system, and by which they strove to raise themselves above all concern about anything but virtue, were fond of saying that he who has that has everything; that he, and only he, is rich, is beautiful, is a king. But no claim of this description is made for the virtuous man by the utilitarian doctrine. Utilitarians are quite aware that there are other desirable possessions and qualities besides virtue, and are perfectly willing to allow to all of them their full

worth. They are also aware that a right action does not necessarily indicate a virtuous character, and that actions which are blameable often proceed from qualities
entitled to praise. When this is apparent in any particular case, it modifies their estimation, not certainly of the act, but of the agent. I grant that they are, notwithstanding, of opinion, that in the long run the best proof of a good character is good
actions; and resolutely refuse to consider any mental disposition as good, of which
the predominant tendency is to produce bad conduct. This makes them unpopular
with many people; but it is an unpopularity which they must share with every one
who regards the distinction between right and wrong in a serious light; and the
reproach is not one which a conscientious utilitarian need be anxious to repel.

If no more be meant by the objection than that many utilitarians look on the
morality of actions, as measured by the utilitarian standard, with too exclusive a
regard, and do not lay sufficient stress upon the other beauties of character which
go towards making a human being loveable or admirable, this may be admitted.
Utilitarians who have cultivated their moral feelings, but not their sympathies nor
their artistic perceptions, do fall into this mistake; and so do all other moralists
under the same conditions. What can be said in excuse for other moralists is equally
available for them, namely, that if there is to be any error, it is better that it should
be on that side. As a matter of fact, we may affirm that among utilitarians as among
adherents of other systems, there is every imaginable degree of rigidity and of lax-
ity in the application of their standard: some are even puritanically rigorous, while
others are as indulgent as can possibly be desired by sinner or by sentimentalist.
But on the whole, a doctrine which brings prominently forward the interest that
mankind have in the repression and prevention of conduct which violates the moral
law is likely to be inferior to no other in turning the sanctions of opinion against
such violations. It is true, the question, What does violate the moral law? is one on
which those who recognise different standards of morality are likely now and then
to differ. But difference of opinion on moral questions was not first introduced into
the world by utilitarianism, while that doctrine does supply, if not always an easy,
at all events a tangible and intelligible mode of deciding such differences.

It may not be superfluous to notice a few more of the common misapprehensions of
utilitarian ethics, even those which are so obvious and gross that it might appear
impossible for any person of candour and intelligence to fall into them: since persons, even of considerable mental endowments, often give themselves so little trouble to understand the bearings of any opinion against which they entertain a prejudice, and men are in general so little conscious of this voluntary ignorance as a
defect, that the vulgarest misunderstandings of ethical doctrines are continually met
with in the deliberate writings of persons of the greatest pretensions both to high
principle and to philosophy. We not uncommonly hear the doctrine of utility
inveighed against as a *godless* doctrine. If it be necessary to say anything at all
against so mere an assumption, we may say that the question depends upon what
idea we have formed of the moral character of the Deity. If it be a true belief that
God desires, above all things, the happiness of his creatures, and that this was his
purpose in their creation, utility is not only not a godless doctrine, but more profoundly religious than any other. If it be meant that utilitarianism does not recognise

the revealed will of God as the supreme law of morals, I answer that a utilitarian who believes in the perfect goodness and wisdom of God necessarily believes that whatever God has thought fit to reveal on the subject of morals must fulfil the requirements of utility in a supreme degree. But others besides utilitarians have been of opinion that the Christian revelation was intended, and is fitted, to inform the hearts and minds of mankind with a spirit which should enable them to find for themselves what is right, and incline them to do it when found, rather than to tell them, except in a very general way, what it is: and that we need a doctrine of ethics, carefully followed out, to *interpret* to us the will of God. Whether this opinion is correct or not, it is superfluous here to discuss; since whatever aid religion, either natural or revealed, can afford to ethical investigation, is as open to the utilitarian moralist as to any other. He can use it as the testimony of God to the usefulness or hurtfulness of any given course of action, by as good a right as others can use it for the indication of a transcendental law, having no connexion with usefulness or with happiness.

Again, Utility is often summarily stigmatized as an immoral doctrine by giving it the name of Expediency, and taking advantage of the popular use of that term to contrast it with Principle. But the Expedient, in the sense in which it is opposed to the Right, generally means that which is expedient for the particular interest of the agent himself; as when a minister sacrifices the *interest* of his country to keep himself in place. When it means anything better than this, it means that which is expedient for some immediate object, some temporary purpose, but which violates a rule whose observance is expedient in a much higher degree. The Expedient, in this sense, instead of being the same thing with the useful, is a branch of the hurtful. Thus, it would often be expedient, for the purpose of getting over some momentary embarrassment, or attaining some object immediately useful to ourselves or others, to tell a lie. But inasmuch as the cultivation in ourselves of a sensitive feeling on the subject of veracity is one of the most useful, and the enfeeblement of that feeling one of the most hurtful, things to which our conduct can be instrumental; and inasmuch as any, even unintentional, deviation from truth, does that much towards weakening the trustworthiness of human assertion, which is not only the principal support of all present social well-being, but the insufficiency of which does more than any one thing that can be named to keep back civilization, virtue, everything on which human happiness on the largest scale depends; we feel that the violation, for a present advantage, of a rule of such transcendant expediency, is not expedient, and that he who, for the sake of a convenience to himself or to some other individual, does what depends on him to deprive mankind of the good, and inflict upon them the evil, involved in the greater or less reliance which they can place in each other's word, acts the part of one of their worst enemies. Yet that even this rule, sacred as it is, admits of possible exceptions, is acknowledged by all moralists; the chief of which is when the withholding of some fact (as of information from a malefactor, or of bad news from a person dangerously ill) would *preserve some one* (especially *a person* other than oneself) from great and unmerited

*i-i*61,63 interests
*j-j*61,63,64 save an individual
*k-k*61,63,64 an individual

evil, and when the withholding can only be effected by denial. But in order that the exception may not extend itself beyond the need, and may have the least possible effect in weakening reliance on veracity, it ought to be recognised, and, if possible, its limits defined; and if the principle of utility is good for anything, it must be good for weighing these conflicting utilities against one another, and marking out the region within which one or the other preponderates.

If utility is the ultimate source of moral obligations, utility may be invoked to decide between them when their demands are incompatible. Though the application of the standard may be difficult, it is better than none at all: while in other systems, the moral laws all claiming independent authority, there is no common umpire entitled to interfere between them; their claims to precedence one over another rest on little better than sophistry, and unless determined, as they generally are, by the unacknowledged influence of considerations or utility, afford a free scope for the action of personal desires and partialities. We must remember that only in these cases of conflict between secondary principles is it requisite that first principles should be appealed to. There is no case of moral obligation in which some secondary principle is not involved; and if only one, there can seldom be any real doubt which one it is, in the mind of any person by whom the principle itself is recognised.

Good and Evil, Good and Bad

Friedrich Nietzsche

I

The English psychologists to whom we owe the only attempts that have thus far been made to write a genealogy of morals are no mean posers of riddles, but the riddles they pose are themselves, and being incarnate have one advantage over their books—they are interesting. What are these English psychologists really after? One finds them always, whether intentionally or not, engaged in the same task of pushing into the foreground the nasty part of the psyche, looking for the effective motive forces of human development in the very last place we would wish to have them found, e.g., in the inertia of habit, in forgetfulness, in the blind and fortuitous association of ideas: always in something that is purely passive, automatic, reflexive, molecular, and, moreover, profoundly stupid. What drives these psychologists forever in the same direction? A secret, malicious desire to belittle humanity, which they do not acknowledge even to themselves? A pessimistic distrust, the suspiciousness of the soured idealist? Some petty resentment of Christianity (and Plato) which does not rise above the threshold of consciousness? Or could it be a prurient taste for whatever is embarrassing, painfully paradoxical, dubious and absurd in existence? Or is it, perhaps, a kind

Source: The Genealogy of Morals [1887], *The Birth of Tragedy and the Genealogy of Morals,* translated by Francis Golffing. New York: Doubleday Anchor Books, 1956, 158–188.

of stew—a little meanness, a little bitterness, a bit of anti-Christianity, a touch of prurience and desire for condiments? . . . But, again, people tell me that these men are simply dull old frogs who hop and creep in and around man as in their own element—as though man were a bog. However, I am reluctant to listen to this, in fact I refuse to believe it; and if I may express a wish where I cannot express a conviction, I do wish wholeheartedly that things may be otherwise with these men—that these microscopic examiners of the soul may be really courageous, magnanimous, and proud animals, who know how to contain their emotions and have trained themselves to subordinate all wishful thinking to the truth—any truth, even a homespun, severe, ugly, obnoxious, un-Christian, unmoral truth. For such truths do exist.

II

All honor to the beneficent spirits that may motivate these historians of ethics! One thing is certain, however, they have been quite deserted by the true spirit of history. They all, to a man, think unhistorically, as is the age-old custom among philosophers. The amateurishness of their procedure is made plain from the very beginning, when it is a question of explaining the provenance of the concept and judgment *good*. "Originally," they decree, "altruistic actions were praised and approved by their recipients, that is, by those to whom they were useful. Later on, the origin of that praise having been forgotten, such actions were felt to be good simply because it was the habit to commend them." We notice at once that this first derivation has all the earmarks of the English psychologists' work. Here are the key ideas of utility, forgetfulness, habit, and, finally, error, seen as lying at the root of that value system which civilized man had hitherto regarded with pride as the prerogative of all men. This pride must now be humbled, these values devalued. Have the debunkers succeeded?

Now it is obvious to me, first of all, that their theory looks for the genesis of the concept *good* in the wrong place: the judgment *good* does not originate with those to whom the good has been done. Rather it was the "good" themselves, that is to say the noble, mighty, highly placed, and high-minded who decreed themselves and their actions to be good, i.e., belonging to the highest rank, in contradistinction to all that was base, low-minded and plebeian. It was only this *pathos of distance* that authorized them to create values and name them—what was utility to them? The notion of utility seems singularly inept to account for such a quick jetting forth of supreme value judgments. Here we come face to face with the exact opposite of that lukewarmness which every scheming prudence, every utilitarian calculus presupposes—and not for a time only, for the rare, exceptional hour, but permanently. The origin of the opposites *good* and *bad* is to be found in the pathos of nobility and distance, representing the dominant temper of a higher, ruling class in relation to a lower, dependent one. (The lordly right of bestowing names is such that one would almost be justified in seeing the origin of language itself as an expression of the rulers' power. They say, "This *is* that or that"; they seal off each thing and action with a sound and thereby take symbolic possession of it.) Such an origin would suggest that there is no *a priori* necessity for associating the word *good* with altruistic deeds, as those moral psychologists are fond of claiming. In fact, it is only after aristocratic values have begun to decline that the egotism-altruism dichotomy takes possession of the human conscience; to use my own terms, it is the herd instinct that now asserts itself. Yet it takes quite a while for this instinct to assume such sway that it can reduce all moral valuations to that dichotomy—as is currently happening throughout Europe, where the prejudice equating the terms *moral, altruistic,* and *disinterested* has assumed the obsessive force of an *idée fixe.*

III

Quite apart from the fact that this hypothesis about the origin of the value judgment *good* is historically untenable, its psychology is intrinsically unsound. Altruistic deeds were originally commended for their usefulness, but this original reason has now been forgotten—so the claim goes. How is such a forgetting conceivable? Has there ever been a point in history at which such deeds lost their usefulness? Quite the contrary, this usefulness has been apparent to every age, a thing that has been emphasized over and over again. Therefore, instead of being forgotten, it must have impressed itself on the consciousness with ever increasing clearness. The opposite theory is far more sensible, though this does not necessarily make it any the truer— the theory held by Herbert Spencer, for example, who considers the concept *good* qualitatively the same as the concepts *useful* or *practical;* so that in the judgments *good* and *bad,* humanity is said to have summed up and sanctioned precisely its unforgotten and unforgettable experiences of the *useful practical* and the *harmful impractical.* According to this theory, the *good* is that which all along has proved itself useful and which therefore may lay the highest claim to be considered valuable. As I have said, the derivation of this theory is suspect, but at least the explanation is self-consistent and psychologically tenable within its limits.

IV

The clue to the correct explanation was furnished me by the question "What does the etymology of the terms for good in various languages tell us?" I discovered that all these terms lead us back to the same conceptual transformation. The basic concept is always *noble* in the hierarchical, class sense, and from this has developed, by historical necessity, the concept *good* embracing nobility of mind, spiritual distinction. This development is strictly parallel to that other which eventually converted the notions *common, plebeian, base* into the notion *bad.*[1] Here we have an important clue to the actual genealogy of morals; that it has not been hit upon earlier is due to the retarding influence which democratic prejudice has had upon all

[1]The most eloquent proof of this is the etymological relationship between the German words *schlecht* (bad) and *schlicht* (simple). For a long time the first term was used interchangeably with the second, without any contemptuous connotation as yet, merely to designate the commoner as opposed to the nobleman. About the time of the Thirty Years' War the meaning changed to the present one.

investigation of origins. This holds equally true with regard to the seemingly quite objective areas of natural science and physiology, though I cannot enlarge upon the question now. The amount of damage such prejudice is capable of doing in ethics and history, once it becomes inflamed with hatred, is clearly shown by the case of Buckle. Here we see the plebeian bias of the modern mind, which stems from England, erupt once again on its native soil with all the violence of a muddy volcano and all the vulgar and oversalted eloquence characteristic of volcanoes.

V

As for our own problem, which we may justly call a *quiet* one, addressing itself to a very restricted audience, it is of interest to note that many of the words and roots denominating *good* still, to this day, carry overtones of the meanings according to which the nobility regarded themselves as possessing the highest moral rank. It is true that, most often, they described themselves simply in terms of their superior power (as the rulers, lords, sovereigns) or else in terms of the visible signs of their superiority, as the rich, the possessors (this is the meaning of *arya,* and there are corresponding terms in the Iranian and Slavic languages); but also in terms of a typical character trait, and this is the case that concerns us here. They speak of themselves as "the truthful"; most resolute in doing this were members of the Greek aristocracy, whose mouthpiece is the Megarian poet Theognis. The word they used was *esthlos,* meaning one who *is,* who has true reality, who is true. By a subjective turn the *true* later became the *truthful.* During this phase the word provided the shibboleth of the nobility, describing the aristocrat, as Theognis saw and portrayed him, in distinction from the lying plebeian, until finally, after the decline of the aristocracy, the word came to stand for spiritual nobility, and ripened and sweetened. The words *kakos* and *deilos* (the plebeian, in contrast to the *agathos*) emphasize cowardice and provide a hint as to the direction in which we should look for the etymology of *agathos,* a word allowing of more than one interpretation. The Latin *malus* (beside which I place *melas*) might designate the common man as dark, especially black-haired ("hic niger est"), as the pre-Aryan settler of the Italian soil, notably distinguished from the new blond conqueror race by his color. At any rate, the Gaelic presented me with an exactly analogous case: *fin,* as in the name Fingal, the characteristic term for nobility, eventually the good, noble, pure, originally the fair-haired as opposed to the dark, black-haired native population. The Celts, by the way, were definitely a fair-haired race; and it is a mistake to try to relate the area of dark-haired people found on ethnographic maps of Germany to Celtic bloodlines, as Virchow does. These are the last vestiges of the pre-Aryan population of Germany. (The subject races are seen to prevail once more, throughout almost all of Europe: in color, shortness of skull, perhaps also in intellectual and social instincts. Who knows whether modern democracy, the even more fashionable anarchism, and especially that preference for the *commune,* the most primitive of all social forms, which is now shared by all European socialists—whether all these do not represent a throwback, and whether, even physiologically, the Aryan race of conquerors is not doomed?) The Latin *bonus* I venture to interpret as warrior; providing that I am justified in deriving *bonus* from an older *duonus* (c.f. *bellum → duellum → duen-lum,* which seems to preserve that *duonus*). *Bonus* would then spell the man of strife, of discord, the warrior: we can now form some idea of what, in ancient Rome, constituted a man's goodness. And might not our German *gut* signify *göttlich,* the man of divine race? And further be identical with the racial term, earlier also a term of rank, *Goth?* My arguments in support of this conjecture do not belong here.

VI

Granting that political supremacy always gives rise to notions of spiritual supremacy, it at first creates no difficulties (though difficulties might arise later) if the ruling caste is also the priestly caste and elects to characterize itself by a term which reminds us of its priestly function. In this context we encounter for the first time concepts of *pure* and *impure* opposing each other as signs of class, and here, too, *good* and *bad* as terms no longer referring to class, develop before long. The reader should be cautioned, however, against taking pure and impure in too large or profound or symbolic a sense: all the ideas of ancient man were understood in a sense much more crude, narrow, superficial and non-symbolic than we are able to imagine today. The pure man was originally one who washed himself, who refused to eat certain foods entailing skin diseases, who did not sleep with the unwashed plebeian women, who held blood in abomination—hardly more than that. At the same time, given the peculiar nature of a priestly aristocracy, it becomes clear why the value opposites would early turn inward and become dangerously exacerbated; and in fact the tension between such opposites has opened abysses between man and man, over which not even an Achilles of free thought would leap without a shudder. There is from the very start something unwholesome about such priestly aristocracies, about their way of life, which is turned away from action and swings between brooding and emotional explosions: a way of life which may be seen as responsible for the morbidity and neurasthenia of priests of all periods. Yet are we not right in maintaining that the cures which they have developed for their morbidities have proved a hundred times more dangerous than the ills themselves? Humanity is still suffering from the after-effects of those priestly cures. Think, for example, of certain forms of diet (abstinence from meat), fasting, sexual continence, escape "into the desert"; think further of the whole anti-sensual metaphysics of the priests, conducive to inertia and false refinement; of the self-hypnosis encouraged by the example of fakirs and Brahmans, where a glass knob and an *idée fixe* take the place of the god. And at last, supervening on all this, comes utter satiety, together with its radical remedy, nothingness—or God, for the desire for a mystical union with God is nothing other than the Buddhist's desire to sink himself in nirvana. Among the priests everything becomes more dangerous, not cures and specifics alone but also arrogance, vindictiveness, acumen, profligacy, love, the desire for power, disease. In all fairness it should be added, however, that only on this soil, the precarious soil of priestly existence, has man been able to develop into an interesting creature; that only here has the human mind grown both profound and evil; and it is in these two respects, after all, that man has proved his superiority over the rest of creation.

VII

By now the reader will have got some notion how readily the priestly system of valuations can branch off from the aristocratic and develop into its opposite. An occasion for such a division is furnished whenever the priest caste and the warrior caste jealously clash with one another and find themselves unable to come to terms. The chivalrous and aristocratic valuations presuppose a strong physique, blooming, even exuberant health, together with all the conditions that guarantee its preservation: combat, adventure, the chase, the dance, war games, etc. The value system of the priestly aristocracy is founded on different presuppositions. So much the worse for them when it becomes a question of war! As we all know, priests are the most evil enemies to have—why should this be so? Because they are the most impotent. It is their impotence which makes their hate so violent and sinister, so cerebral and poisonous. The greatest haters in history—but also the most intelligent haters—have been priests. Beside the brilliance of priestly vengeance all other brilliance fades. Human history would be a dull and stupid thing without the intelligence furnished by its impotents. Let us begin with the most striking example. Whatever else has been done to damage the powerful and great of this earth seems trivial compared with what the Jews have done, that priestly people who succeeded in avenging themselves on their enemies and oppressors by radically inverting all their values, that is, by an act of the most spiritual vengeance. This was a strategy entirely appropriate to a priestly people in whom vindictiveness had gone most deeply underground. It was the Jew who, with frightening consistency, dared to invert the aristocratic value equations good/noble/powerful/beautiful/happy/favored-of-the-gods and maintain, with the furious hatred of the underprivileged and impotent, that "only the poor, the powerless, are good; only the suffering, sick, and ugly, truly blessed. But you noble and mighty ones of the earth will be, to all eternity, the evil, the cruel, the avaricious, the godless, and thus the cursed and damned!" . . . We know who has fallen heir to this Jewish inversion of values. . . .   In reference to the grand and unspeakably disastrous initiative which the Jews have launched by this most radical of all declarations of war, I wish to repeat a statement I made in a different context (*Beyond Good and Evil*), to wit, that it was the Jews who started the slave revolt in morals; a revolt with two millennia of history behind it, which we have lost sight of today simply because it has triumphed so completely.

VIII

You find that difficult to understand? You have no eyes for something that took two millennia to prevail? . . .   There is nothing strange about this: all long developments are difficult to see in the round. From the tree trunk of Jewish vengeance and hatred—the deepest and sublimest hatred in human history, since it gave birth to ideals and a new set of values—grew a branch that was equally unique: a new love, the deepest and sublimest of loves. From what other trunk could this branch have sprung? But let no one surmise that this love represented a denial of the thirst for vengeance, that it contravened the Jewish hatred. Exactly the opposite is true. Love grew out of hatred as the tree's crown, spreading triumphantly in the purest sunlight, yet having, in its high and sunny realm, the same aims—victory, aggrandizement, temptation—which hatred pursued by digging its roots ever deeper into all that was profound and evil. Jesus of Nazareth, the gospel of love made flesh, the "redeemer," who brought blessing and victory to the poor, the sick, the sinners— what was he but temptation in its most sinister and irresistible form, bringing men by a roundabout way to precisely those Jewish values and renovations of the ideal? Has not Israel, precisely by the detour of this "redeemer," this seeming antagonist and destroyer of Israel, reached the final goal of its sublime vindictiveness? Was it not a necessary feature of a truly brilliant politics of vengeance, a farsighted, subterranean, slowly and carefully planned vengeance, that Israel had to deny its true instrument publicly and nail him to the cross like a mortal enemy, so that "the whole world" (meaning all the enemies of Israel) might naïvely swallow the bait? And could one, by straining every resource, hit upon a bait more dangerous than this? What could equal in debilitating narcotic power the symbol of the "holy cross," the ghastly paradox of a crucified god, the unspeakably cruel mystery of God's self-crucifixion for the benefit of mankind? One thing is certain, that in this sign Israel has by now triumphed over all other, nobler values.

IX

—"But what is all this talk about nobler values? Let us face facts: the people have triumphed—or the slaves, the mob, the herd, whatever you wish to call them—and if the Jews brought it about, then no nation ever had a more universal mission on this earth. The lords are a thing of the past, and the ethics of the common man is completely triumphant. I don't deny that this triumph might be looked upon as a kind of blood poisoning, since it has resulted in a mingling of the races, but there can be no doubt that the intoxication has succeeded. The 'redemption' of the human race (from the lords, that is) is well under way; everything is rapidly becoming Judaized, or Christianized, or mob-ized—the word makes no difference. The progress of this poison throughout the body of mankind cannot be stayed; as for its tempo, it can now afford to slow down, become finer, barely audible—there's all the time in the world. . . . Does the Church any longer have a necessary mission, or even a *raison d'être?* Or could it be done without? *Quaeritur.* It would almost seem that it retards rather than accelerates that progress. In which case we might consider it useful. But one thing is certain, it has gradually become something crude and lumpish, repugnant to a sensitive intelligence, a truly modern taste. Should it not, at least, be asked to refine itself a bit? . . . It alienates more people today than it seduces. . . . Who among us would be a freethinker, were it not for the Church? It is the Church which offends us, not its poison. . . . Apart from the Church we, too, like the poison. . . ." This was a "freethinker's" reaction to my argument—an honest fellow, as he has abundantly proved, and a democrat to boot. He had been listening to me until that moment, and could not stand to hear my silence. For I have a great deal to be silent about in this matter.

X

The slave revolt in morals begins by rancor turning creative and giving birth to values—the rancor of beings who, deprived of the direct outlet of action, compensate by an imaginary vengeance. All truly noble morality grows out of triumphant self-affirmation. Slave ethics, on the other hand, begins by saying *no* to an "outside," an "other," a non-self, and that *no* is its creative act. This reversal of direction of the evaluating look, this invariable looking outward instead of inward, is a fundamental feature of rancor. Slave ethics requires for its inception a sphere different from and hostile to its own. Physiologically speaking, it requires an outside stimulus in order to act at all; all its action is reaction. The opposite is true of aristocratic valuations: such values grow and act spontaneously, seeking out their contraries only in order to affirm themselves even more gratefully and delightedly. Here the negative concepts, *humble, base, bad,* are late, pallid counterparts of the positive, intense and passionate credo, "We noble, good, beautiful, happy ones." Aristocratic valuations may go amiss and do violence to reality, but this happens only with regard to spheres which they do not know well, or from the knowledge of which they austerely guard themselves: the aristocrat will, on occasion, misjudge a sphere which he holds in contempt, the sphere of the common man, the people. On the other hand we should remember that the emotion of contempt, of looking down, provided that it falsifies at all, is as nothing compared with the falsification which suppressed hatred, impotent vindictiveness, effects upon its opponent, though only in effigy. There is in all contempt too much casualness and nonchalance, too much blinking of facts and impatience, and too much inborn gaiety for it ever to make of its object a downright caricature and monster. Hear the almost benevolent nuances the Greek aristocracy, for example, puts into all its terms for the commoner; how emotions of compassion, consideration, indulgence, sugar-coat these words until, in the end, almost all terms referring to the common man survive as expressions for "unhappy," "pitiable" (cf. *deilos, deilaios, poneros, mochtheros,* the last two of which properly characterize the common man as a drudge and beast of burden); how, on the other hand, the words *bad, base, unhappy* have continued to strike a similar note for the Greek ear, with the timbre "unhappy" preponderating. The "wellborn" really felt that they were also the "happy." They did not have to construct their happiness factitiously by looking at their enemies, as all rancorous men are wont to do, and being fully active, energetic people they were incapable of divorcing happiness from action. They accounted activity a necessary part of happiness (which explains the origin of the phrase *eu prattein*).

All this stands in utter contrast to what is called happiness among the impotent and oppressed, who are full of bottled-up aggressions. Their happiness is purely passive and takes the form of drugged tranquillity, stretching and yawning, peace, "sabbath," emotional slackness. Whereas the noble lives before his own conscience with confidence and frankness (*gennaīos* "nobly bred" emphasizes the nuance "truthful" and perhaps also "ingenuous"), the rancorous person is neither truthful nor ingenuous nor honest and forthright with himself. His soul squints; his mind loves hide-outs, secret paths, and back doors; everything that is hidden seems to him his own world, his security, his comfort; he is expert in silence, in long memory, in waiting, in provisional self-depreciation, and in self-humiliation. A race of such men will, in the end, inevitably be cleverer than a race of aristocrats, and it will honor sharp-wittedness to a much greater degree, i.e., as an absolutely vital condition for its existence. Among the noble, mental acuteness always tends slightly to suggest luxury and overrefinement. The fact is that with them it is much less important than is the perfect functioning of the ruling, unconscious instincts or even a certain temerity to follow sudden impulses, court danger, or indulge spurts of violent rage, love, worship, gratitude, or vengeance. When a noble man feels resentment, it is absorbed in his instantaneous reaction and therefore does not poison him. Moreover, in countless cases where we might expect it, it never arises, while with weak and impotent people it occurs without fail. It is a sign of strong, rich temperaments that they cannot for long take seriously their enemies, their misfortunes, their *misdeeds;* for such characters have in them an excess of plastic curative power, and also a power of oblivion. (A good modern example of the latter is Mirabeau, who lacked all memory for insults and meannesses done him, and who was unable to forgive because he had forgotten). Such a man simply shakes off vermin which would get beneath another's skin—and only here, if anywhere on earth, is it possible to speak of "loving one's enemy." The noble person will respect his enemy, and respect is already a bridge to love. . . .   Indeed he requires his enemy for himself, as his mark of distinction, nor could he tolerate any other enemy than one in whom he finds nothing to despise and much to esteem. Imagine, on the other hand, the "enemy" as conceived by the rancorous man! For this is his true creative achievement: he has conceived the "evil enemy," the Evil One, as a fundamental idea, and then as a pendant he has conceived a Good One—himself.

XI

The exact opposite is true of the noble-minded, who spontaneously creates the notion *good,* and later derives from it the conception of the *bad.* How ill-matched these two concepts look, placed side by side: the bad of noble origin, and the *evil* that has risen out of the cauldron of unquenched hatred! The first is a by-product, a complementary color, almost an afterthought; the second is the beginning, the original creative act of slave ethics. But neither is the conception of good the same in both cases, as we soon find out when we ask ourselves who it is that is really evil according to the code of rancor. The answer is: precisely the good one of the opposite code, that is the noble, the powerful—only colored, reinterpreted, reenvisaged by the poisonous eye of resentment. And we are the first to admit that anyone who knew these "good" ones only as enemies would find them evil enemies indeed. For these same men who, amongst themselves, are so strictly constrained by custom, worship, ritual, gratitude, and by mutual surveillance and jealousy, who are so resourceful in consideration, tenderness, loyalty, pride and friendship, when once they step outside their circle become little better than uncaged beasts of prey. Once abroad in the wilderness, they revel in the freedom from social constraint and compensate for their long confinement in the quietude of their own community. They revert to the innocence of wild animals: we can imagine them returning from an orgy of murder, arson, rape, and torture, jubilant and at peace with themselves as though they had committed a fraternity prank— convinced, moreover, that the poets for a long time to come will have something to sing about and to praise. Deep within all these noble races there lurks the beast of prey, bent on spoil and conquest. This hidden urge has to be satisfied from time to time, the beast let loose in the wilderness. This goes as well for the Roman, Arabian, German, Japanese nobility as for the Homeric heroes and the Scandinavian vikings. The noble races have everywhere left in their wake the catchword "barbarian." And even their highest culture shows an awareness of this trait and a certain pride in it (as we see, for example, in Pericles' famous funeral oration, when he tells the Athenians: "Our boldness has gained us access to every land and sea, and erected monuments to itself *for both good and evil.*") This "boldness" of noble races, so headstrong, absurd, incalculable, sudden, improbable (Pericles commends the Athenians especially for their *rathumia*), their utter indifference to safety and comfort, their terrible pleasure in destruction, their taste for cruelty—all these traits are embodied by their victims in the image of the "barbarian," the "evil enemy," the Goth or the Vandal. The profound and icy suspicion which the German arouses as soon as he assumes power (we see it happening again today) harks back to the persistent horror with which Europe for many centuries witnessed the raging of the blond Teutonic beast (although all racial connection between the old Teutonic tribes and ourselves has been lost). I once drew attention to the embarrassment Hesiod must have felt when he tried to embody the cultural epochs of mankind in the gold, silver, and iron ages. He could cope with the contradictions inherent in Homer's world, so marvelous on the one hand, so ghastly and brutal on the other, only by making two ages out of one and presenting them in temporal sequence; first, the age of the heroes and demigods of Troy and Thebes, as that world was still remembered by the noble tribes who traced their ancestry to it; and second, the iron age, which presented the same world as seen by the descendants of those who had been crushed, despoiled, brutalized, sold into slavery. If it were true, as passes current nowadays, that the real meaning of culture resides in its power to domesticate man's savage instincts, then we might be justified in viewing all those rancorous machinations by which the noble tribes, and their ideals, have been laid low as the true instruments of culture. But this would still not amount to saying that the *organizers* themselves represent culture. Rather, the exact opposite would be true, as is vividly shown by the current state of affairs. These carriers of the leveling and retributive instincts, these descendants of every European and extra-European slavedom, and especially of the pre-Aryan populations, represent human retrogression most flagrantly. Such "instruments of culture" are a disgrace to man and might make one suspicious of culture altogether. One might be justified in fearing the wild beast lurking within all noble races and in being on one's guard against it, but who would not a thousand times prefer fear when it is accompanied with admiration to security accompanied by the loathsome sight of perversion, dwarfishness, degeneracy? And is not the latter our predicament today? What accounts for our repugnance to man—for there is no question that he makes us suffer? Certainly not our fear of him, rather the fact that there is no longer anything to be feared from him; that the vermin "man" occupies the entire stage; that, tame, hopelessly mediocre, and savorless, he considers himself the apex of historical evolution; and not entirely without justice, since he is still somewhat removed from the mass of sickly and effete creatures whom Europe is beginning to stink of today.

XII

Here I want to give vent to a sigh and a last hope. Exactly what is it that I, especially, find intolerable; that I am unable to cope with; that asphyxiates me? A bad smell. The smell of failure, of a soul that has gone stale. God knows it is possible to endure all kinds of misery—vile weather, sickness, trouble, isolation. All this can be coped with, if one is born to a life of anonymity and battle. There will always be moments of re-emergence into the light, when one tastes the golden hour of victory and once again stands foursquare, unshakable, ready to face even harder things, like a bowstring drawn taut against new perils. But, you divine patronesses—if there are any such in the realm beyond good and evil—grant me now and again the sight of something perfect, wholly achieved, happy, magnificently triumphant, something still capable of inspiring fear! Of a man who will justify the existence of mankind, for whose sake one may continue to believe in mankind! . . . The leveling and diminution of European man is our greatest danger; because the sight of him makes us despond. . . . We no longer see anything these days that aspires to grow greater; instead, we have a suspicion that things will continue to go downhill, becoming ever thinner, more placid, smarter, cosier, more ordinary, more indifferent, more Chinese, more Christian—without doubt man is getting "better" all the time. . . . This is Europe's true predicament: together with the fear of man we have also lost the love of man, reverence for man, confidence in man, indeed the *will to man*. Now the sight of man makes us despond. What is nihilism today if not that?

XIII

But to return to business: our inquiry into the origins of that other notion of goodness, as conceived by the resentful, demands to be completed. There is nothing very odd about lambs disliking birds of prey, but this is no reason for holding it against large birds of prey that they carry off lambs. And when the lambs whisper among themselves, "These birds of prey are evil, and does not this give us a right to say that whatever is the opposite of a bird of prey must be good?" there is nothing intrinsically wrong with such an argument—though the birds of prey will look somewhat quizzically and say, "*We* have nothing against these good lambs; in fact, we love them; nothing tastes better than a tender lamb."—To expect that strength will not manifest itself as strength, as the desire to overcome, to appropriate, to have enemies, obstacles, and triumphs, is every bit as absurd as to expect that weakness will manifest itself as strength. A quantum of strength is equivalent to a quantum of urge, will, activity, and it is only the snare of language (of the arch-fallacies of reason petrified in language), presenting all activity as conditioned by an agent—the "subject"—that blinds us to this fact. For, just as popular superstition divorces the lightning from its brilliance, viewing the latter as an activity whose subject is the lightning, so does popular morality divorce strength from its mani-festations, as though there were behind the strong a neutral agent, free to manifest its strength or contain it. But no such agent exists; there is no "being" behind the doing, acting, becoming; the "doer" has simply been added to the deed by the imagination—the doing is everything. The common man actually doubles the doing by making the lightning flash; he states the same event once as cause and then again as effect. The natural scientists are no better when they say that "energy *moves*," "energy *causes*." For all its detachment and freedom from emotion, our science is still the dupe of linguistic habits; it has never yet got rid of those changelings called "subjects." The atom is one such changeling, another is the Kantian "thing-in-itself." Small wonder, then, that the repressed and smoldering emotions of vengeance and hatred have taken advantage of this superstition and in fact espouse no belief more ardently than that it is within the discretion of the strong to be weak, of the bird of prey to be a lamb. Thus they assume the right of calling the bird of prey to account for being a bird of prey. We can hear the oppressed, downtrodden, violated whis-pering among themselves with the wily vengefulness of the impotent, "Let us be unlike those evil ones. Let us be good. And the good shall be he who does not do violence, does not attack or retaliate, who leaves vengeance to God, who, like us, lives hidden, who shuns all that is evil, and altogether asks very little of life—like us, the patient, the humble, the just ones." Read in cold blood, this means nothing more than "We weak ones are, in fact, weak. It is a good thing that we do nothing for which we are not strong enough." But this plain fact, this basic prudence, which even the insects have (who, in circumstances of great danger, sham death in order not to have to "do" too much) has tricked itself out in the garb of quiet, virtuous resignation, thanks to the duplicity of impotence—as though the weakness of the weak, which is after all his essence, his natural way of being, his sole and inevitable reality, were a spontaneous act, a meritorious deed. This sort of person requires the belief in a "free subject" able to choose indifferently, out of that instinct of self-preservation which notoriously justifies every kind of lie. It may well be that to this day the subject, or in popular language the soul, has been the most viable of all arti-cles of faith simply because it makes it possible for the majority of mankind—i.e., the weak and oppressed of every sort—to practice the sublime sleight of hand which gives weakness the appearance of free choice and one's natural disposition the distinction of merit.

XIV

Would anyone care to learn something about the way in which ideals are manufac-tured? Does anyone have the nerve? . . . Well then, go ahead! There's a chink through which you can peek into this murky shop. But wait just a moment, Mr.

Foolhardy; your eyes must grow accustomed to the fickle light. . . . All right, tell me what's going on in there, audacious fellow; now I am the one who is listening.

"I can't see a thing, but I hear all the more. There's a low, cautious whispering in every nook and corner. I have a notion these people are lying. All the sounds are sugary and soft. No doubt you were right; they are transmuting weakness into merit."

"Go on."

"Impotence, which cannot retaliate, into kindness; pusillanimity into humility; submission before those one hates into obedience to One of whom they say that he has commanded this submission—they call him God. The inoffensiveness of the weak, his cowardice, his ineluctable standing and waiting at doors, are being given honorific titles such as patience; to be *unable* to avenge oneself is called to be *unwilling* to avenge oneself—even forgiveness ("for they know not what *they* do— we alone know what *they* do.") Also there's some talk of loving one's enemy— accompanied by much sweat."

"Go on."

"I'm sure they are quite miserable, all these whisperers and smalltime counterfeiters, even though they huddle close together for warmth. But they tell me that this very misery is the sign of their election by God, that one beats the dogs one loves best, that this misery is perhaps also a preparation, a test, a kind of training, perhaps even more than that: something for which eventually they will be compensated with tremendous interest—in gold? No, in happiness. They call this *bliss*."

"Go on."

"Now they tell me that not only are they better than the mighty of this earth, whose spittle they must lick (not from fear—by no means—but because God commands us to honor our superiors), but they are even better off, or at least they will be better off someday. But I've had all I can stand. The smell is too much for me. This shop where they manufacture ideals seems to me to stink of lies."

"But just a moment. You haven't told me anything about the greatest feat of these black magicians, who precipitate the white milk of loving-kindness out of every kind of blackness. Haven't you noticed their most consummate sleight of hand, their boldest, finest, most brilliant trick? Just watch! These vermin, full of vindictive hatred, what are they brewing out of their own poisons? Have you ever heard vengeance and hatred mentioned? Would you ever guess, if you only listened to their words, that these are men bursting with hatred?"

"I see what you mean. I'll open my ears again—and stop my nose. Now I can make out what they seem to have been saying all along: 'We, the good ones, are also the just ones.' They call the thing they seek not retribution but the triumph of justice; the thing they hate is not their enemy, by no means—they hate injustice, ungodliness; the thing they hope for and believe in is not vengeance, the sweet exultation of vengeance ('sweeter than honey' as Homer said) but 'the triumph of God, who is just, over the godless'; what remains to them to love on this earth is not their brothers in hatred, but what they call their 'brothers in love'—all who are good and just."

"And what do they call that which comforts them in all their sufferings—their phantasmagoria of future bliss?"

"Do I hear correctly? They call it Judgment Day, the coming of *their* kingdom, the 'Kingdom of God.' Meanwhile they live in 'faith,' in 'love,' in 'hope.'"

"Stop! I've heard enough."

XV

Faith in what? Love for what? Hope of what? There can be no doubt that these weaklings, too, want a chance to be strong, to have *their* kingdom come. They call it simply the Kingdom of God—what admirable humility! But in order to have that experience one must live a very long time, beyond death; one must have eternal life to indemnify oneself for that terrestrial life of faith, love, and hope. Indemnify for what and by what means? . . . It seems to me that Dante committed a grave blunder when, with disconcerting naïveté, he put over the gate of hell the inscription: "Me, too, eternal love created." At any rate, the inscription over the gate of the Christian paradise, with its "eternal bliss," would read more fittingly, "Me, too, eternal hate created"—provided that it is fitting to place a truth above the gateway to a lie. For in what, precisely, does the bliss of that paradise consist?

We may have guessed by now, but still it is well to have the thing certified for us by a competent authority in these matters, Thomas Aquinas, the great teacher and saint. *Beati in regno coelesti,* he says, meek as a lamb, *videbunt poenas damnatorum, ut beatitudo illis magis complaceat.* Or, if the reader prefers, here is the same sentiment more forcefully expressed by a triumphant Father of the Church (Tertullian) who wishes to dissuade his Christians from the cruel debauch of public spectacles—on what grounds? "Our faith offers us so much more," he writes in *De spectaculis,* ch. 29 ff., "and something so much stronger. Having been redeemed, joys of quite a different kind are ours. We have martyrs instead of athletes. If we crave blood, we have the blood of Christ. . . . But think what awaits us on the day of his triumph!" And the rapt visionary continues: "Yes, and there are still to come other spectacles—that last, that eternal Day of Judgment, that Day which the Gentiles never believed would come, that Day they laughed at, when this old world and all its generations shall be consumed in one fire. How vast the spectacle that day, and how wide! What sight shall wake my wonder, what my laughter, my joy and exultation as I see all those kings, those great kings, welcomed (we are told) in heaven, along with Jove, along with those who told of their ascent, groaning in the depths of darkness! And the magistrates who persecuted the name of Jesus, liquefying in fiercer flames than they kindled in their rage against the Christians! Those sages, too, the philosophers blushing before their disciples as they blaze together, the disciples whom they taught that God was concerned with nothing, that men have no souls at all, or that what souls they have shall never return to their former bodies! And, then, the poets trembling before the judgment seat, not of Rhadamanthus, not of Minos, but of Christ, whom they never looked to see! And then there will be the tragic actors to be heard, more vocal in their own tragedy; and the players to be seen, lither of limb by far in the fire; and then the charioteer to watch, red all over in the wheel of flame; and, next, the athletes to be gazed upon, not in their gymnasiums but hurled in the fire—unless it be that not even then would I wish to see them, in my desire rather to turn an insatiable gaze on them who vented their rage and fury on the Lord. 'This is he,' I shall say, 'the son of the carpenter or the harlot (*Tertullian here mimics Jewish diatribe, as is shown by what immediately follows as well as by his term for the mother of Jesus, which occurs in the Talmud*), the Sabbath-breaker, the Samaritan, who had a devil. This is he whom you bought from Judas; this is he who was struck with reed and fist, defiled with spittle, given gall and vinegar to drink. This is he whom the disciples secretly stole away, that it might be said he had risen— unless it was the gardener who removed him, lest his lettuces should be trampled by the throng of visitors!' Such sights, such exultation—what praetor, consul, quaestor, priest, will ever give you of his bounty? And yet all these, in some sort, are ours, pictured through faith in the imagination of the spirit. But what are those things which eye hath not seen nor ear heard, nor ever entered into the heart of man (I Cor. 2:9)? Things of greater joy than circus, theater, or amphitheater, or any stadium, I believe."[1] *Per fidem:* so it is written.

XVI

Let us conclude. The two sets of valuations, good/bad and good/evil, have waged a terrible battle on this earth, lasting many millennia; and just as surely as the second set has for a long time now been in the ascendant, so surely are there still places where the battle goes on and the issue remains in suspension. It might even be claimed that by being raised to a higher plane the battle has become much more profound. Perhaps there is today not a single intellectual worth his salt who is not divided on that issue, a battleground for those opposites. The watchwords of the battle, written in characters which have remained legible throughout human history, read: "Rome vs. Israel, Israel vs. Rome." No battle has ever been more momentous than this one. Rome viewed Israel as a monstrosity; the Romans regarded the Jews as *convicted* of hatred against the whole of mankind—and rightly so if one is justified in associating the welfare of the human species with absolute supremacy of aristocratic values. But how did the Jews, on their part, feel about Rome? A thousand indications point to the answer. It is enough to read once more the Revelations of St. John, the most rabid outburst of vindictiveness in all recorded history. (We ought to acknowledge the profound consistency of the Christian instinct in assigning this book of hatred and the most extravagantly doting of the Gospels to the same disciple. There is a piece of truth hidden here, no matter how much literary skulduggery may have gone on.) The Romans were the strongest and most noble people who ever lived. Every vestige of them, every least inscription, is a sheer delight, provided we are able to read the spirit behind the writing. The Jews, on the contrary, were the priestly, rancorous nation *par excellence,* though possessed of an unequaled ethical genius; we need only compare with them nations of comparable endowments, such as the Chinese or the Germans, to sense which occupies the first rank. Has the victory so far been gained by the Romans or by the Jews? But this is really an idle question. Remember who it is before whom one bows down, in Rome

---

[1]Translated by T. R. Glover.

itself, as before the essence of all supreme values—and not only in Rome but over half the globe, wherever man has grown tame or desires to grow tame: before three Jews and one Jewess (Jesus of Nazareth, the fisherman Peter, the rug weaver Paul, and Maria, the mother of that Jesus). This is very curious: Rome, without a doubt, has capitulated. It is true that during the Renaissance men witnessed a strange and splendid awakening of the classical ideal; like one buried alive, Rome stirred under the weight of a new Judaic Rome that looked like an ecumenical synagogue and was called the Church. But presently Israel triumphed once again, thanks to the plebeian rancor of the German and English Reformation, together with its natural corollary, the restoration of the Church—which also meant the restoration of ancient Rome to the quiet of the tomb. In an even more decisive sense did Israel triumph over the classical ideal through the French Revolution. For then the last political nobleness Europe had known, that of seventeenth- and eighteenth-century France, collapsed under the weight of vindictive popular instincts. A wilder enthusiasm was never seen. And yet, in the midst of it all, something tremendous, something wholly unexpected happened: the ancient classical ideal appeared incarnate and in unprecedented splendor before the eyes and conscience of mankind. Once again, stronger, simpler, more insistent than ever, over against the lying shibboleth of the rights of the majority, against the furious tendency toward leveling out and debasement, sounded the terrible yet exhilarating shibboleth of the "prerogative of the few." Like a last signpost to an *alternative* route Napoleon appeared, most isolated and anachronistic of men, the embodiment of the noble ideal. It might be well to ponder what exactly Napoleon, that synthesis of the brutish with the more than human, did represent. . . .

XVII

Was it all over then? Had that greatest conflict of ideals been shelved for good? Or had it only been indefinitely adjourned? Might not the smoldering fire start up again one day, all the more terrible because longer and more secretly nourished? Moreover, should we not wish for this event with all our hearts, and even help to promote it? If the reader at this point begins to develop his own train of thought, he is not likely soon to come to the end of it. All the more reason why I should conclude, assuming that I have made sufficiently clear what I mean by the dangerous slogan on the title page of my last book, *Beyond Good and Evil.* At all events, I do not mean "beyond good and bad."

NOTE   I want to take this opportunity to express publicly a wish which I have hitherto expressed only in occasional conversations with scholars: that the philosophy department of some leading university might offer a series of prizes for essays on the evolution of moral ideas. Perhaps my present book will help to encourage such a plan. I would propose the following question, which deserves the attention of philologists, historians, and philosophers alike, *What light does the science of linguistics, especially the study of etymology, throw on the evolution of moral ideas?* However, it would also be necessary for that purpose to enlist the assistance of physiologists and medical men. This can be most fittingly accomplished by the professional philosophers, who as a body have shown such remarkable skill in the past in bringing about amicable and productive relations between philosophy, on the one hand, and physiology and medicine, on the other. It should be stressed that all tables of values, all moral injunctions, with which history and anthropology concern themselves, require first and foremost a physiological investigation and interpretation and next a critique on the part of medical science. The question "What is this or that table of values really worth?" must be viewed under a variety of perspectives, for the question "valuable to what end?" is one of extraordinary complexity. For example, something obviously valuable in terms of the longest possible survival of a race (or of its best adaptation to a given climate, or of the preservation of its greatest numbers) would by no means have the same value if it were a question of developing a more powerful type. The welfare of the many and the welfare of the few are radically opposite ends. To consider the former *a priori* the higher value may be left to the naïveté of English biologists. All sciences are now under the obligation to prepare the ground for the future task of the philosopher, which is to solve the problem of value, to determine the true hierarchy of values.

The Emotive Meaning of Ethical Terms

Charles Leslie Stevenson

I.

Ethical questions first arise in the form "Is so and so good?," or "Is this alternative better than that?" These questions are difficult partly because we don't quite know what we are seeking. We are asking, "Is there a needle in that haystack?" without even knowing just what a needle is. So the first thing to do is to examine the questions themselves. We must try to make them clearer, either by defining the terms in which they are expressed, or by any other method that is available.

The present paper is concerned wholly with this preliminary step of making ethical questions clear. In order to help answer the question "Is X good?" we must *substitute* for it a question which is free from ambiguity and confusion.

It is obvious that in substituting a clearer question we must not introduce some utterly different kind of questions. It won't do (to take an extreme instance of a prevalent fallacy) to substitute for "Is X good?" the question "Is X pink with yellow trimmings?" and then point out how easy the question really is. This would beg the original question, not help answer it. On the other hand, we must not expect the substituted question to be strictly "identical" with the original one. The original question may embody hypostatization, anthropomorphism, vagueness, and all the

Source: Mind, 46, 1937, 14–31.

other ills to which our ordinary discourse is subject. If our substituted question is to be clearer, it must remove these ills. The questions will be identical only in the sense that a child is identical with the man he later becomes. Hence we must not demand that the substitution strike us, on immediate introspection, as making no change in meaning.

Just how, then, must the substituted question be related to the original? Let us assume (inaccurately) that it must result from replacing "good" by some set of terms which define it. The question then resolves itself to this: How must the defined meaning of "good" be related to its original meaning?

I answer that it must be *relevant.* A defined meaning will be called "relevant" to the original meaning under these circumstances: Those who have understood the definition must be able to say all that they then want to say by using the term in the defined way. They must never have occasion to use the term in the old, unclear sense. (If a person did have to go on using the word in the old sense, then to this extent his meaning would not be clarified, and the philosophical task would not be completed.) It frequently happens that a word is used so confusedly and ambiguously that we must give it *several* defined meanings, rather than one. In this case only the whole set of defined meanings will be called "relevant," and any one of them will be called "partially relevant." This is not a rigorous treatment of *relevance,* by any means; but it will serve for the present purposes.

Let us now turn to our particular task—that of giving a relevant definition of "good." Let us first examine some of the ways in which others have attempted to do this.

The word "good" has often been defined in terms of *approval,* or similar psychological attitudes. We may take as typical examples: "good" means *desired by me* (Hobbes); and "good" means *approval by most people* (Hume, in effect). It will be convenient to refer to definitions of this sort as "interest theories," following Mr. R. B. Perry, although neither "interest" nor "theory" is used in the most usual way.

Are definitions of this sort relevant?

It is idle to deny their *partial* relevance. The most superficial inquiry will reveal that "good" is exceedingly ambiguous. To maintain that "good" is *never* used in Hobbes's sense, and never in Hume's, is only to manifest an insensitivity to the complexities of language. We must recognize, perhaps, not only these senses, but a variety of similar ones, differing both with regard to the kind of interest in question, and with regard to the people who are said to have the interest.

But this is a minor matter. The essential question is not whether interest theories are *partially* relevant, but whether they are *wholly* relevant. This is the only point for intelligent dispute. Briefly: Granted that some senses of "good" may relevantly be defined in terms of interest, is there some *other* sense which is *not* relevantly so defined? We must give this question careful attention. For it is quite possible that when philosophers (and many others) have found the question "Is X good?" so difficult, they have been grasping for this *other* sense of "good," and not any sense relevantly defined in terms of interest. If we insist on defining "good" in terms of interest, and answer the question when thus interpreted, we may be begging *their* question entirely. Of course this *other* sense of "good" may not exist, or it may be a complete confusion; but that is what we must discover.

Now many have maintained that interest theories are *far* from being completely relevant. They have argued that such theories neglect the very sense of "good" which is most vital. And certainly, their arguments are not without plausibility.

Only . . . what *is* this "vital" sense of "good"? The answers have been so vague, and so beset with difficulties, that one can scarcely determine.

There are certain requirements, however, with which this "vital" sense has been expected to comply—requirements which appeal strongly to our common sense. It will be helpful to summarize these, showing how they exclude the interest theories:

In the first place, we must be able sensibly to *disagree* about whether something is "good." This condition rules out Hobbes's definition. For consider the following argument: "This is good." "That isn't so; it's not good." As translated by Hobbes, this becomes: "I desire this." "That isn't so, for *I* don't." The speakers are not contradicting one another, and think they are, only because of an elementary confusion in the use of pronouns. The definition, "good" means *desired by my community,* is also excluded, for how could people from different communities disagree?[1]

In the second place, "goodness" must have, so to speak, a magnetism. A person who recognizes X to be "good" must *ipso facto* acquire a stronger tendency to act in its favour then he otherwise would have had. This rules out the Humian type of definition. For according to Hume, to recognize that something is "good" is simply to recognize that the majority approve of it. Clearly, a man may see that the majority approve of X without having, himself, a stronger tendency to favour it. This requirement excludes any attempt to define "good" in terms of the interest of people *other* than the speaker.[2]

In the third place, the "goodness" of anything must not be verifiable solely by use of the scientific method. "Ethics must not be psychology." This restriction rules out all of the traditional interest theories, without exception. It is so sweeping a restriction that we must examine its plausibility. What are the methodological implications of interest theories which are here rejected?

According to Hobbes's definition, a person can prove his ethical judgments, with finality, by showing that he is not making an introspective error about his desires. According to Hume's definition, one may prove ethical judgments (roughly speaking) by taking a vote. *This* use of the empirical method, at any rate, seems highly remote from what we usually accept as proof, and reflects on the complete relevance of the definitions which imply it.

But aren't there more complicated interest theories which are immune from such methodological implications? No, for the same factors appear; they are only put off for a while. Consider, for example, the definition: "X is good" means *most people would approve of X if they knew its nature and consequences.* How, according to this definition, could we prove that a certain X was good? We should first have to find out, empirically, just what X was like, and what its consequences would be. To this extent the empirical method, as required by the definition, seems beyond intelligent objection. But what remains? We should next have to discover whether most people would approve of the sort of thing we had discovered X to be.

[1]See G. E. Moore's *Philosophical Studies,* pp. 332–334.
[2]See G. C. Field's *Moral Theory,* pp. 52, 56–57.

This couldn't be determined by popular vote—but only because it would be too difficult to explain to the voters, beforehand, what the nature and consequences of X really were. Apart from this, voting would be a pertinent method. We are again reduced to counting noses, as a *perfectly final* appeal.

Now we need not scorn voting entirely. A man who rejected interest theories as irrelevant might readily make the following statement: "If I believed that X would be approved by the majority, when they knew all about it, I should be strongly *led* to say that X was good." But he would continue: "*Need* I say that X was good, under the circumstances? Wouldn't my acceptance of the alleged 'final proof' result simply from my being democratic? What about the more aristocratic people? They would simply say that the approval of most people, even when they knew all about the object of their approval, simply had nothing to do with the goodness of anything, and they would probably add a few remarks about the low state of people's interests." It would indeed seem, from these considerations, that the definition we have been considering has presupposed democratic ideals from the start; it has dressed up democratic propaganda in the guise of a definition.

The omnipotence of the empirical method, as implied by interest theories and others, may be shown unacceptable in a somewhat different way. Mr. G. E. Moore's familiar objection about the open question is chiefly pertinent in this regard. No matter what set of scientifically knowable properties a thing may have (says Moore, in effect), you will find, on careful introspection, that it is an open question to ask whether anything having these properties is *good*. It is difficult to believe that this recurrent question is a totally confused one, or that it seems open only because of the ambiguity of "good." Rather, we must be using some sense of "good" which is not definable, relevantly, in terms of anything scientifically knowable. That is, the scientific method is not sufficient for ethics.[3]

These, then, are the requirements with which the "vital" sense of "good" is expected to comply: (1) goodness must be a topic for intelligent disagreement; (2) it must be "magnetic"; and (3) it must not be discoverable solely through the scientific method.

II.

Let us now turn to my own analysis of ethical judgments. First let me present my position dogmatically, showing to what extent I vary from tradition.

I believe that the three requirements, given above, are perfectly sensible; that there is some *one* sense of "good" which satisfies all three requirements; and that no traditional interest theory satisfies them all. But this does not imply that "good" must be explained in terms of a Platonic Idea, or of a Categorical Imperative, or of a unique, unanalyzable property. On the contrary, the three requirements can be met by a *kind* of interest theory. *But we must give up a presupposition which all the traditional interest theories have made.*

---

[3]See G. E. Moore's *Principia Ethica,* chap. i. I am simply trying to preserve the spirit of Moore's objection, and not the exact form of it.

Traditional interest theories hold that ethical statements are *descriptive* of the existing state of interests—that they simply *give information* about interests. (More accurately, ethical judgments are said to describe what the state of interests is, was, or will be, or to indicate what the state of interests *would* be under specified circumstances.) It is this emphasis on description, on information, which leads to their incomplete relevance. Doubtless there is always *some* element of description in ethical judgments, but this is by no means all. Their major use is not to indicate facts, but to *create an influence.* Instead of merely describing people's interests, they *change* or *intensify* them. They *recommend* an interest in an object, rather than state that the interest already exists.

For instance: When you tell a man that he oughtn't to steal, your object isn't merely to let him know that people disapprove of stealing. You are attempting, rather, to get *him* to disapprove of it. Your ethical judgment has a quasi-imperative force which, operating through suggestion, and intensified by your tone of voice, readily permits you to begin to *influence,* to *modify,* his interests. If in the end you do not succeed in getting *him* to disapprove of stealing, you will feel that you've failed to convince him that stealing is wrong. You will continue to feel this, even though he fully acknowledges that you disapprove of it, and that almost everyone else does. When you point out to him the consequences of his actions—consequences which you suspect he already disapproves of—these *reasons* which support your ethical judgment are simply a means of facilitating your influence. If you think you can change his interests by making vivid to him how others will disapprove of him, you will do so; otherwise not. So the consideration about other people's interest is just an additional means you may employ, in order to move him, and is not a part of the ethical judgment itself. Your ethical judgment doesn't merely describe interests to him, it directs his very interests. The difference between the traditional interest theories and my view is like the difference between describing a desert and irrigating it.

Another example: A munition maker declares that war is a good thing. If he merely meant that he approved of it, he would not have to insist so strongly, nor grow so excited in his argument. People would be quite easily convinced that he approved of it. If he merely meant that most people approved of war, or that most people would approve of it if they knew the consequences, he would have to yield his point if it were proved that this wasn't so. But he wouldn't do this, nor does consistency require it. He is not *describing* the state of people's approval; he is trying to *change* it by his influence. If he found that few people approved of war, he might insist all the more strongly that it was good, for there would be more changing to be done.

This example illustrates how "good" may be used for what most of us would call bad purposes. Such cases are as pertinent as any others. I am not indicating the *good* way of using "good." I am not influencing people, but am describing the way this influence sometimes goes on. If the reader wishes to say that the munition maker's influence is bad—that is, if the reader wishes to awaken people's disapproval of the man, and to make him disapprove of his own actions—I should at another time be willing to join in this undertaking. But this is not the present concern. I am not using ethical terms, but am indicating how they *are* used. The munition maker, in his use of "good," illustrates the persuasive character of the word just as well as does the unselfish man who, eager to encourage in each of us a desire for the happiness of all, contends that the supreme good is peace.

Thus ethical terms are *instruments* used in the complicated interplay and readjustment of human interests. This can be seen plainly from more general observations. People from widely separated communities have different moral attitudes. Why? To a great extent because they have been subject to different social influences. Now clearly this influence doesn't operate through sticks and stones alone; words play a great part. People praise one another, to encourage certain inclinations, and blame one another, to discourage others. Those of forceful personalities issue commands which weaker people, for complicated instinctive reasons, find it difficult to disobey, quite apart from fears of consequences. Further influence is brought to bear by writers and orators. Thus social influence is exerted, to an enormous extent, by means that have nothing to do with physical force or material reward. The ethical terms facilitate such influence. Being suited for use in *suggestion,* they are a means by which men's attitudes may be led this way or that. The reason, then, that we find a greater similarity in the moral attitudes of one community than in those of different communities is largely this: ethical judgments propagate themselves. One man says "This is good"; this may influence the approval of another person, who then makes the same ethical judgment, which in turn influences another person, and so on. In the end, by a process of mutual influence, people take up more or less the same attitudes. Between people of widely separated communities of course, the influence is less strong; hence different communities have different attitudes.

These remarks will serve to give a general idea of my point of view. We must now go into more detail. There are several questions which must be answered: How does an ethical sentence acquire its power of influencing people—why is it suited to suggestion? Again, what has this influence to do with the *meaning* of ethical terms? And finally, do these considerations really lead us to a sense of "good" which meets the requirements mentioned in the preceding section?

Let us deal first with the question about *meaning.* This is far from an easy question, so we must enter into a preliminary inquiry about meaning in general. Although a seeming digression, this will prove indispensable.

III.

Broadly speaking, there are two different *purposes* which lead us to use language. On the one hand we use words (as in science) to record, clarify, and communicate *beliefs.* On the other hand we use words to give vent to our feelings (interjections), or to create moods (poetry), or to incite people to actions or attitudes (oratory).

The first use of words I shall call "descriptive"; the second, "dynamic." Note that the distinction depends solely upon the *purpose* of the *speaker.*

When a person says "Hydrogen is the lightest known gas," his purpose *may* be simply to lead the hearer to believe this, or to believe that the speaker believes it. In that case the words are used descriptively. When a person cuts himself and says

"Damn," his purpose is not ordinarily to record, clarify, or communicate any belief. The word is used dynamically. The two ways of using words, however, are by no means mutually exclusive. This is obvious from the fact that our purposes are often complex. Thus when one says "I want you to close the door," part of his purpose, ordinarily, is to lead the hearer to believe that he has this want. To that extent the words are used descriptively. But the major part of one's purpose is to lead the hearer to *satisfy* the want. To that extent the words are used dynamically.

It very frequently happens that the same sentence may have a dynamic use on one occasion, and may not have a dynamic use on another; and that it may have different dynamic uses on different occasions. For instance: A man says to a visiting neighbour, "I am loaded down with work." His purpose may be to let the neighbour know how life is going with him. This would *not* be a dynamic use of words. He may make the remark, however, in order to drop a hint. This *would* be dynamic usage (as well as descriptive). Again, he may make the remark to arouse the neighbour's sympathy. This would be a *different* dynamic usage from that of hinting.

Or again, when we say to a man, "Of course you won't make those mistakes any more," we *may* simply be making a prediction. But we are more likely to be using "suggestion," in order to encourage him and hence *keep* him from making mistakes. The first use would be descriptive; the second, mainly dynamic.

From these examples it will be clear that we can't determine whether words are used dynamically or not, merely by reading the dictionary—even assuming that everyone is faithful to dictionary meanings. Indeed, to know whether a person is using a word dynamically, we must note his tone of voice, his gestures, the general circumstances under which he is speaking, and so on.

We must now proceed to an important question: What has the dynamic use of words to do with their *meaning?* One thing is clear—we must not define "meaning" in a way that would make meaning vary with dynamic usage. If we did, we should have no use for the term. All that we could say about such "meaning" would be that it is very complicated, and subject to constant change. So we must certainly distinguish between the dynamic use of words and their meaning.

It doesn't follow, however, that we must define "meaning" in some non-psychological fashion. We must simply restrict the psychological field. Instead of identifying meaning with *all* the psychological causes and effects that attend a word's utterance, we must identify it with those that it has a *tendency* (causal property, dispositional property) to be connected with. The tendency must be of a particular kind, moreover. It must exist for all who speak the language; it must be persistent; and must be realizable more or less independently of determinate circumstances attending the word's utterance. There will be further restrictions dealing with the interrelation of words in different contexts. Moreover, we must include, under the psychological responses which the words tend to produce, not only immediately introspectable experiences, but *dispositions* to react in a given way with appropriate stimuli. I hope to go into these matters in a subsequent paper. Suffice it now to say that I think "meaning" may be thus defined in a way to include "propositional" meaning as an important kind. Now a word may *tend* to have causal relations which in fact it sometimes doesn't; and it may sometimes have causal relations which it *doesn't tend* to have. And since the tendency of words which constitutes their meaning must be of a particular kind, and may include, as responses, dispositions to reactions, of which any of *several* immediate experiences may be a sign, then there is nothing surprising in the fact that words have a permanent meaning, in spite of the fact that the immediately introspectable experiences which attend their usage are so highly varied.

When "meaning" is defined in this way, meaning will not include dynamic use. For although words are sometimes accompanied by dynamic purposes, they do not *tend* to be accompanied by them in the way above mentioned. *E.g.,* there is no tendency realizable independently of the determinate circumstances under which the words are uttered.

There will be a kind of meaning, however, in the sense above defined, which has an intimate relation to dynamic usage. I refer to "emotive" meaning (in a sense roughly like that employed by Ogden and Richards).[4] The emotive meaning of a word is a tendency of a word, arising through the history of its usage, to produce (result from) *affective* responses in people. It is the immediate aura of feeling which hovers about a word. Such tendencies to produce affective responses cling to words very tenaciously. It would be difficult, for instance, to express merriment by using the interjection "alas." Because of the persistence of such affective tendencies (among other reasons) it becomes feasible to classify them as "meanings."

Just *what* is the relation between emotive meaning and the dynamic use of words? Let us take an example. Suppose that a man is talking with a group of people which includes Miss Jones, aged 59. He refers to her, without thinking, as an "old maid." Now even if his purposes are perfectly innocent—even if he is using the words purely descriptively—Miss Jones won't think so. She will think he is encouraging the others to have contempt for her, and will draw in her skirts, defensively. The man might have done better if instead of saying "old maid" he had said "elderly spinster." The latter words could have been put to the same descriptive use, and would not so readily have caused suspicions about the dynamic use.

"Old maid" and "elderly spinster" differ, to be sure, only in emotive meaning. From the example it will be clear that certain words, because of their emotive meaning, are suited to a certain kind of dynamic use—so well suited, in fact, that the hearer is likely to be misled when we use them in any other way. The more pronounced a word's emotive meaning is, the less likely people are to use it purely descriptively. Some words are suited to encourage people, some to discourage them, some to quiet them, and so on.

Even in these cases, of course, the dynamic purposes are not to be identified with any sort of meaning; for the emotive meaning accompanies a word much more persistently than do the dynamic purposes. But there is an important contingent relation between emotive meaning and dynamic purpose: the former assists the latter. Hence if we define emotively laden terms in a way that neglects their emotive meaning, we are likely to be confusing. *We lead people to think that the terms defined are used dynamically less often than they are.*

---

[4]See *The Meaning of Meaning,* by C. K. Ogden and I. A. Richards. On p. 125, second edition, there is a passage on ethics which was the source of the ideas embodied in this paper.

IV.

Let us now apply these remarks in defining "good." This word may be used morally or non-morally. I shall deal with the non-moral usage almost entirely, but only because it is simpler. The main points of the analysis will apply equally well to either usage.

As a preliminary definition, let us take an inaccurate approximation. It may be more misleading than helpful, but will do to begin with. Roughly, then, the sentence "X is good" means *We like X.* ("We" includes the hearer or hearers.)

At first glance this definition sounds absurd. If used, we should expect to find the following sort of conversation: A. "This is good." B. "But I *don't* like it. What led you to believe that I did?" The unnaturalness of B's reply, judged by ordinary word-usage, would seem to cast doubt on the relevance of my definition.

B's unnaturalness, however, lies simply in this: he is assuming that "We like it" (as would occur implicitly in the use of "good") is being used descriptively. This won't do. When "We like it" is to take the place of "This is good," the former sentence must be used not purely descriptively, but dynamically. More specifically, it must be used to promote a very subtle (and for the non-moral sense in question, a very easily resisted) kind of *suggestion.* To the extent that "we" refers to the hearer, it must have the dynamic use, essential to suggestion, of leading the hearer to *make* true what is said, rather than merely to believe it. And to the extent that "we" refers to the speaker, the sentence must have not only the descriptive use of indicating belief about the speaker's interest, but the quasi-interjectory, dynamic function of giving direct expression to the interest. (This immediate expression of feelings assists in the process of suggestion. It is difficult to disapprove in the face of another's enthusiasm.)

For an example of a case where "We like this" is used in the dynamic way that "This is good" is used, consider the case of a mother who says to her several children, "One thing is certain, *we all like to be neat.*" If she really believed this, she wouldn't bother to say so. But she is not using the words descriptively. She is *encouraging* the children to like neatness. By telling them that they like neatness, she will lead them to *make* her statement true, so to speak. If, instead of saying "We all like to be neat" in this way, she had said "It's a good thing to be neat," the effect would have been approximately the same.

But these remarks are still misleading. Even when "We like it" is used for suggestion, it isn't quite like "This is good." The latter is more subtle. With such a sentence as "This is a good book," for example, it would be practically impossible to use instead "We like this book." When the latter is used, it must be accompanied by so exaggerated an intonation, to prevent its becoming confused with a descriptive statement, that the force of suggestion becomes stronger, and ludicrously more overt, than when "good" is used.

The definition is inadequate, further, in that the definiens has been restricted to dynamic usage. Having said that dynamic usage was different from meaning, I should not have to mention it in giving the *meaning* of "good."

It is in connection with this last point that we must return to emotive meaning. The word "good" has a pleasing emotive meaning which fits it especially for the dynamic use of suggesting favourable interest. But the sentence "We like it" has no such emotive meaning. Hence my definition has neglected emotive meaning entirely. Now to neglect emotive meaning is likely to lead to endless confusions, as we shall presently see; so I have sought to make up for the inadequacy of the definition by letting the restriction about dynamic usage take the place of emotive meaning. What I should do, of course, is to find a definiens whose emotive meaning, like that of "good," simply does *lead* to dynamic usage.

Why didn't I do this? I answer that it isn't possible, if the definition is to afford us increased clarity. No two words, in the first place, have quite the same emotive meaning. The most we can hope for is a rough approximation. But if we seek for such an approximation for "good," we shall find nothing more than synonyms, such as "desirable" or "valuable"; and these are profitless because they do not clear up the connection between "good" and favourable interest. If we reject such synonyms, in favour of non-ethical terms, we shall be highly misleading. For instance: "This is good" has something like the meaning of "I *do* like this; do so as well." But this is certainly not accurate. For the imperative makes an appeal to the conscious efforts of the hearer. Of course he can't like something just by trying. He must be led to like it through suggestion. Hence an ethical sentence differs from an imperative in that it enables one to make changes in a much more subtle, less fully conscious way. Note that the ethical sentence centres the hearer's attention not on his interests, but on the object of interest, and thereby facilitates suggestion. Because of its subtlety, moreover, an ethical sentence readily permits counter-suggestion, and leads to the give and take situation which is so characteristic of arguments about values.

Strictly speaking, then, it is impossible to define "good" in terms of favourable interest if emotive meaning is not to be distorted. Yet it is possible to say that "This is good" is *about* the favourable interest of the speaker and the hearer or hearers, and that it has a pleasing emotive meaning which fits the words for use in suggestion. This is a rough description of meaning, not a definition. But it serves the same clarifying function that a definition ordinarily does; and that, after all, is enough.

A word must be added about the moral use of "good." This differs from the above in that it is about a different kind of interest. Instead of being about what the hearer and speaker *like,* it is about a stronger sort of approval. When a person *likes* something, he is pleased when it prospers, and disappointed when it doesn't. When a person *morally approves* of something, he experiences a rich feeling of security when it prospers, and is indignant, or "shocked" when it doesn't. These are rough and inaccurate examples of the many factors which one would have to mention in distinguishing the two kinds of interest. In the moral usage, as well as in the non-moral, "good" has an emotive meaning which adapts it to suggestion.

And now, are these considerations of any importance? Why do I stress emotive meanings in this fashion? Does the omission of them really lead people into errors? I think, indeed, that the errors resulting from such omissions are enormous. In order to see this, however, we must return to the restrictions, mentioned in section I., with which the "vital" sense of "good" has been expected to comply.

V.

The first restriction, it will be remembered, had to do with disagreement. Now there is clearly some sense in which people disagree on ethical points; but we must not rashly assume that all disagreement is modelled after the sort that occurs in the natural sciences. We must distinguish between "disagreement in belief" (typical of the sciences) and "disagreement in interest." Disagreement in belief occurs when A believes p and B disbelieves it. Disagreement in interest occurs when A has a favourable interest in X, when B has an unfavourable one in it, and when neither is content to let the other's interest remain unchanged.

Let me give an example of disagreement in interest. A. "Let's go to a cinema to-night." B. "I don't want to do that. Let's go to the symphony." A continues to insist on the cinema, B on the symphony. This is disagreement in a perfectly conventional sense. They can't agree on where they want to go, and each is trying to redirect the other's interest. (Note that imperatives are used in the example.)

It is disagreement in *interest* which takes places in ethics. When C says "This is good," and D says "No, it's bad," we have a case of suggestion and counter-suggestion. Each man is trying to redirect the other's interest. There obviously need be no domineering, since each may be willing to give ear to the other's influence; but each is trying to move the other none the less. It is in this sense that they disagree. Those who argue that certain interest theories make no provision for disagreement have been misled, I believe, simply because the traditional theories, in leaving out emotive meaning, give the impression that ethical judgments are used descriptively only; and of course when judgments are used purely descriptively, the only disagreement that can arise is disagreement *in belief.* Such disagreement may be disagreement in belief *about* interests; but this is not the same as disagreement *in* interest. My definition doesn't provide for disagreement in belief about interests, any more than does Hobbes's; but that is no matter, for there is no reason to believe, at least on common-sense grounds, that this kind of disagreement exists. There is only disagreement *in* interest. (We shall see in a moment that disagreement in interest does not remove ethics from sober argument—that this kind of disagreement may often be resolved through empirical means.)

The second restriction, about "magnetism," or the connection between goodness and actions, requires only a word. This rules out *only* those interest theories which do *not* include the interest of the speaker, in defining "good." My account does include the speaker's interest; hence is immune.

The third restriction, about the empirical method, may be met in a way that springs naturally from the above account of disagreement. Let us put the question in this way: When two people disagree over an ethical matter, can they completely resolve the disagreement through empirical considerations, assuming that each applies the empirical method exhaustively, consistently, and without error?

I answer that sometimes they can, and sometimes they cannot; and that at any rate, even when they can, the relation between empirical knowledge and ethical judgments is quite different from the one which traditional interest theories seem to imply.

This can best be seen from an analogy. Let's return to the example where A and B couldn't agree on a cinema or a symphony. The example differed from an ethical argument in that imperatives were used, rather than ethical judgments; but was analogous to the extent that each person was endeavouring to modify the other's interest. Now how would these people argue the case, assuming that they were too intelligent just to shout at one another?

Clearly, they would give "reasons" to support their imperatives. A might say, "But you know, Garbo is at the Bijou." His hope is that B, who admires Garbo, will acquire a desire to go to the cinema when he knows what play will be there. B may counter, "But Toscanini is guest conductor to-night, in an all-Beethoven programme." And so on. Each supports his imperative ("*Let's* do so and so") by reasons which may be empirically established.

To generalize from this: disagreement in interest may be rooted in disagreement in belief. That is to say, people who disagree in interest would often cease to do so if they knew the precise nature and consequences of the object of their interest. To this extent disagreement in interest may be resolved by securing agreement in belief, which in turn may be secured empirically.

This generalization holds for ethics. If A and B, instead of using imperatives, had said, respectively, "It would be *better* to go to the cinema," and "It would be better to go to the symphony," the reasons which they would advance would be roughly the same. They would each give a more thorough account of the object of interest, with the purpose of completing the redirection of interest which was begun by the suggestive force of the ethical sentence. On the whole, of course, the suggestive force of the ethical statement merely exerts enough pressure to start such trains of reasons, since the reasons are much more essential in resolving disagreement in interest than the persuasive effect of the ethical judgment itself.

Thus the empirical method is relevant to ethics simply because our knowledge of the world is a determining factor to our interests. But note that empirical facts are not inductive grounds from which the ethical judgment problematically follows. (This is what traditional interest theories imply.) If someone said "Close the door," and added the reason "We'll catch cold," the latter would scarcely be called an inductive ground of the former. Now imperatives are related to the reasons which support them in the same way that ethical judgments are related to reasons.

Is the empirical method *sufficient* for attaining ethical agreement? Clearly not. For empirical knowledge resolves disagreement in interest only to the extent that such disagreement is rooted in disagreement in belief. Not all disagreement in interest is of this sort. For instance: A is of a sympathetic nature, and B isn't. They are arguing about whether a public dole would be good. Suppose that they discovered all the consequences of the dole. Isn't it possible, even so, that A will say that it's good, and B that it's bad? The disagreement in interest may arise not from limited factual knowledge, but simply from A's sympathy and B's coldness. Or again, suppose, in the above argument, that A was poor and unemployed, and that B was rich. Here again the disagreement might not be due to different factual knowledge. It would be due to the different social positions of the men, together with their predominant self-interest.

When ethical disagreement is not rooted in disagreement in belief, is there *any* method by which it may be settled? If one means by "method" a *rational* method, then there is no method. But in any case there is a "way." Let's consider the above example, again, where disagreement was due to A's sympathy and B's coldness. Must they end by saying, "Well, it's just a matter of our having different temperaments"? Not necessarily. A, for instance, may try to *change* the temperament of his opponent. He may pour out his enthusiasms in such a moving way—present the sufferings of the poor with such appeal—that he will lead his opponent to see life through different eyes. He may build up, by the contagion of his feelings, an influence which will modify B's temperament, and create in him a sympathy for the poor which didn't previously exist. This is often the only way to obtain ethical agreement, if there is any way at all. It is persuasive, not empirical or rational; but that is no reason for neglecting it. There is no reason to scorn it, either, for it is only by such means that our personalities are able to grow, through our contact with others.

The point I wish to stress, however, is simply that the empirical method is instrumental to ethical agreement only to the extent that disagreement in interest is rooted in disagreement in belief. There is little reason to believe that all disagreement is of this sort. Hence the empirical method is not sufficient for ethics. In any case, ethics is not psychology, since psychology doesn't endeavour to *direct* our interests; it discovers facts about the ways in which interests are or can be directed, but that's quite another matter.

To summarize this section: my analysis of ethical judgments meets the three requirements for the "vital" sense of "good" that were mentioned in section I. The traditional interest theories fail to meet these requirements simply because they neglect emotive meaning. This neglect leads them to neglect dynamic usage, and the sort of disagreement that results from such usage, together with the method of resolving the disagreement. I may add that my analysis answers Moore's objection about the open question. Whatever scientifically knowable properties a thing may have, it *is* always open to question whether a thing having these (enumerated) qualities is good. For to ask whether it is good is to ask for *influence*. And whatever I may know about an object, I can still ask, quite pertinently, to be influenced with regard to my interest in it.

VI.

And now, have I really pointed out the "vital" sense of "good"?

I suppose that many will still say "No," claiming that I have simply failed to set down *enough* requirements which this sense must meet, and that my analysis, like all others given in terms of interest, is a way of begging the issue. They will say: "When we ask 'Is X good?' we don't want mere influence, mere advice. We decidedly don't want to be influenced through persuasion, nor are we fully content when the influence is supported by a wide scientific knowledge of X. The answer to our question will, of course, modify our interests. But this is only because a unique sort of *truth* will be revealed to us—a truth which must be apprehended *a priori*. We want our interests to be guided by this truth, and by nothing else. To substitute for such a truth mere emotive meaning and suggestion is to conceal from us the very object of our search."

I can only answer that I do not understand. What is this truth to be *about?* For I recollect no Platonic Idea, nor do I know what to *try* to recollect. I find no indefinable property, nor do I know what to look for. And the "self-evident" deliverances of reason, which so many philosophers have claimed, seem, on examination, to be deliverances of their respective reasons only (if of anyone's) and not of mine.

I strongly suspect, indeed, that any sense of "good" which is expected both to unite itself in synthetic *a priori* fashion with other concepts, and to influence interests as well, is really a great confusion. I extract from this meaning the power of influence alone, which I find the only intelligible part. If the rest is confusion, however, then it certainly deserves more than the shrug of one's shoulders. What I should like to do is to *account* for the confusion—to examine the psychological needs which have given rise to it, and to show how these needs may be satisfied in another way. This is *the* problem, if confusion is to be stopped at its source. But it is an enormous problem, and my reflections on it, which are at present worked out only roughly, must be reserved until some later time.

I may add that if "X is good" is essentially a vehicle for suggestion, it is scarcely a statement which philosophers, any more than many other men, are called upon to make. To the extent that ethics predicates the ethical terms of anything, rather than explains their meaning, it ceases to be a reflective study. Ethical statements are social instruments. They are used in a cooperative enterprise in which we are mutually adjusting ourselves to the interests of others. Philosophers have a part in this, as do all men, but not the major part.

The Role of Relativism in the Moral Life

Lawrence M. Hinman

When in Rome, so the saying goes, do as the Romans do. Yet what do you do if you are an American executive of a multinational corporation in Rome and income tax time comes around? Many Italians consider an income tax report to be like an opening bid in what often prove to be complex and challenging negotiations. It would be silly to give away your entire hand on the first bid, so typically much is initially concealed. Nor would the Italian government expect complete honesty at this stage. To an Italian, this covert activity does not feel like cheating; it is simply the way business is done. Yet to an American businessperson, to file a false tax return is to cheat. When in Rome, what does the American executive do?

Nor, obviously, is this example just an issue about Rome. What should American business people with factories in South Africa have done during the decades of apartheid? When in South Africa, did one do as the Afrikaaners did and exploit the

Source: Ethics: A Pluralistic Approach to Moral Theory, Chapter 2. Fort Worth: Harcourt Brace, 1994, 26–48.

native population? Should one have actively participated in the oppression, or perhaps just benefited economically from it? Or, to shift locations, how should the American businessperson behave in countries in which a bribe, *la mordida* or the *baksheesh,* is considered a normal and acceptable part of almost any business deal? How are we to act in such situations, especially given the moral restrictions in our own culture against bribes?

Nor are these just questions faced outside our own country. Consider the problems faced by our State Department when a man from Saudi Arabia applies for a visa for himself and his wives. Polygamy is forbidden morally as well as legally in our country, but it is both legal and morally acceptable in Saudi Arabia. Do we issue visas for all his wives, for just one (if so, who chooses which one), or for none? Indeed, do we even issue him a visa, since he is a polygamist? Even closer to home, how would we have dealt with polygamous Mormon families in the United States a hundred years ago when possessing multiple wives was still sanctioned by some of their leaders? More recently, consider the question of the religious use of peyote in Native American religious ceremonies. Should the moral standards of the dominant white society in the United States override the moral and religious standards of the indigenous population?

These are difficult questions, and we will not be able to answer them all in this chapter. However, we will answer that part of the questions which relates to the issue of ethical relativism. **Ethical relativism** is a doctrine that is expressed (inadequately and misleadingly) in adages such as "When in Rome, do as the Romans do." More precisely, it is the belief that moral values are relative to a particular culture and cannot be judged outside of that culture. In examining ethical relativism, we shall be concerned with understanding what makes it attractive to many of us, for it is a doctrine that many people accept, or at least *think* they accept. Yet we shall also ask whether ethical relativism actually succeeds in delivering on its promises, in providing the things that seem to make it attractive. Then we shall look at the standard alternative, moral absolutism, and examine some of its strengths and weaknesses. Finally, we shall suggest a middle ground between relativism and absolutism, one which combines the attractions of both without their liabilities.

THE ATTRACTIONS OF ETHICAL RELATIVISM

Ethical relativism is an attractive doctrine, and in this section we shall see some of the reasons *why* it is attractive. People are drawn to it for any of several possible reasons. First, ethical relativism seems to encourage moral tolerance and understanding, attitudes that most of us find highly desirable. Second, it seems to fit the facts about moral diversity much better than any alternative. Third, it seems that no one has produced a moral system that has commanded universal assent and it seems unlikely that anyone will in the foreseeable future. Fourth, some people hold that everything is relative, and for them ethical relativism is just a corollary of a more general relativism about all beliefs. Finally, we often feel that we have no right to make moral judgment about other people because we ourselves have led far from perfect moral lives. Ethical relativism is often a way of saying, "Don't judge me and I won't judge you." Let us examine each of these lines of argument.

The Need for Tolerance

A Plea for Tolerance and Understanding   Ethical relativism is initially attractive to many of us because it offers the promise of *tolerance* and *understanding,* attitudes most of us value highly. All too often in the past, we have rushed to judgment, letting condemnation eliminate the need for tolerance, allowing superiority to substitute for understanding. Ethical relativism holds the promise of a tolerant attitude of "live and let live."

Moral absolutism, on the other hand, can be a morally intolerant and insensitive position, one which is all too willing to condemn what it does not understand. This argument sometimes is placed within the context of the history of anthropology, which is one of the disciplines most directly involved with issues of cultural relativism. Early anthropology, so the argument goes, was absolutist, measuring the entire world in terms of its own standards and generally finding the rest of the world lacking. So, for example, anthropologists would often refer to the peoples they studied as "barbarians" or "primitive societies." Anthropology made progress, they contend, when it moved toward a more relativistic stance, when it recognized that societies that are different from our own are not necessarily primitive or inferior. Indeed, *we* often appear barbaric to these so-called primitive societies. (When Europeans first reached China, the Chinese were appalled at the Westerners' lack of cleanliness and manners; to the Chinese, it was the Europeans who were the barbarians.) Each society, relativism suggests, should be judged in terms of its own standards rather than be measured in terms of our ethnocentric expectations. We shall return to this comparison with anthropology in the final part of this chapter, and at that point I want again to argue in favor of a third possibility. We shall consider some of the problems with this argument about tolerance shortly.

Tolerance and Understanding   Oddly, given that relativism frequently is associated with a plea for greater understanding as well as tolerance, it often is associated with a belief that we can*not* understand other cultures. Indeed, it is often the conclusion of an argument that begins with a premise such as "We can never (fully) understand another culture." The conclusion then drawn is that we ought not to judge any other culture, and the implicit premise is "We ought not to judge anything which we do not (fully) understand." We will discuss the merits of this argument below.

The Fact of Moral Diversity

Morality and the Ik   For decades, anthropological research has produced countless examples of moral diversity. One of the most striking of recent examples is a mountain tribe in Africa called the Ik. The Ik seem to explode any belief that we have in a universal morality. They do not even bother to cook their food—they just eat it as soon as they find it. They hide from one another so that no one can see them eating and steal their food. The adults do not bring food back to the village for the children, the aged, or the infirm. If they see a weak old man eating, they will sometimes even take the food out of his mouth and eat it themselves. Children are breast-fed until they are about three years old, and then unceremoniously kicked out and left to fend for themselves. The kids form gangs to hunt for food, but they never develop enduring friendships. Even the name of their tribe—the Ik—seems oddly appropriate to English-speakers. Colin Turnbull, whose *Mountain People* is the most detailed study of the Ik, refers to them as the "Loveless People." They pose a deep question to those who believe that there are certain fundamental values common to all societies, since they seem to lack almost all the moral qualities that we admire in people. They appear to provide an almost irrefutable example that proves that moral goodness is not universal and is not found in all societies.

It is worth noting, however, that the Ik were not always this way. Once they were a proud, nomadic tribe of warriors whose hunting grounds were turned into a national park. Their values were hardly unusual for nomadic tribes, and there is little evidence of their current lack of compassion. However, the government forced them to settle in a mountainous area of northern Uganda plagued by droughts and famine. It was during this period that their moral code declined rapidly.

Initially, one of the most attractive aspects of the relativist's position is that it gives adequate recognition to this kind of moral diversity. Different cultures have such widely divergent moral codes that the notion of a universal morality of any kind simply seems to defy the facts: there is radical moral diversity in our world. Indeed, even individuals within a single society seem to exhibit great diversity in the range of moral values they accept. The only adequate way of recognizing this fact, according to the relativist, is by accepting ethical relativism.

The Lack of a Plausible Alternative

Relativists have another argument at their disposal, one which seems to supplement and strengthen the first argument. They issue the following challenge: "If you claim that ethical relativism is mistaken, then show me a plausible alternative. Show me a set of moral values that everyone accepts, or even that everyone plausibly could accept." In other words, they are suggesting that we may come to agree with ethical relativism by default: no alternative moral system has managed to represent everyone. Not only, they continue, is this fact true of the world at large, it is also true of moral philosophers. These are the people one would expect to agree on basic moral principles, if anyone could, because they spend their lives thinking and talking and writing about such things. Yet when we look at the opinions of many moral philosophers today, we see that there is a tremendous amount of disagreement, even about fundamental moral values. Finally, relativists argue, this situation is in sharp contrast to science and medicine. Certainly there is disagreement in those areas, but there is also widespread agreement on many fundamentals. Since morality has never exhibited that kind of consensus, it is pointless to expect that it ever will.

The Relativity of All Understanding

There is yet a fourth route that leads to ethical relativism, and it begins with the conviction that *all* knowledge and understanding are relative. In its strongest version, this position even claims that truth in the natural sciences is relative to the culture and conceptual framework within which it is expressed. Other cultures may develop quite different ways of understanding and controlling the natural world. In some cultures, magic occupies the place that science holds in our society. Strong relativists would claim that we cannot say that science is right and magic wrong; rather, each is appropriate to, and only to be judged in terms of, the culture in which it is situated.

Other more moderate versions of relativism make a slightly more modest claim. They say that *the meaning of human behavior is always relative to the culture in which it occurs.* In one desert society, it is a sign of friendship and respect to spit at the foot of another person; such behavior means something quite different in our own society. In some cultures, eating dogs is as acceptable as eating cows is in Western societies. In our society, we consider killing dogs cruelty to animals; in India, killing cows is a sacrilege. The meaning of the act is different, depending on the society. In India, how we act toward cows is a *religious* issue, and this attitude is what gives it special meaning. In our country, how we treat dogs is a matter of how we relate to pets, which is almost an issue of *friendship*. More generally, the meaning of any action depends on the cultural context within which it is performed. Consequently, the relativist argues, the moral dimension of our actions is similarly dependent on cultural context for meaning.

Don't Cast the First Stone

There is a final consideration that often weighs in favor of relativism, and it centers around doubts whether we have the *right* to judge other people. Often people are hesitant to pass judgment on someone else's actions because they feel that if they had been in that same situation, they might have done the same thing. Since few people like to condemn themselves, it is just a short step to saying that they should not condemn other people either. In one sense, this attitude is a self-protective strategy: if I do not condemn others, then they cannot condemn me. Yet in another sense, it is a position that emphasizes consistency: if I am unwilling to judge myself harshly, then I forfeit my right to judge others in such a manner. In yet a third sense, it is a position of humility, recalling Jesus's injunction, "Let one who is without sin cast the first stone." Whatever way one takes it, it is a position that denies that one has a *right* to pass judgment on other people. It is, moreover, a position that becomes even more plausible in times when there seems to be fundamental disagreement about basic moral values. "Who," my students often ask, "am I to judge someone else?" We will discuss possible answers to this important question below.

THE DEFINITION OF ETHICAL RELATIVISM

We have begun to consider some of the reasons why ethical relativism is attractive, but we have not really looked closely at what ethical relativism maintains. As we shall see, there are several different positions that often are lumped together under this single name. It will be important to distinguish among these various doctrines, for some versions of ethical relativism may prove to be true, while others turn out to be false.

Ethical Relativism: Descriptive and Normative

There is a sense in which there is little disagreement among philosophers about the truth of one type of ethical relativism. It is clear, simply as a matter of fact, that different people have some different moral beliefs—sometimes radically so. Various societies in the past have engaged in such practices as cannibalism or sacrificing human beings to the gods, and those practices were viewed within those societies as morally acceptable, often even as morally commendable. Indeed, even in our own day, there exist some isolated societies that until recently have approved of such actions.

Descriptive Ethical Relativism   Simply to state that different people in fact have different moral beliefs, without taking any stand on the rightness or wrongness of those beliefs, is to accept **descriptive ethical relativism,** which is, as I have already implied, a rather uncontroversial claim, for it does not in any way commit us to saying that these other moral beliefs are also *correct.* Thus someone could be a moral absolutist (that is, someone who believes that there is one and only one true morality) and still accept descriptive ethical relativism, since the absolutist would simply say that those who do not accept this true moral code are wrong. Descriptive ethical relativism does not entail any beliefs about whether the moral codes of various societies are right or wrong.

Normative Ethical Relativism   The more controversial and interesting position is what we can call **normative ethical relativism.** The normative ethical relativist puts forward a crucial additional claim not found in descriptive ethical relativism, namely, that each moral code is only *valid* relative to the culture in which it exists. Thus, for example, if cannibalism is acceptable according to the moral code of society X, then members of that society are right in permitting their people to practice cannibalism, even though it would not be permissible for people in our society to do so. A controversial doctrine, normative ethical relativism suggests that what is right in one culture is not right in another and that members of one culture either should not pass any moral judgments on any other culture or else must endorse the moral judgments of other cultures as right for those cultures. (Because normative ethical relativism is both the interesting and controversial claim and the one we will center our discussion on, when I refer to "relativism" or "ethical relativism" I will mean "normative ethical relativism" unless otherwise noted.)

Types of Ethical Relativism

Descriptive	Claims as a matter of fact that different cultures have different values.
Normative	Claims that each culture's values are right for that culture.

If normative ethical relativism is correct, then the kid of truth that we find in morality is far different from the kind of truth characteristic of everyday factual knowledge, scientific knowledge, or mathematics. If I know that the Morning Star and the Evening Star are the same celestial body (Venus), then I know that it is true for everyone. If some society believes they are two different stars, that society is simply wrong. Similarly, many societies in the past have held that the earth is flat, but we would not hesitate today to state that their belief is false. So, too, we can say with assurance that $2 + 2 = 4$ absolutely, even if some societies do not believe that to be the case. Those who do not believe it are just mistaken. However, if the normative ethical relativist is correct, we cannot say that intentionally killing innocent human beings is always wrong in the same way, because if there is some society that believes that sacrificing innocent victims to the gods is a morally good thing to do, then it is not wrong *for them* according to the normative ethical relativist.

We have now seen one of the basic ambiguities in the claim that morality is relative: it may be either a descriptive or a normative claim. Now we need to get a clearer idea of precisely what we may mean by ethical relativism. We can do so by looking more closely at two important questions: what is morality relative *to,* and *what portion* of our morality is relative? We shall see that there are widely divergent answers to these questions.

Relative to What?

Individuating Cultures So far, we have presumed that the ethical relativist believes that morality is relative to a particular *culture.* That, however, is no easy notion. What, precisely, do we mean by a culture? Typically, we tend to think of some isolated tribe in New Guinea or some other secluded place, and this idea does provide a clear-cut example of another culture that is radically different from our own and which generally is isolated from our own. However, such examples are quickly becoming the exceptions. There are few such isolated cultures remaining in the world today, and it is likely that their number and degree of isolation will rapidly diminish in the near future. The simple fact of the matter is that most cultures interact with and mutually influence other cultures. In fact, the issue is even more complicated because cultures often seem to contain quite a bit of internal diversity.

Consider American culture. We may refer to it as though there were some single culture, but when we look more closely, we uncover much diversity. A generation ago there were many neighborhoods in major cities where one did not need to know English. German, Lithuanian, Polish, Italian, Greek, or any number of other European languages might have sufficed. Were these part of American culture or should they be seen as part of the culture of their original country? Today Vietnamese, Korean, Tagalog, Cambodian, Laotian, and other Asian and Pacific languages predominate, some in these same neighborhoods. Again, should we see the culture as American or as belonging to another country? This problem concerns how we *individuate a culture,* that is, how we draw the lines to separate one culture from another. It is rare in these days of shifting political systems and mass migrations of people that cultural boundaries coincide strictly with geographical ones.

Furthermore, in an age of increasing mass communication and ever-expanding international trade, individual cultures are less and less likely to remain isolated.

The problem of individuating a culture is by no means an abstract issue created solely by philosophers who enjoy drawing logical distinctions. It is very much a problem of everyday living. Consider the moral conflicts that individuals encounter who find themselves on the borderline of two such cultures. For instance, imagine that you were teaching grammar school in an area of the Southwest where a number of the students came from Hopi Indian families. When one student does not know the answer to a question in grammar school, the teacher often calls on other students until one comes up with the correct answer. Yet Hopi schoolchildren would regard it as an insult to provide the answer when the first student did not know it, for they have quite different views on the morality of competition. As a teacher, do you follow the morality of the dominant white group or the morality of the minority Native American group? (Indeed, do we determine which group is "dominant" by sheer numbers or by the power they have in the political and economic system?) Do we have one culture here or two?

In a similar way, think of the problems encountered by American businesspeople in other countries. In South Africa, for example, much of the white population still strongly supports apartheid; some of the white population and virtually all of the black and mixed race population oppose it strongly. If we have businesses with branch offices there, whose values do we follow? Our own? The values of the majority of whites? Those of the majority of blacks and a minority of whites? Again, do we have one culture here or two? These are the questions about the individuation of cultures that are faced every day by people and which directly raise the question of ethical relativism.

From Relativism to Subjectivism   It is easy to see one direction in which this argument can lead. Some people have taken the question "what are our moral values relative to?" and given increasingly specific answers to it until they finally conclude that those values are relative to each individual person. If our values are partially shaped by the culture in which we live, are not our own individual values also shaped by more specific factors such as geographical location, period in history, family background, religion, schooling, early childhood experiences, and so on? Is it not plausible to believe that if our values are shaped by our culture, they are just as significantly influenced by our individual life histories? Soon we reach the point where instead of seeing values as relative to a culture, we see them as relative primarily to individual life histories. Those who maintain this position are claiming that *cultural ethical relativism collapses into ethical subjectivism.* They maintain, in other words, that cultural ethical relativism inevitably leads to a more radical position, **ethical subjectivism,** which claims that moral values are relative to each unique individual.

One of the reasons given in support of the claim that relativism leads to subjectivism already has been discussed; the difficulty in individuating cultures. The other reason usually given has also been hinted at; there are a number of individual factors (such as family background, religious training, economic status, and education) that seem to be at least as powerful as general cultural factors in shaping an individual's moral beliefs. Yet when our argument is stated in this way, something very interesting starts to emerge. We see that the relativist's claim is at least in part about the *causes* of our moral beliefs. Indeed, as we look more closely, we shall see that the relativist can be making several different claims—one about *understanding* and *judging* moral values, one about the *causes* of those values, one about their *justification,* and one about how to *act.* We will look more closely at this distinction when we discuss the nature of the relativist's claim, but first we must address the question of how much of our morality is relative according to the relativist.

When we claim that morality is relative, our claim is still vague. We have not answered the question of *how much* of morality is relative, which is a question of the *scope* of the relativist's claim. There are at least three ways of defining the scope of relativism. It is important to distinguish among these three, for it may well turn out that only one or two of these claims are true.

The Relativity of Behavior   The first thing that the relativist could be saying is that *moral behavior is relative to a particular culture* (or some other aspect of a person's background). This idea is certainly true in non-moral areas. In some cultures, for example, the polite way of expressing approval of the dinner is to belch; in our own society, such behavior would be considered ill-mannered. Approval would properly be expressed in some other way, such as complimenting the host on the meal. Similarly, spitting at another person's feet is a way of expressing respect in some desert cultures; the same behavior in our culture expresses contempt. Notice that there may be agreement here that it is a good thing to show appreciation of a meal, but the *way* in which that is expressed (that is, the behavior) differs from culture to culture. It seems uncontroversial to say that polite behavior is often relative to a particular culture.

The Relativity of Peripheral Values   The second thing that may be said to be relative is what I shall call peripheral values, the non-fundamental or somewhat secondary values of a culture. In our own culture, for example, respect for innocent human life is taken to be a fundamental moral value; individual privacy is a less fundamental one; freedom to smoke cigarettes is becoming comparatively peripheral and low-level. Here, then, is the second claim that the relativist could be making: *peripheral values vary from culture to culture.* So, for example, the value of private property may be quite important in one society and of relatively little significance in another. One culture may value monogamy quite strongly, another may endorse polygamy; but both might value the basic family, especially for child rearing, even though they differ in their respective definitions of the family unit.

Of course, there is no clear-cut line that separates low-level values from fundamental ones, and one point of disagreement between two cultures may be precisely whether a particular value should be taken as fundamental or peripheral. The distinction is unavoidably vague, but nonetheless useful, as we shall now see.

The Relativity of Fundamental Values   Imagine, in discussing ethical relativism, that someone supports the relativist's position by claiming that morally

What Is Relative?

Behavior	How different values are expressed in action varies from one culture to another
Peripheral Values	Secondary or peripheral values vary from one culture to another
Fundamental Values	Basic values vary from one culture to another

acceptable behavior varies from culture to culture and that, furthermore, moral values such as privacy or monogamy are different in various cultures. You easily could imagine someone replying to this assertion in the following way.

> Yes, I agree that there are these differences among cultures. However, while many things are relative, there are some things that are absolute. Virtually no culture believes in torturing and killing innocent children—and if it does, it is simply wrong in holding that value. There are some values, such as respect for innocent human life, which, though they may be few in number, are not relative. Cultures that do not accept these values are simply wrong.

The person who maintains this position is conceding the first two forms of relativism discussed in this section (the relativity of behavior and the relativity of low-level moral values), but disputes the relativity of fundamental values. There are, as I hope to show below, good reasons for rejecting the relativist's claim when it comes to fundamental values.

What Kind of Doctrine Is Ethical Relativism?

There is another kind of ambiguity in the relativist's position, one which can cause serious confusion if not brought to light. When relativists say, "Moral values are relative to culture," they may mean several rather different things. Once again, it is necessary to distinguish among these different meanings because one or two of them may be true while the other(s) may be false. For the sake of clarity, I will present this ambiguity in terms of different versions of the adage "When in Rome, do as the Romans do." In this saying, Rome stands for any culture different from our own.

Action   The first sense in which ethical relativism may be intended is as a doctrine about action, a doctrine that tells us how to act. Here we see the full and straightforward force of the saying "When in Rome, do as the Romans do." It tells us to **always act in a way that is consistent with local customs and values,** which in fact turns out not only to be a guide to behaving in other cultures, but also in our own. It says that we should act in a way that is consistent with the moral standards of whatever culture we are in, including our own when we are at home.

As a doctrine of action, relativism is incomplete in three ways. First, it does not tell us how to act when two cultures overlap—an increasingly important issue, as we shall see below. Second, it does not tell us *why* we should act in this way. In order to do so, relativism as a doctrine of action usually depends on one of the other following versions of relativism for its justification. Third, it does not provide any leverage to convince the majority to change, since by definition whatever the majority believes to be right simply is right.

Understanding   The second claim that the relativist may be making is that *in order to understand a person's values and behavior, we must understand the cultural background out of which they arise.* We must, in other words, understand the Roman's behavior in terms of Roman society. This claim is relatively uncontroversial, at least in regard to behavior. The meaning of most behavior is embedded in a context of social meanings that at least to some extent vary from one culture to another. If we are to understand what a particular action or value means to a person in another culture, it is often necessary to understand that stock of background meanings which underlie its significance. To fail to do so is often to misunderstand and distort the meaning of the behavior we observe in another society.

There is an ambiguity in relativism as a doctrine of understanding, and it is one that is important in our assessment of the relativist's claim. When the relativist claims that behavior can be understood only relative to the specific cultural context within which it occurs, it is unclear whether an outsider to the culture can understand the behavior at all. In its **strong version,** this doctrine claims not only that all behavior must be understood relative to the cultural context, but also that the cultural context can be understood only by participants; consequently, outsiders cannot genuinely understand behavior in a society in which they are not participants and thus they are not entitled to make value judgments about that behavior. In its **weak version,** this doctrine maintains that meaning is relative to culture, but that outsiders can understand other cultures. This weaker version leaves the door open for dialogue between cultures and for mutual understanding. The stronger version seems to close the door to such dialogue and perhaps even precludes the possibility of anthropology.

Judgment   At this juncture, we encounter another ambiguity within relativism as a doctrine of understanding, and this ambiguity rests on the relation between understanding and judgment. Assuming that behavior must be understood relative to its cultural context, what does this assessment tell us about the moral judgments we make about the actions and values of other societies? There are three possibilities: (1) such behavior may not be judged at all by outsiders; (2) it may be judged by outsiders only in relation to the society's own values; and (3) it may be judged by outsiders even in relation to values which the society itself does not share. Relativism as a doctrine of judgment maintains that behavior within a society can be judged only by the standards of that society. We should judge Romans only by Roman standards. Again, this theory has a strong version and a weak version. The **strong version** maintains that only Romans can judge Romans by their own standards; the **weak version** allows anyone in principle to judge Romans as long as they employ Roman standards.

Explanation   In arguing in favor of relativism, some people claim to explain the origins of our moral values by showing that *moral values are caused or determined by cultural forces.* This claim, our fourth possible one, is equivalent to saying that if you were raised in Rome, you would have the values that the Romans have. The fact that people grew up in a particular culture explains *why* they have the specific values they do. Our own culture forces us to accept particular values, while living in another culture would cause us to believe in a different set of values, a concept closely related to what philosophers call **determinism,** that is, the belief that (in this case) our moral values are determined causally. In contrast, some philosophers claim that our values are, at least to some extent, *freely chosen.* They maintain that although our culture may initially shape our values, as we mature we come to make our own independent choices about what our values will be. This notion is a version of the dispute between freedom and determinism, which will be discussed in Chapter Five in our consideration of psychological egoism.

There is little chance that we will be able to unravel all the knotty issues surrounding freedom and determinism here, but we can at least note the following objection to the determinist's position. If we have no choice in our moral values, then there really is not much point in talking about them at all, because we will believe whatever we are determined to believe anyway. If there is not *some* room for freedom of choice, then we will just have whatever values we are determined to have. Yet the whole point of these discussions is that we have to make choices, and making choices presumes some degree of freedom. If determinism is true, there is no point in discussing what we ought to do. (This issue will be discussed in more detail in the chapter on Egoism.)

Justification   There is a fifth claim that the relativist may make: *moral values may be justified only relative to the standards of a particular culture.* In other words, when values are challenged or called into question in some way, the only appropriate way of justifying them is by an appeal to the standards of the culture. When in Rome, the only way of justifying one's actions and values is to appeal to fundamental values accepted by Roman society. This claim is distinct from any of the four preceding claims. One could, for example, maintain that values initially may be understood within the context of a particular culture and yet deny that they can be justified only in relation to that culture.

The question of justification of values is a tricky one, and it is important to realize what the alternatives are. Those who support the claim that moral values can be justified only in terms of the values of that culture encounter a possible problem: the fundamental values of the culture are not themselves open to justification. Those values simply have to be accepted as they are. Yet we can imagine cases, at least as outsiders to a particular culture, where we would want to question some of a society's values and claim that they should *not* be accepted as they are. The anti-Semitism of Nazi

Relativism as a Doctrine about:

Action	People ought to act according to the values of the culture in which they live
Understanding	People's values must be understood within their cultural context
Judgment	People's values can be judged only within their cultural context
Explanation	People's values are causally determined by cultural forces
Justification	People's values can be justified only in terms of their own culture

Germany, for example, became a fundamental value for a number of people in that society, but most of us today would want to deny that that value was justified, even for those in that situation. Yet the relativist's position on justification would seem to leave no basis for those in Nazi Germany to have questioned that value. We shall consider this problem in more detail below when we discuss relativism and moral change.

We have now seen some of the important distinctions that need to be drawn in talking about relativism. They are summarized in the chart on the previous page.

As we shall see by the end of this chapter, relativism as a doctrine of action is largely useless, unable to answer the questions that confront us today. Relativism as a doctrine of judgment, of explanation, and of justification is seriously incomplete. But relativism as a doctrine of understanding has a lot of merit and should be accepted. Let us now turn to a consideration of some of the reasons why ethical relativism will not suffice as a doctrine of action or justification, even though it is partially valid as a doctrine of understanding.

THE LIMITS OF ETHICAL RELATIVISM

Despite its attractiveness, many philosophers have been hesitant to accept ethical relativism. A number of arguments have been advanced against it, some of which are put forward primarily by philosophers, others of which are shared by the general public. In this section, we shall consider five of these arguments: (1) the facts of moral diversity do not actually justify ethical relativism; (2) the refutation of relativism through the defense of one's own absolutist position; (3) the claim that relativism is self-defeating, leading to the acceptance of absolutism or intolerance; (4) the concern that ethical relativism is really a form of moral isolationism or indifference that ignores the fact that moral judgments are unavoidable; and (5) the claim that relativism is unable to provide an adequate basis for moral change. Let us consider each of these arguments in turn.

The Fact of Moral Diversity Reconsidered

We can already see in light of some of the distinctions drawn above that the argument for moral diversity is less strong than it originally appeared to be. First, the fact of moral diversity is certainly sufficient to establish *descriptive ethical relativism,* but taken by itself it does not necessarily commit us to *normative ethical relativism.* We could argue, for example, that there are many bizarre scientific views in the world (today as well as in the past), but the mere fact of different views does not entail the conclusion that each of them is right within its own culture or context. Similarly, there are many people with unusual medical beliefs, but we do not hesitate to label at least some of them quacks. The mere fact of diversity, in other words, does not suffice alone to support the conclusion that we cannot make judgments about the moral values held by other cultures.

Second, we have to be wary of the level of generality on which the relativist's argument is stated. Recall the earlier distinction among behavior, low-level values, and fundamental values. We may well want to concede that respect for the dignity of the person is shown in different ways in different cultures and that other cultures should not necessarily be compelled to manifest this value through the same kinds of behavior that we find appropriate. But most of us certainly would draw the line at *some* point. The Nazis' attempted extermination of Jews, Gypsies, homosexuals, and others is certainly one such point. It may have *seemed* right to some of them within their culture, but I clearly would want to say that they were wrong if they held that belief.

The Appeal to an Absolute Position

Perhaps the most common way of arguing against ethical relativism is to present an alternative, that is, a position that one claims is absolute. We find absolutes in everyday life quite often. Sometimes it is a religiously based viewpoint which is being advocated to the exclusion of all others, at other times it may be grounded in a particular political idealogy. Sometimes it is rooted in philosophical systems, and in the following chapters we shall critically assess five of the primary attempts to provide a philosophical basis for an absolutist morality: the libertarian program of the ethical egoist, Kant's ethics of duty, a utilitarian ethics of consequences, modern attempts to see ethics primarily as rights, and recent attempts to revive Aristotle's approach to the ethics of character. Certainly the strongest refutation of relativism would be the introduction of a moral system which not only claimed to be absolute, but also which everyone actually accepted as such.

There is no simple way of evaluating here all of these attempts at an absolutist morality, although we shall examine several of the strictly philosophical positions in subsequent chapters. Yet there are many other absolutist positions which have not received elaborate philosophical expression, and an examination of these is simply beyond the scope of this book. It is important to note, however, what relativists would say to all of these attempted refutations. None, they would claim, has *in fact* achieved anything approaching universality. While there are groups of people who believe strongly that each of these positions is absolute, relativists see it as simply supporting their claim. Different groups, they would argue, have different sets of moral beliefs, and relativism is the only plausible way of accounting for these differences.

Relativists are not only demanding that an absolutist system of morality *claim* to be absolute, they are also demanding that it be *accepted* by everyone (or at least a very large percentage of people) as absolute if it is to count as a refutation of relativism. Claiming to be absolute is simply not enough, for many moral systems already do that. Indeed, it is precisely the fact that many such systems *claim* to be absolute that creates the problem relativism tries to solve. Until we all agree about which system of morality is absolute, the absolutist refutation of relativism falls short of the mark.

Is Relativism Self-Defeating?

The Relativist in an Absolutist Society   There is a paradoxical implication in relativism as a doctrine of action. If you should do in Rome as the Romans do, what happens if the Romans assume a very absolutist attitude toward everyone else in the world? What if the Romans turn out to be highly ethnocentric, taking their own culture's values and customs as the absolute measure of everyone else's? Then, it would seem, if we are in Rome, and if the Romans are absolutist and ethnocentric, then we should be absolutist and ethnocentric. Yet this absolutism is precisely the kind of culturally chauvinistic attitude that the relativist is trying to convince us to give up. If relativism tells us to do as the Romans do, and if the Romans are not relativists, then relativism tells us to act like non-relativists. Such an injunction appears to be self-defeating.

The Relativist in an Intolerant Society   There is another closely related difficulty with relativism as a doctrine of action. One of the principal attractions of relativism is that it seems to promise tolerance. Yet what if the other culture is intolerant? Do we then accept intolerance as one of our values when in that culture? If, to return to our standard example, the Romans are intolerant, should we also be intolerant when we are in Rome? It would seem that relativism as a doctrine of action commits us to this approach, and that threatens to undermine one of its attractions.

This fault is also true of relativism as a doctrine of understanding and judgment, but in a slightly different way. As a doctrine of understanding and judgment, relativism seems to be the clearest example of tolerance imaginable. It recommends a highly tolerant attitude toward others, and yet it becomes a problem when those others are themselves intolerant. If relativism says do not judge the Romans, be tolerant of them, and if the Romans themselves are very judgmental and intolerant, then relativism commits us to being tolerant toward intolerance.

The Value of Tolerance   As we have seen, one aspect of relativism that makes it initially so attractive is that it promises a more tolerant attitude toward other cultures. We also have seen that this promise may at times be illusory, since relativism as a doctrine of action might oblige us to adopt intolerant values if we were in a society which valued intolerance. Yet there is another difficulty with tolerance which we have not yet addressed here. Granting that tolerance should be an important value for us, should we place it above all others? Should tolerance be our *highest* value?

There are clearly some areas in which most of us are inclined to be tolerant. Other cultures may have different moral codes governing, say, business relations or family obligations, and most of us would probably tolerate and respect those differences, even if we would not personally want to live by them. Yet in other areas, we are more likely to draw the line. Racism in South Africa, for example, is something that calls forth protest from many of us. The Nazis' attempted genocide against the Jews, the Turkish massacre of the Armenians, and Pol Pot's genocide in Cambodia are but a few examples of the wanton killing that outrages almost all of us. When faced with atrocities such as these, tolerance has to take second place to other more important values, such as respect for innocent human life and justice. Tolerance, in other words, is an important value—it just is not appropriate as our *highest* value.

Relativism as Moral Isolationism

There is yet another difficulty with ethical relativism: all too often it seems to lead to a kind of moral isolationism in which we simply do not care about the rest of the world. There are several aspects to this isolationism.

Relativism as a Conversation Stopper   In order to understand relativism, we need to consider not only what relativism actually says, but also the *function* of the appeal to relativism in moral discourse. Consider, in this regard, the typical way that appeals to relativism function in a conversation. Imagine two persons discussing and disagreeing about some moral issue such as abortion or capital punishment. If one of them says, "Well, after all, it's all relative, isn't it?", this serves to bring the conversation to a halt. What, after all, can you say *after* you've said it is all relative? It is crucial to see how the appeal to relativism works in such situations. When someone says, "it's all relative," they are often also *implicitly* saying that something follows from this claim, namely, "therefore, we cannot criticize it." It is this implication which is, I think, most doubtful. If the appeal to relativism were used to begin a conversation rather than end it, we would have quite a different picture of its rhetorical function.

Relativism as a Protection from Criticism   There is another aspect of the way in which relativism is used in conversation which is the opposite side of the implicit claim that we cannot criticize others. If we cannot criticize others because "it's all relative," then neither can *they* criticize *us*. In a sense, this approach may be the payoff that relativism has for many people: it insulates them against criticism from the outside. It nullifies in advance any possible objection to their behavior or values that anyone outside their culture could present.

The full force of this hidden implication of relativism becomes apparent when we recall that relativism often collapses into subjectivism, namely, the belief that values are relative to each individual person. If that were true, then the hidden implication of relativism might be that no one has a right to criticize us. We are each, as it were, worlds unto ourselves, and no one is entitled to criticize a person's choices because no one is in the same situation. The appeal to relativism thereby becomes an insulation against possible criticism, a way of protecting oneself against any possible moral objections to one's behavior or values.

What Is Wrong with Moral Isolationism?

What, one might plausibly ask, is wrong with this hidden implication of the appeal to relativism? There are at least three problems with this isolationist attitude: (1) it fails to provide an answer about how we should resolve moral disagreements between cultures; (2) it ignores the fact that we live in a constantly shrinking world which necessitates inter-cultural moral judgments; and (3) it overlooks the ways in which intra-cultural as well as inter-cultural moral judgments are necessary parts of everyday life.

The Absence of an Answer   First, the appeal of relativism claims to function as a way of dealing with moral conflict and with disagreements about moral values. But the difficulty is that often relativism is not an answer to the question of how to deal with such differences, but is rather *the absence of an answer.* Faced with moral disagreements, the relativist says, in effect, "let's not talk about it," which is not an answer, but instead is the refusal even to search for an answer. But why, we may well ask, are answers necessary?

Relativism in a Shrinking World   Relativism as an attitude toward other cultures made more sense when cultures were in fact much more isolated from one another. A century ago it was not uncommon to find isolated cultures, often tribes that lived in remote jungles or mountains, that had had virtually no contact with our own culture. In such instances, relativism might have expressed an attitude of respect toward those cultures, an unwillingness to interfere with the culture or to judge it too quickly. Such an attitude of non-interference would be particularly appropriate to a scientific, anthropological approach to such a society.

Such societies are increasingly rare today, and it seems highly improbable that they can escape interacting with other more powerful societies. When interaction occurs, the problem is to decide whose values should prevail. And here, precisely where it is needed most, ethical relativism fails to deliver an answer. As different cultures interact more and more, we need to develop rules that govern the *intersection* of two cultures, and this union is what relativism fails to offer. When in Rome, relativism as a doctrine of action suggests, do as the Romans do. Yet there is an area of overlap, an area that is neither purely Roman nor purely American, in which the two cultures meet—and it is here that we need guidance. This overlap emerges most clearly in our world in two ways. First, cultures overlap through trade and commerce. Nations must deal with each other and consequently must develop rules of interaction that are acceptable to *both* cultures. Second, the rapid growth of communications and of the news and entertainment media has increased the amount of influences cultures have on one another. In both of these areas, the larger, more powerful, and more productive cultures threaten to overwhelm the smaller, weaker, and less productive ones. German children grow up watching a number of American television programs; American children watch American programs. We are, in other words, living in a shrinking world, and we need guidance about how to interact with other cultures. To the extent that relativism simply says that each culture is a world unto itself, it fails to give us such guidance.

The Unavoidability of Moral Judgments   Relativism, we have seen, often collapses into subjectivism. Just as cross-cultural moral judgments are increasingly unavoidable in our world, so, too, is it impossible to avoid interpersonal moral judgments. Yet when ethical relativism collapses into moral subjectivism, it is precisely such judgments that it seeks to avoid. To the extent that interpersonal moral judgments are unavoidable, and to the extent that ethical relativism fails to offer us any guidance in making those judgments, relativism does not provide us with an answer to the moral questions that face us.

There can be no doubt that interpersonal moral judgments are unavoidable. We continually make decisions that affect other people, just as their decisions affect us—and in both cases, we need to make moral judgments about the acceptability of such decisions. Nor can we remain neutral about such issues, for we often are forced to make decisions which implicitly take a stance on moral issues. Consider abortion, for example. We may not have to make a personal decision about whether to have an abortion, but we often make decisions that either support or condemn such a practice. The allocation of our tax dollars, the political candidates we support, the kind of sex education we encourage in schools—these are but a few of the ways in which we indirectly take a stand on the morality of abortion.

Even in matters that do not require a decision, we make moral judgments. Recall that moral judgments do not need to be negative. When we say that someone is good, we are making a moral judgment just as much as if we were condemning the person. If we try to avoid moral judgments, then we have to give up positive judgments as well as negative ones. We even have to give up such things as blaming or gossiping, both of which have a significant component of moral judgment. Moral judgments, in other words, permeate our everyday life, and it is hard to imagine what life would be without them.

Relativism and Moral Change

There is an additional set of difficulties associated with ethical relativism, and these relate to the issue of moral progress. Let us examine each of these.

Pressure to Change   There was a cartoon years ago in the *New Yorker* that captured well one of the difficulties with relativism. It showed a group of people marching down a street, carrying signs such as "It's a point of view," "This is just my opinion," "My perspective," and "This is just another way of looking at things." Although the signs were not explicit appeals to relativism, they were close enough to illustrate one of its drawbacks. When we claim that everything is relative, we say that our own point of view is valid only for ourselves. Once we do this, we lose any moral leverage for claiming that other people ought to heed what we say.

Consider the civil rights movement in America. If Martin Luther King, Jr., had been a relativist, in effect he would have said, "I have a dream—but, of course, that's only my limited point of view, valid within my context but not binding on anyone outside of that context." For the full-fledged moral relativist, there is no vantage point from which to exert moral pressure, for each person is considered right relative to his or her culture.

There is, of course, one way in which relativists do have some moral leverage: they are justified in objecting to anything which is *not* consistent with the values of the culture. Yet this makes relativism a profoundly conservative doctrine in ways that may be unacceptable. In a racist society, relativists are justified only in objecting to those who are *opposed* to racism, those who are in favor of equal treatment. This is not to suggest, of course, that relativists are necessarily racists, or anything of the kind. Rather, it is to say that relativists in a racist society can offer no *reasons* why someone should not be a racist, no *justification* for rejecting racism.

Moral Progress   Another difficulty that relates to this issue is whether the relativist can offer a satisfactory account of moral progress. When relativists say that morality is relative to a culture, they usually also are saying that a culture changes over time. Consequently, what might be morally right at one time might be morally wrong at some other time. Just as we cannot legitimately impose one culture's values on another, so, too, we are not permitted to impose one *epoch's* values on those of another epoch. Each era must be understood and judged in terms of its own values.

The difficulty with this claim is that each epoch is, in effect, right unto itself; consequently, it is impossible to say that one is any better than any other. Yet if we cannot make this judgment then it makes no sense to talk about moral progress (or moral decline, either). Just as we cannot say that one society is better than another, neither can we say that one historical period is better than any other. Each has to be judged only in relation to itself. For the relativist, there is no overarching standard in terms of which the various epochs could be judged.

This argument contrasts sharply to our attitude toward, say, science or medicine. A century ago, people were bled with leeches when they had infections; now physicians administer antibiotics. This is progress. Antibiotics are more effective than leeches in eliminating infections. Yet the relativist cannot make similar judgments about moral progress. If we used to hang pickpockets and now we give them a jail sentence, the relativist can say only that we now have different standards, not that we have *better* standards. Similarly, if we used to condone slavery and we now value and strive toward genuine freedom and equality, the relativist can see the development only as change, not as progress. To claim that these changes were improvements would be to claim that there was some standard in terms of which they could both be judged—and it is precisely this understanding which relativism precludes. Each age can be judged only by its own standards.

Where Do We Go from Here?

Where, then, are we left in our attempt to decide whether ethical relativism is true or not? It seems that we have some strong arguments in favor of both sides, and we have some very powerful objections to both sides. Are we to give up, or do we perhaps just ignore the arguments on one side and continue to believe whichever position we prefer? As long as we see ourselves as confined to these two options, relativism and absolutism, there will appear to be no satisfactory answer. However, I think there is a third option, a middle ground between relativism and absolutism that combines the attractive features of both without the liabilities of either. It is to this option that we now turn.

FALLIBILISTIC ETHICAL PLURALISM

Some Preliminary Conclusions

The Inadequacy of Ethical Relativism   Several conclusions emerge from the preceding remarks. First, *ethical relativism is simply inadequate.* As a doctrine of action, it fails to provide us with guidance precisely where we need it most—at the intersection of two cultures. As a doctrine of judgment, it leads to an unacceptable and unrealistic moral isolationism. As a doctrine of causal explanation, it commits us to a determinism that creates more problems than it solves. Yet as a doctrine of understanding, it makes an important contribution, especially through its emphasis on tolerance and the contextuality of our understanding of moral practices. It is precisely this dual emphasis on tolerance and contextuality which we must retain.

The Failure of Ethical Absolutism   Second, *ethical absolutism also fails as a moral theory.* Certainly there are plenty of candidates for such absolutism, but that is precisely the problem. There is no single absolutist position which virtually everyone acknowledges as correct, nor is there any reason to expect that such a consensus will emerge in the near future. Moreover, absolutism seems to carry precisely those dangers that relativism avoids. The twin dangers of intolerance and lack of understanding, although not a necessary part of absolutism, are certainly dangers that often accompany it. It is precisely these which we want to avoid.

The Inevitability of Moral Disagreement   Third, it is reasonable to assume that we will continue to have moral disagreements for the foreseeable future and that, given the shrinking character of our world, such disagreements will become increasingly unavoidable. *Disagreement and difference are standard features of the moral landscape.* We need a moral theory that recognizes this fact and provides an appropriate interpretation of it. Two interpretations seem to me to be unsuitable: (1) those which see such disagreement as a sufficient basis for simply giving up on ethical reflection, for saying the undertaking is futile; and (2) those which see such disagreement simply as an indication of how wrong other people can be. In both cases, disagreement is not something that we can learn from; it is not a positive source of understanding.

Why Should I Be Moral?

F. H. Bradley

Why should I be moral?[1] The question is natural, and yet seems strange. It appears to be one we ought to ask, and yet we feel, when we ask it, that we are wholly removed from the moral point of view.

To ask the question Why? is rational; for reason teaches us to do nothing blindly, nothing without end or aim. She teaches us that what is good must be good for something, and that what is good for nothing is not good at all. And so we take it as certain that there is an end on one side, means on the other; and that only if the end is good, and the means conduce to it, have we a right to say the means are good. It is rational, then, always to inquire, Why should I do it?

---

[1]Let me observe here that the word "moral" has three meanings, which must be throughout these pages distinguished by the context. (1) Moral is opposed to *non*-moral. The moral world, or world of morality, is opposed to the natural world, where morality can not exist. (2) Within the moral world of moral agents, "moral" is opposed to *im*moral. (3) Again, within the moral world, and the moral part of the moral world, "moral" is further restricted to the *personal* side of the moral life and the moral institutions. It stands for the *inner* relation of this or that will to the universal, not to the whole, outer and inner, realization of morality. *Source: Ethical Studies,* Essay II. Oxford: The Clarendon Press, 1876, 3–28.

But here the question seems strange. For morality (and she too is reason) teaches us that, if we look on her only as good for something else, we never in that case have seen her at all. She says that she is an end to be desired for her own sake, and not as a means to something beyond. Degrade her, and she disappears; and, to keep her, we must love and not merely use her. And so at the question Why? we are in trouble, for that does assume, and does take for granted, that virtue in this sense is unreal, and what we believe is false. Both virtue and the asking Why? seem rational, and yet incompatible one with the other; and the better course will be, not forthwith to reject virtue in favour of the question, but rather to inquire concerning the nature of the Why?

Why should I be virtuous? Why should I? Could anything be more modest? Could anything be less assuming? It is not a dogma; it is only a question. And yet a question may contain (perhaps must contain) an assumption more or less hidden; or, in other words, a dogma. Let us see what is assumed in the asking of our question.

In "Why should I be moral?" the "Why should I?" was another way of saying, What good is virtue? or rather, For what is it good? and we saw that in asking, Is virtue good as a means, and how so? we do assume that virtue is not good, except as a means. The dogma at the root of the question is hence clearly either (1) the general statement that only means are good, or (2) the particular assertion of this in the case of virtue.

To explain; the question For what? Whereto? is either universally applicable, or not so. It holds everywhere, or we mean it to hold only here. Let us suppose, in the first place, that it is meant to hold everywhere.

Then (1) we are taking for granted that nothing is good in itself; that only the means to something else are good; that "good," in a word,= "good for," and good for something else. Such is the general canon by which virtue would have to be measured.

No one perhaps would explicitly put forward such a canon, and yet it may not be a waste of time to examine it.

The good is a means: a means is a means to something else, and this is an end. Is the end good? No; if we hold to our general canon, it is not good as an end: the good was always good for something else, and was a means. To be good, the end must be a means, and so on for ever in a process which has no limit. If we ask now What is good? we must answer, There is nothing which is *not* good, for there is nothing which may not be regarded as conducing to something outside itself. Everything is relative to something else. And the essence of the good is to exist by virtue of something else and something else for ever. Everything *is* something else, is the result which at last we are brought to, if we insist on pressing our canon as universally applicable.

But the above is not needed perhaps; for those who introduced the question Why? did not think of things in general. The good for them was not an infinite process of idle distinction. Their interest is practical, and they do and must understand by the good (which they call a means) some means to an end in itself; which latter they assume, and unconsciously fix in whatever is agreeable to themselves. If we said to them, for example, "Virtue is a means, and so is everything besides, and a means to everything else besides. Virtue is a means to pleasure, pain, health, disease, wealth, poverty, and is a good, because a means; and so also with pain, poverty, etc. They are all good, because all means. Is this what you mean by the question

Why?", they would answer No. And they would answer No, because something has been taken as an end, and therefore good; and has been assumed dogmatically.

The universal application of the question For what? or Whereto? is, we see, repudiated. The question does not hold good everywhere, and we must now consider, secondly, its particular application to virtue.

(2) Something is here assumed to be the end; and further, this is assumed *not* to be virtue; and thus the question is founded, "Is virtue a means to a given end, which end is the good? Is virtue good? and why? i.e. as conducing to what good is it good?" The dogma, A or B or C is a good in itself, justifies the inquiry, Is D a means to A, B, or C? And it is the dogmatic character of the question that we wished to point out. Its rationality, put as if universal, is tacitly assumed to end with a certain province; and our answer must be this: *If* your formula will not (on your own admission) apply to everything, what ground have you for supposing it to apply to virtue? "Be virtuous that you may be happy (i.e. pleased)"; then why be happy, and not rather virtuous? "The pleasure of all is an end." *Why* all? "Mine." *Why* mine? Your reply must be, that you take it to be so, and are prepared to argue on the thesis that something not virtue is the end in itself. And so are we; and we shall try to show that this is erroneous. But even if we fail in that, we have, I hope, made it clear that the question, Why should I be moral? rests on the assertion of an end in itself which is not morality;[2] and a point of this importance must not be taken for granted.

It is quite true that to ask Why should I be moral? is *ipso facto* to take one view of morality, is to assume that virtue is a means to something not itself. But it is a mistake to suppose that the general asking of Why? affords any presumption in favour of, or against, any one theory. If any theory could stand upon the What for? as a rational formula, which must always hold good and be satisfied, then, to that extent, no doubt it would have an advantage. But we have seen that all doctrines alike must reject the What for? and agree in this rejection, if they agree in nothing else; since they all must have an end which is not a mere means. And if so, is it not foolish to suppose that its giving a reason for virtue is any argument in favour of Hedonism, when for its own end it can give no reason at all? Is it not clear that, if you have any Ethics, you must have an end which is above the Why? in the sense of What for?; and that, if this is so, the question is now, as it was two thousand years ago, Granted that there is an end, *what* is this end? And the asking of that question, as reason and history both tell us, is not in itself the presupposing of a Hedonistic answer, or any other answer.

The claim of pleasure to be the end we are to discuss in another paper. But what is clear at first sight is, that to take virtue as a mere means to an ulterior end is in direct antagonism to the voice of the moral consciousness.

That consciousness, when unwarped by selfishness and not blinded by sophistry, is convinced that to ask for the Why? is simple immorality; to do good for its own sake is virtue, to do it for some ulterior end or object, not itself good, is never virtue; and never to act but for the sake of an end, other than doing well and

[2]"The question itself [Why should I do right?] can not be put, except in a form which assumes that the Utilitarian answer is the only one which can possibly be given. . . . The words 'Why should I' mean 'What shall I get by,' 'What motive have I for' this or that course of conduct?"—Stephen, *Liberty*, &c., p. 361, ed. ii.

right, is the mark of vice. And the theory which sees in virtue, as in money-getting, a means which is mistaken for an end, contradicts the voice which proclaims that virtue not only does seem to be, but is, an end in itself.[3]

Taking our stand then, as we hope, on this common consciousness, what answer can we give when the question Why should I be moral?, in the sense of What will it advantage me?, is put to us? Here we shall do well, I think, to avoid all praises of the pleasantness of virtue. We may believe that it transcends all possible delights of vice, but it would be well to remember that we desert a moral point of view, that we degrade and prostitute virtue, when to those who do not love her for herself we bring ourselves to recommend her for the sake of her pleasures. Against the base mechanical βαναυσια which meets us on all sides, with its "what is the use" of goodness, or beauty, or truth, there is but one fitting answer from the friends of science, or art, or religion and virtue, "We do not know, and we do not care."

As a direct answer to the question we should not say more: but, putting ourselves at our questioner's point of view, we may ask in return, Why should I be immoral? Is it not disadvantageous to be so? We can ask, is your view consistent? Does it satisfy you, and give you what you want? And if you are satisfied, and so far as you are satisfied, do see whether it is not because, and so far as, you are false to your theory; so far as you are living not directly with a view to the pleasant, but with a view to something else, or with no view at all, but, as you would call it, without any "reason." We believe that, in your heart, your end is what ours is, but that about this end you not

---

[3]There are two points which we may notice here. (1) There is a view which says, 'Pleasure (or pain) is what moves you to act; therefore pleasure (or pain) is your motive, and is always the Why? of your actions. You think otherwise by virtue of a psychological illusion.' For a consideration of this view we must refer to Essay VII. We may, however, remark in passing, that this view confuses the motive, which is an object before the mind, with the psychical stimulus, which is not an object before the mind and therefore is not a motive nor a Why?, in the sense of an end proposed.

(2) There is a view which tries to found moral philosophy on theology, a theology of a somewhat coarse type, consisting mainly in the doctrine of a criminal judge, of superhuman knowledge and power, who has promulgated and administers a criminal code. This may be called the "do it or be d—d" theory of morals, and is advocated or timidly suggested by writers nowadays, not so much (it seems probable) because in most cases they have a strong, or even a weak, belief in it; but because it stops holes in theories which they feel, without some help of the kind, will not hold water. We are not concerned with this opinion as a theological doctrine, and will merely remark that, as such, it appears to us to contain to the essence of irreligion; but with respect to morals, we say that, let it be never so true, it contributes nothing to moral philosophy, unless that has to do with the means whereby we are simply to get pleasure or avoid pain. The theory not only confuses morality and religion, but reduces them both to deliberate selfishness. Fear of criminal proceedings in the other world does not tell us what is morally right in this world. It merely gives a selfish motive for obedience to those who believe, and leaves those who do not believe, in all cases with less motive, in some cases with none. I can not forbear remarking that, so far as my experience goes, where future punishments are firmly believed in, the fear of them has, in most cases, but little influence on the mind. And the facts do not allow us to consider the fear of punishment in this world as the main motive to morality. In most cases there is, properly speaking, *no* ulterior motive. A man is moral because he likes being moral; and he likes it, partly because he has been brought up to the habit of liking it, and partly because he finds it gives him what he wants, while its opposite does not do so. He is not as a rule kept 'straight' by the contemplation of evils to be inflicted on him from the outside; and the shame he feels at the bad opinion of others is not a mere external evil, and is not feared simply as such. In short, a man is a human being, something larger than the abstraction of an actual or possible criminal.

only are sorely mistaken, but in your heart you feel and know it, or at least would do so, if you would only reflect. And more than this I think we ought not to say.

What more are we to say? If a man asserts total scepticism, you can not argue with him. You can show that he contradicts himself; but if he says, "I do not care"—there is an end of it. So, too, if a man says, "I shall do what I like, because I happen to like it; and as for ends, I recognize none"—you may indeed show him that his conduct is in fact otherwise; and if he will assert anything as an end, if he will but say, "I have no end but myself," then you may argue with him, and try to prove that he is making a mistake as to the nature of the end he alleges. But if he says, "I care not whether I am moral or rational, nor how much I contradict myself," then argument ceases. We, who have the power, believe that what is rational (if it is not yet) at least is to be real, and decline to recognize anything else. For standing on reason we can give, of course, no further reason; but we push our reason against what seems to oppose it, and soon force all to see that moral obligations do not vanish where they cease to be felt or are denied.

Has the question, Why should I be moral? no sense then, and is no positive answer possible? No, the question has no sense at all; it is simply unmeaning, unless it is equivalent to, *Is* morality an end in itself; and, if so, how and in what way is it an end? Is morality the same as the end for man, so that the two are convertible; or is morality one side, or aspect, or element of some end which is larger than itself? Is it the whole end from all points of view, or is it one view of the whole? Is the artist moral, so far as he is a good artist, or the philosopher moral, so far as he is a good philosopher? Are their art or science, and their virtue, one thing from one and the same point of view, or two different things, or one thing from two points of view?

These are not easy questions to answer, and we can not discuss them yet. We have taken the reader now so far as he need go, before proceeding to the following essays. What remains is to point out the most general expression for the end in itself, the ultimate practical "why"; and that we find in the word *self-realization.*

How can it be proved that self-realization is the end? There is only one way to do that. This is to know what we mean, when we say "self," and "real," and "realize," and "end," and to know that is to have something like a system of metaphysic, and to say it would be to exhibit that system. Instead of remarking, then, that we lack space to develop our views, let us frankly confess that, properly speaking, we have no such views to develop, and therefore we can not *prove* our thesis. All that we can do is partially to explain it, and try to render it plausible. It is a formula, which our succeeding Essays will in some way fill up, and which here we shall attempt to recommend to the reader beforehand.

An objection will occur at once. "There surely are ends," it will be said, "which are not myself, which fall outside my activity, and which, nevertheless, I do realize, and think I ought to realize." We must try to show that the objection rests upon a misunderstanding, and, as a statement of fact, brings with it insuperable difficulties.

Let us first go to the moral consciousness, and see what that tells us about its end.

Morality implies an end in itself: we take that for granted. Something is to be done, a good is to be realized. But that result is, by itself, not morality: morality differs from art, in that it can not make the act a *mere* means to the result. Yet there is a means. There is not only something to be done, but something to be done by me—*I* must do the act, must realize the end. Morality implies both the something to be done, and the doing of it by me; and if you consider them as end and means, you can not separate the end and the means. If you chose to change the position of end and means, and say my doing is the end, and the "to be done" is the means, you would not violate the moral consciousness; for the truth is that means and end are not applicable here. The act for me means my act, and there is no end beyond the act. This we see in the belief that failure may be equivalent morally to success—in the saying, that there is nothing good except a good will. In short, for morality the end implies the act, and the act implies self-realization. This, if it were doubtful, would be shown (we may remark in passing) by the feeling of pleasure which attends the putting forth of the act. For if pleasure be the feeling of self, and accompany the act, this indicates that the putting forth of the act is also the putting forth of the self.

But we must not lay too much stress on the moral consciousness, for we shall be reminded, perhaps, that not only can it be, but, like the miser's consciousness, it frequently has been explained, and that both states of mind are illusions generated on one and the same principle.

Let us then dismiss the moral consciousness, and not trouble ourselves about what we think we ought to do; let us try to show that what we do do, is, perfectly or imperfectly, to realize ourselves, and that we can not possibly do anything else; that all we can realize is (accident apart) our ends, or the objects we desire; and that all we can desire is, in a word, self.

This, we think, will be readily admitted by our main psychological party. What we wish to avoid is that it should be admitted in a form which makes it unmeaning; and of this there is perhaps some danger. We do not want the reader to say, "Oh yes, of course, relativity of knowledge—everything is a state of consciousness," and so dismiss the question. If the reader believes that a steam-engine, after it is made, is nothing[4] but a state of the mind of the person or persons who have made it, or who are looking at it, we do not hold what we feel tempted to call such a silly doctrine; and would point out to those who do hold it that, at all events, the engine is a very different state of mind, after it is made, from what it was before.

Again, we do not want the reader to say, "Certainly, every object or end which I propose to myself is, as such, a mere state of my mind—it is a thought in my head, or a state of me, and so, when it becomes real, I become real"; because, though it is very true that my thought, as my thought, can not exist apart from me thinking

---

[4]We may remark that the ordinary "philosophical" person, who talks about "relativity," really does not seem to know what he is saying. He will tell you that "all" (or "all we know and can know"—there is no practical difference between that and "all") is relative to consciousness—not giving you to understand that he means thereby any consciousness beside his own, and ready, I should imagine, with his grin at the notion of a mind which is anything more than the mind of this or that man; and then, it may be a few pages further on or further back, will talk to you of the state of the earth before man existed on it. But we wish to know what in the world it all means; and would suggest, as a method of clearing the matter, the two questions—(1) Is my consciousness something that goes and is beyond myself; and if so, in what sense? and (2) Had I a father? What do I mean by that, and how do I reconcile my assertion of it with my answer to question (1)?

it, and therefore my proposed end must, as such, be a state of me;[5] yet this is not what we are driving at. All my ends are my thoughts, but all my thoughts are not my ends; and if what we meant by self-realization was, that I have in my head the idea of any future external event, then I should realize myself practically when I see that the engine is going to run off the line, and it does so.

A desired object (as desired) is a thought, and my thought; but it is something more, and that something more is, in short, that it is desired by me. And we ought by right, before we go further, to exhibit a theory of desire; but, if we could do that, we could not stop to do it. However, we say with confidence that, in desire, what is desired must in all cases be self.

If we could accept the theory that the end or motive is always the idea of a pleasure (or pain) of our own, which is associated with the object presented, and which is that in the object which moves us, and the only thing which does move us, then from such a view it would follow at once that all we can aim at is a state of ourselves.

We can not, however, accept the theory, since we believe it both to ignore and to be contrary to facts . . . , but, though we do not admit that the motive is always, or in most cases, the idea of a state of our feeling self, yet we think it is clear that nothing moves unless it be desired, and that what is desired is ourself. For all objects or ends have been associated with our satisfaction, or (more correctly) have been felt in and as ourselves, or we have felt ourselves therein; and the only reason why they move us now is that, when they are presented to our minds as motives, we do now feel ourselves asserted or affirmed in them. The essence of desire for an object would thus be the feeling of our affirmation in the idea of something not ourself, felt against the feeling of ourself as, without the object, void and negated; and it is the tension of this relation which produces motion. If so, then nothing is desired except that which is identified with ourselves, and we can aim at nothing, except so far as we aim at ourselves in it.

But passing by the above, which we can not here expound and which we lay no stress on, we think that the reader will probably go with us so far as this, that in desire what we want, so far as we want it, is ourselves in some form, or is some state of ourselves; and that our wanting anything else would be psychologically inexplicable.

Let us take this for granted then; but is this what we mean by self-realization? Is the conclusion that, in trying to realize we try to realize some state of ourself, all that we are driving at? No, the self we try to realize is for us a whole, it is not a mere collection of states. . . .

If we may presuppose in the reader a belief in the doctrine that what is wanted is a state of self, we wish, standing upon that, to urge further that the whole self is present in its states, and that therefore the whole self is the object aimed at; and this is what we mean by self-realization. If a state of self is what is desired, can you, we wish to ask, have states of self which are states of nothing . . . ; can you possibly succeed in regarding the self as a collection, or stream, or train, or series,

---

[5]Let me remark in passing that it does not follow from this that it is nothing but a state of me, as this or that man.

or aggregate? If you can not think of it as a mere one, can you on the other hand think of it as a mere many, as mere ones; or are you not driven, whether you wish it or not, to regard it as a one in many, or a many in one? Are we not forced to look on the self as a whole, which is not merely the sum of its parts, nor yet some other particular beside them? And must we not say that to realize self is always to realize a whole, and that the question in morals is to find the true whole, realizing which will practically realize the true self?

This is the question which to the end of this volume we shall find ourselves engaged on. For the present, turning our attention away from it in this form, and contenting ourselves with the proposition that to realize is to realize self, let us now, apart from questions of psychology or metaphysics, see what ends they are, in fact, which living men do propose to themselves, and whether these do not take the form of a whole.

Upon this point there is no need, I think, to dwell at any length; for it seems clear that, if we ask ourselves what it is we should most wish for, we find some general wish which would include and imply our particular wishes. And, if we turn to life, we see that no man has disconnected particular ends; he looks beyond the moment, beyond this or that circumstance or position; his ends are subordinated to wider ends; each situation is seen (consciously or unconsciously) as part of a broader situation, and in this or that act he is aiming at and realizing some larger whole, which is not real in any particular act as such, and yet is realized in the body of acts which carry it out. We need not stop here, because the existence of larger ends, which embrace smaller ends, can not be doubted; and so far we may say that the self we realize is identified with wholes, or that the ideas of the states of self we realize are associated with ideas that stand for wholes.

But is it also true that these larger wholes are included in one whole? I think that it is. I am not forgetting that we act, as a rule, not *from* principle or with the principle before us, and I wish the reader not to forget that the principle may be there and may be our basis or our goal, without our knowing anything about it. And here, of course, I am not saying that it has occurred to every one to ask himself whether he aims at a whole, and what that is; because considerable reflection is required for this, and the amount need not have been reached. Nor again am I saying that every man's actions are consistent, that he does not wander from his end, and that he has not particular ends which will not come under his main end. Nor further do I assert that the life of every man does form a whole; that in some men there are not co-ordinated ends, which are incompatible and incapable of subordination into a system.[6] What I am saying is that, if the life of the normal man be inspected, and the ends he has in view (as exhibited in his acts) be considered, they will, roughly speaking, be embraced in one main end or whole of ends. It has been said that "every man has a different notion of happiness," but this is scarcely correct, unless mere detail be referred to. Certainly, however, every man has *a* notion

---

[6]The unhappiness of such lives in general, however, points to the fact that the real end is a whole. Dissatisfaction rises from the knowing or feeling that the self is not realized, and not realized because not realized as a system.

of happiness, and *his* notion, though he may not quite know what it is. Most men have a life which they live, and with which they are tolerably satisfied, and that life, when examined, is seen to be fairly systematic; it is seen to be a sphere including spheres, the lower spheres subordinating to themselves and qualifying particular actions, and themselves subordinated to and qualified by the whole. And most men have more or less of an ideal of life—a notion of perfect happiness, which is never quite attained in real life; and if you take (not of course any one, but) the normal decent and serious man, when he has been long enough in the world to know what he wants, you will find that his notion of perfect happiness, or ideal life, is not something straggling, as it were, and discontinuous, but is brought before the mind as a unity, and, if imagined more in detail, is a system where particulars subserve one whole.

Without further dwelling on this, I will ask the reader to reflect whether the ends, proposed to themselves by ordinary persons, are not wholes, and are not in the end members in a larger whole; and, if that be so, whether, since it is so, and since all we can want must (as before stated) be ourselves, we must not now say that we aim not only at the realization of self, but of self as a whole; seeing that there is a general object of desire with which self is identified, or (on another view) with the idea of which the idea of our pleasure is associated.

Up to the present we have been trying to point out that what we aim at is self, and self as a whole; in other words, that self as a whole is, in the end, the content of our wills. It will still further, perhaps, tend to clear the matter, if we refer to the form of the will—not, of course, suggesting that the form is anything real apart from the content.

On this head we are obliged to restrict ourselves to the assertion of what we believe to be fact. We remarked in our last Essay that, in saying "I will this or that," we really mean something. In saying it we do not mean (at least, not as a rule) to distinguish a self that wills from a self that does not will; but what we do mean is to distinguish the self, as will in general, from this or that object of desire, and, at the same time, to identify the two; to say, this or that is willed, or the will has uttered itself in this or that. The will is looked on as a whole, and there are two sides or factors to that whole. Let us consider an act of will, and, that we may see more clearly, let us take a deliberate volitional choice. We have conflicting desires, say A and B; we feel two tensions, two drawings (so to speak), but we can not actually affirm ourselves in both. Action does not follow, and we reflect on the two objects of desire, and we are aware that we are reflecting on them, or (if our language allowed us to say it) over them. But we do not merely stand looking on till, so to speak, we find we are gone in one direction, have closed with A or B. For we are aware besides of ourselves, not simply as something theoretically above A and B, but as something also practically above them, as a concentration which is not one or the other, but which is the possibility of either; which is the inner side indifferently of an act which should realize A, or one which should realize B; and hence, which is neither, and yet is superior to both. In short, we do not simply feel ourselves in A and B, but have distinguished ourselves from both, as what is above both. This is one factor in volition, and it is hard to find any name better for it than that of the universal factor, or side, or moment.[7] We need say much less about the second factor. In order to will, we must will something; the universal side by itself is not will at all. To will we must identify ourselves with this, that, or the other; and here we have the particular side, and the second factor in volition, Thirdly, the volition as a whole (and first, as a whole, is it volition) is the identity of both these factors, and the projection or carrying of it out into external existence; the realization both of the particular side, the this or that to be done, and the realization of the inner side of self in the doing of it, with a realization of self in both, as is proclaimed by the feeling of pleasure. This unity of the two factors we may call the individual whole, or again the concrete universal; and, although we are seldom conscious of the distinct factors, yet every act of will will be seen, when analysed, to be a whole of this kind, and so to realize what is always the nature of the will.

But to what end have we made this statement? Our object has been to draw the attention of the reader to the fact that not only what is willed by men, the end they set before themselves, is a whole, but also that the will itself, looked at apart from any particular object or content, is a similar whole: or, to put it in its proper order, the self is realized in a whole of ends because it is a whole, and because it is not satisfied till it has found itself, till content be adequate to form, and that content be realized; and this is what we mean by practical self-realization.

"Realize yourself," "realize yourself as a whole," is the result of the foregoing. The reader, I fear, may be wearied already by these prefatory remarks, but it will be better in the end if we delay yet longer. All we know at present is that we are to realize self as *a whole;* but as to *what* whole it is, we know nothing, and must further consider.

The end we desire (to repeat it) is the finding and possessing ourselves as a whole. We aim at this both in theory and practice. What we want in theory is to understand the object; we want neither to remove nor alter the world of sensuous fact, but we want to get at the truth of it. The whole of science takes it for granted that the "not-ourself" is really intelligible; it stands and falls with this assumption. So long as our theory strikes on the mind as strange and alien, so long do we say we have not found truth; we feel the impulse to go beyond and beyond, we alter and alter our views, till we see them as a consistent whole. There we rest, because then we have found the nature of our own mind and the truth of facts in one. And in practice again, with a difference, we have the same want. Here our aim is not, leaving the given as it is, to find the truth of it; but here we want to force the sensuous fact

---

[7]As we saw in our last Essay, there are two dangers to avoid here, in the shape of two one-sided views, Scylla and Charybdis. The first is the ignoring of the universal side altogether, even as an element; the second is the assertion of it as more than an element, as by itself will. Against this second it is necessary to insist that the will is what it wills, that to will you must will something, and that you can not will the mere form of the will; further, that the mere formal freedom of choice not only, if it were real, would *not* be true freedom, but that, in addition, it is a metaphysical fiction; that the universal is real only as one side of the whole, and takes its character from the whole; and that, in the most deliberate and would-be formal volition, the self that is abstracted and stands above the particulars, is the abstraction not only from the particular desire or desires before the mind, but also from the whole self, the self which embodies all past acts, and that *the abstraction is determined by that from which it is abstracted,* no less than itself is a moment in the determination of the concrete act.

Why Should I Be Moral?   F. H. Bradley

621

to correspond to the truth of ourselves. We say, "My sensuous existence is thus, but I truly am not thus; I am different." On the one hand, as a matter of fact, I and my existing world are discrepant; on the other hand, the instinct of my nature tells me that the world is mine. On that impulse I act, I alter and alter the sensuous facts, till I find in them nothing but myself carried out. Then I possess my world, and I do not possess it until I find my will in it; all I do not find that, until what I have is a harmony or a whole in system.

Both in theory and practice my end is to realize myself as a whole. But is this all? Is a *consistent* view all that we want in theory? Is an *harmonious* life all that we want in practice? Certainly not. A doctrine must not only hold together, but it must hold the facts together as well. We can not rest in it simply because it does not contradict itself. The theory must take in the facts, and an ultimate theory must take in all the facts. So again in practice. It is no human ideal to lead "the life of an oyster." We have no right first to find out just what we happen to be and to have, and then to contract our wants to that limit. We can not do it if we would, and morality calls to us that, if we try to do it, we are false to ourselves. Against the sensuous facts around us and within us, we must for ever attempt to widen our empire; we must at least try to go forward, or we shall certainly be driven back.

So self-realization means more than the mere assertion of the self as a whole.[8] And here we may refer to two principles, which Kant put forward under the names of "Homogeneity" and "Specification." Not troubling ourselves with our relation to Kant, we may say that the ideal is neither to be perfectly homogeneous, nor simply to be specified to the last degree, but rather to combine both these elements. Our true being is not the extreme of unity, nor of diversity, but the perfect identity of both. And "Realize yourself" does not mean merely "Be a whole," but "Be an *infinite* whole."

At this word, I am afraid, the reader who has not yet despaired of us will come to a stop, and refuse to enter into the region of nonsense. But why should it be nonsense? When the poet and the preacher tell us the mind is infinite, most of us feel that it is so; and has our science really come to this, that the beliefs which answer to our highest feelings must be theoretical absurdities? Should not the philosophy which tells us such a thing be very sure of the ground it goes upon? But if the reader will follow me, I think I can show him that the mere finitude of the mind is a more difficult thesis to support than its infinity.

It would be well if I could ask the reader to tell me what he means by "finite." As that can not be, I must say that finite is limited or ended. To be finite is to be some one among others, some one which is *not* others. One finite ends where the other finite begins; it is bounded from the outside, and can not go beyond itself without becoming something else, and thereby perishing.[9]

---

[8]I leave out of sight the important question whether any partial whole *can* be self-consistent. If (which seems the better view) this can not be, we shall not need to say "Systematize *and* widen," but the second will be implied in the first.

[9]We have not to dwell on the inherent contradiction of the finite. Its being is to fall wholly within itself; and yet, so far as it is finite, so far is it determined wholly by the outside.

"The mind," we are told, "is finite; and the reason why we say it is finite is that we know it is finite. The mind knows that itself is finite." This is the doctrine we have to oppose.

We answer, The mind is *not* finite, just because it knows it *is* finite. "The knowledge of the limit suppresses the limit." It is a flagrant self-contradiction that the finite should know its own finitude; and it is not hard to make this plain.

Finite means limited from the outside and by the outside. The finite is to know itself as this, or not as finite. If its knowledge ceases to fall wholly within itself, then so far it is not finite. It knows that it is limited from the outside and by the outside, and that means it knows the outside. But if so, then it is so far not finite. If its whole being fell within itself, then, in knowing itself, it could not know that there was anything outside itself. It does do the latter; hence the former supposition is false.

Imagine a man shut up in a room, who said to us, "My faculties are entirely confined to the *inside* of this room. The limit of the room is the limit of my mind, and so I can have no knowledge whatever of the outside." Should we not answer, "My dear sir, you contradict yourself. If it were as you say, you could not know of an outside, and so, by consequence, not of an inside, as such." You should be in earnest and go through with your doctrine of "relativity"?

To the above simple argument I fear we may not have done justice. However that be, I know of no answer to it; and until we find one we must say that it is not true that the mind is finite.

If I am to realize myself, it must be as infinite; and now the question is, What does infinite mean? and it will be better to say first what it does not mean. There are two wrong views on the subject, which we will take one at a time.

(1) Infinite is not-finite, and that means "end-less." What does endless mean? Not the mere negation of end, because a mere negation is nothing at all, and infinite would thus ≠ O. The endless is something positive; it means a positive quantity which has no end. Any given number of units is finite; but a series of units, which is produced indefinitely, is infinite. This is the sense of infinite which is in most common use, and which, we shall see, is what Hedonism believes in. It is, however, clear that this infinite is a perpetual self-contradiction, and, so far as it is real, is only finite. Any real quantity has ends, beyond which it does not go. "Increase the quantity" merely says "Put the end further off"; but in saying that, it does say "Put the end." "Increase the quantity for ever" means "Have for ever a finite quantity, and for ever say that it is not finite." In other words, "Remove the end" does imply, by that very removal and the production of the series, the making of a fresh end; so that we still have a finite quantity. Here, so far as the infinite exists, it is finite; so far as it is told to exist, it is told again to be nothing but finite.

(2) Or, secondly, the infinite is *not* the finite, no longer in the sense of being more in quantity, but in the sense of being something else, which is different in quality. The infinite is not in the world of limited things; it exists in a sphere of its own. The mind (e.g.) is something *beside* the aggregate of its states. God is something beside the things of this world. This is the infinite believed in by abstract Duty. But here once more, against its will, infinite comes to mean merely finite. The infinite is a something over against, beside, and outside the finite; and hence is itself also finite, because limited by something else.

Why Should I Be Moral?   F. H. Bradley

623

In neither of these two senses is the mind infinite. What then is the true sense of infinite? As before, it is the negation of the finite; it is not-finite. But, unlike both the false infinites, it does not leave the finite as it is. It neither, with (1), says "the finite *is to be* not-finite," nor, with (2), tries to get rid of it by doubling it. It does really negate the finite, so that the finite disappears, not by having a negative set over against it, but by being taken up into a higher unity, in which, becoming an element, it ceases to have its original character, and is both suppressed and preserved. The infinite is thus "the unity of the finite and infinite." The finite was determined from the outside, so that everywhere to characterize and distinguish it was in fact to divide it. Wherever you defined anything you were at once carried beyond to something else and something else, and this because the negative, required for distinction, was an outside other. In the infinite you can distinguish without dividing; for this is a unity holding within itself subordinated factors which are negative of, and so distinguishable from, each other; while at the same time the whole is so present in each, that each has its own being in its opposite, and depends on that relation for its own life. The negative is also its affirmation. Thus the infinite has a distinction, and so a negation, in itself, but is distinct from and negated by nothing but itself. Far from being one something which is *not* another something, it is a whole in which both one and the other are mere elements. This whole is hence 'relative' utterly and through and through, but the relation does not fall outside it; the relatives are moments in which it is the relation of itself to itself, and so is above the relation, and is absolute reality. The finite is relative to something *else;* the infinite is *self*-related. It is this sort of infinite which the mind is. The simplest symbol of it is the circle, the line which returns into itself, not the straight line produced indefinitely; and the readiest way to find it is to consider the satisfaction of desire. There we have myself and its opposite, and the return from the opposite, the finding in the other nothing but self. And here it would be well to recall what we said above on the form of the will.

If the reader to whom this account of the infinite is new has found it in any way intelligible, I think he will see that there is some sense in it, when we say, "Realize yourself as an infinite whole"; or, in other words, "Be specified in yourself, but not specified by anything foreign to yourself."

But the objection comes: "Morality tells us to progress; it tells us we are not concluded in ourselves nor perfect, but that there exists a not-ourself, which never does wholly become ourself. And, apart from morality, it is obvious that I and you, this man and the other man, are finite beings. We are not one another; more or less we must limit each other's sphere; I am what I am more or less by external relations, and I do not fall wholly within myself. Thus I am to be infinite, to have no limit from the outside; and yet I am one among others, and therefore am finite. It is all very well to tell me that in me there is infinity, the perfect identity of subject and object: that I may be willing perhaps to believe, but none the less I am finite."

We admit the full force of the objection. I *am* finite; I am both infinite *and* finite, and that is why my moral life is a perpetual progress. I must progress, because I have an other which is to be, and yet never quite is, myself; and so, as I am, am in a state of contradiction.

It is not that I wish to increase the mere quantity of my true self. It is that I wish to be nothing *but* my true self, to be rid of all external relations, to bring them all within me, and so to fall wholly within myself.

I am to be perfectly homogeneous; but that I can not be unless fully specified, and the question is, How can I be extended so as to take in my external relations? Goethe[10] has said, "Be a whole *or* join a whole," but to that we must answer, "You can not be a whole, *unless* you join a whole."

The difficulty is: being limited and so not a whole, how extend myself so as to be a whole? The answer is, be a member in a whole. Here your private self, your finitude, ceases as such to exist; it becomes the function of an organism. You must be, not a mere piece of, but a member in, a whole; and as this must know and will yourself.

The whole, to which you belong, specifies itself in the detail of its functions, and yet remains homogeneous. It lives not many lives but one life, and yet can not live except in its many members. Just so, each one of the members is alive, but not apart from the whole which lives in it. The organism is homogeneous because it is specified, and specified because it is homogeneous.

"But," it will be said, "what is that to me? I remain one member, and I am not other members. The more perfect the organism, the more is it specified, and so much the intenser becomes its homogeneity. But its "more" means my "less." The unity falls in the whole, and so outside me; and the greater specification of the whole means the making me more special, more narrowed, and limited, and less developed within myself."

We answer that this leaves out of sight a fact quite palpable and of enormous significance, viz. that in the moral organism the members are aware of themselves, and aware of themselves as members. I do not know myself as mere this, against something else which is not myself. The relations of the others to me are not mere external relations. I know myself as a member; that means I am aware of my own function; but it means also that I am aware of the whole as specifying itself in me. The will of the whole knowingly wills itself in me; the will of the whole is the will of the members, and so, in willing my own function, I do know that the others will themselves in me. I do know again that I will myself in the others, and in them find my will once more as not mine, and yet as mine. It is false that the homogeneity falls outside me; it is not only in me, but for me too; and apart from my life in it, my knowledge of it, and devotion to it, I am not myself. When it goes out my heart goes out with it, where it triumphs I rejoice, where it is maimed I suffer; separate me from the love of it, and I perish. . . .

No doubt the distinction of separate selves remains, but the point is this. In morality the existence of my mere private self, as such, is something which ought not to be, and which, so far as I am moral, has already ceased. I am morally realized, not until my personal self has utterly ceased to be my exclusive self, is no more a will which is outside others' wills, but finds in the world of others nothing but self.

[10]'Immer strebe zum Ganzen, und kannst du selber kein Ganzes Wenden, als dienendes Glied schliess' an ein Ganzes dich an.'
—*Vier Jakreszeiten*, 45.

"Realize yourself as an infinite whole" means, "Realize yourself as the self-conscious member of an infinite whole, by realizing that whole in yourself." When that whole is truly infinite, and when your personal will is wholly made one with it, then you also have reached the extreme of homogeneity and specification in one, and have attained a perfect self-realization.

The foregoing will, we hope, become clear to the reader of this volume. He must consider what has been said so far as the text, which the sequel is to illustrate and work out in detail. Meanwhile, our aim has been to put forward the formula of self-realization, and in some measure to explain it. The following Essays will furnish, we hope, something like a commentary and justification. We shall see that the self to be realized is not the self as a collection of particulars, is not the universal as all the states of a certain feeling; and that it is not again an abstract universal, as the form of duty; that neither are in harmony with life, with the moral consciousness, or with themselves; that when the self is identified with, and wills, and realizes a concrete universal, a real totality, then first does it find itself, is satisfied, self-determined, and free," the free will that wills itself as the free will."

Let us resume, then, the results of the present Essay. We have attempted to show (1) That the formula of "what for?" must be rejected by every ethical doctrine as not universally valid; and that hence no one theory can gain the smallest advantage (except over the foolish) by putting it forward: that now for us (as it was for Hellas) the main question is: There being some end, what is that end? And (2), with which second part, if it fall, the first need not fall, we have endeavoured briefly to point out that the final end, with which morality is identified, or under which it is included, can be expressed not otherwise than by self-realization.

Why Be Moral?

A. I. Melden

Our question is notoriously ambiguous and sometimes rather disturbing. It poses what appears to be a reasonable demand for a reason. But the mere demand for a reason provides no assurance that one is possible in principle, and, if it is not, any difficulty which the question occasions is best dispelled by removing the confusions that prompt the question itself. So it is, I shall argue, with that sense of the question that is apt to be most disturbing to the moral theorist because it suggests a skepticism with respect to the foundations of moral theory. To remove any possible misapprehensions concerning my thesis, however, I shall begin by stating those senses of the question with respect to which this thesis is *not* being argued. I shall then attempt to state the precise sense of the question with which I am concerned, and I shall argue that in this sense the question is, appearances to the contrary notwithstanding, impossible.

(1) I am not concerned with the silly question of why I ought to promote the good. That question answers itself. (2) The question I shall discuss is not the empirical

Source: The Journal of Philosophy, 45, 1948, 499–456.

question of what the causes are of the occurrence of the moral attitude. (3) The question is not the pragmatic question whether it is prudent or useful to be moral or to act in those ways commonly described with approval as moral. (4) I shall not discuss the familiar question of whether certain commonly accepted moral principles are morally justified. Such a question is not in general a skeptical attack against the foundations of morality; at the worst, it is a demand for a moral justification of a particular moral code. (5) The question could be construed as a theoretical question that may arise when ordinary attempts to provide moral justifications fail or when intellectual curiosity arises.[1] For what might be intended is a question having to do with the analysis of ethical terms in the light of which assured moral justifications of commonly accepted moral principles can be given. Such a question may be disturbing, for it is not easy to answer; but it poses a reasonable demand which any moral theorist, as theorist, sets out to satisfy.

There is, however, a quite different sense of the question with which I am concerned. It is commonly assumed that there are values and ideals with respect to which there are moral obligations. Now there is a sense of "moral" in which one would be described as a moral being even though the particular values and ideals he selected, and with respect to which he assumed his obligations, were defective. In this sense of the term, the moral is opposed to the non-moral or amoral, and one would be described as an amoralist if he refused to accept any moral obligations at all, however these might be specified or defined. Within this wider meaning of the term "moral" we should then distinguish between the moral in the narrower sense of right or praiseworthy and the immoral. And within the immoral we distinguish between those cases in which a person recognizes what in fact are his duties but acts in a contrary manner because of the superior strength of his inclinations and those cases in which a person acts in accordance with what, erroneously, he takes to be his duties. It follows that being moral in this wider sense is a necessary but not sufficient condition of being moral in the praiseworthy sense. What further conditions are necessary is a matter that has to do with the nature of the values and ideals selected. And whether or not agreement about these further matters is possible it will be well to agree upon a usage of "morality" (and hence of the cognate term "moral") in which we may speak of a morality of which we disapprove, because of the values selected in the determining ideal, e.g., the morality of the Nietzschean superman. For we shall want to be able to contrast an attitude of devotion to ideals of which we do not approve with what in principle at least is possible, namely, an amoral attitude in which, to consider one illustration, the only concern felt is a concern with personal satisfactions and the only attitude felt toward others is that of indifference except when they serve to promote or inhibit personal gratification. We can, therefore, put the question I propose to consider as follows: Is there any reason that can be offered that would suffice to persuade one who was not initially disposed to do so, to be consistent in his valuations by treating as values and dis-values without regard to the locus of their occurrence those things which in his own experience he values and dis-values respectively. For to be more in the wider sense of the term is to be consistent in one's valuations by assuming or accepting *some*

---

[1]This is the question with which Plato is concerned in *The Republic*. A. E. Taylor's discussion of this point in "The Right and the Good," *Mind,* N.S., No. 48.

obligations and by taking something to be good or bad: it is to avoid the attitude that is expressed by saying "What of it?" with respect to those matters in the experience of others about which we are concerned when they occur in our own.[2]

Unless a commitment to this principle of consistency in valuation is given, the story of the costs and consequences of dishonesty, to take one case, serves only to demonstrate that dishonesty is possible if it is not the general rule and painful if found out. Unless it is given, the argument of *The Republic* is gratuitous. For it is contended there that a man can not get away with injustice—he may escape the punishments usually imposed by his society, but he can not escape the costs which his soul must assume—but unless men are concerned with each other's wants and satisfactions, the alleged torments of the soul do not follow. Why not an amoral Gyges who is wholly indifferent to the welfare of others except when it affects his own, smugly cheerful in the harmony of soul obtained by virtue of a clever imposition of constraints upon his desires and appetites—concerned with *his* future but satisfied in his indifference to the fortunes of others? Such a conception is, at any rate, logically possible. If we protest that such a being can not be happy, do we mean anything other than either (*a*) we morally disapprove, (*b*) no man is clever enough so to conceal his total amoralism, or (*c*) men, by nature, can not be cheerful in their injustice because of their essential morality—because they have some propensity to be consistent in their valuations?

That we be consistent with respect to what are in fact the proper values and ideals in our valuations is assumed on any moral theory. Whether goodness be a natural or a non-natural property, it is repeatable and is to be prized for its own sake in whosoever's experience it may occur. No ethicist has, as far as I can see, ever maintained, in any analysis or description of ethical terms or in any statement of the criteria for their proper application, that the names of particular persons are relevant. If there is any reference to persons, it is to all persons or almost all persons (as in Hume's case) or all persons of a certain type. Despite the enormous difference between a Kantian universalism and a Nietzschean ethics of the superman, it would be a mistake to deny that Nietzsche was a moralist and that between you and me, provided that we are both heroic and aggressive members of the knightly community or both weak and submissive members of the supporting class of helots, there is nothing to favor the one or the other with respect to the Nietzschean table of values and disvalues. And if a captious critic will protest that he will be consistent in his valuations, notwithstanding a total indifference to the misfortunes

---

[2] I do not intend the identification of the selfish with the amoral. The unprincipled emotionalism of the chief character in Chekhov's short story *The Darling* serves to remind us that sympathy as a particular feeling or sentiment is not the sentiment of morality, for it may occur capriciously, or, as we sometimes say, without rhyme or reason. What is intended by "amoral" in this context is an attitude in which valuation is capricious or oriented by some capriciously accepted rule or principle. This may be the selfish rule that the values in question count only when they occur in my own experience; it may be the sentimental rule that the values in question must occur in the experience of one to whom I am emotionally attached, or it may be a rule as capricious as any you please. In any case, what will be evidenced in all such cases is an attitude of indifference to values and dis-values except when they occur in arbitrarily or capriciously selected circumstances. For an amoralist will recognize that what he prizes in some special context occurs also outside this context; he will not moralize by arguing that the difference in context makes a moral difference since he will, as I have defined the term, dismiss all moral responsibility with a contemptuous "What of it?"

of others, provided that he defines values as those things which *he* prizes, we shall describe his view as an amoralism, since values, whatever else they may be, are repeatable in a way in which values, as construed by our critic, are not.

For the moralist the question, as I have stated it, is disturbing. The moralist assumes that ethical terms have meaning and application; his task is to explain something given for explanation. What is given is the datum of morality, that there are moral obligations—that, if anything is good, we ought to be consistent in prizing the kind of thing it is simply because it is good. To ask, now, for a reason for being consistent in one's valuations is to ask for something with which the moral theorist as theorist is not concerned for it is to ask in effect why I should treat anything as good or bad and why I should accept any obligation whatsoever. And yet the question is disturbing, for in the absence of a satisfactory answer, the moral theorist's program would seem to be otiose and the moral claims which we make upon one another unreasonable.

Clearly, a reason for our being consistent in our valuations can not be given in terms of logical consistency. Moral consistency is that consistency in action and attitude every breach of which attests to the *logical* possibility and consistency of a perverse *moral* inconsistency or amoralism. The principles of logic are doubly neutral toward ethics: they serve no more as criteria of moral validity than they do of truth, and in themselves they provide no more reason for adopting a moral consistency than for rejecting all consistency of action in a totally perverse, because totally indifferent, attitude to the fortunes and misfortunes of ourselves and others.

The question of the relation between the logical and the moral has been revived by C. I. Lewis in his recent Paul Carus Lectures. Lewis is concerned to repudiate the familiar view, according to which the rational is defined in terms of the principles of logical validity. On the contrary it is, according to Lewis, the converse relation that holds, and this is true where the rationality in question is that rationality that characterizes the moral attitude.

> To be rational, instead of foolish or perverse, means to be capable of constraint by prevision of some future good or ill; to be amenable to the consideration, "you will be sorry if you don't," or "if you do."
>
> Rationality, in this sense, is not derivative from the logical: rather it is the other way about. The validity of reasoning turns upon, and can be summarized in terms of consistency. And consistency is, at bottom, nothing more than the adherence throughout to what we have accepted. . . . Thinking and discoursing are important and peculiarly human ways of acting. Insofar as our actions of this sort are affected with concern for what we may later think or wish to affirm, we attempt to be consistent or rational: and when we achieve this kind of self-accord, then we are logical.[3]

Whether we are concerned with the consistency of thinking or of acting—the former logical and the latter moral consistency—in each case we have that rationality that consists in "this same attempt to avoid any attitude . . . which later must be recanted or regretted."[4] Hence,

> The final and universal imperative, "Be consistent in valuation and in thought and action" . . . is one which is categorical. It requires no reasons; being itself the expres-

---

[3]C. I. Lewis, *An Analysis of Knowledge and Valuation,* Open Court, p. 490.
[4]*Ibid.*

sion of that which is the source of all reason; that in the absence of which there could be no reason of any sort or for anything.[5]

Now I should agree that there is a use of the term "rational" in which a person who is indifferent to his future in his demands on the present is said to be irrational; and there is a use of "reasonable" in which a person who is morally inconsistent by disregarding completely these very things in the lives of others which he values on his own would be said to be unreasonable. "Being reasonable" does often mean being morally consistent. But it would be well to note that the imperative "Be morally consistent" is categorical only on the proviso that the values and ideals selected are adequate, whatever the criteria and analysis of moral adequacy or validity may be; for we should be morally justified in refusing to say to a detzschean "Be morally consistent," knowing the values he prizes and the ideal to which he subscribes. "Be moral!" is categorical only where "moral" is used in the common praiseworthy sense. But it is very doubtful that the rationality that consists in being morally principled can be assimilated with that rationality in whose absence, as Lewis puts it, "there could be no reason of any sort or for anything."

(1) The contention that consistency of thought and of action are "at bottom" the same, namely, "the adherence throughout to what we have accepted" rests upon a confusion of two senses of "consistency of thought." In one sense consistency of thought is a *practical* consistency or consistency of thought—the maintenance, throughout a period of time, of the same attitude of assertion towards a given proposition.[6] In another sense, it consists in a logical relation between the propositions asserted, the absence of which is logical contradiction. In the logical sense it is just false to say that consistency is "at bottom nothing more than the adherence throughout to what we have accepted"; one can be practically inconsistent or inconstant when, for example, one changes one's mind, and in this case there need be no logical inconsistency in any assertion actually made. It is this confusion that leads Lewis to assert that "if it were not that present valuing and doing may later be a matter of regret, then there would be no point and no imperative to consistency of any kind." For supposing our concern with the future provided the only reason for being constant in our willing and doing, it would not follow that without that concern there would be no point to logical consistency. For the imperative "Be logically consistent," all that is necessary is that a person be willing to say anything at all and this could be satisfied by one who is indifferent to the future or by one who is not rational in that sense in which "to be rational means to be capable of constraint by prevision of some future good or ill." (2) But it is misleading, surely, to suggest that our concern for the future does provide us with a sufficient reason for being consistent in any sense. It might well be that in our concern for the future we will be inconstant in our willing and doing by abandoning just those courses of action that jeopardize our future. Indeed, consistency in the sense of constancy is not moral consistency at all. For even if in my concern for my future I avoid any attitude which I shall later recant, by a practical consistency or constancy of willing and doing, I could do this in the manner of an amoral Gyges who orders his appetites by circumspect application of constraints designed with a view to the future.

[5]*Ibid.,* p. 481.
[6]The term "constancy" was suggested to me by Professor D. S. Mackay.

What is required for moral consistency is that we be concerned with what will happen and is now happening to others, as we are with what affects us, whether in the present or in the future. In short, nothing less than a moral concern—a concern consistently applied to all loci of values—will support the moral attitude; and if, as Lewis rightly urges that we do, we look within ourselves for the reasons that impel us to adopt the moral attitude, the only reason that can suffice is that which can not serve as a reason because it is the datum of the commitment to morality itself.

There are those who would appeal to metaphysics at this point. But the mere appeal to an intelligence to see goodness and duty writ large in the nature of the real will not suffice. Indeed, nothing in this respect can be gained that has not already been conceded in the recognition of the truism that we ought to promote the good. A Gyges, however persuaded he may be to accept these demonstrations, will pay his intellectual respects but ignore his moral responsibilities unless he can be shown that the kind of life which he desires is impossible. But the metaphysical arguments designed to demonstrate such impossibility are highly precarious, and the empirical generalization, upon which the arguments for the pragmatic values of the adoption of the moral attitude must rest, presupposes conditions contrary to those given in the case of our hypothetical amoralist and hence are irrelevant to his special case. For if such a person were not concerned with others and hence with the ideal of a community of persons, it would not follow that he would suffer any slights and discomforts by viewing the misfortunes of others. For us, the inducement is genuine; we do want to participate in a community, and given such a concern, happiness, or well-being is not genuinely possible unless we take account of others in our evaluations. But this is not to say that being moral is useful; it serves, rather, as a reminder of our basic morality and of the fact that we will not be able to ignore or expunge it in any attempt to realize any end.

For a thoroughly amoral intelligence, nothing in principle can serve as a reason for *inducing* him to accept any moral responsibilities. Metaphysical elaborations, logical arguments, empirical generalization and data and, finally, all moral discourse with its lavish, complex, and ingenious devices of persuasion are wholly inadequate. No reasons are possible. To conclude, however, that the moral attitude, since it can not be supported by any reason, is unreasonable is to confuse the present case in which no reason in principle is possible with the familiar situation in which reasons, while possible, are not forthcoming. Indeed, the moral attitude requires no reason since it *defines,* implicitly, what it means to be reasonable in our attitude toward others.[7] To be reasonable in one's valuations entails being morally consistent, and it is simply to confuse the meanings of "reason" to suppose that the sense in which people are reasonable when they adopt the moral attitude is reducible to or analyzable in terms of those other senses of "reason" in which logical arguments, causes, purposes, etc., are commonly said to provide reasons. Nothing short of the moral commitment can provide a "reason" for the commitment in question; no reason can be offered for being morally reasonable and none may reasonably be requested.

[7]This indeed, is the contention of Lewis, but it requires no dubious identification of the morally rational with the logically rational to secure its acceptance.

How then shall we argue with one who challenges us to persuade him to adopt the moral attitude? We have, here, no theoretical issue, but a practical problem. He will not incur logical contradiction by resisting the effects of our discourse in the way in which this would occur in the case of one who disputed the principles of logic. And if his discourse is more than a clever intellectual game we shall take all the steps necessary to ensure us from harm. For this we have a reason that is sufficient, namely, a moral justification.

But if a consistent amoralism is to be maintained, no moral attitude must be evidenced by the use of hortative language. As Lewis has rightly observed,[8] the amoralist can not solicit us to share his amoral attitude, for this will betray the so-called amoralist's concern for us; once he does this he has committed himself in practice to what he denies in theory. He must not moralize or apologize. Just as we need only provoke one who denies the principle of logic to an assertion in order to affect his persuasion, so we need only provoke the professing amoralist to express his concern for others in his concern to persuade us. And the fact is that we are social beings. We may fail in our duties and forget our moral commitments, but we will betray our persistent, even though interrupted, moralism in every attempt to rationalize to others our indifference to our obligations. Why then be moral? This is, appearances to the contrary notwithstanding, no theoretical question. For the *practical* problem it poses, we can offer no theoretical compulsion, but only the datum of morality itself, a practical necessity, in the absence of which nothing else will or can do.

[8]*Op. cit.,* p. 482.

PART SIX

Metaphilosophy

The Philosophy of Philosophy

467. I am sitting with a philosopher in a garden; he says again and again "I know that that's a tree," pointing to a tree that is near us. Someone else arrives and hears this, and I tell him: "This fellow isn't insane. We are only doing philosophy."

—Ludwig Wittgenstein
On Certainty, 1969

- Samuel M. Thompson, What is Philosophy?
- R. W. Newell, Philosophical Method
- J. J. C. Smart, The Province of Philosophy
- Bertrand Russell, The Value of Philosophy
- Ludwig Wittgenstein, Philosophy
- A. J. Ayer, The Elimination of Metaphysics and the Function of Philosophy
- R. G. Collingwood, The Reform of Metaphysics
- Richard Rorty, Philosophy Without Mirrors (excerpt)
- Nicholas Rescher, The Mission of Philosophy

It is not surprising that philosophy as an open-minded inquiry into the concepts of all disciplines should also look into the practice of philosophy. The philosophy of philosophy is known as metaphilosophy. Like the philosophy of art, philosophy of language, philosophy of religion, or philosophy of science, metaphilosophy as the philosophy of philosophy investigates among other topics the concept and possibility of philosophy, and the purpose and proper methodology, if any, of philosophy.

What is philosophy? What is a philosophical problem? How are philosophical problems different from problems in history, science, art, or religion? If there are meaningful philosophical questions, are there also meaningful philosophical answers that can be arrived at in ways similar to other modes of inquiry? Philosophers have answered these kinds of questions about the nature of philosophy in different ways. The differences in their metaphilosophies have direct implications for differences in the direction, shape, and content of their philosophies. Indeed, it is no exaggeration to say that metaphilosophical differences between some philosophers are so extreme that there is virtually no common ground on which to discuss their differences as disagreements about philosophy. Some philosophers have maintained while others have flatly denied that philosophy has a special subject matter consisting of propositions about distinctively philosophical concepts. Others have argued that the goal of philosophy is something very different, in a category unlike that of other fields of knowledge. Whether philosophy is concerned exclusively with clarifying ideas, or can make positive contributions to other subjects and human endeavors, substituting improved ideas of its own for mistaken or confused conceptions, are among the important topics of metaphilosophy.

Samuel M. Thompson introduces the central problems of metaphilosophy. In the opening chapter, "What is Philosophy?," of his book *The Nature of Philosophy,* he returns to the Socratic thesis of the examined life as the heart of philosophical inquiry. He distinguishes between analytic and synthetic approaches to philosophy as complementary methods in the search for meaning. He emphasizes the natural intellectual curiosity that motivates the study of philosophy not only for its theoretical value, but more practically as "an essential preparation for self-directed action." Thompson argues that philosophy is different from other kinds of intellectual disciplines because it investigates all of its subjects in relation to basic human interests.

R. W. Newell, in "Philosophical Method," describes philosophy as reasoning about reasoning, in the critical evaluation of the logic of arguments in all reaches of knowledge. He thereby gives more definite shape to the conduct of philosophy and what it is that philosophers try to do in pursuing their quest for the examined life. The idea that philosophy has as its primary charge the scrutiny of arguments gives the philosophy of language special importance in understanding the way in which philosophical problems and arguments are formulated. At the same time, Newell declares, philosophers have assimilated the purposes and some of the methods of modern science. Newell believes that there has been too much emphasis in philosophy both on philosophical semantics and on philosophy as a kind of science. He considers recent philosophical practice, especially in the later philosophy of Ludwig Wittgenstein, whose philosophical views are briefly discussed later, and of John Wisdom and G. E. Moore. By comparing the similar but subtle differences in the practice of these influential twentieth-century philosophers, Newell represents the tasks of philosophy as a critical engagement with the scope and limits of logically correct reasoning.

J. J. C. Smart, in "The Province of Philosophy," from his book *Philosophy and Scientific Realism,* articulates what many philosophers would regard as a reasonable characterization of the aims and methods of philosophy. Smart describes philosophy as any effort to think clearly and comprehensively about the nature of the universe and the principles of conduct. He is, as are most philosophers today, undaunted by the verificationist criterion of meaning that allows only definitions and empirically verifiable statements to count as meaningful. Nor does he share in any special view of philosophy as so different from other ways of questioning the world as to preclude it from truth or relegate it to the status of a therapy. Smart nevertheless regards the elimination of nonsense as one of the ways in which philosophy performs a useful service for other disciplines in clarifying ideas and criticizing vague or poorly defined concepts wherever they occur. Yet he also sees philosophy as something more, as an evaluation of the relative plausibility of alternative hypotheses about subject matters that cannot be decided by empirical scientific methods. In this way, although certainly not all philosophers will join him in this characterization of philosophy's mission, Smart gives philosophy a much more important role to play in the pursuit of truth than many other recent commentators on the philosophy of philosophy.

Russell, in the final chapter, "The Value of Philosophy," from his book *The Problems of Philosophy,* argues that philosophy is not valuable in and of itself. He holds that the study of philosophy is only instrumentally worthwhile for the sake of the questions it poses, which he believes enhance our appreciation of the scope and limits of concepts, and nourish our intellectual imagination. Russell bases this nugatory assessment of the value of philosophy in part on the judgment that definite philosophical answers to philosophical questions are unobtainable, by sharp contrast with scientific answers to scientific questions. A critic might nevertheless observe that, except as an amusing intellectual pastime, it might be difficult to enlist the enormous energy required for philosophy if there is no greater benefit to be expected. If the value of philosophy is only indirect, as Russell proposes, then it is hard to see why the same function could not be fulfilled more directly by studying science instead of philosophy, or, say, by engaging in roughly the same kinds of mental gymnastics encountered in rhetorical or literary diversions. It is nevertheless hard to dispute Russell's observation, coming especially as it does from a philosopher of Russell's impressive stature, with wide experience in logic, mathematics, philosophy, and science, that there are not the same types of widely accepted solutions to philosophical problems as there are in the so-called exact sciences.

In the selection "Philosophy," from his "Big Typescript," Ludwig Wittgenstein offers a variety of reflections on the practice and limitations of philosophy. Wittgenstein personalizes the value of philosophical activity as an effort to clarify thinking. Wittgenstein's philosophy or antiphilosophy is divided into early and later periods. In his early thought, Wittgenstein inadvertently inspired the anti-metaphysics of the verificationist criterion of meaning, which we shall preview below in summarizing the essay by A. J. Ayer. Wittgenstein's *Tractatus Logico-Philosophicus* proposed to eliminate all philosophical questions, concepts, propositions, and problems as nonsensical, because they do not satisfy his arguably narrow theory of meaning, by which only true or false descriptive statements of empirical fact about the world are meaningful. All other uses of language are meaningless in Wittgenstein's early philosophy, even if some, such as those in ethics and aesthetics, religious life and the experience of the mystical, are misguided efforts to make pronouncements about what for Wittgenstein is humanly important nonsense. In his later period, Wittgenstein no longer accepts the theory of meaning that had driven his elimination of philosophy as meaningless in the early (anti-) philosophy.

The remarks on "Philosophy" are from this later time, occurring in a large typescript that was unpublished during Wittgenstein's life. Wittgenstein's later method similarly regards philosophy as a kind of therapy whereby we can lay philosophical preoccupations to rest by investigating what he calls their philosophical grammar.

The task of philosophy on this conception is to identify the contexts of ordinary usage in which philosophically problematic terms and phrases have a definite legitimate part to play in a language game, where they are pragmatically justified by their interconnection in nonphilosophical linguistic and extralinguistic activities. A philosophical problem arises, Wittgenstein states in a famous aphorism, only "when language goes on holiday"—when language is removed from the practical work for which it was introduced and considered philosophically in the abstract. As in his early philosophy, Wittgenstein here seems to distinguish but does not try to clarify the distinction between two different senses of philosophy. There is philosophy as it is wrongly practiced by most philosophers, which is itself or at least a source of anxiety-provoking intellectual disease. And there is the proper method and correct conduct of philosophy, which Wittgenstein in the later period describes as an investigation of philosophical grammar that offers a cure for the ills occasioned by the malpractice of philosophy. It is worth remarking that Wittgenstein, who consistently throughout his career rejected efforts to stratify logical and philosophical theories into hierarchies of disciplines and higher-order disciplines about lower-order disciplines, would have resisted the classification of his ideas about philosophy as any sort of metaphilosophy. Wittgenstein is nonetheless actively engaged in what other philosophers classify as metaphilosophical reflections about the nature and limitations of philosophy, which are appropriately included under this heading, for lack of a better term even in Wittgenstein's writings.

A. J. Ayer carries the attack against the meaningfulness of philosophy specifically to the enterprise of speculative metaphysics. The traditional problems of metaphysics, including the existence of God, and questions about ontology or the study of being, such as the existence of and identity conditions for physical objects, substance, abstract entities, properties, propositions, relations, and mathematical objects; the nature of causation; the concept of mind and freedom of will; the theory of action; and what have otherwise been acknowledged as deep investigations into such metaphysical questions as why there is something rather than nothing, why the universe exists, or why there is existence rather than nonexistence, are all dismissed on different but similar grounds by Ayer.

Ayer, in the first two chapters of his *Language, Truth and Logic,* refutes speculative metaphysics as meaningless because it fails to meet the requirements of a verificationist theory of meaning. Ayer allows only two categories of meaningful questions and propositions as answers. These are sentences that are true or false by definition, including all the mathematics we need for science, and sentences that are true or false by virtue of being subject to confirmation or disconfirmation in principle by a possible experience. This criterion extends meaningfulness to the hypotheses and conclusions of natural science, but denies meaning to metaphysics, as well as ethics, aesthetics, religious belief, and other concerns of philosophy as they are usually conceived.

With implicit but unmistakable reference to the verificationist theory of meaning as a challenge to the meaningfulness of metaphysics, R. G. Collingwood, in his *Essay on Metaphysics,* tries to rescue and resuscitate a special sense of metaphysics. Collingwood views metaphysics not as a speculative effort to answer the deep and fundamental questions of existence, but as a historical science, in which the purpose is to uncover the absolute presuppositions of other disciplines, especially science, in order to achieve greater understanding of their foundations. Collingwood anticipates the objection that merely exposing the presuppositions of science without criticizing or correcting them does not directly contribute to the progress of science. But he argues that to attempt to evaluate absolute presuppositions not only is beyond the resources of metaphysics rightly interpreted as a historical discipline but also is impossible whenever presuppositions are absolute. An absolute presupposition, the sole concern of metaphysics as a historical-philosophical practice, according to Collingwood, cannot be judged true or false by metaphysics or any other branch of philosophy or science. An absolute presupposition, as Collingwood defines the concept, has no truth value but is rather the conceptual ground that makes it possible for relative presuppositions and the superstructure of science built upon them to be true or false. Still, it might be wondered whether it could not be possible to advance a different kind of evaluation of absolute presuppositions within Collingwood's framework, not simply as true or false, but as comparatively acceptable or unacceptable, or comparatively fruitful or unfruitful, as determined by a variety of philosophically considered standards.

Richard Rorty holds up a radically different idea about the aim and proper method of philosophy in the final chapter on "Philosophy Without Mirrors" from his widely discussed book, *Philosophy and the Mirror of Nature.* Rorty conceives of philosophy pragmatically, although not in the sense of classical American pragmatism. He proposes to wean philosophy from its commitment to the truth, which has characterized the Western tradition from the time of the ancient Greeks, through the rise of modern scientific philosophy to the Enlightenment and the present day. The mirror of nature is Rorty's metaphor for the effort on the part of philosophers to represent the facts of the world in philosophy as a main part of its purpose. Philosophy without mirrors is Rorty's controversial recommendation for separating philosophy from the search for ordinary truth. What Rorty would prefer to see is philosophy estranged from its epistemic preoccupations in order to be reconceived as the love of wisdom. Rorty thus stands resolutely against the trend of metaphilosophy that seeks to make philosophy into a science or a continuation of scientific inquiry by other special means or in a special domain of problems. He argues that philosophy should replace its quasi-scientific aims to discover quasi-scientific truths within the mirror of nature with an appreciation for style in continuing the conversations of great philosophical thinkers.

To conclude this presentation of the unending debate among philosophers about the purpose and proper methods of philosophy, we turn to Nicholas Rescher. In "The Mission of Philosophy," the first chapter of volume 3, *Metaphilosophical Inquiries,* of his treatise *A System of Pragmatic Idealism,* Rescher offers a balanced view of the nature of philosophy. Rescher characterizes philosophy with sufficient generality to include virtually all of the recognized schools of philosophy, with their different problems, methods, styles, and types of expression. The succinct formulation he considers is simply to say that: "The mission of philosophy is to ask, and to answer in a rational and cognitively disciplined way, all the great questions about life in this world that people wonder about in their reflective moments." On the relation of philosophy to science, Rescher observes with historical and methodological discernment that: "Philosophy strives after the systematic integration of human knowledge that the sciences initially promised to give us but have never managed to deliver because of their ongoing division of labor and never-ending pursuit of ever more specialized detail." Rescher articulates the metaphilosophy of many practicing philosophers today and in the history of the subject, for whom philosophy in its most general terms is the effort to arrive at a rational understanding of all aspects of our lives and the world in which we live by advancing concepts, principles, and theories to arrive at a correct, comprehensive, and intellectually satisfying worldview.

What Is Philosophy?

Samuel M. Thompson

THE APPEAL OF PHILOSOPHY

It is through wonder that men begin to philosophize, whether in olden times or today. First their wonder is stirred by difficulties of an obvious sort, and then gradually they proceed to inquire about weightier matters. . . . Now the result of wonderment and perplexity is to feel oneself ignorant; if, then, it was to escape ignorance that men began to philosophize, it is evident that they were pursuing this sort of study in order to know and not from any motive of utility.[1]

"Philosophy," combining two words meaning *love* and *wisdom,* is from the Greek language, and is the name given by some early Greek thinkers to the search for truth for its own sake. Thus the source of philosophy is intellectual curiosity, the desire to know the truth about existence and to understand the significance of that truth for man. In this desire, and man's attempt to satisfy it, is the source of all theoretical inquiry; and out of philosophy have come the sciences of nature and man and society, critical history, the criticism of literature and art, and theology. Philosophy itself has lived on, side by side with its offspring, doing its own work; learning from the work of other disciplines, and considering the bearing of their findings on its own problems.

Philosophy springs from wonder, and wonder is aroused by the awareness of difficulties; by the need to understand. The difficulties which not infrequently lead men and women into the province of philosophy are the problems they meet in the attempt to live their own lives intelligently and with discrimination. What makes life worth living? What goals shall I choose? What is the meaning of failure and evil and suffering? What is my place in the scheme of things, if indeed there be a scheme of things? What is the nature of knowledge, and how can I identify truth and distinguish it from what is false? These and many other questions face all of us who take our own existence seriously and are not content to live by other people's rules and to carry out other people's wishes; who believe that life is not merely to be accepted and lived blindly, but is to be examined and its possibilities compared and tested.

According to Plato's account of Socrates' trial, a trial which resulted in his conviction and sentence of death, Socrates based his defense on the proposition that the unexamined life is not worth living. The examination of life is first of all reflection upon whatever it is that we are doing, and it is out of such reflection that many of the problems of philosophy arise. If we are scientists we investigate some aspect of the world of nature, but if we are philosophers of science we turn our attention back

---

[1]Aristotle, *The Metaphysics,* 928b 11–21, translated by Philip Wheelwright, in *Aristotle* (New York, The Odyssey Press, 1951), p. 72. By permission.
Source: The Nature of Philosophy: An Introduction, Chapter 1. New York: Holt, Rinehart and Winston, 1961, 3–28.

upon the process of scientific investigation. As philosophers of science we do not so much study the world of nature directly as we study the study of the world of nature. We seek to understand what scientific knowledge is, its significance and its relation to other modes of knowledge and belief. As the pursuit of scientific knowledge is a part of life, so the examination of that pursuit is a part of the examination of life. The same principle applies to all areas of life: philosophy of religion, philosophy of history, philosophy of the state, philosophy of education, philosophy of art, all include some kind of examination of life.

The more special and limited problems of philosophy lead into inquiries of more general scope. In its broader aspects philosophy examines the various kinds of existence and their interrelationships, in ontology; the general features of the universe as a whole, in cosmology; the nature of knowledge, in epistemology and logic; and the nature of value, in ethics and esthetics. Philosophy may reach very abstract levels and some of its problems may seem far removed from the immediate concerns of life. Yet the most abstruse and technical of philosophical problems arise out of the attempt to understand what we are, what kind of a world we live in; how we know ourselves and our world, and on what basis we select the goals for which we strive.

Why is it important to live an examined life? This itself is a philosophical problem, but we may say here that examination is essential to understanding. Without an attempt to understand we do not live our lives at their full human stretch; we are only half alive, or worse. Without understanding we do not know what we are doing or why; we are like leaves blown about by shifting winds. Without understanding our choices tend to center on the immediate issues that arise as we pursue goals and carry out purposes of which we are only dimly aware. To act as human agents in the fullest sense, to be capable of responsible self-direction, we must be able to choose our final goals and our means of reaching these goals. If we wish to make such choices in the light of knowledge and under the guidance of reason we need as adequate an understanding of ourselves and our place in existence as we can obtain. But to know our goals and how to reach them is not enough for responsible self-direction, nor is it all we need for the examination of life. To live an examined life we need to know why the goals we seek are desirable and why the means we use to reach those goals are appropriate. There are three kinds of people in the world: those who do not know what they are doing, those who do know what they are doing but do not know why they are doing it, and those who know what they are doing and know why they are doing it.

Is there not danger in this that we shall substitute thought for action? On this theme Hamlet soliloquizes:

> And thus the native hue of resolution
> Is sicklied o'er with the pale cast of thought,
> And enterprises of great pith and moment
> With this regard their currents turn away,
> And lose the name of action.

Certainly it is possible and often tempting to substitute thought for action, and the result can be disastrous. But it is also true that we sometimes act impulsively in order to avoid the painful struggle of thinking through our problems—a task we must carry out if we are to arrive at a reasoned conclusion concerning what we ought to do. When a person does not think but acts on impulse, is the act truly his own? If he does not know what he is doing he may not be even legally responsible for his act. Suppose he knows what he is doing but does not know why, or for what end, or how this action accords with the basic policies he accepts for himself. May we not say that the act is only partly his own act? When the time for action comes, when it is too late for reflection, when the pale cast of thought would now turn away the currents of enterprises of great pith and moment, then truly it is too late for thought. But unless thought has already done its work, unless the path of action has been set by thought and confirmed by reflection, we shall find ourselves acting under the control of whatever outside influences happen to be working upon us; and we shall surely be the puppets of circumstance.

Most young people of college age in our culture have lived their lives thus far almost entirely under the control of other people. Most young people are eager for independence, for the opportunity to make their own decisions and to control their own lives. But if they think that this desirable state can be achieved merely by becoming independent of parents and teachers and others who have directed their activities in the past, they are surely deceiving themselves. Merely to escape from earlier controls means only the substitution of new controls. Many who think they are living their own lives are actually the victims of social and psychological pressures of various kinds; and the chief difference between their present and past situations is that now they are pulled this way and that by forces they are not aware of, by anonymous agencies which have no genuine concern for persons. If young people are to attain to personal independence, to a true freedom of choice and decision, they need an understanding of what they are and of what values of life are available to them; they must understand something of the way in which effective decision can be made, and they must have the knowledge and insight which enables them to discover and compare and judge the alternatives open to them. Without philosophy life either is lived blindly or else is lived on trust alone.

WHAT IS PHILOSOPHY ABOUT?

> Philosophical inquiry [says Professor Philip Wheelwright] may be directed toward anything whatever, but its aim will always be to behold and understand the object of inquiry (1) in its whole character and (2) in relation to man's most enduring and most deep-rooted interests.[2]

The special sciences advance by the progressive isolation of the objects of their investigations. Chemists and physicists study the various kinds of materials we find in nature by breaking them down into their molecular components. A molecule is analyzed into its atomic structure; and atoms are understood in terms of electrons,

---

[2]*The Way of Philosophy,* Revised Edition (New York, The Odyssey Press, 1960), p. 7.

protons, neutrons, and other sub-atomic particles and processes. Even the study of the interrelationships of the parts of a complex structure is pursued scientifically by considering each distinguishable relation in isolation. The very heart of the experimental method is in its techniques of varying one factor while holding others constant, and this is a technique of isolation.

Similar strategy is used in other special disciplines. Advances in historical knowledge have come from the intense concentration by specialists upon limited areas and problems. Instead of on the history of a period or place, professional historians often concentrate on such specific aspects as the political or economic or cultural or military. In the social sciences, in the study of literature and art, in every field of investigation which carries knowledge into hitherto unknown areas of fact and value, the same method of isolation and specialization is used.

In contrast with such specialization, one basic aim of philosophy is to bring things together in thought and to try to understand them in their broadest relationships. This aim at wholeness appears in two forms. In the first place it is an attempt to see each object studied in its own unity rather than to study its various parts in isolation from each other. In the second place it is an attempt to see each object in its relations with other objects—an attempt which may lead finally to a consideration of that object in its cosmic setting.

In addition to the concern for wholes and the trend toward synthesis, philosophy has also its analytical side. Preoccupation with synthesis is exposed to the dangers of becoming careless of detail, uncritical of assumptions, and of confusing wishes for reasons. So philosophy needs for its own protection constant and vigorous critical analysis of the process of thinking in terms of wholes, in the attempt to see more clearly the things that may have been distorted or obscure from the perspective of the whole.

> All philosophy [said Alfred North Whitehead] is an endeavor to obtain a self-consistent understanding of things observed. Thus its development is guided in two ways, one is the demand for a coherent self-consistency, and the other is the elucidation of things observed.[3]

These two ways of thinking do not always go along together. Some thinkers aim at synthesis, others are concerned mainly with analysis. Some periods are periods mainly of synthesis, others are periods of analysis. For the late Bernard Bosanquet, for example, philosophy is concerned with totality:

> The essence of philosophy lies in the connected vision of the totality of things, maintaining in every point the subordination of every element and factor to every other element and factor as conditioned by the totality. . . . It includes the direct contemplation—the valuation—of the whole spectacle of life.[4]

Much of the emphasis in present day philosophy is in the contrary direction, upon analysis alone. But there are indications of a renewed interest in problems of wider scope, and it is likely that concern for integration will become stronger. Each aspect

---

[3]*Modes of Thought* (New York, The Macmillan Company, 1938), p. 208. By permission.
[4]*Science and Philosophy* (New York, The Macmillan Company, 1927), pp. 25–26. By permission.

of philosophical inquiry leads naturally to its opposite. The more ambitious and inclusive is the attempt at synthesis, the greater is the need for careful analysis of the structure and method of that philosophy; and the further we go in analysis, the more pressing becomes the need to find some unity and meaning in the scattered results of that method of inquiry.

The entire development of modern science has been in the direction of analysis, and illustrates very well the general principle that analysis without integration leads to specialization. Of course specialization is necessary, for knowledge cannot advance very far without the concentrated pursuit of localized inquiry. But the very success of a limited inquiry often invites uncritical generalizations beyond the area to which the new knowledge properly applies. To overcome this we have to turn again and again to the central organization of our beliefs and to the basic structure of our knowledge, and the problems which face us there are among the chief concerns of philosophy.

> Intellectual analysis and integration are the tasks of the philosopher [says Professor Lewis White Beck]. Philosophy has been defined as "a persistent attempt to think things through." The characteristic attitude of the philosopher is, or ought to be, patient and open-minded inquiry in a serious, disciplined, and ambitious effort to find the general traits of reality, the significance of human experience, and the place of man in the universe as a whole. Philosophy is a vigorous attempt to think about the ultimate questions that are usually "answered" by our emotions and vague hopes and fears. It is a reasoned effort to see facts and ideals, emotions and truths, man and the universe, in such a way that they will, when taken together, make more "sense" than when taken piecemeal.[5]

This suggests that in both its aspects of synthesis and analysis, philosophy is a search for meaning. We discover the meaning of the part when we find its relations with other parts and its place in the whole. To do this we need some degree of analysis, to see the part as a part in its own nature; and we need to see it also in its setting. As Susanne K. Langer has said, the guiding principle which gives to philosophy "a working basis as well as an ultimate aim . . . is the pursuit of meaning."[6]

The pursuit of meaning leads us to inquire concerning the relevance of knowledge for man. What is all this to us, to our enduring interests and basic needs? What is the human situation in relation to the world as we know it? In considering such problems, philosophy can help to open up to us also the meaning of other disciplines. As Erwin Schrödinger, the distinguished physicist, has said:

> It seems plain and self-evident, yet it needs to be said: the isolated knowledge obtained by a group of specialists in a narrow field has in itself no value whatsoever, but only in its synthesis with all the rest of knowledge and only inasmuch as it really contributes in this synthesis something toward answering the demand . . . "Who are we?"[7]

[5]*Philosophic Inquiry: An Introduction to Philosophy* (New York, Prentice-Hall, Inc., 1952), p. 4. By permission.
[6]*The Practice of Philosophy* (New York, Henry Holt and Company, 1930), p. 21.
[7]*Science and Humanism* (Cambridge, Cambridge University Press, 1953), p. 5.

THE SEARCH FOR MEANING

Philosophy is an attempt to grasp in thought the forms of existence disclosed in human experience, the search by thought for the rational structure of existence. It is true that philosophy is not the only kind of search for the rational structure of existence, for the sciences also engage in such a search. But philosophy differs from the natural sciences partly in that its search is by reflective thought alone. Knowledge of existence which requires experiment or the use of mathematical forms as instruments of inquiry belongs to the natural sciences and not to philosophy.

As Susanne Langer insists, philosophy is also a search for the meaning of existence, and in this, like the arts and literature, philosophy belongs with the humanities. As a search for the meaning of existence, philosophy differs from other humanistic disciplines in concerning itself with the meaning that existence has for thought. What do we mean, in our thought about existence? and What meaning has existence for thought? are two sides of the same question. Any attempt to answer this question by means of reflective thinking which is subjected to logical tests of validity and truth is philosophy.

Because of the importance of the search for meaning as a part of philosophy's task, philosophers have usually given considerable attention to language. Some contemporary philosophers, indeed, consider that the main task of philosophy is the analysis of language. The current emphasis upon language analysis is an understandable and a salutary reaction against claims made by many philosophers that they are giving a direct and final report of the ultimate nature of existence and knowledge. The analysis of language is a part of what Whitehead calls "the elucidation of things observed." Language is an expression of thought, and thought that claims to have obtained truth is thought about something. Thus the analysis of language contributes to our understanding of how we think about the things and events we find in experience. As it is a reflection upon the concepts we use in our efforts to understand existence, philosophy is also an examination of the basic structures or forms we find in existence.

A serious philosopher, however, needs assistance from others who are engaged in the same kind of task. To read a philosopher who thinks differently from us about existence is to expose our own thoughts to contact with forms of existence we had missed before. Philosophers may be expected to differ about what forms of existence are basic; for this is a matter of interpretation founded on the individual thinker's own unique pattern of experience. A philosophy is a conceptual interpretation of existence in terms most meaningful to the interpreter, and by discovering what interpretations are significant for other thinkers we expand and transform our own understanding. The process by which this takes place, and its contribution to the discovery of truth, we shall consider later in our study of the method of philosophy.

In human anatomy we study the various structures of the body; and in physiology we study the functions which those structures perform. In psychology we study man's behavior and his modes of experience and adjustment; and in the social sciences we study the various relationships men have with one another in society. The physiologist is concerned with anatomy, but only so far as it has a bearing on physiology; the psychologist takes account of anatomy and physiology, but only so far as those sciences are pertinent to the study of human behavior. Each discipline makes whatever use it can of the results achieved in other disciplines; but no special science studies man as man in an attempt to understand the meaning of human existence.

Sociology and anthropology and psychology give us valuable information concerning human motives and the methods by which men live together; they show us the differences and contrasts among human cultures; they help us understand why some societies have been strong and long-lived while others have been weak and ineffective. But no such studies, so long as they are concerned with discovering and reporting the facts as those facts are observed, can answer the question of what kinds of human life and society are desirable for man. They may be able to tell us much about what man *does* desire but they cannot tell us what man *ought* to desire. To inquire what man ought to desire is to inquire into his place in the whole scheme of things, and this requires some conception of what that scheme is.

To say that philosophy aims at wholeness is to say that philosophy seeks to understand an object not only in terms of its own internal unity but also in terms of its relations to other things. Just as the significance of man's physical make-up can be understood only as we see it in its relations with other aspects of man's nature, so the significance of man's existence can be grasped only by considering man's relations to other existences. In this way alone thought can hope to find the meaning of human life, for the question of the meaning of something is the question of its place in a whole to which it belongs.

Whenever we ask the question of what is the meaning of this or that, we ask the question of how this or that exists in relation to other things. If we wish to understand the meaning of a man's position as an officer of a corporation, for example, we try to discover the relationships he has in that office to other officers and departments. In order to understand this, in turn, we need to know something of the pattern of organization, the kind of business in which the corporation is engaged, and the various relations it has to other industrial and financial organizations. This, in turn, can be understood only in the light of our knowledge of the economy as a whole and even of the world economy together with its historical setting and development.

Even when the pursuit of meaning requires that we break something up into its parts, the attempt to discover the meaning of each part leads into a study of the relation of that part to other things. The search for meaning thus may not always proceed as if in a straight line from the lesser to the more inclusive. It may require frequent steps of analysis, and new attempts which take their point of departure from the products of analysis; but as we push the search for meaning in any single direction we are driven on to wider and wider wholes. If we do not stop short at some point, the search for meaning inevitably leads to questions about the whole of existence, about the various modes of being and their relations with each other. Thus when pursued relentlessly the search for meaning leads to the attempt to find out what is ultimate and final in existence and to understand other things in terms of their relations with these ultimates. Various systems of philosophy are theories concerning ultimates. They are attempts to push our explanations back until we come to something that explains other things but cannot itself be explained in terms of anything else.

If, as some ancient philosophers supposed, the cosmos is ultimately a plurality of material particles ("atoms") in motion in empty space so that everything that happens is understandable as a complex of atomic motions and collisions; then the moving atoms and the empty space in which they move are the ultimates for that philosophy. The existence of these ultimates explains the events of the world, but nothing accounts for the atoms and empty space. If, as some other philosophers have held, the world of nature is the expression or manifestation of a universal mind, then no part of nature accounts for the existence of that mind. The existence of the universal mind is what accounts for the existence of nature; and the universal mind is the ultimate for that philosophy. If the world is the creation of a self-existent God, as Hebrew, Christian, and Muslim versions of theism contend; then God is the ultimate and everything else is dependent on God. The existence of the world is explained by the creative activity of God, but the world in no way accounts for God.

Even those philosophies which deny that there is any ultimate in existence, or deny that we can know such ultimates if they do exist, or deny that the very question of ultimates has any meaning, are setting forth theories of ultimates. The denial of ultimates is itself an ultimate of a sort, for although it denies that there is anything in existence that is ultimate, yet this knowledge is taken to be final. The denial that we can know ultimates is a claim to have a kind of ultimate knowledge. The contention that the questions of philosophy, as traditionally understood, are meaningless is itself a claim to finality in our knowledge of the significance of the traditional questions of philosophy. They turn out to have a meaning after all, even if only as expressions of human misunderstanding and confusion.

When we begin to ask why certain actions are required of us and why certain other things are denied to us we have begun an inquiry which raises philosophical questions if followed out far enough. In this sense most of us are engaged to some degree in philosophical inquiry. Our philosophizing may be well or poorly done, but is a kind of philosophizing nevertheless. The practical importance of the study of philosophy is found in the fact that it is better to do our philosophical thinking with some competence and awareness of what we are doing and of how we are doing it than to do such thinking blindly and incompetently. Any conscious control which a person exerts over his life is exerted with reference to some framework of existence and value. Surely it is worth our while to become familiar with some of the important possible frameworks of life.

PHILOSOPHY AS REFLECTIVE INQUIRY

As the search for the meaning that existence has for thought, philosophy is a *reflective* inquiry. We are directly aware of clouds in the sky, of fields and trees and houses, of living things, of other people and of what they say and do. To increase our knowledge of the nature of any of these things we turn to a special science or special factual discipline. But our awareness that some of the things we think about really exist while others do not is almost sure to be a reflective awareness. We ordinarily judge that the things we see are things that really exist, but we do not in a strict sense *see* their existence as we see, say, their colors and shapes. The distinction between what exists and what does not is a distinction based on experience but made explicit only by thought. We accept as true or reject as false the statements we hear from the lips of others; but only as we turn our attention from the statements themselves and reflect on our way of judging do we become aware of that distinction between truth and falsity we actually use when we agree or disagree with what others say. In our political society we try to establish justice in human relations; but as philosophers we ask, "What is justice?" and "What is the distinction between justice and injustice?" Such reflective inquiries are not pursued primarily by seeking new information but trying to discover the meaning of the facts we already know.

Of course every inquiry is in some sense a search for meaning. Philosophy's search for meaning, however, is in a framework of ultimates. As soon as any inquiry begins to raise questions about ultimates it begins to be concerned with philosophical problems. But the distinction between what is proximate and what is ultimate, between what can be explained by something else and what cannot be explained at all or else is its own explanation, is a distinction that comes into explicit awareness only as we reflect on what we already know. We may *act* in terms of a distinction between the proximate and the ultimate, we may even *feel* such a distinction, but it becomes explicit in our awareness so that we know *what* it is only when we examine it in reflection.

From this we may formulate a brief statement of what is distinctive about a philosophical problem. In the first place, philosophy is concerned with the kind of question which can be investigated by thought alone. This does not mean that we can depend on thought alone for knowledge. In order to learn something by thinking we must already have something to think about. We learn about our world and about ourselves from sense perception, from scientific observation and experiment, and by the use of imagination in art and literary creation. Whatever additional well-grounded knowledge we can obtain by thought alone is philosophical knowledge. We can see what people look like, we can observe their behavior, and we can examine their physical constitution. From such sources we get our common sense and scientific knowledge of man. But if we ask whether man is capable of free choice or is controlled in all his actions entirely by causes beyond his reach, we ask a question that can be investigated only by reflective thought. What we need in order to answer this question is not further factual accounts of how people act but an understanding of the import of the acts we already know about.

Philosophy, like any serious inquiry, is a search for truth. But philosophy differs from other kinds of inquiry in its concern not only to discover what the truth is but also to inquire into the method by which we attempt to find the truth. Philosophy's search for *what* we know always involves the problem of *how* we know. This is the second distinctive character of philosophy. At the point when the question of how we know is raised in any other discipline—such as in a science or mathematics, or history—inquiry becomes philosophical and only the methods of philosophy can be used. The problem of whether or not the method used in a scientific inquiry is a sound one is not a scientific question; the question is one of logic and the philosophy of science. The tests of truth used in historical investigation cannot be examined by the methods of historical inquiry. The problem is one for the philosophy of history. As we shall see later, philosophical inquiry is always unformalized inquiry. As soon as a definite formal procedure is established in any field of inquiry, then investigations can be carried on in that area independently of philosophy.

The third distinctive character of philosophy is its concern with ultimates. We reflect on many questions that face us from day to day, in our work and in our other activities. Someone wants to buy a property I own. Shall I accept his offer or not? A college student must decide upon his major field; a medical student considers whether to specialize or go into general practice; a lawyer is offered appointment as a judge. These are matters of serious concern, and anyone faced with such choices will surely reflect carefully before he decides. But these as they stand are not philosophical questions. Although they may all lead into philosophical questions, each one is limited in scope. Each is limited in scope because it is a question about what is to be done rather than primarily an attempt to discover truth for the sake of knowing what the truth is. When we ask what the truth is and how we know what it is, we are raising the kind of question which remains a problem until our inquiry has taken us to the foundations of our knowledge. We are not through with such a question until we have discovered and recognized our basic assumptions, until we are satisfied that our thinking has reached its ultimate foundations. When our practical problems lead us into such questions as What is the best kind of life for man to live? and Are the values by which I make my choices genuine or counterfeit values? we are seeking not only to decide but to know. We are seeking the kind of knowledge which makes wise decision possible.

Practical questions lead into theoretical questions if we press those practical questions far enough. Of course we seldom have to do so in the ordinary affairs of life, but the affairs of life are not always ordinary. In time of crisis we find ourselves facing questions which can be dealt with adequately only by examining our assumptions concerning what life is about, what goals are truly desirable, and what limits upon our own power and knowledge we need to respect. The question of what the government needs to do when an industrial conflict threatens the national economy may lead into the question of how far the powers of government ought to be used to bring about the settlement of such a conflict. This is a question of political philosophy. Any practical question concerning which is the better course to follow, whether it arises in our personal lives or in business or in politics, can lead into questions concerning what the difference is between the better and the worse, the difference between good and evil, and the basis upon which we can make these distinctions.

Theoretical questions in other fields may also involve philosophical problems. A physicist who is concerned with problems about atomic structure may be forced to reflect on the question of just what a structure is. The scientific search for truth about matter and energy and life may lead into questions of what we mean by truth and how we distinguish what is true from what is not true. These are not scientific questions, and they cannot be investigated by the methods of science. These are philosophical questions and we can get on with them only by using methods appropriate to philosophical questions. Reflection is often philosophical, in the sense that it concerns matters of philosophical import, without reaching to the level of philosophical inquiry. It arrives at some conclusion but neglects the question of how we know the conclusion is sound. Such thinking may be quite revealing; it may communicate discoveries which have far-reaching influence. The sayings of great religious teachers are usually of this character; and the writings of philosophers often contain material of this kind. For example, the following passage from Epictetus is philosophical but not by itself a philosophical inquiry:

> What disturbs men's minds is not events but their judgments on events. For instance, death is nothing dreadful, or else Socrates would have thought it so. No, the only dreadful thing about it is men's judgment that it is dreadful. And so when we are hindered, or disturbed, or distressed, let us never lay the blame on others, but on ourselves, that is, on our own judgments. To accuse others for one's own misfortunes is a sign of want of education; to accuse oneself shows that one's education has begun; to accuse neither oneself nor others shows that one's education is complete.[8]

Here we have perhaps some conclusions reached as the result of philosophical inquiry; or perhaps they are insights which were somehow suddenly recognized by Epictetus as worth recording and communicating. At only one point in this passage does Epictetus give a reason in support of anything he says: "Death is nothing dreadful, or else Socrates would have thought it so." Everything else is either an announcement of what he sees to be true or a recommendation concerning its application to conduct. We are convinced that some statements are true merely by having our attention called to them. Where this happens to us, we are not aware of being confronted by a problem; and inquiry is at an end. Such insights may contribute to the solution of philosophical problems, and they may well be a part of philosophical inquiry; but by themselves alone, merely as something announced, they constitute a philosophy only in part.

To say that this pronouncement by Epictetus is philosophy only in an incomplete sense is not to deny that it is philosophy at all. We here see what a great and discerning mind, reflecting upon his and other men's experience, has discovered to be implicit in that experience. Epictetus gives us one interpretation of the significance of our failures and anxieties, an interpretation which must be understood and taken into account in any serious attempt to evaluate this aspect of life.

Literature is full of philosophical reflection, in this limited sense of "philosophical." Consider the following passage by Joseph Conrad:

> I need not tell you what it is to be knocking about in an open boat. I remember nights and days of calm, when we pulled, we pulled, and the boat seemed to stand still, as if bewitched within the circle of the sea horizon. I remember the heat, the deluge of rain-squalls that kept us baling for dear life (but filled our water-cask), and I remember sixteen hours on end with a mouth dry as a cinder and a steering-oar over the stern to keep my first command head on to a breaking sea. *I did not know how good a man I was till then.* I remember the drawn faces, the dejected figures of my two men, and I remember my youth and the feeling that will never come back any more—the feeling that I could last for ever, outlast the sea, the earth, and all men; *the deceitful feeling that lures us on*

---

[8]"The Manual of Epictetus," #5, *Arrian's Discourses of Epictetus,* translated by P. E. Matheson, in *The Stoic and Epicurean Philosophers,* edited by Whitney J. Oates (New York, Random House, 1940), p. 469. By permission of Oxford University Press.

to joys, to perils, to love, to vain effort—to death; the triumphant conviction of strength, the heat of life in the handful of dust, the glow in the heart that with every year grows dim, grows cold, grows small, and expires—*and expires, too soon—before life itself.*[9]

Much of what Joseph Conrad has to say here is a direct report from experience. But in the three passages which have been printed here in italics, Conrad is not merely reporting the facts about an experience; he is either reflecting upon the experience or reporting an earlier reflection. "I did not know how good a man I was till then," is an order of knowledge quite different from: ". . . the heat, the deluge of rain-squalls that kept us baling for dear life (but filled our water-cask). . . ." We perceive rain-squalls as we perceive clouds and trees, but by no such perception does a man discover how good a man he is. To discover this required reflection upon experience and the discovery in that reflection of the meaning of his strength and endurance. In his reference to the feeling of power as "the deceitful feeling that lures us on to joys, to perils, to love, to vain effort—to death . . . and expires, too soon—before life itself," Conrad is reporting something that can be learned only by reflection. Here is judgment upon that feeling; a statement of its significance and import.

In both of these examples, the one from Epictetus and the one from Joseph Conrad, we see how reflection contributes to our understanding of experience. In both instances reflection brings a grasp of the meaning of certain experiences—the fear of death, and the challenge of a harsh nature to a man's strength and will. In neither of these passages, however, do we have an instance of philosophical thinking as it actually goes on. Each reports what may have been a result of reflective inquiry or, in contrast, may have been nothing more than an intuitive estimate or the expression of a mood. We engage in philosophy only when our reflection leads to inquiry in which we state explicitly the reasons for our conclusions and examine critically their logical relationship to the reasons we give for them. Much thinking is philosophical, in the sense that it concerns problems of philosophical import; but that does not constitute philosophy if it takes no account of the way in which its conclusions are reached, or fails to examine the logical basis for the claim of truth.

THE KIND OF TRUTH PHILOSOPHY SEEKS

Philosophy's search for the meaning existence has for thought is a search for this meaning as knowledge and not merely as satisfactory belief. A philosophy may be interesting or stimulating or inspiring, but its primary concern as philosophy is for truth. Since he uses thought alone as his instrument, the philosopher's test of truth must be a test which can be applied by thought alone. This would be a logical test, and so philosophical thinking is guided and evaluated in terms of its logical soundness.

Whenever we reach a conclusion by thinking alone and base its truth claim on thought, there is only one way to defend that conclusion without appealing to some kind of evidence other than that presented in thought. The only defense open to us

[9]From Joseph Conrad's story, "Youth."

is to show that admitting the basic assumptions upon which our thought is operating, what we claim to be true is true because it *has* to be true. We defend such a truth claim by showing that the conclusion is undeniable without contradiction.

In such cases the standard by which we distinguish between what is true and what is false is a logical standard, and the use of logical standards of course is not confined by any means to philosophy. If I already know that a man prominent in national politics is a naturalized citizen of the United States, and if I know that no one but a native born citizen can be elected President of the United States, then I know also by thought alone that this man is not eligible for the Presidency. The conclusion I draw has such a relation to my other knowledge that it *cannot* be false if the other assertions are true. Its truth follows by necessity from the truth of the other statements. The conclusion is not a new truth generated by a blending of the other statements, as if by some mysterious synthesis, a new item is added to previous knowledge. On the contrary, what thought does here is to bring into the open, where it can be seen directly, some aspect or relationship within the facts already known. Reasoning exhibits something already implicit in what we were aware of before; although what reasoning does thus bring into the open may not have been recognized by us previously as involved in what we knew. We have not seen it before, perhaps, because we have not before organized our knowledge in such a way as to make this further aspect of it apparent.

I may know that the left guard of the football team at Belmont College is to be the captain of the team next year. I may know that Harry Brown, a business acquaintance, has a son on the Belmont team. These are two apparently unrelated, or at best only remotely related, bits of information I happen to have picked up in casual contacts. If, however, someone tells me that young Brown plays left guard, then I see these other facts in a new relationship—a relationship which brings out what before had not been apparent to me, that young Brown is to be the new football captain. I may say to myself, "I wish I had known that when I saw Brown yesterday; I'd have said something about it." I did not know it because I was not aware of the additional fact—that young Brown plays left guard—the fact needed to show the mutual relevance of the facts I already knew.

The process of thinking by which a conclusion is obtained, and its necessary relation with its premises is shown, is *reasoning.* Not all rational knowledge, however, is obtained by this form of reasoning. Some statements we know to be true, and true necessarily, when we become aware of the meanings of the words used to express thought. We have certain *concepts,* and from our understanding of the concepts we can recognize that certain assertions involving those concepts are necessarily true and that certain other assertions cannot be true. If we understand the way in which an ordinary map is constructed we know that there *cannot* be two places on that map with the same latitude and longitude. Our ordinary concept of time *requires* us to deny that the past can be repeated.

There is a further consequence of the fact that truth claims of thought are defended by showing their necessity. These truth claims are also claims of universality. To defend our thinking as true by showing its logical necessity is also to claim that any other person who thinks logically and who uses the same concepts and makes the same assumptions will have to agree with the assertions we contend are involved in

those concepts or implicit in those premises. This does not mean that another's disagreement with our assertions is an indication that those assertions are false; for the
disagreement may be based on misunderstanding or may result from unrecognized
differences in our concepts. It does mean that disagreement cannot survive mutual
understanding except as an indication that at least one position is false.

The kind of truth philosophy seeks is the truth which can be obtained only by
the sustained application of such standards as rational necessity and universality, an
application carried through to the end. We do not reach the end of a philosophical
inquiry until we have found the ultimate reasons for our conclusions and have given
careful consideration to the kinds of reasons we are appealing to and their relevance
to our problem. We may be quite confident that some of the ultimate principles of
any philosophy will be found to be assumptions. Some assumptions are arbitrary,
and are assented to because a thinker has chosen to make a commitment. Sometimes reasons are offered not in support of the truth of an assumption but in defense
of making the assumption, in the same way that a person might offer reasons for
assuming the veracity of a witness although he had no evidence to support the truth
of what the witness had said. That a philosopher makes assumptions is not to his
discredit, for it is a considerable achievement to bring basic assumptions into the
open to see what they are, and to see also what conclusions follow from them. A
systematic philosophy puts such relationships upon public exhibition.

PHILOSOPHY AND OTHER FIELDS OF KNOWLEDGE

Although various fields of inquiry have close relations with each other, and students
in one field use results obtained in other fields, yet each discipline has a certain autonomy. Only confusion can result from failure to respect that autonomy. Indeed the consequence is often much more serious than mere confusion; bitter intellectual controversies, violent political conflicts, and even bloody wars have come from failure to
respect the difference between the questions appropriate to one field of inquiry and
those appropriate to another. As a condition of clarity in our thinking and in the organization of our knowledge we must respect the autonomy of each field of knowledge.

Before the emergence of the natural sciences, as we now know them, philosophers often attempted to solve scientific problems by the use of thought alone. In
the following quotation, note how Lucretius appeals to what "must" be and what
"ought" to be in his discussion of the motions of atoms:

> Again things which look to us hard and dense must consist of particles more hooked
> together, and be held in union because welded all through with branch-like ele-
> ments. . . . Those things which are liquid and of fluid body ought to consist more of
> smooth and round elements; for the several drops have no mutual cohesion and their
> onward course too has a ready flow downwards. All things lastly which you see dis-
> perse themselves in an instant, as smoke mists and flames, if they do not consist
> entirely of smooth and round, must yet not be held fast by closely tangled elements.[10]

[10]*On the Nature of Things*, Book II, translated by H. A. J. Munro, in Oates, *op. cit.*, pp. 99–100. By permission of Oxford University Press.

In contrast with the passage from Lucretius, the following by Marcus Aurelius is at least the beginning of a genuinely philosophical reflection concerning the cosmos:

> Either it is a well-arranged universe or a chaos huddled together, but still a universe. But can a certain order subsist in thee, and disorder in the All?[11]

The rhetorical question is, of course, an appeal to what we must think. Whether the implicit conclusion is true or false, nevertheless the quesion is one that can be investigated only by reflective thought directed upon what we already know and not by collecting further factual evidence.

In spite of the autonomy of each science and intellectual discipline, philosophy is in a unique position in its relation to other fields of inquiry. For every kind of intellectual inquiry makes its own philosophical assumptions and raises its own philosophical problems. Every inquiry makes assumptions about what exists and what does not exist, about the nature of knowledge and the tests of truth, and about the worth of its own existence as an inquiry. If questions are raised concerning the philosophical assumptions or implications of a discipline, those questions can be properly investigated only by the methods of philosophy.

It is easy to see how the very existence of a field of inquiry can lead to important philosophical problems. Although a philosopher does not investigate the problems of a natural science, such as physics, unless he is a physicist as well as a philosopher, he may consider what significance physics has for man. To pursue the problem of the human significance of a science he may ask such questions as how scientific knowledge exists and what is its structure, what are its assumptions and implications for human welfare. Such questions about physics cannot be investigated by the methods used in a physics laboratory any more than we can look at the science of biology through a microscope or examine astronomy with a telescope.

Philosophy differs from the special sciences and disciplines in another respect. The methods and techniques of a special science are governed by the desire to know and understand the object of investigation solely for what it is. The scientist attempts to be completely objective and impersonal. Whatever other desires and interests he may have, his personal likes and dislikes or even his ambitions as a scientist, are kept out of the picture. One basic aim of philosophy, however, is to understand the objects of its inquiry "in relation to man's most enduring and most deep-rooted interests."

This is not to say that a philosopher solves his problems by expressing his preferences and feelings concerning the objects he studies. He may confuse the expression of personal preference with logical thinking, but when he does so he fails as a philosopher; the process of philosophizing is a strictly intellectual activity. But the intellectual problem itself, when it is a philosophical problem, requires the philosopher to take intellectual account of man's wishes and desires in relation to his enduring and deep-rooted interests.

---

[11]*The Meditations of Marcus Aurelius Antoninus,* IV, 27, translated by G. Long, in Oates, *op. cit.,* p. 512. By permission of Oxford University Press.

It is very easy, of course, to say that we must respect the autonomy of each discipline and refrain from trying to solve problems that belong to one by use of the methods of another. In practice this principle is sometimes difficult to apply. As human knowledge pushes back its borders and opens up new problems we do not always know in the early stages just where the new problems belong. It is important, however, to be on guard constantly against the danger of such confusion and to avoid it whenever and as soon as possible. But if we are to err on one side or the other it may be better for a worker in one field of study to trespass on another rather than to be held back by any strictures concerning the danger of confusion and the importance of autonomy. If he goes too far, that error can be corrected later by his critics; but if he holds back, the world may lose something important. This applies of course primarily to those who have something important to say and, as in the arts, to those who know the rules well enough to understand what they are doing when they violate those rules.

PHILOSOPHY AND OTHER QUESTS FOR MEANING

As we have seen, the questions of philosophy are not questions which lead us to push further the frontiers of factual knowledge; they are rather questions which require reflection upon what we already know. Reflection upon what we already know leads to an important extension of our knowledge, but it might well be considered an extension in depth rather than a widening of the field of knowledge. We discover by other methods what the things in our world are like, but philosophy's primary question is what these things mean to thought.

The question of meaning, in the sense in which we have discussed it, is usually a question of special personal interest to the individual thinker. His primary concern is often the meaning of his own existence. What am I? Who am I? What is my place in the scheme of things? These are the questions that perhaps most often lead to philosophical reflection. A scientist's intellectual curiosity as he exercises it in his field of study is objective and impersonal. The first thing he has to learn is to exclude his own wishes and hopes from his inquiry. He presents the results of his study to other scientists, and they undertake to consider those results with the same impersonality and objectivity. The philosopher's intellectual curiosity, however, is more likely to have a deep personal involvement. The knowledge he seeks may be personal in the sense of revealing to him his own existence and the meaning of other existence in relation to himself and to human values. Even if a philosopher attempts no more than the clarification of thought by the analysis of language and concepts, the thought which he analyzes may have a very personal significance and the desire for clarity may be so intense as to be a passion.

Since the search for meaning is likely to be a personal thing, one which involves our attitudes and our deepest concerns, it is not strange that man seeks meaning by other than philosophical methods. Because of this it is important for us to see clearly the difference between philosophy and such other approaches as literature, music, art, and religion. These differ from philosophy in that they are discoveries of what existence means in terms of feeling and imagination and personal encounter. Philosophy is the discovery of what experience and existence mean to thought. It seeks not appreciation or encounter, but understanding; and its tools are concepts. Philosophy will not reveal the meaning of existence for feeling or for imagination, nor will it place us in our proper personal relation to God or to the ground of being; but neither in literature or art or religion can we ever discover the meaning of existence for thought. We may obtain important and even indispensable data from them, data for the reflective inquiries of philosophy, but only by the method of philosophy can that inquiry be pursued.

No one waits until he becomes a philosopher to find some meaning in life. In the very process of growing up we get ideas of what we are and of where we stand in relation to others and to the world. We get these ideas from the beliefs and attitudes we encounter in our families and friends and neighborhood and school. The great difference between philosophy and the schemes of interpretation we find in common sense and popular religion is that philosophy is a conscious search for truth under the control of logical standards. As soon as we question the truth of the beliefs we have acquired in childhood we are beyond the reach of those beliefs to help us. At this point belief is not enough; we need a different kind of assurance of truth. When we begin to think we express the need not merely for something to accept but for intellectual understanding and insight.

SUMMARY

Philosophy arises out of intellectual curiosity, from the need to understand ourselves and our world. The examination of life leads us into the examination not only of our beliefs but also of the ways by which we arrive at our beliefs. Philosophy is not a substitute for action, but philosophy is an essential preparation for self-directed action which is undertaken with some assurance that the course to be followed is wise and sound.

Philosophical inquiry views its object, whatever that object may be, in its whole character and in its relation to man's most basic interests. To accomplish its aim philosophy needs to use the methods of intellectual analysis as well as those of synthesis, and to keep them in proper relation with each other. Philosophical inquiry, however, involves more than merely a point of view or a set of answers to questions. It includes also an explicit presentation and examination of the reasons for the conclusions reached, together with a critical consideration of the method by which thought proceeds. Philosophy is reflective inquiry which includes a concern with the problem of *how* we know as well as an attempt to find *what* we know, and which has no stopping place short of an explicit exposure of the basic assumptions and the ultimate considerations which enter into our thinking.

Inquiry which views its objects in relation to man's basic interests becomes a search for meaning. Philosophy's search for meaning is a search for the meaning which existence has for thought. This cannot be carried very far without an analysis of language, for language is the indispensable instrument of thought. Philosophy's task is a cooperative task; for although thinking is something that goes on only in the individual, yet the individual's own thinking, if it is to achieve results of any importance, needs the help it can get from the work of others. The search for meaning involves us in the search for relations and for wholes; for to discover the meaning of something is to discover its place and its function in the whole to which it belongs. This leads us naturally into a consideration of ultimates.

Philosophical inquiry is reflective inquiry, but not all reflection is philosophy. First of all, philosophical reflection involves, directly or indirectly, a concern with ultimates. Secondly, it is reasoned inquiry in which we examine evidence, become aware of our assumptions, and evaluate our inferences under the control of logical standards. The logical standards which thought employs are necessity and universality, and the kind of truth which philosophy seeks is the kind we obtain by applying those standards rigorously to the very end. One of the important achievements of philosophy is to bring out into the open the basic assumptions we have been making in our thinking.

Each kind of inquiry has its own problems, its own methods, and its own assumptions. Philosophy, science, mathematics, history, and theology are autonomous disciplines, and the problems of one cannot be solved by the methods of another. The position of philosophy, however, is unique in this way: every field of inquiry makes philosophical assumptions and raises philosophical problems, but philosophy alone is in a position to subject such assumptions and problems to rational examination and inquiry. Recognition of this fact thus requires us to distinguish philosophy from other ways by which we seek to find the meaning of things in relation to our fundamental interests. Philosophy differs from literature, music, art, and religion in that it seeks to discover the meaning of life and existence for thought.

Philosophical Method

R. W. Newell

I. REASONING ABOUT REASONING

It is the business of philosophers to mind other people's arguments. The study of physical and mental phenomena, of right and wrong, or of the past or future, is not a part of philosophical practice; these provinces are reserved for physicists and psychologists, moralists and historians. Of interest to a philosopher are the verificational characteristics of statements, questions and disputes which these (and other) studies generate: he is a meta-commentator about first order thinking. To philosophize is to reason about reasoning. This proposition naturally encourages departmental partitioning: the philosophy of science investigates the reasoning of scientists; the philosophy of mathematics the reasoning of mathematicians; the philosophy of psychology the reasoning of psychologists; the philosophy of

Source: The Concept of Philosophy, Chapter 8. London: Methuen & Co. Ltd., 1967, 138–160.

theology the reasoning of theologians; and so on. Cutting across these partitions is the philosophy, or the theory, of knowledge.

Knowledge is anybody's affair. It does not name an occupation or a calling and there are no specialists in knowledge as there are in aerodynamics or art. There is not a philosophy of knowledge as there is a philosophy of physics; to treat the philosophy of knowledge as on a par with the philosophy of mathematics or psychology, differing only in subject matter, is to be guilty of a serious mis-allocation. There is no proper or professional activity called "knowledge" as there are proper and professional activities called "physics" and "mathematics." The competence of Plato and Aristotle to philosophize about knowledge is not diminished by the discoveries of Newton, Darwin or Einstein, and their philosophical reflections are neither more nor less fruitful for the two thousand years between them and contemporary science. The theory of knowledge seems, and is, an especially "philosophical" branch of philosophy, transcending empirical discoveries and professional advances. Yet it deals with exactly the same *philosophical* problems as the philosophy of physics, mathematics, or psychology, when stripped of their non-philosophical specialist uniforms. For the theory of knowledge is a purely *a priori* investigation of the possible types and varieties of reasoning; and reasoning, like knowledge, is not the monopoly of any particular company of reasoners at any particular time. It is a commodity common to every investigation of any problem at any time. On these grounds the philosophy of knowledge is largely taken up with the reasoning of the non-specialist plain man or the specialist in his off-duty thinking. In this book the target has been the reasoning of the specialist in philosophy in his professional moments. The aim has been to give some account of the nature of this reasoning and of philosophical knowledge.

When Newton theorized about the falling apple he was reflecting on things that happen, and his theory is correct or incorrect, appropriate or not, depending upon the facts. There is a difference in excellence, complexity and scope, but not in verification, between the inferences of Newton and those of Sherlock Holmes. Unlike Newton and Holmes, a philosopher's theorizing is concerned with the logical character of reasoning about the facts rather than with the facts themselves. His questions are meta-questions, questions about questions often about matters of fact.

For example. A person may ask whether the height of the Average Constable is six feet. Another person may ask whether the sum of the heights of all constables divided by their number is six feet. A third person may ask whether the first and second persons asked the same or different questions. We can give a right answer to this third question without giving a right answer to the other two; we can know the answer to the third and not know the answer to the first or second. It is impossible to answer the first two by reflection alone and irrelevant in answering the third to investigate empirically the heights of the individual constables: their mode of verification is necessarily different. Philosophical questions are in an analogous position. Sometimes this has been expressed by saying that philosophical questions are "perennial" or "timeless"; or expressed by the remark that they are second-order questions and that the investigations they launch are logically independent of the results of empirical inquiries. However there is nothing in this to separate questions of philosophy from questions of mathematics and formal logic, since both are requests for reflection of a certain sort.

Yet philosophical arguments are not formal demonstrations. There are no philosophical axioms, theorems or postulates and a noteworthy feature of philosophical reasoning is the absence of a Euclidian Q.E.D. A philosopher's reasoning is not dismissed solely on the grounds of its difference from a mathematical proof.

These characteristics have given rise to a chronic self-consciousness among philosophers about the nature and methods of philosophical investigation. One standard move, documented in the first chapter of this book, is to suppose that puzzlement about the position of philosophical method can be overcome by locating the reasoning of philosophers within territories ordinarily assigned to non-philosophical disciplines. Philosophy is thus classified as a kind of science, a department of logic, or a linguistic activity issuing verbal recommendations; and the particular sin is the idea that philosophy can be *sui generis.* The source of the dogma is obvious at once. The proposition that there can be no such thing as distinctively philosophical reasoning is based on the assumption that legitimate reasoning is found only in the sciences and in the formal disciplines of mathematics and logic.

Philosophers who draw a parallel between their own procedures and those of scientists often have in mind that philosophical arguments are grounded in particular concrete instances. Philosophical statements are supported by favourable examples and rejected by counter-cases; the technique is appropriate in psychology or physics, and won the approval of Hume. If the view is old it is not old-fashioned, for Professor Ayer in his Inaugural Lecture "Philosophy and Language" takes a fresh look at philosophical method and the scene he now describes contrasts sharply with his own earlier account. Much of it would not read strangely to Hume. The aim, he says, "is to see the facts for what they are"; philosophers have argued by the presentation of particular cases and particular counter-cases and this is "chiefly a matter of the meticulous inspection of a certain range of facts . . . In this respect the procedure followed in philosophy is like that of the natural sciences."[1]

These remarks leave unclear how like and how different from science Ayer conceives philosophy to be. They are equivocal on an important point brought out by his criticism of Wittgenstein. When in the *Investigation* Wittgenstein describes examples of "reading" he is said not to be engaged in a grammatical investigation and not to be calling our notice to the multiplicity of verbal usage: "We are asked rather to consider what actually happens when, for example, someone reads a newspaper." Wittgenstein's examples "can be taken as showing that what a dictionary might represent as one particular use of the verb 'to read' is in fact a family of uses; but again this would put the emphasis in the wrong place. What is being brought to our attention is the variety of the phenomena in which reading of this sort may consist." The procedure is not linguistic but an effort "to see the phenomena as they really are."

A case can be made for saying that emphasis on its linguistic aspects has distorted Wittgenstein's principal accomplishment, but surely it is wrong to represent Wittgenstein as considering what *actually happens* in cases of "reading." The examples he gives describe mainly fictional or imaginary incidents and are not records of what does, or tends to, occur. Wittgenstein himself understood their

[1]A. J. Ayer, *Philosophy and Language,* Oxford 1960.

nature. "We are not doing natural science; nor yet natural history—since we can also invent fictitious natural history for our purposes." The examples he mentions are not used as instances to support an empirical generalization. But if they do not record events, then what function have examples of this kind? The answer is that they direct our attention to conceptual possibilities. By reviewing conceivable situations and pointing out, let us say, that some overlooked cases are also examples of "reading," Wittgenstein is trying to break the hold of an over-simple picture of what "reading" consists. Whether an instance offered is, or is not, a specimen of "reading" is an *a priori* deliberative question. In order to discredit the idea that philosophical procedure is, in some sense, a special inquiry to do with linguistic usage, Ayer has succumbed to the temptation to say it must be concerned with, not words, but the phenomena to which words refer. The tendency here, once again, is to place philosophy within the province of empirical investigation.

One may underestimate the value of the picture that Hume and (latterly) Ayer have put forward. On the credit side is Hume's insistence on the role of particular instances which he correctly believed to be the bedrock of philosophical reasoning. And Ayer has ventilated an atmosphere of excessive generality by emphasizing the philosophical use of concrete cases. What has not been made plain is that the use of possible cases signals an *a priori* procedure. It is a contingent matter that philosophers sometimes appeal to examples of things that have actually happened, to recorded incidents, events and situations. It is a non-contingent matter that they must appeal to *examples* and that the actuality of an example is a philosophically irrelevant feature. We may easily and mistakenly suppose that the necessity of giving examples to justify philosophical conclusions entails a stronger likeness between philosophical and scientific methods than there is. To say that philosophy proceeds by the comparison and consideration of particular instances is, most certainly, *not* to say, that philosophy is a branch of science.

If the analogy with science breaks down as an explanation of philosophical method the popular alternative is to re-position philosophy within the province of deductive logic. This too is unsatisfactory, but its rejection leaves the (apparently) awkward conclusion that philosophical arguments are entirely reflective even if they are not formally valid. Or, as Dr Waismann remarks, "Philosophic arguments are not deductive; therefore they are not rigorous; and therefore they don't prove anything."[2] This view has an unfortunate consequence, for one might wish to abandon the idea that philosophical arguments are *a priori* if the claim that they are carries with it the rejection of philosophical proof. There is a conflict here between the inclination to think that philosophical proof is possible, and the inclination to think that such proof could not be deductive.

Dr Waismann is right in his premise that philosophical arguments are not logical demonstrations. Much less secure is his conclusion that they are not rigorous, for a rigorous argument can be given even if no deductive steps are invoked. An example striking in its simplicity is McTaggart's argument that a cause need not be like its effect: "Causes do not necessarily resemble their effects. Happiness in A does not resemble the misery it may cause to the envious B. An angry man does not

---

[2]'How I see Philosophy,' *Logical Positivism*, ed. A. J. Ayer, p. 365.

resemble a slammed door. A ray of sunshine does not resemble a faded water-colour."[3] Although rigorous and decisive, McTaggart's argument is untypical. For it consists in directly bringing particular cases to support a philosophical conclusion and is stripped bare of surrounding elucidatory discussion. More typical are arguments of the kind found in Plato and Aristotle, Berkeley and Hume or Ryle and Wittgenstein, where examples are set in a context of discussion and elaboration. Wittgenstein's discussion of "family resemblances" is one such instance and Hume's discussion of causal connections is another; they have in common with McTaggart's reasoning the operative feature that the discussions and conclusions which emerge are backed up by the examples employed. In both, the final justificatory appeal is the reflective consideration of particular instances. Dr Waismann would agree. "What do you find," he asks "in reading Ryle or Wittgenstein? Lots of examples with little or no logical bone in between . . . The real strength lies in the examples." No appeal is made to premises, canons or axioms, and this explains why Dr Waismann is reluctant to use the word "proof" in connection with philosophical arguments. He says forthrightly "proofs require premises," showing that he believes it to be a necessary condition of a proof that its conclusion follows (deductively) from some premises; since philosophical arguments do not fulfil this condition they are not proofs. Of course they are not deductive proofs, and if deduction is a model of proof to which all arguments ought to conform, then Dr Waismann is right. But it is just this supposition which is questionable.

If Dr Waismann's conclusion that "No philosopher has ever proved anything" is paradoxical and less than satisfactory, the reasons for asserting it are logically impeccable. For Waismann's paradox that philosophers' proofs *could not* be proofs has a logical point, comparable to Hume's claim that there is no reason to suppose that past experience is a guide to the future, a paradoxical way of stating that conclusions about the future necessarily cannot be deduced from premises about the past and present. To say that philosophical arguments prove nothing is an unconventional way of stating that necessarily they are not deductive arguments, that a *philosophical* conclusion is necessarily not justified by demonstrative reasoning. Waisman's scepticism signals a logical truth. However, from this truism it does not follow that a person who speaks of a philosopher as having "proved a conclusion" or "given a proof" is thereby mistaken or is, in some sense, using these words incorrectly.

If the analogy with deductive reasoning fails as an explanation of philosophical method valuable and fruitful parallels still remain. The tendency to represent philosophy as a department of logic is an antidote to the opposite tendency to regard it as a branch of empirical science. But the cure is as regrettable as the disease, for the dissimilarities between philosophy and science are revealed at the expense of exaggerating the similarities between philosophy and logic. Philosophers find themselves shuttling between these polar positions because each position pin-points a characteristic feature of philosophical reasoning: there is a likeness to science in that philosophers' arguments are based on a scrutiny of particular instances, and a likeness to logic in that this scrutiny is non-contingent and reflective. Yet one may notice these differences and still present an inadequate picture by

[3]*Some Dogmas of Religion*, p. 89.

representing philosophy as being, in some imprecisely specified sense, a linguistic investigation. This answer is an attractive *general* explanation of the puzzling and frequent conflict between philosophical claims and common sense. It emphasizes that this conflict is *unlike* conflicts between rival empirical conjectures.

This latter point is central to an understanding of the persuasiveness of the linguistic model. If a philosopher says that nobody knows that other people are conscious, a listener can reply "But you and I are conscious, we both know this, so you are mistaken." He is correct in saying the philosopher is mistaken in so far as the evidence supporting his reply is logically appropriate to discredit the proposition ordinarily expressed by the words "Nobody knows that other people are conscious." If the philosopher insists that he has not been shown to be mistaken, and refuses to acknowledge the destructive consequences even of the best evidence that can be brought against him, then his contention is, to say the least, eccentric. The natural question to ask is how this eccentric claim can be explained.

Can we say that he is not asserting an empirical proposition? If we say this we must meet Moore's objection that while the reasons a philosopher gives for his conclusion may not consist of empirical statements, the conclusion which he rightly or wrongly draws from his reasons—that nobody knows that other people are conscious—is nevertheless empirical. Could we reply *a.* that the proposition expressed by the words "Nobody knows that other people are conscious" is not empirical although the form of words would ordinarily express an empirical proposition, for the reason that a philosopher who asserts it does not allow its refutation when presented with facts which would refute it if it were empirical? Could we reply *b.* that a philosopher who concludes "Nobody knows that other people are conscious" is saying something incompatible with the true empirical assertion "You and I are conscious, we both know this" and therefore he is asserting falsely at least some matter of fact? If there is reason to say either *a* or *b* is true there is also reason to say each is inadequate. For it is true that "Nobody knows that other people are conscious" is incompatible with "You and I are conscious, we both know this" so *a* seems false. But it is also true that the philosophical conclusion "Nobody knows that other people are conscious" is asserted on entirely *reflective* grounds, and this is suggested by *a* although concealed by *b*. The puzzle to be dealt with concerns the position of this and similar philosophical claims which despite their falsehood seem on reflection reasonable to assert. It is not to be solved by empirical investigation or the employment of formal logical techniques, and is typical of the kind of puzzles to which Wittgenstein turned in his investigation of the nature of philosophical conflicts.

2. WITTGENSTEIN

In the *Enquiry* Hume argued that there is no new fact to be ascertained once all the circumstances of the case are laid before us; nothing is hidden to be discovered by further investigation. A comparison with Wittgenstein is striking: "Philosophy simply puts everything before us, and neither explains nor deduces anything. Since everything lies open to view there is nothing to explain. For what is hidden, for example, is of no interest to us"; "The problems are solved not by giving new information but by arranging what we have always known." It is Wittgenstein's intention to reveal the nature of philosophical puzzles by exposing their source. Wittgenstein does not draw Hume's conclusions. He turns his back on the belief that philosophy is a kind of science and warns us against just this step which Hume takes; the tendency to ask and answer questions in the way science does "leads the philosopher into complete darkness." Nor does he think that philosophy is logical analysis, and forcefully argues against his own earlier estimation of its role. But if Wittgenstein's conclusions were radically different from Hume's he did not altogether avoid making a typically Humean move in casting about for an alternative place for philosophy. Wittgenstein's reasoning (e.g. "It is not new facts about time which we want to know. All the facts that concern us lie open before us. But it is the use of the substantive 'time' which mystifies us," *The Blue Book*, p. 6) appears to parallel Hume's move from the premise that the facts are all before us to the conclusion that what remains is a matter for the sentiments; with the difference that, in Wittgenstein's case, what remains is a problem to do with the use of words. In the *Blue Book* he says that philosophical puzzlement arises because of a dissatisfaction with a verbal notation: a philosophical conclusion has the character of a linguistic proposal. In the *Investigations* the specific charge that philosophical conclusions are verbal recommendations is not made, yet they are still products of a special kind of perplexity having its origins in language. Being neither science nor logic, he asserts "our investigation is therefore a grammatical one." This kind of investigation is conducted "by clearing misunderstandings away. Misunderstandings concerning the uses of words, caused, among other things, by certain analogies between the forms of expression in different regions of language." Rejecting the conventional alternatives he was drawn to conclude that "we may not advance any kind of theory. There must not be anything hypothetical in our considerations" and "it can never be our job to reduce anything to anything"; that "We must do away with all *explanation,* and description alone must take its place"; "Philosophy really *is* 'purely descriptive'." This description, he says referring to his own philosophical technique, "gets its light—i.e. its purpose—from the philosophical problems." A philosophical problem is based on a linguistic misunderstanding, a "grammatical illusion" standing in need of correction. A philosophical question is a muddle felt as a question: "What we are destroying is nothing but houses of cards and we are clearing up the ground of language on which they stand."[4]

Wittgenstein's remarks about the position of philosophy are vivid, forceful and suggestive. Their exact interpretation is difficult, and if one were to try to say, precisely, what they mean, the loss of their immediate effect is unavoidable: their striking, pointed economy and rich metaphorical expression vividly suggest new tracks of thought in a way that no exegesis however scrupulous could achieve. There is a risk in taking them at their face value; yet the risk must be taken, if only to throw light on Wittgenstein's procedure. A scrutiny of his own philosophical achievement discloses an inadequacy, even a danger, in this characterization of philosophy, since the impression that he is engaged primarily in an imprecisely defined inquiry into

---

[4]*Philosophical Investigations,* sections 126, 109, 118; *The Blue Book,* p. 18.

language—a rough impression his remarks give—conceals what he actually does. Wittgenstein shows us more than ways in which words may confuse. If he draws attention to verbal usages, this is only part of an effort to pull down old misunderstandings and open new conceptions; if he "clears up the ground of language" he also alters traditional *habits* of philosophical thinking; he consistently introduces unsuspected possibilities and relationships; he points out new directions to follow. And this is not, in any ordinary sense, a linguistic operation. It is something else. A more reliable clue to his accomplishment is his remark, "I have changed his *way of looking at things.*"[5]

We can get the feel of Wittgensten's procedure by looking at it somewhat in this way. Often we resort to a comparison to explain a puzzling situation and instruct a person to look, or think, of something as *like,* or as if it were, something else. Suppose a child is puzzled about why the water in the familiar streams he sees always moves in the same direction and why it moves at all. We might tell him to think of it as water running off the roof of a house or flowing down an inclined driveway, to think of the land through which the stream flows as being sloped like the roof or driveway. He will notice at once that the woods and fields of the surrounding landscape are not steeply pitched like the roof and that there are dissimilarities between the landscape and the driveway. Yet this comparison may be enough for him to see for himself the explanation that eluded him; he may go on to comprehend why it is that there are quiet pools, lakes and bogs, as well as torrents and waterfalls. Later on, suppose he questions us about why we speak of electric currents. We tell him to think of electricity in a wire as like the flow of water in a pipe. This may immediately give him a grasp of the operation of the switches, plugs and flexes he finds in his house. But he is likely, on reflection, to be puzzled: why then, he asks, do electric currents flow uphill? The comparisons which so easily removed his puzzlement now create new confusion; we must explain to him that analogies which make things understandable in one situation may not be straight away applicable to another: that differences are as important as similarities, and that the picture of a current in a stream does not in *all* its ramifications do justice to the idea of a current in a wire. The operation of correcting this confusion can be more difficult, more complex and demanding of skill, than that of giving the original simple explanations. Often it is made difficult by the fact that the language we ordinarily and correctly use to describe a situation (e.g. when one speaks of "electric currents") suggests a *view* of that situation which creates philosophical puzzlement.

To take an instance. Wittgenstein remarks that the idea of a "process" carries with it a particular conceptual picture that commits us to looking at processes in a certain way, e.g. we grasp how one goes on to learn things about mechanical processes by further investigation.[6] Mental processes seem in an analogous position and naturally one is puzzled when, guided by the concept of a physical process, one tries to understand the mind in terms of this picture; the question "How is it *possible* to learn about another person's mental processes?" becomes acute, for it seems impossible. One may therefore be driven to deny their hidden

---

[5]*Philosophical Investigations,* 144.
[6]*Philosophical Investigations,* 308.

operation by denying that such "processes" exist and adopt a behaviourist picture of the situation. But this succeeds only in exchanging a new puzzle for the old one. What has happened, Wittgenstein writes, is that we have been misled by a *comparison* and suppose from the start that mental and physical processes are similar in a way in which they are not. In re-positioning these concepts Wittgenstein is attempting to replace (and not merely get rid of) an inadequate view of the likenesses and differences between them by an adequate and correct one. The emphasis here is not on describing ordinary language but on telling or showing us something new. Wittgenstein does not merely *cite* linguistic usages but *points out* overlooked conceptual connections. In his arguments there is surprisingly little documentary appeal to standard forms of speech; there is, instead, constant reference to examples of particular, ordinary and unusual, sometimes incongruous *situations*. The mistakes to which he refers are not like the mistake of a person who confuses (say) "ingenious" with "ingenuous," and not like that of a foreigner who doubts that participles can act as adjectives in an English sentence. They are like the failure of grasp shown by a person who knows the language yet does not see in full the affinities and differences between, to take one of Wittgenstein's examples, a railway ticket, a railway station and a railway law, and so finds himself philosophically puzzled. Stuart Hampshire in his review of Ryle's *Concept of Mind* notices that the "two-worlds" myth is a picture that appears in the forms of common speech only because it first strikes one as a compelling and natural way of presenting the situation. If the metaphor does injustice it is not because of a linguistic oversight but because of a failure to appreciate the ways in which it at once explains and misleads. This is a failure of thought and recognition, and the kind of deficiency which Wittgenstein has frequently made good.

Wittgenstein sometimes began discussions with the words "We have the idea that . . ."—for example, that the mind is like a ghostly person shut up in a house whose activities are known only from seeing what goes on outside it. The *naturalness* of thinking of the mind as a spirit in a house or a pilot in a ship, and its constant historical occurrence in philosophical and non-philosophical writing, is an indication that the comparison is not wholly incorrect. There *is* an affinity and the model *does* tell us something about the mind. But there are differences central and crucial for any adequate account of the mind; on its own, the comparison is misleading. The inadequacy of this *picture* of the mind, Wittgenstein believes, must be exposed before philosophical problems about mind can be understood. Again, when Wittgenstein said we have the idea that the meaning of a word is an object, he was opposing not only an over-simplified philosophical view but also a picture that the plain man readily accepts, not from persuasion, but because it seems to fit in so well with, and to account for, his ordinary verbal practice. In his attack on essentialist theories of universals Wittgenstein goes straight to the source of puzzlement. His claim is not merely that this or that theory of universals is unacceptable, but that behind *all* such theories lies a persuasive comparison whose acceptance constrains a philosopher to adopt a specific, and mistaken, course of reasoning: "The idea of a general concept being a common property of its particular instances . . . is comparable to the idea that *properties* are *ingredients* of the things which have the properties; e.g. that beauty is an ingredient of all beautiful things as alcohol is of beer and wine."[7] His technique is to show the inadequacy of this compelling analogy by pointing to possible cases where it fails to hold. Wittgenstein's central strategy turns on making clear the defects and limitations, as well as the merits, of just such models or "pictures" incipient in the way we regard and talk about our experience. He speaks of his job in philosophy as one of assembling reminders for a particular purpose. While this phrase conveys that there may be more in a philosophical problem than meets the eye it insufficiently conveys that there may be more in it than we have ever thought of. His remarks about "assembling reminders" and solving problems "not by giving new information, but by arranging what we have always known" are modern, original and novel only as descriptions of a philosophical practice already followed by philosophers from Plato to Descartes, from Locke to Hume and A. J. Ayer. The practice itself is not new; it remained for Wittgenstein to drive it home and in this paradoxical way make explicit what his predecessors had not seen clearly, that philosophy proceeds by deliberation.

Wittgenstein constantly returned to the problem of giving an account of how philosophical procedure could be as deliberative as mathematics and as informative as a scientific investigation. There are signs in his work that the reconciliation is less than successful, for his exposition suggests that if philosophy proceeds by deliberation alone then it can disclose nothing new. When Wittgenstein's statement that all the facts lie open before us is read with the remark that philosophy is purely descriptive and does away with explanation, the tendency is strong to suppose that the function of philosophy is wholly critical and clarificatory; and that, accordingly, the job of a philosopher is no more than remedial. What remains, on this view, is the detection and correction on linguistic confusion. But just as Locke caricatured his own procedure by the picture of the under-labourer, Wittgenstein caricatures his work by the picture of therapeutic treatment. Like all good caricatures they convey a truth at the price of distortion. Wittgenstein saw that the method of getting rid of a philosophical puzzle requires more than the refutation of a philosopher's claim, and that a problem can be dissolved only by explaining *why* it happens to be puzzling. This introduces a new dimension to philosophical criticism; for the job is not merely to understand—and accept or reject—a particular philosophical contention, but to understand and explain the influence of a model or comparison through which a philosopher sees the nature of his problem. It is in his sustained attempt to solve philosophical problems by revealing the origins of philosophical perplexity that the inadequacy of the above interpretation becomes clear. Wittgenstein's own practice runs counter to the claim that philosophy discloses nothing new: recognizing and explaining the reasons for the persistence of a philosophical problem is one form of discovery.

Often, Wittgenstein thinks, the explanation of philosophical puzzlement is to be found in an over-simple notion whose acceptance is encouraged simply by the way we ordinarily speak. For example, he writes that in the expressions "He is capable of . . ." or "He can play chess" the verb is used in the present tense, "suggesting that the phrases are descriptions of states which exist at the moment when we speak."[8]

[7]*The Blue Book*, p. 17.
[8]*The Blue Book*, p. 117.

Again, the picture of remembering as an inner process is both suggested by the language we use to describe remembering and also "stands in the way of seeing the use of the word as it is." To break the hold of such suggestions Wittgenstein recommends that we carry out a "grammatical investigation" consisting of looking, unencumbered by preconceptions, at the variety of cases exhibiting the use of the word. But when we see, in fact, what this comes to, it bears little resemblance to anything that ordinarily might be called an investigation of grammar. As he says, ordinary language is "all right as it is"; however its correctness is compatible with its power to introduce a specific though inaccurate picture or notion of the affairs referred to. Wittgenstein's point is that the *correct* use of language can be philosophically misleading, e.g. "A simile that has been absorbed into the forms of our language produces a false appearance, and this disquiets us . . . A *picture* held us captive. And we could not get outside it, for it lay in our language and language seemed to repeat it to us inexorably."[9] It would be a mistake to read Wittgenstein as saying that philosophical problems are always or even usually engendered by errors we make in the usage of words, or by the diffuseness and inexactness of much of common language; it would, therefore, be equally mistaken to suppose that one might remove philosophical puzzlement by redefining ordinary words with more precision. Rather, the problems are created through a failure to "command a clear view" of the complex range of possible situations to which a word can apply, despite the fact that we make no mistakes in its usage. One result of such a failure is to fall victim to an over-simple model, to suppose that a word always functions as it does in a narrow range of conspicuous cases. What is needed is a full and complete view, a "perspicuous representation" which "produces just that understanding which consists in 'seeing connexions.' Hence the importance of finding and inventing *intermediate cases*."[10] Wittgenstein is consistent in saying both that "philosophy may in no way interfere with the actual use of language" and that philosophical problems arise "when language goes on holiday." The forms of ordinary speech frequently suggest a particular though philosophically misleading way of looking at a problem; and by adopting the suggested point of view a philosopher sees a situation as being different from how it actually is, which creates puzzlement when the philosophical requirement to which one is committed by the adopted view clashes with both common sense and common usage ("But *this* isn't how it is!"—we say. "Yet *this* is how it has to *be!*" *Investigations,* 112). In turn, this preconceived view conceals the rich variety of cases that need to be appreciated in order to free oneself from its influence. The solution is to make plain, by the presentation of particular instances, just how misleading the picture is, and how it comes to be adopted. Throughout the emphasis is on changing a person's course of reflection. It is understandable, though a pity, that Wittgenstein's work should be so often included under the popular misnomer of "linguistic philosophy." What is distinctive, perhaps revolutionary, in his philosophy has little to do with verbal problems as such; but lies in the originality of his deliberate attempt to show that the source of philosophical puzzlement is found, not in the language a philosopher uses, but in philosophical habits of thinking.

---

[9]*Philosophical Investigations,* 112, 115.
[10]*Philosophical Investigations,* 122.

3. JOHN WISDOM

In "Philosophical Perplexity" Professor Wisdom remarked that a philosophical answer is really a verbal recommendation. No doubt he would not put the matter in just this way today, and there is a hint even in that article that this claim is not so straightforward as it seems. Although he said "Say which you like" of rival philosophical conclusions he added the warning "but be careful," and to be careful is to hear out the case, to describe tooth and nail the issues on both sides. The slogan "Say which you like" had little of the effect it might have had if it were taken as the literal truth. For it might have been understood as a suggestion to stop listening to philosophical argument, or to any argument which has neither the finality of deduction nor the likelihood of induction. Despite the slogan, Wisdom himself insisted that philosophical disputes must be heard. But to what point? The answer was left obscure.

The point that was missed is that in philosophical controversies rival parties are trying to *gain an understanding* of that which they are talking about. Like juries in the courts it is not only a question of a decision but also a question of knowledge and ignorance. This point can be missed by a failure to appreciate the nature of the process that is employed in discussing and concluding reflective issues. By conventional standards the process is eccentric and informal. What needed to be done was to recognize that this eccentricity does not exclude philosophical debate as a means of reaching the truth. In part what prevented this recognition was the inclination of both Wisdom and Wittgenstein to fasten on examples favourable to the recommendations theory; the idea was to encourage philosophers to agree that it was a question of the choice of a word by comparing philosophical questions with questions like "Is a tomato a fruit or vegetable?" How successful this was can be glimpsed from G. A. Paul's remark that, in a particular philosophical conflict, rival answers can perhaps be decided "by tossing a coin."[11] Besides their triviality questions of this sort, in which there is as much reason to give one answer as another, mislead precisely because, in most cases, either answer will do. Borderline cases of this paradigm kind obscured what was happening in other cases which though borderline were not trivial, like cases in the courts, and so concealed what was happening in philosophical cases. The importance of the difference between them had not been struck home. What is this difference? Wisdom explains by an example:

> Suppose now that someone is trying on a hat. She is studying it in a mirror. There's a pause and then a friend says "My dear, the Taj Mahal." Instantly the look of indecision leaves the face in the mirror. All along she has known there was something wrong with the hat, now she sees what it is. And all this happens in spite of the fact that the hat could be seen perfectly clearly and completely before the words "Taj Mahal" were uttered.[12]

Even though each person sees what the other sees, one of them simply by pointing out a feature of the situation alters and adds to an apprehension of the case.

---

[11] 'Is there a Problem about Sense-Data?,' *Logic and Language* (1st series), ed. Flew, p. 113.
[12] *Philosophy and Psycho-Analysis,* p. 248.

In this instance the remark about the hat is more than a suggestion about what to call it. It is a new comparison and a new discovery. The simplicity of Wisdom's move can hide its far-reaching implications. At once we may see connections between this case and other comparable occasions on which talk and thought finish with a knowledge of the circumstances not present at the start, in spite of the fact that no further investigation is made.

Among these occasions are philosophical discussions. A philosopher's conclusion need no longer be seen as a disguised notational choice, but as the end of an argument in which he seeks to explain a problem comparable in its genuineness to a problem in science or logic, and to be solved by non-deductive reflection alone.

Wisdom's diagnosis of the basis of doubts about other minds is a case in point and complements Wittgenstein's treatment. Like Wittgenstein, he is interested in exposing the source of philosophical puzzlement. But the emphasis is different. For Wisdom it is less a matter of pointing to a philosophical mistake than of disclosing a discovery that has been improperly brought to light in terms of a philosophical paradox; the source of the problem is a feature to do with the verification of statements which has been incorrectly expressed, and its correct expression will add to knowledge. Where Wittgenstein says that philosophical problems should completely disappear, Wisdom remarks that that to which they refer could not have been false. A sceptic's doubts about mind are unconventional expressions of a "logical asymmetry" necessary and peculiar to the verification of statements about mind. If, as a sceptic claims, A knows that B is angry only if it is true that A knows this *as B does* and *in the way B alone does,* then A never does know, never could know, that B is angry. But this is not what "knowing that B is angry" means; and not what is conveyed on particular occasions when one person speaks conventionally of knowing how another feels. Although a sceptic may speak as if A stands in ignorance of the feelings of B, this is not ignorance of any ordinary sort but an "ignorance" which is logically irremediable. In spite of a sceptic's exaggerated claim, Wisdom argues that a sceptic has noticed something that might never have been noticed by one who has had no more than normal doubts about mind. In short, a sceptic's doubt is philosophically valuable since it draws attention to the logically inevitable contrast between *i.* questions to which A's feelings of a certain sort give A *more* authority to answer than do similar feelings give to B, and *ii.* questions to which A's feelings of a certain sort give A *as much* authority to answer as do similar feelings give to B. The former are questions about mind, the latter are not. Moreover, this *logical* difference to which a sceptic paradoxically points does not demonstrate that the ordinary and conventional things one says about the feelings of others are false, or true; to discover their truth or falsehood is to proceed as one ordinarily does proceed when questions about another person's mind arise. The difficulty in opposing a sceptic is not merely one of refuting his conclusion, but of getting him—and others—to recognize the nature of his doubt and the logical truth it expresses.

Wisdom is inclined to take as the starting point of a discussion philosophical problems expressed in the form of paradoxical utterances characteristic of traditional scepticism. At first this approach may seem too one-sided. Might not the issues be clarified at the start by phrasing the problem as a question of analysis or of the usage of words? The answer is, not always. When a problem is thus refor-mulated it is natural to ask whether the analysis or statement about usage is correct, and this can deflect interest from the more important question of *why* an analysis or an examination of usage is felt to be necessary in the first place. The merit of what Wisdom calls the "paradoxical form" of the problem is its very absurdity, which makes us suspect that there is something at issue over and above the truth or falsehood of a sceptic's remarks. And this suspicion is correct.

To take an example. In "A Defence of Common Sense" Moore says, "The strange thing is that philosophers should have been able to hold sincerely, as part of their philosophical creed, propositions inconsistent with what they themselves *knew* to be true." It is evident, Moore goes on, that philosophers who have held to be true such propositions as "None of us knows any proposition which asserts the existence of material things" and "None of us knows any propositions about the existence of other selves, and that they are conscious" *do* know on occasions such propositions as "Here is a table" and "That person is conscious." Characteristically Moore demands a plain answer to a plain question: "When he (Russell) says that no human being has ever known such things, I think he implies that I haven't, and that therefore I am wrong in thinking that I have. And the question I want to dis-cuss is simply this: Was he right in thinking that I haven't, or am I right in thinking that I have"[13] Although Moore's paradox reveals the common sense absurdity of a sceptic's claim, it conceals that a sceptic's literally false remark is the result of a partial insight into the verificational features of the type of statement with which he is concerned. By adopting this technique in which he opposes something which is strictly false with something strictly true, Moore has framed the problem in such a way that the issues at stake are obscured rather than clarified by the extreme clar-ity and simplicity of his question. Strictly, Moore is right; yet his answer misrepre-sents the situation, and all the more for being true. This is to say that there can be a gap between a correct answer and what might be called "seeing the position at issue." Sometimes a situation can be presented in a false light by a statement which describes that situation correctly. A man who has a watch from which the hands are missing still has a watch, and if someone asked "Has he a watch, yes or no?" the answer "Yes" is correct even though no one could tell the time by it. This *true* reply may be of less value in appreciating what is the case than the *false* reply "No" for it suggests that the watch in question is more like a typical watch than it happens to be. Wisdom has spoken of questions like "Is a watch without hands a watch?" (or "Can one play chess without the queen?" to which the correct answer is "Yes") as being *sub-acute* in that they refer neither to typical nor to borderline members of a class. They mislead for often what ordinarily can be said of typical cases can be said also of them without a mistake; the ordinary and correct thing to say conveys no hint of the unordinary situation being talked about. Moore's truthful answer is in a comparable position: it suggests that Russell's doubt is not very different from a typical non-philosophical doubt, that Russell is wrong in the way in which a per-son who is not a philosophical sceptic might be wrong about a matter of fact.

---

[13]'Four Forms of Scepticism,' *Philosophical Papers,* p. 200.

It comes out of this discussion that there may be more to a philosopher's conclusion than the words he uses ordinarily convey. In order to see the character of philosophical questions and answers Wisdom insists we review their logical history rather than rely on the form of words in which they are expressed. The steps which a philosopher takes to reach his answer are of more interest than the answer itself and a scrutiny of his conclusions must be subordinated to a scrutiny of his argument. We cannot tell what he means simply by paying heed to his results: for the *meaning* of his conclusion lies in the arguments he gives for asserting it, and these arguments are the primary objects of philosophical inspection. In short, to understand a philosopher's conclusion is to understand the reasoning behind it.

Again Wisdom places emphasis on *seeing* what is so, not *saying* what is so, a matter of recognizing and coming to apprehend the logical features which a statement of a certain type must have to be a statement of that type. But attempts to see a philosophical situation properly can be hindered by a misapprehension of the nature of one's own inquiries and of philosophical questions and answers. In consequence Wisdom is concerned with the place of philosophical reasoning itself. It would be a mistake to suppose that he lays down a specific procedure to follow. Although there is no recipe or simple nostrum for the conduct of philosophy, the subject is delineated by certain logical ground rules. Philosophers' questions are not settled, like scientists' questions, by investigating what actually happens, but by "reviewing the possible" along non-deductive lines. The investigation is, and could only be, reflective. In the tradition of Wittgenstein and Moore, Wisdom's technique is to deal with an abstract puzzle by putting it in concrete terms.[14] If we wish to understand the philosophically puzzling remarks of philosophers we should "avoid asking them to define their terms, but instead press them to present us with instances of what they refer to contrasted with instances of what they do not refer to, then their pronouncements will no longer appear either as obvious falsehoods or mysterious truths or pretentious nonsense, but as often confusingly presented attempts to bring before our attention certain not fully recognized and yet familiar features of how in the end questions of different types are met."[15]

How can philosophical procedure be as reflective as a purely logical procedure without being deductive? Wisdom has replied somewhat along the following lines. On some occasions people regard what they see before them as a sign of something further to be seen. On other occasions that which people see before them is not regarded as a sign of anything further to be seen. There is an inclination to think that although in the former case a person can ascertain the truth or falsehood of a statement about what is seen, for one can and indeed must investigate further, in the latter case no additional verification is possible for there is no call for further observation. Consequently, if in this case persons disagree about what is before them, there is an inclination to think that they are no longer engaged in an effort to answer a question about what it is; rather, their disagreement concerns a matter of verbal usage, or perhaps reflects only a difference in attitude

[14]See Ch. 4, section 4, of the present book.
[15]'A Feature of Wittgenstein's Technique,' *Aristotelian Society Supplementary Volume,* 1961, p. 13.

among the persons. One may be tempted to think that the dispute here is not a real dispute since there is no conventional way of settling it. All the while, however, that feature of the situation which encourages this response is the fact that their disagreement about what is before them could not be brought to an end in the way in which it could be in the former case where the settlement involves testing one's expectations. It appears, therefore, that there is no way of bringing the dispute to an end. Wisdom urges that it does not follow from this *difference* in mode of investigation that there is no possibility of coming to a right answer when the circumstances are of the latter sort. He calls attention to how people in this position, lawyers, accountants, moralists, novelists, among others, do proceed to give reasons for correct answers despite this feature. The procedure they use may be no more than a matter of rearranging the data, of presenting them differently; often it is a matter of drawing comparisons with possibilities not hitherto considered. What has this to do with philosophy? Although philosophers engaged in debate are not, like lawyers or accountants, attempting to understand the actual, their efforts are none the less directed towards answering questions to which the answers are not known; and the procedures they adopt differ from patterns of typical inductive or typical deductive reasoning. To see that this departure from conventional procedures of reasoning is not a defect, Wisdom recommends that we look at occasions of argument outside philosophy, at specimens of reflective reasoning in which non-philosophical issues are resolved, then move back to specimens of philosophical conflict. To do this is to reason by comparison; and to carry out comparisons across a full range of occasions on which people are conducting reflective investigation is to efface the old, restricting picture of rational argument dominated by the deductive-inductive model.[16]

John Wisdom's philosophy both criticizes and continues the tradition of classical British epistemology, and in significant respects is closer to the spirit of Locke, Berkeley and Hume than to the work of (say) Ryle or Austin. The connection does not lie altogether in his constant return to the topics of mind and the material world, or to the fact that he, like them, has made the problems of philosophical scepticism a central issue. The affinity is more diffuse and more important. In Wisdom's work there is continuing emphasis on philosophical discovery, a desire to reveal what for good reasons is concealed by habits of talk and thought, to use his words. This same emphasis is uniformly found in philosophers from Locke to Hume. They have urged us to notice that things are not quite as we take them to be, that we are often ignorant of the truth. For all Hume's insistence on philosophy as an empirical inquiry he never lost sight of the idea that by drawing upon things one knows the results of philosophy can add to what one knows. Philosophy, to him, was a source of knowledge. The claim is open to misunderstanding, and Hume himself misunderstood it. Most certainly it would be accepted by Wisdom, and the difference between Wisdom and his traditional predecessors comes out most clearly in its interpretation and reveals what is central in his work.

---

[16]See 'The Metamorphosis of Metaphysics,' *Proceedings of the British Academy,* 1961, pp. 55–9; and *Philosophy and Psycho-analysis,* pp. 248–54, 264–70.

The Province of Philosophy

J. J. C. Smart

PHILOSOPHY AND WORLD VIEW

This book is meant as an essay in synthetic philosophy, as the adumbration of a coherent and scientifically plausible world view. A good many philosophers would nowadays question the legitimacy of such an endeavour. It will therefore be as well if I say a few words about the nature of philosophy as I conceive it. No one answer can be given to the question "What is philosophy?" since the words "philosophy" and "philosopher" have been used in many ways. Some people, for example, think of philosophy as offering the consolations of a religion, and of the philosopher as a man who receives with equanimity the buffetings of life. This has very little to do with the way in which academic people, including myself, use the word "philosophy." I do not feel particularly unqualified to be an academic philosopher because I am not "philosophical" when I am bowled out first ball at cricket. As I propose to use the word "philosophy" it will stand primarily for an attempt to think clearly and comprehensively about: (*a*) the nature of the universe, and (*b*) the principles of conduct. In short, philosophy is primarily concerned with what there is in the world and with what we ought to do about it. Notice that I have said both "to think clearly" and "to think comprehensively." The former expression ties up with the prevailing conception of philosophy as linguistic or conceptual analysis, and the latter ties up with another common conception of philosophy as the rational reconstruction of language so as to provide a medium for the expression of total science.*

Thus, a man might analyse biology in a certain way. He might argue, as I shall do, that living organisms, including human beings, are simply very complicated physico-chemical mechanisms. This man might also analyse physics as the ordering and predicting of sense experiences. For the sake of argument let us concede that such a man might be thinking quite clearly in each field. But though he might be thinking clearly, he would not be thinking *comprehensively*. As biologist he would be thinking of man as a mechanism, as very much a part of nature, a macroscopic object interacting with its environment. As physicist, however, he would be thinking of this great world of nature as just a matter of the actual and possible experiences of sentient beings, and so, in a sense, he would be putting nature inside man.[†] To think comprehensively he would have to discover a way of thought which enabled him to think both as a biologist and as a physicist. Presumably a comprehensive way of thought would be one which brought all intellectual disciplines into

---

*In thinking of philosophy as rational reconstruction of language I have been very much influenced by Hilary Putnam and by W. V. Quine. See, for example, Quine's *Word and Object* (Technology Press of M.I.T. and Harvard University Press, 1960).

[†] On this point see Chapter II. It is interesting that theoretical physicists, when they venture into philosophy, commonly tend to be phenomenalists, and biologists tend to be materialists.

Source: Philosophy and Scientific Realism, Chapter 1. London: Routledge & Kegan Paul, 1963, 1–15.

a harmonious relationship with one another. It may turn out that there are some realms of discourse, such as theology, which cannot be brought into a harmonious relationship with the various sciences. Any attempt to do so may result in violence to logic or to scientific facts, or may involve arbitrariness and implausibility. (Consider, for example, the implausibility of a theory which asserts that the mechanistic account of evolution by natural selection and mutation is broadly true, but that there is a special discontinuity in the case of man, to whom was super-added an immortal soul.) If this is so, such anomalous branches of discourse will have to be rejected and will not form part of the reconstruction of our total conceptual scheme.

So much, for the moment, about the "nature of the universe" or "world view" part of philosophy. Let us now briefly consider the second part of philosophy, which is concerned with the principles of conduct. We shall not be much concerned in this book with this part of philosophy, but in the final chapter I shall try to state some of the implications, and some of the non-implications, of my general world view for ethics. As we shall see, and as has been generally recognised in modern philosophy, it is not possible to deduce propositions about what ought to be done purely from propositions about what is the case. It follows that the principles of conduct are by no means unambiguously determined by our general philosophy. Nevertheless, in their laudable objection to those who would deduce ethics from the nature of the world (and in particular to some of those biologists who would base ethics on the theory of evolution and the like) philosophers have tended to obscure the fact that our general philosophical and scientific beliefs may strongly influence our ethical principles. For example, if one of our principles of conduct were that we should do what is commanded by a personal God and if our world view were one which left no place for such a God, then this principle of conduct would have to be given up, or at least we should have to find some other reason for adhering to it. In this book, which will be naturalistic in temper, I do not wish to concern myself with the general question of the legitimacy or illegitimacy of theology. The example of theology was brought up simply to show in a vivid way that metaphysics can be relevant to ethics. We must certainly not jump from the impossibility of deducing "ought" solely from "is" to the untenable position that our general philosophical and scientific views have no bearing on our ethical ones.

PHILOSOPHY AND THE ELIMINATION OF NONSENSE

I have been suggesting a conception of philosophy as the attempt to acquire a synoptic view of the world. On this account of philosophy it shares the tentative character of the sciences. We must never think that we have acquired, even in outline, the final truth, for science inevitably provides surprises for us, and we may have to make important revisions of even our most general notions. We may hope, however, that our synoptic account will be nearer to the final truth than is that of common sense. Now in recent years it has been argued in some quarters that in philosophy we are not concerned, as scientists are, with the distinction between truth and falsity, but with that between sense and nonsense. As philosophers, according to this conception, it is not our business to say what the world is in fact like: we must leave this to scientists and historians. What we can do, and what we are by our training peculiarly fitted to do, is to help to ensure that we, together with scientists and historians, at least utter falsehoods: that we and they do not fall into nonsense which has not even achieved the distinction of an intelligible falsehood. Let me illustrate the notion of nonsense by means of an example based on *Alice in Wonderland*.* Suppose that a man came and said that he had seen a miaowing and blinking cat's head which was unattached to a body. I should be disposed in this case to disbelieve the man, and to say that what he told me was *false*. I should feel that I *understood* him: that I knew what it would be like for such an event as he reported to occur, but that I did not believe that any such event ever had or would occur. His report would contradict various secure beliefs that I possessed, particularly in the field of animal physiology. Now let us suppose that the man had reported not that he had seen a cat's head by itself but that he had seen simply a grin by itself. Not even a grinning mouth unattached to a head, but simply a grin all on its own. In this case I should not know what was meant at all. I should not be disposed to say that I understood what the man said, even though I disbelieved in the truth of his report. I should say, rather, that what he said was nonsense, neither true nor false, and so I could not even disbelieve him.

Now it is indubitable that there are sentences which have appeared to be meaningful and which nevertheless have turned out to be nonsense. I shall mention one such sentence in a moment. And so even though the remarks of traditional philosophers (say, about the famous trio of topics, God, Freedom, and Immortality) may not be obvious nonsense, like the report of the catless grin, they may be nonsense all the same.

Here is a sentence, couched entirely in the respectable terminology of pure mathematics, which at first sight may appear to some readers (assuming that they have not encountered it before) to be perfectly meaningful, though perhaps rather dry and abstract. It was first concocted by Bertrand Russell. (Russell's paradox.) The sentence is: "The class of all classes not members of themselves is a member of itself." There appear to be plenty of classes of objects which are not members of themselves. The class of criminals is not a criminal (the police do not have to seek the *class of criminals* after they have arrested all criminals), and the class of football teams in the league is not a further football team. Most classes therefore appear not to be members of themselves. But some classes do appear to be members of themselves: certainly the class of classes does. For is not the class of classes a class? It would therefore seem to be perfectly intelligible to pose the question of whether the class of all classes not members of themselves is or is not one of those classes which are members of themselves. Unfortunately, this question admits neither the answer "yes" nor the answer "no." For if the class of all classes not members of themselves *is* a member of itself, then it follows that it is one of those classes which are *not* members of themselves. And if it is not a member of itself, then it *is* a member of itself. Either way we get a contradiction. It follows that we can neither say that the sentence "the class of all classes not members of themselves

* Lewis Carroll, *Alice in Wonderland* (Everyman edition, J. M. Dent, London, 1952), p. 56.

is a member of itself" expresses a truth, nor can we say that it expresses a false-hood. We are forced to conclude that it is meaningless.*

The above paradox is particularly important and instructive, because it shows how unsuspected possibilities of nonsense can break out even in the rigorous and austere terminology of mathematics. For those readers who may not find abstrac-tions about classes to their taste I shall mention a similar, though less important par-adox, which may be even more succinctly stated. Consider the sentence "This sen-tence is false." The sentence is about itself. Is it true or false? It can be neither, because if it is true it is false and if it is false it is true. It is important to note that the above paradoxical sentences are not mere contradictions. You can assert the negation of a contradiction. That is, a contradiction is just plain false. "2 + 2 = 5" is a contradiction, and so "2 + 2 ≠ 5" is a truth. Contradictions have their uses, for they occur in proofs by *reductio ad absurdum*. If you can deduce "2 + 2 = 5" you can normally deduce that the negation of one or other of the premises is true. I have said "normally" here, because it is important to use *reductio ad absurdum* methods only when you are reasonably sure of the meaningfulness of the sentence you are trying to prove. If the sentence you are trying to prove is meaningless it may be like one of the paradoxical sentences above and you may be able to deduce a contradiction both from it *and* from its negation. In which case the deduction of a contradiction from its negation does not ensure its truth. This consideration may be of interest to some readers, in that it may throw light on the fact that certain math-ematicians, the so-called "intuitionists," Brouwer and his school, reject proof by *reductio ad absurdum* in circumstances in which classical mathematicians do not. It is, of course, the case that there are sentences which classical mathematicians regard as meaningful and which the intuitionists hold to be meaningless.

The sort of possibility of nonsense to which I have been drawing attention in the last few paragraphs is a subtle and insidious one. Nonsense of a sort has always been recognised: consider "I married a prime number" and "Virtue is triangular." It is an insight of the last fifty years (though foreshadowed by the philosophically subtle humour of Lewis Carroll) that there can be important and non-obvious pos-sibilities of nonsense. This insight was generalised by Wittgenstein and by those much influenced by him into a complete philosophy of philosophy.

It is clear that some technique for recognising non-obvious nonsense is highly desirable, and I should agree that the development and application of such a tech-nique is at least part of the task of philosophy. How does this connect up with my conception of philosophy as the development of a synoptic outlook? Can the elim-ination of nonsense change our world view? At first sight the answer to this is in the negative. If the nonsense really is nonsense it cannot form part of a world view, even a false one. So it looks as though elimination of nonsense removes dead wood

---

* I here neglect the possibility of other ways of dealing with Russell's paradox, such as Zermelo's. The cau-tious reader should consult the essay "The Demarcation between Science and Metaphysics" (especially pp. 263–73) in K. R. Popper's *Conjectures and Refutations* (Routledge and Kegan Paul, London, 1963), which came into my hands while this book was in the press. Popper's argument suggests that we should draw a less sharp line between nonsense and falsehood than I have done. This would strengthen the main argument of this chapter, which is that philosophy is concerned with world view.

but does not affect the living branches of our knowledge. This answer is, however, too hasty. It may well be that by using nonsensical premisses, in addition to a set *A* of meaningful ones, we may be able to deduce a set *B* of meaningful sentences which are not deducible from *A* alone. I shall show how to deduce the false but meaningful sentence "The moon is made of green cheese" from the nonsensical sentence "This sentence is false." Let us represent the sentence "This sentence is false" by the symbol "*S*" for short.

From "This sentence is false" we can deduce "This sentence is not false." That is, from *S* we can deduce not-*S*. However, from *S* we can deduce "*S* or the moon is made of green cheese." But not-*S* (which we have already deduced) together with "*S* or the moon is made of green cheese" enables us to deduce "The moon is made of green cheese."

Thus given the nonsense "This sentence is false" we can deduce that the moon is made of green cheese. We have been able to do this because the nonsense in question issues in a contradiction, and from a contradiction we can, by the method of the last paragraph, deduce any sentence whatever. It is not obvious, however, that all nonsensical sentences issue in a contradiction. Some seem so far off the rails of meaningful discourse that it is not even possible to use them to demonstrate their own senselessness. Thus, it is not obvious that "I married a prime number" or "A bodiless grin appeared in the room" issue explicitly in contradiction. Nevertheless, my derivation of the proposition that the moon is made of green cheese should make it plausible that a philosopher should be able to deduce false conclusions from true premises if he makes his deduction through unrecognised nonsense. The deduction would, of course, be an incorrect one, but it would be incorrect in a very unobvious and subtle way. The detection of its incorrectness would depend on the detection of hidden nonsense. A good example of this sort of thing, in the history of philosophy, suggested to me by D. M. Armstrong, is perhaps Aristotle's deduction of the false, though meaningful, proposition that the heavenly bodies are of a different substance from that of the earth. His deduction is by way of the nonsense that the heavenly bodies obey laws of the same nature as the laws of logic, *i.e.* laws of a sort of logical hardness.

It may be thought that my example of a deduction that the moon is made of green cheese proves too much. For if it proves anything it proves that from "This sentence is false" (or from a simple non-paradoxical contradiction such as "2 + 2 = 5") we could deduce anything whatever. But philosophers, however metaphysical they may be, are not satisfied to assert any proposition whatever. There are some propositions which they wish to assert and there are other propositions which they wish to deny. A system of thought which harboured a contradiction would, on the contrary, degenerate into the happy assertion of anything whatever. To this objection we must reply that in practice a system will degenerate in this way only if the contradiction is detected. If the contradiction is not detected it cannot in practice provide a route for the deduction of any proposition whatever. It is like a way out of prison which is quite unknown to the prisoners:* as far as they are concerned it might as well not exist, and the bolts and bars do not lose any of their effectiveness.

---

*I think that this simile is originally due to Wittgenstein.

I conclude therefore that it must not be supposed that the view that philosophy consists only in the elimination of nonsense implies the proposition that philosophy has no effect on our world view. It may cause us to shed some of our beliefs about the world because it may enable us to see that we have accepted these beliefs only on the strength of a fallacious deduction through a nonsensical part of language. This conclusion is far stronger than another one, which is conceded by most philosophers, that the elimination of nonsense leads to clarity of thought and so helps the progress of the sciences.

PHILOSOPHY AS MORE THAN THE ELIMINATION OF NONSENSE

That philosophy is at least the elimination of nonsense and the clarification of thought is something of which I have not the least doubt. However, I should also wish to argue that philosophy is more than this, and that it is the business of the philosopher to decide between various synoptic hypotheses on grounds of plausibility. Of course, scientists have to decide between hypotheses, and with a slight over-simplification we may say that they do so by means of observation and experiment. It may be, however, that no available method of experiment and observation will decide between two hypotheses. The philosopher may legitimately, I think, feel it within his province to speculate on the relative plausibilities of the two hypotheses if they are of such generality and importance as to affect our overall world view. For example, in the sequel I shall be concerned to argue for the plausibility of the view that the human brain is no more than a physical mechanism, that no vitalistic or purely psychical entities or laws are needed to account for its operations. This type of philosophical thinking links up closely with the purely clarificatory sort of philosophy since part of my strategy will be to try to expose confusions in *a priori* philosophical arguments for the opposite hypothesis. Of course, those who produce such *a priori* arguments will probably deny that what they are arguing for is a "hypothesis": they will hold that their view is true as a matter of logic, just as a mathematical proposition perhaps is. I shall, however, indicate why I think that such philosophers are too sanguine in regarding philosophy as pure logic.

A philosopher might have to decide between two hypotheses for which there not only is no available empirical test but for which there could be no possible empirical test. I shall illustrate this point by reference to the hypothesis that the universe began to exist ten minutes before I began writing this sentence, but with everything just as it was ten minutes ago.* (Fossils in the rocks, photographs in the pocket, memory traces in the brain, light rays in interstellar space, and so on.)† Of course this is not a hypothesis which any philosopher is likely to hold, though the English naturalist and biblical theologian Philip Gosse produced a very similar theory in

---

*If someone raises the relativistic objection that "ten minutes ago" has no unambiguous meaning we can say "ten minutes ago with reference to some specified inertial frame of reference."
†See Bertrand Russell, *Analysis of Mind* (Allen and Unwin, London, 1921), pp. 159–60.

order to reconcile geology and the book of Genesis.‡ Gosse held that the world was created only a few thousand years ago, exactly as stated in the book of Genesis, but that God had also created the various eroded canyons, fossils as if of prehistoric animals and plants, and so on. In short, he held that the world was created a few thousand years ago just as in fact it was (on the usual geological and evolutionary account) at that time. Clearly Gosse's theory was immune to empirical refutation, and he was extremely pained when both the scientific world and the theological world spurned his ingenious reconciliation. Nevertheless, though it is not a live philosophical theory, the hypothesis that the world began ten minutes ago, just as it was ten minutes ago, will serve to illustrate my methodological point. It is clear that no experiment or observation could upset the hypothesis that the world began ten minutes ago just as it was ten minutes ago. If I mention our memories of last week's football match the reply will be that these are not true memories: the football match never happened, but we came into existence ten minutes ago complete with pseudo-memories of the non-existent game. If I point to newspaper photographs of the football match the reply will be that the newspaper, complete with photographs, itself began to exist ten minutes ago. And so on.

Some philosophers would say that since there could be no experimental or observational way of deciding the question whether or not the world came into existence ten minutes ago just as it was ten minutes ago, the assertion or denial that the world began ten minutes ago is without sense. This seems to me to be unplausible. There seems to be nothing contradictory in the notion of a world suddenly springing into existence in this way. Moreover, suppose that I am suffering from an intense toothache. I should not take kindly to the view that in a year's time there would be no meaningful difference between the hypothesis that the world exists now, complete with my toothache, and the hypothesis that the world will spring into existence next year, just as it will be next year, with pseudo-traces, such as memories and empty gums, as if of my present toothache.

It is hard, therefore, without losing all sense of reality, to deny that the hypothesis that the world began ten minutes ago just as it was ten minutes ago is a meaningful one. (Though an unbelievable one.) Indeed, though there are no possible observations or experiments which could distinguish between this hypothesis and the more usual one, there are considerations, hard though they may be to formulate, of simplicity and plausibility, which should determine us to reject the "ten minutes ago" hypothesis. For this hypothesis presents us with a cosmology depending on a highly complex and arbitrary set of initial conditions. If the "ten minutes ago" hypothesis is accepted, then we have to take as a brute fact, for which no explanation could possibly be given, that ten minutes ago there were certain footprints on the beach at Glenelg, South Australia, that there were certain light waves in the depths of intergalactic space, that there were certain definite "photographs" in my breast pocket, that there were certain types of pseudo-prehistoric bones in the rock strata.* All these facts

‡An interesting account of Philip Gosse's theory is given in Martin Gardner, *Fads and Fallacies in the Name of Science* (Dover Inc., New York, 1957), pp. 124–7.
*I am also neglecting the arbitrariness of our choice of criterion of simultaneity at a distance, which is implied by the special theory of relativity.

would have to be taken as just "flat" and in principle inexplicable. Now it is true that on any hypothesis there is an element of arbitrariness in nature. Why have we five fingers rather than four or six? Nevertheless this arbitrariness can be understood as due to the element of sheer accident involved in the large-scale non-accident of evolution by natural selection. This arbitrariness, and other sorts of arbitrariness, such as the occurrence of hard rocks here and soft rocks there, of blue stars here and red stars there, is, on the normal hypothesis that the world has existed for a very long time, much what we should expect. It would be surprising rather if everything were neat and orderly. But this sort of arbitrariness is not like the extraordinary and universal arbitrariness of the initial conditions which we find in the "ten minutes ago" hypothesis.

The example of the hypothesis that the universe began to exist ten minutes ago seems to show that it is possible to choose, on grounds of plausibility, between two hypotheses between which there can be no empirical test. I shall myself consider one important case of this sort in a later chapter, when I shall argue for the view that our conscious experiences are to be *identified* with brain processes. Another possible view would be that our conscious experiences are not identical with brain processes but that they are *correlated* with brain processes. Here once more we have, as we shall see, two hypotheses between which no empirical test could decide. I shall argue on plausible grounds for the former (materialistic) hypothesis against the latter (dualistic) hypothesis. Before I can do this I shall, of course, have to argue that certain *a priori* philosophical arguments against materialism are not so cogent as they seem at first sight to be. The plausible arguments I shall use are of various sorts, but one of these is worthy of specific mention. This is *Occam's razor.* It depends on the precept "Do not multiply entities beyond necessity." This is a familiar maxim not only of philosophical method but also of scientific method. For example, if biochemical reactions will explain a certain phenomenon of cell growth, then there is no need to postulate, in addition to the biochemical reactions which we know to occur anyway, a life force or some irreducibly biological law of nature. (Occam himself is popularly supposed to have applied his razor to the metaphysical problem of universals, though I gather that there is a good deal of doubt about the historical accuracy of this.) It might turn out that in cases where we need to talk of universals, such as justice and whiteness, we could manage equally well by talking of the *words* "just" and "white." If we can think of words as marks on paper and the like (the trouble, of course, is that words, unlike particular inscriptions, themselves turn out to be universals), then we can effect an economy. For we know that ink marks on paper and the like occur anyway, and if they will do all the explanatory tasks that are needed we need not bring in the airy fairy and altogether dubious entities justice and whiteness.

I suspect that considerations of plausibility, turning on the notions of simplicity and arbitrariness, of Occam's razor and the like, have an important and indeed indispensable place in philosophical argument. This is partly because philosophy is carried out in a natural language, not in some artificial language, with rigid formation and transformation rules explicitly laid down as in a formal logical or mathematical system. Hence, though it is often possible to *persuade* another philosopher that he has landed himself in inconsistency or in nonsense, and that he must therefore give up certain of his tenets, it is never possible to *prove* this to him. He can always patch up the inconsistencies and nonsenses in his language by means of supplementary rules and hypotheses. . . . At first sight this theory is easy to refute, for the libertarian seems to hold that acting freely is something intermediate between being determined and acting by pure chance. Logic would seem to leave no room for such an intermediate possibility. The libertarian will reply that if I define "pure chance" as "not being determined," then his "acting freely" is a sub-species of what I call "pure chance."* This sub-species is not properly pure chance, but consists in acting from reasons, not from causes. I then reply to the libertarian with the stock philosophical arguments showing that reasons are not a sort of para-cause and that acting from reasons is not incompatible with acting from causes. The obdurate libertarian is sure to prepare yet another line of defence and get round this objection in some way. (As I well know from inconclusive philosophical discussions on this topic.)

This characteristic inconclusiveness of philosophical argument is a fact familiar to all philosophers. If they were to take it seriously more of them would be favourably disposed to my conception of philosophy as in part depending on merely plausible considerations. If a philosopher keeps on patching up his theory we may try to persuade him that his way of talking is becoming more and more baroque and is ill-fitting to our scientific knowledge. The libertarian philosopher of free-will may, if he is ingenious enough, render himself immune to our logical arguments, but only at the cost of great artificiality in his theory, and at the price of bringing in a great discontinuity in the story of animal evolution. Just where in the line of evolution, the primates, or sub-men, or early men, does this "soul," or power of free choice in the libertarian sense, become superadded to man as he appears in the usual biological story? It would, moreover, have to be a very special creation: it is impossible that the evolution of such a metaphysical entity could be explained in the usual mechanistic terms, natural selection acting on gene pools (a gene being a complex nucleic acid). Of course, if the philosopher is happy with the baroque quality of his theory and with its artificiality of fit with total science, then there is no more to be done. In many cases, however, plausible considerations of the sort I have suggested may have a persuasive force that purely abstract considerations of consistency and the like may not have. With ingenuity these last can be got round, but if the methods of getting round them have to be supplemented every century, or every decade, in order to take account of advances in science, then it will be a very romantically minded philosopher who will not begin to feel uneasy.

SYNOPTIC PHILOSOPHY AND MAN'S PLACE IN NATURE

If philosophy is concerned, in the manner suggested above, with the rational reconstruction of our conceptual scheme, then it quite obviously covers a very wide field.* There will therefore be some important issues which, for the purposes of this book, I shall be content to leave to one side. For example, I shall not be concerned with the much-vexed question of Platonism versus nominalism, that is, whether in addition to the concrete objects or events which exist in space and time we must postulate abstract objects as well. For example, do mathematicians assert the reality of *numbers* and *classes?* The two part of the previous question can indeed be amalgamated if we accept Frege's and Russell's analysis of numbers as classes of classes of objects. In any case, in higher mathematics it is essential to introduce infinite classes, *i.e.* classes of numbers. That a class is an abstract object can most easily be seen if we consider the null class, which can be described, *e.g.*, as the class of twentieth-century terrestrial unicorns. The null class is a perfectly good class, and because it has no members there is no temptation to confuse it with the "heap" of its members. A class, unlike a heap, has a number. Consider the class of students who are in this room at a certain moment. It has, say, 10 members. Contrast the spatially scattered "heap" of human protoplasm in this room. This has no number. It is made up of 10 persons and 10^{15} living cells and goodness knows how many molecules or atoms.[†] Now science, since it includes mathematics, apparently has to mention classes. Does this mean that we must accept classes as real things postulated by science, on a par, perhaps, with electrons or the far side of the moon?[‡] The reason why I shall not discuss this issue of Platonism versus nominalism, or of the reality of abstract entities, is that it has little relevance to the question of man's place in the universe. The connecting theme of this book will be the attack on anthropocentric or near-anthropocentric strains of thought in philosophy. I shall attack phenomenalist and subjectivist theories of mind and matter, space and time. The question of whether the universe contains Platonic entities is neutral to these issues.

*This paragraph was already written and set up in print before I saw the lucid note "Smart on Free-Will," by Richard Acworth, *Mind,* Vol 72, 1963, pp. 271–2. Acworth here replies to a former argument of mine, and points out that the libertarian could defend himself by partitioning the field which I call "pure chance."

*W. V. Quine has recently argued against the tenability of the analytic-synthetic distinction. (See his *Word and Object, op. cit.,* also his *From a Logical Point of View* (Harvard University Press, 1953).) According to this laws of logic and of pure mathematics are not different in kind from very high level laws of physics. It would also seem to follow from his view that there would be an arbitrariness in the formation rules which we lay down for a system. Indeed, there are varying expedients in mathematical logic to eliminate the class of all classes paradox, and some sentences which would be meaningless in Whitehead and Russell's system are allowed in Quine's *Mathematical Logic* (Harvard University Press, 1958). There is perhaps a certain arbitrariness in whether we regard something as meaningless or as a high-level falsehood. (Thus, it could be taken not as meaningless that there are catless grins, but that it follows from certain very high level assumptions that there are none.) If Quine's views on the nature of logic are accepted, then the first of the two conceptions of philosophy that I have sketched in this chapter collapses into the second. If so, this only strengthens my position in this book. Since Quine's views are controversial, I do not wish to commit myself on this issue, which is a highly technical one, and which would in any case lead us away from the main preoccupations of this book.

[†]*Cf.* W. V. Quine, *From a Logical Point of View* (Harvard University Press, 1953), p. 114.

[‡]For a discussion of this issue see especially Quine, *op. cit.*

The Value of Philosophy

Bertrand Russell

Having now come to the end of our brief and very incomplete review of the problems of philosophy, it will be well to consider, in conclusion, what is the value of philosophy and why it ought to be studied. It is the more necessary to consider this question, in view of the fact that many men, under the influence of science or of practical affairs, are inclined to doubt whether philosophy is anything better than innocent but useless trifling, hair-splitting distinctions, and controversies on matters concerning which knowledge is impossible.

This view of philosophy appears to result, partly from a wrong conception of the ends of life, partly from a wrong conception of the kind of goods which philosophy strives to achieve. Physical science, through the medium of inventions, is useful to innumerable people who are wholly ignorant of it; thus the study of physical science is to be recommended, not only, or primarily, because of the effect on the student, but rather because of the effect on mankind in general. Thus utility does not belong to philosophy. If the study of philosophy has any value at all for others than students of philosophy, it must be only indirectly, through its effects upon the lives of those who study it. It is in these effects, therefore, if anywhere, that the value of philosophy must be primarily sought.

But further, if we are not to fail in our endeavour to determine the value of philosophy, we must first free our minds from the prejudices of what are wrongly called "practical" men. The "practical" man, as this word is often used, is one who recognizes only material needs, who realizes that men must have food for the body, but is oblivious of the necessity of providing food for the mind. If all men were well off, if poverty and disease had been reduced to their lowest possible point, there would still remain much to be done to produce a valuable society; and even in the existing world the goods of the mind are at least as important as the goods of the body. It is exclusively among the goods of the mind that the value of philosophy is to be found; and only those who are not indifferent to these goods can be persuaded that the study of philosophy is not a waste of time.

Philosophy, like all other studies, aims primarily at knowledge. The knowledge it aims at is the kind of knowledge which gives unity and system to the body of the sciences, and the kind which results from a critical examination of the grounds of our convictions, prejudices, and beliefs. But it cannot be maintained that philosophy has had any very great measure of success in its attempts to provide definite answers to its questions. If you ask a mathematician, a mineralogist, a historian, or any other man of learning, what definite body of truths has been ascertained by his science, his answer will last as long as you are willing to listen. But if you put the same question to a philosopher, he will, if he is candid, have to confess that his study has not achieved positive results such as have been achieved by other sciences. It is true that this is partly accounted for by the fact that, as soon as definite

Source: The Problems of Philosophy [1912], Chapter 15, with a new introductrion by John Perry. New York: Oxford Univeristy Press, 1959, 153–161.

knowledge concerning any subject becomes possible, this subject ceases to be called philosophy, and becomes a separate science. The whole study of the heavens, which now belongs to astronomy, was once included in philosophy; Newton's great work was called "the mathematical principles of natural philosophy." Similarly, the study of the human mind, which was a part of philosophy, has now been separated from philosophy and has become the science of psychology. Thus, to a great extent, the uncertainty of philosophy is more apparent than real: those questions which are already capable of definite answers are placed in the sciences, while those only to which, at present, no definite answer can be given, remain to form the residue which is called philosophy.

This is, however, only a part of the truth concerning the uncertainty of philosophy. There are many questions—and among them those that are of the profoundest interest to our spiritual life—which, so far as we can see, must remain insoluble to the human intellect unless its powers become of quite a different order from what they are now. Has the universe any unity of plan or purpose, or is it a fortuitous concourse of atoms? Is consciousness a permanent part of the universe, giving hope of indefinite growth in wisdom, or is it a transitory accident on a small planet on which life must ultimately become impossible? Are good and evil of importance to the universe or only to man? Such questions are asked by philosophy, and variously answered by various philosophers. But it would seem that, whether answers be otherwise discoverable or not, the answers suggested by philosophy are none of them demonstrably true. Yet, however slight may be the hope of discovering an answer, it is part of the business of philosophy to continue the consideration of such questions, to make us aware of their importance, to examine all the approaches to them, and to keep alive that speculative interest in the universe which is apt to be killed by confining ourselves to definitely ascertainable knowledge.

Many philosophers, it is true, have held that philosophy could establish the truth of certain answers to such fundamental questions. They have supposed that what is of most importance in religious beliefs could be proved by strict demonstration to be true. In order to judge of such attempts, it is necessary to take a survey of human knowledge, and to form an opinion as to its methods and its limitations. On such a subject it would be unwise to pronounce dogmatically; but if the investigations of our previous chapters have not led us astray, we shall be compelled to renounce the hope of finding philosophical proofs of religious beliefs. We cannot, therefore, include as part of the value of philosophy any definite set of answers to such questions. Hence, once more, the value of philosophy must not depend upon any supposed body of definitely ascertainable knowledge to be acquired by those who study it.

The value of philosophy is, in fact, to be sought largely in its very uncertainty. The man who has no tincture of philosophy goes through life imprisoned in the prejudices derived from common sense, from the habitual beliefs of his age or his nation, and from convictions which have grown up in his mind without the cooperation or consent of his deliberate reason. To such a man the world tends to become definite, finite, obvious; common objects rouse no questions, and unfamiliar possibilities are contemptuously rejected. As soon as we begin to philosophize, on the contrary, we find, as we saw in our opening chapters, that even the most everyday things lead to problems to which only very incomplete answers can be given. Philosophy, though unable to tell us with certainty what is the true answer to the doubts which it raises, is able to suggest many possibilities which enlarge our thoughts and free them from the tyranny of custom. Thus, while diminishing our feeling of certainty as to what things are, it greatly increases our knowledge as to what they may be; it removes the somewhat arrogant dogmatism of those who have never travelled into the region of liberating doubt, and it keeps alive our sense of wonder by showing familiar things in an unfamiliar aspect.

Apart from its utility in showing unsuspected possibilities, philosophy has a value—perhaps its chief value—through the greatness of the objects which it contemplates, and the freedom from narrow and personal aims resulting from this contemplation. The life of the instinctive man is shut up within the circle of his private interests: family and friends may be included, but the outer world is not regarded except as it may help or hinder what comes within the circle of instinctive wishes. In such a life there is something feverish and confined, in comparison with which the philosophic life is calm and free. The private world of instinctive interests is a small one, set in the midst of a great and powerful world which must, sooner or later, lay our private world in ruins. Unless we can so enlarge our interests as to include the whole outer world, we remain like a garrison in a beleagured fortress, knowing that the enemy prevents escape and that ultimate surrender is inevitable. In such a life there is no peace, but a constant strife between the insistence of desire and the powerlessness of will. In one way or another, if our life is to be great and free, we must escape this prison and this strife.

One way of escape is by philosophic contemplation. Philosophic contemplation does not, in its widest survey, divide the universe into two hostile camps—friends and foes, helpful and hostile, good and bad—it views the whole impartially. Philosophic contemplation, when it is unalloyed, does not aim at proving that the rest of the universe is akin to man. All acquisition of knowledge is an enlargement of the Self, but this enlargement is best attained when it is not directly sought. It is obtained when the desire for knowledge is alone operative, by a study which does not wish in advance that its objects should have this or that character, but adapts the Self to the characters which it finds in its objects. This enlargement of Self is not obtained when, taking the Self as it is, we try to show that the world is so similar to this Self that knowledge of it is possible without any admission of what seems alien. The desire to prove this is a form of self-assertion and, like all self-assertion, it is an obstacle to the growth of Self which it desires, and of which the Self knows that it is capable. Self-assertion, in philosophic speculation as elsewhere, views the world as a means to its own ends; thus it makes the world of less account than Self, and the Self sets bounds to the greatness of its goods. In contemplation, on the contrary, we start from the not-Self, and through its greatness the boundaries of Self are enlarged; through the infinity of the universe the mind which contemplates it achieves some share in infinity.

For this reason greatness of soul is not fostered by those philosophies which assimilate the universe to Man. Knowledge is a form of union of Self and not-

Self; like all union, it is impaired by dominion, and therefore by any attempt to force the universe into conformity with what we find in ourselves. There is a widespread philosophical tendency towards the view which tells us that Man is the measure of all things, that truth is man-made, that space and time and the world of universals are properties of the mind, and that, if there be anything not created by the mind, it is unknowable and of no account for us. This view, if our previous discussions were correct, is untrue; but in addition to being untrue, it has the effect of robbing philosophic contemplation of all that gives it value, since it fetters contemplation to Self. What it calls knowledge is not a union with the not-Self, but a set of prejudices, habits, and desires, making an impenetrable veil between us and the world beyond. The man who finds pleasure in such a theory of knowledge is like the man who never leaves the domestic circle for fear his word might not be law.

The true philosophic contemplation, on the contrary, finds its satisfaction in every enlargement of the not-Self, in everything that magnifies the objects contemplated, and thereby the subject contemplating. Everything, in contemplation, that is personal or private, everything that depends upon habit, self-interest, or desire, distorts the object, and hence impairs the union which the intellect seeks. By thus making a barrier between subject and object, such personal and private things become a prison to the intellect. The free intellect will see as God might see, without a *here* and *now,* without hopes and fears, without the trammels of customary beliefs and traditional prejudices, calmly, dispassionately, in the sole and exclusive desire of knowledge—knowledge as impersonal, as purely contemplative, as it is possible for man to attain. Hence also the free intellect will value more the abstract and universal knowledge into which the accidents of private history do not enter, than the knowledge brought by the senses, and dependent, as such knowledge must be, upon an exclusive and personal point of view and a body whose sense-organs distort as much as they reveal.

The mind which has become accustomed to the freedom and impartiality of philosophic contemplation will preserve something of the same freedom and impartiality in the world of action and emotion. It will view its purposes and desires as parts of the whole, with the absence of insistence that results from seeing them as infinitesimal fragments in a world of which all the rest is unaffected by any one man's deeds. The impartiality which, in contemplation, is the unalloyed desire for truth, is the very same quality of mind which, in action, is justice, and in emotion is that universal love which can be given to all, and not only to those who are judged useful or admirable. Thus contemplation enlarges not only the objects of our thoughts, but also the objects of our actions and our affections: it makes us citizens of the universe, not only of one walled city at war with all the rest. In this citizenship of the universe consists man's true freedom, and his liberation from the thraldom of narrow hopes and fears.

Thus, to sum up our discussion of the value of philosophy; Philosophy is to be studied, not for the sake of any definite answers to its questions, since no definite answers can, as a rule, be known to be true, but rather for the sake of the questions themselves; because these questions enlarge our conception of what is possible, enrich our intellectual imagination and diminish the dogmatic assurance which closes the mind against speculation; but above all because, through the greatness of the universe which philosophy contemplates, the mind also is rendered great, and becomes capable of that union with the universe which constitutes its highest good.

Philosophy

Ludwig Wittgenstein

86
DIFFICULTY OF PHILOSOPHY NOT THE INTELLECTUAL DIFFICULTY OF THE SCIENCES, BUT THE DIFFICULTY OF A CHANGE OF ATTITUDE. RESISTANCES OF THE WILL MUST BE OVERCOME.

As I have often said, philosophy does not lead me to any renunciation, since I do not abstain from saying something, but rather abandon a certain combination of words as senseless. In another sense, however, philosophy requires a resignation, but one of feeling and not of intellect. And maybe that is what makes it so difficult for many. It can be difficult not to use an expression, just as it is difficult to hold back tears, or an outburst of anger //rage//.

/(Tolstoy: the meaning (meaningfulness) of a subject lies in its being generally understandable.—That is true and false. What makes a subject difficult to understand—if it is significant, important—is not that some special instruction about abstruse things is necessary to understand it. Rather it is the contrast between the understanding of the subject and what most people want to see. Because of this the very things that are most obvious can become the most difficult to understand. What has to be overcome is not a difficulty of the intellect, but of the will.)/

Work on philosophy is—as work in architecture frequently is—actually more of a //a kind of// work on oneself. On one's own conception. On the way one sees things. (And what one demands of them.)

Roughly speaking, in //according to// the old conception—for instance that of the (great) western philosophers—there have been two kinds of problems in fields of knowledge //twofold kinds of problems. . . .//: essential, great, universal, and inessential, quasi-accidental problems. And against this stands our conception, that there is no such thing as a great, essential problem in the sense of "problem" in the field of knowledge.

Source: [1951], translated by C. G. Luckhardt and M. A. E. Aue, *Synthese,* 43, 1989, 175–203. [Wittgenstein uses "//. . .//" to indicate variant choices of words or phrases; the editors use "/. . ./" to indicate Wittgenstein's inscription of variants typed above a line of his original manuscript.]

87
PHILOSOPHY SHOWS THE MISLEADING ANALOGIES IN THE USE OF LANGUAGE.

Is grammar, as I use the word, only the description of the actual handling of language //languages//? So that its propositions could actually be understood as the propositions of a natural science?

That could be called the descriptive science of speaking, in contrast to that of thinking.

Indeed, the rules of chess could be taken as propositions from the natural history of man. (As the games of animals are described in books on natural history.)

If I correct a philosophical mistake and say that this is the way it has always been conceived, but this is not the way it is, I always point to an analogy //I must always point to. . . .// that was followed, and show that this analogy is incorrect.//. . . . I must always point to an analogy according to which one had been thinking, but which one did not recognize as an analogy.//

The effect of a false analogy taken up into language: it means a constant battle and uneasiness (as it were, a constant stimulus). It is as if a thing seemed to be a human being from a distance, because we don't perceive anything definite, but from close up we see that it is a tree stump. The moment we move away a little and lose sight of the explanations, one figure appears to us; if after that we look more closely, we see a different figure; now we move away again, etc., etc.

(The irritating character of grammatical unclarity.)

Philosophizing is: rejecting false arguments.

The philosopher strives to find the liberating word, that is, the word that finally permits us to grasp what up until now[1] has intangibly weighed down our consciousness.

(It is as if one had a hair on one's tongue; one feels it, but cannot grasp //seize// it, and therefore cannot get rid of it.)

The philosopher delivers the word to us with which one //I// can express the thing and render it harmless.

(The choice of our words is so important, because the point is to hit upon the physiognomy of the thing exactly, because only the exactly aimed thought can lead to the correct track. The car must be placed on the tracks precisely so, so that it can keep rolling correctly.)

One of the most important tasks is to express all false thought processes so characteristically that the reader says, "Yes, that's exactly the way I meant it." To make a tracing of the physiognomy of every error.

Indeed we can only convict someone else of a mistake if he acknowledges that this really is the expression of his feeling.//. . . . if he (really) acknowledges this expression as the correct expression of his feeling.//

For only if he acknowledges it as such, is it the correct expression. (Psychoanalysis.)

What the other person acknowledges is the analogy I am proposing to him as the source of his thought.

---

[1]Handwritten alternative: then.

88

WHERE DOES THE FEELING THAT OUR GRAMMATICAL INVESTIGATIONS ARE FUNDAMENTAL COME FROM?

(Questions of different kinds occupy us, for instance "What is the specific weight of this body," "Will the weather stay nice today," "Who[2] will come through the door next," etc. But among our questions there are those of a special kind. Here we have a different experience. The questions seem to be more fundamental than the others. And now I say: if we have this experience, then we have arrived at the limits of language.)[3]

Where does our investigation get its importance from, since it seems only to destroy everything interesting, that is, all that is great and important? (As it were all the buildings, leaving behind only bits of stone and rubble.)

Whence does this observation derive its importance:[4] the one that points out to us that a table can be used in more than one way, that one can think up a table that instructs one as to the use of a table? The observation that one can also conceive of an arrow as pointing from the tip to the tail, that I can use a model as a model in different ways?

What we do is to bring words back from their metaphysical to their correct[5] use in language.

(The man who said that one cannot step into the same river twice said something wrong; one can step into the same river twice.)

And this is what the solution of all philosophical difficulties looks like. Their[6] answers, if they are correct, must be homespun and ordinary.[7] But one must look at them in the proper spirit, and then it doesn't matter.[8]

Where do //did// the old philosophical problems get their importance from?

The law of identity, for example, seemed to be of fundamental importance. But now the proposition that this "law" is nonsense has taken over this importance.

I could ask: why do I sense a grammatical joke as being in a certain sense deep? (And that of course is what the depth of philosophy is.)

Why do we sense the investigation of grammar as being fundamental?

(When it has a meaning at all, the word "fundamental" can also mean something that is not metalogical, or philosophical.)[9]

The investigation of grammar is fundamental in the same sense in which we may call language fundamental—say its own foundation.

Our grammatical investigation differs from that of a philologist, etc.: what interests us, for instance, is the translation from one language into other languages we have invented. In general the rules that the philologist totally ignores are the ones that interest us. Thus we are justified in emphasizing this difference.

---

[2]In the original typescript: he. The word "who" is a handwritten alteration.
[3]Handwritten marginal note: belongs to "must," "can."
[4]The typescript has: its importance:, the.
[5]Handwritten alternative: normal. There is a handwritten wavy line under "correct": ‿‿‿‿
[6]Handwritten alternative: our.
[7]Handwritten alternative: ordinary and trivial.
[8]At the end of the remark there is the handwriting: <["plain nonsense"].
[9]The parentheses are a handwritten addition.

On the other hand it would be misleading to say that we deal with the essentials of grammar (he, with the accidentals).

"But that is only an external differentiation //an external difference//." I believe there is no other.

Rather we could say that we are calling something else grammar than he is. Even as we differentiate kinds of words where for him there is no difference (present).

The importance of grammar is the importance of language.

One could also call a word, for instance "red," important insofar as it is used frequently and for important things, in contrast, for instance, to the word "pipe-lid." And then the grammar of the word "red" is important because it describes the meaning of the word "red."

(All that philosophy can do is to destroy idols. And that means not creating a new one—for instance as in "absence of an idol.")

89
THE METHOD OF PHILOSOPHY: THE PERSPICUOUS REPRESENTATION OF GRAMMATICAL //LINGUISTIC// FACTS. THE GOAL: THE TRANSPARENCY OF ARGUMENTS. JUSTICE.[10]

Someone has heard that the anchor of a ship is hauled up by a steam engine. He only thinks of the one that powers the ship (and because of which it is called a steamship) and cannot explain to himself what he has heard. (Perhaps the difficulty doesn't occur to him until later.) Now we tell him: No, it is not that steam engine, but besides it a number of other ones are on board, and one of these hoists the anchor.—Was his problem a philosophical one? Was it a philosophical one if he had already heard of the existence of other steam engines on the ship and only had to be reminded of it?—I believe his confusion has two parts: what the explainer tells him as fact the questioner could easily have conceived as a possibility by himself, and he could have posed his question in a definite form instead of in the form of a mere admission of confusion. He could have removed this part of his doubt by himself; however, reflection could not have instructed him about the facts. Or: the uneasiness that comes from not having known the truth was not removable by any ordering of his concepts.

The other uneasiness and confusion is characterized by the words "Something's wrong here" and the solution is characterized by (the words): "Oh, you don't mean that steam engine" or—in another case—". . . . By 'steam engine' you don't mean just a piston engine."

The work of the philosopher consists in assembling reminders for a particular purpose.

A philosophical question is similar to one about the constitution of a particular society.—And it would be as if a society came together without clearly written rules, but with a need for them; indeed also with an instinct according to which they

[10]Under the title, in handwriting: Ⅴ p. 40/3?. This is a reference to page 40 of the typescript. Wittgenstein had apparently wanted to include a remark or a part of one from page 40 on this page.

observed //followed// certain rules at their meetings; but this is made difficult by the fact that nothing is clearly expressed about this and no arrangement is made which clarifies //brings out clearly// the rules. Thus they in fact view one of them as president, but he doesn't sit at the head of the table and has no distinguishing marks, and that makes doing business difficult. Therefore we come along and create a clear order: we seat the president in a clearly identifiable spot, seat his secretary next to him at a little table of his own, and seat the other full members in two rows on both sides of the table, etc., etc.

If one asks philosophy: "What is—for instance—substance?" then one is asking for a rule. A general rule, which is valid for the word "substance," i.e., a rule according to which I have decided to play.—I want to say: the question "What is . . . ." doesn't refer to a particular—practical—case, but we ask it sitting at our desks. Just remember the case of the law of identity in order to see that taking care of a philosophical problem is not a matter of pronouncing new truths about the subject of the investigation (identity).

The difficulty lies only[11] in understanding how establishing a rule helps us. Why it calms us after we have been so profoundly[12] uneasy. Obviously what calms us is that we see a system which (systematically) excludes those structures that have always made us uneasy, those we were unable to do anything with, and which we still thought we had to respect. Isn't the establishment of such a grammatical rule similar in this respect to the discovery of an explanation in physics, for instance, of the Copernican system? A similarity exists.—The strange thing about philosophical uneasiness and its resolution might seem to be that it is like the suffering of an ascetic who stood raising a heavy ball, amid groans, and whom someone released by telling him: "Drop it." One wonders: if these sentences make you uneasy and you didn't know what to do with them, why didn't you drop them earlier, what stopped you from doing it? Well, I believe it was the false system that he thought he had to accommodate himself to, etc.[13]

(The particular peace of mind that occurs when we can place other similar cases next to a case that we thought was unique occurs again and again in our investigations when we show that a word doesn't have just one meaning (or just two), but is used in five or six different ways (meanings).)

Philosophical problems can be compared to locks on safes, which can be opened by dialing a certain word or number, so that no force can open the door until just this word has been hit upon, and once it is hit upon any child can open it. //. . . . and if it is hit upon, no effort at all is necessary to open the door//it// .//

The concept of a perspicuous representation is of fundamental significance for us. It earmarks the form of account we give, the way we look at things. (A kind of "world-view," as is apparently typical of our time. Spengler.)

This perspicuous representation produces just that comprehension //understanding// which consists in "seeing connections." Hence the importance of intermediate cases //of finding intermediate cases.//

[11]Handwritten alternative: now.
[12]Handwritten alternative: deeply.
[13]At the end of the remark there is a handwritten addition: hen and chalkline.

A sentence is completely logically analyzed when its grammar is laid out completely clearly. It might be written down or spoken in any number of ways.

Above all, our grammar is lacking in perspicuity.

Philosophy may in no way interfere with the real //actual// use of language // . . . . with what is really said//; it can in the end only describe it.

For it cannot give it any foundation either.

It leaves everything as it is.

It also leaves mathematics as it is (is now), and no mathematical discovery can advance it.

A "leading problem of mathematical logic" (Ramsey) is a problem of mathematics like any other.

(A simile is part of our edifice; but we cannot draw any conclusions from it either; it doesn't lead us beyond itself, but must remain standing as a simile. We can draw no inferences from it. As when we compare a sentence to a picture (in which case, what we understand by "picture" must already have been established in us earlier //before//) or when I compare the application of language with, for instance, that of the calculus of multiplication.

Philosophy simply puts everything before us, and neither explains nor deduces anything.)

Since everything lies open to view there is nothing to explain either. For what might not lie open to view is of no interest to us. //. . . . , for what is hidden, for example, is. . . .//

The answer to the request for an explanation of negation is really: don't you understand it? Well, if you understand it, what is there left to explain, what business is there left for an explanation?

We must know what explanation means. There is a constant danger of wanting to use this word in logic in a sense that is derived from physics.

When[14] methodology talks about measurement, it does not say which material would be the most advantageous to make the measuring stick of in order to achieve this or that result: even though this too, after all, is part of the method of measuring. Rather this investigation is only interested in the circumstances under which we say that a length, the strength of a current (etc.) is measured. It wants to tabulate the methods which we already used and are familiar with, in order to determine the meaning of the words "length," "strength of current," (etc.)

If one tried to advance theses in philosophy, it would never be possible to debate them, because everyone would agree to them.

Learning philosophy is really recollecting. We remember that we really used words in this way.[15]

The aspects of things //of language// which are philosophically most important are hidden because of their simplicity and familiarity.

(One is unable to notice something because it is always (openly) before one's eyes.)

---

[14]Before the remark, in handwriting in the margin: VII 7.
[15]In handwriting, in the margin: VII 164.

The real foundations of his inquiry do not strike a man at all. Unless that fact has at some time struck him //he has become aware of//. (Frazer, etc., etc.)

And this means he fails to be struck by what is most striking (powerful).

(One of the greatest impediments for philosophy is the expectation of new, deep //unheard of// elucidations.)

One might also give the name philosophy to what is possible //present// before all new discoveries and inventions.

This must also relate to the fact that I can't give any explanations of the variable "sentence." It is clear that this logical concept, this variable, must belong to the same order as the concept "reality" or "world."

If someone believes he has found the solution to the "problem of life" and tried to tell himself that now everything is simple, then in order to refute himself he would only have to remember that there was a time when this "solution" had not been found; but at that time too one had to be able to live, and in reference to this time the new solution appears like //as// a coincidence. And that's what happens to us in logic. If there were a "solution" of logical (philosophical[16]) problems then we would only have to call to mind that at one time they had not been solved (and then too one had to be able to live and think).————

All reflections can be carried out in a much more homespun manner than I used to do. And therefore no new words have to be used in philosophy, but rather the old common words of language are sufficient. //the old ones are sufficient//

(Our only task is to be just. That is, we must only point out and resolve the injustices of philosophy, and not posit new parties—and creeds.)

(It is difficult not to exaggerate in philosophy.)

(The philosopher exaggerates, shouts, as it were, in his helplessness, so long as he hasn't yet discovered the core of his confusion.)

The philosophical problem is an awareness of disorder in our concepts, and can be solved by ordering them.

A philosophical problem always has the form: "I simply don't know my way about."

As I do philosophy, its entire task çonsists in expressing myself in such a way that certain troubles //problems// disappear. ((Hertz.))

If I am correct, then philosophical problems must be completely solvable, in contrast to all others.

If I say: here we are at the limits of language, then it always seems//sounds// as if resignation were necessary, whereas on the contrary complete satisfaction comes, since no question remains.

The problems are dissolved in the actual sense of the word—like a lump of sugar in water.

/People who have no need for transparency in their argumentation are lost to philosophy./

[16]In the typescript presumably mistakenly: Philosophical.

90
PHILOSOPHY.
THE CLARIFICATION OF THE USE
OF LANGUAGE. TRAPS OF LANGUAGE.

How is it that philosophy is such a complicated building //structure//. After all, it should be completely simple if it is that ultimate thing, independent of all experience, that it claims to be.—Philosophy unravels the knots in our thinking; hence its results must be simple, but its activity is as complicated as the knots that it unravels.

Lichtenberg: "Our entire philosophy is correction of the use of language, and therefore the correction of a philosophy, and indeed of the most general philosophy."

(The capacity[17] for philosophy consists[18] in the ability[19] to receive a strong and lasting impression from a grammatical fact.)[20]

Why are grammatical problems so tough and seemingly ineradicable?— Because they are connected with the oldest thought habits, i.e., with the oldest images that are engraved into our language itself. ((Lichtenberg.))

/Teaching philosophy involves the same immense difficulty as instruction in geography would have if a pupil brought with him a mass of false and far too simple //and falsely simplified// ideas about the course and connections of the routes of rivers //rivers// and mountain chains //mountains//./

/People are deeply imbedded in philosophical, i.e., grammatical confusions. And to free them from these presupposes pulling them out of the immensely manifold connections they are caught up in. One must [15] so to speak regroup their entire language.—But this language came about //developed// as it did because people had— and have—the inclination to think in this way. Therefore pulling them out only works with those who live in an instinctive state of rebellion against //dissatisfaction with// language. Not with those who following all of their instincts live within the herd that has created this language as its proper expression./

Language contains the same traps for everyone; the immense network of well-kept //passable[21]// false paths. And thus we see one person after another walking the same paths and we know already where he will make a turn, where he will keep on going straight ahead without noticing the turn, etc., etc. Therefore wherever false paths branch off I should put up signs which help one get by the dangerous places.

One keeps hearing the remark that philosophy really makes no progress, that the same philosophical problems that had occupied the Greeks are still occupying us. But those who say that don't understand the reason it is //must be// so. The reason is that our language has remained the same and seduces us into asking the same questions over and over. As long as there is a verb "to be" which seems to

---

[17]Handwritten alternative (with an unbroken wavy line under the original word): **talent.**
[18]Handwritten alternative (with an unbroken wavy line under the original word): **lies.**
[19]Handwritten alternative (suspending the broken underlining): susceptibility.
[20]Handwritten marginal remark: for 'humor', 'depth'.
[21]In the typescript the word for "passable" was misspelled.

function like "to eat" and "to drink," as long as there are adjectives like "identical," "true," "false," "possible," as long as one talks about a flow of time and an expanse of space, etc., etc., humans will continue to bump up against the same mysterious difficulties, and stare at something that no explanation seems able to remove.

And this by the way satisfies a longing for the supra-natural //transcendental//, for in believing that they see the "limits of human understanding" of course they believe that they can see beyond it.

I read ". . . . philosophers are no nearer the meaning of "Reality" than Plato got. . . .". What a strange state of affairs. How strange in that case that Plato could get that far at all! Or, that we were not able to get farther! Was it because Plato was so smart?

The conflict in which we constantly find ourselves when we undertake logical investigations is like the conflict of two people who have concluded a contract with each other, the last formulations of which are expressed in easily misunderstandable words, whereas the explanations of these formulations explain everything unmistakably. Now one of the two people has a short memory, constantly forgets the explanations, misinterprets the conditions of the contract, and continually gets //therefore continually runs// into difficulties. The other one constantly has to remind him of the explanations in the contract and remove the difficulty.

Remember what a hard time children have believing (or accepting) that a word really has //can have// two completely different meanings.

The aim of philosophy is to erect a wall at the point where language stops anyway.

The results of philosophy are the uncovering of one or another piece of plain nonsense, and are the bumps that the understanding has got by running its head up against the limits //the end// of language. These bumps let us understand //recognize// the value of the discovery.

What kind of investigation are we carrying out? Am I investigating the probability of cases that I give as examples, or am I investigating their actuality? No, I'm just citing what is possible and am therefore giving grammatical examples.

Philosophy is not laid down in sentences but in a language.

Just as laws only become interesting when there is an inclination to transgress them //when they are transgressed// certain grammatical rules are only interesting when philosophers want to transgress them.

Savages have games (that's what we call them, anyway) for which they have no written rules, no inventory of rules. Let's now imagine the activity of an explorer, who travels through the countries of these peoples and takes an inventory of their rules. This is completely analogous to what the philosopher does. ((But why don't I say: savages have languages (that's what we . . . .) . . . . without a written grammar?))[22]

---

[22]In the typescript the parentheses are missing at the end of the remark.

91

WE DON'T ENCOUNTER PHILOSOPHICAL PROBLEMS AT ALL IN PRACTICAL LIFE (AS WE DO, FOR EXAMPLE, THOSE OF NATURAL SCIENCE). WE ENCOUNTER THEM ONLY WHEN WE ARE GUIDED NOT BY PRACTICAL PURPOSE IN FORMING OUR SENTENCES, BUT BY CERTAIN ANALOGIES WITHIN OUR LANGUAGE.

Language cannot express what belongs to the essence of the world. Therefore it cannot say that everything flows. Language can only say what we could also imagine differently.

That everything flows must lie in how language touches reality. Or better: that everything flows must lie in the nature of language. And, let's remember: in everyday life we don't notice that—as little as we notice the blurred edges of our visual field ("because we are so used to it," some will say). How, on what occasion, do we think we start noticing it? Isn't it when we want to form sentences in opposition to the grammar of time?

When someone says "everything flows," we feel that we are hindered in pinning down the actual, the actual reality. What goes on on the screen escapes us precisely because it is something going on. But we are describing something; and is that something else that is going on? The description is obviously linked to the very picture on the screen. There must be a false picture at the bottom of our feeling of helplessness. For what we want to describe we can describe.

Isn't this false picture that of a strip of film that runs by so quickly that we don't have any time to perceive a picture?

For in this case we would be inclined to chase after the picture. But in the course of something going on there is nothing analogous to that.

It is remarkable that in everyday life we never have the feeling that the phenomenon is getting away from us, that appearances are continually flowing, but only when we philosophize. This points to the fact that we are dealing here with a thought that is suggested to us through a wrong use of our language.

For the feeling is that the present vanishes into the past without our being able to stop it. And here we are obviously using the picture of a strip that constantly moves past us and that we can't stop. But of course it's just as clear that the picture is being misused. That one cannot say "time flows" if by "time" one means the possibility of change.

That we don't notice anything when we look around, look around in space, feel our own bodies, etc., etc., shows how natural these very things are to us. We don't perceive that we see space perspectively or that the visual image is in some sense blurred near its edge. We don't notice this, and can never notice it, because it is the mode of perception. We never think about it, and it is impossible, because the form of our world has no contrary.

I wanted to say that it is odd that those who ascribe reality only to things and not to our mental images move so self-confidently in the world of imagination and never long to escape from it.

I.e., how self-evident is the given. Things would have to have come to a pretty pass for that to be just a tiny photograph taken from an oblique angle.

What is self-evident, life, is supposed to be something accidental, unimportant; by contrast something that normally I never worry my head about is what is real!

I.e., what one neither can nor wants to go beyond would not be the world.

Again and again there is the attempt to define the world in language and to display it—but that doesn't work. The self-evidence of the world is expressed in the very fact that language means only it, and can only mean it.

As language gets its way of meaning from what it means, from the world, no language is thinkable which doesn't represent this world.

In the theories and battles of philosophy we find words whose meanings are well-known to us from everyday life used in an ultraphysical sense.

When philosophers use a word and search for its meaning, one must always ask: is this word ever really used this way in the language which created it //for which it is created//?

Usually one will then find that it is not so, and that the word is used against //contrary to// its normal grammar. ("Knowing," "Being," "Thing.")

(Philosophers are often like little children,[23] who first scribble random[24] lines on a piece of paper with their pencils, and now //then// ask an adult "What is that?"—Here's how this happened: now and then the adult had drawn something for the child and said: "That's a man," "That's a house," etc. And then the child draws lines too, and asks: now what's that?)

92
METHOD OF PHILOSOPHY.
THE POSSIBILITY OF CALM PROGRESS.

The real discovery is the one that makes me capable of stopping doing philosophy when I want to.

The one that gives philosophy peace, so that it is no longer //being// tormented by questions which bring itself in question.

Instead, we now demonstrate a method by examples; and one can break off the series of examples //and the series of examples can be broken off//.

But more correctly, one should say: Problems are solved (uneasiness //difficulties// eliminated), not a single problem.

Unrest in philosophy comes from philosophers looking at, seeing, philosophy all wrong, i.e., cut up into (infinite) vertical strips, as it were, rather than (finite) horizontal strips. This reordering of understanding creates the greatest difficulty. They want to grasp the infinite strip, as it were, and complain that it //this// is not possible piece by piece. Of course it isn't, if by "a piece" one understands an endless vertical strip. But it is, if one sees a horizontal strip as a piece //a whole, defi-

[23]Handwritten alternative: (Philosophers) often behave like little children. . . .
[24]Handwritten alternative: some.

nite piece//.—But then we'll never get finished with our work! Of course //certainly// not, because it doesn't have an end.

(Instead of turbulent conjectures and explanations, we want to give calm demonstrations[25] //statements// of linguistic facts //about linguistic facts//.) //we want the calm noting[26] of linguistic facts.//

We must plow though the whole of language.

(When most people ought to[27] engage in a philosophical investigation, they act like someone who is looking for an object in a drawer very nervously. He throws papers out of the drawer—what he's looking for may be among them—leafs through the others hastily and sloppily. Throws some back into the drawer, mixes them up with the others, and so on. Then one can only tell him: Stop, if you look in that way, I can't help you look. First you have to start to examine one thing after another methodically, and in peace and quiet; then I am willing to look with you and to direct myself with you as model in the method.)

93
THE MYTHOLOGY IN THE FORMS OF OUR LANGUAGE.
((PAUL ERNST.))

In ancient rites we find the use of an extremely well-developed language of gestures.

And when I read Frazer, I would like to say again and again: All these processes, these changes of meaning, we have right in front of us even in our language of words. If what is hidden in the last sheaf is called the "Cornwolf" as well as the sheaf itself, and also the man who binds it, then we recognize in this a linguistic process we know well.

The scapegoat, on which one lays one's sins, and who runs away into the desert with them—a false picture, similar to those that cause errors in philosophy.

I would like to say: nothing shows our kinship with those savages better, than that Frazer has at hand a word like "ghost" or "shade," which is so familiar to him and to us, to describe the views of these people.

(This is quite different than if he were to relate, for instance, that the savages imagined //imagine// that their head falls off when they have slain an enemy. Here our description would contain nothing superstitious or magical.)

Indeed, this oddity refers not only to the expressions "ghost" and "shade", and much too little is made of it that we include the words "soul" and "spirit" in our own educated vocabulary. Compared to this it is insignificant that we do not believe that our soul eats and drinks.

An entire mythology is laid down in our language.

Driving out death or killing death; but on the other hand it is portrayed as a skeleton, and therefore as dead itself, in a certain sense. "As dead as death."

[25]Handwritten alternative: reflection.

[26]Originally in the typescript: establishment.

[27]Unclear textual point in the typescript. The typewriting gives the impression that the original words "want to" were overstruck to produce "ought to."

"Nothing is as dead as death; nothing as beautiful as beauty itself!" The picture according to which reality is thought of here is that beauty, death, etc., is the pure (concentrated) substance, whereas in a beautiful object it is contained as an admixture—And don't I recognize here my own observations about "object" and "complex"? (Plato.)

The primitive forms of our language: noun, adjective and verb, show the simple picture into whose form language tries to force everything.

So long as one imagines the soul as a thing, a body, which is in our head, this hypothesis is not dangerous. The danger of our models does not lie in their imperfection and roughness, but in their unclarity (fogginess).

The danger sets in when we notice that the old model is not sufficient but then we don't change it, but only sublimate it, as it were. So long as I say the thought is in my head, everything is all right; things get dangerous when we say that the thought is not in my head, but in my spirit.

The Elimination of Metaphysics
and
The Function of Philosophy

A. J. Ayer

The traditional disputes of philosophers are, for the most part, as unwarranted as they are unfruitful. The surest way to end them is to establish beyond question what should be the purpose and method of a philosophical enquiry. And this is by no means so difficult a task as the history of philosophy would lead one to suppose. For if there are any questions which science leaves it to philosophy to answer, a straightforward process of elimination must lead to their discovery.

We may begin by criticising the metaphysical thesis that philosophy affords us knowledge of a reality transcending the world of science and common sense. Later on, when we come to define metaphysics and account for its existence, we shall find that it is possible to be a metaphysician without believing in a transcendent reality; for we shall see that many metaphysical utterances are due to the commission of logical errors, rather than to a conscious desire on the part of their authors to go beyond the limits of experience. But it is convenient for us to take the case of those who believe that it is possible to have knowledge of a transcendent reality as a starting-point for our discussion. The arguments which we use to refute them will subsequently be found to apply to the whole of metaphysics.

One way of attacking a metaphysician who claimed to have knowledge of a reality which transcended the phenomenal world would be to enquire from what premises his propositions were deduced. Must he not begin, as other men do, with the evidence of his senses? And if so, what valid process of reasoning can possibly

Source: Language, Truth and Logic [1936], Chapters 1, 2. New York: Dover Publications, Inc., 1952, 33–59.

lead him to the conception of a transcendent reality? Surely from empirical premises nothing whatsoever concerning the properties, or even the existence, of anything super-empirical can legitimately be inferred. But this objection would be met by a denial on the part of the metaphysician that his assertions were ultimately based on the evidence of his senses. He would say that he was endowed with a faculty of intellectual intuition which enabled him to know facts that could not be known through sense-experience. And even if it could be shown that he was relying on empirical premises, and that his venture into a non-empirical world was therefore logically unjustified, it would not follow that the assertions which he made concerning this non-empirical world could not be true. For the fact that a conclusion does not follow from its putative premise is not sufficient to show that it is false. Consequently one cannot overthrow a system of transcendent metaphysics merely by criticising the way in which it comes into being. What is required is rather a criticism of the nature of the actual statements which comprise it. And this is the line of argument which we shall, in fact, pursue. For we shall maintain that no statement which refers to a "reality" transcending the limits of all possible sense-experience can possibly have any literal significance; from which it must follow that the labours of those who have striven to describe such a reality have all been devoted to the production of nonsense.

It may be suggested that this is a proposition which has already been proved by Kant. But although Kant also condemned transcendent metaphysics, he did so on different grounds. For he said that the human understanding was so constituted that it lost itself in contradictions when it ventured out beyond the limits of possible experience and attempted to deal with things in themselves. And thus he made the impossibility of a transcendent metaphysic not, as we do, a matter of logic, but a matter of fact. He asserted, not that our minds could not conceivably have had the power of penetrating beyond the phenomenal world, but merely that they were in fact devoid of it. And this leads the critic to ask how, if it is possible to know only what lies within the bounds of sense-experience, the author can be justified in asserting that real things do exist beyond, and how he can tell what are the boundaries beyond which the human understanding may not venture, unless he succeeds in passing them himself. As Wittgenstein says, "in order to draw a limit to thinking, we should have to think both sides of this limit,"[1] a truth to which Bradley gives a special twist in maintaining that the man who is ready to prove that metaphysics is impossible is a brother metaphysician with a rival theory of his own.[2]

Whatever force these objections may have against the Kantian doctrine, they have none whatsoever against the thesis that I am about to set forth. It cannot here be said that the author is himself overstepping the barrier he maintains to be impassable. For the fruitlessness of attempting to transcend the limits of possible sense-experience will be deduced, not from a psychological hypothesis concerning the actual constitution of the human mind, but from the rule which determines the literal significance of language. Our charge against the metaphysician is not that he attempts to employ the understanding in a field where it cannot profitably venture,

[1]*Tractatus Logico-Philosophicus,* Preface.
[2]Bradley, *Appearance and Reality,* 2nd ed., p. 1.

but that he produces sentences which fail to conform to the conditions under which alone a sentence can be literally significant. Nor are we ourselves obliged to talk nonsense in order to show that all sentences of a certain type are necessarily devoid of literal significance. We need only formulate the criterion which enables us to test whether a sentence expresses a genuine proposition about a matter of fact, and then point out that the sentences under consideration fail to satisfy it. And this we shall now proceed to do. We shall first of all formulate the criterion in somewhat vague terms, and then give the explanations which are necessary to render it precise.

The criterion which we use to test the genuineness of apparent statements of fact is the criterion of verifiability. We say that a sentence is factually significant to any given person, if, and only if, he knows how to verify the proposition which it purports to express—that is, if he knows what observations would lead him, under certain conditions, to accept the proposition as being true, or reject it as being false. If, on the other hand, the putative proposition is of such a character that the assumption of its truth, or falsehood, is consistent with any assumption whatsoever concerning the nature of his future experience, then, as far as he is concerned, it is, if not a tautology, a mere pseudo-proposition. The sentence expressing it may be emotionally significant to him; but it is not literally significant. And with regard to questions the procedure is the same. We enquire in every case what observations would lead us to answer the question, one way or the other; and, if none can be discovered, we must conclude that the sentence under consideration does not, as far as we are concerned, express a genuine question, however strongly its grammatical appearance may suggest that it does.

As the adoption of this procedure is an essential factor in the argument of this book, it needs to be examined in detail.

In the first place, it is necessary to draw a distinction between practical verifiability, and verifiability in principle. Plainly we all understand, in many cases believe, propositions which we have not in fact taken steps to verify. Many of these are propositions which we could verify if we took enough trouble. But there remain a number of significant propositions, concerning matters of fact, which we could not verify even if we chose; simply because we lack the practical means of placing ourselves in the situation where the relevant observations could be made. A simple and familiar example of such a proposition is the proposition that there are mountains on the farther side of the moon.[3] No rocket has yet been invented which would enable me to go and look at the farther side of the moon, so that I am unable to decide the matter by actual observation. But I do know what observations would decide it for me, if, as is theoretically conceivable, I were once in a position to make them. And therefore I say that the proposition is verifiable in principle, if not in practice, and is accordingly significant. On the other hand, such a metaphysical pseudo-proposition as "the Absolute enters into, but is itself in capable of, evolution and progress,"[4] is not even in principle verifiable. For one cannot conceive of an observation which would enable one to determine whether the Absolute did, or did not, enter into evolution and progress. Of course it is possible that the author of

[3]This example has been used by Professor Schlick to illustrate the same point.
[4]A remark taken at random from *Appearance and Reality,* by F. H. Bradley.

such a remark is using English words in a way in which they are not commonly used by English-speaking people, and that he does, in fact, intend to assert something which could be empirically verified. But until he makes us understand how the proposition that he wishes to express would be verified, he fails to communicate anything to us. And if he admits, as I think the author of the remark in question would have admitted, that his words were not intended to express either a tautology or a proposition which was capable, at least in principle, of being verified, then it follows that he has made an utterance which has no literal significance even for himself.

A further distinction which we must make is the distinction between the "strong" and the "weak" sense of the term "verifiable." A proposition is said to be verifiable, in the strong sense of the term, if, and only if, its truth could be conclusively established in experience. But it is verifiable, in the weak sense, if it is possible for experience to render it probable. In which sense are we using the term when we say that a putative proposition is genuine only if it is verifiable?

It seems to me that if we adopt conclusive verifiability as our criterion of significance, as some positivists have proposed,[5] our argument will prove too much. Consider, for example, the case of general propositions of law—such propositions, namely, as "arsenic is poisonous"; "all men are mortal"; "a body tends to expand when it is heated." It is of the very nature of these propositions that their truth cannot be established with certainty by any finite series of observations. But if it is recognised that such general propositions of law are designed to cover an infinite number of cases, then it must be admitted that they cannot, even in principle, be verified conclusively. And then, if we adopt conclusive verifiability as our criterion of significance, we are logically obliged to treat these general propositions of law in the same fashion as we treat the statements of the metaphysician.

In face of this difficulty, some positivists[6] have adopted the heroic course of saying that these general propositions are indeed pieces of nonsense, albeit an essentially important type of nonsense. But here the introduction of the term "important" is simply an attempt to hedge. It serves only to mark the authors' recognition that their view is somewhat too paradoxical, without in any way removing the paradox. Besides, the difficulty is not confined to the case of general propositions of law, though it is there revealed most plainly. It is hardly less obvious in the case of propositions about the remote past. For it must surely be admitted that, however strong the evidence in favour of historical statements may be, their truth can never become more than highly probable. And to maintain that they also constituted an important, or unimportant, type of nonsense would be unplausible, to say the very least. Indeed, it will be our contention that no proposition, other than a tautology, can possibly be anything more than a probable hypothesis. And if this is correct, the principle that a sentence can be factually significant only if it expresses what is conclusively verifiable is self-stultifying as

---

[5]e.g. M. Schlick, "Positivismus und Realismus," *Erkenntnis,* Vol. I, 1930. F. Waismann, "Logische Analyse des Warscheinlichkeitsbegriffs," *Erkenntnis,* Vol. I, 1930.
[6]e.g. M. Schlick, "Die Kausalität in der gegenwärtigen Physik," *Naturwissenschaft,* Vol. 19, 1931.

a criterion of significance. For it leads to the conclusion that it is impossible to make a significant statement of fact at all.

Nor can we accept the suggestion that a sentence should be allowed to be factually significant if, and only if, it expresses something which is definitely confutable by experience.[7] Those who adopt this course assume that, although no finite series of observations is ever sufficient to establish the truth of a hypothesis beyond all possibility of doubt, there are crucial cases in which a single observation, or series of observations, can definitely confute it. But, as we shall show later on, this assumption is false. A hypothesis cannot be conclusively confuted any more than it can be conclusively verified. For when we take the occurrence of certain observations as proof that a given hypothesis is false, we presuppose the existence of certain conditions. And though, in any given case, it may be extremely improbable that this assumption is false, it is not logically impossible. We shall see that there need be no self-contradiction in holding that some of the relevant circumstances are other than we have taken them to be, and consequently that the hypothesis has not really broken down. And if it is not the case that any hypothesis can be definitely confuted, we cannot hold that the genuineness of a proposition depends on the possibility of its definite confutation.

Accordingly, we fall back on the weaker sense of verification. We say that the question that must be asked about any putative statement of fact is not, Would any observations make its truth or falsehood logically certain? but simply, Would any observations be relevant to the determination of its truth or falsehood? And it is only if a negative answer is given to this second question that we conclude that the statement under consideration is nonsensical.

To make our position clearer, we may formulate it in another way. Let us call a proposition which records an actual or possible observation an experiential proposition. Then we may say that it is the mark of a genuine factual proposition, not that it should be equivalent to an experiential proposition, or any finite number of experiential propositions, but simply that some experiential propositions can be deduced from it in conjunction with certain other premises without being deducible from those other premises alone.[8]

This criterion seems liberal enough. In contrast to the principle of conclusive verifiability, it clearly does not deny significance to general propositions or to propositions about the past. Let us see what kinds of assertion it rules out.

A good example of the kind of utterance that is condemned by our criterion as being not even false but nonsensical would be the assertion that the world of sense-experience was altogether unreal. It must, of course, be admitted that our senses do sometimes deceive us. We may, as the result of having certain sensations, expect certain other sensations to be obtainable which are, in fact, not obtainable. But, in all such cases, it is further sense-experience that informs us of the mistakes that arise out of sense-experience. We say that the senses sometimes deceive us, just because the expectations to which our sense-experiences give rise do not always accord with what we subsequently experience. That is, we rely on our

---

[7]This has been proposed by Karl Popper in his *Logik der Forschung*.
[8]This is an over-simplified statement, which is not literally correct. . . .

senses to substantiate or confute the judgements which are based on our sensations. And therefore the fact that our perceptual judgements are sometimes found to be erroneous has not the slightest tendency to show that the world of sense-experience is unreal. And, indeed, it is plain that no conceivable observation, or series of observations, could have any tendency to show that the world revealed to us by sense-experience was unreal. Consequently, anyone who condemns the sensible world as a world of mere appearance, as opposed to reality, is saying something which, according to our criterion of significance, is literally nonsensical.

An example of a controversy which the application of our criterion obliges us to condemn as fictitious is provided by those who dispute concerning the number of substances that there are in the world. For it is admitted both by monists, who maintain that reality is one substance, and by pluralists, who maintain that reality is many, that it is impossible to imagine any empirical situation which would be relevant to the solution of their dispute. But if we are told that no possible observation could give any probability either to the assertion that reality was one substance or to the assertion that it was many, then we must conclude that neither assertion is significant. . . . [T]here are genuine logical and empirical questions involved in the dispute between monists and pluralists. But the metaphysical question concerning "substance" is ruled out by our criterion as spurious.

A similar treatment must be accorded to the controversy between realists and idealists, in its metaphysical aspect. A simple illustration, which I have made use of in a similar argument elsewhere,[9] will help to demonstrate this. Let us suppose that a picture is discovered and the suggestion made that it was painted by Goya. There is a definite procedure for dealing with such a question. The experts examine the picture to see in what way it resembles the accredited works of Goya, and to see if it bears any marks which are characteristic of a forgery; they look up contemporary records for evidence of the existence of such a picture, and so on. In the end, they may still disagree, but each one knows what empirical evidence would go to confirm or discredit his opinion. Suppose, now, that these men have studied philosophy, and some of them proceed to maintain that this picture is a set of ideas in the perceiver's mind, or in God's mind, others that it is objectively real. What possible experience could any of them have which would be relevant to the solution of this dispute one way or the other? In the ordinary sense of the term "real," in which it is opposed to "illusory," the reality of the picture is not in doubt. The disputants have satisfied themselves that the picture is real, in this sense, by obtaining a correlated series of sensations of sight and sensations of touch. Is there any similar process by which they could discover whether the picture was real, in the sense in which the term "real" is opposed to "ideal"? Clearly there is none. But, if that is so, the problem is fictitious according to our criterion. This does not mean that the realist-idealist controversy may be dismissed without further ado. For it can legitimately be regarded as a dispute concerning the analysis of existential propositions, and so as involving a logical problem which . . . can be definitively solved. What we have just shown is that the question at issue between idealists and realists becomes fictitious when, as is often the case, it is given a metaphysical interpretation.

[9]Vide "Demonstration of the Impossibility of Metaphysics," *Mind,* 1934, p. 339.

There is no need for us to give further examples of the operation of our criterion of significance. For our object is merely to show that philosophy, as a genuine branch of knowledge, must be distinguished from metaphysics. We are not now concerned with the historical question how much of what has traditionally passed for philosophy is actually metaphysical. We shall, however, point out later on that the majority of the "great philosophers" of the past were not essentially metaphysicians, and thus reassure those who would otherwise be prevented from adopting our criterion by considerations of piety.

As to the validity of the verification principle, in the form in which we have stated it, a demonstration will be given in the course of this book. . . . [A]ll propositions which have factual content are empirical hypotheses; and that the function of an empirical hypothesis is to provide a rule for the anticipation of experience. And this means that every empirical hypothesis must be relevant to some actual, or possible, experience, so that a statement which is not relevant to any experience is not an empirical hypothesis, and accordingly has no factual content. But this is precisely what the principle of verifiability asserts.

It should be mentioned here that the fact that the utterances of the metaphysician are nonsensical does not follow simply from the fact that they are devoid of factual content. It follows from that fact, together with the fact that they are not *a priori* propositions. . . . *A priori* propositions, which have always been attractive to philosophers on account of their certainty, owe this certainty to the fact that they are tautologies. We may accordingly define a metaphysical sentence as a sentence which purports to express a genuine proposition, but does, in fact, express neither a tautology nor an empirical hypothesis. And as tautologies and empirical hypotheses form the entire class of significant propositions, we are justified in concluding that all metaphysical assertions are nonsensical. Our next task is to show how they come to be made.

The use of the term "substance," to which we have already referred, provides us with a good example of the way in which metaphysics mostly comes to be written. It happens to be the case that we cannot, in our language, refer to the sensible properties of a thing without introducing a word or phrase which appears to stand for the thing itself as opposed to anything which may be said about it. And, as a result of this, those who are infected by the primitive superstition that to every name a single real entity must correspond assume that it is necessary to distinguish logically between the thing itself and any, or all, of its sensible properties. And so they employ the term "substance" to refer to the thing itself. But from the fact that we happen to employ a single word to refer to a thing, and make that word the grammatical subject of the sentences in which we refer to the sensible appearances of the thing, it does not by any means follow that the thing itself is a "simple entity," or that it cannot be defined in terms of the totality of its appearances. It is true that in talking of "its" appearances we appear to distinguish the thing from the appearances, but that is simply an accident of linguistic usage. Logical analysis shows that what makes these "appearances" the "appearances of" the same thing is not their relationship to an entity other than themselves, but their relationship to one another. The metaphysician fails to see this because he is misled by a superficial grammatical feature of his language.

A simpler and clearer instance of the way in which a consideration of grammar leads to metaphysics is the case of the metaphysical concept of Being. The origin of our temptation to raise questions about Being, which no conceivable experience would enable us to answer, lies in the fact that, in our language, sentences which express existential propositions and sentences which express attributive propositions may be of the same grammatical form. For instance, the sentences "Martyrs exist" and "Martyrs suffer" both consist of a noun followed by an intransitive verb, and the fact that they have grammatically the same appearance leads one to assume that they are of the same logical type. It is seen that in the proposition "Martyrs suffer," the members of a certain species are credited with a certain attribute, and it is sometimes assumed that the same thing is true of such a proposition as "Martyrs exist." If this were actually the case, it would, indeed, be as legitimate to speculate about the Being of martyrs as it is to speculate about their suffering. But, as Kant pointed out,[10] existence is not an attribute. For, when we ascribe an attribute to a thing, we covertly assert that it exists: so that if existence were itself an attribute, it would follow that all positive existential propositions were tautologies, and all negative existential propositions self-contradictory; and this is not the case.[11] So that those who raise questions about Being which are based on the assumption that existence is an attribute are guilty of following grammar beyond the boundaries of sense.

A similar mistake has been made in connection with such propositions as "Unicorns are fictitious." Here again the fact that there is a superficial grammatical resemblance between the English sentences "Dogs are faithful" and "Unicorns are fictitious," and between the corresponding sentences in other languages, creates the assumption that they are of the same logical type. Dogs must exist in order to have the property of being faithful, and so it is held that unless unicorns in some way existed they could not have the property of being fictitious. But, as it is plainly self-contradictory to say that fictitious objects exist, the device is adopted of saying that they are real in some non-empirical sense—that they have a mode of real being which is different from the mode of being of existent things. But since there is no way of testing whether an object is real in this sense, as there is for testing whether it is real in the ordinary sense, the assertion that fictitious objects have a special non-empirical mode of real being is devoid of all literal significance. It comes to be made as a result of the assumption that being fictitious is an attribute. And this is a fallacy of the same order as the fallacy of supposing that existence is an attribute, and it can be exposed in the same way.

In general, the postulation of real non-existent entities results from the superstition, just now referred to, that, to every word or phrase that can be the grammatical subject of a sentence, there must somewhere be a real entity corresponding. For as there is no place in the empirical world for many of these "entities," a special non-empirical world is invoked to house them. To this error must be attributed, not only the utterances of a Heidegger, who bases his metaphysics on the assumption that "Nothing" is a name which is used to denote something

---

[10]Vide *The Critique of Pure Reason,* "Transcendental Dialectic," Book II, Chapter iii, section 4.

[11]This argument is well stated by John Wisdom, *Interpretation and Analysis,* pp. 62, 63.

peculiarly mysterious,[12] but also the prevalence of such problems as those concerning the reality of propositions and universals whose senselessness, though less obvious, is no less complete.

These few examples afford a sufficient indication of the way in which most metaphysical assertions come to be formulated. They show how easy it is to write sentences which are literally nonsensical without seeing that they are nonsensical. And thus we see that the view that a number of the traditional "problems of philosophy" are metaphysical, and consequently fictitious, does not involve any incredible assumptions about the psychology of philosophers.

Among those who recognise that if philosophy is to be accounted a genuine branch of knowledge it must be defined in such a way as to distinguish it from metaphysics, it is fashionable to speak of the metaphysician as a kind of misplaced poet. As his statements have no literal meaning, they are not subject to any criteria of truth or falsehood: but they may still serve to express, or arouse, emotion, and thus be subject to ethical or aesthetic standards. And it is suggested that they may have considerable value, as means of moral inspiration, or even as works of art. In this way, an attempt is made to compensate the metaphysician for his extrusion from philosophy.[13]

I am afraid that this compensation is hardly in accordance with his deserts. The view that the metaphysician is to be reckoned among the poets appears to rest on the assumption that both talk nonsense. But this assumption is false. In the vast majority of cases the sentences which are produced by poets do have literal meaning. The difference between the man who uses language scientifically and the man who uses it emotively is not that the one produces sentences which are incapable of arousing emotion, and the other sentences which have no sense, but that the one is primarily concerned with the expression of true propositions, the other with the creation of a work of art. Thus, if a work of science contains true and important propositions, its value as a work of science will hardly be diminished by the fact that they are inelegantly expressed. And similarly, a work of art is not necessarily the worse for the fact that all the propositions comprising it are literally false. But to say that many literary works are largely composed of falsehoods, is not to say that they are composed of pseudo-propositions. It is, in fact, very rare for a literary artist to produce sentences which have no literal meaning. And where this does occur, the sentences are carefully chosen for their rhythm and balance. If the author writes nonsense, it is because he considers it most suitable for bringing about the effects for which his writing is designed.

The metaphysician, on the other hand, does not intend to write nonsense. He lapses into it through being deceived by grammar, or through committing errors of reasoning, such as that which leads to the view that the sensible world is unreal. But it is not the mark of a poet simply to make mistakes of this sort. There are some, indeed, who would see in the fact that the metaphysician's utterances are senseless

---

[12]Vide *Was ist Metaphysik,* by Heidegger: criticised by Rudolf Carnap in his "Oberwindung der Metaphysik durch logische Analyse der Sprache," *Erkenntnis,* Vol. II, 1932.

[13]For a discussion of this point, see also C. A. Mace, "Representation and Expression," *Analysis,* Vol. I, No. 3; and "Metaphysics and Emotive Language," *Analysis,* Vol. II, Nos. 1 and 2.

a reason against the view that they have aesthetic value. And, without going so far as this, we may safely say that it does not constitute a reason for it.

It is true, however, that although the greater part of metaphysics is merely the embodiment of humdrum errors, there remain a number of metaphysical passages which are the work of genuine mystical feeling; and they may more plausibly be held to have moral or aesthetic value. But, as far as we are concerned, the distinction between the kind of metaphysics that is produced by a philosopher who has been duped by grammar, and the kind that is produced by a mystic who is trying to express the inexpressible, is of no great importance: what is important to us is to realise that even the utterances of the metaphysician who is attempting to expound a vision are literally senseless; so that henceforth we may pursue our philosophical researches with as little regard for them as for the more inglorious kind of metaphysics which comes from a failure to understand the workings of our language.

Among the superstitions from which we are freed by the abandonment of metaphysics is the view that it is the business of the philosopher to construct a deductive system. In rejecting this view we are not, of course, suggesting that the philosopher can dispense with deductive reasoning. We are simply contesting his right to posit certain first principles, and then offer them with their consequences as a complete picture of reality. To discredit this procedure, one has only to show that there can be no first principles of the kind it requires.

As it is the function of these first principles to provide a certain basis for our knowledge, it is clear that they are not to be found among the so-called laws of nature. For we shall see that the "laws of nature," if they are not mere definitions, are simply hypotheses which may be confuted by experience. And, indeed, it has never been the practice of the system-builders in philosophy to choose inductive generalizations for their premises. Rightly regarding such generalizations as being merely probable, they subordinate them to principles which they believe to be logically certain.

This is illustrated most clearly in the system of Descartes. It is commonly said that Descartes attempted to derive all human knowledge from premises whose truth was intuitively certain: but this interpretation puts an undue stress on the element of psychology in his system. I think he realised well enough that a mere appeal to intuition was insufficient for his purpose, since men are not all equally credulous, and that what he was really trying to do was to base all our knowledge on propositions which it would be self-contradictory to deny. He thought he had found such a proposition in "*cogito*," which must not here be understood in its ordinary sense of "I think," but rather as meaning "there is a thought now." In fact he was wrong, because "*non cogito*" would be self-contradictory only if it negated itself: and this no significant proposition can do. But even if it were true that such a proposition as "there is a thought now" was logically certain, it still would not serve Descartes' purpose. For if "*cogito*" is taken in this sense, his initial principle, "*cogito ergo sum*," is false. "I exist" does not follow from "there is a thought now." The fact that a thought occurs at a given moment does not entail that any other thought has occurred at any other moment, still less that there has occurred a series of thoughts sufficient to constitute a single self. As Hume conclusively showed, no one event intrinsically points to any other. We infer the existence of events which we are not actually observing, with the help of general principles. But these principles must be obtained inductively. By mere deduction from what is immediately given we cannot advance a single step beyond. And, consequently, any attempt to base a deductive system on propositions which describe what is immediately given is bound to be a failure.

The only other course open to one who wished to deduce all our knowledge from "first principles," without indulging in metaphysics, would be to take for his premises a set of *a priori* truths. But, as we have already mentioned, and shall later show, an *a priori* truth is a tautology. And from a set of tautologies, taken by themselves, only further tautologies can be validly deduced. But it would be absurd to put forward a system of tautologies as constituting the whole truth about the universe. And thus we may conclude that it is not possible to deduce all our knowledge from "first principles"; so that those who hold that it is the function of philosophy to carry out such a deduction are denying its claim to be a genuine branch of knowledge.

The belief that it is the business of the philosopher to search for first principles is bound up with the familiar conception of philosophy as the study of reality as a whole. And this conception is one which it is difficult to criticize, because it is so vague. If it is taken to imply, as it sometimes is, that the philosopher somehow projects himself outside the world, and takes a bird's-eye view of it, then it is plainly a metaphysical conception. And it is also metaphysical to assert, as some do, that "reality as a whole" is somehow generically different from the reality which is investigated piecemeal by the special sciences. But if the assertion that philosophy studies reality as a whole is understood to imply merely that the philosopher is equally concerned with the content of every science, then we may accept it, not indeed as an adequate definition of philosophy, but as a truth about it. For we shall find, when we come to discuss the relationship of philosophy to science, that it is not, in principle, related to any one science more closely than to any other.

In saying that philosophy is concerned with each of the sciences, . . . we mean also to rule out the supposition that philosophy can be ranged alongside the existing sciences, as a special department of speculative knowledge. Those who make this supposition cherish the belief that there are some things in the world which are possible objects of speculative knowledge and yet lie beyond the scope of empirical science. But this belief is a delusion. There is no field of experience which cannot, in principle, be brought under some form of scientific law, and no type of speculative knowledge about the world which it is, in principle, beyond the power of science to give. We have already gone some way to substantiate this proposition by demolishing metaphysics; and we shall justify it to the full in the course of this book.

With this we complete the overthrow of speculative philosophy. We are now in a position to see that the function of philosophy is wholly critical. In what exactly does its critical activity consist?

One way of answering this question is to say that it is the philosopher's business to test the validity of our scientific hypotheses and everyday assumptions. But this view, though very widely held, is mistaken. If a man chooses to doubt the truth of all the propositions he ordinarily believes, it is not in the power of philosophy to reassure him. The most that philosophy can do, apart from seeing whether his beliefs are self-consistent, is to show what are the criteria which are used to determine the truth or falsehood of any given proposition: and then, when the sceptic realises that certain observations would verify his propositions, he may also realize that he could make those observations, and so consider his original beliefs to be justified. But in such a case one cannot say that it is philosophy which justifies his beliefs. Philosophy merely shows him that experience can justify them. We may look to the philosopher to show us what we accept as constituting sufficient evidence for the truth of any given empirical proposition. But whether the evidence is forthcoming or not is in every case a purely empirical question.

If anyone thinks that we are here taking too much for granted, let him refer to the chapter on "Truth and Probability," in which we discuss how the validity of synthetic propositions is determined. He will see there that the only sort of justification that is necessary or possible for self-consistent empirical propositions is empirical verification. And this applies just as much to the laws of science as to the maxims of common sense. Indeed there is no difference in kind between them. The superiority of the scientific hypothesis consists merely in its being more abstract, more precise, and more fruitful. And although scientific objects such as atoms and electrons seem to be fictitious in a way that chairs and tables are not, here, too, the distinction is only a distinction of degree. For both these kinds of objects are known only by their sensible manifestations and are definable in terms of them.

It is time, therefore, to abandon the superstition that natural science cannot be regarded as logically respectable until philosophers have solved the problem of induction. The problem of induction is, roughly speaking, the problem of finding a way to prove that certain empirical generalizations which are derived from past experience will hold good also in the future. There are only two ways of approaching this problem on the assumption that it is a genuine problem, and it is easy to see that neither of them can lead to its solution. One may attempt to deduce the proposition which one is required to prove either from a purely formal principle or from an empirical principle. In the former case one commits the error of supposing that from a tautology it is possible to deduce a proposition about a matter of fact; in the latter case one simply assumes what one is setting out to prove. For example, it is often said that we can justify induction by invoking the uniformity of nature, or by postulating a "principle of limited independent variety."[14] But, in fact, the principle of the uniformity of nature merely states, in a misleading fashion, the assumption that past experience is a reliable guide to the future; while the principle of limited independent variety presupposes it. And it is plain that any other empirical principle which was put forward as a justification of induction

[14]cf. J. M. Keynes, *A Treatise on Probability,* Part III.

would beg the question in the same way. For the only grounds which one could have for believing such a principle would be inductive grounds.

Thus it appears that there is no possible way of solving the problem of induction, as it is ordinarily conceived. And this means that it is a fictitious problem, since all genuine problems are at least theoretically capable of being solved: and the credit of natural science is not impaired by the fact that some philosophers continue to be puzzled by it. Actually, we shall see that the only test to which a form of scientific procedure which satisfies the necessary condition of self-consistency is subject, is the test of its success in practice. We are entitled to have faith in our procedure just so long as it does the work which it is designed to do—that is, enables us to predict future experience, and so to control our environment. Of course, the fact that a certain form of procedure has always been successful in practice affords no logical guarantee that it will continue to be so. But then it is a mistake to demand a guarantee where it is logically impossible to obtain one. This does not mean that it is irrational to expect future experience to conform to the past. For when we come to define "rationality" we shall find that for us "being rational" entails being guided in a particular fashion by past experience.

The task of defining rationality is precisely the sort of task that it is the business of philosophy to undertake. But in achieving this it does not justify scientific procedure. What justifies scientific procedure, to the extent to which it is capable of being justified, is the success of the predictions to which it gives rise: and this can be determined only in actual experience. By itself, the analysis of a synthetic principle tells us nothing whatsoever about its truth.

Unhappily, this fact is generally disregarded by philosophers who concern themselves with the so-called theory of knowledge. Thus it is common for writers on the subject of perception to assume that, unless one can give a satisfactory analysis of perceptual situations, one is not entitled to believe in the existence of material things. But this is a complete mistake. What gives one the right to believe in the existence of a certain material thing is simply the fact that one has certain sensations: for, whether one realises it or not, to say that the thing exists is equivalent to saying that such sensations are obtainable. It is the philosopher's business to give a correct definition of material things in terms of sensations. But his success or failure in this task has no bearing whatsoever on the validity of our perceptual judgements. That depends wholly on actual sense-experience.

It follows that the philosopher has no right to despise the beliefs of common sense. If he does so, he merely displays his ignorance of the true purpose of his enquiries. What he is entitled to despise is the unreflecting analysis of those beliefs, which takes the grammatical structure of the sentence as a trustworthy guide to its meaning. Thus, many of the mistakes made in connection with the problem of perception can be accounted for by the fact, already referred to in connection with the metaphysical notion of "substance," that it happens to be impossible in an ordinary European language to mention a thing without appearing to distinguish it generically from its qualities and states. But from the fact that the common-sense analysis of a proposition is mistaken it by no means follows that the proposition is not true. The philosopher may be able to show us that the propositions we believe are far more complex than we suppose; but it does not follow from this that we have no right to believe them.

It should now be sufficiently clear that if the philosopher is to uphold his claim to make a special contribution to the stock of our knowledge, he must not attempt to formulate speculative truths, or to look for first principles, or to make *a priori* judgements about the validity of our empirical beliefs. He must, in fact, confine himself to works of clarification and analysis of a sort which we shall presently describe.

In saying that the activity of philosophizing is essentially analytic, we are not, of course, maintaining that all those who are commonly called philosophers have actually been engaged in carrying out analyses. On the contrary, we have been at pains to show that a great deal of what is commonly called philosophy is metaphysical in character. What we have been in search of, in enquiring into the function of philosophy, is a definition of philosophy which should accord to some extent with the practice of those who are commonly called philosophers, and at the same time be consistent with the common assumption that philosophy is a special branch of knowledge. It is because metaphysics fails to satisfy this second condition that we distinguish it from philosophy, in spite of the fact that it is commonly referred to as philosophy. And our justification for making this distinction is that it is necessitated by our original postulate that philosophy is a special branch of knowledge, and our demonstration that metaphysics is not.

Although this procedure is logically unassailable, it will perhaps be attacked on the ground that it is inexpedient. It will be said that the "history of philosophy" is, almost entirely, a history of metaphysics; and, consequently, that although there is no actual fallacy involved in our using the word "philosophy" in the sense in which philosophy is incompatible with metaphysics, it is dangerously misleading. For all our care in defining the term will not prevent people from confusing the activities which we call philosophical with the metaphysical activities of those whom they have been taught to regard as philosophers. And therefore it would surely be advisable for us to abandon the term "philosophy" altogether, as a name for a distinctive branch of knowledge, and invent some new description for the activity which we were minded to call the activity of philosophizing.

Our answer to this is that it is not the case that the "history of philosophy" is almost entirely a history of metaphysics. That it contains some metaphysics is undeniable. But I think it can be shown that the majority of those who are commonly supposed to have been great philosophers were primarily not metaphysicians but analysts. For example, I do not see how anyone who follows the account which we shall give of the nature of philosophical analysis and then turns to Locke's *Essay Concerning Human Understanding* can fail to conclude that it is essentially an analytic work. Locke is generally regarded as being one who, like G. E. Moore at the present time, puts forward a philosophy of common sense.[15] But he does not, any more than Moore, attempt to give an *a priori* justification of our common-sense beliefs. Rather does he appear to have seen that it was not his business as a philosopher to affirm or deny the validity of any empirical propositions, but only to analyse them. For he is content, in his own words, "to be employed as an under-labourer in clearing the ground a little, and removing some of the rubbish that lies in the way

---

[15]Vide G. E. Moore, "A Defence of Common Sense," *Contemporary British Philosophy,* Vol. II.

of knowledge"; and so devotes himself to the purely analytic tasks of defining knowledge, and classifying propositions, and displaying the nature of material things. And the small portion of his work which is not philosophical, in our sense, is not given over to metaphysics, but to psychology.

Nor is it fair to regard Berkeley as a metaphysician. For he did not, in fact, deny the reality of material things, as we are still too commonly told. What he denied was the adequacy of Locke's analysis of the notion of a material thing. He maintained that to say of various "ideas of sensation" that they belonged to a single material thing was not, as Locke thought, to say that they were related to a single unobservable underlying "somewhat," but rather that they stood in certain relations to one another. And in this he was right. Admittedly he made the mistake of supposing that what was immediately given in sensation was necessarily mental; and the use, by him and by Locke, of the word "idea" to denote an element in that which is sensibly given is objectionable, because it suggests this false view. Accordingly we replace the word "idea" in this usage by the neutral word "sense-content," which we shall use to refer to the immediate data not merely of "outer" but also of "introspective" sensation, and say that what Berkeley discovered was that material things must be definable in terms of sense-contents. We shall see, when we come finally to settle the conflict between idealism and realism, that his actual conception of the relationship between material things and sense-contents was not altogether accurate. It led him to some notoriously paradoxical conclusions, which a slight emendation will enable us to avoid. But the fact that he failed to give a completely correct account of the way in which material things are constituted out of sense-contents does not invalidate his contention that they are so constituted. On the contrary, we know that it must be possible to define material things in terms of sense-contents, because it is only by the occurrence of certain sense-contents that the existence of any material thing can ever be in the least degree verified. And thus we see that we have not to enquire whether a phenomenalist "theory of perception" or some other sort of theory is correct, but only what form of phenomenalist theory is correct. For the fact that all causal and representative theories of perception treat material things as if they were unobservable entities entitles us, as Berkeley saw, to rule them out *a priori*. The unfortunate thing is that, in spite of this, he found it necessary to postulate God as an unobservable cause of our "ideas"; and he must be criticised also for failing to see that the argument which he uses to dispose of Locke's analysis of a material thing is fatal to his own conception of the nature of the self, a point which was effectively seized upon by Hume.

Of Hume we may say not merely that he was not in practice a metaphysician, but that he explicitly rejected metaphysics. We find the strongest evidence of this in the passage with which he concludes his *Enquiry Concerning Human Understanding.* "If," he says, "we take in our hand any volume; of divinity, or school metaphysics, for instance; let us ask, Does it contain any abstract reasoning concerning quantity or number? No. Does it contain any experimental reasoning concerning matter of fact and existence? No. Commit it then to the flames. For it can contain nothing but sophistry and illusion." What is this but a rhetorical version of our own thesis that a sentence which does not express either a formally true proposition or an empirical hypothesis is devoid of literal significance? It is true that Hume does not, so far as I know, actually put forward any view concerning the nature of philosophical propositions themselves, but those of his works which are commonly accounted philosophical are, apart from certain passages which deal with questions of psychology, works of analysis. If this is not universally conceded, it is because his treatment of causation, which is the main feature of his philosophical work, is often misinterpreted. He has been accused of denying causation, whereas in fact he was concerned only with defining it. So far is he from asserting that no causal propositions are true that he is himself at pains to give rules for judging of the existence of causes and effects.[16] He realised well enough that the question whether a given causal proposition was true or false was not one that could be settled *a priori,* and accordingly confined himself to discussing the analytic question, What is it that we are asserting when we assert that one event is causally connected with another? And in answering this question he showed, I think conclusively, first that the relation of cause and effect was not logical in character, since any proposition asserting a causal connection could be denied without self-contradiction, secondly that causal laws were not analytically derived from experience, since they were not deducible from any finite number of experiential propositions, and, thirdly, that it was a mistake to analyse propositions asserting causal connections in terms of a relation of necessitation which held between particular events, since it was impossible to conceive of any observations which would have the slightest tendency to establish the existence of such a relation. He thus laid the way open for the view, which we adopt, that every assertion of a particular causal connection involves the assertion of a causal law, and that every general proposition of the form "C causes E" is equivalent to a proposition of the form "whenever C, then E," where the symbol "whenever" must be taken to refer, not to a finite number of actual instances of C, but to the infinite number of possible instances. He himself defines a cause as "an object, followed by another, and where all the objects similar to the first are followed by objects similar to the second," or, alternatively, as "an object followed by another, and whose appearance always conveys the thought to that other";[17] but neither of these definitions is acceptable as if stands. For, even if it is true that we should not, according to our standards of rationality, have good reason to believe that an event C was the cause of an event E unless we had observed a constant conjunction of events like C with events like E, still there is no self-contradiction involved in asserting the proposition "C is the cause of E" and at the same time denying that any events like C or like E ever have been observed; and this would be self-contradictory if the first of the definitions quoted was correct. Nor is it inconceivable, as the second definition implies, that there should be causal laws which have never yet been thought of. But although we are obliged, for these reasons, to reject Hume's actual definitions of a cause, our view of the nature of causation remains substantially the same as his. And we agree with him that there can be no other justification for inductive reasoning than its success in practice, while insisting more strongly than he did that no better justification is required. For it is his

---

[16]Vide *A Treatise of Human Nature,* Book I, Part III, section 15.
[17]*An Enquiry Concerning Human Understanding,* section 7.

failure to make this second point clear that has given his views the air of paradox which has caused them to be so much undervalued and misunderstood.

When we consider, also, that Hobbes and Bentham were chiefly occupied in giving definitions, and that the best part of John Stuart Mill's work consists in a development of the analyses carried out by Hume, we may fairly claim that in holding that the activity of philosophising is essentially analytic we are adopting a standpoint which has always been implicit in English empiricism. Not that the practice of philosophical analysis has been confined to members of this school. But it is with them that we have the closest historical affinity.

If I refrain from discussing these questions in detail, and make no attempt to furnish a complete list of all the "great philosophers" whose work is predominantly analytic—a list which would certainly include Plato and Aristotle and Kant—it is because the point to which this discussion is relevant is one of minor importance in our enquiry. We have been maintaining that much of "traditional philosophy" is genuinely philosophical, by our standards, in order to defend ourselves against the charge that our retention of the word "philosophy" is misleading. But even if it were the case that none of those who are commonly called philosophers had ever been engaged in what we call the activity of philosophising, it would not follow that our definition of philosophy was erroneous, given our initial postulates. We may admit that our retention of the word "philosophy" is causally dependent on our belief in the historical propositions set forth above. But the validity of these historical propositions has no logical bearing on the validity of our definition of philosophy, nor on the validity of the distinction between philosophy, in our sense, and metaphysics.

It is advisable to stress the point that philosophy, as we understand it, is wholly independent of metaphysics, inasmuch as the analytic method is commonly supposed by its critics to have a metaphysical basis. Being misled by the associations of the word "analysis," they assume that philosophical analysis is an activity of dissection; that it consists in "breaking up" objects into their constituent parts, until the whole universe is ultimately exhibited as an aggregate of "bare particulars," united by external relations. If this were really so, the most effective way of attacking the method would be to show that its basic presupposition was nonsensical. For to say that the universe was an aggregate of bare particulars would be as senseless as to say that it was Fire or Water or Experience. It is plain that no possible observation would enable one to verify such an assertion. But, so far as I know, this line of criticism is in fact never adopted. The critics content themselves with pointing out that few, if any, of the complex objects in the world are simply the sum of their parts. They have a structure, an organic unity, which distinguishes them, as genuine wholes, from mere aggregates. But the analyst, so it is said, is obliged by his atomistic metaphysics to regard an object consisting of parts a, b, c, and d in a distinctive configuration as being simply $a + b + c + d$, and thus gives an entirely false account of its nature.

If we follow the Gestalt psychologists, who of all men talk most constantly about genuine wholes, in defining such a whole as one in which the properties of every part depend to some extent on its position in the whole, then we may accept it as an empirical fact that there exist genuine, or organic, wholes. And if the analytic method involved a denial of this fact, it would indeed be a faulty method. But, actually, the validity of the analytic method is not dependent on any empirical, much less any metaphysical, presupposition about the nature of things. For the philosopher, as an analyst, is not directly concerned with the physical properties of things. He is concerned only with the way in which we speak about them.

In other words, the propositions of philosophy are not factual, but linguistic in character—that is, they do not describe the behaviour of physical, or even mental, objects; they express definitions, or the formal consequences of definitions. Accordingly, we may say that philosophy is a department of logic. For we shall see that the characteristic mark of a purely logical enquiry is that it is concerned with the formal consequences of our definitions and not with questions of empirical fact.

It follows that philosophy does not in any way compete with science. The difference in type between philosophical and scientific propositions is such that they cannot conceivably contradict one another. And this makes it clear that the possibility of philosophical analysis is independent of any empirical assumptions. That it is independent of any metaphysical assumptions should be even more obvious still. For it is absurd to suppose that the provision of definitions, and the study of their formal consequences, involves the nonsensical assertion that the world is composed of bare particulars, or any other metaphysical dogma.

What has contributed as much as anything to the prevalent misunderstanding of the nature of philosophical analysis is the fact that propositions and questions which are really linguistic are often expressed in such a way that they appear to be factual.[18] A striking instance of this is provided by the proposition that a material thing cannot be in two places at once. This looks like an empirical proposition, and is constantly invoked by those who desire to prove that it is possible for an empirical proposition to be logically certain. But a more critical inspection shows that it is not empirical at all, but linguistic. It simply records the fact that, as the result of certain verbal conventions, the proposition that two sense-contents occur in the same visual or tactual sensefield is incompatible with the proposition that they belong to the same material thing.[19] And this is indeed a necessary fact. But it has not the least tendency to show that we have certain knowledge about the empirical properties of objects. For it is necessary only because we happen to use the relevant words in a particular way. There is no logical reason why we should not so alter our definitions that the sentence "A thing cannot be in two places at once" comes to express a self-contradiction instead of a necessary truth.

Another good example or linguistically necessary proposition which appears to be a record of empirical fact is the proposition, "Relations are not particulars, but universals." One might suppose that this was a proposition of the same order as, "Armenians are not Mohammedans, but Christians": but one would be mistaken. For, whereas the latter proposition is an empirical hypothesis relating to the religious practices of a certain group of people, the former is not a proposition about "things" at all,

---

[18]Carnap has stressed this point. Where we speak of "linguistic" propositions expressed in "factual" or "pseudo-factual" language he speaks of "Pseudo-Objektsätze" or "quasi-syntaktische Sätze" as being expressed in the "Inhaltliche," as opposed to the "Formale Redeweise." Vide *Logische Syntax der Sprache,* Part V.

[19]cf. my article "On Particulars and Universals," *Proceedings of the Aristotelian Society,* 1933–4, pp. 54, 55.

but simply about words. It records the fact that relation-symbols belong by definition to the class of symbols for characters, and not to the class of symbols for things.

The assertion that relations are universals provokes the question, "What is a universal?"; and this question is not, as it has traditionally been regarded, a question about the character of certain real objects, but a request for a definition of a certain term. Philosophy, as it is written, is full of questions like this, which seem to be factual but are not. Thus, to ask what is the nature of a material object is to ask for a definition of "material object," and this, as we shall shortly see, is to ask how propositions about material objects are to be translated into propositions about sense-contents. Similarly, to ask what is a number is to ask some such question as whether it is possible to translate propositions about the natural numbers into propositions about classes.[20] And the same thing applies to all the other philosophical questions of the form, "What is an *x*?" or, "What is the nature of *x*?" They are all requests for definitions, and, as we shall see, for definitions of a peculiar sort.

Although it is misleading to write about linguistic questions in "factual" language, it is often convenient for the sake of brevity. And we shall not always avoid doing it ourselves. But it is important that no one should be deceived by this practice into supposing that the philosopher is engaged on an empirical or a metaphysical enquiry. We may speak loosely of him as analysing facts, or notions, or even things. But we must make it clear that these are simply ways of saying that he is concerned with the definition of the corresponding words.

The Reform of Metaphysics

R. G. Collingwood

Metaphysics has always been an historical science; but metaphysicians have not always been fully aware of the fact. This was not altogether their fault, because it is only within the last half-century that the aims and methods of history have defined themselves with the same sort of precision that those of natural science achieved round about the year 1600. Until that happened people did not understand that history is a kind of thinking whereby absolutely cogent inferences about the past are drawn from interpretation of the evidence it has left behind. Or rather, the people who understood this were rare even among historians, and the occasions on which they understood it were exceptional. The ordinary belief was that history is a repeating of statements about the past which are found ready-made in the writings or on the lips of persons whom, because the historian believes what they tell him, he calls his authorities. This repetition of ready-made statements which the historian is allowed within limits to decorate with comments of his own devising I call scissors-and-paste history: a phrase in which the word "history" means "history improperly so called."

[20]cf. Rudolf Garnap, *Logische Syntax der Sprache,* Part V, 79B, and 84.
Source: Essay on Metaphysics, Chapter 7. Chicago: Henry Regnery Company, 1972, 58–77.

Some readers of this book will reject my statement that metaphysics is an historical science because, being half a century out of date in their notions as to what history is, they fancy it to be an affair of scissors and paste. I hasten to assure them of my sympathy. I should never dream of suggesting that metaphysics was a scissors-and-paste affair. For it does not proceed by the scissors-and-paste method of accepting testimony; . . . it proceeds according to a method called metaphysical analysis, by which the metaphysician discovers what absolute presuppositions have been made in a certain piece of scientific work by using the records of that work as evidence. It is because people until lately regarded history as a scissors-and-paste affair that they could not realize the historical character of metaphysics.

But history to-day is no longer a scissors-and-paste affair. Instead of repeating statements accepted on the testimony of authorities, the historian of to-day makes his own statements on his own authority according to what he finds the evidence in his possession to prove when he analyses it with a certain question in his mind. And I know perfectly well that people who understand the nature of historical thought, as historical thought exists to-day among even the rank and file of quite ordinary historians, will not need to be convinced that metaphysics is an historical science. They will need only to understand the statement in order to see at once that it is true.

Dissatisfaction with the state of metaphysics has been endemic among philosophers ever since at least the time of Kant. It has been partly the fault of metaphysicians and partly the fault of those who have been dissatisfied. I will not say whose fault I think has been the greater. My business is to show how the dissatisfaction can be removed.

It can be removed by taking seriously the proposition that metaphysics is an historical science. Let it be understood both by metaphysicians and by their critics that metaphysics is the science of absolute presuppositions. Let the distinction between metaphysics and pseudo-metaphysics be firmly grasped. Let it be understood that the business of metaphysics is to find out what absolute presuppositions have actually been made by various persons at various times in doing various pieces of scientific thinking. Let it be understood that if a certain absolute presupposition has been made on one occasion by one person this fact makes it probable that the same presupposition has been made by other persons having in general what may be called the same cultural equipment as himself: the same outfit of social and political habits, the same religion, the same sort of education, and so forth; but correspondingly improbable that it has been made by persons whose cultural equipment was noticeably different. At the same time let it be understood that probabilities are not history, which demands proof; and that the only way to prove that somebody has made or has not made a certain absolute presupposition is to analyse the records of his thought and find out.

When this is done the peculiar perplexities and obscurities that have always been felt to surround the work of the metaphysician will disappear. At the same time the scope of metaphysical inquiry will be greatly enlarged. New and interesting problems will arise, not hitherto envisaged because the possibilities of metaphysical thinking have been as imperfectly understood as its methods. I will make a few observations on each of these two heads.

I. PERPLEXITIES REMOVED

(*a*) As to subject. What is metaphysics about? Ever since the time of Aristotle this has been a perplexing question. I have shown that the perplexity goes back to Aristotle himself. Aristotle knew well enough that the science he was creating was a science of absolute presuppositions, and the text of his *Metaphysics* bears abundant witness to the firmness with which he kept this in mind and the perspicacity with which he realized its implications; but Aristotle is also responsible for having initiated the barren search after a science of pure being, and for the suggestion that a science of pure being and a science of absolute presuppositions were one and the same. This perplexity has never been overcome. The history of metaphysics since Aristotle shows that at no point have people become quite clear in their minds as to what metaphysics was about. With this perplexity has gone another, as to how the metaphysician should train himself for his work. In the Middle Ages it was supposed that his preliminary training should consist chiefly of logic; in the seventeenth century, of physics; in the nineteenth, of psychology.

These questions can now be answered. Metaphysics is about a certain class of historical facts, namely absolute presuppositions. Its subject-matter is as clearly defined as if it had been, for example, the history of mathematics or metallurgy. Because the metaphysician is a special kind of historian, his training should consist first in a general historical education; secondly in special attention to the history of science; and finally in concentrating on problems of the following type: Here is a document providing evidence about the history of science; what light does it throw on the question what absolute presuppositions have been made?

(*b*) As to method. The perplexity as to what metaphysics is about has naturally bred perplexity as to how it should proceed. The ghost of Aristotle's science of pure being has always haunted it with the suggestion that some part at least of its proper method consists in groping blindly for what is not in fact there. If its object is inaccessible the search for that object can only consist in doing something futile; and although no metaphysician has ever taken this inference quite seriously, it cannot be denied that most of them have been to some extent daunted by it into half thinking that their proper place is among the shades, and that a little flitting, a little gibbering, are among the duties of their profession.

This again is now cleared up. The problems of metaphysics are historical problems; its methods are historical methods. We must have no more nonsense about its being meritorious to inhabit a fog. A metaphysician is a man who has to get at facts. He must be quite clear in his mind what facts he wants to get at and by means of what evidence he proposes to get at them. We live in the twentieth century; there is no excuse for us if we do not know what the methods of history are.

Another perplexity as to method, or perhaps only the same one over again, arises from the recognition that metaphysics investigates presuppositions. Surely, it is argued, a science that investigates presuppositions must avoid making presuppositions in the course of its own work; for how can you detect a presupposition in your neighbour's eye if you have a whole faggot of them in your own? So the idea got about that metaphysics must be a science with no presuppositions whatever, a science spun out of nothing by the thinker's brain.

This is the greatest nonsense. If metaphysics is a science at all it is an attempt to think systematically, that is, by answering questions intelligently disposed in order. The answer to any question presupposes whatever the question presupposes. And because all science begins with a question (for a question is logically prior to its own answer) all science begins with a presupposition. Metaphysics, therefore, either has presuppositions or is no science. The attempt at a metaphysics devoid of presuppositions can only result in a metaphysics that is no science, a tangle of confused thoughts whose confusion is taken for a merit. Not only has metaphysics quite definite presuppositions, but every one knows what some of them are, for as metaphysics is an historical science it shares the presuppositions of all history; and every one, nowadays, has some acquaintance with the principles of historical thought.

(*c*) As to form, two different perplexities may be instanced. First, should a metaphysician aim at completeness? Is there a certain repertory of problems which are "the" problems of metaphysics; and is it the duty of a metaphysician who takes his work seriously to tackle the whole set?

I call this a perplexity because a great many metaphysicians, as any one can see from their writings, have been troubled by it: conscious of an attraction always drawing them towards the idea that there is what I have called a repertory of metaphysical problems and that the proper way of going about their business is to solve the whole lot systematically, and yet conscious that when they come closer to grips with this idea it fails to fulfil its promises, for either their problems will not make up into a really systematic form, or the desire to make them up into such a form fails to survive a closer acquaintance with the problems themselves. All science undoubtedly is systematic; and metaphysics, if metaphysics is to be a science, will be systematic too; but does this imply that metaphysical thinking should aim at system-building? Thus doubts arise, as with the other problems I have enumerated; and these in practice lead for the most part to compromises that satisfy nobody: repertories of problems which are not quite closed, systems that are not quite systematic, and a general air of pretence to do what hardly anybody firmly believes to be worth doing.

These doubts can now be resolved. Metaphysics aware of itself as an historical science will be systematic in the sense in which all historical thought is systematic and in no other. Its systematic character will be exhibited in the clear-cut and orderly manner in which it states problems and marshals and interprets evidence for their solution. But the idea that these problems form a closed repertory, or even a repertory with the door ajar, is the purest illusion. So, therefore, is the corresponding idea that the metaphysician's business is to "cover the ground" of this repertory, to deal with all the problems, and thus to build a system. *Nil actum reputans si quid superesset agendum,* Kant quoted, stuck fast in the grip of this illusion. The historian's work is never finished; every historical subject, like the course of historical events itself, is open at the end, and however hard you work at it the end always remains open. People who are said to "make history" solve the problems they find confronting them, but create others to be solved, if not by themselves, by their survivors. People who write it, if they write it well, solve problems too; but every problem solved gives rise to a new problem.

A second perplexity as to form arises from the question whether the various problems of metaphysics are so related that a correct solution of one would lead to the correct solution of others: whether, in technical language, there are relations of implication or entailment between their various solutions. This is the question often asked in the shape of the question whether metaphysics is a "deductive" science.

The answer is, unhesitatingly, No. Let us suppose that the metaphysician is trying to analyse out one single set of absolute presuppositions, namely those of ordinary science in his own society and his own time. I speak of a set of absolute presuppositions, because if metaphysics is an historical science the things which it studies, namely absolute presuppositions, are historical facts; and any one who is reasonably well acquainted with historical work knows that there is no such thing as an historical fact which is not at the same time a complex of historical facts. Such a complex of historical facts I call a "constellation." If every historical fact is a constellation, the answer to the question "What is it that such and such a person was absolutely presupposing in such and such a piece of thinking?" can never be given by reference to one single absolute presupposition, it must always be given by reference to a constellation of them.

What is the logical relation, then, between the presuppositions making up this constellation? The constellation, complex though it is, is still a single fact. The different presuppositions composing it are all made at once, in one and the same piece of thinking. They are not like a set of carpenter's tools, of which the carpenter uses one at a time; they are like a suit of clothes, of which every part is worn simultaneously with all the rest. This is to say that, since they are all suppositions, each must be *consupponible* with all the others; that is, it must be logically possible for a person who supposes any one of them to suppose concurrently all the rest.

It need not, however, be anything more than this. It need not be a relation of such a kind that a person supposing any one of them is logically committed to supposing all or indeed any of the others. Metaphysicians have often thought it was; but that is because they thought of metaphysics as a kind of quasi-mathematics, and did not realize that it was a kind of history.

I say that the relation between the constituents in a single constellation of absolute presuppositions need not be of this kind; but actually it cannot be. For if any one of these constituents logically necessitated any other, the first would be a presupposition of the second, and therefore the second would not be an absolute presupposition. Taken together, the constellation forms a single historical fact; but any constituent within it taken separately is also a single historical fact, discoverable by the metaphysician only in the way in which any historian discovers any historical fact, by the interpretation of evidence. If a given person in a given piece of thinking makes the absolute presuppositions AP_1, AP_2, AP_3, AP_4 . . ., each of these is a genuinely independent presupposition which can no more be deduced from the rest than waistcoat can be deduced from trousers or from trousers and coat together. Metaphysics, aware of itself as an historical science, will abandon once for all the hope of being a "deductive" or quasi-mathematical science.

It follows that the literary form of a treatise in which a metaphysician sets out to enumerate and discuss the absolute presuppositions of thought in his own time cannot be the form of a continuous argument, leading from point to point by way of quasi-mathematical demonstration, as in the *Ethics* of Spinoza. It must be the form of a *catalogue raisonné,* as in the fourth book of Aristotle's *Metaphysics* or in the *Quaestiones* of a medieval metaphysician.

(*d*) As to the effect which a metaphysician hopes to produce on the minds of his readers, there is a foolish idea that his business is to found a "school," if he is a great enough man, and if not, to bring recruits into the "school" to which he himself belongs, the school of Platonists, Aristotelians, Thomists, Scotists, Cartesians, Hobbists, Spinozists, Leibnitians, Berkeleians, Humians, Kantians, Hegelians, or whatever it may be. This once more I call a perplexity because a great many people can see, when they think, how foolish it is and yet cannot entirely rid themselves of it. They find themselves on the whole agreeing with A's doctrines rather than B's; why not say so?

Metaphysics, aware of itself as an historical science, will abolish in one clean sweep not only the idea of "schools" but the idea of "doctrines." It will realize that what are misdescribed as A's "metaphysical doctrines" are nothing more than the results of A's attempt to discover what absolute presuppositions are made by scientists in his own time. Thus it is not a "metaphysical doctrine" or "metaphysical theory" of Spinoza's that Nature is the same as God. If you understand the metaphysical rubric when you read what he says about this you will see that what he is doing is to state an historical fact about the religious foundation of seventeenth-century natural science. When I accept what Spinoza says on this subject I am no more going Spinozist in a war of metaphysical sects than I am going Tacitean in a war of historical sects when I accept Tacitus's statement that Agricola conquered southern and central Scotland. What I am doing in either case is to say: "Here is a statement as to certain facts made by a contemporary writer. The evidence at my disposal proves that it is true."

Sometimes a metaphysician will make a mistake and say that an absolute presupposition is made which in fact is not made. It is still being said to-day, for example, in spite of a public and altogether right protest made several years ago by Earl Russell,[1] that "all events have causes." His protest was altogether right because the point he made was the point that mattered: that the idea of causation is not presupposed in modern physics. In such cases it would be *suggestio falsi* to call the mistake a "metaphysical doctrine" of the persons who make it. It is not a doctrine, it is a blunder.

Sometimes we find a metaphysician of the past correctly describing an absolute presupposition made in his own times which is still being made to-day; sometimes one which is to-day obsolete. No one who understands that metaphysics is an historical science will be so silly as to say in the first case that his "doctrine" or "theory" is true, and in the second that it is false.

All this stuff about schools, doctrines, theories, agreement and disagreement, useful though it certainly is for amusing the minds of would-be metaphysicians who cannot get ahead with their work because they do not know how, has nothing to do with metaphysics. It belongs to the apparatus of pseudo-metaphysics.

---

[1]"On the Notion of Cause." *Proc. Arist. Soc.,* 1911–12; reprinted in *Mysticism and Logic,* 1918.

2. SCOPE ENLARGED

Metaphysicians up to now, so far as they have evaded the perplexities mentioned above and have attended to their own proper business, the study of absolute presuppositions, have been working no doubt at history; but their unawareness that history was what they were working at has narrowed the scope of their work. It has prevented them from studying the absolute presuppositions that have been made in the so-called past, because that would be history, and has confined their attention to those made in the so-called present, because that is not history but metaphysics. I say the "so-called" present and past because the "present" referred to in that antithesis is not really a present, it is a past, but a relatively recent past. The "so-called present" means the more recent past, the "so-called past" means the remoter past.

Metaphysics not aware of itself as an historical science; accordingly, has been in the habit of confining its attention to the absolute presuppositions made in that recent past which is loosely called the present. Aristotle describes us the absolute presuppositions of Greek science in the fourth century B.C.; St. Thomas those of European science in the central Middle Ages; Spinoza those of European science in the seventeenth century, or rather those of them which he thinks relevant to his special purpose. This habit of attending only to the recent past cannot survive the discovery that metaphysics is an historical science. That discovery enlarges the scope of metaphysical study by opening to it no longer the merest antechamber of the past, but the past in its entirety.

(*a*) The first consequence of this enlargement is that the metaphysician, instead of being confined in his studies to one single constellation of absolute presuppositions, has before him an indefinite number of them. He has as many worlds to conquer as any conqueror can want. He can study the presuppositions of European science at any phase in its history for which he has evidence. He can study the presuppositions of Arabic science, of Indian science, of Chinese science; again in all their phases, so far as he can find evidence for them. He can study the presuppositions of the science practised by "primitive" and "prehistoric" peoples. All these are his proper work; not an historical background for his work, but his work itself.

If he is a lazy or a stupid man, he may find this enlargement embarrassing; but no one is asking him to eat all the thistles in his field, only the kind he likes best, and so many of them as he has a stomach for. The ordinary metaphysician will treat this field very much as any ordinary historian treats any historical field. He will recognize that it is inexhaustible and will decide for reasons of one sort or another what part of it he will make peculiarly his own. In this part he will do genuine, first-hand historical work. In the parts that impinge on it he will be content to know the first-hand work that others have done, without doing any himself. In remoter parts he will be content to look at second-hand work: compilations and text-books and what are called, *a non lucendo,* "histories"; and where the penumbra shades off into complete darkness he may even sink so low as to consult the encyclopaedia.

(*b*) When he has some knowledge about several different constellations of absolute presuppositions, he can set to work comparing them. This is not a high class of historical work, but it has its uses. For one thing it will convince the metaphysician, if it is honestly done, that there are no "eternal" or "crucial" or "central" problems in metaphysics. It will rid him of the parish-pump idea that the metaphysical problems of his own generation or, more likely, the one next before his own are the problems that all metaphysicians have been worrying about ever since the world began. For another thing it will give him a hint of the way in which different sets of absolute presuppositions correspond not only with differences in the structure of what is generally called scientific thought but with differences in the entire fabric of civilization.

(*c*) But all this is still a very superficial kind of historical study, based as it is on the false assumption that an historical "phase"—a civilization, a phase of scientific thought, a set of absolute presuppositions—is a static thing, whose relations with others can be adequately studied by comparing them and noting resemblances and differences. The essential thing about historical "phases" is that each of them gives place to another; not because one is violently destroyed by alien forces impinging on its fabric from without by war or from within by revolution, but because each of them while it lives is working at turning itself into the next. To trace the process by which one historical phase turns into the next is the business of every historian who concerns himself with that phase. The metaphysician's business, therefore, when he has identified several different constellations of absolute presuppositions, is not only to study their likenesses and unlikenesses but also to find out on what occasions and by what processes one of them has turned into another.

This is the only legitimate (that is, historical) way in which he, or anybody else, can answer the question "Why did such and such people at such and such a time make such and such absolute presuppositions?" Like all questions in metaphysics, this is either a nonsense question or an historical question. It is a nonsense question if the answer it expects is one which identifies the cause of the historical fact in question with something outside history, like the geographical or climatic environment of that fact or the psycho-physical characteristics of the human beings concerned in it. It is a significant question if it expects an answer in the form: "Because they or the predecessors from whom they inherited their civilization had previously made such and such a different set of absolute presuppositions, and because such and such a process of change converted the one set into the other." If any one is dissatisfied with this kind of answer his dissatisfaction shows that the question, as he was asking it, was a nonsense question.

(*d*) The dynamics of history is not yet completely understood when it is grasped that each phase is converted into the next by a process of change. The relation between phase and process is more intimate than that. One phase changes into another because the first phase was in unstable equilibrium and had in itself the seeds of change, and indeed of that change. Its fabric was not at rest; it was always under strain. If the world of history is a world in which *tout passe, tout lasse, tout casse,* the analysis of the internal strains to which a given constellation of historical facts is subjected, and of the means by which it "takes up" these strains, or prevents them from breaking it in pieces, is not the least part of an historian's work.

Thus if Gibbon seems out of date to a modern student of the Roman Empire it is not because Gibbon knew fewer facts than the modern student knows; it is because Gibbon was not sensitive enough to the internal strains of what he wrote about. He begins by depicting the Antonine period as a Golden Age, that is, an age containing no internal strains whatever; and from the non-historical or anti-historical tone of its opening his narrative never quite recovers. If Hegel's influence on nineteenth-century historiography was on the whole an influence for good, it was because historical study for him was first and foremost a study of internal strains, and this is why he opened the way to such brilliant feats as that analysis of internal strains in nineteenth-century economic society which entitles Karl Marx to the name of a great historian. If Oswald Spengler, who was so much talked about a few years ago, is to-day deservedly forgotten, it is because whenever he set himself to describe a constellation of historical facts (what he called a "culture") he deliberately ironed all the strains out of it and presented a picture in which every detail fitted into every other as placidly as the pieces of a jig-saw puzzle lying at rest on a table.

Where there is no strain there is no history. A civilization does not work out its own details by a kind of static logic in which every detail exemplifies in its own way one and the same formula. It works itself out by a dynamic logic in which different and at first sight incompatible formulae somehow contrive a precarious coexistence; one dominant here, another there; the recessive formula never ceasing to operate, but functioning as a kind of minority report which, though the superficial historian may ignore it, serves to a more acute eye as evidence of tendencies actually existing which may have been dominant in the past and may be dominant in the future. And even an historian whose eye is not acute enough to detect this recessive element may have feelings sensitive enough to savour the peculiar quality which its presence imparts to the whole. The historian in his study can perhaps afford to neglect these strains, because he does not really care about being a good historian; but the man of action cannot afford to neglect them. His life may depend on his ability to see where they are and to judge their strength. It was not by gunpowder alone that Cortez destroyed Montezuma; it was by using gunpowder to reinforce the strains which already tended to break up Montezuma's power.

The same characteristic will certainly be found in any constellation of absolute presuppositions; and a metaphysician who comes to his subject from a general grounding in history will know that he must look for it. He will expect the various presuppositions he is studying to be consupponible only under pressure, the constellation being subject to certain strains and kept together by dint of a certain compromise or mutual toleration having behind it a motive like that which causes parties to unite in the face of an enemy. This is why the conception of metaphysics as a "deductive" science is not only an error but a pernicious error, one with which a reformed metaphysics will have no truce. The ambition of "deductive" metaphysics is to present a constellation of absolute presuppositions as a strainless structure like a body of propositions in mathematics. That is all right in mathematics because mathematical propositions are not historical propositions. But it is all wrong in metaphysics. A reformed metaphysics will conceive any given constellation of absolute propositions as having in its structure not the simplicity and calm that characterize the subject-matter of mathematics but the intricacy and restlessness that characterize the subject-matter, say, of legal or constitutional history.

This is the answer to the somewhat threadbare question "How can metaphysics become a science?" The answer is: "By becoming more completely and more consciously what in fact it has always been, an historical science." The reform of metaphysics, long looked for and urgently needed, can be brought about by nothing more abstruse or difficult than its adoption of principles and methods which are now common form among historians. And the extent to which metaphysics has already been a science in the past is governed by the extent to which it has already been history.

By this reform metaphysics will find a complete and conclusive answer to the various criticisms which at various times have been brought against it, so far as those criticisms have been justified by defects in its own practice. And so far as they have not been justified it may help people to clear them out of their minds.

Philosophy Without Mirrors (excerpt)

Richard Rorty

1. HERMENEUTICS AND EDIFICATION

Our present notions of what it is to be a philosopher are so tied up with the Kantian attempt to render all knowledge-claims commensurable that it is difficult to imagine what philosophy without epistemology could be. More generally, it is difficult to imagine that any activity would be entitled to bear the name "philosophy" if it had nothing to do with knowledge—if it were not in some sense a theory of knowledge, or a method for getting knowledge, or at least a hint as to where some supremely important kind of knowledge might be found. The difficulty stems from a notion shared by Platonists, Kantians, and positivists: that man has an essence—namely, to discover essences. The notion that our chief task is to mirror accurately, in our own Glassy Essence, the universe around us is the complement of the notion, common to Democritus and Descartes, that the universe is made up of very simple, clearly and distinctly knowable things, knowledge of whose essences provides the master-vocabulary which permits commensuration of all discourses.

This classic picture of human beings must be set aside before epistemologically centered philosophy can be set aside. "Hermeneutics," as a polemical term in contemporary philosophy, is a name for the attempt to do so. The use of the term for this purpose is largely due to one book—Gadamer's *Truth and Method.* Gadamer there makes clear that hermeneutics is not a "method for attaining truth" which fits into the classic picture of man: "The hermeneutic phenomenon is basically not a problem of method at all."[1] Rather, Gadamer is asking, roughly, what conclusions might

---

[1]Hans-Georg Gadamer, *Truth and Method* (New York, 1975), p. xi. Indeed, it would be reasonable to call Gadamer's book a tract against the very idea of method, where this is conceived of as an attempt at commensuration. It is instructive to note the parallels between this book and Paul Feyerabend's *Against Method.* My treatment of Gadamer is indebted to Alasdair MacIntyre; see his "Contexts of Interpretation," *Boston University Journal* 24 (1976), 41–46.
Source: Philosophy and the Mirror of Nature, Chapter 8. Princeton: Princeton University Press, 1979, 357–379, 389–394.

be drawn from the fact that we have to practice hermeneutics—from the "hermeneutic phenomenon" as a fact about people which the epistemological tradition has tried to shunt aside. "The hermeneutics developed here," he says, "is not . . . a methodology of the human sciences, but an attempt to understand what the human sciences truly are, beyond their methodological self-consciousness, and what connects them with the totality of our experience of the world."[2] His book is a redescription of man which tries to place the classic picture within a larger one, and thus to "distance" the standard philosophical problematic rather than offer a set of solutions to it.

For my present purposes, the importance of Gadamer's book is that he manages to separate off one of the three strands—the romantic notion of man as self-creative—in the philosophical notion of "spirit" from the other two strands with which it became entangled. Gadamer (like Heidegger, to whom some of his work is indebted) makes no concessions either to Cartesian dualism or to the notion of "transcendental constitution" (in any sense which could be given an idealistic interpretation).[3] He thus helps reconcile the "naturalistic" point I tried to make in the previous chapter—that the "irreducibility of the *Geisteswissenschaften*" is not a matter of a metaphysical dualism—with our "existentialist" intuition that redescribing ourselves is the most important thing we can do. He does this by substituting the notion of *Bildung* (education, self-formation) for that of "knowledge" as the goal of thinking. To say that we become different people, that we "remake" ourselves as we read more, talk more, and write more, is simply a dramatic way of saying that the sentences which become true of us by virtue of such activities are often more important to us than the sentences which become true of us when we drink more, earn more, and so on. The events which make us able to say new and interesting things about ourselves are, in this nonmetaphysical sense, more "essential" to us (at least to us relatively leisured intellectuals, inhabiting a stable and prosperous part of the world) than the events which change our shapes or our standards of living ("remaking" us in less "spiritual" ways). Gadamer develops his notion of *wirkungsgeschichtliches Bewusstsein* (the sort of consciousness of the past which changes us) to characterize an attitude interested not so much in what is out there in the world, or in what happened in history, as in what we can get out of nature and history for our own uses. In this attitude, getting the facts right (about atoms and the void, or about the history of Europe) is merely propaedeutic to finding a new and more interesting way of expressing ourselves, and thus of coping with the world. From the educational, as opposed to the epistemological or the technological, point of view, the way things are said is more important than the possession of truths.[4]

[2]Gadamer, *Truth and Method*, p. xiii.
[3]Cf. ibid., p. 15. "But we may recognize that *Bildung* is an element of spirit without being tied to Hegel's philosophy of absolute spirit, just as the insight into the historicity of consciousness is not tied to his philosophy of world history."
[4]The contrast here is the same as that involved in the traditional quarrel between "classical" education and "scientific" education, mentioned by Gadamer in his opening section on "The Significance of the Humanist Tradition." More generally, it can be seen as an aspect of the quarrel between poetry (which cannot be omitted from the former sort of education) and philosophy (which, when conceiving of itself as super-science, would like to become foundational to the latter sort of education). Yeats asked the spirits (whom, he believed, were dictating *A Vision* to him through his wife's mediumship) why they had come. The spirits replied, "To bring you metaphors for poetry." A philosopher might have expected some hard facts about what it was like on the other side, but Yeats was not disappointed.

Since "education" sounds a bit too flat, and *Bildung* a bit too foreign, I shall use "edification" to stand for this project of finding new, better, more interesting, more fruitful ways of speaking. The attempt to edify (ourselves or others) may consist in the hermeneutic activity of making connections between our own culture and some exotic culture or historical period, or between our own discipline and another discipline which seems to pursue incommensurable aims in an incommensurable vocabulary. But it may instead consist in the "poetic" activity of thinking up such new aims, new words, or new disciplines, followed by, so to speak, the inverse of hermeneutics: the attempt to reinterpret our familiar surroundings in the unfamiliar terms of our new inventions. In either case, the activity is (despite the etymological relation between the two words) edifying without being constructive—at least if "constructive" means the sort of cooperation in the accomplishment of research programs which takes place in normal discourse. For edifying discourse is *supposed* to be abnormal, to take us out of our old selves by the power of strangeness, to aid us in becoming new beings.

The contrast between the desire for edification and the desire for truth is, for Gadamer, not an expression of a tension which needs to be resolved or compromised. If there is a conflict, it is between the Platonic-Aristotelian view that the *only* way to be edified is to know what is out there (to reflect the facts accurately— to realize our essence by knowing essences) and the view that the quest for truth is just one among many ways in which we might be edified. Gadamer rightly gives Heidegger the credit for working out a way of seeing the search for objective knowledge (first developed by the Greeks, using mathematics as a model) as one human project among others.[5] The point is, however, more vivid in Sartre, who sees the attempt to gain an objective knowledge of the world, and thus of oneself, as an attempt to avoid the responsibility for choosing one's project.[6] For Sartre, to say this is not to say that the desire for objective knowledge of nature, history, or anything else is bound to be unsuccessful, or even bound to be self-deceptive. It is merely to say that it presents a temptation to self-deception insofar as we think that, by knowing which descriptions within a given set of normal discourses apply to us, we thereby know ourselves. For Heidegger, Sartre, and Gadamer, objective inquiry is perfectly possible and frequently actual—the only thing to be said against it is that it provides only some, among many, ways of describing ourselves, and that some of these can hinder the process of edification.

To sum up this "existentialist" view of objectivity, then: objectivity should be seen as conformity to the norms of justification (for assertions and for actions) we find about us. Such conformity becomes dubious and self-deceptive only when seen as something more than this—namely, as a way of obtaining access to something which "grounds" current practices of justification in something else. Such a "ground" is thought to need no justification, because it has become so

---

[5]See the section called "The Overcoming of the Epistemological Problem . . ." in *Truth and Method,* pp. 214ff., and compare Martin Heidegger, *Being and Time,* trans. John Macquarrie and Edward Robinson (New York, 1962), sec. 32.

[6]See Jean-Paul Sartre, *Being and Nothingness,* trans. Hazel Barnes (New York, 1956), pt. two, chap. 3, sec. 5, and the "Conclusion" of the book.

clearly and distinctly perceived as to count as a "philosophical foundation." This is self-deceptive not simply because of the general absurdity of ultimate justification's reposing upon the unjustifiable, but because of the more concrete absurdity of thinking that the vocabulary used by present science, morality, or whatever has some privileged attachment to reality which makes it *more* than just a further set of descriptions. Agreeing with the naturalists that redescription is not "change of essence" needs to be followed up by abandoning the notion of "essence" altogether.[7] But the standard philosophical strategy of most naturalisms is to find some way of showing that our own culture has indeed got hold of the essence of man—thus making all new and incommensurable vocabularies merely "noncognitive" ornamentation.[8] The utility of the "existentialist" view is that, by proclaiming that we have no essence, it permits us to see the descriptions of ourselves we find in one of (or in the unity of) the *Naturwissenschaften* as on a par with the various alternative descriptions offered by poets, novelists, depth psychologists, sculptors, anthropologists, and mystics. The former are not privileged representations in virtue of the fact that (at the moment) there is more consensus in the sciences than in the arts. They are simply among the repertoire of self-descriptions at our disposal.

This point can also be put as an extrapolation from the commonplace that one cannot be counted as educated—*gebildet*—if one knows *only* the results of the normal *Naturwissenschaften* of the day. Gadamer begins *Truth and Method* with a discussion of the role of the humanist tradition in giving sense to the notion of *Bildung* as something having "no goals outside itself."[9] To give sense to such a notion we need a sense of the relativity of descriptive vocabularies to periods, traditions, and historical accidents. This is what the humanist tradition in education does, and what training in the results of the natural sciences cannot do. Given that sense of relativity, we cannot take the notion of "essence" seriously, nor the notion of man's task as the accurate representation of essences. The natural sciences, by themselves, leave us convinced that we know both what we are and what we can be—not just how to predict and control our behavior, but the limits of that behavior (and, in particular, the limits of our significant speech). Gadamer's attempt to fend off the demand (common to Mill and Carnap) for "objectivity" in the *Geisteswissenschaften* is the attempt to prevent education from being reduced to instruction in the results of normal inquiry. More broadly, it is the attempt to prevent abnormal inquiry from being viewed as suspicious solely because of its abnormality.

---

[7]It would have been fortunate if Sartre had followed up his remark that man is the being whose essence is to have no essence by saying that this went for all other beings also. Unless this addition is made, Sartre will appear to be insisting on the good old metaphysical distinction between spirit and nature in other terms, rather than simply making the point that man is always free to choose new descriptions (for, among other things, himself).

[8]Dewey, it seems to me, is the one author usually classified as a "naturalist" who did not have this reductive attitude, despite his incessant talk about "scientific method." Dewey's peculiar achievement was to have remained sufficiently Hegelian not to think of natural science as having an inside track on the essences of things, while becoming sufficiently naturalistic to think of human beings in Darwinian terms.

[9]Gadamer, *Truth and Method*, p. 12.

This "existentialist" attempt to place objectivity, rationality, and normal inquiry within the larger picture of our need to be educated and edified is often countered by the "positivist" attempt to distinguish learning facts from acquiring values. From the positivist point of view, Gadamer's exposition of *wirkungs-geschichtliche Bewusstsein* may seem little more than reiteration of the common-place that even when we know all the objectively true descriptions of ourselves, we still may not know what to do with ourselves. From this point of view, *Truth and Method* . . . are just overblown dramatizations of the fact that entire com-plaince with all the demands for justification offered by normal inquiry would still leave us free to draw our own morals from the assertions so justified. But from the viewpoints of Gadamer, Heidegger, and Sartre, the trouble with the fact-value dis-tinction is that it is contrived precisely to blur the fact that alternative descriptions are possible in addition to those offered by the results of normal inquiries.[10] It sug-gests that once "all the facts are in" nothing remains except "noncognitive" adop-tion of an attitude—a choice which is not rationally discussable. It disguises the fact that to use one set of true sentences to describe ourselves is already to choose an attitude toward ourselves, whereas to use another set of true sentences is to adopt a contrary attitude. Only if we assume that there is a value-free vocabulary which renders these sets of "factual" statements commensurable can the positivist distinction between facts and values, beliefs and attitudes, look plausible. But the philosophical fiction that such a vocabulary is on the tips of our tongues is, from an educational point of view, disastrous. It forces us to pretend that we can split ourselves up into knowers of true sentences on the one hand and choosers of lives or actions or works of art on the other. These artificial diremptions make it impos-sible to get the notion of edification into focus. Or, more exactly, they tempt us to think of edification as having nothing to do with the rational faculties which are employed in normal discourse.

So Gadamer's effort to get rid of the classic picture of man-as-essentially-knower-of-essences is, among other things, an effort to get rid of the distinction between fact and value, and thus to let us think of "discovering the facts" as one project of edification among others. This is why Gadamer devotes so much time to breaking down the distinctions which Kant made among cognition, morality, and aesthetic judgment.[11] There is no way, as far as I can see, in which to *argue* the issue of whether to keep the Kantian "grid" in place or set it aside. There is no "nor-mal" philosophical discourse which provides common commensurating ground for those who see science and edification as, respectively, "rational" and "irrational," and those who see the quest for objectivity as one possibility among others to be taken account of in *wirkungsgeschichtliche Bewusstsein*. If there is no such com-mon ground, all we can do is to show how the other side looks from our own point of view. That is, all we can do is be hermeneutic about the opposition—trying to

---

[10]See Heidegger's discussion of "values" in *Being and Time,* p. 133, and Sartre's in *Being and Nothingness,* pt. two, chap. 1, sec. 4. Compare Gadamer's remarks on Weber (*Truth and Method,* pp. 461ff.).

[11]See Gadamer's polemic against "the subjectivization of the aesthetic" in Kant's Third Critique (*Truth and Method,* p. 87) and compare Heidegger's remarks in "Letter on Humanism" on Aristotle's distinctions among physics, logic, and ethics (Heidegger, *Basic Writings,* ed. Krell [New York, 1976], p. 232).

show how the odd or paradoxical or offensive things they say hang together with the rest of what they want to say, and how what they say looks when put in our own alternative idiom. This sort of hermeneutics with polemical intent is common to Heidegger's and Derrida's attempts to deconstruct the tradition.

2. SYSTEMATIC PHILOSOPHY AND EDIFYING PHILOSOPHY

The hermeneutic point of view, from which the acquisition of truth dwindles in importance, and is seen as a component of education, is possible only if we once stood at another point of view. Education has to start from acculturation. So the search for objectivity and the self-conscious awareness of the social practices in which objectivity consists are necessary first steps in becoming *gebildet*. We must first see ourselves as *en-soi*—as described by those statements which are objectively true in the judgment of our peers—before there is any point in seeing ourselves as *pour-soi*. Similarly, we cannot be educated without finding out a lot about the descriptions of the world offered by our culture (e.g., by learning the results of the natural sciences). Later perhaps, we may put less value on "being in touch with reality" but we can afford that only after having passed through stages of implicit, and then explicit and self-conscious, conformity to the norms of the discourses going on around us.

I raise this banal point that education—even the education of the revolutionary or the prophet—needs to begin with acculturation and conformity merely to provide a cautionary complement to the "existentialist" claim that normal participation in normal discourse is merely one project, one way of being in the world. The caution amounts to saying that abnormal and "existential" discourse is always parasitic upon normal discourse, that the possibility of hermeneutics is always parasitic upon the possibility (and perhaps upon the actuality) of epistemology, and that edification always employs materials provided by the culture of the day. To attempt abnormal discourse *de novo,* without being able to recognize our own abnormality, is madness in the most literal and terrible sense. To insist on being hermeneutic where epistemology would do—to make ourselves unable to view normal discourse in terms of its own motives, and able to view it only from within our own abnormal discourse—is not mad, but it does show a lack of education. To adopt the "existentialist" attitude toward objectivity and rationality common to Sartre, Heidegger, and Gadamer makes sense only if we do so in a conscious departure from a well-understood norm. "Existentialism" is an *intrinsically reactive* movement of thought, one which has point only in opposition to the tradition. I want now to generalize this contrast between philosophers whose work is essentially constructive and those whose work is essentially reactive. I shall thereby develop a contrast between philosophy which centers in epistemology and the sort of philosophy which takes its point of departure from suspicion about the pretensions of epistemology. This is the contrast between "systematic" and "edifying" philosophies.

In every sufficiently reflective culture, there are those who single out one area, one set of practices, and see it as the paradigm human activity. They then try to show how the rest of culture can profit from this example. In the mainstream of the

Western philosophical tradition, this paradigm has been *knowing*—possessing justified true beliefs, or, better yet, beliefs so intrinsically persuasive as to make justification unnecessary. Successive philosophical revolutions within this mainstream have been produced by philosophers excited by new cognitive feats—e.g., the rediscovery of Aristotle, Galilean mechanics, the development of self-conscious historiography in the nineteenth century, Darwinian biology, mathematical logic. Thomas's use of Aristotle to conciliate the Fathers, Descartes's and Hobbes's criticisms of scholasticism, the Enlightenment's notion that reading Newton leads naturally to the downfall of tyrants, Spencer's evolutionism, Carnap's attempt to overcome metaphysics through logic, are so many attempts to refashion the rest of culture on the model of the latest cognitive achievements. A "mainstream" Western philosopher typically says: Now that such-and-such a line of inquiry has had such a stunning success, let us reshape all inquiry, and all of culture, on its model, thereby permitting objectivity and rationality to prevail in areas previously obscured by convention, superstition, and the lack of a proper epistemological understanding of man's ability accurately to represent nature.

On the periphery of the history of modern philosophy, one finds figures who, without forming a "tradition," resemble each other in their distrust of the notion that man's essence is to be a knower of essences. Goethe, Kierkegaard, Santayana, William James, Dewey, the later Wittgenstein, the later Heidegger, are figures of this sort. They are often accused of relativism or cynicism. They are often dubious about progress, and especially about the latest claim that such-and-such a discipline has at last made the nature of human knowledge so clear that reason will now spread throughout the rest of human activity. These writers have kept alive the suggestion that, even when we have justified true belief about everything we want to know, we may have no more than conformity to the norms of the day. They have kept alive the historicist sense that this century's "superstition" was the last century's triumph of reason, as well as the relativist sense that the latest vocabulary, borrowed from the latest scientific achievement, may not express privileged representations of essences, but be just another of the potential infinity of vocabularies in which the world can be described.

The mainstream philosophers are the philosophers I shall call "systematic," and the peripheral ones are those I shall call "edifying." These peripheral, pragmatic philosophers are skeptical primarily *about systematic philosophy,* about the whole project of universal commensuration.[12] In our time, Dewey, Wittgenstein, and Heidegger are the great edifying, peripheral thinkers. All three make it as difficult as possible to take their thought as expressing views on traditional philosophical problems,

---

[12]Consider the passage from Anatole France's "Garden of Epicurus" which Jacques Derrida cites at the beginning of his "La Mythologie Blanche" (in *Marges de la Philosophie* [Paris, 1972], p. 250):

. . . the metaphysicians, when they make up a new language, are like knife-grinders who grind coins and medals against their stone instead of knives and scissors. They rub out the relief, the inscriptions, the portraits, and when one can no longer see on the coins Victoria, or Wilhelm, or the French Republic, they explain: these coins now have nothing specifically English or German or French about them, for we have taken them out of time and space; they now are no longer worth, say, five francs, but rather have an inestimable value, and the area in which they are a medium of exchange has been infinitely extended.

or as making constructive proposals for philosophy as a cooperative and progressive discipline.[13] They make fun of the classic picture of man, the picture which contains systematic philosophy, the search for universal commensuration in a final vocabulary. They hammer away at the holistic point that words take their meanings from other words rather than by virtue of their representative character, and the corollary that vocabularies acquire their privileges from the men who use them rather than from their transparency to the real.[14]

The distinction between systematic and edifying philosophers is not the same as the distinction between normal philosophers and revolutionary philosophers. The latter distinction puts Husserl, Russell, the later Wittgenstein, and the later Heidegger all on the same ("revolutionary") side of a line. For my purposes, what matters is a distinction between two kinds of revolutionary philosophers. On the one hand, there are revolutionary philosophers—those who found new schools within which normal, professionalized philosophy can be practiced—who see the incommensurability of their new vocabulary with the old as a temporary inconvenience, to be blamed on the shortcomings of their predecessors and to be overcome by the institutionalization of their own vocabulary. On the other hand, there are great philosophers who dread the thought that their vocabulary should ever be institutionalized, or that their writing might be seen as commensurable with the tradition. Husserl and Russell (like Descartes and Kant) are of the former sort. The later Wittgenstein and the later Heidegger (like Kierkegaard and Nietzsche) are of the latter sort.[15] Great systematic philosophers are constructive and offer arguments. Great edifying philosophers are reactive and offer satires, parodies, aphorisms. They know their work loses its point when the period they were reacting against is over. They are *intentionally* peripheral. Great systematic philosophers, like great scientists, build for eternity. Great edifying philosophers destroy for the sake of their own generation. Systematic philosophers want to put their subject on the secure path of a science. Edifying philosophers want to keep space open for the sense of wonder which poets can sometimes cause—wonder that there is something new under the sun, something which is *not* an accurate representation of what was already there, something which (at least for the moment) cannot be explained and can barely be described.

The notion of an edifying philosopher is, however, a paradox. For Plato defined the philosopher by opposition to the poet. The philosopher could give reasons,

---

[13]See Karl-Otto Apel's comparison of Wittgenstein and Heidegger as having both "called into question Western metaphysics as a theoretical discipline" (*Transformation der Philosophie* [Frankfurt, 1973], vol. 1, p. 228). I have not offered interpretations of Dewey, Wittgenstein, and Heidegger in support of what I have been saying about them, but I have tried to do so in a piece on Wittgenstein called "Keeping Philosophy Pure" (*Yale Review* [Spring 1976], pp. 336–356), in "Overcoming the Tradition: Heidegger and Dewey" (*Review of Metaphysics* 30 [1976], 280–305), and in "Dewey's Metaphysics" in *New Studies in the Philosophy of John Dewey,* ed. Steven M. Cahn (Hanover, N.H., 1977).

[14]This Heideggerean point about language is spelled out at length and didactically by Derrida in *La Voix et le Phénomène,* translated as *Speech and Phenomenon* by David Allison (Evanston, 1973). See Newton Garver's comparison of Derrida and Wittgenstein in his "Introduction" to this translation.

[15]The permanent fascination of the man who dreamed up the whole idea of Western philosophy—Plato—is that we still do not know which sort of philosopher he was. Even if the *Seventh Letter* is set aside as spurious, the fact that after millenniums of commentary nobody knows which passages in the dialogues are jokes keeps the puzzle fresh.

argue for his views, justify himself. So argumentative systematic philosophers say of Nietzsche and Heidegger that, whatever else they may be, they are not *philosophers*. This "not really a philosopher" ploy is also used, of course, by normal philosophers against revolutionary philosophers. It was used by pragmatists against logical positivists, by positivists against "ordinary language philosophers," and will be used whenever cozy professionalism is in danger. But in that usage it is just a rhetorical gambit which tells one nothing more than that an incommensurable discourse is being proposed. When it is used against edifying philosophers, on the other hand, the accusation has a real bite. The problem for an edifying philosopher is that qua philosopher he is in the business of offering arguments, whereas he would like simply to offer another set of terms, *without* saying that these terms are the new-found accurate representations of essences (e.g., of the essence of "philosophy" itself). He is, so to speak, violating not just the rules of normal philosophy (the philosophy of the schools of his day) but a sort of metarule: the rule that one may suggest changing the rules only because one has noticed that the old ones do not fit the subject matter, that they are not adequate to reality, that they impede the solution of the eternal problems. Edifying philosophers, unlike revolutionary systematic philosophers, are those who are abnormal at this meta-level. They refuse to present themselves as having found out any objective truth (about, say, what philosophy is). They present themselves as doing something different from, and more important than, offering accurate representations of how things are. It is more important because, they say, the notion of "accurate representation" itself is not the proper way to think about what philosophy does. But, they then go on to say, this is not because "a search for accurate representations of . . . (e.g., 'the most general traits of reality' or 'the nature of man')" is an *in*accurate representation of philosophy.

Whereas less pretentious revolutionaries can afford to have views on lots of things which their predecessors had views on, edifying philosophers have to decry the very notion of having a view, while avoiding having a view about having views.[16] This is an awkward, but not impossible, position. Wittgenstein and Heidegger manage it fairly well. One reason they manage it as well as they do is that they do not think that when we say something we must necessarily be expressing a view about a subject. We might just be *saying something*—participating in a conversation rather than contributing to an inquiry. Perhaps saying things is not always saying how things are. Perhaps saying *that* is itself not a case of saying how things are. Both men suggest we see people as saying things, better or worse things, without seeing them as externalizing inner representations of reality. But this is only their entering wedge, for then we must cease to see ourselves as *seeing* this, without beginning to see ourselves as seeing something else. We must get the visual, and in particular the mirroring, metaphors out of our speech altogether.[17] To do that

[16]Heidegger's *"Die Zeit des Weltbildes"* (translated as "The Age of the World-View" by Marjorie Grene in *Boundary II* [1976]) is the best discussion of this difficulty I have come across.
[17]Derrida's recent writings are meditations on how to avoid these metaphors. Like Heidegger in "Aus einem Gespräch von der Sprache zwischen einem Japaner und einem Fragenden" (in *Unterwegs zur Sprache* [Pfullingen, 1959]), Derrida occasionally toys with the notion of the superiority of Oriental languages and of ideographic writing.

we have to understand speech not only as not the externalizing of inner representations, but as not a representation at all. We have to drop the notion of correspondence for sentences as well as for thoughts, and see sentences as connected with other sentences rather than with the world. We have to see the term "corresponds to how things are" as an automatic compliment paid to successful normal discourse rather than as a relation to be studied and aspired to throughout the rest of discourse. To attempt to extend this compliment to feats of *ab*normal discourse is like complimenting a judge on his wise decision by leaving him a fat tip: it shows a lack of tact. To think of Wittgenstein and Heidegger as having views about how things are is not to be wrong about how things are, exactly; it is just poor taste. It puts them in a position which they do not want to be in, and in which they look ridiculous.

But perhaps they *should* look ridiculous. How, then, do we know when to adopt a tactful attitude and when to insist on someone's moral obligation to hold a view? This is like asking how we know when someone's refusal to adopt our norms (of, for example, social organization, sexual practices, or conversational manners) is morally outrageous and when it is something which we must (at least provisionally) respect. We do not know such things by reference to general principles. We do not, for instance, know in advance that if a given sentence is uttered, or a given act performed, we shall break off a conversation or a personal relationship, for everything depends on what leads up to it. To see edifying philosophers as conversational partners is an alternative to seeing them as holding views on subjects of common concern. One way of thinking of wisdom as something of which the love is not the same as that of argument, and of which the achievement does not consist in finding the correct vocabulary for representing essence, is to think of it as the practical wisdom necessary to participate in a conversation. One way to see edifying philosophy *as* the love of wisdom is to see it as the attempt to prevent conversation from degenerating into inquiry, into an exchange of views. Edifying philosophers can never end philosophy, but they can help prevent it from attaining the secure path of a science.

3. EDIFICATION, RELATIVISM, AND OBJECTIVE TRUTH

I want now to enlarge this suggestion that edifying philosophy aims at continuing a conversation rather than at discovering truth, by making out of it a reply to the familiar charge of "relativism" leveled at the subordination of truth to edification. I shall be claiming that the difference between conversation and inquiry parallels Sartre's distinction between thinking of oneself as *pour-soi* and as *en-soi,* and thus that the cultural role of the edifying philosopher is to help us avoid the self-deception which comes from believing that we know ourselves by knowing a set of objective facts. In the following section, I shall try to make the converse point. There I shall be saying that the wholehearted behaviorism, naturalism, and physicalism I have been commending in earlier chapters help us avoid the self-deception of thinking that we possess a deep, hidden, metaphysically significant nature which makes us "irreducibly" different from inkwells or atoms.

Philosophers who have doubts about traditional epistemology are often thought to be questioning the notion that at most one of incompatible competing theories can be true. However, it is hard to find anyone who actually does question this. When it is said, for example, that coherentist or pragmatic "theories of truth" allow for the possibility that many incompatible theories would satisfy the conditions set for "the truth," the coherentist or pragmatist usually replies that this merely shows that we should have no grounds for choice among these candidates for "the truth." The moral to draw, they say, is not that they have offered inadequate analyses of "true," but that there are some terms—for example, "the true theory," "the right thing to do"—which are, intuitively and grammatically, singular, but for which no set of necessary and sufficient conditions can be given which will pick out a unique referent. This fact, they say, should not be surprising. Nobody thinks that there are necessary and sufficient conditions which will pick out, for example, the unique referent of "the best thing for her to have done on finding herself in that rather embarrassing situation," though plausible conditions can be given which will shorten a list of competing incompatible candidates. Why should it be different for the referents of "what she should have done in that ghastly moral dilemma" or "the Good Life for man" or "what the world is really made of"?

To see relativism lurking in every attempt to formulate conditions for truth or reality or goodness which does not attempt to provide uniquely individuating conditions we must adopt the "Platonic" notion of the transcendental terms . . . . We must think of the true referents of these terms (the Truth, the Real, Goodness) as conceivably having no connection whatever with the practices of justification which obtain among us. The dilemma created by this Platonic hypostatization is that, on the one hand, the philosopher must attempt to find criteria for picking out these unique referents, whereas, on the other hand, the only hints he has about what these criteria could be are provided by current practice (by, e.g., the best moral and scientific thought of the day). Philosophers thus condemn themselves to a Sisyphean task, for no sooner has an account of a trascendental term been perfected than it is labeled a "naturalistic fallacy," a confusion between essence and accident.[18] I think we get a clue to the cause of this self-defeating obsession from the fact that even philosophers who take the intuitive impossibility of finding conditions for "the one right thing to do" as a reason for repudiating "objective values" are loath to take the impossibility of finding individuating conditions for the one true theory of the world as a reason for denying "objective physical reality." Yet they should, formally the two notions are on a par. The reasons for and against adopting a "correspondence" approach to moral truth are the same as those regarding truth about the physical world. The giveaway comes, I think, when we find that the usual excuse for invidious treatment is that we are shoved around by physical reality but not by values.[19] Yet what does being shoved around have to do with objectivity, accurate representation, or correspondence? Nothing, I think, unless we confuse *contact* with reality (a causal, non-intentional, non-description-relative relation) with *dealing with* reality (describing, explaining, predicting, and modifying it—all of which are things we do under descriptions). The sense in which

[18]On this point, see William Frankena's classic "The Naturalistic Fallacy," *Mind* 68 (1939).
[19]What seems to be a sense of being shoved around by values, they reductively say, is just physical reality in disguise (e.g., neural arrangements or glandular secretions programmed by parental conditioning).

physical reality is Peircean "Secondness"—unmediated pressure—has nothing to do with the sense in which one among all our ways of describing, or of coping with, physical reality is "the one right" way. Lack of mediation is here being confused with accuracy of mediation. The absence of description is confused with a privilege attaching to a certain description. Only by such a confusion can the inability to offer individuating conditions for the one true description of material things be confused with insensitivity to the things' obduracy.

Sartre helps us explain why this confusion is so frequent and why its results are purveyed with so much moral earnestness. The notion of "one right way of describing and explaining reality" supposedly contained in our "intuition" about the meaning of "true" is, for Sartre, just the notion of having a way of describing and explaining *imposed* on us in that brute way in which stones impinge on our feet. Or, to shift to visual metaphors, it is the notion of having reality unveiled to us, not as in a glass darkly, but with some unimaginable sort of immediacy which would make discourse and description superfluous. If we could convert knowledge from something discursive, something attained by continual adjustments of ideas or words, into something as ineluctable as being shoved about, or being transfixed by a sight which leaves us speechless, then we should no longer have the responsibility for choice among competing ideas and words, theories and vocabularies. This attempt to slough off responsibility is what Sartre describes as the attempt to turn oneself into a thing—into an *être-en-soi.* In the visions of the epistemologist, this incoherent notion takes the form of seeing the attainment of truth as a matter of *necessity,* either the "logical" necessity of the transcendentalist or the "physical" necessity of the evolutionary "naturalizing" epistemologist. From Sartre's point of view, the urge to find such necessities is the urge to be rid of one's freedom to erect yet another alternative theory or vocabulary. Thus the edifying philosopher who points out the incoherence of the urge is treated as a "relativist," one who lacks moral seriousness, because he does not join in the common human hope that the burden of choice will pass away. Just as the moral philosopher who sees virtue as Aristotelian self-development is thought to lack concern for his fellow man, so the epistemologist who is merely behaviorist is treated as one who does not share the universal human aspiration toward objective truth.

Sartre adds to our understanding of the visual imagery which has set the problems of Western philosophy by helping us see why this imagery is always trying to transcend itself. The notion of an unclouded Mirror of Nature is the notion of a mirror which would be indistinguishable from what was mirrored, and thus would not be a mirror at all. The notion of a human being whose mind is such an unclouded mirror, and who *knows* this, is the image, as Sartre says, of God. Such a being does *not* confront something alien which makes it necessary for him to choose an attitude toward, or a description of, it. He would have no need and no ability to choose actions or descriptions. He can be called "God" if we think of the advantages of this situation, or a "mere machine" if we think of the disadvantages. From this point of view, to look for commensuration rather than simply continued conversation—to look for a way of making further redescription unnecessary by finding a way of reducing all *possible* descriptions to one—is to attempt escape from humanity. To abandon the notion that philosophy must show all possible discourse naturally converging to a consensus, just as normal inquiry does, would be to abandon the hope of being anything more than merely human. It would thus be to abandon the Platonic notions of Truth and Reality and Goodness as entities which may not be even dimly mirrored by present practices and beliefs, and to settle back into the "relativism" which assumes that our only useful notions of "true" and "real" and "good" are extrapolations from those practices and beliefs.

Here, finally, I come around to the suggestion with which I ended the last section—that the point of edifying philosophy is to keep the conversation going rather than to find objective truth. Such truth, in the view I am advocating, is the normal result of normal discourse. Edifying philosophy is not only abnormal but reactive, having sense only as a protest against attempts to close off conversation by proposals for universal commensuration through the hypostatization of some privileged set of descriptions. The danger which edifying discourse tries to avert is that some given vocabulary, some way in which people might come to think of themselves, will deceive them into thinking that from now on all discourse could be, or should be, normal discourse. The resulting freezing-over of culture would be, in the eyes of edifying philosophers, the dehumanization of human beings. The edifying philosophers are thus agreeing with Lessing's choice of the infinite *striving for* truth over "all of Truth."[20] For the edifying philosopher the very idea of being presented with "all of Truth" is absurd, because the Platonic notion of Truth itself is absurd. It is absurd either as the notion of truth about reality which is not about reality-under-a-certain-description, or as the notion of truth about reality under some privileged description which makes all other descriptions unnecessary because it is commensurable with each of them.

To see keeping a conversation going as a sufficient aim of philosophy, to see wisdom as consisting in the ability to sustain a conversation, is to see human beings as generators of new descriptions rather than beings one hopes to be able to describe accurately. To see the aim of philosophy as truth—namely, the truth about the terms which provide ultimate commensuration for all human inquiries and activities—is to see human beings as objects rather than subjects, as existing *en-soi* rather than as both *pour-soi* and *en-soi,* as both described objects and describing subjects. To think that philosophy will permit us to see the describing subject as itself one sort of described object is to think that all possible descriptions can be rendered commensurable with the aid of a single descriptive vocabulary—that of philosophy itself. For only if we had such a notion of a universal description could we identify human-beings-under-a-given-description with man's "essence." Only with such a notion would that of a man's *having* an essence make sense, whether or not that essence is conceived of as the knowing of essences. So not even by saying that man is subject as well as object, *pour-soi* as well as *en-soi,* are we grasping our essence. We do not escape from Platonism by saying that "our essence is to have no essence" if we then try to use this insight as the basis for a constructive and systematic attempt to find out further truths about human beings.

---

[20]Kierkegaard made this choice the prototype of his own choice of "subjectivity" over "system." Cf. *Concluding Unscientific Postscript,* trans. David Swenson and Walter Lowrie (Princeton, 1941), p. 97.

That is why "existentialism"—and, more generally, edifying philosophy—can be *only* reactive, why it falls into self-deception whenever it tries to do more than send the conversation off in new directions. Such new directions may, perhaps, engender new normal discourses, new sciences, new philosophical research programs, and thus new objective truths. But they are not the point of edifying philosophy, only accidental byproducts. The point is always the same—to perform the social function which Dewey called "breaking the crust of convention," preventing man from deluding himself with the notion that he knows himself, or anything else, except under optional description. . . .

5. PHILOSOPHY IN THE CONVERSATION OF MANKIND

I end this book with an allusion to Oakeshott's famous title,[21] because it catches the tone in which, I think, philosophy should be discussed. Much of what I have said about epistemology and its possible successors is an attempt to draw some corollaries from Sellars's doctrine that

> in characterizing an episode or a state as that of *knowing,* we are not giving an empirical description of that episode or state; we are placing it in the logical space of reasons, of justifying and being able to justify what one says.[22]

If we see knowing not as having an essence, to be described by scientists or philosophers, but rather as a right, by current standards, to believe, then we are well on the way to seeing *conversation* as the ultimate context within which knowledge is to be understood. Our focus shifts from the relation between human beings and the objects of their inquiry to the relation between alternative standards of justification, and from there to the actual changes in those standards which make up intellectual history. This brings us to appreciate Sellars's own description of his mythical hero Jones, the man who invented the Mirror of Nature and thereby made modern philosophy possible:

> Does the reader not recognize Jones as Man himself in the middle of his journey from the grunts and groans of the cave to the subtle and polydimensional discourse of the drawing room, the laboratory, and the study, the language of Henry and William James, of Einstein and of the philosophers who, in their efforts to break out of discourse to an ἀρχή beyond discourse, have provided the most curious dimension of all? (p. 196)

In this book I have offered a sort of prolegomenon to a history of epistemology-centered philosophy as an episode in the history of European culture. Such philosophy goes back to the Greeks, and goes sideways into all sorts of non-philosophical disciplines which have, at one time or another, proposed themselves as substitutes for epistemology, and thus for philosophy. So the episode in question cannot simply be identified with "modern philosophy," in the sense of the standard textbook sequence of great philosophers from Descartes to Russell and Husserl. But that

---

[21]Cf. Michael Oakeshott, "The Voice of Poetry in the Conversation of Mankind," in his *Rationalism and Politics* (New York, 1975).

[22]Wilfrid Sellars, *Science, Perception and Reality* (London and New York, 1963), p. 169.

sequence is, nevertheless, where the search for foundations for knowledge is most explicit. So most of my attempts to deconstruct the image of the Mirror of Nature have concerned these philosophers. I have tried to show how their urge to break out into an ἀρχή beyond discourse is rooted in the urge to see social practices of justification as more than just such practices. I have, however, focused mainly on the expressions of this urge in the recent literature of analytical philosophy. The result is thus no more than a prolegomenon. A proper historical treatment would require both learning and skills which I do not possess. But I would hope that the prolegomenon has been sufficient to let one see contemporary issues in philosophy as events in a certain stage of a conversation—a conversation which once knew nothing of these issues and may know nothing of them again.

The fact that we can continue the conversation Plato began without discussing the topics Plato wanted discussed, illustrates the difference between treating philosophy as a voice in a conversation and treating it as a subject, a *Fach,* a field of professional inquiry. The conversation Plato began has been enlarged by more voices than Plato would have dreamed possible, and thus by topics he knew nothing of. A "subject"—astrology, physics, classical philosophy, furniture design—may undergo revolutions, but it gets its self-image from its present state, and its history is necessarily written "Whiggishly" as an account of its gradual maturation. This is the most frequent way of writing the history of philosophy, and I cannot claim to have avoided such Whiggery entirely in sketching the sort of history which needs to be written. But I hope that I have shown how we can see the issues with which philosophers are presently concerned, and with which they Whiggishly see philosophy as having always (perhaps unwittingly) been concerned, as results of historical accident, as turns the conversation has taken.[23] It has taken this turn for a long time, but it might turn in another direction without human beings thereby losing their reason, or losing touch with "the real problems."

The conversational interest of philosophy as a subject, or of some individual philosopher of genius, has varied and will continue to vary in unpredictable ways depending upon contingencies. These contingencies will range from what happens in physics to what happens in politics. The lines between disciplines will blur and shift, and new disciplines will arise, in the ways illustrated by Galileo's successful attempt to create "purely scientific questions" in the seventeenth century. The notions of "philosophical significance" and of "purely philosophical question," as they are currently used, gained sense only around the time of Kant. Our post-Kantian sense that

---

[23]Two recent writers—Michel Foucault and Harold Bloom—make this sense of the brute factuality of historical origins central to their work. Cf. Bloom, *A Map of Misreading* (New York, 1975), p. 33: "All continuities possess the paradox of being absolutely arbitrary in their origins and absolutely inescapable in their teleologies. We know this so vividly from what we all of us oxymoronically call our love lives that its literary counterparts need little demonstration." Foucault says that his way of looking at the history of ideas "permits the introduction, into the very roots of thought, of notions of *chance, discontinuity* and *materiality."* ("The Discourse on Language," included in the *Archaeology of Knowledge* [New York, 1972], p. 231) It is hardest of all to see brute contingency in the history of *philosophy,* if only because since Hegel the historiography of philosophy has been "progressive," or (as in Heidegger's inversion of Hegel's account of progress) "retrogressive," but never without a sense of inevitability. If we could once see the desire for a permanent, neutral, ahistorical, commensurating vocabulary as itself a historical phenomenon, then perhaps we could write the history of philosophy less dialectically and less sentimentally than has been possible hitherto.

epistemology or some successor subject is at the center of philosophy (and that moral philosophy, aesthetics, and social philosophy, for example, are somehow derivative) is a reflection of the fact that the professional philosopher's self-image depends upon his professional preoccupation with the image of the Mirror of Nature. Without the Kantian assumption that the philosopher can decide *quaestiones juris* concerning the claims of the rest of culture, this self-image collapses. That assumption depends on the notion that there is such a thing as understanding the essence of knowledge—doing what Sellars tells us we cannot do.

To drop the notion of the philosopher as knowing something about knowing which nobody else knows so well would be to drop the notion that his voice always has an overriding claim on the attention of the other participants in the conversation. It would also be to drop the notion that there is something called "philosophical method" or "philosophical technique" or "the philosophical point of view" which enables the professional philosopher, *ex officio,* to have interesting views about, say, the respectability of psychoanalysis, the legitimacy of certain dubious laws, the resolution of moral dilemmas, the "soundness" of schools of historiography or literary criticism, and the like. Philosophers often do have interesting views upon such questions, and their professional training as philosophers is often a necessary condition for their having the views they do. But this is not to say that philosophers have a special kind of knowledge about knowledge (or anything else) from which they draw relevant corollaries. The useful kibitzing they can provide on the various topics I just mentioned is made possible by their familiarity with the historical background of arguments on similar topics, and, most importantly, by the fact that arguments on such topics are punctuated by stale philosophical clichés which the other participants have stumbled across in their reading, but about which professional philosophers know the pros and cons by heart.

The neo-Kantian image of philosophy as a profession, then, is involved with the image of the "mind" or "language" as mirroring nature. So it might seem that epistemological behaviorism and the consequent rejection of mirror-imagery entail the claim that there can or should be no such profession. But this does not follow. Professions can survive the paradigms which gave them birth. In any case, the need for teachers who have read the great dead philosophers is quite enough to insure that there will be philosophy departments as long as there are universities. The actual result of a widespread loss of faith in mirror-imagery would be merely an "encapsulation" of the problems created by this imagery within a historical period. I do not know whether we are in fact at the end of an era. This will depend, I suspect, on whether Dewey, Wittgenstein, and Heidegger are taken to heart. It may be that mirror-imagery and "mainstream," systematic philosophy will be revitalized once again by some revolutionary of genius. Or it may be that the image of the philosopher which Kant offered is about to go the way of the medieval image of the priest. If that happens, even the philosophers themselves will no longer take seriously the notion of philosophy as providing "foundations" or "justifications" for the rest of culture, or as adjudicating *quaestiones juris* about the proper domains of other disciplines.

Whichever happens, however, there is no danger of philosophy's "coming to an end." Religion did not come to an end in the Enlightenment, nor painting in Impressionism. Even if the period from Plato to Nietzsche is encapsulated and "distanced" in the way Heidegger suggests, and even if twentieth-century philosophy comes to seem a stage of awkward transitional backing and filling (as sixteenth-century philosophy now seems to us), there will be something called "philosophy" on the other side of the transition. For even if problems about representation look as obsolete to our descendants as problems about hylomorphism look to us, people will still read Plato, Aristotle, Descartes, Kant, Hegel, Wittgenstein, and Heidegger. What roles these men will play in our descendants' conversation, no one knows. Whether the distinction between systematic and edifying philosophy will carry over, no one knows either. Perhaps philosophy will become purely edifying, so that one's self-identification as a philosopher will be purely in terms of the books one reads and discusses, rather than in terms of the problems one wishes to solve. Perhaps a new form of systematic philosophy will be found which has nothing whatever to do with epistemology but which nevertheless makes normal philosophical inquiry possible. These speculations are idle, and nothing I have been saying makes one more plausible than another. The only point on which I would insist is that philosophers' moral concern should be with continuing the conversation of the West, rather than with insisting upon a place for the traditional problems of modern philosophy within that conversation.

The Mission of Philosophy

Nicholas Rescher

THE TASK OF PHILOSOPHY

Philosophizing represents the human mind's attempt to bring intelligible order into our often chaotic experience of the world's doings. The history of philosophy constitutes the ongoing process of people's attempts to deploy ideas to make the seemingly endless diversity and complexity that surrounds us on all sides rationally comprehensible. Philosophy's instruments are concepts and theories—ideational structures—and it deploys them in quest of understanding, in the attempt to create a thought structure that provides us with an intellectual home that affords a habitable thought shelter in a complex and difficult world.

The mission of philosophy is to ask, and to answer in a rational and cognitively disciplined way, all the great questions about life in this world that people wonder about in their reflective moments. Aristotle was right on target when, in the first book of the *Metaphysics,* he said that "it is through wonder that men now begin and originally began to philosophize, wondering first about obvious perplexities, and then gradually proceeding to ask questions about the greater matters too, such as

Source: A System of Pragmatic Idealism, Volume III—*Metaphilosophical Inquiries,* Chapter 1. Princeton: Princeton University Press, 1994, 3–16.

. . . the root origin of it all" (982b10).[1] Philosophy deals largely with *how* and *whether* and *why* questions: how the world's arrangements stand in relation to us, whether things are as they seem, and why things should be as they are (e.g., why we should do "the ethically right" things). Ever since Socrates pestered his fellow Athenians with puzzling issues about "obvious" facts regarding truth and justice, philosophers have probed for the reason why behind the reason why. What characterizes philosophy is its mission of grappling with the "big questions" regarding ourselves, the world, and our place within its scheme of things. Philosophy strives after the systematic integration of human knowledge that the sciences initially promised to give us but have never managed to deliver because of their ongoing division of labor and never-ending pursuit of ever more specialized detail.

Philosophy accordingly excludes no subject matter altogether. It is too inclusive and all-encompassing to rest content with any delimited range of preoccupation. For virtually *everything* is in some way relevant to its synoptic concerns, its task being to provide a sort of traveler's guidebook to the lay of the land in reality at large. Dealing with being and value in general—with possibility, actuality, significance, and worth—the concerns of philosophy are universal and all-embracing. Moreover, philosophy does not limit itself to specific mechanisms and routine methods but makes opportunistic use of whatever means come to hand to get the job done.

Those "big questions" that preoccupy philosophy—questions on the order of "Why is there anything at all? Why are things-in-general as they actually are? Why is the law structure of the world as it is?"—clearly move beyond the range of the standard framework of causal explanation. For causal explanations need inputs: they are essentially transformational, rather than formational. They address themselves to specific issues emplaced within an environing manifold of process and cannot proceed holistically to look from an external vantage point at the framework itself. If we persist in posing such global questions, we cannot hope to resolve them in orthodox causal terms.

Does this mean that such questions are improper? Throughout the history of the discipline there have been those who thought that philosophy was asking for too much. This book's principal aim is to show why this is not so—or at any rate need not be.

THE NEED FOR PHILOSOPHY:
HUMANS AS *HOMO QUAERENS*

At the base of the cognitive enterprise lies the fact of human curiosity rooted in the need to know of a weak and vulnerable creature emplaced in a difficult and often hostile environment in which it must make its evolutionary way by its wits. For we must act—our very survival depends upon it—and a rational animal must align its actions with its beliefs. We have a very real and material stake in securing viable answers to our questions as to how things stand in the world we live in.

---

[1]Oxford translation (modified). Actually, Plato's Socrates already maintained that wondering (*thaumazein*) is the beginning (*arché*) of philosophy (*Theaetetus* 155D).

The discomfort of unknowing is a natural human sentiment. To be ignorant of what goes on about one is unpleasant to the individual and dangerous to the species from an evolutionary point of view. As William James wisely observed: "The utility of this emotional affect of expectation is perfectly obvious; 'natural selection,' in fact, was bound to bring it about sooner or later. It is of the utmost practical importance to an animal that he should have prevision of the qualities of the objects that surround him."[2] There is good reason why we humans pursue knowledge—it is our evolutionary destiny. Humans have evolved within nature to fill the ecological niche of an intelligent being. We are neither numerous and prolific (like the ant and the termite) nor tough and aggressive (like the shark). Weak and vulnerable creatures, we are constrained to make our evolutionary way in the world by the use of brainpower. It is by knowledge and not by hard shells or sharp claws or keen teeth that we have carved out our niche in evolution's scheme of things. The demand for understanding, for a cognitive accommodation to one's environment, for "knowing one's way about," is one of the most fundamental requirements of the human condition. Our questions form a big part of our life's agenda, providing the impetus that gives rise to our knowledge—or putative knowledge—of the world. Our species is *Homo quaerens*. We have questions and want (nay, *need*) answers.

In situations of cognitive frustration and bafflement we cannot function effectively as the sort of creature nature has compelled us to become. Confusion and ignorance—even in such "remote" and "abstruse" matters as those with which philosophy deals—yield psychic dismay and discomfort. The old saying is perfectly true: philosophy bakes no bread. It is no less true, however, that man does not live by bread alone. The physical side of our nature that impels us to eat, drink, and be merry is just one of its sides. *Homo sapiens* requires nourishment for the mind as urgently as it does nourishment for the body. We seek knowledge not only because we wish but because we must. For us humans, the need for information, for knowledge to nourish the mind, is every bit as critical as the need for food to nourish the body. Cognitive vacuity or dissonance is as distressing to us as hunger or pain. We want and need our cognitive commitments to compose an intelligible story, to give a comprehensive and coherent account of things. Bafflement and ignorance—to give suspensions of judgment the somewhat harsher name they deserve—exact a substantial price from us. The quest for cognitive orientation in a difficult world represents a deeply practical requisite for us. That basic demand for information and understanding presses in upon us, and we must do (and are pragmatically justified in doing) what is needed for its satisfaction. For us, cognition is the most practical of matters. Knowledge itself fulfills an acute practical need. Philosophy comes in precisely at this point of attempting to grapple with our basic cognitive concerns.

Philosophy seeks to bring rational order, system, and intelligibility to the confusing diversity of our cognitive affairs. It strives for orderly arrangements in the cognitive sphere that will enable us to find our way about in the world in an effective and satisfying way. Philosophy is indeed a venture in theorizing, but one whose

[2]William James, "The Sentiment of Rationality," in his *Will to Believe and Other Essays in Popular Philosophy* (New York, 1897), pp. 63–110 (see pp. 78–79).

rationale is eminently practical. A rational animal that has to make its evolutionary way in the world by its wits has a deep-rooted need for speculative reason.

But why pursue rationalizing philosophy at all? Why accept this enterprise as an arena of appropriate human endeavor? The answer is that it is an integral and indispensable component of the larger project of rational inquiry regarding issues important to us humans. This, to be sure, simply pushes the question back: Why pursue reasoned inquiry? This question splits into two components.

The first component is, Why pursue *inquiry?* Why insist on knowing about things and understanding them? The answer is twofold. On the one hand, knowledge is its own reward. On the other hand, knowledge is the indispensable instrument for the more efficient and effective realization of other goals. We accordingly engage in philosophical inquiry because we must, because the great intellectual issues of humanity and its place in the world's scheme, of the true and the beautiful and the good, of right and wrong, freedom and necessity, causality and determinism, and so on, matter greatly to us—to all of us some of the time, and to some of us all of the time. We philosophize because it is important to us to have answers to our questions. After all, a philosophical work is neither a work of fiction nor a work of history. Its mission is not so much to enlighten or to inform as it is to persuade: to convince people of the appropriateness of a certain solution to a certain problem. What is at issue is, at bottom, an exercise in question resolution, in problem solving. It roots in human curiosity—in the "fact of life" that we have questions and may need to obtain cognitively satisfying answers to them.

The second component of our question is, Why *reasoned* inquiry? The answer is that we are *Homo sapiens,* a *rational* animal. We do not want just any answers, but answers that can satisfy the demands of our intelligence—answers that we can in good conscience regard as appropriate, as tenable and defensible. We are not content with information about which answers people would like to have (psychologism), nor with information about what sort of answers are available (possibility mongering). What we want is cogent guidance regarding which answers to adopt—which contentions are correct or at any rate plausible. Reason affords our prime standard in this regard.

Philosophy, then, is an inquiry that seeks to resolve problems arising from the overall incoherence of our extraphilosophical commitments. To abandon philosophy is to rest content with incoherence. One can, of course, cease to do philosophy (as skeptics of all persuasions have always wanted). But if one is going to philosophize at all, one has no alternative but to proceed, by means of arguments and inferences, to the traditional vehicles of human rationality.

Yet why pursue such a venture in the face of the all-too-evident possibility of error? Why run such cognitive risks? For it is only too clear that there *are* risks here. In philosophizing, there is a gap between the individual indications at our disposal and the answers to our questions that we decide to accept. (Science faces the same gap. In philosophy, however, the gap is far wider because the questions are of a different scale.) The positions we take thus must be held tentatively, subject to expectation of an (almost certain) need for amendment, qualification, improvement, and modification. Philosophizing in the classical manner—exploiting the available indications of experience to answer the big questions on the agenda of traditional philosophy—is predicated on the use of reason to do the best we can to align our cognitive commitments with the substance of our experience. In this sense, philosophizing involves an act of faith. When we draw on our experience to answer our questions, we have to proceed in the tentative hope that the best we can do is good enough, at any rate for our immediate purposes.

The question of intellectual seriousness is pivotal here. Do we care? Do we *really want* answers to our questions? And are we sufficiently committed to this goal to be willing to take risks for the sake of its achievement—risks of potential error, of certain disagreement, and of possible philistine incomprehension? Such risks are unavoidable, an ineliminable part of the philosophical venture. If we lose the sense of legitimacy and become too fainthearted to run such risks, we must pay the price of abandoning the inquiry.

This of course can be done. But to abandon the quest for answers in a *reasoned* way is impossible. For in the final analysis there is no alternative to philosophizing as long as we remain in the province of reason. We adopt some controversial position or other, no matter which way we turn. No matter how elaborately we try to avoid philosophical controversy, however, it will come back to find us. The salient point was well put by Aristotle. Even if we join those who believe that philosophizing is not possible, "in this case too we are obliged to inquire how it is possible for there to be no Philosophy; and then, in inquiring, we philosophize, for rational inquiry is the essence of Philosophy."[3] To those who are prepared simply to abandon philosophy, to withdraw from the whole project of trying to make sense of things, we can have nothing to say. (How can one reason with those who deny the pointfulness and propriety of reasoning?) But with those who *argue* for its abandonment, we can do something— once we have enrolled them in the community as fellow theorists with a position of their own. F. H. Bradley hit the nail on the head: "The man who is ready to prove that metaphysical knowledge is impossible . . . is a brother metaphysician with a rival theory of first principles."[4] One can abandon philosophy, but one cannot *advocate* its abandonment through rational argumentation without philosophizing.

The question "Should we philosophize?" accordingly receives a straightforward answer. The impetus to philosophy lies in our very nature as rational inquirers—as beings who have questions, demand answers, and want these answers to be as cogent as the circumstances allow. Cognitive problems arise when matters fail to meet our expectations, and the expectation of rational order is the most fundamental of them all. The fact is simply that we must philosophize; it is a situational imperative for a rational creature such as ourselves.

AGAINST DISMISSING SYNOPTIC QUESTIONS

On what might be called the rejectionist approach, the entire project of seeking for a reason for the existence of things is simply dismissed as illegitimate. Even to

---

[3]*Aristotelis Fragmenta Selecta,* ed. W. D. Ross (Oxford, 1955), p. vii; for the text, see p. 28. But see also Anton-Hermann Chroust, ed., *Aristotle: Protrepticus, a Reconstruction* (Notre Dame, Ind., 1969), pp. 48–50.
[4]F. H. Bradley, *Appearance and Reality,* 2d ed. (Oxford, 1897), p. 1.

inquire into the existence of the universe in the manner of traditional metaphysics is held to be somehow inappropriate. It is just a mistake to ask for a causal explanation of existence per se; the question should be abandoned as improper in failing to constitute a legitimate issue. In the light of closer scrutiny—so it is said—the explanatory "problem" vanishes as meaningless.

Dismissing the legitimacy of synoptic explanation is generally based on the idea that the issue involves an illicit presupposition in that it looks to answers of the form "Z is the (or *an*) explanation for the existence of things." Seen as committed to this response schema, the question is held to presuppose that "there indeed is a ground for the existence of things—existence-in-general is the sort of thing that has an explanation." This presumption—we are told—is inappropriate on grounds of deep general principle inherent in the very "logic" of the situation. A discussion of C. G. Hempel's has forcefully advocated this point of view:

> Why is there anything at all, rather than nothing? . . . But what kind of an answer could be appropriate? What seems to be wanted is an explanatory account which does not assume the existence of something or other. But such an account, I would submit, is a logical impossibility. For generally, when the question "Why is it the case that *A*?" is answered by "Because *B* is the case" . . . *[A]n answer to our riddle which made no assumptions about the existence of anything cannot possibly provide adequate grounds.* . . . The riddle has been constructed in a manner that makes an answer logically impossible.[5]

But this plausible line of argumentation has its shortcomings. The most serious of these is that it fails to distinguish appropriately between the *existence of things* and the *obtaining of facts*[6]—and supplementarily also between specifically substantival facts regarding existing *things* and nonsubstantival facts regarding *states of affairs* that are not dependent on the operation of preexisting things.

We are here confronted with a principle of hypostatization, to the effect that on grounds of logical principle the reason for anything must ultimately always inhere in the operations of things. At this point we come to a prejudice as deep rooted as any in Western philosophy—the idea that things can originate only from things, that nothing can come from nothing (*ex nihilo nihil fit*) in the sense that no *thing* can emerge from a thingless condition.[7] Now this somewhat ambiguous principle is quite unproblematic when construed as saying that if the existence of something real has a correct explanation at all, then this explanation must pivot on something that is really and truly so. For, clearly, we cannot explain one *fact* without involving other *facts* to do the explaining. However, the principle becomes highly problematic when construed in the manner of the precept that "*things* must come from *things*," that

---

[5]Carl G. Hempel, "Science Unlimited," *Annals of the Japan Association for Philosophy of Science* 14 (1973): 187–202 (see p. 200), italics supplied.

[6]Note too that the question of the existence of facts is a horse of a very different color from that of the existence of things. There being no things is undoubtedly a possible situation; there being no facts is not (since if the situation were realized, this would itself constitute a fact).

[7]Aristotle taught that every change must emanate from a "mover," i.e., a substance whose machinations provide the cause of change. This commitment to causal reification is at work in much of the history of Western thought. That its impetus is manifest at virtually every historical juncture is clear from William Lane Craig's interesting study *The Cosmological Argument from Plato to Leibniz* (London, 1980).

substances must inevitably be invoked to explain the existence of *substances*. For we now become committed to the thesis that everything in nature has an efficient cause in some other natural thing that is its causal source, its reason for being.

The stance that is implicit in Hempel's argument is actually explicit in much of the Western philosophical tradition. Hume, for one, insists that there is no feasible way in which an existential conclusion can be obtained from nonexistential premises.[8] The principle is also supported by philosophers of a very different ilk on the other side of the Channel—including Leibniz himself, who writes with characteristic explicitness that "the sufficient reason [of contingent existence] . . . must be outside this series of contingent things, and *must reside in a substance which is the cause of this series*."[9] Such a view amounts to a thesis of genetic homogeneity that says (on analogy with the old but now surely untenable idea that "life must come from life") that "things must come from things," or "stuff must come from stuff," or "substance must come from substance."

Despite its surface appeal, the plausible principle that only real (existing) causes can have real (existing) effects has major problems. It presupposes that there must be a type homogeneity between cause and effect on the lines of the ancient Greek principle that "like must come from like." This highly dubious idea of genetic homogeneity has taken hard knocks in the course of modern science, which teaches that matter can come from energy, and living organisms from complexes of inorganic molecules. If such a principle fails as regards matter and life, need it hold for substance as such? The claim that it does so would need a very cogent defense. None has been forthcoming to date.

Is it indeed true that only things can engender things? Why must a ground of change always inhere in a thing rather than in a nonsubstantival "condition of things-in-general"? Must substance inevitably arise from substance—rather than, say, from a law or principle or "mere abstraction" of some sort?[10] Even to assert such a requirement is in effect to challenge its credentials. Why must the explanation of facts rest in the operation of *things?* To be sure, fact explanations must have inputs (*all* explanations must). Facts must root in facts. But why in thing-existential ones? A highly problematic bit of metaphysics is involved here. Dogmas about explanatory homogeneity aside, there is no discernible reason why an existential fact cannot be grounded in nonexistential ones, and the existence of substantial things be explained on the basis of some nonsubstantival circumstance or principle. Once we give up the principle of genetic homogeneity and abandon the idea that existing

---

[8]David Hume, *Dialogues Concerning Natural Religion,* ed. N. K. Smith (London, 1922), p. 189.

[9]G. W. Leibniz, "Principles of Nature and of Grace," sec. 8, italics supplied. Cf. Saint Thomas: "Of necessity, therefore, anything in process of change is being changed by something else" (*Summa Theologica,* Ia, q. 2, art. 3). The idea that only substances can produce changes goes back through Thomas's master, Aristotle. In Plato and the pre-Socratics, the causal efficacy of principles is recognized (e.g., the love and strife of Empedocles).

[10]One of the very few voices ever raised in opposition to the idea that only existing causes can have existing affects is that of Speusippus, Plato's nephew and successor as head of the Academy, who is sometimes interpreted as having taught that the world of existing things depends upon a principle, the One, that is not itself an existing thing. See R. M. Dancy, "Ancient Non-Beings: Speusippus and Others," *Ancient Philosophy* 9 (1989): 207–43.

things must originate in existing things, we remove the key prop of the idea that asking for an explanation of the existence of things in general is a logically inappropriate demand. The footing of the rejectionist approach is gravely undermined.

There are, of course, other routes to the destination of rejectionism. One of them turns on the thesis of Kant's First Antinomy that it is simply illegitimate to try to account for the phenomenal universe as a whole (the entire *Erscheinungswelt*). Explanation on this view is inherently partitive: phenomena can be accounted for only in terms of other phenomena, so that it is in principle improper to ask for an account of phenomena-as-a-whole. The very idea of an explanatory science of nature at large—its structure, its volume, its laws, its composition, and so forth—is inappropriate. And so is the issue of its *existence* as well. Such an approach insists that explanatory discussion is necessarily partial and cannot deal with the whole. But this position is also deeply problematic. For why should a question be inappropriate just because it is difficult to resolve? Aesop's story of the fox and the grapes leaps to mind.

The question of "the reason why" behind existence is surely an important one. If there is *any* possibility at all of getting an adequate answer, there is no question but that we would very much like to have it. Dismissing synoptic questions is not only unsatisfying and incompatible with our standing in the world's scheme of things as *Homo quaerens,* but it is unfruitful in a way that presents substantial problems. For there is nothing patently meaningless about this "riddle of existence." It does not seem to rest in any obvious way on any particularly problematic presupposition—apart from the epistemically optimistic yet methodologically inevitable idea that there are always reasons why things are as they are (the "principle of sufficient reason"). Rejectionism seems a mere device for sidestepping embarrassingly difficult questions—and not a very satisfactory one at that. Simply rejecting the question as improper or illegitimate is fruitless. Try as we will to dismiss the problem, it comes back to haunt us.[11]

RATIONALITY IS THE INSTRUMENT OF PHILOSOPHY

The ancients saw man as "the rational animal," set apart from other creatures by capacities for speech and deliberation. Under the precedent of Greek philosophy, Western thinkers have generally deemed the use of thought for the guidance of our proceedings to be at once the glory and the duty of *Homo sapiens.*

Rationality consists in the intelligent pursuit of appropriate ends. It calls for the appropriate use of reason to resolve choices in the best possible way. To behave rationally is to make use of one's intelligence to figure out the best thing to do in the circumstances. It is a matter of the recognizably effective pursuit of appropriately appreciated benefits. Rationality thus has a crucially economic dimension,

---

[11]For criticism of ways of avoiding the question "Why is there something rather than nothing?" see chap. 3 of William Rowe, *The Cosmological Argument* (Princeton, 1975), and also Donald R. Burrill, ed., *The Cosmological Argument* (Garden City, N.J., 1967), esp. the piece entitled "The Cosmological Argument" by Paul Edwards.

seeing that the impetus to economy is an inherent part of intelligent comportment. Rationality is a matter of deliberately doing the best one can with the means at one's disposal—of striving for the best results that one can expect to achieve within the range of one's resources, specifically including one's intellectual resources. Optimization in what one thinks, does, and values is the crux of rationality. Costs and benefits are the pivotal factors. Whether in matters of belief, action, or evaluation, rationality demands a deliberate endeavor to optimize benefits relative to the expenditure of available resources. Reason requires the cultivation of intelligently adopted objectives in intelligent ways.

Rationality is not an inevitable feature of conscious organic life. Here on earth, at least, it is our specifically human instrumentality, a matter of our particular evolutionary heritage. Rational intelligence—the use of our brains to guide action by figuring out what is the apparent best—is the survival instrument of our species, in much the same way that other creatures have managed to ensure their survival by being prolific or tough or well sheltered. It is a means to adaptive efficiency, enabling us (sometimes at least) to adjust our environment to our needs and wants rather than conversely.

The maintenance of rational coherence and consistency is a key task of philosophy. But is such consistency itself not simply a mere ornament, a dispensable luxury, the hobgoblin of little minds? Rousseau wrote to one of his correspondents that he did not wish to be shackled by narrow-minded consistency; he proposed to write whatever seemed sensible at the time. In a writer of belles lettres, this sort of flexibility may seem refreshingly open-minded. But such an approach is not available to a philosopher. Philosophy in its very nature is a venture of systematization and rationalization, of rendering matters intelligible and accessible to rational thought. Its concern is for the rational order and systemic coherence of our commitments. The commitment to rational coherence is a part of what makes philosophy the enterprise it is.

But why not embrace contradiction in a spirit of openness rather than flee from it?[12] The answer is that rejecting inconsistencies is the only road to comprehension and understanding. To the extent that we do not resolve an issue in one definite way to the exclusion of others, we do not resolve it at all. Only a coherent, alternative-excluding resolution is a resolution at all. Moreover, intelligence has, for us, an evolutionary dimension, and only a consistent and coherent mode of action can provide for evolutionary efficacy.

The presence of an inconsistency in framing an answer to a question is self-destructive. To respond "yes *and* no" is in effect to offer no response at all, answers that do not exclude manage to achieve no useful inclusions either. Only where some possibilities are denied is anything asserted: "All determination is negation" (*omnis affirmatio est negatio*). A logically inconsistent theory of something is thereby self-defeating—not just because it affirms an impossibility but because it provides no information on the matter at issue. An inconsistent position is no position at all.

---

[12]Paul K. Feyerabend embraces the concurrent use of mutually inconsistent scientific theories within a "theoretical pluralism." See his essay "Problems of Empiricism" in *Beyond the Edge of Certainty,* ed. R. G. Colodny (Englewood Cliffs, N.J., 1965), pp. 145–260 (see esp. pp. 164–68).

Keeping on good terms with *all* the possibilities requires that we embrace *none.* But the point of having a position at all is to have some answer to some question or other. If we fail to resolve the problem in favor of one possibility or another, we do not have an answer. To whatever extent we fail to resolve the issue in favor of one alternative or another, we also fail to arrive at some answer to the question. Unrelieved yea-saying is socially accommodating but informatively unhelpful. (Cf. Aristotle's defense of the law of noncontradiction in book gamma of the *Metaphysics.*) As long as and to the extent that inconsistencies remain, our goal of securing information or achieving understanding is defeated.

To be sure, while we ever strive to *improve* our knowledge, we never manage to *perfect* it. The stage for our present deliberations is itself set by the aporetic cluster of individually plausible but collectively incompatible theses represented by the following inconsistent triad:

1. Reality is adequately cognizable. (Thought can characterize reality in a way that achieves *adaequatio ad rem*—not fully, to be sure, but at any rate in essentials.)
2. Our knowledge of reality is consistent; it constitutes a logically "coherent whole." Rational inquiry can in principle depict reality adequately in a coherent system of true propositions.
3. Experience shows that our ventures at devising knowledge of reality eventually run into inconsistency as we work out their ramifications and implications more fully.

Denial of thesis (3) is not a promising option here, since, to all appearances, this simply represents a "fact of life" regarding the situation in philosophy. Rejecting (2) also has its problems. Perhaps it is conceivable (just barely) that reality will, whenever offered a choice of alternatives, decide to have it both ways and accept inconsistency—a prospect envisaged by thinkers from the days of Nicholas of Cusa to contemporary neo-Hegelians. This is a theory that we might, in the end, feel compelled to adopt. But clearly only as a last resort, "at the end of the day"—and thus effectively never. In philosophy, we want to make sense of things. A theory that says they just cannot be made sense of coherently and consistently may well have various merits, but it is nevertheless decisively flawed. Its defect is not just a lack of rationality but a lack of utility as well. For such a theory simply aborts the aim of the cognitive enterprise—it impedes any prospect of gathering information.

Denying thesis (1) thus affords the most readily available option. We must concede that philosophical thought can at best make a rough and imperfect approximation of adequacy—that reality refuses cognitive domestication, so that our best cognitive efforts represent a valiant but never totally satisfactory attempt to "get it right." Such a position is not a radical skepticism that denies the availability of any and all useful information about reality but a mitigated skepticism that insists that thought at best affords rough information about reality—not by way of definitive and indefeasible *epistēmē,* but by way of a "rational belief" that is inevitably imperfect and defective (its rationality notwithstanding). An element of tentativeness should always attach to our philosophical theories, for we can never rest assured that they will not need to be revamped and shored up by our successors. (Quite to the contrary, we can count on it!)

As this line of thought indicates, two basic goals set the scene for philosophical inquiry: (1) the urge to know, to secure answers to our questions, to enhance our
cognitive resources, to enlarge our information, to extend the range of accepted theses, to fill up an intellectual vacuum. But this in the nature of the case—given the
character of its "data"—inexorably leads to overcommitment, to informational
overcrowding, to inconsistency. And now comes (2), the urge to rationality: to have
a coherent theory, to keep our commitments consistent and harmoniously coordinated. The first impetus is expansive and ampliative, the second contractive and
eliminative. Both point in the direction of systematization, with its characteristic
concern for comprehensiveness and harmonization.

PHILOSOPHOBIA

Philosophy, then, is the enterprise of using the resources of reason to resolve, as
best we can, the "big questions" regarding the nature of human beings and the
ramifications of their thoughts and actions within the world's scheme of things.
But throughout the long history of this subject there have been schools of thought
antipathetic to this endeavor and concerned to urge its abandonment. In particular, the skeptics have, from classical antiquity onward, maintained the impotence
and incapacity of reason. Philosophy's big questions, so they insist, simply lie
beyond the reach of reason, placed outside the range of questions that human reason can answer. Any attempt to resolve them is inescapably futile. Analogously,
the *sophists* always maintained that while reason can indeed provide answers to
these questions, it will provide too many of them. An equally cogent case can be
made out from each and every one of various alternative answers. What reason
cannot do is to decide between them, no one of them admitting of a justificatory
case any stronger than that for the others. Again, *deconstructionism* (or *logical
positivism*) maintains that the questions are inherently meaningless. The reason
why we cannot resolve them lies not in limitations of human reason but in the
nature of the issues. The questions involved are inherently flawed though involving literally senseless terms (*legal* positivism) or false presuppositions (Kant) or
mistaken preconceptions ("postmodernism" or deconstructionism). By contrast,
post-Enlightenment *scientism* (or *scientific positivism*) insists on reducing or
transforming the traditional big questions into orthodox scientific issues. It is not
that the questions are intractable but rather that when their sense is appropriately
understood—duly analyzed and "clarified"—they reduce to scientific issues of
the familiar sort. When science has done its work, there is no residual work left
for philosophy. Finally, *historicism* insists that at this stage, there is no work left
for philosophy itself because the residual work should be accomplished, not by
science, but by history. At this time and in this era we should not address philosophical issues directly but rather should see the issues in an altogether historical
light. The appropriate course consists in surveying the history of philosophical
theorizing of all sorts. For philosophy itself we can and should substitute the history of philosophical theories and ideas. Each of these very different doctrinal
positions agrees that philosophy as traditionally conceived should be abandoned

and that something very different (perhaps only a vacuum) should take its place. All of these positions propose to abolish philosophy as practiced in the traditional mainstream of the subject.

What is striking about these positions, however, is their self-inconsistency—the fact that each of them violates its own prescriptions. Skeptics are not skeptical about the correctness of their own position. Sophists do not think the positions that rival their own are equally meritorious. Deconstructionists do not regard their own strictures against philosophy to be meaningless. Adherents of scientism are clearly unable to characterize the issue of philosophy's possibility as itself somehow representing a scientific question. Finally, historicists are not prepared to replace their own position with discussions exclusively devoted to surveying what people have thought and said about the topic.

The ironic fact is that all of these philosophy-rejecting doctrinal positions come to grief through the selfsame circumstance that metaphilosophy—the consideration of the nature, scope and methods of philosophy—is an integral part of philosophy itself. Given this circumstance, it is clear that even these who try in a reasoned way to maintain and substantiate the position that philosophy is not possible are thereby engaged—albeit self-defeatingly—on a project of philosophical investigation. To engage in rational argumentation designed to establish the impossibility of philosophizing is in fact to be engaged in doing a bit of it.

One may conceivably manage to argue cogently by philosophical means against the traditional ways of understanding or of practicing philosophy, or against the feasibility of a successful practice of this or that particular sector or sort of philosophy. But given that metaphilosophy is an integral component of philosophy itself, one cannot argue for the abortion of philosophy as such without succumbing to self-inconsistency. It lies in the very nature of the subject that a philosophical philosophobia has no rational justification.[13]

But is it not a very meager result that such an analysis provides? For does it not allow the prospect that, conceivably, the only viable kind of philosophy is a negativistic metaphilosophy that envisions the destruction of everything else in this domain?

Admittedly, the one-liner at issue—"Metaphilosophy is, after all, a branch of philosophy itself"—can of itself underwrite no further large and weighty result. But it does, at least, suffice to reverse the burden of proof. For if *any* part of philosophy, however small, can be secured against the philosophobes, then it is clear that the sort of wholesale and across-the-board argumentation to which they traditionally resort will not do the job, and that they cannot avoid the painstaking and laborious task of providing a detailed, sector-by-sector invalidation of the philosophical enterprise. The facile across-the-board approach of all-or-nothing doctrines like those of traditional skepticism or positivism cannot achieve its intended aims.

---

[13]As the very etymology of the matter indicates, *philo-sophia-phobia* involves a contradiction in terms.

Index